Forgotten: Scotland's Former Football League Clubs

Robin Holmes

ISBN 979-8-64059-851-3

To Nic, Josh and Eve...for their love, patience and understanding during those times when I went to the library and was on the laptop – you are my world...To Paul Gray for his encouragement...and to all my former colleagues at Nationwide Building Society, where I spent 30 happy years.

Contents

Introduction 1

Abercorn 19

Armadale 45

Arthurlie 69

Ayr FC 85

Ayr Parkhouse 93

Bathgate 102

Beith 115

Berwick Rangers 123

Bo'ness 169

Broxburn United 196

Cambuslang 213

Clackmannan 224

Clydebank I (1914–1931) 230

Clydebank II (1966-2002) 253

Cowlairs 283

Dumbarton Harp 294

Dundee Hibernian 300

Dundee Wanderers 313

Dykehead 319

East Stirlingshire 326

ES Clydebank 397

Galston 401

Gretna 408

Helensburgh 421

Johnstone 431

King's Park 442

Leith Athletic 461

Linthouse 502

Lochgelly United 509

Meadowbank Thistle 519

Mid-Annandale 536

Nithsdale Wanderers 542

Northern 551

Peebles Rovers 557

Port Glasgow Athletic 564

Renton 580

Royal Albert 613

St Bernard's 619

Solway Star 667

Third Lanark 673

Thistle 756

Vale of Leven 762

Appendix 804

Bibliography 812

Introduction

This book tells the story of the Scottish football clubs that once played in the Scottish Football League. This includes the Glasgow clubs: Cowlairs, Linthouse, Northern and Thistle; the Edinburgh clubs of Leith Athletic and St Bernard's; and the other founding League club from Paisley - Abercorn. What happened to the other original founding members Cambuslang, Renton and Vale of Leven? It also includes King's Park of Stirling whose demise was precipitated by the German Luftwaffe; the four missing clubs of West Lothian: Armadale, Bathgate, Bo'ness and Broxburn United; the name changes of Meadowbank Thistle, Dundee Hibernian and ES Clydebank; the financial intrigues at Third Lanark, Clydebank and Gretna; and the clubs of the ill-fated Third Division whose abandonment in 1926 saw eleven further clubs drop out of the League never to return. All the stories behind the bankruptcies, name changes and failed re-elections of over forty clubs that have dropped out of the Scottish Football League. Over a dozen of these clubs have their name etched on a domestic Scottish trophy and their honours include eight Scottish Cup wins and one overall Scottish League championship. Extensively researched and drawing heavily on the prosaic newspaper reports of the day it charts the rise and ultimately fall of these former League clubs.

The journey for this book has its origins in a real journey, my move to Scotland in 2003. Well, actually it pre-dates this by some considerable time going back to my time as a kid following the football results! This was an era of cardboard tabs coloured for each team that you moved and put into slots to represent their place in the tables of the respective divisions. The four English League divisions were represented along with three divisions in Scotland and it was around this time that I developed my love of Scottish football clubs. They were so colourful, not just their actual colours but also their names.

In terms of colours in England I was used to a preponderance of blues (of various shades), reds and whites - in Scotland there was yellow and red stripes, greens of all shades, striped patterns and overall a greater variety and mix. As a young boy I played the table football game Subbuteo and can remember painting over Notts County to create an Airdrieonians with its red diamond and Leeds United were also painted over to create Hibernians.

In terms of names, I lived in Shropshire, and the local team was Shrewsbury, and they were a "Town". When the family moved to Norfolk the local team was Norwich, who are a "City" and the local derby was against Ipswich, another "Town". If you were lucky you got an appendage like a "United". Maybe that is why clubs like Aston Villa and Chelsea held so much appeal for me. In Scotland you get "Thistles" and "Academicals" and you even get a club with a combination of second names like Albion Rovers. At school my favourite subjects were history and geography and I loved pouring over a map (still do). I can remember being intrigued that I couldn't find a St Mirren, a St Johnstone or a Queen of the South on a map. Likewise I couldn't find a Celtic or a Rangers until my elder brother said they were really called "Glasgow" Celtic and Rangers.

My interest in history was rekindled in 2002 when my future father-in-law was mourning the loss of his beloved Airdrieonians. They had gone out of business and we were talking about Third Lanark being the last Scottish club to have gone bust and this got me interested in finding out more about clubs that had once featured. I could also remember a Meadowbank Thistle from my time of tracking the football clubs and wondered what had happened to them. As a result I started researching some of the early Scottish Cup matches and came across names like Vale of Leven, St Bernard's and Renton. And then along came an episode of the *BBC's Pointless* quiz show that had a final question around the founding members of the English and Scottish Leagues, with one of the pointless answers being Cambuslang. I started following the formation of the Scottish League in 1890 and the founding clubs and then the movements in and out of the League. I also uncovered the existence of a Third Division in the 1920s which only lasted three seasons with only a few of the founding teams still in existence.

The definition of "forgotten" is something that is unremembered, beyond recall, a bygone, something that is lost, in the past, irrecoverable and irretrievable. My mission is to bring these clubs back into the conscious of the communities they represented and for them to be remembered again.

A note on inclusion: I've only sought to include clubs no longer in existence who completed at least one season in the League. I am deliberately body-swerving the issues of clubs immediately reforming, and of "newcos". So for me, the current Rangers is a continuation. Airdrieonians have also been excluded even though there was a short period when they played as Airdrie United following the demise of the original club and it's reincarnation by taking over Clydebank and changing their name. Some name changes have been included, even though the club was a continuation.
I have also included East Stirlingshire and Berwick Rangers. They might not yet be "forgotten" but they are worthy of inclusion as they introduced a new category for

leaving the League when in 2016 East Stirlingshire became the first club to be relegated out of the Scottish Football League. In doing so they also knocked out a planned entry as Edinburgh City were due to be included for their tenure in the 1930s. Berwick Rangers also suffered the same fate in 2019 and required a hasty inclusion.

A note on fallibility: I've tried to ensure that the information contained in this work is as accurate as possible. I've painstakingly poured over web pages, newspapers, books and microfiches in pursuit of this aim. I've tried to use multiple sources and cross-check information and statistics to make this a reality. However, I am only human. Any mistakes, omissions and errors are not intentional. They are a result of human error.

I make no apology for quoting directly from the newspaper reports of the day. Their colourful prose is much better than any descriptive text I could come up with and the language used, complete with scrimmages, strangers and custodians, evokes a bygone era.

*   *   *   *   *   *   *   *

The story of Scottish football really begins in 1873. Prior to this date games were played but the various clubs played ad hoc friendly matches. But at a historic meeting held on the 13th March 1873, at Dewar's Hotel, Bridge Street in Glasgow, Queen's Park FC invited a number of clubs to join with them in the formation of a Football Association. Seven other clubs joined the new Scottish FA including Glasgow clubs Clydesdale, Dumbreck, Glasgow Eastern, Granville, Rovers, and 3rd LRV (Third Lanark), along with Vale of Leven. Officials were appointed and the president of the new organisation was Mr A Campbell and the first secretary was Mr A Rae. The other members of the first committee were Messrs W Ker, W E Dick, R Gardner, W Gibb, E Hendry, D McFarlane, J McIntyre, J McKay and J Turnbull.

Other clubs soon followed and the original members were joined by Alexandra Athletic, Southern, Blythswood, Western, Renton, Dumbarton, Kilmarnock and Callender. The clubs then subscribed towards the purchase of a challenge trophy, which got underway in October, with Queen's Park of Glasgow becoming the first winners.

Friendlies continued to be played, as they were a source of valuable revenue for the clubs, and it was this desire for regular income that led to the idea of a league competition, based upon English lines. This time it was Renton who invited the clubs to a meeting, held on the 20th March 1890 at Holton's Commercial Hotel, Glassford Road, Glasgow. *The Scotsman* reported that "a meeting of football club representatives, convened for the purpose of taking into consideration the proposal to form a Football League for Scotland, was held...After some discussion, in the course of which it was pointed out that although on the lines of the English one, the League was to have no sympathy with the introduction of professionalism, the following resolution was passed:- 'that a committee be appointed from this meeting to draft rules and constitution of the proposed League, and submit it to the various clubs determined upon this meeting, and that these clubs be requested to send representatives with full powers to a meeting to be afterwards convened'."

The Scottish Football League (SFL) was officially formed a month later on the 30th April. The eleven founder members were Renton, Dumbarton, Abercorn, St Mirren (both from Paisley), Glasgow Celtic, Glasgow Rangers, Cowlairs (from the Springburn area of north Glasgow), Third Lanark (Glasgow south side), Cambuslang (Glasgow), Heart of Midlothian and Vale of Leven. Of the original eleven members, only Celtic, Dumbarton, Hearts, Rangers and St Mirren survive.

On Tuesday 3rd June 1890 the Scottish Football League was formally constituted at a meeting held in Aitken's Hotel, Glasgow. The original office-bearers elected were Mr A Lawrence of Dumbarton as Chairman; Mr George Henderson of Cowlairs as Vice-Chairman; Mr John H McLaughlin of Celtic as Secretary and Mr William Wilton of Rangers as treasurer and the first set of League fixtures were agreed.

Before the recent introduction of the pyramid system in Scotland there were re-election votes at the SFL's Annual General Meeting (AGM) and a number of teams left the League by this reason - some applied successfully to come back but others never returned and were confined to historical footnotes and obscurity. Re-election was the main reason for leaving the Scottish Football League. Right from the outset the provision for the bottom three clubs (later changed to two) to stand for re-election meant that the possibility of a club not being voted back in and therefore leaving the League was a possibility. The initial success of the League meant that when the first re-election vote was held thirteen clubs competed for five places (the three places up for re-election and League expansion from a ten team to a twelve team League). As organised football grew in Scotland and a number of non-League competitions were organised, the number of clubs aspiring to join the SFL also grew. Established clubs were therefore subject to challenge from other clubs. At the 1906 AGM eleven clubs from two different non-Leagues challenged the two clubs up for re-election.

The other main reasons for dropping out of the Scottish Football League are:

- Financial: bankruptcy, liquidation, and being wound up having entered administration. In recent times this was one of the main reasons and includes, most famously Third Lanark and most recently Gretna.
- Disbanded: often due to no ground or no competition.
- Expelled: due to an infringement, often linked to the failure to fulfil a fixture or pay a financial obligation.
- Resigned: generally due to financial difficulties.
- Relegated: the last re-election vote took place in 1951. Since 2015 two clubs have left this way.
- League reconstruction: usually a way of introducing new members, there were occasions in the early years when the League reduced the number of teams from 12 to 10 and this also happened in 1922.
- Name changes: often linked to a change in location, such as with Meadowbank Thistle but also in the case of broadening appeal with Dundee Hibernian.
- Division Three collapse: this experimental division only lasted three seasons between 1923 and 1926 and collapsed due to financial considerations. Nevertheless it introduced some colourful names to the annals of Scottish football history and was the single largest exodus of clubs in any one event.
- Merger: Ayr FC & Ayr Parkhouse, both SFL clubs at the time, merged to form Ayr United.

The one notable omission from the clubs forming the Scottish Football League was Queen's Park. Winners of a record nine Scottish Cups by 1890, they declined to join due to their strictly amateur code, whereas the League was seen as the onset of professionalism. It was this issue of professionalism that prevented one of the key advocates for the League, Renton, from completing their fixtures in the first year of competition. St Bernard's, from Edinburgh, had already been excluded for payment to players and when they played a fundraising game, under the name of the 'Edinburgh Saints' against a sympathetic Renton, the Dunbartonshire club found themselves excluded as well.

The first SFL matches were played on Saturday 16th August 1890. Eight of the eleven clubs kicked off - not Abercorn, Third Lanark or St Mirren – with Rangers scoring five against Hearts but with Cambuslang setting the standard with an 8-2 victory over Vale of Leven. The early rulebook was nowhere near as extensive as today and the early rulemakers made no provision for the situation that arose when all of the League fixtures had been completed. Dumbarton and Rangers were tied on 29 points, each having won 13 games, drawn 3 and lost only 2. Nowadays teams level on points are separated by a process involving goal difference, goals scored, number of wins and head to head results. But in this case no process existed. Goal average, the forerunner of goal difference wasn't introduced until 1922. If some of these methods had been employed Dumbarton would have taken the title on account of having scored 61 and conceded 21 (compared to 58-25 by Rangers). As it was a one-off, play-off game was held, but once again the two couldn't be separated, drawing 2-2 and as a result the first ever League title was 'shared'. Dumbarton narrowly missed out on the very first 'double', beaten 1-0 by Hearts in the Scottish Cup final.

At the end of the season the bottom three clubs faced a re-election vote at the SFL's AGM held at the Union Hotel in Glasgow. They were Cowlairs, Vale of Leven and St Mirren. The first club to be impacted was Cowlairs, with *The Scotsman* reporting on 5th June 1891 that "the teams selected for next season are the same as last, with the exception that the Cowlairs are deleted from the list, and the Leith Athletic and Clyde are added, twelve clubs in all competing."

Dumbarton won the League title outright the following year, finishing two points ahead of Celtic. Renton were admitted this time, having threatened legal action (St Bernard's were admitted in 1893), and they were joined by Clyde of Glasgow and Leith Athletic of Edinburgh - so the League expanded to twelve teams. Dumbarton inflicted some heavy defeats on their opponents along the way, including an 8-2 win over the newcomers Clyde in November 1891, an 8-1 win over Vale of Leven the following month and a 6-0 win over Rangers in May 1892 to claim the title. At the SFL AGM on the 3rd June 1892 it was voted that the number of competing clubs would reduce this time, from 12 to 10 for the next season. Two of the original founding clubs, Cambuslang and Vale of Leven, left the SFL as a result of the vote, Cambuslang never to return.

The year 1893 was a momentous one for the League. After a series of suspensions, expulsions, court cases and points deducted the thorny issue of professionalism was accepted. And so began the turning of the tide away from the amateurs of Queen's Park and the Dunbartonshire clubs towards the Glasgow sides of Celtic and Rangers. Dumbarton, having won the first two championships, finished bottom of the 1894-95 table. 1893 also saw the formation of a Second Division, although no automatic promotion or relegation existed until 1921, despite several debates at the League's AGM. Prior to this clubs moved between divisions on the basis of an "election". This led to some anomalies whereby some of the teams going up actually finished below other teams that did not. Hibernian were the first winners of the new Division but were denied promotion, whereas Clyde who finished third, five points behind the leaders, were elected back into the First Division. Hibs also won the Second Division the following year and went up at the second time of asking, at the expense of neighbours Leith Athletic.

Two of the sides that entered into the Scottish League with the formation of the Second Division only lasted the one season. Glasgow clubs Northern and Thistle finished in the bottom two at the end of the 1893-94 season and failed to be re-elected to the League. They were replaced by Airdrieonians and Dundee Wanderers. One of these clubs went on to have a long career while the other also only lasted a season.

The year 1897 saw the loss of two of the founding clubs, albeit one on a temporary basis. At the end of the 1895-96 season Dumbarton, playing in the First Division, had finished in the re-election places for the second successive season and were subsequently placed in the Second Division. The club finished bottom and were now required to go through the election process for continued membership of the Scottish League. At the League's AGM in June they lost their place by seven votes. The other two sides up for re-election, Motherwell and Port Glasgow Athletic were both comfortably re-elected and retained their League Status but Dumbarton, five years after retaining the overall League championship, lost out to Ayr FC of the Ayrshire Combination by 24 votes to 17. Dumbarton were successfully re-elected to the Scottish League in 1906. Just four games into the new 1897-98 season founder members Renton, unable to meet their financial guarantees, tendered their resignation and their place was taken by Hamilton Academical.

During the 1900s the number of clubs competing in the League slowly grew. In 1900 Queen's Park bowed to the inevitable and joined the League, although they retained their highly valued amateur status. Given their history and pedigree they were fast-tracked straight into the top flight. Not long after a rule was introduced making new entrants play in the lowest division first. By the time of the 1906-07 season 18 teams were now competing in the top flight, as opposed to the original ten.

Despite the operation of two divisions there was no automatic promotion and relegation between them. At the League's AGM on the 27th May 1907 a motion proposed by Hearts to reduce the number of clubs in the First Division to 16 was defeated. Hearts also proposed that the top club of the Second Division be automatically promoted to take the place of the bottom club of the First Division but this was motion also defeated. At the 1910 AGM there was another failed motion for automatic promotion and relegation and the following year Hearts had another automatic promotion motion defeated, although at the SFA's AGM it was decided that Scottish Cup Semi-finals would now be played at neutral grounds.

Further motions were submitted in the run up to 1914. At the SFL AGM held on the 3rd June 1912 *The Scotsman* reported that "the Celtic put forward a motion to the effect that the highest club in the Second Division should automatically pass into the first Division, and that the lowest club in the First Division should drop into the Second Division. The necessary two-thirds majority supported the motion, but it was ultimately agreed that in view of the fact that the motion involved the relegation of St Mirren, who had committed themselves to the First Division wage bill and other expenditure for next season, to the Second Division, it was decided to hold the matter over till next annual meeting. It was understood, however, that the meeting virtually decided for automatic promotion, twelve months hence." However, a year later this rule wasn't enforced as the decision was taken to expand the First Division from 18 to 20 clubs. At the end of the 1913-14 season Cowdenbeath won the Second Division but did not replace St Mirren who had finished bottom of the First. A motion put forward by Hearts at the League's AGM for automatic promotion was defeated.

By the outbreak of the Great War in 1914, Linthouse, Ayr Parkhouse and Port Glasgow Athletic had all come and gone. In April 1915 *The Scotsman* reported that 202 players had enlisted and 114 were employed on government work and the League decided to suspend the Second Division, affecting the membership of a number of clubs including founders Abercorn and Vale of Leven, plus the likes of St Bernard's and Leith Athletic. During the War Aberdeen, Dundee and Raith Rovers were asked to step down in 1917 to help reduce the travelling incurred by the rest of the clubs and Clydebank were offered a place to bring up the numbers to 18 clubs. These three clubs returned for the 1919-20 season but this now made for a 21 club division and so an election was held to fill the vacancy. On 3rd April 1919, Albion Rovers beat Cowdenbeath by 11 votes to 10 to take the position. Clydebank, who had been 'co-opted' in 1917, had their place in the League confirmed.

The Second Division was not reformed immediately after the War and after much agitation, at the League's AGM on the 10th May 1921, *The Scotsman* reported that "a meeting of the Scottish Football League was held in Glasgow last night, when it was unanimously agreed, subject to the confirmation of the annual general meeting, that a Second Division be formed with the following clubs:- Arbroath, Alloa, Armadale, Bathgate, Cowdenbeath, Bo'ness, Dunfermline Athletic, East Fife, East Stirlingshire, Clackmannan, Dundee Hibs, Forfar Athletic, Johnstone, King's Park, Lochgelly United, St Bernard's, Stenhousemuir, Broxburn, Vale of Leven and St Johnstone." The newly reinstated Division comprised of 20 clubs but did so on the understanding that the bottom two clubs would drop out as part of League reconstruction and a reduction in the overall number of clubs from 42 to 40. This planned reduction led to Clackmannan and Dundee Hibernian leaving, although both clubs subsequently found a route back in.

Of even more significance was the decision that at the end of the season the three bottom clubs of the First Division would be relegated to the Second Division and the top club of the Second Division would be promoted to the First Division. Thereafter the two bottom clubs of the First Division would be relegated and the top two clubs of the Second Division promoted to the First, thereby establishing the principle of automatic promotion and relegation between the two Divisions for the first time.

Not everyone agreed with this new arrangement though and at the League's AGM in 1922 *The Scotsman* reported, under the headline "Promotion and Relegation in Scotland: Attempt to Wreck Last Year's Agreement" that "at the annual general meeting of the Scottish Football League in Glasgow last night, an attempt to wreck the new system of promotion and relegation was unsuccessful. Consequently, as agreed last year, the League next season will consist of two divisions, twenty clubs in each. Alloa step into the First Division and Queen's Park, Clydebank and Dumbarton will be relegated to the Second Division." Alloa Athletic were the first team to be promoted on merit at the end of the 1921-22 season.

The issue of how to separate teams level on points continued to rear its head from time to time. Back in 1905 Celtic and Rangers had finished tied on points. Celtic won the play-off and the title, yet Rangers had a better goal difference, had scored more goals and had recorded more wins. In the 1909-10 Second Division campaign Leith Athletic and Raith Rovers finished level on points but did not contest a play-off match for the championship so were declared joint winners. Eventually a change came about for the 1921-22 season with the introduction of goal average. This was arrived at by simply dividing the goals scored by the number conceded, so that a team scoring 100 and conceding 50 would have an average of 2.0. This change not only helped to separate teams but also encouraged goalscoring. In 1953 the League title was decided in favour of Rangers over Hibernian by a margin of 0.23 and in 1965 by an even narrower margin when Kilmarnock finished ahead of Hearts by 0.04. Goal average was replaced for the 1971-72 season by goal difference.

Two years after the reinstatement of the Second Division the League undertook the largest expansion of the number of Scottish League clubs with fifteen teams joining relegated East Stirlingshire in forming a Third Division. The number of new entrants surpassed the foundation of the SFL in 1890 when eleven teams joined and the creation of the Second Division in 1893 when nine new teams joined.

The question of a Third Division was discussed at the League's AGM on the 17th May 1923 and a Management Committee was formed with full power to consider and take action. This was then debated at a Management Committee meeting on the 18th June 1923 and ratified on the 28th June. Automatic promotion of the leading two clubs to the Second Division was agreed upon. Eighteen clubs were invited but three of those didn't reply; Helensburgh (who did eventually join), Hurlford (who were practically defunct) and Leith Athletic (who didn't join until 1924). Arbroath Athletic were interested, but the League refused their application as Arbroath already had a League club despite Dumbarton, a town of similar size, now having two clubs. Eleven teams joined from the Western League (Arthurlie, Beith, Dykehead, Dumbarton Harp, Galston, Helensburgh, Nithsdale Wanderers, Peebles Rovers, Queen of the South, Royal Albert and Solway Star) and these were joined by five further teams to form a sixteen team league. Three of the other five came from the Eastern League (Brechin City, former League side Clackmannan, and Montrose), one from the South Counties League (Mid-Annandale) and one team was demoted from the Second Division (East Stirlingshire). These clubs were not granted full membership of the SFL but were instead granted associate membership status which did not carry with it any voting rights.

This new division only lasted 3 seasons and collapsed due to financial considerations as it proved unsustainable and unviable for a number of the clubs. The high cost of travel and match guarantees were more than the clubs could afford. With average gates counted in the hundreds the revenues generated were not enough to cover the costs involved and in 1926 the competition was abandoned in chaos, with fixtures incomplete.

The first season progressed as normal. Queen of South top scored with 64 goals in 30 games but this was not enough to secure promotion for the Doonhammers, as two of the team with an existing pedigree, Arthurlie and East Stirlingshire won promotion. Vale of Leven and Lochgelly United were relegated and joined the Third Division for the 1924-25 season. They were joined by former League member Leith Athletic, making for an unwieldy division of 17 teams. The second season in the Third Division was a regional affair, with the top three positions occupied from teams from Dumfriesshire – Nithsdale Wanderers, Queen of the South and Solway Star. Queen of the South piped Solway Star for the second promotion berth on goal average. Star had sold their centre-forward Dick to Celtic for £150 in the close season.

But in a sign of things to come Dumbarton Harp dropped out of the Scottish Football League in February 1925 and their record was expunged. The economic downturn was a contributory factor, as was the need to provide a financial guarantee to the visiting team. In a town already supporting one senior club, Harp struggled to attract sufficient crowds to their Meadow Park home. *The Sunday Post* on the 8th February 1925 commented "Dumbarton Harp's resignation from the Third Division was accepted after discussion. It was agreed that to subsidise the club in order to enable the programme of fixtures to be carried through would create a precedent with which the League could not cope satisfactorily. This gives an indication of the financial conditions existing in Division III."

Other clubs, such as Galston were also in financial difficulties and contemplated resigning from the League without fulfilling all of their fixtures. Bottom club Montrose were one of those struggling financially but they were able to stay afloat as a result of a money-spinning Scottish Cup tie against Rangers on the 7th February 1925, which they lost 2-0. The club was still haemorrhaging money and at a crisis meeting held in June the club directors asked the players to take a wage cut. The problem was also alleviated when they sold centre-forward Benny Yorston to Aberdeen for £35.

The 1925-26 season kicked off as usual, with Johnstone and Forfar Athletic joining the Division in place of Nithsdale Wanderers and Queen of the South, having been relegated from the Second Division. As winter approached many of the teams found themselves facing a worsening financial situation. The general economic situation was still poor and clearly was a mitigating factor. However, from the outset it became apparent that the small clubs involved would struggle to survive on meagre gate receipts given the travel costs and match fee guarantees required. Clubs like Galston, which had managed perfectly well in regional competitions attracting a few hundred spectators, now had to travel as far afield as Peebles and Annan in the south, Montrose and Brechin in the north. In January 1926 Galston folded after playing 15 matches and their record was expunged and it was this episode that precipitated a general collapse. *The Sunday Post,* on the 17th January 1926 made this prophetic comment: "withdrawal from the Third Division was the ultimate finding of a meeting of the club's members and supporters held during last week. Finance is the whole trouble. In their recent game with Johnstone at Galston the receipts were only a few shillings over £10, and the guarantee was £15. It has practically been failure all along the line. Had it not been for the efforts of an enterprising Supporters' Club (which has come to the rescue with about £100 since the season opened), Galston would have had to give up long ago....Apparently the Third Division is a bogey as far as Galston is concerned (and many other clubs, too, I fear), and Galston may have given to others the lead to follow."

With reality biting this ill-conceived competition eventually collapsed towards the end of the 1925-26 season with a number of fixtures unfinished or guarantees unpaid. In one example, Montrose were only offered half the gate by Dykehead after their midweek game, which amounted to just over £2. Montrose refused and requested payment of the official guarantee of £15. Dykehead said they couldn't pay, pointing out they had taken nothing like that sum in gate receipts. Montrose subsequently reported the matter to the League authorities. The League Management Committee met resulting in Dykehead being ordered to pay the "Gable Endies" the stipulated guarantee.

On the 10th April 1926 *The Scotsman* reported that "the Vale of Leven were unable to fulfil their fixture with Montrose at Montrose. Owing to the dull trade in the Vale of Leven and the extra expense caused by the long railway journeys, the directors of the club have found it difficult to carry on this season. Last Saturday week, against Mid-Annandale at Alexandria, they did not draw the guarantee, with the result that several of the players who did not receive their wages for that game refused to travel to Montrose on Saturday. The following day the *Sunday Post* reported on the players' revolt at Vale of Leven over unpaid wages: "Vale of Leven, after their long history, are in a very bad way. Yesterday they were unable to muster a team, the reason being given as 'financial difficulties'. The cause of the trouble is that the players, not having been paid for their last week's services, are in revolt. Last Saturday the Vale played Mid-Annandale, and drew as gate money the sum of £13 2s 19d. From this they paid the visiting club £10, £5 short of the Third Division guarantee, and after meeting the referee's fee and other expenses they were left with 2s 10d to pay the players' wages. A hurried search was made, but the wherewithal could not be found, so the players had to depart empty-handed. On Tuesday evening the players held a meeting to consider what action they should take, and apparently they decided to go on strike, for yesterday four players turned up at Buchanan Street Station in time for the ten o'clock for the North, and these four were not present at the players' meeting earlier in the week. The Supporters' Club also held a meeting on Thursday evening, but feverish activity on the part of this organisation, which has done much to help the finances of the football club, failed to find any means to alleviate the club's pecuniary embarrassment." A week later Clackmannan didn't fulfil one of their fixtures and seven days after that Beith didn't travel to Forfar either.

To bring matters to a head, F W McMillan, President of Helensburgh FC called for a meeting of the Third Division teams in Central Halls, Glasgow. This was to discuss the worsening financial situation as gate money generated was proving insufficient to meet the guarantees and travelling expenses. *The Scotsman* reported that "the Chairman had explained that the clubs in the Division were in sore straits, partly on account of the expenses incurred in traveling, and partly on account of the bad arrangement of fixtures. In the course of a long discussion many suggestions relating to a possible solution of the difficulties in which the clubs found themselves were made, and eventually the proposal put forward by Mr George Cumming (Brechin City FC) was adopted. The suggestion was that a sub-committee consisting of Messrs Cumming, McMillan and W. Paterson (Royal Albert FC) be appointed to make representation to the League Management Committee requesting them to offer means of help to the Third Division, and to report at a later date to a meeting of the Third Division representatives." A subsequent proposal was made to amalgamate the Second and Third divisions along regional lines and a number of clubs, including Clackmannan, Dykehead, Peebles, Royal Albert and Vale of Leven stated that they had made up their minds not to participate in any Third Division next season.

On the 25th April 1926 under the headline "Last Days of the Third Division", *The Sunday Post* was quite damning in its assessment: "it is time the Third Division of the League was dead. It does not deserve to be alive. Many of its members would like to see it done for. It is an incumbrance and a nuisance. This season its existence has been tragic - no enthusiasm, no real effort to make the competition a success, evasions, procrastinations, a mockery of League football. At the headquarters of the Scottish League the Third Division's existence has been the cause of much vexation, and there will be no weeping when it gives, as it will give this week, its final, feeble kick....The feeling in football circles grows that in Scotland a Third Division is almost an absurdity, a waste of time, money, and energy, and that local Leagues, run at quarter the cost, should be revived. We are being provided with concrete examples of the regard held by Third League clubs for that Division. Galston, as a competitive club, have thrown up the sponge. Clackmannan could not receive Leith Athletic last Saturday. The guarantee was beyond them. Vale of Leven have succumbed as a League entity. Beith declined to travel to Forfar yesterday."

Third Division representatives McMillan (Helensburgh), Cumming (Brechin) and Patterson (Royal Albert) met Messrs Liddle, Duffy and McAndrew, representatives of the Scottish League in Glasgow. McMillan stated that all 16 clubs were willing to carry on if conditions could be met to suit local requirements. Cumming was asked to expand on his proposed scheme for reorganisation which had the unanimous support of the clubs. Cumming identified the issues as too much travelling and not enough concentration of clubs to build up local rivalries. He cited that, apart from Aberdeen, every club in the Third Division paid more in travelling than any First or Second Division club. As an example his own club Brechin had paid out something like £200 for travelling whereas for Aberdeen it was £135 for the same number of matches. He concluded by saying that "it would be a serious matter if these sixteen clubs of good standing went to the wall." He strongly advocated a breakup of the Second and Third Division and their reorganisation into two regional Second Division sections. An alternative proposal was to take in the Scottish Alliance teams and split the enlarged

Third Division into two regional sections. Mr Liddle, President of the League sought to reassure them offering sympathy for their plight and stating he wanted to see them be successful. He kind of passed the buck though saying that the first proposal depended on the agreement of the Second Division clubs.

Various solutions were being offered up. Lochgelly proposed that the Third and Second divisions be absorbed into two regional sections - a South & West and a North & East. Brechin proposed the same, but along North-South lines. At the end of April the League Management Committee suggested instead a regional competition for next season involving the Third Division clubs and the Scottish Alliance. This was agreed to in principle by the clubs although assurances were sought around the prospect of promotion. And on that note, the League decided at its AGM that there would be no promotion from the Third Division for the current season, *The Scotsman* reporting that "In view of the fact that 14 clubs had not completed the competition the Scottish Football League Management Committee, at a meeting in Glasgow, decided that in accordance with the rules, that no Third Division Club was entitled to promotion and also that in view of the unsatisfactory state of the competition that no championship flag would be awarded."

Helensburgh actually topped the table, but only on account of having completed all of their fixtures. Leith Athletic finished in second, one point behind but having played a game less. They had come with a late eight game unbeaten run which included six wins to lift them from seventh place to second. Forfar Athletic came in third, but were the likely winners of the Division if they had completed their programme, as they still had two matches to play. As a result they were favoured by many of the clubs at the subsequent voting at the Scottish League AGM.

Bathgate and Broxburn United, the two bottom sides in the Second Division escaped automatic relegation at the end of the 1925-26 season and a re-election vote took place instead. Four of the defunct Third Division sides applied including the top three sides - Leith Athletic, Forfar Athletic, and Helensburgh - along with Dykehead – for the two vacant spots. Broxburn, Helensburgh and Dykehead were eliminated as it became a three way tussle for the two vacant spots. In an extraordinary tight contest only one vote separated the top three clubs on the first ballot. The second ballot was slightly more definitive with Bathgate securing re-election with 23 votes to Forfar's 21 and Leith's 20. In the run-off the two clubs were tied on 16 apiece, Forfar getting the nod on the Chairman's casting vote.

The Third Division therefore came to a somewhat ignominious end after just three seasons. Three of the original clubs continue to be members of the Scottish League today – Brechin City, Montrose and Queen of the South, and a fourth, East Stirlingshire, only recently lost their SFL status. The demise of the Division was the biggest single exodus of teams from the SFL. Fifteen teams left the League with only Forfar Athletic surviving. Leith Athletic were the first to return in 1927 and Montrose and Brechin City came back in 1929. However twelve of the original teams never returned. A large number of clubs found a place in the Scottish Alliance, so much so that for one season the competition was split into regional sections. This split lasted only one season, after which the Alliance was re-formed as one division. The Alliance was against any large scale expansion and not every club was offered a place. Those clubs excluded were Vale of Leven, Solway Star, Clackmannan, Mid-Annandale and Galston.

On the 12th June Vale of Leven representatives met with Mr McMillan in Helensburgh to protest at their exclusion. Southern clubs Mid-Annandale and Solway Star continued to lobby for their clubs participation and the Alliance's actions came in for widespread criticism. In early July *The Scotsman* reported that the Alliance had reconsidered, and at a meeting in Glasgow they agreed to let these three clubs in, which meant that all the clubs from the defunct Third Division had been found places with the exception of Clackmannan and Galston, the team that precipitated the collapse. The Alliance now operated in Northern and southern sections and Dykehead and Peebles Rovers were not happy to have been placed in the Northern section, which included trips to Aberdeen, Dundee, Montrose and Brechin. Never really happy with the influx of the former Third Division the Alliance expelled the majority of them a season later, with the clubs going on to form the ill-fated Provincial League.

Less than ten years after the reinstatement of the Second Division, several clubs, including Arthurlie, Clydebank and Bathgate had left the Scottish League, all resigning owing to financial difficulties, and Bo'ness had become the first to be expelled for failing to meet financial guarantees. The economic depression that had such an impact on the viability of the Third Division continued to adversely affect a number of clubs. In reviewing the 1930-31 season, the Glasgow Herald commented that "for some clubs the season has been a good one; for the majority it has been one of worry, as the industrial depression has curtailed their income to such an extent that they have only been able to carry on at a loss. Many players have not been re-signed by their clubs as a consequence, and the number of players granted free transfers must border on a record."

Following the start of the Second World War the Scottish League officially suspended its competition on the 13th September 1939 and set up a committee to investigate the possibility of regional league competitions. The League was not officially competed for again until the 1946-47 season. Instead, football was arranged on regional lines with two divisions, Eastern and Western, each consisting of 16 clubs. Organised football restarted at the end of October with *The Scotsman* noting that "football undergoes a severe test today, for with the start of regional league tournaments, it will be seen whether any real public interest is maintained in the sport. Many clubs, of course, are already in difficulties regarding players, since there are travelling difficulties, and many players are now in full-time employment in their home towns."

Two clubs failed to re-emerge after the war - St Bernard's of Edinburgh and King's Park of Stirling. Both clubs were unable to resume due to a lack of a ground although a phoenix club, Stirling Albion, emerged to take King's Park's place. Post-war seasons saw the divisions renamed 'A', 'B' and 'C' with the last section also including reserve sides. The First Division or Division A had 16 teams, the Second Division had 14 teams and the remaining seven sides in Division C were supplemented by reserve sides. In 1949, Division C was expanded to two regional sections – North-West and South-East. Re-election votes continued up until 1951.

The withdrawal of the reserve sides from Division C in 1955 saw a return to two divisions with the five non-reserve or first teams in Division C being given automatic promotion to an expanded 19 club Division B and the Division C was abolished. Berwick Rangers and Stranraer joined the League around this time which settled into an 18 club Division A and a 19 team Division B, so 37 League clubs in total. In 1956 the divisions were renamed the First and Second Divisions.

In 1964 we had the strange case of a relocation and name change, where, in a move akin to franchise changes in US sport, the owners of East Stirlingshire upped sticks and moved the club to Clydebank, calling themselves ES Clydebank. Under legal challenge they were forced to reverse this decision but a new Clydebank came back for the 1966-67 season to even up the numbers in the Second Division, so there were now 38 clubs. Things reverted back to an odd number just a year later with the sad demise of Third Lanark, the biggest and most high profile of the names to disappear from the League and also the most successful of the ex-League clubs. Founder members of the Scottish League, Third Lanark had won the League title in 1904 and made six appearances in the Scottish Cup Final, winning it twice in 1889 and 1905.

In 1974, the SFL made the decision to have three divisions comprising 10-14-14 clubs in place for the start of season 1975-76. Since 1967 the SFL had consisted of 37 clubs, so a vacancy had to be filled and applications were invited to be the 38th club. Meadowbank Thistle were successfully admitted but their name disappeared twenty years later with a relocation and name change to Livingston in 1995.

The three tier setup continued until the 1994–95 season, when a four divisional structure was introduced, along with a new Third Division, with all four divisions consisting of ten clubs. Two new teams entered the League at this point, Inverness Caledonian Thistle and Ross County.

On the 8th September 1997, the Premier Division clubs decided to split from the Scottish Football League and form the Scottish Premier League (SPL), following the example of the English Premier League.

Further League expansion took place in 2000, and a further two teams entered the SFL, Elgin City and Peterhead. The promotion/relegation play-off format between Scottish Football League divisions was introduced five years later, in 2005. The play-offs are contested between the ninth placed (second bottom) club in the higher division and the second, third and fourth placed clubs in the lower division. It is therefore possible for a team finishing fourth in the Second Division or Third Division to be promoted, rather than the clubs finishing immediately above them in the standings.

Back in 2010 the former First Minister of Scotland Henry McLeish conducted a review of how Scottish football was organised and recommended that Scottish football should have a single League body. After months of wrangling a merger between the Scottish Premier League and the Scottish Football League was formally agreed on 28th June 2014 and this created the Scottish Professional Football League (SPFL).

Scottish League football has lost four clubs this century. First to go was Clydebank, but only by a tortuous and convoluted route that actually started with the demise of the original Airdrieonians in 2002. Airdrieonians went out of business but quickly reformed as Airdrie United and sought to remain in the League applying for the vacancy created by the demise of the old club. However, they surprisingly lost out 16-11 in the voting as the other clubs preferred the bid submitted by Gretna. In a desperate attempt to keep senior football in the town the Airdrie Board sought approval to buy over Clydebank, who were both homeless and in administration, and gained agreement to relocate and rename the club, with Airdrie United taking their place in the SFL, and thereby starting a division higher than the newly elected Gretna.

Gretna had a dramatic but short-lived League career. Bankrolled by millionaire Brooks Mileson they won three successive divisional championships and promotions and made a Scottish Cup Final appearance but over stretched themselves in reaching the Premier League in 2007. When Mileson withdrew his funding due to illness the club collapsed in 2008.

2015 saw the introduction of a pyramid system in Scotland to replace the practice of clubs being voted into the League. For the first time teams from the Highland and Lowland Leagues could be promoted on merit to the Scottish Football League and thereby, by definition, clubs could be relegated too. The first round would see the winners of the two regional competitions play-off over the two legs, with the victors taking on the team that finished bottom of the SFL, also in a two-legged affair. This mechanism has seen the relegation of two further League clubs.

Montrose, East Stirlingshire, Cowdenbeath twice and then Berwick Rangers have been the League clubs involved in the play-offs. Three of the first four ties were settled by a single goal and the other by penalties. In 2015 Montrose became the first club to face a play-off to stay in the League. They beat the Highland League champions Brora Rangers in the two legged play-off, winning 3-2 on aggregate, twice coming from behind.

In May 2016 East Stirlingshire became the first Scottish League side to be relegated out of the League, ending a 61 year stay, when they were beaten 2-1 on aggregate by the Lowland league champions Edinburgh City. This club was going to have a chapter all of its own after leaving the League in 1949 but instead they became the first non-League club to earn promotion to the Scottish Football League.

After East Stirlingshire had lost their place in 2016 Cowdenbeath faced two consecutive playoffs, beating Lowland League champions East Kilbride 5-3 on penalties in 2017, and then Highland League Cove Rangers 3-2 on aggregate in 2018. In May 2019 Berwick Rangers' 68 year stay ended when they were beaten by the Highland League champions Cove Rangers.

In the spring of 2020 Angus based club Brechin City were firmly anchored at the bottom of the League in the 2019-20 season and facing a relegation play-off. They entered the League in 1923 as one of the sides to join the new and ill-fated Third Division. When this was disbanded in 1926 they left but returned shortly afterwards in 1929 when other teams dropped out. In 2017 they were playing in the second tier of Scottish League football having been surprisingly promoted via the play-offs. However, they then suffered the ignominy of becoming the first senior Scottish side in 126 years to go a whole League season without a win, matching Vale of Leven. Brechin ended the 2017–18 season with 0 wins, 4 draws, 32 defeats and no away points at all. They were expected to bounce back but instead suffered back to back relegations. They survived the prospect of a third successive relegation which would have ended their Scottish Football League status altogether, when the COVID-19 Coronavirus brought a premature end to the season.

Abercorn

Formed: 1877

Colours: White shirts, blue shorts

Grounds: Underwood Park (1890-99); Old Ralston Park (1899–1909); New Ralston Park; (1909–1920)

Entered League: 1890. Founder members of the Scottish Football League

Number of League Seasons: 25

Highest League Finish: 7th in Division One

Honours: Second Division Champions 1895-96, 1908-09

Left League: 1915 Due to the War. Joined the Western League. Did not re-join. Wound up 1922

Our tour of the former members of the Scottish Football League starts in the town of Paisley, Scotland's fifth most populous urban centre, located ten miles west of Glasgow. Followers of Scottish football would be aware that Paisley is currently represented by St Mirren, who were founded in 1877 and who are named after Saint Mirin, the founder of a church at the site of Paisley Abbey and Patron Saint of Paisley. In 1883 they moved to what was their third ground, Westmarch, and in 1894 they moved to Love Street, which is the ground they are most often associated with, staying there until 2009. St Mirren are one of the original founders of the Scottish Football League. What many people might not be aware of was that Paisley had a second representative, as a founding member. Abercorn, known as 'The Abbies' were based in the east end of Paisley and were formed in November 1877, just a couple of months after St Mirren.

Prior to the formation of the Scottish Football League Abercorn reached the Semi-final stage of the Scottish Cup only to be thrashed 10-1 by Cambuslang. One of the eleven original members of the Scottish Football League, they suffered the indignity of having to apply for re-election in each of their first three seasons. Abercorn were also founder members of the Second Division when they failed re-election in 1893, being placed in the new Second Division when it was formed for the 1893-94 season. There was no automatic promotion or relegation at that stage, the issue being decided by a vote of the First Division clubs. In 1896 Abercorn won the Second Division championship and replaced Dumbarton in the top division, but the following season they went back down again.

In 1909 the club won the Second Division championship but this time they failed to be elected to the First Division. They went on to win the Scottish Qualifying Cup in 1912. In 1915 the Second Division was suspended and the members formed two regional competitions, Abercorn joining the Western League where they competed until 1920 when the lease on their New Ralston Ground expired. Unable to secure a new home, the club resigned from the Western League and the following season (1920-21) played only one fixture, a heavy defeat at the hands of Vale of Leven in the Scottish Cup. This was to be their last match but the club continued to exist until 29th March 1922 when they were expelled from the Scottish FA because they had no home ground and were unable to fulfil any fixtures. Overall they competed in the Scottish League for 25 seasons, between 1890 to 1915, four of which were in the top flight, and they were twice Second Division champions. Six Abercorn players also went onto represent their country while at the club, five of them prior to the formation of the Scottish Football League.

During their short existence, Abercorn played at five different homes. Their home matches were initially played at East Park on the corner of Seedhill Road and Mill Street, in the area around Bank Street and Cochrane Street. Abercorn played their first match at East Park on the 16th February 1878 against St Mirren. It wasn't to be a good occasion for them as they went down 7-0! In the two years at East Park most matches were against local opposition and there were no competitive matches played before they moved to Blackstoun Park in Well Street in 1879 where they played for the next ten years. Following Abercorn's departure, East Park was home to Paisley Athletic for a number of years.

In 1878 Abercorn were founder members of the Renfrewshire Football Association who competed for their own trophy independent of the Scottish Cup. The Renfrewshire Cup is the third longest running competition in Scottish football behind the Scottish Cup and the East of Scotland Shield. Abercorn went on to win the trophy five times (1885-86, 1886-87, 1888-89, 1889-90 and 1891-92)

Their new ground, Blackstoun Park was located near the gasworks at Lonewells and was opened on the 6th September 1879 for a game against Western of Glasgow, the Abbies recording a 2-0 win. Blackstoun Park was to see the first national competitive competition for the Abbies when they entered the Scottish Cup in 1880-81. The first match was a First Round tie against Barrhead in 1880 which was memorable for Abercorn as they ran out 7-1 winners. The Abbies knocked out Greenock Morton in the next round before losing the Paisley derby game in the Third Round, losing at home to St Mirren 4-1 on the 23rd October 1880. In both the 1882-83 and 1883-84 seasons they made it to the Fourth Round. In the first of these they recorded a big win in the opening round, beating Ladyburn of Greenock 10-0 on the 10th September 1882.

In January 1884, John Goudie, the club's centre-forward and William Fulton, a back, became Abercorn's first Scotland internationals, both winning their one and only cap in a 5-0 win over Ireland in Belfast in which Goudie scored the third goal.

The 1885-86 season was a memorable one for the Abbies as they reached the Fifth Round of the Scottish Cup and won their first Renfrewshire Cup. In the national competition Abercorn secured Paisley boasting rights by knocking St Mirren out in the First Round, winning 2-0 at Blackstoun Park. After knocking out Renfrew, Thornliebank and Strathmore (of Arbroath) they lost narrowly to Cambuslang by a solitary goal. Consolation came in the form of a thrilling 6-5 win over Morton in the semi-finals of the Renfrewshire Cup. A month later, on the 20th March, Abercorn beat Port Glasgow Athletic, the holders, 4-0 in the final at Cappielow Park, Greenock before a crowd of 7,000 to win their first Renfrewshire Cup. After a goalless first half Abercorn opened the scoring ten minutes into the second half. As Port pushed for an equaliser they left gaps at the back which Abercorn exploited to add two more. One of the members of the team, Robert McCormick, playing at outside-right, was capped for Scotland a month later, scoring the first goal in a 4-1 win against Wales at Hampden. He subsequently moved to England in 1889 and played for Stoke City.

Port Glasgow got a modicum of revenge by knocking Abercorn out of the Scottish Cup the following season, winning 5-1 in Paisley. However, the Abbies went on to retain the Renfrewshire Cup, beating Arthurlie 5-1 at St Mirren's Westmarch ground. The club were thwarted in going for three Renfrewshire Cups in a row when they were beaten in the final by their arch-rivals St Mirren in the 1887-88 competition. The first final, played at Cappielow was drawn 2-2. In the replay St Mirren won comfortably by 4-1. Abercorn opened the scoring after already having hit the crossbar but Saints hit back to lead 2-1 at half-time. Their opponents started the second half the stronger and scored a third, adding a fourth five minutes from time.

In the Scottish Cup Abercorn reached their first Semi-final, although their marvellous Cup run came to a rather ignominious end, as they lost to Cambuslang by a 10–1 scoreline, which is a joint record margin of defeat for the Semi-final stage of the Scottish Cup. On the way to the semis the Abbies dished out some thrashings of their own, beating Johnstone Harp 9-0, Neilston 6-0 and in the Fifth Round, St Bernard's 9-0. In the last of these games the St Bernard's 'keeper had made half a dozen saves before he was eventually beaten by a low shot from Neil Munro. This opened the floodgates and the same player quickly scored a second, third and fourth. Martin scored a fifth and Robert McCormick a sixth before Munro added to his tally. McCormick got his second and his side's eighth before the two teams crossed over. On the resumption McLardie scored Abercorn's ninth goal. St Bernard's had to play much of the match with ten men. Having then disposed of Arbroath in the Quarter-finals, after a replay, Abercorn were drawn at home to Cambuslang, in a time when the Semi-finals weren't played on a neutral ground.

In an evenly matched contest at Blackstoun in front of a crowd of 7,000, Abercorn's McCormick unselfishly set up Buchanan for the opener and only goal of the first half. Cambuslang made determined efforts to equalise on the resumption but found Clark in the Abercorn goal in inspired form. Maintaining their pressure though, their opponents did succeed and then pushed on for the winner. Some heroic but anxious defending by the home team meant that the match ended in a draw.

A week later the clubs met at Whitefield Park, the home of Cambuslang for the replay. Abercorn started the stronger but it was their hosts who opened the scoring after 25 minutes. Abercorn responded almost immediately to level matters but Cambuslang restored their lead just before the interval. Early in the second half a breakaway led by McLardie nearly resulted in Abercorn drawing level but in end-to-end action Cambuslang immediately went down the other end and extended their advantage. Almost from the restart Cambuslang scored again to now lead 4-1 and the Abercorn heads went down. It soon turned into a rout as their hosts scored six more times to win 10-1.

A couple of months later outside-left Neil Munro was capped for Scotland in a 5-1 victory against Wales on the 10th March 1888. He scored the second goal. The only Abercorn player to be capped more than once he also featured against England at the Oval in April 1889. He also scored in this game, Scotland's first in a 3-2 defeat. He left the club in May 1890 to go to the USA. Also in the Scotland side that played Wales at Easter Road was Abercorn's right-half, James Johnston, who won his only cap.

In the 1888-89 Scottish Cup completion Abercorn again had a good Scottish Cup run. After a bye in the First Round they knocked out Morton 4-1 and Thornliebank 8-0, both away from home, before being drawn at home to Our Boys of Dundee. The two sides met on the 3rd November 1888 and with the wind in their favour Abercorn scored nine goals in the first half through McLardie (3), Raeside (3), Munro (2) and McCormick. The *Glasgow Herald* commented that "the striking contrast between the two teams was shown by the Abercorn being able to exhibit good work against the wind, in which their opponents had failed." McCormick made it ten with his second. Our Boys got a well-earned consultation before Raeside made it 11-1 to complete the rout.

They were knocked out by the eventual winners Third Lanark, but only after four matches. Regional Cup success continued with their fourth Renfrewshire Cup final in a row. For the second successive season Abercorn and St Mirren reached the final, offering up to the Abbies a chance for revenge. On the 23rd Mach 1889 Abercorn won 3-2 at Cappielow Park to lift their third Renfrewshire Cup in four seasons. In the game the Abbies scored first but Saints led 2-1 at the interval. On the hour mark Abercorn got on level terms and they took the lead 15 minutes later. Saints strived to equalise themselves but to no avail.

After ten years at Blackstoun Park it was a short 200 yard move to Underwood Park, located near the cleansing department on St James' Street. The 1889-90 season was their last before the formation of the Scottish Football League and it was another successful season as they successfully defended their Renfrewshire Cup and won through to a second Scottish Cup semi-final. In the First Round of the Scottish Cup Abercorn beat Lochwinnich 10-1 after their opponents had surrendered home advantage. In the Second Round they amazingly matched this score at Underwood Park, beating Thornliebank 10-1. In this match Harry Raeside scored after five minutes and scored a second soon after. From the re-start Raeside notched his hat-trick and two minutes later Nicol made it four. Raeside quickly scored a fifth. Thornliebank now raised their game and hit the crossbar after enjoying a good passage of play. But just in the stroke of half-time Raeside scored again. The two teams crossed over with Abercorn leading 6-0, and Raeside personally had five. Thornliebank started the brightest in the second half but their shooting let them down. No such problems for Abercorn as McLardie scored a seventh, and soon after an eighth. Thornliebank now succeeded in getting a goal but Abercorn retaliated and Raeside scored a ninth and a tenth was scrambled in near the close.

Having disposed of Stevenson Thistle and Airdrieonians they then beat Cowdenbeath away 8-2 in the Fifth Round. The home team opened the scoring within three minutes of the start of the game. Abercorn equalised about ten minutes later and went on to score three more times before the interval and four in the second half. Cowdenbeath got a second goal and Harry Raeside scored five goals in the match. Abercorn went on to beat Hibs 6-2 in the Quarter-finals but lost to the eventual winners Queen's Park in the Semi-final. Back in the Renfrewshire Cup they had better fortune in this Semi-final, beating arch-rivals St Mirren 6-1 despite conceding first. The sides were level at the break but McLardie scored a second half hat-trick, to reach their fifth Final in a row. In the final, played at St Mirren's Westmarch ground, Abercorn beat Port Glasgow

Athletic to lift the trophy for the fourth time in five seasons. In a tight game, Abercorn scored the only goal of the game with fifteen minutes remaining.

In March 1890 Underwood Park was chosen to host the first international football match held in Paisley when Scotland entertained Wales. Scotland won the game 5-0. A few days before Abercorn had sent a representative to Holton's Hotel in Glasgow, to join a meeting convened to discuss the proposal to form a Scottish Football League along the lines of the English League, with the exception of professionalism. The motion was passed and a committee was formed. On the 3rd June the Scottish Football League was formally constituted at a meeting held in Aitken's Hotel, Glasgow. The original office-bearers elected were Mr A Lawrence of Dumbarton as Chairman; Mr George Henderson of Cowlairs as Vice-Chairman; Mr John H McLaughlin of Celtic as Secretary and Mr William Wilton of Rangers as treasurer. Abercorn entered the League as one of the founder members and the fixtures for the inaugural season were agreed. On the 16th August 1890 eight of the eleven clubs founding the League kicked off but Abercorn were not involved.

Abercorn played their opening League game on the 30th August 1890, a 2-1 reverse at Milburn Park against Vale of Leven, who recorded their first win having already played twice. A full report on the match appeared in *The Scotsman*: "these teams met on the Vale's ground at Alexandria, and were both strongly represented. This was Abercorn's first match in the League competitions. Rankin kicked off for the Vale, and immediately thereafter Murdoch tried a long shot at Wilson's goal, but it was too long to be dangerous. The Paisley men, however, brought the ball back to close quarters, and for a few seconds the Vale goal was in some danger, but Murray with a strong kick opened up the play, and Rankin, getting possession, set off at a rattling pace, and was only brought up – or, more correctly, brought down – at the opposite goal by having his feet opportunely knocked from under him. The free kick given only resulted in the ball being sent through without any one touching it. From the kick-off the Vale left wing opened negotiations with Duff, the goal-keeper, but Rankin closed for the time by sending the ball somewhere between the crossbar and the sun. The Abercorn forwards, with a nice bit of combined play, transferred play to the opposite end, where Raeside when about to shoot was neatly deprived of the ball...A corner fell to the Vale which Cuthbert headed out, but McNicol was in a good position, and with a hard shot beat Duff. From the kick-off the visitors had a good look in, and Murray, falling, gave Buchanan a splendid chance to equalise, but he shot wide. A minute later Bruce got a similar chance at the opposite end, but bungled it in the same way. The Abercorn men strove hard to equalise, and Raeside and Buchanan sent in some splendid shots, which Wilson stopped magnificently. Half time was called without further scoring. The second half was just begun when a misunderstanding between the Vale backs again gave Buchanan an opening; he lost no time in taking advantage of it, and a goal was only averted by Wilson's wonderful saving. The Paisley men hovered round the Vale goal, but Murray was on the alert, and several times saved with his head when a goal seemed imminent. Three corners fell to the visitors in quick succession, but neither of them was productive. A corner fell to the Vale, and the ball, being dropped into the goal mouth, was headed through...Ten minutes later, from a corner kick, Raeside reduced the Vale majority by one point. Both teams struggled hard to add to their score, and each goal was in turn strongly assailed; but time was called with the positions unchanged, the Vale winning by two goals to one." The first ever Abercorn team to take the field in an SFL match was: Andrew Duff; Cuthbertson, Bisland; Reid, James Bowie, Johnstone; John Bonnar, Robert Buchanan, Harry Raeside, Tom Nicol and Murdoch.

The first SFL game played at Underwood Park was on the 13th September 1890 against Renton. Abercorn made two changes – James Fleming replaced Duff in goal and Wallace replaced Murdoch amongst the forwards. Renton opened the scoring in the first few minutes which roused Abercorn, the *Glasgow Herald* commenting that "the point was so quickly taken that even the spectators were surprised at the suddenness of the goal obtained. Annoyed at this, the Abercorn endeavoured...and strove hard indeed." Their reward soon came and Wallace equalised following a fine pass by Bonnar. This was followed shortly afterwards by Robert Buchanan putting Abercorn into the lead. Renton tried hard to force an equaliser but following a long kick out of defence by Cuthbertson, Raeside scored his side's third goal. Following a goalmouth scramble the referee contentiously awarded Renton a second goal, ruling the ball had crossed the line and two minutes later he blew for half-time with the home team 3-2 up. Taking up the story of the second half, the *Glasgow Herald* reported that "there was to be no falling off in the high chase style of play which had characterised the opening portion. In the midst of a scrimmage Buchanan beat Gow for the fourth time. All round, the Abercorn were playing a magnificent game, and their play was giving great satisfaction to their supporters. Equally must it be said for the once Scottish champions that they were playing well and pluckily, though they could not further score. A good game ended – Abercorn, 4 goals; Renton, 2 goals." Unfortunately following Renton's expulsion from the League a few weeks later the record of games involving them were expunged.

A week later Abercorn lost the first Paisley derby League game losing to St Mirren 4-2 at Westmarch. Saints opened the scoring and just before half-time doubled their lead when Fleming, in goal for Abercorn, let a shot slip through his hands. Play was more even in the second half with both teams scoring twice. On the 11th October they lost to League leaders and eventual joint champions Dumbarton 5-1 away, despite opening the scoring after ten minutes. Dumbarton immediately pegged them back and despite some stoic defence were not to be denied, at first equalising and then going ahead two minutes before the break. In the second half Abercorn were overran by their opponents and eventually lost 5-1, having also lost Bowie to injury before the close.

Disregarding the Renton match Abercorn effectively lost their first seven League fixtures up to the 2-1 home defeat against Dumbarton on the 27th December. They dominated early in this game and Nicol opened the scoring. They made lots of attempts to add to their score, coming close on a number of occasions. They were to rue those missed chances as Dumbarton equalised before half-time and then took the lead early in the second period. Picking up on the match *The Scotsman* reported that "from this time till the close of the game the home team showed superior play to that of the strangers, but were unable to score, and a fast and exciting game ended in favour of the Dumbarton by two goals to one."

Abercorn were knocked out of the Renfrewshire Cup by St Mirren in the Second Round but fared better in the Scottish Cup and reached their third Semi-final. Along the way they beat Irvine 8-0 and Cathcart 12-0. After knocking out Linthouse in the next round three they beat Bathgate Rovers 8-0, Tom Nicol scoring a hat-trick. After a bye in Round Five they met Leith Athletic away at Bank Park in the Quarter-final. Raeside scored early and Bonnar added a second for the Abbies to lead 2-0 at the break. Leith improved in the second half and got back on level terms and had a third disallowed for handball. Abercorn also had third ruled out when the referee ruled that the ball had not crossed the line, and shortly afterwards Leith hit a post, McQueen one of the Leith backs was then sent off for kicking an opponent number. The numerical advantage counted and Abercorn scrambled a winner in added time. Leith subsequently protested at the result, citing numerous grounds including the state of pitch, the disallowed goal and the sending off, but the SFA ruled against them and the result stood. On the 17th January 1891 Abercorn were beaten in the Semi-final by eventual runners up Dumbarton 3-1 who proved too strong at Boghead and who led 3-0 before a late consolation by Raeside.

A week later Abercorn recorded their first League win and it was a sweet one as it came in the reverse fixture of the Paisley derby. Saints created the first opening but then found themselves under a period of sustained pressure which ultimately paid dividends when Buchanan scored the opening goal for Abercorn. This early reverse stirred up the St Mirren team who responded with a period of dominance of their own which also resulted in a goal, and the two sides went into the break on level terms. Within a minute of the restart Raeside had restored Abercorn's advantage and the *Glasgow Herald* commented that "following up the advantage they had gained, the Abercorn pressed with all their eagerness and dash against the Westmarch men.

26

Johnstone, Bowie and Reid were doing excellent work in confining the Saints to their own half, whilst the forward lot were not giving the St Mirren defenders time to steady themselves." With their tails up Buchanan added a third, and a fourth came from a headed own-goal, before a long range effort from Wallace gave Abercorn a fifth and completed the scoring. The result would prove to be their best ever SFL win over St Mirren.

The Abbies followed this up with a creditable 1-1 draw at home to second placed Rangers, who would end up being joint champions at the end of the season. Their next game was an entertaining one against bottom club Cowlairs. Their hosts dominated first period and going into the interval led 4-0. Abercorn scored three quick goals in succession at the start of the second half but late goals from Cowlairs gave them the points as they won the game 7-5. The result took Cowlairs above Abercorn in the table but Cowlairs were subsequently docked four points for fielding an ineligible player. The defeat marked Harry Raeside's last game, as he was then transferred to Preston North End.

In their next game they recorded a season's best win, as they beat Vale of Leven 6-0, who were missing half a dozen regulars. Cree was promoted from the second eleven to take the place of Raeside. Half an hour's play had gone before Nicol opened the scoring and shortly afterwards the same player scored again. *The Scotsman* commented that "Cree, whose smartness and clever passing were largely instrumental in bringing about the win for the home team, was highly commended by the spectators as a successor to Raeside. He scored a third goal shortly after restarting, and Bowie, a few minutes later, registered a fourth point. During this half the Vale only visited the Abercorn goal three times, and before the call of the time the latter had increased their score to six goals, whole the Vale had nothing to their credit."

A fortnight later they beat Cowlairs 1-0, although they were missing Robert Buchanan, at inside-right, who was on international duty. He is the only Abercorn player to be capped during their tenure as a League club. He scored Scotland's third goal in a 4-3 win over Wales in Wrexham. The League win was the start of a run of four games unbeaten, in which they won three of them, including a nine goal thriller at Cambuslang. Initial play was in the Abercorn half but they survived this period with their goal intact and in the 15th minute took the lead through Bonnar. A minute later Nicol added a second and after their hosts had briefly threatened to get back into the game they scored two more goals in quick succession. Undeterred, Cambuslang, continued to press and were rewarded for their efforts with their opening goal just before the break. On resuming Cambuslang continued their comeback from four-nil down and scored two goals to get within one of Abercorn. Buchanan provided some breathing space with a well-directed shot for number five but Cambuslang were not finished and scrambled in a fourth to set up a tense finish, but Abercorn held out to edge the nine-goal thriller. At the end of April Thomas Nicol got the only goal of the game in a home win over Hearts but Abercorn lost their two remaining games to eventually finish in seventh place, which would prove to be their best League finish.

For the second SFL season the First Division was expanded to 12 teams. Clyde and Leith Athletic came in, as did the previously expelled Renton, and Cowlairs dropped out. This time Abercorn finished in ninth place. They again took the local bragging rights as St Mirren were one place lower. Abercorn had two more points than their Paisley rivals, who faced a re-election vote along with Cambuslang and Vale of Leven. The Saints survived, the other two didn't. The new season didn't get off to a great start as they lost 8-1 against joint champions Dumbarton on the 22nd August 1891. By the end of the season Dumbarton would be champions in their own right. 3,500 fans were present to see the home team unfurl the joint championship flag. Back on the pitch, the home team scored four in each half. Abercorn beat one of the new clubs, Leith Athletic, in their next game, winning 3-2 after leading 3-0 at one point. They followed this up with a 3-0 win away at Vale of Leven, with Robert McClung scoring a hat-trick. A week later Abercorn's highest League attendance at Underwood Park was set when 6,000 saw a 5–2 defeat to Celtic on the 12th September 1891.

A month later Abercorn recorded their best result of the season, a 6-3 win over Vale of Leven, who were winless during the season. The Abbies had trailed 2-0 before getting it back to 2-2 before going behind again before the break. They equalised within three mins of the restart and had matters their own way for the rest of the match. At the end of January they suffered a 7-2 loss at Clyde but back-to-back wins in February, including a 3-0 derby win at Westmarch, took them up as high as sixth but they failed to win any of their remaining five fixtures. Fortunes were mixed in the Cup competitions.
They made a First Round Scottish Cup exit at the hands of Queen's Park but did win their fifth and final Renfrewshire Cup. Abercorn came from behind to beat St Mirren 2-1 at Cappielow.

For the 1892-93 season the League reverted back to a ten team division, with Vale of Leven and Cambuslang having dropped out, town rivals St Mirren having survived at the League's AGM. Abercorn again came ninth, but this time that was second bottom, which meant a re-election vote of their own. St Mirren were much improved, finishing in third place. Abercorn got off to a terrible start, losing eight of their first nine games. They lost 4-0 at home to Rangers in the opening game at Underwood Park in front of 5,000. Undone by playing against a strong breeze they were 3-0 down when ends were switched. The second half was much more even and Rangers only got a fourth in the

85th minute. In mid-September they lost 4-0 in the Paisley derby. Abercorn dominated the early play and McLardie, Munro and McGee passed up good opportunities. St Mirren then scored and got a second ten minutes before half-time. Their hosts dominated the second half to run out 4-0 winners, meaning Abercorn had lost all four League matches they had played. This then became five straight losses, conceding 20 goals in the process, before getting their first points with a narrow 1-0 win over Leith Athletic. They scored in the 47th minute after a goalmouth scramble following a rare corner. The visitors continued to press but Jamieson was up to it and the Leith men's efforts were all in vain. Abercorn lost heavily in their next game against Third Lanark. Play was fairly even initially but once Thirds got the first goal they scored at regular intervals to lead 5-0 at half-time and Abercorn went on to lose 8-0. They lost their next game 5-1 against Dumbarton, but then beat Clyde by the same score to register their second win and move off the bottom, above their vanquished opponents.

In late November they beat Renton 6-0 in the First Round of the Scottish Cup, but lost a nine goal thriller at home to Third Lanark in the next round. In this Cup tie Abercorn started well and rained efforts in on the Third Lanark goal and eventually taking the lead through Harry Millar. After some pressure by the away team Bonnar broke away and scored a second so that Abercorn went into the interval with a two goal lead. After the restart Bonnar scored a third but a long range effort got a goal back for Thirds and two minutes later it was 3-2. McLardie then made it 4-2 but it was almost immediately back to 4-3 and a few minutes later 4-4. The excitement was intense with ten minutes left to play as both sides pushed for a winner. Near the end Abercorn had a corner, but Third Lanark cleared their lines and broke fast and scored the winner.

Back in the League St Mirren did the double over them and the home loss left them in ninth place, with only Clyde below them. Abercorn scored first and kept up the pressure but found the St Mirren goalkeeper, Patrick, in inspired form. He kept his team in it and St Mirren then scored two goals in two minutes against the run of play. In the last ten minutes Abercorn strove hard to get on level terms but ultimately lost 2-1.

At the end of March Abercorn got an unexpected point away at Leith Athletic, their equalising goal through McLardie having a touch of handball in the build-up. The *Glasgow Herald* reported that "the game was evenly contested; but on both sides the shooting was wretched, and neither team added to their score." This was the only point they earned away from home in the whole of the campaign.

Abercorn surprisingly won their last two League fixtures. They beat Dumbarton 4-0, which was a terrific result as they were missing McLardie and Kirkwood who had been chosen to play against Ireland in the Irish International League match. Miller scored against the run of play for a 1-0 half-time lead. Then, after early Dumbarton pressure Boyd made it 2-0, immediately followed by Barr for 3-0. A fourth came from an own goal following a goalmouth scramble. They then beat Third Lanark 5-2. After an uneventful first twenty minutes Abercorn scored two through Barr and McLardie. In the second half Barr made it 3-0 before Thirds came back into it. Boyd scored a fourth and McLardie the fifth. Despite these two late wins Abercorn only picked up 11 points. Leith Athletic in seventh place had 17 points so the Abbies were six points adrift from avoiding the vote.

At the League's AGM on the 2nd June 1893 Abercorn came in a poor fifth and bottom in the re-election vote. Renton who had finished in eighth place got 12 votes. Dundee, who were a new club formed by the amalgamation of Our Boys and East End also got 12. St Bernard's got 8, bottom side Clyde got 7, and Abercorn could manage only 2 votes and dropped out of the League, along with Clyde.

Their League status was preserved however. At the June AGM, Hibernian, Cowlairs, Morton, Partick Thistle, Port-Glasgow Athletic, and Thistle had all expressed an interest in joining the League, although they didn't participate in the actual voting. With sufficient interest from clubs the Scottish Football League decided to form a Second Division on the 7th July 1893. The principal non-League competition, the Scottish Alliance, wanted their members to automatically form the new section but the League themselves took on the responsibility of selecting the clubs. On the 10th July, Abercorn and Clyde, who were not re-elected at the initial AGM, were granted a place in the new section, along with Hibernian. Abercorn thus became founder members of the Second Division with these two clubs and with ex-League club Cowlairs, and then Greenock Morton, Motherwell, Northern (Glasgow), Partick Thistle, Port Glasgow Athletic and Thistle (Glasgow) making up the remaining sides.

Abercorn's first season in the Second Division was something of a disappointment. The prospects of a good campaign, a possible title and the chance of being elected back to the top flight were undermined by a poor start to the 1893-94 season. Whilst Clyde were re-elected back to the First Division in place of Renton, despite only finishing in third behind champions Hibernian and Cowlairs, Abercorn struggled and could only manage seventh place in a ten team division, only one place from participating in another vote.

Their first game in the new second tier was a 3-2 home defeat against Motherwell on the 29th August 1893. Goalkeeper William McCann made a series of saves to keep them in it after Motherwell had taken an early lead and McLardie had got an equaliser before the break. After the resumption Munro put the home team ahead. Motherwell equalised and got a soft goal as the winner, a few minutes from time.

In all, Abercorn lost four of their first five games in the new division including a 7-2 loss at Easter Road against Hibernian in mid-September. *The Scotsman* reported that "both elevens were powerfully represented, and as on all former occasions the Paisley eleven has managed to give a good display in the eastern capital, a very close game was looked for. In the first period the contest was a very even one, ends being changed with the score two goals each, but in the second half the Hibernian soon asserted their superiority, and eventually ran out winners of an interesting game by seven goals to two." Abercorn actually led 2-1 through goals by Miller and McLardie at one stage. Their first win came against Partick Thistle, 3-0 away. The home team had a goal disallowed for offside before McLardie scored. The same player got his second after the sides had switched ends and Barr added a third late on. Abercorn had a good Scottish Cup run, reaching the Third Round, only going out to ten time winners and eventual Semi-finalists Queen's Park after a second replay. Their League form remained poor and in late February 1894 they lost to Cowlairs 7-1 and ultimately finished seventh with only five wins and two draws.

There was no real improvement in the 1894-95 season as they finished a place lower in eighth, and as they were in the bottom three this meant they faced a re-election vote. They won their opening game 3-0 against Cowlairs but then lost the next four games heavily, 5-1 at home to Hibs, 7-0 away at Motherwell, 5-1 away at Morton and also 5-1 at Port Glasgow Athletic. These results left them joint bottom with Cowlairs with just two points.

In December Renton beat Abercorn 8-2 who "turned up minus their goalkeeper and had to play a substitute. The player, unfortunately, was not much of a goalkeeper, and in the first half of the game lost six goals" (*The Scotsman*). 1895 saw an upturn in their fortunes and they went on a seven match unbeaten run. Included in this was their record SFL win, a 9-2 victory over Dundee Wanderers, a new side in the division, on the 13th April 1895. In a one-sided contest Abercorn opened the scoring after five minutes through McGuire but a mistake by their 'keeper, Clark, allowed the visitors back on level terms. Abercorn then scored four goals to make it 5-1 at half-time. Ten minutes of constant home pressure after the break resulted in McClung making it 6-1. Dundee Wanderers got another back before Abercorn scored three more. The run had lifted them up to eighth place, above Wanderers, with Cowlairs at the bottom. Abercorn were now level on points with the other new club Airdrieonians and were five ahead of Dundee Wanderers. The run came to an end the following Saturday losing 4-0 at Airdrieonians. This defeat consigned them to finish in the bottom three and face a re-election vote along with Dundee Wanderers and Cowlairs. At the Scottish Football League's AGM on the 3rd June 1895 Cowlairs (3 votes) and Dundee Wanderers (3) were not re-elected and were replaced by Kilmarnock (24) and Linthouse (24). Abercorn got 22 votes, well ahead of Raith Rovers who got 10.

The 1895-96 season saw a turnaround in fortunes as the club won the Second Division title and were elected back into the First Division. They carried their strong form from the beginning of 1895 into the new season, losing only one of seven games played in the rest of that calendar year. They won their first three games before losing 3-1 at Leith, who would be their championship rivals. In October they beat Airdrieonians 5-1. They led 3-1 at the interval and Airdrie were making a fight of it when they had a player retire hurt following a collision. In December they beat second placed Leith 4-0. This was only their seventh League fixture whereas current leaders Renton had played twice that number.

Abercorn had a bit of wobble in early 1896 but on the 29th February, and lying in mid-table, they beat Linthouse 6-1 away at Langlands Park. This was the first win in a run of six consecutive victories through to the end of the season which propelled them to the championship crown. They overtook Leith Athletic to take their first League honour by four points, having lost only three League games all season.

At the League's AGM held on the 26th May the bottom three clubs from the First Division – Dumbarton, Clyde and Paisley rivals St Mirren – were challenged by Abercorn, Leith Athletic and Renton (who got third place after a play-off against Kilmarnock). In the voting Abercorn regained their place in the First Division at the expense of the first ever League champions Dumbarton. Clyde got 14 votes, St Mirren 13 and Abercorn 8. Leith Athletic got 4 votes, Dumbarton could manage only 2 and Renton got 1.

Abercorn's return to the top flight was shortlived and their return was an unmitigated disaster. They finished tenth and bottom and came straight back down again following a re-election vote. What made it so bad was that the club set a new record for the lowest points total ever, securing just three points from their 18 matches. They recorded one win, one draw, and 16 losses, conceding 88 goals in just 18 games.

They opened their First Division campaign on the 22nd August 1896 against eventual champions Hearts and were thrashed 6-1, despite Bobby Walker getting an equaliser to Hearts' opening goal. Trailing 2-1 they conceded four goals in the last ten minutes with Willie Taylor getting a hat trick for Hearts. A week later they lost their second game 6-0 at home to Celtic, largely due to an injury to John Harvey sustained in the 20th minute, meaning they had to play the remainder of the game with ten men. Having conceded six in each of their opening matches they then preceded to let in eight in their third game, going down 8-3 at Third Lanark, having made a number of changes. They were bottom, pointless and had conceded 20 goals in just three matches.

In their fourth game, played on the 12th September, they secured their first point back in the top flight, a 2-2 draw at home to Hibernian. The Abbies came from behind to lead 2-1 before being pegged back. Their next game was the Paisley derby, which they lost 4-2. They then suffered two more heavy losses. The first of these, a 9-2 loss at home to Rangers was a club record SFL defeat. In this match they conceded after only five minutes but Walker equalised just two minutes later, much to the surprise of the crowd. Rangers quickly restored their lead but from a goalmouth scramble James Cleland, signed from St Bernard's, made it 2-2. However, the visitors then notched three goals in quick succession before half-time to lead 5-2. The second half was all one way traffic and when Rangers scored early on the *Glasgow Herald* commented that "the Paisley club seemed entirely disorganised after this, although it may be stated that the weather conditions were entirely against them." A week later they lost 6-2 away at Clyde and were now firmly at the bottom of the table, with one point from seven games, having let in 41 goals.

Their first, and only win, came at the end of October in the reverse Paisley derby. The game kicked off in a snowstorm with Saints making most of the running and forcing Traynor into a series of saves. Eventually the Abercorn 'keeper was beaten but two minutes later Hamilton equalised from a free kick. Parity only last a minute though as St Mirren restored their advantage but again they couldn't hold their lead as Hamilton again equalised and the teams went in level at the break. Saints had much of the early play after the restart and hit the woodwork. McKim scored the winning goal for the Abbies following a great through ball from Hamilton. *The Scotsman* reported that "the Saints now played desperately to get on level terms, and a little force was put into the play. Hamilton had to retire for some time through an injury. Till the close the game was fast and exciting, and ended in the Abercorn's first League victory by three goals to two." This was their first win of the campaign, at the tenth attempt.

Abercorn followed up the win with eight straight League losses. They lost 5-0 at Celtic in early November having conceded after a minute, and were losing 3-0 at the interval although *The Scotsman* commented that "on resuming the visitors exhibited rare dash." A fortnight later their biggest defeat came away at Hibs when they lost 9-0. In December they lost 6-1 at Rangers and then 6-0 at St Bernard's to end the year firmly at the bottom. The destination of the League title was getting interesting with only one point separating Celtic, Hearts, Hibs and Rangers. Not so at the bottom where the

Abbies only had three points from 17 games, five less than Clyde and nine off avoiding a re-election vote.

In between various Scottish Cup ties their disastrous League season concluded with an ignominious 7-1 home defeat against Dundee on the 16th January 1897. Abercorn had the better of the first quarter of an hour but then conceded. Dundee added a second and five minutes from the crossover a third. From the restart Abercorn scored. *The Scotsman* reported that "the second portion was resumed with great dash on both sides, and for fully twenty minutes neither side could claim the advantage." Dundee scored and Abercorn heads went down and they added three more. Abercorn's League record was: P18 W1 D1 L16 F21 A88 Pts3.

Unsurprisingly, after such a dreadful season, they were not re-elected to the First Division at the League's AGM held on the 1st June 1897, although it was a close run thing. They stood for re-election along with Clyde and Third Lanark against Second Division champions Patrick Thistle, Kilmarnock and Leith Athletic. In the final reckoning they only lost out by one vote. Third Lanark came first with 14 votes, Partick were elected into the top flight with 13, and Clyde took the last place with 8 votes to Abercorn's 7, the other two sides attracted no support. Despite winning the Second Division title a dozen years later Abercorn would never return to Scotland's top flight and spent the rest of their League history in the Second Division.

In the 1897-98 season they came a disappointing seventh place on their return to the Second Division, equal on points with Linthouse and Ayr. Despite winning their opening game 2-0 at home to Airdrieonians a dose of reality followed in the next game when they lost 7-1 to Kilmarnock - Killie would go on to win the championship. They recovered to be third but had a serious setback in mid-December when they lost 8-2 against Port Glasgow Athletic. Lappin opened the scoring for the Abbies but after that Port Glasgow pretty much had things their own way and they went into the break 3-1 down. Worse was to follow after the interval as the home team scored five more goals to Abercorn's one. After this Abercorn went on to only win one of their last six games, which was a 2-1 away win at Hamilton. The last three of these games were all at home and they only picked up one point.

The 1898-99 season was even worse as Abercorn finished tenth and bottom to record their lowest League placing ever, gaining only nine points from their 18 matches, losing 13 of them. They lost their opening game at Airdrie 3-2 despite leading 2-0 and went on to lose their opening four games before beating Hamilton 4-2, coming from 2-1 down. In their next game they lost to Ayr 7-4 to leave them bottom of the table, although level on points with Linthouse. Overall they 12 of their first 14 games including further heavy defeats against Leith Athletic (8-1) and Hamilton (6-1). They beat fellow strugglers Linthouse on Christmas Eve, recording their best win, in a 7-1 win, thanks to goals from McLay (2), Topping (2), Hunter, Adam and Bell. They also secured a fourth win of the season in mid-February 1899, beating Airdrieonians 3-1. Their final League match of the season was played at Underwood Park on the 8th April 1899, and ended in a 3–3 draw against Ayr. The Abbies had led 3-0 at half-time but blew their lead. They finished with only nine points, two less than Linthouse and four fewer than Ayr. Only the bottom two clubs were up for re-election to the League and these sides faced competition for the places from Raith Rovers, Arthurlie, Dundee Wanderers and Orion of Aberdeen. At the League's AGM held on the 30th May 1899 in Glasgow both teams were comfortably re-elected, Linthouse getting 37 votes, Abercorn 32 and their nearest challengers, Raith, only got 13 votes.

Abercorn moved to Ralston Park (later known as Old Ralston) for the start of season 1899-1900 and stands were built on either side of the pitch, one covered and one uncovered, with a pavilion brought from Underwood Park and an embankment on the eastern side of the pitch. The Abbies went on to play at the ground for the next ten seasons. The first League match was played on their new field on the 26th August 1899 when Abercorn beat Leith Athletic 3-0, Currie scoring two first half goals and McCrone adding a third late on.

In December the Abbies recorded two big wins, first, winning 6-0 away against Linthouse at Govandale, having only been in front 1-0 at the interval from a goal by Robertson. In the second half Abercorn scored five times through Campbell (2), Robertson, McIntyre and McDonald. The win lifted them out of the bottom two, above Ayr. They then beat Hamilton 5-0 at home. The Accies were bottom and winless, with only one point. Abercorn won a one-sided game to move up to sixth in the table and with plenty of games in hand on four of the teams above them. However, after a 4-1 win over Airdrieonians in mid-January 1900 they then lost five in a row to drop down and finished in sixth place.

The following season was quite a topsy-turvy one. After taking five points from their opening three games they then lost five in a row, scoring only one goal in a 5-1 defeat at Airdrie. This result left them second from bottom, just two points above Hamilton at the foot of the table. On the 1st December Abercorn beat Port Glasgow Athletic 3-0, which was the start of a run in December that brought three wins and a draw including a 5-1 win over Leith Athletic. On the 5th January 1901 they surprisingly lost 5-0 away at bottom club Hamilton. The game was played at Fir Park Motherwell due to storm damage at Douglas Park so perhaps the Paisley team lost their bearings! Abercorn then came with a charge winning seven and drawing two of their last ten games but they had left themselves too much to do and they finished in third place behind champions St Bernard's and Airdrieonians.

The next six seasons were poor as the club finished 11th, 10th, 10th, 11th, 10th and 9th and they went no further than the Second Round of the Scottish Cup. They started a run of five consecutive seasons where they always finished in the bottom three in the 1901-02 season, finishing eleven. Although they won their opening game 5-2 against on the 17th August 1901 they didn't win again until 30th November when they beat Leith. In that sequence of 13 games without a win they did pick up their one and only point on their travels, in a 1-1 draw against St Bernard's. They registered back-to-back wins against St Bernard's and East Stirling in early 1902 and finished joint bottom with Clyde. The First Division was increased to 12 clubs by promoting the top two of Port Glasgow and Partick. Abercorn were re-elected along with Clyde as two new clubs joined – Raith Rovers and Falkirk.

In the 1902-03 season they finished one place higher. They lost 15 out of 22 matches, earning fewer points but finishing higher. They beat fellow strugglers Clyde 5-1 away as part of an opening set of games where they won three out of their first six games but only won two more games and went winless from mid-November to early April. Clyde got their revenge winning 6-0 away at Old Ralston Park in the penultimate League game of the season. The only bright spot during this period was another appearance in the Renfrewshire Cup Final. Having monopolised the competition in the 1880s the competition in the 1890s and early 1900s had come to be dominated by St Mirren, Port Glasgow and Morton and it was the Greenock based side that Abercorn met, in what was a now two-legged Final in 1903. Morton won the first leg at Cappielow 2-1 and Abercorn won the return 1-0. Away goals weren't a factor so a play-off game was arranged at St Mirren, with Morton winning 4-0.

In the 1903-04 season Abercorn failed to win any of their first four matches but then won, in some style, beating Raith Rovers 7-3 on the 24th October, scoring five goals in the first half. The Abbies won three in a row from mid- November to early December to be seventh in the table but only won two more game to eventually finish in tenth place out of 12 teams, although they avoided a re-election vote which was now confined to just the bottom two.

There was no such luck the following year as they finished in the bottom two this time. Abercorn won four of their first seven matches, including a rare away win at Arthurlie, so that by the end of October they were third in the table. But a 5-1 defeat at Hamilton in early November started a poor run of results as they lost six out of the next seven. Following that away win at Arthurlie they lost their next ten away games. Following a 2-

1 win over Ayr on the 31st December 1904 Abercorn were in eighth place. They only won once more, in their last game of the season, against Aberdeen. They were still in eighth but East Stirlingshire and Aberdeen had games still to play. In the case of Aberdeen, they still had seven games to go when Abercorn had finished. Aberdeen were five points behind and beat Albion Rovers 7-2, Ayr 2-0 and then had three consecutive goalless draws to overhaul Abercorn and condemn them to a re-election vote along with St Bernard's.

The First Division was being expanded again so once again the odds were in Abercorn's favour as two new places were available in the Second Division along with the two retiring clubs. In total ten clubs were up for the four spaces. Abercorn and St Bernard's were both re-elected and were joined by Cowdenbeath and the returning Vale of Leven. Abercorn came second in the voting, getting 19 votes. St Bernard's topped the poll with 23. Cowdenbeath got 18 and Vale of Leven 17, with the next nearest being Ayr Parkhouse with 7 and Stenhousemuir with 6 votes.

The 1905-06 season was a modest improvement, finishing one place higher in tenth, and so avoiding another re-election vote. They made a poor start though, recording only three draws in their first eight matches and propping up the table by mid-November. They eventually recorded a win on the 18th November, winning 3-1 away at fellow strugglers East Stirlingshire at Merchiston Park. They then lost 5-1 at Raith and 4-1 at Vale of Leven before recording a second win just before Christmas, beating Arthurlie 4-2. They made it back-to-back wins with a 2-0 win over Ayr FC the following Saturday and ended 1905 in the bottom two, in eleventh place, one point ahead of East Stirling, but only a point behind both Vale of Leven and Cowdenbeath ahead of them. Abercorn won their first game of 1906, to make it three wins in a row, beating Clyde 1-0. They won four out of five at beginning of 1906 including a 4-0 win over Cowdenbeath, in which they scored two in each half and the visitors had a man sent off. They lost their last two matches to finish in ninth place, avoiding being involved in a re-election vote by one point.

The 1906-07 season saw another slight improvement as the Abbies lost only ten matches but then they won only five, picking up seven draws to finish in ninth place. They made another poor start, despite edging a seven goal thriller against East Stirlingshire in late August, and they lost five out of their first six matches including a 5-0 home defeat against Dumbarton and a 4-0 loss away at Albion Rovers. These results left them with just two points from six games, lying second from bottom, a point above winless Ayr FC. These two clubs met the following month at Somerset Park with Abercorn scoring in the first minute. Ayr had drawn level early in the second half but a few minutes from the close Abercorn scored a soft and lucky goal. They failed to win again in 1906 and at the turn of the year only one point separated the bottom six sides of Raith, Arthurlie, Abercorn, Ayr, Ayr Parkhouse and East Stirlingshire.

The year 1907 started well for the Abbies as re-election fears were eased by a 4-3 win at Arthurlie, in which they completed a remarkable turnaround having been 3-0 down at half-time. This was followed by a 3-1 home win over Leith Athletic and then three consecutive draws. A 2-0 win over Cowdenbeath on the last day of the season took them out of the bottom two and thus avoided another re-election vote by one point.

The end of the 1906-07 season had hinted at an improvement and they carried this form into the new season, making a good start for a change. Abercorn started brightly winning their first five games and were the only League side with a 100% record by the end of September. Key to their start was the goal scoring partnership of Caig and Curran, and a defence that was the best in the country. Things turned in the autumn though and the club didn't win a game during October and most of November and they dropped out of the top two, eventually winning again on the 30th November, when they won 1-0 at Arthurlie.

A brief recovery in a December was followed by a poor start to 1908. A 5-0 Scottish Cup exit at the hands of Hibernian was part of an eight game run without a win. Three consecutive draws in February saw them placed fourth and even though they won their last match, 3-2 away at Albion Rovers, they finished seven points off the top and four short of second place. Still, after six seasons of struggles a fourth-placed finish represented a much improved performance.

At the League's AGM on the 1st June, Abercorn, along with the top three sides in the Second Division, Raith Rovers, Dumbarton and Ayr challenged the two First Division sides facing re-election, Clyde and Port Glasgow Athletic. Perhaps their recent history of struggles counted against them as the Abbies secured only one vote. The Second Division champions, Raith, were the most popular of the challengers with 8 votes. Clyde, with 12 votes, and Port Glasgow with 9, were duly re-elected.

If a challenge for promotion failed to materialise after a good start in the previous season Abercorn came good in the 1908-09 season. They failed to win in any of their first three matches but a narrow 1-0 win over Raith Rovers at the beginning of October started an unbeaten run of six games, the highlight being a 5-2 win over Arthurlie on Halloween. The run took them up to second and in pursuit of leaders Raith Rovers. In mid-December they recorded a season's best 6-0 win over Cowdenbeath, scoring four in the first 25 minutes in a one-sided affair. The same teams met a week later in the Boxing Day fixture, Abercorn winning 2-0 away whilst leaders Raith lost 2-1 at

Dumbarton. The gap was now down to three points and the Abbies had two games in hand. The gap was narrowed to one point on the 9th January 1909 when Abercorn won 2-1 at Leith and Raith went down at home to Ayr by the same scoreline. Abercorn won their game in hand the following week to hit the front, leading by a point, and with a game in hand, and with four games left to play.

On the 6th February Abercorn drew 1-1 at home against third placed Vale of Leven, whilst Raith weren't in action. The result stretched their lead to two points with three games left apiece. The following Saturday Abercorn beat Ayr 1-0 whereas Raith could only draw 0-0 at home to Leith Athletic. The lead was now four points with two games to go. A week later Abercorn were not in action but a top two finish was confirmed when Raith lost 2-1 in Alexandria against Vale of Leven.

Abercorn completed their programme on 20th March, their final game at Old Ralston Park, with a 4-0 win over Ayr Parkhouse to finish on 31 points. Raith in second had 26 points but only one game left to play whereas Vale of Leven had 25 points but still had four to play and could therefore still claim the championship flag. However, Vale, having won the first of these games, lost at East Stirling and drew at Ayr Parkhouse to hand Abercorn the Second Division title by three points.

At the League's AGM Abercorn made the decision not to apply for membership of the First Division, perhaps discouraged by their lack of support the previous year. Runners-up Vale of Leven reached the same decision. Despite being the Second Division champions for the second time in their history Abercorn would continue to play in the second tier for the 1909-10 season.

Abercorn would be starting the new season at another ground. After the lease had expired at Old Ralston Park, Abercorn secured a new ten year lease on a park just to the west of their old pitch, across the Lady Burn, which became known as New Ralston Park. A new wooden stand was built but the pavilion at the old ground was continued to be used. The first League match at New Ralston Park was played on the 11th September 1909, with 2,000 spectators watching Abercorn win 2–1 against Ayr Parkhouse, who had also been their final opponents at Old Ralston Park. The old site was taken over by the neighbouring claypit and brickworks.

Abercorn were joint top at the end of October having won four out of five games played that month (and drawing the other) but they only won one game in November to drop to fourth and their challenge fizzled out and they eventually finished ten points adrift in fifth place. Abercorn reached another Renfrewshire Cup final having knocked

Morton out in the Semi-final. They faced St Mirren, now well established as the premier Paisley side in senior football, and lost the Final over two legs.

Rather bizarrely, Abercorn did put themselves forward for election this year but unsurprisingly they gathered little support. Morton were re-elected but the other First Division side, Port Glasgow accepted a place in the Second Division. Four teams were after the one remaining place, though not the champions Leith Athletic. Raith Rovers were elected to the top flight with 13 votes, one more than Ayr United. Abercorn only got one vote although Dumbarton got none.

After a couple of good seasons the 1910-11 season was a bit of a disaster as Abercorn's form slumped. They lost five of their six opening games of the new season including a 4-1 loss at Tannadice against new club Dundee Hibernian. They did win four in a row towards the end of the year but lost the first four matches of 1911, including a 4-1 home defeat against Leith Athletic and 5-1 away loss at Merchiston Park against East Stirlingshire. They were one of five clubs to finish at the bottom with 19 points. Port Glasgow Athletic decided to resign from the League and St Johnstone were the only applicants for the vacancy and so no re-election vote was held.

For the 1911-12 season Duncan Gribben, who had been secretary/manager between 1900-04, and who had presided over three re-election votes returned with the club's fortunes again at a low ebb and he got them to second place in his first season back. Abercorn lost their opening game against the eventual divisional champions Ayr United 4-2 on the 19th August 1911. They then went on a run of seven games unbeaten, including a 5-1 away win at Dumbarton, and by the end of October they were joint leaders with Leith Athletic and Ayr United.

At the turn of the year only one point separated a top four of Ayr, Abercorn, St Bernard's and Cowdenbeath. Abercorn beat St Bernard's in Edinburgh on the 6th January 1912 by one goal to nil but then lost by the same score line at home to Ayr United, missing a penalty that would have drawn the scores level. Ayr ultimately ran away with the championship, finishing five points ahead of Abercorn who were Second Division runners-up, themselves finishing three points above third placed Dumbarton.

The Scotsman, at the League's AGM, reported that "Celtic put forward a motion to the effect that the highest club in the Second Division should automatically pass into the First Division,and that the lowest club in the First Division should drop into the Second Division. The necessary two-thirds majority supported the motion, but it was ultimately agreed that in view of the fact that the motion involved the relegation of St Mirren, who had committed themselves to the First Division wage bill and other expenditure for next season, to the Second Division, it was decided to hold the matter over till next annual meeting." The decision was also taken to increase the Second Division to fourteen clubs. The bottom two sides – Albion Rovers and Vale of Leven - were unanimously re-elected and they were joined by Dunfermline Athletic and Johnstone.

Abercorn had another good campaign, this time coming in fourth in a close finish where only three points separated the top four teams. The new campaign started very promisingly with a 2-0 away win at champions Ayr United on 17th August 1912, *The Scotsman* reporting that "prior to the commencement of the match at Somerset Park, Ayr, Provost Hunter unfurled the League Championship flag. Play was very uninteresting for a time, neither team impressing. At length, following an attack by Abercorn, Wallace scored from a free kick. The second half favoured the United so far as outfield play was concerned, but in point of shooting the Ayr forwards were outclassed. A mid kick by Thomson gave Carson a chance, and he was not slow to accept it, Massey having no chance to save. Abercorn retired deserved winners by two goals to nothing."

Abercorn went the first ten games of the season unbeaten in a League programme disrupted by weather. This took its toll later as they had to play nine games in the month of April having taken from 17th August 1912 to the 4th January 1913 to play their first nine. Going into April they were lying in sixth, ten points behind leaders Ayr United and six behind East Stirlingshire but having played seven fewer games. The Abbies won two but lost two of the first four games but the three defeats against promotion rivals would prove costly - a 1-0 home loss and a 3-0 defeat in the reverse against Dunfermline and a 5-1 thrashing away at East Stirlingshire so that they eventually came in fourth.

At the League's AGM the decision to automatically promote and relegate the top and bottom side was overlooked due to an expansion in the number of First Division clubs, which went from 18 to 20 clubs, with the Second Division reverting back to 12 teams. Partick and Queen's Park were unanimously re-elected and Ayr United, who won the Second Division title again joined them in the First Division. Dumbarton, who finished in sixth place, two below Abercorn, were elected over Cowdenbeath on the chairman's vote. Dunfermline Athletic and Dundee Hibs got 4 and 3 votes respectively, whereas Abercorn, along with St Bernard's, didn't figure in the voting.

The 1913-14 season would be Abercorn's penultimate season in the League. They started well with four wins out of five in their opening games, which suggested another challenge, but they lost three out of four in November and suffered two further defeats in December to sit in fourth at the turn of the year, but already eight points behind leaders Cowdenbeath and four behind second placed Dunfermline. They lost heavily 6-1 'at home' to Dunfermline on the 7th February 1914 which left them back in fifth. *The Scotsman* noted that the "match was transferred from Paisley to Dunfermline owing to the St. Mirren-Dundee cup tie monopolising attention in the thread town." Despite a strong finish to the season they were eventually placed sixth.

The 1914-15 season would prove to be their last as a League club. They had a poor final season in which they only won five games. They had started well enough and were placed fifth at the end of October but they then suffered a heavy 6-1 away defeat at new club Clydebank. Further bad defeats came with a 5-0 loss against Cowdenbeath, 4-0 against St Johnstone, 5-1 against Vale of Leven and 4-0 at St Bernard's so that by the end of February 1915 they had dropped to eleventh. They lost ten out of their last 12 games, picking up their last ever League point on the 6th March 1915. In what would turn out to be their last home SFL game, they drew 1-1 with Leith Athletic at New Ralston Park in front of a crowd of only 500. Leith did most of the pressing in the first half but missed several chances before Kennedy scored what would be Abercorn's last League goal, albeit against the run of play, with a swift counter-attack. The second half followed the same pattern as the first but the home team were denied a victory when Leith justifiably equalised a minute from the end. Their last ever League game was played a fortnight later, a 4-0 loss away at Lochgelly United, who had been admitted to the League for that season, in which the team from Paisley were thoroughly outplayed and the score might have been worse.

At the end of the season the League took the decision to disband the Second Division for the duration of the war. Abercorn played five seasons in the Western League, as the Second Division did not resume at the end of hostilities, with a best finish of fourth in the 1916-17 season. In the 1919-20 season they enjoyed a run to the Semi-finals of the Renfrewshire Cup where they lost to eventual winners Morton.

At the end of the 1919-20 season the club's lease at their ground ended and it was not renewed by the land owner, as plans were in place to build an ice rink on part of the ground. This was the catalyst that started the demise of the club. History would show that the ice rink did not actually appear for a further four years. It has been speculated that Paisley rivals St Mirren had used their connections with the town council to kill off their rivals. Unable to secure another ground within the town, this effectively spelled the end of Abercorn.

Despite not being entered in any league competition they played one game in season 1920-21, a Scottish Qualifying Cup defeat away to Vale of Leven on the 4th September 1920. 2,000 spectators witnessed this, the last game that Abercorn played, which resulted in an 8-2 victory for Vale of Leven. There was no Renfrewshire Cup for 1920-21 and Abercorn scratched from the 1921-22 competition, giving their First Round opponents Paisley Academical a walkover.

Abercorn retained membership of the SFA until the 29th March 1922, when they were disbarred for failing to secure their own private home ground. Effectively though the club were defunct in 1920 when it played its last game.

Over the years there were 34 competitive Paisley derbies between Abercorn and St Mirren across all competitions (Scottish Football League, Scottish Cup, Renfrewshire Cup, Paisley Charity Cup and Renfrewshire Victoria Cup). The head to head count was played 34; Abbies wins 13; Saints wins 16; Draws 5. The only occasions they met in the SFL was in the four seasons that Abercorn were in the First Division and so the sides met eight times in the League – four games hosted by Abercorn at Blackstoun Park, three home matches for St Mirren at Westmarch, and one at Love Street. The head to head count in the SFL was played 8; Abbies wins 3; Saints wins 4; Draws 1. The two sides met twice in the Scottish Cup, both at Blackstoun Park with honours even.

The name still features in the town. Abercorn Street runs north out of the town running parallel with the White Cart Water, part of the River Cart (which itself is a tributary of the River Clyde). There is an Abercorn Bridge, a wide, high arched red sandstone bridge at Old Sneddon Street which was built in 1881. There was an Abercorn railway station which originally opened in 1866 and which closed permanently to regular passenger services in June 1967. There is an Abercorn industrial estate and a number of businesses in Paisley continue to use the name. New Ralston Park was eventually used for a skating rink and is now a supermarket, with primary schools to the west and playing fields to the south.

SEASON	LEAGUE	P	W	D	L	F	A	P	POS
1890-91	SCOT	18	5	2	11	36	47	12	7/10
1891-92	SCOT	22	6	5	11	47	59	17	9/12
1892-93	SCOT	18	5	1	12	35	52	11	9/10
1893-94	SCOT-2	18	5	2	11	42	60	12	7/10
1894-95	SCOT-2	18	7	3	8	48	65	17	8/10
1895-96	SCOT-2	18	12	3	3	55	31	27	1/10
1896-97	SCOT-1	18	1	1	16	21	88	3	10/10

1897-98	SCOT-2	18	6	4	8	33	41	16	7/10
1898-99	SCOT-2	18	4	1	13	41	65	9	10/10
1899-00	SCOT-2	18	7	2	9	46	39	16	6/10
1900-01	SCOT-2	18	9	3	6	37	33	21	3/10
1901-02	SCOT-2	22	4	5	13	27	57	13	11/12
1902-03	SCOT-2	22	5	2	15	35	58	12	10/12
1903-04	SCOT-2	22	6	4	12	38	55	16	10/12
1904-05	SCOT-2	22	8	1	13	31	45	17	11/12
1905-06	SCOT-2	22	6	5	11	29	45	17	10/12
1906-07	SCOT-2	22	5	7	10	29	47	17	9/12
1907-08	SCOT-2	22	9	5	8	33	30	23	4/12
1908-09	SCOT-2	22	13	5	4	40	18	31	1/12
1909-10	SCOT-2	22	7	8	7	38	40	22	5/12
1910-11	SCOT-2	22	9	1	12	39	50	19	11/12
1911-12	SCOT-2	22	13	4	5	43	22	30	2/12
1912-13	SCOT-2	26	12	7	7	33	31	31	4/14
1913-14	SCOT-2	22	10	3	9	32	32	23	6/12
1914-15	SCOT-2	26	5	7	14	35	65	17	12/14

Armadale

Formed: 1910
Colours: Navy Blue shirts, white shorts
Ground: Volunteer Park
Entered League: 1921. Founder member of the reformed Second Division
Number of League Seasons: 11
Highest League Finish: 3rd in Division Two
Honours: None
Left League: 1932. Expelled. Wound up in 1935

The council area of West Lothian is currently represented solely by Livingston but a 100 years ago there were four West Lothian towns playing in the Scottish Football League – Armadale, Bathgate Bo'ness and Broxburn. All four featured in the 1920s and by 1932 all had lost their League status.

Armadale joined the Scottish Football League in 1921 and played for 11 seasons with a best placed finish of third in 1922. They finished bottom of the League in 1928 and 1929 and over the next three years they continued to struggle, with a best-placed finish of 15th. They were eventually expelled from the League during the 1932-33 season for non-payment of guarantees to visiting clubs. They were thrown out on the 3rd December 1932 after completing 17 fixtures. During this time they had won only one game and lost 14, although their record was expunged. No teams replaced them (or Bo'ness who had been kicked out the month before) and the division continued as an 18 team league. Armadale's last first-class fixture came in the first round of the Scottish Cup on the 21st January 1933 when they lost against Dundee United. After this the club made no further appearances and eventually folded.

Armadale is an ex-mining town which is also known for its brick manufacturing. Formerly known as Barbauchlaw, it is named after Armadale in Sutherland, this estate being owned by Sir William Honeyman, who later acquired the land of Barbauchlaw. Some of the street names in the town retain the original name and owner i.e. Barbauchlaw Avenue and Honeyman Court. In more recent times, due to its location between Edinburgh and Glasgow, it has become a commuting hub.

Armadale grew rapidly from the mid-nineteenth century onwards and in 1879 the first Armadale FC was formed. In 1889 the club took over the home of Armadale Volunteers FC whose members were allowed to use the ground provided they joined the local Volunteer Regiment. The ground, Volunteer Park, takes its name from this Royal Scots Volunteer battalion. It is located off North Street and is still in use today.

The name of West Lothian is a modern replacement for the original county of Linlithgowshire and in 1884 Armadale were one of the original founders of the Linlithgowshire FA who instigated their own county cup competition. In its first season Armadale reached the final, losing to Mossend Swifts 3-2. Mossend is a village near West Calder, itself south-west of Livingston. They went one better the following year beating Broxburn Shamrock in the final on the 22nd May 1886.

In the 1886-87 season they made their first appearance in the Scottish Cup where they reached the Third Round in what was called the Edinburghshire section. On the 11th September they played their first game, beating West Calder 3-1 away. Playing with the wind, Armadale had much the best of the play in the first half, opening the scoring after twenty minutes and adding two more before the interval. With the assistance of the wind in the second half West Calder created more chances but it took them until the 75th minute to open their account and Armadale were able to see out the game.

In the next round they beat Newcastleton, from the Scottish Borders, who had got a walkover in the previous round. The *Edinburgh Evening News* reported that "Armadale appeared promptly on the field, but only seven of the local team turned out. [The referee]...did not allow the game to proceed until ten of the local team were on the field, the eleventh man turning up five minutes after the kick-off. Newcastleton played up pluckily at first, but were far too light for the West Country men, who won...by five goals to one."

The Linlithgow Cup holders were then drawn to play St Bernard's of Edinburgh at their Powderhall ground. They lost an exciting game 5-2, the *Edinburgh Evening News* reporting that "the Armadale had evidently made up their minds to die hard, and they certainly gave the Stockbridge team a good deal more trouble than they bargained for. The Saints started lazily, while, on the other hand, the Linlithgowshire men put in all they could." Armadale scored first as a result but their opponents grew into the game and soon equalised. Armadale, returning to the attack, created a number of opportunities and eventually their efforts were rewarded as they retook the lead. This new setback seemed to weaken up the Edinburgh Saints who again equalised before half-time. Armadale must have come out for the second period thinking they could more than hold their own but their opponents seemed to have raised their game. From the restart they scored and this seemed to settle the game as after that there was only one team in it. The Saints added two more before the call of time. Commenting on the Armadale team, the paper said "Love, who kept goal for Armadale, is a custodian of no mean merit...The backs played a fairish game, Walker at times kicking very strongly. The halfs, if not brilliant, are made of the right stuff, and stick to their work with a dogged determination....The forward line combined badly. The centre, Johnston, has the cut of a good player, and but for careful watching he would have been very dangerous. The right wing pair worked very fairly together...The left wing, McKenzie, is undoubtedly the best forward in the team. The Armadale team that featured in these Scottish Cup matches was: Love; Walker, Green; Stewart, Simpson, Sneddon; John MacKenzie, Chalmers, Johnston, Mathieson and James MacKenzie.

Armadale retained the Linlithgowshire Cup against Durhamtown Rangers, from the south of Bathgate, although it took three matches. The original final, played at Broxburn on the 12th March 1887, was played as a friendly due to the state of the ground. No-one told the spectators and they broke in and halted the game after being refused a refund. A fortnight later the two sides drew 2-2 at Bo'ness. Armadale eventually prevailed a month later winning 2-0.

In the 1887-88 Scottish Cup Armadale drew St Bernard's again this time in the First Round. They twice came from behind to level in the first half but eventually lost 3-2. The following year they again reached the Third Round of the Cup. They recorded a record 12-0 win in their first home tie, against Champfleurie, named after a house and estate to the east of Linlithgow near the village of Kingscavil. They were fortunate to secure a bye in the next round but then lost 5-2 at Mossend Swifts. The home team raced into a two goal lead within the first five minutes. Armadale recovered and pulled a goal back soon after and continued to press and scored a second to go into the break level at two apiece. Love kept Armadale in the game with some good saves and Swifts had a goal disallowed before determined play saw them score not once, but twice. Armadale again tried to press but their hosts scored a fifth in the final minute of the game. In the same season they reached the final of the Linlithgow Cup but lost 1-0 against Bo'ness in a match played at Bathgate's Boghead Park.

In the 1889-90 Scottish Cup Armadale were drawn at home to Hibernian in the First Round. In the tie played on the 7th September Hibs scored after just seven minutes and then missed an open goal. They made amends shortly afterwards and extended their lead. Soon afterwards they made it three and appeared to have put the tie to bed. Rousing themselves, the home forwards poured forward and Fleming pulled a goal back for Armadale. Hibs came out the strongest in the second half and Love was called upon to keep his side in the game. Play slackened as the match wore on and the game threatened to peter out. Before the close Armadale scored their second goal, but could not get on equal terms. The Armadale team was: Love; G Simpson, T Brown; J Simpson, T Brown, McDonald; Chalmers, Walker, Boise, Fleming and Mathieson. In their team was a teenage John Walker. Playing at inside-forward he would go on to join Hearts in 1893 and then go on to play for both Liverpool and Rangers. He was capped five times for Scotland from 1895 onwards.

In the 1890-91 season Armadale won the Linlithgow Cup for the third time, beating Bo'ness 2-0 at Boghead Park in Bathgate on the 21st March. A couple of months later Armadale joined the Eastern Football Alliance, an early league formed by clubs based in West Lothian, Edinburgh and Fife. Armadale won only three of their twelve matches but the league was abandoned anyway with only two other clubs completing their fixtures.

In 1894 the original Armadale FC collapsed and was wound up. An Armadale Volunteers side briefly appeared in the Linlithgow Cup, winning it in 1897 and reaching the final the following year but by the turn of the century their involvement had ceased. The town was without a senior side until 1910 when a new Armadale Football Club was formed, taking up residency at the Volunteer Ground. The club joined the Scottish Union for the 1910-11 season, which was considered one of the strongest of the non-League competitions, but in 1911 they switched to the Central League, where they finished 11th out of 12 teams. It was whilst playing in this competition that this new club played in the Scottish Cup, reaching the Second Round. They won their first tie at home to Peterhead, 2-1, before going out to Aberdeen, who were not yet in the Scottish Football League.

In the 1912-13 season the club improved to finish fifth in the Central League and they then went on to win the competition in the 1913-14 season, finishing six points ahead of Bathgate and Dundee A. They successfully defended their title the following year, winning it by five points from Arbroath. In the 1912-13 season the new Armadale club had also won the Linlithgow Cup beating Broxburn United 2-1 and the following year they had reached the final again, against the same opposition, although this time the scoreline was reversed.

When non-league football was restructured following the suspension of the Second Division of the SFL in 1915, Armadale joined the Eastern League. They won both the Eastern League and Cup competitions in the 1915-16 season and also won the Linlithgowshire Cup beating Bathgate 1-0. They retained the trophy in April 1917 when they beat Broxburn United 2-1.

In 1919 they re-joined the Central League, now much strengthened by the addition of former members of the SFL. D H Young was appointed as secretary/manager in 1919 and he led the club for five of the League seasons across two spells - 1921-23, 1924-27. In his first season Armadale knocked three League clubs - Clyde, Hibs and Ayr United – out of the Scottish Cup, narrowly losing 2-1 to eventual winners in Killie in the quarter-finals. The club finished 6th in the Central League and also reached the final of the Linlithgow Cup that season, losing a replayed final against Bathgate, but it was their Scottish Cup run that drew the attention.

In the First Round a crowd of 5,000 at Volunteer Park on the 24th January 1920 watched Armadale knock out Clyde 1-0. Clyde were one of four First Division clubs to be knocked out that day, the others being Hamilton, Motherwell and Airdrieonians. Armadale had most of the play but couldn't make the breakthrough and the scoreline was goalless at half-time. Clyde resumed a man short due to an injury to Allan, their centre-forward. Armadale again dominated and they finally got a reward for their efforts when John Fleming scored seven minutes before time.

In the next round Armadale got a glamour tie against Hibernian at Volunteer Park. The two sides met on the 7th February 1920 in front of a crowd of 8,000 this time. The visitors started strongly and play was largely confined to the Armadale half, with the occasional breakaway by the home forwards. With practically their first counter Armadale took the lead, Prentice getting on the end of a cross from Smith to beat Scott in the Hibernian goal. Although the visitors kept up a constant pressure, and forced numerous corners they couldn't find an opening and went in 1-0 down. The second half was more evenly contested. Hibs spurned a couple of chances but Armadale had opportunities of their own to increase their lead. As it was, they progressed 1-0, causing a major upset. The Armadale side was: Robb; Dick, Kiernan; Harris, Kirkbride, Gardner; Spiers, Sullivan, Prentice, Fleming and Smith.

Armadale drew 1-1 with Ayr United at home in the next round. The home side had the better of the exchanges in a goalless first half. On the resumption Ayr monopolised the play but from a breakaway Smith opened the scoring for Armadale in the 65th minute. Ayr were awarded a penalty for handball and equalised. From this point to the final whistle Ayr had the better of the play and but for magnificent goalkeeping by Robb, they would have secured the victory and progressed. Goalkeeper Willie Robb joined Rangers at the end of the season and stayed there for six years, making over 250 appearances. In 1925 he was capped for Scotland and the following year he joined Hibernian, where he won a second cap.

Armadale caused a major sensation when they won the replay. *The Scotsman* reported that "the unexpected happened at Ayr, where Armadale engaged the United of that town in their undecided third round Scottish Cup tie. Ayr played their usual side, but Armadale had several changes that made for strength. One of the newcomers was Gordon, Heart of Midlothian. Armadale started with great dash, and in the opening minutes gave Kerr plenty of work to do. Gradually, however, they slackened off, and the home forwards took a grip of the game....Ten minutes or so from the interval Armadale got a corner through a mis-kick by McLaughlan, and in the melee which followed Gordon scored the only goal of the match. The second half was largely a case of Ayr searching in vain for openings. None did better on the Armadale side than Dick, Kiernan, and Scoular, to whose coolness the victory is largely due. The attendance came to over 10,000...Armadale have now knocked out Clyde, Hibernians, and Ayr United out of the Scottish ties."

Their amazing Scottish Cup run ended in March 1920 when they lost their Quarter-final tie 2-1 at home to Kilmarnock. Another sizeable crowd at Volunteer Park witnessed a contentious opening goal for the visitors, the referee ruling that the ball had crossed the line. There was no doubt about the second that soon followed so Armadale were two down at half-time. The second half was more evenly contested. In the 50th minute Gordon scored and for a time the equaliser looked like it was coming but Killie held firm. It was a very creditable performance though, especially in the light of Kilmarnock going on to beat Albion Rovers in the final to lift the Scottish Cup.

The following year Armadale reached the Third Round knocking out St Mirren and Bo'ness along the way. It took four games for Albion Rovers, the beaten finalists from the previous year, to knock them out. On the 22nd January they caused the surprise of the day at Paisley, knocking out League side St Mirren. Their hosts opened the scoring but Short, in the Armadale goal, prevented any further scoring and Armadale grew into the game and got an equaliser through Wardrop before the interval. St Mirren restored their lead but Armadale hit back through goals from Dunsire and then Wardrop scored his second and the winning goal. The Armadale team that caused the Cup shock was: Short; Harris, Dunsmuir; Lamb, Kirkbride, Gibson; Speirs, Weir, Wardrop, Dunsire and Kelly.

They were drawn away at county rivals Bo'ness in the Second Round and took 2000 fans to Bo'ness in early February where they drew 0-0. They produced a fine defensive display plus had a bit of luck when their opponents hit the post. The replay took place the following Saturday, with the right to host last year's beaten finalists Albion Rovers at stake. There was an attendance of 8000 at Volunteer Park, who watched a keenly contested which they deservedly won. Armadale opened the scoring through

Williamson in the first half. After the break Wardrop increased their lead.

On the 19th February 1921 the ground's record attendance of 12,600 was set when they played League side and last year's runners-up Albion Rovers. Armadale were struggling towards the bottom of the Central League and gave their opponents a real fright. Inspired by the crowd they raced into a 2-0 lead inside the first twenty minutes, Spiers and Sneddon finding the net with good shots. Albion Rovers settled down after that and before half- time was reached had levelled the score. The second half was very even-steven and there was no further scoring. The replay was played the following week in front of a crowd of 21,000 at Coatbridge. Armadale were grateful to an inspired display by Short in goal who kept them in it. Armadale grew in confidence and had the best of the second half and a 0-0- draw was a fair result. The replay was scheduled for the following week and was played at Hampden as a neutral venue. During the week the draw was made for the Quarter-finals with the winners scheduled to play away at Dundee. On the 2nd March a crowd of 12,000 watched the two sides play out another goalless draw. *The Scotsman* reported that "the game made up in keenness and excitement what it lacked in the finer points of football. After ninety minutes' play neither team had succeeded in scoring. An extra half-hour was played, but by this time both teams were practically done, and it was not surprising there was no scoring. At the close it was intimated that the replay would take place today on the same venue." The following day they met for a fourth time and this time the League side won through. Albion monopolised the play and went into the break 2-0 up. The second half was more even but there were few clear cut chances. Armadale took a League club to a third replay and came out with an enhanced reputation. The gate receipts helped fund the building of a new grandstand at Volunteer Park, which coincided with their admittance to the Scottish Football League.

In 1921 the SFL eventually reformed the Second Division and incorporated the Central League into the new structure. Armadale were thus admitted to the newly expanded Second Division. Armadale made a promising start to their League career, finishing third at the end of their first season. This was not to last though and Armadale slowly declined, consistently finishing in the bottom three in their last five seasons.

On the 20th August 1921 they played their first ever Scottish Football League match, a home game against St Bernard's. The game generated much excitement and a crowd of 4000 was present to see Armadale take early control and dominate the play, but they only scored near to the end of the first half. McLean one of the Saints backs slipped and McNeilage was able to square to Fleming to score their first ever League goal. It was not until fifteen minutes from time that Glen added a second and in the 85th minute Campbell made it 3-0. The Armadale line up for their League debut was: McLeod;

Hopewell, Dryburgh; Atkinson, McInally, Gibson; Stalker, Glen, Fleming, McNeilage and Campbell.

The following week a 0–0 draw with local rivals Bathgate was watched by a large crowd of over 3000. *The Sunday Post* reported on the match and gave an appraisal of the Armadale team: "It was a dour struggle between those two great local rivals, Bathgate and Armadale, and a no goals result was a fair reflex of the game...In the first half Armadale had the better of the attack, but Wilkinson gave a delightful performance, and shots that came his way were smartly saved. In the second half it was Bathgate's show, but here there was greatly required an opportunist. The feature of the match was the splendid defence of each team."

Armadale went their first eight games unbeaten which included six wins, with Arthur McInally impressing at centre-forward, which attracted transfer interest from Patrick Thistle. They topped the table by the end of September as a result, with the defence being particularly miserly with only two League goals conceded in those first eight matches. McLeod in goal was in great form. It was a surprise then when they lost in October to mid-table Linlithgowshire rivals Bo'ness by a single goal. They were typically strong in defence but the attack was off colour.

In December they beat leaders Alloa Athletic in an evenly contested game in front of 5,000 spectators, to move to just a point behind them. Fleming beat Caldwell with a fine shot ten minutes from time and added a second a minute later. But defeats away against Broxburn and St Johnstone saw them drop to fourth place, five points behind the leaders. In February 1922 they went three games without scoring. Two goals from Fleming and one from Stalker in a 3-1 midweek win over Vale of Leven ended this barren spell and had them placed third but Alloa and Cowdenbeath by this time had built up a gap in pursuit of the championship flag. Any lingering hopes of a challenge were dashed on the 11th March when they lost 4-0 at Dunfermline, although didn't deserve to lose by such a margin. Armadale got off to the worst possible start conceding shortly after kick off and were two down within ten minutes. Armadale came into the game but just before half-time they conceded again. Armadale continued to press for a goal, especially through McInally, but Dunfermline scored a fourth with a counter attack.

On the 1st April they beat strugglers Clackmannan 8-1 although at half-time the score was only 1-1. Armadale scored a remarkable seven goals in the second half in a result that flattered them, with Clackmannan equal to the home team in a tame first half. After 25 minutes Chalmers opened the scoring for Armadale and just five minutes later Bain equalised after McKinlay in the Armadale goal had first saved from Gettins. In the second half it took Armadale twenty minutes to retake the lead through Fleming. Ten minutes later Hopewell scored. Muir saved from Campbell but Croal bundled in the rebound to make it 4-1. With a quarter of an hour left to play Fleming found the net for the second time and there then followed a deluge of goals as Fleming got his hat-trick and Campbell added two more.

Armadale eventually finished third and that would prove to be their highest placed finish in their eleven seasons as a League club. They capped off a fine season by lifting the Linlithgowshire Cup for the seventh, and final time, when they beat Bo'ness 1-0 at Mill Park, Bathgate on the 17th April 1922. A crowd of 5,000 saw Fleming score the only goal of the match.

Armadale went into their second campaign with a number of team changes. The most significant departure was Arthur McInally, the centre-half, who joined newly promoted Alloa in the First Division. The club signed a mix of youth and experience. Three youngsters came from Parkhead - Cant, Dempster and Beattie, Jolly was signed from Yoker and the experience came in the form of goalkeeper Jim Watson, formerly of Hamilton and Dundee; Ben McLaren, a forward from Hamilton Accies; and Kay, a back from Third Lanark.

Armadale came sixth in the 1922-23 season. They were particularly strong at Volunteer Park where they only lost one game all season (against King's Park) and recorded some big victories on their home ground. The biggest of these was on the 23rd December 1922 when they beat Johnstone 7-2. Two players scored hat-tricks in front of 2000 spectators. *The Scotsman* reported that "Armadale won handsomely and rather easily against Johnstone...The opening stages suggested that the visitors would give Armadale a run for the points; in fact they opened the scoring. Thereafter Armadale were the superior lot and monopolised play." McDonald opened the scoring for the visitors after 10 minutes. Chalmers, playing at centre-forward equalised five minutes later, running into a measured through ball from Brown and two minutes later McLaren put them ahead. In the remainder of the first half Chalmers got his hat-trick by netting two more. In the second half Irvine got a second for Johnstone in the 65th minute to make it 4-2 before Gibson made it five a minute later, scoring in off the bar. McLaren added the remaining two to also score a hat-trick. *The Sunday Post* commented that "the score does not do Johnstone credit. Johnstone had quite a full share of the game but had no luck at close quarters....it is safe to predict that when the teams meet in the Scottish Cup, there will not be such a difference in the scores." Johnstone won that match 2-0 but went out in next round to Falkirk.

A week after exiting the Cup Armadale beat Lochgelly United 5-1. Young, their centre-forward, accepted a cross from Alec Wales (signed the previous evening from Airdrieonians) and evading numerous defenders shot home giving Paterson in the Lochgelly goal no chance. After 40 minutes Young got his second and a minute before the interval Danny Muir netted a long range effort. In the 63rd minute Wilson forged ahead for Lochgelly and evading challenges from Reid and Jolly, scored with Watson well beaten. Near the end Williams, one of the Lochgelly centre backs slipped, to allow Chalmers in to score and just on time Muir scored from close range. The result left them a mid-table 10th place but a mini-run of four wins out of five in early March saw them up to sixth place.

Towards the end of the season they finished with another fine home win, beating Forfar Athletic 5-0 in early April 1923. Fleming, the centre-half headed in a corner kick from Willie Dick after five minutes and then Dempster scored from a pass by Young after a quarter of an hour. Wales added a third on 25 minutes, Bruce, in the Forfar goal, failing to catch the ball cleanly and Young scored a fourth just before the interval. The second half saw an improved display by the visitors and it wasn't until the last minute that Dempster made it 5-0 from a corner. The club eventually finished sixth and rounded off another good season by reaching the final of the Linlithgowshire Cup, although they were beaten by Broxburn United, who had finished a couple of places lower than them in the League.

After these two good seasons Armadale's fortunes gradually declined and in their remaining nine seasons in the SFL they finished in the bottom half of the 20 team division including the bottom three in four out of their last five last seasons. Armadale started the 1923-24 season with three wins and a draw in their first four matches and topped the table on the 1st September. Over the next two months their form was inconsistent but they were still well placed in fourth place just a couple of points off the top when they came a cropper away at St Johnstone (who would win the Second Division) in late November. Conceding two penalties, they lost 5-0, *The Sunday Post*, under the headline "Severe Shock for Armadale" reported that "St Johnstone rose to the occasion with a vengeance against Armadale, dubbed the 'shock' team of the Second League...Saints showed their best form, and were good enough for anything a Second League team can produce. They were helped to reach their total of five goals by awards of two penalties, Fleming being fouled on the first occasion when going through to score, and an Armadale defender handling the second, just before the final whistle....The game was fought with much keenness before the season's record attendance of about 8000....Armadale's half's were entirely unable to cope with the smart home forwards....The visitors strove manfully against a superior lot."

Armadale then failed to win any of their next four games and dropped to 12th in the table. In March 1924 they recorded their best ever away win in the SFL, beating Forfar 5-1 at Station Park. Bill Paterson, a centre-forward formerly of Cowdenbeath, and loaned from Derby County, scored four and Ashton the other, as Armadale won four games out of five in March to finish a place higher in eleventh. They reached the Final of the Linlithgow Cup again, and in a repeat of the previous season's Final, lost out once more to Broxburn United.

The 1924-25 season saw a much changed team with only two players starting the new campaign who had featured the season before, one of these being Willie Dick. One of the departures was Danny Muir who left to join Dumbarton where he made over 100 appearances. Armadale could boast of an English FA Cup winner amidst their ranks though. Goalkeeper Alex Hunter joined for the season from Tottenham, with whom he won the FA Cup in 1921. He, along with Willie Dick, went to play in the USA at the end of the season. Armadale lost their opening game, with *The Sunday Post* commenting that "Armadale, once they have settled down, should knit into a fine all-round team."

The new look side experienced mixed fortunes and were lying in mid-table before a 5-2 defeat to division leaders Dundee United in mid-November. An even first half ended 1-1 after Cullen had given Armadale the lead after 30 minutes but Dundee United had equalised just a minute later through Bauld. United took the lead early in the second half through Mackie before Cullen equalised from a penalty. But the leaders raised their game and three more goals were scored by Oswald, Mackie and Gilmour.

At the end of January a season's best 5-1 win over St Bernard's lifted them up to ninth place. The Edinburgh Saints took the lead and led until the half hour mark. Chisholm equalised rushing in and forcing Weir, the Saints keeper, who had claimed a cross, over the line. Leitch, on loan from Celtic made it 2-1 and Chisholm added a third before half-time. Chisholm, who usually played outside left, but who was playing at centre forward went on to complete his hat-trick. McAdam, a junior playing from Kirkintilloch Rob Roy, scored a fifth. However, this good win was soon followed by a run of six games without a win. This run ended surprisingly when they beat Dundee United 1-0 at the end of March, Graham scoring with a long range drive in off the woodwork fifteen minutes from time and they eventually finished in 14th place. They reached the Final of the Linlithgow Cup for the last time. They were leading 1-0 at half-time against Bo'ness on the 29th April when a snowstorm caused the game to be abandoned. A further attempt to replay the game was also called off due to the weather so the two sides eventually met on the 19th August, after the summer break, to play the delayed final, which Bo'ness won 4-1.

The remaining seven seasons of the club's League history saw Armadale firmly ensconced in the bottom half of the Second Division, finishing in the bottom three on four of those occasions. Armadale lost seven of their first nine fixtures in the 1925-26 season including a 7-1 away defeat against Dunfermline Athletic in late October. Skinner for the Pars scored twice in the first half, and got a second half hat-trick, scoring five in all (for the second time that season). Davies, the Armadale 'keeper was only at fault for one of the goals. Martin got a goal for Dale with virtually the last kick of the game. The result saw them in 18th place in the twenty team division, just one point off the bottom.

A week later they surprisingly scored six in beating Dumbarton 6-2. Grove, then a triallist, scored the second as they led 2-0 at half-time. Dumbarton levelled the score early in the second period but Grove then headed his second to restore the lead. Morgan netted from a corner and Grove added two more to get four for the match. This win was the start of three consecutive wins for Armadale, which temporarily lifted them up to 16th place in the table.

On the 19th December they lost 5-0 at home to Dunfermline in the reverse fixture, Skinner scoring a hat-trick. A week later, in the Boxing Day fixture, their game against Arthurlie saw 11 goals with Armadale losing 7-4 at Dunterlie Park, Barrhead, where there was a thin covering of snow on the pitch. Arthurlie scored first before Martin equalised. Arthurlie scored two more before Armadale got back on level terms for a second time through Dougan and Martin's second. Just before the break Jessiman again established the lead for Arthurlie. Armadale equalised yet again in the first minute of the second half, Bain deflecting a shot from Dougan into the net. Arthurlie though scored all of the remaining goals, scoring three without reply.

In the New Years' Day game of 1926 Armadale beat local rivals Bathgate 5-1 at Volunteer Park. They went a goal down after just five minutes but Dougan soon equalised. Morgan then scored a hat-trick and Hunter scored just before the close. Just over a week later they scored five again, this time beating St Bernard's of Edinburgh, again at home. *The Scotsman* reported that "St Bernard's deserved a better fate against Armadale than the score would indicate. The honours of the first portion were certainly in their favour but Armadale took the shortest road to goal and grasped every opportunity which came their way. Consequently they secured the necessary goals. It would have occasioned no surprise, however, if the visitors had opened the scoring, so promising were they. Yet it was the Dale who drew first blood through Martin, who rushed in to net, following a rebound of the ball off the crossbar. No sooner had this point been registered then an offside goal was scored by Grove. As a result of the referee's decision a section of the home supporters invaded the field, and play was suspended for two minutes. Before the interval arrived McGrogan emerged from a scrimmage to score his side's second point. Goals came rapidly in the second half, Dougan scoring two and Grove one, while the Saints' solitary point was notched by Simpson, a few seconds before the end." Armadale had mixed fortunes after that, for example conceding four one week but then scoring four themselves the next. By the time they finished their League programme with a 4-3 away win against bottom side and local rivals Broxburn United, Morgan scoring a hat-trick, they were in 15th place, their lowest since entering the League.

Armadale were similarly placed the following year although briefly topped the Division in early October 1926. Having lost their opening game 4-2 away at Bo'ness – who would go on to win the Second Division – Armadale followed this with a seven game unbeaten run, which included a 4-0 over King's Park. A 2-0 reverse at Arthurlie saw the home team go top with Dale now down to third but they bounced back with a 5-1 win over promotion chasing East Fife. McMillan, returning to the side after a three week absence scored a hat-trick. The win took them back to the top as the sides around them lost. They followed this up with another win over a promotion rival, this time Raith Rovers. In this game Dale dominated the first half and Raith did likewise in the second, but the points weren't shared because the Raith forwards were not as decisive in front of goal. McMillan, the Dale inside-right scored after 15 minutes and shortly afterwards Morgan added a second, Muir failing to hold the ball although he made up for his error with some fine stops from then on until half-time. Raith dominated the second half but rarely tested the Armadale goalkeeper. The result left Armadale top, one point ahead of Bo'ness and two in front of East Stirlingshire and East Fife.

In November things started to unravel, as they lost three out of four matches starting with 4-3 defeat at home to Dumbarton. The visitors were hopelessly outclassed during the first half although they scored first. Morgan equalised and he scored a second following a solo run and the leaders dominated the rest of the half. Only four minutes had elapsed of the second half when Dumbarton drew level and a few minutes later the away team took the lead but almost immediately Grove restored parity following a goal mouth scramble. Armadale pushed for the winner but in doing so left their defence exposed and near the end Dumbarton snatched both points when a draw was a fair result. In November they also lost away at Alloa and lost another seven goal thriller away at Forfar to drop to fourth place, now six points behind the leaders Bo'ness.

December followed the same pattern with defeats in three out of four games which included a 6-0 drubbing away against Queen of the South, by which time Armadale had slipped to 7th and out of contention for promotion. For this game they had a weakened forward line, missing three regulars due to injury - Morgan, Duff and Martin. A 5-1 win over bottom club Nithsdale Wanderers on the 3rd January 1927, in which the returning Morgan scored four, could not paper over the cracks and they didn't win another game until April as they plummeted down the table to 14th place.

The 1927-28 season brought the first threat to their League status as they finished 20th and bottom and faced a re-election vote. They failed to win away all season and conceded a club record 112 goals for the League season, including eight in a game on three separate occasions. They lost their opening game 4-1 at home to Queen of the South. Wardrop scored but also missed a penalty. They got their first point in their next game, a 3-3 draw at Alloa Athletic in which each side's centre-forward scored a hat-trick - Barr for Alloa and Wardrop for Armadale. They obtained their first win in their fifth game, a 2-1 win over St Bernard's with goals from Wardrop and Grove before the Edinburgh Saints got a late goal.

On the 1st October 1927 they were on the receiving end of a drubbing from Arthurlie, in which Owen McNally scored a League record eight goals, the *Daily Record* previewing the game commented that "Armadale ought to leave both points at Dunterlie," despite the Lothian club fielding Gray, an ex-junior Shawfield forward with Chelsea experience. Ten minutes play had elapsed when McNally opened the scoring, applying the finishing touch to a sweeping move down the left-hand side. Armadale nearly added a second shortly afterwards and Dale's McLaren flashed a ball across the Arthurlie six yard area as the two teams continued to spar, the *Glasgow Evening Times* noting that "the encounter was proving a keen one and play fluctuated from end to end." The woodwork came to the rescue of Dale as an Arthurlie free-kick hit the upright and the ball rebounded into play. Soon after they converted a penalty after 25 minutes. A beautiful cross allowed McNally to head home his second to make it 3-0 with half an hour played and before half-time McNally completed his hat-trick by scoring Arthurlie's fourth goal. The second period began quietly with neither 'keeper unduly troubled before McNally netted his fourth, beating King with an angled shot. And then on the hour mark McNally scored a sixth for his team. The Arthurlie forwards continued to aid their centre and McNally scored three more to take his individual tally in the game to eight and the match ended 10-0 to Arthurlie. The *Daily Record* headlined with "Armadale Victims at Dunterlie of New Scoring Record" and went on to say that "Arthurlie ran riot at the expense of Armadale, who wilted before the hurricane scoring of McNally, a record breaker in very truth. Eight goals in all did he put past the hapless King. Black and Armstrong made up the ten. The West Lothian men were completely outclassed, it is almost unnecessary to add." The unfortunate Armadale team was: King, Finlayson, Reid, McCracken, McBurnie, Calderwood, McLaren, Hunter, Wardrope, Gray and Turner. The result was Armadale's biggest ever Scottish League defeat.

This heavy reverse began a sequence of nine games without a win, which also included 5-0 defeats away at Leith Athletic and Ayr United. The defeat against League leaders Ayr United at the end of November, in which Jimmy Smith scored a hat-trick, saw them drop to the bottom on eight points, as Clydebank surprisingly beat Queen of the South to go a point ahead of them. King, the Armadale 'keeper prevented his side from experiencing an even heavier defeat.

There were mixed fortunes in December, as Armadale registered a couple of wins, but also conceded eight in an 8-5 loss at Palmerston Park against high flyers Queen of the South. *The Sunday Post* reported that "a more sensational game that that at Dumfries between Queen of the South and Armadale is hardly conceivable. In all, 13 goals were scored, a fact which plainly indicates the weak nature of the defences, but any glory there was went to Queen's by reason of their miraculous recovery. Twice they made up a two goal deficit only for the Dale to regain the lead at five, but brilliant work by the forwards during the last twenty minutes produced no fewer than four counters, and gave success to the home team by eight goals to five." Four goals were scored in the first half and nine in the second at Palmerston Park. Gray, the opposition centre-forward was in fine form, scoring four second half goals. Dale actually led 2-0 after 25 minutes (the goals scored by a triallist and Wardrop) but were pegged back by the interval. In the first 15 minutes after the interval six goals were scored - at one point the score was 4-2 to Dale (Hunter and Wardrop) and then 4-4, 5-4 to Dale (Hunter) and then 5-5 before the home team added three more. Torrance was deputising in goal for Smith for Queen of the South and his lack of experience was noticeable. King played well in goal for Armadale despite being beaten eight times.

A 3-2 home defeat against Albion Rovers on New Years' Eve left them three points adrift at the bottom of the table at the beginning of 1928. Dale's goals came from Wardrop and Grove and they deserved a draw. Wardrop was injured in the second half but stayed on, but this undermined their attempts to get back into the game. They only recorded two draws in January which left them seven points adrift of Dumbarton and Morton at the bottom by the end of the month. A fifth win of the season at the beginning of February, 2-0 at home to Arthurlie, saw them close the gap to six points, but they then lost the rest of their matches in the month where their opponents each had a goal scorer who got a hat-trick - a 5-0 defeat at Arbroath (Gentles scored a hat-trick) and a 5-1 home defeat against East Fife (Weir scored a hat-trick). These results left them eight points adrift at the bottom with eight games to play.

Three consecutive 1-0 score lines followed in March, two of them in favour of Dale. Hunter scored in a 1-0 win over Alloa Athletic and Tonner scored against Leith Athletic, but on each occasion it was the defensive performance of Muir who was a rock at the back, which made sure of the points. However, on the 24th March it all came crashing down with a 10-3 thrashing at the hands of promotion chasing Third Lanark, which confirmed them with the wooden spoon. Thirds raced into a 3-0 lead before David Cochrane, a newly signed centre-forward, and Love reduced the arrears for Dale. But Thirds then hit back and scored three, one from a penalty, to lead 6-3 at the interval. The second half was only four minutes old when Thirds made it seven and two more followed. Armadale, in a breakaway secured a penalty following a handball, Tonner converting. With two minutes to go McNeil of Thirds finished off a second half hat trick for a final score of 10-3.

Armadale amazingly beat runaway leaders Ayr United 3-1 in their next game but perhaps the fact that the leaders couldn't be caught had something to do with it. Nevertheless Ayr took the lead through their goal machine Jimmy Smith, and they had the chance to go two up when Muir fouled Fitzpatrick, but King saved Smith's penalty. With 20 minutes gone in the second half Ayr were still good for their lead but Love then equalised. Five minutes later Cochrane, after eluding three opponents, put Armadale ahead. Then from a Cochrane corner Love netted Armadale's third goal. Ayr's collapse could have been worse but Hepburn saved Tonner's penalty. The following week Armadale lost 6-2 at Dumbarton. According to *The Sunday Post* "Armadale fielded a stranger goalkeeper in Muir - King arriving too late to strip...it was Urquhart's day out. Five of the six goals were to his credit." They finished their campaign with two draws to finish seven points adrift of Bathgate.

These two sides faced a re-election vote on the 17th May 1928 at the Scottish League's AGM as they were challenged by three sides including former League side Nithsdale Wanderers, who had themselves lost a re-election vote the year before. In the first ballot Bathgate secured 28 votes, Armadale 22, Nithsdale Wanderers11, Brechin City 8 and Montrose 7. Bathgate were re-elected. A second ballot followed which eliminated the bottom two. In the run-off Armadale secured 23 votes, nine more than Nithsdale and they continued to play in the League.

During the Great Depression unemployment throughout Scotland's central belt hit record levels, which in turn led to a fall in attendances. The SFL had refused to allow struggling sides to reduce admission fees for the unemployed and the club slid into debt. On the 4th July 1928 the *Edinburgh Evening News* reported on the club's AGM, where the Chairman, W Nimmo, reported that for the season 1927-28 they had lost the sum of £857. Income had been £1923, expenditure £2780, wages and match costs £1378, and guarantees for visiting clubs £900. It was reported that "the loss is accounted for mainly by the poor home gates." During the 1921-22 season the club had averaged gates around the 2500 mark. By the end of the 1927-28 season this was down to 500. It was further reported that four directors of the club had left during the season and their places were unable to be filled at the club's AGM.

Armadale kept going for the 1928-29 season with W C Forsyth taking over the reins as manager. They finished 19th and effectively bottom for a second time as Bathgate had resigned mid-season and had their records expunged. Arthurlie, who were in 17th place also resigned near to the end of the season. Dale's fortunes didn't improve on the pitch, going winless in the first ten League matches, losing seven of them. They eventually won on the 20th October 1928, a 2-1 victory over Bathgate but this was ultimately expunged from the record books when Bathgate resigned in January 1929. During the Autumn they conceded five goals on three occasions, losing 5-1 away at St Bernard's, 5-2 at Alloa and 5-2 at Dumbarton, so that by the end of November they were bottom with just six points from 16 games, with just the solitary win over Bathgate, who were two points ahead of them.

Having only won one game in the first four months of the season Armadale then won three in a row in the month of December. All of the matches were played at Volunteer Park and they beat King's Park 2-0, East Stirlingshire 2-1 and Leith Athletic 1-0 to lift themselves off the bottom. In January 1929 they had a morale boosting win in the Scottish Cup, recording their best ever win, a 9-2 First Round victory against Moorpark of Renfrew, in which Heigh scored four. They followed this up with a 3-1 League win over Forfar and by the end of January they were out of the bottom two. Their Scottish Cup run was ended in the next round with a heavy 5-1 defeat away at Ayr United. Their League form took a turn for the worse, especially from the end of February. On the 27th February they lost 5-1 at top of the table Dundee United and during March they lost 6-1 at third placed Arbroath, 9-1 at fourth placed Albion Rovers and 7-3 at Queen of the South. With Bathgate's withdrawal from the League and all of their results expunged Armadale now found themselves bottom, one point behind Stenhousemuir and three behind Alloa Athletic.

A 1-1 draw with Dumbarton on the 30th March 1929 brought them level with Stenhousemuir but the following week they lost 4-0 at King's Park whereas Stenhousemuir beat Bo'ness 3-2. However, later in April, Arthurlie became the second team to leave the Division. They resigned but their record was allowed to stand and it became clear that no re-election vote would take place and that, instead, two new clubs would be voted in to fill the vacancies. Ultimately they finished on 23 points, one short of Stenhousemuir and in 19th place, having conceded 99 goals in the matches that were counted.

61

Brechin City and Montrose came in as new clubs for the 1929-30 season, both elected from the Scottish Alliance in preference to Nithsdale Wanderers. Armadale opened against a fellow struggler from the previous season in Stenhousemuir and won 2-1 but came down to earth with a bump in the second round of matches when they were thrashed 6-0 at Firs Park against East Stirlingshire. However they bounced back with a 6-0 win over new club Montrose, who had not conceded a goal in their first three matches in the League. Form was inconsistent during September and October although they had a shocker on the 26th October when they went down 7-1 at East End Park against Dunfermline. Performances improved in November with Dale winning three and drawing one of their five fixtures which took them up to 12th in the table. Inconsistency continued to plague them as they lost 8-0 at Raith in early December and 5-1 at St Bernard's in the first game of 1930. Armadale were knocked out of the Scottish Cup by non-League Inverness Citadel in January 1930 and won only two more League games to the end of the season as they eventually finished in 15th position.

This poor form was carried into the new season as they lost their opening game 4-1 at home to Dundee United, the *Glasgow Herald* observing that "Armadale's blend of professional and amateur talent did not show up well." They then lost 5-1 away at Arbroath (McAleer scored all five), the same paper noting that "Armadale were outclassed, their finishing and defensive work being woefully weak." Dale did then win 4-0 at home to Bo'ness (who would finish in the bottom two). However this was followed by six consecutive defeats across the rest of August and the whole of September that left them with just two points and only one win in nine games, and second from bottom in the table above pointless Clydebank.

Armadale recorded their second win of the season on the 4th October 1930 with a 4-0 victory over Albion Rovers but during November and December they suffered a series of heavy defeats where 27 goals were conceded across seven games with only seven scored, so that by turn of the year they were in 18th place with just 9 points, one ahead of Bo'ness and two ahead of Clydebank. And that is how the bottom three ended with Armadale avoiding a re-election vote.

Back to back wins in the League in early January 1931 was followed by a record 7-1 Scottish Cup defeat at home to Rangers, although a crowd of over 5,500 boosted the financial coffers. This was the last truly big game that Armadale played and the team that day was: Watson; Findlay, Hamilton; Joe Polland, Fyfe, Hailstones; Fleming, Stout, Brannan, Livingstone, and John Polland. Armadale suffered something of a Cup hangover with a 6-2 loss against Dumbarton followed by a 5-2 defeat against Albion Rovers and then another defeat by the same scoreline versus fellow strugglers Clydebank. Form picked up after that and they won six of their remaining eight games, including 5-1 against Alloa Athletic, 5-1 against Montrose and 5-2 against East Stirlingshire as they finished six points clear of the bottom two. Both Bo'ness and Clydebank survived the re-election vote but a month later Clydebank resigned and were replaced by Edinburgh City. This club was going to have a chapter all of its own after leaving the League in 1949 but returned in 2016, becoming the first non-League club to earn promotion to the Scottish Football League.

The 1931-32 season was their last full season in the Scottish Football League and they started it badly with seven straight losses. They picked up their first point in a 1-1 draw with Hibernian on the 12th September. *The Scotsman* reported that "the West Lothian men should have been well beaten once more, but they kept the Edinburgh side from settling, and though generally on the defensive, the home lot were always just as likely to score, and the game ended at one goal each" Barclay scored for the home team. Their first win of the season eventually came in their tenth game when they beat Brechin City 3-1 at Volunteer Park to lift themselves off the bottom of the table, going above Edinburgh City who only had two draws to their credit.

Dale failed to win in any of their next six games and lost heavily at leaders East Stirlingshire in early November by 6-1, although *The Scotsman* reported that "Armadale put up a much better fight than the score would seem to indicate." Having conceded two early goals they "stiffened up perceptibly and, not only did they prevent the home team from adding further to their score before the interval, but they themselves succeeded in reducing the leeway by means of a penalty kick converted by Russell. Play in the second half was of a scrappy nature, the heavy and sodden condition of the ground militating against accurate football. East Stirlingshire, however, adapted themselves better to the conditions" and scored four more goals. Armadale now found themselves bottom of the table with just four points from 16 fixtures.

Armadale won a ten goal thriller 6-4 away at Edinburgh City the following week to leapfrog their opponents. *The Scotsman* reported that "companions in misfortune, Edinburgh City and Armadale provided one of the best games seen at Powderhall since the season opened. The match was remarkable for the number of goals scored, no fewer than ten being registered of which the West Lothian side claimed six. Considering the miserable weather conditions, and the consequent sodden state of the pitch, the football was of a good quality, and interest was maintained to the last kick." Weir, a new centre-forward from Norwich City, led the line and scored a hat-trick. The score was 4-4 at one point before Russell and Barclay claimed the points.

The club's struggles continued though and they failed to win in December, including a 6-1 loss away at promotion challengers St Johnstone. The New Years' Day game brought a surprising result, as Armadale registered a 7-1 win over Bo'ness. Under the headline "Shock for Bo'ness" *The Scotsman* reported that the first half of the game was "very ordinary. Armadale succeeded in keeping a clean sheet against the wind. There was a complete transformation after the interval. Bo'ness certainly scored first, but their lead lasted only a minute, Weir equalising. After that it was all Armadale. Bo'ness were never in the picture. They were unfortunate to meet Armadale when the latter were at the peak of form. Such a fine display has not been given by the West Lothian club for a long time. The team played cleverly as a combination, but reference must be made to the feat of Weir at centre-forward, in scoring five goals, in addition to sharing in the scoring of a sixth." However, later in the same month they lost 9-0 away at King's Park, being completely over run and being on the receiving end of one of Alex Haddow's hat tricks for the Stirling club.

Following this heavy defeat they preceded to win six out of their last eleven games to move off the bottom, going ahead of Edinburgh and Brechin City. Included in this were two high scoring games early in February, a 4-3 away win against Brechin was followed by a 5-4 home win over East Fife. Armadale actually led this game 5-0 at half-time with two apiece from Weir and Barclay. East Fife nearly rescued a point in a fine comeback and it was a shame only 500 spectators witnessed the game. Armadale lost only one of their last five games including a 5-1 home win over Montrose in early April 1932, and finished what was to be their last full season as a Scottish Football League club in 18th place.

Armadale were continuing to struggle off the pitch as well. They had wanted to reduce the gate price to 6d to try and increase the size of crowds but this had been vetoed by the League. They were using their ground for greyhound racing to generate more income but the League were not happy in how it impacted on the playing surface at Volunteer Park. The summer of 1932 saw a big turnover in players, a number of new faces signing on for the club on amateur terms.

They lost their opening game of the 1932-33 season 4-1 at home to Arbroath on the 13th August. There was no Weir or Barclay among the forwards, or Steele in goal and the line-up featured a triallist. They secured a 1-1 draw at King's Park the following week but then went down 6-0 at Alloa. In mid-September they lost 4-2 at home to Hibs. Dale scored first and it was 2-2 at the break but they faded after a bright start. The gate of over 1,000 was a small consolation though.

A few days later they lost 4-3 at strugglers Edinburgh City but they eventually recorded their first League win of the season on the 24th September when they beat Dundee United 5-3. The team line-up continued to hint at problems though as there were two

'Newman's' and a 'Junior' playing. The game was level at half-time, 1-1, with one of the triallists scoring. Dale were then 2-1 down before Scoular equalised. This was followed by another goal for a triallist and also for Scoular. United made it 4-3 before Scoular got his third and his side's fifth.

On the 1st October Armadale lost 9-1 at Dunfermline Athletic. The Pars scored after 12 minutes and added a second soon after. Scoular then skimmed the bar for Dale before Dunfermline scored a third in the 25th minute. A fourth followed from the restart and a fifth came on 35 minutes. Meek, in the Armadale goal again prevented a much larger deficit, but at this stage had to retire injured following a goalmouth scramble and his place between the sticks was taken by Scott. Before the half was over Dunfermline added a sixth. Armadale's main aim in the second half was to keep down the margin of defeat and they showed no attacking ambition being a man down. Dunfermline toyed with their opponents, eventually scoring a seventh before Michie surprised everyone, including the Athletic 'keeper Steele, by scoring for Armadale. Dunfermline added two more in between which Scoular was brilliantly denied by Steele. The Armadale team was listed as: Meek, Scott, Kerr; Forrester, Young, "Newman"; Fleming, McDonald, Scoular, Michie and "Junior". Interestingly, the full-back Kerr was a 19 year old Jerry Kerr, best known as the manager of Dundee United from 1959 to 1971. He joined Motherwell at the end of the season before going on to play for Alloa, St Bernard's and Dundee United themselves.

A week later Dale drew 2-2 with Leith, taking their points total to four thanks to two goals from Scoular and also that Leith played a man down for most of the game due to injury. However, six successive defeats followed, kick-started by an 8-1 defeat against East Fife. Again the Dale team evidenced player turnover with two triallists listed. Armadale scored first through Scoular in the first minute of the game but the lead didn't last long when Marshall equalised after eight minutes. Marshall had a hand in both of the next two goals for the men from Methil, each time McCartney scoring from the assist. McCartney got his hat trick before half time to make the score 4-1. Four more goals were scored in the second half with McCartney taking his tally to four soon after the restart.

At the end of the month Armadale hosted Stenhousemuir at Volunteer Park but were unable to pay the visiting club the £50 match guarantee. This was eventually paid late but newspaper reports circulated after their next home game saying that Alloa, the visiting team, had failed to report to the League that Dale had not paid the £50 guarantee. Mr McDonald, the club secretary, also denied a report that the club had approached former Bo'ness players with a view to them turning out for the club.

On the 12th November 1932 the *Edinburgh Evening News* ran with the headlines "The Dale Downed!" and "Hibernians Nearly Run Into Double Figures", as Hibs beat an Armadale side featuring two more triallists by eight goals to two at Easter Road. *The Scotsman* reported that "the meeting of the Hibernians and Armadale provided no surprise, and the 4000 spectators at Easter Road were regaled with a perfect riot of goal-scoring by the home team, eight times they found the net, and the West Lothian men were only able to reply twice. Right from the beginning it was obvious that the Hibernian would consolidate their position as league leaders…The goalkeeper [Meek] gave a polished display of custodianship, and but for him the score would probably have mounted into double figures. Time after time he prevented the ball from entering the net when the odds seemed to be against him doing so, and he well deserved the ovation which the sporting Easter Road spectators gave him for his great work. Five minutes sufficed to see the Hibernians take the lead." Hibs added two more before Scoular scored for Armadale before the interval. Hibs scored five more in the second half before "Junior" headed home a second Armadale goal just before the end.

Perhaps more significantly, two off pitch events, seemed to accelerate the demise of the club. First, on the same day, came news of the expulsion of Bo'ness from the Scottish Football League. They too, had fallen behind with match guarantees, the minimum payment to visiting sides required by SFL rules. They had been given an ultimatum by the League to clear the arrears, but were unable to raise the money. Secondly, on Wednesday the 16th November the Scottish League Management Committee met to discuss the practice of hosting greyhound racing at football stadiums. Armadale were one of those clubs using their ground in this way as a means to supplement their income. This additional income stream soon dried up when the racing was ordered to stop as it breached guidelines set by the League which stated that the racing should not interfere with the football pitch. Barely able to meet the visiting match day guarantees and fielding weakened teams this was the beginning of the end for the club.

On Saturday the 19th November 1932 Armadale played what would turn out to be the last home game at Volunteer Park. Only 300 watched a 5-1 home defeat against Raith Rovers, their lowest ever SFL crowd. The *Edinburgh Evening News* reported that Armadale started well and for a time besieged Raith's goal. The visitors gradually assumed the upper hand and scored two in quick succession. Though two goals down Armadale were still putting up a fight but couldn't find a way past the Raith 'Keeper Wallace, who denied both Fleming and Michie. Cowan, the Raith centre-forward finished the half with a hat-trick as the visitors went into the interval 4-0 up. In the second half Raith scored again before Harry Michie scored what would be Armadale's last ever SFL goal. The last Armadale team to take the field was: Meek; Boyle, Kerr; Donnelly, Brown, Hamilton; Fleming, Thomson, "Newman", Michie and McDonald.

By now Armadale were being pursued for guarantee payments and by Sheriffs Orders. An expulsion order from the League arrived for club secretary William McDonald a few days later and the planned visit to Forfar Athletic was cancelled. The League Management Committee had decided on Wednesday that unless Armadale paid on Thursday the guarantee in respect of Saturday's game with Raith Rovers they would cease to be members of the Scottish League. At the meeting a representative of Armadale put before the members a proposal that at the close of each home match they would give the visiting clubs an IOU for £50, which would be liquidated at their next away match. The proposal was turned down. The *Press and Journal* later reported that "Armadale F.C. made a move in connection with their £50 guarantee to Raith Rovers. The club approached the league secretary and offered to pay £30 meantime, but Mr McAndrew could do nothing in the matter, as, according to rule, failure to pay the full guarantee by midnight on Thursday meant automatic expulsion. It is only four weeks ago since Bo'ness were expelled from the league following their failure to pay guarantees due, and the default of Armadale means the closing down of the Lothians for league football. Not so long ago there were four clubs closely linked up - Bathgate, Broxburn, Armadale and Bo'ness. Armadale have been members of the Second Division of the Scottish League since 1921. This season they have played seventeen league games, nine at home and eight away, and have a total of four points - one win and two draws. Their only win was against Dundee United at Volunteer Park."

Unable to meet their financial obligations, the club was formally served with expulsion papers on the 3rd December 1932. Armadale's demise brought SFL representation from West Lothian to a close. It would take a name change and a relocation to bring senior football back to West Lothian over 60 years later with the emergence of Livingston.

Armadale fulfilled one last commitment, a home Scottish Cup tie with Dundee United, played on the 21st January 1933, which they lost 2-0. The last eleven to represent Armadale in a senior match was: Wilkinson; Boyle, Scott; Hamilton, Forrester, Fleming; Connelly, McInally, Michie, Miller and Imrie.

Armadale's records for the 1932-33 season were subsequently expunged on the 5th April 1933. They had played 17 games, winning only one and drawing two and therefore had gained just four points. At the time of expulsion they were six points adrift at the bottom. At the Scottish League's AGM the following month it was decided not to replace Armadale and Bo'ness. No new teams were admitted and it was decided to reduce the Second Division to 18 clubs.

In 1935 Armadale FC was finally wound up. Armadale Thistle JFC were formed shortly afterwards in 1936 and continue to represent the town at junior level and they play their games at Volunteer Park.

SEASON	LEAGUE	P	W	D	L	F	A	P	POS
1921-22	SCOT-2	38	20	5	13	64	49	45	3/20
1922-23	SCOT-2	38	15	11	12	63	52	41	6/20
1923-24	SCOT-2	38	16	6	16	56	63	38	11/20
1924-25	SCOT-2	38	15	5	18	55	62	35	14/20
1925-26	SCOT-2	38	14	5	19	82	101	33	15/20
1926-27	SCOT-2	38	12	10	16	69	78	34	14/20
1927-28	SCOT-2	38	8	8	22	53	112	24	20/20
1928-29	SCOT-2	36	8	7	21	47	99	23	19/19
1929-30	SCOT-2	38	13	5	20	56	91	31	15/20
1930-31	SCOT-2	38	13	2	23	74	99	28	18/20
1931-32	SCOT-2	38	10	5	23	68	102	25	18/20

Arthurlie

Formed: 1874
Colours: Black and white horizontal striped shirts and white shorts
Ground; Dunterlie Park
Entered League: 1901. Elected to Second Division Two. 1923 Founder members of the Third Division
Number of League Seasons: 20 (over two spells)
Highest League Finish: 3rd in Division Two
Honours: Third Division Champions 1923-24
Left League: 1915. League Suspended. Did not re-join in 1921. 1929. Resigned.

We head back to Renfrewshire for our third former League club. Arthurlie were based in Barrhead, a textile town also known for the sanitary engineers Shanks, and located seven miles from Glasgow. West Arthurlie is a suburb of Barrhead where there was a cotton mill and also the South Arthurlie printworks. Arthurlie were formed in 1874 and played in the Scottish Cup that year along with two other teams from Barrhead. These clubs eventually amalgamated and had combined success in the Renfrewshire Cup and also reached the Quarter-finals of the Scottish Cup three years in a row between 1880-83. In January 1897 they famously knocked Celtic out of the Scottish Cup, running out 4-2 winners. (Celtic got their revenge, beating Arthurlie 7-0 in the same competition a year later.) They gained admission to the Scottish Football League in 1901, playing in the Second Division until 1914. They finished as joint runners-up in 1907, their highest ever placing but they were not elected to the First Division. They lost their League status after the war but returned to the newly created Third Division in 1923. They had made a successful return to the League, winning the title and promotion to the Second Division in their first season back. In the late 1920s they were one of a number of clubs to suffer from the general economic downturn and they resigned their membership of the League in April 1929. In total they competed in 20 seasons in the SFL over two spells; fourteen seasons between 1901 and 1915 and then six seasons between 1923-29.

Arthurlie played their matches at Dunterlie Park from 1882 having moved there from their original Cross Arthurlie Street ground. In 1906 they relocated to the second Dunterlie Park. This was located to the north of Barrhead, in the shadow of the Shanks

Victorian Pottery Works, with the Glasgow to Kilmarnock railway adjacent to the south-east and Blackbyres Road to the north-east, across the railway line from Commercial Road.

The club made their Scottish Cup debut in the year of their formation, playing on the 17th October 1874 in a First Round tie against Dumbarton which they lost 3-0. In the 1876-77 competition they reached the Third Round, going out to three-time winners Queen's Park 7-0. In May 1879 Arthurlie reached the final of the very first Renfrewshire Cup, losing to Thornliebank in a replay. In the 1879-80 season they recorded their highest scoring win in the Scottish Cup, beating Morton 8-3 on the 11th October 1879.

In the 1880-81 Scottish Cup they had the first of three consecutive runs to the Quarter-finals, beating local teams Johnstone, Cartvale, Pollock and South Western before drawing Hearts in the Fifth Round. On the 11th December they knocked out Hearts 4-0, scoring two in each half and drew three-time winners Vale of Leven. The game, played at Barrhead on a cold and bitter day, was evenly balanced in the first half and was goalless at the interval. Vale raised their game in the second half and scored twice in the second half to progress. The Arthurlie side is listed as: Thomas Turner; McCowat, Stevenson; Clark, Neil, John McAulay; Kitterson, Robert McPherson, McNab, Duncan and Melvin. There was a rowdy crowd, with the *Glasgow Herald* commenting that "in the course of the game the onlookers were remarkably demonstrative of their leanings towards the respective teams, and even the most virtual members of the teams. There is not perhaps much to be found fault with in this when the approbation or disapprobation intended to be conveyed to the players is expressed in a rationed, commonsense way. When, however, the spectators, or a large number of them, think it the proper thing to indulge in rounds of profane, disgusting language - at the top of their voices, too - it is surely right that the matter should be called attention to. And we are sure it has only to be pointed out to be discouraged at all Football gatherings."

At the end of the season they club won the Renfrewshire Cup beating St Mirren 3-1 and retained the trophy the following year with a 2-0 win over Cartvale. They would reach the final on a further eight occasions yet never win the competition again. They also reached the Quarter-finals of the Scottish Cup again, losing to Kilmarnock Athletic. Along the way they had beaten Paisley Athletic 7-1 in the Third Round. In March 1882, Robert McPherson became the club's first ever international player when he made his sole appearance for Scotland against England. McPherson scored the third goal in a 5-1 win.

In the 1882-83 season they reached their third consecutive Scottish Cup Quarter-final, recording a 7-0 win over Bute Rangers in an early round and beating Hibernian 6-0 in a

Fifth Round replay at Kinning Park, after the original game was abandoned. They again lost out to Kilmarnock Athletic, but it took four games for them to be eliminated.

The following season Arthurlie made it to the Fifth Round, eventually going out to three time winners and beaten finalists that year, Vale of Leven. A month after their Cup exit forward John MacAulay was capped for Scotland against Ireland in Belfast. Scotland won the game 5-0. A couple of months after that, on the 29th March 1884, the club's goalkeeper Thomas Turner was capped against Wales. He was beaten in the first five minutes of play but Scotland went on to win 4-1. Two years later left back Andrew Thomson was also capped for Scotland in the side that thrashed Ireland 7-2.

In the 1886-87 season Arthurlie were knocked out of the Scottish Cup in the First Round by Renfrewshire rivals St Mirren. They did, however, reach their fourth Renfrewshire Cup final, losing 5-1 to the other Paisley based side Abercorn in May 1887. The club continued to enjoy runs to the later rounds of the Scottish Cup, although in the 1888-89 season they lost 7-0 at home to St Mirren, the third time in a row they had been knocked out by them.

Following the formation of the Scottish League in 1890 Arthurlie became founder members of the Scottish Federation in 1891. The won the competition in its first year, finishing four points clear of Albion Rovers. The following year they came in third but then the competition was disbanded and its members supplemented the Scottish Alliance, who had lost clubs to the newly formed Second Division. They competed in the Alliance between 1893 and 1896 and in the 1894-95 season they reached their fifth Renfrewshire Cup final, losing to Port Glasgow Athletic 6-1 at Cappielow Park, in Greenock.

In the 1896-97 competition they caused a major Scottish Cup upset, knocking Celtic out in the First Round by running out 4-2 winners. To put that into perspective Celtic were the reigning Scottish League champions. In the match, played on the 9th January 1897 their illustrious visitors were out-fought and out-played. The final scoreline did not flatter Arthurlie who at one point led 4-1. The back story was one of Celtic infighting over pay, newspaper criticism and general dressing room unrest, which meant that Celtic would start the game with only seven regular players. *The Scotsman* reported on the match: "At Barrhead, The Arthurlie team was the strongest that could be produced, while that of the Celtic was composed of seven first-eleven players and four reserves. The home team kicked off, and for a little the Celtic looked rather dangerous; but the pressure being relieved, the Arthurlie had then a good run up the field, and Hannigan placed the ball between the uprights amidst great cheering. The Celtic then succeeded in breaking away, and after a brilliant rundown the Arthurlie goal the home custodian cleverly stopped a well-directed ball from going through. Celtic, continuing to press their opponents hard, next succeeded in putting on an equalising point, which was loudly cheered by their followers. Again assuming the aggressive, the strangers made a hot attack on the Arthurlie goal, but the danger was soon averted, and after some give-and-take play in midfield the Arthurlie had a look in at the Celtic goal, and Hannigan again sent the ball through, giving Arthurlie again the lead. On resumption of the second half of the game, the Arthurlie continued to show their supremacy, and within 20 minutes succeeded in increasing their previous score by another 2 goals. Nothing daunted, the Celtic played up most determinedly, and were ultimately rewarded with a goal just a few minutes from the finish. In the remaining few minutes the game was stubbornly fought, but no further scoring was made on either side, the game, which was one of the hardest ever played at Barrhead, ending in the defeat of the Celtic by four goals to 2 goals." The Arthurlie giantkilling team was: Airston, Smith, Hirst, Miller, Tennant, Boyd, Hannigan, Tait, Ovens, Speir, and McGregor. Hannigan scored a hat-trick and McGregor got the other goal. Celtic got their revenge, beating Arthurlie 7-0 in the same competition a year later.

In 1897 Arthurlie joined the Scottish Combination, a competition where ambitious non-League clubs competed alongside the reserve teams from established Scottish Football League clubs. In the October of that year Renton, one of the founder members of the League suddenly resigned. The League decided to elect a replacement club to fulfil the remaining fixtures and Arthurlie was one of the clubs under consideration. In the end, Hamilton Academicals, who were also playing in the Scottish Combination, were elected.

At the end of the 1898-99 season Arthurlie had finished as runners-up to Rangers A in the Scottish Football Combination and made another bid to join the Scottish Football League at the AGM held on the 30th May. As it was the club was unable to get a seconder so they didn't take part in the round of voting. Arthurlie went one better in the 1900-01 season and won the Scottish Combination League and this prompted another bid. With the Second Division expanding to 12 clubs there was the need to elect one new member after Partick Thistle dropped down from the First Division which reduced to 10 clubs. Arthurlie were up against Albion Rovers, also from the Combination, Raith Rovers from the East of Scotland League and Ayr Parkhouse from the Ayrshire League. Raith were their strongest rivals having made a number of recent failed bids and in the end, after the other two clubs were eliminated, Arthurlie beat Raith Rovers by 12 votes to 10 in a final ballot, and were elected to the Scottish Football League. *The Scotsman* summed up all of the movements in the League, reporting that "the proposal of Dundee FC to increase the number of clubs in the First Division was negatived, while the proposal of Hamilton Academicals to increase the

Second Division to twelve clubs was carried....Partick Thistle were relegated to the Second Division. Leith Athletic, Hamilton and Motherwell were re-elected to the Second Division, while Arthurlie defeated Raith Rovers for the remaining place."

On the 17th August 1901 Arthurlie played their first ever Scottish Football League game at Fir Park against Motherwell which ended in a 2-2 draw. The first SFL match staged at Dunterlie Park was a 3-1 win over the future Second Division champions that season, Port Glasgow Athletic. *The Scotsman* reported that "Arthurlie were the first to find an opening and scored, which was followed by the Athletic equalising, and before half-time Arthurlie notched another goal. In the second half Port Glasgow put forth every effort, but were unable to augment their score, whilst the home team were successful in obtaining another goal." An unbeaten run in October saw them up as high as fifth in their debut season but they lost all of their games during November. By the time of a 3-0 defeat away at Airdrieonians in the first game of 1902 they had slipped to ninth place and they eventually finished tenth, narrowly avoiding a re-election vote.

They avoided the same fate in an uneventful 1902-03 season when they finished ninth. Bob Currie scored 12 goals in 16 games in that season and was signed mid-season by Middlesbrough. But the following season they did come in the bottom two and therefore faced a vote. The new season began badly with just a single point gained from their first four fixtures. A 5-0 loss at leaders Hamilton early in November left them just two points above Abercorn at the bottom. The following week they themselves scored five in a 5-2 win over Ayr Parkhouse and it would be with their vanquished opponents that they faced the re-election vote at the SFL AGM. This was held on the 30th May and Arthurlie were re-elected on the first ballot with the most votes. They secured 14 votes, Aberdeen 11, Ayr Parkhouse 9 and Royal Albert and Cowdenbeath 7 apiece. Aberdeen beat Ayr Parkhouse in the next round of voting to secure the second available place.

The 1904-05 season didn't get off to a great start either with a 4-0 loss away against Ayr FC but by the end of the campaign Arthurlie had finished in sixth, their best SFL finish to date. Arthurlie went through both September and October undefeated and following a 3-1 win over Hamilton at the end of October they were placed fifth in the table which they were able to sustain to the end of the season. Six teams from the Second Division applied to join the top flight at the League's AGM, but Arthurlie weren't one of them. Aberdeen and runners-up Falkirk went up to newly expanded First Division but Second Division champions Clyde didn't get elected and Albion, Hamilton and Leith didn't get a single vote between them which perhaps justified Arthurlie's decision. They reached the Final of the Renfrewshire Cup in the 1904-05 season, although they received a walkover in the Semi-final when St Mirren scratched after Arthurlie had been granted a time extension. In the Final played over two legs they lost both matches against Morton, losing 4-1 on aggregate.

The following season they matched their sixth place finish in the League. Although they lost heavily to Rangers in the First Round of the Scottish Cup, 7-1, a record crowd was set at the first Dunterlie Park of 6000. At the end of the season Arthurlie played their last game at this original ground, losing 3-1 to Hamilton Academicals. They also reached their seventh Renfrewshire Cup Final having defeated Port Glasgow Athletic 2-0 in the Semi-final. In a repeat of the 1905 Final they drew the first leg 2-2 away at Morton and in the return leg the two sides couldn't be separated in a goalless game. There was no away goals rule so a replayed Final was held at Port Glasgow's Clune Park on the 12th May, with Morton winning 4-3.

In the 1906-07 season Arthurlie finished third, their highest ever League placing. They missed the runner-up spot on goal average (although this is a subsequent classification as goal average wasn't introduced until 1922). Things didn't start so well with a 3-0 opening day defeat away against Albion Rovers, then playing at Meadow Park, Whifflet. On the 25th August 1906 they played their first SFL game at the new Dunterlie Park against Vale of Leven. The two teams served up a nine goal thriller with the men from Barrhead prevailing 5-4.

The club's form was inconsistent during the remainder of 1906 and they entered 1907 in a lowly eighth position with no hint of what was to come. The New Year started with a season's best 5-1 win against St Bernard's on the 5th January. Arthurlie put an amazing run together in the last two months of the season winning seven out of their eight last fixtures, and drawing the other, their run underpinned by the goalscoring of Clark, their centre-forward. A 5-2 away win at Cowdenbeath on the 9th March, in which they scored three goals in the opening ten minutes, lifted them to fifth. A 3-1 home win over Ayr on the 23rd and a 2-1 away win against Raith a week later confirmed their second place on points, level with Vale of Leven. St Bernard's the champions, and Vale of Leven were two of five teams from the Second Division to unsuccessfully apply for membership of the First Division that year. Arthurlie again declined to out themselves forward and the 1906-07 season was the closest they ever came to competing in Scotland's top flight.

Arthurlie couldn't repeat the feat and in the next two seasons they finished in the bottom two and on each occasion successfully survived a re-election vote. In the 1907-08 season they lost four of their five opening games including a 6-2 loss at Dumbarton. They failed to win away from home and finished in 11th place, three points above Cowdenbeath and a point behind Vale of Leven. At the League's AGM on the 1st June,

Johnstone were the only challenging club that applied, and they were the Combination runners-up. The two clubs up for re-election were voted back in with Cowdenbeath getting 25 votes, Arthurlie 22, and Johnstone 9.

The 1908-09 season was a similar story with the same bottom two facing re-election, although this time it was Arthurlie who finished bottom of the table, with just 11 points. Arthurlie again failed to win on their travels although their away form was even worse, as they only picked up a solitary point. At the AGM Arthurlie topped the poll this time and Cowdenbeath were second (21 and 17 votes respectively). Johnstone were again the nearest challenger with 11. Renton, Wishaw Thistle and Dundee Hibernian also applied (Renton 8, Wishaw Thistle 5 and Dundee Hibernian 3).

In the next six seasons Arthurlie finished no higher than eighth place in the League. One bright spot was an eighth appearance in the Renfrewshire Cup final but this ended in a sixth loss. In the first leg they went down 2-0 in Greenock against Morton and could only draw the return one each.

In the 1912-13 season they again faced re-election after finishing second from bottom in a now expanded division of 14 teams. They had lost six of their first seven matches but three consecutive wins from the end of November closed the gap on the teams above them and by the end only four points separated the bottom five clubs. At the AGM on the 2nd June Arthurlie survived a re-election vote once more. They stood, along with Leith Athletic against six hopefuls including East Fife and three of the clubs that would join the newly created Third Division in 1923: Dumbarton Harp, Galston and Peebles Rovers. This was their sixth vote at an AGM and their fourth re-election vote.

The following season saw a slight improvement in fortunes as they finished in ninth place (in a 12 team division), although they did concede six against both Dunfermline Athletic and St Johnstone throughout the course of the season. They ended the season in final style beating Leith Athletic 5-0, Barnett scoring a hat-trick.

Clydebank and Lochgelly United joined the League as the Second Division reverted to 14 teams for the 1914-15 season. Arthurlie had a terrible start and didn't win their first game until the 5th December. In January 1915 the club lost 6-0 at both Clydebank and St Bernard's and were five points adrift at the bottom. The club won four out of their last six fixtures to overtake Vale of Leven but finished a point behind Abercorn. On the 3rd April 1915 they played their last SFL game for nearly a decade, a 5-3 win over Lochgelly United.

At the League's AGM they were re-elected unopposed as no applicants were received from any non-League clubs. Later in the year though the Second Division was abandoned due to the Great War and Arthurlie joined the Western League. At the end of the War Arthurlie moved to a new location near the railway line at Barrhead in 1919 and brought the name Dunterlie Park with them but they didn't play their first SFL match at this ground until August 1923. At the League's AGM on the 2nd June 1919, Arthurlie were one of twelve clubs to lose their League status when the Second Division was not resumed.

Arthurlie played in the Scottish Cup in January 1920 (losing 4-0 in the First Round away at East Fife) and then again in 1922 (losing 2-1 in the First Round against Hearts having taken an early lead). They did not re-join the finally re-formed Second Division in 1921 and continued to play in the Western League until 1923, despite Johnstone and Vale of Leven leaving this competition to go back to the League. A year later they unsuccessfully applied for election to the Second Division, participating in a seventh vote. They were one of five clubs challenging Arbroath and East Stirlingshire who faced re-election. At the League's AGM held on the 17th May 1923 they only came fourth in the first ballot with eight votes and were eliminated. Arbroath were re-elected with 29 votes and East Stirlingshire and Dundee Hibs went to a second ballot with East Stirlingshire dropping out. The League's AGM discussed the possibility of a Third Division and this was left in the hands of the League Management Committee.

Just under a fortnight later the management committee of the SFL, at a meeting in Glasgow, proposed the formation of a Third Division comprising 16 clubs and met with representatives from the proposed clubs including Arthurlie. A meeting the following month confirmed Arthurlie as one of the participants, along with the majority of the Western League. Arthurlie were one of only three clubs joining the new division with SFL experience – the others being Clackmannan and East Stirlingshire.

On the 18th August 1923 Arthurlie began their second spell as a Scottish Football League club as founder members of the new Third Division. Arthurlie finished as champions of the new division in its first season and were automatically promoted to the Second Division. In a terrific campaign they only lost four of their thirty matches. Goals from Clark and George Jessiman gave them a 2-0 away win against Helensburgh at Ardencaple in their opening game following re-admittance. Arthurlie were unlucky to lose by the odd goal in five in their opening League game at the third ground to be called Dunterlie Park against East Stirlingshire the following weekend. After a 0-0 draw against Queen of the South in their third League game Arthurlie then went on a run of six consecutive wins which placed then second on 15 points, three points behind early pacesetters East Stirlingshire but having played three fewer games.

The run was surprisingly ended at bottom club Brechin City but on the 2nd January 1924 they beat struggling Helensburgh 5-0 and together with East Stirlingshire's surprise 2-0 defeat at Beith, Arthurlie usurped East Stirling at the top of the table. Later that month they secured a vital 1-0 away win at Nithsdale. On the 8th March they played Dykehead, *The Sunday Post* reporting that "Arthurlie finished their home engagements in good style by defeating Dykehead. The home team pressed from the start and Johnstone and Agnew scored in the first half, Dykehead failing to make any show at goal. In the second half Arthurlie were still the better team." Arthurlie won 3-0 to move six points clear of East Stirlingshire.

They followed up this result with a 2-0 away win at Dumbarton Harp, wrapping up the victory in curious circumstances. *The Sunday Post* headline was "Arthurlie make sure of their lead" and the match report went on to say "Arthurlie consolidated their position as Third Division champions by beating Dumbarton Harp at Meadow Park. The visitors were the superior team throughout, and it was only the solid defence by the Harp which kept the score so low against them. Agnew scored early in the second half, after a great shooting effort by Clark and Jessiman. Miller missed Harp's best chance when he failed to make use of a miskick by Nicol. Ten minutes from time there was a curious incident. Arthurlie were given a penalty kick. It was taken by McGowan who shot wildly past, but immediately protested that the ball had been interfered with. A break-in of spectators followed, and it was a few minutes before the field was cleared. The Harp goalkeeper admitted the ball had been moved, and the referee repeated the kick, which McGowan netted." Arthurlie were now eight points clear at the top and 14 points ahead of Montrose in third place and assured of promotion.

On the 22nd March Arthurlie won 3-0 against Galston. Clark scored in the first half. Jessiman scored two in the second half and Galston missed a penalty. East Stirlingshire lost, 2-1 at Montrose and these results crowned Arthurlie as the Third Division champions. Sadly, just five years later the club would leave the Scottish Football League. Key to Arthurlie's success was the goalscoring trio of William Clark, Billy Agnew and George Jessiman. Agnew scored a lot of goals and eventually attracted interest from a number of English clubs, eventually signing for Luton Town in 1925. Jessiman was an ever-present and contributed thirteen goals. Arthurlie drew their last game, 1-1 at third placed Montrose to end the season five points ahead of East Stirlingshire, who were promoted with them, with Montrose a further four points back. They also reached the final of the Renfrewshire Cup for a ninth time , where they drew a two legged final against St Mirren before losing decisively, 6-1, in a play-off match.

Back in the Second Division Arthurlie finished a commendable 12th place in a 20 team division in the 1924-25 season. They drew their opening fixture on the 16th August, a 1-1 draw with recently relegated Clydebank. Commenting on the Arthurlie line-up *The Sunday Post* noted "the home club had only one change from last season's flag-winning side, the team including J Jessiman, of Shettleston, a very much fancied junior." James Jessiman, no relation to his namesake George, who was ever-present again, contributed 11 goals, playing for Arthurlie for this season only, before joining Morton, where he made over 100 appearances.

After scoring five against St Bernard's in September Arthurlie conceded five themselves against Clyde in the November. The club went six League games without a win in early January-February but then pulled off another Cup shock. This time they knocked out First Division Cowdenbeath, who would come fifth in the League. *The Scotsman* reported that "Cowdenbeath's defeat at the hands of Arthurlie at Barrhead was one of the surprises of the day, for though it was realised that the Barrhead team would give the Fifers a good run, it was generally felt that the First League club were safe for a draw at least. But they were beaten - quite decisively - by a team whose dash and vigour were prime factors in turning the scale in their favour." James Jessiman opened the scoring and Arthurlie led 1-0 at half-time. In the second period Billy Agnew scored a stunner immediately after the resumption but the visitors got one back straight away. Clark scored a third goal and Rundell made some good saves as Arthurlie ran out 3-1 winners. In the next round they lost at struggling First Division side Motherwell. They put up a stubborn fight at Fir Park but had a bad ten minutes in the first half and lost 2-0. A run of six games without defeat back in the League from the beginning of March saw Arthurlie finish in 12th place.

The new season opened with a 2-2 draw at Armadale but their opening home League game against Third Lanark on the 22nd August 1925 was marred by crowd trouble. *The Scotsman* reported on the incident, saying that "there was an ugly incident at Barrhead, where the spectators invaded the field, and the referee had to get police protection." The cause of the incident was a hotly disputed last minute penalty. Smith had scored for Thirds and Agnew had scored for Arthurlie. In the last minute a whistle was blown, but not by the referee. This led to McMeekin, Arthurlie's left back, picking up the ball in the belief that the time had been called. The referee subsequently granted a penalty for handball much to the dismay of the Arthurlie players. The spot kick was converted by Green. This led to spectators invading the pitch and the referee had to be escorted to safety before he could blow the final whistle. The referee, a Mr Gray from Coatbridge, was kicked and mauled before he got to safety. Sam Brown, the Thirds right back, went to his assistance, receiving cuts and bruises for his troubles. The club were censured by the SFL and their ground was closed for a month, leading to two 'home' League games being switched to Beith's Bellsdale Park. The change of venue didn't seem to affect them as Arthurlie won both games, scoring four goals on each occasion, first, in a 4-0 win over Broxburn United and then in 4-1 victory against East Stirlingshire. They returned to Dunterlie Park on the 17th October where they beat Bathgate 2-1 to move into fifth place, just three points off the top.

Mixed fortunes followed but in mid-November they beat East Fife 5-0, thanks to an injury to the opposing goalkeeper. On Boxing Day eleven goals were scored at Barrhead in a thrilling encounter with Armadale, Arthurlie emerging victorious 7-4. However, on the 9th January 1926 they suffered their heaviest ever home League defeat, losing 6-2 to Dunfermline Athletic. They conceded six again, but also scored six, in a remarkable game with Nithsdale Wanderers, played on the 13th February. The two sides shared a dozen goals in a remarkable match at Barrhead with *The Sunday Post* reporting that "Arthurlie and Nithsdale played very different types of football at Barrhead, but the result would indicate that both were equally successful. Twelve goals were equally divided. Nithsdale adapted the open game, and kept the ball swinging...Arthurlie played a more intensive game. The draw was the fair result in a match in which each team scored three goals in each half. Arthurlie at one time had a two goal lead at 3-1. The Arthurlie goalscorers were Jessiman, who scored a hat-trick, Armstrong, who scored twice but was injured early in the second half and Sproule, who scored on debut.

Just a week later Arthurlie conceded one more, going down 7-1 at East Fife, but they went on to win five out of their remaining seven fixtures to finish in seventh place and they would match this placing over the course of the next two seasons. Arthurlie also reached the Final of the Renfrewshire Cup for the tenth time but lost against St Mirren, meaning they had now lost their last seven Finals.

Arthurlie won their opening game of the 1926-27 season, 3-1 at home to Forfar Athletic and in their next home game scored seven, as they beat Stenhousemuir 7-2, George Jessiman scoring a hat-trick. Later in the year they scored seven again, this time against Nithsdale Wanderers. Played on the 13th November 1926 Arthurlie won 7-1, with Malloy, signed from Celtic, scoring two. Arthurlie deserved to win, but not by such a wide margin. Arthurlie took their chances whereas Nithsdale were weak in front of goal. Arthurlie built up a substantial 4-0 lead by the interval. Jessiman, who had scored one of the first half goals, added two more to register a hat-trick, and would go on to notch up 20 goals for the season.

Arthurlie were up to third in the table when they crashed to earth with another 7-1 defeat at East Fife, getting off to the worst possible start by conceding two in the first eight minutes. By the turn of the year they were actually up to second, but with just two points separating them and Clydebank in seventh. A good Scottish Cup run followed where they knocked out fellow Second Division sides Nithsdale Wanderers, St Bernard's and Alloa Athletic before succumbing to another, East Fife – who would go on to reach the Final. A poor run of results on their return to League action saw the club slip down the table to finish in seventh place again. At the end of the season Arthurlie beat Moorpark 4-1 in the Semi-final of the Renfrewshire Cup to reach the Final for the last time. The two legged Final was held over until August where they met old rivals St Mirren, losing the first leg 3-1 at home before being thrashed 5-0 in the return on the 30th August.

The new League season had kicked off ten days before this, and on the Saturday before the return leg, Arthurlie suffered their heaviest ever SFL defeat, losing 8-0 at Firs Park against East Stirlingshire. *The Scotsman* ran the headline "East Stirlingshire Sharpshooters" and reported that "as the score suggests, the game was of a one-sided nature, but the bright play of the 'Shire was sufficient in itself to maintain interest at a high level...Arthurlie were a disjointed and disappointing lot, weak at half-back, and with little thrust in their forward rank." Arthurlie were missing George Jessiman, who after 120 appearances and 58 goals had signed for First Division Clyde.

Arthurlie won four of their first seven fixtures, and despite the 8-0 defeat at East Stirling, were lying in ninth in the table when they hosted Armadale at Dunterlie Park on the 1st October 1927. Armadale were down in 18th place, although had beaten Morton 2-1 at home the week before. *The Daily Record* previewing the game commented that "Armadale ought to leave both points at Dunterlie", despite the Lothian club fielding Gray, an ex-junior Shawfield forward with Chelsea experience. Of more significance was a player included in the Arthurlie ranks. Owen McNally was born on the 20th June 1906 in Denny, near Falkirk. He had joined Celtic from local club Denny Hibs in March 1927 and was on loan at Arthurlie, a certain Jimmy McGrory blocking his path to a regular starting berth at centre-forward. Three months before McGrory would himself hit eight in an SFL game, Owen McNally became the first player to score eight goals in a Scottish Football League match.

Arthurlie beat Armadale 10-0 to record their best ever SFL win. *The Sunday Post*, under the headline "McNally's Octette at Barrhead Festival" noted that "but for the excitement of the spectators as McNally reached and exceeded the record six goal limit, there was nothing to enthuse over. Arthurlie started the brightest and a flowing movement culminated in McNally's shot striking the crossbar, with King in the Armadale goal well beaten. Armadale came more into the picture, but a free-kick opportunity was wasted by McLaren. Ten minutes play had elapsed when the 20 year old McNally opened the scoring, applying the finishing touch to another sweeping move down the left-hand side. Semple nearly added a second shortly afterwards and McLaren flashed a ball across the Arthurlie six yard area as the two teams continued to spar, the *Glasgow Evening Times* noting that "the encounter was proving a keen one and play fluctuated from end to end."

The woodwork again came to the rescue of the away team as a Black free-kick hit the upright and rebounded into play. But the same player was soon on the scoresheet, converting a penalty after 25 minutes after a handball. Black, soon to be overshadowed by his colleague's goalscoring, was making his own mark on the game and turned provider five minutes later. He delivered a beautiful cross for McNally to head home his second to make it 3-0 with half an hour played. "The homesters about this period were having matters pretty much their own way, and it came as no surprise when McNally completed his hat-trick by scoring Arthurlie's fourth goal. To the interval the Arthurlie forwards continued to hover around King without increasing their score."

Scouts from English side Burnley were at Dunterlie to watch Arthurlie's half-back Allan Sliman but all of the talk at the interval was about Owen McNally. The second period began quietly with neither 'keeper unduly troubled before McNally netted his fourth, beating King with an angled shot. And then on the hour mark McNally scored a sixth for his team. Semple and Black continued to aid their centre and McNally scored three more to take his individual tally in the game to eight. Tommy Armstrong also got the scoresheet for the Barrhead team as they got stuck into their opponents and the match ended in their favour by ten goals to nil. The Arthurlie team was: Hilligan, McGowan, Dunlop, Wyllie, Sliman, Ballantyne, Armstrong, Semple, McNally, McInnes, and Black.

McNally's goalscoring feat was not really acknowledged on the day but in the next few days the new record drew comment from the newspapers. *The Daily Record* headlined with "Armadale Victims at Dunterlie of New Scoring Record" and went on to say that "Arthurlie ran riot at the expense of Armadale, who wilted before the hurricane scoring of McNally, a record breaker in very truth. Eight goals in all did he put past the hapless King. Black and Armstrong made up the ten. The West Lothian men were completely outclassed, it is almost unnecessary to add." *The Glasgow Herald*, under the banner of "Arthurlie's Record" noted that "in the Second League the outstanding feat was the victory over Armadale by ten goals to none. McNally, the centre-forward for the winners, was responsible for eight of the goals, probably a record in senior league football."

The win propelled Arthurlie up the table, and it was followed by three further straight wins in which 12 goals were scored, so that by the end of the month the club sat in second, behind leaders Ayr United. A 6-1 defeat to the leaders in the New Year's Eve game, in which Jimmy Smith scored four, saw the Barrhead men slip down the table. In total they won 13 of their home games but suffered badly on their travels losing the same number away from home including a 9-2 defeat to Dundee United in January 1928, their highest scoring SFL loss. United were chasing promotion and were in second place in the Second Division. *The Scotsman* reported that "Arthurlie began in fine style against Dundee a United at Dundee, before 8,000 spectators, but the game ended with the surprising score of nine goals to two in favour of the home team. For the first fifteen minutes, Arthurlie were the superior side, Black being particularly prominent at outside left. Black scored from a penalty kick. The equalising goal came from a similar award, and was scored by Walker. From that point onwards the United played splendid football, and before the interval Hart, McGregor and Hutchison had scored goals. In the second half the United were easily masters of the game...in the last minute Black converted a penalty kick. "In February they also lost the return fixture to Armadale at Volunteer Park 2-0 and they eventually finished the season in seventh place.

Despite his goalscoring exploits McNally still found his way barred into the Celtic first team, especially as Jimmy McGrory had matched his goal-scoring feat just three months later. In addition, his one-off feat was somewhat overshadowed by Jimmy Smith's record goalscoring season for divisional champions Ayr United. At Arthurlie he scored 32 goals and was their top scorer for the 1927-28 season. He played only 11 league games for Celtic in total, scoring four times and in 1929 was loaned out again, this time to fellow First Division side Hamilton, for whom he scored seven times in ten starts. McNally eventually left Celtic and played six matches for Cardiff City in the 1931-32 season and 16 games for Leicester City in the mid-1930s, scoring seven times. In a cosmopolitan career he also played for Lausanne of Switzerland, Racing Club of Paris and Calais in France and Sligo, Bray and Distillery in Ireland. He died in 1973 and remains a joint record holder for the most goals scored in a Scottish Football League game. Sliman, who the scouts had come to watch eventually joined Bristol City in September 1928 for a fee of £280 and made 136 appearances for them before signing for Chesterfield where he made a further 240 appearances.

Arthurlie's 20th season in the Scottish Football League would surprisingly turn out to be their last. The general economic conditions and falling income from reduced gates caused the club to resign from the SFL before the end of the season. Whilst they did attract over 8000 spectators to Dunterlie Park for a Scottish Cup Quarter-Final against East Fife in March 1927, they averaged under 1500 for League games and in their final season this had dropped to around 500. Arthurlie opened their 1928-29 League campaign on Saturday 11th August 1928 at home to Arbroath. The match ended in a 1-1 draw in what *The Sunday Post* described as "a drab game". Their first win of the season came a fortnight later when they beat Queen of the South 4-0, with Hodgson, making his debut at centre-forward, scoring a hat-trick.

Form was indifferent and they lost 6-1 at Leith in October and in November lost 5-1 at Clydebank and by the same scoreline at St Bernard's. They lost 5-1 away at Dunfermline in the New Year's Day game of 1929, although on the following Saturday they unexpectedly beat Queen of the South to sit in 15th place. A 5-1 First Round Scottish Cup exit at the hands of Celtic precipitated a run of five League games without a win during which time bottom club Bathgate resigned from the SFL due to financial difficulties.

On the 16th March 1929 Arthurlie beat Clydebank by a solitary goal and this would turn out to be their last ever SFL win. A fortnight later they played their last ever League game at Dunterlie Park, a 1-1 draw with St Bernard's. Their last ever League game was a 4-1 away defeat at East Stirling at Firs Park on the 6th April, with the club sitting in 17th place and four games away from fulfilling their fixtures.

On the 17th April 1929 Arthurlie were forced to resign from the Scottish Football League, three months after Bathgate. Unlike Bathgate, who had themselves resigned in February 1929 and who had their record expunged, Arthurlie's results were allowed to stand. *The Glasgow Herald* reported on the situation: "a meeting of the Scottish Football Management Committee was held in Glasgow yesterday, when the resignation of Arthurlie FC from the Second Division was accepted. It was decided not to interfere with the points won or lost by the club. The registration of the Arthurlie players was cancelled. The annual general meeting was fixed for May 23." No re-elections took place at the SFL AGM on the 23rd May. Instead, Montrose and Brechin City were elected as replacements, Nithsdale Wanderers missing out on the ballot for a third time.

After two seasons as an amateur team Arthurlie became a junior side in 1931 and they continue to compete at this level to this day. By 1938 the pottery works had expanded onto the site of the former pitch. Dunterlie Park is now industrial wasteland, with the nearby Dunterlie community centre providing the only reference to its existence. The junior side's ground is also called Dunterlie Park and is located on Carlibar Road.

SEASON	LEAGUE	P	W	D	L	F	A	P	POS
1901-02	SCOT-2	22	6	5	11	32	42	17	10/12
1902-03	SCOT-2	22	6	8	8	34	46	20	9/12
1903-04	SCOT-2	22	5	5	12	37	50	15	11/12
1904-05	SCOT-2	22	9	5	8	37	42	23	6/12
1905-06	SCOT-2	22	10	2	10	42	43	22	6/12
1906-07	SCOT-2	22	12	3	7	50	39	27	3/12
1907-08	SCOT-2	22	6	5	11	33	45	17	11/12
1908-09	SCOT-2	22	5	1	16	29	55	11	12/12
1909-10	SCOT-2	22	6	5	11	34	47	17	10/12
1910-11	SCOT-2	22	7	5	10	26	33	19	10/12
1911-12	SCOT-2	22	7	5	10	26	30	19	8/12
1912-13	SCOT-2	26	7	5	14	37	49	19	13/14
1913-14	SCOT-2	22	8	4	10	35	37	20	9/12
1914-15	SCOT-2	26	6	4	16	36	66	16	13/14
1923-24	SCOT-3	30	21	5	4	59	24	47	1/16
1924-25	SCOT-2	38	14	8	16	56	60	36	12/20
1925-26	SCOT-2	38	17	5	16	81	75	39	7/20
1926-27	SCOT-2	38	18	5	15	90	83	41	7/20
1927-28	SCOT-2	38	18	4	16	84	90	40	7/20
1928-29	SCOT-2	32	9	7	16	51	73	25	17/19

Ayr FC

Formed: 1879
Colours: Red and gold hooped shirts and white shorts
Ground: Somerset Park
Entered League: 1897. Elected to Second Division
Number of League Seasons: 13
Highest League Finish: 3rd in Division Two
Honours: None
Left League: 1910. Merged with Ayr Parkhouse to form Ayr United

Ayr FC are the predecessors of the current Ayr United. In 1910 they merged with another Ayr-based club, Parkhouse, to form Ayr United, which is said to be the only Scottish Football League club to have been formed from a merger of two pre-existing League clubs.

Ayr FC were themselves formed in 1879 by a merger of the Ayr Thistle and Ayr Academicals football clubs. Their initial home ground was Springvale Park, which they left in 1884 to play home fixtures at Beresford Park, located in the town centre, near to the current Beresford Terrace and the train station. They made their first appearance in the Scottish Cup in the 1879-80 competition, going out in the First Round 6-0 at home to Kilmarnock Athletic. In October 1881 the lost to the same opposition by 7-1, this time in a Second Round match.

In the 1884-85 Scottish Cup competition, having recently moved to Beresford Park, Ayr FC had a run to the Fourth Round, knocking out Lugar Boswell, Cumnock and Kilmarnock Thistle, before losing to Hibernian. The following season they repeated the feat, this time knocking out Maybole, Monkcastle and Dalry. It took three matches before they were knocked out by Third Lanark. In the same season they reached the Ayrshire Cup final for the first time, losing 2-1 to Kilmarnock in the final staged at Rugby Park.

The 1887-88 Scottish Cup campaign was arguably one of their best although it ended in a heavy defeat. Having received a walkover in the First Round, Ayr thrashed Maybole 13-0 away on the 24th September 1887 in the next round. In the Third Round they beat Port Glasgow Athletic 4-0 to draw one of the early powerhouses of Scottish football,

Vale of Leven, in the next round. Vale of Leven were three-time winners and had appeared in six finals altogether. In the match played on the 5th November 1887 Ayr beat Vale 3-2 "in the presence of the largest turn-out of spectators ever seen in a football field in the town" (*Glasgow Herald*). Vale took an early lead but Ayr came back strongly and were denied by the post. In the second half Ayr lay siege to the visitors' goal and their pressure paid off with an equaliser on the hour mark. In the 71st minute Ayr took the lead and increased their advantage six minutes later. Vale got an immediate goal back but couldn't force an equaliser and lost 3-2. "The Vale of Leven did not play anything like good form" (*Glasgow Herald*). In the next round they were thrashed by beaten finalists Cambuslang. They went behind after six minutes and were two down after a quarter of an hour. Later in the half they conceded two more in the space of two minutes to go into the break four-nil down. Cambuslang ran riot in the second half to win 10-0.

At the end of the 1887-1888 season they decided to move to a new ground at Somerset Park, beside the Walkers Chemical Works and adjacent to Somerset Road. They did not have exclusive use of Beresford Park, which from time to time was used as a venue for the Ayr Cattle Show, which can't have helped the pitch condition. In February 1889 they reached the Ayrshire Cup final, losing to Hurlford 2-0. Later in the same year, in the Scottish Cup they registered a record win, beating Beith 16-0 on the 7th September, the report in *The Scotsman* simply saying that Beith "broke down after a quarter of an hour's play". They again made it to Fourth Round, going out to Leith Athletic after a replay.

The following year they made it to the Fourth Round again. By this time the Scottish Football League had started and Hearts had the honour of being the first League club to play at Somerset Park in a Scottish Cup tie. Ayr started well and scored after ten minutes. Fortunes ebbed and flowed. After 25 minutes it was 1-1 and ten minutes later they were two-one down. Early in the second half, a mistake by the home 'keeper Steele saw Hearts go 3-1 up. Ayr then pressed and made it 3-2 before Hearts scored again. Ayr got another one back to trail 4-3. Soon after Ayr's third "one of the Hearts' men violently struck the Ayr goalkeeper on the stomach and felled him. The crowd, infuriated, rushed over the ropes, and threatened the Hearts' man with violence, and would certainly have done him injury if the police had not given him protection." (*The Scotsman*)

On the 21st March 1891, James "Jimmy Logan" became the first, and only, Ayr FC player to gain international recognition, scoring the opening goal for Scotland in a 4-3 win over Wales at the Racecourse Ground in Wrexham. After the international he was briefly signed by Sunderland for the remainder of the 1891-92 season but then re-joined Ayr in October 1892 before signing for Aston Villa. He became famous for scoring a hat-trick in the 1894 FA Cup Final for Notts County in a 4–1 victory over Bolton Wanderers. Sadly he died prematurely at the age of 25 of pneumonia.

For the 1891-92 season Ayr joined the Scottish Alliance, set up as an alternative to the Scottish Football League. In 1893, having turned professional, they joined the Ayrshire Combination League. They came second in their first season and then won it for the next three years. The club were elected to the Scottish League's Second Division Two in 1897 at the second attempt. They first applied in May 1896 from the Ayrshire Combination having finished as champions in the 1895-96 season but they failed to find a seconder and were thus excluded from the vote. They applied again, as the Ayrshire Combination champions at the end of the 1896-97 season. At the League's AGM on the 1st June 1897 Motherwell (34 votes) and Port Glasgow Athletic (27 votes) were re-elected to the Second Division but Ayr, with 24 votes, beat Dumbarton who only got 17. So, only five years after being SFL champions, Dumbarton found themselves replaced by Ayr. Other clubs putting themselves forward to join the SFL were Victoria of Aberdeen, Falkirk, East Stirlingshire, Hamilton Academicals and Dundee Wanderers. Hamilton subsequently did join the SFL, taking over Renton's place four games into the season.

Ayr FC had 13 seasons as a League club, all in the Second Division, and they achieved three third place finishes, in the 1902-03, 1903-04 and 1907-08 seasons. They never finished in the bottom two and therefore avoided any re-election votes. In their first season, 1897-98, they finished a creditable sixth place. On the 4th September 1897 they played their first ever League game, at home to Glasgow-based Linthouse. A crowd of 850 saw Ayr concede two goals in each half in a 4-1 loss. They got their first points and first victory in their next game, another home fixture, on the 25th September against Port Glasgow Athletic. They won 3-0, scoring 25 minutes after the start and 10 minutes later they scored a second. A third was scored after the interval to round off a convincing display. Port Glasgow would go on to finish as runners-up to Kilmarnock.

Their third match was a 5-2 defeat against Kilmarnock. They also conceded five in their next game, a 5-1 defeat away against Airdrieonians, before scoring five themselves in a 5-3 victory against Leith Athletic. This took place on the 13th November and *The Scotsman* reported on the game, whilst also giving some insight into the impact of the town supporting two clubs. The report stated that "this fixture came off on Somerset Park on Saturday, in presence of an attendance that would doubtless have been larger but for a match on Beresford Park, the ground of the Parkhouse. Ayr have made such a poor show thus far in the present season that the game was at the commencement looked upon as likely to furnish a sure win for the visitors. This feeling was strengthened when about the quarter-hour Fotheringham sent a neat shot into the net for his side. Ayr were, however, not long in equalising by Aitken. At half-time, when each side had scored three goals, local opinion was still against the ground team. Soon after they entered on the second half Ayr had the luck to be awarded a penalty kick, but Hamilton failed to score. About the twenty minutes the locals were again on the ascendant, very pretty combination completely baffling the Athletic. The strangers made strenuous efforts to get on equal terms again, but they were met with such a strong opposition that they were not only not able to effect this, but they suffered another point to be scored against them. Eventually the Athletic were defeated by five goals to three. Parkhouse played a friendly against Maybole."

Ayr only picked up one more win in 1897 and finished the year in eighth place (in a 10 team division) with just six points. However, they then went on a five game unbeaten run during January and February that lifted them up to fifth. They suffered a couple of bad defeats in March but did record a season's best win on the 26th March with a 6-1 win over Morton (who finished third) and eventually they finished in sixth place.

The next couple of seasons saw them flirt with the re-election places, finishing eighth, in a ten team division, twice in a row. They again opened their campaign at home to Linthouse, this time winning 4-0. In October 1898 they registered one of their best wins, beating Abercorn 7-3. Ayr scored two in the opening fifteen minutes and added a third before their visitors pulled one back. Ayr scored two more in the first half to lead 5-1 at half-time. In the second half play was more even with each side scoring two goals. They were undone by their away form, as they lost eight of their nine away games, picking up a solitary point on their travels in a 3-3 draw with Abercorn.

The 1899-1900 season saw them plagued by inconsistency as they recorded some big wins and losses. The heavy defeats came early in the season where they had a disastrous start losing their first five games, including an opening day home defeat against Port Glasgow Athletic by three goals to one. On the 2nd September they lost 5-1 at home to Linthouse and a fortnight later they lost 7-1 away against Morton. By mid -December they were second from bottom in ninth but at the end of the month, on the 30th they recorded a good 5-0 win over Airdrie, a major factor being that the visitors played a man short. On the 6th January 1900 they beat Port Glasgow Athletic at Clune Park 8-2, their opponents putting out a weakened team.

The 1900-01 season was much improved, and they started by winning six out of seven of their opening fixtures. The last of these, a 3-1 win over Motherwell on the 8th December, moved them into fourth place. They then twice conceded five goals in the next two away games in losses against Airdrieonians and Port Glasgow Athletic. New

Year's Day win at home against Clyde, saw them in fifth at the start of 1901 but they lost five of their last six matches to eventually finish a place lower. Their improved showing spilled over into the Ayrshire Cup, which they won for the first time, beating Stevenson Thistle 2-1 in a replayed Final, following a 1-1 draw the week before.

The 1901-02 season saw another mid-table finish in an otherwise uneventful season but Ayr then secured two successive third place finishes, their highest ever placing in the Scottish Football League. In the 1902-03 season their third place was underpinned by a strong home performance, in which they won ten of their eleven games at Somerset Park. They had a brief flirtation with the top two, defeating promotion rivals Motherwell 1-0 in front of 4,000 fans at the end of February and the following week, when they beat Falkirk, they temporarily moved into second place. Airdrieonians were the runaway leaders but crucially Motherwell in fourth place were only two points behind, but with three games in hand. It was vital, therefore, that having beaten 'Well at home they also had to beat them away, but they lost 2-0 and were eventually pipped by a point. Due to the First Division being expanded to 14 clubs both Lanarkshire clubs were promoted.

The following year they again finished third, and once again were just one point off second. They were joined in the Second Division by local rivals Ayr Parkhouse who were elected to the League in May 1903. Ayr made a strong start to the new season and were unbeaten in their first six games. A 4-3 away win against Leith Athletic in early November saw them in fourth place, having played four games less than the teams in second and third, but only two points behind them. A 3-1 away win in the derby game against Ayr Parkhouse in February 1904 saw them five points of second but with five games in hand. Hamilton ran away with it this time, winning the Second Division championship by eight points. Ayr suffered a surprise home defeat against by now perennial strugglers Abercorn but perhaps more crucially, they lost 2-0 against promotion rivals Clyde. Going into the game they were just a point behind Clyde, having played a game more. As a result of their defeat they were now three points behind with just two to play. Clyde eventually finished a point ahead but neither them nor division champions Hamilton were elected to the First Division. At the end of the season their rivals Parkhouse, who had finished bottom, failed to be re-elected and dropped out of the League after just one season.

The 1902-03 and 1903-04 seasons represented the high point for the club, although there would be another third place finish in the 1907-08 season. H G Murray took over the managerial reins for the 1904-05 season and would be in charge of the club up to 1910 and then of the newly merged Ayr United from 1910-1914. In his first season in charge the club finished in fifth and also won the Ayrshire Cup for the second time, beating Kilmarnock 1-0.

Ayr began the 1905-06 season with three straight wins to start and on the 14th October beat Vale of Leven 5-1 to make a statement of intent. This game was played in rough stormy weather and it was the visitors who took the lead following a mistake and there was no further scoring in the first half. On the resumption of play Ayr attacked and Garry equalised after just five minutes. Keeping the pressure up the same player then scored a second. From this point Ayr were in total control, helped by their opponents going down to ten men due to injury, and they scored three more goals. The result left Ayr top of the table, having played six, won five and drawn the other. Any hopes of a promotion challenge soon petered out as they suffered heavy losses to Leith Athletic (5-1), St Bernard's (5-1) and Hamilton (6-0). They lost their last four League matches to eventually finish seventh although they did retain the Ayrshire trophy, beating rivals Ayr Parkhouse 1-0.

Parkhouse returned to the Scottish League for the 1906-07 season. Unfortunately Ayr carried their poor form into the new season and after an opening game 1-1 draw away against East Stirlingshire they lost their next five matches before beating Ayr Parkhouse 2-1 at the beginning of November. They played out two entertaining fixtures against Dumbarton, first losing 6-1 away in December before winning 5-0 at home in January, and eventually finished eighth, their joint lowest placing in the League. Rivals Ayr Parkhouse again finished bottom, although this time they were re-elected.

The 1907-08 season saw an improvement in Ayr's fortunes with another third place finish and an unsuccessful attempt to gain election to the First Division. After an indifferent start to the season they went on a nine game unbeaten run, so that by mid-December they were top, three points clear of Dumbarton who had two points deducted for fielding an ineligible player. The run ended when they lost at home to Dumbarton on the 21st December 1907 and they suffered consecutive defeats across the festive period, the second of these away against Ayr Parkhouse, their first League defeat to their town rivals. These results ultimately cost them as Raith Rovers won the Second Division championship and Dumbarton came in second.

On the 1st June 1908, the club made a failed bid to be elected to the First Division, attracting an embarrassing no votes in a six way contest in which they were one of four Second Division teams (along with Raith Rovers, Dumbarton and Abercorn) who were aiming to displace Clyde and Port Glasgow Athletic. The result prompted speculation and debate around the possibility of a merger between Ayr and Parkhouse and many believed that First Division football could be brought to the town of Ayr if both clubs put aside their differences and amalgamated.

Ayr weren't able to reproduce their form of the previous year and settled into the usual mid-table finish, although they did put five past Dumbarton, Albion Rovers and Arthurlie before finishing in fifth. The following season they finished seventh and Parkhouse finished 12th and bottom. This would be the last season as separate entities as the two clubs merged at the end of the season. Ayr opened what would prove to be their last season with an entertaining 4-3 win over Albion Rovers. In November they won the derby game 2-0, a keenly contested match before a large crowd. Ayr took the lead in the first half through Allan but the win wasn't assured until Muir scored a second a few minutes before the close of play. The last Ayr derby was played on New Year's Day 1910, with Ayr doing the double in a 3-1 away win.

Under the headline "Ayr Football Clubs and Amalgamation", *The Scotsman*, on the 1st March 1910 reported that "since the New Year proposals have been on foot to amalgamate the Ayr and Ayr Parkhouse Football Clubs with the view to a united team entering the First League. At a recent public meeting the prevailing feeling was for amalgamation, and it was decided then to appoint three gentlemen to acquaint the clubs of the resolution so unanimously adopted. The Parkhouse Club were the first to move, and they decided in favour of amalgamation. A meeting of the shareholders of the Ayr Club was held last night to ballot on the question. The motion was that the club was agreeable to the principle of amalgamation, and the amendment was to the effect that there should be no amalgamation under any conditions. The result of the ballot was that the motion and amendment each received 120 votes, and as the chairman refused to give his casting vote, no decision was arrived at. It was ultimately agreed to postpone further consideration till the annual general meeting of the club in April."

On the 2nd April 1910 the club played what would turn out to be there last League game as Ayr FC at Somerset Park, 1,000 spectators were present to see a 2-2 draw with Arthurlie. A week later the two Ayr sides met in the Final of the Ayrshire Cup at Somerset Park, with Ayr lifting the trophy for the fourth time. *The Scotsman* reported that "play was fast and keen, with the Parkhouse distinctly superior in the first half, but the finishing efforts of the forwards was very poor. The interval arrived without any scoring. When about twenty minutes of the second half had gone, Ayr scored through Allan. After Ayr had looked like adding to their score, the Parkhouse rallied in the last few minutes and almost made a draw of it."

By now it was generally accepted that the town of Ayr could not support two senior sides and there was certainly no prospect of First Division football coming to the town unless the two joined forces. Parkhouse were facing re-election again having finished bottom and so at the end of April it was agreed that the clubs would amalgamate. This is the only example to date of a merger between two existing League sides. The Inverness Thistle/Caledonian merger in 1994 occurred when both clubs were in the Highland League.

On the 4th May 1910 Celtic played the newly merged club, called Ayr United, in a friendly at Somerset Park, winning 3-2. A month later, the new club applied for a First Division spot but they won just two votes. Morton were re-elected with 16 votes. Port Glasgow Athletic resigned their First Division place and the vacant spot was claimed by Raith Rovers, the joint Second Division Champions, who got 13 votes. The newly merged club instead continued in the Second Division.

In a vindication of the merger, the new club finished as runners-up in the 1910-11 season. Ayr United also reached the final of the Ayrshire Cup, losing to Hurlford 2-1, although they won it a year later. The following year they won the Second Division championship but did not apply for promotion. In the 1912-13 season they were the Second Division champions again, and were elected into the First Division when it was increased to 20 clubs.

SEASON	LEAGUE	P	W	D	L	F	A	P	POS
1897-98	SCOT-2	18	7	2	9	36	42	16	6/10
1898-99	SCOT-2	18	5	3	10	35	51	13	8/10
1899-00	SCOT-2	18	6	2	10	39	48	14	8/10
1900-01	SCOT-2	18	9	0	9	32	34	18	6/10
1901-02	SCOT-2	22	8	5	9	27	33	21	8/12
1902-03	SCOT-2	22	12	3	7	34	24	27	3/12
1903-04	SCOT-2	22	11	6	5	33	30	28	3/12
1904-05	SCOT-2	22	11	1	10	46	37	23	5/12
1905-06	SCOT-2	22	9	3	10	43	51	21	7/12
1906-07	SCOT-2	22	7	6	9	34	38	20	8/12
1907-08	SCOT-2	22	11	5	6	40	33	27	3/12
1908-09	SCOT-2	22	10	3	9	43	36	23	5/12
1909-10	SCOT-2	22	9	3	10	37	40	21	7/12

Ayr Parkhouse

Formed: 1886
Colours: Navy blue and white hooped shirts and white shorts
Ground: Beresford Park
Entered League: 1903. Elected to Second Division Two. 1906. Elected to Second Division
Number of League Seasons: 5
Honours: None
Highest League Finish: 6th in Division Two
Left League: 1904. Failed re-election. 1910. Merged with Ayr FC to form Ayr United

Ayr Parkhouse were the other Ayr based football club that merged to form today's Ayr United. They were formed in 1886 and took their name from the Parkhouse farmhouse where the club's players trained. Known as 'The Parkies', they initially played their home games at Ballantine Drive, before moving to the Ayr Racecourse ground. In 1888 Ayr FC vacated the better developed Beresford Park, and Ayr Parkhouse moved in, where they played for the remainder of their existence. Ayr Parkhouse spent five seasons as members of the SFL across two separate spells before merging with Ayr FC in 1910 to form Ayr United.

They made their debut in the 1890-91 Scottish Cup final and beat Kilbirnie of North Ayrshire 6-1 in a First Round tie held on the 6th September 1890. In the first half play was pretty even, even though Parkhouse managed to go into the break two up. In the second half the home team dominated play and scored another four goals. Kilbirnie scored a late consolation. Parkhouse lost to Summerton Athletic of Govan in Glasgow in the next round.

In the 1894-95 Scottish Cup competition they reached the Third Round. Having accounted for Polton Vale (of Loanhead, Midlothian) and Mossend Swifts (of West Calder, West Lothian) they came up against one of the early powerhouses of Scottish football in Renton, but only lost 3-2. They also reached the Third Round in the 1897-98 competition, knocking out Dundee Wanderers, who had played a season in the League), before losing to Kilmarnock 7-2.

In the 1898-99 season they achieved their best Scottish Cup result to date when they knocked out Dundee in the First Round. Dundee had reached the Semi-finals the year before and were playing in the First Division. The match, played on the 14th January 1899, attracted 2,000 spectators and the crowd saw the home team take a surprise lead when McCosh's shot was deflected in for an own goal. Dunsmore made it two after nice build up play from Baird and Boyd. With fifteen minutes to go Dundee pulled a goal back but just before the final whistle Spence made it 3-1. The giant-killing Parkhouse team was: Brown; Dick, Orr; Mellon, Paton, Munnehen; McCosh, Spence, Baird, Dunsmore and Boyd. In the Second Round Parkhouse drew the holders Rangers, again at home, and this time a crowd of 5,000 came to the match. Any hopes of keeping it tight at the start were quickly banished when Rangers scored within the first two minutes. With Parkhouse still reeling their opponents quickly added a second and a third came after a quarter of an hour. Shortly before the interval a mistake by Riley, the Parkhouse 'keeper allowed a fourth. In the second half, after a series of corners, Milne scored for Parkhouse in the 60th minute. Rangers lost a player to injury and played the rest of the game with ten men, happy to shut up shop and protect their lead, and winning 4-1.

Parkhouse were founder members of the Ayrshire League in 1891 and they played in the competition for two seasons, coming in second and then third. They were then one of a number of clubs that broke away to form the rival Ayrshire Combination in 1893 and they played there up to 1897. Kilmarnock had left to join the Scottish Football League in 1895 and when Ayr FC did the same in 1897, the loss of the two biggest clubs brought the competition to an end. A revised Ayrshire League was formed in 1900 by Ayr Parkhouse, Beith, Galston and, Maybole and ran for two seasons. During this time Ayr Parkhouse also competed in the Ayrshire Cup, reaching three Semi-finals before eventually getting to the Final in 1900, where they lost to Kilmarnock. They again reached the Final in 1902, this time lifting the trophy, defeating Galston 1-0 in a match played at Kilmarnock's Rugby Park.

In 1901 they first applied to join the Scottish Football League but were unsuccessful. Due to League expansion one place was available after the two clubs facing re-election (Hamilton and Motherwell) had won their places. Parkhouse competed against Scottish Combination sides Arthurlie and Albion Rovers and Raith Rovers from the East of Scotland League. Ayr FC were already in the SFL which diminished the chances of a second club from the town and it is said that their rivals campaigned against their inclusion. Parkhouse were eliminated in the first ballot and Arthurlie beat Raith Rovers by 12 votes to 10 in the final vote.

Following their triumph in the Ayrshire Cup Parkhouse made a second attempt at the SFL AGM held on the 19th May 1902. Again, due to League expansion, there were two additional places this time up for grabs. Parkhouse were up against Albion Rovers and Raith Rovers again, the latter now playing in the Northern League. Falkirk from the Central Combination were a new applicant. Ayr Parkhouse were again unsuccessful with Raith and Falkirk being elected to the League.

In January 1903 Parkhouse sold their best player, Sandy Bell, to Manchester United for £700. Bell would go on to make nearly 300 appearances for his new club and be capped for Scotland in 1912. More significantly 1903 was third time lucky for Parkhouse as they were finally elected to the SFL. The First Division expanded with two clubs promoted, so four places were up for grabs at the AGM held on the 18th May 1903. Both Raith and Clyde were re-elected and Albion Rovers also finally made it into the SFL with 21 votes. Ayr Parkhouse took the fourth and final position, beating St Johnstone of the Northern League by 1 vote (15-14).

Their initial season in the League was a disaster. They only won three games and finished 12th and bottom of the Second Division and therefore had to reapply. James Murray was the manager for their first season and they opened their League campaign on the 15th August 1903 with a visit to Shawfield to play re-elected Clyde. *The Scotsman* reported that "Ayr Parkhouse made their first appearance as Second Leaguers on Saturday, when they opposed Clyde at Shawfield, Glasgow. The ground was very heavy and rain fell heavily at the start...The amateurs kicked off before about 1000 spectators, but Clyde settling down from the start, Walker scored the first goal in three minutes. Play thereafter was contested on even lines, and although Walker again put the ball through, off-side was given against him, and half-time found Clyde leading by one goal to nothing. On resuming, Clyde again took up the running and Walker notched a second and Monteith a third goal. These further reverses had a good effect on the play of the Parkhouse men, who were lasting the pace very well and Ball almost scored, McArthur bringing off a splendid save. Towards the close the amateurs pressed hard, and R. Young at length beat McArthur." The Parkhouse line-up for their first ever SFL match was: Thomson: S Cairns, Hill: Williams, Menzies: W Cairns, R Young, Bell, G Young, Finlay and Garven.

They played their first League home game the following Saturday, the 22nd August, when 1,200 spectators watched them entertain Albion Rovers. Despite taking a 2-0 lead into the half-time break and which they continued to hold until the 75th minute, they eventually lost 5-2. *The Scotsman* reported that "this League match was played on Beresford Park, Ayr, before a large attendance. The initial stage of the first half was in favour of the visitors but for the first thirty minutes there was no scoring. Parkhouse then pressed their opponents and Muir allowed a soft one, kicked by Bell for Parkhouse, to slip through his hands into the net. A few minutes afterwards Garven headed the second goal for Ayr, and as the Albion Rovers failed to score the teams changed ends with Parkhouse leading by two goals. When they crossed over, the game was without incident, though decidedly in favour of the strangers for nearly half an hour. From that time onwards the Rovers got completely the better of their opponents and during the last quarter of an hour they scored no fewer than five goals." Conlin, the Albion outside-left, scored four of his side's goals.

Ayr Parkhouse's first League points came a week later when they beat Raith Rovers at Starks Park by the odd goal in five. They bagged the points by surprise, coming back from 2-1 down. In the first period Rovers had the major share of the play, although Parkhouse were the first to score through Garven. Raith hit back and went into the half-time break with a 2-1 lead. In the second period Raith continued to dictate play but failed to score. Muir drew the visitors level and Cameron ensured Parkhouse took both points with the winner.

Parkhouse picked up a third point with a draw at home to Falkirk before reality bit home and they lost five in a row, including a 6-1 reverse defeat at Brockville against Falkirk on the 10th October and a 5-1 defeat at Douglas Park against Hamilton on the 24th October. In all, Parkhouse conceded 25 goals in their first eight matches and had the division's leakiest defence. These results left them just a point above a group of four teams at the bottom.

Their third win came at the beginning of November with a narrow win over East Stirlingshire but they then went the remainder of the season - twelve games - without a win, losing their final game on the 12th March against Albion Rovers 5-1. Parkhouse finished adrift at the bottom, five points behind Arthurlie. Rivals Ayr FC finished third. The first Ayr League derby had taken place on the 9th January 1904, with Ayr FC hosting Parkhouse with the match ending in honours even. Ayr FC won the return a month later 3-1.

The rivalry between the two Ayr sides also manifested off the pitch. At the SFA's AGM on the 17th May the Parkhouse candidate, Thomas Steen beat the sitting Ayr representative, J Copland, for a place on the committee. At the SFL AGM at the end of the month it is said that the directors of Ayr FC campaigned vigorously against Parkhouse's application for re-election and the club duly lost their place. In the first ballot Arthurlie, also facing re-election, topped the poll with 14 votes, Aberdeen got 11, Parkhouse 9, Royal Albert 7, and Cowdenbeath, then of the Northern League also got 7 votes. Newly formed Aberdeen had tried unsuccessfully to be fast tracked into the First Division. In the second ballot Aberdeen got 14 to Parkhouse's 6 and so after just one season Ayr Parkhouse dropped out of the League.

For the next two seasons Parkhouse played in the Scottish Combination. They also played in the Scottish Cup of 1904-05, giving a good account of themselves in going out to Rangers in the First Round by just 2-1. At the end of their first season as a non-League club they made an immediate attempt at returning to the League. Due to the promotion to the First Division of Falkirk and Aberdeen as means of expanding that division, there were four places available – the usual two re-election places plus the two vacant spots. St Bernard's and Abercorn faced re-election and eight other teams also applied at the League AGM held on the 22nd May 1905. St. Bernard's and Abercorn were both re-elected, topping the voting. Cowdenbeath, who finished second behind Dundee 'A' in the Northern League were elected with 18 votes along with Vale of Leven who were Combination champions and got 17. Ayr Parkhouse came fifth in the voting with 7.

This second rejection caused a lot of soul searching at the club. Originally a strictly amateur club like Queen's Park, the board, at a meeting held on the 20th October 1905, unanimously decided to signal their intent by turning professional. They reached the final of the Ayrshire Cup in April 1906, losing to deadly rivals Ayr FC 1-0, but better news came the following month, when, after two seasons outwith the League, Ayr Parkhouse were accepted back into the Second Division in 1906. At the SFL AGM held on the 21st May 1906 a record thirteen clubs applied for four available spaces – the two clubs facing automatic re-election and two new places following the First Division again expanding. Seven teams applied from the Scottish Combination and four from the Northern League. Former SFL clubs Dumbarton, Renton and Dundee Wanderers were among the applicants. Surprisingly, Ayr Parkhouse were elected over the others from the Combination despite finishing eighth out of eleven clubs. The two clubs facing re-election, Vale of Leven and East Stirlingshire, were voted back into the League along with Ayr Parkhouse and Dumbarton. Parkhouse actually came second in the voting. Vale of Leven came top with 22 votes, then Parkhouse with 14, East Stirlingshire with 13 and Dumbarton with 12. The unsuccessful clubs, with their votes in brackets were: Alloa Athletic (8), Dunfermline Athletic (8), Royal Albert (7), Stenhousemuir (4), Beith (3), Lochgelly United (3), Renton (3), Dundee Wanderers (1), and East Fife (1).

Ayr Parkhouse re-joined the Scottish Football League for the 1906-07 and in this second spell performed without much distinction for the next four seasons. Their second appearance in the SFL was just as a much a disaster as their first, although they did win two more games. They finished bottom again in their first season back, winning five of their 22 matches and finishing with 12 points. Rivals Ayr FC came in eighth place. Parkhouse began life back in the League with a 2-1 home win over Abercorn on the 18th August 1906. Trailing 1-0 at half-time having conceded a penalty, the score remained the same until 15 minutes from time when Parkhouse equalised through McCall and they snatched the winner right at the death through Gemmell. They came backdown to earth with a bump though against Dumbarton in their next game, losing 6-0 at Boghead, although they were only one down at the interval.

After beating Albion Rovers 1-0 on the 22nd December Parkhouse failed to win another game losing seven of their last eight matches. On the 6th April 1907, in their last game of the season, they beat the newly crowned champions St Bernard's, although the Edinburgh side fielded a reserve team. *The Scotsman* reported that "St Bernard's tried the experiment of placing two teams on the football field, and that which met Ayr Parkhouse at the Gymnasium under Second League auspices was decisively beaten by five goals to three. The Ayr team was strongly represented and the forwards were not slow to take advantage of openings. When twenty minutes of the game had gone the visitors had the strong lead of three goals, but the Saints scored twice before half-time. Parkhouse obtained another two goals in the second half, while the Saints raised their total to three. It was a poor game throughout, the Saints' reserves being for the most part outplayed."

On the 27th May 1907, at the League's AFGM, Ayr Parkhouse contested their seventh successive vote. They faced re-election with East Stirlingshire, who had tied on 16 points with Raith. As goal average wasn't used to separate clubs in important league positions the two sides met in a play-off game, Raith beating East Stirlingshire 3-2 on the 11th May at Logie Green in Edinburgh. East Stirlingshire, with 24 votes, and Ayr Parkhouse, with 16, were both re-elected to the SFL. They were opposed by two clubs, Renton of the Scottish Union, who got 8 votes, and Dunfermline Athletic of the Northern League who got 6 votes.

There was a marked improvement in their third season in the League. A 50:50 record, won 11, lost 11 with no draws saw them finish mid-table in sixth. Their best result was a 5-1 win against East Stirlingshire in December 1907, *The Scotsman* reporting that "Parkhouse were first dangerous, and kept the Shire busily defending. After twenty minutes play Skillen ran in and scored, Cameron adding a second a few minutes later. Before half-time the Shire goal fell a third time, Skillen beating Caldwell with a fast shot. Five minutes after resuming Skillen rushed in with the ball and raised the Parkhouse total to four. Shire now improved but Parkhouse returned to the attack again, and Cameron shot, Caldwell caught the ball, but in attempting to fling it out he dropped it into the goal. Before time was called Shire scored."

In the New Year's game of 1908 Parkhouse recorded their first ever League win over Ayr FC, at the sixth attempt, by two goals to nil. They had lost the three away games and in the two previous seasons they had drawn both games at Beresford Park. *The Scotsman* reported on the game: "At Beresford Park, Ayr, before a record crowd for a Second League game. The ground was hard and slippery, and miskicking was frequent. Ayr were the better team in the first half, but, despite several good chances. They failed to score, and half-time found the teams level. A hard game took place in the second half, Ayr having several chances, but the first goal fell to Parkhouse. From a breakaway, Skillen scoring. Ayr now lost heart, and Skillen again scored. Again Parkhouse pressed to the end, but failed to add to their score." For the first time in seven years Ayr Parkhouse were not involved in the voting at the League's AGM. Ayr FC were though. They had finished in second, runners-up to Raith, and the whole of the top four unsuccessfully applied to join the First Division, Raith missing out by one vote.

Parkhouse produced another mid-table finish in the 1908-09 season, coming in seventh this time, just two places behind Ayr FC. In a largely uneventful season there were two noticeable results. First, on the 2nd January 1909 they won the Ayr derby match 2-1, this time away at Somerset Park. *The Scotsman* reported that "at half-time neither team had scored, though Parkhouse had missed a penalty. Shortly after resuming Parkhouse scored from a penalty, and Lynch added a second with a good shot. Another penalty was awarded Parkhouse, but Gilhooley saved. Anderson scored for Ayr near the close. The Ayr men deserved the equaliser, which, however, they could not get." The other result was a 9-0 thrashing at Dundee in the First Round of the Scottish Cup. The First Division side, with home advantage, were vastly superior and there was a huge gulf in class. A crowd of 10,000 watched the game in which Hunter and Bellamy each scored a hat- trick for Dundee. Although their opponents were knocked out in the next round by Rangers, in the League they finished as runners-up to Celtic by just one point.

In their fifth (and last) season they again finished 12th and bottom, their third bottom place finish in five seasons. They lost their opening game 1-0 at Cowdenbeath, and only picked up one point from their first four games before beating Arthurlie (4-1) and Albion Rovers (3-1) away, with the home team reduced to nine men having had two players sent off. These two wins in early October were followed by a run of five defeats in a row, part of a longer sequence where they went twelve games without a win. The last of these was a 5-0 defeat at Dumbarton, where they conceded two in the first seven minutes and were 4-0 down at half-time having also given away two penalties. With just four games of the season remaining they were bottom with just seven points. Arthurlie were ahead of them with 11 and Cowdenbeath had 14 and so another re-election vote looked inevitable.

On Saturday 26th February 1910 Ayr Parkhouse ended their disastrous run by beating Dumbarton in the return fixture by 4-2, but the other results went against them, meaning they were guaranteed to face re-election. However, events off the pitch were also moving to bring about the end of the Parkhouse Club. Under the headline "Ayr Football Clubs and Amalgamation", *The Scotsman*, on the 1st March 1910 reported that "since the New Year proposals have been on foot to amalgamate the Ayr and Ayr Parkhouse Football Clubs with the view to a united team entering the First League. At a recent public meeting the prevailing feeling was for amalgamation, and it was decided then to appoint three gentlemen to acquaint the clubs of the resolution so unanimously adopted. The Parkhouse Club were the first to move, and they decided in favour of amalgamation. A meeting of the shareholders of the Ayr Club was held last night…It was ultimately agreed to postpone further consideration till the annual general meeting of the club in April."

On 9th April 1910, Ayr beat Parkhouse by the only goal of the game at Somerset Park to win the Ayrshire Cup. It proved to be the last match for both sides as independent clubs. On April 29th it was agreed in principle for the clubs to amalgamate and at the following meeting, with backing from both sets of shareholders, the only amalgamation to date by two Scottish League clubs was completed. The merged club made an unsuccessful bid to join the First Division at the SFL AGM on the 7th June. The following season Ayr United made their debut while Dundee Hibernian filled the vacancy. The newly merged club finished as runners-up in the 1910-11 season and then won the Second Division title for the next two seasons, finally being elected to the First Division in 1913.

Ayr Parkhouse and Ayr FC competed against each other in each of the five seasons that Parkhouse were in the League. The overall head-to-head record is two wins for Ayr Parkhouse, five wins for Ayr FC and three draws.

Although Ayr United's home ground was Ayr FC's Somerset Park, they continued to use Beresford Park for training and reserve team fixtures until 1926 when the ground was sold. Subsequently it was redeveloped for housing and Parkhouse Street and the adjacent Beresford Terrace now stand on the former site of the ground.

SEASON	LEAGUE	P	W	D	L	F	A	P	POS
1903-04	SCOT-2	22	3	4	15	23	61	10	12/12
1906-07	SCOT-2	22	5	2	15	32	64	12	12/12
1907-08	SCOT-2	22	11	0	11	38	38	22	6/12
1908-09	SCOT-2	22	8	5	9	29	31	21	7/12
1909-10	SCOT-2	22	4	3	15	27	43	11	12/12

Bathgate

Formed: 1893
Colours: Maroon shirts and white shorts
Ground: Mill Park
Entered League: Founder member of the reformed Scottish Division Two 1921.
Number of League Seasons: 7
Honours: None
Highest League Finish: 3rd in Division Two
Left League: Resigned 1929. Wound up October 1938

After our trip to Ayr we return to West Lothian and to the second of the four West Lothian towns that played in the Scottish Football League in the 1920s – Bathgate. Historically Bathgate was a centre of coal mining and then later for the distilling of paraffin from shale. The landscape around Bathgate is still dotted with the reddish-orange spoil heaps from this era. Later it developed into a centre for brickworks and steel-making plants.

A football team from Bathgate was first formed in 1879 but disappeared soon after. Bathgate FC were formed in July 1893 and competed in the Eastern League between 1893 and 1902 when they joined the Central Combination. It was at this time that Bathgate moved to Mill Park and they played all of their games there until they folded in 1938. Mill Park took its name from the adjacent Mill Road and saw-mill to the west and was bordered by Russell Row and the gasworks to the south, and Cochrane Street and a spade and shovel works to the north.

Their original ground, Boghead Park, located near to the golf course, hosted the Linlithgowshire Cup final in 1889 and 1891 and Mill Park was then used for the 1894 final. In the 1894-95 season Bathgate won this county competition, for the first time, beating Bo'ness 5-4 in the final played at Linlithgow. They would go on to lift the trophy another five times, the last one being in 1920.

Bathgate made their debut in the Scottish Cup in January 1897, losing 5-0 in the First Round to Blantyre. They also went out at the same stage the following year and didn't compete again until 1905. After playing in the Central Combination for the 1902-03 season Bathgate moved to the Midland League for the 1903-04 season, but this competition only lasted a year as a number of clubs left to reform the Eastern League. Bathgate were one of them and they played the 1904-05 season here before continuing their roaming existence by joining the Scottish Combination for the 1905-06 season.

In February 1905 they reappeared in the Scottish Cup, beating Arbroath 2-1 in the First Round but were heavily beaten 6-1 away at Aberdeen in the next round. In 1906 Bathgate were among some of the members of the Scottish Combination who formed a new league, the Scottish Union, which included within its ranks the reserve teams of some Scottish League clubs including Rangers, Hearts and St Mirren. Rangers 'A' were declared the first champions when Bathgate declared that they were unwilling to contest a play-off after finishing level with the Glasgow club. The following season Bathgate won the competition outright. Bathgate did win the Linlithgowshire Cup again after a marathon final. The match against Broxburn was eventually settled in their fourth game, played in the September, after the first three finals, played across April and May had failed to settle the contest due to a pitch invasion, a protest, and a drawn game (including extra-time). Bathgate retained the trophy the following year, beating Bo'ness 4-2 after the first match had ended with one goal apiece.

In 1909 Bathgate transferred to the reformed twelve team Central League which included Alloa Athletic, Arbroath, St Johnstone, Stenhousemuir, Dunfermline Athletic and East Fife. In their first season they finished fifth. In the same season they qualified for the Scottish Cup but exited in the First Round, losing 4-0 at home to Hearts, but in front of a crowd of 5,000.

In both 1911 and 1912 Bathgate won the Linlithgowshire Cup, beating Bo'ness and Broxburn Athletic respectively. In 1912 Bathgate made an unsuccessful bid to join the Scottish Football League, the catalyst being the decision to increase the Second Division to fourteen clubs. The bottom two clubs Albion Rovers and Vale of Leven were unanimously re-elected and a second vote was taken to fill the two vacancies. At the League's AGM held on the 3rd June Dunfermline Athletic, also from the Central League, were voted into the League but Johnstone of the Scottish Union took the other place. The other two clubs missing out were Galston and Peebles Rovers. All three of the disappointed clubs would eventually join the Scottish Football League.

Bathgate finished fourth in the Central League for the 1912-13 season and when they finished as runners-up the year after they made another unsuccessful bid to join the SFL. Johnstone and Vale of Leven were up for re-election and two new clubs were being admitted. In a first round of voting Bathgate survived an elimination ballot and were tied in third place. The results were: Clydebank 26, Vale of Leven 25, Bathgate 17, Johnstone 17, Lochgelly United 17, East Fife 13 and Forfar Athletic 2. The bottom two clubs were eliminated and another ballot was held with the top two to be elected. Vale of Leven and Lochgelly were the principal beneficiaries and Vale of Leven, with 29 votes, and Clydebank, with 26 votes were elected. Lochgelly had increased their vote to 22, Bathgate to 20 whereas Johnstone remained the same on 17 votes. It now went into a third round of voting with only the top club earning a place in the League. This went to Lochgelly who got 23 votes. Bathgate got 17 votes, beating Johnstone who had 15. It was now a straight fight for the fourth and final place and it was Johnstone who were re-elected, beating Bathgate by five votes. Bathgate had tied with Johnstone on the first ballot and beat them in ballots two and three, but lost out on the crucial fourth and final ballot.

As it was, the Second Division only ran for one more season and was suspended due to the War. Seven of the Second Division clubs combined with five of the Central League sides, including Bathgate, to form the Eastern League in 1915. In 1916 they lost in the Linlithgowshire Cup against Armadale but got their revenge in the 1919-20 season when they beat them to win the competition, for what would be the last time. In 1919 they rejoined the Central League and in 1921 this competition was incorporated into the SFL as the newly-reformed Second Division.

On the 20th August 1921 Bathgate played their first ever Scottish Football League game, a 2-1 away win at Bayview against East Fife. *The Scotsman* reported that "Henretta opened the scoring for Bathgate, and after Stewart had missed one penalty, T Neish equalised from a second. East Fife had Bathgate comfortably beaten on play in the next period, till taking an advantage of an open field Chalmers dashed off and scored. Burton shook the upright in an immediate response, but there was no more scoring."

The first SFL match was played at Mill Park on 27 August 1921, a 0–0 draw with local rivals Armadale, watched by a large crowd of over 3,000. *The Sunday Post* reported on the match and gave an appraisal of the Bathgate team: "It was a dour struggle between those two great local rivals, Bathgate and Armadale, and a no goals result was a fair reflex of the game. Bathgate by the inclusion of Robertson, of Motherwell, signed the previous evening, added to their strength, for he did especially good work in opening up play. In the first half Armadale had the better of the attack, but Wilkinson gave a delightful performance, and shots that came his way were smartly saved. In the second half it was Bathgate's show, but here there was greatly required an opportunist. The feature of the match was the splendid defence of each team. Bathgate had in Stein a lad who will soon achieve success, for he has both speed and adroitness in distributing play...McNeil and Robertson proved easily the better wing, and Robertson was especially clever at outside right. At outside left Chalmers was anxious, but he lacked method. Brown, his partner...had some pretty touches. Bathgate have a powerful half-back line, and in the Brothers Fleming ideal backs. Wilkinson, as custodian, will not be easily beaten." The Bathgate line up was therefore: Wilkinson; W Fleming, A Fleming; McGibbon, Duncan, Johnstone; McNeil, Robertson, Stein, Brown and Chalmers.

A 4-2 win over Dundee Hibernian on the 24th September kicked off a ten game unbeaten run over the next two months which took them up to second place, behind leaders Alloa Athletic. Three defeats though in the next four matches scuppered their promotion hopes and they went into 1922 in seventh place. On the 2nd January 5,000 spectators watched a 0–0 draw with leaders and eventual champions Alloa Athletic and double that attended a Second Round Scottish Cup tie against Falkirk the following month. Bathgate had knocked out Helensburgh in the First Round and faced the Bairns on the 11th February at Mill Park and produced the shock of the day, winning 1-0. *The Scotsman* reported that on their own ground "Bathgate sprang a surprise upon Falkirk by defeating the First Division team by one goal to nothing. Ten thousand spectators watched a thrilling encounter in which both sides played cup-tie football...Bathgate scored the one goal of the match ten minutes from time, Robertson, the old Motherwell forward, beating the opposing defence, and scoring from a difficult angle. Falkirk strove hard to retrieve their fallen fortunes, but the home defence refused to be beaten, and the Second Division team made history be a notable win." Bathgate were knocked out by First Division Partick Thistle in the next round and went on to finish in fifth place in their first season as a League club. At the end of the season their goalkeeper John Wilkinson was enticed away to join Partick Thistle.

In the 1922-23 season they again finished in sixth place. They were unbeaten in the first five games, but three of these were draws. The best result in this sequence was a 5-1 home win over Forfar Athletic. Bathgate played most of the game with ten men, but even with this numerical disadvantage they were too much of a match for their visitors. Their form then took a turn for the worse as they lost five out of their next six matches, getting a draw in the other. On the 2nd December 1922 they delighted their supporters with a 5-0 win at home to mid-table Lochgelly United. For the first twenty minutes or so honours were even but then Bathgate took control with Drummond scoring a hat-trick and McAllister scoring the other two. A fortnight later they beat Stenhousemuir 4-0 at home with Drummond and McAllister each getting a brace. The record League attendance at Mill Park was equalled when a crowd of 5,000 watched a 4–2 derby win over Armadale on the 1st January 1923, with Drummond scoring a hat-trick. A 5-0 defeat at second placed Clydebank later in the same month saw Bathgate slip to seventh and they recovered a bit to finish in fifth place.

The 1923-24 season was the high point of Bathgate's SFL career as they achieved a best placed finish of third, although they never really challenged the top two of St Johnstone and Cowdenbeath who finished over ten points clear at the top. They lost their opening game 1-0 at Lochgelly and then drew three out of the next four, so that by mid-September they were languishing in the bottom half. On the 17th November they beat Bo'ness 3-2 away, with a brace from Forsyth, which would signal the start of a run of four consecutive wins and a 12 game unbeaten streak. They scored four goals in a match for four games in a row. By the time the Scottish Cup competition got underway in late-January 1924, and in doing so interrupted the League programme, Bathgate had risen up to second place, two points behind leaders St Johnstone, having lost only three fixtures out of 25 matches played. When they eventually lost in the League on the 2nd February they had gone 13 games undefeated.

Involvement in the Scottish Cup, where they were knocked out after a replay by Bo'ness, seemed to knock them off their stride, as they then lost back-to-back fixtures against St Bernard's and, crucially, third placed Cowdenbeath. The following Saturday, and now in third place, they drew with leaders St Johnstone. Another home draw, this time against East Fife was followed by a crushing blow - a 5-1 defeat at Stenhousemuir - who subsequently leapfrogged them in the table. A further defeat mid-March away at Arbroath saw them drop down to fifth. Although they got revenge for their Scottish Cup exit by eating Bo'ness 2-0 at the end of March, a 1-0 loss at Alloa in the first game in April meant that neither St Johnstone nor Cowdenbeath could be caught. Bathgate did cement third place but the eventual gap to Cowdenbeath in second grew to 11 points by the end of the season.

After three good seasons the 1924-25 campaign signalled a decline in the club's fortunes, which would eventually led to the demise of the club. The season started with four consecutive draws, starting with a 4-4 draw on the opening day against East Stirlingshire. They then surprisingly won 4-1 away at Dunfermline, with Muir netting a hat-trick, to move into second place. They then went the next five games without a win. Inconsistency was their watch word as they won four games in a row in November only to lose four in a row in January. A 5-0 loss at Forfar in mid-March saw them slip to 16th place which is where they eventually finished, six points above what were now the relegation places to the relatively new Third Division.

Efforts to keep Britain in the Gold Standard, and in particular, the decision in 1925 to return to the pre-war level meant UK exports were overvalued and the steel, coal and iron industries faced difficulties from global oversupply and falling prices. As these industries were a mainstay of the local economy this began to impact on clubs like

Bathgate, who saw gates and therefore income drop. In the 1925-26 season Bathgate finished in 19th place, with Broxburn United bottom.

The season started alright with five points from the first four games and then four straight wins at Mill Park. After eight games they were ninth in the table and in a tight Division, just two points off the top, after defeating the then leaders Third Lanark 2-1. October brought the first signs of problems as they lost three out of the next four games including a 4-0 loss at St Bernard's on the 31st. This was followed by another 4-0 loss on the 7th November, against local rivals Bo'ness. A 2-1 home win over Ayr United was then followed by a disastrous run of eight consecutive defeats and Bathgate didn't win again until mid-January 1926. Included in this sequence was another 4-0 loss at Arbroath, a 5-1 loss at neighbours Armadale and 7-3 hammering at East Fife. *The Sunday Post's* appraisal of the Bathgate side after this game was quite scathing: "the losers were not an impressive side. Gilchrist kept a good goal, but the backs were very weak, and could never cope with the attack. The half-backs were workers, but their movements were often without aim or purpose. The forwards were clever and thrustful."

The run of eight successive League defeats was also part of a longer sequence of fourteen League games without a win which ran from the end of November 1925 to the beginning of March 1926 and which was eventually ended by a 4-0 home win over Arbroath on the 3rd March. *The Scotsman* reported on this game, noting "Bathgate registered their first League win since 21st November last by defeating Arbroath yesterday. The greater part of the game was contested under miserable weather conditions, heavy showers of sleet and snow falling at frequent intervals. Arbroath were the likelier lot to begin with, and subjected the home goal to severe pressure. A little luck and Gilchrist's fine saving helped Bathgate to keep their goal intact. After Scoular scraped the ball over the line from a corner for Bathgate's first goal eight minutes after the start the team gathered confidence, and gave a good display. Scoular scored a capital second goal, and Lindsay followed on with a third before the interval. Arbroath showed good football in the open, but they had no luck at close quarters. For a time after the resumption they looked like reducing the leeway, but Gilchrist was unbeatable. A fourth goal for Bathgate, got by McKinlay, robbed the closing stages of any real interest."

The club fared better in the Scottish Cup where they did record victories over East Stirlingshire and Bo'ness. A crowd of 8,000 was at Mill Park for the Third Round tie against Airdrieonians, on the 20 February 1926, with the visitors winning 5–2. They also reached the final of the last ever Linlithgowshire Cup, losing 3-1 to Bo'ness.

Barely a fortnight after ending their terrible winless run Bathgate suffered a record League home defeat against Clyde. Ten goals were scored at Mill Park but the four goal margin in Clyde's favour flattered them. In a game that pitted second from bottom versus fourth, the opening stages suggested a keenly fought contest and this seemed validated when Clyde's early goal was quickly followed by the equaliser from Scoular. During the next half an hour, however, Clyde took their opportunities while Bathgate squandered their own. Clyde put on five goals, while "Junior", a triallist for Bathgate reduced the arrears so that at half-time the score was 6-2 to the visitors. Bathgate started the brightest after the interval but again failed to take their chances and Clyde scored a seventh before Scoular again found the net for Bathgate. Bathgate pushed for more goals until the end but the opposing defence stood firm.

A week later Bathgate bounced back with a 5-0 win over mid-table Dumbarton. *The Scotsman* under the headline "Bathgate in Scoring Vein" reported that "in striking contrast to recent experiences they enjoyed a little luck. They opened the scoring in the first minute, and went further ahead at the end of twenty minutes. Between the scoring of these goals the visitors played the more attractive football, and more than once the home goal escaped downfall. Both Bathgate's goals were got by Scoular. Up to the interval Bathgate held the upper hand but failed to add to their score. Four minutes after the resumption, following a bombardment of the Dumbarton goal, McKinlay scored again for Bathgate. For a short spell after that the visitors put forth a strong effort to reduce the leeway, but without success. During the last twenty minutes or so the Bathgate men let themselves go, and Scoular brought their goals total up to five and his own up to four. But for Britton's fine display in the Dumbarton goal the win might have been even more decisive."

The result left Bathgate in 19th place as East Stirlingshire above them also won and they only picked up one further point to eventually finish second from bottom, having failed to win away all season. They were spared relegation by the demise of the Third Division at the end of the season. Instead they faced a re-election vote against four of the defunct Third Division sides - Leith Athletic, Forfar Athletic, Helensburgh and Dykehead – for the two vacant spots - in which they were joined by Broxburn United. They survived the first ballot, unlike Broxburn, who dropped out of the League, and went into a second round of voting against Forfar and Leith. In an extremely tight vote they won with 23 votes (Forfar 21, Leith 20) and retained their place in the League, Forfar joining them.

The new season kicked off on the 14th August 1926 and after being two goals down at one stage at home to Ayr United Bathgate made a great recovery and eventually ran out worthy winners. Wilkie, a new player signed from St Andrews United, scored a hat-trick on debut. Ayr strove hard for an equaliser but had a man sent-off just before time and a minute later Pearson scored a fourth goal for Bathgate.

After a second win at the end of the month Bathgate then only won once more in the next two months. Attendances slumped during the miners' strike which followed the General Strike of May 1926 and at the beginning of November they were beaten by leaders Bo'ness 7-0. Bathgate were unfortunate to find the forward line of the leaders in irresistible form. In a one-sided affair they conceded four first half goals. *The Scotsman* reported that "Taylor, the Bathgate custodian, was reliable, and was in no way to blame for the tall scoring. The visiting backs and halves were weak and an easy prey to the clever and enterprising Bo'ness vanguard."

The following week Bathgate and the bottom side Arbroath shared ten goals at Mill Park. The home team were behind 4-3 with ten minutes to go, *The Scotsman* taking up the story: "with nine minutes to go Watson made the score equal, and Broadley followed up by once more placing Bathgate ahead. The excitement was intense in the closing minutes, when Taylor, the home goalkeeper, had to be carried off after Edwards had rushed both him and the ball over the line for the equalising goal. The referee was subjected to shouts of disapproval from the home crowd for allowing the point."

A week later they conceded five again, although this time only scoring one in return as they went down 5-1 to Clydebank, a result that left them just two points off the bottom. In mid-December they scored five goals of their own once again, defeating second-placed Athurlie 5-2, Houston and McKinlay each scoring two, although the gate was only about 1,000.

On the 8th January 1927 they recorded an 8-3 win at home to Queen of the South. The visitors were handicapped by the absence of four of their regular players. Wales scored after 13 minutes and goals were added by Gardner, Wilkie and Houston (2) to bring Bathgate's first half total up to five with no reply. Gardner, making his debut for the club at centre-forward having signed from Kirkintilloch Rob Roy the day before, scored his second and his side's sixth shortly after the resumption, but that was countered by one from Gilmour, the opposing centre- forward. Gardener then got his hat-trick on debut and Wilkie scored an eighth, before Gilmour and McCall brought the margin down to five.

Bathgate didn't win again until the end of February and dropped from mid-table to 15th by the beginning of April. Their safety was ensured in their final home game, a 1-0 win over Albion Rovers, and they eventually finished in 17th place, one point ahead of both

Dumbarton and Arbroath, with Nithsdale Wanderers finishing bottom and being replaced by Leith Athletic at the League's AGM.

Having narrowly avoided facing re-election there was no escape the following season as the club finished in the bottom two along with Armadale and faced a strong challenge from Nithsdale Wanderers who had themselves lost a re-election vote the year before. They lost their opening game of the 1927-28 season 4-2 at Dundee United having taken an early lead through Houston. They won their first home game a week later, in defeating East Stirlingshire 3-1 with Houston scoring two and setting up Pearson for the third. Although they lost 5-0 at Arbroath at the beginning of October the club was picking up sufficient points to so that by the end of November they sat comfortably in tenth place.

On the 14th January 1927 Ayr United hosted Bathgate and ran out 7-2 winners. *The Glasgow Herald* noted that "Ayr Utd's success, as usual, was largely contributed by their centre-forward, Smith, who scored five goals." A month later Bathgate lost 6-1 at Third Lanark but they then won 5-0 against Clydebank, *The Scotsman* noting "that Bathgate won so decisively against Clydebank was not due so much to any outstanding qualities of their own as to the weakness of their opponents." Bathgate opened the scoring after 24 minutes and held their one goal advantage until the interval. A second goal, scored by McArthur, one of two players transferred from Clyde, inspired them with confidence and they went on to score three more, with McArthur getting a second and a triallist or "Junior" getting the other two.

Bathgate failed to win another game all season and struggled in front of goal, drawing a blank in five of their next seven games. They plummeted down the table to 18th place by the end of March, and with three games to go they were level on 31 points with St Bernard's and Morton, with Armadale nine points adrift at the bottom. St Bernard's beat them 2-0 on the 7th April and Morton picked up a point and Bathgate slipped into the bottom two for the first time all season. A week later, as Rangers were winning the Scottish Cup final, Bathgate went down 2-1 at Albion Rovers, whereas Morton won to condemn Bathgate to a re-election vote. At the Scottish Football League's AGM held on the 17th May 1928 Bathgate survived by topping the ballot with 27 votes, four ahead of Armadale and 13 more than Nithsdale. They were re-elected and Armadale were also successfully retained following a run-off ballot.

On the 9th June *The Sunday Post*, under the headline "Bathgate FC show £900 profit. But the club may cease to function" reported that "the failure of a sufficient number of gentleman to come forward to make up the Board of Directors for Bathgate Football Club, Ltd, at the annual meeting the other day came as no surprise." Although the club had turned a profit, this was because they had received £1500 from transfer fees from five deals. The main issue was the insufficient number of directors, with long standing directors Messrs Donoghue and Telfer, wanting to retire and the report in the paper suggested that the shareholders would need to wind up the club.

A month later, the *Edinburgh Evening News* reported that "the perilous position of Second Division football in Scotland was demonstrated by the decision which was come to at a meeting of the shareholders of Bathgate FC last night. The club, as is well known, has been struggling under a heavy financial handicap for some time, and, at a previous meeting difficulty was found in securing directors to carry on the club's activities. At the meeting in question, it was decided to postpone coming to a definite decision until steps had been taken to enlist the sympathy of the local trades-people with the hope of completing a directorate. This effort, apparently, failed, for at last night's meeting, the position was rapidly outlined, and without any possibility of securing directors, it was reluctantly decided to notify the League secretary of the club's retirement from the League."

Bathgate did take their place for the 1928-29 season and kicked off on the 11th August, losing 4-0 at home against Dundee United, but during the course of the season the club's financial position deteriorated so badly that they were unable to fulfil their fixtures and with 28 matches played they resigned their place in the Scottish Football League.

In their opening game against Dundee United their team featured two triallists, a new goalkeeper, and they started the match with only ten men as Gribbon, one of the forwards, arrived ten minutes after the start. No surprise then that *The Sunday Post* said the team "lacked cohesion." Duncan "Hurricane Hutch" Hutchieson scored a hat-trick on debut for their opponents and went on to be the division's top scorer over the next two seasons.

Bathgate won their next two matches, scoring four in each. They first beat Queen of the South, scoring early, which seemed to give them confidence. At half-time they led 2-0, both goals scored by Drummond. They scored early again in the second half and with ten minutes to go it was 3-0, then 3-1 and then Drummond got his hat-trick. They withstood a late fightback where their opponents got two more goals back to ensure a tight finish. They then beat East Fife 4-1 at home and when they beat Alloa on the 1st September they were as high as fourth in the table following those three straight wins.

Bathgate then failed to win another game in 1928, going on a disastrous run of 17 games without a win, recording just two draws. In the next six weeks they dropped from fourth to fourth bottom, having picked up only one more point. Their poor run then got worse as they suffered a string of heavy losses. On the 13th October they lost 8-2 at Forfar. *The Sunday Post* commented that "despite the heavy scoring against them, Bathgate put up a good show, but unfortunately for them there was a twelve-minute spell in the first period when the Forfar forwards ran riot, and netted five times." In the second half Forfar lost the services of their centre-forward who went off injured. They were missing Drummond, their goalscoring centre-forward, who had signed for Morton and who scored a hat-trick on debut for his new club.

A fortnight later they lost 5-0 at home to Leith, the score flattering the visitors who were better at taking their chances and to whom rebounds fell more kindly. A month later they lost by the same scoreline at East Stirlingshire, and Alloa's win on the same day dropped them into the bottom two along with Armadale. A week later they conceded five again, this time losing 5-3 at home to Bo'ness, handicapped by the loss of Higgins, their right-back to injury.

On the 29th December 1928 Bathgate lost 6-1 at leaders Dundee United, who also missed two penalties. The club's new goalkeeper, James Dempster, was an ex-United player, and he kept the score down, *The Sunday Post* commenting that Bathgate "were a poor team, [with] no outstanding player except Dempster." By this time Bathgate were bottom of the League. They had been overtaken by Armadale and were six points adrift, having not won in three months.

On Wednesday 2nd January 1929 their terrible winless run finally came to an end. They won away 2-1 at mid-table Leith Athletic, who had been unbeaten at their Marine Gardens home. This was their first win since 1st September 1928. Bathgate hinted at some incredible recovery when they won their next game as well, beating Alloa 3-1. They made it three consecutive wins, although not in the League, when they beat St Andrews University 3-0 away in the First Round of the Scottish Cup. In the next round they held First Division Raith Rovers to a 1-1 draw in front of a crowd of 3,000, but lost the replay 5-2.

This little run did not mark the start of some incredible renaissance as Bathgate went down 8-0 at Dunfermline in early February. They played what would prove to be their last home match on the 16th February 1929, a 3–1 defeat by King's Park. The paltry crowd of 200 was the club's lowest recorded attendance during their time in the SFL. On Saturday 23rd February 1929 they played their last ever SFL game, losing 3-0 at Dumbarton. On the eve of their next game *The Scotsman* reported under the headline "Bathgate and Scottish League – Club to Withdraw": "a sensation has been caused in Scottish football circles by the decision of the directors of the Bathgate Football Club to withdraw the club from the Second Division of the Scottish League. This decision, reached at a special meeting on Thursday night, has been arrived at owing to the club being in financial difficulties." Their game against Forfar, due to be played on Saturday 2nd March was subsequently postponed.

On the 12th March their records for the season were expunged. *The Scotsman* reporting that "Bathgate's resignation from the Scottish Football League was accepted at a meeting of the League Management Committee held yesterday afternoon in Glasgow. It was agreed to ignore all results of games previously taken part in by Bathgate. In consequence of this decision, the League table requires alteration." Top of the table Dundee United lost four points as did third placed Morton. Second placed Arbroath only lost two so the main impact was that United lost their two point lead at the top. In the end it didn't seem to have lasting impact as Dundee United were crowned champions and Morton came in second.

Bathgate weren't the only casualty as Arthurlie also resigned in mid-April, although their record was allowed to stand. No re-elections took place at the AGM on 23 May 1929, instead Montrose and Brechin City were voted in from the Scottish Alliance to fill the vacancies.

Bathgate spent two seasons in the East of Scotland League winning both championships, before leaving for the Edinburgh & District League, winning that before disbanding soon after. They also made two further appearances in the Scottish Cup. In the 1929-30 season they lost 6-2 at King's park, playing as the Qualifying Cup winners. In January 1931 they were thrashed 6-0 by a Motherwell side that was competing with Rangers and Celtic for the SFL title having been runners-up, and who subsequently made it to the final where they were beaten by Celtic.

The club was finally dissolved in October 1938 and Mill Park was subsequently redeveloped for housing. Bathgate has subsequently been represented in junior football by Bathgate Thistle, who play their matches at Creamery Park, off Hardhill Road, to the west of the town centre.

SEASON	LEAGUE	P	W	D	L	F	A	P	POS
1921-22	SCOT-2	38	16	11	11	56	41	43	5/20
1922-23	SCOT-2	38	16	9	13	67	55	41	5/20

```
1923-24  SCOT-2  38  16  12  10  58   49  44   3/20
1924-25  SCOT-2  38  12  10  16  58   74  34  16/20
1925-26  SCOT-2  38   7   6  25  60  105  20  19/20
1926-27  SCOT-2  38  13   7  18  76   98  33  17/20
1927-28  SCOT-2  38  10  11  17  62   81  31  19/20
```

Beith

Formed: 1876
Colours: Black and white horizontal pin striped shirts and white shorts
Ground: Bellsdale Park
Entered League: 1923. Founder members of the Third Division
Number of League Seasons: 3
Honours: None
Highest League Finish: 7th in Division Three
Left League: 1926. Division Three abandoned. Disbanded 1938

Beith is a small town situated in the Garnock Valley of Ayrshire, approximately 22 miles south-west of Glasgow and they had a football team that participated in the three seasons of the ill-fated Third Division of the 1920s. The town of Beith is situated on the crest of a hill and was known originally as the 'Hill o' Beith', which means the 'hill of the birches' and wood features prominently in the town's history. From 1845 until the 1980s Beith was an important furniture-manufacturing town and this gave the football team their nickname - 'the cabinet makers'.

Beith Football Club were originally founded in 1876 and played in the Scottish Cup for seven consecutive seasons between 1876-1883, reaching the Fifth Round on three occasions. They played at a variety of grounds including Netherhill Field, Gateside Toll, Muirfield Park and between 1920 and 1938, at Bellsdale Park.

They entered the Scottish Cup in their founding year, debuting in the Cup's fourth year, and played on the 30th September 1876, losing in the First Round away to Ayr Thistle 1-0. In the 1877-78 competition they went as far as the Fifth Round, beating Catrine, Portland, Maybole Carrick in regional ties and they then had a walkover in the Fourth Round when St Clement of Forfarshire scratched. On the 5th January 1878 they lost 3-0 at home to eventual beaten finalists Third Lanark (then playing as 3rd LRV). The following season they again reached the Fifth Round, beating Hurlford, Ayr Thistle and Barrhead in regional ties, the latter by 7-1. In the Fourth Round they beat Kilmarnock Thistle 9-1, which earned them a tie against two-time winners and current holders Vale of Leven, which was played on the 8th March 1879.

The match against the Cup-holders and one of the early powerhouse of Scottish football, attracted press attention and an account of the game was reported in the *Glasgow Herald* – "This tie was played off at Alexandria in the presence of 1500 spectators. The strangers kicked off against a stiff breeze, and for a considerable time play consisted of a series of unsuccessful assaults on the Visitors' goal, which was remarkably well defended by Smith. The contest was afterwards transferred to midfield, with occasional incursions on the home ground. Before half-time, however, the Beith colours were twice lowered, the immediate agents in this being J C Baird and Ferguson. In the second half play had scarcely been resumed when McFarlane added a third success for his team. The game now became very fast and exciting all round. The strangers made strong efforts to score, and Parlane got some sharp work to do, which he did to the best advantage - saving his charge intact. Fortune held the balance very even for a time, till McDougall got on the ball, and ended a fine run with goal No. 4. After this, through a false kick by one of the Leven backs, the Ayrshire team were credited with a goal – their only one of the game. Before the close two more goals were added to the score of the Dumbarton-shire players by Ferguson and McDougall respectively, the 'tie' thus ending in a win for the Vale by six goals to one." The Beith team was, in goal, W Smith; the backs were Miller and Edmonstone; the half-backs were Peddie and Gilmour; and the forwards were Brodie, K Gilmour, McGuire, Innes, Weir and Stevenson. Included in the line-up was William McGuire, who, still as a Beith player, would be capped for Scotland twice in March 1881. Vale of Leven went on to lift the trophy for a third consecutive year, thereby matching the achievement of Queen's Park, who had won the first three competitions.

The 1879-80 season saw the club exit early, in the Second Round, but in the 1880-81 competition they made it to the Fourth Round. They got there by recording their biggest win, as they beat the 5th Kirkcudbrightshire Rifle Volunteers (based in Maxwelltown, Dumfries) 17-2 on the 23rd October 1880. Such a scoreline was reported on by the *Glasgow Herald:* "Played at Netherhill Field, Beith. A large number of spectators were present to witness the match which turned out a most hollow affair, although at the beginning the game promised to be a well-contested one, as at the end of five minutes' play the game stood equal with one goal each. After this the Volunteers had very little chance, the home team before ends were changed having scored five additional goals. During the second half the strangers secured one goal, by Wallace, and against this Beith supplemented their previous score by no less than eleven goals, Beith thus won by seventeen goals to two."

Beith were drawn against the holders and most successful Cup side, Queen's Park, in the nest round and themselves lost heavily. Beith scored first and went into the interval only one down with the score at 2-1. Commenting on the game, *The Scotsman* wrote:

116

"the Beith showed up well at the beginning of the game, but their backs being very weak, disorganised the team, and near the close of the game the Queen's Park had the Ayrshire men entirely at their mercy." Nine more goals were scored against them whilst they managed to secure a second goal, the final score being 11-2. Beith again had the consolation of going out to the eventual winners, as Queen's Park went on to lift the trophy for the fifth time.

In the 1881-82 competition Beith made it to the Fifth Round yet again. Having got through three regional ties, and received a bye in the next round, they were drawn away at Kilmarnock Thistle and lost 2-0. Kilmarnock Thistle made it to the semi-finals where they lost to Queen's Park, who went on to beat Dumbarton in the final, after a replay, to claim their sixth trophy.

The tenth Scottish Cup competition, 1882-83, was the original club's last appearance. They beat Beith Thistle before losing to Lugar Boswell (based in the village of Lugar, near Cumnock). The club then briefly closed down in 1883 and there was a five year hiatus before they returned to the Scottish Cup from 1888 onwards. Things did not go well on their return. They lost their first Cup game back, a 3-2 home defeat against Irvine, but worse was to come in the following year when they suffered a heavy and embarrassing defeat, losing 16-0 on the 7th September 1889, away against Ayr FC. The match report in *The Scotsman* simply saying that Beith "broke down after a quarter of an hour's play."

In 1891 the club joined the Ayrshire League, stepping up to the Scottish Combination in 1903 and winning the title in 1905, a success which prompted them to make their first unsuccessful bid to join the Scottish League. They'd also had a good run in the Scottish Cup, reaching the Third Round, and knocking out First Division League side Kilmarnock after a replay. On the 28th January 1905 Beith travelled to Kilmarnock and aided by a strong wind in the first half, shocked their hosts by scoring two goals in the first fifteen minutes. Killie got one back before half-time and then lay siege to the Beith goal, but only scored once. The replay took place on the 4th February in front of a 4,000 crowd at Beith and *The Scotsman* reported on the game: "Kilmarnock played a strong game at the start, and scored after twenty minutes had elapsed. The home team retaliated, and equalised in five minutes. Beith in the second half held the upper hand, and first harper and then Walker scored. Five minutes from time a section of the Kilmarnock crowd rushed the barricades, but the police adopted strong measures, and after an arrest had been made the game was finished." Beith had won 3-1, registering a notable victory. Having disposed of Cowdenbeath 4-0 in the next round Beith were drawn away to Rangers, where they lost 5-1 to the eventual losing finalists, Beith were described in *The Scotsman* as being "at least equally as earnest and determined" as their opponents. For half an hour Beith put up a good fight but after that fell away. Walker scored their consolation goal but Cameron, their centre-forward was later sent off for showing too much "fighting" spirit.

With the growth and expansion of the SFL a record thirteen clubs applied for a place at the 1906 AGM, seven of which were members of the Scottish Combination, including Beith. Unfortunately the club secured the joint lowest votes of the teams from this league, with just three. No further attempts were made and the club joined the Western League after the First World War.

Up to 1914 Beith continued to feature in some notable Scottish Cup ties. With no penalty shoot-outs it took five matches to separate them and Broxburn United in a First Round tie in the 1908-09 competition, before they eventually prevailed. The following year they were drawn away against Dundee in the First Round. Dundee were the SFL runners-up from the previous year so were expected to progress easily but on the 22nd January 1910 Beith held them to a 1-1 draw in front of a crowd of 9000. *The Scotsman* reported that "Dundee were easily the superior team in the first half, and poor shooting alone prevented them scoring. Bellamy missed a penalty kick, and Monteith, the Beith goalkeeper, afterwards defended well. Close upon the interval Comrie opened the scoring for Dundee with a good shot. In the second half Beith were seen to better advantage and Dundee were completely surprised when Smith beat Crumley with a clever shot. Dundee strove hard to regain the lead, but Beith responded in good style, Monteith saving well." Beith surrendered home advantage for the replay which took place the following Saturday. Monteith was again the hero but was eventually beaten just before the interval. In the second half Dundee attacked almost continuously but failed to add to their score, progressing 1-0. Replays were a feature of Dundee's Cup run, as it needed three games for them to get past Hibernian in the Semi-finals and in the Final itself, they eventually beat Clyde in a second replay, to lift the Scottish Cup for the first time. Beith made one last appearance in the Scottish Cup in the 1911-12 competition, losing 6-0 against Broxburn Athletic in the First Round, and this would be their last appearance for over 10 years.

In 1923 teams from the Western League formed the bulk of the new Scottish Third Division, contributing 11 of the 16 teams and Beith joined the Scottish Football League. Beith finished seventh in their first season, their highest League placing, winning eleven out of fifteen games at Bellsdale Park. They made their SFL debut on the 18th August 1923, playing away against recently relegated East Stirlingshire. They went down by two goals to one, Crosbie scoring their first ever SFL goal with a long but powerful drive, equalising just two minutes after their hosts had scored in the 20th minute. But East Stirlingshire went ahead again just before the interval and in the second half missed a penalty. A week later the first SFL match at Bellsdale Park was played on 25 August 1923, a 1–0 win over Royal Albert. McCracken scored just before half-time. In the second period Royal Albert strove hard for parity but the Beith defence held firm to record their first League win.

Beith were strong at home but weak on their travels as Arthurlie and East Stirlingshire took the top two places. A notable result during their inaugural season was a 6-2 home win over Dumbarton Harp on the 8th March 1924. In this match Stevenson scored for Beith five minutes after the start, but Harp equalised twenty minutes later. Scoular gave Beith the lead before half-time. In the second half Smith scored for Harp, whilst Walters scored two, Cameron converted a penalty and a sixth goal was scored by a triallist playing at centre-forward. A month later, on the 28th April, Beith suffered their heaviest defeat of the season, losing 5-1 against Dykehead. In the Scottish Cup the club narrowly went out in the First Round away at First Division St Mirren 3-2.
In the following two SFL seasons Beith finished 13th and 12th only registering one away win across these two seasons. In the 1924-25 season they failed to win any of their away games and got off to a poor start, losing their first three games of the new season and they were winless in six before an 8-3 home win over Mid-Annandale on the 4th October. Both teams had failed to register a win going into the match and the result would prove to be Beith's highest scoring SFL win.

Unfortunately another winless streak followed, of eight games this time, which included an 8-4 loss at fellow strugglers Helensburgh on the 6th December. Beith had to play with only ten men during the second half, as McAllister, the right back, had to retire after the ball struck him hard on the head. At one point Helensburgh led 6-0, but then Beith scored three before it ended 8-4. Beith did eventually pick up some wins over the winter, including a 7-1 win over Brechin City on the 10th January 1925. This was their biggest ever SFL win although the score flattered them. McLean opened the scoring for Beith but Brechin then equalised. Grieve was causing problems on Beith's left and he set up further goals for McLean and Walker for Beith to lead 3-1 at the interval. 3-1. Four more goals were scored in the second half - Melville (2), Cameron and an own goal. This was only their only their fifth win, and it left them tenth in the 16 team table. Towards the end of the season, on the 11th April, they beat the Third Division leaders and eventual champions Nithsdale Wanderers 3-0, with goals scored by Walker, McLean and a Walters penalty. Their fickle form continued though as the following week they lost 7-1 away at Peebles Rovers. This was to be their biggest ever defeat in the SFL and all the damage was done in the first half as then went into the interval 6-0 down having conceded as early as the first minute. They finished the season with two home wins but having only picked up two points all season on their travels.

The 1925-26 season also started poorly as they lost six of their opening seven games. On the 14th November they lost 7-3 at Clackmannan, a defeat that left them bottom of the table. *The Sunday Post* match report noted that "Beith proved an easy hurdle for Clackmannan at Chapelhill Park, but it was not due to any excessive degree of brilliancy that such a convincing victory was recorded." Their hosts opened the scoring in the first minutes and got a second soon after, going into the interval 3-0 up. Play in the second half was keener and although their hosts scored two more, Beith then scored three goals through Walters (2) and Walker. Towards the end Clackmannan finished off the game.

Beith won three games on the trot in early January 1926 but around this time things began to unravel and the Third Division was abandoned with fixtures outstanding. Beith's last ever SFL game was a midweek affair, on the evening of Wednesday 21st April, where they hosted Leith Athletic at Bellsdale Park and lost 4-2. The match was moved to midweek as Beith were playing in the first leg of the Ayrshire cup final on the Saturday against Ayr United. Beith failed to complete all of their League fixtures, with three games not played. In one of these, Beith deliberately choose not to fulfil a fixture with Forfar Athletic, preferring to play instead a local cup tie. *The Sunday Post* reported that "on Thursday night Beith FC informed the secretary of the Athletic that they were unable to fulfil the fixture. The Forfar secretary at once communicated with Beith, offering them every financial inducement if they would carry through their obligation….The Beith club's reply to Forfar Athletic's extra offer was a refusal, and yesterday Beith FC took the field in the final for the Ayrshire Cup against Ayr United."

Beith left the Scottish Football League as the Third Division was disbanded but continued to play as a senior club and joined the Scottish Football Alliance. They also continued to feature in the Scottish Cup between 1926 and 1937. On the 22nd January 1927, they recorded a big 7-1 win in the First Round of the Cup against Huntly in front of a crowd of 1200. Under the headline "Beith's Runaway Victory" *The Sunday Post* reported that "Huntly fell rather softly at Beith. The home men took up the attack right away and Watson put them ahead after five minutes play with a shot from twenty yards out. The visitors put up a poor show, and it was well on before they got over the halfway line. Watson put in some great work in the home attack, and it was from his efforts that the second goal came, Geddes heading home a beautiful cross. Watson added the third goal with a fine shot, although the point was hotly disputed by the visitors. Beith were again the aggressors on the resumption, and after a spell of play in midfield they brought strong pressure to bear on the Huntly defence. Shots came from all directions, and five minutes after the interval MacLean, from a corner, scored a grand goal. A brilliant piece of individual play by Higgins ended in a fifth goal, the inside man beating the defence on his own and scoring with a rising shot. Play was still confined to the Huntly area, and from another corner Patrick added a sixth. The visitors began to get a greater share of the game now, but Beith were not finished, Maclean adding a seventh goal after Geddes had struck the bar. In the closing stages Huntly pressed and J Munro scored. Beith were not stretched to gain the victory, the home halfs being easily able to cope with the feeble attack opposed to them."

On the 30th January, 1937 Beith made their last Scottish Cup appearance in the 1936-37 competition, a 4-0 loss in the First Round away at St Mirren. Watched by a crowd of 6,000 *The Scotsman* reported that "it was a result that flattered the Saints...Beith had their chance to go ahead in the first half, when they had a strong wind in their favour, but they did not finish as they should, and it was all against the run of things when Saints turned about with a lead." In the first 30 minutes Beith were the more convincing side at Love Street, seemingly adapting quicker to the hard, icy conditions. However, before the interval they conceded a penalty that was converted by the St Mirren centre-half Cunningham and then a second just before the half-time whistle. In blizzard conditions St Mirren scored two more goals in the second half, both from Cunningham who thus scored a hat-trick. The first was another penalty and the second from a free kick just outside the penalty area. The Beith team to take the field was: Blyth; Auchenclose, Lindsay; Morrison, Narrowmore, Paterson; Pope, Bell; Walker, Cameron and Stoddart.

In 1938 the Scottish Football Alliance took the decision to become an exclusively reserve team league. In the 1937-38 season only Beith and Galston were remaining from the former Third Division teams. Both sides had found it increasingly difficult to compete and Beith had finished bottom twice in the last three years. As a result the original club disbanded and Beith were transformed into Beith Juniors, and this new club continued to use the ground. In recent times this side has featured in the early rounds of the Scottish Cup, and won the Scottish Junior Cup in 2016. The Semi-final first leg at Bellsdale Park attracted a crowd of nearly 1,500.

SEASON	LEAGUE	P	W	D	L	F	A	P	POS
1923-24	SCOT-3	30	14	4	12	49	41	32	7/16
1924-25	SCOT-3	30	9	6	15	62	74	24	13/16
1925-26	SCOT-3	27	9	4	14	58	68	22	12/16

Berwick Rangers

Formed: 1884
Colours: Black & gold vertical striped shirts, black shorts
Ground: Shielfield Park
Entered League: 1951. Admitted to Division C
Number of League Seasons: 68
Honours: Second Division Champions 1978-79. Third Division Champions 2006-07
Highest League Finish: 6th in Second Division (2nd tier)
Left League: 2019. Relegated to Lowland League

Berwick Rangers are the most recent club to have lost their Scottish Football League status, when in 2019 they became the second club to be relegated from the SFL as part of the pyramid structure. Having finished bottom of the Third Division at the end of the 2018-19 season they faced a play-off with the winners of the Highland League, Cove Rangers, of Aberdeen. Cove had won the right to challenge for a League placing having beaten the Lowland League champions East Kilbride in an earlier play-off. Cove had already made four attempts to join in 2000, 2002 and 2008 by election, and in 2016 (via the playoffs, losing to Edinburgh City in the semi-final). On the 18th May 2019, Berwick Rangers became the second club after East Stirlingshire to be relegated out of the Scottish League pyramid and into the Lowland Football League, after a 7-0 loss on aggregate to the Highland League champions.

Berwick Rangers are renowned for their various run-ins with the other Rangers – on and off the pitch - and most famously with what some regard as the greatest Cup shock in Scottish football, when they beat the Glasgow side 1-0 in 1967. More quirkily, and often the subject of a quiz question, Berwick-upon-Tweed is a town in England and yet their football team, due to their geographical position with the border, play in Scotland. Berwick-upon-Tweed is just over two miles south of the Scottish border and is closer to the Scottish capital Edinburgh than to Newcastle upon Tyne. Berwick Rangers are one of a handful of clubs that play in a league outside their own country and others include the Welsh clubs Cardiff City, Swansea City and Newport County playing in the English League, Monaco playing in the French Ligue One and FC Andorra who play in the Spanish League and FC Vaduz of Liechtenstein who play in the Swiss League.

Formed in 1884 the club largely played a series of local matches and didn't become a member of the Scottish Football Association until 1905. Right from the outset they had a closer affiliation with Scotland and joined the Scottish Border League, winning it in 1899. Berwick were founder member of the East of Scotland League in 1923 and won it 1927-28 and 1946-47 as well as finishing as runners-up in 1923-24 (to Coldstream) and 1928-29 (to Peebles Rovers). In the 1947-48 season they participated in the Scottish Cup, losing 4-2 at home to Division B Cowdenbeath in front of a crowd of 2,285. Berwick gave as good as they got and it was only in the last fifteen minutes that Cowdenbeath achieved the ascendancy. They next played in the competition in the 1950-51 season where they lost 3-2 at League side Brechin City. At the end of the season the club applied for election to the Scottish Football League. At the League's AGM, held on the 4th June 1951, Division B clubs Stenhousemuir and Alloa Athletic were challenged by four Division C clubs plus Berwick. The club received no support in the voting but at the same meeting Berwick Rangers were admitted to the Scottish League Division C (North & East). This third tier, made up largely of reserve sides, had been created in 1946 and was regionalised in 1949.

Known as the Borderers or the 'Wee Rangers' they originally had a nomadic existence. A move to Bull Stob Close came about in the early 1900's before a move to Union Park. In the 1930's they moved again, this time to the original Shielfield Park which was adjacent to the current ground. The ground was named after land owned by local butcher William Shiel Dods. In 1954 aided by the gate receipts from a Scottish Cup Quarter final tie at Ibrox Berwick made their move to a new Shielfield Park. Berwick bought Bradford City's old stand in 1954 and it was dismantled, driven north and reassembled. The ground is situated on the south side of the River Tweed, in the Tweedmouth district of the town.

Berwick finished eighth out of 16 teams in their first season as a Scottish Football league club under manager Bobby Ancell, winning 12 of their 30 matches. In this first year of League competition they had a run to the Third Round of the Scottish Cup. In bitterly cold conditions they beat Peebles Rovers 7-0 in the First Round, Albert Juliussen scoring a hat-trick. They then drew away at Alloa 0-0 in which Hogg and Moffat at the back were immense and Juliussen was always a threat up front. Berwick won the replay 4-1 to set up a Third Round tie against Dundee. Former Dundee favourite Juliussen nearly scored against his former club in a lively start, shooting just inches over from 25 yards out. Dundee took the lead in the 13th minute when Pattillo accepted a pass from Flavell and fired gone past Maddison. Dundee did most of the attacking after that and their finishing was poor, and they progressed 1-0.

Berwick played four seasons in the regionalised Division C with a best placed finish of third in the 1952-53 season. Reserve teams won each of the sections in each of the seasons played and Berwick came in behind Aberdeen A and Hibernian A in winning 13 and losing only 5. Jerry Kerr was now the manager and his side knocked out Second Division Dundee United in the Scottish Cup on the 24th January. The two sides had drawn 3-3 in the first game and Berwick won the replay 3-2. They were beaten by Queen of the South, then of the First Division in the next round.

In the 1953-54 season they came in fifth place but they finished bottom the year after. The highlight of the opening years of League life was a run to the Scottish Cup Quarter-Finals which culminated in a tie at Ibrox on the 13th March 1954. In the First Round they swept past fellow Division C side East Stirlingshire 7-0. They scored four goals in the first 23 minutes and in scoring the fourth an injury resulted in their opponents' goalkeeper having to leave the field. Inside-right Jimmy Muir scored three and centre-forward Brian Kingsmore two in front of a crowd of 3,500. In the Second Round they caused the shock of the day on the 13th February 1954 when they beat Ayr United 5-1. Kingsmore opened the scoring and added a second half hat-trick. A bigger Cup shock was to follow as in the Third Round Berwick beat top flight side Dundee 3-0 on the 27th February in front of a bumper crowd of 8,500. There was an early chance for their visitors, who put an effort just over the crossbar. Then Berwick has two good chances, one cleared off line and the other hit the woodwork. Alec Devanney, the former Celtic 'keeper then made a good save to keep Berwick level. After half an hour McGovern headed home from a corner to give Berwick the lead. Chances at both ends followed before Kingsmore shocked Dundee with a second and Muir scored a third. Berwick had produced an 'ABC' backwards as they had beaten C and then B Division opponents and now knocked out a Division A team. Reflecting on their achievement, the Glasgow Herald noted that "Berwick Rangers, who caused the surprise of the third round of the Scottish Cup by beating Dundee, one of the leading clubs in Division A of the Scottish League, 3-0 at Shielfield Park on Saturday, are only the second club from Division C to reach the last eight in the national tournament." In doing so they matched the feat of Montrose in the 1947-48 season.

Berwick met Rangers at Ibrox in the Quarter-Final of the Scottish Cup on the 13th March. This would be the first of many notable run-ins with them, both on and off the pitch. Bob Taggart was the stand out performer for Berwick in the first 30 minutes. He slipped in Muir who sent a shot across goal and Jimmy Blaikie just missed connecting with the ball as he slid in. This was Berwick's one real chance and they were made to rue their miss when five minutes later Rangers took the lead when a shot rebounded off the post but was followed up and fired onto the net. Five minutes later Rangers made it two and they doubled their advantage in the second half running out comfortable 4-0 winners. The Cup run financed ground improvement at the new Shielfield Park.

A number of clubs in Division C continued to agitate for an expansion of Division B and eventually, at the League's AGM in June 1955, League reconstruction came about. The First Division was expanded from 16 clubs to 18 with the top two sides from Division B being promoted and no relegation occurring from Division A. This left 14 clubs in Division B and five Division C teams were moved up to create a 19 team Division B. Berwick Rangers were effectively promoted, along with Dumbarton, East Stirlingshire, Montrose and Stranraer.

Berwick finished the 1955-56 season in 14th place, finishing above Forfar Athletic, East Stirlingshire, Albion Rovers, Arbroath and Montrose. They started the new season on the 24th August 1955 with a 3-3 draw at Hamilton Academicals at Douglas Park. They had to play without their goalkeeper Alex Patterson for practically all of the game, Alan Runciman deputising. They led after four minutes and despite their handicap were ahead 3-1 at half-time. The Berwick Rangers line-up was: Alex Patterson; Runciman, Arnott; Taggart, Barclay, Mitchell; Morton, Tommy Paterson, Laird, Campbell and Robertson.

On the 10th of September they lost 6-0 at home to East Stirlingshire, the first of four consecutive defeats which left them bottom. However, they recorded their first win later in the same month, beating Cowdenbeath 2-1. Their second win came at the end of October when they beat Third Lanark 3-1. Lawrence opened the scoring for Berwick after a quarter of an hour. In the 35th minute a high cross from Airlie was then fumbled by the visiting goalkeeper into the net. Their opponents got a goal back just before half-time but Berwick eventually made sure of the points. This result left them as one of four clubs at the bottom on five points (the others being Alloa, Montrose and Forfar).

The win started a run of only one defeat in nine games so they went into the New Year in 15th place. They eventually finished a place higher, but not before losing 8-1 against Dundee United at Tannadice at the end of April. They were only two down at half time, trailing 3-1, Runciman their scorer from a penalty. McLaren saved numerous times but was beaten on five more occasions, but not until the hour mark.

The divisions were rebranded at the start of the 1956-57 season with Division A becoming the First Division and Division B becoming the Second Division. The change in name didn't do them any good as in the next two seasons they finished in the bottom two. After the sectional League Cup games Berwick lost six out of their first seven League games at the start of the new season, including another big defeat away at

Dundee United (6-1). In early November they beat Hamilton 6-2 but the following month they lost badly again versus Dundee United, this time 6-0 at home and this was followed by a 5-1 home defeat against St Johnstone and a 5-1 loss at Arbroath. When they lost 6-0 at leaders Clyde in early January the 'Wee Rangers' were joint bottom with East Stirling with just nine points from 21 matches. A mini-revival followed as they went four games without defeat to move two ahead of East Stirling and four ahead of bottom side Forfar. However, they subsequently lost 6-1 against Forfar although they did beat East Stirling 5-2. A week later they suffered their worst defeat of the season, losing 7-1 against Stirling Albion and eventually finished second bottom, three points ahead of East Stirlingshire and a point behind Montrose, having conceded a club record 114 League goals for the season.

The 1957-58 season was much worse. Although they only conceded 109 goals this time, they only scored 37. They won only five times and ended up ten points adrift of Stranraer at the bottom. Berwick only earned a solitary draw in their opening dozen games and lost 6-0 against Ayr United and 5-1 versus Dunfermline, both of these defeats coming in games hosted at Shielfield. By mid-November they only had one point. The team nearest to them in the table was Stranraer on seven, and then came East Stirling and Forfar on nine. Danny McLennan took over the managerial reins and at the end of November they recorded their first win, beating St Johnstone 2-0 (a triallist scored in the first half and Bartle in the second) and in early December they beat Stranraer 2-1 for second win. They then lost 8-0 at Morton having been two down after just three minutes. Eddie Beaton scored four first half goals and then set up the other. Beaton got a fifth in the second half. Tommy McQueen was the unfortunate goalie. Although they then beat Hamilton on New Year's Day, they lost 5-0 at leaders Stirling Albion to leave them bottom with just nine points. Berwick conceded 15 goals in their first three games of March. A rare away win, 2-1 at Montrose, at the end of March still left them six points adrift of Stranraer at the bottom. In their last four games they lost 3-0 at Stranraer and then 5-0 against East Stirling. The second goal against them in a 4-1 loss at Brechin City marked the unwanted century of goals against and in their last game they conceded seven without reply at Dundee United to end a truly miserable season.

In the 1958-59 season Berwick Rangers achieved their best League placing to date, finishing ninth, which was a considerable improvement on their previous showings. They started well in the League Cup sectional games, winning their first two games, although they failed to qualify once again. After drawing their opening League game they were thrashed 5-0 at East Fife and also lost 4-0 at home to Ayr United. By the end of October the season was shaping up to be just like all the others, with Berwick in 16th, with the second worst defensive record in the division and with the third lowest number of goals scored. A better run of form across November and December saw Berwick rise up the table and following a 2-0 win over East Stirlingshire in their first game of 1959 they moved up to 14th place. Berwick won three consecutive League games in February, including an 8-2 win over Dundee United on the 21st February. Eric Addison scored after just four minutes, Dougan added a second after a quarter of an hour's play and Addison got Berwick's third five minutes before half-time. In the second half Addison scored three more past the United goalie Bill Lucas. Addison went on to score 37 goals in 50 appearances for the club between 1957 and 1960 before moving to Falkirk and then Stirling Albion, returning to the club for the 1962-63 season where he added 6 goals in 20 appearances. The club went unbeaten in their last five games (three wins and two draws) and finished in ninth place.

Berwick matched this finish over the next two seasons, before going one better in the 1961-62 season by finishing eighth. They started the 1959-60 season well and were unbeaten in their first four games. They beat Dumbarton 4-0 away on the 19th September and four days later they beat East Stirling 5-3. A 4-0 win over Brechin City on the 10th October saw Berwick in joint second, a point behind leaders St Johnstone. However, they then lost against the leaders 2-0 and inconsistent form saw them drop out of contention, and by the end of January they were in seventh, although only six points off second. Four wins on the bounce across February and March kept them in it but they lost each of their last four fixtures to slip down to ninth place.

Berwick matched their points tally, goals scored and final position in the following season. Highlights were a 4-0 win over Morton in September and a 5-2 victory over Forfar in December. Lowlights were a 4-0 loss at Falkirk in November, 7-2 at Stenhousemuir in January and 5-0 at Alloa Athletic. In the 1961-62 season they edged up a place. Berwick opened with a 3-0 win at Cowdenbeath but lost their first home League game 5-2 against Brechin City. In September they recorded back-to-back 5-1 wins over Stenhousemuir and East Stirling. One week they were losing 4-0 at Stranraer, the next they were beating Albion Rovers by the same score. In early February they beat Stranraer 6-0 only to lose 7-1 at Clyde three weeks later. Still, eighth place was their highest League finish to date across their eleven seasons so far.

The 1962-63 season saw a return to the poor performances of their early seasons as they finished in 17th place, just two off the bottom. Things started well with three wins and two draws from their six sectional League Cup games meaning they were involved in a two legged play-off versus Dumbarton. Berwick held them 0-0 away at Boghead but lost 2-1 at Shielfield. The league campaign kicked off with three wins out of five, with draws in the others, and included a 5-1 win over Forfar, Addison scoring a hat-trick. At this point the club was in seventh place, and just two points off the top.

However, they then lost 4-0 at Arbroath and 6-0 away at Forfar. Rangers went nine games without a win from the beginning of October and when they finally recorded another win against bottom side Brechin City on the 8th December they had fallen to 16th place and they eventually finished one place lower.

The 1963-64 season was an eventful one. On the pitch there was an appearance in a major Cup Semi-final and a record individual goalscoring performance for the season and off it there were threats to their League status. Former Stirling Albion and Raith Rovers inside-forward Ian Spence joined the club as player-manager in August having played the previous season at Third Lanark. Berwick Rangers lost their opening game on the 10th August, a League Cup sectional game, going down 3-0 at Montrose. They won their other three fixtures though against Brechin, Stenhousemuir and Forfar and entered a play-off. In the first leg they drew 2-2 at St Johnstone before winning the return 4-2 in front of a crowd of over 2,000 to go through 6-4 on aggregate. League form wasn't as good as they lost their first three League games before earning their first point at home to Stenhousemuir on the 21st September. Their first win in the League came a week later, 2-1 at Alloa. In between these games they had played their League Cup Quarter-Final, which was another two-legged affair. They drew 2-2 at Stirling Albion before edging the return 4-3 to go through 6-5 on aggregate to reach the League Cup Semi-final. Berwick Rangers got the hardest draw, although the glamour tie, when they got Rangers, the other teams being Morton and Hibernian. On the 2nd October 1963 Berwick Rangers travelled to Hampden park to play the biggest game in their history, acquitting themselves well in only losing 3-1. Trailing 1-0 and approaching half-time centre-forward Ken Bowron received the ball on the halfway line with his back to goal. He flicked the ball round the corner and out-pacing the Rangers centre-half Dave McKinnon ran towards the goal, firing past the goalkeeper Richie and into the net. Rangers went on to win but it was a massive achievement for the club to get to a Semi-final after only twelve years of League football.

There was no immediate Semi-final hangover as in their very next League they beat Stirling Albion 6-0, although a week later they lost 7-1 at Morton. They then only picked up one point from their next five League games, which included a 6-0 defeat at East Fife. At the end of December they beat Ayr United 6-1 but in early January lost 8-2 at Stenhousemuir. There would be no extended run in the Scottish Cup. Having beaten St Cuthbert Wanderers of Kirkcudbright they went out in the next round to Falkirk. They actually held them 2-2 at Brockville before losing the replay at home 5-1. Berwick then went on a nine game unbeaten run from March and included in that was a 3-1 win over Montrose in which Ken Bowron scored a hat-trick. Bowron started his footballing career as a goalkeeper with Newcastle Juniors but converted to a striker and in the 1956-57 season scored 41 goals in 29 games for Newcastle Juniors. He later played in the Northern League for Durham City, Spennymoor and Crook Town and joined the club for the 1963-64 season. Bowron scored a club record 50 goals for the club, 38 in the League, and altogether finished with 114 goals in 136 games for the club. In December 1965 he signed for Workington, who at that time played in the English Football League. Despite his goalscoring prowess Berwick Rangers finished in 12th place.

At the end of the season Rangers tabled a motion that the League be reorganised which would have resulted in five clubs, including Berwick Rangers, being expelled from the League. The motion was successfully fought through the courts. In recent years efforts had been made by members to reorganise the League but never had they been able to secure the necessary two-thirds majority. On the 23rd March 1964 the Scottish League Management Committee proposed a reorganisation and soon afterwards Rangers FC convened a meeting of 12 of the First Division clubs where it was agreed to reduce the number of League clubs from 37 to 32. It was not known why the specific five clubs were selected. Rangers then circulated details of their plans to all the other members of the League except the five clubs identified for exclusion (Berwick Rangers plus Albion Rovers, Brechin City, Stenhousemuir and Stranraer) and asked the clubs to appoint a representative to come to a further meeting. Of the 30 clubs represented at the meeting 27 voted in favour. The five teams went to court to fight this proposal, but the High Court found in Rangers' favour. The teams then appealed to the Court of Session.

On Tuesday 26th May the *Glasgow Herald* reported under the headline "Rangers FC Interdicted on League Reform Plan" that Lord Cameron had granted the interdict, prohibiting Rangers from putting forward proposals for reorganisation or that the League be dissolved at the AGM on Thursday. The paper reported that "Rangers Football Club were banned under an order of interim interdict from introducing at tomorrow's annual meeting of the Scottish Football League, a new rule which would have led to a reorganisation of Scottish Football. Under the scheme Berwick Rangers, Brechin City, Albion Rovers, Stranraer, and Stenhousemuir would have ceased to be members of the League. In addition, 26 other clubs regarded as likely to support Rangers, were prohibited from voting in their favour. The respondents were the other members of the First and Divisions of the Scottish League, excluding Celtic, East Stirlingshire, Hamilton Academicals, Airdrieonians and Third Lanark. The respondents were not represented in Court. Lord Cameron ruled that a caveat lodged by the Scottish League did not apply, and Mr Robertson QC, made his submissions on behalf of the petitioners without opposition. Mr Robertson recalled that the Scottish Football League was a voluntary organisation, founded 74 years ago with the object of promoting and extending Football, and he emphasised, guarding the interests of member clubs. Members derived financial benefit from the League to an ever-increasing extent and there was no doubt that if membership of the petitioners ended, irreparable damage would be suffered...The rules made no provision for reduction in membership or for exclusion of a member other than on the ground of objectionable conduct. None of the five petitioners had been so guilty....Mr Robertson said that Rangers circularised all members of the League [with their proposal] and according to the letter, those member clubs who were prepared to guarantee the scheme would themselves be guaranteed a place in the new set-up. 'In other words', Mr Robertson said, 'to coerce them into supporting the scheme Rangers said that if they did not agree with the proposals the place of the club addressed would be offered to one of the five petitioners.' Rangers now proposed to introduce a new rule to dissolve the League [but Mr Robertson] submitted that this could only be done by all members and not merely a majority. If carried through the scheme would constitute a breach of contract with the five petitioners." The League structure remained unaltered but the case certainly added a bit of spice to future matches involving Rangers.

By comparison the 1964-65 season was uneventful, although Berwick did match their best finish of eighth place. They made a poor start in the League Cup, conceding 16 goals across three of the sectional matches but a 5-1 win over Brechin in September kick-started a good run of form. Following a 4-1 home win over Cowdenbeath at the beginning of October Berwick were as high as sixth in the table. However, they slipped back a bit to finish in eighth.

In the 1965-66 season the 'wee Rangers' went unbeaten in their first four sectional League Cup matches, including a 6-1 win over Cowdenbeath but lost their last two and failed to progress. They made a reasonable start in the League to sit in fifth place after the first eight games. However, after a 3-0 home win over Airdrieonians on the 2nd October they failed to win again until the 13th November when they beat Queen of the South 3-1. This in turn started a run of ten League games without defeat which included a club record League win of 8–1 at home to Forfar Athletic on Christmas Day 1965. By early March, and following a 4-1 win over Albion Rovers, they were up as high as fifth place, just six points off second. However, they subsequently lost all five games they played in the rest of March and only won one of six fixtures in April and slipped back to finish a disappointing eleventh place.

For the 1966-67 season the Second Division was increased to twenty clubs with the inclusion of Clydebank. This would be a momentous season for Berwick Rangers as they famously beat Rangers 1-0 in the Scottish Cup in one of the biggest cup upsets of all time. The new season didn't get off to a great start as they failed to win any of their sectional League Cup games – drawing four. Their League campaign also started with a draw, 1-1 at home to Queen of the South. Draws were an early feature in the League as well as they drew three of their first five matches. Following a 2-0 win over Cowdenbeath in mid-September they failed to win again in their next six matches and therefore had only won once in their first ten League games. Ian Spence left as manager in November and was succeeded by Jock Wallace. Wallace, the club's goalkeeper, was in his second spell at the clubs, having originally played for the team in the 1950s before moving, first to Airdrieonians and then onto, amongst others, West Bromwich Albion. He returned as a player in 1966 and combined playing with his managerial duties.

In mid-December Berwick entered the Scottish Cup in the preliminary rounds. On the 17th December 1966 they achieved a club record Scottish Cup win when they beat Vale of Leithen 8-1 away from home. At the end of December they beat Stenhousemuir 6-0, which started a run of five League games without defeat. A month later the club produced arguably the greatest Cup shock of all time. Having beaten Forfar Athletic in the next preliminary round of the Cup the club had been drawn at home to the mighty Rangers in the First Round proper. The two clubs met on the 28th January 1967 and the *Glasgow Herald*, previewing the match, noted that "anything other than a comfortable Rangers victory must be deemed a surprise." The mis-match was obvious. The Rangers team featured nine players with international caps and at the time of the match, Rangers were in second place in the First Division and Berwick were tenth and mid-table in the Second.

A crowd of 13,365 packed into Shielfield Park, a record attendance for the ground. Rangers were on the offensive right from the kick-off and forced a string of early corners. The Berwick goal survived intact though despite numerous chances. Rangers claimed a penalty when Willie Henderson went down in the box under a challenge from Jim Kilgannon but nothing was given. Rangers continued to press but good work by Doug Coutts prevented Alex Smith from opening the scoring. It had been all one way traffic so far, however, in the 32nd minute Berwick scored. Kenny Dowds and George Christie ran at the Rangers defence and the latter passed to Sammy Reid, who blasted it past Norrie Martin and in off the post. Stunned, another chance fell to Berwick where Christie had an opportunity to make it two, but he couldn't connect properly with his shot and Martin made a comfortable save in the end. Rangers failed to replicate their early onslaught and only had a John Greig shot to show for their efforts since falling behind.

In the second half, Berwick continued to trouble Rangers with a number of chances. In the 65th minute, following a collision with Jock Wallace, Willie Johnston was stretchered off with a broken leg, to be replaced by Davie Wilson. As the match progressed the Rangers play became more frenetic. Rangers had a few chances to equalise but Berwick's Alan Ainslie also had opportunities, including hitting the post. Wallace's tactical attention to detail and ability to motivate his side for the battle was a key factor as Berwick held on to win 1-0 and to send shockwaves around Scotland and beyond. The defeat of Rangers was the first time they'd been knocked out in the First Round in over 30 years and *The Scotsman* described it as "the most ludicrous, the weirdest, the most astonishing result ever returned in Scottish football." The famous giant-killing Berwick team was: Jock Wallace, Gordon Haig, Jim Kilgannon, Ian Riddell, Russell Craig, Doug Coutts, Tommy Lumsden, Sammy Reid, George Christie, Kenny Dowds and Alan Ainslie.

Sammy Reid is the most famous of the team, having scored the winning goal. Reid was a diminutive inside-forward who had played for Motherwell and then Liverpool. Doug Coutts was the captain and defender, who had made 100 appearances for Aberdeen before joining Berwick in 1965. He left the club in 1969, going on to join Wigan Athletic. Ian Riddell, the full back had spent eight years at St Mirren and had two seasons with the club. Fellow full-back Gordon Haig had joined the club from Raith Rovers in 1964 and had a ten year spell at the club, making over 250 appearances, before becoming the player-manager at Dunbar United at the end of his career. He later returned to the club as manager during the 1975-76 season. Jim Kilgannon had previously played for Montrose, Dumbarton, East Stirling and then ES Clydebank, but he didn't re-join the Shire, but signed instead for Berwick where he spent two seasons. Russell Craig was a tough-tackling midfielder who had joined from Blantyre Victoria and who left in 1969 to play for Cambuslang Rangers. Inside forward Tommy Lumsden had two spells at the club with a spell in South Africa inbetween. In 1972 he left the club for good and joined Forfar. George Christie joined in 1966 from East Fife and scored 16 goals in 38 appearances. He was tragically injured in a friendly against South Shields shortly after the Rangers game and never played again. Kenny Dowds left the club in 1970 and joined Stirling Albion having made over 160 appearances for the club and scored 35 goals. Alan Ainslie was a 19 year old winger and the youngest player in the side. In 1969 he emigrated to Australia, playing for a number of Sydney based clubs, and he played international football for his adopted country, first being capped in 1971. Two years later, Berwick manager Jock Wallace left to become coach at Hearts and subsequently left the Jambos to join Rangers as Willie Waddell's number two becoming their manager in 1972. Wallace went on to capture the treble of all three Scottish trophies on two occasions, 1975–1976 and 1977–1978. After leaving in 1978 he later returned for a second spell in charge but couldn't replicate his success and was sacked in 1986. Dave Smith, one of the Rangers players that day, managed Berwick between 1976 and 1980, leading them to their first League championship in 1979. Exactly 11 years later, the teams met again at Shielfield in the 1977-78 Scottish Cup, with Smith and Wallace on opposite teams from 1967. This time the result went to form with Rangers winning 4-2.

Berwick were drawn against Hibernian in the Second Round away at Easter Road, but lost 1-0 in front of a crowd of nearly 31,000, though Berwick had a goal by Kenny Dowds disallowed in the first half and Wallace saved a penalty. Berwick had an inconsistent end to their League season following their Cup exit. A 4-0 loss at Morton in March was followed, a month later, by a 6-0 thrashing of Forfar. They lost the return at Forfar a fortnight later, 4-0, having beaten East Fife 4-1 three days earlier and eventually finished in a mid-table tenth place, but all the talk of the 1966-67 season was about 'that' game.

Berwick failed to make it out of their League Cup group in the 1967-68 season, a group which included St Mirren, Ayr United and Stranraer. They convincingly won their opening League game, 5-1 at Alloa but went on to lose five in a row across September and October. When they lost 4-1 at second placed Queen of the South on the 21st October they were in the bottom three in 17th place. They recorded a couple of wins in early November to climb a few places and eventually finished in 14th place. In the Scottish Cup they had to negotiate a couple of preliminary rounds before losing to Clyde in the First Round proper.

For the 1968-69 season they once again failed to get out of their League Cup group and they lost their first four games of the League season as well, including a 7-3 defeat at East Stirlingshire. Their first win though started a mini-run of four games without defeat. However, in early November they were thrashed 7-1 by run way leaders Motherwell. Two months later they were dealt a further blow when Jock Wallace left the club to take up the Number Two post at Hearts under John Harvey. Harry Melrose, the former Dunfermline and Aberdeen winger joined as player-manager in March 1969 and although they ended the season with a 5-0 win over Clydebank they finished two places lower than the year before, in 16th place. In the Scottish Cup they lost 3-0 in the First Round away at Aberdeen.

The 1969-70 season saw a step forward in terms of their League performance as the club finished in ninth place. They didn't progress out of a five team Group Nine in the League Cup, coming in fourth, and they lost their opening League game 3-0 at Cowdenbeath on the 30th August. However, they won their next game by the same score, at home to Alloa, which was the start of a run of six games without defeat. In mid-October they beat Stenhousemuir 6-1 and in early November they beat East Fife 4-0 and East Stirling 4-1 and they reached the end of 1969 in seventh place. They failed to qualify for the Scottish Cup, going out in the second preliminary round, and lost their first four games of 1970 to slip down the table. On the 28th March 1970 they beat Hamilton 5-1, with Eric Tait scoring two. Tait would go on to be a club legend. Tait joined Berwick from Coldstream in 1969, and holds the club records for most appearances made, with 526, of which 435 were made in League action, and most goals scored, having netted 114 times. He later went on to combine playing with managing the club in the 1980s.

The following season saw the club regress in terms of League placing. Having failed to progress from their League Cup section they lost their opening League game before beating Stenhousemuir 6-2. They then lost 6-2 themselves at Dumbarton and only won once in their next ten games, leaving them down in 16th place by the end of 1970. At this time they were also knocked out of the Scottish Cup by Highland League side Elgin City 2-0. Despite winning their first League game of 1971 they lost each of the next five to drop to second from bottom. From mid-February they then went seven games unbeaten (two wins and five draws) which pulled them away and up to 13thplace.

The 1971-72 season was largely a repeat of the season before. They started with a poor performance in their League Cup group where they won only one of their six games, and lost one of them 5-0 against Clydebank. They did, however, win their first two League fixtures, scoring seven goals, but by the end of October they had only four wins from twelve matches and had dropped down to 13th place which is where they eventually finished. In the Scottish Cup they entered and exited at the Second Round stage, going out to Queen of the South. They held their opponents first in a 0-0 draw before losing the replay at home 1-0.

Having won only one of six group matches in the League Cup and having been eliminated they started their 1972-73 League campaign poorly, being thrashed 5-0 at Cowdenbeath at the beginning of September. Their poor form continued as they lost each of their next five matches as well, and were beaten 8-1 by Raith and so had now played six, and lost six. They had scored only two goals and conceded 21. Their first point eventually came with a 1-1 draw at Queen of the South on the 23rd September, 1972 and their first win came a fortnight later when they beat Hamilton 3-0. The Berwick side featured two new signings and they scored all of their goals in the first half. They took the lead as early as the ninth minute and were two up before the half hour mark. The win started a run of seven games without defeat and when the run ended towards the end of November they had moved from bottom to a mid-table tenth. They eventually finished one place higher. In the Scottish Cup Berwick enjoyed some success reaching the Third Round. They had entered in the First Round and knocked out non-League Babcock & Wilcox and then fellow Second Division side Alloa -

both ties away from home. In the Third Round they secured a home tie against First Division Falkirk but lost 3-1 on the 3rd February 1973.

The 1973-74 season saw a much improved performance. Berwick's six games in their League Cup group yielded two wins and a draw and they failed to progress to the later stages of that competition once more but in the League they put in an improved showing and finished sixth, their best finish since entering the League nearly a quarter of a century ago. After an indifferent start things really clicked won they won 3-2 away at Kilmarnock at the beginning of October. The win came at the start of an unbeaten run of 13 games that was eventually ended on the 12th January. By this time they were up to second behind leaders Airdrieonians. A defeat at the leaders in early March and a loss at Montrose saw them drop out of contention. In the Scottish Cup they were knocked out in the First Round against Albion Rovers after a replay.

Due to the introduction of a new Premier Division in Scotland for season 1975-76 the top six teams from the Second Division were to be promoted to the First Division and Berwick couldn't replicate their final placing from the previous year and finished three places lower. They only won one of their six sectional League Cup matches before starting their League campaign with a 2-1 victory over Brechin City at the end of August. A 5-1 home defeat against St Mirren followed but Berwick won five and lost three of their first eight matches to sit in fourth place at the end of September. Inconsistency plagued them for the next few months and at the turn of the year they were in sixth place, although only four points separated second and ninth places. In the Scottish Cup they were drawn against last year's beaten finalists Dundee United and held the First Division side to a replay at Tannadice 1-1, narrowly losing the replay 1-0. Three draws and a win in March saw them slip down to seventh, two points off the top six before they lost 2-1 at home to second placed Falkirk. They failed to win any of their remaining five fixtures to slip further down to ninth place and eventually missed out on being placed in the First Division by six points.

Berwick began the 1975-76 season with two wins and three defeats in their first five fixtures. They were now playing in the third tier in a Second Division consisting of 14 clubs. Although they won 6-2 against new club Meadowbank Thistle Harry Melrose left as manager at the end of September. Walter Galbraith, the former Hibs manager took over but he had a disastrous stint in charge. The club picked up only one point in nine games and ended up being joint bottom with Stenhousemuir with just five points. They then recorded back to back wins but Galbraith left to be replaced by former player and 1967 legend Gordon Haig, who in a ten years span at the club had made over 250 appearances. Their form picked up a bit and a 2-1 away win at Stranraer at the end of February, with a brace from Ian Smith, saw them up to 11th place, although only four points off the bottom, which is where they eventually finished. In the League Cup they won only one of their six group games and failed to progress. In the Scottish Cup it took three matches before Brechin City knocked them out.

The 1976-77 season saw a slight improvement albeit after a poor start and another managerial change. Berwick failed to score in their two opening League matches and when they lost 5-1 at Alloa at the end of September they were bottom of the table, winless and with just two points to their name. This poor run had led to Gordon Haig leaving as manager and he was replaced by Dave Smith the former Rangers and Aberdeen player who had twice been capped for Scotland. Smith became player-manager in October and he would go on to transform the Shielfield Park club's fortunes, guiding them to the Second Division championship in 1979. Smith had a successful playing career at Aberdeen and Rangers (1966-74) making over 300 appearances and being part of the European Cup Winners Cup side of 1972. He joined Berwick, aged 32, and played between 1976 and 1980, making over 150 appearances as player-manager. The turnaround wasn't immediate and only two more draws followed in the next eight matches and they didn't win until a 1-0 away victory over Cowdenbeath on the 6th November. Remarkably this was the first in a run of five consecutive wins that saw them achieve a 100% record in November. This fine run moved them off the bottom and up the table into eighth place and they sustained this position until the end of the season. There was no improvement though in the Cups. They did draw four of their sectional League Cup matches but finished fifth out of six teams. In the Scottish Cup they made a First Round exit, losing 1-0 at Stranraer.

The 1977-78 season saw Smith's side continue their improved showing and the club put in a rare promotion challenge. They opened with a 2-2 draw at home to Dunfermline in mid-August and a month later thrashed East Stirlingshire 7-2 at Firs Park on the 24th September 1977. The League Cup moved to a two-legged tie and Berwick entered in the Second Round, losing 4-0 at Dundee before holding them 1-1 in the return to go out 5-1 on aggregate. Their big League win over East Stirling was the second game in a run of 18 matches without defeat which lasted until January 1978 and included a 4-0 win over Cowdenbeath and 4-1 over Forfar Athletic. In December 1977 they beat Burntisland Shipyard 4–1 away in the First Round of the Scottish Cup before thrashing fellow Second Division side, and promotion rivals, Raith Rovers 6-0 on the 7th January 1978, a result that led to the resignation of Raith's manager Andy Matthew. Their reward was a home tie against Rangers, played on the 28th January 1978 in front of a crowd of 10,500. Jock Wallace, who had been in goal for Berwick on that day in 1967, as well as being the Manager, was now in charge of Rangers, and Smith, who had played for Rangers, was now managing Berwick. The club was unable to reproduce the heroics of 1967 and this time the result went to form with Rangers winning 4–2. Raith, now under the charge of Bobby Reid, took revenge for their heavy Cup defeat by ending Berwick's fine unbeaten League run, dishing out a heavy beating of their own as Berwick lost 7-1 at Stark's Park. Berwick bounced back and went on a mini-run of five games without defeat before losing 3-1 at leaders Clyde. Another defeat followed at Forfar as Berwick lost ground on the leading pair of Clyde and Raith. By mid-April, and with five games left, Clyde had 47 points, Raith 45 and Berwick 41. Dunfermline in fourth place, two points further back, had an additional game to play. Their next fixture saw them host second-placed Raith Rovers. Berwick's promotion hopes were dashed as they lost 2-1 at home in front of a crowd of 1,600, double their previous home gate. They were now six points behind their opponents with four games left. Three days later they drew 1-1 at Stenhousemuir, in a game they had to win. The following Saturday, despite winning, Raith also won to earn promotion. Berwick eventually finished five points behind Clyde and Raith, the Bully Wee taking the title on goal difference. The same measure placed Dunfermline, level on points with them, into third place and Berwick were classified as fourth.

It had been progress under Dave Smith and after finishing fourth, Berwick went on to win the Second Division championship in 1979, claiming their first major honour. To put that success into some context, they beat Dunfermline Athletic and Falkirk to the title. Key to their success was the goals scored by Peter Davidson, who had been a FA Vase winner with Newcastle Blue Star, and who was eventually sold to Queens Park Rangers for £30,000. He stayed for less than one season making one solitary appearance in West London before returning in 1980, this time staying until 1986. In total he made 215 appearances netting 45 goals, after which he returned from whence he came to Newcastle Blue Star. Jimmy Morton, also starred in the championship winning side, having signed from Brechin City the previous year. He contributed 20 goals from midfield but actually left the year after picking up his medal to sign for St Johnstone. In his all too brief spell he appeared 54 times scoring an impressive 25 goals.

Berwick got off to an inauspicious start, thrashed by Falkirk 6-0, on the opening day of the season. They then scored six of their own in their next League game, beating Stenhousemuir 6-2. Inbetween they knocked St Johnstone out of the League Cup, a two legged affair won 2-0 on aggregate before going out to Premier Division St Mirren, 8-2. After a couple of League defeats in early September Berwick went on a run of eleven games without defeat, including a 5-0 victory at Meadowbank. At the end of October they sat in third place on 18 points, two behind Falkirk and a further point behind leaders Dunfermline Athletic.

During January and February 1979 Berwick Rangers were in Scottish Cup action and knocked out Forfar Athletic and East Fife, both matches played away from home, before going out to Celtic 3-0 in the Fourth Round. By Mid-March little had changed in the League standings, although Falkirk were the new leaders on 36 points, Dunfermline had 34 points in second, and Berwick also had 34 points, having played two more games. At the end of the month they beat Albion Rovers 5-1, in the early stages of a run of 17 games without defeat, and they also beat East Stirling 5-1 as part of this run.

This run saw them overtake their two promotion rivals and on Saturday the 28th April they extended their lead at the top to four points in a decisive set of results, as they drew with Queen's Park 1-1 and both Falkirk and Dunfermline lost. The other sides had games in hand but failed to capitalise, only drawing them. On Wednesday the 2nd May 1979 Berwick won their penultimate fixture 2-1 at Cowdenbeath to earn promotion. They had 54 points with Falkirk on 50 and Dunfermline 49. Falkirk still had two to play and Dunfermline three matches but as one of these was against each other it meant that Berwick couldn't be caught by both of them and Dave Smith's team were definitely going up. At the weekend only Dunfermline were in action and they lost at Alloa. On the 8th May Falkirk surprisingly lost 3-0 at home to Cowdenbeath and as a result Berwick were crowned the champions without kicking a ball! Five days later Dunfermline beat Berwick 1-0 to leapfrog over Falkirk into second and when Dunfermline drew with the Bairns three days later they confirmed that they would accompany Berwick to the First Division.

Many people's tip for an immediate return, Berwick surprised a number of pundits by avoiding relegation. It was still a season of struggle in the higher division but they finished three points clear of Arbroath, who accompanied Clyde to the Second Division. Berwick drew their opening League game 2-2 with Airdrieonians, who would be promoted as runners-up at the end of the season, and then won away 2-1 at Dunfermline Athletic. They then lost 3-1 at home to Hearts, for who Derek O'Connor scored a hat-trick, and the Jambos would go on to win the division and return to the Premier Division. This loss against Hearts was the start of a bad run of six games without a win. They then experienced a mini revival as they beat Stirling Albion 3-1 and then strugglers Arbroath 7-2 – a win that lifted them three places to eighth. They then made it three wins on the trot by winning 2-1 at Hamilton. Berwick then became the draw specialists, drawing seven out of eight games across November and December. In early January 1980 they beat St Johnstone 5-0 and were still in eighth and looking fairly comfortable to retain their First Division status. However, after beating Dumbarton 3-0 in mid-March they failed to win any of their remaining League fixtures to drop down to 12th, finishing three points clear of the relegation zone. In the cup competitions the Wee Rangers had contrasting fortunes. In the League Cup they went out in the First

Round, 5-4 on aggregate against Forfar Athletic. In the Scottish Cup they beat Peterhead and then giant-killing Keith, who had beaten Hamilton Accies, to reach the last eight and set up a Quarter-Final tie at home to Hibernian. On the 8th March 1980, in front of a crowd of over 7,000 at Shielfield the club fought out a 0-0 draw and acquitted themselves well in the replay four days later, narrowly losing 1-0, with Hibs being thrashed 5-0 in the Semi-finals against Celtic, who went on to lift the trophy.

Having survived relegation Berwick were unable to consolidate their position and were relegated after two seasons back to the Second Division. The bad omens came early with a club record SFL defeat on the opening day of the season and they went down 9-1 at Hamilton Academicals on the 9th August 1980. The following week they drew 1-1 at home to Dunfermline but later in August they were thrashed 8-1 at Aberdeen in a League Cup First Round first leg tie and lost the return 4-0 to go out 12-1 on aggregate. Shortly afterwards they lost 6-0 at Falkirk and didn't win in the League until the 20th September, when they beat Motherwell 3-2. They only recorded one more win to the end of 1980 and only five wins across the course of the whole League season. A 5-1 loss at East Stirling at the end of September saw the departure of manager Dave Smith. He was replaced by former goalkeeper and one-time player-manager of Cowdenbeath Frank Connor. He was unable to effect any turnaround in the club's fortunes on the pitch and they only won three more times. Towards the end of March 1981 they lost 6-2 at St Johnstone and on the 11th April, Berwick lost at Clydebank to effectively relegate the club. Dunfermline drew that day to move six points clear of the 'Wee Rangers' with three to play. Berwick were bottom with 20 points, Stirling Albion has 23 points and Dunfermline now had 26 points. On the 18th April Berwick lost 2-1 at home to Falkirk and although the two sides above them also lost, they had run out of games. Four days later Dunfermline and Berwick drew 1-1 and Berwick ended the season losing 4-1 at Hamilton, finishing bottom, two points behind Stirling Albion and six behind Dunfermline.

Berwick made an immediate attempt to bounce back and signalled their intent, both in progressing out of their League Cup group and in emphatically winning their opening League game. In the League Cup they qualified out of their group to reach the Quarter-Finals, although they lost 5-0 at Aberdeen and then 3-0 at home to go out 8-0 on aggregate. In the League they opened with a 4-0 win over Montrose and following a defeat at Forfar they then won three out of their next four matches, drawing the other. On the 5th December a 6-1 win over Albion Rovers was the first of four consecutive wins to sit in third, behind leaders Clyde and Brechin City. A 3-1 defeat at Clyde in mid-February was followed by a six game unbeaten run, although this included four draws. On the 1st May their promotion hopes suffered a blow when Brechin City beat them 1-0. Clyde were the runaway leaders at this point, with a nine point gap at the top. Five clubs were chasing the remaining promotion slot and with two games left Alloa had 47 points, Arbroath 46, Berwick and Forfar had 45 and Brechin had 44. A week later Berwick beat Forfar 2-1, Alloa drew, and Arbroath beat Brechin. The two beaten clubs – Brechin and Forfar now dropped out of contention and with a game to play both Alloa and Arbroath now had 48 points and Berwick had 47 points. Berwick's goal difference was the best of the three clubs and Alloa's was 12 goals better than Arbroath's. Berwick needed to win and for the other two to not win. As it was they drew 0-0 at Stirling Albion. The other two sides both won with Alloa securing the final promotion spot and Berwick were placed fourth. Their failure to secure a return to the First Division saw manager Frank Connor depart the club.

Jim McSherry, formerly of Kilmarnock and Ayr United was appointed the new player manager for the 1982-83 season but it was a disappointing campaign as the club failed to mount another promotion challenge and the new boss left in February 1983. Club legend Eric Tait then took over as player-manager. At the beginning of the season Berwick won three and lost three of their League Cup group games, failing to progress. They started well in the League, winning five and drawing five of their first eleven fixtures and at one point they were as high as fourth, although they slipped back to seventh place by the beginning of 1983. They then failed to win any of their next five matches and were beaten 5-0 by leaders Meadowbank, dropping to ninth place, which is where they finished. In the Scottish Cup Berwick beat Stirling Albion but then lost to Forfar Athletic.

In the 1983-84 season they did mount a promotion challenge. They opened their League campaign with a 3-0 win over Queen's Park and won their next two games as well, without conceding a goal, to top the division. They then lost the next two and four consecutive draws in November saw them drop to fourth. Inconsistent form followed and by mid-March they had dropped to seventh. Forfar had a ten point lead at the top and East Fife were seven points behind in second place. Berwick then put a strong run together, only losing one of their remaining fixtures. The best result in this sequence was a 6-1 win over Stenhousemuir at the end of April, with O'Hara scoring four. This run in saw Berwick move into third place, two points behind East Fife with two games to play. Saturday the 5th May was their one defeat, losing 2-1 at Montrose. East Fife won 3-0 to be promoted, and Berwick finished third. It had been a fine run but ultimately they came up just short. In the League Cup the club beat Stranraer 3-1 on aggregate before going out 4-0 on aggregate to Motherwell. In the Scottish Cup they entered at the Second Round stage and beat then Highland League side Peterhead 2-1 away. They drew Celtic at home where a crowd of five and a half thousand saw them lose 4-0.

The 1984-85 season was terrible. On the pitch the club slipped dramatically back and finished second from bottom, winning only eight League games out of 39 matches. The season started with a 2-1 win over Raith in the League but they then lost their next four on the trot. Five consecutive draws in November saw them drop to eighth in the fourteen team division. In mid-December they beat second bottom Arbroath 5-0 away but they failed to win in 1985 until the 26th February. Towards the end of March they beat Queen of the South 4-0 to rise as high as tenth place but they then failed to win any of their remaining eight fixtures to plummet to second from bottom, only three points above bottom side Arbroath. Berwick made early exits in both Cup competitions. In the League Cup they went out on penalties to East Stirlingshire in the First Round. In the Scottish Cup they beat Albion Rovers 2-1, then lost a marathon tie against non-League Inverness Caledonian after three matches. Off the pitch there were problems as well. Due to a worsening financial situation the club was forced to sell Shielfield Park to the local council, who then leased it back to the club.

The 1985-86 season saw little improvement as the club won only seven times in the League, one less than the year before, although they finished a place higher in 12th. They made a terrible start, winning only one of their first nine fixtures. They continued to struggle into 1986 and on the 18th January they lost 5-0 at home to Queen's Park, their worst home defeat for 28 seasons since Ayr United beat them 6-0 in 1957. The campaign ended in dismal fashion as they lost their last two fixtures both by the same 4-0 scoreline. In the Scottish Cup Berwick lost to Cowdenbeath after a replay and in the League Cup they went out in the First Round, losing 3-1 at home to the same opposition.

The 1986-87 season was their third poor season in a row where they won only eight games and finished bottom. They made an even worse start going their first nine games without a win. Berwick eventually won on the 11th October, 2-0 over Arbroath, thanks to goals from Stuart Romaines and Derek O'Connor to end a 17 game winless run in total dating back to the end of March 1986. They didn't win again until late November when two more wins followed and the club ended the year in 12th place, but tied on 13 points at the bottom with East Stirling and Stenhousemuir. They only won one of their first five games of 1987 but subsequently recorded a couple of wins in February. At the end of March they recorded a 1-0 win over Queen's Park and with six games left the club was four points clear of East Stirling at the bottom. However, they didn't win again and only gained one further point to the end of the season and finished bottom, level on points with East Stirling but with a much worse goal difference. In the Scottish Cup the club reached the Third Round. Having beaten Forres Mechanics and then Stenhousemuir they lost 2-0 at home to First Division Morton. In the League Cup they lost in the First Round, 3-1 at Albion Rovers.

The following season saw a marginal improvement in their final placing but they also recorded their lowest points tally of just 16. Although they won two fewer games, just six, and lost 29 out of 39 League games, they avoided finishing bottom again, goal difference being in their favour this time, as they finished above Stranraer. They failed to score in any of their first three matches, losing all of these games. Their first goals and point came at the end of August when they drew 2-2 against Cowdenbeath. They lost their next three before their first win when they beat Montrose 2-1 with goals from Graham Buckley and Mark Main. As a result of their first win they drew level with Montrose at the bottom with just three points. However, they lost their next five before they beat Stranraer 2-0 away at the end of October. By this time manager Eric Tait had left and in November was replaced by Jimmy Thomson as manager, the former St Mirren, Dunfermline and Raith player, who would also manage the club for a second spell in 1996. At the end of November they lost 4-0 against Montrose and as a result were now five points adrift at the bottom with just six points. The club continued to struggle and in early January 1988 they lost 5-3 at Cowdenbeath and a few weeks later lost 4-0 at home to Stirling Albion. A week later they did beat Albion Rovers 2-0 away from home but from early March the club experienced a run of six games where they only scored two goals and picked up just a single point. Going into the final League game of the season Berwick were bottom, two points behind Stranraer and a marginally inferior goal difference. In the final round of matches, played on the 7th May, Stranraer lost 2-0 whereas Berwick beat Arbroath 4-0 and the six-goal swing in goal difference meant the club avoided finishing bottom again. In the Scottish Cup the club entered at the Second Round stage but lost 1-0 at home to Brechin City. Earlier, in the League Cup First Round they had lost 2-1 at home to Stirling Albion.

Berwick made it a quintet of poor seasons in the 1988-89 campaign when they finished in the bottom three yet again. This time they finished second bottom, in 13th place, four points ahead of Stenhousemuir. They made yet another terrible start losing their first seven League games and they only scored once in their first five matches and this sequence of results led to the departure of manager Jimmy Thomson. Jim Jefferies was appointed as the new manager. Best known for both playing and managing at Hearts, he ended his playing career at Berwick between 1981 and 1983 and returned to take on his first Scottish League club in a management role, having previously been in charge at non-League Gala Fairydean.

Berwick's first points and win came on the 1st October when they beat Dumbarton 1-0. This was followed by another poor run of nine games without a win which included a 5-0 home defeat against East Stirling at the end of November. On the 31st December they had an entertaining 4-4 home draw against Brechin City, by which time they were well adrift at the bottom. The club then became the division's form team going unbeaten in the first three months of 1989. They gradually reined in Dumbarton and Stenhousemuir and moved ahead of the latter. On the 8th April they beat Dumbarton 4-0 at Boghead to move levels on points with their hosts and five ahead of Stenhousemuir. Scott Porteous with two and Ralph Callachan and John Hughes got the goals as the club extended their unbeaten run to 17 games. The club went four more games unbeaten to set a club record 21 games, before losing their last game of the season. In both Cups the club went out at the First Round stage to fellow Third Division opposition. In the Scottish Cup they lost to Alloa Athletic after a replay and in the League Cup they were knocked out by Stenhousemuir.

After five seasons at the foot of the table the 1989-90 season saw a massive improvement as the club carried their good form of 1989 into the new season. They made a good start to the new campaign, for once. They opened the season in the League Cup with a 3-0 win at Stirling Albion before going out 2-0 at home to St Mirren of the Premier Division. They won their opening League game 2-0 against Cowdenbeath and at the beginning of September beat Dumbarton 5-1 away to go fifth. Their performances on the pitch were even more commendable given the distractions and disruptions off it. Northumberland County Council closed Shielfield due to safety concerns and gave the club 28 days to get the ground up to the required standard. The club was therefore forced to look at alternative "home" venues. At the end of November they beat promotion chasing Kilmarnock 3-2 in a match played at Tynecastle, although they were given a scare as they were 3-0 with ten minutes to go. In early December they conceded home advantage to Stenhousemuir in the First Round of the Scottish Cup and played their "home" tie at Ochilview, drawing 1-1 before losing the replay 1-0. They returned to Shielfield at the beginning of January 1990 and beat Queen's Park 2-0. From mid-January they played four out of five games at home, winning three, to climb up the table. They won each of their last five matches, including beating Arbroath 5-0 in their last fixture to finish as high as fifth. At the end of the season though manager Jim Jefferies left to take the vacant managerial role at Falkirk.

Ralph Callachan, the ex-Hearts, Hibs, Meadowbank and Berwick player then became player manager for the next two seasons. In the 1990-91 season the club slipped back a bit to a mid-table finish in the League. They won three and lost three of their first half dozen matches and this trend was continued throughout the whole season. Their best result was a 4-0 away win at East Stirling in September and their worst result was a 5-0 defeat at Alloa in November. In the Scottish Cup they beat Albion Rovers 1-0 and in the Third Round they held St Johnstone of the Premier Division 0-0 in Perth but lost the replay 4-3 at Shielfield. In the League Cup Berwick were knocked out 4-3 in the First Round by Stranraer.

The following season saw a further decline and there were problems off as well as on the pitch as the club nearly went out of business. On the pitch they only won two of their first ten League matches and continued to struggle throughout the season. Off the pitch the club were kicked out of Shielfield once more, this time after they failed to keep up with the rent. Berwick were locked out of the ground, forcing the club to groundshare with other Second Division clubs. From February 1992 they lived a nomadic existence and played their "home" games at the Meadowbank Stadium in Edinburgh, Cliftonhill in Coatbridge, the Recreation Park in Alloa, at East Fife's Bayview and Stenhousemuir's Ochilview. Meanwhile, Shielfield was staging greyhound racing and later speedway. In the circumstances a 12th place finish was commendable. In the Scottish Cup Berwick beat Ross County, then of the Highland League, 7-4, but then lost 6-0 at Premier Division Dundee United. In the League Cup the club lost 1-0 at home to Dumbarton in the First Round. At the end of the season Callachan left and was replaced by former player Jimmy Crease as manager, who would go on to have four spells in charge of the 'Wee Rangers'.

The opening game of the 1992-93 season was a 3-0 loss at Queen of the South in the League Cup and in the League Berwick played their first six fixtures away, in which they secured two wins and a draw. After spending a number of months in exile, Berwick Rangers returned back to Shielfield Park on the 19th September 1992, when they hosted and beat Queen's Park 1-0. On the 3rd of October they beat Arbroath 5-1 but they then conceded five themselves in their next two games, a 5-3 defeat at Forfar and a 5-2 home defeat against East Stirling. In November they conceded four at Queen's Park and also at home to Queen of the South. They recorded four consecutive wins in March before a 6-0 loss at Arbroath and eventually finished in eighth place. In the Scottish Cup Berwick reached the Third Round. They beat Inverness Thistle 1-0 before going out to Premier side Falkirk 5-2.

There was a massive improvement in the club's fortunes on the pitch in the 1993-94 season. They finished as runners-up in the Second Division but were cruelly denied promotion due to League reconstruction. The League moved to four divisions of ten teams which meant the introduction of a new Third Division (fourth tier). Five teams were to be relegated from the First Division and only the Second Division champions would be promoted to the First Division. The bottom eight teams of the old Second Division were to be "relegated" to the new Third Division. Teams placed second to sixth would stay in the Second Division.

In the League Cup Berwick went out narrowly to Alloa Athletic 1-0 on the opening day of the season. In the League they failed to win any of their first three League games and won only three of their first ten League matches. In their next League game, on the 9th October, they beat Queen's Park 6-0, but then they didn't win again until the beginning of December. Manager Jimmy Crease left his role and was succeeded by Tom Hendrie. He had made over 300 appearances for Meadowbank over a 12 year period and had joined Berwick as a player for the 1992-93 season where he made 30 starts. In January 1994 Berwick beat East Fife 1-0 in the Scottish Cup but lost in the next round by the same score to Stirling Albion. From mid-January they went seven games unbeaten in the League to move into the top six. At the end of March Berwick beat Cowdenbeath 5-1 away, which was the second game in a run of nine games through to the end of the season where they went unbeaten. Despite this run they couldn't catch leaders Stranraer and on the 14th May, on the last day of the regular season, they beat Arbroath 5-0 to make sure of second place. Despite their improved performances on the pitch financial problems resurfaced at the end of the season.

Under the new League format Berwick finished fifth in the ten team division in the 1994-95 season. They finished five points behind the runners-up, Dumbarton, and Greenock Morton were the champions. The season opened with a League Cup tie against Montrose and the game ended 0-0 but Berwick went out on penalties. In the League the club went their first eight games without defeat, before losing 5-4 at Queen of the South. However, they then only won once from mid-November to the end of the year. The club were then in Scottish Cup action where they beat Buckie Thistle 4-1 away, before losing out to Meadowbank in a replay, also on penalties. Back in the League they only lost once in eleven matches from mid-February to mid-April but this contained six draws. In off the pitch news, the club's supporters bought the lease out in August 1995 to ensure the club would not be evicted from their ground in the future.

The mid-table finish of the 1994-95 season was followed up by with an excellent third place in 1995-96 under Tom Hendrie. Having lost their last two penalty shootouts in the cup competitions the previous year they made it third time lucky, beating Inverness Caley Thistle (then of the Third Division), 5-3 on spot kicks after a 1-1 draw. They were thrashed 7-0 at home by Premier League Partick Thistle in the next round. In the League they won two and drew the other of their first three League fixtures and only lost two of their first ten matches. In January they were in Scottish Cup action where they drew 3-3 at home to then non-League Annan, but they won the replay 2-1 to earn a home tie against Dundee United. In this Cup-tie they took the lead in the ninth minute due to a deflected own goal but Owen Coyle scored two first half goals, one a penalty to give their visitors victory. Back in the League their form stumbled as they lost three out of four from mid-January. Worse was to follow when Hendrie's two years in charge came to an end when he left Shielfield in February for Alloa Athletic, where he experienced some success before then moving on to St Mirren, winning the First

Division title in 2000 and taking them back to the top flight. Ian Ross, the former Liverpool and Aston Villa player, who as a manager in Iceland had won two domestic league titles took over as manager in March. Berwick lost 3-0 at home to leaders Stirling Albion, and this was followed by a 5-0 loss at Ayr United, as they dropped out of contention. Stirling Albion ran away with the Third Division title finishing 14 points clear of East Fife in second. Berwick were seven points behind the men from Methil.

The 1996-97 season was disastrous as the club won only won four League matches, their lowest total in a League campaign to date, and finished bottom and were relegated to the Third Division. Berwick lost their opening game 2-1 at Clyde on the 17th August. This was followed by two successive 6-0 thumpings at home to Stenhousemuir and then away to Ayr United. They picked up their first point in match day four, a 2-2 draw at home to Queen of the South and their first win came towards the end of September when they beat Dumbarton 3-1. However, they then failed to win any of their next 16 matches which led to the departure of Ross at the end of October. Jimmy Thomson returned for his second spell in charge but the club didn't win again until the 1st February 1997, when they beat Stranraer 2-0. A mini-unbeaten run of four games in March (one win, three draws) was already too little, too late, and they lost 5-0 at home to Hamilton in April and finished bottom, 12 points behind Dumbarton who accompanied them to the fourth tier. In the Scottish Cup they beat Peterhead 2-1 to set up a tie against First Division Falkirk. They held them to a 1-1 draw but lost the replay at home 2-1. Falkirk went all the way to the final, where they were beaten 1-0 by Kilmarnock. In the League Cup they were knocked out in the first Round by First Division St Mirren 4-0.

The 1997-98 season was the first of three seasons they spent in the Third Division and in their first season in this fourth tier they finished sixth in the ten team division. They won only one of their first six League matches which led to the departure of manager Jimmy Thomson. Two months after his arrival at Shielfield Park as a player Paul Smith was appointed manager. As a player Smith had a journeyman career, encompassing spells with Raith, Motherwell, Dunfermline Athletic (twice), Falkirk, Heart of Midlothian, Ayr United and Berwick Rangers. His managerial rein lasted seven years, one of the longest managerial stints in the club's history, and he got the club promoted to the Scottish Second Division in 2004.

Smith made an immediate impression and the team went unbeaten in October with Paul Forrester knocking in the goals. However, the improvement wasn't long lasting at this stage and the club's form deteriorated. From the end of March to the end of April the team went 13 games without a win, although that included eight draws. In the Scottish Cup Berwick went out early, 2-1 versus Livingston. In the League Cup they beat

Brechin City in the First Round to set up a glamour tie at home to Celtic. However there would be no cup shock as Celtic thrashed them 7-0 in front of a crowd of over 6,000 at Tynecastle - Regi Blinker, Henrik Larsson and company were five up by half-time.

The following season Berwick finished one place higher in fifth, but were fifteen points behind the runners-up Stenhousemuir, with Ross County as the runaway leaders. The club only won one of their first ten matches to be in the bottom two, but crucially kept faith with the manager. From early November to the end of January they went ten games without defeat, to climb to mid-table. Although they were thrashed 6-0 by leaders Ross County there were encouraging signs towards the end of the season as they went undefeated in their last six League fixtures. In the two major domestic cups the team were knocked out early on. In the Scottish Cup Berwick entered at the First Round stage losing 2-0 against Queen's Park. In the League Cup they beat Clyde on penalties in the First Round but lost 5-1 at home to Falkirk in the next round.

In the 1999-00 season Berwick Rangers won promotion back to the Second Division after three seasons in the Third Division. Further League reconstruction was taking place with the Premier League being increased to 12 and the divisions below were all having three sides up and one down, with two new teams joining the League at the end of the season as backfill. Berwick were promoted under Paul Smith as runners-up as they finished three points behind the champions Queen's Park, five ahead of Forfar Athletic, and seven ahead of fourth placed East Fife. Berwick made a good start to the season only losing two of their first ten matches. A 4-1 away at eventual champions Queen's Park on the 20th November was the start of a ten game unbeaten run, which was ended at third placed Forfar on the 7th March.

With four League games left Berwick led the table with 59 points, two ahead of Queen's Park, with Forfar a further point back. These three clubs occupied the promotion places with East Fife the leading challengers on 52 points. On the 15th April Berwick beat East Stirling 3-0. Queen's Park also won but the other two sides drew. This meant the club were now nine points ahead of East Fife, with three games left, and thus only needed one more point to be assured of promotion. They hosted East Fife in their next game, a week later, but lost 1-0. Forfar also lost but Queen's Park won to move one point ahead at the top of the table. On the 29th April the promotion nerves were finally settled when Berwick drew with Albion Rovers to get the point needed to guarantee promotion. Queen's Park won to extend their lead at the top to three points. Forfar drew and East Fife won, with the last two trading places. In the final game of the season Berwick beat Montrose 2-1. Queen's Park secured the title with 3-2 win over Cowdenbeath. Forfar won and East Fife lost so Forfar took the last of the promotion spots. Only one team came down (Hamilton - due to a points deduction) and Elgin City and Peterhead joined the League.

In the League Cup Berwick went out on the opening day of the new season, losing 2-1 at Queen's Park. They faced the same opposition in the Second Round of the Scottish Cup, this time winning 2-1. They also won 2-1 away at Stranraer in the next round to reach the Fourth Round (last 16) where they were drawn at home to First Division Falkirk. A crowd of 2,000 saw them hold their higher League opposition to a 0-0 draw but they lost the replay 3-0.

Berwick almost made it back-to-back promotions in the 2000-01 season when they finished third in the Second Division. Partick Thistle won the Second Division by 17 points and Berwick finished four points behind second placed Arbroath. They lost their opening game of the season but were unbeaten in their next four before a 4-0 home loss to Queen of the South. At the beginning of October they scored five, away from home at Forfar in a 5-3 victory and later in the month beat Arbroath 2-0 away before narrowly losing to leaders Partick 2-1 at Shielfield, with 1,240 spectators present. On the 2nd January 2001 Clydebank avenged two earlier defeats with a 2-1 win at Shielfield, which was far more comfortable than the final score line suggests, despite Garry Wood giving the home side an early lead, scoring from the rebound after his initial penalty had been saved. On the 4th February Berwick were leading Forfar 3-1 away when the game was abandoned at half time in blizzard conditions. At this point there was no talk of a promotion push but from mid-March Berwick went nine games unbeaten in the League (including a rearranged 1-0 win at Forfar). The run surprisingly came to an end when they lost 1-0 away at struggling Stirling Albion, and a 2-0 defeat at Arbroath a fortnight later effectively ended any lingering promotion hopes.

A successful League campaign was backed up by a good showing in the Scottish Cup. Earlier in the season they had made a First Round exit in the League Cup at the hands of Montrose. In the Scottish Cup they squeezed past Cowdenbeath after a replay to earn a home Third Round tie against Hearts. On the 27th January 2001 Berwick produced a magnificent performance to deny Premier League Hearts at Shielfield Park, and secured a fully deserved replay in Edinburgh, the match ending in a goalless draw. The 'Wee Rangers', watched by a home crowd of over 3,000, were more than a match for their opponents with Alan Neill a colossus at the heart of the defence and with Garry Wood and Barry Elliot a constant threat upfront. The Berwick team that day was: McLean, McMartin, Gray, Ritchie, Alan Neill, Anthony, Forrest, Neil, Wood (Whelan 89), Elliot (Findlay 80), and Darren Smith (Duthie 71). Garry Wood had two spells at Shielfield, the first from 1999 to 2003 when he signed from Ross County and ultimately departed for Queen of the South. During this period at Shielfield he clocked up 101 appearances scoring 44 times. He returned three years later from Dumfries and this time stayed for a further two seasons before retiring from the game adding another 38 starts and 10 goals to his tally. Darren Smith had signed up in 1998 from local side Berwick Rangers Colts and stayed for seven seasons before leaving for Brechin City in 2005. He clocked up 192 appearances scoring 35 goals.

Berwick lost the replay on the 7th February 2-1 but not after giving Hearts a fright. There were chances for both sides early on before an 18th minute strike from Barry Elliott gave Berwick the lead. Wood produced a fine defence splitting pass and the player, on loan from Dundee, ran through before calming picking his spot. Hearts now pressurised the Berwick defence and only a string of fine saves by goalkeeper Mark McLean kept them out. Hearts started the second half as they had finished the first and hit the post after just 60 seconds of play. Berwick then had a penalty claim waved away after Elliot went down after contact with Stephen Pressley. The Hearts pressure continued to mount and eventually paid off as they scored twice in three minutes through goals by Gary McSwegan and Juanjo.

Paul Smith completely overhauled his squad in the summer of 2001, bringing in seven players as another ten moved out. Former loanee from Falkirk, striker Colin MacDonald joined on a permanent basis; Derek Rae joined from Stranraer; defender Gerry Farrell came from Alloa; former Hearts defender Davie Murie, having been released by Morton also joined; as did Neil Bennett from Stirling and former Leeds United teenage striker Dale Crawford. Despite the signings the club finished in mid-table. Berwick made an inauspicious start to the new season, losing 4-0 at home to Alloa Athletic and they lost the next three as well, finally winning for the first time on the 2nd September, beating Morton 2-0. They then lost three out of their next four matches and in mid-October conceded five at home to Cowdenbeath in a 5-2 loss. At the end of October they won 1-0 away at Hamilton, which started a run of 12 League games without defeat, lasting until mid-February 2002, ended by Clydebank, who would fold at the end of the season.

Berwick lost in the First Round of the League Cup 3-0 at home to Partick Thistle but in the Scottish Cup they beat Cowdenbeath in the Second Round to set up a another meeting with Rangers, 35 years on from their famous giant-killing performance. Berwick came close to another major upset when they drew 0-0 with Rangers on the 15th January 2002. The club, then sitting bottom of the Second Division, went into the tie given little hope of repeating that historic 1-0 victory over Rangers but they held Alex McLeish's Premier League side. Watched by a crowd of over 4,000 at Shielfield, the visitors started well but goalkeeper Willie McCulloch made several important saves. After half an hour Berwick finally threatened themselves, Craig Feroz passing up a good opportunity. McCulloch then turned a low drive around the post using his feet and Michael Mols and Neil McCann both had good chances, with Berwick holding out to earn a replay. The Berwick side was: McCulloch, Farrell, Murie, Neill, Wood, Bennett, Forrest, Anthony, Smith, McDonald and Feroz. The two sides then met at Ibrox on the 21st January for the right to host Hibernian. Rangers won 3-0 but the win did not come easily, with the opening goal not coming until the hour mark when Lorenzo Amoruso's free kick beat Willie McCulloch. Rangers went on to score two more quick goals, to make it three in a ten minute period.

The 2002-03 season brought with it another mid-table finish. In a tight division they finished six points short of the promotion places and five points ahead of the relegation zone. In a largely uneventful season they won 4-2 away at Brechin City (who would go up as runners up) on the opening day. They also faced a new opponent in Airdrie United, the new entity that had replaced Clydebank. In the League Cup the club got beyond the First Round for a change when they beat Arbroath 4-2, but they lost to Partick Thistle for the second season running, and by the same scoreline, 3-0 at home. In the Scottish Cup they lost 2-1 to Montrose in the First Round.

They following season Berwick Rangers achieved their third mid-table finish in a row, in being placed in fifth position. Two highlights were the gates at Shielfield, which continued to average over 500 spectators, and the goalscoring of 30 year old striker Gareth Hutchison, formerly of Stenhousemuir, Falkirk and Alloa, who finished as the Second Division top goalscorer with 22 (scoring 25 across all competitions from 40 appearances). Berwick only won once in their first four League games and conceded four without reply at home to Forfar in October. They took revenge on the Loons winning 5-1 away at the end of December. In between Hutchison scored eight League goals in nine games, including a hat-trick in a 3-0 win over Arbroath on the 1st November. Hutchison went on to score eight goals in seven matches across February-March 2004, although the club lost 6-0 at the beginning of April to the eventual champions Airdrie United, conceding five goals in the opening 25 minutes, Alan Gow and Owen Coyle each scoring two and Coyle completed his hat-trick in the 88th minute. In the League Cup Berwick lost in the opening round, 1-0 at Forfar. In the Scottish Cup a Hutchison hat-trick saw off Huntly, 4-2, which brought Smith the manager, as a former Jambo, up against his old side once more. Berwick lost to Hearts 2-0 at Tynecastle with substitute Joe Hamill firing home from close range. His goal, in the 65th minute, was set up by Alan Maybury, whose wicked first-half cross had been turned into his own net by Berwick defender Mark Cowan after 28 minutes. Berwick never threatened to pull off a shock, as they had done in 2001 when they took an early lead. *The Scotsman* reported that "the 2-0 win was not pretty to watch and not a performance which will be remembered with any great affection by the supporters. But it was a win and at the end of the day that's all that matters in cup competitions. Having your name in the hat for the next round is the bottom line for all managers. The conditions made it almost impossible to produce the kind of football which was pleasing to the eye, a strong swirling wind combined with squally showers making life difficult for both sets of players from the outset....Riding high in the second division, the visitors had arrived in Gorgie full of confidence. And boss Paul Smith, as expected, had his troops well drilled and primed for battle. The wee Rangers made a lively start to proceedings, no doubt buoyed by memories of their last visit to Tynecastle three years ago when they were leading 1-0 with 20 minutes remaining of their third round replay after the teams had fought out a 0-0 draw at Shielfield Park. But while Berwick were again well organised and competitive throughout the proceedings, they never really threatened ...with Craig Gordon hardly having a save of note to make."

After five seasons Berwick Rangers were relegated to the Third Division at the end of the 2004-05 season, finishing bottom of the ten team Second Division. The League season started on the 7th August with a 2-1 win over Morton. In the League Cup they beat Elgin City and drew Aberdeen, unsurprisingly losing 3-0 at Pittodrie on the 24th August 2004. In the fourth minute Darren Smith's drive shaved the Dons crossbar minutes before the home side took an early lead over Berwick from a corner, and they extended their lead before the interval. Minutes after the resumption Aberdeen scored a third past Berwick goalkeeper Gary O'Connor. Ian Little then had a couple of half chances before Aberdeen were denied what would have been a wonderful fourth goal when O'Connor produced a fabulous fingertip save, and the keeper was called upon again to save another effort late on. After this reasonable start they lost their next five League matches and failed to win in 13 games, prompting the departure of Smith who left in October 2004. He was replaced by Airdrieonians legend and former Rangers and Hearts player Sandy Clark, who had management experience at Partick Thistle, Hamilton, Hearts and St Johnstone.

Berwick recorded their next win on the 20th November, 1-0 away at Stirling Albion. This was followed by a 1-0 win over Forfar and a mini-run of four games without defeat. In the Scottish Cup they entered in the Second Round and knocked out fellow Second Division Dumbarton after a replay. In the next round they were drawn to play the divisional leaders Brechin City, losing 3-0 at home. Back in League action they won three of their next six games to close the gap on the teams above them, and in March went five games without defeat, although four of those were draws. This lack of victories continued to plague them and in their remaining six fixtures in April they won only once. On the 9th April they lost 2-1 at home to Stranraer, the visitors going ahead in the 11th minute from a corner and they extended their lead shortly after half-time. With five minutes left Kevin McLeish hooked in a Kevin Gordon cross to give Berwick hope, but despite a grandstand finish they could not equalise and relegation was now virtually certain. On the 16th April they lost 2-0 at fellow strugglers Arbroath, and although they then drew with eventual champions Brechin City and then beat Ayr United 2-1 at home they lost their final game 4-2 at Morton to finish eight points from safety.

Clark was only a temporary appointment and former player John Coughlin was appointed as the new manager in May 2005. Berwick started life in the Third Division (or fourth tier) on the 6th August 2005 with a 4-0 win at East Fife, which was the first of eight consecutive League victories, a club record. As a result Coughlin won the Manager of the Month prize for August and September. They eventually lost on the 12th November at Arbroath, the Shielfield side having no answers to a determined Arbroath who ran out 4-0 winners. They lost their next three as well, including 2-0 at home to promotion rivals Stenhousemuir and went a total of six games without a win, across two months. During this time they were also knocked out of the Scottish Cup by non-League Spartans. The two sides met on the 26th November 2005 and the then Third Division leaders crashed out 1-0. Spartans from Edinburgh, and members of the Lowland League, had tried to join the Scottish League in 2008. They scored in the 61st minute and the home team had the best of the game and deserved to go through. They went on an extended run, reaching the last 16, where they held St Mirren to a 0-0 draw, before losing the replay at Love Street 3-0.

The Third Division title race was now wide open. Back to back League defeats in February threatened to derail their promotion bid but they won six games on the trot from mid-March, with Coughlin picking up a third Manager of the Month award for the season. The Wee Rangers went the rest of the regular season unbeaten, a run of nine games, winning eight of these. They finished as runners-up, on the same points total as champions Cowdenbeath, but with an inferior goal difference, having set a new club record of 23 wins in a League season. However they were not automatically promoted as this was the first year of the SFL play-offs which were contested between the ninth placed (second bottom) club in the higher division and the second, third and fourth placed clubs in the lower division. It was therefore possible for a team finishing fourth to be promoted, rather than the clubs finishing immediately above them in the standings. In the first stage of the play-offs they played third placed Stenhousemuir, winning 1-0 away. Gareth Hutchison scored the only goal of the game, against his old club, to put Berwick in the driving seat. Stenhousemuir's goalkeeper spilled a Kevin McLeish free-kick from 30 yards out and Hutchison was on hand to sweep home the loose ball fifteen minutes from time. The two clubs drew 0-0 three days and Berwick then faced Alloa Athletic from the higher division for a place in the Second Division. On Wednesday 10th May they were thumped 4-0 at Alloa, conceding two goals just before the break, and two in the last quarter of an hours play. They came from one-nil down in the return to win 2-1, thanks to two goals from Robbie Horn and Kevin McLeish also had a penalty saved, as they lost 5-2 on aggregate.

John Coughlin's side put the disappointment behind them and made sure the following year, finishing as Third Division champions in 2007, their first title since 1979. Berwick won 24 League matches in the campaign although they didn't start that well this time and were knocked out of the League Cup in the First Round by Ayr. They won five of their first ten games to settle into mid-table but on the 11th November they beat East Fife 2-1, which was the start of a run of eight consecutive wins, matching the club record. The months of December 2006 and January 2007 saw Coughlin awarded the Manager of the Month award again before the run came to an end on the 27th January 2007. They lost three of their next four games as well but then won four on the trot during the remainder of March. In the Scottish Cup fellow Third Division sides East Fife and Arbroath were knocked out before Berwick lost 2-0 at home to SPL side Falkirk.

On the 7th April they dropped points at home to Elgin City, drawing 0-0 after having Kevin Haynes sent off. A week later an early Stuart Fraser goal gave them a 1-0 win At Albion Rovers and this set up a championship decider when Berwick faced their closest challengers Arbroath at Shielfield on the 21st April. The two best teams in the division went head to head in front of a 2,000 plus crowd. In a nervy match Iain Diack shot home after 20 minutes following an Ian Little free-kick. Arbroath thought they had equalised 15 minutes after Diack's goal when they had the ball in the net, but it was disallowed for a foul on goalkeeper Gary O'Connor. Berwick took charge after the interval and Arbroath's 'keeper made two good saves from David Greenhill before O'Connor was called upon to save when their opponents launched a late challenge. With five minutes left to go Arbroath were reduced to ten men for a second yellow and Berwick eased out the game to win 1-0. The victory was their 24th win and set a new club record for most wins in a League campaign. The Third Division trophy was presented to captain Grant McNicoll after the game. The Berwick team that day was: O'Connor, Manson, McGroarty, Horn, Smith, Fraser, Thomson, Notman (McNicoll 89), Haynes (David Greenhill 65), Diack and Little (Gary Greenhill 75).

Berwick were relegated after only one season in which a number of unwanted records were set, including the fewest wins in a League campaign (3), and their lowest points tally (16). They also conceded more than a 100 goals in a season for the third time in their history, and the first since the 1957-58 season. On the 4th August 2007 they drew their opening game 1-1 with Cowdenbeath. They lost their next game but then beat Airdrie United 2-0 with goals from McLeish and Scott Gemmill to register their first League win of the season. They then conceded four in each of the next two games - 4-0 at Ayr and 4-3 at Peterhead - which came at the beginning of a run of 13 games without a win. During the middle of this run John Coughlin resigned as Berwick Rangers manager after a 3-0 home loss to Alloa Athletic on the 6th October 2007 and bemoaned the lack of investment in the squad and inadequate training facilities. He left with Berwick at the foot of the table with only five points after nine games. Former player Jimmy Crease, who had returned to the club in 2005 as a general manager, took over as caretaker boss.

With Berwick in a relegation dog-fight the club went against the prevailing wisdom of appointing an experienced manager with a track record of relegation scraps and went instead for a youthful coach with no management experience. Michael Renwick, a coach at Cowdenbeath, took over on the 25th October and suffered a 4-0 loss at Airdrie in his first game in charge. His spell in charge was an unmitigated disaster and Berwick eventually won again on Boxing Day, beating Raith 2-1, Iain Diack scoring both goals. They only won one more League fixture after that, in mid-March, 2-1 away at Cowdenbeath. They finished bottom, conceded over 100 goals and lost 9-2 at Peterhead and conceded five against Brechin, Cowdenbeath and Raith. Renwick was sacked after the last of these, on the 19th April, with Jimmy Crease taking temporary charge again for the last game of the season. In the 2007-08 League Cup they beat Stenhousemuir in the First Round stage before going out to Hamilton. They entered the Scottish Cup at the Third Round stage and went out 2-0 at Third Division Dumbarton.

In May 2008 non-League Camelon manager and former East Stirlingshire striker Allan McGonigal was appointed as the new permanent manager. His was also a short and unsuccessful tenure with the club making little progress on the pitch. Berwick started the 2008-09 season with a 2-1 win over East Stirlingshire on the 2nd August but then didn't win again until the end of September. A 5-2 loss at Dumbarton at the beginning of November was followed a 3-0 home defeat against Albion Rovers. Shortly afterwards a fan-based consortium, led by the Supporters Trust, took over the club with a significant change in the composition of the board. Brian Porteous became the new chairman of the club and the announcement coincided with the departure of Allan McGonigal after just six months in charge. He resigned after the loss of five straight games and Jimmy Crease took charge as a caretaker for the third time and was appointed manager on a full-time basis a month later, becoming the club's fourth manager in little over a year. Berwick were second bottom of the Third Division, although they were 12 points clear of Elgin City. Crease's spell in charge started well and four consecutive wins saw him win December's Manager of the Month award. December's success was a flash in the pan as Berwick didn't win in 2009 until the end of February. On the 21st March they beat Elgin City 2-1 but they failed to win any of their remaining seven games to finish second from bottom, although they still finished nine points ahead of Elgin. In the League Cup they had gone out to Ayr United in the First Round and in the Scottish Cup they entered at the Second Round stage and went out to Albion Rovers, 2-1 at home.

The 2009-10 season saw a marked improvement as Berwick briefly challenged for a place in the end of season promotion playoffs, finishing in sixth place, although only one point off fourth spot and the final playoff place. Berwick won five of their first seven matches and followed this up with a six game unbeaten run in the autumn. In January 2010 they beat struggling Elgin City 5-1 away but a month later lost 4-0 at home against promotion chasing Forfar Athletic. They only lost one of their last six matches but three draws in that scuppered any hopes of nicking a playoff place. On the 24th April, in their penultimate game of the League season they went down 2-1 at home to promotion rivals Albion Rovers. Queen's Park occupied the last play-off place on 50 points, Albion Rovers had 49 points and Berwick had 47, with a five goal worse goal difference. In the last round of matches Berwick needed to win and the other two to lose to claim the last spot in the play-offs. Damon Gray scored in the 44th minute at Annan to give Berwick the lead and although Jay Shields was sent off on the hour mark, the Wee Rangers held on for a 1-0 win. Unfortunately both of their rivals drew so the victory was in vain. In the League Cup Berwick went out in the First Round to Partick Thistle 5-1 (then playing in the second tier). In the Scottish Cup they beat Civil Service Strollers in the Second Round before going out 5-1 to then First Division (second tier) Ross County.

In the 2010-11 season they again finished short of the playoff places, with the same classification of sixth, but this time they were ten points shy of fourth place. They started the new season with a trip to Peterhead in the League Cup where they went down 1-0. Their League programme kicked off with a 2-2 draw in Coatbridge against Albion Rovers before they won 6-2 against Elgin City in their first home match of the season. Darren Gribben, a former Cowdenbeath and Forfar striker, and in his second spell with the club, scored a hat-trick and scored 17 League goals for the season. They also recorded 4-1 wins at Clyde and at home to Arbroath (Gribben scoring a second hat-trick) and went the first eleven games of the League season without defeat. Jimmy Crease was named Manager of the Month for August and by the end of October they were in third place in the division.

A couple of defeats in December and a 4-0 loss at home to future champions Arbroath in mid-January began to undermine their promotion challenge and following this setback they lost their next four as well to drop out of contention. In early March, Damon Gray, another striker in his second spell with the club, scored a hat-trick against Elgin in a 4-0 victory but ten days later they lost 6-1 at home to promotion challengers

Albion Rovers, Scott Chaplain scoring a hat-trick for the visitors. Berwick only earned two draws in their last three matches, the first of these against Clyde all but ending their promotion play-off hopes. They were six points adrift of Stranraer, who occupied the final playoff place with only two games remaining. In the Scottish Cup Berwick entered in the Second Round where they beat fellow Third Division side Clyde 2-1 away from home. In the next round they travelled north to play Highland League side Cove Rangers, who would ultimately go on to replace them in the League, and won 3-0. This set up a glamour tie against Celtic, played on the 9th January 2011. A crowd of just under 4,000 saw them go down 2-0 at home. Berwick emerged with a lot of credit having made their illustrious opponents work hard for their victory. Celtic took the lead in the 17th minute, but the visitors toiled for long spells and Scott Brown only sealed the tie in the 81st minute. Gribben had the ball in the net prior to the second goal, but it was ruled out for an infringement. The Cup run and tie against Celtic gave the club a financial boost and they reported a £150,000 profit for the season.

The 2011-12 season saw the club regress on the pitch leading to a further managerial change. The season started well on the 30th July when Berwick produced a cup shock in the First Round of the League Cup when they knocked out Partick Thistle 3-1 at Firhill. Berwick came from behind to beat their opponents who ended with nine men. Patrick took the lead but Gray soon equalised. Partick were reduced to ten men soon after the interval. Stuart Noble put Berwick ahead midway through the second half. With ten minutes left Partick gave away a penalty and had a man sent off, Paul Currie converting from the spot for a 3-1 win. Berwick lost their opening League game 4-1 at Elgin, whose striker Craig Gunn scored all four of his side's goals. A week later Paul Currie bagged a brace as Berwick beat East Stirlingshire 4-2. At the end of August Berwick travelled through to Easter Road to play Hibs in the Second Round of the League Cup, but were comprehensively beaten 5-0.

A 4-1 away victory at Clyde in mid-September, in which Gribben scored two, briefly took Berwick up to fifth in the table. On the 22nd October they suffered a Scottish Cup exit at the hands of Highland League Deveronvale, losing 4-0. Berwick were two down after half an hour and conceded two in three minutes midway through the second half plus had a man sent off. In the wake of the defeat Jimmy Crease resigned as manager. Ian Little, the ex-Alloa, Livingston and Stenhousemuir player, who had signed for the club in 2004 and had made over 160 League appearances, took over as player-manager on a caretaker basis and the club went unbeaten in his first four League matches in charge, which included a 5-3 win at Montrose in which Darren Gribben and Stuart Noble each bagged a brace. Ian Little was named as Manager of the Month for November and Gribben took the Player of the Month award. At the end of the year the club announced that he would remain as manager until at least the end of the season and he subsequently had his contract extended to the end of the 2012-13 season. This mini-run took them up to fifth again, but this was the highest League placing they would achieve during the season. Berwick only won once in the League in the first two months of 2012 but finished strongly, only losing two of their last ten. On the 17th March the club announced Little had been appointed as manager on a permanent basis. Danny Handling was brought in on loan from Hibs and scored two goals on his Berwick debut, a 2–1 win at Peterhead on the 24th March and went on to score seven goals in as many games, including two in a 5-0 win over Alloa Athletic. Berwick scored all of their goals in the first hour of play and although Handling was recalled by his parent club, Berwick eventually finished in seventh place.

Little's first full season in charge was a success as Berwick reached the playoffs and achieved their best League placing in the five years since being relegated to the Third Division. In the summer they lost the services of top goalscorer Darren Gribben who went to Arbroath but the big news was the placing of the mighty Rangers into the Third Division alongside the 'Wee Rangers'. The club appointed a skipper with genuine leadership qualities in Chris Townsley and signed former Hearts midfielder and playmaker Neil Janczyk from East Fife. Berwick played Rangers early on, in only the second round of matches, securing a 1-1 draw at home in front of a crowd of over 4,000 at Shielfield Park. Berwick had just about edged the first half but fell behind in stoppage time when they conceded. Fraser McLaren broke clear to find the far corner after 62 minutes and had another effort saved by keeper Neil Alexander. Chris Townsley found the net for Berwick, but his effort was disallowed.

The club won for the first time on the 1st September, beating perennial strugglers East Stirling 3-0 and later in the same month they beat Stirling Albion 4-1. However, they failed to win any of their fixtures in the month of December and this included a 6-3 loss away at Stirling Albion. Back to back wins in early January improved their position before a 4-2 loss at Ibrox started a run of five games without a win, the last of these being on the 23rd February when they lost 3-1 at home to the leaders Rangers, despite taking an early lead. They won their next game, 2-1 at home to Elgin City, which was the first of a run of six games without defeat, a sequence that included five wins. In one of these, a 4-0 win over Montrose, Fraser McLaren scored a hat-trick.

In the League Cup the club had gone out at the first stage, losing 4-3 to Raith, the winner being scored in the 85th minute. In the Scottish Cup they went out in the Third Round to Stenhousemuir. By the end of the regular season they were involved in a three way battle for the last playoff spot. Rangers were confirmed as champions after a goalless away draw with Montrose on the 30th March and Peterhead and Queen's Park had claimed the first two play-off places. On the 20th April the 'Wee Rangers' beat Elgin

City 2-1 at Borough Briggs. They gave away an early penalty but goals from Darren Lavery and Kevin McDonald in the second half gave them a vital win against one of their rivals. Although they lost their last two games, at home to Annan and away to Rangers (where the Ibrox club were presented with the Third Division championship trophy in front of a crowd of over 50,000, the largest crowd for a Third Division match), Berwick claimed the last play-off spot, finishing on 49 points with Elgin, but with a better goal difference of six.

In the play-offs Berwick played the ninth placed team in the Second Division which was East Fife. In the first leg the two sides met at Shielfield Park in front of a crowd of 732. They conceded just before half-time but Lavery equalised in the 72nd minute, although the advantage lay with the men from Methil. In the second leg Berwick took the lead after an hour thanks to a Lavery penalty, his 20th goal of the season. However, a MacDonald own goal 12 minutes from time levelled things up, both in the match, and on aggregate. The game went into extra-time and looked destined for penalties when, in the 119th minute, Liam Gormley volleyed in Robert Barr's cross and broke Berwick's hearts. East Fife went on to play Peterhead in the two-legged final which they won narrowly 1-0 on aggregate after the two matches.

For the 2013-14 season and the formation of the Scottish Professional Football League the First Division was rebranded as the Championship and the Third Division as League Two (still the fourth tier). More significantly, the introduction of a pyramid system for the following season, provided a gateway for non-League clubs to enter the League and therefore the possibility of relegation from it. Berwick started the season well in the League and in mid-August recorded a 4-0 win over Queen's Park. However, they were thrashed 5-0 at home to Cowdenbeath in the League Cup and poor form across the rest of 2013 saw Little sacked as manager on the 12th January, with the club citing its lowly league position, third from bottom, as the reason for making a managerial change. Little subsequently went on to become the manager of Lowland League side Whitehall Welfare.

Following the sacking of Ian Little, Colin Cameron was appointed player-manager on the 14th January. He had made his name first at Raith Rovers and then Hearts, Wolves and was capped for Scotland. He had subsequently been player-manager at Cowdenbeath. Cameron's impact was immediate and four days after his appointment the club matched their best win of the season when they beat Stirling Albion 4-0. He went on to be named the Manager of the Month for January as the club slowly started to climb the table. In the Scottish Cup the club reached the Fourth Round (last 32) having beaten Peterhead, Culter, from a suburb of Aberdeen, after a replay, but they then went out to Dumbarton 3-1, despite taking an early lead through Lee Currie. In the League they eventually finished five points behind Clyde who occupied the last play-off place.

After two moderately successful League campaigns the club slipped back to eighth place but they did enjoy a successful run to the last eight of the Scottish Cup and a money spinning game at Easter Road against Hibernian. Things started well in the League and on the 23rd August Berwick beat East Stirling 5-0. Lee Currie hit a superb 30-yard effort into the top corner and player-manager Cameron bagged a goal with a 20-yard drive after the break. Darren Lavery added a third off the inside of the post before Shire were reduced to ten men. Scott Dalziel and John Fairburn scored goals four and five to add to East Stirling's misery. After this big win Berwick didn't win again until the 8th November when the reverse fixture against East Stirling came around. On the 6th December they beat Clyde 4-0 and finished the year in seventh place.

The club made a good start to 2015 and climbed as high as sixth but only won two of their last ten games and ended the season with a 5-0 thrashing against Arbroath on the 2nd May. All the goals came in the second half. The club finished ten points clear of the bottom, in eighth place. Montrose came bottom but survived relegation by beating Highland League side Brora Rangers 3-2 on aggregate. In the League Cup Berwick lost to Morton 2-1 in the First Round but they had much better fortune in the Scottish Cup, equalling their best ever Scottish Cup performance, reaching the Quarter-finals for the third time, yet in four years they would be out of the League! Highland League Formatine United, East Fife, Albion Rovers and Spartans (the last two both after replays) were accounted for and Berwick were drawn away, at then Championship side Hibernian. The two sides met on the 8th March 2015 at Easter Road and Colin Cameron's side held out for 25 minutes, before Hibs scored two goals in three minutes and ran out comfortable 4-0 winners.

The 2015-16 League season started well with three wins and a draw in their first five games, although the one defeat was 5-0 at East Fife. By mid-September Berwick were in second place but they only won once in their next five matches, losing 4-1 at Montrose on the 31st October, a result that led to the sacking of Colin Cameron as manager. In November John Coughlin returned as manager but the 'Wee Rangers' lost six games in a row, which included a 5-0 home defeat to Clyde. The last of these was a 3-2 home defeat against Elgin City. The hosts went in front when Michael McKenna drove a rebounded shot past the 'keeper. Elgin then scored three before Darren Lavery gave Berwick a late consolation when the visiting goalie spilled a Steven Notman cross. Berwick were now bottom of the table on 15 points, the same as Arbroath, but with a worse goal difference, and a further point behind East Stirling. They finally won again in mid-December, 4-0 at East Stirling, Finn Graham scoring two first half goals, a result that lifted them off the bottom and into eighth place. This was the first of three wins in a row, as they climbed back up the table. In April 2016 Coughlin was awarded the division's Manager of the Month award following three wins and a draw from their last five matches, which included a 3-0 win over Clyde, Blair Henderson scoring two, and taking his season's tally to 17 goals. Berwick eventually finished in sixth place, with bottom club East Stirling being relegated out of the League having lost the play-off against Edinburgh City.

In the League Cup David Banjo scored an extra-time winner as Berwick Rangers came from two goals down to surprise Championship side Alloa Athletic. The Wee Rangers had gone 2-0 down after 21 minutes and looked down and out at half-time. Lavery got a goal back in the 56th minute before substitute David Morris headed an equaliser 23 minutes from time. In extra time Banjo headed Berwick into the lead for the first time and Berwick held on to win. They went out 4-1 at Premier League Kilmarnock in the next round as three goals in the final 20 minutes helped Kilmarnock finally ease past them. Lavery cancelled out Kris Boyd's first half penalty with a brilliant effort on 55 minutes, but goals in the 70th and 77th minutes, and a sensational 30 yarder last-minute goal from Kallum Higginbotham sealed the victory. In the Scottish Cup Berwick slumped 4-1 at Annan.

At the end of the season Chairman Brian Porteous stepped down to be replaced by Len Eyre. Back on the pitch the club were still struggling and finished in eighth place in the 2016-17 season. They only lost two of their first ten League fixtures although that included five draws. However, they then struggled and on the 10th December they were thrashed 6-0 at second-placed Elgin City. Trailing two-nil at half-time they conceded four in fifteen minutes in the second half. The club steadily dropped from fifth to bottom but fortunes picked up in March, and striker Greg Rutherford was named Player of the Month. At the end of the month they beat Forfar 3-2 away, but didn't win any of their next five matches. Going into the last round of matches Berwick were in ninth place on 37 points, the same as Clyde, in eighth, but with a one goal difference margin, and crucially, three points ahead of Cowdenbeath. A point would be enough to avoid the dreaded play-off, regardless of what Cowdenbeath could achieve. On the 6th May victory for Berwick Rangers over Edinburgh City, and a draw for Clyde at Montrose, condemned Cowdenbeath, who drew away to Elgin City, to the relegation play-off. A 2-0 lead calmed Berwick's nerves, with goals by Lavery and Rutherford, until Edinburgh brought it level and anxiety levels rose once more. A David Verlaque strike, on as a substitute, in the 92nd minute, secured the three points and survival was assured. Berwick finished five points ahead of bottom side Cowdenbeath, who narrowly retained their League status by beating Lowland league champions East Kilbride on penalties.

In the League Cup Berwick were placed in Group H along with Albion Rovers, Clyde, Morton and Premier League Kilmarnock. They beat Albion Rovers on penalties but their best performance came against the Premier League opposition. They were leading Killie 2-0 after an hour with goals from Johnny Fairbairn and Sean Mackie and threatening an upset but eventually lost 3-2. In the Scottish Cup they were on the receiving end of a surprise, losing 3-2 at home to Hawick Royal Albert of the Lowland League on the 22nd October 2016. To rub salt into their wounds, former player Josh Morris scored all three Hawick goals, two inside the first ten minutes as the visitors raced into an early two goal lead and led 3-1 at half-time. Rutherford got another back on debut as the second half was all one way traffic but Berwick spurned numerous chances and the day belonged to Hawick.

Off the field, the club reported a loss of nearly £90,000 for the trading year up to the 31st May 2017. This was an even higher figure than in the previous season (£80,000) which gave a combined deficit of around £170,000 over the last two years. In another blow, centre-forward Rutherford asked to be released at end of the season for personal reasons in order to return to his native north-east.

The club had stuck with manager John Coughlin but August 2017 saw his departure early on following a couple of heavy defeats, 4-0 at Stirling and then 5-1 at home to Annan. The board moved quickly to appoint Robbie Horn to replace Coughlin. Horn was well known to Berwick fans having played a pivotal part in Coughlin's title winning team of 2006-07 and also served in the management team alongside Ian Little and his successor Colin Cameron. Horn returned to the club after a successful stint at Bonnyrigg Rose, where he made the headlines by guiding them to a shock Scottish Cup win over Championship side Dumbarton which had earned them a tie against the then Cup holders Hibs.

Horn was unable to turn the club's fortunes around and a heavy defeat 5-1 defeat at Elgin in November was followed by an eleven game run without a win between February and early April 2011. The club only won nine League matches out of their 36 fixtures but fortunately for them Cowdenbeath were even worse, only winning four. With two games to play Berwick were assured of safety as they were eight points ahead of the bottom side. Berwick beat Cowdenbeath 1-0 in their penultimate League game. The victory was only Berwick's second in 20 League games. Rangers took the lead in the 12th minute when a Darren Lavery corner found its way to the back post where Jamie Todd, who had come in on the blind side, headed in from close range. The following week Berwick also won, beating Clyde 2-1 away in their final League match of the season. Cowdenbeath again survived the play-off, beating Highland League side

Cove Rangers 3-2 on aggregate. In the League Cup the club were drawn in a group with Morton, Edinburgh City, Queen's Park and Motherwell and lost all their matches, although they drew against Edinburgh City 2-2 after extra-time but lost the penalty shootout 4-2. In the Scottish Cup they beat Annan Athletic 1-0 but lost 3-0 against Arbroath in the next round. The poor performances on the pitch were reflected in the finances of the club as the accounts to the year ending May 2018 revealed another loss of £50,000.

After years of struggle fate finally caught up with Berwick Rangers as they became the second club to be relegated from the Scottish Football League. They only won five League games all season but the main cause of their demise was a terrible run of results from March 2019 onwards. The 'Wee Rangers' kicked off what would be their last campaign on the 4th August with a home match against Stirling Albion which they won 1-0 through a Ross Brown goal. The following Saturday they travelled to Hampden to face Queen's Park, who had been relegated the year before, and narrowly lost 1-0. A second away game in succession saw them travel to Cowdenbeath on the 18th August where they went down heavily 4-0. On the 1st September they came from 3-2 down to beat bottom side Albion Rovers 5-3. This was a solitary win in a run of ten games where the other nine matches ended in defeat. In the League cup the club had been placed in Group F and lost all four of their matches (two at home, two away) without scoring a single goal. Budgetary constraints led to Robbie Horn resigning as manager in early October after a 3-0 loss to Edinburgh City, with the club lying second from bottom in the League after nine games. He was replaced by 36 year old former player Johnny Harvey. He was the manager of non-League Penicuik Athletic, having previously been in charge of other East of Scotland sides like Edinburgh United and Haddington Athletic. His first match was Scottish Cup tie against Gretna 2008 which the club won 3-1, although they lost in the next round, 2-1 at home to East Fife, conceding two inside the first 11 minutes.

On the 8th December Berwick lost 5-0 at home to Peterhead, having been three-nil down at half-time. The following month they lost 7-1 at Queen's Park, with goalkeeper Kyle Allison sent off for violent conduct in the 45th minute. These defeats were part of a run of fifteen games without a win. Despite this run the club were seven points clear of Albion Rovers with a game in hand in March, but the Cliftonhill side were handed a lifeline when they were awarded three points after Clyde had fielded an ineligible player against them. Berwick had managed to get the better of Albion Rovers, their main rivals for the drop, over the first three encounters – including 5-3 and 2-0 wins, and a late equaliser which, at the time, appeared to have ensured Berwick's survival. But then this administration error by Clyde helped swing momentum in the opposite direction. The reversal of Rovers' result versus the Bully Wee gave the previously doomed Coatbridge outfit an extra three points, which they added to with a win over Stirling on the same day. The statement issued by the Scottish Football League read: "at a disciplinary hearing yesterday (Friday, 8 March) a sub-committee of the SPFL Board charged Clyde Football Club with playing an ineligible player (Declan Fitzpatrick) in two Ladbrokes League Two matches: Saturday, 16 February 2019 – Clyde v Albion Rovers (1-0) and Saturday, 23 February 2019 – Queen's Park v Clyde (1-1). Clyde FC admitted breaching SPFL Rules and were sanctioned as follows: 1. Club reprimanded, warned as to future conduct and fined £1,500 (£1,000 suspended until 30 June 2020), 2. The original match results were also annulled and the outcome of the matches recorded as follows: 16 February 2019 – Clyde v Albion Rovers (0-3) and 23 February 2019 – Queen's Park v Clyde (3-0). The three points for a win were awarded to Albion Rovers and Queen's Park respectively, and the points previously awarded to Clyde were withdrawn."

Days later Berwick recorded their fifth and final League win of the season when goals from Lewis Barr and Cameron Blues gave them a 2-0 win over Peterhead and a five point advantage over bottom side Albion Rovers, with seven games to play. Few would have predicted that the victory would be their last ever as a Scottish Football League club or even that they would fail to score again. On the following Saturday they narrowly lost 1-0 at Stirling Albion, the winning goal coming in the 80th minute. Albion Rovers won 2-0 at Elgin City to move to within two points, and with the results their goal difference went three better than Berwick's. Both sides lost the following Saturday, Berwick 2-0 at home to Edinburgh City but Albion Rovers only lost 1-0 at home to Clyde.

Going into April and the final five fixtures Berwick held a slender two point advantage over Albion Rovers, but their goal difference was -45 compared to -41. On the 6th April both clubs suffered heavy defeats, although Berwick's goal difference worsened significantly as they went down 6-0 at Annan Athletic, whereas Albion lost 4-0 at home to Queen's Park. The half-time score at Galabank was goalless, but Annan scored within a minute of the restart and five minutes later from a penalty after a foul by Rob Wilson. Annan scored four more in 13 second half minutes as it turned into a rout.

The following Saturday Berwick also lost at home to Queen's Park, 3-0. Albion though, picked up a precious point at leaders Peterhead when they scored a 92nd minute equaliser. With just a point now separating them Berwick travelled to Clyde and Albion Rovers hosted Edinburgh City. Both opponents had already qualified for the play-offs, although Clyde still had an outside chance of winning the title and automatic promotion. Berwick quickly fell behind after five minutes but reached half-time only the one goal down. At Cliftonhill Albion had also gone behind after five minutes but had equalised shortly afterwards and were level at the break, meaning that if things stayed as they were they would move above Berwick on goal difference. Edinburgh City retook the lead at Albion early in the second half. Meanwhile, Clyde quickly increased their advantage over Berwick to 3-0 and it looked like it would be a case of 'as you were' but just after the hour mark Albion Rovers equalised. In the 77th minute as Berwick were falling further behind Albion took the lead. They went on to win 3-2 as Berwick ultimately lost 5-0. The impact of these two results was that Albion moved off the bottom for the first time since the middle of August. They now had a two point lead over Berwick, which was effectively three, due to their superior goal difference. Both sides had two matches left but crucially and most importantly, their next game was against each other.

Berwick hosted Albion Rovers on Saturday the 27th April in what was essentially a relegation playoff. A crowd of almost 1,000 saw the visitors take the lead midway through the first half and appeared to settle it with a penalty right on the stroke of half-time following a foul in the box by Andy Forbes. The issue was put beyond doubt five minutes after the restart. The result confirmed Berwick as finishing bottom and in the relegation playoff spot. Albion Rovers had put up a fight and had won five of their last nine matches, eventually finishing eight points above the bottom spot. By contrast, Berwick finished the League campaign with a run of one win from 24, having failed to find the net since the 19th March. It left the Shielfield club facing a play-off against either Highland League champions Cove Rangers or Lowland League winners East Kilbride to preserve their unique status as the only English club playing in the Scottish League.

Manager Johnny Harvey left after the club before the play-offs. Chairman Len Eyre, in a statement on the club's social media pages, said: "We'd like to thank Johnny for his absolute commitment to Berwick Rangers and his tireless work to improve matters...He inherited a difficult situation and unfortunately has been unable to get the results we needed to stay clear of the foot of League Two. We sincerely wish him every success for the future." The club moved quickly and appointed former managers John Brownlie and Ian Little to the positions of manager and assistant respectively. Former Scotland full-back Brownlie, 67, played for Berwick Rangers at the tail end of his career, while Little, 45, managed the club from October 2011 to January 2014. (Little gave up his job as manager of Lowland League side Whitehill Welfare).

On the 18th May 2019, Berwick Rangers became the second club after East Stirlingshire to be relegated out of the Scottish Football League and into the Lowland League, after a 7-0 loss on aggregate to Highland League champions Cove Rangers. The two sides initially met on the 11th May in Aberdeen for the first leg of their play-off tie and the matter was more or less settled after the first game as goals from Sam Burnett, Mitch Megginson, Jamie Masson and Jordon Brown gave the Highland League champions a comfortable 4-0 victory. The result, and even the margin of Cove's victory, shouldn't have been a surprise given the respective form of the two clubs. Berwick had lost seven in a row, while Cove have won seven in succession and were unbeaten in 19 games. Cove had 21 shots and hit the bar twice, while Berwick could only muster 3 shots. Cove led 2-0 at half-time which didn't reflect their dominance, and their last two goals only came in the final quarter of an hour. Berwick now faced a mountain to climb to extend their 68 year tenure in the Scottish League and to preserve their distinction of being the only non-Scottish club in the SFL.

A crowd of 1,300 gathered at Shielfield Park for the second leg on Saturday the 18th May. It was vital for their League survival that Berwick scored first but Jamie Masson's deflected shot gave Cove a first-half lead. Masson cut inside on his right foot and saw his shot deflected beyond goalkeeper Ryan Goodfellow. Declan O'Kane felt he had cleared the ball off the line but the referee allowed the goal to stand. Things got worse for Berwick when just on half-time Ross Brown was sent off for a last-man challenge on Mitch Megginson. Cove scored a second just two minutes after the break and with 15 minutes to go they made it 3-0, and 7-0 on aggregate. In doing so, the previous season's beaten finalists (who lost to Cowdenbeath) become the first Highland League side to enter the Scottish Football League since the introduction of the pyramid system and its play-off in 2015. Berwick's last League line-up was: Ryan Goodfellow; Aidan McIlduff, Jack Cook, Craig Hume, Ross Brown; Jack Ogilvie, Cameron Blues, Lewis Barr, Declan O'Kane; Ouzy See, Grant Rose. Subs used: Andy Forbes, Ahmed Aloulou and Calum Adamson

A new chairman, John Bell, a former Chairman of the Supporters' Trust and club director took over in May 2019. The new man in charge was quick to urge community support for the club as it faced life outside of the SFL. Ian Little returned as manager in June 2019 but the prospect of a quick return was soon dashed and it looks increasingly likely that the 'Wee Rangers' will follow East Stirlingshire in terms of a prolonged spell outside of the Scottish Football League.

SEASON	LEAGUE	P	W	D	L	F	A	P	POS
1951-52	SCOT-CNE	30	12	7	11	66	68	31	8/16
1952-53	SCOT-CNE	28	13	10	5	70	34	36	3/15
1953-54	SCOT-CNE	24	9	8	7	53	46	26	5/13
1954-55	SCOT-CNE	24	6	1	17	35	61	13	13/13
1955-56	SCOT-B	36	11	9	16	52	77	31	14/19
1956-57	SCOT-2	36	7	6	23	58	114	20	18/19
1957-58	SCOT-2	36	5	5	26	37	109	15	19/19
1958-59	SCOT-2	36	16	6	14	63	66	38	9/19
1959-60	SCOT-2	36	16	5	15	62	55	37	9/19
1960-61	SCOT-2	36	14	9	13	62	69	37	9/19
1961-62	SCOT-2	36	16	6	14	83	70	38	8/19
1962-63	SCOT-2	36	11	7	18	57	77	29	17/19
1963-64	SCOT-2	36	10	10	16	68	84	30	12/19
1964-65	SCOT-2	36	15	9	12	73	70	39	8/19
1965-66	SCOT-2	36	12	11	13	69	58	35	11/19
1966-67	SCOT-2	38	16	6	16	63	55	38	10/20
1967-68	SCOT-2	36	13	4	19	34	54	30	14/19
1968-69	SCOT-2	36	7	9	20	42	70	23	16/19
1969-70	SCOT-2	36	15	5	16	67	55	35	9/19
1970-71	SCOT-2	36	10	10	16	42	60	30	13/19
1971-72	SCOT-2	36	14	4	18	53	50	32	13/19
1972-73	SCOT-2	36	16	5	15	45	54	37	9/19
1973-74	SCOT-2	36	16	13	7	53	35	45	6/19
1974-75	SCOT-2	38	17	6	15	53	49	40	9/20
1975-76	SCOT-2	26	7	5	14	32	44	19	11/14
1976-77	SCOT-2	39	13	10	16	37	51	36	8/14
1977-78	SCOT-2	39	16	16	7	68	51	48	4/14
1978-79	SCOT-2	39	22	10	7	82	44	54	1/14
1979-80	SCOT-1	39	8	15	16	57	64	31	12/14
1980-81	SCOT-1	39	5	12	22	31	82	22	14/14
1981-82	SCOT-2	39	20	8	11	66	38	48	4/14
1982-83	SCOT-2	39	13	10	16	47	60	36	9/14
1983-84	SCOT-2	39	16	11	12	60	38	43	3/14
1984-85	SCOT-2	39	8	12	19	36	49	28	13/14
1985-86	SCOT-2	39	7	11	21	45	80	25	12/14
1986-87	SCOT-2	39	8	7	24	40	69	23	14/14
1987-88	SCOT-2	39	6	4	29	33	78	16	13/14
1988-89	SCOT-2	39	10	13	16	50	59	33	13/14

1989-90	SCOT-2	39	18	5	16	66	57	41	5/14
1990-91	SCOT-2	39	15	10	14	51	57	40	8/14
1991-92	SCOT-2	39	10	11	18	50	65	31	12/14
1992-93	SCOT-2	39	16	7	16	56	64	39	8/14
1993-94	SCOT-2	39	18	12	9	75	46	48	2/14
1994-95	SCOT-2	36	15	10	11	52	46	55	5/10
1995-96	SCOT-2	36	18	6	12	64	47	60	3/10
1996-97	SCOT-2	36	4	11	21	32	75	23	10/10
1997-98	SCOT-3	36	10	12	14	47	55	42	6/10
1998-99	SCOT-3	36	12	14	10	53	49	50	5/10
1999-00	SCOT-3	36	19	9	8	53	30	66	2/10
2000-01	SCOT-2	36	14	12	10	51	44	54	3/10
2001-02	SCOT-2	36	12	11	13	44	52	47	6/10
2002-03	SCOT-2	36	13	10	13	43	48	49	5/10
2003-04	SCOT-2	36	14	6	16	61	67	48	5/10
2004-05	SCOT-2	36	8	10	18	40	64	34	10/10
2005-06	SCOT-3	36	23	7	6	54	27	76	2/10
2006-07	SCOT-3	36	24	3	9	51	29	75	1/10
2007-08	SCOT-2	36	3	7	26	40	101	16	10/10
2008-09	SCOT-3	36	10	7	19	46	61	37	9/10
2009-10	SCOT-3	36	14	8	14	46	50	50	6/10
2010-11	SCOT-3	36	12	13	11	62	56	49	6/10
2011-12	SCOT-3	36	12	12	12	61	58	48	7/10
2012-13	SCOT-3	36	14	7	15	59	55	49	4/10
2013-14	SPFL-L2	36	15	7	14	63	49	52	5/10
2014-15	SPFL-L2	36	11	10	15	60	57	43	8/10
2015-16	SPFL-L2	36	14	7	15	45	50	49	6/10
2016-17	SPFL-L2	36	10	10	16	50	65	40	8/10
2017-18	SPFL-L2	36	9	10	17	31	59	37	8/10
2018-19	SPFL-L2	36	5	4	27	27	91	19	10/10

Bo'ness

Formed: 1882
Colours: Blue shirts and white shorts
Ground: Newtown Park
Entered League: 1921. Founder member of the reformed Second Division
Number of League Seasons: 11
Highest League Finish: 19th in Division One
Honours: Second Division Champions 1926-27
Left League: 1932. Expelled

Bo'ness is the third of the former Scottish Football League clubs originating from the old county of Linlithgowshire, or modern day West Lothian. They are also the most successful of these clubs, having played in the top flight, albeit for one season only, having earned a place in the record books as the Second Division champions for the 1926-27 season. Like the other clubs in the area they suffered financially during the economic recession and they were ignominiously expelled by the League in November 1932, one month before Armadale suffered the same fate.

Bo'ness is one of a few teams with an apostrophe. This normally donates "possession of" as in Queen's Park but in this case it is used in place of missing letters to shorten the name. Bo'ness is short for Borrowstounness. The town's full name is rarely used though, and is nowadays almost always contracted to Bo'ness. The town is located on the southern bank of the Firth of Forth, on an elevated site seven miles east of Falkirk and 17 miles west of Edinburgh, Bo'ness has important historical links to the Roman period and marks the eastern extent of the Antonine Wall which stretched from Bo'ness to Old Kilpatrick on the west coast of Scotland on the way to Dumbarton. Due to its location on the southern bank of the Firth of Forth the town became a major port and centre of industry including coal mining, pottery, shipbreaking and ironmongery and examples of the Bo'ness Iron Company's work are to be found in many places, especially on drainage covers. A harbour was constructed during the 18th century and a dry dock was added in the 1880s. The port eventually closed in 1959, badly affected by silting and a decline in the industries served by the port.

Bo'ness Football Club were formed in 1882 and played in blue shirts and white shorts and were known as 'the Blues'. They played their games at Newtown Park from 1886 onwards located just off the road in from Linlithgow. Bo'ness were founder members of the Linlithgowshire Football Association and played in the County Cup's first competition in the 1884-85 season. The won their first game 10-0 against Linlithgow, but were beaten in the Semi-final by Armadale. They also made their debut in the Scottish Cup that year when they hosted Hibernian in a First Round match on the 13th September 1884, which Hibs won 2-0.

The following year they advanced to the Third Round of the Scottish Cup, where they were again knocked out by Hibs, this time 6-0. In the earlier rounds they had knocked out Broxburn Shamrock 5-1, after a replay and on the 3rd October 1885 they registered an 8-1 win over Norton Park of Leith. They reached the Fourth Round of the 1887-88 Scottish Cup competition and in the same year they won the Linlithgow Cup for the first time. They beat Erin Rovers of Bathgate 4-3, on the 28th April 1888, in a match played at Champfleurie Park, Kingscavil, near to Linlithgow.

In the 1888-89 Scottish Cup competition they acquitted themselves well in only losing to Hearts by a solitary goal in a First Round tie which Bo'ness hosted. The two sides had met in a drawn friendly a fortnight previous. Hearts dominated the first half and had a string of corners but any chances created were put high or wide, or both. On the stroke of half-time though they took the lead. Bo'ness came out strongly in the second half but Hearts weathered the storm and thought they had got a second but it was ruled out for offside. Chances now came at both ends but none were taken, Hearts winning by the solitary goal. *The Scotsman* commented that "the game was roughly contested, the country players being no less than five times checked for rough play." They retained the County Cup that season, beating Armadale 1-0 in the Final in April 1889, played at Boghead Park in Bathgate. Armadale got their revenge the following year as the same two sides met in the Final, at the same venue, Bo'ness going down 2-0.

The 1890-91 season saw the formation of the Scottish Football League. Bo'ness weren't included but they again reached the final of the Linlithgowshire Cup but lost 2-0 against Armadale. They also continued to play in the Scottish Cup that season and were involved in a couple of high scoring matches. On the 11th October 1890 they beat Bellstane Birds 7-0 in a Second Round match. The Birds were based in Queensferry and played in the Scottish Cup for five seasons between 1886 and 1891. *The Scotsman* reported on the game, first explaining that "the Birds failed to appear a fortnight ago owing to the death of one of their players, and Bo'ness claimed the tie. Ultimately they withdrew their claim. Bo'ness were not at their full strength, while the Birds' team included only three of last year's eleven, and through the entire game they played with only ten men. The home team, playing with the wind, put the ball through within ten minutes, and Hamilton shortly afterwards followed up with a second.

Bo'ness still kept up the pressure, and a shot was sent in. The ball striking the post, rebounded into play, and Robertson, of the Birds, inadvertently breasted it through his own goal. Scrimmages in front of goal resulted in Bo'ness raising their total to five goals in the first period, while the Birds were unable to score. The Ferry boys in the second half had occasionally a look in at the Bo'ness goal, but during the greater part they had to act on the defensive."

In the next round Bo'ness were on the receiving end, losing 9-1 on the 25th October against Mossend Swifts in a replay, after the first match had ended 1-1. Their opponents were from the shale mining village of Mossend, just to the north of the town of West Calder, West Lothian. Their hosts completely overran them in the first half and led 4-0 at the break. *The Scotsman* noted that "Bo'ness continued to play up in a plucky manner...but...playing with great dash, the Swifts now completely outplayed their opponents at every point." Sadly they didn't qualify for the Scottish Cup again until 1897.

Bo'ness didn't make it to another Linlithgowshire Cup Final until 1895 when they lost a nine goal thriller by the odd goal. Bathgate beat then 5-4 before a large crowd in a match played at Captain's Park, Linlithgow. The following season they finally won the trophy again, beating Armadale Volunteers 3-0 at Linlithgow. The *Glasgow Herald* reported on the final, saying that "play at the outset was pretty equal, although Armadale were smarter on the ball. They were, however, lamentably weak in shooting, and before many minutes had gone had lost several chances...Bo'ness soon showed them the way, and Bowman at length opened the scoring for that team after 17 minutes' play. Bo'ness continued to play better, and Bowman helped through a second point after 30 minutes had gone, and when half-time was called no change had been made on the score. On resuming, play was of a very equal nature, but Bo'ness by a sudden rush slapped on a third goal." Armadale Volunteers got their revenge when they beat Bo'ness 5-1 in the Semi-final of the competition the following year. The two sides met yet again at the Semi-Final stage in the 1897-98 competition, Bo'ness winning through after a replay. Bathgate won the other Semi-final but for some reason refused to play Bo'ness in the Final. The Linlithgowshire FA then arranged a further Semi-Final featuring the two beaten teams, with the winners meeting Bo'ness in the Final. Armadale Volunteers won through but Bo'ness beat them again in the Final, 3-0, going on to lift the Linlithgowshire Cup for a record fourth time. Back in Scottish Cup action they were perhaps unfortunate to draw ten time winners Queen's Park in the First round. The match was played at Bo'ness on the 8th January 1898 and from the outset Queen's Park dominated and quickly established a two goal lead. Bo'ness came in the game a bit more and Anderson had a shot saved but ten minutes from half-time the tie was effectively over when the visitors added a third. The second half followed the same pattern and only the splendid goalkeeping of Bell in the home goal kept the score unchanged. Eventually Queen's Park broke through and added two more goals near the end to complete the rout.

Bo'ness retained the Linlithgowshire Cup the following season, beating Bathgate 2-1 at Linlithgow, but they didn't fare any better in the Scottish Cup, going out in the First Round to League side St Bernard's of Edinburgh. Bo'ness hosted the Edinburgh side on the 14th January 1899 and within the first minute Grant, formerly of Leith Athletic, scored for the home team. From the restart though the visitors immediately drew level. Bo'ness, aided by the wind in their favour, had a sustained period of pressure but just couldn't seem to get the ball in the net. A bit of magic from Grant, scoring with an overhead kick, eventually restored their lead. Myles then scored from a corner to give Bo'ness a 3-1 lead at half-time. In the second half the pattern of play was reversed, with St Bernard's doing all the pressing. Fifteen minutes from time their opponents eventually got one back. With time running out St Bernard's had an equaliser ruled out for handball but they were not to be denied and they finally brought the scores level and took the tie to a replay. Having shared six goals the two sides met a week later at Logie Green before a crowd of 3,000. Six goals were also scored in this game. The first half was very even with chances on both sides, *The Scotsman* commenting that "both goalkeepers had good shots to deal with, but they proved equal to the calls made on them." The score was goalless at half-time and on the resumption it was Bo'ness who scored the first goal through Gallacher. This led to a period of sustained pressure from their opponents and from a corner they drew level. Having got on equal terms their hosts weren't long in taking the lead and a third soon followed. Bo'ness then pulled one back from a corner, again from Gallacher, to make it 3-2 to set up an interesting last quarter of an hour. However, right on time it was St Bernard's who got the sixth goal of this game to win through 4-2

In the 1899-1900 Scottish Cup competition Bo'ness continued their misfortune of drawing top teams in the First Round when they came out of the draw to play away at Celtic, losing the game 7-1. In the 1900-01 competition they drew League opposition in the shape of Morton, who would finish fourth in the First Division that season. The two sides met on the 12th January 1901 in Greenock, *The Scotsman* reporting that "the visitors made headway shortly after the start, but...Morton then took the game in hand, and four goals were scored in quick succession....On resuming, the visitors, though playing hard, were unable to cope with the tactics of the home men, who, before the finish, had added another six goals." Bo'ness won the Linlithgowshire Cup for a sixth time in 1901, defending their trophy as it wasn't played for in the 1899-1900 season, so effectively making it three times in a row. In the Final they triumphed 3-0 over Bathgate at Linlithgow.

For the 1901-02 season Bo'ness joined the Central Combination league where they played for two seasons. In the first season they came third behind Stenhousemuir and Falkirk, positions that were repeated in the 1902-03 season. During this time they also won the Linlithgowshire County Cup for the fourth time in a row, and seventh time overall when they beat Broxburn in a replayed Final. Both matches were played at Mill Park, Bathgate and a large crowd saw them draw 1-1 with Broxburn, which was a fair result, Broxburn having to play the second half a man short. Broxburn refused to play extra time with a man short and after consultation with the officials it was agreed to replay the game on the Tuesday. Bo'ness won the replay 3-1. They were prevented from making it five in a row by the same opposition. Two thousand spectators at Boghead Park, Bathgate, saw a poor game in which Broxburn beat Bo'ness 1-0.

For the 1903-04 season Bo'ness played in the Midland League. This competition only lasted a year before six of the eastern clubs, including Bo'ness left to reform the Eastern League. Bo'ness were the champions of the Midland League. The Blues played in the Eastern League for the 1904-05 season, finishing third behind Hearts A and Bathgate. When the second Scottish Alliance was formed in 1905 Bo'ness joined that competition. It was during this season that they returned to the Scottish Cup after an absence of five years. They knocked Arbroath out in the First Round, 4-1, to set up a glamour tie away against League champions Celtic. The two sides met on the 10th February 1906 where a crowd of 5,000 at Parkhead saw them concede three first half goals to effectively seal the tie for their hosts. Prentice for Bo'ness had a goal ruled out for an earlier infringement. According to *The Scotsman* "the second half was more or less of a scramble, and at times temper was shown on both sides. No further scoring was effected and the game ended Celtic three goals; Bo'ness nothing." During the same season they reached the Final of the Linlithgow Cup, where they came up against old rivals Bathgate. The Final was played at Albion Park, Broxburn and McGhee was sent off for Bo'ness near the end, the match finishing in a 1-1 draw. The replay was again held in Broxburn a week later, this time at Shamrock Park, with Bathgate winning 4-2 before a crowd of 2,000.

At the end of the season all the clubs with the exception of Broxburn Shamrock combined with some clubs from the Scottish Combination to form the Scottish Union where Bo'ness played for two seasons. In the 1906-07 season they came fourth behind Rangers A, Alloa Athletic and Bathgate. In the same season they also triumphed in the Linlithgowshire Cup, which again went to a replay. They played against Broxburn at Mill Park, Bathgate, with *The Scotsman* reporting that "the ground was treacherous, and neither team seemed to rise to the occasion. Taken all over, the draw - with neither team scoring - was the most satisfactory result that could have been desired." They then won the replay 2-1 at Winchburgh, although they made the worst possible start as Broxburn were awarded and converted a penalty in the first minute. This stung Bo'ness into action and McGhee soon levelled and the two sides went into the break at a goal apiece. In the second half Bo'ness continued to hold the upper hand and ten minutes from time the holders retained the Rosebery trophy when Brown scored the winning goal.

The following year was not as good as they came bottom of the Scottish Union. They featured in the opening round of the Scottish Cup, losing 4-0 to Partick Thistle. In the 1908-09 season they were victorious once again in the County Cup, beating Bathgate 2-1. The Central League reformed in 1909 when Northern League clubs Arbroath, Dunfermline, Kirkcaldy United, Lochgelly United and St Johnstone joined with a number of Scottish Union clubs, including Bo'ness, to form a new 12 team competition. It would be as members of this competition that the club would ultimately gain admission to the Scottish Football League. At the end of the first year's competition Bo'ness finished tied top with Alloa Athletic. A championship play-off match between the teams was arranged for the start of the following season which Bo'ness won to be crowned champions. In the same season they lost to First Division League side Aberdeen in the First Round of the Scottish Cup but retained the Linlithgowshire Cup by beating Broxburn Athletic, after a replay, lifting the trophy for the tenth time overall. They finished runners-up in 1911 and there was then a ten year gap before they appeared in the Final again, winning it in 1921 when they beat Bathgate 2-0, with Cobban scoring both goals. In 1921 they also made an appearance in the Scottish Cup, still as a non-League team, knocking out Galston, from Ayrshire before losing to local rivals Armadale after a replay.

In the remaining seasons of the Central League up to 1915 they generally finished mid-table. When the competition was resurrected after the war Bo'ness won it twice in a row. They were the 1919-20 champions, finishing two points ahead of Dunfermline and East Fife and in the 1920-21 season, the last year of the competition, they retained their title by a point from Hearts 'A' and three ahead of Cowdenbeath.

In 1921 the Central League was incorporated as the reformed Second Division with Bo'ness among them and the club entered the Scottish Football League as the Central League champions. For their first five seasons the club regularly finished in the top half of the table, finishing in 6th, 7th, 12th, 6th and 8th places. Their first League manager was Andrew Wylie who led the team until April 1926.

Their first ever Scottish Football League game was a 2-2 draw at Tannadice against Dundee Hibs played on the 20th August 1921. The brilliance of Miller in the Bo'ness goal, prevented Dundee Hibernian from scoring in the first half. Gilchrist opened the scoring for Bo'ness after 18 minutes' play, and Cobban added a second in the first half. After the interval the home team pressed and Bo'ness were handicapped through the loss of Reid, their left-back, who was injured in a collision with Williams, the Hibs centre. It was he who scored from the penalty spot after 70 minutes and ten minutes from time he scored the equalising goal. *The Sunday Post* gave their appraisal of the Bo'ness players, commenting that "Miller...was a grand custodian, who disposed of every dangerous shot in great style. Spiers, the ex-Armadale player and Gilchrist, late of King's Park, formed the finest wing on the field, but Bennie, who formerly wore the Falkirk colours, was a splendid defender for Bo'ness. Moffat was especially brilliant in the mid-line." The Bo'ness line-up for their first ever League game was: Miller; Bennie, Reid; Scott, Cahill, Moffat; Spiers, Gilchrist, Cobban, Robb and Clark.

A week later, the 27th August 1921, Bo'ness hosted their first League game at Newtown Park, a 3-1 win over county rivals Broxburn United, watched by a crowd of 3,000. United scored first but Cobban equalised before half-time before adding a second with fifteen minutes left to play and Stewart scored a third. A detailed report on the game was provided by the *The Sunday Post*: "stirring football was served up at Newtown Park, Bo'ness, and if yesterday's standard is maintained, the Second League will indeed be a live and profitable institution. By reason of their superior forward play and early success, Sutherland scoring in the opening minutes, the Broxburn team gave the Bo'ness supporters a fright. To add to their display, the backs were wavering, and the half-backs alone saved the situation. It may be said that Bo'ness won the match in the closing minutes of the first portion, when against the wind, Cobban scored the equaliser. The second goal was long in coming. Cobban heading out of the reach of Kerr fifteen minutes from the close from a corner. When Stewart followed this up a few minutes later with a long shot, the points were lost and won, and the concluding incident in an exciting game was an accident to Harris, which left Broxburn to finish with ten men. Kerr, in goal [for Broxburn] got more to do than Miller, and the Broxburn custodian was in luck's way in more than one scrimmage in the second half. Crichton [for Bo'ness] was injured early in the game, but stayed on. Bennie rallied as the game progressed. Moffat and Scott were outstanding and Clark, Cobban and Stewart were prominent forwards. Speirs and Baxter were strange to each other's mode of play, and the touchline man stood idle. Bo'ness acted wisely in putting Cobban in centre, and his two goals were got by sheer determination." The Bo'ness team for this game was: Miller; Bennie, Crichton; Scott, Milehall, Moffat; Speirs, Baxter, Cobban, Stewart and Clark.

Cobban later scored a hat-trick in their best League result, a 5-1 win over St Johnstone in October. However, this result was followed by them gaining only one further point

174

from their next four matches. Following a 2-0 win over King's Park on the 26th November they failed to win in the month of December, again only picking up one point from five games. All this meant was that by the turn of the year they were as low as 16th in the table, just two points off the bottom. Bo'ness surpassed the 5-1 SFL victory with a 6-0 win over Stranraer in the First Round of the Scottish Cup, but were themselves on the receiving end of a big score line in the Second Round, going down 5-1 to Clyde. There was already a warning of financial difficulties to come as *The Scotsman* reported "Bo'ness would hardly clear themselves from the gate drawings in their tie with Stranraer, the attendance not exceeding the 1,500 mark." Back in League action Bo'ness won three games on the trot in early January and then back to back wins in February against East Stirlingshire and Bathgate to climb up the table. In early March they beat East Fife at Newtown Park and eventually finished a very creditable sixth place in their debut League season.

During the close season Bo'ness sold a number of players which financed new dressing rooms and a drainage scheme to improve the playing surface at Newtown Park. The first five games of the new season were all drawn, the first three 0-0, with the first win not coming until a 2-1 away win at Broxburn United on the 23rd September 1922. In early October they beat Stenhousemuir 6-2, but this was followed up by four consecutive 1-1 draws during November. Centre-forward Jimmy Mackie scored four in the 5-0 win over bottom side Forfar Athletic in the last game of 1922, although only 1,500 watched the game. Mackie, originally from Ayr, had moved to Bo'ness from Wales just six weeks previously, making his club debut on the 25th November. At this stage of the season, twenty League games had been played and the club had only lost three - but then again they had only won five, with the other dozen matches drawn.

In January 1923 Bo'ness embarked on a great Scottish Cup run eventually reaching the Quarter-finals of the competition. After beating Inverness Clachnacuddin 6-0 in the First Round, with Mackie again scoring four, their moment of glory came with 3-2 giant-killing win over Hearts in the next round on the 27th January. Under the headline "Sensational Defeat of the Hearts", *The Sunday Post* noted that "there were broken hearts and broken heads...as the Tynecastle club made an inglorious exit from the Scottish Cup competition." Hearts scored first through John "Jock" White, beating David Stevenson in the Bo'ness goal. Two players, Jock Ramage of Hearts and John Kelly of Bo'ness, then collided and both had to go off to have head injuries dressed. Tempers then flared when John Clark was injured by a Hearts player and also had to go off. Bo'ness were down to nine players and Hearts down to ten!

On the resumption both teams reappeared at full strength, Kelly, his head swathed in bandages getting a great reception from the home support. Nine minutes after the interval the same player equalised for Bo'ness. Now playing with the wind at their backs Bo'ness put the Hearts defence under sustained pressure which paid off when Willie Moffat put them ahead. They didn't lead for long though when White scored his second a few minutes later to bring the sides level at two apiece. Ten minutes from the end Bo'ness regained their lead, John Gilfillan, the Hearts goalie, being at fault in dealing with a 30 yard shot from John Rayne, failing to hold the ball which slipped into the net. This seemed to knock the stuffing out of Hearts who never threatened to get back on level terms again and who had to defend to prevent conceding a fourth. *The Scotsman* wrote that "there was very little pretty football...[but]...what the game lacked in that direction was more than balanced by the keenness of the exchanges, thrilling cup-tie football being served up for the full ninety minutes." The giant-killing Bo'ness team that day was: David Stevenson; Peter Brown, Harris; John Rayne, Thomas Anderson, Willie Moffat; John Clark, John Kelly, Jimmy Mackie, Dawson and Stewart.

Bo'ness knocked out Nithsdale Wanders in the next round 2-0 before losing 4-2 to First Division Motherwell in front of 17,000 spectators at Fir Park. Back in League action the club went on a six game unbeaten run between March and early April to more or less match their final placing from the previous year in finishing in seventh place. *The Sunday Post* in July 1923, reported that the club were able to clear a £200 overdraft and end the year with a credit balance of £100, which was probably attributable to their Cup run.

The 1923-24 season saw a decline in their performance as they came in 12th, their lowest final position since joining the League. More significantly, the club became embroiled in a bribery case towards the end of the season, which overshadowed events on the pitch. Despite losing their opening game 3-1 away at Cowdenbeath, consecutive wins in September lifted Bo'ness into fourth place, just two points behind early leaders King's Park. By the end of October the gap was down to just a point as Bo'ness lay in third place. However a 4-0 reverse at the beginning of November at Albion Rovers precipitated a dramatic loss in form as they went on a run of five games without a win which saw them drop to tenth place.

On the 8th March 1924 Bo'ness hosted bottom club Lochgelly United, who were a massive 14 points adrift at the bottom of the division having only gained seven points from thirty games played. Under the headline "Surprise Win for Lochgelly" *The Scotsman* reported that Lochgelly had won 2-0, thanks to a penalty awarded for a handball and a second goal near the end. Sometime later, Bo'ness player Peter Brown, who both *The Scotsman* and *The Sunday Post* had reported as being one of the best players for Bo'ness, alleged that ex-players John Browning and Archie Kyle had offered him a bribe to throw the game. Browning was an ex-Celtic player with over 200 appearances between 1911 and 1919, including four League titles, and Archie Kyle was a former Rangers player.

Arrests were subsequently made and on the 10th June the case came to court with *The Scotsman* reporting on the case: "there appeared at the Northern Police Court, Glasgow yesterday, the football player, John Browning, ex-Celtic, Chelsea, Dumbarton and Vale of Leven outside left. He had been arrested the previous day in Alexandria. Along with him was Archibald Kyle, once a notable Rangers' player, who had been taken into custody when he called at the Police Office a short time before. They were charged with having, on 3rd March, in a house at Bo'ness, occupied by Peter Brown, a member of the Bo'ness team, corruptly offered him a bribe, as an inducement for failing to exercise his skill, so that Bo'ness Football Club might be defeated by Lochgelly United Football Club in a match to be played on 8th March 1924. A second charge referred to an offer alleged to have been made to two Bo'ness players on 5th March in connection with the same match, and a third charge against Browning and Kyle was to the effect that they, at a later date, in a public house in Dundas Street, Glasgow, gave a bribe of £30 to the said two professional players, in furtherance of, and in compliance with, the said offers. They were remitted to the Sheriff, and later in the day appeared before Sheriff Lyell. No declaration was made. Bail was fixed at £25."Both players were charged under the terms of the Prevention of Corruption Act 1906. The other player referenced was Thomas Anderson.

The case was heard before the court on the 24th June 1924. Both men pleaded guilty and their legal representative asked for a monetary penalty to be imposed. *The Scotsman* reported on the sentencing outcome: "the Sheriff said they had pleaded guilty to a practice dishonourable from first to last, and he could not see his way to impose a fine, as he was fully convinced there was someone behind. Football was no worse than any other sport, and he should do his best to clear the sport when any such cases came before him. The sentence would be sixty days' imprisonment, with hard labour, and he hoped it would be an example to others."

The new 1924-25 season represented a considerable improvement in terms of a final League standing with the Blues finishing in sixth place. More importantly, this was the season when Christy Martin first came to prominence as a goal scorer with Bo'ness, scoring 34 goals during the season. His goal scoring would later inspire the club to win the Second Division title in 1927 and gain promotion to the top flight of Scottish League football. *The Scotsman* commented at the start of the season that "Bo'ness have got together a promising set of forwards, and with practically the same defence should do well in the coming struggle for promotion." The team were particularly strong at Newtown Park as they lost only one game at home.

Bo'ness signed Irishman Christy Martin from the Glasgow Junior League, where he was playing for St. Anthony's. His goal scoring prowess earned him international recognition. He was a dual internationalist who played for both Northern Ireland at Windsor Park against Scotland on the 28th February 1925 and then for the Irish Free State against Italy in 1927. His 29 goals in the 1926-27 season were key to the club's success but he was limited to just seven goals in the First Division the following season. Martin briefly played with Falkirk in the 1928-29 season, making two appearances in April 1929 before he joined the exodus of players from the British game to the American Soccer league. He had a spell with Brooklyn Wanderers before returning in 1931 to finish his career at Bo'ness. Unfortunately his career was brought to a premature end by a non-footballing injury, when he sustained a fractured skull.

After a somewhat indifference start to the 1924-25 season things began to click in the autumn as the club put together some impressive results. On the 11th October they beat Clyde 4-1, *The Scotsman* noting that "the game at Newtown Park, Bo'ness, where the local team encountered Clyde, was marked by an outstanding display on the part of Martin, the home centre-forward who scored four goals for his team." Only the heroics of Shingleton in the Clyde goal kept the score down. A week later they beat St Bernard's 6-0. In this match the first half was evenly contested and gave no hint of the eventual score line. However, a brilliant second-half display by the Bo'ness forwards resulted in the rout of their opponents. Martin opened the scoring just a minute before half-time and he scored another four minutes after the resumption. McDonald scored a third and Rayne added a fourth, before Kelly scored two towards the close. In late November Bo'ness beat Johnstone 6-1 with Martin scoring four and Graham getting the other two Bo'ness goals.

In early 1925, on a waterlogged pitch, Bo'ness beat Forfar Athletic 5-0. The visitors held out for half-an-hour before Kelly opened the scoring following a fine cross by Graham. Martin, who had been well marked up to now, got free, and scored two goals before the interval. Forfar fought hard in the early stages of the second half but towards the end began to fade and Kelly added two more, with Graham supplying the crosses.

In the last game of the League season, played on the 25th April, Bo'ness beat Dunfermline Athletic 3-1. Martin scored two, the first from a penalty to end the season on 34 goals. Goodwin scored the other Bo'ness goal. Dunfermline got their goal with ten minutes remaining. *The Sunday Post* commented that "by adding a couple of goals to his total against Dunfermline Athletic, Chris Martin, the Bo'ness centre, showed himself the pre-eminent marksman of the Second Division."

Bo'ness made it a dozen wins in the Linlithgowshire Cup, but they had to wait until August 1925 to lift the trophy. On the 29th April Bo'ness met Armadale at Bathgate but the game had to be abandoned at half-time due to a snowstorm, with Armadale leading 1-0. Further attempts to hold the replay were also postponed by the weather. The replay was eventually held nearly four months later, this time as a new season curtain raiser. The game was played on the 19th August 1925, with Bo'ness winning 4-1, with the goals coming from Cottingham, Graham and Martin (2). Between these two matches, captain Willie Moffat, who had featured in the first ever Bo'ness team to play a League fixture in 1921 was signed by Portsmouth, for whom he went on to make over 120 appearances.

The 1925-26 League season opened with a 3-0 defeat at Boghead against Dumbarton. Bo'ness then won their first home game 3-1 against Dunfermline with two goals from Kelly and one from Martin. A 5-0 home win over Queen of the South at the end of November saw Bo'ness in mid-table, in tenth place, but in a tight division they were only three points behind leaders Stenhousemuir. When they played the leaders next, Martin scored two, as Bo'ness won 2-1 in Larbert. However, Bo'ness couldn't capitalise as they lost their next two games but in the Boxing Day game against St Bernard's they won 6-3 in snowy conditions, with Martin scoring five, *The Sunday Post* describing "his goals being masterpieces." In January 1926 a 4-0 loss at Shawfield against promotion chasing Clyde and a 6-0 defeat at relegation threatened Alloa left them down in 13th place. They recovered a bit to finish in eighth place but finished poorly losing 4-0 to East Stirlingshire at Newtown Park in front of barely a 1,000 spectators.

On the 24th April 1926 Bo'ness won the Linlithgowshire Cup for the 13th and last time. They beat Bathgate 3-1 in the Final played at Armadale's Volunteer Park. Bo'ness were the better side but didn't score until just before half-time through McDonald, who nodded home from an Oswald cross. Five minutes after the resumption Cottingham made it two and Kennedy added a third. Five minutes from time Bathgate were awarded a penalty which they converted. Bo'ness decided to leave the Linlithgowshire FA and join the Stirlingshire FA instead, and this brought about the demise of the competition. At the end of the season manager Andrew Wylie left to take over the reins at Reading, where he stayed until 1931, before returning to Scottish football to manage Hamilton. His brother Bob Wylie took over at Bo'ness.

Christy Martin scored 29 goals during the 1926-27 season and this helped Bo'ness win the Scottish Second Division title and gain promotion to the First Division. Bo'ness started the season with a West Lothian derby game at home to Armadale on the 14th August 1926 and six goals provided the 2,000 spectators with good entertainment. Bo'ness scored two goals within the first twenty minutes, through Martin and Hair. *The*

Sunday Post noted that "Martin, the home centre, was very deadly, and he rounded off a fine afternoon's work by performing the hat trick." Armadale showed some fight early on in the second half and pulled one back and threatened to equalise. This seemed to rouse Bo'ness back to life and Martin scored twice more to put the issue beyond doubt, before Armadale got a late consolation. Bo'ness lost their next game at Stenhousemuir but won the next three. Martin scoring in all three games and getting two against Queen of the South in front of 1500 "including 500 unemployed admitted free" (*The Scotsman*).

On Saturday the 16th October 1926 a 3-2 away win at East Stirlingshire started a club record run of nine consecutive League wins (16th October to 11th December) which was only ended by a 0-0 draw at Arbroath on the 18th December. Included in this sequence was a 5-3 win over Albion Rovers, followed by a 7-0 win over Bathgate which sent them clear at the top. *The Scotsman* commented that "five goals against Albion Rovers and seven against Bathgate in successive Saturdays is a record for Bo'ness, and one which will be difficult to beat. Deadly shooting by the forwards is accountable for the recent spate of goals. The feature is that the goals have been pretty evenly distributed among the quintette. Cottingham showed the way to goal on Saturday when he walked into the net a perfect pass by Martin. Oswald rounded off with a goal another clever movement by the home centre. An express drive by Gribbin brought out the third goal, while Watson headed past his own custodian for the home team's fourth and last goal of the first half. The second half was equally one-sided, and additional goals were scored by Martin, Oswald, and Hair. Taylor, the Bathgate custodian, was reliable, and was in no way to blame for the tall scoring. The visiting backs and halves were weak and an easy prey to the clever and enterprising Bo'ness vanguard." The 7-0 win over Bathgate on the 6th November was their biggest ever home League win. As well as Martin, the Bo'ness forward line included Robert "Bert" Oswald, who had been on the books at Hearts but made only one appearance before transferring to his home town team in February 1926. In June 1928 he followed manager Andrew Wylie to Reading, who paid £400 for him. After two seasons he joined Sheffield United for a fee of £4,000. He later played for Southend United. Thomas Cottingham also regularly contributed goals and was assisted by Jimmy Gribben, who later joined Celtic as a scout and was a key member of Jock Stein's backroom staff.

Following the draw with Arbroath they went a further eleven games without defeat, so a total run of 20 games unbeaten between 2nd October 1926 and 12th March 1927. Included in this latest run was a 6-0 win over Forfar Athletic on the 8th January 1927, in which Cottingham scored a hat-trick. Forfar were missing players due to flu. At this point Bo'ness were now a massive eight points clear of Raith, having won 17 out of 23 games.

Bo'ness reached the Fourth Round of the Scottish Cup, knocking out Cowdenbeath and Buckie Thistle before losing to Celtic at home. A record crowd of 9,000 watched them lose 5-2 on the 5th March 1927. Under the headline "Bo'ness Buckle Under Steady Celtic Pressure - rout follows a plucky opening display" *The Sunday Post* compiled a punctuation mark and biblical themed match report: "I don't know who put the apostrophe in Bo'ness, but I do know that Celtic put a coma over the Bo'ness forwards whenever they got within shooting distance; and also put a full stop to their Scottish Cup pretensions by beating them by 5-2 at Newtown Park. So David did not this time slay Goliath. One of the main reasons was that pebbles which were simply made for administering fatal wounds to giants did not leave the sling properly. In other words, balls that screamed to be put into the Celtic net in the first half were sent futilely past, over, round, or across the posts." Quite simply, Bo'ness failed to take the early opportunities that came their way before Celtic had felt themselves into the match. Early on the Celtic 'keeper John Thomson flapped at a corner and Cottingham missed an open net by sending the ball wide. Smith spurned a couple of chances and when Cottingham was given the chance to redeem himself he shot over. Midway through the first half Celtic took the lead but Bo'ness continued to create chances. A poor back pass was pounced on by Martin who slipped the ball inside to Cottingham but with the goal at his mercy he again shot over. Just on the stroke of half-time Celtic gave their hosts an object lesson in taking your chances when they doubled their advantage. Within five minutes of the restart Jimmy McGrory made it three and he scored another inbetween an effort from McInally. Picking up the match report, *The Sunday Post* commented that "Celtic were now indulging in fancy stuff but nevertheless pressing, and Bo'ness got two goals as consolation." From a free kick Smith crossed for Martin to open the home team's scoring and just on the call of time Smith crossed again for Martin, who this time teed up the ball for Oswald to score. Reviewing the individual performances within the Bo'ness team the paper added that "Martin was dominated throughout...Smith did not justify the fervent hopes of the Bo'ness supporters, and apart from his closing runs, did nothing of note. Oswald played very nicely, but with a lack of verve that was necessary to pass a 'first-time' defence. Cottingham was clever but marred his display with his misses at goal. Walker was the hero for the Bo'ness side, and the amount of work he put in was prodigious. He alone of the middle men did not lose heart, no matter the state of the scores. Young and Ramsay opened well, but when the middle line broke they were simply overwhelmed. Muir's 'keeping did not give confidence, and his inability, or disinclination, to grasp a high ball was fatal."
The Bo'ness team was Muir; Young, Ramsay; Falconer, Walker, Thomson; Smith, Gribben, Martin, Cottingham and Oswald.

Three weeks later, a 2-1 win over St Bernard's assured the Bo'ness Blues of promotion. The following week they played second-placed Raith and came from 3-1 down with two goals from Cottingham and one from Martin to earn a 3-3 draw. *The Scotsman* commented that "Bo'ness are to be congratulated on their pluck in facing a situation which at one time seemed well-nigh hopeless for them." The draw was significant and as it left them eight points ahead of Raith Rovers with just four games to play.

On Saturday the 9th April a 1-1 draw away at bottom club Nithsdale Wanderers secured the championship although it was far from straightforward. Reporting on the game, *The Scotsman* said "Bo'ness had to go the whole ninety minutes to secure the all-important point which makes the Second Division Championship secure, and even then they freely admit that fortune favoured them when a last-minute goal, scored during a blinding hailstorm, gave them the equaliser." Nithsdale gave their best display of the season and led after a quarter of an hour. Nithsdale deservedly held their lead until the 85th minute when Oswald's corner, taken amidst a blinding snowstorm, was only partially cleared by Armour and Cottingham equalised.

Bo'ness finished the season seven points clear of Raith and eleven ahead of third placed Clydebank. They also went the whole season unbeaten at home in the League. They were promoted to the First Division as Scottish League Division Two Champions and were joined by Raith in replacing Morton and Dundee United who were relegated. The *Glasgow Herald* lamented the relegation of Morton and their replacement by Bo'ness "the descent of the Greenock club will be deplored generally and the closing of so populous a district to first-class football will not weaken the opposition to automatic promotion. In the West at any rate it can be understood there is little enthusiasm for a system that has driven out of first class football such clubs as Third Lanark, Albion Rovers, Ayr United, and now Morton and while Dunfermline Athletic, Raith Rovers and Bo'ness are entitled to plume themselves on their achievement it can scarcely be said that their substitution of the clubs named has added to the attractiveness of the senior League."

The Athletic News, which later merged with *The Sporting Chronicle*, previewed the season ahead for the Blues: "Bo'ness, carrying the colours of a West Lothian club in the First Division for the first time, will differ materially from the eleven which earned promotion except in the forward line, where an element of complexity has been introduced through the engagement of Duncan Walker, the old Bo'ness centre forward, who made a great name as a scoring centre forward when with St. Mirren, and has since done duty for Nottingham Forest. C. Martin, the little Irish internationalist, has occupied the position for some season, and is still with Bo'ness. One or other may be played on the right wing. The half-backs and backs have all their spurs to earn, all of them being young players, in fact, the single man of any experience to speak of among the defenders is Dempster, who lost his place in the Airdrie goal to Jock Ewart, and in the St. Johnstone to Samuel Page, but is a good goalkeeper for all that." Bo'ness only lasted one season in Scotland's top flight. They finished in 19th place, above Dunfermline who were bottom, and just two points behind Hamilton in 18th, and three behind fellow promoted side Raith Rovers. Hopes of staying in the First Division were undermined by their poor away form, where they lost 16 out of 19 matches away from Newtown Park.

Things started promisingly enough on the opening day of the season with a 2-1 win over Falkirk on the 13th August 1927 in front of a crowd of 9,000. Before the match the Second Division championship flag was unfurled by Mrs Cochrane, wife of the Bo'ness Club President, who was introduced by Mr James Kidd, the MP for West Lothian. Falkirk were prominent early on and had a shot cleared off the line with the 'keeper prostrate on the ground. A penalty was then awarded to Falkirk for handball against Crichton, who fisted away a corner. The resulting kick though was saved by Dempster. Midway through the second half Lynas scored for Bo'ness, causing "all hats, caps and sticks of the Bo'ness supporters being thrown in the air in a frenzy of delight." (*The Sunday Post*) However, Falkirk equalised in the 79th minute and threatened to spoil the party but Martin got the winner two minutes later, meeting a cross from Lynas and heading home. When time was called Bo'ness were pressing for a third. *The Scotsman* covered the game and reported that "the game was a very fair test of football ability, and the young Bo'ness team came out of it with considerable credit....Good half-back play was a factor in their success. Duff, Walker and Thomson were an untiring, and often aggressive trio. The forwards played so well that it is doubtful if places can be found in the meantime for Oswald and Duncan Walker, and the defence was generally good."

The Bo'ness team that took the field for the first time in a top flight League match was Dempster; Crichton, Ramsay; Duff, A Walker, Thomson; Lynas, Cottingham, Martin, Hart and Clark. The *Glasgow Herald* commented that "Boness's initial performance was especially noteworthy in view of the fact that six of their team that opposed Falkirk were making their first appearance as seniors, while of the eleven who served the club in Second League football last season only two were retained." The two retained players were Christy Martin and Thomas Cottingham. In the close season Bo'ness had signed James Dempster, the goalkeeper, who came from Dundee United and played for the club in the 1927-28 season only. He had previously played for Sunderland, Airdrieonians and St Johnstone. Outside-right John Clark came from Luton Town and Alex Duff was picked up from Armadale. The rest came from non-League clubs: David Ramsay, Archie Thomson, John Lynas and John Hart all came from Shettleston,

Glasgow, Thomas Crichton came from Strathclyde and Andrew Walker joined from Renfrew Victoria.

Although beaten in each of their opening six away games Bo'ness picked up four wins and a draw and only one loss in the corresponding number of home games. Crowds had settled down around the 4,000 mark. By the end of October, and after the first dozen games, they were 14th in the table. Their first big loss came on 3rd December with a 5-0 defeat at Tynecastle, with opposing player Tim Morgan scoring a hat-trick. A week later they conceded four at home to Patrick and a fortnight later they again lost 5-0 away at St Mirren, McCrae scoring four. By now they had dropped into the relegation places. On the 7th January 1928 they lost 7-0 at Hamilton, their heaviest defeat. The result would be significant given the final placing in the table. *The Scotsman* reported on the game saying that "there were few indications of such a distinctive score in favour of the Hamilton Academicals in the early stages of their match with Bo'ness at Douglas Park, Hamilton. With Cottingham as leader-out the Bo'ness forwards made several pointed attacks on the Hamilton goal, but their work was far too much of an individualistic kind to bring them anything tangible." Hamilton scored through Dick after ten minutes and scored four more times in the first half, Tollan scoring two and Dick scoring another. Bo'ness came out strong in the second half but after fifteen minutes of all out attack without reward they appeared to run out of steam. Hamilton added two more, both from Dick who made it four for the match. The paper concluded that "there was no dubiety about the superiority of the Academicals in every department."

Bo'ness went on a mini unbeaten run in February winning three out of the four games they played. Martin scored two first half goals in a 2-0 home win over Queen's Park and this was followed by away wins at Dunfermline and Cowdenbeath. At the end of the month Wardrope scored two early goals against Airdrieonians but Bo'ness were pegged back to 2-2. Nevertheless, by the end of the month they were up as high as 16th and four points above the relegation places.

However, Bo'ness then failed to win any of their games in March. Heeps scored as early as the 11th minute away at Celtic on the 31st, but Bo'ness went on to lose 4-1, a result that left them in 18th place, just above the relegation places, with four games left. On the 7th April Bo'ness led Hearts 2-0 with just 15 minutes left but then conceded two goals to draw. Still, the point took them ahead of Hamilton who had lost. With Dunfermline relegated a long time ago the last place had become a three way battle between Bo'ness, Hamilton and Raith, and only one point separated the three teams. In order to avoid a clash with the Scottish Cup Final, Hamilton hosted Clyde on the Friday night and drew 1-1. On the Saturday Bo'ness lost 2-1 at Partick, *The Sunday Post* commenting that "Bo'ness often showed nice combination, and frequently brought the ball to within shooting range of Thistle's goal, but their lack of force coupled with a very vigilant defence was revealed in the final score." Partick led 2-0 midway through the second half before Lynas scored for Bo'ness. They then made desperate efforts to draw level but the home defence held firm. Elsewhere, Raith won 3-0, which meant that Bo'ness had now dropped into the last relegation place, a point behind the other two teams, although Hamilton only had one match left to play.

On the 21st April 1928 the relegation situation was effectively settled. Hamilton won at Falkirk and Raith grabbed a point at Shawfield against Clyde, which ensured their survival, part of a run of four wins and two draws in their last six games. Bo'ness fell three goals behind in Paisley against St Mirren and despite a spirited comeback in the second half lost 3-2, the goals coming from Oswald and Walker. *The Sunday Post* reported that "by reason of their defeat at Newtown Park Bo'ness go down with Dunfermline. That was made manifest to Bo'ness directorate before they left the field, and there were some sad hearts. If blame has to be attributed to any department of the team it must be to the forwards. Lynas played very well, and might have had the match won yesterday in the first quarter of the game, during which time he missed two gilt-edged opportunities. When midway through the second half Bo'ness were three goals down, everything pointed to a run-away victory to St Mirren. Bo'ness then made a desperate rally and scored twice. In the closing minutes they tried hard to save a point at least, and Cottingham, from a corner kick, almost scored direct. Goals seemed to come easy to St Mirren, who had in McCrae an opportunist of the first water. He scored two goals in the first half. In the second half it seemed as if the visitors were marking time Then it seemed all up when McCrae rounded off a clever individual run by a third goal. Although the game seemed lost and won at this stage, Bo'ness plucked up courage and rattled on two goals, one by Oswald and the other by G Walker." Both Bo'ness and Raith still had one match to play with the gap at two points but Raith's goal average was vastly superior. The last games were Raith against Celtic and Bo'ness against newly crowned champions Rangers, which they actually drew, *The Sunday Post* reporting that "had the seaport team given as good an exhibition in recent home matches they would not have been relegated." Oswald scored first for Bo'ness and the champions only equalised ten minutes from time.

Relegation saw a number of players leave the club. The most high profile departure was Bert Oswald. In June 1928 he followed manager Andrew Wylie to Reading, who paid £400 for him. There would be no immediate bounce back from relegation or promotion challenge for Bo'ness in the 1928-29 season mainly due to changes in personnel. When they opened the new season on the 11th August 1928 only three players were left that ended the season - Hume, Ramsay and Martin. Andrew Walker

185

had joined Oswald at Reading and the transfer fees the club received helped put Bo'ness on a finer financial footing. Thomas Cottingham, James Dempster and Archie Thomson also left. They won their opening game in the Second Division 4-1 against East Fife, *The Sunday Post* reviewing the team in the following way: "Boness's reconstructed team made a successful appearance against East Fife although their forwards might have combined ether. Strange to each other's company, nether shortcomings were excusable, and doubtless an improvement will be effected in the future. Dunn, late of Denbeath Star, excelled in crossing the ball, and he had a big say in several of the goals scored. The new half back line exceeded expectations, especially Fife, at centre-half, and it was particularly gratifying that the first goal should come from that division, Harkins beating Garth from 30 yards with a terrific shot. The second goal was scored by the Portobello Junior Internationalist, Hutchinson, who was very deadly." Hart and Martin scored the other goals. In their next game Bo'ness lost by the same score, away at eventual champs Dundee United. Following that result they then went six games unbeaten during September and October so that by the time they beat Dumbarton 3-0 away in mid-October they were up as high as fourth in the table, four points behind leaders Dundee United but only two behind Morton in the other promotion spot.

Bo'ness scored five in two consecutive games, starting on the 24th November against Bathgate. Their opponents were unlucky not to get a share of the points. After three minutes, following clever play by Fleming, Russell, the Bo'ness centre-forward opened the scoring. Bathgate dominated the rest of the first half but it was Bo'ness who got the game's next goal when Hutchison scored a second just before the interval. In the second half Henry Haggerty got a third before Bathgate got one back. Bathgate then went down to ten men due to injury but put up a good fight for the remainder of the game, so much so they actually got back on level terms at 3-3. But before the close Russell and Fleming each scored and Bo'ness won a hard fought contest 5-3. Unfortunately this game was ultimately removed from the record books when Bathgate left the League in March 1929. A week later Bo'ness scored five again in a 5-1 win over Stenhousemuir. Their visitors put up a good fight in the first half but crumbled in the second. Fleming scored the only goal of the first half but in the second half scored three goals in quick succession through Kelly, Russell and Hutchison. Stenhousemuir from a rare raid were awarded a penalty which they converted, but this was immediate followed by a fifth goal from Fleming.

Early in 1929 Bo'ness scored five once more, this time at home to Queen of the South in a 5-1 victory. However, they then lost by the same score line away at mid-table Forfar to lie in seventh place and even though they won 6-0 v Dumbarton (who were eighth) in their next game they eventually finished a disappointing tenth, which would be as good as it got in their remaining seasons in the Scottish League.

The records show that Bo'ness played 35 League games for the season as opposed to 38. The missing games were the two against Bathgate and they only played once against Arthurlie. Bathgate resigned in February 1929 and had their record expunged on the 12th March 1929. Although Arthurlie also resigned, on the 17th April 1929, their record was allowed to stand as they had completed their matches against the leading clubs. A ballot was taken at the Scottish League's AGM to replace both clubs and Montrose and Brechin City joined from the Scottish Alliance.

Bo'ness made a mixed start to the 1929-30 season. They scored four against Brechin and Armadale in successive wins in September but with four wins and four defeats from the opening eight games by the end of September they were in 12th place. Having beaten Dumbarton 5-2 away from home on the 5th October 1929 they were then beaten 5-0 by second placed East Fife a week later. They also conceded five the following month losing 5-1 at leaders Leith and 5-0 at Dunfermline in November. This erratic form continued as they beat new club Montrose 5-0 in December only to then be beaten by Albion Rovers 6-0 in the January and they eventually finished in 13th place.

The 1930-31 season was the worst in the club's League history as they finished 20th and bottom. They conceded exactly 100 goals and lost 17 out of 19 away games and scored only thirteen goals away from home. The Blues lost their opening match against Montrose, the *Glasgow Herald* commenting that "Bo'ness showed a dash and combination which should carry them well up the table later on." In their fourth game of the season the club got their first win against pointless Clydebank and they recorded two further successes in September. A 3-2 win over an illness and injury deflated Raith Rovers on the 27th September briefly saw the club up as high as 12th place.

However, after the win against Raith, Bo'ness lost a club record eleven League games in a row (from the 4th October to the 13th December 1930), including a 5-1 loss at King's Park and 5-0 at both Arbroath and Queen of the South. This terrible sequence of results was eventually ended by a 3-3 home draw against Montrose on the 20th December. Bo'ness were now in 18th place with eight points, one point ahead of Armadale and three ahead of bottom side Clydebank. But a week later they lost 6-2 at Stenhousemuir and in January 1930 they suffered their biggest SFL home defeat when they were beaten 6-0 by East Stirlingshire. By mid-February they had dropped to the foot of the table, two points behind Clydebank and three behind Armadale.

The much changed team was struggling on the pitch and the club was struggling financially off it as well, especially in relation to meeting the match guarantees for visiting teams. One bright note was the club's Scottish Cup run to the Quarter-Finals. Bo'ness beat non-League Peterhead 3-0 and then knocked out fellow Second Division side Alloa Athletic 4-2, to draw First Division strugglers Ayr United in the Third Round. These two sides met on the 14th February 1931 at Newtown Park with Bo'ness winning 1-0. They then drew First Division Kilmarnock at home, the tie being played on the 28th February. A bumper crowd of over 6,000 witnessed Bo'ness looking set for another shock result, as they led until the 89th minute. Bo'ness took the lead after just seven through Pratt and had W Aitken limping through the game because of an injury. Bo'ness were temporarily down to ten men as W Aitken finally left the field when a free kick was headed in. The rest of the game was a prolonged siege of the Bo'ness defence by the Kilmarnock forwards. The *Glasgow Herald* commented that "Bo'ness took the honours of the game. Fraser kept a good goal, the backs kicked well, and McLaren was a very fine half-back in a good line." Bo'ness lost the replay 5-0 at Killie, who got Celtic, the eventual Cup winners in the Semi-final.

On the 28th March Bo'ness lost 4-1 at new club Brechin City, conceding all four goals in the first half. The result left them at the bottom, eight points adrift of 18th place. Bo'ness won their next two games, 3-1 against Arbroath (Lumsden scoring twice) and 4-0 against Queen of the South, their largest win of the season. Pratt scored twice and Fraser saved a penalty. They ended the season by equalling the score line by beating Brechin. They finished equal on points with Clydebank – both with 22 points, six points behind Armadale. Bo'ness were placed bottom on goal average (Bo'ness 54/100=0.540; Clydebank 61/108=0.565). Both sides faced a re-election vote and faced a challenge from ex-League side Nithsdale Wanderers and also from Edinburgh City of the Edinburgh & District League. At the League's AGM on the 27th May both were re-elected, although Clydebank subsequently disbanded a month later.

The 1931-32 season was the club's last full season in the SFL. They made a much better start winning their first three games against Forfar Athletic, Edinburgh City and East Fife before a loss against eventual champions East Stirlingshire. Stewart, a centre half, had been signed from Alloa and still playing were Duncan Walker at centre-forward, Alex Heeps and ex-Norwich city goalkeeper Simpson. By the end of September Bo'ness were second in the table, just a point behind East Stirlingshire, having won seven and drawn one of their opening ten games. On the 3rd October they hosted Montrose, *The Scotsman* reporting that "Bo'ness, at home, did not find Montrose light opposition. Far from it, for the Newtown Park team had to pull their weight man for man to secure the points. There were many fine movements in the game, and it said a lot for the defences that the scoring was kept so low. Carruthers, the home outside right, had both goals to his credit. He was the most enterprising player afield, and, in consequence, fully deserved the success with which he met. The old Heart of Midlothian and Leith Athletic player was ever ready to cut in and gave a shot at goal." This win, together with East Stirlingshire's 1-1 draw away at Hibs took them, took them level on points at the top.

Mixed fortunes across the next half dozen matches saw them drop to fifth, although they were only three points off second place. However, a 6-2 defeat at struggling Dumbarton at the end of November was followed by a 4-0 loss at East Fife a week later, neither result justifying their position in the league table. They lost the New Year West Lothian derby against bottom club Armadale to drop to ninth. The score was 0-0 at half-time and Bo'ness scored first, yet somehow contrived to lose 7-1, Weir the Armadale centre-forward scoring five.

Their form continued to be poor in 1932, as they conceded five at leaders East Stirlingshire, Montrose and King's Park. For the last game of the season they travelled to Perth to play St Johnstone. Their opponents entered the last game knowing they needed to win 7-0 in order to pip East Stirlingshire for the title. They led 2-0 at half-time having missed three other clear cut chances. They scored again in the 49th minute but then Carruthers scored for Bo'ness, and although St Johnstone scored three more to win 6-1, they didn't get the goals they needed for the championship. The heavy loss meant that Bo'ness conceded 103 goals for the season, although due to their good start they actually finished in 14th place.

The club was by now facing serious financial problems. In a sign of mounting difficulties Alex Heeps and two other players - A Pratt and J Gray – resigned, although they were subsequently reinstated once arrears of wages were paid. Manager Wyllie, left it until the last minute to sign Richard Bell, Andrew Fagan, C Tallis and T Trotter in order to put out a side, which contained a number of triallists, for the opening League fixture on the 13th August against Dumbarton. They lost the game 5-1 with Parlane scoring four, Heeps scoring the Bo'ness goal.

At the end of September the club was down in 15th place with three wins and a draw from nine matches. Things went sorely wrong in October and by the end of the month they had played their last ever League game. On the 1st of October they were routed 10-0 by fourth-placed Queen of the South, who went top as a result of their big win. In a team featuring two triallists, Bo'ness were four down after half an hour and six down at the interval. On the resumption play was more even and Heeps, Trotter and Pratt all passed up good opportunities for Bo'ness. As it was their hosts took control and added four more. A week later the Blues suffered another debacle as they lost 7-0 against Hibernian. It took their opponents fifteen minutes to open the scoring but once they did the goals came at regular intervals. Four goals came before the break and three more were added after that. *The Scotsman* noted that "none of the visiting players was outstanding, but all deserve credit for battling bravely to the end against an infinitely better combination."

On the 15th October they played a home game against Stenhousemuir and it was this game which would ultimately prove significant in the demise of the club. In the game itself Bo'ness lost 3-2. They fielded a heavily changed team and gave a debut to a goalkeeper called Newlands, who did not inspire confidence and who let the first Stennie goal in, scored by Hart. Trailing 1-0 at half-time Hart scored two more goals in quick succession on the resumption of play and thus registered a hat-trick. Trotter reduced the leeway for Bo'ness. Heeps then scored a penalty for Bo'ness, but was later carried off injured, which scuppered any further attempts by the home team to draw level. A poor crowd of around 500 turned up and at the end of the game Bo'ness were only able to pay Stenhousemuir £10 instead of the £50 match guarantee – which should have been paid from the gate receipts.

A fortnight later, on the 29th October 1932 Bo'ness played what would turn out to be their last ever Scottish Football League match. They hosted Brechin City at Newtown Park but didn't pay the visiting side any of the £50 match guarantee. Pratt opened the scoring for Bo'ness after seven minutes. "Newman", a centre-forward on trial for Bo'ness scored a second with a snap shot. Buoyed by their success Bo'ness piled forward and after 30 minutes the triallist scored a third goal. Brechin played better and got a goal back before the triallist got his hat-trick, following a fine solo run. A mistake by one of the Bo'ness backs, Gray, let in the visitors to score a second and at half-time Bo'ness led 4-2. Only one further goal was added in the second period, going to the visitors, near to the end. Bo'ness therefore won what would turn out to be their last ever SFL game 4-3. The last Bo'ness team to take the field in a League game was: Bernard; Foy, Gray; Sharkey, Muir, Bell; Trotter, Baxter, "Newman", Heeps and Pratt.

Events now moved quickly. Two days later on the Monday, the *Edinburgh Evening News* reported that Bo'ness still had not paid Stenhousemuir the major portion of the match guarantee arising out of their game at Newtown Park and that this would be raised at a meeting of the League Management Committee the following day. On the 3rd November an ultimatum was given to Bo'ness. Under the headline "Pay Up or Pack Up" and "£90 Tonight or Quit" the *Edinburgh Evening News* reported that "the guarantee question has raised another crisis in the affairs of the Bo'ness FC, with the future of the club threatened by the Scottish League Management Committee. The Committee decided that unless Bo'ness pay the £50 guarantee money due to Brechin City and the balance of £40 to Stenhousemuir, the Bo'ness club will automatically cease to be members of the League from tonight. This means that the club, which has lately been troubled severely by financial worries and poor attendances, must produce £90 to permit them to fulfil their engagement with Leith Athletic at the Marine Gardens on Saturday. Bo'ness were reported to the Committee by both Brechin City and Stenhousemuir arising out of matches played at Newtown Park on October 29th and 15th respectively. On Saturday last the gate amounted to £7. The club have had 50 years of senior football of one kind or another. They won the Central League championship on three occasions and the Second Division championship in season 1926-27, but the fleeting fame as a First Division club in season 1927-28 was a costly failure. One of the most sensational victories scored by the seaport club was in the Scottish Cup competition of season 1922-23, when they beat the Heart of Midlothian 3-2 at Newtown Park in the second round of the competition. The directors were to meet today to see what could be done to pilot the club over its latest crisis, but the position was not regarded as hopeful."

The deadline came and went and no monies were paid over and so Bo'ness were expelled. Under the headlines "Bo'ness Forced to Quit" and "The Sword Falls – Bo'ness Fail to Save Themselves" the *Edinburgh Evening News* reported that "the sword has fallen on Bo'ness FC. The 24 hours ultimatum presented by the Scottish League Management Committee to the club for the payment of £90 to Brechin City and Stenhousemuir expired without the Bo'ness officials being able to raise the money , so that under the terms of the Management Committee's resolution the club are no longer members of the Second Division. This means that Leith Athletic will have an idle day tomorrow, for Bo'ness were due at Marine Gardens. Last minute efforts by the directors to save the club failed. The Supporters' club were reluctantly compelled to inform the directors last night that they could find no immediate financial support, and the directors announced that they would have to accept the Scottish League Management Committee's order to withdraw. Since the formation of the Second Division ten years ago several clubs, including Arthurlie, Clydebank and Bathgate, have resigned owing to financial difficulties, but Bo'ness are the first to be expelled....The League will require to decide what is to be done about the points which have been won and lost by Bo'ness. In this matter they have precedent to go by. When Bathgate fell out of season 1928-29 the League decided that the points table should be adjusted as if Bathgate had never played at all...Poor gates at home matches, caused by industrial depression and the competition of dog racing in neighbouring towns, are the chief causes of the club's demise. The game still appeals to many inhabitants of Bo'ness, a fact testified by the existence of seven juvenile clubs and one junior club in the town, which has a population of only 10,000." Mr John Cochrane, president of the club, interviewed after last night's meeting, said "Anything we could have done would only have put off the evil day. Every avenue was explored by the directors before we came to our regrettable decision that we would have to accept defeat. We shall, of course, compete in the Scottish Cup, for which we are still eligible."

With 14 fixtures played, Bo'ness were expelled for not meeting gate guarantees and ultimately it was decided that their results be declared void and their records expunged. This was not a resignation, this was an expulsion. Their record at the point of expulsion was played 14, won four, drawn two and lost eight, with ten points. Rather bizarrely Newcastle United offered to play their remaining fixtures but this was not taken up.

In their edition on Saturday the 12th November, the *Edinburgh Evening News* reflected and lamented on the state of Senior football in West Lothian under the headline "Is it Played Out": – "A few years ago West Lothian possessed some very good senior football teams. That is now a thing of the past and today she only has one club in the Second Division. The name of Broxburn United still lingers in the minds of all lovers of the sport. The United were a team of repute, but the decline in the shale trade and the gradual cessation of work in and around Broxburn hastened the end of the club. Bathgate, Armadale and Bo'ness were all well-known and well supported in those days but the number who attend senior matches in the county has greatly decreased for various reasons. Unemployment is undoubtedly the main one. West Lothian has lost its place as the industrial centre, and the lack of work has caused many men to forsake the pleasure derived from attending the game on a Saturday afternoon. Then one must remember the provision of buses and trains. The football fans formerly had to content themselves with the local matches, which were of a fairly high standard. Modern travel has helped to abolish the provincial club. Now, too, the junior and juvenile combinations are serving up football which is worth watching…Yes! Senior football has had its day in West Lothian, and it is questionable if it will ever come back again." Broxburn United had left in 1926 and Bathgate resigned in 1929. Bo'ness were expelled in November 1932 and just one month later Armadale suffered the same fate. Senior football was finished in West Lothian, and it would take a controversial relocation and name change to bring it back. Bo'ness were the most successful of the four West Lothian clubs playing between the wars as they reached the top flight in 1927 having won the Second Division championship.

Bo'ness did indeed play on in the 1932-33 season and took their place in the First Round of the Scottish Cup. On the 21st January 1933, just over two months after their expulsion from the SFL they drew 1-1 at Stranraer (not yet a League club). Stranraer took the lead after five minutes. Dudgeon saved a second but at the expense of an injury. Whitters headed the equaliser after an hour. A week later they hosted the replay, with the victors earning the right to visit Dens Park, Dundee on the following Wednesday. Bo'ness won the replay 3-0 and would have won by more but for the efforts of Hannah in the Stranraer goal. Stranraer had the better of the first half an hour. Murdoch was brought down and Bell's penalty was saved brilliantly by Hannah. Later, a punched clearance by the 'keeper, dropped nicely at the feet of T McDonald, who rifled home. The change of ends saw Bo'ness assert their superiority and their pressure was rewarded by further goals from M McDonald and Main. The attendance was listed as 1,700 and the gate receipts as £50.

On the 1st February 1933 Bo'ness fulfilled their Scottish Cup tie against Dundee. Under the headline "Bo'ness Beaten at Dundee. Their Gate Money Arrested", *The Scotsman* reported that "after a plucky fight in the early stages, Bo'ness faded out of the picture against Dundee...and were beaten by four goals to none. The ground was heavy, and ball control was difficult, but there was some good football. Fine goalkeeping by Dudgeon, the Bo'ness custodian, kept the scoring down to a reasonable figure. The Dens Park side scored just before half-time, and in the second half Bo'ness allowed Dundee to make all the running. The visiting players tired visibly towards the end, and it came to a question of the margin by which the home team would pass on to the next round...The attendance was 3000, and the drawings £150. The Bo'ness share of the gate money was arrested after the match. Bo'ness was expelled recently from the Scottish League for failure to pay certain guarantees."

Bo'ness continued to play in regional leagues such as the Edinburgh & District League and made five further Senior appearances in the Scottish Cup, never going beyond the First Round. In the 1934-35 season they lost 9-0 against Morton in late January 1935. In this tie Morton went two up inside three minutes and scored two more before the break. Dudgeon, the Bo'ness 'keeper was beaten nine times, Calder scoring four. *The Scotsman* commented that "the Bo'ness players were hard workers, and in the open showed a lot of clever football, but at close quarters they were overpowered by an astute defence." A year later they lost a home tie against Airdrieonians, 3-1, before a 2,000 crowd. They also lost at home in the 1936-37 competition against Cowdenbeath by six goals to nil, this time in front of a crowd of 1,200. Their visitors had the upper hand from start to finish and were superior in every department. The *Glasgow Herald* reported that "the defence of the home eleven was far from sound, and the forwards, though clever in the outfield, found the Cowdenbeath defence an insuperable obstacle." Cowdenbeath scored after just four minutes and continued to dominate without adding to their score. When they did score again they added three in as many minutes and they added a fifth just before the interval. More was seen of the home team in the second half but they rarely looked capable of scoring and the visitors got a sixth right at the end. The following year they lost a First Round home time 4-0 against Hamilton and they drew the same opposition for their last ever Scottish Cup tie. This match was played at Newtown Park on the 21st January 1939 in front of a bumper crowd of 3,451. Under the headline "Bo'ness's Fine Fight" *The Scotsman* reported that "the surprising thing about the game at Bo'ness was the courageous display given by Bo'ness against their experienced First League opponents. In the first half the teams were level with a goal apiece, Keddie scoring for Hamilton and Peat for Bo'ness. Hamilton lost the services of King, when he had his nose broken, and Drumgoole, the home inside-left, strained his leg in a tackle, and had to retire also. Both teams began the second half with ten players, and Bo'ness crowded on all sail, and for twenty-five minutes did everything but score, Hoy missed a golden opportunity from five yards. Then Hamilton staged a rally, and Wilson gave them the lead. Bo'ness slacked off after this reverse, and Wilson snatched another two goals. The last Bo'ness team to play a senior fixture was: Hunter; Patrick, R Miller; Kennedy, Higgins, W Miller; Hay, Innes, Peat, Drumgoole and Holt.

In 1945 the club was formally wound up and merged with Bo'ness Cadora Juniors to form Bo'ness United and joined the Scottish Junior FA. They are now one of the strongest Junior sides in Scotland.

Newtown Park is still in use as their ground and made headlines in June 2019 when the astro-turf was set alight, although thankfully the resulting fire caused minimal damage to the ground.

SEASON	LEAGUE	P	W	D	L	F	A	P	POS
1921-22	SCOT-2	38	16	7	15	57	49	39	6/20
1922-23	SCOT-2	38	12	17	9	48	46	41	7/20
1923-24	SCOT-2	38	13	11	14	45	52	37	12/20
1924-25	SCOT-2	38	16	9	13	71	48	41	6/20
1925-26	SCOT-2	38	17	5	16	65	70	39	8/20
1926-27	SCOT-2	38	23	10	5	86	41	56	1/20
1927-28	SCOT-1	38	9	8	21	48	86	26	19/20
1928-29	SCOT-2	35	15	5	15	62	62	35	10/19
1929-30	SCOT-2	38	15	4	19	67	95	34	13/20
1930-31	SCOT-2	38	9	4	25	54	100	22	20/20
1931-32	SCOT-2	38	15	4	19	70	103	34	14/20

Broxburn United

Formed: 1912
Colours: Maroon shirts and white shorts
Ground: Sports Park
Entered League: 1921. As part of the newly re-formed Second Division
Number of League Seasons: 5
Honours: None
Highest League Finish: 7th in Division Two
Left League: 1926. Failed re-election

Broxburn United are the fourth and final of the former West Lothian (or Linlithgowshire) towns (Armadale, Bathgate and Bo'ness are the others) that played in the Scottish Football League in the 1920s. They completed the fewest number of seasons of the four clubs, playing five seasons between 1921 and 1926.

The name Broxburn is a corruption of "brock's burn", brock being an old name for a badger and burn being a stream. In the mid to late nineteenth century the town was being transformed from a largely agricultural based community into an industrial one centred around mining and the developing shale oil industry.

Broxburn Football Club was founded in 1883 as Broxburn Thistle. When the first Linlithgowshire Cup competition was played for in 1884 three teams entered from Broxburn – Harp, Shamrock and Thistle. Shamrock reached the final of the 1885-86 competition, losing to Armadale in the Final. By 1890 Harp had dropped out. Thistle changed their name to simply Broxburn FC and this club won the Linlithgow Cup that year. In 1891 Broxburn FC and Shamrock were two of the eight clubs that made up the Eastern Football Alliance. This competition was abandoned after just one season and only three clubs completed all of their fixtures.

In the 1892-93 season Broxburn won the county cup for the second time, albeit in controversial circumstances. In the Final against Bathgate Rovers, played at Uphall on the 15th April 1893, the two sides were level at 2-2 with 15 minutes to go. Broxburn scored a third goal but the Rovers' players left the field in protest. Broxburn remained on the field until the referee blew for time. A gale force wind was blowing from end to end and Bathgate Rovers had the benefit of it in the first half. As a result play was largely confined to the Broxburn end. The Broxburn defence held firm but Rovers eventually worked an opening but could only add one more to their score before the change of ends. Playing with the wind Broxburn quickly got back in level terms with goals from Walker and McLeod. *The Glasgow Herald* then described the curious end to the game: "when the second half was about half-an-hour gone, Broxburn added a third goal from a scrimmage. This point, however, the Rovers disputed, and they refused to play any further, ultimately leaving the field with the ball in their possession, with a quarter of an hour to go. Broxburn remained till the referee (Mr Archer, Armadale) blew the whistle for time, the game standing in favour of Broxburn by three goals to two. Numerous fouls were given throughout the game against the Rovers for rough play." The referee was, coincidentally, Mr James Archer, Chairman of the Linlithgowshire Football Association and he hastily called a special meeting in the nearby pub! The Rovers protested against the awarding of the third goal on the grounds of offside and also in the giving of the first goal, saying it had not crossed the line. The referee, and chairman, responded, saying he had acted conscientiously. The *Herald* reported that "after a great deal of discussion the matter was voted upon, when four voted for the replay and four that the cup be awarded to Broxburn, the chairman refusing to give his casting vote for either side. Mr Young (Broxburn), vice-president, intimated that he could no longer remain in an association that could upset the decision of a referee appointed by them and consider the protest of a team that refused to play the recognised time of the game." The matter was subsequently referred to a further meeting which awarded the trophy to Broxburn.

Shamrock were the first of the Broxburn clubs to appear in the Scottish Cup, making their first appearance in September 1885 when they lost to Bo'ness after a replay. Their finest hour came in the 1892-93 competition but before that, in the 1891-92 season, they took Cup-holders Hearts all the way in an epic 5-4 Second Round defeat in December 1891. *The Scotsman* reported that the match had "created quite an exceptional amount of interest in Association football circles. Under ordinary circumstances such would not have been the case, but the fact of the match being played at Broxburn was supposed to introduce an element of doubt as to the result. In the earlier stages of the competition the Shamrock had shown excellent form, while in the very latest round they had defeated such a representative team as the Northern by the large score of seven goals to two. The weather, bar a strong wind, was not unfavourable to football, though the field, for many reasons was ill-adapted for so important a contest. There was a very large attendance of spectators present to witness the contest, including many of the regular followers of the cup-holders, who had journeyed to the scene of the action by special train. So much had been heard of forcible play on the part of the home team that the visitors were naturally on the alert for rough play. Contrary to expectation, however, the Broxburn lads played a game with which no fault could be found. As the result of a hard and fast match, the Heart of Mid-Lothian claimed a victory by the narrow majority of five goals to four." Hearts took the early lead and kept up their initial dominance by adding two more. Shamrock responded and succeeded in reducing the deficit to one by half-time, Gribbin scoring both goals. In the second half Hearts scored a fourth and despite an injury to one of their players, who remained on the field, but was of little use, they added a fifth. Again back came Shamrock, *The Scotsman* reporting that "two goals were put on and amid a scene of unwanted excitement the Scottish Cup-holders pulled through and no more. Though defeated, the Broxburn gained hosts of friends by reason of their fine display. Brady, O'Bryne and Gordon were the best of a most capable team." The full Broxburn Shamrock team that day was: Gordon; John and James McCabe; J McCann, O'Bryne, E Hughes; Brady, Cannon, Millar, E McCann and Gribbin.

In the 1892-93 season Broxburn Shamrock famously had a run to the Semi-finals of the Scottish Cup. They knocked out Dunblane and King's Park before drawing League side St Mirren. The match was played at played at Shamrock Park, located on Pyothall Road in the town, on the 21st January 1893 but there was only a small crowd as Broxburn were hosting Hearts in an East of Scotland Shield tie, and this drew spectators away. Frost and thaw meant soft ground and within a minute of kick-off Shamrock had surprised their League opponents when they scored through Brady. St Mirren, sitting as high as third place in the First Division slowly got accustomed to the playing conditions and eventually drew level. Shamrock responded and Brady missed a chance to restore their lead by a matter of inches but did eventually succeed, again putting his team in the lead before half-time. Saints dominated the second half and eventually equalised after about 20 minutes of play. This seemed to break the resolve of the Shamrock and a few minutes later the visitors took the lead for the first time. The Shamrock hopes seemed over but a cross from the left was turned in by O'Byrne. The equaliser saw momentum switch and the home team took charge, with Miller scoring the winning goal with five minutes to go. The Broxburn Shamrock team that beat League opposition was: Walker; McCabe, Docherty; Hughes, O'Byrne, J McCann; Brady, Moreland, Miller, O'Brien and E McCann.

Following their 4-3 triumph Shamrock drew the mighty Queen's Park, nine-time winners. Their opponents had the home advantage so Broxburn travelled through to Hampden on the 18th February 1893. In a fairly even start with chances at both ends, Shamrock were holding their own until their hosts opened the scoring after 25 minutes. The Spiders continued to press and doubled their advantage. Just before half-time a blatant handball by one of the home defenders was missed by the referee as he cleared a goalbound shot. This led to a crowd disturbance during the interval. The raised temperature spilled onto the pitch with *The Scotsman* commenting that "forcible tactics were resorted to on both sides, and in these circumstances scientific play was impossible." An injury saw Queen's Park go down to ten men but soon after they actually increased their lead. A goalmouth scramble from a corner saw Shamrock pull a goal back but just as the Broxburn team were playing with renewed vigour their hosts scored again. Taking up the commentary *The Scotsman* reported "all hope of the Shamrock entering the final was now lost, but they, nevertheless, played gamely to the end, and a few minutes from time E McCann scored their second goal. The visitors showed superior staying power and were pressing when the whistle blew." Queen's Park when on to lift the Scottish Cup for their tenth and final time which is well documented. Less well known is that a team from Broxburn made it to the Scottish Cup Semi-finals.

Rivals Broxburn Thistle had first played in the Scottish Cup in the 1886-87 competition, where they beat Bellstane Birds of South Queensferry after a replay. They drew Hearts in the next round, in a match played at Albyn Park on the 2nd October 1886. Play was even for the first twenty minutes before Hearts took the lead. Broxburn Thistle grew into the game and got a deserved equaliser five minutes before the break. Hearts had most of the play in the second half but the Broxburn defence was resolute until it was eventually breached fifteen minutes from time. Thistle tried in vain to get back on terms but the game ended in a win for Hearts by two goals to one. The *Edinburgh Evening News* was quite scathing of the Hearts performance, commenting that "this is certainly another case of a first-class club allowing an inferior team to be their equal, and it is ridiculous to suggest that the Hearts are only a couple of goals better than the Thistle. If these matches have done little good, they have at least taught our senior clubs to play the winning game in the first half, and not take it late into their heads that they can run through teams at any time and score."

The following season Broxburn Thistle drew Hibernian and the two sides met in September 1887 at Easter Road. Thistle had the first chance of the game and after that it was balanced in terms of play. After 25 minutes Hibs scored past Docherty in the Broxburn goal. Eight minutes later they got a second and immediately after that they added a third. Eight minutes before the interval it was four and a fifth was added on the stroke of half-time. No scoring took place in the second half. *The Scotsman* reported that "the Broxburn men were not a match for their experienced opponents. They had frequently speedy runs to the Hibernian goal, and they might have scored had they been more careful in their shooting, which, as is usually the case with junior teams, was faulty. However, in this they were little worse than the Hibernians, who lost some very easy chances. Docherty, also, did his share in keeping down the scoring, and played much better in the second half than in the first."

Later, playing simply as 'Broxburn', the club beat Adventurers of Edinburgh 9-3 in the First Round of the 1888-89 competition. In the Second Round they were drawn at home to Hearts and held them to a 2-2 draw. A crowd of 2,000 saw Marr open the scoring for Broxburn. This roused Hearts who made efforts to equalise but it was Broxburn who scored next through Russell. Hearts got one back before half-time. The home team dominated the beginning of the second half but were handicapped by going down to ten men due to injury. Hearts put the Broxburn goal under siege and eventually got a late equaliser. The Broxburn team that held Hearts to a draw was: Docherty; A Cuthbertson, D Cuthbertson; Hamilton, Wardrope, McCann; McLean, Mitchell, Paterson, Russell and Marr. Broxburn took 400 supporters to Tynecastle for the replay. A very evenly contested first half ended goalless. The second period resumed and followed a similar pattern before Hearts took the lead in the 65th minute. Not long afterwards Docherty in the Broxburn goal was beaten again. The *Scotsman* reported that "Broxburn now made it lively for the Hearts for a time, but luck seemed against them when in front of goal."

In the 1889-90 Scottish Cup Broxburn recorded a 9-2 away win against West Calder. Played at Burngrange Park they scored five in the first half, Marr scoring four. They added four more in the second, with their hosts also scoring two. In the next round they hosted Leith Athletic. In a hard fought game that they should have won, they were wasteful in front of goal and the game ended 2-2. Leith won the replay in what *The Scotsman* described as "a very hard game, in which the finer points of football were conspicuous by their absence." The match ended in a victory for the home team by the narrow margin of two goals to one.

Broxburn also featured in the 1890-91 Scottish Cup competition, reaching the Third Round. In the Second Round they beat Clackmannan 5-2, eventually prevailing after twice being pegged back. They suffered a heavy 6-0 defeat at the hands of Bathgate Rovers in the next round, *The Scotsman* noting that "the Broxburn team was largely made up of second eleven men, while the Rovers were very strong."

Both Broxburn clubs played in the East of Scotland Football League which was created in for the 1893-94 and was subsequently abandoned with not all fixtures complete. Shamrock had played the most matches, nine, and were unbeaten, winning seven. They went on to lift the Linlithgow Cup for the one and only time, beating Linithgow Athletic 4-0 at Mill Park, Bathgate on the 21st April 1894. They also appeared in the Scottish Cup that season, where they were beaten 8-3 by Arbroath. Broxburn disbanded in 1894 but a second Broxburn team came back into existence in 1901.

Inbetween these years Broxburn Shamrock reached another county cup final, this time losing to Armadale Volunteers after a replay in March 1897.

The reformed Broxburn re-entered the Linlithgowshire Cup for the 1901-02 season, reaching the Final which they lost against Bo'ness 3-1 in a replay, after the first Final had been drawn 1-1. The following year they got revenge, beating Bo'ness 1-0 on the 9th May 1903 at Boghead Park, Bathgate. They also participated in the Scottish Cup that year, losing to Leith Athletic in the First Round. Broxburn also competed in the Central Combination league for the 1902-03 season only. Broxburn retained the County Cup the following year beating Bathgate 2-0. Both they and Shamrock joined the Midland League for the 1903-04 season but this competition only lasted a year as a number of clubs left to reform the Eastern League.

In the 1904-05 season Broxburn beat Shamrock in the Linlithgowshire semi-finals to reach their third successive final. This was a repeat of the previous season's final against Bathgate and it took four matches to settle the final in favour of their opponents. Bathgate were leading the first match 1-0, being played at Newtown Park, Bo'ness, when the game was abandoned late in the second half due to a pitch invasion. The re-scheduled game a week later, played at Shamrock Park, Broxburn, was goalless. The two sides met for a third time, on the 13th May 1905 but this game ended 1-1, after extra-time. The fourth match didn't get played until the September of 1905, when Bathgate beat Broxburn 3-2 at Shamrock Park.

The Eastern League had been reformed in 1904 and featured both Broxburn clubs plus Bathgate, Bo'ness, West Calder Swifts and a reserve team from Hearts amongst others. Broxburn finished fifth and Broxburn Shamrock came seventh. Early in the following season, the Scottish Alliance was reformed. Bo'ness, Broxburn and Broxburn Shamrock who were still Eastern League members left for this league. A new Broxburn entity, Athletic, joined the Eastern League in their place and competed for two seasons until its demise in 1907.

In the 1906-07 Linlithgowshire Cup considerable interest was caused in the town when Broxburn and Broxburn Athletic met each other in the Semi-final. Broxburn won 2-0 but lost the Final after a replay against Bo'ness. The following year they did win the County Cup for the fifth time. By this time Broxburn had joined the new Scottish Union, playing there between 1906 and 1911. Shamrock returned to the Eastern league for the 1906-07 and competed alongside Athletic for a time until they left to join the Scottish Combination for the 1907-08 season, playing there for two seasons.

In the 1908-09 season Broxburn Athletic made their debut in the Scottish Cup where they were involved in a marathon cup tie against Beith, which took five games to settle. The two sides first met on the 23rd January 1909 at Broxburn where they drew 1-1. *The Scotsman* summarised the game thus: "the game was stiffly contested but produced little good football." Clark scored for Broxburn midway through the second half and ten minutes later Beith equalised. A week later they met in Ayrshire, and this one was described as "stubbornly contested" by the same paper and yielded no goals. The two sides then played three games in as many days. They met for the second replay on Wednesday the 3rd February. This match was staged at the neutral Ibrox, although only 500 were present. Broxburn opened the scoring but Beith equalised from a long range effort despite playing the second half with ten men due to injury. Beith were marginally the better side but were wasteful in front of goal. Extra time was played but there was no further scoring. At the end of the game it was decided to try again the following day at Cathkin Park, but it wasn't available, so the sides returned to Ibrox. This third replay also ended in a draw, although for much of the game it appeared that Beith would prevail. A defensive mix up led to them giving away an early goal. Beith were then awarded a penalty in the second period but Laing threw himself to the side and tipped the ball around the post. Just on the call of time McKnight equalised for Broxburn amid great excitement. The extra half an hour was played, which was dominated by Broxburn, but again the two sides couldn't be separated. At the close of the match it was agreed to replay at Paisley the following day on the ground of St Mirren, who the winners were due to play on the Saturday. So, on Friday the 5th February the two sides met for the fifth time, and the third time in three days. Broxburn started the strongest and Cadman scored after fifteen minutes which was followed shortly afterwards by a second from Meek. Beith responded well and by the half-time interval had restored parity. On resuming the momentum was with Beith and they scored twice. With fifteen minutes to go Broxburn got a lifeline when a penalty was awarded but they failed to convert it. Beith, therefore, finally progressed 4-2 and played their fourth game in four days the following day, the Saturday, losing 3-0 at Love Street.

Broxburn Athletic joined the Central League for the 1909-10 season, finishing second bottom. They also made it to the Linlithgow Cup Final, where they lost to Bo'ness. In the 1911-12 season they featured in the Scottish Cup, beating Beith 6-0 before losing 6-1 to Third Lanark. They also made it to the final of the county cup for the second year in a row. This time they lost 5-2 to Bathgate in a match played at Armadale's Volunteer Park on the 20th April 1912. In the same season Broxburn FC joined Athletic in the Central League, finishing in seventh place in the twelve team competition.

Broxburn was still too small a community to support multiple teams and in 1912 Broxburn FC and Broxburn Athletic amalgamated to form Broxburn United. Both teams wore blue shirts so the choice of colours for the new team was nice and easy although by the time of their admittance to the League they had changed to maroon shirts and white shorts. The new club continued in the Central League but in their first year as United they finished a disappointing second bottom. They had more joy though in the Linlithgowshire Cup, reaching the Final in their first season, where they lost 2-1 against Armadale at Boghead Park in Bathgate.

The wisdom of merging the two clubs continued to be demonstrated by success in the regional county competition. Broxburn United won the trophy the following season, gaining revenge by beating Armadale 2-1 in the Final. Armadale had beaten Broxburn Shamrock 6-0 in the First Round and this was the last appearance made by Shamrock. They made it three Finals in a row in the 1914-15 season when they beat Bo'ness by the same score in May 1915 to retain the trophy.

Broxburn United first featured in Scottish Cup in December 1913, losing 5-0 at home to Raith Rovers, who were a First Division side at the time. They reached the Third Round the following year going out to Motherwell.

The club originally played their games at Albion Park but moved in 1914 to Sports Park where they played all of their matches as a League club. The present Albyn Park, home of the junior side Broxburn Athletic, sits on the site of the original ground. Sports Park was located where the sports centre is now.

In 1915 Broxburn United joined the new Eastern League formed by members of the suspended Second Division of the Scottish Football League. In 1919, largely due to the refusal of the SFL to reinstate these former members, the Central League was re-established as a rival competition with Broxburn United among the membership. In the immediate post First World War years they again featured in the Scottish Cup. In the 1919-20 competition they reached the Third Round, putting up a good fight going out against Rangers 3-0 at Ibrox in front of a crowd of 16,000. The following season they got a home tie against First Division Hamilton Academicals. The match, played on the 5th February 1921, attracted about 5,000 spectators to Sports Park. The match was evenly contested but near to the end of the first period the visitors began to assert themselves and justifiably took the lead. Hamilton extended their lead in the second half, *The Scotsman* reporting that "from that point the Broxburn team had rather the better of matters, and after scoring from a scrimmage following a penalty kick, they pressed their opponents continuously till the close." They couldn't find a way through though and lost the tie 2-1, having put up a good performance against a Scottish League side.

In 1921 the 16 member of the Central League, including Broxburn United and the three other West Lothian clubs, plus four other teams drawn from the Alliance and West of Scotland League were invited by the Scottish Football League to re-form the Second Division. Thomas Heatlie was appointed manager and the club made it's debut in the SFL on the 20th August 1921. They hosted Dunfermline Athletic at Sports Park, and won 3-2 in front of a bumper crowd of 3,500. Broxburn United came from one-nil down to score three second half goals before a second was scored for the Pars via the penalty spot five minutes from time. The first ever Broxburn United team to play an SFL match was: Kerr; Harris, McLeod; Coyle, Allan, Cairns; Hendry, Davies, Sutherland, Williamson and Dunn. The Broxburn goals were scored by Williamson and Sutherland, who scored two. *The Sunday Post* commented that "the directors of Broxburn have every reason to be pleased with the players they have signed. Their defence is steady and consistent, and Harris in the position of right back was particularly outstanding. The halfs, if not brilliant, were good, and their front ranks should enable the club to go far. Sutherland, the centre-forward, proved a bit slow, but the wings are a nippy lot, especially Dunn and Williamson on the left, who also caught the eye with their energetic and resourceful play."

Their next game was away at Bo'ness, which they lost 3-1. United scored first through Sutherland but Bo'ness equalised before half-time before scoring two goals in the last fifteen minutes. *The Sunday Post* gave their assessment on the Broxburn team: "Broxburn have a fine front rank, and of the quintette, Davies stood out prominently. In the mid-line Coyle filled the eye, and the rear defence stood the strain well to within fifteen minutes from the close.

A strong finish to 1921 and three consecutive wins in early January 1922 saw them as high as fourth place but they then won only one of their remaining fifteen fixtures to eventually finish a very creditable seventh place, although they had no local bragging rights as the three other West Lothian clubs finished above them. This seventh place finish would be matched again in the 1924-25 season and was their highest ever finish in the Scottish League. Part of this poor run at the beginning of 1922 was controversial. Broxburn were censured in 1922 for fielding only two first team players in a League match against St Bernard's. They had drawn Hearts in the Scottish Cup and had played them on the 11th and 15th February, both games ending in 2-2 draws. On Saturday the 18th February they fielded a weakened team away at St Bernard's, so that they could rest players for the replay two days later. They lost the League game 4-0. *The Scotsman* reported that "after their arduous games with the Heart of Midlothian, Broxburn played only two of their Cup-tie side, the remainder being replaced by reserves, a local junior, and three players borrowed from Armadale. This scratch side was hardly a match for the St Bernards, who dominated the game almost from first to last. Broxburn went on to lose the replay 3-1, *The Scotsman* noting that they were "troublesome opponents" and "fell fighting." Only a late penalty for handball had enabled Hearts to salvage a draw in the first game and Broxburn had led twice in the first replay. The Tynecastle club were obviously impressed as they returned to the club in the close season and signed Andrew Jamieson, the left-back, Terry Coyle at right-half and Willie Williamson, the inside-left.

The Cup run enabled the club to erect a new 450 seat grandstand for the new 1922-23 season. Broxburn United once more performed well, finishing once again in the top half, this time in eighth, although they still were the bottom ranked of the West Lothian teams. They opened with a 2-2 draw at rivals Bathgate before hosting Cowdenbeath, *The Scotsman* reporting that the "game at Broxburn attracted between 3000 and 4000 spectators. The club's new stand, built to accommodate 450, was opened for the occasion, and it was filled." The game ended 0-0. Broxburn followed up these two opening games with three consecutive wins to go joint top by mid-September. Form dipped after that and a month later they lost 5-0 at Stenhousemuir and by the end of 1922 they had slipped to eighth, where they subsequentrly finished. The only other results of note during this season were a 5-0 defeat against Kilmarnock in the First Round of the Scottish Cup and a heavy defeat to Queen's Park, the eventual Seciond Division champions, by the same score. On a brighter note United won the Linlithgowshire Cup, beating Armadale 3-0 at the end of April 1923 in the Final played at Bathgate's Mill Park.

The following season was a poor one by their early standards, as they finished in 15th place, only three points above what were now relegation places to the Third Division. They started badly, losing five of their first six matches. When they lost 3-0 at Cowdenbeath at the end of September they were second from bottom. A mini-run in December where they picked up five points out of a poosible eight, lifted them away from the relegation dogfight as they recovered to finish in 15th place. They had qualified for the Scottish Cup but suffered a First Round exit against Raith. The highlight of the season was that they retained the Linlithgowshire Cup, winning it for the fourth time overall. In a repeat of the previous year's Final, they beat Armadale 1-0.

In stark contrast to the previous season Broxburn United made a strong start to the new League campaign, going unbeaten in their first six games, winning four of them. By the end of October the joint leaders of the Second Division were "Uniteds" – Broxburn and Dundee. Dundee United would go on to be the champions whereas Broxnurn would slip back, although they would equal their best ever finish of seventh place. Both Bo'ness and Alloa beat them 3-0 during November and December and new leaders

Clyde beat them 6-0 in mid-December, in a run of nine games without a win as they slipped into the bottom half of the table.

The club's form picked up in the New Year and 1925 also saw the beginning of their best showing in the Scottish Cup, as they made a run to the Quarter-finals. In the first two rounds they desposed of Third Division League sides Nithsdale Wanderers and Royal Albert, before drawing First Division opposition in the shape of Falkirk in the Third Round. The probable record attendance for Sports Park was set for this tie, played on the 21st February 1925, which Broxburn won 2-1. This was one of two shocks heavily reported, the other being the Cup holders Airdrieonians being knocked out by Dundee. *The Scotsman* reported that "a record crowd of about 9500 saw Broxburn United administer the knock out to Falkirk at Broxburn. Doubtless the nature of the ground and the absence of Townsley were both contributory factors to Falkirk's defeats, but even after making due allowance for these things, there was no doubting the merit of Broxburn United's win. The fact that Falkirk did most of the pressing was a peculiar feature of the game, but while the sustained attacks of the visitors gave McKinlay, in the home goal, comparatively few anxious moments the possibility of a goal coming at the Falkirk end loomed up almost every time the United forwards got on the move. The marksmanship of the Falkirk forwards was weak....The Broxburn United forwards, although possibly not combining so well as a whole, showed far more dash and enterprise than their opponents, and both goals were well taken, Hair in the first half converting a cross from Walker, which he might well have missed, and Graham near the end flashing a header past Ferguson from a centre by Coyle. Coyle himself had a great try which Ferguson brought down on the line, and a claim for a goal was refused. Graham led the United attack in fine style, and distributed the ball with great cleverness, but David was the outstanding player of the match. He played splendidly at inside-right, and he and Hair provided the best wing on the field." Tom Townsley, the Falkirk centre-half was missing, having been placed on the transfer list at his own request, following an approach from Hearts. Broxburn scored after ten minutes through Hair but Todd equalised in the second half. Graham scored the winning goal near the end. The giant killing Broxburn team was: McKinlay; Reid, Fordyce; Coyle, McBeth, McIllvenny; Hair, Davies, Graham, Wardrope and Walker.

Broxburn United drew Dundee away in the Quarter-final and put up another great display, only narrowly losing by the only goal of the game. *The Scotsman* noted that "it cannot be said that Dundee made an impressive entry into the semi-final of the Scottish Cup competition. With Broxburn United as opponents at Dundee, they were understood to have the easiest task of the round, but, as it turned out, they had greater difficulty in shaking off Broxburn than they had in knocking out the Cupholders a fortnight earlier." A solitary goal decided the contest which only came with fifteen minutes remaining - from a corner, scored by Halliday. Broxburn put in a heroic defensive effort with McKinlay in goal performing well, and with Reid and Fordyce shielding him, although Broxburn offered little up front. *The Sunday Post* said "to the end Broxburn played in plucky style in their attempt to force a replay in the Lothians, but were unsuccessful. They are, however, due every credit for their fine display, and especially their defence." Dundee went to the final where they were beaten by Celtic 2-1.

Their Cup form appeared to galvanise them as they only lost one of the five League matches played between the opening round and the quarters. At the end of February they sat in eleventh place but they finished the season strongly, going unbeaten in their last seven fixtures, and eventually finished seventh.

Their spell as a Scottish Football League club came to an abrupt end at the conclusion of the 1925-26 season. The season was a disaster from start to finish as they won only four out of 38 fixtures and lost 28, conceding 127 goals in the process as they finished bottom. The demise of the Third Division after three seasons meant that there was no relegation so they faced a re-election vote instead, which was hotly contested by a host of leading Third Division clubs anxious to preserve their League status.

Broxburn United lost their opening game, narrowly, 1-0 at home to Kings Park. They conceded in the second minute but deserved a share of the spoils. They were then thrashed 8-0 away in Edinburgh against St Bernard's in only the second match of the new campaign. Under the headline "St. Bernard Slaughter Broxburn" *The Sunday Post* reported that "with both teams on the losing side last week, it was no surprise to find St Bernard and Broxburn United going all out for victory at the Gymnasium. Play was even enough in the first half, but afterwards the Broxburn men collapsed like a pack of cards, and the Saints found goals easier to get than they have done for many a long day. Eight they got past McKinlay, seven of these in the second half, Simpson, at centre proved himself a rare opportunist, and had half of the goals. It is difficult to account for Broxburn's rout. The forwards certainly were very poor, and this threw a lot of extra work on the half-backs, and allowed the Saints to push on the game uninterruptedly. McKinlay in the Broxburn goal, had not much chances with any of the shots that beat him. It can at least be said for Broxburn that they never lay down." The result was Broxburn's heaviest ever SFL defeat.

On match day three they picked up their first points, beating county rivals Bo'ness 3-2. Despite fielding a weakened side that was missing McIlwraith, at outside-left and McBeth, at centre-half, due to injuries, goals from Hair and Wardrope (2) gave them the win. In late October they beat East Stirlingshire 6-5. Broxburn had two triallists in the forward line listed as 'Junior' and 'Newman' - both who scored. Wardrope got two and McBeth got the winning goal coming from 4-5 down.

Across the next six months, from the end of October 1925 to April 1926 they won only one more game, a terrible run that included a sequence of nine consecutive defeats. Broxburn conceded six on successive Saturdays in November, losing 6-1 at Dunfermline and then 6-2 against new leaders Stenhousemuir. At this point Broxburn were in 18th place, a point above Alloa Athletic and four ahead of bottom club East Stirlingshire. Things got worse with back-to-back defeats where seven goals were conceded in January 1926. On the 2nd January they lost 7-4 against St Bernard's at home, although they were only 3-2 down at half-time. East Stirlingshire won that day which meant Broxburn we're now bottom, Two days later they lost 7-1 at King's Park.

Against this background Broxburn got a creditable 1-1 draw against Hibernian at Easter Road in the Scottish Cup thanks, in part, to an early wonder strike. *The Scotsman* under the headline "A Scare for Hibernians" reported that "the Hibernians made a very unimpressive start in the Cup ties. They could only draw with Broxburn United, and were a trifle lucky to do even that. The Broxburn men played up to the club's reputation as Cup-tie fighters. All through they were dashing and spirited, and lasted the pace of a strenuous game as well as, if not better than, their First Division opponents. A goal scored three minutes after the start went far to encourage the visitors. It was the result of a free kick taken by Raeburn from a point thirty yards out and close to the touchline, the shot hitting a post on its way to the net. Subsequently the Hibernians did a lot of vigorous attacking, but beyond a shot or two by Ritchie and Kerr, the finishing was never so dangerous as that by the opposition, among whom Taylor was a prominent figure at outside-left. On two occasions Sharp had to stretch himself full length to save from the Broxburn left-wing. The equalising goal eight minutes after half-time was neatly headed through by Miller from a corner. It seemed to mark a turning point for the Hibernians, but again they had to give way to fine defending, and in a close finish they had one outstanding let-off when Lindsay hit the cross-bar. Ritchie, on the other hand, lost a chance for the Hibernians by a slip at the crucial moment. The absence of Halligan, hurt a week earlier, had probably an adverse effect on the Hibernian forward play...Broxburn United had credit by their plucky display. They had a fine goalkeeper in Walker, and a couple of sturdy backs in Reid and Gillespie."

Broxburn surrendered home advantage for the reply. On the eve of the match *The Scotsman* reported the terms of the switch, reporting that "the conditions regarding the replay at Easter Road include free admission to all Broxburn members, and to accommodate them and other supporters the United will convey all to Easter Road by motor buses, free of charge. There is, of course, some grumbling on the part of a section of the public that the replay should have been arranged for Easter Road; but it is felt that, owing to the present condition of the club's finances and owing to the industrial depression in the district, the directors have done the right thing."

Hibs won the replay 1-0. In another keenly contested affair the scoreline was goalless at the interval with *The Scotsman* commenting that "United had revealed greater dash and penetration, and with better finishing on the part of the forwards might have been on the lead." After the break though, Hibs started to take control of the game and Broxburn seemed to tire as Walker became the busier of the two goalkeepers. Eventually he was beaten and although they tried hard to equalise their efforts were in vain.

Back in the League their poor form continued. At the beginning of February they lost 5-0 at home to Alloa although it looked like Lady Luck was against them. They had to play the entire second half a man short through injury to Fordyce and two of the goals had a suspicion of off-side about them. Things were also taking a turn for the worse off the pitch as the club became entangled in a bribery controversy when a Stenhousemuir player alleged that a Glasgow bookmaker had offered him £50 (a very substantial sum at the time) to throw their game with Broxburn. On the 9th January Broxburn had hosted leaders Stenhousemuir. Later, the Stennie goalkeeper, Joe Shortt, reported to the League that he had been offered £50 by the representatives of a bookmaker from Glasgow to play poorly in a match against Broxburn United. There were lots of speculative theories and it was even suggested that Stenhousemuir didn't want to be promoted and had tried to throw the game. The facts of the matter were that Broxburn lost 2-1, conceding two soft goals. Their opponents could be considered lucky to come away with the win, and the newspaper reports of the match said that Shortt had played a good game. Broxburn were later cleared of any involvement but the affair was a distraction and did further damage to their reputation.

On the 13th February 1926 Broxburn finally broke their long sequence of losses when they beat Albion Rovers 4-3. They showed great character as they twice went behind, but Davis, a new centre-forward recently transferred from Falkirk, equalised on both occasions. Dunsire put Broxburn ahead in the second half but Rovers equalised. Taylor scored the winning goal ten minutes from time to end a winless run stretching back to October 1925. Broxburn United drew two and lost eight of their remaining ten fixtures and so failed to win again in the League. On the 3rd April they lost 8-2 at Firs Park against East Stirling, conceding a penalty after just three minutes, that was actually missed, but it didn't prove costly as just two minutes later their hosts scored. Broxburn came into the game and Davis scored a brilliant equalising goal but before the interval

Shire scored two more. Within five minutes of the restart the hosts had added two more and a sixth followed soon after. Broxburn got a second goal, again through Davis, before Shire got two more, this time converting a penalty.

By the mid-1920s the shale trade, which had been responsible for the growth of the team in the first place, was now in decline. The general economic situation didn't help either. Attendances declined and for their last home game of the season only 500 came. This was a 4–3 defeat against Armadale on the 24th April 1926, a game which also turned out to be the club's final match in the Scottish Football League.

Broxburn United finished bottom with just 14 points, six points adrift of Bathgate and 13 behind East Stirlingshire in 18th place. The recorded a number of unwanted club records during the season including fewest points and number of wins, most defeats and most League goals conceded in a season (126). They went 16 games without a win and within that suffered nine straight losses. They also recorded their highest home scoring loss and their biggest ever defeat at home.

Broxburn United, along with Bathgate, escaped automatic relegation due to the demise of the Third Division, a re-election vote taking place instead. On the 20th May 1926 four of the defunct Third Division sides applied including the top three sides - Leith Athletic, Forfar Athletic, Helensburgh - along with Dykehead – for the two vacant spots. Broxburn United, (along with Helensburgh and Dykehead) were unfortunately eliminated in the first ballot. Their poor form and the bribery affair had damaged their reputation and they failed to gather much support. Bathgate were re-elected and Forfar Athletic were elected to replace them.

Broxburn United joined a number of the ex-Third Division clubs who joined the Scottish Alliance for the 1926-27 season. The big influx of clubs meant this competition split along regional lines and United played against other ex-League clubs such as Lochgelly United, Dykehead and Leith, as well as the reserve teams from Hearts and Hibs. When the Scottish Alliance took the decision to expel the majority of the ex-League clubs the following season Broxburn decided to adopt Junior status and eventually disbanded in 1932.

Broxburn continued to play in the Scottish Cup during this time and were drawn at home to local rivals Armadale, who were still a League club. In the match played in January 1927 the visitors took the lead from a corner after just six minutes. Roared on by a crowd of 2,500 Broxburn soon equalised through Reid, via a long range shot. Home pressure paid off in the second half when Simpson scored the deserved winner from a long range effort, *The Scotsman* saying that "the game was fought out thereafter in a determined manner, but the Broxburn team were the superior lot, and the score did not indicate their all-round superiority over the Second Leaguers." In the next round they got a home tie against fellow Alliance side Montrose but were held to a 2-2 draw as a result of a last minute goal from their opponents. Reid scored two, one from a penalty. Montrose got a penalty as well prior to their last gasp equaliser. Broxburn United lost the replay 1-0 at Links Park. Montrose scored after just two minutes from a corner and Broxburn strove hard for the equaliser but just couldn't the draw they at least deserved.

After the Second World War local businessmen got together with the aim of reforming Broxburn and in 1947 the Broxburn Athletic Football Club was formed, playing their home games at Albyn Park, off Greendykes Road and the site of the original Albion Park. The club is part of the Senior set up in Scottish football, and they play in the East of Scotland League. In the 2019-20 season this new club made headlines with a run to the Fourth Round of the Scottish Cup. In the First Round of the competition they beat former League side East Stirling 3-2 and were then drawn away at League Two opposition in the form of Cowdenbeath. On the 19th October 2019 an 87th minute equaliser by Nick Locke saw them draw 1-1 at Central Park. A week later a gate of just over 1,000 at Albyn Park saw them win the replay 3-0. The first half of the tie was quite even before a Zander Miller penalty in the 43rd minute gave them the half-time lead, after Greg Binnie had been brought down in the box. Their League opponents made a strong start to the second half but after an hour Broxburn had the opportunity to get some breathing space when Miller was brought down in the box this time, but Miller failed to capitalise as his shot was well saved. However, with less than 20 minutes to go, and the game still in the balance, Craig Scott's high shot from outside the area made it 2-0 and ten minutes later Ross Nimmo set up Conor Kelly for number three. At the end of November Broxburn Athletic travelled north to play Highland League side Inverurie Loco Works and despite the home team dominating possession they snatched an 87th minute winner through Miller. Goalkeeper Conor Wallace made a fine save and Broxburn broke up the other end in a sweeping move that culminated in Miller firing in. Their reward was an away tie at Premier League St Mirren. This Fourth Round tie took place on the 18th January 2020, and while they rarely threatened their opponents, they did hold out until the 55th minute before going behind, and conceded two very late goals to go out 3-0.

SEASON	LEAGUE	P	W	D	L	F	A	P	POS
1921-22	SCOT-2	38	14	11	13	43	43	39	7/20
1922-23	SCOT-2	38	14	12	12	40	43	40	8/20
1923-24	SCOT-2	38	13	8	17	50	56	34	15/20
1924-25	SCOT-2	38	16	9	13	48	54	41	7/20
1925-26	SCOT-2	38	4	6	28	55	126	14	20/20

Cambuslang

Formed: 1879
Colours: Navy blue shirts and white shorts
Ground: Whitefield Park
Entered League: 1890. Founder members of the Scottish Football League
Number of League Seasons: 2
Honours: None
Highest League Finish: 4th in Division One
Left League: 1892. Failed re-election. Wound up in 1897.

A little known fact, and indeed a celebrated *Pointless* answer on the BBC quiz show, Cambuslang were founder members of the Scottish Football League, although they only managed two seasons. Prior to that their most notable achievement was being the runners-up of the Scottish Cup in 1888. However, their 6-1 loss in the final at the hands of Renton remains the joint-worst defeat in a Scottish Cup Final (matched by Celtic beating Hibernian in 1972).

Although today part of South Lanarkshire, the suburban town of Cambuslang is more closely associated with Glasgow. The town is located just south of the River Clyde and is about six miles south-east of the city centre. However, going back in history, Cambuslang was a standalone settlement and has a long history of coal-mining, iron and steel making and engineering works dating back to the late 19th century.

The club was formed in 1879 and were known as 'The Villagers'. They originally played at Westburn Park but moved to Whitefield Park in 1888 and played here until their demise in 1897. The park was named after 18th century preacher George Whitefield, whose *'Cambuslang Work'* religious revival events had attracted thousands to the area in 1742. The ground was located between the Vicarland and Howieshill areas just off modern day Croft Road. The ground is famous for being the scene of the first ever hat-trick in the Scottish Football League in August 1890, when John McPherson scored four goals for Rangers.

At a meeting at the Cross Hotel in Hamilton the secretary of Cambuslang was joined by the secretaries of Airdrie, Coatbridge Drumpellier, Hamilton Academicals, Uddingston and many other clubs where it was agreed that each club would pay 10 shillings (50p) towards a county cup and Cambuslang were early winners of the Lanarkshire Cup in 1884 and 1885. They also made eleven successive appearances in the Scottish Cup between 1879 and 1890 including reaching the final in 1888.

They made their first appearance in the 1879-80 Scottish Cup competition where they reached the Fifth Round. They got a walkover in the first round as opponents Uddingston scratched. They beat a team from Airdrie 4-1 in their first senior fixture, and eventually lost to beaten semi-finalists Pollockshields Athletic 4-0. In the 1880-81 competition they again went deep, this time reaching the Fourth Round where they were beaten by Hearts and they matched this in the 1882-83 season, this time being beaten by six time winners and holders Queen's Park 5-0.

In the 1883-84 season Cambuslang reached the Quarter finals where they were beaten by Rangers. They knocked out Bellshill, Tollcross and Hamilton Accies, scoring 21 goals in their first three matches. In the Fourth Round they knocked out Kilmarnock Athletic, 3-2 away, and were given a bye in the Fifth Round. On the 22nd December 1883 they played Rangers, conceding five goals in the first half. In the second half, according to the *Glasgow Herald* "the local team pressed their opponents pretty severely, and were several times within an ace of scoring, but the Rangers' backs and goalkeeper performed their difficult work brilliantly, and the ball was often cleared away. At length, however, a good run by the forwards enabled R. Dalrymple to get the better of the Rangers' backs, and a good shot from his right foot put on record the only point gained for Cambuslang during the entire game." Their strong Cup showing crossed over in their regional competition as they won the Lanarkshire Association Cup at the end of the season.

The following season the Villagers went one better, reaching the Scottish Cup Semi-finals, going out to three time winners Vale of Leven after a replay. In a Second Round replayed tie on the 11th October 1884 they beat Airdrieonians 10-2. They then went on to knock out Hamilton Academical and the 1880 runners-up Thornliebank. On the 10th January 1885 they met Battlefield of Glasgow in their Quarter-final tie, the *Glasgow Herald* commenting that "unusual interest was taken in the meeting of these clubs at Cambuslang to play off their Cup tie. The Caledonian Railway Company ran a special train from Glasgow; and altogether there was a large attendance around the ropes. The excitement from the beginning to the end of the match ran high. The weather was of the most unpropitious description, alternate showers of hail and rain falling during most of the match. The home team lost the toss, and kicked off with a strong wind against them. It was therefore very difficult for them to make any headway against the Battlefield, and the extremely soft nature of the ground prevented good play. Not long after the start one of the strangers' backs sent down a long shot, which Sellars in the centre managed to head through the posts, thus drawing the first blood for his side. The rest of the play in the first half requires little description. The ball was generally kept in the home team's territory, but all the efforts to score were rendered futile. On change of ends it was evident that the Cambuslang meant to press their opponents hard, and, indeed, the play was for the most part in the latter's ground. After about 25 minutes' play, Buchanan sent in a nice shot, which passed the goalkeeper amidst great enthusiasm. Encouraged thus by their success, the Cambuslang played in more determined style, and in about eight minutes afterwards Hamilton secured the second goal. On the kick-off, the ball was again sent back to the strangers' goal, and Low shortly afterwards did the needful, registering the third point. It was now apparent that the Battlefield could do nothing to equalise matters, and, in fact, the game ended without further scoring on either side. The Cambuslang were thus hailed the victors by three goals to one. Both teams played a hard and fast game throughout, but before the close the strangers were pretty much exhausted." The listed Cambuslang team was: James Dunn; William Semple, William Smith; Andrew Jackson, N Black; James Gourlay, James Plenderleith, John Hamilton, James Low, James Dalrymple and James Buchanan.

On the 31st January Cambuslang travelled to Alexandria to play their first ever Scottish Cup Semi-final. An injury to McLeish of Vale after 30 minutes handicapped their more illustrious hosts who had won the trophy three times and reached the final in the past two seasons. The score was goalless at half-time, with the *Glasgow Herald* taking up the story from here: "when play was resumed by the Vale against the wind, although they were without the aid of one of their best men, they not only succeeded in preventing the strangers scoring, but confined play very much in Cambuslang territory. Repeatedly the Vale forwards brought the leather down to the strangers' uprights, and but for the magnificent goalkeeping of Dunn and the effective back play of Semple and Smith their efforts would have proved successful."

The replay was held a week later with the right to meet Renton in the final. A crowd of 5,000 was present, and playing the first half with the breeze behind them Cambuslang lay siege to the Vale goal for the first 20 minutes. Hamilton scored for Cambuslang but nearing half-time Dunn was beaten by a shot from Galloway. With the wind now in their favour, the Vale dominated the second half and Galloway poked in a second. Cambuslang tried hard to score but were kept at bay by the Vale backs and nearing the close their opponents scored a third. Cambuslang again had the consolation of regional cup success, retaining their Lanarkshire Cup in 1885.

In the 1885-86 season the Villagers had another good Cup run, reaching the Quarter-finals where they were beaten by Hibernian and in the following season they reached the Fifth Round. In doing so they won 3 matches by the same 6-1 scoreline - against Motherwell in the First Round, Rutherglen in the Second and Albion Rovers in the Fourth. They held Queen's Park to a 1-1 draw but lost an exciting replay 5-4.

In the 1887-88 Cup competition Cambuslang made it all the way to the Scottish Cup Final. They are one of six ex-Scottish League clubs to have reached a final, the others being Vale of Leven, Renton, Third Lanark, St Bernard's and Gretna. In the early rounds they knocked out Hamilton, Royal Albert and East Stirlingshire before receiving a bye in the Fourth Round. In the Fifth Round they were drawn at home to Ayr. In the match played on the 26th November 1887 Cambuslang recorded a club record Scottish Cup win beating Ayr 10-0. They took the lead after just five minutes through Hugh Gourlay and were two up after a quarter of an hours' play, the goal this time scored by James Gourlay. Cambuslang extended their lead through John Buchanan and a few minutes later James Buchanan gave Cambuslang a 4-0 lead at half-time. In the second half Cambuslang lay siege to the Ayr goal and scored at regular intervals.

In the Quarter-finals Cambuslang were drawn at home against Our Boys of Dundee in a match played on the 17th December 1887. James Plenderleith opened the scoring for Cambuslang who kept pressing and added a second through an own goal. Cambuslang lay siege to their opponents goal but couldn't add to their score before half-time. The same pattern continued in the second half and they added four goals to win 6-0. The *Glasgow Herald* appraised the teams to have reached the last four - Queen's Park, Renton and Abercorn being the others – and when they got to Cambuslang they commented that: "the Cambuslang, as has been demonstrated by their recent performances, are at present in their very best form, and, if they could only keep it up - and there is no reason why they should not - they will prove a hard nut to crack."

The previous Cup winners Queen's Park and Renton were drawn against each other which meant that Cambuslang probably got the most favourable draw they could have hoped for in being paired with Abercorn of Paisley. Their opponents had home advantage in an era before neutral venues and the two sides met at Blackstoun Park, Paisley before a crowd of 7,000 on the 14th January 1888. In a very even game Abercorn took the lead but Cambuslang came back strongly, although, according to the *Glasgow Herald* "the visitors threw away their chances by apparent over anxiety in front of goal." Half-time found the score unaltered with Abercorn having the only goal of the first half. Cambuslang dominated play and Hugh Gourlay hit the bar and Clark in the hosts' goal pulled off a couple of great saves from Plenderleith and James Gourlay. "Still maintaining their pressure, the Cambuslang, from a really splendid attack, succeeded in equalising, the credit of the goal lying between James Buchanan and

James Gourlay." Both teams pressed for a winner but the match ended in a draw which was a fair result.

The two clubs met a week later at Whitefield Park to decide who would meet Renton in the Final. Abercorn had the better of the replay in the early minutes twice forcing saves from James Dunn. After 25 minutes, and somewhat against the run of play, Plenderleith beat Clark with an unstoppable shot from ten yards out. Abercorn immediately brought the ball up the other end and equalised but James Buchanan restored Cambuslang's lead before half-time. On the resumption Abercorn strove to again get back on equal terms but a fast counter-attack by the Cambuslang forwards saw the home team go 3-1 up. Incredibly, this was the start of a deluge of goals, which the *Glasgow Herald* described: "immediately following this, Gourlay, by a clever free kick, evaded Clark once more, and increased Cambuslang's score to four goals. James Buchanan put on an easy fifth goal, and from a scrimmage a sixth point was registered. John Buchanan scored a seventh goal, Hugh Gourlay an eighth, J Gourlay the ninth, and Plenderleith the tenth. Cambuslang thus won by 10 goals to 1." The result is a Scottish Cup record win in a Semi-final.

Unfortunately Cambuslang would go on to be on the wrong end of a record scoreline in the Scottish Cup, this time in the Final. On the 4th February 1888 they lost by a joint record score of 6-1 against Renton. Before the Scottish Cup final the club had received a boost when they had won the inaugural Glasgow Cup earlier in the same year. They had caused a major surprise by beating Queen's Park on their own ground in the Semi-final. They scored after eight minutes and Semple increased their lead in the second half. Queen's Park scored in the 87th minute but Cambuslang won 2-1 at Hampden. The final was played at the same venue and Cambuslang faced Rangers on the 28th January 1888. James Plenderleith gave Cambuslang the lead on 25 minutes but Rangers equalised before half-time. Plenderleith scored a second and Hugh Gourlay's goal ensured Cambuslang would lift silverware.

The Scottish Cup Final was played a week later, on the 4th February 1888. Renton started as favourites and indeed were unbeaten in all matches that season. Renton, playing in their third final had the wind at their backs and had the better of the early play. After fifteen minutes a goalmouth scramble developed in front of Dunn's goal and McNee forced the ball over for the opening goal. Keeping up the pressure their opponents added a second following a string of corners. Just before the interval Hugh Gourlay gave his side hope by pulling a goal back following a fine run by John Buchanan. However, that hope was quickly extinguished within a minute of the restart when Renton made it 3-1. Cambuslang now hit back, The *Glasgow Herald* commenting that "the Glasgow cupholders were now playing a much more brilliant and effective game than during the first half, and were conspicuously in the ascendant for some time...but without being able to find an opening." Against the run of play Renton broke away to score, their effort just creeping over the line beyond the despairing Dunn. Cambuslang's heads went down at this stage with twenty minutes left to play, the *Herald* noting that "from this time the Cambuslang seemed to lose heart." Five minutes later Renton had made it 5-1 and they scored near the end to win 6-1. The Cambuslang Cup final team was: James Dunn; William Smith, William Semple; James Gourlay, McKay, Andrew Jackson; James M. Gourlay, Hugh Gourlay, James Plenderleith, James Buchanan, and John Buchanan.

As can be seen, the Cambuslang team contained three Gourlays: Hugh Gourlay who scored; James Gourlay at half-back, and James M Gourlay on the wing. James Gourlay had played for the club since 1884 and had been capped for Scotland against Ireland in 1886. Unrelated was James McCrorie Gourlay, who played for the team in the 1887-88 season only. His cousin, Hugh Gourlay was their Cup final goalscorer. There were two other Scottish internationals in the team besides James Gourlay and they were Andrew Jackson and William Semple. Semple had captained Scotland in 1886, in his one and only international appearance, when he led Scotland to a 4-1 win over Wales. Andrew Jackson had also featured for Scotland in that game. He went on to be the most capped Cambuslang players when he featured again in March 1888 in a 10-2 win over Ireland. John Buchanan, brother of James, was later capped once for Scotland in March 1889 against the same opposition.

A few months later, Cambuslang had a chance for revenge when they played Renton in the final of the Glasgow Merchants Charity Cup – a sort of annual end of season football festival. They had beaten Hibs 3-0 in the semi-final but lost to Renton 4-0.

In the new season Cambuslang made a poor defence of their Glasgow Cup trophy, being thrashed 6-0 by Third Lanark in the First Round in September 1888. *The Scotsman* had noted that "a close game had been expected" and the *Glasgow Herald* expanded on this, saying that "the only tie in which any doubt was felt was that between Cambuslang, the present holders of the handsome trophy, and the 3rd LRV, at Cathkin Park. The suburban team have been showing pretty good form since the beginning of the season, but there was just a feeling that after all they would not be able to pull through, the Volunteers having lately been so much strengthened. This supposition proved to be correct, although even the most enthusiastic supporters of the 3rd scarcely anticipated such a victory as six goals to nothing....the Cambuslang did not show the combination expected of them - indeed there was an entire absence of the dash which generally characterises their play." This Third Lanark team went on to lift the Scottish Cup. Cambuslang had another opportunity to get revenge on Renton as the two sides met in the Third Round of this competition in October, in a repeat of the final. Unfortunately, despite being level 1-1 at the break Renton were far superior in the second half and ran out 4-1 winners. Third Lanark beat Renton in the Semi-final and went on to beat Celtic in a replayed Final.

 In the 1889-90 season Cambuslang reached the Fourth Round of the Scottish Cup, where they were beaten by East End of Dundee after a replay. In the Glasgow Cup they reached the Semi-final where they were beaten by Celtic. Near the end of the season though two more of their players were capped for their country. John Russell was capped once in March 1890 against Ireland. A week earlier, Robert "Bob" Brown, playing at inside-right was capped once against Wales.

At the end of March 1890 the original meeting to form the Scottish Football League was held and Cambuslang were one of the eleven founder members. They finished a very respectable fourth in 1891 in what ended as a ten team Division following the expulsion of Renton. On the 16th August 1890 their opening League fixture was played at Whitefield Park. Cambuslang hosted the three-time winners of the Scottish Cup, Vale of Leven, in front of a 3,000 crowd. *The Scotsman* reported on the match saying: "the opening period saw Cambuslang well in, and ultimately the ball was rushed past McCallum, being the first goal for Cambuslang. The visitors were kept well at home, mainly through the strong half-back play of the homesters, and Hugh Gourlay put on number 2 for his team. The Vale now had some of the play, and kept the Cambuslang backs busy. Through good play by James Gourlay the Cambuslang forwards transferred play, and McCallum had to hold two warm ones from Brown, but five minutes later he was beaten by Plenderleith…Low had the credit of a fourth goal…Plenderleith, with a fine low shot, added a fifth goal for Cambuslang…Half-time: Cambuslang, five; Vale, nothing. The home team restarted the play, and Plenderleith, running up the centre, put on number six. Cambuslang still kept the visitors within their bounds, and Plenderleith had another to his credit, being the seventh goal for the home team. Towards the finish the strangers improved in their play, and through the instrumentality of their left wing two points were put past Ross. Just on call of time James Gourlay notched the eighth goal for Cambuslang, and the game ended in a win for Cambuslang by eight goals to two." It wouldn't get any better than this as the 8-2 victory would prove to be their record SFL win. The Cambuslang team taking the field in their first ever SFL match was: Ross; Smith, Collins; Russell, Jackson, Buchanan; Low, Brown, Plenderleith, Hugh Gourlay, and James Gourlay.

The following week a crowd of 4,000 watched the first-ever hat-trick in the SFL. This was scored at Whitefield Park on the 23rd August 1890 but unfortunately it wasn't a Cambuslang player that got the goals. Instead, John McPherson scored four goals for

Rangers in a 6-2 win. Cambuslang then lost on the road, 5-2 away at Celtic before winning their next three games. This included a 4-0 win over Cowlairs of Glasgow. Their opponents had much of the early play forcing a succession of corners but they failed to make anything of them. They were made to pay when Low forced the ball home to give the home side the lead. Bob Brown then added a second and Hugh Gourlay, according to *The Glasgow Herald* "lowered the colours of Cowlairs for the third time." In the second half Cowlairs again started strongly, but as in the first period could not take their chances and it was Cambuslang who got the only goal of the half to win 4-0. This result saw Cambuslang sitting in third place in the table, behind the two early pacesetters Dumbarton and Rangers.

Dumbarton were their next opponents but the gulf in class was exposed, even though Dumbarton were missing two regulars. Dumbarton opened the scoring on fifteen minutes following a header from a corner. Ross, in goal, thought he had scooped the ball out but the referee decided it had crossed the line. Dumbarton scored two more in the first half, the third goal being a penalty kick following a foul by Buchanan. Cambuslang, despite being three down at the break, put on a spirited display in the second half before they conceded a fourth in the 70th minute, somewhat against the run of play. A fifth followed soon after with the final score at Boghead 5-0 to Dumbarton, who would go on to be the eventual joint champions with Rangers.

Towards the end of the season, in early March 1891, Cambuslang entertained Celtic at Whitefield Park hoping for revenge for their earlier defeat. Good work by Gourlay and Brown set up James Low for a tap-in. According to *The Scotsman* "the excitement was renewed when another goal was added to the villagers' score" and half-time found Cambuslang leading by two goals to none. In the second half Celtic played much better and pulled a goal back but Cambuslang were not to be denied and restored their two goal lead. End to end action ensued but there was no further scoring and Cambuslang beat Celtic 3-1. One of the scorers, James Low, was capped by Scotland later in the month. He played on the 28th March 1891 against Ireland and scored the opening goal after six minutes in a 2-1 win.

Cambuslang's last game of the League season was played on the 2nd May when they recorded a 2-0 win over Hearts, Bob Brown scoring both goals. The result confirmed Cambuslang as finishing in a very respectable fourth place in the first season of the League. Only Dumbarton and Rangers, as the joint champions, and Celtic, finished above them. Cambuslang reached the Third Round of the Scottish Cup, where they were knocked out by fellow League side St Mirren. They fared better in the Glasgow Cup, where they reached the Semi-final again, this time beaten 4-3 by Third Lanark.

The 1891-92 season was Cambuslang's second and last League season. Cowlairs dropped out but Renton returned and two new clubs joined – Clyde and Leith Athletic – to make a 12 team division. On the 15th August 1891 they kicked off the new season with a home fixture against joint champions Dumbarton. *The Scotsman* reported that "unfortunately the villagers were not at their strongest, Collins, among other changes, having departed to Everton." After 27 minutes Dumbarton took the lead and added a second before half-time. "In the second half, the hardest of lines were experienced by Cambuslang, as time after time they sent in shots...Despite repeated endeavours of the villagers' front rank, the Dumbarton defence could not be broken and the Dumbarton retired with a victory of two goals to nothing to their credit."

The Collins referred to as moving to Everton is James Collins. The paper alluded to the club not being at their strongest and others changes. Only six players started the opening game of the new season who had played the equivalent fixture 12 months previously – goalkeeper Sydney Ross, centre-back Billy Smith and forwards John Buchanan, James Low, Bob Brown and Hugh Gourlay. Perhaps this goes some way to explain the poor season that followed. Having finished fourth in the inaugural competition they won only two games (both against bottom club Vale of Leven) and lost 14 and were only kept off the bottom by Vale who went the entire season without winning a League game.

The first of those two wins came in their second fixture, a 1-0 away win against Vale of Leven. Cambuslang scored early through James Ramsay, and despite chances at both ends there was no addition to the scoreline, Cambuslang securing a narrow victory. Cambuslang only picked up three more points, from draws, before they hosted Vale of Leven in the return fixture at the end of November 1891. They won this game 1-0 as well, thanks to a goal in the 65th minute by John Buchanan.

The club then went the remaining twelve games without a win including seven consecutive losses between December 1891 and March 1892 which was finally ended with a 1-1 draw with Third Lanark. Included in that sequence were two heavy home defeats, 4-0 to Celtic and 6-0 against Rangers. The defeat against Rangers on the 27th February 1892 was their biggest SFL defeat. *The Glasgow Herald*, covering the game reported that "the villagers for a time gave Haddow [in the Rangers goal] and his colleagues a hard time of it, in fact they had hard lines in not notching a point." However Rangers steadied themselves and put on two goals before the break. On resuming the visitors added a third and added goals at regular intervals to run out 6-0 winners.

Cambuslang managed to get two draws in their last four games, their last League point coming on the 30th April 1892 in a 1-1 draw with Renton at Whitefield Park, Muir scoring their last ever League goal. They ended their League career on Thursday 5th May 1892 when they lost 3-0 away against Leith Athletic.

At the SFL Annual General Meeting on the 3rd June 1892, it was voted 12 to 4 that the number of competing clubs would reduce from 12 to 10 for the next season. The bottom three clubs had to retire as per the rule and re-apply and these were St Mirren, Cambuslang and Vale of Leven. These three clubs faced opposition from four new applicants: Kilmarnock, Cowlairs, Northern and St Bernard's. None of the aspiring clubs received a single vote and nor did Vale of Leven after a particularly disastrous season. The one place available essentially came down to a straight choice between St Mirren and Cambuslang and the Paisley club prevailed by 11 votes to 7 and so after just two seasons Cambuslang dropped out of the Scottish Football League. The loss of their League status saw a number of players leave, with a number following the lead of James Collins by going to play in England. One of these was goalkeeper Sydney Ross, who along with left back Bernard Coyle, signed for Liverpool.

Cambuslang joined the rival Scottish Football Alliance where they played the 1892-93 season, although they had another disastrous season, finishing bottom, winning only three out of eighteen matches. They also performed poorly in the Scottish Cup, equalling their record Cup loss sustained in the Final against Renton when they lost 6-1 away in Larkhall, against Royal Albert, in November 1892 in a First Round tie. They conceded within the first five minutes and although Cambuslang then pressed, the home team on the counter scored a second. Their opponents added two more before the interval. The second half was more evenly contested, both sides scoring, although just on the call of time Albert scored a sixth. This was Cambuslang's last appearance in the Scottish Cup.

At the end of the season Cambuslang did not seek election and were not invited to membership of the new Second Division. The Alliance, widely regarded as the principal non-League competition had wanted its members to form the new division but the Scottish Football League decided to select and invite clubs. In the event, six Alliance clubs were invited but Cambuslang weren't one of them.

They played on in the Scottish Alliance and came second behind Royal Albert in the 1893-94 competition. These two clubs, along with three others from the Alliance (Albion Rovers, Wishaw Thistle and Airdrieonians) applied for SFL membership and election to the Second Division at the AGM on the 1st June 1894. However, Cambuslang couldn't get a seconder and didn't take part in the actual voting.

The Alliance disbanded in 1897 and Cambuslang were wound up soon after. They had continued to play on in the Glasgow Cup but at the end of 1897 they informed the Glasgow FA of their financial difficulties. At a meeting of the Glasgow Association on the 19th October, where they were making the draw for the Semi-final of the Glasgow Cup, the Committee agreed unanimously to grant Cambuslang a donation of £25 to assist them in their financial difficulty. They did so, acknowledging they were the first club to have their name inscribed in the Glasgow Cup. The club were in debt to the tune of £100 and the club was wound up before the end of the year.

Whitefield Park is now used for lawn bowling and the club carries the name of the old ground. Cambuslang's history as a Scottish Football League club was all too brief. But should you ever need to come up with a list of all of the founding clubs of the Scottish Football League, remembering Cambuslang could make all the difference.

SEASON	LEAGUE	P	W	D	L	F	A	P	POS
1890-91	SCOT	18	8	4	6	47	42	20	4/10
1891-92	SCOT	22	2	6	14	22	53	10	11/12

Clackmannan

Formed: 1885
Colours: Blue and white hooped shirts, white shorts
Ground: Chapelhill Park
Entered League: 1921. Founder member of the reformed Second Division. 1923. Founder members of the Third Division
Number of League Seasons: 4
Honours: None
Highest League Finish: 20th in Division Two
Left League: 1922. League reconstruction. 1926. Division Three abandoned. Disbanded 1931

Clackmannanshire is one of the smallest municipal area in Scotland at 60 square miles and the smallest mainland council by population size at 50,000. Senior football in the county is associated with Alloa Athletic but the town that gives the county its name has also featured in the Scottish Football League, competing in four seasons in the 1920s, including three of those in the ill-fated Third Division that ran between 1923 and 1926. Clackmannan was the principal town of Clackmannanshire, the smallest county in Scotland, until the second half of the 18th century when it was overshadowed by the growing manufacturing community of Alloa. It sits on the north shore of the Firth of Forth at the north-eastern corner of Scotland's central belt.

Clackmannan Football Club was formed in 1885, initially playing at Tower Park and Glebe Park, before settling at Chapelhill Park in 1886 which was located to the south of the town. The club played in various league competitions in the years leading up to the Great War, winning a remarkable Midland League game against Dunfermline Athletic 17-2 in 1891. They were Midland League champions in 1897 and later competed in the Central Combination, Eastern League and from 1914-15, the Central League. This competition was suspended for the duration of the First World War in 1915 when Clackmannan appear to have closed down. They resumed membership when the Central League was revived in 1919, now playing alongside many former Scottish Second Division sides.

In 1921 Clackmannan joined the Scottish Football League when the Central League clubs were absorbed into the newly-reformed Second Division, consisting of 20 clubs. This was the first season of automatic promotion and relegation and with the First Division having 22 teams the SFL wanted to even up the divisions with 20 teams in each. It was decided at the outset that three teams would be relegated from the First Division but would only be placed by the Second Division champions. Additionally, the bottom two clubs in the Second Division would retire from the League. Unfortunately, Clackmannan finished 20th and bottom, and along with Dundee Hibernian, lost their League place at the end of the season.

On the 20th August 1921 Clackmannan played their first ever SFL game at St Johnstone and came away with a 3-1 win. The report from *The Scotsman* said that "bad luck had a great deal to do with St Johnstone's defeat in their opening match of the season against Clackmannan at Perth. A goal down early in the game, they played very poor football throughout the first half, but after the resumption improved. Time and again, with the visitors' goalkeeper beaten, the ball was scraped clear by the Clackmannan defence, and then to crown all, a breakaway gave the visitors a second, and again a third point. Almost on time St Johnstone notched their only point." Gettins, at inside left, opened the scoring on 15 minutes with a low shot. Ferguson and Bulloch scored the counter-attacking goals.

The first SFL match at Chapelhill Park was played a week later, on the 27th August 1921, with Clackmannan being beaten 2–1 by local rivals Alloa Athletic in front of 4,000 spectators. This gate remained the club's highest recorded home attendance during their time in the League.

This defeat started a run of ten games without a win which lasted until the 5th November. During this time they suffered a heavy 7-1 defeat away at Dundee Hibernian, which left them bottom of the 20 club division. They could count themselves unlucky to be so heavily beaten. For the majority of the game they were without the services of Forsyth, their right half, who sustained a knee injury, and they played practically the whole game with ten men. Dundee Hibs opened the scoring before Ferguson equalised, but before the interval Hibs regained the lead. The home team easily had the better of things in the second half and put on five goals. *The Sunday Post* commented that "although decisively beaten, Clackmannan played gamely, and gave the home defence plenty of work."

Clackmannan eventually won again, with a 2-0 victory at home to Dunfermline Athletic on Saturday 5th November, in front of a crowd of 2,500. Hutchison scored in the first half after a fine solo run and a breakaway in the second half saw Bulloch get the second. The result lifted them off the bottom of the table with seven points, leapfrogging St Johnstone on six, and level with their vanquished opponents and also Lochgelly United.

A second away win of the season the following week at Ochilview against Stenhousemuir, by 2-1, with first half goals from Cowan and Bennett (from a spot kick), briefly hinted at better fortunes as they moved out of the bottom two. However, five losses out of the next six fixtures saw them drop back to the bottom of the table on 13 points, albeit level on points with Forfar and Lochgelly and only one point behind King's Park and St Johnstone.

A New Year's Eve victory over Forfar Athletic, courtesy of an own goal and a strike from Gettins, saw the club go up two places into 18th as they went into 1922. Despite a 3-1 win over East Stirlingshire on the 3rd, they lost the other four games played in the month of January and were then dumped out of the Scottish Cup in the First Round by Inverness Citadel, 5-3 at Chapelhill Park (a game in which they were losing 5-1 at one point). This was followed by a 4-0 defeat away at fellow strugglers Lochgelly and although they continued to pick up a few points, by the end of March they were again at the foot of the Second Division table.

The month of April kicked off with a heavy defeat on the 1st. This was no April Fool as they went down to their highest scoring loss, 8-1 away at promotion chasing Armadale at Volunteer Park. *The Scotsman* reported that "Armadale scored a great win over Clackmannan defeating the 'wee county' team by eight goals to one. The first half was a tame affair, though Clackmannan gave occasional glimpses of clever football. In this period Chalmers scored for Armadale and Bain for Clackmannan. On changing ends Armadale were masters of the situation, and goals came to them rather easily. Fleming had the 'hat-trick', Campbell two goals, the other marksmen being Hopewell and Croal."

In their next game, played in midweek, they picked up a fortuitous 3-2 victory over Stenhousemuir, who were forced to play much of the game with ten men due to their outside left, David Maitland, breaking his right leg. A 2-2 draw at home to Broxburn United on the Saturday left them three points off Dundee Hibs at the bottom, but more importantly six adrift of King's Park in the safety spot of 18th place, with only three games to play. They had led the game despite going down to ten men but the visitors equalised before the close. A 2-0 defeat at Bo'ness on Saturday 15th April 1922 condemned them, as they conceded two goals in the first five minutes. They finished the season with two draws to end on 26 points, two behind Dundee Hibs and five behind Lochgelly United.

At the League's AGM on the 16th May 1922, a proposal by Airdrieonians to maintain the 22-20 divisions which would have saved the club from dropping out of the League altogether failed, and the decision to lose two members to even up the numbers in the two divisions was implemented. Clackmannan, along with Dundee Hibernians, were denied the chance to apply for re-election.

Clackmannan played the 1922-23 season in the Eastern League and were knocked out of the Scottish Cup by Hibernians. 4-0, in the First Round. The club were confident that a strong campaign at the end of the season would see them elected back into the Scottish Second Division. As it was, it was Dundee Hibs that were welcomed back to the fold as Clackmannan could not muster sufficient votes. In the ballot held on the 17 May 1923 Arbroath were re-elected on the first ballot and Clackmannan, along with three other clubs were eliminated. Dundee Hibs replaced East Stirlingshire in the SFL after a second ballot. The club received a second chance though when it was decided to form a Third Division with clubs drawn primarily from the Western League with Clackmannan, Brechin City and Montrose from the Eastern League, and the rejected East Stirlingshire, making up the numbers.

Their experience of one season of League football counted for nothing as they finished a lowly 12th place in the new 16 team division. Back in the League, they lost their opening game of the 1923-24 season 3-1 at home to Nithsdale Wanderers on 18th August 1923. The following week they picked up their first points playing at Meadow Park, Dumbarton, against Harp. Clackmannan won by the odd goal in five. Reid and Brookes scored for the home team in the first half whilst in the second Roy had a couple and Cameron the other. They suffered a couple of heavy defeats towards the end of the year, losing 5-0 away at East Stirlingshire and 6-1 at Mid-Annandale and by the turn the year they were a mid-table eighth place. Form continued to be inconsistent into 1924 and towards the end they suffered a heavy 5-0 loss away at Queen of the South and eventually finished 12th.

The 1924-25 season saw a modest improvement as this time they finished two places higher in tenth. Clackmannan won their opening game, a 1-0 home win over Beith, but they followed this up with only one point from their next five games, so that by the end of September they had only accumulated three points from their first six fixtures. Back to back wins over Galston and Royal Albert hinted at an improvement in fortunes but they then came down to earth with a bump with a 6-0 loss away at Third Division leaders Vale of Leven on the 1st November 1924. Clackmannan got revenge in the New Year reverse fixture, winning 3-0, a result that lifted them up to eighth place. This win kicked off a run of three successive victories and a six game unbeaten run that temporarily lifted them up as high as sixth by the end of February 1925. However, they only won one of their remaining fixtures to eventually finish in tenth place. In November 1924 Chapelhill Park was closed by the authorities following crowd trouble at a Scottish Qualifying Cup match between Clackmannan and Peebles Rovers. As punishment their ground was temporarily closed by the authorities and their next League game, at home to Brechin City on the 15th November was played at Alloa's Recreation Ground.

The following season was both their worst and their last as an SFL club. They effectively finished 15th out of 16 but a number of games were not played. In a sign of things to come on the pitch they lost their opening game of the 1925-26 season 7-1 away at Royal Albert. This would be the first of five occasions in which they would concede five or more goals away from home. In the September they lost 5-0 away at Forfar Athletic but they also lost heavily at home as well, losing 7-1 at Chapelhill Park to Vale of Leven on the 24th October 1925. Across the season they conceded an average of three goals per game. The highlight of the season was a record 7-3 win on the 14th November 1925 against Beith. *The Sunday Post*, under the headline "Beith Badly Beaten", reported that "Beith proved an easy hurdle for Clackmannan at Chapelhill Park, but it was not due to any excessive degree of brilliancy that such a convincing victory was recorded. Davidson opened the scoring for Clackmannan within a minute of the game by catching up a rebound off Gillespie and netting. Several minutes later Forsyth burst away and scored, while just on half-time Ingram beat Gillespie with a long range effort. Play in the second half was keener, and following two goals scored by Walls and Higgins, Beith redoubled their efforts, and Macdonald had to admit defeat to Walters (2) and Walker. Towards the close Forsyth secured the hat trick. For the winners, Macdonald, Fyfe and Ingram were best." Overall though, Clackmannan only gathered 18 points from 25 of the scheduled 30 games, and were officially placed 15th out of 16, but they only avoided being bottom because Galston had completed just 15 games (gaining 12 points). The last ever SFL game at Chapelhill Park was at home to Leith Athletic on Saturday 24th April 1926 and honours were even in a thrilling 3-3 draw.

Clackmannan left the Scottish Football League as the Third Division collapsed but did not join the Scottish Alliance. They continued to play in the Scottish Cup, although with little success. They were beaten heavily by Third Lanark at Cathkin Park 10-0 in January 1928; Albion Rovers beat them 8-1 at home in 1929; and Ayr United thrashed them 11-2 in 1931. The club closed down for good shortly after this. After the Second World War their former ground became housing development and a road through the estate is called Chapelhill, located south of the current Clackmannan primary school.

SEASON	LEAGUE	P	W	D	L	F	A	P	POS
1921-22	SCOT-2	38	10	7	21	41	75	27	20/20
1923-24	SCOT-3	30	10	7	13	37	54	27	12/16
1924-25	SCOT-3	30	10	6	14	35	48	26	10/16
1925-26	SCOT-3	25	5	8	12	42	74	18	15/16

Clydebank I (1914–1931)

Formed: 1914
Colours: White shirts with red horizontal band in the centre and white shorts
Ground: Clydeholm
Entered League: 1914. Elected to Second Division
Number of League Seasons: 15
Highest League Finish: 5th in Division One
Honours: None
Left League: 1931. Resigned. Disbanded July 1931

Two separate entities have existed as Clydebank FC. Between 1914 and 1931 the original team from Clydebank participated in the Scottish Football League, playing matches at Clydeholm Park. At the time of their entry shipbuilding was booming and economics no doubt played a part in their elevation. And it did so again in their demise. The harsh realities of the depression in the late 1920s meant the club suffered from financial difficulties and they dropped out of the League in 1931.

Clydebank is a town in West Dunbartonshire, situated, as the name suggests on the north bank of the River Clyde. Clydebank borders Dumbarton and the villages of Old Kilpatrick and Bowling to the west, as well as the town of Milngavie in East Dunbartonshire, and the Yoker and Drumchapel districts of Glasgow. The burgeoning growth of Glasgow resulted in additional shipping quays and boatyards being built in Clydebank with a railway line constructed in 1882 to connect them. In the 1880s the Singer Manufacturing Company built a large factory producing sewing machines in Kilbowie and it was around this time that the first Clydebank FC was formed. This club played their fixtures at Hamilton Park and closed down in 1895. Another club was formed in 1899 and went out of business in 1902. This team entered the Scottish Cup twice in 1901 and 1902 but scratched from the First Round on both occasions.

The first club to represent the town in the Scottish Football League was formed in 1914 and was immediately elected to the League. This was quite a remarkable feat, gaining admittance to the League without kicking a ball. Most other clubs built up a reputation in non-League competitions and/or the Scottish Cup. The club participated in the sole division of the League during the War due to their geographical location but on the resumption found themselves relegated to the Second Division. During their time in the League, they were runners-up in the Second Division twice, in 1922-23 and 1924-25. They yo-yoed between the First and Second division with five consecutive seasons of relegation and promotion. After suffering from financial difficulties, they resigned from the League and disbanded in 1931. Throughout their existence, they played at Clydeholm Park, which continued to exist after their demise as a venue for greyhound racing up to the 1960s.

On Friday 5th June 1914 at the AGM of the Scottish League, a proposal by Celtic and Third Lanark to increase the number of clubs in the Second Division from 12 to 14 was carried. Johnstone and Vale of Leven were eventually re-elected and Clydebank, along with Lochgelly United, were admitted to the Second Division as the new clubs. Clydebank had only been formed in the February and were overwhelmingly elected despite their lack of competitive football or a track record. They topped the first ballot: Clydebank 26; Vale of Leven 25; Bathgate 17; Johnstone 17; Lochgelly United 17; East Fife 13; Forfar Athletic 2. The first vote eliminated the bottom two teams (East Fife and Forfar) and they were elected to the League on the second ballot, with the same number of votes, although Vale topped this second round of voting with 29. The key factor behind the club's election was economic, as the shipyards of Clydebank were booming due to the threat of war.

Under the stewardship of Alex Maley, the ex-Clyde manager, and the younger brother of Celtic managerial legend Willie Maley, they played their first League fixture on the 15th August 1914, a 3-1 victory over East Stirlingshire. The first ever Clydebank line-up was: McKenna; Clark, Ireland; Neish, Rennie, Thomson; Norton, Reid, Smart, Howie and Goldie. This win was the first of four consecutive victories and by the end of September only they and Cowdenbeath were unbeaten in the division.

They suffered their first defeat on the 3rd October away at Abercorn 4-2, but bounced back with a 5-1 win over Johnstone that took them joint top. Under the headline "Clydebank's Nap Hand", the *Daily Record* reported that "Johnstone started in aggressive fashion, but Clydebank put up a gallant defence....McKenna's save of a stinging shot was superb...[and]...Ireland stood sentinel-like over the home goal....When twenty-five minutes had been played, Reid opened the scoring from a fine pass from Goldie, and twelve minutes later O'Kane emulated his comrade by netting a pass by Norton. Then Irvine [of Johnstone] was brought down inside the penalty area, and he himself scored from the accruing kick. At half-time Clydebank led by 2 goals to 1. With the resumption Clydebank pressed severely, and within three minutes O'Kane forced [a] point...O'Kane added a fourth goal for Clydebank from long range...A scramble in the Johnstone goal followed, and in the general mix up the ball found its way into the net. Clydebank were superior in all departments, the forwards showing their best early season form."

At the end of October 1914 they secured a thumping 6-1 revenge win over Abercorn in which, according to the *Daily Record*, "there was an appalling number of serious accidents...Heggie (Abercorn) was lamed ten minutes after the start and was useless afterwards; Reid (Clydebank) was off the field almost an hour with a leg injury; while to crown all, Ireland, the home left-back had a leg broken." The injuries took their toll as they lost their next two matches to slip to third but in early December they scored nine, as they beat Leith Athletic 9-2. The wind was a factor and the Bankies exploited this to the full in the first half netting seven times. The Yoker men beat Cowdenbeath 1-0 in the New Year's Day fixture to start 1915 in second place, just three points behind their beaten foe. In mid-January they beat bottom club Arthurlie 6-0 but the gap to Cowdenbeath was now five points with only six games to go. A 1-0 defeat away at Johnstone effectively ruined any chance of winning the Championship flag, especially with Cowdenbeath winning by the same score away at Dunfermline. Leith's win at Arthurlie saw them go second. A 4-1 loss at St Bernard's in the run-in saw this Edinburgh club also leapfrog them. The following week they lost 2-1 at leaders Cowdenbeath, *The Edinburgh Evening News* reporting that "Clydebank had themselves to blame for their defeat at Cowdenbeath. A poor defence considerably weakened the whole team, and though the Fife forwards were not of the same class as those of the Glasgow eleven, they prevailed over the visiting backs, who were anything but steady." Clydebank eventually finished in fifth place – not bad for their first season.

Great Britain had declared war on Germany on the 4th August 1914, barely a fortnight before Clydebank made their debut in the Scottish League. At the end of the season although the First Division continued the Second Division was disbanded and Clydebank joined the Western League, which they won in the 1916-17 season. At a special meeting of the Scottish Football League held on the 6th June 1917 three clubs from the north and east of the country, Aberdeen, Dundee and Raith Rovers, were forced to stand down for the duration of the war due to travel restrictions. Clydebank were then invited to join the First Division to even up the numbers to make an 18 team division. No doubt the economic boost the war had given to Clydebank's shipyards and factories was a contributory factor to them being chosen.

Clydebank started only their second season in the League as a First Division club on the 18th August 1917. They didn't made a very auspicious start, losing 4-0 at home to Clyde, although the size of the crowd must have provided some sort of consolation. *The Sunday Post* reported that "12,000 onlookers were at Clydeholm to see Clydebank duly baptised into the First Division by Clyde...Clydebank fielded only five of last year's lot, the newcomers being Fullarton (Celtic) at right back, Forrest (Fulham) centre half, and Travers (Dumbarton) left half. Jarvis (Celtic) filled the right wing berth, O'Kane (Celtic) was at centre, and Croot (Rangers) was at outside left. For thirty minutes Clydebank filled the bill, and then Clyde applied the screw. The forwards bore down on McTurk in purposeful fashion, and under the pressure a home defender handled within the area and McGowan's penalty drive passed into the net over McTurk's head. Clydebank's defence shook after this...and Clyde's forwards, coming in a body...finished a nice movement with a shot which beat McTurk all ends up for a second counter. Within ten minutes of the resumption Shimmon added further to the Bankies' discomfiture with a third goal after the ball had twice rebounded from the cross bar, and within five minutes the same player completed the quartet. Till the finish Clyde were masters of the situation. Clydebank failed to finish. The halves were not good enough to hold a clever Clyde quintette." The Clydebank team was: McTurk; Fullarton, Ferguson; Neish, Forrest, Travers; Jarvis, Shortt, O'Kane, Martin and Croot. Clydebank picked up their first point in a 1-1 draw at home to Falkirk on the 1st September and their first win came a week later when they won 1-0 at Easter Road against Hibs. They beat neighbours Dumbarton 3-2 away and another away win, this time 1-0 at bottom side Third Lanark, saw them go into ninth place, where they eventually finished up.

The following season Clydebank finished a place lower in tenth and at the end of this season the three northern clubs who had dropped out during the war - Aberdeen, Dundee and Raith Rovers – returned to the League. Clydebank had their League place confirmed and Albion Rovers were elected to make a new 22 team First Division. Controversially, the League decided not to re-instate the Second Division.

The new 1919-20 season was Clydebank's most successful in terms of a highest placed finish. Despite a poor start in which they lost four out of their first five matches they eventually finished as high as fifth place. Crucial to their success was the goal-scoring of Joe Anderson. He originally played for Vale of Leven and then Airdrieonians and joined for the new season. Playing at centre-forward he scored 31 League goals before leaving in March 1920 to join Burnley. He spent four years at Burnley, then one of the top sides in English Football League. They finished as English League runners-up in the 1919-20 season, and thanks to Anderson's goal were champions for 1920-21. Anderson top scored with 25 League goals (31 in total for the season from 44 appearances).

On the 4th October Anderson scored a second half hat trick in a 5-2 win over new side Albion Rovers. The men from Coatbridge twice led before Anderson's intervention. The following month Anderson scored eight goals in four games, two in each match during November. In January 1920 he did even better, scoring in six consecutive matches. On the 21st February he scored two in a 5-1 win over Motherwell, who would finish in third, and on the 6th March he scored a hat-trick including two spot-kicks against Falkirk. This took his recent tally to 14 goals in ten games. But he didn't play again as his goal-scoring prowess had attracted interest from England.

A 1-0 loss at home to Hearts at the end of March left Clydebank in seventh place with seven games to play. The title race was between Rangers (who won), Celtic and Motherwell but the Bankies were only three points behind fourth placed Dundee. The club won their first three games in April but lost 1-0 at Dundee who were above them and eventually finished in fifth place. The team that played most of the 1919-20 season and secured their highest placed league finish was: Morton; Stevenson, Ferguson, Walker, Gilhooly; Neish, McMillan, Fulton; Anderson, Paton and Goldie. Whilst Anderson's goals were key to the successful season significant contributions also came from Michael Gilhooley, the centre half, who left at the end of the season to join Hull City, and who was eventually capped by Scotland in 1922; and also from Malcolm Goldie, the outside left, who, although born in Dumbarton, went on to acquire US citizenship and was capped by his adoptive country in 1925.

Although only Anderson and Gilhooly were missing from line-up that started the 1920-21 season against Clyde, the club went down 4-0, which was the start of a poor campaign. They clearly missed Anderson's goals but the problem was more the defence where they conceded 32 more goals across the course of the season. They got their first point in a 1-1 home draw with Partick Thistle and their first win at the beginning of September, 1-0 against Clyde. They didn't win again until mid-October when they beat Third Lanark 3-0 and at the end of the month they beat Albion Rovers 4-1, their best win of the season, with Goldie scoring two. The Bankies drew all four games in the month of December but then failed to win in both January and February 1921, going down 5-1 at Ayr as part of that sequence. They eventually won for the first time in 1921 on the 12th March, in a 3-1 win over Morton, thanks to two goals from Michael McLavin. On the 2nd April they beat Queen's Park 2-0 but they then only gained one more point from their last five games (a 1-1 draw at Celtic) to finish in 20th position in the 22 team League.

JB Prentice took over the managerial reins for the 1921-22 season as Alex Maley had left to take over at Hibernian. For this season the Second Division was finally re-formed and automatic promotion and relegation was introduced for the first time. For this season three teams would be relegated as part of a reorganisation, creating two divisions of 20 teams. This meant that a repeat of their performance would see the club drop out of the First Division.

On the 16th August 1921 the Bankies kicked off the new season away against Partick Thistle at Firhill, going down 1-0. There was not much between the teams in the first half. After the interval Thistle took the game in hand and for the remainder of the game they kept up a steady attack and edged a close game. Disaster followed with a 7-1 thumping by champions Rangers in their opening home game. A crowd of 22,000 at Clydeholm saw Henderson score a hat-trick. Michael McLavin scored Clydebank's goal, the third goal of the game. They got their first League point in their third game, a 0-0 draw with Falkirk in midweek, Johnny Morton in goal pulling off a string of marvellous saves for his side. On the 3rd September they got their first win, beating Ayr United 2-0. Remarkably this was only the second game in the first eight matches where they actually scored a goal. Martin and David Chalmers were the goalscorers. They then went three games without a goal and by the end of the month they were second bottom with just four points, with only winless Queen's Park behind them with a solitary point. They eventually scored again in a 1-1 home draw with Aberdeen, where they were again indebted to the brilliance of Morton in goal.

Clydebank only picked up one more point from their next eight games before eventually recording their second win of the season in mid-November, a 3-2 away win at Airdrieonians, that lifted them off the bottom. *The Scotsman* reported that "the Airdrieonians on their own ground were caught on the hop and staggered by the loss of two points to Clydebank. The win of the Clydebank team was all the more meritorious because of the fact that owing to the indisposition of Bradford they found themselves without a regular goalkeeper, whose place was filled by Stevenson, their right back. Early in the game the Airdrie team looked like winning with ease, judging by the number of fine balls crossed by Ellis, off one of which Gallacher scored the first goal. Chalmers equalised, and then Reid gave the home team the lead again, when Stevenson missed punting out an easy shot. The second half began in favour of Clydebank, and Chalmers and King scored for them. The latter's shot was from thirty yards out, and caught O'Hagan napping. From that point to the end the Airdrieonians besieged The Clydebank goal but the visitors put up an impregnable defence." A week earlier, Johnny Scraggs had made his debut at centre-half. Signed from Glentoran he would go on to be a mainstay of the club's defence for the next five years and was the club's designated penalty-taker.

On the 17th December Clydebank lost 6-0 at Celtic, who would wrestle the league title from Rangers by a point. They successfully held out for 22 minutes against the championship contenders but once the deadlock was broken the floodgates opened and their forwards offered little in return. The result left them bottom with ten points, three points from safety. They won their first game of 1922, a well merited 2-0 win over Motherwell, and drew their following game but then lost eight in a row including a

6-1 away defeat at Rangers in midweek. The Bankies were now five points adrift at the bottom and eight points from safety. On Saturday the 4th March a 3-1 defeat at Hamilton saw them now 12 points from safety with nine to play. A 2-0 win over Airdrieonians merely delayed the inevitable and on the 25th March a 3-0 loss at Morton relegated the club.

On the 8th April they beat St Mirren 3-2, boosted by the return of Scraggs from injury after a month's lay off following injury at Clyde. They trailed 2-0 to the visitors before Chalmers reduced the arrears scoring with a header from a corner kick by Goldie. This seemed to boost the home team and three minutes after the resumption McLavin, accepting a pass from Goldie and equalised. The home team continued to dominate play and McLavin benefitted from a deflected ball to steer home to take the points. This was their last win of the campaign and they only picked up one further point, in a drab 0-0 draw with fellow strugglers Queen's Park. They ended the season with a 6-0 thumping by Hibs at Easter Road. The Bankies finished eight points adrift at the bottom and twelve points from safety and were relegated along with Queen's Park and Dumbarton. They conceded 103 goals, over twenty more than the next worst club and won only six League games all season.

Former Celtic, Newcastle United and Scotland player James 'Dun' Hay was appointed manager in April 1922. One player leaving though was outside-left Malcolm Goldie. After the club was relegated he joined the exodus to the nascent US Soccer League, joining Bethlehem Steel and playing nearly 200 games for them over the next eight years, scoring over 50 goals. Goldie took US citizenship and earned one cap with the US national team in a 6-1 win over Canada in 1925.

The three relegated clubs finished in the top four the following season, with St Johnstone completing the quartet. The divisional flag was won by Queen's Park who finished five points ahead of Clydebank, who themselves were two ahead of St Johnstone. Clydebank thus returned to the First Division at the first time of asking. The club experienced mixed fortunes at the start of the new season, winning two, drawing two and losing two of their opening six games to sit in eighth place, but it was all very tight as only two points separated them and joint leaders Dunfermline Athletic and Broxburn United. One of those games, a 2-1 defeat at Vale of Leven on the 23rd August, would have severe consequences at the end of the season for the club, when the eligibility of one of their players was called into question.

In a sign of better things to come they recorded a 4-1 win over Stenhousemuir, their first home victory, and this was followed by further wins against East Stirlingshire and Lochgelly. From the beginning of November to the end of 1922 they went eleven games unbeaten. The run was eventually ended by a 1-0 defeat at Bathgate on the 6th January 1923, but a fortnight later they took their revenge in the reverse fixture, with a 5-0 win, scoring three second half goals in seven minutes, Chalmers scoring a brace. The result placed them second, three points behind leaders Queen's Park and one ahead of St Johnstone in third and two ahead of Dumbarton in fourth place.

This win over Bathgate was the start of a run of five wins in six games (the other match drawn) and included a 4-0 win over Bo'ness. *The Scotsman* reported that "the outstanding feature of the encounter between Clydebank and Bo'ness at Clydeholm was the successful debut made by Smith, late of Dunfermline Athletic, and loaned to Clydebank to fill the centre forward berth. He scored twice in the opening five minutes...[and]...in the early stages of the second portion he completed the "hat trick" and was also the prime mover in the movement which enabled Chalmers to secure Clydebank's fourth goal."

This victory was followed by two consecutive 5-0 wins in early April, away at Lochgelly United and at home to East Stirlingshire, in which Smith, their on loan striker scored another hat trick. A 1-0 loss away at St Johnstone on the 14th April 1923, in front of 12,000, killed off any chance of winning the divisional championship from Queen's Park, but crucially it also took promotion matters out of their own hands. If St Johnstone won away at Forfar and then at home to Broxburn they would accompany Queen's Park to the First Division, whereas Clydebank, leading the Perth team by a solitary point only had only one game left at home to East Fife.

The promotion pendulum then swung back in their favour both on and off the pitch. On Friday 20th April, *The Scotsman* reported that "at a meeting in Glasgow yesterday of the Management Committee of the Scottish Football League...two points and a fine of £20 was imposed on the St Johnstone FC, who committed an irregularity in respect of A S Reid, who was transferred from the Airdrieonians FC after 16th March and played on four occasions after that date...The decision means that Queen's Park win the Scottish Second League championship, as St Johnstone were the only club that could equal the amateurs' present total of 53 points. St Johnstone's prospects of gaining promotion are now very small. By winning their remaining two matches they would aggregate 51 points, while Clydebank, with one match to play, total 50." This penalty appeared to have come out of the blue and the press certainly felt that St Johnstone had been dealt with harshly, especially as it came to light that a League official had known of the transfer and the player had appeared not once, but four times, as the club were not aware of his illegibility. The fine was broken down into £5 per game.

The following day, the Saturday, St Johnstone went 2-0 down at Forfar Athletic and Clydebank were promoted. The Scotsman wrote that "St Johnstone fell before Forfar Athletic, and in consequence Clydebank will accompany Queen's Park into the First Division next season....The loss of two League points by St Johnstone for a professional irregularity made their chance of promotion to the First Division almost hopeless, but their defeat by 2 goals to 0 by Forfar Athletic made it certain that not yet will they go up." Commenting on the situation, the *Glasgow Herald* said "it is unfortunate that a competition so completely satisfying was marred in its closing stages by the penalty inflicted upon St Johnstone by the Management Committee of the League, who on Friday...gave the Perth club a fine and the deduction of two points that practically deprived the club of its reasonable chances of promotion. Assuming that St Johnstone were guilty of a technical infringement of an ambiguous rule, the punishment meted out was altogether harsh and unreasonable, and a censure or at the most the monetary penalty would have sufficiently met the case. St Johnstone lost their game on Saturday by 2-0 and finally their chances of promotion, and there is widespread feeling that their defeat was contributed to by the League's action on the eve of the game. Clydebank were not engaged on Saturday and have one game to play, but St Johnstone's defeat and penalty ensures that Clydebank accompany Queen's Park to the Senior Division next season."

This wasn't the end of the matter though. On Friday 27th *The Scotsman* reported that not only were St Johnstone appealing but they were also saying Clydebank were guilty of the same thing. Under the headline "The St Johnstone Decision - Reported Protests against Clydebank" the paper revealed that the club were "appealing to the Scottish League Management Committee against a recent decision regarding an infringement of rules...[and]...intend to supplement that appeal with a protest against Clydebank, alleging an infringement by the latter club. Clydebank, it is held, signed on an ex-Anthony player, who turned senior and played for a prominent Belfast club. The player returned to junior circles in Scotland, after which he was picked up by Clydebank. Should the contentions of the Perth Club be correct the question of which second division club will accompany Queen's Park into higher circles will yet have to be settled."

On the following day, Saturday the 28th, in front of a crowd of 3,000 at Clydeholm, Clydebank beat East Fife 3-2 whereas the men from Perth were held 1-1 at home to Broxburn. Smith scored in the first three minutes and Chalmers got a second on the half-hour mark before East Fife got one back. Smith got his second to restore the two goal lead and the visitors got a second in the last five minutes. Queen's Park finished as champions with 57 points, Clydebank had 52 points and St Johnstone, with their two point deduction, had 48 points. A successful appeal by St Johnstone and a penalty handed out to Clydebank might yet provide a late dramatic twist to the promotion battle.

On Wednesday the 2nd May the Management Committee of the SFL met in Glasgow and considered the St Johnstone protest. St Johnstone alleged that Clydebank had played John Swan on the 23rd August against Vale of Leven before the player had been transferred and registered and that to cover this up, the club had committed a more serious offence of impersonation by playing Swan under the name of James Stafford, another player already registered with Clydebank. The first complaint was held proved and the Management Committee decided that two points be deducted from Clydebank, and that they be fined £25 for playing an unregistered player. For the second offence they were also found guilty. There was no further points deduction but a £100 fine was imposed. The decisions of the Management Committee therefore did not affect the placings and Clydebank still finished ahead of St Johnstone, and were promoted to the First Division.

Some commentators thought Clydebank lucky. *The Sunday Post*, under the headline "The Scandal of Clydebank FC's Punishment" stated that "in our view, Clydebank's punishment is nothing more than a scandal. It is lacking in justice as is the punishment inflicted on St Johnstone. For having covertly played an unregistered player, they have had two points deducted from their total and been fined £25. St Johnstone made no attempt to conceal A S Reid, yet their punishment was the same. And for having pretended that their unregistered player was another player altogether, Clydebank have been let off with a fine of £100. There is no comparison between the offences. St Johnstone took every precaution not to offend. They went the length of consulting the League secretary before they played Reid. What did Clydebank do? They, knowing what they were doing, sought to cover up their tracks by impersonation. And but for the Management Committee's unsatisfactory handling of the case against St Johnstone, Clydebank's offence would not have come to light. A fine of £100 for impersonation in an important League game! It was not enough to play an ineligible man. The ineligible man had to take the identity of one who was eligible. Thus was the primary offence aggravated. Clydebank must be tickled almost to death! The more we consider these cases, the smaller grows our respect for the equitableness of the Management Committee. They have hidden the scales of justice, and roused the gorge of all fair-minded sportsmen." Strong words indeed!

On the 8th May a special general meeting of the SFL was held to hear the appeal of St Johnstone. The meeting was held in private but the following statement was issued to the Press by the League Secretary: "in virtue of Rule 23 the Management Committee, being of the opinion that this transfer secured an unfair advantage to the St Johnstone

Club in the season's competition, refused to sanction the transfer. The Club set to prove that they had the authority of the League to play this man, and alleged that one of their directors had been given that authority by the secretary of the League at an interview on March 22. The secretary denied having granted any such permission, and explained to them that the transfer was contrary to the rules, and they could please themselves whether they played the man or not. The secretary's denial was borne out by the fact that on March 30 a letter was sent to the St Johnstone Club to the effect that the transfer required the approval of the Committee. The meeting, after hearing the whole argument, agree to dismiss the appeal by 31 votes to 5."

Earlier in the day a special meeting of the Management Committee was held to investigate the circumstances under which Clydebank had played John Swan without supplying his name on the official team sheet. *The Scotsman* reported on this hearing, explaining that Clydebank "were under the impression that the player was entitled to play under rules contained in the agreement whereby second division clubs are entitled to play one man in any match without registration, and that their infringement really consisted in omitting to change the name in the team sheet. They further explained that they had only 12 players, and that they had a transfer arranged of the man they had played, but that the papers had not actually come through and his name was printed in their team sheet. It was pointed out that this was verified, and in the whole circumstances the Management Committee decided that the Board of Management of the Clydebank Football Club should be severely censured."

Clydebank duly regained their place in the top flight of Scottish football but were now in a period where they see-sawed between the two divisions in the League. Having been relegated at the end of the 1921-22 season and promoted in 1922-23 they went straight back down again in the 1923-24 season, relegated along with Clyde, having finished bottom, four points adrift at bottom and five from safety. They started with a 1-1 draw away at Patrick on the 16th August 1923, *The Scotsman* reporting that "an exciting game was witnessed at Firhill Park, Glasgow, last night, when Clydebank made an auspicious re-entry into the First League by drawing with Partick Thistle...Clydebank played their captures, Murphy and McGrory (Celtic). The play served up was of a high standard, and Clydebank were full value for their point." Partick took the lead in the first half but Clydebank came back strongly in the second and McGrory missed a great chance to equalise. With just two minutes to go, and the Partick goal under siege, a penalty was awarded for handball, which was converted by Scraggs. Clydebank only scored once in their next five matches, although their goalscorer was a certain Jimmy McGrory, who was referenced as having missed an easy chance in that opener at Partick. Perhaps the most famous player to appear for the club, Jimmy McGrory went on to be a Celtic legend and the Scottish League's all-time record goalscorer, scoring

410 League goals. He spent the 1923–24 season on loan to Clydebank from Celtic, scoring 13 League goals while at Clydeholm.

Clydebank eventually won their first League game of the season in their eleventh match. On the 20th October they hosted Hamilton, *The Scotsman* reporting that "the game had a sensational opening. Clydebank pressed for five minutes, at the close of which Fleming rounded Johnston, and, steadying for a second, kicked the ball into the roof of the net." The Yoker eleven held firm against an immediate response from Hamilton and were unlucky in the second half not to win by more than the single goal margin.

The win took them above Hamilton and the club was further boosted by the return of goalscoring legend Joe Anderson from Burnley the following month. Anderson scored on his return and a goal from David Chalmers gave Clydebank a 2-1 win over Queen's Park. The club went on to record five straight wins across the end of December 1923 and January 1924. This fine run culminated in Clydebank's biggest ever Scottish Cup win, as McGrory scored a hat-trick in an 8-2 win against Blairgowrie on the 26th January. Clydebank opened the scoring after just three minutes through Anderson but were then surprised when Blairgowrie equalised. Two goals from McGrory and a second for Anderson made it 4-1 at the break. Chalmers headed two in quick succession, and an own goal and McGrory's hat-trick made it eight. Their opponents got a late consolation. Arbroath were dispatched 4-0 in the Second Round, with Anderson scoring two but they were knocked out by fellow First Division side Ayr United in the Third Round.

Back in the League they lost 5-1 at home to Third Lanark on the 1st March. The game was over for all intents and purposes when their scored four times in the opening twenty minutes, all scored by McInally. The result left them bottom, two points behind both Hamilton and Queen's Park. Four consecutive defeats followed, including a 6-2 defeat at St Mirren, where Wood, the Saints' centre-forward scored five. At the end of March they secured a 1-1 draw at Queen's Park, with McGrory scoring, but they really needed more. With four games left to play they were three points behind Queen's Park and four from safety.

On the 5th April a 2-0 home defeat against Motherwell left their chances of avoiding relegation as remote. Queen's Park had won so they were now five points from safety with a maximum of six points available. The following Saturday they did their bit, beating Aberdeen 2-1 at Clydeholm with goals from McGrory and a penalty converted by Scraggs. There was no margin for error though and a week later they hosted Dundee. Clydebank totally bossed the game but found the Dundee 'keeper

Fotheringham in inspired form. Try as they might they couldn't get the goal their performance deserved and the game ended in a 0-0 draw. Draws elsewhere for their rivals meant relegation back to the Second Division.

Alec Bennett took over the managerial reins for the new season. He had played for both Celtic and Rangers and had been capped eleven times for Scotland. He had been the manager at Third Lanark, who had been in the relegation battle with Clydebank, and had been released by them. Under his leadership the club bounced back up again, this time as runners up to Dundee United. They struggled initially back in the second tier failing to win any of their three opening games and were joint bottom after a 4-1 loss at Bo'ness. They registered their first win mid-September beating East Stirlingshire 3-2 and scored four goals in successive matches in October with wins over Bathgate and Forfar that lifted them up to fifth. On the 13th December they met leaders Dundee United at Clydeholm and emphatically knocked them off their perch, winning 5-0.

Clydebank ended 1924 in third place behind Dundee United and Clyde, but at the end of January they beat promotion rivals Clyde 1-0, Dave McEachran, a winger signed from Vale of Leven scoring the all-important goal. They subsequently went unbeaten during February to close the gap on Clyde in second to just a point. Fortunes ebbed and flowed and on the last Saturday in March both Dundee United and Clyde lost whereas Clydebank beat St Bernard's 3-2. Chalmers headed an early goal before their opponents levelled. Chalmers restored their lead and a penalty converted by Scraggs following a handball gave them a 3-1 half-time lead. St Bernard's got a goal back and the Yoker men became nervy and flustered but ultimately held on. These results left them two points behind Dundee United but two ahead of Clyde, with four matches left.

The following weekend matches were played on a Friday evening to avoid a clash with a Scotland versus England international being played at Hampden. Clydebank drew 0-0 away at Albion Rovers and Dundee United won. Clyde weren't in action, playing away at Stenhousemuir the following day, but when they did play they lost 2-1. Clyde then played the coming Friday and won to narrow the gap to a point and put the pressure back on Clydebank. The next day the men from Yoker comfortably beat Johnstone 4-1 to re-establish the three point lead. Their visitors gave them an early fright by scoring first after just seven minutes, a lead they still held at half-time. In the second half Anderson equalised within a minute of the restart and then Houston headed home after a cross by McEachran. Abrams made it three and near the end McKendrick ran the length of the field and scored with a drive that deflected in off the post. Dundee United also won to guarantee themselves promotion and the top three sides had the following points totals with two games to play: Dundee United 49, Clydebank 46, Clyde 43.

On the 18th April Clydebank hosted top six side Bo'ness whereas Clyde were away at bottom side Forfar. Clydebank needed a win or to better Clyde's result but in the event were held to goalless draw while Clyde won 3-1. Halligan the visitor's keeper kept them at bay in the first half. Reporting on the rest of the game, *The Scotsman* observed that "towards the end, Clydebank made great efforts to get a goal, for victory was essential to make sure of promotion, and in the last fifteen minutes an exciting time occurred round Halligan's goal. In one raid, Chalmers was fouled in the penalty area...and the referee's award was hotly disputed by the visitors who surged round him. Halligan kicked the ball behind his goal, and on it being returned again, deliberately drove it across the field. Referee Galloway ordered him to go for it, and he walked slowly across the ground. Just as he was near the ball he fell full length, and as he did not rise, other players went to his assistance. He was carried off, and in the dressing room complained that he had been hit with a stone. It is stated that the referee picked up one or two small stones on the field, but no one appears to have seen a missile flung that would have caused the player to collapse. Farmer took up the goalkeeper's position, but Scraggs, who was entrusted with the penalty try, drove over. There was plenty of excitement in the closing minutes, first one goal and then the other being attacked, but the end came with neither team having scored."

Going into the last round of games Clydebank needed a point and they travelled to Armadale. They initially went all out to try and put the outcome beyond doubt, but as the game remained goalless and time went on they became increasingly nervous. The game ended 0-0 and Clydebank got the point they needed. In a bold but ultimately futile effort Clyde won 4-0 at Dumbarton. Clydebank's promotion winning team was: James Gallacher; John Murphy, Charlie McKendrick; Caldwell, Joe Scraggs, Alex Fleming; Abrams, Alex Houston, Joe Anderson, David Chalmers and Dave McEachran.

The promotion-relegation yo-yo continued in the 1925-26 season as Clydebank went straight back down again, finishing in 20th place and bottom with 22 points, six points from safety. The club began life back in the top tier of Scottish League football with a 2-1 reverse away against Motherwell on the 15th August 1925. *The Scotsman*, commenting after the narrow loss, said "newly promoted from the Second Division, the Clydebank side pressed as one likely to give a good account of themselves in the First Division. They were a bustling if not an over-skilful combination, and by sheer grit, combined with dash, they led the scoring after fifteen minutes." Motherwell soon equalised and took the lead from a penalty before the interval. The Clydebank goalscorer was Sam Evans.

They lost their first home game back, against Celtic 2-1, in front of over 20,000. The score was goalless at the break and the shipbuilders scored two minutes into the second half. Celtic got level and when Fleming got injured McGrory, against his old club, got the winner. Their first point of the new season came in the next game, a 2-2 draw at Kilmarnock but they then lost 7-0 at Hearts in mid-September. Neither side had registered a League win in their opening four games. *The Scotsman* described the match as "a one-sided game in which the Clydebank defence went all to pieces, losing four goals in the first half and three more in the second. The collapse was due in some measure to lack of understanding between the backs and goalkeeper....Apart from their unstable defence, Clydebank looked a capable enough side. Scraggs was a fine worker at centre-half, and the forwards showed a lot of clever play without enjoying any luck.

Clydebank got their first win of the season on the 3rd October and they did it in emphatic style against fellow promoted Dundee United, winning 6-1. They dominated from the outset and eventually opened the scoring through Reid, who was injured in the process, and had to go off with concussion. Dundee United subsequently equalised. Smith, however, put Clydebank ahead shortly before the interval. Despite being a man short Clydebank extended their lead through Smith and McEachran added a fourth. The same player scored a fifth from a cross from Evans and near the finish Smith scored Clydebank's sixth goal. The Smith referenced was Jimmy Smith, who they had signed from Dunfermline. A few years later, in the 1927-28 season when playing for Ayr United, he scored a record 66 League goals in 38 appearances, which remains a British record for most League goals in a season. He subsequently joined Liverpool and he was the club's top scorer during the 1929–30 season, scoring 23 goals in all competitions.

A 3-0 win over Queen's Park at the end of November was followed by a creditable 1-1 draw at Celtic but they found themselves bottom, by a point, from Queen's Park, St Johnstone and Partick Thistle. Clydebank failed to gain any more points during December but did beat St Johnstone and draw with Partick in early January 1926. They failed to win in the next six weeks and by the time that they beat Morton 2-1 in mid-February they and Queen's Park were four points adrift at the bottom.

On the 20th February they gave themselves some hope, deservedly beating Kilmarnock 5-1. Reid scored first for Clydebank but Kilmarnock equalised within three minutes from a corner kick. Caldwell made it 2-1 and in the second-half Smith scored from close range, which was followed by another from a drive from 20 yards out. Chalmers headed in from an Evans cross to complete the scoring. The club were still bottom of the First Division, but there was now only two points separating the bottom five teams. However, Clydebank failed to win any of their remaining League fixtures, losing 4-1 at

Queen's Park, 5-0 at Dundee United and 5-1 at home to Hearts and relegation was confirmed on 3rd April with three games left to play when they lost 2-0 at Hamilton. At the end of the season a number of key players left, most noticeably Jimmy Smith, who went to Ayr United, but also Dave McEachran, who left to go and play in America, and Joe Anderson.

Clydebank missed out on a third cycle of relegation from the First Division followed by promotion straight back by finishing third behind Bo'ness and Raith Rovers (who had been relegated the previous season as well). They drew their opening two games back in the Second Division but then surprisingly lost two heavily, conceding four goals in each game. Three more draws followed so they were winless by the end of September and in the bottom five.

They won their first game on the 2nd October, beating bottom side Alloa Athletic 2-0 away from home. They followed this up with three more wins to lift themselves into the top half of the table by the end of October. A 4-1 win over St Bernard's at the beginning of the next month, thanks to a G Thomson hat-trick, was soon followed by a 5-1 victory over Bathgate and Clydebank were up to sixth. In early December they suffered a setback with back-to-back losses, going down to promotion challengers Arthurlie and then at home to the leaders Bo'ness. However, they ended the year on a brighter note, beating Dumbarton 6-2 on the 31st December to go into the New Year in fourth place, behind Bo'ness, who were eight points clear at the top, Raith Rovers and Arthurlie.

The men from Yoker conceded four at East Stirling in their first game of 1927 but bounced back by recording four goals themselves on two occasions in the League in January, beating Stenhousemuir and Armadale by the same 4-1 scoreline. G Thomson scored another hat-trick against Stenhousemuir. In between they beat Douglas Wanderers 6-0 in the First Round of the Scottish Cup. They were knocked out in the next round, 5-1 at Hamilton, but scored five themselves the following week, as back on League duty they beat Alloa Athletic 5-1. Two draws followed before another big win, this time 6-1 over second bottom Arbroath, on the 5th March. The strugglers scored first and the sides were level at half-time at Clydeholm but the Bankies scored five goals in 14 second half minutes. Clydebank were now in fourth, a point behind Raith Rovers and Ayr United, with Bo'ness eight points clear. However, this result was followed by a couple of losses as they lost ground in the promotion race. Going into the last month of the season and with six games to play Bo'ness were way out in front on 50 points. They were followed by five sides, separated by just four points: Raith Rovers 41, Clydebank 38, Ayr United also 38, and then Third Lanark and East Stirlingshire both on 37 points.

At the beginning of April 1927 Clydebank drew at Bathgate and then lost 5-4 at Forfar but did bounce back with a 5-2 win over Arthurlie. Of the seven goals, four were registered in the last seven minutes of play, with Clydebank leading 3-0. But Raith now had a four point advantage over Clydebank with only three games left to play. Their next game was away against champions-elect Bo'ness. They lost 3-2 whereas Raith won 6-3 to take the final promotion spot and to leave Clydebank facing another season in the Second Division. Clydebank won their two remaining games to finish in third place, four points behind Raith in second. At the end of the season the club suffered two high profile departures. Johnny Scraggs left and returned to Glentoran to finish his playing days and David Chalmers also left. His son Stevie was the Celtic legend and one of the Lisbon Lions.

After narrowly missing out on promotion in 1927, the economic downturn took its toll in the late 1920s and the club went into terminal decline as the recession hit shipbuilding and over the next three years they progressively finished in a lower position - 14th, 16th and then 18th place. The Bankies lost the opening game of the new season 4-0 at Third Lanark, Wilson on debut scoring all of the goals. *The Sunday Post* called Clydebank's display "erratic" and went on to critique the team, saying "the defence was too easily flustered, and the forwards were not strong enough physically." They won their next game, 2-1 at home to Dundee United but then lost four out of the next five games they played, a run which left them bottom of the Second Division.

In October 1927 former club manager Alex Maley left Crystal Palace, somewhat ironically because of their poor start to the season in England, and took up the managerial reins once more at Clydeholm. He quickly transformed the club's fortunes and having beaten Morton 6-5 in a thriller in which Thomson scored a hat-trick, Clydebank subsequently went on to beat Queen of the South 6-3, Forfar Athletic 5-1 and St Bernard's 7-1. The first of these was an unexpected win over the then leaders Queen of the South in their best home display of the season. They undeservedly were behind 1-0 at half-time but on the resumption, and following two corners, Chalmers equalised. However, their visitors scored almost straight away but this was quickly cancelled out by Thomson. Chalmers fired in a long range effort to give Clydebank the lead for the first time and Crawford made it 4-2, with five goals having been scored in the first quarter of an hour of the second half. Further goals were added with Clydebank winning 6-3.

At the beginning of December the men from Yoker beat Forfar Athletic 5-1. Clydebank deservedly won the points but the margin of the victory slightly flattered them. The Forfar centre-forward injured his knee after just ten minutes and had to retire from the game. Shortly afterwards Wilson headed Clydebank in front and they increased their lead from a Thomson penalty. At the beginning of the second half Forfar scored but it only took Clydebank five minutes to restore their two goal advantage, Chalmers scoring with a fine drive. Forfar kept going though despite the numerical disadvantage and it was only with a quarter of an hour to go that Thomson and Chalmers added further goals. However, despite the fine win the club remained second from bottom in the table.

Their purple patch continued as later in the same month they beat St Bernard's of Edinburgh 7-1 at Clydeholm, a season's best result. In this match outside-left Crawford scored after 15 minutes and added a second ten minutes later. Their opponents got one back, but Crawford went on to complete a first half hat-trick. An injury to one of the St Bernard's forwards saw their opponents reduced to ten men for the second half. In the second half Thomson scored a hat-trick of his own and Chalmers added a seventh near the end. This run of wins saw them climb way from the bottom and up to 16th place.

By this time, the general economic slowdown and recession was starting to bite, especially the shipbuilding industry, and the club was struggling financially. Back on the 14th November 1927 *The Scotsman* had reported that Clydebank "has sold its ground to a greyhound racing syndicate. The club has been performing indifferently for several years…Trade depression has hit the club very badly, gates being extremely low. The acute state of Clydebank's finances may be realised by the fact that the gate on Saturday amounted to only £35. Following Saturday's game, a delegation of London and Glasgow business men went over the pitch, and the deal was completed later for the sale of the ground at £12,000, so that racing may commence in the new year." Two days later, the same paper reported that "a vigorous protest against the proposed introduction of greyhound racing to Clydebank was made at a large public meeting in the Town Hall, Clydebank, last night, by Councillor P McDevitt, who declared that Clydebank had plenty of opportunity for gambling already without starting the sink of iniquity now proposed. The establishment of dog racing would simply mean that the worst element of every town and village in the neighbourhood would come to the burgh with the 'bookies' who would seek to drain away the hard-won earnings of the people…Continuing, Councillor McDevitt said the people of Clydebank had been hearing bleatings from the Clydebank FC directors that the town would not, or could not, support a first-class football team. That was not true. Let the directors give the town a real football team and the citizens would soon show them that they could support one." The same paper also reported that "members of Clydebank Football Club yesterday received a circular calling an extraordinary general meeting of the club for Thursday of next week, at which a resolution will be moved that the company cannot, by reason of its liabilities, continue its business, and that it is advisable to wind it up. In the event of the resolution being passed, a further resolution to appoint a liquidator is to be submitted." A week later *The Scotsman* reported that at the meeting it was decided to defer matters for a few more months and that the club in the meantime had decided to carry on. On the 30th November Clydebank's situation was discussed at a special meeting of the Scottish Football League's Management Committee in Glasgow. The paper reported that "it was intimated that the Clydebank Club had given an assurance that it was their present intention not to withdraw from the League, but if circumstances compelled them they would give at least one or two months' notice. Brechin City, Montrose and Nithsdale Wanderers had intimated their willingness to enter the League in the event of Clydebank withdrawing." By the turn of the year, although Clydebank had moved up to 16th place, they were still very much under the threat of a re-election vote. Clydebank continued through to the end of the season and eventually finished as high as 14th, four points clear of Bathgate in 19th place.

Concerns over their financial situation and their ability to continue rumbled on. On the 19th June 1928 *The Sunday Post* under the headline "Clydebank on verge of collapse", reported on the precarious position of the club with manager/secretary Alec Maley not sure if the club would carry on next season. Only nine players from the squad had been offered new terms and the club had made no new signings. The paper reported that the club was in a bad way financially and was in debt to the tune of several thousand pounds. The paper commented that "the football public of Clydebank are quite unconcerned regarding the fate of the club. They gave it miserable support last season, and for some reason or other are still unsympathetic in their attitude."

Clydebank stumbled on for three more seasons. In the 1928-29 season they finished in 16th place and in a sign of the financial situation affecting League clubs, Bathgate resigned part way through the season. The club had actually started reasonably well on the pitch and by the beginning of October were as high as seventh place, just two points off second place. However, they failed to win any of their next four games and slipped to 12th. The run ended with a 5-1 win over Arthurlie. At the end of December they lost 6-1 at home to Dumbarton and Third Lanark put six past them in the Scottish Cup. In February Queen of the South went one better, beating them 7-2. They won their next two games to move up to 14th but picked up only one more point to eventually finish 16th. By this time another club had also succumbed, Arthurlie resigning from the League near the end of the season.

Brechin City and Montrose joined the League for the 1929-30 season to restore the twenty team Second Division. Clydebank made a disastrous start losing 6-1 at Arbroath on the 10th August and only picked up a single point from their first five matches. When the leaders Leith Athletic overwhelmed Clydebank at the beginning of October, winning

5-0, they were the only winless team after nine rounds of matches. On the 12th October they recorded their first victory. They had only scored seven goals in their first nine games but somehow contrived to score five in beating Stenhousemuir 5-2. This result was followed by five straight losses before a ten goal thriller with Forfar where the spoils were shared. They ended 1929 in 17th place and started 1930 well, with three straight wins including a 6-2 win over bottom side Brechin City. They also put up a brave showing in the Scottish Cup, only going out to Hearts 1-0 at Tynecastle. They eventually finished in 18th place, outside of the two re-election places, level on points with Alloa in 19th but with a far superior goal average, and six points ahead of bottom side Brechin City. Off the pitch the greyhound racing saga was brought to a conclusion and a greyhound racing track was installed, with the first race taking place in May 1930.

The 1930-31 season turned out to be the club's last in the Scottish Football League. Economic conditions that had brought about their sudden emergence and inclusion as a League club were also a factor behind their decline as the recession hit shipbuilding. The club was caught in a vicious circle of declining income from gates leading to a reduction in the quality of the players and a less attractive proposition on the field. They conceded 108 goals, the worst defensive record in the division and finished in the bottom two, level on points with Bo'ness, but placed above them on goal average. They survived a re-election vote but came to the realisation that they couldn't continue as a viable club and took the decision to resign from the League.

They lost their opening game on the 16th August, 2-1 at home to a King's Park, and then travelled through to Edinburgh to play St Bernard's, where they were thrashed 6-1, the *Glasgow Herald* noting that "the Yoker team contained no fewer than seven amateurs and, although they held their own in the first half, they lacked the staying power of the Saints." At the end of the month they lost for the fourth weekend in a row. Although they got three goals, their hosts, Bo'ness doubled that to win 6-3, with both centre-forwards scoring hat-tricks. In mid-September they were beaten 5-0 at fourth-placed Queen of the South and on the 11th October they suffered their tenth consecutive League defeat, 5-2 at Albion Rovers, and were still pointless.

A week later they finally earned their first point in a 3-3 draw at second from bottom Armadale. Their poor form continued though and in late November, in snowy and icy conditions, they were thrashed by the leaders Third Lanark. At this point they had played 16 games and lost 15 of them, and had only one point, and were six points adrift at the bottom. Their first win of the season was finally achieved on the 29th November when they beat Alloa Athletic 3-0, the *Glasgow Herald* noting that "the bottom-markers adapted themselves better to the slippery ground and foggy atmosphere than did the Alloa players and won well." Their first victory cut the gap to Armadale and

Bo'ness to four points, but two more defeats followed, including a 5-0 loss at Raith in mid-December.

Clydebank then surprisingly recorded three consecutive victories, from the 20th December to the New Years' Day fixture. The first of these, a surprise 2-1 away win at King's Park, was followed by a home win against St Bernard's by the same score line. They then beat Dumbarton 2-0 with the *Glasgow Herald* reporting that "it is a truism that in football the unexpected often happens, and it was certainly the case when Clydebank, who were the first-footers at Boghead, annexed both points from Dumbarton. The pitch was frost bound, and any good football shown was by the home men. On the other hand, Clydebank had a defence which adapted themselves to the ground conditions throughout, and it is to this stonewall defence that they really owe this victory. Coen was invincible in goal, and Ramsay played great havoc with the home forwards' excellent work. Dumbarton had sixty minutes out of the ninety attacking, and fruitless corners and ill-luck were all that fell to them. It can be said for the Clydebank forwards, particularly the wingers and Thomson that they were snappy when chance offered, and both goals were well taken." Both goals were scored by Thomson, both in the first half. On the 10th of January their revival continued when they beat fellow strugglers Bo'ness 1-0. The club was in Scottish Cup action the week later, losing 3-1 at St Mirren, and they didn't win in the League again until Valentine's Day when they beat Albion Rovers 4-1.

A week later they won again, this time 5-2 at home to Armadale to move off the bottom, the *Glasgow Herald* noting that "a remarkable comeback is being staged by Clydebank, who capped their win over Albion Rovers the previous week with another well merited victory at the expense of Armadale, who are now in a somewhat desperate position. The Clydeholm men made good in the first half, and led at the interval by four clear goals." However, they came down to earth with a bump when they were beaten 6-1 by East Stirling at the end of the month, but they recorded their third win in four games with a narrow 1-0 win over Montrose at the beginning of March. These results meant they were now second bottom, three ahead of Bo'ness and a point behind Armadale.

However, Clydebank failed to win any of their next four games and with just three matches left, although still second bottom, they were now six points adrift of Armadale in 18th place and more or less guaranteed to face a re-election vote along with Bo'ness. They won two of their remaining three fixtures, 2-0 at Alloa and 3-2 at home to Forfar before losing what turned out to be their last ever SFL match against Raith. They hosted the men from Kirkcaldy at Clydeholm on the 25th April in front of a paltry crowd of 300 and lost 5-1. They finished equal on points with Bo'ness – both with 22 points, six points behind Armadale. Bo'ness were narrowly classified as bottom on goal average (Bo'ness 54/100=0.540; Clydebank 61/108=0.565).

On the 2nd May the *Glasgow Herald* ran a report suggesting that the club would drop out before any re-election vote with Bo'ness. Nevertheless, on the 27th May at the League's AGM Clydebank contested an election vote along with Bo'ness, Nithsdale Wanderers and Edinburgh City and were successfully re-elected to the League. However, a month later, they submitted their resignation from the SFL and closed down for good. On the 24th July, a special meeting of the Scottish Football League was held in the Kenilworth Hotel, Glasgow to discuss the vacancy caused by their withdrawal, and Edinburgh City were elected by 25 votes to 7 for Nithsdale Wanderers.

Their resignation marked the end of 15 seasons of senior football in Clydebank but the end of the club wouldn't be the end of Senior League football in Clydebank. Over thirty years later, in 1964, the Steedman brothers, the owners of East Stirlingshire, moved this club from its Falkirk base to Clydebank. Although ultimately thwarted in this move following a legal challenge, their resolve to bring football back to Clydebank was ultimately successful when a new Clydebank club entered the Scottish Football League in 1966.

Clydeholm Park continued to exist after the club's demise as a venue for greyhound racing up to the 1960s. The final greyhound racing meeting took place in November 1963. The stadium was subsequently demolished and the site used to build a shopping centre and housing, with one of the roads through it named Clydeholm Terrace.

SEASON	LEAGUE	P	W	D	L	F	A	P	POS
1914-15	SCOT-2	26	13	4	9	68	37	30	5/14
1917-18	SCOT	34	14	5	15	55	56	33	9/18
1918-19	SCOT	34	12	8	14	52	65	32	10/18
1919-20	SCOT	42	20	8	14	78	54	48	5/22
1920-21	SCOT	42	7	14	21	47	72	28	20/22
1921-22	SCOT-1	42	6	8	28	34	103	20	22/22
1922-23	SCOT-2	38	21	10	7	69	29	52	2/20
1923-24	SCOT-1	38	10	5	23	42	71	25	20/20
1924-25	SCOT-2	38	20	8	10	65	42	48	2/20

1925-26	SCOT-1	38	7	8	23	55	92	22	20/20
1926-27	SCOT-2	38	18	9	11	94	75	45	3/20
1927-28	SCOT-2	38	16	3	19	78	80	35	14/20
1928-29	SCOT-2	36	11	5	20	70	86	27	16/19
1929-30	SCOT-2	38	7	10	21	66	92	24	18/20
1930-31	SCOT-2	38	10	2	26	61	108	22	19/20

Clydebank II (1966-2002)

Formed: 1965
Colours: Originally red shirts with a white sash and black shorts. Then white shirts with various red and black trims and white shorts.
Ground: Kilbowie Park. Then ground sharing at Boghead (Dumbarton) and then Cappielow Park (Greenock Morton)
Entered League: 1966. Elected to create a 38th member
Number of League Seasons: 36
Honours: Second Division Champions 1975-76
Highest League Finish: 10th in Premier Division
Left League: 2002. Administration. Taken over by Airdrie United

Following the demise of the original Clydebank FC in 1931 the name of Clydebank re-entered the Scottish Football League in 1964 when East Stirling were relocated by their owners to Kilbowie Park in Clydebank. The owners of East Stirlingshire had negotiated a merger with Clydebank Juniors and moved the club from its Falkirk base to Clydebank. The team was called East Stirlingshire Clydebank. This doesn't exactly roll off the tongue or lend itself to chants does it so the name was abbreviated to ES Clydebank. This team played during the 1964-65 but only lasted one season. The move was strongly opposed by supporters of East Stirlingshire and led to a legal challenge. At the Court of Session on the 7th May 1965 Lord Hunter ruled that the transfer of shares which resulted in the move of East Stirlingshire to Clydebank was invalid and should be nullified. An Extraordinary General Meeting took place days afterwards and it was decided to move East Stirlingshire back to Falkirk and return to the name East Stirlingshire. Charles Steedman was deposed as Chairman and Jack Steedman voted out of office as Secretary.

The Steedman brothers, remained convinced that the Clydebank area offered better prospects for a football club and so reincarnated a Clydebank team. The second Clydebank FC to play Scottish League football was technically established as a brand new club in 1965. However, the new club was now in limbo. Having vacated their position in the Junior ranks they had now lost their place in the Scottish Football League. However, with the Scottish League having 37 teams, leaving one team sitting idle each week in the Second Division, it was hoped that their application to join as a new entity would be accepted. The League Management Committee called a special meeting and Clydebank's application was approved by a slender majority of 19 votes to 18. However, the proposal needed a two-thirds majority to be carried. Clydebank had to wait a year in the Combined Reserve League before being elected to the SFL in 1966. A vote was taken to even up the Second Division to twenty clubs and this time they were victorious, becoming the 38th member of the Scottish Football League, securing 30 out of 37 votes in a contest involving Gala Fairydean and Hawick Royal Albert from the Borders.

Clydebank took their place in the League for season 1966-67 and within ten years they were in the First Division. They won the Second Division title in 1976 and finished runners-up in the First Division in 1977 and 1985, securing promotion to the top flight of Scottish League football. However, they shared the same fate as the original Clydebank club, facing severe financial difficulties, although the circumstances were very different. In 2002 the club went into administration and was bought out by the newly formed Airdrie United and relocated to play in Airdrie under the new identity.

Clydebank played their games at Kilbowie Park, notable for being one of the first all-seater stadiums in Britain. It had been built in 1939 for Clydebank Juniors and was also the home of ES Clydebank during the 1964-65 season. Jack Steedman managed the club from 1967 to 1975 and by a quirk of fate, their first game of the new season was against East Stirlingshire in a sectional League Cup game on the 13th August 1966. As the *Glasgow Herald* stated "an interesting fixture is that between Clydebank, now associate members of the SFA, and East Stirlingshire, in view of the legal controversy which raged before the Clydebank club was revived." Clydebank opened the scoring after seven minutes through McCallum. Rankine from 20 yards out scored in the top left ten minutes later and the home team went on to win 3-0. A gate of 2,060 demonstrated the support for senior football in Clydebank.

They made their Scottish League debut on the 24th August 1966, losing 3-0 at home to Arbroath, with an attendance of 2,586. This was an early indication of their struggles which became even more apparent when they lost the next eight games as well. Included in this disastrous run was a 4-0 home defeat against Montrose and a 6-0 loss at Morton. Their first League point eventually came on the 15th October, a 1-1 draw away against Berwick Rangers. This result was followed by two further draws. On Saturday the 19th November they finally registered their first victory, a 4-2 win over fellow strugglers Brechin City.

Clydebank beat East Stirlingshire 3-1 in early December to record their second win, which lifted them off the bottom, above the vanquished Shire, and this win was part of a run of six games without defeat, a run that was only ended by a narrow 1-0 home defeat against division leaders Morton. At the end of February they notched up a 4-0 win over Stranraer and their best win came near the end of the season when they beat East Stirlingshire 5-1 away, doing the double over the Shire, much to the delight of the Steedman brothers. On the 15th April they were beaten 1-0 by Third Lanark, which would be that club's last ever League victory. They finished third from bottom in their inaugural season, above Stenhousemuir and East Stirlingshire, who came bottom. Tony Moy top-scored with 26 goals. On the books of Celtic when he was younger, Moy was one of the best goalscorers the club has ever had and only six players have scored more goals than him.

Between 1967 and 1975 Clydebank generally finished mid-table with a best placed finish of fifth in the 1970-71 season and a lowest of 17th in the 1972-73 season. The 1967-68 season was something of an improvement as they came in ninth, with Moy again topping the goalscoring charts with 29 goals. Fixtures involving East Stirlingshire continued to throw up some interesting matches, including a 5-5 draw on the last day of season, but this match was watched by only 381 spectators. Two 13th place finishes followed. In the 1969-70 season the club suffered a record home SFL defeat, losing 7-0 at home to Falkirk on the 20th September 1969. By now they had a new strikeforce partnership in Jimmy Caskie and Alan Munro who regularly combined to score 30 plus goals a season. Jimmy Caskie made his debut for the Bankies in January 1968 having joined from Dumbreck Amateurs. He eventually moved to Patrick Thistle but he failed to break into the first team and he subsequently moved to Stirling Albion. After a short period at Annfield Jimmy returned to Kilbowie in January 1975 where he was part of the Second Division championship winning side. Caskie went on to make over 200 appearances for the club and scored 66 goals. Alan Munro had made his debut in August 1968 and went on to make 186 appearances, scoring 69 goals and had four consistent seasons where he scored between 15 and 19 goals.

For the 1970-71 season they were joined by Peter Kane who came from St Mirren, and between them the three of them scored 50 goals in that season as Clydebank finished a best to date fifth place in the Second Division. Kane scored four goals in a 7-1 victory over Queen's Park in March 1971. The following season the trio notched up 42 goals as the club slipped back to ninth. Kane scored a hat-trick in a 7-1 win over Hamilton but left at the end of the season to join Barrow, although he returned for the 1974-75 season. With Jimmy Caskie agitating for a move away from the club a new goalscorer emerged in the shape of Mike Larnach, who would go on make over 300 appearances for the club and score over 100 goals. He top scored with 19 goals in the 1972-73 season, but the next highest total was Andy Roxburgh's seven, as the club finished a lowly 17th place (out of 19 clubs). Goals were also a problem the following year as

Roxburgh and Jim Fallon were joint top-scorers with nine goals apiece, although the club did finish tenth. For the 1974-75 season Meadowbank Thistle joined the League to become the 20th club in the Second Division and Clydebank finished a creditable seventh place. At the end of this season, the League was reconstructed into three divisions of 10, 14 (8+6) and 14. This meant that the top ten teams in the First Division entered the new Premier Division, while the rest of the First Division One clubs entered the new First Division. The top six in the Second also went into the second tier, so Clydebank just missed out by a place. They missed the slot by two points and were placed in the new Second Division, which was now the third tier. They had come with a late charge winning six out of their last seven matches but crucially lost against Alloa. A 2-0 home win over leaders Falkirk a week later wasn't enough.

For the new season Bill Munro took over as manager and his side earned back-to-back promotions, including winning the Second Division title in 1976 and promotion to the top flight Premier Division in 1977. Munro had worked with the Steedman's at East Stirlingshire and was the club's trainer. With Jack Steedman deciding to take more of a back seat role Munro stepped up and was appointed manager in August 1975.

Clydebank entered the new phase of League construction as the highest placed team and only conceded 13 League goals and lost only three League matches as they won the Second Division title. It was a close-run thing though as they were matched all the way by a Raith Rovers side that lost only once. Both sides ended on 40 points but Clydebank had a plus eight better goal difference. Their League campaign began on the 30th August 1975 against Brechin City after the usual League Cup sectional games and they beat their opponents, who would struggle, 3-0 in front of a crowd of 1,400. This was the first of a run of five straight League wins in which they didn't even concede a goal. The fifth of these games was a 4-0 away win at Berwick Rangers on the 27th September meaning they were the only team in Britain with a 100% record at the start of October. They naturally topped the division with unbeaten sides Raith and Alloa two points further back and with next best defence having conceded five. Their winning streak was ended against Raith at home with a 1-1 draw in which they came from behind with a late equaliser. This was part of a larger sequence where they went unbeaten in their first 13 games and were five points clear at the top until they surprisingly lost 1-0 at home to bottom club Berwick on the 29th November. They also lost their next game against promotion rivals Raith 1-0 and also lost on the 20th December to Stenhousemuir but this third League defeat would be their last.

Clydebank went unbeaten for the rest of the SFL season, effectively for four months, and only conceded a further five League goals during this time. The goals scored came from Cooper and McCallan. 19 year old Davie Cooper, who had made his debut the year before, and who would go on to be a club legend, making 182 appearances and scoring 45 goals (over two spells), scored 22 goals for the season, one more than Joe McCallan, who would go on to make 224 appearances for the club and score a total of 78 goals. A McCallan goal on the 21st February at Firs Park away at East Stirling left them four points ahead of Raith and six ahead of Alloa. The following week they got the one point the needed to make sure of promotion, when they beat Forfar 2-0, thanks to second-half goals by Cooper and McCallan.

Raith kept up the challenge for the title by winning their games in hand. With one game left each, Clydebank were on 39 points and Raith on 38. A ten plus superior goal difference meant that Clydebank effectively only needed a point. Each of their last games was against third placed Alloa. Raith played first and won 1-0 away at Alloa. On Tuesday 6th April Clydebank became Second Division champions when they drew 0-0 with Alloa at the Recreation Ground. It was a nervous 90 minutes, made worse by their right back Norrie Hall missing a penalty in the first half, after Cooper had been brought down. Davie Cooper finished the season as top scorer with 22 goals, with Joe McCallan contributing 21 and Mike Larnach 13.

Their year in the First Division was a huge success, as they finished in second place to earn back to back promotions and gained entry to the Premier Division. They started off strongly with consecutive 3-0 League wins and went unbeaten throughout September in their first eight games (six wins, two draws) topping the division with 14 points, one point ahead of Dundee and two ahead of St Mirren. They reached the Quarter-finals of the League Cup where they played Rangers across two legs. They drew 3-3 at Ibrox and 1-1 at Kilbowie but there was no away goals rule so the tie went to a replay. This was drawn 0-0 before they lost the second replay at Firhill 2-1.

Back in the League the Bankies kept six consecutive clean sheets after that and at the beginning of December beat East Fife 6-0 away from home. Mike Larnach, another club legend who would score over 100 goals and make over 300 appearances scored a hat-trick. In the first game of 1977, played on the 3rd January, Clydebank beat Arbroath 8-1. The match ended as a contest within the first twenty minutes, when Clydebank hit Arbroath with three goals in as many minutes. Joe McCallan scored four, Davie Cooper three and Mike Larnach got the other one. The result was a club record SFL win.

The result against Arbroath was part of a ten game unbeaten run which was eventually ended at the beginning of March 1977 when they lost 3-1 at Alex Ferguson's League leaders, St Mirren, a result which left them four points behind. Clydebank were eight points ahead of third placed Dundee, having played two matches more. After the games played on Saturday the 9th April Clydebank were six points clear of Dundee with four games to go, having played one more game than Dundee. The two sides met in a vital midweek game on the 12th April, from a fixture postponed from mid-December. Crucially Clydebank beat the Dens Park team 3-2 to guarantee promotion. A 2-1 loss against Raith on the Saturday gave St Mirren the title. Joe McCallan top scored with 31 goals, just ahead of Mike Larnach with 29 and Billy McColl contributed 20. McColl went on to make over 150 Scottish League appearances for Clydebank before a transfer to Ayr United in 1978. Clydebank were thus promoted to the Premier Division, becoming the first club to play in all three Scottish League divisions since League reconstruction in 1975.

The Bankies spent three seasons in the Premier Division in total across two stints but they were immediately relegated back to the First Division at the end of the 1977-78 season. Clydebank began life in the top flight with an away trip to the First Division champions St Mirren where they drew 1-1, Larnach scoring their goal. They made their home debut against Aberdeen on the 20th August in front of a crowd of 4,500, losing 3-1. They lost their next four in a row without scoring and this was then followed by a 4-1 defeat against Rangers at Ibrox. They eventually recorded their first win on the 8th October with a 2-1 win over Motherwell but only won once more in 1977 (across ten games) and then only one more across the first three months of 1978, coming right at the start when they beat Partick 1-0 on the 7th January 1978. By this time they were nine points adrift at the foot of the Premier Division.

Their best form came in April 1978 when relegation was already assured, doubling their total of League victories for the season by winning three matches - the highlight being a 3-2 win over Jock Stein's Celtic on the 8th April, Celtic's first ever defeat against the Bankies. John McCormack scored first for the home team on five minutes after Celtic goalie Peter Latchford had spilled a corner from Gerry O'Brien. Celtic equalised soon after and led 2-1 at half-time. Jim Lumsden got the Bankies on level terms when he drove in on the hour mark. Gerry Colgan scored a shock winner four minutes from time. The club only scored 23 League goals in 36 games with Larnach and McColl being joint top scorers for the season with just six apiece. In their promotion year the club had scored 89 times in 39 matches.

Clydebank just missed out on an immediate return to the top flight as they finished third, level on 54 points with Kilmarnock but with a minus eight worse goal difference. Dundee were the First Division champions, finishing a further point ahead. The Bankies won their opening game of new campaign back in the First Division on the 12th August 1978 beating Kilmarnock 2-1. Dundee went the first eleven games unbeaten to take an early lead with a chasing pack of six teams, including Clydebank, only separated by two points. Significantly, across November and December, promotion rivals Kilmarnock recorded wins of 5-0, 4-0, 4-0 and 4-1. And yet, by the end of March 1979, Clydebank led the division with 43 points, two ahead of Kilmarnock and five ahead of Dundee although it was a false position as Dundee had five games in hand!

On the 31st March Clydebank lost a crucial promotion game at home to Killie 2-1. On Wednesday the 25th April, whilst Nottingham Forest were coming through a European Cup Semi-final on their way to beating Malmo, two crucial games were taking place in the Scottish First Division. Kilmarnock beat Dundee 2-1 and Clydebank beat Dumbarton 3-1 and the two victorious clubs opened up a two point lead at the top of the division. On the following Saturday, with Clydebank not in action, Kilmarnock finished their programme with a 3-1 win at Dumbarton and Dundee beat Montrose 1-0. Clydebank finished their League fixtures on Wednesday 2nd May with a 2-1 win at Raith, Frank McDougall scoring his fifth goal in as many games, to end the season on 29 goals. McDougall had joined in August 1978 and played just this season, joining St Mirren for £150,000 at the end of the season. Blair Millar had joined in February and top scored with 31 goals in the 1978-79 season. He went on to score 97 goals in 197 appearances across four and a half seasons and was the club's top scorer for four consecutive seasons. St Johnstone did the Bankies a favour by beating Dundee 3-2 but matters were still in their own hands for the Dens Park club. Clydebank's win meant they had the same number of points as Kilmarnock but their goal difference was worse. Dundee were two points behind both clubs but still had three games to play. Dundee lost the first of these at home to Arbroath but then beat Raith 2-0 to go ahead of Clydebank on goal difference, but were behind Kilmarnock on the same measure. A 2-2 draw at home to Ayr in their last game was enough to give them the title, with Clydebank missing out on the second spot.

The next two seasons saw Clydebank finish in the bottom half of the 14 team First Division, coming in ninth and then tenth. In the second of these seasons, 1980-81, they did reach the Quarter-finals of both cup competitions. In the League Cup they went out to eventual winners Dundee United and in the Scottish Cup they went out to Morton after a replay (which they lost 6-0 at home having drawn the first tie at Cappielow 0-0, suffering their heaviest Scottish Cup defeat).

The 1981-82 season didn't start well as the Bankies lost three out of four League Cup games. These disappointing results prompted the resignation of manager Bill Munro. Former player and assistant Sammy Henderson was appointed Munro's successor on the 21st August 1981. Under his tenure the club were regular promotion candidates and his team eventually reached the top flight in 1985. In his first season in charge Clydebank finished in fourth, five points off the promotion spots. In the following 1982-83 season the club was again up there, finishing one place higher, but again missing out on promotion. Top goalscorer Blair Millar left for Airdrieonians but Bobby Williamson emerged from the youth ranks and top scored with 24 goals. Clydebank got off to a good a start, scoring five against Dumbarton and Clyde in the space of four days to lie in fourth but then had come a cropper against second placed Airdrie with a 4-0 home loss. Their best win of the season came on the 12th March 1983 when they beat top of the table St Johnstone 6-1 to go third. Tommy Coyne scored a hat trick and went on to notch 19 goals for the season. With two games to go they were still in third, just two points behind Hearts in second. Both clubs won away from home in their penultimate games. Hearts had a plus 15 better goal difference so Clydebank needed some dramatic score lines in the last set of games. As it was Hearts won 2-0 at home to Hamilton whereas Clydebank lost 2-1 at home to Partick.

Tommy Coyne scored ten goals in eleven games at the start of the 1983-84 season, and was enticed away in October to join Dundee United for a fee of £60,000. He had scored 38 goals in 80 appearances for the Bankies and would later be capped for the Republic of Ireland. He later managed the club as player-manager from August 2000 but lost his job in early 2001 when the club entered administration. Bobby Williamson also left the club, in January 1984, when he was sold to Rangers for £100,000. He later successfully managed Kilmarnock, winning the Scottish Cup with them in 1997. At the turn of the year Clydebank sat in a mid-table seventh place but a nine game unbeaten run across February and March got them up to fourth, but that still left them six points behind second placed Morton and seven behind leaders Dumbarton. Their run came to an end away at Dumbarton and their last four games all ended in draws as once again Clydebank fell just short, finishing in the top four for the third successive season.

Clydebank finally succeeded in returning to the Premier Division in the 1984-85 season finishing as runners-up to Motherwell. They opened the new campaign with a 3-0 win over St Johnstone. After winning 5-0 at home against Kilmarnock on 15th September, thanks to an Alan Bain hat-trick, they went on a run of nine games without defeat to lie in second place behind then leaders Airdrie at the beginning of November. The top two met on New Year's Day with Clydebank winning 1-0, thanks to a goal from Larnach, and the Bankies went level on points at the top (Airdrie had a superior goal difference).

Clydebank then surprisingly lost at home to mid-table Brechin City leaving the table delicately poised with only two points separating a top five of Clydebank, Hamilton, Motherwell, Airdrie and Forfar. Following this set back the club went on another unbeaten run, this time of seven games, across February and early March. By the time this run was ended with a 1-0 away defeat to Motherwell on the 16th March the number of clubs challenging for promotion was done to three: Clydebank, Motherwell and Airdrie - with just one point separating them, although Clydebank had played one more game than Airdrie, and two more than Motherwell.

Another loss, the following weekend, 2-1 at home to Partick, was lessened by losses also for Airdrie (surprisingly beaten 5-3 at home to Meadowbank) and Motherwell (beaten 1-0 by Clyde). Airdrie then lost again in midweek, again at home, this time to Ayr, and dropped out of the promotion race, to be replaced by Falkirk who were coming with a late run. At the beginning of April Clydebank recorded convincing wins, 3-0 and 5-1 away at Meadowbank and at home to Brechin respectively. In the second of these Brechin scored first after 25 minutes before Martin Hughes equalised just before half-time. Two goals in five minutes early on in the second half through Conroy and Larnach put the Bankies in the ascendancy and Larnach and Hughes each got their second goals towards the end.

Things were starting to get tense with Falkirk waiting to pounce on any slip-ups. Clydebank's next game was away at Forfar and on the eve of game the *Glasgow Herald* produced a scathing assessment of their top flight credentials lamenting their lack of support. The article wrote: "so Clydebank are almost there. Against all the odds they are poised again to enter the big time world of the premier division. It has been a long distance slog rather than a spectacular campaign but the Bankies are still due a round of applause. Unfortunately they are more likely to be greeted with cries of 'so what?' and 'who cares anyway?' Not even the promise of top-10 entertainment has done much to win Clydebank friends in their own corner of the world. Hardly anyone seems to want to know and that is a pity. The absentees are denying themselves some exciting times. Backed by a mere handful of loyalists, the Bankies are somehow managing to outrun outfits which have healthier resources and command more respectable numbers. We can only wonder at what they could achieve had they a decent support of their own. At the very least they would be entitled to feel secure in the knowledge that premier-division survival would be within their capabilities. As things stand, the Kilbowie side realise that life upstairs will be traumatic, perhaps even short. But since they are bold enough to have a go surely they merit more attention from their own people. They cannot go much farther without it. Although those who are already doing quite nicely out of the premier division will be thinking that the Bankies represent easy points, though they will not be happy with he thought of meagre gates. After all, if the people of Clydebank can't be bothered the supporters of bigger clubs may not see the need to recognise them either." The Bankies drew 1-1 at Forfar, giving away a penalty before Conroy scored for them. They still had the lead in the division though, although Motherwell moved to within one point, with a game in hand, having won 1-0 at Partick.

Clydebank did slip up, losing 3-2 at Ayr having been two goals up after seven minutes, and Falkirk pounced, winning their match. Reporting on the situation the *Glasgow Herald* noted that "old habits do indeed die hard, particularly in football. Consider Clydebank's desperate struggle to become first-class citizens again and you will see what I mean. It appears they are so used to finishing on the fringe of promotion from the first division that their senses have been scattered by the realisation that they are only a few points from actually going up. On Saturday they travelled to the seaside for a match with Ayr United and, despite having been two goals up after seven minutes, lost 2-3. It looks like the Bankies have forgotten the first commandment for those working at great heights which says; 'don't look down'. Now they are swaying rather precariously at the top of the league, two points behind Motherwell, who themselves are showing slight signs of vertigo, but only one in front of Falkirk, who have shouldered past an impotent Airdrie outfit. The Brockville side, it must be said, are looking good and waiting to pounce should the Bankies falter again. Clearly these are difficult days for Clydebank. A couple of weeks ago it looked as though their place in the premier division had been secured but they reckoned without Falkirk and, of course, the spirited resistance of teams like Ayr. However, their target remains clear, they have two matches left – against St Johnstone at home and East Fife away – and they must win both. Surely that is not asking too much more of weary legs. Saints are already doomed and East Fife too, are flagging."

With two games left Motherwell led the division on 47 points, Clydebank had 45 and Falkirk had 44. Falkirk then lost at home to Ayr United and the Bankies beat St Johnstone 2-1. Motherwell also won and both sides were promoted. If Clydebank could beat East Fife away by a big score and Motherwell lose at Forfar, the Bankies could have claimed the title but as it was both games ended goalless. After three relatively close shaves they were back in the top flight of the Scottish League.

Their latest stint in the top flight lasted two season in which they struggled in both. At the end of the 1985-86 season they finished tenth and bottom of the Premier Division but were not relegated due to League reconstruction. The following season they finished second from bottom in an expanded top flight of twelve teams and were relegated. Clydebank struggled back in the top flight and amassed only 20 points in their first season back, and scored just 29 goals, with David Lloyd top-scoring with 9, Conroy scored 7 and Larnach 6. The season opened promisingly enough with a goalless draw at Motherwell, who had come up with them as the First Division champions, in the first game. 34 year old 'keeper Jim Gallacher produced a superb performance to earn them a point and when he was beaten Gerry McCabe was on hand to clear the ball off the line. The Clydebank line up on their return was: Gallacher, Treanor, Given, Fallon, McGhie, Shanks, Ronald, Moore, Larnach, Conroy and McCabe. Subs: Hughes and Dickson. The Bankies followed this up with a 4-0 win at home against Dundee. They made a dream start to the game, opening the scoring after a minute. Mike Conroy intercepted a loose pass and ran through to score. Conroy then turned provider to put Mike Larnach through to chip the second goal. Larnach took a Dickson cross under control and set up Vinnie Moore for an easy third. Seven minutes from time, and almost a repeat of their first, Conroy ran through and fired home. The only downside to the match was young centre-half Willie McGhie being taken off with broken ankle. Although only two games in, the Bankies were the only Premier Division team yet to have conceded a goal.

Clydebank followed this up with narrow home defeats against Celtic and Rangers. They then won away at St Mirren and a home victory over Hearts, saw them in sixth place at the end of September. They then suffered a 5-0 loss against Hibs on 1st October and didn't win again until the 10th December, a 2-1 win over Aberdeen by which time they had slipped back to ninth place, four points ahead of bottom side Motherwell but four behind eighth placed Dundee. A poor run saw them caught at the bottom and at the end of March they hosted Celtic, going into the game having lost all of their last five and scored only two goals in the process. They lost 5-0 at Kilbowie to Celtic although the score was 0-0 at half-time, Brian McLair scoring a second half hat-trick. They lost their last game of the season 6-0 at home to Aberdeen, a poor way for Jim Fallon, a Bankies legend, who was making last appearance for the club after 19 years and 800 games, to bow out.

Motherwell, who had also gone up, were ninth with the same number of points as them, but with a much better goal difference. At the other end of the table Celtic pipped Hearts to the title on the same measure. Both clubs were saved from relegation by the expansion of the Premier Division from 10 to 12 teams. In the League Cup Clydebank beat Raith 7-2, thanks in part to a Larnach hat-trick, but went out in the next round to Dundee United 2-0. In the Scottish Cup they went out to First Division Falkirk after a replay.

Hamilton and Falkirk joined the now twelve team Premier Division but the Bankies continued to struggle and they were involved in a relegation scrap with the two new clubs. They kicked off the new season with a narrow 1-0 win away at the newly promoted First Division Champions Hamilton. Accies fielded six new players having been on a modest spending spree in the close season. At Douglas Park Clydebank spoiled the party atmosphere and were the more cohesive and purposeful side, emerging as 1-0 winners. After just four minutes Jim Given scored the only goal of the game having been sent clear by Stuart Gordon. Thereafter chances fell to the home side but opportunities were spurned on a regular basis and they did not get the equaliser which their play deserved. Manager Sam Henderson remarked that he was happy with the result if not the performance, commenting that there was a lot of work to do.

The next four games brought a home goalless draw with Dundee United, a creditable 1-0 home defeat against Celtic, a 3-0 home win over St Johnstone in the League Cup and then a 1-0 victory at Love Street against St Mirren that saw Sam Henderson's side sitting proudly in the top half of the table in fifth place. At this point the two newly promoted teams occupied the bottom two places with just a solitary point between them. The Bankies then lost four in a row and a 6-0 defeat at the end of October to Celtic, who bounced back from a 2-1 League Cup Final defeat, left them in tenth place. It could be argued that worse was to follow when Falkirk beat them 1-0 to go ahead of them in the table and push them into eleventh. The *Glasgow Herald* commented that "Clydebank, after a good start to the season, have slipped to the dreaded second bottom position. They have some good players - notably full back Joe Dickson who often makes penetrating runs from defence - but the signs are beginning to look ominous."

After beating Falkirk 2-1 in the New Years' Day game the club suffered two 5-0 defeats against Rangers and Aberdeen, the latter at home. They fared a little better in the Scottish Cup, knocking out both Falkirk and Hibernian, before losing in the Quarter-finals to Dundee. A four game unbeaten run at Easter, albeit with three draws, saw them briefly overtake Falkirk and with four games to go they were two points ahead of Falkirk and five ahead of Hamilton. However, two consecutive three goal margin defeats at the hands of Rangers and Dundee saw them slip back into the relegation zone. On the same day that there were losing to Rangers, Hamilton lost 1-0 at home to Falkirk, the Bairns going level on points with them, but above them thanks to a vastly superior goal difference. In the game against Dundee Clydebank scored first through Stuart Gordon but a Tommy Coyne hat-trick against his old club condemned them to defeat. Falkirk lost at home to Dundee United but Hamilton kept their slim hopes alive by getting a point at Hibs. Three days later Hamilton lost 2-1 at Dundee United and were relegated. With two games left it now came down to a straight fight between Clydebank and Falkirk for the remaining relegation place. Falkirk were one point ahead, which realistically was two, given a massive goal difference advantage (19 goals). In the penultimate round of games Clydebank appeared to have the easier of the two fixtures. They were at home to eighth placed Motherwell while Falkirk were away at second placed Celtic, who still had a slim chance of catching Rangers for the title.

Clydebank drew 0-0 with Motherwell. They created some decent chances but couldn't quite apply the finishing touch, with the *Glasgow Herald* reporting that "what we witnessed at Kilbowie was football in the raw, a bloody fight for survival. The Bankies took a draw only to learn that they had lost. The players trudged off the pitch believing they could still save themselves by beating Hibernian in next week's final match of the season, but shocking news awaited in the dressing room, Falkirk, who had been only one point in front of them, had beaten Celtic at Parkhead. All around the home dressing room jaws fell slack and heads drooped into cupped hands...Clydebank deserved the right to try again next Saturday. They had fought well and hard. David Shanks and Alan Bain won Purple Hearts. Blinded by their eagerness to succeed those two went for the same ball and banged heads. Bain was assisted from the pitch to have a head cut stitched but displayed bravery above and beyond the call of duty by returning to his front-line position 10 minutes later. Shanks was more seriously wounded. He was taken off on a stretcher dazed and clutching his nose which had been badly broken. The willingness of Clydebank's players cannot be doubted. Only last week Stuart Gordon ended up in Paisley's Royal Alexandra Infirmary after having fractured his skull playing against Dundee. Perhaps it is a blessing in disguise that they have run out of time. These lads really are ready to die for the cause." Clydebank were relegated with news of Falkirk's surprise 2-1 win at Parkhead. Falkirk scored after 40 seconds but Celtic got back on terms before a late winner saved Falkirk. In the League Cup Clydebank had beaten St Johnstone before going out at Motherwell. In the Scottish Cup they reached the last eight. They knocked out Falkirk after a replay and then beat Hibs 1-0 thanks to a Gordon effort after a quarter of an hour. They then lost 4-0 at home to Dundee, where a crowd of over 5,000 saw them go 3-0 down after 22 minutes.

In their following season back in the First Division a reduction of the Premier Division back from twelve clubs to ten saw only one promotion place available for the First Division champions. Clydebank, alongside fellow relegated side Hamilton Academicals, competed against Meadowbank Thistle and Forfar Athletic for this single spot. The Bankies had an abysmal start to the 1987-88 season, but recovered to finish in third position, the first of three seasons of coming in third! Clydebank were held to a 1-1 home draw against Queen of the South on the opening day, followed by back-to-back defeats at promotion rivals Hamilton and Forfar. They went a further four games without a win, picking up a solitary point and this poor run culminated in 5-1 loss against Clyde on the 12th September. The Bankies were leading 1-0 before both Dave Shanks and Ian Grant were sent off. According to reports Jack Steedman stormed into the dressing room at half-time and told both players that they would never play for the club again. After the defeat Clydebank were bottom and winless after seven games and were already 12 points behind the leaders Hamilton. In midweek they finally registered their first win, a 2-0 victory over Kilmarnock. Their form started to pick up after that and they won five in a row during October which lifted them up to seventh in the table, and in a tight league, they were crucially only five points behind leaders Hamilton.

In the Scottish Cup they caused a sensation by knocking out the holders and Premier Division side St Mirren at Love Street 3-0. Two goals from striker Ken Eadie and another by Brian Wright ended the Paisley side's defence of the trophy. There was no extended Cup run though as the Bankies went out to fellow First Division side Partick Thistle after a replay in the next round. They drew at home 2-2 but lost the replay 4-1 after conceding two in the first ten minutes. In another blow, top scorer Mike Conroy left mid-season to join St Mirren.

By the beginning of March Clydebank were in sixth place, eleven points behind leaders Hamilton. They won three in a row at the end of the March/beginning of April and in the third of these, Chic Charnley scored a hat-trick in a 3-2 win over Forfar Athletic. These victories moved them up to third, five points behind leaders Hamilton with four games to play. However, their promotion hopes were snuffed out when they lost 2-0 at home to rivals Meadowbank Thistle and they finished third, behind their opponents with seven points less than Hamilton. Tommy Bryce ended up as top scorer with 12, Mike Conroy who left in January notched 11, Chic Charnley scored 10 and Ken Eadie, who joined in January scored 8 in 17 appearances.

Manager Sam Henderson decided to step down citing outside work pressures and former player and Bankies legend Jim Fallon took up the managerial reins. Following the League's reorganisation movement between the Premier Division and First Division was now only one up and one down. Now in an extended 14 team First Division the Bankies mounted a stronger challenge to get back into the top flight, despite being up against the three relegated Premier Division sides of Falkirk, Dunfermline Athletic and Morton. Airdrieonians also managed a challenge and so five clubs competed for the First Division championship and the sole place promotion place on offer.

Once more the Bankies didn't get off to a good start, a 6-0 thumping by Rangers early in in the League Cup not helping, and it took until the 10th September before they registered their first League win, and they did it in spectacular style, thrashing Clyde 5-0 away from home. This started a run of 12 games without defeat, which eventually ended with a 3-2 loss at Brockville against promotion rivals Falkirk on the 3rd December. By the end of January 1989, with two-thirds of the fixtures completed, Clydebank were third in the table on 33 points, one point ahead of Falkirk in fourth; one behind Airdrie in second; but four points behind leaders Dunfermline Athletic on 37 points.

Crucially Clydebank suffered narrow 1-0 home defeats to both Dunfermline and Falkirk in March which severely dented their promotion challenge. Reporting on the second of these, *The Glasgow Herald,* under the headline "Bankies Last Line Just Had to Crack" wrote that "the meaning of last line of defence became all too clear as Jim Gallacher, veteran Clydebank keeper, regularly thwarted the Brockville team's efforts to score...then Gallacher made a mistake after 83 minutes. He brought down Peter Hetherston in the box. His penalty was Stuart Burgess thundering towards him to take the spot kick. Not a pretty sight, and even more heart- stopping as the ball played ping-pong with both posts before the keeper bravely stopped Burgess scoring from the rebound. Unfortunately, 60 seconds later Gallacher was beaten for the only goal of the game - from Burgess, who volleyed a poor clearance into the net from the edge of the penalty area." After the game the Bankies' coach Jim Fallon conceded that First Division football would still be at Kilbowie next season. Clydebank were now four points behind second-placed Airdrie and three behind Falkirk, in fourth place, with Dunfermline the outright leaders. Clydebank won five of their last six games but finished in third place, with Dunfermline as champions. Falkirk who had also come down finished in second place. Ken Eadie top scored with 23 goals, Owen Coyle scored 17 and Tommy Bryce scored 16. Eadie had signed for £35,000 in January 1988 from Falkirk and went on to make over 300 appearances for the club, and scored 152 goals. He was top scorer for four consecutive seasons and is the club's all-time leading scorer.

In the 1989-90 season Clydebank came in third place for the third year in a row, although this time they were a distant third. This was another frustrating season where their promotion challenge just fell short. St Johnstone were the champions, Airdrie came second but Clydebank finished a massive 14 points behind the champions. Any lingering disappointment was tempered by a fine run in the Scottish Cup which was only ended at the Semi-final stage. Their League campaign started with three wins and two defeats in their first five fixtures, but they then went seven games without a win, until they beat Alloa 4-1 away at the end of October - a brace each for Eadie and Coyle. By this point though they were down in ninth place in the 14 team division, only three points above the relegation zone. Performances picked up from here and they ended the calendar year with a 4-0 home win over the leaders St Johnstone. They carried this form into 1990 and recorded good away wins at the two key promotion challengers Airdrieonians and St Johnstone. They subsequently climbed up the table, but they finished poorly, winning only won once in their last three matches. Once again Ken Eadie finished as the club's top scorer with 25 goals and his strike partner Owen Coyle notched 18. Airdrie subsequently paid £175,000 for the services of Coyle.

The club had a terrific Scottish Cup run that saw them reach the Semi-final for the first time in their history. They entered at the Third Round stage and beat Albion Rovers 2-0 away and then drew Premier Division side St Mirren. They drew 1-1 at Love Street and a crowd of over 6,000 at Kilbowie saw them win the replay 3-2, with two goals from Ken Eadie and the other from John Davies. They drew Stirling Albion in the last eight, who were going well in the Second Division. The Bankies were held 1-1 at home but they won the replay four days later 1-0, Pat Kelly getting the winner in the 83rd minute, to set up a Semi-Final against Celtic. This tie was played at Hampden on the 14th April and any hopes of an upset were dashed as early as the 11th minute when 39 year old goalkeeper Jim Gallagher seemed late in getting down to a low shot which he could then only parry, Celtic forcing home the rebound. The 'keeper atoned for his error, many times over, as he preceded to make a number of important saves that kept his side in the game. In fact he was only beaten again four minutes from time, and on this occasion he had no chance. This second goal came shortly after the Bankies had spurned a great opportunity to equalise. A free kick was swing over and Bonner in the Celtic goal came to collect but missed the ball. The Clydebank defender Sean Sweeney, perhaps surprised by the arrival of the ball, failed to make a clean contact, and the ball bounced off his knee and wide.

The early nineties saw an end to any lingering hopes of the club reclaiming a spot in the top flight. Instead, the Bankies languished in the bottom half of the First Division. The Premier Division was going back to a 12 team top flight so two promotion places were up for grabs. They were taken by Falkirk, and Airdrie who finished one point behind the Bairns. The Bankies failed to mount a challenge and finished a disappointing eighth. The most notable result of the season came on the last day of the season when they beat Partick Thistle 7-1. In this match Eadie won the Golden Boot, clinching it with four second half strikes to pip Gordon Dalziel and finish the season with 30 goals. At the end of the season he followed Owen Coyle and joined Airdrieonians.

In the 1991-92 season they continued to remain in the lower half of the table. They lost their first three games in the League and exited the League Cup early, losing 3-0 at Hearts, all three goals coming in the first half. They first won on the 24th August, beating Montrose 4-1. Their opponents took the lead after 11 minutes before Ken Eadie equalised after half an hour. George Rowe gave Bankies the lead in the 68th minute and Clydebank made sure of the victory with two goals in the last five minutes from Paul Harvey and another from Eadie. A week later they recorded their best ever away SFL win, beating Morton 7-1 at Cappielow on the 31st August. John Henry opened the scoring for Clydebank after just six minutes although their hosts soon equalised. Eadie scored a penalty not far off half-time and in the second half the Bankies scored five goals in the last 25 minutes through Brian Wright (65), Eadie (67), Rowe (77), John Traynor (84) and then Eadie got his hat-trick with a second penalty in the 86th minute. However, the club then went on a poor run of six games without a win before beating

Patrick Thistle 3-0 away in early October, Rowe and Eadie (2), scoring in the last quarter of an hour. Form picked up after this and they themselves went six games unbeaten across November. By the turn of the year they were in ninth place, comfortably clear of the relegation places and this is where they finished. Ken Eadie was again the club's top scorer, with 24 goals, with John Henry netting 10. In the Scottish Cup they beat Cowdenbeath 3-1, who were going well in the Second Division, and who would be promoted. In the next round they lost 5-1 at home to Hibs.

The 1992-93 season was a very similar season to the one that went before, even down to going out of the League Cup against Hearts once more. This time the Bankies only lost by one goal, which came ten minutes from time. In the League they were beaten heavily early on by Morton, 5-1, despite Tommy Bryce opening the scoring after just two minutes. They failed to win any of their first eight games but then won three out of the next four and climbed away from the foot of the table. Their best result of the season came in early March when they beat bottom of the table Cowdenbeath 5-0, leading 4-0 at the interval. Their worst result came a month later when they lost 6-0 at Kilmarnock, who earned promotion to the Premier Division, having conceded two in the first three minutes. The club eventually finished one League place higher up, in eighth place, with Ken Eadie top scoring again with 25 goals, although he was pushed all the way by Craig Flannigan who netted 23 times.

The highlight of their season was a run to the Scottish Cup Quarter-finals. They entered at the Third Round stage and knocked out last year's beaten finalist Airdrieonians, after a replay. The first game was goalless and in the replay Clydebank won 2-0, Eadie scoring at the end of each half. They then beat East Stirlingshire before drawing Aberdeen in the last eight. They drew 1-1 at Pittodrie, despite falling behind after just two minutes. Martin McIntosh equalised in the 82nd minute to earn a replay at Kilbowie on the night of Tuesday the 16th March 1993. The match attracted a crowd of 8,000 who saw the Dons go two up after just 25 minutes. However, on the stroke of half-time Eadie got one back and just before the hour mark John Maher brought the Bankies level. The Kilbowie crowd were in raptures when John Henry put Clydebank 3-2 up ten minutes later. However, Scott Booth scored twice in the last fifteen minutes to give Aberdeen a 4-3 victory.

After three disappointing League seasons club legend Jimmy Fallon was replaced as manager by Brian Wright for the start of the 1993-94 season. The former midfielder player, who made over 500 appearances, the majority for Hamilton, had also made over 50 starts for the club between 1990 and 1992. Further League reconstruction would be introduced for the 1994–95 season resulting in four divisions of ten teams. This meant that there would be a new Scottish Third Division, so this season the bottom five teams would be relegated from the First Division and only one club promoted. Any repeat of the last two seasons would see Clydebank drop down to the third tier.

They needn't have worried as they made a fabulous start to the new season winning seven League matches in row from the start of the season. Craig Flannigan scored six goals in those games and would end up as top scorer for the season, albeit with 13 goals. Only one win in the next seven games undermined any promotion bid and they failed to score for five consecutive League games between mid-December and mid-January and they eventually finished in fifth place. In the
League Cup they were thrashed 5-0 by Aberdeen, Duncan Shearer scoring a hat-trick against them. In the Scottish Cup they were knocked out by Premier side Dundee after a replay. In the first match at home they were leading 1-0 with less than ten minutes to go but conceded in the 84th minute.

For the 1994-95 season the division now consisted of ten teams and Clydebank finished in eighth place, avoiding relegation by six points from Ayr United with Stranraer adrift at the bottom. The Bankies only won eight League games, although their points total was boosted by the introduction of three points for a win. They beat Stranraer in their opening game and in early September hit five against Dundee in a 5-2 win. On the 5th November they lost 4-1 at Dunfermline, which was part of a run of 14 League games without a win. They eventually won again on the 14th February 1995 when they recorded a 2-0 victory over Airdrie. In the League Cup the club had been knocked out by Premier League Motherwell. In the Scottish Cup they went out to Hearts, but only after a replay. In March 1995 the club was stunned by the sudden death of club legend Davie Cooper, aged 39, after suffering a brain haemorrhage. He was still on the club's books and had contributed four goals in what was to be his final season.

There was more misery off the field as well. The club had sustained heavy losses over the previous two seasons and the club accounts for the period ending June 1995 showed a deficit of about £120,000. Based on missives dated mid-July 1995 the club agreed to sell Kilbowie Park to Vico Projects Limited, a development company, for £2.3 million, subject to obtaining planning consent for a mixture of leisure and retail purposes. However, this was strongly opposed by local residents and was refused. An appeal to the Secretary of State against that refusal was also unsuccessful.

Back on the pitch the 1995-96 season was another one of struggle although the club was able to maintain its First Division status. They finished one place higher in seventh but were only four points ahead of Hamilton who were relegated in ninth, along with Dumbarton who came bottom with only 11 points. The club started reasonably well, going undefeated in their first three League games. At the end of October they were beaten 3-0 by Dundee United and then 4-0 at home to Dunfermline and from Mid-December they went two months and nine games without a win. On the 23rd March they lost 6-0 at Dundee United, with Craig Brewster scoring a hat-trick and former player Owen Coyle scoring the last. By this time the club had also been on the wrong end of a Cup shock, losing 1-0 at home to Second Division Stirling Albion in the Scottish Cup. On the 13th April 1996 a crowd of just over 800 attended their penultimate home League game against Airdrie. A fortnight later a crowd over four times that size attended their final home game. By this time news had broken that the sale of Kilbowie Park was now going through. Clydebank played its last competitive game at Kilbowie against Hamilton on the 27th April 1996 watched by a staggering crowd of 3,665, with the Bankies losing 3-1 and Ken Eadie scoring the club's last goal at their home.

The club made a substantial loss of close to £250,000 for the season but this was offset when Vico made a loan of £600,000 set against the proposed purchase price of Kilbowie of £2.3 million, which remained subject to planning consents. The result was that a surplus of £145,000 appeared in the balance sheet as at 30 June 1996. Far from easing the club's ills the sale of Kilbowie accelerated the club's decline. Clydebank spent the next six years playing "home" games at first Boghead Park, Dumbarton, followed by Cappielow Park, Greenock. Fans were mucked about as the club became nomadic and the change of locations were not popular with Clydebank fans, many of whom deserted the club. While the redevelopment of Kilbowie Park was under planning considerations the property, including the social club premises located there, were seriously damaged by vandalism and as the vacant buildings began to decay demolition orders were ultimately served in respect of several of the structures.

On Saturday 10th August 1996 Clydebank kicked off the new season at Boghead against East Stirlingshire, playing out a 0-0 draw in a Challenge Cup match in front of a crowd of about 600. They played their next game, a League Cup fixture against Rangers at Firhill, losing 3-0 and they started their League campaign with a 1-0 victory over Stirling Albion on the 24th August. Inconsistent early form gave way to a poor run during the last three months of 1996 where they won only two League games out of twelve. The second of these, at home to East Fife on the 21st December, saw a crowd of just 350 turn up. Having drawn Rangers in the League Cup, the Bankies drew Celtic in the Scottish Cup. The tie was once again switched to Firhill where a crowd of 16,000 saw Celtic win 5-0. By this time East Fife were well adrift at the bottom of the First Division, having been promoted the year before, and they finished bottom with only 14 points and two wins. Unfortunately Clydebank were also in trouble as a big gap opened up between them in ninth place and the rest. The Bankies only won seven games and finished on 28 points, well behind Morton and Second Division champions Stirling

Albion on 45 and 46 points respectively. With the writing on the wall manager Brian Wright resigned and player Davie Irons, in his second spell at the club, assumed management responsibilities as caretaker until the end of the season.

Halfway through the season a significant step towards a change in ownership of the club occurred. In January 1997 representatives of Dr John Hall, a Glasgow millionaire based in Bermuda, had approached the club and offered £150,000 on the basis that the existing shareholders "would retain ownership of the heritable assets and liabilities of the Company, including any planning gain." With the club now relegated to the Second Division and much of the club support having melted away the prospect of a new stadium seemed remote, and this was confirmed when discussions were initiated around ground sharing with the West of Scotland Rugby Football Club based in Milngavie.

The Steedman family proceeded to sell the club to Hall and a press statement drafted on behalf of the purchaser was issued, which included the following: "A company controlled by Dr John Hall has today acquired a controlling interest in Clydebank Football Club Limited. Dr Hall is a Scot, who is currently working in Bermuda who has been appointed Chairman of Clydebank subject to approval of The Scottish Football Association and The Scottish Football League. Dr Hall, with his fellow directors, intend to instruct management consultants with a view to determining the best means of provision of first class football to the Clydebank supporters, whose loyalty will not be taken for granted. The new player-manager Ian McCall and his squad have already demonstrated their skills and enthusiasm..."

McCall was appointed as the new manager and under his guidance the club bounced right back finishing as runners-up in the Second Division. They were just pipped to the title by Stranraer by a single point. Playing at Boghead, in front of a paltry crowd of just 316 spectators, they opened their League campaign on the 5th August with a 3-0 win over Brechin City. They picked up two wins and two draws in their first four fixtures and although they then lost to East Fife they followed this with a run of 15 games in the League without defeat and in the first six of these they didn't concede a single goal. The club had exited the League Cup at the first hurdle, losing 2-0 against St Mirren. In the Scottish Cup though they thrashed Montrose 6-0, with six different goalscorers, to set up a tie against Hearts at Tynecastle, which they lost 2-0.

Events off the pitch continued to dominate though. The Steedman's and the other directors set up a company for the heritable assets of the club in December 1997, most noticeably Kilbowie Park. When the sale of this asset finally went through the sum was £2.3 million, out of which the Vico loan of £600,000 fell to be repaid. Thus Kilbowie realised a net sum of £1.7 million for the previous owners. Kilbowie was subsequently redeveloped and became a retail development with shops and restaurants. Around this time rumours started to circulate about the intentions of the new owners to relocate the club to Dublin, although to continue to play in the Scottish League. The club's supporters were understandably furious and protest groups were soon set up. At the end of February 1998 the away fans invaded the pitch at Forfar and staged a protest. There was also a walk out at home to Livingston and then a fan boycott in their next home game against East Fife when only 186 spectators watched the game. Unfortunately the effect of these protests was more keenly felt by the performance of the team. Leading the table at the beginning of February they won only two games in their next ten matches and during this time they failed to score in five consecutive matches.

At the beginning of April they lost 2-1 at promotion rivals Stranraer and then 1-0 at home to Forfar. On the 18th April they beat East Fife 2-0 thanks to goals by top scorer Colin McDonald and Gary Teale and at this point the Bankies were in second place, two points behind the leaders Livingston and a point ahead of Stranraer in third. A week later they went down 2-0 at Clyde but Stranraer also lost while Livingston drew. In the penultimate round of games Clydebank were held 1-1 by fourth placed Queen of the South but Stranraer beat the leaders Livingston 2-0 to leapfrog into second place. Livingston remained top on 59 points, Stranraer had 58, and Clydebank had 57, but the Bankies had the worst goal difference of the three sides. With only two points separating the top sides and with goal difference likely to be a factor the Bankies needed a big away win at Brechin City on the last day of the season to have any chance of promotion. On Saturday 9th May Clydebank thrashed Brechin 6-1 at Glebe Park with goals from Kenny Ward and Derek Williams, who both scored two, and also from Joe McLaughlin and Gary Teale. Stranraer won 1-0 away at Clyde to secure the Second Division championship but it was Livingston's 2-1 home defeat at the hands of Inverness Caledonian Thistle that ensured the Bankies were promoted on 60 points, finishing one behind the champions but one ahead of Livingston.

Clydebank made a creditable return to the First Division and finished in seventh place. They were never under any threat of relegation, as they started well, losing only one of their first five League matches, and recording three wins in a row from the end of September. They had a little wobble in November when they failed to win any of their four League fixtures, although that did include three draws. In the Cups they made an early exit in the League Cup against Raith Rovers. In the Scottish Cup they beat Ross County after a replay. They then drew 2-2 at home to Dundee United, before losing the replay 3-0. Colin McDonald was again the top scorer, this time with ten, although the next best contribution was just three. Gates continued to be poor though, averaging between 250 and 300 and the season drew to a close.

Off the pitch the new owners sued the Steedman's and the other former directors in connection with the sale of Kilbowie. At the same time the folly of the Dublin plan began to unravel and subsequent attempts were made to investigate the feasibility of relocating the club. None of these came to fruition and there was a complete breakdown in trust between the owners and the fans. This was further exacerbated when the club switched their home games from Dumbarton to Greenock Morton's Cappielow ground.

For the 1999-2000 season the club's performances on the pitch reached a new nadir. Clydebank were relegated from the First Division earning only ten points. The Bankies won just one League game all season and lost 28 (although they at least avoided matching the unwanted record of Vale of Leven in 1892, who went the whole of the season without winning a game. This feat was eventually matched by Brechin City in 2018). They had to wait until March and their 27th League fixture before recording their one and only win. In a truly dreadful season they scored only 17 League goals in 36 matches, conceding 82.

The new season opened on the 31st July 1999 with 2-1 home defeat to East Stirling in the League Cup. This was their first game at Cappielow and was subject to a fan boycott with only 69 spectators present, although the gate is recorded as only 29 on the resurrected club's website. The *Glasgow Herald* clears up the confusion: "Dr John Hall, the Bermuda-based owner of Clydebank FC, was urged to sell the club last night after they went into the record books for staging a game where the crowd barely outnumbered the players. Just 29 people paid to see the first-division side lose 2-1 to East Stirling in the first round of the CIS Insurance Cup on Saturday - the smallest attendance at a senior game in Britain. Of these only 13 were Bankies fans. The crowd was swollen to 69 when spies from other clubs plus guests with complimentary tickets were taken into account."

Their League campaign kicked off in similar fashion, losing at home to Airdrie 2-0 on the 7th August, this time with a gate of 425. The next two games were both drawn – away at Morton and home to Raith - but the Bankies lost nine League games in a row during September and October for the second time in the club's history (although they did record some victories in the Challenge Cup). This sequence was eventually ended with a goalless draw at Ayr United on the 6th November. By this time Clydebank were firmly rooted to the bottom of the Second Division, having played 13, won nil, drawn two and lost 11. By the time January came the Bankies had not won any of their 21 matches and only had four draws to their credit. Manager Ian McCall then took the opportunity to jump the sinking ship and took over at Greenock Morton. He was replaced by Steve Morrison, a midfielder who had a long playing career with a number of League clubs, most noticeably Dunfermline Athletic, but also Clyde and Dumbarton.

Clydebank did beat Stirling Albion in the Scottish Cup on the 29th January 2000, thanks to a goal by defender Fraser Wishart, and they then held Hibs away in the next round, drawing 1-1 at Easter Road on the 19th February. With the club struggling, a massive shock was on the cards when Clydebank took the lead in 63rd minute from a penalty converted by Lee Gardner but their lead was short-lived when their hosts equalised just three minutes later. Hibs went on to comfortably win the replay 3-0 at Cappielow in front of a crowd of 2,500. Due to player shortages manager Steve Morrison was required to play, in goal. This was the not the first time he had been called upon in this respect, it was actually his fourth go between the sticks. Hibs took the lead six minutes before half-time. Bankies stayed in the tie until there was twenty minutes left when Hibs scored twice in eight minutes. Hibs went on to reach the Final where they lost 2-1 to Aberdeen.

Going into March the Bankies had still failed to record a League victory. At this point they had played 26 matches which had produced four draws and 22 losses. On the 4th March only 168 spectators were present at Cappielow to see the club lose 1-0 to Inverness Caley Thistle. However, a few days later, on the evening of Tuesday the 7th March, the Bankies avoided the ignominy of going an entire campaign in the Scottish First Division without a victory, when they recorded a narrow 2-1 win over Raith Rovers. *The Herald* reported on this momentous and rare event, saying that "mere mathematics separate Clydebank from confirmation of their relegation, but last night the debt-ridden club at last had something to celebrate after a nightmare season, when two goals from Ian Cameron led them to their first league win of the season." It was a miserable night, and only 250 supporters braved the unrelenting rain to watch the game. Cameron, the veteran former Aberdeen winger struck twice within the first twenty minutes to give Clydebank a healthy lead and his goals lifted the spirits of the crowd. The first was a free-kick, taken from 30 yards out and which was swept superbly into the top corner of the net, as Guido van de Kamp in the Raith goal "flailed uselessly to his right." His second came from a Murray Hunter assist, who nodded the ball in the penalty area into the path of Cameron who struck a low drive into the net. Raith came right back into the game and mid-way through the first half Paul Tosh scored. Craig Dargo made good progress down the left and his centre eluded Colin Scott in the Clydebank goal and fell to Tosh who scored from a few yards out. Scott made amends by saving bravely at the feet of Dargo but suffered a head injury as a result. Done to the bare bones, Clydebank had no substitute goalkeeper. Derek McWilliams, a midfielder replaced Scott at half-time but it was Hunter who went into goal for the second half. Clydebank held out for the second half to record their first League win and the team were applauded off the pitch.

Prophetically, the United Clydebank Supporters chairman Gordon Robertson, while pleased with the result was worried about the future of the club off the park, commenting that "what has overshadowed everything on the park - even when they have done well - is the long term future of the club. We are all scared witless that there won't be a club there in future years so it doesn't matter if we are winning the First Division or at the bottom without a win. Ultimately the only thing which is worrying the supporters is where the club will be in two or three years' time."

Hopes of a longer term recovery and relegation Houdini-act were quickly dashed on the Saturday (the 11th March). It was a case of normal service being resumed as the Bankies came down to earth with a bump, crashing 8-0 to St Mirren. Clydebank's goalkeeping crisis was a contributory factor. With Colin Scott injured against Raith on the Tuesday night, Clydebank manager Steve Morrison had been forced to quickly search for a replacement. Ben Plevey, a 24 year old former RAF man and physical training instructor, and once on the books of Aston Villa, was signed on a one-match deal. The deal was struck at the eleventh hour so Plevey had no opportunity to train with his new team and in fact only met his new team mates ninety minutes before the kick-off. Plevey confessed after the game that he didn't even know the names of the defenders in front of him and so shouted instructions by calling out their shirt numbers. This point was quickly seized upon by the *Daily Record* who led with the headline "Battered Ben couldn't tell the difference between Bankies defenders". The circumstances surrounding Plevey's disastrous debut overshadowed the performance of St Mirren's Barry Lavety, who came on as an early substitute and scored a hat-trick. Lavety came on in only the seventh minute as a replacement for Junior Mendes who had suffered a back injury. A couple of minutes later the league Leaders opened the scoring through Steve McGarry, who picked up the ball and turned and shot into the top left. An Iain Nicolson effort was then cleared off the line before Barry 'Basher' Lavety opened his account on twenty minutes by bundling the ball in at the back post. St Mirren's third goal was both comical and embarrassing. A chance fell to their leading scorer Mark Yardley, but he miscued his shot. But Plevey dived anyway in the direction he thought the ball was going. The mis-kicked ball fell to Ian Ross, and with Plevey still prone on the ground, he somewhat apologetically kicked the ball into the empty net. The Bankies reached half-time without suffering any further losses but after only six minutes of the second half they went four down. First, Murray juggled the ball past two defenders and then rifled in from six yards. Just five minutes later Lavety bagged his second. He was played in by McGarry's pass and slotted the ball past Plevey into the bottom right hand corner. Things then began to go from bad to worse. Plevey missed the ball as he flapped and flailed at Ian Ross's cross and Murray volleyed in his second to make the score 6-0. Just four minutes later Clydebank's poor defending of set pieces cost them again as Scott Walker headed in from Ross's corner. And then St Mirren made it five in twenty second half minutes when Lavety got his hat-trick. Again a weakness in defending crosses was Plevey's undoing as Lavety met a cross from Ross with a glancing header to make it 8-0. As the *Herald* noted "the only surprise was that Saints didn't go on to reach double figures as their eighth goal came after only seventy minutes." Ironically St Mirren's failure to add to their score was attributable to Plevey who made a couple of good saves later in the game. As he revealed later "I was determined not to become a quiz question in pub trivia games."

As it was St Mirren scored eight for the first time since beating Third Lanark in the Scottish Cup in 1961 and the Saints, under Tom Hendrie would go on to win the League by five points. Lavety's hat-trick took his tally to 15, one behind Yardley who drew a blank. The eight goals conceded by the Bankies was their record defeat. As for Ben Plevey, this was to be his one and only appearance, strangely enough, and he headed back to Birmingham.

At the end of the game Clydebank were 15 points adrift at the bottom of the table, having played 28 games and won just one and losing 25 times. In the remaining eight games of the League season their relegation was confirmed, as they picked up three points, from three 0-0 draws, but also suffered a 6-0 defeat at division runners-up Dunfermline. They lost 4-0 at Ayr the following week before drawing 0-0 with St Mirren at home. They then lost 1-0 at home to Falkirk before losing 2-1 at home to Livingston, Cameron scoring the club's only goal in their last six League matches. On the 15th April they lost 6-0 at Dunfermline. Kick off was delayed by half an hour after the Bankies' coach got caught up in roadworks and by half-time they must have wished that they hadn't made it all when they were four-nil down, Stevie Morrison commenting that "we should have turned back at Cumbernauld!"

The Bankies drew two of their remaining three fixtures 0-0 and finished the season with just ten points, earned from one win and seven draws. They finished 19 points adrift of Airdrie and scored just 17 goals all season, failing to score in 23 out of 36 League games. After two years back in the First Division the homeless club returned to playing in the Second Division. The season ended with the club being advertised for sale in *The Scotsman* by the club owners for £250,000.

The following two seasons in the Second Division saw the Bankies finish mid-table on both occasions. By this time their financial problems had become acute. Home support had melted away after they left Kilbowie Park and falling gates meant reduced income and the club had to enter administration. Ex-player Tommy Coyne became the new player-manager for the new 2000-01 season. The club got a point in their opening game, a 2-2 draw away against Stirling Albion, followed by a 1-0 home win over Stenhousemuir, with Coyne scoring the goal. However, a crowd of only 236 was present at Cappielow to see them win.

Worse was to follow. When they hosted Berwick Rangers on Saturday 4th November the crowd was down to 196. A fortnight later at home to Forfar it was 153 and on Tuesday 5th December only 126 fans came to the home game against Stranraer. Back in the courts, at the end of September, the club's present owners lost their court case against the Steedman's over the sale of the ground, with the judge ruling that he was "satisfied that the shareholders of the Company had sufficient information before them and that the passing of the resolution at the Extraordinary General Meeting constituted a valid approval by them of the arrangement which was subsequently carried through." In December the club had no option but to enter administration. In February the club conceded four goals in successive week against the top two sides in the Division - Partick and Arbroath. The administrators took the decision to sack Coyne just six months into his tenure. The club were sitting in fourth place at the time, but were well off the promotion places. Tony Fitzpatrick and Fraser Wishart were placed in temporary charge before Derek Ferguson was appointed as manager. Ferguson would be the club's last ever manager in the Scottish League. Ferguson, a creative midfield player, most noticeably for Rangers and Hearts, joined from Ross County as player-manager. Capped twice for Scotland he went on to make over 50 appearances for the club.

Towards the end of March reports started to circulate expressing doubts over the club's ability to fulfil their forthcoming League match against Berwick Rangers. Unnamed club officials were quoted as hoping that the game would fall victim to the weather so they would not have to seek a postponement from the League authorities. It was reported on *BBC News* that administrator Bryan Jackson had said "I have given the creditors a final chance to reconsider and have given them until Tuesday. If they do not, then I will resign and the club will most likely be wound up. We were very close to an agreement, that's the aggravating thing. Everybody said they did not want to see the demise of the club but their actions have not backed that up." Glasgow businessman David McGhie wanted to buy the club but couldn't agree terms with the main creditors, with owner Hall reportedly owed £600,000. The game against Berwick was postponed and a few days later a deal was reportedly agreed. A spokesman for McGhie told the *Sunday Mail*: "We are delighted an agreement has been reached. We have been trying our very best for several months to sort it all out. The settlement means we can look forward to a bright future for the club and we will do everything possible to get Clydebank back to where they belong." Ultimately the ownership deal unravelled and the club remained in administration although they did finish a comfortable mid-table fifth place in the Second Division.

The 2001-02 would prove to be their last ever season in the Scottish Football League. Bankies boss Ferguson remoulded his side for the new season and although there was a large turnover of players the club started as one of the favourites for promotion. They won their opening game at Forfar 2-1 and their first home game against Hamilton, 3-2, watched by a crowd of 367. Their "home" game against Morton at Cappielow attracted 1,142 fans on the 8th September but their home game versus Cowdenbeath less than a fortnight later attracted only 154. The club was knocked out of the League Cup by Dumbarton and made a disappointing exit in the Scottish Cup. Having beaten Third Division Peterhead they went out at home to fellow Second Division side Stranraer 1-0. This turned out to be their last Cup game and victory would have given them a lucrative home tie against Hibernian. They then beat Stranraer away, in the League, the following Saturday by the same score.

By the beginning of March the Bankies were making a strong promotion push alongside Queen of the South and Alloa Athletic. On the 16th March they travelled to Alloa and were leading 2-1 until their hosts equalised in the last minute. The result allowed Queen of the South to pull three points clear of Clydebank at the top, with Alloa one point behind but with a game in hand. However, the Bankies only won one of their last ten League matches as their promotion push petered out. Queen of the South finished as the Second Division champions and Clydebank finished in fourth place, eight points behind Alloa in second. Morton, their hosts, were relegated in last place.

What would turn out to be last ever League game was the rescheduled match at home to Berwick Rangers on the 27th April 2002. The club's League history ended in defeat as they lost 2-1 in front of a paltry crowd of 209. The Bankies ended the match with ten men after Mark Nicholls was sent off 16 minutes from time for taking a kick at an opposing player. The visitors took the lead as early as the 18th minute and doubled their advantage seven minutes later. Clydebank hit back with an Eric Paton header after 30 minutes, but any chances of a late revival disappeared with Nicholls' dismissal. Clydebank's last ever goal League was thus scored by Paton, who ended up with nine for the season, one less than Alex Burke. The last Clydebank starting eleven for a Scottish League fixture was: Henry Smith, Andy Whiteford, Neil McGowan, Simon Vella, Liam McVey, Brian McColligan, Mark Nicholls, Eric Paton, Alan Gow, Ally Graham and Paul Shields.

Less than three months later the club's identity disappeared. The end came on the 11th July 2002 and it came indirectly as a result of the demise of First Division Airdrieonians. When that club went bust local businessman Jim Ballantyne set up Airdrie United as a phoenix club and immediately applied for membership of the League. However, the reincarnated Airdrie club surprisingly lost the vote to Gretna on the 18th June 2002 by 16 votes to 11. Ballantyne then turned his attentions to the ailing Clydebank. He offered to buy the club's few assets from the administrators if the Scottish Football League would agree to let him change the name of Clydebank to Airdrie United, change the strip to an Airdrieonians strip and play games at New Broomfield, the former Airdrieonians stadium.

The football authorities decided to authorise this rare move given Clydebank's declining support, their lack of progress in securing a new home and especially given their protracted time in administration plus the perceived financial unviability of the club. The Bankies had been in administration for two years and prospective buyer David McGhie had now withdrawn his interest after 12 months of negotiations had ultimately proved fruitless. By this time player manager Derek Ferguson had left to join Alloa as a player and a number of players had been released, including Eric Paton, as the club announced its intention to switch to part-time football.

On Monday 1st July Ballantyne was given the go-ahead for the buyout by the SFL. The League's Management Committee unanimously gave the green light for Clydebank to undergo a change of name, strip and stadium. Ballantyne met with the Clydebank's administrators the following day to try to conclude the takeover. At the end of the week and although the writing appeared to be on the wall for the Bankies, the Supporters group fighting to save Clydebank from takeover were given a lifeline when the administrator informed the United Clydebank Supporters group that they had until Monday to come up with the £160,000 needed to continue in their present guise. Administrator Bryan Jackson of PKF told *The Scotsman*: "The Clydebank people are trying to put the funds together to come in and retain Clydebank as a club. I have now set a deadline of close of business on Monday for them to do that. I am still progressing with the Airdrie United bid for Clydebank at the moment, but there are a few administrative and technical problems to overcome before it can be completed. No-one has preferred bidder status but, as we speak, I would say the Airdrie United bid is still the front-runner. Having said that, I have no doubt about how genuine the intentions are of the Clydebank people and they are trying hard to come up with the necessary finance. My agenda is simply to get a dividend back to Clydebank's creditors." The *Sunday Mail* then reported that a source had confirmed that the fans consortium had failed to match the Airdrie bid but when the deadline passed the administrator confirmed the Airdrie takeover based on their consortium submitting a higher bid of £170,000. The Supporters Group were furious but time was against them as they debated whether to pursue a legal injunction. Bryan Jackson of the administrators said the decision to accept Ballantyne's offer was simply because they were the highest bidders. He said: "I received two offers, the highest one being from Airdrie Football Club Limited. As Nominee of Clydebank FC Limited, my primary duty is to the creditors and, accordingly, having taken legal advice, I accepted the highest offer received."

On the 11th July 2002 the new Airdrie club were included in the draw for the SFL Challenge Cup and Clydebank's name disappeared from the fixture list. SFL secretary Peter Donald admitted he was sorry to see the name of Clydebank disappear, saying that "the name Clydebank will not continue in Scottish football and that is a matter of great regret as Clydebank had a great role to play for many years."

The Clydebank Supporters group moved quickly to constitute a new club but it was too late for them to join the Junior ranks, while the East of Scotland and South of Scotland Leagues had also approved their fixture lists so there was no competition for them to enter for the 2002-03 season. Airdrie United did at least agree to transfer their unwanted ownership of the name and insignia of Clydebank FC to the new club. For the 2003-04 season, the resurrected club, playing at Drumchapel Amateurs' Glenhead Park ground in Duntocher, entered the Scottish Junior Football Association, West Region. Former player Billy McGhie was appointed manager of the club in July 2003 and was in charge until December 2016. During his long tenure the club enjoyed a successful run to the Final of the Scottish Junior Cup and they also worked their way up through the regional leagues gaining promotion to the West Region Premiership. Back in June 2008 they entered into a ground share at Yoker Athletic's Holm Park.

SEASON	LEAGUE	P	W	D	L	F	A	P	POS
1966-67	SCOT-2	38	8	8	22	59	92	24	18/20
1967-68	SCOT-2	36	13	8	15	62	73	34	9/19
1968-69	SCOT-2	36	6	15	15	52	67	27	13/19
1969-70	SCOT-2	36	10	10	16	47	65	30	13/19
1970-71	SCOT-2	36	17	8	11	57	43	42	5/19
1971-72	SCOT-2	36	14	11	11	60	52	39	9/19
1972-73	SCOT-2	36	9	6	21	48	72	21	17/19
1973-74	SCOT-2	36	13	8	15	47	48	34	10/19

1974-75	SCOT-2	38	18	8	12	50	40	44	7/20
1975-76	SCOT-2	26	17	6	3	44	13	40	1/14
1976-77	SCOT-1	39	24	10	5	89	38	58	2/14
1977-78	SCOT-P	36	6	7	23	23	64	19	10/10
1978-79	SCOT-1	39	24	6	9	78	50	54	3/14
1979-80	SCOT-1	39	14	8	17	58	57	36	9/14
1980-81	SCOT-1	39	10	13	16	48	59	33	10/14
1981-82	SCOT-1	39	19	8	12	61	53	46	4/14
1982-83	SCOT-1	39	20	10	9	72	49	50	3/14
1983-84	SCOT-1	39	16	13	10	62	50	45	4/14
1984-85	SCOT-1	39	17	14	8	57	37	48	2/14
1985-86	SCOT-P	36	6	8	22	29	77	20	10/10
1986-87	SCOT-P	44	6	12	26	35	93	24	11/12
1987-88	SCOT-1	44	21	7	16	59	61	49	3/12
1988-89	SCOT-1	39	18	12	9	80	55	48	3/14
1989-90	SCOT-1	39	17	10	12	74	64	44	3/14
1990-91	SCOT-1	39	13	10	16	65	70	36	8/14
1991-92	SCOT-1	44	12	12	20	59	77	36	9/12
1992-93	SCOT-1	44	16	13	15	71	66	45	8/12
1993-94	SCOT-1	44	18	14	12	56	48	50	5/12
1994-95	SCOT-1	36	8	11	17	33	47	35	8/10
1995-96	SCOT-1	36	10	10	16	39	58	40	7/10
1996-97	SCOT-1	36	7	7	22	31	59	28	9/10
1997-98	SCOT-2	36	16	12	8	48	31	60	2/10
1998-99	SCOT-1	36	11	13	12	36	38	46	7/10
1999-00	SCOT-1	36	1	7	28	17	82	10	10/10
2000-01	SCOT-2	36	12	11	13	42	43	47	5/10
2001-02	SCOT-2	36	14	9	13	44	45	51	4/10

Cowlairs

Formed: 1876
Colours: White shirts, dark blue shorts and then red shirts and navy blue shorts
Ground: Springvale Park
Entered League: 1890. Founder members of the Scottish Football League. 1893. Founder members of Second Division
Number of League Seasons: 3
Honours: None
Highest League Finish: 10th in Division One
Left League: 1891. Failed re-election. 1895. Failed re-election

Cowlairs were a Glasgow based club and one of the founding members of the Scottish Football League in 1890. They only lasted one season before dropping out of the League but they returned shortly afterwards when the SFL introduced a Second Division in 1893. They only played two further seasons in this division before dropping out of the League altogether.

Cowlairs were based in the Springburn district of the city, north of the River Clyde. The team was a works team, formed in 1876 by craftsmen from the Hyde Park and Cowlairs Railway works which later became the North British Railway's main workshop. As Glasgow experienced industrial expansion around its shipbuilding, so associated industries such as iron and steel works flourished. There was also a growth in the railways with a number of locomotive works based in this area of Glasgow producing rolling stock.

Cowlairs originally played their games at Gourlay Park between 1876 and 1890. They moved to Springvale Park, located on Cowlairs Road, following their admission to the SFL although they returned to Gourlay Park after leaving the SFL.

Cowlairs entered the Scottish Cup for the first time in 1880 where they reached the Fourth Round, beating Glasgow and Dunbartonshire teams in the early regionalised rounds. They beat another Springburn based team Petershill 4-3, Oxford of Glasgow 4-3 and Alexandria Athletic 2-1 (twice after the first game was subject to a protest), before losing to St Mirren.

The following season they were drawn against the all-conquering Queen's Park in the Second Round and held them to a 2-2 draw, the *Glasgow Herald* commenting "the result of which surprised more than the players in the match." Cowlairs went from one down to two-one up. "The match was one of the best seen for some time, and the Cowlairs team is certainly the most formidable that has as yet come against the Queen's Park in their matches this season. The play-off will be worth seeing." The replay was indeed worth seeing, if you were a Queen's Park fan, as they won the replay 9-0. In later rounds they beat Partick Thistle 10-0 and Shotts 15-0 in the Quarter-finals, going on to lift the trophy for the sixth time.

The following year Cowlairs scored a big victory of their own. On the 30th September 1882 Cowlairs beat fellow Glaswegians Apsley at Gourlay Park in a second round tie 13-0. The visitors kicked off but Cowlairs in their first attack scored through a Weir header. After ten minutes play the one-sided nature of the game was apparent with Cowlairs having scored another two goals. Before half-time the home team had added another five goals to lead 8-0 at the interval and they added a handful before time was called. They were knocked out by Partick Thistle in the next round

In the 1887-88 competition Cowlairs progressed as far as the Fifth Round, recording two 9-1 victories en-route. The first of these came in the Second Round when they beat Southern Athletic on the 24th September. The *Glasgow Herald* reported on the game saying "this tie in the second round of the Scottish Cup was played at Gourlay Park, the ground of the Cowlairs. The strangers kicked off 25 minutes late, when the ball was returned and sent past. Five minutes from the time of starting Bishop was successful in scoring a goal. Scott added another point to the score. Matters were looking serious for the Athletic, play being principally conducted in their half of the field. The strangers, however, had an excellent goalkeeper, who saved many a well-directed shot. From a foul the Athletic passed the ball down to their opponents' goal, but were repulsed, the Cowlairs taking the ball back, scoring two goals in five minutes. An exciting scrimmage occurred in front of the Cowlairs posts, and a goal would have been the result but for an unfortunate foul. No more points were gained and the result at half-time was Cowlairs 4 goals, Athletic nil. At the commencement of the second half the Athletic assumed the offensive but the Cowlairs turned the tables and scored the first goal. A high, swift shot was then delivered at the strangers' goal, but the goalkeeper saved in splendid style. After some play, a scrimmage took place...and Cowlairs almost scored. They returned, however, and were successful in putting on two more points, and then shortly after, another. About eight minutes before time the strangers secured a soft goal, which rather surprised the Cowlairs. The home team retaliated by putting on another goal. No more points were gained, and the result was –Cowlairs 9 goals, Southern Athletic 1 goal." The Cowlairs team that day was: in goal, Hunt; backs,

McLeod and McCartney; half-backs, McPherson, Sinclair, Sommerville; forwards, Carson, Scott, Reynolds, McInnes and Bishop. Three of this team played for their country. William McLeod had already been capped for Scotland while playing for Cowlairs, playing in March 1886 against Ireland in a 7-2 win. Tom McInnes would go on to be capped once in March 1889, scoring in the 88th minute in a 7-0 rout of Ireland. He was eventually lured down south and played for Notts County. John McPherson, won two of his nine caps while at Cowlairs, in March and April 1890. He joined Rangers in August 1890 for the first SFL season and made nine appearances for Scotland up to 1897, scoring six goals.

In the next round, on the 15th October 1887, they played Campsie. Cowlairs opened the scoring after ten minutes and after a series of corners Campsie equalised. Cowlairs restored their lead and at half-time led 2-1. From the restart Cowlairs scored again and totally dominated the second forty-five, running out 9-1 winners. The Cup run was ended by a 5-1 defeat to Arbroath.

The following year Cowlairs notched up their biggest victory to date. On the 1st September 1888 they beat Temperance Athletic 18-2. The *Glasgow Herald* reported on the match: "The Athletics had the first try but set the ball wide. With a nice low shot McPherson made the first decisive point, and a minute or two afterwards Small registered a second goal for Cowlairs. Nothing daunted, the strangers came up the field in fine style and shooting smartly, eluded Duff. A third goal in favour of Cowlairs enabled the juniors to get to close quarters, but McLeod speedily relieved all anxiety. From a foul the right wing of the Athletics succeeded in laying siege to the home citadel, but unfortunately at the critical moment they kicked wide. Their front division was in beautiful form, and would have done much better had they been at all ably supported, but almost every time the Cowlairs got near the posts they scored. Latterly the Springburns men simply amused their opponents and displayed an amount of indifference in taking goals that is not usual with them. Time after time the ball went over the bar, but it was hardly away till it was back again. A smart run by the Temperance left managed to pass McLeod, and compelled Duff to fist out. A corner next fell to their lot, but it only ended in the ball being once more transferred to the other end, where McInnes sent it over the line. At half-time the score stood – Cowlairs 7 goals; Athletics 1. On changing ends, the Cowlairs continued pressing, till their opponents broke away, and had a good run down the field. This was followed by another goal for the ground team. The visitors now made a determined effort, but their inefficiency was shown by the ball being sent through once more. Two fouls were given in succession against Springburn, which brought the Temperance men nearer to their opponents' goal but they failed to improve their chance. McPherson sent in a beautiful shot from mid-field through the centre of the goal, making the fourteenth. When time was called the scores stood: Cowlairs, 18 goals; Athletics, 2 goals." There would be no extended Cup run though as Cowlairs lost heavily in the next round 8-0 against Celtic.

The record win didn't last long – just over a year in fact, for on the 7th September 1889 Cowlairs beat Victoria of Helensburgh 21-1 in a First Round Scottish Cup tie.
The Glasgow Herald merely commenting that "the Cowlairs playing against the Victoria almost accomplished a record performance, beating their opponents by 21 goals to 1."

Cowlairs were one of the clubs at the original meetings in the spring of 1890 looking at the establishment of a League and they became one of the founder members. They finished bottom of the table at the end of their first season, winning only three games of the 18 played, but they were not helped by having four points deducted for fielding an ineligible player. They made their debut in the SFL on the 16th August 1890 and drew their first game, a 1-1 draw at Boghead against eventual joint champions Dumbarton. *The Scotsman* commented that "the Cowlairs accomplished a creditable performance in drawing". The match report went on to say that "the afternoon was wet and stormy and against accurate play, Dumbarton kicked off, and following up had a try or two, and ultimately secured a corner which proved fruitless. Cowlairs had a brief look in, but Dumbarton soon returned to the vicinity of Duff's charge. The latter and his backs kept them at bay for a bit, but ultimately, after 15 minutes' play, Taylor had a goal for Dumbarton. Shortly afterwards Cowlairs visited the home goal. A misunderstanding between the backs allowed the ball to pass, and McLeod [the Dumbarton goalkeeper] slipped, and the score was equalised. It stood thus at half-time. Play in the second half was almost exclusively contained to the vicinity of the Cowlairs' goal, but the backs and goalkeeper played brilliantly, and the shooting of the home forwards was very indifferent." *The Glasgow Herald* taking up the story, commented on the sustained pressure put on the visitors, saying "every now and again it looked as if Cowlairs must be beaten; but no. The ball repeatedly struck the uprights or cross bar but it could not be got through", with *The Scotsman* concluding that "a favouring fortune and a strong defence enabled the Cowlairs to keep their goal intact, and the game ended in a draw of one goal each, much to the chagrin of Dumbarton." Dumbarton got their revenge, winning the reverse fixture 6-1 in October. The Cowlairs team taking to the field for their first ever SFL game was: Thomas Duff; McCartney, William McLeod; Masterton, James McPherson, Campbell; Binks, Dickson, Dempsey, Mathieson and Blake.

The following Saturday, the 23rd August 1890, Cowlairs won their first 'home' game, 3-2 against Vale of Leven with a last minute winner, although the game was played at Celtic Park, in front of 1,000 spectators. *The Scotsman* reported that "this League fixture was decided at Celtic Park before a fair crowd. The Vale were out in force and Cowlairs had also a strong team, though McCartney was on the accident list. Aided by the wind,

Cowlairs rushed off and scored in the first minute of the game. The Vale responded gamely, and though they got twice past the backs, Duff was equal to the occasion and sent them off bootless. The play was stubbornly maintained, the Alexandria men, despite the wind, forcing the game finely. The Cowlairs played a strong game, their left pair, Dickson and Mathieson, combining very finely. The Vale played up, and had a fair share in the run of the game. In heading out, Sinclair put the ball through his own goal, and the Vale were thus equal. At half-time the score stood one goal each, on crossing over the chances were all in favour of the Vale, who soon made it hot for Cowlairs. McLeod, McPherson and Duff averted danger for a long time, till a combined rush ended in the Vale forwards blocking the goal-mouth and scoring. The Cowlairs desperately strove to equalise, and clever play by Dickson and Mathieson ended in the former beating Wilson with a cross shot. Additional interest was thus aroused in the contest, and, despite the slippery ground, fast play was exhibited...Time was drawing nigh and the excitement was intense. Just as time was up, Cowlairs luckily put on a third goal, and thus won by three goals to two." The winning Cowlairs team that day was: Duff; Sinclair, McLeod; Masterton, Kennedy, McPherson; Bishop, Binks, Dempsey, Dickson and Mathieson.

Cowlairs lost their next League game against St Mirren and were then knocked out of the Scottish Cup by Airdrieonians. Shortly afterwards they were then beaten 4-0 at Hearts, but matters also took a turn for the worse off the pitch. Along with Celtic, Cowlairs had four points deducted for fielding an ineligible player, *The Scotsman* reporting on an SFA Meeting on the 25th September that "for playing Munro, Cowlairs club was ordered to appear before the committee." The impact of the points deduction was that they were now bottom of the table on minus one point. Less than a week later Renton were expelled from both the SFA and SFL for professionalism.

Things got worse for Cowlairs in October. First, one of their better players, James McPherson left to join Celtic on loan. Then, the club were placed under investigation by the SFA, the allegation being that the financial affairs of the club had been mismanaged. Cowlairs were unable to produce any evidence of financial record-keeping and this would ultimately lead to their temporary suspension. On the 17th October *The Scotsman* reported on an SFA Meeting: "in pursuance of their crusade against professionalism, the sub-committee of the SFA met...when the Cowlairs Club officials were examined relative to the financial position of the club. The case was not finished, and was further adjourned for a week. McPherson, the international forward, was also under examination, and came through the ordeal well."

Back on the pitch a creditable 1-1 draw was followed by a second game at Hyde Park, the home of Glasgow Northern, who were playing in the Scottish Alliance, and who would themselves join the SFL in 1893. Their opponents, Dumbarton, took an early lead but Cowlairs had their chances at only 1-0 down before Dumbarton took total control and were 4-0 up at half-time. The Glasgow Herald reported that "on restarting, Cowlairs assumed the offensive, and seemed as if they meant to make up for lost ground...Cowlairs were having hard lines in not scoring. Keeping at it, they were rewarded by a goal after 25 minutes of this half had gone. This altered the aspect of the game, which became most exciting." However, more profligate finishing cost the hosts and Dumbarton eventually took the upper hand and scored two more goals.

On the 18th November 1890 Cowlairs were temporarily suspended from the SFA and the League. *The Scotsman* reporting on an SFA Meeting noted that "the committee came to the conclusion that the affairs of the club had been mismanaged; that Mr G Henderson was actually the Cowlairs club during the past season, and that several club books were examined and returned." The club faced accusations of professionalism and that alleged illicit payments had been made to players. Cowlairs didn't play in the League again until January 1891. Their suspension ended in mid-December and they were due to host Hearts, but owing to the state of the pitch a friendly game was played instead.

They resumed League matches on the 17th January 1891 with a 4-0 loss at Cambuslang, which was followed up by a 2-1 defeat away at Vale of Leven. On the 28th February 1891 they played their third 'home' game, their first at Springvale Park. The match was a 12 goal thriller against Abercorn which Cowlairs won 7-5. The bottom two clubs kicked off half an hour late and after a fairly even start the hosts eventually took control with their swift passing and put four past Fleming in the Abercorn goal before the break without reply. Following the resumption Abercorn immediately put on pressure and scored three times in quick succession. *The Scotsman* commented that "the play of Abercorn was very rough, time after time fouls being given against them". Abercorn added another two but Cowlairs, having added three more to their score were victorious by 7 goals to 5.

Cowlairs then lost four more games before draws against Third Lanark and Cambuslang in April. They won their third game, 4-2 at home to St Mirren but concluded their season with a 5-0 defeat at home to Celtic and a 3-0 loss at Third Lanark. They ended the season bottom with six points and faced a re-election vote, along with Vale of Leven and St Mirren. Abercorn, who finished in seventh place had 12 points so the outcome would have been the same for the club even without the points deduction.

On the 30th April the SFA reported on their investigation into professionalism and gave an update on their ongoing court case against Renton. They had inspected the accounts and examined the books of nearly 50 clubs and concluded that professionalism was not widespread. A number of clubs were censured for inadequate bookkeeping though as a result of their investigation. Cowlairs received specific condemnation for what *The Scotsman* described as "specially written up books" i.e. they cooked the books. Not unsurprisingly they failed re-election at the League AGM on the 5th June, *The Scotsman* reporting that "the teams selected for next season are the same as last, with the exception that the Cowlairs are deleted from the list, and the Leith Athletic and Clyde are added, twelve clubs in all competing." St Mirren and Vale of Leven were re-elected and Renton were reinstated.

Despite not being in any league competition the following season, the club enjoyed its longest Scottish Cup run reaching the Quarter-finals. On the 19th December 1891 they beat Mid-Annandale 11-2 in the Second Round, the *Glasgow Herald* reporting on the match: "Mitchell [of Mid-Annandale] set the ball in motion, and the visitors made off with a rush, but McLeod cleared. Bishop got on the ball, and from a beautiful pass Campbell scored first. Keeping up the pressure, and in two minutes more, Burke scored again. A third point was gained by Shanks immediately after. This was too much for the visitors, and Adamson got away in fine style, and carried the ball right through the goal. Getting into close quarters again, Campbell defied the efforts of Adamson. A penalty kick for Cowlairs came to nothing. Play for a time was confined to the visitors' territory, and they had hard lines in not adding to the score. Two corners in succession were fruitless. The Annandale defended grandly at this point. They found an opening at last. After the ball had been passed across the field twice, Shanks managed to head it through. Nothing daunted, the Dumfries men kept pegging away, and J Steele, after a smart run, sent in a beauty which rather surprised McLelland. A foul in the goal mouth saved the strangers and half-time was called before the kick could be taken, the result standing – Cowlairs, 5 goals; Mid-Annandale, 2. On restarting, the home team again took up the running, and in less than five minutes Bishop rushed the ball through. The home forwards were in fine form, and simply carried all before them. Result:-Cowlairs, 11 goals; Mid-Annandale, 2 goals." Cowlairs were knocked out by eventual winners Celtic in the quarter finals, Celtic winning 4-1. Celtic were winning 3-0 at half-time and played a man short for part of the second half. Lambie scored a 90th minute consolation for Cowlairs.

At the end of the 1891-92 season the club failed in an attempt to be reinstated in the League. The SFL was going from 12 clubs to 10 and with three League clubs also going for the single place on offer it was no surprise when they received zero votes. Cowlairs joined the rival Scottish Alliance competition for the 1892-93 season and won it at a canter, finishing seven points clear of St Bernard's in second place. The club made a further attempt to re-join the League at the AGM on the 12th June 1893 but failed.

288

Instead, a month later, the League decided to form a Second Division. The Scottish Alliance was the leading non-League competition and provided six of the clubs for the new division, including Cowlairs.

Cowlairs had their most successful season in the new Second Division for the 1893–94 season, finishing as runners-up, by two points, to Hibernian. They made a positive start winning their opening game 4-2 and then thrashing Glasgow rivals Northern 7-0 on the 9th September 1893. *The Scotsman* reported on the match, saying that "Cowlairs kicked off, and immediately made a raid on Burnside, who saved cleverly. The Northern next had a trial; but Kyle grazed the post. From a free kick McPherson scored for the home team. The game then became lively. The Northern strove hard to equalise, but half-time was called without further scoring. On resuming the Cowlairs began pressing, but the strong defence of the Northern's backs kept them well in check. About twenty minutes from the start Burnside was the means of scoring against his own side by striking the ball against the post and sending it through. During the rest of the game Cowlairs seemed to settle down for scoring, Scott adding two goals within a few minutes. A hard game ended Cowlairs, seven goals; Northern, nil."

On the 7th October they played eventual champions Hibs at Easter Road, winning by the odd goal in a seven goal thriller. The home team were at full strength but put in their worst display of the season to date and Cowlairs fully deserved their win. The following month Cowlairs enhanced their championship credentials with an 8-1 thrashing of Partick Thistle. The *Glasgow Herald* commented that "it was evident the game would be a hard one" and the visitors had the better of the early exchanges and had a goal disallowed for charging the goalkeeper. Lynch beat Crossan in the Partick goal to open the scoring and Watson, after a goalmouth scramble poked home for 2-0. Partick got one back before the break but after the interval it was all one way traffic. Scott scored Cowlairs' third goal and two more swiftly followed by Edgar and Scott respectively. Three more followed for the hosts before the final whistle was sounded.

Cowlairs then got a reality check of what life might be like back in the First Division when they suffered a heavy defeat in the Scottish Cup a fortnight later, losing 8-0 to Rangers, the eventual winners. Rangers opened the scoring early on before Lynch missed a chance to equalise for Cowlairs. The *Glasgow Herald* reported that "the game was being well contested, considering the slippery nature of the ground, and against the wind Cowlairs were making a good display." Rangers went two up in the 20th minute, whilst "Cowlairs played as hard as ever, but were woefully slack in front of goal." Rangers kept creating the best of the chances and headed home a third to lead 3-0 at half-time. An early injury to Scott, who "remained on the field, although of little use" was compounded when James McPherson, who had previously twisted his leg "met with another accident, and had to be carried off the field." Down to nine men Cowlairs quickly succumbed and Rangers ran out 8-0 winners.

Cowlairs reached the turn of the year in fifth place in the ten team division, but having played between two and four games less than all of the teams above them. On the 24th February 1894 they beat Abercorn 7-1 and they followed this up with a 4-1 win away at Northern. Partick Thistle, Clyde and Hibernian were now all tied at the top with 20 points and Cowlairs had 17 points, with games in hand on the first two, but not Hibs. On the 17th March Cowlairs hosted Hibs and a large crowd of 2,500 saw Cowlairs take an early lead through Smith. Hibs equalised in the 40th minute and went ahead five minutes after half-time. They then added a third before Cowlairs got one back from a goalmouth scramble. Soon afterwards Cowlairs thought they had scored again but it was disallowed and Hibs won 3-2 to go top. Cowlairs stayed in fourth but with games in hand on Partick and Clyde in second and third respectively.

Cowlairs then went on a good run, winning all five of their remaining games, putting seven past Morton and five past Port Glasgow Athletic. They couldn't catch Hibernian though, who won two of their three remaining games to finish two points clear and claim the first Second Division championship, but they did overtake the other clubs to finish three points ahead of Clyde in second place.

Surprisingly both Hibs and Cowlairs missed out in the election vote, with third placed Clyde going up instead. Renton, Leith and Dundee from the First Division all faced a vote and were challenged by the top three clubs from the Second. In the voting at the AGM on the 1st June Dundee (14), Clyde (14) and Leith Athletic (8) were all elected to the First Division. Cowlairs got 4 votes, Renton 3 and Hibernian, the champions only got 1 vote. A subsequent motion by John McLaughlin of Celtic that future Second Division champions be automatically promoted didn't find a seconder.

Automatic promotion had to wait another 25 years and for Cowlairs the chance was gone. The following season proved to be their last as they couldn't repeat their form and they ended up finishing tenth and bottom and facing a vote at the wrong end. In the 1894-95 season they only won two games and lost 13 out of their 18 matches.

Cowlairs lost the first three games of the new season conceding 15 goals in the process. A 4-3 win over Motherwell at the end of September gave them their first points. They only picked up two more to the end of the year and their final game of 1894 was an 8-2 defeat against Hibs. *The Scotsman* wrote that "the Hibernians had an easy task at Easter Road against the Cowlairs...The match, especially in the first half, when the home men had the game at their backs, was merely a case of shooting at goal and half-time found them leading by seven goals to nothing. They only turned out ten men in the second half, but despite this drawback they held their own, and ultimately ran out easy winners." Thorburn and Simpson scored for Cowlairs to make it 7-2 before Hibs got an eighth. Breslin was absent for Hibs due to sickness. It was also reported that Cowlairs only turned up with seven players and put out a scratch team. The reverse game ended in exactly the same scoreline. Played on the 16th March 1895 Hibs beat Cowlairs 8-2 at Springvale Park. The result left Hibs seven points clear at the top whereas Cowlairs, still with only four points, were eight points away from avoiding a re-election vote.

In early April they conceded six, twice, against Dundee Wanderers (6-3) on the 6th and then 6-0 versus Morton on the 20th. Later that month they played what would be their last SFL game at Springvale Park. On the 27th April 1895 they beat Dundee Wanderers 2-1, registering only their second win in a hard fought game. Their team that day was: McPherson; Sharp, Shanks; Marshall, Binks, Melrose; Thorburn, Ewing, Boag, Gilchrist and Gibbon.

On the 18th May 1895 they played their last ever Scottish League game, a 4-0 loss at Dalziel Park away at Motherwell. *The Scotsman* recorded that "these teams finished their Second League engagements at Motherwell, the home team winning by four goals to nil. Motherwell takes second place on the League table, while Cowlairs are the 'wooden spoonists'."

Cowlairs, bottom with only seven points, and Dundee Wanderers (9) and Abercorn (17) faced a re-election vote at the League's AGM on the 3rd June. They were challenged by Kilmarnock, Linthouse, Raith Rovers and Alliance champions Wishaw Thistle. The club, known to be beset by financial and administrative problems were voted out of the League. Abercorn got 22 votes and were re-elected but Cowlairs (and Dundee Wanderers) only mustered 3 votes each. Kilmarnock and Linthouse each secured 24 votes to take their places.

The club subsequently left Springvale Park and returned to Gourlay Park. Cowlairs played a few games in the 1895-96 season but, under pressure from their creditors, they closed down before the season ended and in August 1896 the club was wound up.

SEASON	LEAGUE	P	W	D	L	F	A	P	POS
1890-91	SCOT	18	3	4	11	24	50	6 *	10/10
1893-94	SCOT-2	18	13	1	4	75	32	27	2/10
1894-95	SCOT-2	18	2	3	13	37	77	7	10/10

* 4 points deducted

Dumbarton Harp

Formed: 1894
Colours: Green shirts and white shorts
Ground: Meadow Park
Entered League: 1923. Founder members of the Third Division
Number of League Seasons: 1
Honours: None
Highest League Finish: 10th in Division Three
Left League: 1925. Resigned mid-season

The town of Dumbarton has a proud football heritage and Dumbarton FC have been members of the Scottish Football League for well over 100 years, sharing the inaugural League competition in 1891 and winning it outright in 1892. They have collected many honours including the first two League titles, the Scottish Cup in 1883 and the Second Division title in 1911. However, they haven't always been the town's sole representative in the League, as another team from Dumbarton competed for a season and a half in the 1920s.

The early successes of Celtic and Hibernian inspired Irish communities across Scotland to form their own teams, often with the suffix of 'Hibernian' or 'Harp'. The first Dumbarton team, drawn from the Irish community was Dumbarton Hibernian who were formed in 1885 but closed down in 1887. Shortly afterwards the first Dumbarton Harp was founded but they did not prosper and were wound up at the end of the season. Among the few matches they played was a 9-1 defeat at the hands of Kirkintilloch Central in the first round of the Dunbartonshire Cup. The second Dumbarton Harp was formed in 1894, playing their games at Meadow Park, and between 1908 and 1912 they played in the Scottish Union, considered to be one of the strongest non-League competitions, which they won in 1910. Between 1912 and 1915 they played in the Scottish Reserve League, and as members of this League they applied to join the Scottish Football League at the 1913 AGM. They failed in the vote in which eight teams were involved, with Arthurlie and Leith Athletic both being re-elected. At the same AGM Dumbarton were elected back into the First Division.

In 1915, members of the suspended Scottish Second Division decided to form two regional competitions, the Western and Eastern Leagues. Dumbarton Harp joined six former Scottish League clubs and five other non-League sides in the Western League and in 1919 they won the championship.

In 1920 they featured in the Scottish Cup for the first time, narrowly going out to Alloa Athletic in the First Round after a replay. They next played in the 1921-22 competition when they lost 7-0 in the First Round in January 1922 against the Cup holders Partick Thistle (who had beaten Rangers 1-0 in the 1921 final to lift the trophy for the one and only time). Harp, for half an hour, put up a fight, but were let down by poor finishing. Before the interval the Jags scored three times. In the second half the Harp were outplayed.

In 1923 the Scottish Football League was extended with the addition of a Third Division made up largely of members of the Western League. Harp were one of the clubs to be invited, joining Dumbarton FC (now in the Second Division) in the SFL. Harp made their League debut on the 18th August 1923, a 3-0 defeat at Raploch Park away against Royal Albert. Their name was a headline writers dream and *The Sunday Post* reported on their opening fixture under the headline "Harp Unstrung". The following Saturday they played their first home game at Meadow Park against Clackmannan. Their opponents won by the odd goal in five. Reid and Brookes scored for the home team in the first half whilst in the second Roy had a couple and Cameron the other as Clackmannan came from 2-0 down to win 3-2.

Harp's first League point came in their third game, a 0-0 draw at home to Beith, but this was watched by only 500 spectators. Dumbarton, in the Second Division were attracting crowds of 1,500-2,000 at Boghead and Harp were struggling to compete with their more illustrious neighbours. On the 22ⁿᵈ September 1923 Harp recorded their first League victory with a 3-1 win over Solway Star, *The Sunday Post* reporting that "on the run of play the Harp were easily the better lot, more especially in the second half, but Solway's defence was stubborn, and not readily beaten. A. Smith put the Annan lads on the lead after twenty minutes, but Reid levelled the score shortly after. Early in the second half McKenzie put Harp on the lead from a Miller cross, and shortly before the close G. Fotheringham settled the issue with a smartly taken goal."

Form continued to be inconsistent. On the 19th January 1924 they suffered their biggest SFL defeat at Meadow Park, losing 5-0 to promotion chasing Queen of the South. Six weeks later they recorded their highest winning margin at home, beating Galston 4-1, with a triallist, a young Glasgow junior, scoring two. A week later they lost 6-2 at Beith. On the 15th March they played their last home game of the season, hosting the newly crowned champions of the new Division, Arthurlie. Solid defence by the Harp kept the score down to just 1-0. Miller missed Harp's best chance, failing to capitalise on an error. Near the end a strange incident occurred, as recounted by *The Sunday Post*: "Ten minutes from time there was a curious incident. Arthurlie were given a penalty kick. It was taken by McGowan who shot wildly past, but immediately protested that the ball had been interfered with. A break-in of spectators followed, and it was a few minutes before the field was cleared. The Harp goalkeeper admitted the ball had been moved, and the referee repeated the kick, which McGowan netted." A week later Harp recorded their best SFL win, beating Nithsdale Wanderers 4-0 away (a scoreline that was said to flatter them), with goals from Miller, Smith, Reid and Brooks. Harp finished their programme of games sitting 8th but eventually were placed 10th once the other teams had completed their fixtures.

Dumbarton Harp failed to complete the 1924-25 season, resigning half way through the season and having their records expunged. They didn't get off to a very auspicious start, losing their opening game of the new season on the 16th August 1924 against Galston. After a disastrous start, in which they were two down after the first five minutes, they went on to lose 5-0. Things didn't get any better as they also lost the next three games as well, scoring only one goal in those first four games whilst conceding 13. They also failed to score away at Nithsdale Wanderers on the 27th September, but also prevented the home team from scoring, hence securing their first point of the season. *The Sunday Post* reported that "although Dumbarton Harp managed to force a draw at Sanquhar, they were forced to play a practically a defensive game right through the piece...An outstanding man was Chalmers in the Harp goal. He made not one single mistake and he certainly had a trying time of it, especially in the second half, when his goal was simply bombarded. An accident to Kennedy deprived the local side of a grand player, and this handicap naturally upset calculations. No goals were scored in a game which on play the Wanderers should have won."

The following Saturday they suffered their worst SFL result, losing 6-0 against Lochgelly United, giving away a penalty within four minutes of the start and conceding three in each half. Now, after six games, they had just a single point, having scored only one goal (by Robertson), and conceded 19. Their first win of season came in their eighth game, on the 18th October, a 3-1 win over fellow strugglers Mid-Annandale, who they overtook in the table as a result. *The Sunday Post* commented that "the Harp have not had the best of luck this season, but the fates were kind to them for once, and their 3-1 victory should provide them with the encouragement which may take them quickly up the points ladder." This didn't happen though, and after a further defeat and a draw they lost heavily away against Solway Star, the men from Annan scoring two hat tricks in a 7-1 victory. The result left Harp joint bottom with Helensburgh and Mid-Annandale with just five points.

During this period were the first signs of things to come. Harp failed to fulfil a fixture with Leith Athletic on 1st November. The SFL Management Committee ordered Harp to pay Leith the usual £15 match guarantee for visiting teams. A representative of Harp declared that they didn't have fifteen pence!

Dumbarton Harp beat Brechin City 1-0, Roberts converting a penalty after fifteen minutes, and then also won against Galston 3-2, in what *The Sunday Post* described as "one of the hardest and most exciting seen at Meadow Park for a long time. The visitors put up a splendid fight. They were forced to play the whole of the second half with ten men, Law, their left back, receiving a thigh injury that required the attention of a doctor." The consecutive victories took them off the bottom and into 15th place (in a now 17 team division, Leith Athletic having joined at the start of the season). Unfortunately the run couldn't be sustained and they went down 4-1 away at Clackmannan. Halloran scored first for Harp against the run of play but they then conceded four second half goals.

Their best win came in the last match of 1924, when they hosted promotion challengers Queen of the South at Meadow Park on the 27th December. Their opponents were second in the table and going strong but Halloran scored four as Harp led 5-0 at the interval. The Dumfries men showed great fight and determination and scored three in the second period, harp eventually winning 6-3. *The Sunday Post* reported that "Dumbarton Harp's remarkable victory over the Queen of the South was the feature of yesterday's proceedings. Halloran was the hero of the game. All his goals were cleverly taken and thoroughly deserved on the quality of play that led up to them. Five times was the Queens' keeper beaten before the interval, and this heavy handicap proved too much for them. Still, they made a real plucky stand, as is convincingly indicated by the fact that they had three goals to their credit before the close." Campbell and Roberts had the other goals for Harp.

On the 5th January 1925 Dumbarton Harp played what would be their last SFL fixture. It was a Monday night and they lost against Dykehead 3-1. Harp didn't play on Saturday the 10th and Secretary/Manager Smyth leaked the news of the club's demise to *The Sunday Post* the following day. Under the headline "Dumbarton Harp Resigns" the report continued, explaining that "this step has been forced owing to lack of support. Matters have reached such a pass that the officials could do nothing else but throw up the sponge. This places the other Third Division clubs in a quandary, and threatens the tournament with disorganisation unless the League comes to the financial assistance of the Harp, and enables them to carry on until the end of the season."

In mid-January and under the headline "Dumbarton Harp's Serious Position," *The Glasgow Evening Times* reported: "The hopes of the management of Dumbarton Harp that they will be able to continue their Third League fixtures till the end of the season are likely to fail, and the question 'continue or disband' is at present under consideration, following on the club's failure to gather around them the necessary support in the New Year fixtures. The match against Queen of the South at Meadow Park was fairly well attended and against Vale of Leven a little over the £15 guarantee was drawn at the gate, but anything gained was lost on Monday last, when only £7 was taken at the match against Dykehead. Meanwhile, Secretary P. Smyth has wired off the match which was fixed for Saturday last with Royal Albert. Besides the difficulty of not being able to raise the necessary guarantee, the club has been hit by the recent strong weather, when a large part of the park barricade at the north end was blown down. There seems no prospect of greater support in the town until trade revives."

At a meeting of the SFL Management Committee on 4th February 1925 it was decided that "the fixtures played by them in the competition are to be ignored" (*The Scotsman*) and their records were expunged, having played 17 games, won four, drawn 3 and lost 10. *The Sunday Post* on the 8th February commented "Dumbarton Harp's resignation from the Third Division was accepted after discussion. It was agreed that to subsidise the club in order to enable the programme of fixtures to be carried through would create a precedent with which the League could not cope satisfactorily. This gives an indication of the financial conditions existing in Division III."

Harp resigned because their receipts did not cover their increased running and travel costs. The economic downturn was a contributory factor, as was the need to provide a financial guarantee of £15 to the visiting team. In a town already supporting one senior club, Harp struggled to attract sufficient crowds to their Meadow Park home. Dumbarton Harp's entry into the new division sums up the lack of thought that went into its composition. How could a town so small sustain two League clubs? Dumbarton FC were already well established and Harp were barely able to attract a few hundred supporters to their Meadow Park ground and they were the first to fold. The following season the Third Division itself was abandoned as more and more members fell into financial difficulty.

The name Dumbarton Harp lives on as a Social Club located on the High Street, and also as a local amateur football club Dumbarton Harp Celtic. Meadow Park remained in use as a playing field until 1950 when it was built on and is now part of the Broadmeadow industrial estate.

SEASON	LEAGUE	P	W	D	L	F	A	P	POS
1923-24	SCOT-3	30	10	8	12	40	51	28	10/16
1924-25	SCOT-3	RECORD EXPUNGED							

Dundee Hibernian

Formed: 1909
Colours: Green shirts, white shorts
Ground: Tannadice Park (renamed from Clepington Park)
Entered League: 1910. Elected to Second Division. 1921. Founder member of the re-formed Second Division. 1923. Elected to Second Division
Number of League Seasons: 6
Honours: None
Highest League Finish: 4th in Division Two
Left League: 1915 League suspended due to Great War. 1922. League reconstruction. 1923. Name changed to Dundee City and then Dundee United

During the late 1870s and 1880s Irish communities throughout Scotland, inspired by the examples of Hibernian in Edinburgh and then later Celtic in Glasgow, formed their own teams. In Dundee two such clubs were formed in 1879 - a Dundee Hibernian and a Dundee Harp but neither lasted very long. In 1894 a new Dundee Hibernians club was formed but they lasted only two seasons before going the way of their predecessors in 1896.

In the spring of 1909 the third Dundee Hibernian club was formed with the express purpose of gaining admittance to the Scottish Football League. Although they represented the city's Irish/Catholic population, the club adopted a non-sectarian approach to the recruitment of players and backroom staff. They moved into Clepington Park, the former home of Dundee Wanderers, and renamed it Tannadice, this being the name of the street where the ground was located, and Clepington was the district.

After a single season in the Northern League Dundee Hibs were elected to fill the vacancy in the Scottish Second Division created by the amalgamation of Ayr and Ayr Parkhouse. They competed at this level without distinction until 1915 when the Second Division was suspended. The member clubs then formed regional competitions and Dundee Hibs joined the Eastern League. In 1921 Dundee Hibernian re-joined the SFL as members of the newly reformed Second Division. At the same time automatic promotion and relegation was introduced for the first time. A condition of the arrangement was that the two bottom clubs in the SFL would drop out at the end of the season in order to even up the numbers across the two divisions. Unfortunately, Dundee Hibernian finished the season in one of these positions and lost their place.

In 1923 the club secured election back into the Second Division. In a plan to widen the club's appeal the club sought to distance itself from its Irish roots by seeking a name change to Dundee City and the green colours were discarded. Following objections from Dundee FC, the club's name was changed to Dundee United in October 1923. While this matter was in dispute, the club continued to be known as Dundee Hibernian and their new club crest featured the letters "DH" superimposed on the city's coat of arms.

Dundee Hibernian completed in six seasons in the Scottish Football League, all in the Second Division – five seasons before the Great War between 1910-15 and then one on the resumption of the Division in 1922 and they achieved a best finish of fourth in the 1913-14 season. One of the driving forces behind the formation of Dundee Hibernian Football Club was local businessmen Pat Reilly, who became their first manager in June 1909. He held the post until 1915 and resumed his duties between 1919 and 1922. He consolidated the new club in the Second Division up until the outbreak of the First World War before handing over managerial duties to Herbert Dainty in 1915, Reilly remained as the club secretary, but returned to the joint role again in 1917 up until 1922.

At the Scottish League's AGM held on the 31st May 1909, Dundee Hibernian challenged for membership of the League. Arthurlie and Cowdenbeath faced re-election and they were also challenged by three Scottish Union non-League clubs: Johnstone, Renton and Wishaw Thistle. Although Celtic had pipped Dundee to the championship by one point, Dundee had led the table for much of the season and the new club was hopeful that the League would admit a second team from the city. Dundee Wanderers had only played one season in 1894-95 and perhaps their lack of success carried more weight for in the voting Dundee Hibernian came bottom, attracting only 3 votes. Arthurlie, with 21 votes, and Cowdenbeath, with 17, were both re-elected, with Johnstone the best of the challengers with 11 votes.

Dundee Hibs joined the Northern League instead for the 1909-10 season and finished third, behind the Dundee 'A' team and Brechin City. At the end of the League season Cowdenbeath again faced re-election but this time there was a vacant spot as Ayr Parkhouse, who had finished bottom, didn't seek re-election as they were merging with Ayr to form Ayr United. At the Scottish League's AGM on the 7th June Cowdenbeath were re-elected. Dundee Hibernian beat St Johnstone, then of the Central League, by 20 votes to 10 to claim the vacant place.

Dundee Hibernian joined the Scottish League's Second Division for the 1910-11 season and finished eighth out of 12 teams in their first season. They made their League debut on the 20th August 1910, a home tie at Tannadice against Leith Athletic. They lost the game 3-2, in front of 3,000 fans. Leith opened the scoring after five minutes and then added a second before the home team got their act together and got on level terms through Peter Yuill and James O'Gara before half-time. Dundee Hibs tried for the winner but their opponents were resolute in defence and it was Leith who got the winner near the end. The first ever Dundee Hibernian team to play in the SFL was: Bill Tullis, William Welsh, John Robertson, Tommy Miller, James Loney, John Collins, Tom Collins, Tom Boland, George Fyfe, James O'Gara and Peter Yuill. The first Dundee Hibs goalscorers were Yuill and O'Gara. Yuill had signed from West End FC. A centre forward, he was converted to play centre half in the latter stages of the season. He was released the end of 1910-11 and soon after signed for Dundee Wanderers. O'Gara was a former Middlesbrough and Airdrieonians player signed from Clapton Orient who later played for Portsmouth.

Dundee Hibs lost their next game, 4-3 away at St Bernard's in a match played in wet conditions. Yuill scored two and Willie Swan the other. Once again they came from behind to level at 3-3 before losing to a late goal. In their next match they registered their first League points with a 4-1 win over Abercorn, despite conceding in the first few minutes. O'Gara got them on equal terms to be level at half-time. The second half belonged to the Hibs and two goals were scored by Swan and before the close Swan got his hat-trick. Willie Swan had signed from Arbroath and despite scoring seven goals in nine games he fell out of favour and was used in the side less frequently as the season progressed.

This win started a run of seven games without defeat which took them up to second in the table, a point behind leaders Albion Rovers, and one point ahead of St Bernard's and Port Glasgow Athletic. However, in November they lost all three games played, without scoring a goal, to drop to third and four points adrift from the top. The poor run continued throughout December where they failed to win and the 3-0 defeat at Cowdenbeath on the 31st December saw them drop into the second half of the table.

On the 18th March 1911 Charlie Dunnian scored a first half hat-trick as Dundee Hibs beat Port Glasgow Athletic 4-1. Dunnian was a former Irish international who had previously played for Carfin Shamrock and the Edinburgh Hibs. The hat-trick was scored on his debut and whilst he added a further goal in his next three matches to make it four goals in four games he wasn't retained and was released. This result was the highlight of the second half of the season and the club eventually finished in eighth place, losing their last game of the season away at the divisional champions Dumbarton.

The club's second season in the League was a poor one, as they won only five games out of the 22 played, scoring only 21 goals, or less than a goal a game. O'Gara re-signed just days into the new campaign but left in November 1911 to join to Portsmouth. They particularly struggled away from home losing ten of their eleven games on the road. Dundee Hibs only won once in their opening ten games and suffered two heavy defeats. On the 21st October they lost 6-0 away at Ayr United and on the 4th November they were beaten 7-1 by St Bernard's despite opening the scoring through centre-forward David Scrimgeour. Jim Crumley, the goalkeeper, missed just one game throughout the season but at the end of the campaign he moved to Canada.

Defeat at home to Vale of Leven on the 30th December left them joint bottom (with Albion Rovers) on just nine points. A strong finish to the season saw them win three of their last four games including a 5-2 win over Cowdenbeath, in which Willie Linn and Dan Gibson each scored two. This was their last fixture and the win led to them escaping the second bottom position in the League table and they thus avoided the need to seek re-election.

In the 1912-13 season Dundee Hibs again finished in tenth place although this was an improved showing in a now 14 team division. They again failed to win away but at least this time they secured five draws. The club won only one of their first eight games (including a 5-1 defeat away at Albion Rovers) to be bottom by mid-November with only three points and the they were still bottom after the games over the festive period.

In late January 1913 they secured back-to-backs wins over Ayr United and Johnstone. The game against Johnstone, played on the 25th January 1913, saw them run out 7-1 victors. Kennedy, the Johnstone goalkeeper was injured and retired and Mercer kept goal for the second half, conceding four goals. David Scrimgeour scored a hat-trick. The two wins kicked off a run of nine games without a defeat. A 3-0 win over Abercorn in mid-February lifted them off the bottom and above their defeated opponents and Leith. Scrimgeour scored 11 goals, which attracted attention and he was transferred to Portsmouth in April 1913. Willie Linn, who had signed from Dundee North End the previous year finished as top scorer for the season. In his first four seasons he was a regular in the line-up and made over 100 appearances and scored over 30 goals. In April 1915 he signed up for military service but remained a registered Hibs player during the Great War, leaving at the end of 1918-19.

At the Scottish League's AGM the decision was taken to expand the First Division from 18 to 20 teams and the two clubs facing re-election, Partick and Queen's Park, were voted back in. Seven Second Division sides stood for election for the two new places, and somewhat curiously, Dundee Hibs were one of them. They were the lowest finishers of the seven clubs having come in tenth place. They were up against Ayr United (the Second Division champions), Dunfermline Athletic (runners-up in their first season), Abercorn (who had finished 4th), Cowdenbeath (5th), Dumbarton (6th) and St Bernard's (who had finished 7th). Ayr United and Dumbarton were the two successful clubs. Dundee Hibernian secured only three votes, although St Bernard's and Abercorn both got zero votes. Based on their League placing their case was weak, but it was a statement of intent and ambition.

The 1913-14 season saw them finish in fourth place, their best since joining the League. They showed strong home form at Tannadice, losing only once. They started well, losing only one of their opening five fixtures and winning their sixth match 5-0 at home to Johnstone. Key to their improved showing was the goalscoring of Collie Martin who scored two of the goals against Johnstone. Signed in July 1913, having played for Brechin City, Hearts and Dundee, he had made his club debut on the 16th August in a 0-0 draw at St Johnstone on the opening day of the season. He scored his first goal a week later in 1-0 win over Arthurlie and would go on to score 18 goals for the season and finish as top scorer.

Following the result against Johnstone in early October Dundee Hibs sat third in the table, with Cowdenbeath the early pace setters. However they then lost four of their next games so that following a 3-1 home defeat against St Bernard's at the beginning of January 1914 they had slipped all the way down the table and were now 11th and second bottom, although they had played as many as seven games fewer than some other teams in the division.

Strong form in the early months of 1914 saw them climb back up to mid-table and Martin scored both goals in a 2-1 win over second-placed Dunfermline before a crushing 7-0 defeat away at league leaders Cowdenbeath on the 14th March. Cowdenbeath, as the newly crowned champions, closed their League programme with an emphatic victory, storming into a 5-0 lead at half-time. Philip the Cowdenbeath centre-forward scored five of the goals. Dundee Hibs won their remaining three fixtures to finish in fourth but had never really challenged for the top places and finished five points behind the leaders.

Collie Martin finished as the top scorer in the Second Division for the 1914-15, scoring 30 goals, but his contribution was the highlight in an otherwise poor season, in which the club finished eleventh. The club only picked up three points on their travels all season and they started poorly, picking up a solitary draw in their opening six games before gaining their first win against fellow strugglers Lochgelly United on the 3rd October. In the battle of the basement, with both sides winless with a solitary point each to their name, they met at Tannadice with Hibs edging a seven goal thriller. *The Sunday Post* reported that "Martin, an ex-Dundee centre-forward scored within sixty seconds of the start with a rifling long range effort. Lochgelly were having the better of the play but the better scoring opportunities were going the way of the Hibs and they added a second, against the run of play through Linn, who scored in the top corner. Early in second half Pattison scored for Lochgelly and the same player levelled the scores twenty minutes later. Martin got his second and restored the lead for the home side converting from a cross from Low. McDonald scored a fourth with a driven shot and Dundee Hibernian ran out comfortable winners despite a third goal for the men from Fife right at the end."

Dundee Hibs followed this up with a second win at home to St Bernard's, 1-0, thanks to a Martin goal and Alex Grieve heroics in goal. Grieve had signed towards the end of the 1913-14 season and after his debut he had an uninterrupted run in the side until January 1915 when he left Dundee Hibs, to volunteer for military service. The win briefly took them up to 10th but they then lost four in a row to slip back down to 12th in the table, just two points ahead of Arthurlie and Lochgelly at the bottom.

By this time the First World War had started and on the 19th December Collie Martin scored a club record five goals in a single match, in a 6-1 win over Albion Rovers. Only a couple of hundred spectators were present and the disappointing crowd led manager Reilly to note "the Germans may send their blooming bombs here whenever they like. There won't be many to kill."

Dundee Hibernian completed their fixtures on the 13th February at Tannadice Park, where they defeated Vale of Leven 4-1, a good finish in a not too successful season. Martin finished as the division's top goalscorer. Martin scored 53 goals in 59 games over two seasons for Dundee Hibs. With the advent of war he later enlisted and was killed in action serving as a corporal with the 5th Black Watch near Ypres.

The League suspended the Second Division and Dundee Hibernian played on in the regional Eastern League between 1915 and 1920. At the Scottish League's AGM held on the 3rd April 1919 the league management committee put forward a proposal that the Scottish League should continue with 22 rather than 18 clubs in a single division.

Aberdeen, Dundee and Raith Rovers were to be readmitted automatically, leaving one vacancy. Dundee Hibs applied but were unsuccessful and subsequently resigned their membership of the SFL in protest at the refusal of the League's decision not to reinstate the Second Division.

Jim Crumley, their former goalkeeper, re-joined the club during the first half of the successful 1919-20 where they won the Eastern League. Lured by the prospect of what was then a substantial £6 weekly wage, he joined Swansea Town in December 1920. The club then joined the Central League for the 1920-21 season but finished joint bottom of the 18 team competition.

In 1921 Dundee Hibs returned to Scottish League football as the Second Division was finally reinstated. Automatic promotion and relegation was also introduced, but more significantly, the bottom two clubs in the Second Division would drop out to even up the number of clubs to 20 in each division. There were 22 clubs in the First Division and 18 in the Second. Three teams would go down from the First with only the Second Division champions going up, with the bottom two in the Second Division dropping out altogether. Dundee Hibernian's restoration to the Scottish League was short-lived as by finishing 19th and second bottom they dropped out of the League, along with Clackmannan.

Pat Reilly was back as manager and on the playing side Willie Linn returned. They played their first game back on the 20th August 1921 when they drew 2-2 at home to Bo'ness. *The Scotsman* reported that "Dundee Hibs' opening Scottish League Second Division fixture was played at Tannadice Park, Dundee, against Bo'ness before about 4000 spectators. It proved an extremely hard struggle. The brilliance of Miller, the Bo'ness custodian, prevented the home team scoring in the first half. Gilchrist opened the scoring for Bo'ness after 18 minutes' play, and Cobban added a second in the first half. After the interval, Dundee Hibs, pressed on numerous occasions, though Bo'ness were handicapped through the absence of Reid, their left-back, who was injured in a collision with Williams, the Hibs centre, who, after 25 minutes' play, scored from a penalty, and ten minutes from the close equalised with a splendid shot. At the same time, however, Hibs were well worth their draw...Dundee Hibs' best were Mulholland, Macdonald, Wilkie, Linn and Williams." The full Dundee Hibernian taking to the field on their restoration to the League was: Henderson; Adams, Mulholland; Wilkie, Bannister, McDonald; Hogg, Linn, Williams, Braidford and Ritchie.

Their goalscorer was Horace Williams who was making his debut for the club. A centre - forward, he had been with St Johnstone and the Edinburgh Hibernian before he came to Dundee Hibs for a fee of £30. He played regularly and finished the 1921-22 season as top scorer. Also in the team was Lowingham Braidford, playing at inside-half and also making his debut. He had joined the club during the Central League season of 1920-21 initially as a trialist. When Dundee Hibs were restored to the Scottish League he re-signed and missed just one game in that campaign. He was released in May 1922 and then signed for Hartlepool United. A former Dundee player, Tom Bannister, at centre-half, was another new recruit for the 1921-22 season and missed just two League matches over the campaign. Willie Hogg, playing at outside-right had been with Sunderland, Rangers, Dundee, Raith Rovers and Montrose before signing for Dundee Hibs. He made a good start but was dropped in October and then released in November 1921. In goal was Andy Henderson. He had joined Dundee Hibs from Falkirk in April 1920 and was first choice goalkeeper throughout most of the season. A fortnight later their ranks were boosted by the addition of half-back George Stuart. He was an ex-Dundee player signed from Leeds United. He played for most of the season but in May 1922 he was released.

Dundee Hibs followed up their opening draw with three consecutive wins and over 6,000 spectators watched their 3-0 win over St Johnstone on the 10th September. The result left the club in fourth place but a couple of defeats in late September saw them lose momentum. They bounced back in some style though, thrashing bottom club Clackmannan 7-1 on the 1st October. For the greater part of the game the visitors were a man down following an injury. The *Sunday Post* reported that "Dundee Hibs piled up seven goals against Clackmannan, but the visitors were worthy of more than their solitary goal. Individually they played well, and Hendricks, their right back, was one of the best players on the field. The side lacked balance and combination, largely due to the fact that they lost Forsyth (injured) early in the game, and played practically the whole time with ten men. The Hibs' left wing sparkled, and Horace Williams was again a big factor in his side's success. He scored two goals, and had a share in at least two others. William's goal just before the finish was brilliant, as the result of a first-time effort from a cross by Hogg. It was the type of goal that should be seen much more frequently in higher class football, where in Williams would undoubtedly shine if given the opportunity. He is considered in Dundee to be one of the best centres in Scotland just now, and the opinion is not far off the mark. Ritchie and Gibson were in ramping form. Indeed, the whole of the Hibs' front line played well, and were well supported by Stuart. Hogg was also very prominent. Although decisively beaten Clackmannan played gamely, and gave the home defence plenty of work. McNeill, Ferguson, and Cowan showed good form, and Balloch, at right half, did well. Clackmannan's goal in the first half, during which they often played quite as well as their opponents, was attributed to Ferguson, but one of the home defenders appeared to help the ball into the net." The goalscorers for Dundee Hibs were Williams (2), Braidford (2) and one apiece for Gibson, Hogg and Bannister.

A month later Horace Williams scored a hat-trick against struggling Lochgelly United in a 4-0 win. However, *The Sunday Post's* prophecy that Williams should be seen playing in "higher class football" soon came to pass. The player was transfer listed at £200 in December 1921 and soon after moved to Gillingham. He finished as Dundee Hibs' top scorer despite leaving before the end of the season, scoring 13 goals in 25 appearances.

In-between these two results against Clackmannan and Lochgelly Dundee Hibs suffered a run of five games without a win, scoring only once, in a 4-1 defeat at Dunfermline Athletic, in which only the brilliance of Henderson in goal prevented a higher score against the Hibs. Close on 10,000 spectators at Tannadice saw Dundee Hibs lose unfairly 4-0 to leaders Alloa. This time Henderson was at fault for two of the goals. On the 31st December 1921 they lost 2-0 at home to third-placed Vale of Leven, Henderson again at fault after being surprised by a 40 yard free kick for the visitors' first goal. Dundee Hibs moved into the New Year in 12th, although only four points ahead of bottom placed Forfar Athletic.

1922 started badly and Dundee Hibs lost all four games in January, going down 6-2 at home to second-placed Cowdenbeath. Second choice keeper Joe Kinsella was deputising for Henderson in goal. J R Smith, the visitors' centre-forward scored a hat-trick, and Cowdenbeath led 3-0 at half-time, and then 4-0, before the Hibernians came back into the game through Bannister and Stuart. Cowdenbeath got two more goals, with Smith making his total four, and they were perhaps fortunate to win by such a large margin. February didn't see much of an improvement with only two draws in five games and as a result of this sequence they found themselves bottom of the Second Division, level on 19 points with Clackmannan and King's Park.

Now facing a battle for their League survival Dundee Hibs drafted in some new players and their first win of 1922 eventually came on the 4th March when they beat St Bernard's 2-0. Henderson kept the Hibs in the game with some good early saves. Low, the new Hibs centre-forward signed from Dundee Violet, scored twice. The side featured two other debutants. David Duncan, a centre-half, arrived from Hearts, probably on loan. After his arrival he played in all of the remaining League matches of 1921-22. Alex McCulloch was the other new face and he featured at inside-left. He had been with Leith Athletic and a number of English sides before joining Raith Rovers. After signing for Dundee Hibs and making his debut, he also played in all the remaining league matches of 1921-22. At the end of the season it appears that he retired. This, their first win since December, lifted the club two places off the bottom, despite a win for fellow strugglers Kings Park and a draw for Clackmannan. Dundee Hibs followed this with two consecutive 3-0 defeats away at Stenhousemuir and League leaders Alloa. The results left them joint bottom with Clackmannan on 21 points although Hibs had played two games more. Crucially, the gap to King's Park in 18th place and safety was now five points.

On the 25th March they beat Broxburn United 1-0 to lift themselves off the bottom as Clackmannan lost. Joe Kinsella, again back in goal in place of Henderson, made a number of good saves and George Stuart scored the only goal of the game from close range. Entering April and with five games left to play the club again tried new players, drafting in Joe Bibby from Blackburn Rovers and Farquharson from Dundee Violet. They narrowly lost 3-2 at East Stirlingshire, having come from 2-0 down to level at 2-2, but then won 1-0 over Dunfermline, centre-half John Rae's only goal of the campaign, having joined the club from Albion Rovers in the January. With King's Park being held to a draw at home the gap to safety was now four points, but with only three games remaining.

Two days later, and in front of a crowd of 4,000, they suffered a 1-0 home defeat to East Fife, in a game brought forward to avoid the Scottish Cup Final, despite more heroics from Kinsella. This result effectively sealed their fate. King's Park in 18th place played on the Saturday and drew 1-1 away at the newly crowned Second Division champions Alloa, which condemned Hibs to drop out of the League. They were now five points behind the Stirling club but with only two games to play, so couldn't catch them.

On the 22nd April the two condemned sides met and played out a 1-1 draw. Under the headline "Clash of the Pigmies: Divided Points At Clackmannan" The *Sunday Post* reported that "fewer than one thousand spectators witnessed one of the poorest games of the season at Chapelhill Park....weak finishing was the undoing of both sides. "The rivals for the wooden spoon played out a dour first half. Cowan, an ex-Falkirk winger scored past Joe Kinsella with 10 minutes to go but close to the call of time Lowingham Braidford equalised.

A week later they played their last home League game prior to dropping out of the Scottish Football League. The visitors were Armadale and Dundee Hibs ran out 4-1 winners, with two goals from Willie Oswald, one from Willie Linn and the fourth from Alex McCulloch. With Lochgelly United losing Dundee Hibs ended up finishing three points behind the Fifers and safety. The last team was Joe Kinsella, Tom Bannister, David Duncan, William McDonagh, James Headrick, John Rae, Willie Linn, Lowingham Braidford, Alex McCulloch, Willie Oswald and Peter Kelly.

Tom Bannister, centre half, missed just two league matches over the campaign. One of just three players who stayed with the club after their Scottish League status was lost, he was released in April 1923. Andy Henderson also stayed on. He spent his third season at Tannadice in the Scottish Alliance with Hibs but left in January 1923. James Headrick, who had played 31 matches and scored twice was initially retained, but left soon afterwards and joined promoted Alloa Athletic. Lowingham Braidford was amongst those players released at the end of the season and he then signed for Hartlepool United. Willie Linn was also released at the end of the season. His total appearances in all competitions is unsurpassed by any other Dundee Hibs player, making 129 appearances and scoring 33 goals. He was the first and only Dundee Hibs player to receive a benefit from the club.

The club dropped into the Scottish Alliance for the 1922-23 season and a campaign was launched to secure election back into the Second Division. On the 12th May, and a few days before the Scottish League's AGM, the club announced the signing of Jimmy Brownlie as player/manager for the new season. Brownlie was an experienced goalkeeper and had been with Third Lanark for 19 years and had international experience, winning 16 caps for Scotland. On Wednesday the 16th May *The Scotsman* reported on the AGM, noting that "Dundee Hibernians and Arbroath, the latter one of the two clubs obliged to seek re-election, were admitted to the Second Division. East Stirlingshire, who were at the foot of the Second Division League table, on the same mark as Arbroath, failed to retain their place." The *Sunday Post* later in the week commented that "Dundee Hibs have been readmitted to the Second Division of the League. The first vote revealed:- Arbroath 27, East Stirlingshire 19, Dundee Hibs 17; and the second:- Dundee Hibs 23, East Stirlingshire 15. We hope that the Hibs will live up to the talk of those now at the head of affairs of the Tannadice club, and build a team capable of taking the club into the First Division. Another Dundee club in Division I would be the best thing that could happen to senior Tayside football, which has languished sadly of late years. Dens Park used to be the home of a brilliant combination, but for many seasons there has been little over which to enthuse and nothing in the playing line in which to place firmly one's confidence. Let us trust that the Hibs' venture will be the beginning of a new era of real, live football in Dundee. We understand that the Hibs are busy about a team for next season. They have at present a large number of players under consideration. It is said that perhaps one of the old lot will be in the League team next season. Help is being sought freely in the West of Scotland."

Brownlie needed to put a new team together and recruited Jock Kay and Bobby Knox from his old club Third Lanark; striker Joe O'Kane was signed from Celtic, and would be the club's top scorer in the 1923-24 season; James Porter and Sandy Gilmour came from Hearts; Eddie Gilfeather was loaned from Celtic; defender Dave Richards came from Port Vale; half-back Ed Stirling had been playing for Dundee reserves and Bobby McEwan was signed from Dumbarton.

On the 18th August 1923 the new season got underway with a 0-0 draw against Cowdenbeath at Tannadice. A crowd of 10,000 watched their League return in a game they were unlucky not to win. The team line up was: Jimmy Brownlie, James Porter, Dave Richards, Jock Kay, Ed Stirling, Bobby Knox, Bobby McEwan, Tom Cottingham, Joe O 'Kane, Sandy Gilmour and George Hannah. This game had the side still referred to as 'Dundee Hibernian' but a week later the club beat Alloa Athletic 1-0 away, with a goal scored by Gilmour, with the newspapers referring to them as 'Dundee City.' Essentially, a consortium of local businessman had stepped in with a plan to broaden the club's appeal by abandoning its Irish roots. The reformed club was now named Dundee City and the green jerseys had been discarded in favour of white and black.

A week later and the newspapers were back to calling them Dundee Hibernians after objections from Dundee FC. On Saturday 20th October 1923 the club played its last game as Dundee Hibernian, beating leaders King's Park 3-2, James Mackie, signed from Bo'ness the month before scoring two and Gilmour getting the third. Following this game the club's name was changed to Dundee United, with their new club crest featured the letters "DH" superimposed on the city's coat of arms. After several weeks of discussion, agreement on the new name had been reached and then approved by the football authorities. On the 27th October the club played as Dundee United for the first time against Dumbarton and were reported as such in the newspapers.

The club started the 1923-24 season as Dundee Hibernian and ended it as Dundee United. The club's new name is familiar to all and its subsequent success must be seen as a vindication of the name change. In only his second season in charge, Brownlie led Dundee United to the Second Division championship and promotion to the top flight. Although relegated in 1927 they won the Second Division again in 1929 and went on to secure much greater success in the 1980s, winning the overall League title and experiencing successful European campaigns.

SEASON	LEAGUE	P	W	D	L	F	A	P	POS
1910-11	SCOT-2	22	7	5	10	29	36	19	9/12
1911-12	SCOT-2	22	5	5	12	21	41	15	10/12

```
1912-13  SCOT-2  26   6  10  10  34  43  22    10/14
1913-14  SCOT-2  22  11   4   7  36  31  26     4/12
1914-15  SCOT-2  26   8   3  15  48  61  19    11/14

1921-22  SCOT-2  38  10   8  20  47  65  28    19/20
```

Dundee Wanderers

Formed: 1894
Colours: Maroon and white striped shirts and navy blue shorts
Ground: East Dock Street and Clepington Park
Entered League: 1894. Elected to Second Division
Number of League Seasons: 1
Honours: None
Highest League Finish: 9th in Division Two.
Left League: 1895. Failed re-election. Disbanded April 1913

The city of Dundee has a great footballing tradition, punching way above their weight. The two principal clubs – Dundee (who joined the League's top flight in 1893) and Dundee United (who entered the League in 1910 as Dundee Hibernian) have over 175 seasons between them in the Scottish Football League. Their records includes a Championship each (Dundee 1961-62, Dundee United1982-83), a Scottish Cup win each (Dundee 1910, Dundee United 1994) and five League Cups (Dundee 3, Dundee United 2). Dundee is also one of a select band of European cities that have had two representatives reach the European Cup semi-final stage – a list which includes Glasgow, London, Madrid and Milan – all with substantially greater populations. Consequently both teams are well-known, as is the proximity of their grounds Dens Park and Tanandice. Lesser known within the city are the team who were called Dundee Wanderers. This team had a very brief Scottish Football League career, spending a solitary league season in the Second Division in the mid-1890s.

For the 1894-95 season two new clubs entered the Scottish Football League to replace the Glasgow clubs - Northern and Thistle. In those times there was no automatic promotion or relegation and clubs were elected into the League. Seven teams contested the three places available with Morton being successfully re-elected to the Second Division. Dundee Wanderers were successfully elected along with Airdrieonians. They got 23 votes and Airdrieonians got 19. For both clubs this was their first season in the League and the two clubs would go on to have contrasting fortunes. One would go on to have a League career lasting over a hundred years and including numerous cup final appearances. The other would sink into obscurity and ultimately disappear after just one season.

Dundee Wanderers entered the League to widen its appeal, which at the time was largely confined to the central belt. They were formed by the merger of Johnstone Wanderers and Strathmore in 1894, with the expressed intention of joining the League, and in doing so became the city of Dundee's second League club. Wanderers had originally been formed in 1885 as an offshoot of Our Boys, who would later merge with another local team to become Dundee FC.

The original Wanderers played their games at Morgan Park and in 1886 they first featured in the Scottish Cup, losing 7-2 in a regionalised match against Broughty Ferry. In the following season, they made it all the way to the Quarter-finals, knocking out Lochee United (7-0), Aberdeen Rovers (10-0), Coupar Angus (8-0), Queen of the South Wanderers and Carfin Shamrock along the way. In the last eight they were eventually beaten 5-1 by the 1885 Cup winners Renton. Wanderers took an early lead but Renton equalised just before the interval and then immediately scored again to go into the break 2-1 up. *The Glasgow Herald* reported that "throughout the game the Wanderers played as well as their most ardent supporters could desire, and made a much more obdurate resistance than expected by their opponents. But the Vale men were too much for them, and latterly had matters all their own way." Three more goals were added by Renton who went on to lift the trophy for the second time.

Across the next three seasons the club played in the Cup competition but didn't make it beyond the Second Round. They became known as Johnstone Wanderers in 1891 and in 1894 they merged with Strathmore FC, who were considerably older, having been formed as far back as 1876. The original name of the new merged club was Dundonians FC but after objections from Dundee they adopted the title of Dundee Wanderers.

Dundee Wanderers played their games, first at East Dock Street, between June to December 1894 and then at Clepington Park. They played in maroon and white striped shirts and blue shorts and were known as 'The Forkies', possibly because they had split, or forked off from Our Boys.

The club played their first SFL game away at Partick Thistle on the 11th August 1894. The game was played at Meadowside and they lost 5-2 with their line up being Coventry; Murray, Brown; McIntosh, McDermid, Donnachie; Fleming, Moodie; Proudfoot, Craik and Abbot. Their first ever League goal was actually an own goal scored by Ross, the left back of Partick, early on in the second half. Craik was the first ever Dundee Wanderers goal scorer when he got their second in the 65th minute.

Their first League points came in their second fixture, a 2-2 draw with Motherwell at East Dock Street on the 25th August, a game in which they twice led (which incidentally was their only draw in their whole League campaign). In their third match, on the 8th September, they suffered the first of a number of heavy defeats losing 8-2 away at Hibernian. *The Scotsman* was underwhelmed reporting that "the visit of the Dundee Wanderers to Edinburgh created very little interest in local circles, and although the weather was first-class, the attendance at no time would exceed 1500. The match was the poorest seen in Edinburgh this season...the Hibernians simply holding the game in hand from the first moment." Hibs put five past Coventry in the Wanderers goal in the space of ten minutes with the away team grabbing a goal just before the interval to trail 5-1. The second half was quite scrappy with both sides adding a goal before incessant pressure from Hibs towards the end saw them add two more to end this one-sided game 8-2.

A week later they recorded their first win in emphatic style beating Port Glasgow Athletic 9-1. In front of a crowd of 1,000 Wanderers had seven different scorers, with Craik scoring two and with an own goal. However, Dundee Wanderers would go on to win only three games all season. They were poor travellers, losing every away game they played, including a 2-1 defeat against bottom team Cowlairs at Gourlay Park, in Glasgow. They were kept off the bottom of the Division by being awarded an away win by default. On Saturday 29th September 1894 Dundee Wanderers were due to visit Renton but their opponents organised a lucrative friendly with Queen's Park instead. Dundee Wanderers were eventually awarded the two points at a meeting of the SFL Management Committee in mid-October.

On the 10th November they lost 6-0 at home to Hibs, who would go on to win the Second Division, but worse was to follow. On the 1st December 1894 they visited Broomfield for a return fixture against Airdrieonians, having already lost 2-1 at home to Airdrie on the 20th October. Dundee Wanderers were missing five of their best players- Coventry, Roberts, Tosh, Ireland & Abbot – and they were thrashed. The club's 15–1 away defeat against Airdrie remains the heaviest ever away defeat in Scottish Football League history.

A detailed match report survives from the local *Airdrie & Coatbridge Advertiser* and it records that - "The Dundee men kicked off against a slight wind and started as though they meant serious business against Traynor. Doubtless they did but the home club's defenders were alert and play was diverted with a run up the left which culminated in Martin capturing the first goal with a perfectly unsaveable shot."

From the re-start Wanderers were immediately pegged back and put under pressure. Airdrieonians forced a corner from which Bob Scott, the Scotland international who was renowned for hitting the ball hard and fast, fired home their second and he soon followed this up with his second, Airdrie's third. The game was still in its infancy and the home side were already three up! "This sort of thing looked serious for the Northern eleven, and their right wing made great efforts to get into goal, but as a team they simply failed at every effort to get beyond the home captain and his redoubtable partner, so that Traynor was purely a spectator."

The paper goes on to report that: "by this time the spectators were beginning to see that the visitors were a soft mark – an opinion which was verified when the home team rushed on goal and got a corner for their trouble twenty minutes after the start. This was well placed by R. Scott, and landed eventually to Inglis who promptly put it in the net for the fourth time. The Wanderers meantime were simply 'not in the show', and out of many sieges were caught again by R. Scott, who lay out and got the ball as Baird threw it away in a hurry, to rid himself of Martin. It only remains to be said that Scott put his foot on the ball, and in a twinkling it was past Baird."

The score was now 5-0 and barely half an hour of the game had been played. The Airdrie forwards were dominating the game and Bob Scott had secured his hat-trick. Kyle had a number of opportunities to join Scott on the score sheet before McDonald, who was married the week before, celebrated by steering a shot past Baird, whilst under pressure from the Wanderers' defence. The Dundee side responded to going six down in half an hour with some attacks of their own but the Airdrie defence were up to the task. When they did carve out a shooting opportunity Traynor in the Airdrie goal was equal to it. Just before half-time McDonald received a delightful cross from Inglis in a great goal-scoring position but was ruled off-side. No matter, for moments later Kyle jinked his way past Taylor and unleashed a shot which Baird, in the Dundee goal, got a touch on but was unable to keep out. After a brief spell of possession, Dundee had suffered a further blow and went into the interval with the score at 7-0 in favour of the home side.

"If there was fun during the first portion, the second half started more sensationally and promised to end in a record score. McDonald and Scott at once ran through the defence when the former passed into the centre, and Martin, with all the ease imaginable had leave to steady himself and shoot in the eighth goal. Talk about the cat and the mouse, the play shown described that splendidly as the home team waltzed round the poor Wanderers, and inside of ten minutes Martin had scored another three, bringing the register up to eleven." In a manic period at the beginning of the Second Half Martin had scored four goals at the rate of one every two minutes. Dundee

Wanderers were stunned. And there was to be no let-up and no mercy as the Airdrieonians players kept pushing forward seeking even more goals.

Both Martin and Bob Scott now had hat-tricks to their name. The youngster, Inglis, not to be out shone by the more senior players, then secured his own with two more goals. First he raced between Taylor and McHardy before finishing with a clever shot and then he fired past Baird. The local paper records that "the spectators looked on the game as a pure farce, and appeared to enjoy the 'fancy' passing of the Airdrieonians, as they slid the ball from forward to back at times, and altogether demonstrated that it was a genuine 'one horse show' ". In between his goals ironic cheers had "announced that off a free kick Traynor was next beaten." The Dundee scorer is not recorded.

"Nearing the end the Airdrieonians could hardly do anything else but score." The Wanderers left-back Taylor "scored against himself" to make the score 14-1 and then Bob Scott completed the scoring – "as a fitting end, Airdrie's grandest forward closed the record, the final score being Airdrieonians 15 Dundee Wanderers 1." Scott had scored four, Martin finished with five, a divisional record and Inglis with three. It's not known who got the match ball! The result is a record win in the old Second Division and for a Scottish League fixture overall. The Dundee Wanderers line up for the game was: Baird, Burgess, Taylor, Shepherd, Crawford, McHardy, Peat, Cust, Bryan, Craig and Sutherland.

Wanderers conceded 32 goals in their next six fixtures, although one of these was a rare victory, a thrilling 6-5 win over Partick Thistle on the 9th March 1895. In this game Wanderers made most of the early running and established a 3-0 lead before Partick were successful. In the second half Wanderers increased their lead but Thistle came storming back scoring four goals in quick succession. The *Glasgow Herald* noted that "towards the close the Wanderers made a vigorous effort, and scored twice, thus winning 6 goals to 5."

On Saturday 6th April 1895 they won their penultimate home game, beating bottom club Cowlairs 6-3 "at the outset the Wanderers played in brisk fashion" (*Glasgow Herald*) and opened the scoring through an own goal. The visitors equalised but the hosts then scored three times. "In the closing stages the game was almost wholly devoid of the finer points, and the result was a victory for Dundee by 6 goals to 3."But they lost their last ever home SFL game against Morton 1-0, a late winner scored by Drysdale with a low shot.

On the 13th April they lost 9-2 at Abercorn before finishing their SFL campaign in the reverse fixture against Cowlairs on the 27th April 1895. They lost the game narrowly 2-1 and their final line up was Coventry; Wilson, Taylor, Matthew, Crawford, McHardie, Peat, Graham, Sutherland, Docherty and Gray. Only the goalkeeper Coventry was a survivor from their opening fixture.

Although they attracted a gate of 3,000 spectators for their win over Partick Thistle, Wanderers attracted little support in the re-election vote. Whilst Abercorn of Paisley secured 22 votes in the voting, Wanderers, along with Cowlairs could muster only a paltry 3 votes. Kilmarnock and Linthouse (from Govan, Glasgow) were elected in their places with 24 votes each

Dundee Wanderers dropped down into the Northern League where they had some success, finishing as runners-up for three seasons in row between 1987-99, before winning it in the 1899-1900 season. They made occasional appearances in the Scottish Cup, their last being in December 1900 when they lost 3-0 at home to Aberdeen in the First Round. At the end of the 1905-06 season they had finished bottom of the Northern League and they got the wooden spoon again in 1907-08. They played for their last few seasons at St Margaret's Park having lost the tenancy of Clepington Park to the newly formed Dundee Hibernian in 1909. The 1911-12 season was their last in the Northern League, finishing second from bottom. On the 7th September 1912, Dundee Wanderers were hammered 8-0 at Arbroath in a Scottish Qualifying Cup tie. There are no records of the team playing any further fixtures and in April 1913, the club was formally wound up.

SEASON	LEAGUE	P	W	D	L	F	A	P	POS
1894-95	SCOT-2	17	3	1	13	44	86	9 *	9/10

*Awarded the points when Renton failed to turn up for fixture

Dykehead

Formed: 1880
Colours: Black and white vertical striped shirts and white shorts
Ground: Parkside
Entered League: 1923. Founder members of the Third Division
Number of League Seasons: 3
Honours: None
Highest League Finish: 4th in Division Three
Left League: 1926. Division Three abandoned. Wound up 1928

Dykehead is a scattered settlement lying close to Shotts in Lanarkshire, a former industrial village located between Glasgow and Edinburgh. It grew to prominence in the nineteenth century as a centre for the extraction and smelting of iron ore with locally mined coal supplying the foundries. Somewhat surprisingly for a village, a team from here joined the Scottish Football League and played for three seasons, as part of the new, but short-lived Third Division.

Although founded in 1880 they didn't register with the Scottish FA until 1884 when they made their debut in the Scottish Cup. They originally played at Dykehead Park before moving to their Parkside home in 1886, which was located just off Rosehall Road, to the south-west of the village.

Although they entered the Scottish Cup in 1884 they didn't progress from a match until 1921. It is recorded that they played on the 27th September 1884, losing 5-2 in Shotts to Wishaw Swifts, but this was not exactly their first Scottish Cup match. As the *Glasgow Herald* reported, "these clubs met on the ground of the former in a protested Association Cup tie. In the first match, which was played at Wishaw, the Swifts gained a victory by two goals to one. Dykehead lodged an appeal, which was obtained. The Swifts maintained their reputation, defeating the home team by five goals to two."

The following year they played in the Second Round, but only after receiving a First Round bye. They did 'beat' Tollcross in the next round but were subsequently disqualified. In the 1886-87 season they again got a bye into the Second Round but were beaten 7-0 by Albion Rovers. In the 1887-88 competition they lost 8-0 against

Airdrieonians, in what *The Scotsman* described as "a very one-sided character, the play of the Airdrieonians being throughout of a decidedly superior kind." Played in torrential rain, with the home team scoring four goals in each half, this was their biggest ever Cup defeat.

Dykehead didn't play in the Scottish Cup again until 1909 when they lost to Clyde 4-0 in the First Round. In 1895 they briefly joined the Scottish Alliance and in 1898 the Scottish Federation before playing in the Scottish Combination between 1905 and 1909. In 1909 they joined the rival Scottish Union which they won in the 1912-13 season. In 1915, following the suspension of the Scottish Football League's Second Division they joined with clubs from this division, and other non-League clubs, to form the Western League. They temporarily withdrew from this competition in 1917 due to the War but returned in 1919.

Between 1920 and 1922 they had three seasons participating in the Scottish Cup. On the 31st January 1920, a First Round replay against Albion Rovers attracted an incredible record crowd of 4,000 to Parkside. Dykehead had drawn the first game 0-0 the week before against their SFL opponents, Eadon, their goalkeeper was the hero, while Geddes and Watson performed Herculean work in front of him. Dykehead lost the replay 2-1. The Rovers got an early goal and in the second half increased their lead. Rennox, the centre-forward, got the goal for Dykehead. The following year, on the 22nd January 1921, they finally won a Scottish Cup tie when they beat Peterhead away 3-0. Allander scored all of the goals for Dykehead. One of the Peterhead's backs had his leg broken. They went out in the next round at Ayr United losing 4-0. Finally, in January 1922 a crowd of 5,000 spectators saw Airdrieonians beat Dykehead by the narrowest of margins. Airdrie took the lead after ten minutes but then spurned several chances to extend their lead. *The Scotsman* commented that "Dykehead, for a period put up a strong fight, and were unlucky not to equalise. The second half was one-sided, but the Shotts team put up a great defence against almost continuous bombardment, and held out to a narrow defeat." Under the alliterative headline "Dour Dykehead Defence" *The Sunday Post* noted that "Somerville was fine in goal, and there was no better back than Abernethy. Hardin upheld his name...The best of the Dykehead attack came from Watson, King and Sneddon. That was their weak spot, however, and the narrow win was due to their fine defence."

In 1923 the bulk of the Western League were invited to join the Scottish Football League as founder members of the new Third Division. Dykehead made their debut as a League club on the 18th August 1923, losing 2-0 away against Queen of the South at Palmerston Park in front of 4000 spectators. Commenting on the Dykehead team *The*

Sunday Post noted that "Taylor was clever in goal and Tumulty a great worker in the middle line."

The first SFL match at Parkside was played on the 25th August 1923, a 3–1 win over Ayrshire side Galston. Whilst the reports suggested the visitors were a bit unlucky and had the better of the play, a strong home showing by the team from Shotts was going to be a feature of their debut season. They went on to win 13 out of 15 home fixtures. They drew 2-2 versus Queen of the South, their only draw in the whole of the season, and the club's only home defeat came against leaders (and eventual champions) Arthurlie. This strong home form was undone on their travels where they lost 12 out of 15 matches and they eventually finished a very good fifth place in their debut season, albeit nine points off the promotion places.

Their second season was very disappointing, finishing a lowly 12th. They started with a 1-1 home draw against Peebles but their form was erratic. A 5-1 defeat at Lochgelly was followed by a 4-1 home win over Vale of Leven and a 3-0 win away at Dumbarton Harp. But these were then followed by a 4-0 defeat against Nithsdale Wanderers. On the 13th December 1924 they suffered their heaviest ever SFL defeat, losing 7-0 at Larkhall's Royal Albert, who were below them in the table. *The Sunday Post* reported that "Royal Albert were in rampant form against Dykehead at Raploch Park yesterday and simply overwhelmed their Lanarkshire rivals. In the first half Dykehead put up a good fight, but Albert were superior in all departments, and led at the interval by two goals...There was no holding the Albert forwards after the cross-over and goals came rapidly...Dykehead failed to convert a penalty...Finlayson and Allan for Dykehead tried hard to put a better face on the state if matters, but their defence could not tackle the part they had in hand." Dykehead struggled to score, especially on their travels, drawing a blank in half of their away games. In contrast to their League performances, Dykehead had their best run in the Scottish Cup, reaching the Third Round. They beat Second Division strugglers Forfar Athletic and then fellow Third Division side Peebles Rovers before losing 5-0 to Kilmarnock.

In early 1925 one of the Third Division sides, Dumbarton Harp, resigned from the SFL due to financial problems. Dykehead, amongst other clubs, were not immune from the general economic downturn, nor the financial viability of the new division. On Saturday 21st March Dykehead hosted Helensburgh but had to owe the visiting club £5 from the £15 match guarantee paid to visiting clubs. On Saturday the 18th April Dykehead called off their home tie against Brechin City as they couldn't afford the match guarantee payment and on the 28th April, when they did host Montrose, they only offered the visiting club £2 4s, half the takings, instead of the full match guarantee. On the 29th April *The Scotsman* reported on the meeting of the Management Committee of the SFL, stating that "in a claim by Brechin City against Dykehead in connection with postponed league games, the former club were awarded the points, and are to receive £7, 10s from Dykehead."

The 1925-26 season was a much better one on the pitch for Dykehead as they mounted a promotion challenge. However, this was completely overshadowed by the overall collapse of the division, with lots of matches not being completed, as some teams were suffering financial difficulties. The new season started well with an opening 2-1 win over Johnstone. Under the headline "Dashing Dykehead" *The Sunday Post* reported that "Dykehead made an auspicious start against Johnstone, scoring in five minutes. Rankin headed through cleverly from a cross by Robb. Johnstone were not long in arrears, Bickerstaffe equalising with a great drive which beat Stewart all ends up. Dykehead opened the second period in dashing style, but nothing came from all their raids. Whiteside stopping some tries that were on the mark but lacking in sting. Twenty-five minutes after the restart Rankin again gave his side the lead, this time from a pass by Senior." Three consecutive wins in September, all at home, left them joint second in the table.

On the 7th November 1925 they entertained Peebles. They led 1-0 at half-time, from a penalty by Rankin. Peebles equalised but Dykehead soon regained the lead through O'Hare and Robb and McCourt scored to make it 4-1. At this point they were in fourth place, six points off first place and only two points off second. They had also played four fewer games than the leaders and had a game in hand on the team in second and so were very much in contention. They played their last game of 1925 on the 19th December. Lots of games were postponed due to snow, but they beat leaders Helensburgh 2-0 to move within four points of new leaders Vale of Leven, but with three games in hand. Hepburn in the Shotts goal kept the visitors out in the early stages as they had the better of the play. Rankin was brought down in the area and picked himself up to score from the spot. O'Hare scored from a long range strike in the second half.

On the New Year's Day fixture of 1926 they dropped a point away at bottom side Galston in a game that ended in a 2-2 draw. *The Sunday Post* on 10th January reported on an incident that occurred in that recent Dykehead v Galston game: "the story, as told in official circles, is to the effect that as the players were leaving the field at half-time…Rankin, the Dykehead outside-left, is reported to have said -"there are some fine referees in this Division". The referee, who was within hearing, immediately turned to the player and said – "you remain in the pavilion during the second half of the game." Consternation reigned when this became known, and on a prominent official of the Dykehead club interrogating the player, the latter is alleged to have said that his remark was made to one of his own players and not to the referee. When the teams returned to the field in the second half, Rankin was advised to go out also, which he did, but on seeing him the referee is reported to have said – "did I not tell you to remain in the pavilion during the second half? Off you go!" And the player had to go. Galston only played two more games after this before resigning from the League due to financial problems.

In their next game Dykehead suffered a 3-2 home defeat against the latest leaders Forfar Athletic despite leading twice. The result left them in fourth but with games in hand on the teams above them - the other two being Helensburgh and Vale of Leven. The men from Shotts bounced back from the setback against the leaders, going the next seven games unbeaten. Included in this sequence was a 5-1 win over Clackmannan, in which the centre-half McCourt opened the scoring with a superb goal, beating several opponents to find an opening and then firing off a beauty which left the goalkeeper no chance. Rankin, the Dykehead centre added two before the interval and their opponents got one back. In the second half Allan added a fourth and Rankin got his third, taking his season's tally to 24.

On the 6th February Dykehead shared the spoils in an eight goal thriller away at Lochgelly. This was a remarkable comeback as the home team were 4-1 up with half an hour to go. Rankin scored all four of his side's goals. Overall Dykehead only lost once across December 1925 and the first two months of 1926. They were very strong at home again and recorded their biggest SFL win on the 13th February 1926 over Royal Albert, gaining revenge for that heavy defeat the previous season. Under the headline "Dykehead Drub Royal Albert", *The Sunday Post* reported that the men from Larkhall scored first before Dykehead scored two in a minute and they added two more before the interval. They scored another four in the second half through Forgan, McCourt and O'Hare (2) with Albert getting a second thereby making the score 4-1 in each half. After this result Forfar were top with 29 points having played 22 and there were three clubs on 28 points – Dykehead (played 20), Vale of Leven (played 21) and Helensburgh (played 23). Some way back were Leith Athletic who had accumulated 21 points and who were still in contention on account of only having played 16 matches.

On the 20th February Dykehead secured a key win away at promotion rivals Helensburgh. A cagey affair was goalless until a faulty clearance by the home defence allowed Rankin to score the only goal of the game. With Vale of Leven losing at Beith and Forfar not playing, the results meant Dykehead now topped the Division by a point and had a game in hand. The following week a 2-2 draw away at Beith was enough to keep them top as Forfar lost at Helenburgh. But the unbeaten run was surprisingly ended by a 2-1 loss in Annan on 13th March against a struggling Solway Star. Despite leading at half-time through another Rankin goal, Solway equalised in the second half and scored the winning goal five minutes from the end.

Dykehead then met follow promotion challengers Vale of Leven at Parkside and drew 1-1. Their promotion hopes then suffered a major blow when they surprisingly lost 3-1 away at bottom side Peebles Rovers. A triallist put them ahead but before the interval Ramage and Turner put Peebles into the lead. Findlay registered a penalty for the Rovers in the second half which seemed to stir the men from Shotts but their efforts were too little too late. Dykehead's challenge then collapsed as they failed to win any of their last seven games, picking up only three points, including just one point from their last three fixtures.

In what would ultimately prove to be their last ever SFL game at Parkside, Dykehead drew 2-2 with Solway Star on Saturday 10th April 1926, coming from 2-0 down. Goals by Knox and Ross gave Solway Star an early lead but before the interval O'Hare had reduced the deficit. In the second half Rankin missed the chance to restore parity with a missed penalty but before the close McCourt equalised and the game ended 2-2. The draw left them in second place, just two points behind Forfar, level on points with Helensburgh and one ahead of Mid-Annandale, two ahead of Vale of Leven and four ahead of Leith (who had three games in hand).

The key result was in the second of these last three fixtures, a 3-0 away defeat against Leith Athletic at Logie Green In front of 3,000 on Wednesday 14th April. The result strengthened Leith's chances of promotion. McCourt failed to convert a penalty kick for Dykehead earlier in the game. While Dykehead had no game on the Saturday, both Leith and Helensburgh had good wins. Helensburgh now had 38 points (having completed all of their 30 fixtures); Forfar had 34 points (from 27 games); Dykehead had 33 points from 25 games (one of the remaining fixtures was supposed to be the home game against Galston); and Leith Athletic had 32 points, with four games to play. Leith then played games on the 19th and 21st April winning both to go second with 36 points.

Clackmannan cancelled their game scheduled for the 17th April and Saturday 24th April saw the last round of games. Dykehead's last ever SFL game was a disappointing 4-1 loss at Links Park against Montrose with Arthur Rankin scoring their last ever SFL goal. Leith played and drew finishing with 37 points (from 29 matches), Helensburgh had 38 (from 30 matches) Forfar had 35 points (from 28 matches) and Dykehead were in fourth with 33 points (from 28 matches). Dykehead were unable to play a reverse home fixture against Galston who had resigned in the January and they also never got to play away at Clackmannan.

The worsening economic situation in 1926 meant that the gate money generated was proving insufficient to meet the guarantees and travelling expenses. At the SFL AGM in May it was noted that because only one club had completed all of its fixtures, no club was entitled to promotion or to have the championship flag awarded. The Third Division was abandoned and as this meant no automatic promotion or relegation a re-election vote was held instead. The bottom two clubs from the Second Division, Bathgate and Broxburn United, were challenged by the top four sides of the now defunct Third Division: Helensburgh, Leith Athletic, Forfar Athletic and Dykehead. Dykehead were eliminated, along with Broxburn and Helensburgh, in the early rounds of voting. Bathgate were re-elected and Forfar Athletic beat Leith Athletic on the Scottish Football League chairman's casting vote after tying on 16 votes apiece.

Dykehead spent the following season in the Scottish Alliance and then spent 1927-28 in the Provincial League. They featured in the Scottish Cup in each of these seasons. In the 1926-27 competition they were knocked out by Montrose after a replay. They drew the first game 3-3 with their centre-forward Allan scoring a hat-trick. *The Scotsman* described the replay at Links Park as "grim". After 90 minutes the score was level with Stewart having scored first for Dykehead. No goals were scored in the first 15 minutes but three minutes after the resumption Montrose took the lead and less than two minutes later they added a third. This was the last ever senior fixture because although they were drawn away at Hibernian in the first round the following year, they scratched and gave Hibs a walkover on the 21st January 1928.

The Provincial League only lasted for the one season before it was disbanded and at this time Dykehead were wound up. The site of Parkside remains in use as a football pitch

SEASON	LEAGUE	P	W	D	L	F	A	P	POS
1923-24	SCOT-3	30	16	1	13	55	41	33	5/16
1924-25	SCOT-3	29	7	11	11	30	47	25	12/16
1925-26	SCOT-3	28	14	5	9	62	47	33	4/16

East Stirlingshire

Formed: 1881
Colours: Black and white horizontal hooped shirts and white shorts
Ground: Merchiston Park (1881-1920). Firs Park (1921-2008). Then groundsharing at Ochilview (Stenhousemuir).
Entered League: 1900. Elected to Second Division. 1921. Reformed Second Division. 1965. Court Case.
Number of League Seasons: 61
Highest League Finish: 18th in Division One (top flight), 1963-64
Honours: Second Division Champions 1931-32. Third Division Champions 1946-1947
Left League: 1915. League suspended due to Great War. 1964. Name change and relocation. 2016. Relegated to Lowland League

In 2016 East Stirlingshire became the first Scottish Football League club to be relegated from the League. Other clubs had dropped out due to re-election, or League reconstruction but East Stirling were the first club to be actually relegated. The introduction of a pyramid system in Scotland to replace the practice of clubs being voted into the League was introduced for the 2014-15 season. For the first time teams from the Highland and Lowland Leagues in Scotland could be promoted on merit to the SFL. The winners of these two Leagues would first play-off and would then undertake a two-legged playoff against the team finishing bottom of League Two or the fourth tier. It was therefore now possible for a League club to be relegated. East Stirling suffered this fate in the second season of the playoffs. They have one of the longest tenures and are one of most successful of the ex-Scottish League clubs, having won two divisional titles, and they competed in two seasons in the top flight - 1932-33 and 1963-64.

East Stirlingshire originated in 1881 when a cricket team called Bainsford Bluebonnets decided to form a football team. Bainsford is a village, one mile north of Falkirk, near to the Forth and Clyde Canal. They originally took the name of Bainsford Britannia but changed their name to East Stirlingshire FC in 1881. The Shire are therefore a Falkirk based team and have no connection with the city of Stirling. At the time Falkirk was located in the east of the historic county of Stirlingshire and that is how the club gets its name.

They originally played at a playing field in Bainsford which was rented from James Young, the owner of Mungal Farm, and a club director. It was located just north of the Forth and Clyde Canal at Bainsford Bridge and was originally called Bainsford Park. It later formally adopted the name of Merchiston Park. In 1906 the whole ground was moved a few hundred metres south to make way for a new railway line, the Bainsford Branch, with the railway line to the north and the Burnbank Iron Foundry to the south. The ground was closed completely in 1920 when the Burnbank Iron Foundary acquired the Merchiston Park grounds for expansion.

The club joined the Scottish Football Association in 1882 and in 1888 they reached the Quarter finals of the Scottish Cup before losing to Celtic. They reached the last eight again in the 1890-91 season, this time going out to Hearts. The club joined the Scottish League in 1900, spending most of their time in the lower leagues, although they did play two seasons in the top division after winning the Second Division title in 1931-32. In 1964 the club briefly went out of existence when the club was forcibly moved to Clydebank, playing under the name of ES Clydebank. After a court case the club regained its identity and independence and returned home to Firs Park. In July 1974 East Stirlingshire briefly became the first managerial post of one Alex Ferguson. After a number of dire performances in the League at the start of the new millennium a rule change was introduced that led to the possibility of relegation from the League and Shire ultimately succumbed, ending over 60 years in the SFL.

East Stirlingshire first entered the Scottish Cup in the 1881-82 where they were knocked out in the First Round 2-1 by Milngavie Thistle on the 9th September 1881. They played in the Cup for 18 successive seasons prior to League admission. In the 1883-84 competition they reached the Third Round before going out 6-1 away to Partick Thistle, played at Muirpark. In the following season they reached the Second Round where Shire came up against the eventual winners Renton at Bainsford. It was no surprise when Shire were thrashed 10-2 on the 4th October 1884. In the 1885-86 competition East Stirlingshire again reached the Third Round where they again drew an early powerhouse of the Scottish game, this time Queen's Park. A crowd of over 3,000 turned up at Merchiston Park on the 24th October to watch the home team lose 3-0, *The Scotsman* reporting that "the strangers had the best of the game all through." Shire reached the Third Round stage of the competition in each of the next two seasons, going out to Clyde 3-1 at Merchiston Park. And the following year this time in a replay to Cambuslang.

East Stirlingshire were founder members of the Stirlingshire Football Association in December 1883. The inaugural tournament, played for during the remainder of the 1883-84 season, was won by Falkirk who defeated East Stirlingshire 3–1 in a replayed final after an initial 1–1 draw. Shire played their first match in this tournament on the 9th February 1884 when they beat Comely Park of Falkirk 9-1. In the Second Round they beat Tayavalla (of Tamfourhill, West of Falkirk and south Camelon) 7-1 and in the Semi-final beat Strathblane (of Blanefield) 2-1. The final, played on the 29th March at Tayavalla's Lock 16 Ground, ended in a 1-1 draw. The replay, staged a week later at same ground was won by Falkirk 3-1. East Stirling first won the Stirlingshire Cup in its third year of competition, in the 1885-86 season. They beat King's Park of Stirling 3-1 in a replay, at Victoria Park, the home of Camelon FC. This was the first of four wins in a row, to make them the most successful club at that time. In the 1886-87 competition they defended the trophy by beating Falkirk 1-0 at the same ground. They repeated this against the same opposition, although this time winning by an incredible 9-0 and in 1889 they secured their fourth win by thrashing Slamannan 7-0, also at Victoria Park, Camelon.

The 1888-89 season also saw the club's great Scottish Cup run to the Quarter-finals with some notable victories along the way. In the First Round, played on the 1st September, they met local Larbert rivals Stenhousemuir at Merchiston Park. Their visitors actually scored first, very early on, which seemed to rouse the home forwards who promptly equalised and then went on to score another five before half-time to lead 6-1 at the break. In the second half Shire eased off, still scoring another four goals to win 10-1. This was followed up in the Second Round with an 11-2 home win against Vale of Bannock (from Bannockburn, Stirling). Play was fairly even for the first ten minutes before Simpson scored for Shire and this was followed by another three goals with Shire leading 4-0 at the interval. In the second half the home team continued to have the best of the play and scored seven more goals. Towards the close their opponents managed to score twice with the final score being 11-2.

In the Third Round King's Park of Stirling were easily defeated 4-0 at Bainsford. This game was played on the 13th October and nearly 2,000 spectators turned up. The Shire took up the early running and Stewart scored after ten minutes. Not long after, Dunn added a second and a superb shot from Jones, the half-back, made it 3-0 at half-time. Ten minutes after the re-start Dunn scored a fourth and although the home team created a number of fresh chances they failed to add to their score and won 4-0.

East Stirlingshire drew Dunblane in the Fourth Round with the *Glasgow Herald* reporting that "at Dunblane the holders of the Stirlingshire Cup and the holders of the Perthshire Cup faced each other before a large turnout of spectators. Ever since these teams have been drawn great interest has been taken in the tie. A special train was run from Grahamston with the supporters of East Stirlingshire." Their hosts had the better of the first half and led 4-2 at the break. Shire drew level in the second half and the game ended in a 4-4 draw. Shire won through 4-0 at home in the replay, although this was subject to a protest. The *Glasgow Herald* reported that "the Dunblane protested against awarding East Stirlingshire their tie...on the ground that the East Stirlingshire had played Kirkwood, who had played a month under the English Association."

The protest against Dan Kirkwood, the former Broxburn Shamrock player who would later play for Everton, was thrown out and Shire received a bye in the Fifth Round and so on the 15th December Celtic travelled to Merchiston Park to play their Quarter-final tie. Celtic had only been formed in November 1887 but had instantly become a major player in the game. In front of a 3,000 crowd Shire went in at the break 1-0 up through a goal from Shire legend Laurie McLachlan but two late goals in the last four minutes won the game for the Glasgow club. *The Scotsman* covered the match, reporting that "the visitors losing the toss, Groves started the ball for them, and for the next few minutes had the best of the play. The Shire, however, broke away, and had one or two likely tries at the Celts' goal. Both teams now played up hard, each visiting the others goal in turn. Maley, by an awkward mistake missed a very likely chance. A corner also fell to the Celts, but they failed to improve it. After play had gone on for forty minutes, McLachlan scored the first point on the game for East Stirlingshire. Half-time was called with the Shire leading by one goal to nil. On resuming, the Celts made a determined effort to score, but the Shire retaliated and play was for a time pretty even. A foul fell to the Celts within a few feet of the home goal, but they failed to improve on it. The visitors put up a strong pressure within three minutes of time and notched their only two goals and thus won a hard game." The East Stirlingshire side that reached the quarter-finals was: Sharp, Keddie, Reid, Ritchie, Wilson, Humphrey Jones, Dan Kirkwood, Jocky Stewart, Wull Dunn, Laurie McLachlan and Harry Simpson. Amongst the line-up was forward Laurence "Laurie" McLachlan, who was an early club legend. The team also included Humphrey Jones, who became the first Shire player to receive International Honours when he represented Wales against England and Ireland. He was already a Welsh international when he played for the club in the 1889-90 season and earned five of his 24 caps for Wales while at the club, and subsequently moved to Queen's Park. In 1889 club record goalscorer William "Wull" Dunn moved down to England to play for Stoke along with teammate Harry Simpson.

In the 1890-91 season East Stirlingshire had another great run in the Scottish Cup, reaching the Quarter-Final for the second time in three seasons. Grangemouth were the visitors in the First Round and they opened the scoring at Merchiston Park after just two minutes. Carty equalised a few minutes later. Each team scored another goal in the first half and so the score stood at 2-2 at half-time. In the second half Shire completely dominated scoring six goals without reply to win 8-2. Campsie were knocked out in the next round but in the Third Round Shire were held to a 3-3 draw against Camelon. On the 25th October 1890, at Victoria Park, 1,500 spectators watched the replay produce an amazing 16 goals. Eleven goals were scored in the second half as East Stirlingshire won 10-6. Carty opened the scoring before the home team equalised. Howden (2) and Reid made it 4-1 at the interval. On resuming Carty and Alexander made it 6-1 before the hosts scored two to make it 6-3. The scoreline then went to 8-3, then 8-5 before it ended 10-6. In the Fourth Round they beat Inverness Caledonian 2-0. 5,000 fans watched in a downpour as Alexander set up Reid for the opening goal. Their hosts had a goal ruled offside, before in the 65th minute Johnston made it 2-0. Shire got a bye in the next round and for the Quarter-final were drawn against Hearts. The Quarter final took place on the 20th December at Bainsford but despite going in at half-time 1-1 the 2,000 home crowd went home disappointed when two further goals in the second period won the tie for the Edinburgh team. Hearts took the lead after ten minutes but Carty equalised fifteen minutes later. The Shire team that day was: John Mercer; Archie Ritchie, Wull Dunn; Andrew Inch, William Keddie, John Hastings; Davie Alexander, Tom Howden, Reid, Carty and Johnston. Defender Archibald "Archie" Ritchie was the first player from East Stirlingshire to be capped from Scotland when he was picked to play on the 21st March 1891 against Wales in Wrexham in the British Home Championship, Scotland winning 4-3. He later joined Nottingham Forest and won the FA Cup with them in 1898. Davie Alexander was capped a few years later, in March 1894, also against Wales in the Home Championship 5-2 win at Rugby Park Kilmarnock. Alexander scored Scotland's fourth goal as they came from 2-0 down to win. He played a week later against Ireland in Belfast, Scotland winning 2-1.

In the 1890-91 Stirlingshire Cup competition Shire failed to make it five in a row as Falkirk beat them 5-2 in the First Round. Falkirk went on to win the competition and Merchiston Park staged the final. They regained the Stirlingshire Cup the following season though, beating Grangemouth 4-1 at Victoria Park, Camelon. In 1891 Shire joined the Scottish Alliance, a rival competition to the Scottish League and in the first season finished 10th out of 12 clubs. Their defence of the county Cup ended in the Quarter-Finals as Grangemouth took their revenge, winning 2-0. They switched to the Scottish Federation for the 1892-93 coming in seventh place out of ten teams. In the same season they won back the Stirlingshire Cup, beating Kilsyth Wanderers 2-1 at Brockville, Falkirk.

When the Scottish Alliance, as the senior non-League body, was used as the backbone for the new Second Division in 1893 four Federation clubs transferred to the Alliance. Hurlford and Kilmarnock Athletic joined the Ayrshire League so Falkirk and East Stirlingshire entered the Midland League, for its third season, and the Federation closed down. Shire won the Midland League, at the first time of asking, finishing four points ahead of King's Park and five in front of Falkirk and Stenhousemuir. They also retained the Stirlingshire Cup trophy, beating Gairdoch 5-0 at Brockville. In March 1894 Davie Alexander played for Scotland in the wins against Wales and Ireland, scoring against Wales.

In the 1894-95 the club came third in the Midland League, Falkirk winning it this time and for the 1895-96 season they came third again - this time Stenhousemuir were the champions. They failed to reach the final of the county Cup in each of these seasons, although Merchiston Park went on to stage the finals. At the end of the season they applied to join the Scottish League for the first time (along with Falkirk), but were unsuccessful, both clubs failing to get a seconder and they were therefore excluded from the vote.

The club subsequently left the Midland League and were founder members of the Scottish Football Combination, along with Falkirk and Stenhousemuir. At the end of the 1896-97 season East Stirlingshire beat Stenhousemuir 4-1 at Brockville to win the Stirlingshire Cup for an eighth time, twice as many as Falkirk. At the League's AGM held on the 1st June 1897 Shire applied again to join the Scottish Football League, along with Falkirk and Hamilton. Ayr FC were elected instead and replaced Dumbarton. At the same time they left the Scottish Football Combination, along with Falkirk and Stenhousemuir, to form the nine team Central Combination. On 20th October 1897, during the 1897-98 season, Renton resigned for financial reasons. The SFL decided to elect a replacement at this early stage in the season. East Stirlingshire, along with Hamilton, Falkirk, Albion Rovers, Raith Rovers and two other clubs all applied but it was Hamilton, who were successfully elected on the 27th October. Shire performed well in the new Central Combination and went through the season unbeaten, winning 14 of their 16 matches to win the competition in its inaugural season. Buoyed by this success they made a fourth bid to join the League. At the AGM on the 30th May 1898. Falkirk and Raith were unsuccessful in getting a seconder at the AGM whereas Shire did, making them the sole challenger to Airdrieonians, Hamilton and Motherwell. They secured 16 votes but Motherwell took the third spot with 20 votes. On a brighter note, two months earlier centre-forward James McKie became the Shire's third Scottish International (after Ritchie and Alexander) when he played in the Scotland team which defeated Wales 5-2, scoring Scotland's third and fourth goals. He subsequently joined Bolton Wanderers in 1900.

In the 1898-99 season Shire finished as runners-up to Stenhousemuir and then left the Central Combination after two seasons to join the Falkirk & District League. In the Scottish Cup Shire comfortably beat then non-League Dumbarton 4-1 at Bainsford in the First Round. In the next round the club were drawn against Kilmarnock and a large crowd of 6,000 turned out on the 11th December to watch a 1-1 draw. The replay the following week at Rugby Park was drawn 0-0 and therefore a second replay was required, which was staged a week later at Third Lanark's Cathkin Park, in Glasgow. This game was played on the 25th February and the tie was settled at the third attempt. Shire were again competitive and took an early lead through James McKie, but lost heart when their goalkeeper, Hastings, allowed a couple of soft shots to beat him and at half-time Kilmarnock led 3-1. Shire scored within a minute of the restart and buoyed by this early success put their opponents under continued pressure as they sought an equalising goal. Kilmarnock held firm and towards the end put the result of the game beyond doubt with a fourth.

In the 1899-1900 season Shire came second in the Falkirk & District League, again finishing behind Stenhousemuir. Stenhousemuir won the Stirlingshire Cup although East Stirling, along with Falkirk, didn't take part, protesting at the inclusion of the Clackmannanshire clubs. At the Scottish League's AGM held on the 16th May 1900 Linthouse of Glasgow decided not to seek re-election. East Stirlingshire went up against Raith Rovers of the East of Scotland League for the vacant place and Shire were successfully elected at their fifth attempt.

East Stirlingshire entered the Scottish Football League for the 1900-01 season, two years before local rivals Falkirk. Walter Clarkson took charge and would be the team's manager for over 500 games and a quarter of a century. Shire played their first ever Scottish League game on Saturday 18th August 1900. They lost 3-2 at home to Airdrieonians at Merchiston Park in front of a 2,500 crowd. Shire were two-nil down at half-time and missed a second half penalty that could have given them a share of the spoils. Shire's team in that first Scottish League game was: William Allan, Peter Hunter, Jimmy Johnston, Andrew Prentice (the captain), Wull Morris, Peter Steele, John Dobbie, Thomas Laidlaw, James Shearer, David Gillespie and John Reid. Wull Morris was the scorer of Shire's first ever Scottish League goal.

Shire's first League points and first win came in the very next round of matches. Shire won 3-0 away at Motherwell the following Saturday, which turned out to be only one of only two away wins in the League that season. They suffered a heavy 6-0 defeat in the First Round of the Scottish Cup against fellow Second Division side Clyde and this seemed to adversely affect them as they then suffered back-to-back 5-0 defeats in the League against Hamilton and then St Bernard's. By the end of January 1901 they were in eighth place with ten points, just one point ahead of bottom placed Motherwell, although they had played considerably fewer games. A strong finish, including wins over Leith and Hamilton (5-2) saw them finish above both these clubs, and Motherwell, in a commendable seventh place in their inaugural season. After a gap of four years East Stirlingshire won the Stirlingshire Cup, beating Camelon 3-2 at Brockville.

The club generally finished in the bottom half for the next four seasons, with a best finish of sixth out of 12 in the 1903-04 season. The 1901-02 season was not a great one for the club. In an expanded Second Division of 12 teams Shire were placed ninth, and they didn't record a win until their seventh League game of the season. The season had started on the 17th August 1901 with a 4-2 defeat at Clyde. Shire led 2-1 at the interval. Reid had opened the scoring for East Stirlingshire but Clyde had quickly equalised. Just before the interval Speedie had made it 2-1. On the resumption Clyde again equalised. The game was played in a downpour of rain which made the pitch heavy and towards the end of the game the players naturally showed signs of flagging. Clyde went on to score two in the last fifteen minutes. The Shire team starting the club's second League season was: C Hastings; Hunter, Johnstone; Prentice, Morris, Rae; Mitchell, Speedie, Reid, Shearer and Bauchope. The following week Shire hosted Motherwell and lost 3-1. Again they scored first, through Speedie and had the better of the first half. Motherwell equalised fifteen minutes from time and went on to score twice more. Their first point came in the fourth match, a 0-0 home draw with St Bernard's. Shire had to hold on after Prentice had to leave the field injured.

After six games they had a record of drawn one, lost five and were bottom and already three points adrift. In the next match they recorded their first win of the season, beating Hamilton 4-1. Bowman opened the scoring for Shire after a quarter of an hour but minutes later Hamilton equalised and the sides were level at the break. East Stirlingshire had the better of the second half; Bowman added two more for a hat trick and Mitchell scored the other. Shire only picked up one more point from their next three games but in early November recorded back-to-back wins over Hamilton and Abercorn (two goals apiece for Laidlaw and Bowman). This was followed by a heavy 6-2 defeat away to Port Glasgow Athletic but a third win in the month came with a 3-1 win over Airdrieonians which lifted them off the bottom. By now only two points separated the bottom five clubs. Three consecutive wins in January, two of them away from home, pulled them away and they finished in ninth, six points ahead of the bottom two clubs, Abercorn and Clyde. They failed to defend their Stirlingshire Cup although Merchiston Park as a result, staged the final. At the League's AGM on the 19th May 1902 rivals Falkirk were elected, following League expansion, bringing the prospect of local derby games for the 1902-03 season.

The first ever SFL Falkirk derby took place on the 30th August 1902, in the third round of games, when a crowd of 4,000 at Merchiston Park witnessed the Brockville team win 2-0. There was an early penalty awarded to the Bairns which was blazed over the bar, but Falkirk weren't made to rue the miss when they took the lead a few minutes later. In the second half Shire pressed their opponents and pushed for an equaliser. Just three minutes from time Falkirk broke away and scored a second goal to win the first ever Scottish League Falkirk derby.

The return fixture was played on the 28th February 1903, in the penultimate game of the League season, and ended in a 2-2 at a Brockville. Falkirk had to do most of the defending during the opening passage of play but they opened the scoring after 20 minutes. Two minutes later Baird thought he had put Shire level but the goal was disallowed. After repeated attacks East Stirlingshire did eventually equalise through Prentice, from a corner. In the second half Shire continued to dominate the play and Baird did score this time. Shire thought that Whyte had made it 3-1 but the goal was ruled out for offside. Just as East Stirlingshire thought they had won, a Falkirk breakaway, led to a ricocheted effort finding its way into the net. Both teams finished in mid-table but bragging rights went to Falkirk who finished two points, and two places higher. In the Stirlingshire Cup East Stirlingshire triumphed, beating Stenhousemuir 3-0 at Falkirk's Brockville, after replay (0-0) to record their tenth win in the competition.

In the 1903-04 season Shire ended up sixth in the 12 team Division, their best season so far in the SFL. Highlights included a 3-0 home win against Raith Rovers and a first ever League win against Falkirk on 9th January when a 2-1 result was achieved at Merchiston Park. They were beaten finalists in the Stirlingshire Cup, losing to arch rivals Falkirk and both clubs tried to get elected to the First Division. However, at the League's AGM held on the 30th May 1904, Motherwell and Kilmarnock were re-elected to the First Division. Second Division sides Hamilton and Clyde also stood alongside Falkirk and Shire but only the champions Hamilton got any votes.

The next season Shire only achieved ninth place, winning just seven of their games. Home form remained competitive and included wins against Falkirk (2-0), St, Bernard's (4-0) and Albion Rovers (5-2) but away performances were very poor with only one win achieved against Leith Athletic in the penultimate away match. They once more finished as runners-up in the Stirlingshire Cup, this time losing out 1-0 against Alloa Athletic at Brockville.

Following their respective individual failed bids to join the top flight East Stirlingshire and Falkirk held Special General Meetings to discuss the proposed merger of the two clubs with a view to forming a new club and applying for membership of the First Division. The Falkirk board agreed but the Shire directors decided against it on the casting vote of the Chairman. Falkirk subsequently applied to join the First Division and at the League's AGM on the 22nd May were successful. Although Clyde were four points clear at the top of the Second Division, runners-up Falkirk and seventh place Aberdeen were elected into the expanded First Division. The election of their neighbours was a bit of a body blow to Shire as the lure of First Division football at Brockville took away both fans and players.

The 1905-06 season was a low point for Shire as they finished rock bottom in the League and consequently faced a re-election vote. Shire only won one League game all season, drawing ten and went the first nine games without a win, drawing four but losing five. Included in this sequence was an entertaining 4-4 home draw with Clyde, in which Whyte (2), Baird and Murray scored for Shire, all in the first half. Their only win came on the 11th November when they beat Ayr FC 4-2 away from home. Whyte scored the only goal for the visitors in an otherwise dull first half. After the break Strang scored a second for Shire before Ayr got one back. Almost immediately Shire restored their two goal lead through Whyte. Murray made it 4-1 before the home team got a second. Towards the end of the game Shire were awarded a penalty but this was saved. Shire failed to win again during the season although they drew six of their remaining 12 League fixtures. Their biggest defeat in this run was a 5-1 away defeat at leaders Albion Rovers, at Meadow Park, Whifflet. Due to League expansion there were four vacancies and 13 clubs applied. At the League's AGM held on the 21st May 1906 Shire came third in the voting, with 13 votes, five votes ahead of Alloa in fifth place, and their League status was preserved.

East Stirlingshire leased Merchiston Park and when plans for a railway expansion went through the site it was clear that their tenure was up and the lease wouldn't be renewed. They moved just a short distance to a new site and this ground was named New Merchiston Park, to differentiate it from the old ground, although it wasn't too long before it was just called Merchiston Park. The ground was located near Main Street, just north of the Forth and Clyde Canal at Bainsford Bridge. On the 16th August 1906, two weeks before the League season got underway, in a pre-season friendly, they entertained Clyde to mark the opening of the ground. *The Scotsman* reported that "East Stirlingshire's new field, which has been named New Merchiston Park, was opened last night by Dean of Guild Stevenson, ex-president of the Scottish Football Association. The directors were compelled to look out for a new field owing to a railway having taken up their old ground. A game was afterwards played with Clyde. During the first half the game was a typical friendly match, neither team showing very great earnestness...McNair opened the scoring [for East Stirling]. The second half, while dull at times, contained some exciting moments. Grier brought the score level...and the game proceeded to the call of time in semi-darkness."

The League season proper got underway with a home match against Ayr FC. *The Scotsman* reported that "this Second League game took place on the new ground of

East Stirlingshire, in the presence of fully two thousand spectators. The home team started in splendid style, and tested the Ayr defence for some time. A break away by the visitors' left wing ended in Main opening the scoring. Half-time: Ayr, one; East Stirlingshire, nothing. The second half was not long in progress when East Stirlingshire were awarded a penalty kick. Morris undertook it, but Bone saved his attempt to convert it. After repeated attempts, Orrock at length equalised the scores, and although the home team pressed persistently they had to be content with a division of the points." Shire continued to struggle on the pitch though and they lost their next five games in a row, before a 2-1 home win over Vale of Leven in mid-October.

In mid-February Shire lost 7-3 at Albion Rovers and were tied second bottom on 12 points with Raith Rovers and Abercorn of Paisley, with Ayr Parkhouse bottom with just nine points. The following week they drew 3-3 with Raith, who reached the Quarter-finals of the Scottish Cup, only going out after a third replay against Hearts. The week after that they beat struggling Ayr Parkhouse 6-2. On the 23rd March they ended their League programme with a 1-1 draw against St Bernard's in Edinburgh. It was only in the closing minutes that their hosts equalised and that dropped point would prove to be highly significant. Shire had finished their League fixtures and had finished with 16 points. Raith were a point behind, and due to their Cup involvement still had four games left. Abercorn had 14 points and still had three matches to go. Ayr Parkhouse still had a game left but only had ten points and so were guaranteed to finish bottom and face a re-election vote.

On the 30th March Abercorn and Raith both lost. East Stirlingshire were in action in the final of the Stirlingshire Cup and they beat Alloa 2-0 at Brockville in front of a crowd of 5,000. In the first half play was fairly even, although Shire scored twice through Baird and McMillan, the two goal lead not representing the balance of play. Shire had the better of the second half though, but could not add to their score, running out 2-0 winners. On the Monday Raith played a rearranged fixture and drew 1-1 at home to St Bernard's to draw level with East Stirling in the table. On the Saturday Raith lost at Cowdenbeath but Abercorn picked up a point. Shire and Raith both had 16 points and Abercorn had 15. The final fixtures were completed on Saturday 13th April - Abercorn were at home to Cowdenbeath and Raith were away to the champions St Bernard's. Abercorn won 2-0 to move ahead of the other two on 17 points. Raith lost 3-2 in Edinburgh. Raith and East Stirling thus tied. Raith's goal average and goal difference were both superior but neither measure was in operation.

At a Scottish Football League Management Committee meeting it was decided that the two teams should play-off to decide who would face the re-election vote along with bottom side Ayr Parkhouse. In the play-off, Raith Rovers beat East Stirlingshire 3-2 on

Saturday the 11th May at Logie Green in Edinburgh to avoid re-election. In the first half Raith scored twice and Chalk scored for Shire. In the second half McMillan quickly made it 2-2 but Raith were awarded a penalty from which they scored to take the lead, which they held until the end. At the League's AGM held on the 27th May Shire topped the voting with 24 votes and were re-elected with Ayr Parkhouse who got 16. The two challengers were Renton and Dunfermline Athletic, who got 8 and 6 votes respectively.

There was a marked improvement in the 1907-08 season and Shire achieved their best SFL placing to date of fifth, in their eighth season as a League club. Results included two draws against the eventual champions, Abercorn, and a win and draw against third placed Vale of Leven. The Stirlingshire Cup final was a repeat of the previous year although this time Alloa prevailed after a replay.

The following season was uneventful, save for a local Scottish Cup tie when East Stirling were drawn away to Falkirk in the First Round. This was Shire's first appearance since the 1900-01 competition and they went down narrowly 2-1 to their local rivals, who were then a First Division side and who went onto reach the Semi-final. In the League Shire came in ninth and although they would only finish one place higher in the League the following season, they were only three points off fourth place.

In the 1910-11 season they achieved a comfortable mid-table placing of seventh place. The following season they finished ninth, although they did defeat the champions, Ayr United, 1-0 at home in April. East Stirling also won their first game in the Scottish Cup since 1899, defeating Dumbarton 3-0 at home in the First Round. Ironically Dumbarton had been team the team that Shire had last beaten in the Scottish Cup. The club drew Celtic in the next round (the last 16), who would go onto win the Cup that season and also end up as First Division One runners up. This game took place at Celtic Park on the 10th February, in front of a crowd of 4,000, and Shire lost 3-0, although they gave a good account of themselves according to The *Scotsman,* who reported that "the Shire [played] vigorously but were unable to penetrate the home defence...the visitors played desperately...but were far too scraggy in combination to be effective...The East Stirlingshire men played gamely...[and]...were at least value for one goal."

For the 1912-13 season the Second Division was increased to 14 clubs with the addition of Dunfermline Athletic and Johnstone. East Stirlingshire secured their highest ever League placing to date, finishing in third place, and only two points off the top. For the first time they mounted a serious and sustained challenge for honours and remained in contention until they lost two of their three last games. They opened with a 3-2 away win against Dundee Hibs on the 17th August 1912. In this match Shire generally had the better of the play, Martin scoring first, but their hosts soon equalised. In the second half Martin restored their lead but Dundee Hibs again got themselves level. Parity didn't last long though and Couper put East Stirling ahead once more. Dundee Hibs forced a string of corners in attempt to get level once more but failed to score, Shire running out 3-2 winners. This was then followed by a 2-0 home win over St Johnstone. Following a home 2-1 defeat against Vale of Leven on the 12th October they went the rest of 1912 unbeaten, a run of eight games, and they ended the year second in the table, just a point behind leaders Ayr United.

On the 11th January 1913 the top two met at Somerset Park but Shire lost 3-0. Ayr's victory established a three point lead at the top for them and Cowdenbeath were now level on points with Shire in second place following their 2-0 win over St Bernard's. A week later Shire beat Arthurlie 4-2, Couper scoring a hat-trick, while the leaders surprisingly lost 1-0 at bottom club Dundee Hibs to close the gap to a single point. However, consecutive defeats away at St Johnstone, and crucially at home to Cowdenbeath, in February severely dented their championship chances. In this latter game the visitors, third in the table, took an early lead. East Stirling then laid siege to their opponent's goal. *The Scotsman* reported that "East Stirlingshire pressed in a fashion which time and again seemed likely to result in their securing the equaliser, but the splendid work of the visitors' defence, and particularly of Robertson in goal, prevented them from scoring."

Shire were fortunate to receive a bye in the First Round of the Scottish Cup and then were drawn against First Division Clyde in the Second Round. In a very close tie East Stirling lost out 2-1 in a second replay. Despite two consecutive League draws at the beginning of March, Shire still occupied second place, although they were now four points behind leaders Ayr United, but two ahead of Cowdenbeath in third. On Saturday the 15th March Shire closed the gap at the top to two points as they beat Dunfermline Athletic 4-2, while Ayr lost 2-1 at fourth placed Johnstone. The following Saturday, the 22nd, Ayr United lost again, this time 3-0 at St Bernard's but Shire failed to capitalise, losing at home 1-0 to Albion Rovers. *The Scotsman* reported that "at the conclusion of the match a break-in, caused, it is presumed, by the dissatisfaction of a section of the spectators with some of the referee's decisions occurred. The players and referee were surrounded by a large crowd, but were escorted off the field by the police without mishap." On the 29th March Ayr beat Dunfermline in their penultimate game 1-0 to move four points clear so Shire could not afford any further slip ups. The destination of the Second Division title was settled on Saturday 5th April when Shire lost again, beaten 1-0 at Dunfermline, who eventually overtook them into second by a point.

In the 1913-14 season East Stirling dropped back in terms of a League placing, coming in eighth in a reduced twelve team division. An early 5-0 win over Johnstone hinted at better times but a poor run of only one win in seven matches saw them drop to eighth place by the turn of the year. In the 1914-15 season that followed Shire ended up in fourth place in the once again expanded 14 team division, although they were six points behind the top three. As the season progressed Britain went to war with Germany and Shire lost Charles Stirling to the war effort and as the season went on forward Dan McNeilage enlisted too. On the 17th April 1915 East Stirling completed their League fixtures with a 3-0 win over Arthurlie.

In the summer of 1915 the League was suspended and two regional competitions were set up, East Stirlingshire joining the Eastern League and they played there for two seasons, finishing seventh on each occasion. At the East Stirlingshire AGM on the 23rd July 1917 it was agreed that the club would stop playing football until the termination of the war due the heavy travel costs in the Eastern League.

After the Great War the Second Division was quietly dropped by the League at their AGM on the 2nd June and 12 clubs lost their status as a League club including East Stirlingshire. When the Scottish League failed to re-start the Second Division East Stirlingshire, along with other displaced teams, reformed the Central League. The East Stirlingshire secretary, Walter Clarkson, was elected president of the Central League and he became a key player in lobbying the SFL to reinstate the Second Division with the teams comprising this League.

In the 1919-20 season East Stirlingshire finished 12th out of 14 teams in the Central League. They also featured in the Scottish Cup. A 6-0 home win against Thornhill of Falkirk was achieved before a marathon Second Round tie took place against Scottish League side Raith Rovers, which took four games to settle. The first tie, a home match, ended 0-0 with Shire having had the better of the game. The replay, played the following Saturday, ended 1-1. Shire took the lead late on through Sime in the 75th minute but Raith responded almost immediately, with another draw a fair result. The following Wednesday the second replay was staged at the neutral venue of Tynecastle, in front of a 12,000 crowd. This match ended in yet another draw, even after extra time had been played. *The Scotsman* reported that "after long discussions and an endeavour to get into touch with the Scottish Football Association officials, it was mutually agreed to re-play the tie at Tynecastle this afternoon." So, the fourth match was played the very next day, also at Tynecastle. Only half as many spectators this time, some 6,000, watched a completely different game to the previous three matches, as this was a very one-sided affair. After Raith got an early goal in the third minute the result was never in doubt. *The Scotsman* attributed the different nature of the contest down to changes in personnel: "the East Stirlingshire team had to take the field without Caldwell, their goalkeeper in the previous game - he had been hurt on Wednesday- but the real difference between the sides, as compared with the other meetings, was in the substitution of Baldie and Dunn for Cant and Wilson in the Rovers' forward line. That pair were not only fresh, but played good football, and the presence of a new centre-forward made all the difference in the attack." Raith were 2-0 up at the break, and although the Shire strove hard to get into the game in the second period, Raith broke away and put themselves further ahead and sometime later they made it 4-0. At the East Stirlingshire AGM in June 1920 it was announced that the club's lease for Merchiston Park was due to expire and that the club were now having to look for yet another new ground.

In the 1920-21 season Shire finished 14th in the Central League, a competition now consisting of 18 teams. In the Scottish Cup Shire received a bye in the First Round before winning a Second Round tie 5-1 in Annan against Solway Star. This set up a tie at home to Partick Thistle. Shire refused Partick's offers of several hundred pounds to switch the game from Merchiston Park. In the end a record crowd for New Merchiston Park of 8,000 saw Shire go down narrowly 2-1. *The Scotsman* reported that "by the odd goal in three, East Stirlingshire fell before Partick Thistle in their tie at Merchiston Park, Falkirk, but a chapter of accidents which befell the Central League team accounted in some measure for their narrow defeat. The opening minutes saw the Thistle pressing as though they intended to carry all before them, but after some tricky play by Blair and Kinloch, the home team gave evidence of their powers as an attacking force. Twenty-five minutes had gone when [Partick scored]. From that point East Stirlingshire showed to advantage. Early in the second half, however, they lost the services of both Johnston and Meaney, who were carried to the pavilion injured. During their absence Partick pressed most persistently, and...succeeded in securing a second goal. With Johnston's return to the field, East Stirlingshire became more aggressive, and received a hard-earned reward in the closing minute, when N Wilson, profiting by a mistake by Crichton, promptly [scored]. The home side, in all the circumstances, were slightly unfortunate to lose. Partick went on to lift the Scottish Cup, beating Rangers 1-0 in the Final.

On the 23rd April 1921 the *Falkirk Herald* announced that the club had leased a new ground which would become known as Firs Park. The new site was located on Firs Street, less than half a mile north-east of the town centre, off Thornhill Road, with the Callendar Iron Works to the South (now the Central Retail Park) and a goods and mineral railway depot to the west, now derelict waste ground. Shire's new ground was formally opened on the 16th August 1921 with a friendly match in front of a crowd of nearly 6,000 against Hearts.

At the League's AGM in June 1921 it was decided to reform the Second Division incorporating the 16 teams from the Central League, plus a further four teams, two from the Scottish Alliance and two from the West of Scotland League. The League now consisted of 42 clubs with 20 teams in the First Division and a new 22 team Second Division. In order to even up the two divisions to have twenty clubs in each three teams would be relegated from the First with only the Second Division champions going up. At the end of the 1921-22 season the bottom two sides would drop out of the League altogether.

East Stirlingshire's first two seasons back in the Scottish Football League were disappointing. After a six year hiatus they kicked off on the 20th August 1921 in Stirling against King's Park, which ended in a 1-1 draw. A week later they recorded their first win, beating Vale of Leven at home 3-1. They were 1-0 down at half-time but a brace from Mackie, formerly of Dumbarton and a goal by Brown, a new signing, gave them victory. However, this was followed by only one win in their next six games. A 4-1 defeat at Lochgelly United at the beginning of October left them down in 16th place, just two points off the bottom. A narrow 1-0 win over bottom side Clackmannan pulled them away though. They then failed to win any of their first seven League games of 1922 to get sucked back in again. During this time they had a Scottish Cup run to the Third Round. They knocked out Douglas Wanderers and Dunfermline Athletic before going down away at Queen of the South (who were not yet a League club). Three wins in early spring boosted their League situation and they eventually finished 15th out of the twenty clubs.

Things got worse the following season as Shire finished in the bottom two. Again they opened their campaign against King's Park, this time losing 1-0. They lost their next three as well, including a 5-1 loss at early leaders Dunfermline. The club secured their first point of the season in their fifth match, a 1-1 home draw versus St Johnstone. In total Shire went their first eight games without a win until the 14th October 1922 when they beat Arbroath 3-0, a result which took them off the bottom, above their opponents. Burns scored two in a one-sided win. Under the headline "East Stirlingshire's First Win, *The Scotsman* reported that "East Stirlingshire, for the first time since the season opened, finished on the winning side, full points being gained from the meeting with Arbroath at Firs Park. An early attack by the home forwards was successfully repulsed...East Stirlingshire...gradually forced play back towards Jenkins, and after twelve minutes Burns opened the scoring with a good shot. Play thereafter was more evenly distributed, but Arbroath failed badly when in front of goal, and a few minutes from the interval Shearer got through to score a second goal for East Stirlingshire. In the second half the bulk of the pressing was done by the home side. The issue was put beyond doubt when Burns, from a beautiful cross by Hillcoat, cleverly headed a third goal." The disappointing form continued and by the end of 1922, following a 3-0 loss at home to East Fife, they ended the year second from bottom, level on points with Forfar on 13 points and one behind Stenhousemuir and Arbroath.

The prospect of a re-election vote was looming large but Shire gave themselves some hope by putting together a late run, winning three out of their last five fixtures. On the 31st March they beat a resurgent Forfar 2-0 to go level at the bottom with Arbroath and two behind St Bernard's with four games to go. But the following week they lost at second placed Clydebank 5-0. *The Scotsman* noted that "East Stirlingshire's misfortunes were added to by Hunter retiring after a collision with an opponent. A shaky defence and bad finishing were large factors in the heavy defeat." With Arbroath and St Bernard's both securing draws Shire went back to the bottom, a point behind Arbroath and three behind the Edinburgh Saints. On the 14th April Shire entertained Armadale, with *The Scotsman* reporting that "East Stirlingshire surprised even their own supporters by defeating Armadale in the game at Falkirk by five goals to two, but on play the decisive victory was fully merited." Shire raced into a two goal lead with goals from Logan and Docherty, but were then pegged back to 2-2. Just before the interval Docherty got his second and the home team led 3-2. Goals in the second period from Logan and Docherty (for his hat-trick) gave them the win. St Bernard's also won to guarantee their safety but Shire went back above Arbroath who lost 7-4 at Cowdenbeath.

The following Saturday Shire beat Vale of Leven 1-0 in what was their opponent's last fixture. Arbroath won 2-1 at Dunfermline and St Bernard's drew. These results meant that with one round of matches to go for the bottom three sides Arbroath were bottom with 27 points, East Stirling had 28, Vale of Leven 30 and St Bernard's 31. Arbroath drew 1-1 with Stenhousemuir and Bathgate beat St Bernard's 2-0. Shire travelled to Bo'ness and *The Scotsman* reported that "just when everything seemed in favour of East Stirlingshire collecting a vital brace of points at Bo'ness, the game suddenly veered round in favour of the home team, who won on the tape. They were a goal down with twenty minutes to go, Docherty having scored for the 'Shire twenty-three minutes after the start. It was then that the visitors' defence, which had been hard pressed this half, gave way, and first Kelly and then later Neil scored for the home side. The 'Shire were all out for a win, and Stevenson by his brilliant work in goal, had a large say in the victory." East Stirling finished level on points at the bottom with Arbroath, but avoided being placed bottom of the table on goal average and both clubs faced a re-election vote. St Bernard's subsequently incurred a two point deduction for an infringement of rules to finish just a point above the two sides.

At the League's AGM held on the 17th May 1923 Shire, along with Arbroath, had to re-apply for re-election to the Second Division and Shire's application was rejected though bottom club Arbroath were re-elected. Reporting on the meeting *The Scotsman* said that "the annual general meeting of the Scottish Football League was held last night at 175 West George Street, Glasgow...Dundee Hibernians and Arbroath, the latter one of the two clubs obliged to seek re-election, were admitted to the Second Division. East Stirlingshire, who were at the foot of the Second Division League table, on the same mark as Arbroath, failed to retain their place." *The Sunday Post* reported with more details of the vote: "Dundee Hibs have been readmitted to the Second Division of the League. The first vote resulted:- Arbroath 27, East Stirlingshire 19, Dundee Hibs 17; and the second:-Dundee Hibs 23, East Stirlingshire 15.

East Stirlingshire looked set to relinquish their League status after just two seasons back but a month later they were offered a reprieve. The formation of a new Third Division was debated at a Management Committee meeting on the 18th June and ratified later in the same month. Although Shire had not been re-elected they were placed in the newly formed Third Division and so were effectively relegated instead.

East Stirlingshire now found themselves in the new third tier of Scottish League football, facing some unfamiliar names such as Dykehead, Galston and Peebles Rovers. Shire got off to a great start winning their first four games including 5-0 at home to Clackmannan (goals from Mooney, Logan (2), a Stoddart penalty and Chalmers) but then lost heavily 5-1 away in the reverse fixture against Clackmannan. *The Scotsman* noted that "this was a surprising result, in as much as the home club went down at Falkirk a fortnight ago by 5 clear goals. The game was exciting and tempers seemed always on edge, which led at a point of the game to the field being invaded by an angry crowd, who were, however, promptly dispersed by a handful of police." Balloch, for Clackmannan, scored four and Shire's solitary goal was scored by their centre-half Mooney. This result was followed by a 3-0 win over Montrose and then a fine 6-2 away win against Peebles. In a truncated League programme due to Cup action, Anderson scored a hat-trick, Callan two and Mooney got the other. The result moved Shire four points clear at top, with six wins from seven fixtures. Shire went undefeated throughout October but at the beginning of November suffered a surprise 4-0 loss at Dykehead. Trailing 1-0 after an hour's play a hail storm caused the game to be played in poor visibility during which Dykehead scored three further goals.

The top two sides in the new division, Shire and Arthurlie, played out a 1-1 draw on New Year's Day at Firs Park and the remainder of the season was effectively an ongoing battle between these two clubs for the championship flag. East Stirlingshire had a great run to the Third Round (last 16) of the Scottish Cup before losing out at Aberdeen 2-0. In the earlier Rounds Shire easily despatched Newton Stewart away 8-1 and then fellow Third Division side Mid Annandale 1-0 at Firs Park. Following their Cup exit East Stirling found themselves six points behind the leaders Arthurlie, with a game in hand, and in terms of promotion a comfortable seven points ahead of third place. The two sides matched each other in terms of results on the 8th March with Shire recording a 4-1 away win at Galston but Arthurlie won as well. They had three games left whereas Shire had four. A week later, with East Stirlingshire not in action Arthurlie won to extend their lead to eight points. On the 22nd March Shire lost at Montrose in a bad tempered game. Arthurlie won and were crowned champions. Shire's conquerors, Montrose, were now in third place, four points behind, but with a game in hand, and so were a real threat to Shire's promotion ambitions. On the 29th March East Stirlingshire beat Galston 3-1 and Montrose were held 1-1 by the champions. Shire were now five points ahead having played 28 out of 30 matches. Montrose had played 27. On the 5th April Shire secured promotion by beating Queen of the South 2-1. They came from behind having been 1-0 down at the interval. Anderson equalised and then a sloppy back pass allowed Christie to nip in to score the goal that confirmed his side's promotion back to the Second Division at the first attempt. As it was, Dykehead beat Montrose 1-0. Shire's success continued in the Stirlingshire Cup, which they won for the first time since 1913-14, beating Alloa Athletic 1-0 at Brockville in the Final, the first of four wins during the 1920s.

Back in the Second Division Shire kicked of the 1924-25 season with a League game away to Bathgate which was drawn 4-4. *The Sunday Post*, under the headline "Tall Scoring at Bathgate" reported on the game saying "a crowd of 3000, including 600 East Stirlingshire supporters saw a glut of goals at Bathgate, as well as a keen and exciting struggle for supremacy. The result, a draw of four goals each, was on the whole lucky for Bathgate, the East Stirling men showed throughout a far better idea of combined play than the home lot, and more enthusiasm in attack. The visitors opened the scoring through Anderson, the Harthill junior, who played a fine game. Shirlaw, who shaped well, equalised, and before half-time Christie, the 'Shire's great leader, netted with a header from McKechnie's cross. A misunderstanding between the Bathgate backs enabled Christie to rush in and put his side two on the lead. Forsyth reduced the leeway, and Sharp, keen worker for his side, netted, and the teams stood even. Two minutes from the finish, Kerr, following a wing attack, again put 'Shire on the lead, but just on time Bathgate burst through, and Sharp headed the equaliser. It was a thriller finish to a hard game. East Stirlingshire had a grand front line, Christie made an ideal leader, and the wing men worked in fine unison." The Shire team making a return to the Second Division was: Wilkinson; Monnoch, Devine; Kerr, Mooney, Kemp; McKechnie, Kilgun, Christie, Anderson and Stoddart.

Their first couple of seasons back in the Second Division were struggles and they had two close shaves with relegation, finishing 18th in both seasons (in a twenty team division). On each occasion Shire could have ended back in the ill-fated Third Division and therefore excited the Scottish Football League when this Division was abandoned in 1926. Shire went unbeaten in the first four games of the 1924-25 season, although three of them were draws. However, they then only picked up one further point from their next four fixtures. Three consecutive losses in December saw them joint bottom on 14 points with Forfar and then there was a gap to four teams on 17 points.

On the 3rd January 1925 they beat Bathgate 3-0 but then lost their next three games. On the 21st February Shire lost 5-1 at Clyde to sit second bottom on 20 points, five from safety. They had a real fight on their hands to avoid the bottom two places in the League and face relegation back to the Third Division. In the end Shire won four and drew three of their last eight games to avoid this and ended up in 18th place in the 20 team League by two points. They started a run of four games without defeat by beating East Fife 5-2 on the last day of February and by the 21st March the gap was down to one point behind Johnstone in 18th, with four games to go. The following week they suffered a setback, losing 2-1 at home to bottom club Forfar. *The Scotsman* reported that "although monopolising three-quarters of the play, East Stirlingshire were forced to surrender the points at home to Forfar Athletic. The result was not in accordance with the run of the game...The Grahamston team were visited with a good deal of bad luck in their efforts, but on the whole their finishing was poor and undeserving of result." Johnstone also lost so the gap remained at a point.

On the first Saturday in April things turned in their favour. Johnstone lost again but Shire beat Dunfermline 2-0 to leapfrog them and move one point ahead themselves. Under the headline "East Stirlingshire's Safety Win" *The Scotsman* reported that Shire were "worthy winners." Wood gave Shire the lead. Brown then saved a Dunfermline penalty to keep the lead intact before the break. In the second half another penalty kick was awarded, this time to East Stirling, and Wood made no mistake. A week later they lost 2-1 at leaders Dundee United, who gained promotion and the Second Division title as a result of their victory. Shire scored a late consolation in a match where they were always second best. However, there was no detrimental effect as Johnstone lost once more.

On the 18th April, needing a win to assure themselves of safety, East Stirlingshire beat St Bernard's 2-0. Under the headline "Precious Points for East Stirlingshire" *The Scotsman* reported that "by their victory over St Bernard's at Firs Park, East Stirlingshire made sure of their position in the Second Division of the League next season. The game was keenly contested throughout, the Shire showing an eagerness which reflected their determination to secure the points which were to mean so much to the club." Shire dominated the play but failed to score, the two sides going into the interval goalless. In the second half another sustained period of pressure from Shire led to the opening goal being scored by Wood, who scored a brilliant free kick from 30 yards out. Shortly afterwards Shire were given the chance to make the game safe when they were awarded a penalty but Wood's shot was superbly saved. However, soon afterwards Kemp scored a second goal following good work by Christie. Johnstone weren't in action but were now three points behind so were unable to catch Shire. A week later Johnstone drew 2-2 with Alloa to finish two points behind. East Stirling put up a strong defence of their Stirlingshire Cup reaching the Final, but this time losing to Alloa Athletic.

After a quarter of a century in charge Walter Clarkson retired as manager, although he remained as part of the Board. He was replaced as manager by John 'Jock' Morrison, a former centre-forward for Falkirk before the Great War. To mark his service to the club Clarkson was awarded a benefit game, which took place on the 8th September. Shire entertained Hearts at Firs Park, the visitors winning 5-3. Morrison's first season was similar to the previous one, with Shire still continuing to struggle and they again ended up third bottom. Shire had a terrible first half of the season only winning once before the New Year. They started with a 2-2 draw with Bathgate. In this game they were 2-0 down but rescued a point thanks to two penalties, scored by Wood. In mid-September they lost 6-1 at St Bernard's which was then followed by a 7-1 hammering at Clyde. After six games, Shire were winless, and with just two points to their name. Only pointless Alloa were beneath them in the table.

Shire secured their first win of the 1925-26 season on the 26th September, beating East Fife 2-1. Wood scored after just four minutes and then scored a second seven minutes later. The visitors were awarded a penalty before the interval but shot wide. It wasn't until the last minute of play that East Fife scored their only goal. However, Shire didn't win again until January 1926, going 13 games without a win. Their last game of 1925, a 3-0 derby home defeat against Stenhousemuir, left them three points adrift at the bottom of the Second Division and four points from safety, having gathered just six points from 19 matches (one win and four draws).

On the 2nd January 1926 they beat Queen of the South 4-2 for only their second win of the season. One down after just three minutes, a triallist listed as "Junior" equalised after nine minutes. Wood scored, then "Junior" and then Wood again as Shire dominated. Their opponents only got their second goal towards the end. East Stirling also beat Arbroath a fortnight later to move off the foot of the table. Back-to-back wins in early March over Nithsdale Wanderers and Dumbarton took them two points clear of the relegation zone, the bottom two places now occupied by Bathgate and Broxburn United. A further win at the end of March, 2-1 over Third Lanark was followed by an 8-

2 thumping of bottom side Broxburn on the 3rd April. Their visitors started badly giving away a penalty after just three minutes but Stoddart failed to convert it. An own goal gave them lead but Broxburn equalised. "Newman", a triallist Stirlingshire junior, then scored two to make it 3-1 at the break. Within five minutes of the restart goals from McKay and Stoddart had taken the score to 5-1. Docherty then made it six before Broxburn scored again. The scoring was not yet complete and the goal count reached ten for the match when first McKay from the spot, and then Stoddart, made it 8-2. According to *The Sunday Post,* "the game was not so one-sided as the score would indicate. Broxburn played surprisingly well, particularly in the first half...For the winners, Calder, McRoberts, Stoddart, 'Newman', and Bickerstaffe were outstanding." Their nearest rivals Bathgate lost so the gap was now four points with three games left to play. A few days later Bathgate drew 1-1 with East Fife. In a lively game Bathgate had two goals disallowed and although they closed the gap to three points with the draw they really needed both points. On the 10th April their safety was assured. Although they lost 3-1 at Albion Rovers, Bathgate also lost at home to leaders Dunfermline, who were crowned champions. The gap remained at three points but Bathgate only had one game left. As it was Shire finished with a flourish, winning their last two games, beating Bo'ness 4-0 away from home and then securing a 2-0 win over St Bernard's.

Finlay Potter, the club chairman, took over after the short tenure of John Morrison, and managed the club between 1927 and 1936 before moving back to the post of club secretary. In the 1926-27 season, Potter's first, Shire secured their highest finish since returning to the Scottish League after the Great War, coming in fifth, and set a new club record of 18 wins in a League season. The club made a poor start in the first game away to Arbroath losing 5-0 but after that results picked up and Shire began to challenge for promotion. A home draw against King's Park was followed by a fine 4-1 away win at Clydebank. In the fourth round of matches played on the 4th September they hosted Nithsdale Wanderers, with *The Scotsman* reporting that "East Stirlingshire followed up their fine win at Clydebank the previous week by a sweeping victory at home over the Nithsdale Wanderers, the Sanquhar team being defeated by the heavy score of seven goals to two. Play favoured East Stirlingshire practically throughout, but in the first half their forwards did not finish to the best advantage. Russell, however, gave them the lead with a nicely-taken goal, but near the interval, McConnell, the Nithsdale centre, completed a fine bit of work by registering the equaliser. In the second half East Stirlingshire amply made up for their first half deficiencies in the matter of goal-scoring, and within the brief space of ten minutes they counted five times. Docherty led the way with two goals, then McKay intervened with a score before Docherty completed the rout by contributing a 'hat-trick' and bringing his own total for the afternoon to five, W Ballantyne scored Nithsdale's second goal just on time."

East Stirling went eight games unbeaten following on from that opening day defeat and they reached the turn of the year in the running for promotion. Bo'ness were the runaway leaders, eight points clear, but behind them only one point separated six clubs – Ayr United, Arthurlie, East Fife, Raith Rovers, Clydebank and East Stirlingshire. Shire lost the New Years' Day derby game away at King's Park but three more wins in January kept them in contention. During this month Shire went out in the Scottish Cup First Round, although it was a narrow 1-0 home defeat to First Division Dumbarton. Consecutive League defeats against St Bernard's and Arthurlie followed their Cup exit and a defeat away at leaders Bo'ness at the end of March left Shire five points adrift of the second promotion place. This gap was maintained to the season's end with Shire securing a fifth place finish.

The next four seasons saw a series of mid-table finishes, with a best placed finish of seventh in the last of these, the 1930-31 season. In the 1927-28 season they recorded an 8-0 victory over Arthurlie in the third round of matches. Under the headline "East Stirlingshire Sharpshooters" *The Scotsman* reported that "as the score suggests, the game was of a one-sided nature, but the bright play of the 'Shire was sufficient in itself to maintain interest at a high level...Only six minutes had been played when McKay opened the scoring by driving home a cross from Kennedy. Soon after this Stoddart got a second goal from a penalty kick. Arthurlie tried hard to beat off the attack, but to no avail, and before the interval the score against them had been raised to five, McKay, Stoddart and Kilear each counting. In the second half the visitors showed slight improvement, but still they were no match for the sprightly 'Shire, for whom further goals were added by McKay, Kennedy and Russell." The big win failed to kick start any promotion challenge and Shire finished in ninth place. In the Scottish Cup they were knocked out at the First Round stage by Rangers, "the triumph being achieved under deplorable weather conditions and on a ground that was flooded with rain water to such an extent that it resembled a pond" (*The Scotsman*). They did, however, secure their third Stirlingshire Cup of the 1920s, beating First Division Bo'ness 1-0 at Brockville Park.

In the 1928-29 season Shire finished 12th, a placing they repeated the following year. In the Scottish Cup they progressed to the Second Round after knocking out Alloa Athletic, after a replay. Despite losing their opening game of the 1929-30 season 4-2 at Queen of the South East Stirling recorded two big victories before the end of August. On the 17th of that month they entertained Armadale and ran out 6-0 winners and a fortnight later they beat Brechin City 7-0. After that the season settled into a pattern of win at home but lose away which effectively meant a mid-table placing. When they beat King's Park 3-2 in the New Years' Day game they occupied 11th place. Soon after they were knocked out of the Scottish Cup 6-0 by Motherwell. Two heavy League defeats followed, 6-2 at home to Albion Rovers, and 5-3 at Dumbarton and Shire eventually finished in 12th place.

The 1930-31 season saw a marked improvement. Inconsistent form during the first few months saw them reach the end of 1930 in tenth place. Shire then won all six matches played in January 1931 including 7-1 against Dumbarton and 6-0 away at Bo'ness. By the end of the month they had shot up to third place, two points behind second placed Dunfermline. Although they then lost against leaders Third Lanark they bounced back a week later to beat Clydebank 6-1. They now sat in joint third with eight games left. Any lingering hopes at promotion were then undone by a run of four consecutive defeats and they failed to win any of their remaining seven matches to drop to seventh place.

Season 1931-32 was a major highlight in the club's history as they lifted their first senior honour. In an amazingly tense finish to the season they finished season equal on 55 points with St Johnstone, with East Stirlingshire winning the championship on a superior goal average and gaining promotion to the First Division for the first time. Shire set a new club record for the most wins in a League season (26) and notched up a club record 111 League goals, the first time and only time they recorded a century of goals scored.

The League season kicked off on the 8th August 1931. Shire didn't make a great start though, with a 5-1 away defeat to Queen of the South. The match was closer than the result would suggest and not a fair reflection on the difference between the two sides. Turnbull scored after just a minute for Shire after being set up by Latimer. The Dumfries men made a quick reply but Shire had the lion's share of possession and it was somewhat against the run of play when their hosts took the lead just before the interval. Early in the second half Hart missed a chance to equalise and Queens then went up the other end and scored to make it 3-1. A fourth followed and a fifth was added five minutes from time. This was just a minor setback though and a week later they beat Albion Rovers 5-1 at Firs Park. *The Scotsman* reported that "East Stirlingshire atoned for the defeat they sustained by a similar score in their opening game at Dumfries. The victory was well merited...the home men were the stronger, more impressive, and effective side. Their superiority was pronounced in every division." Shire went three up after the first quarter of an hour's play. After five minutes Black converted Kemp's cross from the left. In the 12th minute Hart headed home another cross by Kemp and just two minutes later Black made it 3-0. Rovers improved after the break and reduced the leeway, however, Black and Hart added further goals. On the 22nd August East Stirlingshire won 5-2 at Bo'ness with *The Scotsman* commenting that "in team work the visitors were distinctly superior. Their defenders were sound without being brilliant, while they possessed five forwards who could work the ball to advantage. In addition, their attack possessed two sharpshooters in Hart and Latimer, the latter being particularly deadly with his work." Hart scored a hat-trick and Latimer got one and Turnbull the other.

These victories came at the start of a run of seven consecutive wins, the last of these, a 3-0 win over Dumbarton in mid-September, put them two points clear of St Johnstone at the top. Hart scored a hat-trick, bringing his total to eight goals from the last three games. Key to their success was the goalscoring partnership of Jamie Hart, an ex-Charlton Athletic and Chester City player, who would score 37 League goals during the 1931-32 season and Johnny Latimer, formerly of Portsmouth.

 Shire's run came to an end with defeat against East Fife but they then set off on another run, going nine games unbeaten, including a 6-1 win over Armadale and a 5-0 win over Forfar. When they took revenge and beat Queen of the South 5-0 at Firs Park on the 19th December, Hart scoring four, they were top by five points, and had only lost two out of 21 games played.

Shire scored five, twice in January, in a 5-2 win over Bo'ness (Hart hat-trick) and a 5-1 win over East Fife. In between they conceded five themselves, against fellow Second Division side Dunfermline in the First Round of the Scottish Cup. A defeat at Arbroath and a League defeat this time against Dunfermline cut their lead to just three points over St Johnstone. Three wins followed, including a 6-4 win over Edinburgh City before the top two met on the 12th March at Firs Park, St Johnstone winning 1-0, breaking the club's unbeaten home record. *The Scotsman* wryly noted that "for their defeat the Shire men had themselves largely to blame through their inability to turn their chances to account." Shire then suffered a mini-wobble. Two further defeats followed at the hands of struggling Armadale and Forfar, with the gap reduced to three points, with St Johnstone having a game in hand.

Entering April, Shire got back on track, defeating St Bernard's of Edinburgh 5-1. *The Scotsman* reported that "territorially the exchanges were fairly even, but the winners were clearly sounder in defence and faster and more enterprising in attack." Mason scored early on, followed by Black. St Bernard's got one back but then Fraser scored from a penalty. The game became an ill-tempered one and from a free-kick Crichton made it 4-1. Watson brilliantly saved a penalty to keep intact their three goal advantage at the interval. The only goal of the second half was scored by Mason. Significantly, on the same day St Johnstone beat third placed Raith Rovers 2-0 to guarantee promotion for both sides. Who would win the championship? Shire still led by three points with two to play. St Johnstone had three fixtures left.

On the 9th April it was Shire's turn to host Raith and they scored five for a second time in as many matches, winning 5-1. *The Scotsman* reported that "East Stirlingshire kept themselves ahead of St Johnstone in the race for the Second Division championship by reason of their convincing win over Raith Rovers at Falkirk. The game was played under extremely trying conditions, the ground being heavy and water-logged, and it looked as it would be a case of the survival of the fittest. Actually, however, it was the Shire's superiority in attack, and particularly in finishing power, which were the deciding factors. Raith dominated the first ten minutes but were given a lesson in taking their chances when a breakaway saw Tallis score for Shire against the run of play. A superb run and cross by Latimer on the right was headed in by Kemp for number two. Soon afterwards, and again as a result of good work by Latimer, Black shot a third goal from a narrow angle. Raith now had a period of pressure but again couldn't take their chances and just before the interval Mason made it 4-0. Raith dominated the early part of the second half and this time had something to show for it when they got one back but any hope of a fight back was soon extinguished when Kemp got a fifth. St Johnstone won 7-1 at Edinburgh City but Shire's two consecutive 5-1 results would ultimately prove to be significant in terms of goal average.

On the 16th April, and needing to win to make sure of the title East Stirlingshire were held 1-1 by local rivals Stenhousemuir. Watched by a crowd of 5,000 Shire were 1-0 down at half-time. They played desperately for the equaliser which was eventually scored by Tallis. On the same day St Johnstone won 4-0 against Montrose. The 1-1 draw in their last game meant Shire were not quite mathematically confirmed as champions. With a point dropped Shire finished on 55 points and St Johnstone now had 53 points, with a game to play. Shire had scored 111 goals and conceded 55 and finished with a goal average of 2.018. St Johnstone had scored 96 goals and conceded 51 and had a goal average of 1.882. St Johnstone needed to not only win their game in hand, but to win by seven clear goals (a 7-0 win would mean 103 goals divided by 51 = 2.019).

On the 23rd April St Johnstone gave it a really good go! Needing to win 7-0 they beat Bo'ness 6-1. Under the headline "St Johnstone's Plucky Effort", *The Scotsman* reported that "St Johnstone entered upon their last League game of the season with the knowledge that they required seven goals without reply, to wrest the Second Division Championship from East Stirlingshire, and if they failed to achieve their object, the team made a valiant effort to secure the goals. Bo'ness provided the opposition and for most of the time they were defending. The score of six goals to one in no way exaggerated the Saints' superiority." St Johnstone raced into a two goal lead but missed a number of chances to increase their lead. It only took four minutes of the second half to make it three but in pushing for more goals they exposed themselves at the back and Bo'ness scored a breakaway goal. This temporarily took the wind out of their sails, but they pressed on and added three more. Near to the end they made a number of desperate appeals for penalties and the game ended with St Johnstone three goals short. Both teams finished on 55 points each, nine clear of Raith in third. Shire's goal average was 2.018 (111/55) and St Johnstone ended on 1.962 (102/52). Having conceded they had needed to win 9-1 (105/52 would equal 2.019). Shire's Second Division championship winning team was: Willie Watson; Willie Fraser, William McMillan; Willie Crichton (c), Jim McCabe; Willie Black, Rabbie Kemp, Johnny Latimer, Jimmy Turnbull, Jamie Hart and Geordie Mason. Shire also added the Stirlingshire Cup to their League title, beating Stenhousemuir 4-2 in the Final.

East Stirlingshire spent only one season in its first spell in the top flight, ending the season bottom of the First Division in 20th with seventeen points, conceding a club record 115 goals and suffering a record 28 defeats. Shire struggled from the off and were never out of the bottom two after Christmas. They started the 1932-33 season on the 13th August by unfurling the Second Division championship flag at Firs Park, on the opening game of the new season. Bailie Alexander and Finlay Potter conducted the ceremony, Morton were the visitors and they left with both points. Reporting on the match the *Glasgow Herald* said that "East Stirlingshire's display in their opening game in the First Division was a big disappointment to their followers, and Morton, without being brilliant, won the points with comparative ease. Taken as a whole the game provided the 6000 spectators present with little to enthuse over. The Shire football was a good bit below First Division standard. They had not a craftsman in their ranks, and never at any time did they reveal that they had any definite plan of campaign. Their energy was boundless, but the bulk of it was misapplied." Play was fairly level for the first twenty minutes before the visitors took the lead in the 24th minute. They increased their lead just four minutes later from the penalty spot after a handball. Their third wasn't scored until the 78th minute.

Shire lost their next two First Division fixtures as well before eventually recording their first point on the 27th August with a 1-1 draw at home to Queen's Park. Their first win came on the 17th September away at Aberdeen when they came from 1-0 down at the interval and scored three second half goals. The *Glasgow Herald* commented that "it is fair to assume that East Stirlingshire's victory is indicative of their progressive improvement through experience." The turning point came 20 minutes from the end when, trailing 1-0, Watson saved a penalty kick. Shire broke away and centre-forward Craigie equalised. The Dons made an immediate attempt to restore their lead but Craigie, picking up a clearance, ran through in his own to give his side the lead. In the last minute of the match Fraser scored from a penalty to give Shire a 3-1 victory at Pittodrie. The victory moved Shire off the bottom and above Partick and Falkirk.

It was a month later when the club secured their second win and first home victory when they beat St Mirren 2-1. An overhaul of the team was already underway at this stage and the line-up featured two new players. One of these, McAulay from Camelon Juniors made an impressive debut at centre-forward. He scored Shire's second in the first half after Crichton had given them the lead after a quarter of an hour. St Mirren only got one back late in the game. A third win and a season's best came in November with a 4-0 victory over Ayr United but by the turn of the year Shire were second from bottom with ten points. Morton were two points ahead of them and Airdrieonians were below them on nine points.

During January Shire won only one of five League fixtures and were also knocked out of the Scottish Cup by struggling Second Division side Montrose. Following their Cup exit they lost five in a row. On the 18th March they beat Third Lanark 2-0 to secure their first points since they had defeated Aberdeen on the 3rd January. *The Scotsman* commenting that "their success was undoubtedly deserved, but it was not achieved in any particularly inspiring fashion." Thirds played all but ten minutes of the second half a man short following a facial injury to one of their players. The second half was only four minutes old when Turnbull headed in from a Latimer cross. Ten minutes later Smith scored a second. By this time though Airdrieonians had turned a corner and moved into a position of safety on 21 points, Morton had 17 and East Stirlingshire had only 14 – seven points from safety with six games to go. Shire put up a dismal fight, conceding six, seven, and then eight goals in their next three match – losing 6-3 against Patrick, then 7-2 at home against the same opposition and finally 8-1 away at Airdrieonians – and relegation was confirmed. They picked up just one point from five matches although they did win their final fixture, beating Dundee 3-2.

Although they won their first two games of the new 1933-34 season, including a 5-1 win over Raith Rovers, there would be no promotion challenge to make an immediate return to the top flight. Two defeats followed those two opening games and Shire settled into mid-table, and eventually finished a disappointing ninth place. At the beginning of October they lost 6-1 at Arbroath and at the end of December they were thrashed 10-3 away at leaders Dunfermline. There were mitigating factors in the loss, *The Scotsman* revealing that "this heavy defeat was in a considerable measure due to an injury to Falconer, the East Stirlingshire goalkeeper, sustained in making a brilliant save just after thirty minutes' play. Up to then the East Stirlingshire men had made a great fight." Shire took the lead through Smith before Dunfermline scored two. It was with the score only at 2-1 that Falconer left the field and at the break Shire were 3-1 down. In the second half the Pars scored seven, Turnbull scoring two breakaway goals for Shire. In Scottish Cup action, after having beaten Nithsdale Wanderers, Shire got revenge on Arbroath, knocking them out after a replay, before going on to lose 5-0 against Motherwell. By the end of March they were as low as 15th in the table, just four points from the bottom. However, they won three of their four remaining games in April, drawing the other one, to eventually be placed in ninth position. Shire reached the Final of the Stirlingshire Cup and the tie against Alloa Athletic was played over two legs, East Stirling losing 5-4 on aggregate.

East Stirling opened the 1934-35 season with a win and a draw but then lost heavily at Morton, 9-2, Kayes, the Greenock centre-forward scoring six. The following week Shire bounced back with a 5-1 win over Forfar, *The Scotsman* commenting that they "made atonement for their extraordinary collapse at Greenock the previous week." Cameron at centre-forward scored a hat-trick, including two in the opening minutes. The victory started a run of six games without defeat and by the end of September they were second in the table, a point behind leaders Third Lanark. Indifferent form followed across the three remaining months of 1934 and a 3-3 draw away against leaders Thirds (in which they recovered from 3-0 down thanks to a hat-trick from a diminutive forward called Peat, formerly of Falkirk), in the last match of the year, saw them now down in eighth place.

Only one point from their first three games of 1935 followed before they won 6-2 against Dumbarton in mid-January, *The Scotsman* reporting that "East Stirlingshire played what was one of their best games at Firs Park this season. The reconstructed home forward line, in which Peat appeared at outside right, partnered by 'Newman', with Cameron at centre, was an unqualified success." After a Brown penalty had been cancelled out by their opponents, Cameron and A Thomson gave Shire a 3-1 lead. The two sides then traded goals, Cameron getting his second. It was only near the end that Thomson and then Cameron, with his third, added two more goals. Inconsistency continued to plague them. At the beginning of March they won 5-1 at Leith, Peat scoring a hat-trick. However, a month later they lost their last game of season, 7-0 at St Bernard's, and finished a lowly 14th place.

The 1935-36 season brought about a modest improvement and Shire opened the new season with a 1-1 draw at home to Dumbarton and then registered a 6-1 away win at Stark's Park against Raith Rovers on the 31st August, *The Scotsman* reporting that "although the final result...exaggerated the visitors' superiority, there was nothing of a fluke about their win. The Rovers were surprisingly weak in defence, while the visitors were absolutely sound in that department. Therein lay the principal difference between the elevens....Easily the most impressive footballer in the game was Muir, of East Stirlingshire, the centre-half playing a fine game." Home wins followed over Morton, Brechin (5-1) and King's Park but their win in Kirkcaldy was the highlight of games on their travels. They recorded back to back wins over the festive period in the local derbies against Stenhousemuir and King's Park but then lost 5-0 at home to leaders Falkirk, in front of a 9,000 crowd, to sit in seventh place. This defeat started a poor run of form where they only won once in their next eight games and their season reached a nadir in the penultimate game, where they lost 12-1 at Tannadice against Dundee United, despite taking an early lead. United equalised minutes later and by half-time were 5-1 up. Their opponents scored four times in the opening five minutes of the second half and added three more near the end for a 12-1 victory - United's record League victory. Shire had a triallist in goal. Shire did, however, win the county cup for the first time in four seasons beating Alloa Athletic 5-1 on aggregate in the two-legged Final.

Director Peter Galbraith took over the managerial reins up until League suspension in 1939. Shire opened the 1936-37 season on the 8th August 1936 with a 2-0 win at Alloa. Kemp punted the ball forward from the centre circle and it bounced over the advancing keeper and into the next. Borland, formerly of Hibs, headed the second a few minutes later. East Stirling won six on the trot across October and November, including a 6-4 away win at Tannadice, Turnbull scoring four and a 5-3 victory over leaders Morton, in which they scored four goals in the opening 25 minutes, saw them move up to fifth place, three points off the top. However, Shire ended 1936 poorly, losing 5-0 against promotion rivals Raith and then on the 2nd January 1937 they lost 7-2 at new leaders Ayr United, who recorded a twelfth successive win. By the time of a 7-2 win over Stenhousemuir on the 13th March they had only dropped a place but were now ten points off second place. They won three of their remaining four games eventually finishing in seventh place.

Shire drew seven of their first dozen games at the start of the 1937-38 season, with their best result coming when Beath scored a hat-trick in a 6-0 win over King's Park in September. Financial problems surfaced in November characterised by pay cuts and a number of released players. On the 18th November Meechan was granted a free transfer and joined St Johnstone and Alexander Cochrane left for Dumbarton. On the 25th November, William Brown left for Falkirk after four seasons and Beath joined Albion Rovers. What *The Scotsman* called a "somewhat makeshift team" then went down 6-1 against Dundee United and the club went on to lose five in a row. On the 8th January 1938, what *The Scotsman* called an "under strength" team lost 8-1 at home to leaders Raith. Shire got an undeserved 4-3 victory against Edinburgh City in mid-February which they followed up with a narrow win over bottom club Brechin City. They then lost 6-0 at Cowdenbeath and 7-0 against Albion Rovers (having had a man sent off) and ended a dismal campaign in 13th place.

Things got worse in the last full season before the Second World War. They opened with a 4-0 loss at Dumbarton and lost their next two as well, conceding seven at East Fife. Things then picked up as the club went six games without defeat. At the end of September they beat Montrose 5-4 away from home and discovered a new goalscorer. Malcolm Morrison scored a hat-trick against the Gable Endies and would go on to score a club record 36 goals in a poor season where they would ultimately finish second from bottom. In early October they beat Dundee 6-5 at Dens Park. In a sensational game the score was 2-2 at half-time, 5-2 for Dundee twenty minutes later, and 6-5 for Shire at the finish with Morrison having scored another hat-trick. Their form was very erratic though. At the end of the same month they lost 7-1 at Dunfermline. At the beginning of November they beat Edinburgh City 7-2 in the capital, Morrison once again scoring three, but in mid-December they went down 8-1 at Airdrie and ended 1938 in 15th place.

In January they made a First Round Scottish Cup exit 7-0 at St Mirren. The following month they beat Dumbarton 6-4, Morrison scoring two. Dumbarton's goalkeeper was injured after 20 minutes and had to retire. At the end of March they lost 10-0 at Dundee United, fielding a team that featured two triallists. On the 15th April they beat Leith Athletic 5-2 to leapfrog their opponents into 16th place. Morrison scored four times to take his season's tally to 36 goals. Leith drew level on points in midweek following a draw but on the following Saturday Shire lost at home to Stenhousemuir, whereas Leith won. In the last round of matches, and needing to win, Shire lost at home to bottom club Edinburgh City, with both sides therefore facing re-election. The visitors had a three goal lead at the interval but Shire scored two penalties in the second half. At the League's AGM held on the 24th May East Stirling were successfully re-elected along with Edinburgh City.

The 1939-40 season kicked off as normal on Saturday 12th August with Shire beating Montrose 4-1. They then lost 3-0 at Morton before drawing 1-1 with Dundee United at Firs Park. On the 2nd September they played what would turn out to be their last Scottish Football League game for a while, which was a 2-2 draw with King's Park in Stirling. 'Junior' gave Shire the lead after just three minutes and Roughead put them two-up after eight minutes but King's Park fought back to earn a draw. The East Stirlingshire makeshift line up was listed in *The Sunday Post* as: Newman; Allan, J Young; A N Other, T Anderson, W Anderson, Morrison, Junior, Roughead, Whittington and R Young. On the 1st September Germany had invaded Poland and Britain declared war on Germany two days later. World War Two saw the suspension of the Scottish Football League for a short while. In October the League restarted with two regional divisions of 16 clubs apiece although East Stirlingshire were not included in the new setup and they closed down for the duration of the War.

The 1946–47 season was the first season of competitive football in Scotland after the Second World War. The League was organised into three Divisions, now called 'A' 'B' and 'C'. Divisions A and B had 16 and 14 teams respectively. Division C was the smallest, comprising the six teams that had not been included in the regional divisions during the war, which included East Stirlingshire, plus Stirling Albion (who replaced King's Park) and three reserve sides.

Shire thus found themselves in the third tier of the League on the resumption and they played their first Scottish Football League game since 1939 on Saturday 10th August 1946 when they travelled to Glebe Park to play Brechin City. East Stirling took the lead after just eight minutes through McCormack and this was followed by a first half hat-trick by their centre-forward Crawford. Brechin had pulled one back so Shire led 4-1 at half-time. Only one further goal was scored, early in the second half, when Louden made it 5-1 after 51 minutes. The East Stirlingshire team was: Hastings; Kelly, Costello; McMillan, Collins, Scott; Cook, Burke, Crawford, McCormack and Louden. The following week League football returned to Firs Park with Edinburgh City the visitors. A crowd of 1,500 saw Shire sweep into a three goal lead after just six minutes. Burke scored after thirty seconds without an opponent having kicked the ball. Ian Crawford scored after three minutes and Louden after six. Edinburgh City then staged an amazing comeback scoring three of their own in eight minutes to draw the contest level at 3-3 after 17 minutes. City added two more, either side of the interval before Cook scored for Shire with fifteen minutes left. City held on to win an amazing match 5-4.

East Stirlingshire eventually fnished in fourth place. Stirling Albion topped the Division, with Dundee 'A' second and Leith Athletic third. At the end of the season Stirling Albion as champions were promoted to Division B. They should have replaced Cowdenbeath who had finished bottom but it had already been decided to expand Division B to 16 clubs. Cowdenbeath were re-elected and a ballot was held at the League's AGM on the 30th June 1947 To decide the sixteenth club. Five teams from Division C stood - Shire, Leith Athletic, Montrose, Edinburgh City and Brechin City. Leith won with 25 votes. Shire came a distant second with 9 votes.

The following season East Stirlingshire won their second honour, winning the Division C or Third Division championship, thus winning promotion to the Second Division (Division B). Automatic promotion and relegation was in force between the winners of Division C and the bottom side in Division B. Shire won 18 of their 22 matches, losing only one, and finished four points clear of East Fife 'A', and with reserve sides not being eligible for promotion, the more significant gap was seven points ahead of Forfar Athletic in third.

356

East Stirlingshire took the place of Leith Athletic for the 1948-49 season but unfortunately they won only six matches and finished bottom, four points adrift, and therefore immediately returned to the third tier. Forfar and Leith had a battle for the championship title in Division C, Forfar ultimately preventing Leith making an immediate return, by winning the title by two points. Shire had started the season with a 3-2 loss at Kilmarnock, Allan scoring both of the goals. *The Sunday Post* reported that "the finest patch of real honest-to-goodness endeavour came after East Stirling netted. This goal spurred Killie into a frenzied attack which brought them three goals in fifteen minutes." Shire only picked up one point from their opening six League games. They then took a break from League action, playing six games in the sectional League Cup, where they recorded their first win of the season, 2-1 over Kilmarnock. Their first win in the League didn't come until the 27th November, when they beat fellow strugglers Cowdenbeath 2-0. The win followed a freshening up of the side with new signings Samuel and Hazelton joining, after rumours circulated that promotion and relegation to and from Division B would cease after this season. The result moved them above their beaten opponents into 14th place, with Hamilton in 16th and bottom. By the time of their Scottish Cup exit First Round exit at the hands of Queen of the South, at the end of January 1949, only one point separated Shire, Cowdenbeath and Hamilton at the bottom, in a three-way fight to avoid relegation to Division C. Disaster followed as Shire lost away at both of these rivals in the coming weeks, and following a 4-0 home defeat against Ayr United the club found themselves bottom, two points behind the other two teams, with only four games left to play. On the 2nd April Shire lost 5-1 at Arbroath and the following Saturday they lost 1-0 at home to Queen's Park and their fate was sealed. A first half injury to Crawford hadn't helped their cause. On the same day Cowdenbeath pulled off a spectacular 9-2 win over Ayr United and Hamilton continued to pick up points. Both of these teams were now safe and Shire found themselves four points behind Dumbarton, with just two games to play, but with a vastly inferior goal average. A goal from Allan in their penultimate fixture gave them a 1-0 win at home to Hamilton, but Dumbarton won anyway.

Another step in the reorganisation of Scottish League football took place at the League's AGM held on the 24th May 1949. It was decided by 33 votes to 4 to expand Division C by the inclusion of the reserve teams of the Division A and B clubs. Division C was split into two sections – North and East and South and West. Shire were placed in the former (although they subsequently moved), and to even up numbers Stranraer were unanimously admitted to membership of the League, by joining Division C, South & West Section. East Stirlingshire had protested but finding little support withdrew their objection. As rumoured, automatic relegation from Division B was abolished and the bottom two sides were required to stand for re-election instead.

East Stirlingshire played six seasons in the regionalised Division C and made two bids to re-join the League in 1950 and 1951. Reserve teams won each of the sections in each of the seasons played and Shire came in 12th place out of 16 teams in the 1949-50 season. The League's AGM was held on the 2nd June 1950 and *The Scotsman* reported that "a matter before the meeting was the composition of next year's B Division. It was agreed that the division should consist of exactly the same clubs as were included last year – Dumbarton and Alloa Athletic being re-elected. East Stirlingshire pursued a notice of motion that Brechin City, Leith Athletic, East Stirlingshire, and Montrose (there was no mention of Stranraer) should be incorporated into B Division to make that division consist of 20 clubs instead of 16. The President, Mr Robert Kelly, Celtic, moved the status quo, and said the system of two Leagues each of 16 clubs had been eminently successful. He did not remember a period when so many clubs were in such a sound financial position. East Stirlingshire's resolution, which, in any event, required a two-thirds majority, was defeated by 22 votes to 15."

Shire played on in Division C and made a further attempt to re-join at the League's AGM held on the 4th June 1951. Alloa Athletic again faced re-election, this time along with Stenhousemuir. Shire, along with fellow Division C clubs Brechin City, Leith Athletic and Montrose contested the two places, as did Berwick Rangers from the East of Scotland League. Stenhousemuir, 30 votes, and Alloa, 29 votes were both re-elected by a wide margin. Leith Athletic were the best of the Division C sides, attracting only 6 votes. Brechin City got 4, East Stirlingshire only got 3. Completing the voting, Montrose got 2 and Berwick got none. This was the last ever re-election vote taken by the Scottish Football League.

A number of clubs in Division C continued to agitate for an expansion of Division B. Leith Athletic were expelled in September 1953 for refusing to play any fixtures. They had wanted the League restructured to enable them to play in Division B. Eventually, at the League's AGM in June 1955, League reconstruction came about. A number of clubs intended to withdraw their reserve sides and reform the Reserve League. The First Division was expanded from 16 clubs to 18 with the top two sides from Division B being promoted and no relegation occurring from Division A. This left 14 clubs in Division B and five Division C teams were moved up to create a 19 team Division B. East Stirlingshire were effectively promoted, along with Dumbarton, Montrose, Stranraer and Berwick Rangers.

Shire finished the 1955-56 season in 16th place, finishing above just Montrose of the new entrants, plus Arbroath and Albion Rovers. They started well, including a 6-0 away win against Berwick Rangers, Allan scoring a first half hat-trick. The result took them top but at the end of November they lost 8-1 at second placed Ayr, part of a run of six games without a win, and they started to slip down the table. Three 5-1 defeats in the space of five games in early 1956 saw them drop to eleventh place. They failed to score in any of their last five games, picking up just a single point, to drop even further, and finished in 16th place.

The Scottish League divisions were rebranded at the start of the 1956-57 season with Division A becoming Division One (or the First Division) and Division B becoming Division Two. The change in nomenclature did them no favours as they finished the season in 19th place and bottom of the Scottish Football League. East Stirling lost their first four games, including a 6-2 home defeat against Clyde, and three 5-0 defeats - away at Arbroath and St Johnstone and at home to Hamilton - at the end of 1956 left them joint bottom with Berwick Rangers with just seven points from 18 matches. Worse was to follow as they lost 7-1 at Albion Rovers, the start of a run of only one win in 16 games. Also within that sequence was a 5-2 loss at Berwick Rangers which meant they finished three points behind them and bottom of the League, having conceded 121 goals, their second worst ever defensive performance. At the end of the season brothers Jack and Charles Steedman acquired a controlling stake in East Stirlingshire and they would have a significant part to play in Shire's history.

Jack Steedman took on the managers role and over the next four seasons Shire finished 15th, three times in a row, and then 16th. The 1957-58 season had an improved showing, albeit after a slow start where Shire won only two of their first 13 fixtures. They lost 5-0 at home to St Johnstone in October and also lost 7-0 at Dundee United in their first game of 1958. They also suffered a heavy loss, 7-3 at home to Motherwell in the Scottish Cup and in March went down 6-0 at Cowdenbeath. They did, however, win three in a row after that including a season's best 5-0 at home to Berwick Rangers.

In contrast to the previous season Shire started well in the 1958-59 season with four wins out of four, scoring sixteen goals. They then lost 5-0 at Hamilton in mid-October and a month later 8-0 away against Albion Rovers. This defeat started a run of 14 games without a win which saw them slide down the table to 17th. Shire didn't win again until they faced the same opposition in early March, 1959, when they won 1-0.

Shire were unbeaten in their first five League games of the 1959-60 season, including a 3-2 win at Falkirk and a 6-3 win over Alloa Athletic. However, in mid-September they lost 5-0 at Montrose. They went on a 12 game run without a win from the 31st October to the 23rd January, which included a 5-1 defeat at Firs Park against Falkirk on New Years' Day. They also lost 6-1 against Dundee United in February and finished in 15th place for the third year running.

In the third round of League matches in the 1960-61 season Shire earned a home 0-0 draw with Falkirk (who would be promoted as runners-up), but they then suffered heavy defeats at Montrose, (6-0) and East Fife (8-1). On the 2nd January 1961 they lost the return Falkirk derby game 6-0. They went on to concede four goals in four out of five matches during February and March, and won only one of their last 15 matches.

After four mediocre seasons the 1961-62 campaign saw the first signs of an improvement as the club finished in eleventh place, their highest finish since returning to the Second Division in 1955. Their League campaign didn't get off to the best of starts with just two wins and four defeats in their first six games. After 13 games they had won six and lost seven and sat in mid-table where they eventually finished. Shire's biggest win of the season was an easy 8-2 home win against bottom club, Brechin City, at the end of March 1962. Shire won the Stirlingshire Cup for the first time since 1935-36, beating Stenhousemuir 3-1 in the Final, having knocked out Falkirk and Dumbarton along the way.

The 1962-63 season brought an unexpected promotion and vindication for the Steedman's. Shire made an indifferent start in the League, beating Berwick Rangers 2-1, but conceding five against both St Johnstone and Arbroath in their next two games. They then went on an eleven game unbeaten run which included eight wins, so that by the end of November East Stirling were in second place in the League table just a point behind St. Johnstone. They then lost their next two games away against Cowdenbeath and Montrose, but bounced back to thrash Stranraer 6-0 in mid-December, scoring five in the second half, although they had by now dropped to fourth behind St Johnstone, Hamilton Accies and Stranraer.

The winter of 1962-63 was known as the 'Big Freeze' and was one of the coldest winters on record in the United Kingdom. The widespread snow and frosts impacted severely on the League programme until the thaw in early March. East Stirlingshire played on the 26th January but then didn't play again until the 6th March in the Scottish Cup, when they knocked out First Division Motherwell. Reporting on this Cup upset, the *Glasgow Herald* commented that "throughout the first half play had swept from end to end, as first one team and then the other seemed set to open the scoring but were thwarted by a final interception. At the start of the second half East Stirlingshire became more dangerous as the Motherwell defence showed signs of slackness and indecision. Suddenly Willie McIntosh, who had looked the most dangerous forward on the field, received the ball five yards inside the Motherwell half, beat Aitken and Thomson, and passed to Jimmy Kemp, who scored from 10 yards."

When the League campaign finally restarted on Saturday the 9th March Shire beat promotion rivals Hamilton 3-1 away from home which was the start of an eight game unbeaten run which included six victories. During this League run Shire travelled away in their Third Round Scottish Cup tie to face Rangers, who would go onto win the League and Scottish Cup double that season. Shire lost 7-2 in front of a 35,000 crowd, Ralph Brand scoring four for the Gers.

After a defeat against Forfar ended their unbeaten run Shire set off on a mini-run this time, recording another three wins and two draws by the end of April. The season had been extended due to the severe winter and Shire still had five games left come the 1st May. By this time they were in second place, a point behind leaders St Johnstone, having played a game more. In terms of securing promotion they were themselves a point ahead of Greenock Morton, with two games in hand on them.

On Wednesday the 1st of May Shire travelled to Albion Rovers but suffered a 2-0 reverse. St Johnstone also lost and Morton weren't in action. On the following Saturday, Shire hosted Greenock Morton in a virtual promotion decider. An incredible crowd of over 7,000 witnessed Shire beat Morton 2-0, with both goals coming in the second half. St Johnstone also won so the top three looked like this: St Johnstone 48 points, Shire 47, Morton 44. This left Shire needing just two points from their last three games to guarantee promotion. The games were coming thick and fast and on the Monday Shire hosted the leaders, with another crowd of about 6,000 turning out. St Johnstone just needed a point to secure promotion and were content to play out a 0-0 draw. Shire still needed one point from their last two fixtures to join them. The result also meant that Shire had remained undefeated in the League at home for the full season. On the Saturday the 11th May Morton thrashed Cowdenbeath 6-1. Shire had travelled to Alloa Athletic and secured the required point with another 0-0 draw. St Johnstone won to take the title. Shire had won promotion to the First Division for the first time since 1932, exactly thirty years ago, and for only the second time in the club's history.

The promotion winning team was made up of: Ronnie Swan; Tommy McNab, Jackie McQueen; Jimmy Kilgannon or Joe Frickleton, Tommy Craig, Jackie Coburn; Arthur Hamill, Jimmy Kemp, Ernie Collumbine, Frank Sandeman and Willie McIntosh. Goalkeeper Ronnie Swan left at the end of 1964 having lost his place and moved to England where he played for Oldham Athletic and then Luton Town. Tommy McNab also left in 1964, emigrating to New Zealand, for who he was capped five times between 1967 and 1969. Jimmy Kilgannon went to ES Clydebank for the 1964-65 season but then joined Berwick Rangers. Ernie Collumbine also went to ES Clydebank but then moved to St Johnstone for a season before returning to Clydebank. Tommy

Craig went on to make over 250 appearances for the club having moved across to ES Clydebank. Frank Sandeman was picked up by Hearts but failed to settle and left in May 1965 and joined Arbroath and then Brechin City, who he later also managed.

Just as with thirty years ago East Stirlingshire's stay in the top flight of Scottish League football was brief, as they made an immediate return to the Second Division at the end of the 1963-64 season. Shire played their first League game back in the First Division on the 21st August 1963 at Firs Park against Kilmarnock. They were drawing 0-0 at the interval but eventually went down 2-0. The *Glasgow Herald* covered the match, reporting that "East Stirlingshire, marking their return to the first division after an absence of 30 years, were beaten at home by Kilmarnock. For much of the game, however, the lighter home team played as attractive football as the visitors and for a period of almost a quarter of an hour in the second half were in command. Sandeman at this stage was plying Hamill and a McIntosh with the ball, and the Kilmarnock defence was tested by the darting raids of Coburn and Kemp. But the picture changed dramatically when first McIlroy and then Brown, exploiting slips by Swan and Craig, scored for Kilmarnock. Thereafter the game quietened down...The home team must, however, have been heartened by their display during the first 60 minutes, in which McQueen, Sandeman, and the two wingers were outstanding." The East Stirling line up for their first League game back in the First Division was: Swan; McNab, McQueen; Collumbine, Craig, Kilgannon; Hamill, Sandeman, Coburn, Kemp and McIntosh.

Next up was the much anticipated derby against Falkirk at Brockville but Shire went down to a narrow 1-0 defeat, conceding after just four minutes. Their first win and points came in mid-September in a 4-0 win achieved at Firs Park against Queen of the South, who were also relegated at the end of the season. They would only record four more League wins all season and they lost 27. Shire won twice in the month of October, beating St Mirren and Partick Thistle. At the beginning of November they lost 5-1 at home to Celtic and lost the first four games of the month before concluding it with a 2-1 away win at Third Lanark, Jimmy Kemp giving them an early lead and Hamill getting the winner in the 66th minute. Shire now had eight points, two more than Airdrie and one less than Hibs and Thirds. Shire then lost six in a row, including a 2-1 home defeat against Falkirk in the New Years' Day derby game. They eventually picked up a point at home to Dundee United but subsequently lost 4-0 at Hearts and 5-1 at home to Dundee. Jim Murphy scored all four for Hearts. Shire played a 17 year old goalkeeper called Johnny Arrol. The Jambos must have been impressed by Frank Sandeman as they went on to sign him in mid-March.

A rare victory, and their first of 1964, came in the Second Round of the Scottish Cup, when they beat East Fife 1-0. However, they lost in the next round 6-1 at home to Dunfermline. This was followed by a 5-0 home defeat against Rangers in the League. In total the club went 14 League games of 1964 without a win. Relegation was confirmed as early as the 14ᵗʰ March, with a further five matches to go, when they lost 4-1 away at Dunfermline. The result left them on just nine points, 11 points adrift of safety with just five games left. They finally recorded a first League win of 1964, and only their fifth of the whole campaign in their penultimate game, when they beat Aberdeen 2-1.

The Steedman's had gambled on being full time but ended the season bottom of the division. The average attendance for the 1963-64 season was around 3,000. It was during this season that the Steedman's had their first thoughts about relocating, as they came to realise that in order to sustain football in Falkirk, the team needed a minimum home attendance of 5,000. With Falkirk FC already established they began making enquiries and looked at places without senior football such as nearby Grangemouth and Cumbernauld. Clydebank had been without a senior football club since 1931 and the brothers met with Clydebank Junior officials in March 1964 and subsequently proposed a merger of the two clubs, with the new club to inherit East Stirlingshire's place in the Second Division, following their relegation.

A board meeting was called at Firs Park for 8ᵗʰ April 1964. At that meeting the directors unanimously approved the merger proposal. The next day, at the Clydebank Juniors AGM, their members voted 21 votes to 7 in favour of merging. A week later Charles and Jack Steedman, held a press conference in Glasgow to announce that a merger between East Stirlingshire and Clydebank Juniors had been agreed. The governing bodies had no reason to block to the merger as there was nothing in the constitution of either the SFA or the Scottish League to bar the amalgamation and the playing of the amalgamated team in the League, with the merger of Ayr and Ayr Parkhouse in 1910 cited as an example.

In May the Steedman's released a statement confirming that the merger between the two clubs, which would be known as East Stirlingshire Clydebank, shortened to ES Clydebank, had been confirmed. The new entity took their place in the Scottish Football League for the 1964-65 season. Eight of the Shire team subsequently played for ES Clydebank: Arrol, McQueen, Collumbine, Craig, Munro, Coburn, Kemp and Hamill. Arthur Hamill had the distinction of scoring the first goal for this new club.

Meanwhile, protest meetings were held in Falkirk and an East Stirlingshire Shareholders Protection Association was formed, led by local businessman, and former East Stirlingshire Chairman James Middlemass. He organised a legal challenge to the move on the basis that the Steedmans' transfer of shares to individuals outwith the company was in contravention of the club's articles and associations. Lord Hunter ruled that there was a case to answer. In March 1965 the court case was brought forward to begin in front of Lord Hunter so that the issue could be resolved for the 1965-66 season. The hearing ended on Friday 26th March 1965, with Lord Hunter promising his decision within four to six weeks.

On the 7th May 1965 at the Court of Session, Lord Hunter ruled that the transfer of shares which resulted in the move of East Stirlingshire to Clydebank was invalid and should be nullified. East Stirlingshire and Clydebank were subsequently de–merged. At an EGM that followed the court ruling the Steedman's were deposed from the Board and Middlemass was elected as Chairman. The Shire returned to their Firs Park home and resumed their identity and playing colours. The Steedmans decided to remain associated with Clydebank who were reconstituted as a senior club and later secured a place in the Second Division in 1966. The Shire were welcomed home on the 18th August 1965 by a parade through Falkirk led by a piper.

Previously the Steedman's had continued the trend of being both directors and managers. On the club's return to Falkirk for the 1966-67 season manager Lawrence Binnie was appointed the club's first manager outside of the directors, although he only lasted until December before being replaced by former player Ian Crawford. Given all of the upheaval and off the field shenanigans it wasn't a surprise that Shire struggled on their return and they finished 17th (out of 19 teams) in the 1965-66 season. On the 14th August 1965 they played their first fixture, losing 2-1 at Dumbarton in a sectional League Cup match. Their first game back at Firs Park was against Alloa Athletic, also in a sectional League Cup match. This game was played on Wednesday the 18th August in front of a large crowd of 3000 and Shire won 1-0.

Shire failed to win any of their first six League games, eventually beating Cowdenbeath 5-4 on the 9th October. They lost 6-2 at Montrose at the end of the same month which was the start of a poor run of eight consecutive defeats, which finally ended in a 1-1 home draw with East Fife on the 8th January 1966. A month later they held Motherwell 0-0 in the Scottish Cup, before losing the replay 4-1. In-between they finally recorded another win, 3-1 over Dumbarton. Three more wins followed as they started to pull away from the bottom, moving ahead of Forfar and Stenhousemuir.

The dozen seasons from 1966-67 to 1978-79 saw Shire confined to the Second Division with only two eighth placed finishes as the height of their achievements. The 1966-67 season saw the inclusion of the Steedman's Clydebank in the Scottish Football League, taking their place to make the Second Division up to twenty teams. In a twist of fate the first game of the new season was away against Clydebank in a sectional League Cup game on the 13th August 1966. As the *Glasgow Herald* stated "an interesting fixture is that between Clydebank, now associate members of the SFA, and East Stirlingshire, in view of the legal controversy which raged before the Clydebank club was revived." Clydebank were two up after twenty minutes and went on to win 3-0.

In the League the club made an even worse start than the year before, failing to win any of their first dozen League matches and picking up only three points. Shire lost 6-3 at Stenhousemuir, 4-0 at Morton, 5-1 at Albion Rovers and 5-0 at home to Stranraer. On the 5th November they finally recorded a win, beating Brechin City 3-1. The only comfort was that Clydebank were also struggling. Shire then went another ten games without a win, including a 3-1 loss at Clydebank which saw the Bankies leapfrog Shire. By the end of March East Stirling were bottom of the table with 16 points. Ahead of them were Stenhousemuir, on 18, Brechin City with 21, and Clydebank with 22 points. Shire won four of their last six fixtures, although one of the others was a 5-1 home defeat against Clydebank of all people, much to the delight of the Steedman brothers. Brechin finished bottom on 23 points. Shire and Clydebank were tied on 24 points but Shire were placed below Clydebank on goal average (Clydebank 59/92 = 0.64; East Stirlingshire 44/87 = 0.51).

The next two seasons were ones of steady improvement as the club started to move forward and Shire finished, first in 15th and then in ninth place. The 1967-68 season saw the Second Division return to 19 clubs following the sad demise of Third Lanark. Shire started promisingly for a change with a 5-0 win over Stenhousemuir but their early form slipped away and they failed to win in the League from mid-November to the end of December. In the Scottish Cup they secured a home draw with Hibs which attracted a crowd of 4,000, although they lost the match 5-3. Notable results towards end of the season included heavy losses at Arbroath (5-0) and East Fife (6-0) and also an entertaining 5-5 draw at Clydebank.

Shire were unbeaten in the first seven League games of the next season, including six consecutive wins. During this spell they beat Berwick Rangers 7-3 and followed this up with a 6-0 win over Stenhousemuir to briefly top the division. The club reached the Second Round of the Scottish Cup, knocking out Stirling Albion to set up a home tie with St Johnstone. A bumper crowd of 6,500 witnessed a 1-1 draw, although Shire lost the replay at Muirton Park 3-0. Back in the League the club suffered three defeats in March to drop out of contention and inconsistent form in the run in saw them fall to ninth place. Shire won the Stirlingshire Cup for the 20th time. The final was held over until the 7th October and East Stirling beat Alloa 3-2 at Brockville.

After a couple of seasons of steady progression on the pitch the next two seasons saw a decline, finishing back in 12th in the 1969-70 season and then 17th the following season. They lost their opening three League games of the season and suffered a 6-1 home derby humiliation against Falkirk in December. They also lost 6-0 at home to Cowdenbeath to sit just three points off the bottom, which led to the departure of manager Ian Crawford, who was replaced by Jim Rowan, a former Stirling Albion, Airdrieonians and Falkirk player. Under him Shire recovered and finished well with eight wins in their last 12 matches.

Shire weren't able to carry this form unto the 1970-71 season and they won only one League game from the start of the season to the end of 1970, across a total of 18 games. The solitary victory came in September in a 3-1 win over Stirling Albion. By the start of 1971 they had nine points, with one win and seven draws. Brechin were bottom with seven points and Hamilton Accies were ahead of them on 14. They had also been knocked out of the Scottish Cup in the First Round, losing 2-0 at home to Clydebank. On the 9th January 1971 Shire beat Queen of the South 5-4 in Dumfries. In a well reported incident Shire 'keeper George Wood opening the scoring after two minutes. Gathering a pass back, Wood punted the ball downfield. Aided by a strong wind the ball floated deep into the opposition half. As home 'keeper Allan Ball moved out to collect it the wind swirled it over his hands and into the empty net. This victory was the first of three on the trot that closed the gap at the foot of the table. However, they conceded six at both East Fife and Dumbarton in the spring to remain in the bottom two. Three wins in their last five games saw them move out of the bottom two and they eventually finished in 17th four points clear of Hamilton and eight ahead of Brechin City. They reached the Final of Stirlingshire Cup, but the match was again held over and this time they lost 3-2 versus Stenhousemuir at Brockville, having led 2-0 at half-time.

Jim Rowan left the club in August 1971 and Bob Shaw, director and club secretary took over as manager. The club showed a big improvement, securing their highest finish since the de-merger. They made an unbeaten start to the 1971-72 season, and after four matches, with two wins and two draws, they sat in sixth place. However, they then lost heavily, 5-0, at one of the early pacesetters, Cowdenbeath. Inconsistent form followed but a strong run from late December to mid-February, in which they won five and drew the other saw them move back up the table. Included in this run was a 5-0 win over Arbroath that featured a brace each for Ian Scanlon and Alan Miller. However, the inconsistency returned and they eventually finished in eighth place.

The next two seasons saw a decline in Shire's performances which led to Shaw giving up his managerial role in at the end of the 1973-74 season. The club was unbeaten in their first three games (a win and two draws) of the 1972-73 season but only won twice in the following three months. Shire lost 5-0 at home to Clyde and 5-1 at home to Montrose to lie in 17th place with ten points, a point ahead of Brechin City and

Stranraer. They did beat then Highland League side Ross County 1-0 in the First Round of the Scottish Cup, which kick started a run of five League games without defeat and they eventually finished in 13th place. Back in the Cup they disappointingly went out to Brechin City in the next round. They did reach the Final of the Stirlingshire Cup, but lost 6-0 at Dumbarton's Boghead Park, despite only being one down at the interval, and Dumbarton's T McAdam scored four.

After narrowly losing to Alloa 3-2 in the opening game of the 1973-74 season, Shire won the next five, scoring five against Cowdenbeath both home and away to sit in fourth. However, Shire won only four more League games after that. A 2-0 defeat away at leaders Airdrieonians at the beginning of October started a poor run of form. After a 2-0 win against Clydebank at the beginning of 1974 they went eleven games without a win and in their final few games suffered some heavy defeats including 4-0 at Kilmarnock, 5-0 at Raith Rovers and 6-0 at Stirling Albion on the last day of the season and they finished in 16th place.

For the 1974-75 season the Second Division was restored to 20 teams by the election of Meadowbank Thistle into the SFL. Stepping aside, Shaw appointed a certain Alex Ferguson as manager in June 1974. Aged 32, this was his first managerial role. Under Ferguson Shire made a good start. A nine game unbeaten run from late September culminating in a 4-0 win over Alloa on the 19th October saw Shire up to fifth place, just three points off second. Ferguson's rein came to a premature end after four months in charge when he was poached by fellow Second Division side St Mirren. Ian Ure took over the managerial reins in November. The former Dundee, Arsenal, Manchester United and Scotland centre-half had recently joined the coaching staff at Cumnock Juniors and jumped at the chance to make the step up into senior football.

Shire reached the Third Round of the Scottish Cup, knocking out Stenhousemuir and Ferguson's St Mirren before going out to Arbroath, then of the First Division. In the League Shire's promotion challenge fell away as they went winless in February, starting that month by losing heavily 6-1 at Falkirk. One final consolation came in their last game of the season, a 5-0 win over Ferguson's St Mirren at Firs Park. Shire eventually finished in tenth place, six points off sixth place. This was of significance because at the end of the season the top ten teams in the First Division moved into the new Premier Division. The remaining eight teams, together with the top six from the Second Division went on to make up the new First Division (now the second tier). The remaining 14 teams became the new Second Division (third tier).

For the 1975-76 season East Stirling were therefore now playing in the third tier. There were 14 teams in the new set up and they only played them each home and away, so the League programme only consisted of 26 matches. Shire finished a disappointing eighth place. They won their first two opening League games but results were patchy after that. They were knocked out of the Cup 5-0 at home to Alloa in Mid-December and Dan McLindon, a former Dunfermline, Partick and St Johnstone player, with managerial stints at Alloa and Cowdenbeath replaced Ure in December. They scored four, twice in a row, at the end of December, 4-2 at home to Cowdenbeath, to give McLindon his first win, against his old club, and then a week later, away at new club Meadowbank, who they beat 4-0. They only won one of their remaining fixtures across the start of 1975 though. They did reach the Final of Stirlingshire Cup but lost 1-0 against Stenhousemuir.

For the 1976-77 season the programme of only playing each team home and away was changed. The number of games was increased to 39 with each team having either one or two home games against the other teams in the division. Shire made a good start, only losing one of their first eight games, to be joint second at the end of September. They then surprisingly lost 3-1 at Meadowbank, which was the start of a run of only one League win in 12 which ran for four months which saw them plummet to second from bottom. From mid-February they recovered and chalked up nine wins to move up to a final place of tenth. In the Scottish Cup they reached the Third Round. They received a bye before beating Meadowbank but then lost 3-0 at home to Albion Rovers.

The club made a poor start to the League campaign in the 1977-78 season which included a terrible 7-2 home defeat to Berwick Rangers on 17th September, which resulted in McLindon leaving and being replaced by Billy Lamont, who had played in goal, most notably for Hamilton Accies and also Albion Rovers. Inconsistent form plagued them for the remainder of the season until a fine unbeaten run in their last seven games of the season, when they won five and drew the other two games to finish in ninth place. Shire for the second season in a row received a bye in the First Round of the Scottish Cup and for the second season drew Meadowbank Thistle away in the next Round. Unfortunately this time they lost. East Stirling also received a bye in the First Round of the League Cup. This competition was re-organised for the 1977-78 season and the sections removed. Instead a two legged tie was played against Stirling Albion, Shire narrowly losing out on aggregate.

The 1978-79 season saw a decline in fortunes with Shire finishing 12th in the 14 team Second Division. They opened in the League with a 2-0 win away at Stenhousemuir, although they were beaten 5-0 at East Fife in their third game. They scored four in two successive wins over Queen's Park and Cowdenbeath to briefly challenge but then won only one game in ten. At the end of February they lost 6-2 at Stranraer and a week later lost 5-0 at Stenhousemuir. In the Scottish Cup East Stirling were on the receiving end of a Cup upset going out to non-League opposition. In the First Round Shire won 2-0 at Castle Douglas against Threave Rovers before being drawn against The Spartans in the Second Round at Firs Park. Due to a fixture pile up caused by bad weather Shire played the tie just 24 hours after being in League action and crashed out 3-2. In the League Cup the club went out to Montrose 2-0 on aggregate, after extra time at Firs Park.

The 1979-80 season saw a dramatic upturn in the club's fortunes. The campaign was a Falkirk duopoly as Shire and the Bairns went head to head for promotion and the divisional title. Billy Lamont's side had an indifferent start to the season only winning one of their first five games but something clicked and they then went on a great run, winning 11 out of their next 13 games, including a 3-2 win at Brockville at the end of October. Shire also got the better of Falkirk in the New Year derby game at Firs Park when a crowd of over 2,500 turned out to watch them win 2-1. Shire and Falkirk battled it out for top spot throughout the season. On Wednesday the 16th April Shire beat Montrose 2-1 with goals from Ian Robertson and Kenny Ashwood and three days later, in their penultimate League game, Shire beat East Fife 1-0 at Firs Park to guarantee promotion. Falkirk were also promoted when they drew at Brechin City 1-1, and going into the last round of matches the two sides were level on points but Shire had an inferior goal difference. East Stirling needed to better Falkirk's result to win the championship but could only draw 1-1 against Brechin, while Falkirk won to take the title by a point, even though Shire had won two more games than them. Their 21 League victories was their best for a season since the 1931-32 Second Division championship winning season.

In the League Cup Shire met Albion Rovers in August in the two-legged First Round tie. The first leg at Firs Park ended 1-1 but the return at Cliftonhill proved to be newsworthy when the second leg ended goalless and instead of playing extra-time the referee incorrectly proceeded straight to a penalty shoot-out, which East Stirling won 9-8. Due to the referee's error a replay was ordered despite Shire's appeal to the League Management Committee for the result to stand. In the replayed second leg East Stirling conceded two own goals in the first quarter of an hour and went on to lose 4-1. In the Scottish Cup it took three meetings against Brechin City before the Angus club prevailed.

On the two previous occasions that East Stirlingshire had earned a promotion they had been immediately relegated the following season but they managed to avoid that fate this time. Not only that, they also reached the Quarter-Final stage of the Scottish Cup for the third time in their history. Significantly both of these were achieved in Shire's centenary season. They made an indifferent start losing 4-0 at home to Queen's Park in a League Cup tie before losing by the same scoreline in the League at home to Dunfermline Athletic at the beginning of September. At the end of the month they beat Berwick Rangers 5-1 and although they only won six League games, they also picked up points earned from seventeen draws. Two of these draws came in the derby games against Falkirk.

Shire entered the Scottish Cup at the Third Round stage beating non-League Inverness Thistle 4-1 to draw Cowdenbeath from the Second Division. They won this tie 2-1 away from home and got a glamour tie in the next round, drawn away at Celtic. A crowd of 18,500 on the 8th March witnessed Shire's first game at Parkhead since 1964. Shire came to defend and offered no attacking threat. Celtic only had a Mike Conroy goal to show for all their first half dominance and didn't score a second until Murdo MacLeod thundered in a 25 yard drive with less than twenty minutes to go. After their Scottish Cup exit Shire won only one of their remaining 12 League matches, including none of their last seven fixtures. Nevertheless, for the first team in their history, the club avoided relegation the season after winning a promotion, as they finished in eleventh place in the second tier 14 team First Division.

Their stay was brief though, as they were relegated to the Second Division in the following season. Billy Lamont left to go to Dumbarton and Martin Ferguson, brother of Alex, took over as manager for a year and a half. The signs weren't good from the start as the League Cup reverted back to sections and Shire lost all six fixtures. They won their opening game of the League season, 3-0 at Dumbarton, but then didn't win again for a month. In mid-October they lost 5-1 at Ayr United but at the end of the month pulled off a surprise 1-0 win at Tynecastle, against Hearts, Billy Howitt scoring the only goal of the game after 56 minutes. The result left them in tenth place. In December they lost 6-0 at home to Motherwell and this was followed by a 4-1 Scottish Cup exit at home to Hearts, where they conceded three first half goals.

In February Shire lost 5-1 at home to Hamilton and this defeat was part of a run of eleven games without a win. This was eventually ended with a 3-0 midweek win at Falkirk but by now the club was in the bottom two. They narrowly lost their next home game 1-0 to Clydebank to leave Shire in 13th place, ahead of Queen of the South but crucially five points behind Raith Rovers, who also had a game in hand. At the end of April they lost 7-1 at St Johnstone. With Raith picking up a point they were now six points from safety with just five games to play. Three days later they lost 2-0 at Hearts and on the 1st May relegation was confirmed when they lost 5-1 at home to Kilmarnock.

The next five seasons saw Shire finish towards the bottom of the Second Division with a highest placed finish of eleventh. Any thoughts that East Stirling would make a quick return to the First Division were quickly dispelled as it took until early November for them to record their first League win, a 2-1 win over Stenhousemuir, a winless run of 12 games. Ferguson vacated the manager's seat and former player Billy Little took over, in what would be a number of managerial spells at the club. A solitary draw in eight matches across February and March followed, but a vital 3-1 away win against Berwick Rangers ensured Shire finished one point ahead of bottom side Montrose.

The 1983-84 season saw only a marginal improvement as the club finished two places higher. They again started poorly with only one win in their first fourteen League games but form improved, including three consecutive wins at the end of November. The highlight of the season was a Scottish Cup run where they reached the Third Round. Stenhousemuir and Fraserburgh were both dispatched to set up a tie against Greenock Morton at Cappielow. Shire were level 0-0 at the break but eventually went down 2-0.

The following season saw yet another poor start. This time it took until the 3rd of November before Shire finally won a League game. The club exited both Scottish and League Cups at the Second Round stage and a 5-1 defeat at Cowdenbeath at the beginning of February 1985 left them joint bottom with Albion Rovers on just 14 points. Little left and physio Angus Williamson assumed the role of caretaker manager to the end of the season. Goalscoring was a particular problem as the side scored only 38 League goals, their lowest total for nearly a decade. Shire failed to score in six consecutive League games from the 6th March to the 6th April, Paul Leetion ending the drought. There was cause for celebration though as after a gap of 13 years they won the Stirlingshire Cup. The final against Stirling Albion was played on the 14th May at their opponents' Annfield ground and despite the venue disadvantage goals from Ian Rennie and Russell Doig saw Shire win 2-0 and lift the trophy once more.

In May 1985 former player David Whiteford was appointed as the new manager. Shire made a good start for a change and recorded four wins and a draw in their first six League games of the 1985-86 season and they briefly topped the table. They then failed to win any of their next eight games before beating bottom side Albion Rovers 5-1 in mid-November, Steven Maskrey scoring a hat-trick. By this time they had slipped all the way down to eleventh place which is where they eventually finished.

The 1986-87 season saw another close shave with the bottom of the League. Shire won only six games all season, and only avoided last place on goal difference. The club only won two games to the turn of year and goalscoring was again a problem with only 33

League goals scored from 39 matches. They lost their opening game 3-0 at Stirling Albion and failed to win any of their first eleven League games. This included a 5-0 defeat at home to Raith, with Paul Smith being sent off and manager Dave Whiteford bemoaning the lack of effort from his players. Shire finally won on the 25th October when they beat Queen's Park 2-0, their visitors missing a penalty. Under the headline "Strange Day for Shire" the *Glasgow Herald* played on the goalscorers name, reporting that "strange goals were responsible for East Stirling's 2-0 win. Queen's found themselves a goal down in only four minutes when David Strange ran on to a through ball and shot past [the keeper]. Seventeen minutes later Strange put the finishing touch to a good move by John McLindon, whose pass gave the scorer a simple task...East Stirling may well have turned the corner with this initial success. The arrival of Strange should make a difference to their midfield strength. He had four starts last season for Stenhousemuir, when he impressed on the right side...and it will be a bonus for Shire if he continues to score as well." However, the win didn't lead to any change in fortune and East Stirling failed to win again in the next two months, eventually beating Alloa Athletic 1-0 on the 27th December. The year 1987 didn't start well either, losing their first six games of the New Year and Whiteford left on the 10th February to be replaced by David Connell. Form improved a bit and Shire secured back to backs wins in early April. With one match to play Shire were one point behind Berwick Rangers. On the 9th May Berwick lost at Stenhousemuir 3-1 while East Stirling drew 2-2 with Queen's Park. The two sides were now level on points but Shire avoided finishing bottom with a six goal better goal difference. Future manager John Sludden was the division's top goalscorer for Ayr United with 31 goals. In the League Cup Shire won 2-0 away at Stranraer and then narrowly lost 1-0 at Hibs. In the Scottish Cup they went down 1-0 at Peterhead.

Under the new leadership of Connell, Shire had an improved showing although they failed to win in their first three games. A 2-0 win over Stenhousemuir at the end of August was the first of four consecutive wins that took them up to third place. After this positive start Shire's form took a dip and a run of no wins in eleven matches saw them drop to tenth place by the end of November. They went winless until a 3-1 win over Alloa on the 19th December. They made a fine unbeaten start to 1988 which was only ended by a 2-0 defeat at leaders Ayr. Reporting on the game, the *Glasgow Herald* commented that "if there is criticism that can be made of Ayr United this season it is that some of their players are prone to indiscipline, mostly of the petulant variety. It came as no surprise, therefore, that there was trouble during their meeting at Somerset Park on Saturday with East Stirlingshire, who have probably the second division's worst disciplinary record. Ayr's 2-0 victory, ending East Stirling's 11-game unbeaten run, was devalued also by the fact that their opponents played the second half with only nine men." Shire started strongly with Joe Woods twice going close but

Ayr took the lead against the run of play. Gary Murray picked up two yellow cards for bad tackles and forward Tom Ward was red carded at half time for raising an arm. Despite their two man advantage Ayr only added one more goal. Three wins in a row in early March lifted them up and they finished in sixth place.

In the Scottish Cup Shire went on a run to the last 16. Visits to Non-League side's Inverness Caledonian, Buckie Thistle and Gala Fairydean were safely negotiated. In the game against Gala their hosts took lead after just eight minutes. Garry Murray equalised and Shire went ahead through John Irvine before the home team drew level by half-time. Irvine scored two in the second half for his hat-trick, before Gala scored again, Tom Ward settling things five minutes from time. In the Fourth Round Shire got a home draw against First Division Clyde. In a very close game, East Stirling put up a fine showing and led 2-1 before a hotly disputed penalty led to their opponents getting level just before half time. Clyde scored the only goal of the second half to progress 3-2. In the League Cup back in August Shire beat Stenhousemuir 3-1 in the First Round but were knocked out by Premier League Dunfermline Athletic by the same scoreline.

In the 1988-89 season the club failed to build on the progress made the year before. The new season got off to an eventful start on the 10th August when a floodlight failure at Firs Park caused the abandonment of their home League Cup tie against Arbroath with the tie delicately balanced at 1-1 after ninety minutes and with extra time due to be played. The rearranged tie was played the following night but Shire lost 1-0. The League season started a few days later and Shire lost only one of their first seven fixtures. Form became inconsistent after that although they did beat Berwick Rangers 5-0 away from home at the end of November. In the Scottish Cup Shire met Gala Fairydean again, this time at home, and won a tight game 1-0, but went out to fellow Second Division side Montrose at home in the next round. A 4-2 win over East Fife on the 1st April saw Shire in eleventh place and the goalscoring of Billy McNeill and Tommy McEntegart ensured they finished in ninth place.

During the summer of 1989 Alan Mackin became the major shareholder and appointed himself player manager, dispensing with the services of David Connell. The move was a disaster. Under him Shire lost their opening match of the season in the League Cup away at Arbroath and also their first five League games. Three draws followed before a first win on the 7th October, 3-1 over Berwick Rangers. With only one win in their last fifteen matches it was no surprise that Shire finished bottom of the 14 team division, six points adrift of second bottom Montrose. This was the first time that the club had finished bottom of the whole of the SFL since 1957. In the Scottish Cup Shire entered at the Second Round stage and beat Vale of Leithen in Innerleithen but lost at home to Stirling Albion in the next round.

The new season started with a 2-1 away win at Queen of the South and was followed up with a home 2-2 draw against Stenhousemuir. However, the results from the next nine games yielded only one draw and eight defeats, including 4-0 losses against Queen's Park and Berwick Rangers. Defeats in early November, 3-0 at Stirling Albion and 4-1 at Stenhousemuir saw Mackin resign as manager, although he remained on the Board. Dom Sullivan, the former Clyde, Aberdeen, Celtic, Morton and Alloa midfielder was appointed as the new manager although he was unable to effect a significant turnaround in the club's fortunes. They did avoid finishing bottom for a second season, finishing four points ahead of bottom club Arbroath. In February 1991 they had lost 6-1 at home to Alloa but at the beginning of April beat East Fife 5-1. In the Scottish Cup they lost to Queen of the South 3-1 at home in the First Round. They fared a little better in the League Cup where they beat Dumbarton on penalties and drew Rangers away, losing 5-0. They reached the final of Stirlingshire Cup, which had long been expanded, and lost against Dumbarton.

A redevelopment of Firs Park took place and a new stand was opened on the 25th July 1991, part-funded by the sale of land for the Central Retail Park. Costs overran though and this was a time of boardroom disputes. The new season started well and the club scored five on the opening day of the season as they beat Stranraer 5-3 at Stair Park. However, they didn't win again for a month after which they beat Berwick Rangers 4-1. Inconsistency was their issue. One week they lost 5-1 at Queen of the South, and the next they were beating East Fife 4-2. They only lost once in eight matches across December and January, but had a particularly bad February, losing 4-0 at Cowdenbeath and suffering two heavy home defeats, 4-0 against Berwick Rangers and 5-0 versus Arbroath and they eventually finished in sixth place. In the League Cup they beat East Fife on penalties but lost to Falkirk 3-0 in the next round. In the Scottish Cup they went out at home to Dumbarton 2-0 in the First Round.

The club were unable to sustain this improved showing and it was a familiar tale in the 1992-93 season as the club slipped back and finished a disappointing second from bottom, winning only eight of 39 League matches. They lost their first two games before making an amazing comeback away at Arbroath. Shire were 4-2 down after an hour before scoring three late goals. The first of these didn't come until the 83rd minute and then Shire drew level two minutes later. Paul Roberts then sealed a famous win for the Shire with a goal in the 89th minute to win the game 5-4. However. Further victories were hard to come by. Shire lost 7-3 at home against Stenhousemuir on the 10th October and a 6-1 home defeat against East Fife and a 4-1 loss at Montrose saw manager Dom Sullivan leave the club in mid-December after two years in charge. Former player Bobby McCulley took over as manager. McCulley had made over 250 appearances for the club over a ten year period and later played for Falkirk. He returned as a player and made six further appearances before becoming the manager. East Stirlingshire only recorded two more wins across the rest of the season, and only scored one goal in their last six league fixtures, finishing in 13th place, only three points above bottom placed Albion Rovers. In the Scottish Cup Shire entered at the Second Round stage knocking out non-League Vale of Leithen and Cove Rangers, both after replays. This set up a last 16 home tie against Clydebank which Shire narrowly lost 2-1. In the League Cup the club went out in the First Round, losing 1-0 at home to Alloa Athletic. Off the pitch, Mackin resigned from the board although remained the majority shareholder.

The 1993-94 season saw a modest improvement as the club finished four places higher in ninth place. With a planned reorganisation taking place at the end of the season, with the League moving to a four Division set up, there was an added incentive to finish sixth to avoid relegation to the new Third Division, but Shire finished five points off sixth place. At the start of the season they beat Montrose in the opening round of the League Cup but they lost their opening League game 3-1 at Stenhousemuir. The exited the League Cup in the next round, losing 2-0 at Dunfermline after extra time, but recorded their first League victory in mid-August with a 2-1 win over Berwick Rangers. They then failed to win any of their next five, including a 5-0 loss at Queen of the South on 11th September, which prompted the departure of Bobby McCulley. Billy Little was appointed as the replacement, managing the club for a second spell, having been in charge between 1983 and 1985. Fortunes slowly improved and the club went on a six game unbeaten run during November and the start of December in which they recorded their best win of the season, 5-1 away to Albion Rovers. They had another good run in March, which included a 4-0 home win against Cowdenbeath but they only won one point from their last four matches to finish in ninth place. In the Scottish Cup Shire received a bye and then played Cove Rangers again, beating them 4-1 to set up a Third Round tie against Aberdeen. The match was switched to Brockville and a crowd of nearly 4,000 saw East Stirling go down 3-1.

Due to their League placing East Stirlingshire were placed in the Third Division for the 1994-95 season, which was now the fourth tier. The SFL was now reorganised into four divisions, each with ten teams. The bottom eight off the Second Division were supplemented with two new teams - Ross County and Inverness Caledonian Thistle. The 1994-95 season also saw the introduction of three points for a win to greater incentivise teams. Shire started well in the new set-up and by mid-October an eight game unbeaten run had taken the club to the top of the table. Shire continued to be in the mix for promotion into 1995 but their challenge eventually ran out of steam. From April they lost five of their remaining eight fixtures to finish in fourth place, eight points behind Montrose, and a whopping 21 points behind the new champions of the Third Division, Forfar Athletic. Shire were knocked out of both major Cups at the First Round stage. In the Scottish Cup they were beaten by Stenhousemuir and in the League Cup by the new entrant Inverness Caledonian Thistle.

The following season got off to a poor start and any hopes of a promotion challenge were quickly dispelled. Shire went winless in the first eight games eventually winning 2-1 at Albion Rovers. Form improved as they registered a further ten wins and they had a great end of season run which included wins against the teams who would finish second to fourth in the League (Brechin City, Inverness Caledonian Thistle and Ross County) and a 1-1 away draw with the Champions Livingston. Their poor start had left them with an uphill struggle though, and they ended up three places lower, in seventh place. In the League Cup the club beat Second Division Clyde 2-1 at Broadwood and drew First Division Dundee in the next round. This tie was also switched to Brockville and Dundee thrashed East Stirling 6-0, going on to reach the Final. In the Scottish Cup the club entered at the Second Round stage and met Stenhousemuir at Firs Park, losing 1-0. The club did reach the Final of The Stirlingshire Cup once more, knocking out Falkirk and Clydebank along the way. They travelled to play Dumbarton at their home ground for the Final, narrowly losing 2-1.

The 1996-97 season was a struggle and the club only recorded eight wins from their 36 League matches. They opened with a 3-3 draw at Queen's Park but only recorded two wins in their first ten games. They had another poor patch, recording only one win in the last three months of 1996 and by the end of January only had three League wins. Performances picked up a little and in early March they achieved back-to-back away wins against Arbroath and Montrose. They were now in a battle with Arbroath to avoid bottom place in the Third Division. It all came down to a last day showdown with Arbroath on the 10th May at Firs Park to decide the bottom two League positions with Shire having to win. East Stirling were 1-0 up at half time and scored twice in the second half to finish on 33 points, two points ahead of Arbroath. In the League Cup Shire suffered a First Round home defeat to Alloa Athletic losing 3-1. In the Scottish Cup the club met Highland League Brora Rangers winning a close match 4-3. They drew Premier league opposition in the shape of Kilmarnock, and gave a good account of themselves, only losing 2-0. Kilmarnock would go on to win the Cup that season defeating Falkirk in the Final. Manager Billy Little had left the club in March and Angus Williamson acted as caretaker once more until John Brownlie was appointed at the beginning of April. Brownlie, the former Hibs and Newcastle defender had previously managed Cowdenbeath and Meadowbank.

The 1997-98 season saw a notable improvement after a poor start, with the club doubling the number of League wins in the campaign. East Stirling lost their opening couple of matches but then won 11 out of their next 17 League games before the turn of the year including back-to-back 4-0 home wins against Cowdenbeath and Berwick Rangers in November. John Brownlie left as manger on the 17th January 1998 and later managed Arbroath and Berwick Rangers and returned to Shire as an assistant. A few days later former player Hugh McCann, who also played for Alloa and Berwick and who had managed Alloa and Queen's Park, took charge. Shire didn't concede a goal in five League matches for a month from the 10th February to the 14th of March, recording three 1-0 wins and two goalless draws. However, at the end of the season they suffered two 5-2 defeats, at the hands of Alloa and then Ross County and finished in fourth place, although they were eleven points from second place and a promotion place.

In the Cup competitions Shire reached the second round of both, albeit in different circumstances. In the League Cup they knocked out Stranraer, who would win the Second Division title that season, 3-1 at Firs Park. In the next round they came up against Dundee once more and narrowly lost 1-0 to a side who also won their divisional championship, the First Division, that year. After receiving a bye in the First Round of the Scottish Cup shire met Edinburgh City at Firs Park in the next round, drawing the game 1-1. The replay staged at the Meadowbank Stadium was goalless after 120 minutes and Shire lost on a penalty shootout. Behind the scenes the club's major shareholder, Alan Mackin, again put forward his plan to sell off Firs Park and split the profits between the shareholders. An EGM was held in June and the motion was defeated.

The following season Shire failed to push on and instead returned to their recent history of lower half placings, coming in eighth place finishing ten points above bottom team Montrose. They made a poor start, failing to win any of their first half dozen games and picking up a single point. A 2-1 win away against Berwick Rangers on the 19th September kick started an unbeaten eight game run which included a 4-0 away win against Queen's Park. These victories were followed by five straight draws and Shire then won four in a row from the end of January through February, including consecutive 4-1 wins over Albion Rovers and Brechin City. Form then dipped a bit but they finished strongly, only losing one of their last five games.

In the League Cup Shire lost 1-0 at fellow Third Division and local rivals Stenhousemuir. In the Scottish Cup the club faced two trips to Dumfries and Galloway. In the First Round they beat Dalbeattie Star 2-1 and they then travelled to First Division Stranraer where they narrowly lost 1-0. In the Stirlingshire Cup the club progressed from a section including Stenhousemuir, Alloa Athletic and Clydebank to reach the Final. The Final was played at Ochilview against Stirling Albion but they lost 4-1.

There was another poor performance in the 1999-2000 season as Shire finished in seventh place in the ten team division. Shire only won two games in the first three months of the season. They failed to win any of their first four League games, before recording consecutive 2-1 away wins against Montrose and Brechin respectively. However, they didn't win again until mid-November in the reverse home fixture against Montrose, who at this time were bottom of the division.

Boardroom struggles continued and Secretary George Ronald resigned in November at the club's AGM. Majority shareholder Alan Mackin raised a successful court action at the Court of Session in Edinburgh contesting previous share transfers made by the club board at a time when he had been denied the right to transfer his own shares. The court ruled the club's share transfers were ineligible for the AGM which meant that Mackin was in a position to win control of the board. Manager Hugh McCann resigned on the 2nd December, citing that he was unable to work with the new board and was replaced by George Fairley. By the end of December Alan Mackin took over as Chairman of the club. In March Alan Mackin announced that the club were now looking into the possibility of moving the Shire to Grangemouth.

Shire won their first two League matches of the new millennium and they continued to pick up regular points and eventually finished seventh, 18 points ahead of bottom side Albion Rovers. In the League Cup Shire played against Clydebank at Cappielow Park, Greenock. East Stirling won 2-1 but the game is best remembered for the paltry crowd of just 69, caused by a protest of the homeless Bankies' supporters. The next round was a local derby against Falkirk which was switched to Ochilview Park to accommodate the 1,200 crowd. East Stirling took their First Division neighbours to extra-time after the ninety minutes ended goalless and they were eventually beaten 2-0. Shire travelled Aberdeenshire to play Huntly in the First Round of the Scottish Cup, narrowly winning 1-0 thanks to a late goal. They drew Partick Thistle in the next round and were knocked out 2-1.

East Stirling lost their opening League game of the 2000-01 season at home to Cowdenbeath but won away at Montrose the following week, before again losing at home, this time 5-2 by East Fife. A mini run of four games unbeaten was ended by a 4-1 loss at Brechin City, which was the first of five consecutive defeats. This run extended to eight games without a win until they beat bottom side Elgin City 2-1 at the end of November. Manager George Fairley departed after 14 months in charge and moved to Clyde, citing the atmosphere at the club as a reason. He subsequently left Clyde and joined the board at Hamilton. The club moved quickly, appointing his assistant, and former Airdrieonians and Shire defender Brian Ross. A 1-0 win over Elgin in early February was the start of seven game unbeaten run but this was also ended by Brechin, this time 5-1. Shire eventually finished one place lower than the year before, coming in eighth place. In off the pitch events, former Club Secretary George Ronald took the Club to court to try and stop a development deal arranged by Chairman Alan Mackin.

In the League Cup Shire knocked out Hamilton 2-1 before going out to Dunfermline Athletic. In the Scottish Cup they went out at the first hurdle to Dumbarton, after a replay. In the September, George Fairley took on brother Brian, who was managing Second Division Stenhousemuir, in the Challenge Cup. In the battle of the brothers George won out, with East Stirling winning 4-0, although they were beaten by Livingston in the Semi-Final. On a brighter note, fifteen years after their last win, Shire lifted the Stirlingshire Cup for the 22nd and last time (only Falkirk have more). Shire progressed past Stirling Albion and a young Falkirk side in their section. The Final against First Division Alloa Athletic took place at Alloa's Recreation Park on the 6th September. Shire twice led only for the game to end 2-2. The Cup was settled on a penalty shootout with Gordon Russell being the Shire hero, hitting the winning penalty to give them a 6-5 win on penalties. Russell holds the record for the most number of League appearances for the club with 415 between 1983 and 2002, and played a total of 513 games for the club. He also went on to become the manager of the club for a short period in 2002.

Shire lost their opening fixtures of the 2001-02 season home and away before beating East Fife 4-0 away from home. A month later they repeated the score line, this time away at Albion Rovers. From mid-October to the beginning of February they failed to win in the League, and this sequence included a 5-1 defeat by Albion. This poor run led to the departure of Brian Ross in February 2002 after a year in charge. He was eventually replaced by Danny Diver, who had played for the club between 1989 and 1992 before going on to Stranraer, Arbroath and Alloa. In the meantime club playing legend Gordon Russell took over as caretaker manager until the end of the season. Shire then beat Stirling Albion 3-0, which was the first of three wins in four matches. After a poor run they won four games in April to finish in seventh place.

For the next five consecutive seasons between 2002 and 2007 the club finished bottom of the Scottish League. For the first of these seasons they won only two games, amassed only 13 points and conceded 105 goals, their worst defensive record for over forty years. Shire failed to win any of their first five matches, their first win coming in mid-September when they beat Queen's Park. A 4-0 loss at home to Gretna, a 5-0 defeat at Peterhead and a 6-0 defeat by Albion Rovers were part of a run of 13 games without a win. In mid-January they beat Queen's Park again, their second and final victory of the season. Things were desperate for Danny Diver, and he even made a rare appearance on the field himself, before resigning as manager on the 16th February after less than a year in charge. He had been in charge for 35 matches and won just two, with a win percentage of just 6%. He was replaced by his former assistant Stevie Morrison on the 20th March. The midfielder had made over 250 appearances for Dunfermline and had later played for Dumbarton and Clyde and had managed Clydebank for eight months. Disastrously, Shire went winless for the remainder of the season, a run stretching 16 matches and four months, and in February they lost 6-0 at Peterhead, and finished with just 13 points, 15 behind Elgin City.

If the 2002-03 season was bad then East Stirlingshire were truly awful in the 2003-04 season. Their woeful performances attracted national media attention; became the subject of a book entitled *Pointless*, and prompted the Scottish Football League to review its procedures on re-election to the League. The previous season East Stirlingshire had finished bottom of the Third Division with a paltry 13 points – with only 2 wins in 36 league games, and had conceded 105 goals. The new season started a little better. Okay, they were not setting the world on fire or capturing any headlines but there was an improvement. Two draws from their first four games represented a modest return but gave no hint of what was to come. From November 2003 through to May 2004 East Stirlingshire lost 24 consecutive League games – a new record. They narrowly avoided the lowest points total ever in collecting just eight, but over the course of the season conceded 118 goals, a new record for the Third Division.

First round cup exits in the League Cup (2-1 at home to Ross County) and the Scottish League Challenge Cup (5-2 at home to Raith Rovers) sandwiched the first four SFL games of the 2003-04 season. Back in the League and during September and October, East Stirling lost 4-0 at Stranraer, 5-0 at Albion Rovers and 5-1 at Montrose. The defeat against the Gable Endies came in their tenth League fixture and left them with a record of no wins and just two draws from these matches. On the 1st November they got the proverbial monkey off their back by winning 3-1 at home to Elgin City, thanks to two goals from Derek Ure and one from Sean McAuley.

The following week East Stirlingshire suffered the first of 24 consecutive League defeats, going down 4-1 at home to Stranraer, despite scoring first through Paul Rodden. They also scored first in their next game away at Cowdenbeath, thanks to an own goal, but eventually lost 2-1. Three goals were then conceded against both Peterhead and Queen's Park before Shire had the audacity to go two up in the first quarter of an hour at home to Albion Rovers before eventually losing by the odd goal in seven.

The sequence now stood at five consecutive League losses and the team were firmly anchored at the bottom of the league. The Second Round of the Scottish Cup against Cowdenbeath therefore came as a welcome distraction but there was to be no escape. Having picked up a point at home to the same opposition in the League and having only lost narrowly away from home in the return their supporters probably expected better than the 5-0 home gubbing handed out to them. A 2-1 defeat at Gretna in the League, to end the year, consequently represented something of an improvement.

2004 started as the previous year had ended. However, in their first game of the new year, at home to promotion seeking Stirling Albion, Shire came tantalisingly close to pulling off a shock home win. They took a 2-0 lead, thanks to a brace from Derek Ure, however, with 20 minutes to go Brian Mulholland was sent off. Stirling then pulled a goal back and piled on the pressure. In an amazing finale Stirling scored two goals in two minutes to take the lead, both Craig Reid and Graham McLaren were sent off as tempers frayed and, just to top it all off, Scott Livingstone scored an own goal to make it 4-2! Three goals were conceded and two red cards received in the space of two incredible minutes. During those first two months East Stirlingshire conceded 25 goals in six League fixtures and in doing so extended their losing sequence to a dozen games. Included in the run were a 6-0 defeat at Peterhead, where Shire were four down in little over a quarter of an hour, and a 7-1 defeat at pacesetters Stranraer in their very next game.

March saw the losing streak extended still further and Shire also lost their manager during the month. Two home defeats, in which four was conceded in each, was followed by a 5-1 away defeat to Albion. It was this result, their 15th consecutive League defeat that prompted the resignation of manager Steve Morrison, who had been in charge since Danny Driver had stepped down in March 2003. Diver's win percentage as a manager had been a paltry 6% but Morrison's was even lower with just two wins in 46 matches, which was just 4%. Worse was to follow as managerless Shire then lost 6-0 at Stirling before ending March with defeats number 17 and 18 against Stranraer and Cowdenbeath respectively. Former Albion Rovers coach Dennis Newall was appointed as the new manager but he couldn't perform a King Canute act and stem the tide of defeats. A narrow loss to Queen's Park and defeats to Peterhead and Gretna took the tally of consecutive League losses to 21 games.

On the 24th April East Stirling suffered their 22nd straight loss and recorded their heaviest defeat of the campaign, conceding eight against Albion Rovers, at home. Rovers, under former player Kevin McAllister, had expected to win, although they came into the match having lost their previous five. A paltry crowd of just 223 saw Shire get off to the stronger start - Jordan Leishman shooting straight at Neil Bennett in the Albion goal when well placed; Darren Miller, on-loan from Airdrie United then fluffed a shot from just six yards out; and Derek Ure headed powerfully wide. Shire would ultimately be made to pay for their profligacy in front of goal. Rovers now came back into the match and showed some attacking mettle of their own. A Paul McManus volley from 25 yards out struck the post and the same player had an effort saved by goalkeeper Chris Todd. The home 'keeper then twice denied striker Mark Yardley before Shire opened the scoring, slightly against the run of play. On 25 minutes the ball fell loose to Stuart Kelly who struck a shot from outside the area past the despairing Bennett. But the Rovers pressure finally paid off and they scored twice before half-time to take a 2-1 lead into the interval. First, Rovers drew level when John Bradford fired home from close range having been set up by Paul McManus. Then Jered Stirling curled in a 20 yard free-kick past the helpless Todd in the Shire goal.

It all went pear-shaped for East Stirling at the start of the second half as Albion Rovers racked up three goals in five minutes. Two minutes into the second period Mark Yardley laid on the ball for Paul McManus to crack home from 25 yards. Then the Wee Rovers assistant player-coach Scott Crabbe fired into the corner of the net and this was followed up Bradford's second after a good sequence of passing involving Yardley and Jim Mercer. From trailing 2-1 at the interval Shire now found themselves 5-1 down within a matter of minutes. Not long after the hour mark a header from McManus from Crabbe's cross made it 6-0. Ten minutes later young striker Marc McKenzie, on as a substitute for Paul McManus, scored his first senior goal for the club to make it 7-1. Shire manager Newall made three substitutions, the best of these being Graham McLaren who had a couple of good chances. But with five minutes left Rovers got their eighth, when a corner from young Jamie Valentine, on for the veteran Crabbe, was flicked on by Yardley and Mercer steered the ball fortuitously into the net off some part of his anatomy other than his foot. Amazingly, Mark Yardley, the Rovers playmaker didn't get in on the scoring act.

Albion scored eight, for the first time in the League since the 1958-59 season when they beat, who else, but Shire at Cliftonhill. Albion also recorded their biggest ever League victory away from home. As for East Stirling, the defeat now made it 22 in a row. With just three League games left of the season the club was faced with the prospect of being labelled the worst ever in the history of Scottish football by earning a clutch of unwanted records. Third Lanark had lost their last 21 League games in the 1964-65 season and the first two in the following season for a total of 23 in succession. With just one win out of 33 games so far, East Stirling were on course to match the worst League results by a Senior club in Scottish football history. That record was held jointly by Dundee, who in 1898-99 recorded just one win and two draws and Clyde, who in 1900 also scored just four points, this time from two wins. At least with only three fixtures remaining there was no way that Shire could end up with the record of most League defeats in a season. Cowdenbeath's record of League defeats in a season, in 1992-93, featured 34 defeats. However, supporters of the Blue Brazil will point out that they played more games, 44, so lost 77.27% of their league games. East Stirling had lost 30 out of 33, a much higher percentage at 90.90%.

East Stirling's remaining three games in May were at home to promotion chasing Stirling Albion, away at mid-table Montrose and they would end their League campaign with a home game against Elgin City. Elgin sat one place above Shire in the table and were the only team they had beaten all season. On the 1st May Shire lost the first of these games to equal Third Lanark's 23 consecutive league defeats. The following Saturday the record was their own, but in somewhat cruel circumstances. The Firs Park club looked sure to end their 24-match losing run in the away game against Montrose. As full time approached Shire were holding out for a 0-0 draw. But a Craig Smart goal in injury time gave the Gable-Endies a 1-0 win.

On the last Saturday of the season Shire's record breaking run finally came to an end. The final game saw the return to Firs Park of Elgin City, the only team Shire had beaten all season. But things started badly as Elgin took the lead, an Alex Bone cross fell for Willie Martin to fire home from the edge of the six-yard box in the 23rd minute. But 13 minutes later the home team were level when Derek Ure shot low past Elgin keeper Martin Pirie, to record his eighth League goal of the season. A crowd of 363 was on hand to see Shire take the lead early in the second half, thanks to an own-goal by Elgin's Hugh Dickson. This goal would prove decisive but East Stirlingshire thoroughly deserved their win. In the words of manager Dennis Newall, his team finally "got the monkey off our back" with their rare victory and escaped being labelled the worst team ever in Scotland.

The club ended the season 17 points adrift at the bottom, with a paltry eight points and a record of just two wins, two draws and 32 losses, with 118 goals conceded. So why were they so poor? Beleaguered managers are often keen to point to the fact that it's the players who are ultimately responsible. But the playing squads have changed during this period with the same results. And the club had also had four managers during this time without any noticeable sign of improvement. Both of these point to more fundamental problems at the club and in the modern era that tends to come down to finance. With gates of just a couple of hundred the club has struggled commercially. The adage of 'you get what you pay for' is as true with footballers as it is with wine. The club famously introduced a wage cut, paying their players a paltry £10 a week, and prompting an exodus of more senior players. This in turn has made it difficult to attract and retain players. Unrest behind the scenes off the pitch at a club can also have an unsettling effect on the pitch. And during this time boardroom difficulties had surfaced over apparent plans to sell Firs Park for housing development and move to a new location away from Falkirk at Grangemouth.

The year after their dismal record-breaking season East Stirling again finished bottom, this time 12 points adrift of ninth-placed Albion. This was their third consecutive bottom placed finish and it led to League authorities to consider either automatic relegation or to reinstate the use of re-election procedures, last used in 1951. Shire were beaten 5-0 by Peterhead on the 7th August and a fortnight later Stenhousemuir beat them 6-0. The club lost all seven of their opening League fixtures and eventually earned their first point on the 25th September with a 3-3 draw at Albion Rovers. They were thrashed 8-1 by future champions Gretna in mid-October and their first win eventually came on the 6th November 2004 when they beat Elgin City 3-1 away from home. A second win was registered at the end of January 2004 when they beat Queen's Park at home and Shire surprisingly recorded three consecutive wins in March, to make it five victories for the season, although they still finished 12 points behind ninth placed Albion Rovers.

At their meeting in May 2005, the Scottish League voted to introduce play-offs for the second promotion spots and at the same meeting decided that any club finishing bottom for two seasons in a row would run the risk of being downgraded to associate member status. As a result they would lose their voting rights and be effectively placed on probation for two years. Any further appearances at the bottom would result in the club facing a re-election vote.

During the 2005-06 season, the first one under this new rule, East Stirling again found themselves at the foot of the table, although not always bottom. However, they did eventually finish tenth and bottom, five points behind Montrose. Newall left on the 1st December 2005, sacked by Chairman Alan Mackin in December and was replaced by his assistant Gordon Wylde, who as a midfielder had played for Shire between 1983 and 1988 before spells at Kilmarnock and Clyde.

The 2006-2007 season was now crucial and the club got off to a reasonable start, winning two of their first four fixtures to sit in fifth place. From mid-September to February they were in ninth place. But three consecutive home defeats in March and a sequence of results that saw them lose their last eleven games sealed their fate. This poor run coincided with an upturn in fortunes for Elgin City, who were bottom from August to early March. They produced a late rally, which included a 2-1 defeat of East

Stirling on the 14th April and so it was East Stirling who finished bottom for the second successive season under the new rules and also the fifth year in a row in total.

East Stirlingshire's performances had been so dire that the Scottish League had decided to reintroduce a re-election of sorts. Any club that finished in last place twice in succession would lose their vote and be allowed to play for two more seasons after which members would vote on whether their membership should be terminated. At a meeting of the Scottish Football League on the 25th May 2007, the League's Management Committee voted against reducing the Falkirk club to associate members. An impassioned plea by club secretary Les Thomson, together with news of additional investment into the club, saved the club, although they were warned that they would lose their full member status if they finished bottom again the following season. The club effectively had their punishment suspended. Commenting later, Thomson said "we have been given one more year to improve, but I left the meeting telling them that I didn't think I would be back in front of them next year."

In the 2007-08 season Shire scraped ninth place, avoiding finishing bottom for a sixth consecutive time. After an opening defeat East Stirling quickly ran off four League wins in a row earning manager Gordon Wylde the accolade of Manager of the Month for August with the team sitting in third place. However, the club failed to make the most of their great start and a run of poor results saw the club slowly slip down the table and the pressure began to tell on Wylde, who resigned in February, citing health and stress in terms of trying to prevent the club finishing bottom for a sixth season in succession. He was replaced by Jim McInally, who had resigned as manager of Morton. The former Dundee United player, who would go on to manage Peterhead, was unable to stop the rot, and in fact, things got worse as the club went 12 games without a win, which included ten consecutive defeats.

With six games to go the club were in a small group of four teams at the wrong end of the table. They then won two and drew two before losing to Dumbarton. The battle to avoid last place developed into a three-way tussle and went to the very last game of the season. Shire were bottom with 31 points, a point behind Forfar and had to better Forfar's result, who hosted eighth place Dumbarton. East Stirlingshire entertained promotion-chasing Montrose, on the 26th April 2008, which would turn out to be their last ever game at Firs Park. Due to rising maintenance costs and the cost of upgrading the ground the club had decided to leave Firs Park. It had been confirmed that East Stirlingshire would be ground sharing with Stenhousemuir at Ochilview Park from the start of the following season. Things didn't look good when David King put through his own net to give Montrose the lead, but Andy Rodgers headed in an equaliser. Joe Savage then accepted a pass from Rodgers after 65 minutes to fire home from 20 yards out. Michael Bolochoweckyj headed the third to secure a win, with Forfar finishing bottom after drawing with Dumbarton. East Stirlingshire therefore avoided the bottom spot in the Scottish Football League for the first time in six years by a single point and more importantly, avoided losing their full member status of the Scottish League. In the same season Shire once again had a run in the Scottish Cup. They knocked out Meadowbank Thistle and then Albion Rovers 5-1 to secure an away tie at Ibrox against Rangers which they duly lost 6-0. In the League Cup they travelled to Hamilton, who would go on to win the First Division that season, and put in a creditable performance, only losing 2-1 with the winning goal coming in the last quarter of an hour.

By the middle of May 2008 the news came through that Spencer Fearn's buyout of Alan Mackin and his supporters had been completed. In the deal Fearn took ownership of the club but crucially Mackin retained control of the club's assets and specifically the ground. Fearn invited a representative from the supporters trust onto the board. Things started promisingly as a result of financial backing from the new Chairman as the club finished third and reached the play-offs to complete a remarkable transformation from no-hopers to promotion hopefuls. It took a while though, and the team made a poor start, losing five of their first seven matches. A nine game unbeaten run followed, including a 5-2 win over Dumbarton and a 5-0 victory against Montrose as McInally won the Third Division Manager of the Month award in both November 2008 and February 2009. During the season Shire faced new opposition in the shape of Annan Athletic who had been voted into the League to replace Gretna.

Aided by the goal scoring of Andy Rodgers and Brian Graham, who each scored 14 goals, East Stirling won 19 games won during the campaign, equalling the most by any team in the League that season (champions Dumbarton also having won the same number) and their best number of wins in thirty years. They finished in third place, six points behind the champions, their highest placed finish in 15 seasons and their best since being placed in the Third Division in 1994. In the play-offs they faced second placed Cowdenbeath. They lost 2-1 at Ochilview but scored within the first five minutes of the second leg to level the aggregate score. In the 84th minute Cowdenbeath scored and a number of Shire players lost the plot resulting in a double red card. Still, it had been a successful season where attendances had risen significantly from the 250 mark to around 450.

The club had another good run in the Scottish Cup where they reached the Fourth Round, the highlight being a 2-1 win over First Division Livingston which set up a home tie against Premier League Dundee United. A crowd of over 2,000 saw their opponents outclass them 4-0. The club were also drawn against Livingston at home in the First Round of the League Cup, this time losing 2-1, although only in extra-time.

In the 2009-10 season East Stirling repeated their achievement, again winning 19 games in finishing third, but again losing in the play-offs. Livingston had been demoted from the First Division to the Third having entered administration and were the runaway winners of the title, finishing 15 points clear of Forfar, with East Stirling two points further back. At the start of the season there was confusion over the position of Livingston and Shire's opening fixture, supposedly against the West Lothian club, was cancelled, as their opponents took legal action against the SFL. When their League campaign did get underway they made a great start and eight wins in a row saw manager McInally win another two Manager of the Month awards. A 2-0 home loss against Livingston in mid-February ended the fine run and was the first of three consecutive defeats in which they failed to score. The club played nine matches in the month of March and only won two of them and eventually finished in third. They met Forfar Athletic in the play-offs, with the first leg taking place at Ochilview, where Shire narrowly lost 1-0. In the return East Stirling produced a fine comeback after their hosts had moved further ahead after just four minutes. Andy Rodgers pulled one back in the 49th minute and then levelled the tie in the 75th minute. However, with the prospect of extra-time looming Stephen Tulloch's late goal took Forfar through and defender Eddie Forrest was sent off for a second yellow at the end for Shire.

The same side did for East Stirling in the Scottish Cup, the club going out 4-2. The opening game of the season was in the League Cup where East Stirling met Premier League St. Mirren at Ochilview. The game turned out to be eventful one when St. Mirren rushed into a 3-0 lead after 20 minutes before Shire staged a comeback to draw level at 3-3. St. Mirren scored another goal before the break and two more in the second half, to win 6-3. Later in the month owner Spencer Fearn sold his majority shareholding to the chairman Les Thomson for a £1, with the intention of then passing on ownership to a supporters trust.

It could be said that normal service resumed on the pitch as in the next six seasons the club was never out of the bottom three and finished last in three of these six campaigns. In the 2009-10 season the club finished second-bottom in ninth place. After two wins and two defeats they failed to win any of their next six games as they slide down the table. They lost all six SFL matches in February and only 178 spectators came to a 5-1 home defeat against Annan Athletic on the 15th March, the lowest attended game in the Third Division all season. By the time leaders Arbroath beat them 5-2 in mid-March they had recorded only one draw from eleven matches, a run which had seen then drop to the foot of the table. With three games left, Shire were three points behind ninth placed Clyde, with a worse goal difference. On the 23rd April East Stirling beat Elgin City 2-1, thanks to a late winner by David Dunn. Clyde drew so Shire were now just a point behind. A week later they lost 3-0 at Montrose, where they let in three goals inside the first twenty minutes. Clyde also lost so the gap remained at a point, and Shire had a four goal deficit on the club's respective goal differences. On the 7th May East Stirlingshire played Annan, who had secured a place in the promotion playoff. Clyde were at Stranraer who had nothing to play for. Stranraer took the lead against Clyde after twenty minutes. Needing to win, Kevin Cawley put Shire ahead just before half-time. Stranraer increased their lead with less than twenty minutes to play and they made it three near to the end. Entering added on time Shire still led but an equaliser by Annan would mean they would finish bottom. In the 92nd minute Cawley got his second, and eighth of the season, to ensure East Stirling leapfrogged Clyde and avoided finishing bottom.

In the 2010–11 Scottish Cup, East Stirlingshire initially reached the Fifth Round of the tournament, having beaten Forres, Spartans and then with a 1–0 victory against Buckie Thistle at Ochilview Park. However, they were expelled a week later for failing to register the loan extension of Falkirk goalkeeper Michael Andrews to the Scottish Football Association, who therefore became ineligible to play for the club. McInally left at the end of the season and was replaced by John Coughlin, best known for his two spells in charge of Berwick Rangers with whom he won the Third Division in 2006-07. By this time Firs Park had still not been sold and was still being used by the club for administrative purposes, the pitch having lain idle since 2008. In July 2011 the Board agreed to sell the club's home to former owner and current director Mackin for £50,000 with a further payment of £50,000 to be made on any re-sale of the land.

In the 2011-12 season East Stirlingshire finished bottom for the sixth time in ten years. They finished 11 points adrift of Clyde and won only six times in the League all season. They were bottom after five games and stayed there all season. They actually won their opening League game of the season on the 6th August, beating Montrose 1-0 at Ochilview, courtesy of a Steve Jackson penalty in the 79th minute, but they then lost ten games in a row, stretching to early November. Two draws followed to extend the run to 12 games without a win, before they beat Annan Athletic 1-0 on the 3rd December, Bradley Coyne scoring the all-important goal, atoning for missing an earlier penalty. Defeats in the ten match run included a 7-1 loss at Clyde, where five goals were scored in the last fifteen minutes. Having beaten Annan to end their disastrous run Shire lost 6-0 at Stranraer the following week and didn't win again until mid-January. On the 25th February then won 2-0 away at Berwick and recorded back-to-back wins a week later when they beat Peterhead 6-3 in the highest scoring game of the season. In this game Shire led 5-1 at half-time before a second yellow for Scott Maxwell just after the hour mark let their opponents back into the game. The following week Shire lost 5-1 at leaders Alloa and only won once more before the end of the season.

In the League Cup Shire went out 3-0 at home to Ayr United in the First Round. In the Scottish Cup they entered at the Second Round stage with a home tie against Highland League Buckie Thistle. The first game ended 1-1 in which a stoppage time penalty was missed and in the resulting melee Shire had two players sent off. In the replay they went 2-0 up after half an hour but were pegged back to 2-2. The match went to extra time and substitutes Nico Gibson and Fraser Team scored to give Shire a 4-2 win. In the Third Round they were drawn away to Second Division East Fife, losing 5-0.

The following year saw no improvement as the club lost 23 of their 36 league games and finished 11 points adrift at the bottom. Rangers were demoted to the Third Division and won the title easily. Having lost their League opener 2-0 against Queen's Park Shire lost heavily 5-1 at Ibrox. After four consecutive League defeats they then recorded back-to-back wins against Stirling Albion and Clyde. A 6-2 home defeat against Rangers in mid-November, in which Lee McCulloch converted two penalties, was the start of a run of eight games without a win. Three consecutive wins in February lifted Shire off the bottom but they lost all of their ten remaining games. The second of these was a 9-1 thrashing by Stirling Albion. Jordan White scored four for their opponents and Shire had Steven Jackson red carded just before the interval. In the League Cup the club suffered a First Round exit 5-1 at home to Morton. In the Scottish Cup they won 2-1 away at Fraserburgh, scoring two early goals. However, they went out in the next round, 4-1 at Dumbarton.

For the 2013-14 season the Scottish Premier League merged with the Scottish League to form the Scottish Professional Football League and the divisions were renamed, with the Third Division becoming League Two in the new competition. East Stirling started well in the League and won three in a row to top the division at the end of August, Couglin winning the Manager of the Month award. They held the top spot until late November, when they went six games without a win. By the beginning of March they had dropped to fifth and a run of five defeats in six matches saw them drop further and they finished in eighth place, above Elgin City and Queen's Park. In the League Cup they lost 2-0 at home to Dunfermline. In the Scottish Cup the thrashed non-League Threave Rovers 6-0, four goals coming in the last quarter of an hour, before losing 2-0 at home to Raith Rovers in the next round. At the end of the season, amid discussions around developing a new ground in Grangemouth, Couglin's contract was not renewed and the club appointed former Elgin, Peterhead and Shire defender Craig Tully as their new manager.

Significantly, the 2014-15 season saw the implementation of relegation from the League and the introduction of a pyramid system to replace the practice of clubs being voted into the League. For the first time teams from the Highland and Lowland Leagues could now earn promotion on merit. The winners of the two Leagues would play off over two legs with the victor taking on the team finishing bottom League Two, or the fourth tier of the Scottish Football League. Shire avoided finishing bottom, coming in ninth place, above Montrose, who survived against the Highland League champions Brora Rangers.

East Stirling actually lost their opening League game 4-1 at Montrose and shortly afterwards went down 5-0 at Berwick Rangers. By mid-November they were bottom but two wins and a draw saw the club briefly up to seventh place, but they lost all their games in December, winning only once in seven matches. They won three out of four in February and that good form continued into March where they picked up 13 out of a possible 18 points, which moved them up to sixth, and saw Craig Tully named as the division's Manager of the Month. However, they had a poor finish to the season and in mid-April, a 4-0 home loss to Berwick Rangers saw them slip to eighth place. On the 2nd May they suffered another poor home defeat, this time losing 5-1 to eventual champions Albion Rovers. The result saw them drop a place but safety was already assured as they were ten points clear of bottom side Montrose. The club made early exits in both major cup competitions. In the Scottish Cup, having beaten Whitehill Welfare 1-0 they lost 4-1 at home to Dunfermline. In the League Cup they made a First Round exit 4-0 at home to Ayr United, having held them in the first half. David McKenna was sent off after an hour and Shire conceded three when a player down. East Stirlingshire reached the Final of the Stirlingshire Cup, for the last time. Their opponents in the Final at Ochilview was Stenhousemuir and the game ended in a 1-1 draw. Andrew Kay put Shire ahead but Stennie equalised with only a few minutes remaining and went on to lift the trophy after a penalty shoot-out.

At the end of the 2015-16 season East Stirlingshire were relegated from the SPFL ending their 61-year tenure in the Scottish League. The club finished seven points adrift at the foot of League Two and met Lowland League champions Edinburgh City in a two legged play-off. After securing a 1-1 draw in the away leg, the return was heading for extra-time when Shire conceded a penalty in the 86th minute. The visitors scored to consign the Shire to the Lowland League, the first time that an existing Scottish League member had lost its place under the new structure.

The new season started with Shire being beaten 5-0 by Falkirk in the opening round of the League Cup. The club then won two of their opening three League fixtures but then proceeded to lose the next six. In late October they were knocked out of the Scottish Cup by Highland League Huntly 2-1. Two wins in November temporarily lifted them off the bottom but by the end of January 2016 they were bottom again. On the 1st March they recorded a surprise 1-0 away win at second-placed Clyde. David McKenna scored after just two minutes and Shire then defended resolutely for the rest of the game. However, they then only gathered one more point from their next seven games, the last of these, a 3-0 home loss against Queen's Park guaranteeing they would finish bottom and face a play-off for their League survival, as they were now ten points behind Montrose with only three games left to play. On the 16th April they recorded what would turn out to be their last League win when they beat Annan Athletic 3-1 away. The score was 1-1 after an hour but East Stirling were down to ten men after their goal scorer Max Wright had been sent off. However, goals from Kris Faulds and Gavin McMillan gave them the win. They lost their final home game 3-0 against Elgin City, watched by a crowd of only 234, and a week later they drew 1-1 at East Fife and they eventually finished seven points behind Arbroath.

The first round of the play-offs was contested between Cove Rangers and Edinburgh City, the winners of the Highland League and Lowland League respectively. Edinburgh City won 4-1 on aggregate and the two sides met at City's Meadowbank Stadium on Saturday the 7th May for the first leg of their League Two play-off. Gary Jardine's hosts came into the play-offs on the back of a twenty game run without defeat, whereas Shire had only won once in their last eleven matches. A crowd of 1,090 was present and the battle for a place in Scottish League Two remained in the balance after the two sides drew the first leg. The Lowland league champions took the lead when Douglas Gair fired home a penalty when Kris Faulds handled inside his own box. Shire equalised just before the break when Max Wright forced home after the home defence had failed to clear. With less than fifteen minutes to go City defender Joe Mbu was sent off and then, in stoppage time, Shire's Reece Donaldson was also red carded.

A week later Edinburgh City became the first club to be promoted to the Scottish Football League through the pyramid system after a dramatic win over East Stirlingshire. Shire had the better of the opening half with Max Wright and Tommy Orr both coming close to giving them the lead. In the second half City came much more into the game and Mark McConnell forced a fine save from goalkeeper Darren Dolan. The tie looked destined for extra-time before the contest turned on a moment of drama. With four minutes left Edinburgh City's Ross Allum was put through on goal when he was brought down by Donaldson, who had successfully appealed against his red card in the first leg. He was sent off again and veteran Dougie Gair, who had scored from the spot in the first leg, hammered the ball down the middle of the goal. The 2-1 aggregate score brought to an end East Stirlingshire's 61-year tenure in Senior football with Shire now entering the Lowland League, swapping places with Edinburgh City. Shire's last ever League line up was: Dolan; Donaldson, McMullin, Townsley, Kinnaird; Wright, McCabe, Fisher, Faulds (Lynas); Orr (McMillan) and McKenna.

Edinburgh City thus made a return to the League having played there between 1931 and 1949. Originally formed in 1928 the club closed down in 1955 but reformed in 1966 as Postal United before adopting their original name in 1986. They had made a failed bid to join the League in 2002 from the East of Scotland League. They tried again in 2008 to replace Gretna, but secured only one vote and were eliminated, Annan Athletic being voted into the League instead. In 2013 they entered the newly created Lowland league and were champions in the 2014-15 season, but were beaten by the Highland League champions Brora Rangers in the play-off.

Craig Tully was replaced as Shire manager by former Ayr United and East Fife player John Sludden. Shire played in the sixteen team Lowland League for the 2016-17 season and put in a strong title bid in their first season after relegation, finishing as runners up, seven points behind champions East Kilbride. Despite being the League's top scorers with 107 goals the following year, they came in fourth, nine points behind the champions Spartans.

Former Chairman Alan Mackin had left the club in October 2017 but hit the headlines again in August 2019 when he was found guilty of harassing two lawyers linked to his divorce case. In the 2018-19 season Shire they slipped to sixth in the Lowland League, a whopping 33 points behind champions East Kilbride. Their performance is trending down and they now look destined to remain outwith the Scottish Football League for some time.

Their ground-share at Ochilview Park was only supposed to last for five years whilst a new ground was developed. Alternative sites had been looked at, in Grangemouth for example, but in 2018 they ended a decade of ground sharing with Stenhousemuir by returning to Falkirk and playing at the Falkirk Stadium. In January 2012, after lying unused and derelict the old ground was demolished.

SEASON	LEAGUE	P	W	D	L	F	A	P	POS
1900-01	SCOT-2	18	7	4	7	35	39	18	7/10
1901-02	SCOT-2	22	8	3	11	36	46	19	9/12
1902-03	SCOT-2	22	9	3	10	46	41	21	8/12
1903-04	SCOT-2	22	8	5	9	35	40	21	6/12
1904-05	SCOT-2	22	7	5	10	38	38	19	9/12

```
1905-06  SCOT-2   22   1  10  11  26  47  12   12/12
1906-07  SCOT-2   22   6   4  12  37  48  16   11/12
1907-08  SCOT-2   22   9   5   8  30  32  23    5/12
1908-09  SCOT-2   22   9   3  10  28  34  21    9/12
1909-10  SCOT-2   22   9   2  11  38  43  20    8/12
1910-11  SCOT-2   22   7   6   9  28  35  20    7/12
1911-12  SCOT-2   22   7   3  12  21  31  17    9/12
1912-13  SCOT-2   26  12   8   6  43  27  32    3/14
1913-14  SCOT-2   22   7   8   7  40  36  32    8/12
1914-15  SCOT-2   26  13   5   8  53  46  31    4/14

1921-22  SCOT-2   38  12  10  16  43  60  34   15/20
1922-23  SCOT-2   38  10   8  20  48  69  28   19/20
1923-24  SCOT-3   30  17   8   5  63  36  42    2/16
1924-25  SCOT-2   38  11   8  19  58  72  30   18/20
1925-26  SCOT-2   38  10   7  21  59  89  27   18/20
1926-27  SCOT-2   38  18   8  12  93  75  44    5/20
1927-28  SCOT-2   38  14  10  14  84  76  38    9/20
1928-29  SCOT-2   36  14   4  18  71  75  32   12/19
1929-30  SCOT-2   38  16   4  18  83  75  36   12/20
1930-31  SCOT-2   38  17   7  14  85  74  41    7/20
1931-32  SCOT-2   38  26   3   9 111  55  55    1/20
1932-33  SCOT-1   38   7   3  28  55 115  17   20/20
1933-34  SCOT-2   34  14   7  13  65  74  35    9/18
1934-35  SCOT-2   34  11   7  16  57  76  29   14/18
1935-36  SCOT-2   34  13   8  13  70  75  34    8/18
1936-37  SCOT-2   34  18   2  14  81  78  38    7/18
1937-38  SCOT-2   34   9   7  18  55  95  25   13/18
1938-39  SCOT-2   34   9   4  21  89 130  22   17/18
1939-40  SCOT-2    4   1   2   1   7   7   4   ABAND

1946-47  SCOT-C   18  10   2   6  54  40  22    4/10
1947-48  SCOT-C   22  18   3   1  72  26  39    1/12
1948-49  SCOT-B   30   6   6  18  38  67  18   16/16
1949-50  SCOT-CNE 30   9   8  13  51  62  26   12/16
1950-51  SCOT-CSW 30  11   6  13  57  66  28   11/16
1951-52  SCOT-CSW 30  10   7  13  53  72  27   11/16
1952-53  SCOT-CSW 26   7   3  16  38  75  17   14/14
1953-54  SCOT-CSW 26   9   2  15  46  82  20   10/14
1954-55  SCOT-CNE 24   8   4  12  58  75  20   10/13
```

393

1955-56	SCOT-B	36	9	10	17	66	94	28	16/19
1956-57	SCOT-2	36	5	7	24	56	121	17	19/19
1957-58	SCOT-2	36	12	5	19	55	79	29	15/19
1958-59	SCOT-2	36	10	8	18	50	79	28	15/19
1959-60	SCOT-2	36	10	8	18	68	82	28	15/19
1960-61	SCOT-2	36	9	7	20	59	100	25	16/19
1961-62	SCOT-2	36	15	4	17	70	81	34	11/19
1962-63	SCOT-2	36	20	9	7	80	50	49	2/19
1963-64	SCOT-1	34	5	2	27	37	91	12	18/18
1965-66	SCOT-2	36	9	5	22	59	91	23	17/19
1966-67	SCOT-2	38	7	10	21	44	87	24	19/20
1967-68	SCOT-2	36	9	10	17	61	74	28	15/19
1968-69	SCOT-2	36	17	5	14	70	62	39	9/19
1969-70	SCOT-2	36	14	5	17	58	75	33	12/19
1970-71	SCOT-2	36	9	9	18	57	86	27	17/19
1971-72	SCOT-2	36	17	7	12	60	58	41	8/19
1972-73	SCOT-2	36	12	8	16	52	69	32	13/19
1973-74	SCOT-2	36	9	5	22	47	73	23	16/19
1974-75	SCOT-2	38	16	8	14	56	52	40	10/20
1975-76	SCOT-2	26	8	8	10	33	33	24	8/14
1976-77	SCOT-2	39	12	8	19	47	63	32	10/14
1977-78	SCOT-2	39	15	8	16	55	65	38	9/14
1978-79	SCOT-2	39	12	8	19	61	87	32	12/14
1979-80	SCOT-2	39	21	7	11	55	40	49	2/14
1980-81	SCOT-1	39	6	17	16	41	56	29	11/14
1981-82	SCOT-1	39	7	10	22	38	77	24	13/14
1982-83	SCOT-2	39	7	9	23	41	79	23	13/14
1983-84	SCOT-2	39	10	11	18	51	66	31	11/14
1984-85	SCOT-2	39	8	15	16	38	53	31	12/14
1985-86	SCOT-2	39	11	6	22	49	69	28	11/14
1986-87	SCOT-2	39	6	11	22	33	56	23	13/14
1987-88	SCOT-2	39	15	13	11	52	48	43	6/14
1988-89	SCOT-2	39	13	11	15	54	58	37	9/14
1989-90	SCOT-2	39	8	10	21	34	66	26	14/14
1990-91	SCOT-2	39	9	11	19	36	72	29	13/14
1991-92	SCOT-2	39	15	11	13	61	70	41	6/14
1992-93	SCOT-2	39	8	9	22	50	85	25	13/14
1993-94	SCOT-2	39	13	11	15	54	57	37	9/14
1994-95	SCOT-3	36	18	5	13	61	50	59	4/10

1995-96	SCOT-3	36	11	11	14	58	62	44	7/10
1996-97	SCOT-3	36	8	9	19	36	58	33	9/10
1997-98	SCOT-3	36	17	6	13	50	48	57	4/10
1998-99	SCOT-3	36	9	13	14	50	48	40	8/10
1999-00	SCOT-3	36	11	7	18	28	50	40	7/10
2000-01	SCOT-3	36	10	7	19	37	69	37	8/10
2001-02	SCOT-3	36	12	4	20	51	58	40	7/10
2002-03	SCOT-3	36	2	7	27	32	105	13	10/10
2003-04	SCOT-3	36	2	2	32	30	118	8	10/10
2004-05	SCOT-3	36	5	7	24	32	88	22	10/10
2005-06	SCOT-3	36	6	5	25	28	89	23	10/10
2006-07	SCOT-3	36	6	3	27	27	78	21	10/10
2007-08	SCOT-3	36	10	4	22	48	71	34	9/10
2008-09	SCOT-3	36	19	4	13	57	50	61	3/10
2009-10	SCOT-3	36	19	4	13	50	46	61	3/10
2010-11	SCOT-3	36	10	4	22	33	62	34	9/10
2011-12	SCOT-3	36	6	6	24	38	88	24	10/10
2012-13	SCOT-3	36	8	5	23	49	97	29	10/10
2013-14	SPFL-L2	36	12	8	16	45	59	44	8/10
2014-15	SPFL-L2	36	13	4	19	40	66	43	9/10
2015-16	SPFL-L2	36	9	5	22	41	79	32	10/10

ES Clydebank

Formed: 1964
Colours: White shirts and shorts with a black trim
Ground: Kilbowie Park
Entered League: 1964. Name change. East Stirlingshire changed name
Number of League Seasons: 1
Highest League Finish: 5th in Division Two
Honours: None
Left League: 1965. Name change. Name reverted to East Stirlingshire

In 1964, in a move more akin to the movement of franchises in American sport, Falkirk-based East Stirlingshire and Clydebank Juniors, whose grounds were over 30 miles apart, controversially merged to form East Stirlingshire Clydebank (or E.S. Clydebank for short), with the new club basing themselves in Clydebank. The club was the brainchild of brothers Jack and Charlie Steedman who had acquired a controlling stake in East Stirlingshire in 1957. Frustrated at their attempts to secure First Division football and a perceived lack of local support, the brothers turned their attentions to alternative locations.

Although East Stirlingshire had been promoted to the top flight in 1963, for the first time in 30 years, their stay didn't last long and they were relegated in 1964. The club had gambled on being full time but ended the season bottom of the division. The average attendance for the 1963-64 season was around 3,000. It was during this season that the Steedman's had their first thoughts about relocating, as they came to realise that in order to sustain football in Falkirk, the team needed a minimum home attendance of 5,000. With Falkirk FC already established they began making enquiries and looked at places without senior football such as nearby Grangemouth and Cumbernauld. Clydebank had been without a senior football club since 1931 and the brothers met with Clydebank Junior officials in March 1964 and subsequently proposed a merger of the two clubs, with the new club to inherit East Stirlingshire's place in the Second Division, following their relegation.

A board meeting was called at Firs Park for 8th April. At that meeting the directors unanimously approved the merger proposal. The next day, at the Clydebank Juniors

AGM, their members voted 21 votes to 7 in favour of merging. A week later Charles and Jack Steedman, held a press conference in Glasgow to announce that a merger between East Stirlingshire and Clydebank Juniors had been agreed.

The governing bodies had no reason to block to the merger as there was nothing in the constitution of either the SFA or the Scottish League to bar the amalgamation and the playing of the amalgamated team in the League, with the merger of Ayr and Ayr Parkhouse in 1910 cited as an example. In any case, League authorities were pre-occupied with moves to reduce the SFL from 37 to 32 clubs and faced a legal challenge by the potentially impacted clubs – Berwick Rangers, Brechin City, Albion Rovers, Stranraer and Stenhousemuir. In May the Steedman's released a statement confirming that the merger between the two clubs and the new entity took their place in the Scottish Football League. Protest meetings were held in Falkirk and an East Stirlingshire Shareholders Protection Association was formed, led by local businessman, and former East Stirlingshire Chairman James Middlemass.

On the 8th August 1964 ES Clydebank made their first appearance in a sectional League cup game against Stenhousemuir at New Kilbowie Park. The Clydebank public welcomed the return of senior football and their first game attracted a crowd of nearly 5000 and ended in a 2-2 draw, with Arthur Hamill scoring both goals. Their next home game in the same competition attracted a healthy 3000 crowd against Hamilton.

On the 19th August the new club made its debut in the SFL, beating Alloa Athletic 4-1. The first was an own-goal and the other three were scored by Kemp, Hamill and Roxburgh, and these three goalscorers would share 40 goals across the season. The first League line-up for ES Clydebank was: Johnny Arrol; Jackie McQueen, Munro, Tommy Craig, Ernie Columbine, Stobo; McPhee, Jimmy Kemp; Arthur Hamill, Coburn and Andy Roxburgh (who would go on to coach the Scottish national team at the 1990 FIFA World Cup). Eight of those lining up had played in East Stirlingshire's last game of the 1963-64 season.

On the 5th September the new club played their first home League game, a 3-0 win over Dumbarton at Kilbowie Park, which attracted a crowd of 2,599. The goals were scored by Kemp, Coburn and Roxburgh. The last home gate for East Stirlingshire at the end of the 1963-64 season had been 983 and the Steedman's saw this as a vindication of their strategy.

In a midweek game on the 16th September the new club beat Montrose 5-0 thanks to a Hamill hat-trick, and they followed this up with an eight game unbeaten run, so that by the end of October 1964 they were level on points at the top with Stirling Albion. The run surprisingly came to an end when they lost 3-0 at struggling Raith Rovers but a fortnight later they beat the leaders 4-1 at Annfield. Successive 2-1 home defeats against Hamilton and East Fife saw them drop six points behind Stirling and now only two points separated the next four places. A 3-0 loss at Dumbarton in the New Year's Day game saw them drop to fourth.

By this time a legal challenge was underway brought by supporters and former Board members of East Stirlingshire. Their leader, James Middlemass argued that the Steedmans' transfer of shares to individuals outwith the company was in contravention of the club's articles and associations. Lord Hunter ruled that there was a case to answer. Meanwhile, in the Scottish Cup, the new entity were drawn away against Hibernian in the First round but came away from Easter Road with a surprise 1-1 draw. The replay, held on the 10th February attracted a record attendance of 14,900. Hibs won the game 2-0.

On the 20th February 1965 ES Clydebank recorded their best League victory, beating bottom club Brechin City 6-1, with goals from Munro (2), Jones, Kemp, McPhee and Roxburgh. They remained in fourth place, 11 points behind runaway leaders Stirling Albion, but only one point off second place. However, they failed to register a win in their next six games, including a 5-0 loss away against promotion challengers Hamilton, which would be their heaviest League defeat. They only recorded one win during the whole of March and April and failed to score in their first three games of April. Perhaps off the field events were a distraction. The court case was brought forward to begin in front of Lord Hunter on 16th March, in order that the issue could be resolved for the 1965-66 season. The hearing ended on Friday 26th March 1965, with Lord Hunter promising his decision within four to six weeks.

With promotion now out of the questions gates for their last two home games dropped to an average of 600. They had started life against Stenhousemuir and they ended it against the same opposition, playing their last League game of the season on the 27th April 1965, losing 2-1. Stirling Albion finished as champions and Hamilton came in second. ES Clydebank came fifth, finishing ten points behind the Accies.

In front of a packed Court of Session on Friday 7th May 1965 Lord Hunter ruled that the transfer of shares which resulted in the move of East Stirlingshire to Clydebank was invalid and should be nullified. East Stirlingshire and Clydebank were de–merged from E.S. Clydebank after the successful court case brought by shareholders. At an EGM that followed the court ruling the Steedman's were deposed from the Board and Middlemass was elected as Chairman. The Shire returned to their Firs Park home and resumed their old identity and playing colours. The name of ES Clydebank was short-lived but the Steedmans decided to remain associated with Clydebank, who were reconstituted as a senior club and later secured a place in the Second Division in 1966.

SEASON	LEAGUE	P	W	D	L	F	A	P	POS
1964-65	SCOT-2	36	15	10	11	64	50	40	5/19

Galston

Formed: 1891
Colours: Originally red and black horizontal striped shirts and white shorts but changed to light blue shirts after the first season
Ground: Portland Park
Entered League: 1923. Founder member of the Third Division
Number of League Seasons: 3
Honours: None
Highest League Finish: 11th in Division Three
Left League: 1926 (resigned February). Disbanded 1940.

Located just four miles away from Kilmarnock, the small town of Galston, population 5,000, seems an unlikely place for a senior football team. But in 1923, the town's football team was one of those invited by the Scottish Football League to join their new Third Division. Ultimately this new competition turned out to be economically unviable. In January 1926 Galston folded after playing only fifteen matches and it was their demise that ultimately precipitated the collapse of the new Division.

Galston FC was formed in 1891, initially performing at Riverside Park before playing at Portland Park from 1922. They made 18 appearances in the Scottish Cup, never going beyond the Second Round. They made the first of six pre-War appearances in the 1894-95 season, losing 2-1 away at Dumbarton on the 24th November 1894. This was a very creditable result as Dumbarton at this time were twice SFL champions. Dumbarton had 75% possession in the first half and scored twice. Galston scored from a free kick to make things interesting with *The Scotsman* commenting wryly that "Dumbarton should have scored oftener."

In the 1905-06 season they were beaten 5-0 by the Cup holders Third Lanark, *The Scotsman* saying that "the Ayrshire men...put in some strenuous work. Their energy and determination never flagged, even when it was evident that all hope of success was gone; and if their play lacked finish in comparison with the style of their more experienced city opponents, they deserve credit for their pluck."

The following year they won their first Scottish Cup match and achieved their first giant-killing act as well, beating First Division Motherwell 2-1 on the 9th February 1907. After a goalless first half Galston went on to win 2-1, *The Scotsman* noting that "the home men played a strong rushing game all through." Their reward was a home tie against Rangers, played a week later. Over 4,000 spectators watched them go down 4-0, although they were only trailing 1-0 until the last fifteen minutes. 1907 was a very successful year for the club, and not just for their Cup exploits, as they went onto to win the non-League title for the competition they were participating in, the Scottish Football Combination.

Back in 1891 Galston had become founding members of the Ayrshire League, and finished third in its inaugural year. In 1893 the competition was weakened by a split, with a number of clubs going off to form the Ayrshire Combination. In 1904 the club became members of the Scottish Football Combination and won the title three years in a row between 1907 and 1909 (the first title was actually shared with Johnstone). They didn't defend their title for the 1909-10 season, preferring instead to take on a new challenge in the Scottish Football Union. The Union was regarded as the strongest of the non-League competitions and its membership was much more broader, fielding sides across the central belt. They won the competition in the 1911-12 season, the ten team league featuring eight clubs that at one time or another would be members of the SFL. In 1911 they also beat Lochgelly United in the First Round of the Scottish Cup by 8-0. They scored three in the first half and five in the second. Interestingly, Lochgelly were elected to the SFL just a few years later. They drew Celtic away in the Second Round and only went down 1-0. *The Scotsman* reported that "Celtic did all the pressing, but were met by a stubborn defence, who cleared their goal in fine style. Dickie, in goal, saved splendidly on many occasions, and all the Parkhead forwards made unsuccessful attempts to beat him." The only goal of the game was scored via a free kick. The second half was one way traffic but somehow the Galston defence wasn't breached. The Galston team was: Dickie; Stevenson, Fraser; Fullarton, Young, Richmond; McLean, Morrison, Morton, Clark and Brown. This was their last appearance in the Cup until after the Great War. In the regionalised Ayrshire Cup, Galston lifted the trophy in 1903, 1904 and 1908.

As a result of their non-League and Cup successes Galston made a couple of bids to join the Scottish Football League. In 1912 they were unsuccessful in a vote to join an expanded Second Division, with Dunfermline Athletic and Johnstone being elected instead. The following year they failed in the vote in which eight teams were involved. Arthurlie and Leith were both re-elected instead. To improve their election chances they joined the Scottish Reserve League in 1913. This strong League was largely dominated by, as the name suggests, the reserve sides of the top senior sides such as Rangers and Hearts, but also featured a handful of non-League teams. In 1913 and 1914 they also won the Ayrshire Cup again (in the first of these beating Ayr United in the final). The Reserve League was disbanded in 1915 and in 1919 Galston joined the Western League. In 1923 when the SFL formed the new Third Division, 10 of the 16 teams came from this competition.

In the few years prior to SFL admission Galston took the scalp of a Second Division League club in the Scottish Cup and also took Hibs to a replay. First, in the 1919-20 season they held Hibs to a 0-0 draw in First Round. On the 24th January 1920, a crowd of 5,000 gathered at Riverside Park in wet and stormy weather, *The Scotsman* reporting that "the Hibernians got a fright at Galston. Repeatedly in the first half the local side came near to scoring, playing up against the wind surprisingly well. Then in the second half the wind increased to half a gale, and the Hibernians, try as they might, could make little or no headway....In the end no goals were scored, and the tie falls to be replayed at Edinburgh. To their defence are the Hibernians largely indebted for Galston having to appear at Easter Road...All round Galston gave a good account of themselves, and were quite worthy of another try." The replay was held a week later at Easter Road, this time in front of 15,000 spectators. Again Galston did not make it easy for Hibs who struggled to break down the Ayrshire men. Hibs did eventually make the breakthrough after about half an hour. The second half followed the same pattern but from a breakaway W Young set in a shot that the Hibs 'keeper spilled. Following up, Cook made sure the ball had crossed the line and scored the equaliser. Galston nearly got another but then Cook, their left winger got injured with ten minutes left and had to be carried off. Playing with ten men eventually proved too much of a handicap and their gallant resistance was ended when Hibs regained the lead six minutes from time. The Galston team in both ties was: Murdoch; Fleming, Wylie; Young, W Connell, A Connell; W Young, Purdie, Clark, Neil and Cook.

In the 1922-23 season Galston knocked out League opposition in the form of Second Division Stenhousemuir. Played at Portland Park on the 13th January 1923, in front of a crowd of just 1,000, Galston won 1-0. This was a hard fought game and a narrow margin of victory which was nonetheless deserved. Cook scored the only goal of the game after the interval. The team that day was: Christie; Walker, MacHallum; Fulton, Banks, Edwards; McGarvie, Watson, Cook, Shankland and Cowan. Disappointingly there was no extended Cup run as they lost to Peterhead in the next round.

On the 19th August 1923 Galston made their debut as a Scottish League club with a home tie. *The Sunday Post* reported that "Galston opened with Solway Star as their opponents. In the opening stages Galston had all the play, and Watson beat Little with a fine header. In the second half play continued strong and McGarvie scored a second for Galston. The best players for Galston were Harris, Shankman, Watson and Smith." Galston finished 13th in the 16 team League, winning 11 but losing 16 matches. In November they recorded their biggest win, 8-2 away at bottom of the Division Brechin City at Glebe Park, although the home team was weakened due to a number of injuries. At this point they were actually up as high as fourth in the table. However, the following Saturday they lost 6-1 in Dumfries against Queen of South. In the Scottish Cup they lost 6-0 to Hearts at Tynecastle in front of a 14000 crowd in the Second Round of the Scottish Cup. Hearts opened the scoring after 10 minutes and scored at regular intervals; three in each half.

The 1924-25 saw a modest improvement as they finished in eleventh place. *The Sunday Post* reported on their opening game, played on the 16th August 1924 under the headline "Galston's Glorious Start" - "Galston surely made history yesterday when they actually finished highest scorers in the Scottish League. A nap hand against Dumbarton Harp, which was very much out of time, is a wonderfully encouraging start...The feature of the game at Galston was the smart scoring of the locals in the first half. With only three minutes gone, Bolland took full advantage of a penalty, and two minutes later Munro added a second. Bolland, shortly after, with a magnificent drive, added a third, and Munro added a fourth. The visitors showed up better in the later stages, and frequently got in touch with Haggo, but their finishing efforts lacked sting. Bolland, after a clever individual run, scored a fifth goal for the locals, who were entire masters of the game." As the season progressed though Galston suffered a number of heavy defeats. They conceded five twice (against Leith and Helensburgh), six against Lochgelly - all without reply - and on the 21st March 1925 they suffered their biggest ever SFL defeat, losing 8-0 at promotion chasing Queen of the South, not helped by giving away two penalties in the first half. In the Scottish Cup they lost 6-3 against First Division Motherwell in the First Round but lifted the Ayrshire Cup for a sixth and final time by beating Kilmarnock, also a First Division side, 4-1 in the final.

The 1925-26 season was their last and they were lying in 16th and bottom when they resigned midway through the season having completed only 15 of 30 matches. On the pitch, Galston started the season poorly, losing their first home game of the season 5-1 against Royal Albert. *The Sunday Post* reported that "Galston were weak in attack, just where Royal Albert excelled, and their defence was consequently overwrought." Gordon headed the opening goal for Galston, but Christie in their goal was soon beaten by McMillan. A penalty converted after handball gave the visitors the lead and they added a third before the interval. In the second half they scored twice more and McMillan completed his hat-trick.

As winter approached during the 1925-26 season, many of the teams found themselves facing a worsening financial situation. The general economic situation was poor and clearly was a mitigating factor. However, from the outset it became apparent that the small clubs involved would struggle to survive on meagre gate receipts given the travel costs and match fee guarantees required. Clubs like Galston, which had managed perfectly well in regional competitions attracting a few hundred spectators, now had to travel as far afield as Peebles and Annan in the south; Montrose and Brechin in the north. At this time Galston were censured by the SFL for reducing entrance fees below the minimum agreed in a vain attempt to boost crowds.

On Saturday 2nd January 1926 Galston lost 9-2 against Brechin City in a bottom of the table clash. The result saw Brechin leapfrog them off the bottom. Two players scored hat-tricks - Brown (4) and Milne (3). Cook scored both the Galston goals. *The Sunday Post* commented that "the game was quite keen throughout, with a little bit of bitterness, resulting in one of the visitors having to walk to the dressing room five minutes before the whistle sounded."

On Saturday 9th January Galston played what was to be their last game. They hosted Johnstone and incredibly they thrashed them recording their best SFL win at home. Leading 3-1 at half-time they went on to win 8-2. The goalfest started five minutes after the start when Bolland notched the first goal for Galston. Chalmers soon equalised but Watson then scored two for the home team who went into the interval 3-1 up. On resuming, Hillhouse scored a fourth for Galston, while Chalmers scored his and his side's second. Then Cook (2) and Bolland (2) scored goals in quick succession, Bolland completing his hat-trick. Their team for this last game was: Christie, McHarrow, White, Murdoch, Howitt, Gordon, Boyd, Watson, Bolland, Cook and Hillhouse.

On the 14th January 1926 Galston submitted a letter to the management committee of the League meeting being held in Glasgow intimating their resignation from the Scottish Football League. On the eve of their next game the following Saturday, away at Clackmannan, the *Glasgow Evening Times* reported that the club's financial difficulties had "led the club to sever its connection with the Third Division of the League. This decision, which was come to at a meeting of the club's supporters held during the week, at which Mr Abbott, the Secretary, made a statement on the position of the club's finances, has not come as a surprise. Kilmarnock is only five miles away, and large numbers of the Galstonians naturally prefer witnessing First League to Third League football. Although retiring from the League competition, it is the intention of the club to take part in this season's Ayrshire Cup competitions."

Galston didn't fulfil their fixture away at Clackmannan on Saturday the 16th and *The Sunday Post*, the following day, under the headline "Galston's Position Today", explained the position: "Withdrawal from the Third Division was the ultimate finding of a meeting of the club's members and supporters held during last week. Finance is the whole trouble. In their recent game with Johnstone at Galston the receipts were only a few shillings over £10, and the guarantee was £15. It has practically been failure all along the line. Had it not been for the efforts of an enterprising Supporters' Club (which has come to the rescue with about £100 since the season opened), Galston would have had to give up long ago....Apparently the Third Division is a bogey as far as Galston is concerned (and many other clubs, too, I fear), and Galston may have given to others the lead to follow."

Galston had completed 15 fixtures, which was exactly half of their programme, winning four, drawing four and losing seven. The rest of the Third Division clubs soldiered on but several teams were unable to complete their fixtures due to financial difficulties. At the end of the season the championship was withheld, and the Third Division was dissolved, with the bulk of the clubs being absorbed into the Scottish Alliance for a single season.

Galston continued as members of the Scottish Football Association and played in the Amateur League up to 1932 and then the Alliance before disbanding when war broke out. The Scottish Football Alliance in 1932 was a reserve league for senior teams but which also fielded a small number of other clubs. Galston left in 1938 when this League became exclusively a reserve team League.

During this time they played in the Scottish Cup on seven occasions, the last one in the 1937-38 season. On the 19th January 1929 they lost 7-1 at Albion Rovers, their biggest ever Cup defeat. The following year they lost 6-1 at Arbroath. In the 1933-34 competition they made it to the Second Round, beating Keith 8-2 at home on front of an 1100 crowd, but they lost to Ross County 3-1 in the next round. In January 1935 they went down 1-0 at home to Kilmarnock, in a match that attracted over 4,000 spectators. Their last appearance in the Scottish Cup came on the 22nd January 1938, when they lost 2-0 at Queen's Park. Under the headline "Galston's Gallant Fight", *The Scotsman* reported that "although never revealing the balance and precision of Queen's Park, Galston made a courageous stand in the tie at Hampden Park. They kept the amateurs at bay until close on the interval, and with more repose and confidence in front, might have crossed over with equality. Their strength, however, was chiefly concentrated in the rear. Upward, an agile cool, and daring goalkeeper, gave a display without a blemish, while Powell shielded his charge with determination...With McGhee in the pavilion, having collapsed through sheer exhaustion, Queen's Park threw the handicapped Galston side back, and shortly before the interval, Kinghorn scored. The amateurs' second goal was registered...half an hour after the restart. Shortly before this, Andrew, the Galston outside left, was carried off on a stretcher with a badly wrenched knee."

The Scottish Alliance was briefly re-formed in 1939 and Galston were invited to join, along with Nithsdale Wanderers and Vale of Leven but the competition was disbanded after only a few games because of the War. Galston FC subsequently disbanded. The A71 bypass now passes over the original site of their ground, although just to the south is a new public park bearing the same name.

SEASON	LEAGUE	P	W	D	L	F	A	P	POS
1923-24	SCOT-3	30	11	3	16	53	70	25	13/16
1924-25	SCOT-3	30	10	6	14	39	70	26	11/16
1925-26	SCOT-3	15	4	4	7	38	46	12	16/16

Gretna

Formed: 1946
Colours: All white with black trim
Ground: Raydale Park
Entered League: 2002. Elected to replace Airdrieonians
Number of League Seasons: 6
Highest League Finish: 12th in the Scottish Premier League
Honours: First Division Champions 2006-07, Second Division Champions 2005-06, Third Division Champions 2004-05
Left League: Resigned June 2008 following entering administration

It's hard to believe but at the turn of the new millennium Gretna FC were playing football in the non-League in England. At this time the town was better known for its staging of runaway weddings at the nearby Blacksmiths at Gretna Green. The club, formed in 1946, were playing south of the border in Division One of the English Unibond League. They had unsuccessfully applied for membership of the Scottish Football League in both 1994, securing only two votes (Inverness and Ross County elected) and then in 2000 (Peterhead and Elgin elected). They eventually entered the Scottish League for the 2002-03 season after successfully applying to replace the bankrupt Airdrieonians.

Within the space of a few years Gretna had made rapid progress through the divisions, winning the Scottish Football League Third, Second and First Division titles in successive seasons and reaching the final of the Scottish Cup in May 2006. Their fairy tale trip to Hampden was cruelly ended by a penalty shoot-out defeat to Hearts, but European qualification was secured on account of the Jambos entry into the qualifying rounds of the Champions League. Who would have thought that just five years after entering the Scottish Football League, Gretna would be playing in the top flight of Scottish football; would have been the first team from the third tier of the League to reach the final of the Scottish Cup since its reintroduction in 1975; and would have been playing in Europe, albeit the qualifying rounds of the UEFA Cup?

Gretna's rapid rise was bankrolled by their millionaire backer, entrepreneur Brooks Mileson. He essentially took a team from a village with a population of 3,000 and lived the dream. But their demise was even swifter after Mileson withdrew his support following an illness and they went out of business after relegation from the Scottish Premier League in 2008.

For the 1982-83 season Gretna joined the English Northern League's Second Division and were promoted at the first attempt. They then spent nine seasons in the First Division of the Northern League and were crowned champions in 1991 and 1992. For the 1992-93 season they entered into the Northern Premier League Division One and during this time they also entered the English FA Cup, taking Rochdale to a replay in the 1991-92 competition. They held the English Football League side to a 0-0 draw at home in November 1991 before losing the replay 3-1 at Spotland.

In 1994 their eyes turned north and over the border into Scotland. The Scottish League was being expanded from 38 clubs to 40 to allow for league reconstruction and a move from three divisions to four. The newly merged Inverness Caledonian Thistle topped the poll with 68 votes and fellow Highland League side Ross County secured the second spot with 57 votes. Rather embarrassingly Gretna came fifth and bottom in the voting gaining just two votes. Six years later they tried again. The top flight or Premier League was increased to twelve clubs and so in order for the Scottish League to continue with three divisions of ten clubs each, it had to admit two additional clubs. In a case of déjà vu two more Highland League clubs were chosen. Peterhead topped the ballot in this first round of voting and Elgin City obtained the second place on offer.

Gretna made it third time lucky when, at a meeting of the Scottish Football League on the 18th June 2002, Gretna were admitted to the League to replace the now-defunct Airdrieonians. Chairmen from the 27 SFL clubs entitled to vote chose the English Northern Premier League side ahead of six other applicants, including the new Airdrie United, Gala Fairydean, Cove Rangers, Huntly, Edinburgh City and Preston Athletic of the East of Scotland League. It basically came down to a straight choice between Gretna and Airdrie United. In the second ballot Gretna prevailed by 16 votes to 11. Gretna, having spent their career playing in England, now found themselves members of the Scottish Football League.

Gretna's rapid ascent up the leagues did not start immediately on joining the SFL. In their first season they finished mid-table in sixth. They played their first SFL game on Saturday 3rd August 2002, and they took just 19 seconds to mark their entry into the Third Division as they held one of the promotion favourites, Morton. Matt Henney collected a poor goal-kick from Morton's keeper Craig Coyle before firing low into the net to give them a dream start and to score their first ever Scottish League goal. But the visitors responded and a couple of crosses caused goalkeeper David Mathieson trouble before wing-back Derek Collins' ball was bundled into the net by Warren Hawke. The late introduction of Gretna player-boss Rowan Alexander sparked new life into the match, although the few chances created by both teams were spurned. The game ended in a 1-1 draw and the Gretna starting line-up for their first ever Scottish League game was: Mathieson, McGuffie, Skelton, Turner, Hewson, Henney, Skinner, Irons, Gordon, Dobie and Hore. A bumper crowd of 1,566 came to Raydale Park to witness the game, the game no doubt swelled by the novelty of the occasion and because they were playing the biggest team in the division. Future crowds would settle down around the 350-400 mark. Gretna made their debut in the Scottish Cup in the same season, beating Cove Rangers 3-0 in January 2003 before going out to Clyde in the next round.

The following season Gretna improved, rising up to third, although finishing nine points behind second placed Stirling Albion and eleven points behind champions Stranraer. It was after these first couple of seasons that Gretna really announced themselves. They won the Third Division title by a country mile in the 2004-05 season, securing promotion as early as March and the title in the first week of April. In the process they amassed 104 points, beating the previous record of 80 set by Forfar Athletic in the 1994-1995 season. In doing so they finished a massive 20 points ahead of Peterhead in second place and 47 points in front of the third placed team Cowdenbeath. They scored a total of 130 goals, just two short of matching Hearts' post-war record of 132. Their total was a new record for the Third Division, absolutely smashing the previous record of 87, jointly held by Ross County (1998-99) and Stranraer (2003-04). Their new record total was a massive 47 goals more. They more than doubled their tally from the previous season, when they scored 59 times in finishing third. They averaged 3.6 goals per game and won all 18 of their home games. Finally, they recorded a new record for the most consecutive League wins in the Third Division by winning 13 in a row, and then incredibly topped their own feat later in the season by winning their last 14 games.

The real turning point for the club had come when they were bought by a Durham-based businessman by the name of Brooks Mileson. This larger than life character was born in Sunderland in 1947 and made his fortune from a number of business ventures including various branches of the insurance, construction and property business. The chain-smoking millionaire, complete with his ponytail, looked more like an aging hippie than the usual image associated with a football chairman. As a devotee of grass-roots football he had given generously to other small clubs whilst bankrolling a team that generated crowds of less than a thousand. Mileson also endeared himself to the fans by shunning the directors' box and sitting in amongst the rank and file supporters. One significant factor, that would have an enormous bearing on the eventual outcome, was

Milseon's health. He had lost a kidney in childhood, had already suffered two hearts attacks and was also suffering from a debilitating chronic fatigue condition.

Gretna were managed by former Morton striker and Queen of the South manager Rowan Alexander. With Mileson's money behind him he was able to assemble a squad of players, which in terms of both quantity and quality was the envy of the division. Squads at this level are typically no more than 20 players and are characterised by the part-time nature of the players. Gretna had a squad of 30 and amongst these were a number of seasoned professionals. In an age when fees aren't really paid in the lower divisions, Alexander's pre-season signings included the veteran 35 year old striker David Bingham from Inverness Caledonian Thistle for £20,000 and defender Brian Gilfillan from Cowdenbeath for £10,000. In addition, Mileson's money meant the salary budget could accommodate more players and in a significant move striker Kenny Deuchar joined on a free from East Fife. Gretna's policy appeared to be based on the buying up of experienced players, some with an SPL pedigree and blending these with the best players outside of the top flight.

Other teams cried foul as Gretna stormed to the top amid calls that they had 'bought' promotion and that it was an unlevel playing field. But this has always been the case in football. It isn't equal. Teams have always had bigger transfer kitties or larger player salary budgets. It certainly didn't harm their cause when in the January transfer window – when already flying in the League – they went on a spending spree and bought David Graham, who joined from Stranraer for £75,000 and Dene Shields joined from Cowdenbeath for £30,000. In addition they signed the experienced midfielders Davie Nicholls from Falkirk and Steve Tosh from Aberdeen plus defenders Chris Innes from Dundee United and Derek Collins from Morton. Most of these new signings spent the second half of the season warming the subs bench and making occasional appearances, which only served to build up the resentment towards Mileson and the club.

Gretna set the tone for their 2004-05 campaign right from the off when they recorded a 6-0 win over Albion Rovers on the first day of the League season. However, they then experienced an early season stumble when they lost at Queen's Park and drew 1-1 with Peterhead, the latter topping the table. The Black and Whites of Gretna then went on a lengthy winning run. Between the 4th September and the New Year Gretna recorded 13 successive victories, smashing the record for the most consecutive wins by a Third Division team, surpassing Inverness Caledonian Thistle's record of 11. The sequence came to an end on the 3rd January 2005, when Queen's Park popped up again to hold them to a 1-1 draw. Included in this winning streak was a 5-1 win over East Fife, two 6-2 wins over Albion Rovers (home and away) and a narrow win over promotion rivals

Peterhead that took them to the top of the table – where they stayed for the rest of the season.

Gretna also scored eight goals on two occasions during this amazing sequence and it was around this time that people began to sit up and take notice. On the 16th October 2004 they met perennial strugglers East Stirling and thrashed them 8-1. The visitors took a surprise lead in the 9th minute when Derek Ure scored. Parity was restored just before the half hour mark when Mark Birch made it 1-1 and just two minutes later Gretna were ahead through Bryan Gilfillan. Then up stepped Kenny Deuchar. The part-time doctor, who had put his career on hold to join Gretna during the summer scored a hat-trick, his second of the season. Deuchar had been mainly used as a substitute in the early games of the season but got his chance against former club East Fife in late September. He featured in the starting line-up due to regular striker Andy Smith suffering from bruised ribs. He didn't disappoint scoring three in the 5-1 win. Deuchar scored twice in three minutes to give his club a half-time lead of four goals to one. Gavin Skelton made it 5-1 in the 54th minute and Deuchar completed his hat-trick just after the hour mark. Shire held out for a further twenty minutes before Brian Wake scored past the unfortunate Shire 'keeper, 19 year old Ross Gilpin, to make it seven in the 82nd minute. There was still time for one more as Ryan Baldacchino added an eighth in the last minute to complete the rout.

Soon after, on the 6th November, Gretna travelled to Central Park to take on Cowdenbeath. Gretna had narrowly won the corresponding home fixture 2-1 back in September but were now on a roll. Central midfielder Ryan McGuffie set Gretna on their way with the opener in the 12th minute. Full back Mark Birch then grabbed an unlikely eight-minute hat-trick, the middle one from the penalty spot and Ryan Baldacchino then made it five, and only half an hour had been played. In the 36th minute David Bingham got himself on the scoresheet and with no further goals the teams went into the interval with Gretna having put six past Cowden goalkeeper Andrew Carlin, and remember, this was away from home. Only two further goals were added, Bingham's second in the 52nd minute and Kenny Deuchar's in the 86th minute. Playing for the home side that day was Dene Shields who would later sign for the Black and Whites. This was Gretna's seventh successive win in which 37 goals had been scored and also a club record away win.

The week before Christmas the record for consecutive wins was claimed with a 3-0 home win over Stenhousemuir. David Bingham opened the scoring after only four minutes, with Ryan McGuffie and Bryan Gilfillan getting the others. The win also earned the players a Christmas present from Brooks Mileson consisting of a trip to La Manga in

Spain. The colourful chairman had promised them the trip earlier in the season if they were top of the league by Christmas.

The run of wins came to an end at Queen's Park on the 3rd January 2005 when Gretna drew 1-1. Two games later the unbeaten run was also ended, when they lost 4-2 away at Peterhead. But Gretna bounced right back, winning the next 14 League games in a row, a sequence which took them right through to the end of the season. During this run they scored 54 times and conceded just six. Averaging nearly four goals a game in this sequence they scored just one away at Cowdenbeath on the 5th March 2005. However, the goal was priceless as it was the one that secured promotion for them – after just 27 games. Steve Tosh, the former Aberdeen midfielder scored with a spectacular first half strike. The win took them to an unassailable 35-point lead over their third-placed hosts and in the process confirmed the fastest-ever promotion from the Third Division and the earliest from any Scottish division since Morton won the Second Division title in 1964.

Mid-way through March, and as if to emphasise their superiority in the League, Gretna thrashed second placed, and one-time rivals Peterhead by 6-1. Kenny Deuchar grabbed a hat-trick as Gretna stretched their lead to 13 points at the top of the Division with a rout of their title rivals. Deuchar's first, as early as the fourth minute, brought up the century of goals for the club and took him to a personal tally of 33, which was more than the entire squads at East Fife, Albion Rovers and East Stirling had managed between them.

On the 9th April 2005 Gretna secured the Third Division title in style, thrashing Stenhousemuir 7-0. It took Gretna half an hour to open the scoring from a header from captain Andy Aitken, but once they did the proverbial floodgates opened. Gavin Skelton made it two just four minutes later and then a stunning strike from leading scorer Kenny Deuchar made it three at half-time. Rowan Alexander's men went into the game needing just a point to take the title and the three points were effectively gained in the first period of play. Gretna introduced Northern Irishman Bryan Gilfillan and Mark Birch after the break to replace Steve Tosh and Derek Collins but the shuffling of the pack did not affect the team as they put four more past Willie McCulloch in the Stennie goal in the second half. Three goals in eight minutes from Deuchar, David Bingham and Bryan Gilfillan and then a late goal from Andy Smith (also on as a substitute) made the final result 7-0. Deuchar's double took his goal tally to 38 with strike partner Bingham sitting on 25. A crowd of 908 at Raydale, double the divisional average, watched the game and celebrated the title win.

Ten further goals in two games now took their league tally to 124. On the 30th April 2005 Gretna completed their home League fixtures for the season against bottom club East Stirling. A high scoring home win was no doubt expected but in the end the Black and Whites only won 1-0. In an otherwise dull encounter, Ryan Baldacchino's 16th-minute goal secured the club the remarkable feat of winning every single home game during the season. But the solitary goal meant that any lingering hopes of the club securing a new overall League goalscoring record were quashed. The club now stood at 125 league goals for the season and needed to score an improbable eighteen goals in their final fixture. The Gretna goal avalanche did continue right to the last day of the season as the team thumped Albion Rovers 5-0 at Cliftonhill (in four fixtures against Rovers they scored 23 goals without reply). While both Ryan Baldacchino and Ryan McGuffie fired in two each and Gavin Skelton also got on the scoresheet, Gretna's win over Albion Rovers left them on 130, a dozen short of the total achieved by Raith Rovers in the Second Division during season 1937-38. Raith played 34 games, two fewer than Gretna. Striker Kenny Deuchar easily shattered the Third Division scoring record of 24 previously held by Michael Moore of Stranraer and David MacFarlane of Hamilton by scoring 38 League goals and 41 overall (including six hat-tricks). Fellow striker David Bingham ended up with 28 goals.

Success in the Second Division swiftly followed and the title was won with a massive 18 point cushion. They opened the League season with a 5-1 win over Forfar Athletic In August. Barry Sellars put Forfar ahead after 15 minutes, before Ryan McGuffie levelled from the spot after David Bingham was pulled down in the box. Bingham chipped Colin Meldrum for the second and lethal marksman Kenny Deuchar made it 3-1 before half time with a well-taken effort. Substitute James Grady marked his debut with a 73rd-minute goal, with David Nicholls completing the rout two minutes later.Gretna went the first 17 games unbeaten before surprisingly losing at home to Forfar in December. They then won seven out of eight matches including beating Partick Thistle 6-1 in January 2006, and a month later they beat Stirling Albion 5-0 away from home. On the 25th March Gretna secured the Second Division title and promotion at the first time of asking after coming back from a goal behind to defeat Alloa Athletic. A few weeks later they beat Stirling Albion 6-0 thanks to a first-half hat-trick by Steve Tosh and they eventually finished a massive 18 points clear of Morton.

The 2005-06 season was also the year of their famous Scottish Cup run, which saw them account for First Division leaders St Mirren and also St Johnstone. The remarkable Gretna story continued as they swept Dundee aside 3-0 in the Semi-final to reach the Scottish Cup final. In doing so they became the first team from the Second Division to reach the Final since a third tier was introduced in the 1975-76 season. Their defeat of Dundee meant that they reached the final without meeting a top flight side but this shouldn't distract from their achievement. As for the Semi-final match itself, Kenny Deuchar opened the scoring on the stroke of half-time from a tight angle. Ryan McGuffie scored from the penalty spot and Dundee, who posed little threat, conceded an own goal on 82 minutes.

In the Final played on the 13th May 2006 they gave a great account of themselves against Hearts, only losing out in a penalty shoot-out, the cruellest of endings to their fairytale march to the Scottish Cup Final. A penalty shoot-out looked unlikely after Hearts made an impressive start. Rudi Skacel tucked away a close-range strike six minutes before the break to give Hearts a deserved lead. Gretna caused a sensation by getting back on level terms after John O'Neil was tripped by Cesnauskis to win a 75th minute penalty kick. McGuffie's spot-kick was saved by Craig Gordon but the same player followed up to hit home the rebound and the match went to extra-time. Hearts dominated the extra half hour's play and Skacel hit the post and Main was called upon to make a super save to block a fierce Hartley effort. Hearts had Paul Hartley sent off towards the end of extra time, dismissed after picking up a second yellow card, and the game went to a penalty shoot-out. Hearts scored all four going first. Grady and Birch scored but Derek Townsley and Gavin Skelton missed from the spot to give Hearts the trophy 4-2 on penalties.

The one consolation was that as Hearts had finished third in the SPL and qualified for Europe via the League, Gretna now found themselves in Europe, although their campaign was short-lived, eliminated by Derry in a qualifying round. The Gretna Scottish Cup final line-up was: Main, Birch, Townsley, Innes, Nicholls (Graham 55), McGuffie, Tosh, O'Neil, Skelton, Grady and Deuchar (McQuilken 103).

The First Division or the Championship as it is now known was, and still is, a very competitive division and at the time featured Livingston, Hamilton, Dundee and St Johnstone. Nevertheless, Gretna also stormed through this division, especially in the early to mid-part of the season. They opened the 2006-07 League season on the 5th August, delivering a warning to the rest of the First Division with a 6-0 demolition of Hamilton at Raydale Park. The newly-promoted side opened the scoring after just 14 minutes when a Steve Tosh blasted in a shot. Bad goalkeeping then allowed Tosh to fire in from a tight angle and James Grady chipped in before half time. Tosh completed his hat-trick with a superb 15-yard strike after 48 minutes. New-boy Brendan McGill and David Graham completed the rout.

Gretna won their first four games and although they then subsequently lost 4-0 at home to Dundee they emphatically thrashed Patrick Thistle 6-0 away at the end of

September to top the First Division. They then failed to win in the next four matches before winning five in a row including all four games played in the month of November.

By mid-January 2007 they had a 12 point lead of over second placed St Johnstone but they somehow contrived to squander this lead, winning only three more games from the end of January to the end of March. Perhaps of a sign of things to come, economic considerations started to come more to the fore in the shape of the release of the experienced players, albeit on the pretext of lowering the age of the squad. In another twist, manager Rowan Alexander, rewarded with a five year contract extension in May 2005, suddenly went off work with an apparent stress-related illness in March 2007. Mystery surrounded his absence and head-coach Davie Irons stepped up and it was during this time that Gretna's 12 point lead at the top of the division was whittled away by Owen Coyle's Perth side.

A dour midweek 0-0 draw at Airdrie United at the beginning of April was followed up by a disastrous 2-0 home defeat to the chasing St Johnstone, in which Jason Scotland scored both goals in the first half. Gretna's points advantage was now down to five points with three to play. The following week Gretna drew 0-0 at Hamilton whereas the Saints won against Clyde to whittle the lead down to three points. The following weekend saw the same sequence of results as Gretna were held 0-0 at home to Clyde whereas St Johnstone beat Queen of the South 4-0.

Gretna's title challenge therefore went to the final game of the season. They had to travel to Dingwall to face a Ross County side that had to win to avoid relegation. Second-top St Johnstone were away to third-placed Hamilton Academical where they swept into a three-goal. Meanwhile, up in Dingwall, Michael Gardyne had blasted County into the lead from the edge of the box, but Gretna had drawn level four minutes later when Grady's flick from a Nicholls free-kick was saved by Craig Samson and Nicky Deverdics scrambled the ball home. Grady then broke clear to slip the ball through the advancing goalkeeper's legs to give Gretna the half-time lead. Early in the second half the pendulum swung St Johnstone's way when Ross County drew level. A Gardyne cross was headed on by Don Cowie and O'Carroll bundled in the equaliser. St Johnstone increased their own lead to 4-2 before a third goal for their hosts in the 88th minute set up a tense finale. As their game finished with a 4-3 win the game at Dingwall was still going and St Johnstone were denied promotion in a dramatic finish. Gretna were a matter of seconds away from finishing second to St Johnstone before James Grady scored in the final minute of the final game to hand Gretna an amazing victory that clinched a third consecutive promotion. David Graham set up Grady to score which promoted Gretna to the SPL for the first time in their history with their third title in a row.

Gretna's meteoric rise had not proved universally popular and some were quick to point out that the existing SPL clubs would undoubtedly have preferred a club able to attract a greater number of fans, such as St Johnstone. Plans to redevelop their Raydale Park into a 6,000 all-seated stadium to meet SPL standards, were revealed in 2006 but they were forced into a groundsharing agreement in terms of playing their home matches at Motherwell's Fir Park as their Raydale ground did not meet SPL rules demanding a minimum 6,000-capacity.

Life in the SPL proved a step too far for Gretna. Their SPL debut was overshadowed by a bizarre appearance at the game by former manager Alexander. He had been airbrushed out of Gretna's history and was refused entry into Fir Park apparently seeking to do his job. Out on the pitch the club struggled with the step up in class, winning only one of their first 16 games, losing 12. Attendances for their home matches were embarrassingly low. On the 27th October 2007 Gretna hosted Inverness and only 1,092 fans attended – a new SPL record. The game was lost 4-0 prompting claims of 'No fans, no goals and no fight'.

Things were beginning to unravel and turn sour. In November 2007 Rowan Alexander was formally dismissed, with the club releasing a statement, saying: "Gretna FC can confirm that Rowan Alexander has been dismissed after an extensive investigation and internal procedure." Alexander immediately announced he would contest the decision, with the case to go before an employment tribunal.

In the January transfer window the club started off-loading players, replacing experienced pros with youth players and loan signings. They sold Colin McMenamin to Dundee and Danny Grainger to Dundee United. One high profile departure was Kenny Deuchar, who left to join Major League Soccer team Real Salt Lake in the US. They also released nine players including Ryan McGuffie, David Graham, and Niall Henderson, and sent some senior players out on loan like David Bingham and brought in a load of youth players in their places.

In February 2008 rumours of unpaid wages surfaced and uncertainty was fuelled by the illness of the club's benefactor Brooks Mileson, with a brain infection. Mileson went into hospital on the 12th, and as he was responsible for the payroll, no wages were paid. On the 22nd Mileson came out of hospital and the delayed payments were made on the 25th. However, during this time Manager Davie Irons jumped ship to join Morton, with Mick Wadsworth taking over the reins. By this time they were nine points adrift at the bottom, having accumulated only 13 points from 25 games.

On the 6th March 2008 Gretna set a further unwanted record with another all-time low crowd for an SPL game. Only 501 turned up for the midweek game against Dundee United, although there were mitigating factors as the game had been postponed twice already in six days. (This record was reduced still further, when on the 5th April Gretna hosted Inverness Caledonian thistle at Fir Park; the game being watched by only 431 people).

A few days later Brooks Mileson formally withdrew his funding for the club and things began to unravel pretty quickly. An administrator was called in as it emerged that the club had debts estimated at £4 million, including over £350,000 which was said to be owed to the Inland Revenue. Former boss Rowan Alexander also had an outstanding claim for £800,000 and the club was in arrears on its ground-sharing payments with Motherwell.

The silence from the Mileson camp was deafening and no explanations or statements were issued on his behalf. Instead the Administrators confirmed the club was running at a substantial weekly loss, which had been funded out of Mileson's pocket over the years, to the tune of £8 million. Obviously they couldn't allow this to continue and 27 staff in total, including a number of first team players were made redundant on the 26th March. One of the early casualties was Scottish Cup captain Chris Innes and other notable players forcibly leaving were David Bingham, Mark Birch and David Mathieson.

On the 20th March a six figure cash advance from SPL chiefs meant that the club were able to see themselves through to the end of the season and fulfil their fixtures although they were docked ten points for entering administration, which effectively sealed their fate on the pitch and condemned them to relegation. Summing up the situation, former Chief Executive Graeme Muir was quoted as saying that "we relied on one man; on his health and his wealth." Rather less charitably, St Johnstone chairman Geoff Brown was quoted as saying "they talked about living the dream and some people bought it...As far as I'm concerned, people were misled by an ego-tripper who was looking after number one." Gretna's meteoric rise was not universally popular and their collapse in 2008 is seen by their critics as the consequence of the club overreaching itself. On the 23rd April details emerged of almost £4m debt with over 130 creditors.

Gretna finished the season with a 0-0 draw at St Mirren and, on the 13th May 2008, in what would turn out to be their last ever fixture, they beat Hearts at Fir Park 1-0. Gavin Skelton's 90th minute goal gave Gretna victory over 10-man Hearts. The last Gretna side to take the field was: Fleming, Barr, Griffiths, Hall, Naughton, McGill, Osman, Meynell, Skelton, Deverdics, Hogg. Ironically, in their last six games, they had experienced their best run, losing only once in six games. A few days after this game the remaining 40 staff were laid off by the administrators.

At the Scottish Football League's AGM Gretna applied for membership due to their relegation from the Scottish Premier League. But with doubts about the loss-making operation and the club not being able to fulfil a full season's worth of fixtures the SFL took the decision to demote them two divisions and place them whence they came – back into the Third Division. Sadly, when the only potential buyers' business plan was rejected, the administrators concluded that the club was no longer viable as an ongoing concern and they duly resigned from the Scottish Football League on the 3rd June 2008, bringing to an end their six year adventure as a senior club.

Things then turned full circle as the SFL then called a special general meeting for the 3rd July 2008 and invited clubs to apply to take the vacant spot, just as Gretna had done to replace the defunct Airdrieonians in 2002. Five clubs put themselves forward: Spartans, Edinburgh City and Preston Athletic from the East of Scotland League; Annan Athletic from the South of Scotland League; and Cove Rangers from the outskirts of Aberdeen, the Highland League champions.

Spartans were the bookies' favourites, but the Edinburgh outfit dropped out of the running after the second round, having amassed just six votes. Fellow East of Scotland League teams Edinburgh City and Preston Athletic had already been eliminated in the first round of voting so that in the end it came down to a choice between Annan and Cove. With a minimum of 15 votes required from the 29 clubs, Annan had polled 14 in the earlier rounds, just one short of the required number and in the deciding round they polled 17 votes with Cove collecting 12 votes.

Annan were therefore chosen ahead of three clubs who finished ahead of them in that season's East of Scotland League. Annan finished seventh, 19 points behind third-top Spartans, with Edinburgh City in fourth and Preston in fifth. Crucially it was felt that Annan were, at present, the most capable of meeting the League's criteria, having already had in place their 3,500-capacity Galabank Stadium. Once bitten, it is perhaps understandable that the Scottish Football League's members were not shy in adopting a safety-first policy by voting Annan Athletic into their ranks. One further factor was a possible desire to keep football in the area as Annan are only seven miles away from the defunct club.

On 2 July 2008, the Gretna Supporters' Society, a trust, founded a new Gretna club. This club was not a continuation of the old club, and technically, as the old Gretna was not formally wound up until the 8th August, the two clubs briefly existed side by side.

To distinguish the club, its founding year was incorporated into the name, and they are known as Gretna 2008. At the end of July the new club joined the East of Scotland League, taking the place of Annan Athletic but with Raydale Park bound up in the administration of the old club, the new club based themselves in...Annan, playing their home matches at the Everholm Stadium. In the following May the new owners of Raydale allowed the new club to return and in 2011 the ground was sold back to the club. In 2013 the club entered the new Lowland League, which, via the new pyramid system, offers a route back to the SFL. In December 2019 former manager Rowan Alexander made a surprise return to the new Gretna club to take up the managerial reins once more.

In one last tragic act, five months to the day that the club had resigned, former benefactor Brooks Mileson passed away. He was found unconscious at his home at Blackford, near Carlisle, on the morning of the 3rd November and later died at the Cumberland Infirmary in Carlisle. He undoubtedly was a colourful character, who 'lived the dream' or unkindly indulged his fantasy. He was the epitome of a successful businessman who comes to discover that all business acumen and rationale disappear out of the window when it comes to owning a football club. He may have been naïve but he did things with the best of intentions. His death brought to an end one of the most colourful passages of Scottish football history.

2002-03	SCOT-3	36	11	12	13	50	50	45		6/10
2003-04	SCOT-3	36	20	8	8	59	39	68		3/10
2004-05	SCOT-3	36	32	2	2	130	29	98		1/10
2005-06	SCOT-2	36	28	4	4	97	30	88		1/10
2006-07	SCOT-1	36	19	9	8	70	40	66		1/10
2007-08	SCOT P	38	5	8	25	32	83	15	*	12/12

* Points deducted for entering administration

Helensburgh

Formed: 1896
Colours: Red shirts, navy blue shorts
Ground: Ardencaple Park
Entered League: 1923. Founder members of the Third Division
Number of League Seasons: 3
Honours: None – see below
Highest League Finish: 1st in Division Three. The club were leading the Third Division but as not all the games were played, no Championship was awarded
Left League: 1926. Division Three abandoned. Wound up 1928

The town of Helensburgh was founded in 1776 as a planned spa town by Sir James Colquhoun who named it after his wife Helen. Helensburgh became a favourite place of residence for the industrial barons from Glasgow and one of these, the publishing tycoon Walter Blackie, had a house designed and built for him in 1903 by the renowned architect Charles Rennie Mackintosh, the Hill House, now cared for by the National Trust for Scotland. Situated on the northern coast of the Firth of Clyde at the mouth of the Gareloch and a short distance from Loch Lomond, Helensburgh later became a holiday resort for Glaswegians.

Football in the area was dominated in the early days by the likes of neighbouring Vale of Leven, Renton and Dumbarton but a Helensburgh club first appeared in 1874 and entered the Scottish Cup, in its second season. The played their first Cup-tie on the 17th October 1874, beating the 3rd Edinburgh Rifle Volunteers 3-0 in the First Round, before losing to eventual beaten finalists Renton 2-0 in the next round.

This original club continued to feature in these early Scottish Cups and in the 1875-76 season they reached the Third Round. In the 1878-79 competition the club knocked out Hearts and Hibs in a run to the Semi-finals where they were eventually beaten by holders and local rivals Vale of Leven 3-0. Yes, Helensburgh, Scottish Cup Semi-finalists! In the first three rounds they accounted for Kilmarnock Thistle 4-0, Alexandria 4-1 and Shaugran of Campsie 2-0. In the next two rounds they knocked out the top Edinburgh clubs.

In the Fourth Round they beat Hearts 2-1, on the 30th November 1878. *The Scotsman* reported that "the champion Association club of the East of Scotland, having lost the toss, had to journey to Helensburgh to play off the tie with Helensburgh. The game was very fast, remarkable for rough play, and was played from beginning to end under protest, Helensburgh objecting to the referee brought by the Hearts from a neutral club in Glasgow, and insisting on playing with the referee chosen by themselves. Pullen scored a goal for the Heart in the first half, while the first goal got by Helensburgh in the second half was disputed on the ground of the player being offside. Close on time Helensburgh scored a goal." The victorious Helensburgh team was: MacMillan; Lumsden, MacGregor; McEwan, Boyle; Boyle, Paton, Patterson, MacLeod, MacKinlay and Goodwin.

There was a bit of a break before they played Hibs, away in Edinburgh at the Powderhall grounds, on the 8th March 1879. Helensburgh had a goal disallowed before Hibs took the lead. Helensburgh responded by storming the Edinburgh goal and McLeod equalised. In the second half Hibs had a goal ruled out before Boyle scored the winner. The Helensburgh team that beat Hibs was: Smith; Lumsden, MacGregor; Strachan, McEwan; Boyle, Paton, Patterson, MacLeod, MacKinlay and Goodwin. Helensburgh secured a bye in the Quarter-finals and in the Semi-finals drew the holders and two time winner Vale of Leven, losing out 3-0.

Other early notable Scottish Cup ties included a 7-0 loss to Dumbarton in October 1879, a 4-1 Third Round loss to Vale of Leven in 1880 and a 6-2 win over a team from Loch Lomond in the 1881-82 competition. This club then disappeared in 1882 and two other very short-lived clubs were formed in 1885 and 1886.

A fourth incarnation was born in 1896 and competed in the Dunbartonshire Cup. Initially a straight knockout competition, at the end of the 19th Century, the competition adopted a league format with the top two playing off in a final. Nicknamed 'The Burgh', the club's colours were red shirts and blue shorts, and they played their games at Ardencaple Park, the ground drawing its name from a nearby castle/tower and a wood and farm. The ground was located north of Rhu Road Higher. A cricket ground was adjacent to this road and the football ground was a short distance away to the north-west.

After a lengthy absence Helensburgh made another appearance in the Scottish Cup in 1922, drawn away at Second Division Bathgate. Bathgate opened the scoring from a penalty kick but Hamill equalised for Helensburgh just before half-time. Bathgate got another penalty at the start of the second half which they scored from and then went further ahead. In the closing stages Helensburgh pushed on and Hamill scored a second but they couldn't get on level terms before the game ended. Although they lost, the performance and result showed they could compete with a team from the Second Division.

In 1922 Helensburgh joined the Western League and just a year later were playing in the Scottish Football League, when the majority of clubs from this competition were incorporated into the new Third Division. They made a poor start to their League membership, finishing 15th, or second from bottom, with only Brechin City below them. They won just five of their thirty fixtures. On the 18th August 1923 they played their first ever SFL game, a home match at Ardencaple. A crowd of a 1,000 saw Helensburgh lose 2-0 against Arthurlie. The visitors scored after ten minutes but it was a game of few chances after that, with defences generally on top. Arthurlie scored a second, with *The Sunday Post* reporting that "Mercer, Roberts and Wharrier were best for Helensburgh."

The following Saturday they scored their first League goals in 4-3 defeat away against Mid-Annandale at Kintail Park. Mids took an early lead after just seven minutes. Murray then scored Helensburgh's first SFL goal before a quarter of an hour had passed. Mids scored twice more, either side of the interval before Roberts got another for Burgh from the penalty spot following a handball. Helensburgh thought they had claimed their first League point when Murray equalised seven minutes from time but Groves of the Mids was brought down in the box and had to be carried off. Robb stepped up to score from the spot and won the game for the hosts.

Two further defeats followed but in their fifth League match they finally got their first points, a 4-3 win at Beith at Bellsdale Park on the 6th October 1923. Beith were inferior in the first half but played better in the second period and nearly snatched a draw. As a result of the two points earned Helensburgh moved off the bottom, above Brechin City who were still pointless. Burgh picked up further wins against Galston and Brechin but then went 13 games without a win between the 1st December 1923 and the 1st March 1924, when they finally beat Montrose 4-0. Included in this sequence was a 5-0 loss to eventual champions Arthurlie, their biggest ever SFL defeat.

On the 29th March 1924 they recorded their best win of the season, a 6-1 victory over Royal Albert of Larkhall. *The Sunday Post* reported that "Helensburgh were in great scoring form against Royal Albert and the one goal lead at half-time did not suggest the debacle that was in store for the Royalists. Shaw was the marksman, but it was after the cross-over the goals came thick and fast. The Larkhall lads went through it, the goalscorers being McKechnie (2), Lawrie, Shaw and Wyllie for Helensburgh." This was the highlight of an otherwise poor season in which they finished second from bottom, just three points above last place.

The 1924-25 season represented a big improvement as they finished a mid-table seventh place. They got off to another bad start though. They lost their opening game at home against Vale of Leven, *The Sunday Post,* under the headline "No Vale of Tears" reporting that "Helensburgh proved no match for Vale of Leven in their opening game at home, and were well beaten by four goals to one. Burns opened the scoring for the Vale, and although Lawrie netted for Helensburgh from a penalty kick the Vale never allowed their opponents to seriously threaten the issue." They only picked up two draws from their first four games and by the end of November they were again second from bottom, with only five points from their first ten fixtures, with only winless Mid-Annandale beneath them.

Their first game of December 1924 was the start of a turnaround in fortunes. Helensburgh scored eight times in an 8-4 win over Beith, their biggest score but not their biggest winning margin that would come a year later. *The Sunday Post* reported that "although Helensburgh made a pretty tame start in the Third Division, they have been doing some wonderful things recently...and yesterday they trounced Beith to the tune of eight goals to four. This was a home achievement, of course, but it convincingly indicates that they have sharpshooters to aid them....It must be explained, of course that Beith had to play with only ten men during the second half....Helensburgh, after the first twenty minutes, had little difficulty in rising superior to their opponents. The first goal was the outcome of a nice bit of play on the part of the home forwards, Lawrie and Miller carrying the ball up the left wing, Fleming into the centre, and Blair opened the scoring for Helensburgh, giving Gillespie no chance. Play was no sooner kicked off before Blair had it in the net for a second time after a pass by Miller....Shortly before half-time Blair added a third goal for Helensburgh after a fine solo run. Beith started the second portion with ten men, McGlasson, the right back, having to retire during the first half, owing to the ball striking him hard on the head. It was all Helensburgh for a time, and they added another three goals before Beith counted...[and scored three]...The last fifteen minutes were brisk, the home team scoring twice and Beith once. The scorers for Helensburgh were Blair (5), Lawrie (2) and Kesson." The win lifted them up a place above Dumbarton Harp and they were now only one point behind three other clubs, including the vanquished Beith. Burgh then won three of their next four matches and by the end of 1924 they were up to 12th place.

On the 17th January 1925 Helensburgh lost 5-0 at Peebles to equal their heaviest ever SFL defeat. It was 0-0 at half-time but then Peebles rearranged their front line, putting

Gossman to centre-forward and he duly scored a second half hat-trick in a 5-0 thrashing. They responded well to this set back and later in the month they took Second Division Bo'ness to two replays in the Scottish Cup. Bo'ness, who were going well in fourth place in their division, were held to a 1-1 draw at their Newton Park ground, with a number of papers calling it a "surprise". *The Scotsman* commented that "Helensburgh made a plucky fight at Bo'ness, and forced a replay. A goal scored by Smillie for the western team in the closing minutes of the first half was more than Bo'ness had bargained for, and, although they equalised shortly after the resumption, they never appeared to recover from the shock. It was something unusual for Bo'ness to be a goal down on their own ground. Bo'ness were the masters of their opponents in speed and craft, but the Third Division League team struggled on until the finish. Their defence, and notable McSkimming and McLellan, were the mainstays for the visitors."

The replay, staged a few days later, attracted a record gate of 2,500 at Ardencaple Park, with the winners drawn at Raith. Under the headline "Still Undivided" *The Scotsman* reported that "from start to finish the game was fast and keen, and ended in a goalless draw, even although half an hour's extra play was allowed in the hope of a decision being reached. On the afternoon's showing the home lot were value for a win, being superior in almost every department to their opponents, and taking into account ground advantage, it looked for a considerable time as if they would qualify for entry into the next round. Their forward line were, however, slow to make use of the many opportunities which came their way, and when they did put forth an effort lack of finishing and over-anxiety caused their attempts at goal-scoring to prove of no avail. On many occasions Helensburgh proved dangerous, but Hilligan, who had charge of the Bo'ness goal, showed himself to be a keeper of no mean ability by warding off many well-directed tries. The visiting defence, however, readily held the home team in check, and were responsible in great measure for saving their team from defeat."

The second replay was held on the 3rd February and this time Helensburgh were beaten 2-0, in a game they should have won. Playing at the neutral ground of Firhill, in front of 4,000 spectators, they were let down by poor finishing. *The Scotsman* noted that "Bo'ness were decidedly fortunate in overcoming Helensburgh in the Scottish Cup first round replay at Firhill Park, Glasgow. Helensburgh's failure is attributable to two facts – weak finishing on the part of their forwards, and the dour, determined defence of Hilligan, Anderson and Girvan [of Bo'ness]. Only four minutes had gone when Bo'ness took the lead. Goodwin forced a corner; his flagkick found the Helensburgh defence in a tangle, and before they could recover Goodwin dashed in, and headed the ball into the net. Splendidly supported by a clever and resourceful half-back line, the Helensburgh forwards made determined efforts to get on level terms again, but although they sorely harassed the Bo'ness defence, all their efforts went for nothing.

Twenty minutes after the restart Stewart put the issue beyond doubt when he lobbed the ball over the heads of the opposing defenders into the net." The Helensburgh line-up for the games was: McDonald; Thomson, McClellan; Wilson, McSkimming, Fraser; McKechnie, Kesson, Shaw, Smillie and Miller.

Although out of the Cup Helensburgh had a strong finish to the League season. They recorded a 5-0 win over Montrose and then beat eventual champions Nithsdale 4-0. *The Sunday Post* noted that "Helensburgh were in happy mood against Nithsdale Wanderers, and the latter will not readily forget their visit to the West. No goals were recorded in the opening half, a state of affairs principally due to splendid goalkeeping on the part of Armour in the visitors' goal. Once Helensburgh got on the lead, however, they made no mistake about keeping it. Smillie got the first goal, Fraser a second, Shand the third and Blair, after failing at a penalty, the fourth. It was a clever victory for Helensburgh." They ended the season with another 5-0 win, this time over Galston. In this game Kesson opened the scoring after just five minutes. Blair, their new centre-forward scored two but missed a chance of his hat-trick when his spot kick hit the bar, after McKechnie had been fouled. Fraser made it four just before the interval and Blair did eventually get his hat-trick, scoring the only goal in the second half. The season had been one of progress on the pitch and the club went into the 1925-26 harbouring realistic promotion ambitions.

The new season would prove to be their best, but also their last. They were leading the Third Division when it was abandoned but as not all games were played, no Championship was awarded, and there was no automatic promotion. Leading club official and President Frank McMillan took charge for the new season and after an opening day defeat away at Forfar the club won four of the next five and drew the other. By mid-October they were fourth in the table, four points off the top but having played three games less.

Burgh then went on to win six out of their next seven games including a record margin win of 6-0 over Galston on the 5th December. *The Sunday Post* under the headline "Helensburgh's Day" reported on the game: "The opening stages of the game at Helensburgh gave the impression that Galston would carry off the honours, as their forwards during that period hovered round the home area. But the Helensburgh goal remained intact. It was a different story with the Garelochside team, who, whenever a chance was presented, took advantage of it, with the result that ere the interval three goals had been registered. The first fell to Cowan, who easily netted after clever forward combination. Smillie was credited with the other two, obtaining them both from a couple of rare passes by Miller. The second half was a repetition of the first, Galston playing a good game in the open, but failing miserably at goal. Three goals were added, the marksmen being Cowan, Miller and Kesson. The big margin, however, was not quite a true reflection of the play." In a sign of things to come though their vanquished opponents would resign from the League in mid-season just over a month later. The result saw Helensburgh go top for the first time, level on points with Forfar Athletic, who had played two games less as their match away at Peebles was postponed due to frost.

The following weekend Burgh won away 2-0 at Solway Star, Roberts and Peters taking their chances when the Annan forwards did not. Forfar also won though, edging a close game 3-2 over Royal Albert. Both teams were being pursued by Vale of Leven who were just a point further back. On Saturday 19th December only three games survived the winter snow, with the top three all in action. Burgh went down 2-0 at Dykehead in circumstances similar to their big win over Galston. This time it was they that dominated the play but who missed their chances. *The Sunday Post* reported that "clever forward play by the whole Helensburgh front line marked the opening stages of their game with Dykehead at Shotts, but though they had the better of matters in the outfield for a time, they could not get goals. Faulty elevation on the one hand, and good saving on the art of Hepburn, kept them out. Thomson, the Helensburgh right-back, gave away a penalty by forcibly bringing down Rankin, and the latter beat Wallace from the spot. The goal got by O'Hair in the second half was a good one...Fraser was the pick of the halfs on the Helensburgh side. Near the end Wallace was not too sure in his clearances." It was mixed fortunes for their promotion rivals. Forfar also lost, 2-1 at Mid-Annandale but Vale thumped Lochgelly 8-2 and therefore leapfrogged to the top, one point above the other two, although Helensburgh had a game in hand on them.

All of the Boxing Day games were postponed due to the snow but it had cleared as the teams entered 1926. In the New Year's Day games Forfar beat the new leaders Vale 6-2, whilst Helensburgh went down 1-0 in Lockerbie against Mid-Annandale. Forfar now led with 23 points, Vale of Leven were second with 22 points and Helensburgh were third with 21; the games played by the respective sides also counting down sequentially: 18, 17,16. Wins for Helensburgh, over Montrose (coming from behind with goals from Smillie and Stirling) but also for Forfar now established these as the top two with Vale not playing.

On the 9th January 1926 Helensburgh thrashed Royal Albert 5-1 win, coming from behind to do so. Helensburgh hit the crossbar and post before the visitors took an unexpected lead. Wilson equalised for Burgh from a corner and a few minutes later another corner saw Helensburgh take the lead through Roberts. Due to an injury sustained to Kesson in the first half Burgh emerged with only ten players but that didn't seem to affect them, as Stirling, their centre-forward scored three goals in quick succession. The table remained unchanged with both their rivals winning.

On the 14th January fellow Third Division side Galston submitted a letter to the Management Committee of the League meeting being held in Glasgow intimating their resignation from the SFL. The following Saturday Helensburgh hosted Vale of Leven at Ardencaple and the meeting of the county rivals drew a large crowd, who witnessed Helensburgh's first home defeat this season, and their heaviest ever SFL home defeat. The Burgh were the first to attack but the Vale defence held firm and after ten minutes the visitors took the lead through Crawford. Helensburgh made many attempts to equalise but O'Neill in the opponent's goal was having a fine game. Vale added two more before Peters scored for the home team right on the call for half-time. The second half was strongly fought out and Crawford, for Vale, completed a hat-trick. *The Sunday Post* match report summarised by saying that "the home team were not in luck's way. They had almost as much of the play as the visitors, but O'Neill was a hero in the Vale goal."

While their rivals were in Scottish Cup action the following weekend Helensburgh played out a 2-2 draw at Clackmannan. A poor run of form followed with two further draws and two losses from the next four games including a 1-0 home defeat against new leaders Dykehead, where Burgh were unlucky, conceding a late goal. All of these results meant that Dykehead now led the Third Division with 30 points, Forfar had 29, Vale of Leven 28 and Helensburgh were three points off the top, in fourth place with 27 points, but also now having played more matches than their rivals.

Helensburgh's next game was against promotion rivals Forfar Athletic at Ardencaple, which they won 3-0, although the game was more evenly contested than the final scoreline suggests. The game's first goal didn't come until fifteen minutes from time when Smillie broke the deadlock. As Forfar pressed forward for an equaliser they left gaps at the back and from a swift counter-attack Noble got a second and the same player got a third in similar circumstances in the final minute. Leaders Dykehead dropped points, drawing 2-2 at Beith, twice coming from behind, and also having two goals disallowed.

Two draws followed with points dropped, especially in a 1-1 home draw with Lochgelly United. However, Burgh's goalkeeper, Wallace, injured his shoulder in this match and had to leave the field before the interval. The visiting team took advantage and scored but despite their numerical disadvantage Helensburgh forced the draw through Peters. On the 20th March Helensburgh got a vital 3-2 win over Leith Athletic, Noble scoring a hat-trick. In the other key promotion games Forfar lost at Lochgelly and Dykehead drew with Vale of Leven. Excluding the results against Galston, who had resigned, Forfar now topped the table with 32 points from 25 matches; Dykehead had 31 points (23 matches); Mid-Annandale 30 (25); Helensburgh 30 (26), Vale of Leven 29 (24) and Leith 25 (from just 22 games).

The following Saturday Helensburgh didn't have a game but Dykehead lost at Peebles, Mid-Annandale lost at Beith, but Forfar extended their lead by beating Vale of Leven. A week later they were back in action and secured a vital 3-2 win away at Peebles, thanks to a surprise late goal. Forfar weren't in action and Mids and Vale drew with each other meaning Helensburgh moved up to second, two points behind the leaders, but having played one more game.

On Saturday 10th April Helensburgh again didn't play although their situation improved with Forfar losing their game in hand at Peebles, 2-1, and Dykehead being held at home by Solway Star. However, more concerning was that promotion rivals Vale of Leven were unable to fulfil their fixture due to financial problems. F W McMillan, President of Helensburgh FC, called for a meeting of the Third Division teams in Central Halls, Glasgow. This was to discuss the worsening financial situation as gate money generated was proving insufficient to meet the guarantees and travelling expenses. On the 14th April 1926 the *Helensburgh & Gareloch Times* reported "the affairs of the third division of the Scottish Football League appear to be in a serious condition. The long railway journeys to away games have killed this league. Mr FW McMillan (Helensburgh FC) called for a meeting of the teams to be held in Glasgow." An appeal to the Scottish League Management Committee was not sympathetically received and the division was wound up, its fixtures incomplete.

Helensburgh completed their programme at home on the 17th April 1926 by beating Montrose 5-1. In what would prove to be their last ever League game Smillie (2), Peters (2) and Coutts scored the goals. The victory took them joint top on 34 points with Forfar (excluding their result against Galston) although Leith won again and were now just two behind with games in hand. Leith then beat Dykehead 3-0 to emerge as championship contenders. Leith subsequently gained further points to move ahead but including the fixtures against Galston, Helensburgh, actually topped the table, but only on account of having completed all of their fixtures. Leith Athletic finished in second, one point behind but having played a game less. They had come with a late eight game unbeaten run which included six wins to lift them from seventh place to second. Forfar Athletic came in third, but were the likely winners of the Division if they had completed their programme, as they still had two matches to play.

At the Scottish League's AGM in May 1926 it was decided that no championship would be awarded due to the number of fixtures unfinished. The Third Division was abandoned despite attempts led by Helensburgh to keep it going in a regionalised format, with a south-western and north-eastern divisions, augmented by teams from the Second Division. The end of the Third Division meant no automatic promotion/relegation but instead a re-election vote was held. Bathgate and Broxburn United, the two bottom sides in the Second Division escaped automatic relegation, a re-election vote taking place instead. Four of the defunct Third Division sides applied including the top three sides – Helensburgh, Leith Athletic, Forfar Athletic, along with Dykehead – for the two vacant spots. Broxburn, Helensburgh and Dykehead were eliminated as it became a three way tussle for the two vacant spots. Bathgate were victorious in the second ballot and Forfar beat Leith in the third ballot. Forfar were favoured by many of the clubs in the subsequent voting, as they were seen as the 'moral' victors of the old division.

Having lost out in the voting for a place in the Second Division, Helensburgh joined the Scottish Alliance for the 1926-27 season, and F W McMillan was elected to the management committee of Alliance. When they travelled to Pittodrie to play Aberdeen (in a Scottish Cup tie on the 27th January 1927 cup game), 14,000 people came to watch, by far the biggest crowd the club ever played in front of. When the majority of the ex-Third Division clubs were expelled from the Alliance they decided to set up their own league, known as the Provincial League. At this point Helensburgh became a junior club but even at this level they struggled and in 1928, they closed down and their ground was incorporated into the cricket and rugby club.

SEASON	LEAGUE	P	W	D	L	F	A	P	POS
1923-24	SCOT-3	30	5	7	18	46	72	17	15/16
1924-25	SCOT-3	30	12	7	11	68	60	31	7/16
1925-26	SCOT-3	30	16	6	8	66	47	38	1/16

Johnstone

Formed: 1891

Colours: Originally black and gold striped shirts with black shorts. For the last season in the Third Division they played in all white

Ground: Newfield Park

Entered League: 1912. Elected to Second Division. 1921. Founder member of the reformed Second Division.

Number of League Seasons: 8

Highest League Finish: 7th in Division Two

Honours: None

Left League: 1915. League suspended due to Great War. 1926. Division Three abandoned. Disbanded 1928.

Johnstone were a team from Renfrewshire that completed eight seasons in the Scottish Football League. They completed three seasons before the First World War having been elected to the League in 1912. When the Second Division was reinstated in 1921 they competed for a further five seasons. In 1925 they were relegated to the Third Division, which was abandoned at the end of the following season and at that point the club left the Scottish Football League, never to return.

The town of Johnstone lies three miles west of neighbouring Paisley and twelve miles west of Glasgow. Johnstone is a small industrial town that grew up around cotton mills and coal mines. The first Johnstone FC was formed in 1878 during the boom in popularity that swept through the working class communities in western Scotland in the late 1870s and early 1880s but this club folded in 1887 and a new club was formed in 1891.

The first Johnstone FC had made its debut in the Scottish Cup on the 4th September 1880, losing to nearby Arthurlie of Barrhead 2-0 in the First Round. The following season the club reached the Fourth Round, narrowly going down to Queen's Park, the holders and five time winners. In the First Round they had beaten Greenock Southern 9-1. The following year they reached the Fourth Round again, recording a 6-2 win over Paisley Athletic in the first round and then 7-2 over the neighbouring village of Kilbarchan. In the 1884-85 season they recorded a big win in the First Round, beating

Lyle Athletic of Greenock by 9-1 on the 13th September 1884. The *Glasgow Herald* reported that the game was "played at Cartbank, Johnstone, in presence of a large turn-out of spectators; but from the first it was evident that the visitors were no match for their older opponents, the Johnstone, who defeated them by nine goals to one." Johnstone lost to St Mirren, 3-0, in the next round. There was also a Johnstone Athletic who competed in the Scottish Cup for five seasons in the 1880s.

The second Johnstone FC came into being in 1891 and they moved to Newfield Park in 1894 to coincide with them joining the Scottish Alliance, a league competition set up to rival the Scottish Football League. The ground was located to the north, just beyond the train station on the Dalry-Johnstone line (now the A737) near to the Barbush flax mill and gasworks. Johnstone subsequently left the Alliance to play in the North Ayrshire League. In 1897 they played once more in the Scottish Cup, going out in the First round to Morton, and the following year they joined the Scottish Combination, which they won jointly with Galston in the 1906-07 season. Both teams finished level on points and no play-off match was arranged so the title was shared. In the same season they held Hibernian to a 1-1 draw at Easter Road in a Second Round Scottish Cup tie in front of 10,000 spectators. McCormick their goalkeeper was the hero and kept the score down to 1-0 at the interval. Bowie equalised five minutes after the break to give the club a shock result against the 1902 Scottish Cup winners and the 1903 Scottish Football League Champions. They lost the replay 5-0.

The following year they finished as Scottish Combination runners-up (to Galston of Ayrshire) and this prompted a first bid to join the Scottish Football League. At the League's AGM, held on the 1st June 1908, they were the only non-League club to challenge the two clubs from the Second Division up for re-election: Cowdenbeath and Arthurlie. The two current League clubs were comfortably re-elected, Cowdenbeath getting 25 votes, Arthurlie 22 while Johnstone got 9.

In 1908 Johnstone joined the Scottish Football Union, which was considered to be one of the strongest non-League competitions in central Scotland. They finished runners-up to Falkirk 'A' and made a fresh challenge to join the SFL. At the AGM on the 31st May it was a case of déjà vu as they came up against the same two SFL sides facing re-election. Although this time they were accompanied by three other non-League teams. Again the existing SFL teams were re-elected but this time Johnstone were closer and were the best of the non-League challengers: Arthurlie 21, Cowdenbeath 17, Johnstone 11, Renton 8, Wishaw Thistle 5 and Dundee Hibs 3.

Johnstone didn't apply at the end of the next two seasons. In the 1911 Scottish Cup they took First Division strugglers Hamilton to a replay in the Second Round. Johnstone took the lead and came close to a Cup upset. The match took place on the 11th February and resulted in a 1-1 draw. *The Scotsman* reported on the match: "at Hamilton, before 5000 spectators, 1000 of whom travelled from Johnstone per special train. In the first half play was mostly confined to the Johnstone quarters. The Academicals forwards were, however, weak in finishing, and half-time arrived without a score. After crossing over the Academicals pressed persistently, yet the easiest of chances went abegging for lack of good finishing. Connor broke off for Johnstone, and scored a goal some twelve minutes after the resumption. The remainder of the game was a long persistent pressure on the Johnstone goal, yet past the club goalkeeper the ball could not be got. Some five minutes from time, however, the Johnstone right back gave away a penalty kick, and amid great excitement, Davie scored the equalising goal. The remaining minutes were full of exciting passages, and Johnstone were near scoring more than once. The end came, however, without further scoring, and the Academicals must travel to Johnstone. The weakness of the Academicals forwards, and the brilliance of McDonald in the Johnstone team goal contributed largely to the unexpected draw - one goal each." Johnstone lost the replay a fortnight later. Each side scored in the first half with the visitors opening the scoring. Hamilton went ahead early in the second half and made sure of going further to meet Motherwell in the third round by going two goals up later in the second period, winning 3-1. Hamilton went on to contest the final where they were beaten by Celtic 2-0 in a replayed final after the first match ended goalless.

At the 1912 SFL AGM Falkirk put forward a motion to increase the number of clubs in the Second Division from 12 to 14 which was agreed to. The bottom two clubs, Albion Rovers and Vale of Leven were re-elected and the meeting then heard applicants for the two additional positions. Johnstone were up against two recent champions of the Scottish Union, Galston and Peebles, as well as Central League champions Dunfermline Athletic and also Bathgate. On the 3rd June 1912 Johnstone were successfully elected to the SFL along with Dunfermline, no doubt aided by their strong Cup showing the previous year.

Johnstone made their Scottish Football League debut on the 17th August 1912, losing 3-1 against Albion Rovers at Whifflet. The 1912-13 season was the first of three pre-war seasons and they finished a creditable eighth place in a 14 team division. They played their first home SFL match at Newfield Park on 24th August 1912, a 2–1 win over Dumbarton, in front of a 1,500 crowd. This was followed by good form that took them up to fifth in the table but they ended 1912 with a 5-0 away defeat against Ayr United on the 28th December 1912. In January 1913 they suffered a surprise heavy defeat against bottom club Dundee Hibs, losing 7-1. This was caused by Kennedy, their goalkeeper, suffering an injury and one of the outfield players, Mercer, having to keep goal. They finished their first campaign at home with a 2-1 win over Ayr United and were placed eighth in the final table.

Their second season was a poor one as they finished 12th (which was now also bottom following an expansion to the First Division). Johnstone lost all eleven away games including defeats against Dunfermline Athletic (7-1) Dundee Hibernian (5-0), East Stirlingshire (5-0), Albion Rovers (5-1) and Leith Athletic (5-1). When they lost to Dunfermline Athletic on the 3rd January 1914 they had lost 13 out of 17 games played, with only one win and five points on the board. They were cut adrift at the bottom, five points behind Dundee Hibs and seven behind Vale of Leven and Arthurlie. Wins over Dundee Hibs and Vale of Leven helped close the gap and they eventually finished only one point behind Vale. Both clubs faced a re-election vote although their prospects were both enhanced by the League's decision to restore the Second Division to a 14 team competition. Nevertheless, the voting at the AGM on the 4th June went to a fourth ballot, where Johnstone eventually beat Bathgate of the Central League 15-10 in a run-off for the last place available. Johnstone had survived the initial elimination ballot which reduced the teams from seven to five, but then came in bottom in the second ballot of the five clubs going for four places. Vale of Leven and new club Clydebank were elected and Johnstone went into a third round of voting with Lochgelly and Bathgate for a further place. Johnstone came bottom in the voting with 15, Bathgate got 17 and Lochgelly United were elected with 23. Johnstone then went in a fourth and final ballot and a straight fight with Bathgate who they beat by five votes to preserve their League status.

Having had a narrow escape Johnstone turned things around on the pitch in the 1914-15 season, achieving their highest ever League placing, coming in seventh in the restored 14 team division. They started with a seven goal thriller where they lost 4-3 in Perth against St Johnstone. Key behind their improvement was their excellent home form, winning 10 out of 13 games (and losing just one) at Newfield. They went seven games unbeaten from Saturday 9th January to February 20th, a run that took them up four places to seventh, although they were badly beaten in the last game, a 6-0 loss away against Lochgelly United.

The Second Division was suspended in 1915 and later dropped altogether and during the First World War Johnstone played in the Western League, which they won in the 1920-21 season. In 1921 the Second Division was finally reinstated with four Western League clubs including Johnstone joining 16 clubs from the Central League. Johnstone spent a further five seasons in the SFL and in this first year back they finished in eleventh. Johnstone lost their opening fixture on the resumption, 3-1 at Arbroath, in a match played on the 20th August 1921. Johnstone seldom posed a threat in a first half where Arbroath took the lead. On resuming Johnstone were immediately on the attack and equalised through McDonald. They were now in the ascendancy but a corner resulted in a second goal for Arbroath which seemed to impart new life to the hosts who made sure of the points with a third goal. The Johnstone team line-up for their return to League action was: Eadon; McClellan, Watkins; Stewart, O'Donald, Lawson; Gray, Crawford, McDonald, Duncan and Wylie.

A week later they played their first home game back. Keen interest was taken in their game against Dundee Hibs with a crowd of 3,000 in attendance. Their opponents started the stronger and scored after ten minutes, Bannister guiding the ball past the helpless Eadon. Johnstone responded well but found Henderson in the Hibs goal in inspired form. Crossing over with a 1-0 lead their opponents extended their lead after just five minutes and seemed assured of both points. It needed something special for the home team and Crawford duly supplied it with a beauty from 30 yards out. Five minutes later the equaliser was obtained by Wylie. Hibs dominated the first period but were outplayed in the second and a 2-2 draw was a fair result.

Their first win of the resumption came on the 10th September, a 4-1 victory over King's Park. *The Sunday Post* headline was "Joyful Johnstone" as they reported that "Johnstone thoroughly deserved their four to one victory over King's Park. Playing against almost a hurricane in the first half, they forced the game into the visitors' quarters. The home eleven were the more aggressive, and when Scott and Wylie got going on the left, and Crawford scored from a well-directed cross, Johnstone were justly entitled to the lead. A second soon followed. By dint of good work on the part of Wylie, McDonald fastened on to his pass, and with a shot thirty yards out gave Buchanan no chance. This looked bad for the visitors, who after having the aid of wind and sun, had to cross over two goals in arrear, but the King's Park forwards would have fared better had they shot, rather than attempted to walk the ball through the goal. The second half was largely in favour of Johnstone, the visitors seldom being over midfield. On their first visit to Eadon's end Cullen reduced the leeway with a smartly-taken goal. Johnstone reasserted themselves, Stewart from twenty-five yards out scoring a third goal with a great drive. Another immediately followed, the point being gained by Crawford." The Johnstone team that day was: Eadon; McClellan, Armstrong; Stewart, Lawson, Watkins; Craig, Crawford, McDonald, Gray and Wylie.

Johnstone entered 1922 just below mid-table but on the 7th January they lost heavily in Edinburgh at Old Logie Green against St Bernard's. Despite Eadon's heroics in goal they conceded six, which was probably a wider margin than the balance of play warranted. Later in the same month they suffered a heavy loss in the Scottish Cup, beaten 6-0 by First Division Albion Rovers. Willie Reid, the Rovers' player-manager scored two goals in each half. Two goals were scored when two of the Johnstone players had to leave the field through injury. After this game they continued to pick up points at regular intervals and eventually finished in eleventh place.

The 1922-23 season saw the club regress on the field, finishing a lowly 16th place. They got off to a poor start, only scoring once in their first five fixtures, before a 4-1 derby home win over Cowdenbeath. This match, played on the 23rd September 1922, led *The Scotsman* to simply say that "the home men rearranged their team, and struck their best form of the season." Under the headline "Johnstone Jazz" *The Sunday Post* reported that Johnstone fully merited their biggest win of the season...they were easily the better lot, and scored in three minutes through McDonald, and with this lead, which did not represent their superiority, they crossed over at half-time. The homestead included Rutherford, of Kilmarnock, and Greenhorn, of Stenhousemuir. In the second half Johnstone increased their lead through Kirk, but the visitors replied with a breakaway, and Noble lobbed over a ball that Carson let slip through his goal. Further goals were added for Johnstone by Greenhorn and McDonald."

This performance was a rare ray of brightness in an otherwise dull campaign. In December they lost 7-2 at Volunteer Park against Armadale but gained revenge in the Cup, beating them 2-0 in front of 4,000 spectators on the 13th January 1923. They drew First Division Falkirk, who were flying high (eventually finishing fourth) in the next round. Played on the 27th January, a probable record attendance of 7,000 fans watched them lose narrowly 1-0. *The Scotsman,* under the headline "Falkirk Scrape Through" reported that "Falkirk did not cover themselves with glory at Johnstone by only scraping through in their tie. The point was got early in the game by McNair, who headed through from a corner. Falkirk had a strong breeze with them that half, and their lead was not considered by any means a safe one, although it proved to be. Johnstone made a better show in the second-half, and the game was strenuously contested. Ferguson in the Falkirk goal and Carson in the Johnstone goal had both a great deal to do, and, if anything, the latter was the better. Twice in particular he saved from Puddefoot when all seemed lost. It was in defence rather than attack that Falkirk proved to be strong. Their forwards seemed to find the small field a handicap. *"The Sunday Post* said "if Johnstone had equalised instead of being defeated by the only goal it would not have been more than they deserved." The Cup game must have taken a lot out of them, for just two days later they travelled to Boghead to play Dumbarton and were trounced 6-0. They won at home to Bo'ness the following Saturday but then lost four of the next five, picking up a solitary point, to drop perilously close to the re-election places. Home wins against Armadale and King's Park though lifted them away from danger and they eventually finished in 16th place in the twenty team division.

The following season was their best since re-admittance, finishing in the top half in eighth place and setting a new club record for most wins in a season (16). They won their opening game away against Arbroath, and made a good start overall, going the first six matches unbeaten. One of these matches was a 4-0 away win against Vale of Leven, although the score flattered Johnstone. Houston opened the scoring for Johnstone after a quarter of an hour. Fifteen minutes after the restart McNaught beat O'Neill in the host's goal for a second time. A couple of minutes later Neave added a third, and close on time Houston had a fourth. The result took Johnstone into third after the early leaders Armadale lost. Johnstone now sat just a point behind new leaders King's Park but having played a game fewer. It all proved to be a bit of a false dawn though. After this result their form was a bit erratic and they were unable to string any sort of run together and they eventually finished eighth, only five points off third place, but 16 points from the promotion places.

The 1924-25 season was the beginning of the end for Johnstone as a League club. At the end of the season they were relegated to the new, but ill-fated Scottish Third Division and lost their place in the Scottish Football League when this division was abandoned in 1926. An opening loss against Stenhousemuir at home on the 16th August 1924 did not augur well. *The Sunday Post* commented that "Johnstone sadly disappointed their supporters when they went under to Stenhousemuir in their opening League game at Newfield Park. Both teams played well in the first portion, despite wretched overhead and ground conditions. Both were awarded penalty kicks early, but the respective 'keepers saved. Crossing over on equal terms, the visitors forced the pace in the second half, and scored in fifteen minutes. After this Johnstone were awarded a penalty, but Bruce again saved. The visitors thereafter took the game in hand and scored twice." Johnstone lost their next two games as well, including a 5-1 defeat at Stirling against King's Park. After three games they were pointless, having scored only one goal but conceded eleven.

After these three consecutive defeats Johnstone got their first win, although in controversial fashion. In a lively game, Armadale were unlucky to come away from Newfield Park with nothing. Johnstone's second goal was controversial as it was doubtful that the ball completely crossed the line. McNaught, in a sparking display for Johnstone opened the scoring. McDonald then set him up for the second. Armadale were good value for their goal but were hampered in their attempts for an equaliser by an injury to one of their players, Johnstone winning 2-1.

Johnstone were bottom of the table by the end of October but four wins in November lifted them up to 13th in the 20 team division. However, they had a poor winter and festive period, losing 6-1 at Bo'ness and 5-1 at Dunfermline on the 27th December. In early March they lost 5-1 at St Bernard's and with five games left, after a 3-1 win at home to Bo'ness, they were in 18th place, just above the two relegation places.

Johnstone ended the season with a disastrous run, contriving to lose four in a row and only gain one more point, in the last game at home to Alloa Athletic. They lost the last two games in March and then lost 2-0 at home to Dundee United on the 3rd April, a Friday game to avoid the Scotland v. England international at Hampden. In this match they started with only ten men before Cameron put in an appearance and conceded the two goals in the first 12 minutes. They remained in 18th place on 27 points, but East Stirlingshire, on 26 points still had to play. Forfar were bottom, three points behind, but with two games in hand. On the Saturday East Stirlingshire won 2-0 (and Forfar got a home draw) and Shire leapfrogged Johnstone, putting them in the bottom two, with two games to play.

On Saturday 11th April Johnstone lost 4-1 at second placed Clydebank. They actually opened the scoring after seven minutes play through their outside-left Kirk and had a chance to increase their lead when McDonald, their centre-forward was through and one on one with the 'keeper but somehow contrived to miss. Soon after Clydebank got back on level terms and then went ahead. A third settled the issue but Johnstone kept at it and were unlucky to hit the post. Near the end Clydebank broke away and scored a fourth. Rivals East Stirlingshire also lost, at leaders Dundee United and Forfar also went down at Broxburn. All these results meant Johnstone were 19th with 27 points and one game left. Forfar were bottom on 25 points with two games. East Stirlingshire were one point ahead of Johnstone, with a game left.

The following Saturday Johnstone did not have a fixture. Forfar played their game in hand but lost 3-1 at home to Clyde to relegate themselves. More importantly though, East Stirlingshire completed their fixtures, beating St Bernard's 2-0 to finish on 30 points and relegate Johnstone (on 27 points) along with Forfar. Johnstone played their last game a week later. Only 500 turned up to see this meaningless game at Newfield Park that ended in a 2-2 draw with Alloa Athletic. Johnstone had lost a club record 22 League matches that season and also conceded a record 85 goals.

Any thoughts of an immediate rebound were soon dashed. The new season opened on the 15th August 1925 and Johnstone lost their opening fixture 2-1 in Shotts against Dykehead. They got their first point of the new campaign a week later in a 2-2 home draw with Leith, throwing away a two goal lead. They only recorded one win in their first seven games in the Third Division, a 4-0 victory against fellow relegated club Forfar, so that by the end of the first two months of the new season they were fourth from bottom.

On the 24th October 1925 things took a turn for the better when they recorded their biggest ever SFL win, beating Mid-Annandale 6-2. Mids were bottom with only one win in seven and under the headline "Joy for Johnstone" *The Sunday Post* reported that "Johnstone secured their biggest victory at Newfield Park, when they beat Mid-Annandale by six goals to two. The visitors started in spirited fashion, and after ten minutes Maleney opened their account. McWhinnie, after a spell equalised, and soon afterwards Nairn put them ahead. Harvie scored a third, and before the interval was reached McNaught added a fourth. After the resumption Nairn and Harvie, from a penalty, added to the home team's total. The visitors were reckless finishers. Before the end Dawson scored a second goal for the visitors."

On the 5th December 1925 Johnstone snatched a 1-0 win over then bottom club Brechin City, despite not being able to put out a full team. This was a sign of difficulties at the club as the low gate receipts and general economic situation began to take their toll. On the 9th January 1926 matters got even worse on the pitch as they lost 8-2 at Galston, their biggest SFL defeat. This would turn out to be Galston's last game as they resigned shortly afterwards. Chalmers scored both goals for Johnstone, his second making it 4-2, before the home team ran in four quick goals. The result left them second from bottom, in 15th place, and now only one point ahead of Brechin, having played two games more.

On the 14th January 1926, Johnstone were fined by the Scottish Football League for the circumstances surrounding the match against Brechin the month before. *The Scotsman* takes up the story: "At a meeting in Glasgow yesterday of the Management Committee of the Scottish Football League, an unusual offence was recorded against the Johnstone Football Club. The report was that the club, in their match with Brechin City on December 5, had played two men belonging to their opponents under names of players registered for the Johnstone club. D. Carlton of the Johnstone Club was suspended until the end of the season, and a penalty of £10 was imposed on the club." At the same meeting a letter was received from Galston FC, formally resigning from the League.

A few days later *The Sunday Post* continued the story, and the reporter revealed that "Johnstone FC resigned some time ago, but, after remaining out of the tournament for a few weeks, the club's supporters came to the rescue, and they are now carrying on the club – a thankless and thorny task. Will they, however, continue to perform that task much longer? Consider what happened to the club at the meeting last week of the Management Committee of the League. Johnstone FC, for having, in a quandary, played two Brechin City players at Brechin against the local club on 5th December under the names of players registered by the Johnstone club, were fined £10, and Mr D.

Carlton, who was looking after the team that day, was suspended till the end of the season. In comparison with recent punishments imposed by the Management Committee of the League, this punishment appears to be terribly heavy. I make no excuse for the Johnstone club. They erred and have got it in the neck, but in all the circumstances, and there were extenuating circumstances, surely a little mercy might have been shown to this poor and struggling club. A member suspended till the end of the season, and the club, in whose purse it is deepest winter, fined £10 - that is a punishment calculated to make the Johnstone club again throw up the sponge, and any day their resignation may be announced."

Johnstone soldiered on, completing their remaining fixtures with the exception of the reverse game against Galston. A good run of four games without defeat around the end of March lifted them up the table. On the 10th April 1926 they played what would turn out to be the final SFL match at Newfield Park, going down to defeat 3–2 against Brechin City. Nairn scored twice as they came from 0-2 down to draw level before a Brechin breakaway gave the visitors the win. A week later they played their last ever League game, losing 4-1 at Leith Athletic with Galbraith scoring their last ever League goal. They are listed as finishing 13th but not all fixtures were completed and the two teams below them had all played fewer games. Galston, the club that had resigned were placed bottom.

In May, at the League's AGM, the Third Division was scrapped. Johnstone then joined the Scottish Alliance where they played for just one season before going out of business in 1928. They featured in the Scottish Cup for two seasons, going out in the First Round on each occasion. In the second of these, they were on a receiving end of a thrashing. On the 21st January 1928 Cowdenbeath beat Johnstone 12-0, and this remains the Blue Brazil's record win. *The Scotsman* noted that "little interest was shown in the tie between Cowdenbeath and Johnstone, and with heavy rain falling at the time of starting, only 700 spectators were present, the drawings amounting to £30. The game calls for little comment, Cowdenbeath having matters entirely their own way from start to finish and, without exerting themselves after the first 20 minutes, scoring 12 goals without reply from Johnstone. As a match, indeed, the tie was a farce, and it is no exaggeration to say that Cowdenbeath could have doubled their big score had they been so inclined. They led at the interval by 7 goals, and their scorers were Lindsay (6), Leonard (3), Pullar, Connaboy and Dixon." The Johnstone team to take the field was: Armstrong; Craig, McAlpine; Irving, Thom, Jameson; Ritchie, McCutcheon, Lang, Howe and Gibson.

There was a prophetic commentary in *The Sunday Post:* "Johnstone's coming to life has not passed the coma stage, and Cowdenbeath's dozen goals will doubtlessly cause a fatal relapse" – and so it came to pass, as the club was disbanded shortly afterwards. The ground continued to be used until it was eventually demolished to make way for the A737 bypass. In 1956 a new football club was formed called Johnstone Burgh and they play in the Junior leagues.

SEASON	LEAGUE	P	W	D	L	F	A	P	POS
1912-13	SCOT-2	26	9	6	11	31	43	24	8/14
1913-14	SCOT-2	22	4	4	14	20	55	12	12/12
1914-15	SCOT-2	26	11	5	10	41	52	27	7/14
1921-22	SCOT-2	38	14	10	14	46	59	38	11/20
1922-23	SCOT-2	38	13	6	19	41	62	32	16/20
1923-24	SCOT-2	38	16	7	15	60	56	39	8/20
1924-25	SCOT-2	38	12	4	22	53	85	28	19/20
1925-26	SCOT-3	29	7	6	16	55	74	20	13/16

King's Park

Formed: 1875
Colours: Mauve and white striped shirts and white shorts
Ground: Forthbank Park
Entered League: 1921. Founder member of the reformed Second Division
Number of League Seasons: 19
Highest League Finish: 3rd in Division Two
Honours: None
Left League: 1939. League suspended due to war. Failed to re-join when the SFL restarted in 1946. Wound up in 1953

King's Park were based in Stirling and were that town's representative in the Scottish League between the wars and therefore pre-date Stirling Albion. They took their name from the biggest and most popular park in the city where they played until 1881. Had it not been for the unintentional actions of the German Luftwaffe in 1940 football supporters in Stirling might still be following the 'Parkers' as opposed to the 'Albion'.

Formed in 1875 they were admitted to the Scottish Football League's Second Division in 1921 and retained their membership of the Division until the League closed down in 1939. The club is one of only two teams not to re-emerge after the Second World War, St Bernard's of Edinburgh being the other. King's Park generally finished in the middle of the table, although they narrowly missed out on promotion in 1928 when they finished in third place, just one point behind promoted Third Lanark. They played their games at Forthbank Park, not to be confused with the modern stadium of the same name, located just north of the Kerse Road and to the east of the railway line.

They club first entered the Scottish Cup in 1879, playing at Brassburn Park against Milton of Campsie on the 6th September in a First Round tie, losing 3-1. The following year they knocked out Strathblane 1-0 to progress to the Second Round where they lost to Falkirk 2-1. In the 1882-83 competition they received a bye into the Second Round where they were roundly trounced by Dumbarton, the eventual winners, 8-0. The following year they dished out a thrashing themselves, when, on the 15th September 1883, they beat Lenzie 11-0 in a First Round tie, the *Glasgow Herald* simply noting that "the strangers had only ten men." They lost in the next round

6-1 to Renton, one of the early dominant forces in Scottish football. In the 1888-89 competition, having knocked out Alloa Athletic, they were drawn away against Slamannan and drew 3-3. In the replay on the 29th September they recorded their record Cup win, beating their opponents 13-1. They were knocked out by East Stirlingshire in the next round.

In the 1894-95 season the Parkers had their best Scottish Cup run to date, as they reached the Quarter-finals, producing a giant killing act in order to progress. Having beaten Lochee United they were drawn at home to the Scottish League champions of 1891 and 1892, and current First Division side Dumbarton. The two sides met on the 15th December 1984 and the *Glasgow Herald* reported that "Dumbarton had to contend with the sun in their eyes in the first half, and King's Park kept them almost continuously on the defensive...Donald McInnes opened the scoring with a fine overhead kick, and the score at the interval was unchanged. Jackson equalised shortly after the restart, and King's Park wavered before the determined pressure of Dumbarton. Nothing but the fine defence of Broad, Kinross and Thomson kept the visitors from taking the lead. From a breakaway King's Park again scored from a scrimmage, amid a scene of the greatest enthusiasm. The concluding twenty minutes of the game was of the most exciting description. Dumbarton played desperately, completely hemming in the home team. Kinross and Brand, however, turned aside all manner of shots, and all the efforts of the Dumbarton team to defeat Thomson were unavailing. The whistle sounded amidst intense excitement, with the score King's Park 2; Dumbarton 1". On the 12th January 1895 they played top of the table Hearts at Tynecastle in the last eight. To the surprise of the crowd King's Park took the lead through David Marshall and he then extended it. Stung into action and roared on by the home support Willie Michael scored two goals to draw Hearts level by half-time. Hearts dominated after the break but couldn't find a way through and their supporters began to grow impatient. There was more relief than jubilation when Bob McLaren scored and then Michael completed his hat-trick as Hearts ran out 4-2 winners. Hearts went on to win the League Championship but were beaten in the Semi-finals of the Scottish Cup by fellow Edinburgh side, and eventual winners St Bernard's.

In 1891 King's Park had become founder members of the Scottish Alliance, one of several leagues set up after the Scottish League was formed in 1890. They then joined the Scottish Football Union in 1906 although they struggled, finishing in the bottom three. In 1909 they joined the Central League, finishing bottom in their first season. They continued in this competition until 1915 and resumed their membership in 1919. In 1921 the Central League was incorporated into the Scottish League as the new

Second Division and King's Park took up their place in the Scottish Football League for the 1921-22 season.

In their first League season they struggled, eventually finishing 17th out of the 20 teams. Due to planned League reconstruction the bottom two clubs would drop out of the League to leave an 18 team division for the following season so the club had a narrow escape. They drew their opening League game on the 20th August 1921, 1-1 against East Stirlingshire at Forthbank, watched by a crowd of 4,000. In this match their opponents had the better of the game but King's Park took the lead from a penalty kick scored by Cullen, the club's first ever League goal. Shire equalised and the scores were level at the interval. King's Park improved in the second half and forced their opponents onto the defensive but there were no further goals and the points were shared. The club's first ever League win came on the 3rd September with a 2-1 win over Clackmannan. The winning goal was scored by Tommy Mannion although the visitors protested that the ball had not crossed the line.

The following month the club had a brush with the authorities following crowd trouble at a home match against St Johnstone. In this game, played on the 8th October, St Johnstone raced into a two goal lead before Tommy Mannion pulled one back and then fifteen minutes from time King's Park equalised. The crowd trouble was caused by two potentially winning goals being disallowed. *The Scotsman* takes up the story: "King's Park got a penalty for handling, but Buchanan, the goalkeeper, who took it, shot into the Perth custodian's hands. The latter dropped the ball, and Cullen netted, but the point was disallowed. Mannion then got the ball into the net for King's Park, but a prior infringement nullified the effort. The crowd invaded the playing pitch, and the game was stopped for some minutes. At the close of play there were some disorderly scenes around the pavilion, and the police had to draw their batons." The SFA met on the 19th October and closed the King's Park ground from the 24th October to the 7th November. This led to King's Park playing a home match against Vale of Leven at Dunblane's Duckburn Park on the 5th November. This game ended 0-0 before a crowd of 4,000, which was around the average gate at Forthbank.

A fortnight later they were back at Forthbank but lost 8-1 at home to League leaders Alloa Athletic. *The Scotsman* reported that "with Alloa as visitors the attendance at Stirling was the largest of the season, 5,000 being present. Alloa forced the pace from the start, and with the exception of occasional bursts by King's Park, play was in Stirling territory. Crilley scored after fifteen minutes, and the clever centre, lying well in on Buchanan, had another two goals before the interval, Gaffney scoring a fourth. Between the third and fourth goals, King's Park got their only point through Paterson. The second half was largely a repetition of the first, Alloa getting another four goals;

Crilley bringing his own total to five. The ground was very heavy and the King's Park defence gave out long before the finish." This was their biggest ever League home defeat in their history and left them 14th in the table.

This defeat was part of a run of six games without a win which was finally ended with a 3-2 home win over Arbroath in mid- December. They also went winless for seven games in early 1922. This particular run featured a nine goal thriller where they lost by the odd goal in a nine against East Fife on the 11th February. By this time they were fighting for their survival having dropped to the bottom of the table. As part of League reconstruction, and a return to an 18 team Division, the bottom two clubs would drop out of the SFL at the end of the season. At this stage King's Park were bottom with 17 points, level with Clackmannan, but with a worse goal average, which had been introduced as a means of separating teams level on points. Dundee Hibs, in the 18th and safe spot, were a further point ahead.

In their next game on the 22nd February the Parkers entertained second placed Cowdenbeath. In a hard fought match there was little between the teams but the only goal of the first half fell to the hosts, Devlin heading home after half an hour. In the second half, Martin scored a second and 'Newman' or a 'new man' scored a third. The visitors were awarded a penalty for handball but Buchanan saved it. Near the end they did score as a result of a misunderstanding between the 'keeper and defender, both leaving it for each other. The game ended 3-1 to King's Park who thus ended their winless run by securing an unexpected but vital victory. The win breathed new life into the club as they battled to retain their SFL status. They then went on a seven game unbeaten run from early March which included a 5-2 away win at Arbroath, in which Devlin scored four. By this time they were out of the bottom two with a five point gap over Dundee Hibs and Clackmannan.

On the eve of matches on Saturday 15th April King's Park were 18th, four points ahead of Dundee Hibs, needing just a point to guarantee their League status. Their fixture, though, was away against the newly crowned champions Alloa. The hosts led for much of the match but Devlin scored the vital equalising goal towards the close of play that secured the vital point. With Clackmannan losing this result guaranteed their safety. On the same day Greenock Morton won the Scottish Cup surprisingly beating Rangers 1-0.

For the 1922-23 season the club strengthen and signed J McDonald of Clackmannan in goal, Waugh from Falkirk and Raitt from Johnstone, but on-loan Devlin, who had scored freely, was recalled by Clyde. *The Sunday Post*, appraised their new team thus: "King's Park have got together a fine defence, particularly the backs and goalkeeper. The half-backs were fair, and the forwards were the poorest division of the team, particularly the centre." They started well going unbeaten in their first four matches and jointly topped the division with Dunfermline before indifferent form culminated in a 5-1 loss at Vale of Leven. When they drew the New Years' Day game 2-2 at East Stirlingshire they were sixth in the table. They didn't win a game in 1923 until the 28th February, a run of eight games, which saw them slide down to twelfth place where they eventually finished.

The following season was their best since League admittance, finishing in sixth place. After losing the opening game they won the next four and went nine games unbeaten before losing to the renamed Dundee United. A 4-2 away win at Armadale the week before had taken the club to the top of the Second Division. Key to their success were the wingers McLavin and McLachlan, and the forwards Lamond, Scullion and Raitt. Indifferent form followed this loss and when they were soundly beaten by promotion rivals Cowdenbeath, 5-0, at the beginning of December, they lost top spot. They conceded five the following week as well, away at new leaders St Johnstone, and it would be them, and Cowdenbeath, who would break away at the top and gain promotion to the top flight.

King's Park beat Dumbarton 5-0 on the 1st January 1924 but by this time they had slipped to fourth. A month later they recorded their best ever SFL away win, beating Lochgelly United 8-3. The Fife team were anchored at the bottom, 12 points adrift. The Stirling team scored two goals within the first five minutes through Lamond and McRobbie. A junior centre-forward on trial added a third before Lochgelly got one back from the penalty spot. After the interval the trialllist added a fourth goal and Lochgelly scored another spot kick to make it 4-2. McLachlan scored a fifth, Stainers the sixth and seventh, and the junior got his hat-trick. A series of draws undermined any lingering hope of a promotion push and they eventually finished in sixth place, which was six places higher than the season before.

The next three seasons saw a series of mid-table finishes (10th, 13th and 12th). The only fixture of note was the club being drawn against the Scottish Cup holders Airdrieonians in the First Round. They lost 4-0, but the game, played on the 24th January 1925, attracted a record attendance of 8,911. After three mediocre seasons King's Park achieved their best ever League placing, coming third in the Second Division in the 1927-28 season. Ayr United easily won the championship and Third Lanark were promoted along with them, finishing just one point ahead of King's Park, although with a far superior goal average. Only two points separated the teams from second to sixth place making for a thrilling run in. Things didn't start to well for King's Park as they lost 4-1 at Leith Athletic on the opening day of the season and then 5-1 a fortnight later against Third Lanark. In between though they beat eventual champions Ayr United 2-1.

445

After two consecutive draws they scored five goals in three consecutive games, beating Armadale 5-2, Dumbarton 5-4 away and Arbroath 5-1. Their winger turned centre-forward Frank Toner scored a hat-trick against Dumbarton and all five of the goals against Arbroath. King's Park also scored five in a 5-1 win over Clydebank on the 19th November, with Toner notching another hat-trick. The game caused some controversy as a newspaper report before the game had suggested that their opponents were about to go out of business and as a result the attendance at the match was reduced. As a consequence King's Park held back Clydebank's cut of the gate until the Scottish League intervened.

At the beginning of December 1927 King's Park scored five in a match for the fifth time, beating third-placed Arthurlie 5-1, Toner recording yet another hat-trick. The result left them fourth in the table, three points behind Ayr United and two behind Arbroath. By the time they drew with East Stirlingshire in the New Years' Day game they were up to second place, although leaders Ayr had now pulled away and were seven points clear at the top. On the 7th January 1928 they beat promotion rivals Third Lanark 4-2, with Scoular scoring a hat-trick, to cement their challenge. The following week they were held 1-1 at lowly Armadale, although they did beat the same side 4-2 in the Scottish Cup Second Round to set up a Third Round tie away at Rangers, which they lost 3-1. Watched by a crowd of 20,000 they gave their illustrious opponents a wee fright, taking the lead through Lennon after 28 minutes, which they held until the second half.

Following their Cup heroics King's Park failed to win any of their next five League games, drawing three, and their promotion challenge started to fade. The last of these, a 5-0 defeat at Clydebank on the 24th March, where they conceded three goals in the last five minutes, saw them drop to sixth place, although only three points off second place. Ayr United were crowned champions with four games to go. King's Park secured three points from the first two fixtures and on the 14th April they beat St Bernard's 8-1, to register their record victory up to that point. *The Sunday Post* reported that "King's Park had the record victory of their League career when, at Forthbank yesterday, in the last home match of the season, they trounced St Bernard to the tune of eight goals to one. Three of the eight came in the first half and five in the second, and all were due to the dashing tactics of the home front rank, who time and again went through the defence, the home halfs and backs giving no hope to the Edinburgh club's forwards, who only made occasional attempts at scoring with no combination or method in them." Toner continued his fine goalscoring form scoring four of his side's goals. Second placed Third Lanark didn't play to avoid a clash with the all Glasgow Scottish Cup final, in which Rangers beat Celtic 4-0. Thirds remained on 43 points with two games to play. East Fife won to have 42 points with a game left. King's Park were fourth, also on 42 points, as were Dundee United, who had been thrashed 7-1 by the champions. Any hopes of taking the promotion battle into the last day of the season were scuppered when Thirds played their rearranged home fixture against Stenhousemuir in midweek, winning 3-1 to guarantee the runners-up spot. On the following Saturday they lost at Arbroath, with King's Park ending their programme with a 3-2 win at Morton, to close the gap to just one point by the end. East Fife and Dundee United both drew ensuring third place for King's Park.

Despite holding on to their prize goalscoring asset in the shape of their centre-forward Toner and the majority of their team, the Parkers were unable to mount another promotion challenge the following season. After an opening day defeat at Forfar they opened their League account with a narrow win over Arthurlie, one of two clubs in the division not to complete the season due to financial problems, but this was the only win in their first six games. A 6-1 loss at Queen of the South and a 5-2 defeat away at East Stirlingshire left them languishing in 15th, where they eventually finished the season.

The 1929-30 season saw an improvement and was one where two club records were set – their longest run without a win and their biggest ever League win. They got off to a cracking start, winning their first four games, including a 7-3 win over Stenhousemuir and victory over Armadale by four goals to nothing. A 6-1 reverse at Albion Rovers halted their progress but they continued to accumulate points and by the end of October they were in seventh place. They then went on to set an unwelcome club record of nine games without a win that saw them drop down the table to 13th place. The run was ended in emphatic style went they beat Alloa 9-0, although the size of this victory was soon surpassed.

On the 2nd January 1930 King's Park recorded their biggest ever Scottish League win, beating Forfar Athletic 12-2. This particular match has entered the annals of history due to the scoring prowess of one man - Jim Dyet. In this match he equalled the record of the most League goals scored in a game, set first by Owen McNally in October 1927 and subsequently matched by Jimmy McGrory in January 1928. What makes his achievement all the more special is that he achieved this incredible feat on his debut!

The festive season is a busy time for football fixtures. On Saturday 28th December 1929 ex-Falkirk winger Hugh Martin had scored four for King's Park in that 9-0 win over Alloa Athletic. Martin was injured in the 3-2 defeat against East Stirling at Firs Park on the 1st January and this presented the Stirling club with a problem, for the team had another fixture the very next day - Thursday 2nd January versus Forfar Athletic at Forthbank. At the last minute, Jim Dyet of Cowlie Juveniles, a Bonnybridge club was signed to fill the vacant jersey. James "Jim" Dyet was born in Dailly, Ayrshire on 14th June 1908 and moved to Bonnybridge aged three. He supported Falkirk as a boy and played for a local team before joining Cowlie Juveniles. He was signed on trial as a replacement centre-forward for the injured Martin on the recommendation of his brother Gilbert, who was the King's Park left-half.

Forfar Athletic started the New Year in fifth place, six points and six places ahead of King's Park. They had in their midst, the League's current top goalscorer in Davie Kilgour. He had scored in their previous game, a 4-3 win over Arbroath which had taken his season's tally up to 24 goals for the season. But Forfar, like King's Park, had suffered some injuries and went into the game with a weakened line up, especially in defence, where they were missing four of their regulars.

Under the headline "Extraordinary Scoring at Stirling" *The Scotsman* reported that: "Despite the heavy scoring the game was always interesting to watch, and although the ground resembled a quagmire, the football by King's Park was of a high standard. Forfar...lacked cohesion and depended too much on individual effort. King's Park on the other hand were in rampant form and every movement bore fruit. The whole forward rank moved with machine-like precision and was well supported by the halves." Scoring got under way as early as the third minute, Dyet winning a 50:50 ball with the Forfar 'keeper, before knocking the ball into the net. It was a dream start for the debutant. And things got better when he then made it two on the quarter of an hour mark, firing home a low shot from six yards out. Forfar greatly missed the steadying influence of their veteran McLean, who was on the injured list, and quickly conceded two further goals, one from Duffy and then a third from Dyet via a header.

With half an hour gone the score stood at 4-0 and Dyet had a hat-trick on debut. Not satisfied he completed his double hat-trick in the fifteen minutes left before the interval. He scored his fourth with another header, his fifth with a well-placed shot into the corner and just on stroke of half-time Dyet rounded a defender and shot inside the left post with his right foot to secure his double hat-trick. The score stood at 7-0 and Dyet was given a standing ovation as he left the field.

Forfar fought back at the beginning of the second period, and pulled a goal back through a Davie Kilgour penalty. Kilgour's goals would be the highlight of Forfar's campaign, establishing a club record of 45 goals in the 1929-30 season. He still sits third on the club's all-time goalscoring list, having netted 107 times in 106 appearances between August 1928 and April 1932. The King's Park defence was proving to be more redoubtable, with Baird at centre-half outstanding for the home team. Baird would score his team's ninth goal, sandwiched in-between strikes from Ross and Murphy. With the score now standing at 10-1 Forfar were reduced to ten men with the sending off of Smith. However, they scored for the second time, thanks to an effort from Forbes. At this point the match report in *The Scotsman* noted the lack of a contribution from the first half hero Dyet. "Conspicuous by his absence so far in the second half action was Jim Dyet but his great day was not over yet." Awakening from his second half slumber, the centre-forward sprang the offside trap, running 25 yards towards goal before unleashing a blistering shot that was so delicious you could have put it inside a buttered roll and eaten it. This goal was Dyet's seventh and King's Park's eleventh.

As the game drew nearer towards its conclusion Anderson was brought down in the penalty area. The ball was offered to Dyet who stepped forward and converted the spot kick, to make it 12-2 – and in doing so he scored his eighth – thereby equalling the record of Owen McNally and Jimmy McGrory. In the last minute of the game Dyet had a chance to make the record his own but his shot was saved by "the Forfar custodian" at the post. When the final whistle blew, the crowd of almost 4,000 spectators, who had endured a cold wet day, showed their appreciation. The young centre-forward walked off to the sounds of cheering and clapping and universal acclaim from his new team mates.

The game itself finished 12-2 to King's Park, a new club record victory, secured just five days after setting the previous benchmark with the 9-0 win over Alloa. But why the apparent mis-match between two mid-table sides? Well, first of all there was the Forthbank pitch, which reassembled a quagmire. But then it was the same for both sides. Second, the Forfar defence was clearly weakened. They were fielding a makeshift defence and rumours later surfaced that some of their players had over-indulged on New Year's Day. But the main reason must lie with the performance of Jim Dyet. Dyet, on his debut, clearly had something to prove and it's well-known that debutants raise their game. Scoring eight on his debut was a remarkable feat and unsurprisingly King's Park wasted no time in signing him on a permanent basis, paying Cowlie Juveniles the princely sum of £3! The full King's Park line-up that day was: Arnott; Crickett, Soutar: Regan, Baird, G Dyet; Duffy, Anderson, J Dyet, Murphy and Ross.

Dyet continued to score goals over the remainder of the season, finishing the season with 25 from 16 games. King's Park finished sixth with a club record of 109 goals in a season, only promoted East Fife scoring more (114). Dyet's goalscoring prowess did not go unnoticed and in July 1930 he was signed by Falkirk for £750 (an excellent piece of business by the Stirling club, making a £747 profit in seven months!) and on a wage of £5 a week. He finished as the Bairns top goalscorer for the 1930-31 season and was then sold onto Dundee United in March 1932. His later career was blighted by injuries and he was never able to emulate his remarkable goal scoring debut. He eventually returned to King's Park, albeit on a part-time basis, before hanging up his boots. He died peacefully in Falkirk Royal infirmary in July 2005, aged 97.

The eventful 1929-30 season was followed by two seasons of little note in which the club finished 14th and 15th. The start of the 1931-32 season saw the club sitting in fourth place at the beginning of September but their early season form soon deteriorated and they won only two of their next 16 League fixtures, and these were against the lowly amateurs of Edinburgh City and Brechin City. They matched the unwelcome club record of nine games without a win and after the New Year's 3-1 defeat at East Stirling the club had slumped to 18th place.

Cometh the hour, cometh the man! Step forward one Alex Haddow! Sometimes referred to as Johnny Haddow, he started his career with Rangers in 1927, making his one and only appearance for them in a 2-1 win over Partick Thistle on the 3rd January 1928. At the end of the 1927-28 season he joined Dumbarton and became a Boghead favourite, regularly topping the club's goalscoring charts. In August 1931 he signed for King's Park and by the turn of the year he had rediscovered his scoring boots. During January and February 1932 Haddow scored five hat-tricks in five consecutive matches, helped by the fact that he also took his side's penalties, but that should not take anything away from his achievement.

Haddow started his amazing sequence by notching four against bottom club Armadale at Forthbank on the 23rd January 1932. In a one-sided affair the home team virtually camped in their opponents half and scored goals at regular intervals. Tracey opened the scoring for the home team after ten minutes. The next ten minutes saw Haddow twice break through but each time his shots were easily saved by Steele in the Armadale goal. Haddow made it third time lucky when he headed home a Tracey cross in the 20th minute to make it 2-0. Ten minutes later Stewart made it 3-0 from a free-kick taken by Regan. In the second half Haddow scored three more times and his side scored six more in total as they easily crushed Armadale 9-0. The full King's Park line up was: Milton, Temple, Soutar, Anderson, Baird, Stewart, Duffy, Regan, Haddow, Hart and Tracey.

The following weekend saw Scottish Cup action with King's Park going out to Airdrie after a replay. In this game played at Broomfield Haddow scored the second goal to put his side 2-1 up (Duffy had scored the first) before the First Division side equalised. King's Park lost the replay at home 3-1, the game played on the 3rd February. When the League programme resumed on the 6th February, the Stirling club hosted promotion hopefuls Stenhousemuir. Both teams took time to settle, the Larbert club having marginally the better of the opening exchanges. And it was the visitors who opened the scoring after 12 minutes through their centre-forward Hart. Robertson's run took him to the bye-line and his cross was met by Hart who beat Kerr, restored to the Parkers goal. King's Park restored parity through Haddow six minutes later. Duffy's crosses had already caused Newman in the visitors' goal some anxious moments, and from his corner Haddow was able to scramble in an equaliser. King's Park were now very much on the offensive and only some stout defence kept the Stirling side out. But King's Park were very much in the ascendancy and Hillan's right-footed drive made it 2-1 with Duffy once more the supplier. The Stenhousemuir defence was floundering now and Haddow scored his third soon after with a cute back-heel and Duffy was rewarded for his efforts when the winger scored to make it 4-1 at half-time. Duffy was a constant threat with his runs down the line and the opposition cause wasn't helped with an injury to Corrie, although Turnbull and Prior did well in the visitors' defence. They held out for a further twenty minutes before Haddow notched up his hat-trick in the 65th minute. Haddow scored two more before the final whistle to make it five in the game and to complete a 7-1 rout of Stenhousemuir, severely denting their promotion credentials. The headlines on the Monday were all about Haddow but Duffy was a constant menace and the backs, Baird, Soutar and Anderson had been commanding in the home defence.

The next round of matches saw King's Park travel to the capital to take on the amateurs of Edinburgh City. They were struggling in their inaugural season and had been on the receiving end of some heavy defeats. However, on this occasion the amateurs put on a good show in a seven goal thriller and were unfortunate not to share the points. Haddow opened the scoring for the visitors before an eventual passage of play saw three penalties awarded. Edinburgh City notched the first of these through Parry before Haddow converted the other two past Arbuthnot for a first half hat-trick. This was his third consecutive league hat-trick. Cumming and Robson scored further goals for the home team but Hillan added a fourth for the visitors who won 4-3.

The following Saturday King's Park played host to Montrose, who were in the bottom four in the table. Despite their recent good form the home team got off to a shaky start and White for the visitors forced Kerr into a good save. But after just five minutes play the Stirling side went ahead. Duffy was the supplier and Regan gave Gerrard in the visitor's goal no chance with a fierce drive. After ten minutes King's Park doubled their lead, Hillan this time scoring from close range and they quickly made it three in just twelve minutes when Duffy scored after good work from Hart. Haddow finally got on the scoresheet himself, converting a first half penalty to give King's Park a 4-0 lead at the interval. All four of the home scorers in the first half scored again in the second half, with Haddow going one better than his colleagues in scoring two, giving him a fourth hat-trick. The King's Park line up was: Kerr, Baird, Soutar, Anderson, Dyet, Hart,

Duffy, Regan, Haddow, Hillan and Tracey; and the goalscorers were: Regan (2), Hillan (2), Duffy (2), Haddow (3, 1 pen).

King's Park's nine goals against Montrose took their tally in their last four games to an amazing 29 goals, which was just one less than the total they had managed in their previous seventeen games. Haddow had scored fifteen of these goals in the four games – each time scoring a hat-trick - and he made it five hat-tricks in as many games the following week. On the 27th February 1932 King's Park travelled to Glebe Park to take on strugglers Brechin City and they won easily, with Haddow scoring three. Haddow's goalscoring feats coincided with an upturn in fortunes for King's Park. At the turn of the year they had been languishing in 18th place having lost eight out of ten games. They were now up to 13th in the division as a result of this remarkable winning sequence, although four of these games were against teams also at the bottom, the exception being the win over fourth placed Stennie. Alas King's Park still only finished 15th, undone by poor form in the autumn of 1931 when they picked up only one point in nine games.

Haddow stayed with the club for one more season and on the 24th December 1932 he scored all six as King's Park beat Raith Rovers 6-0, before returning to Boghead in the summer of 1933. His return proved a success as he scored 33 goals in the 1933-34 season as Dumbarton finished in sixth place, one above King's Park. In November 1935 he moved to Falkirk, and scored a hat-trick against his old club and notched up 21 goals in his six months there. His spell was brief though and in May 1936 he moved to Leith Athletic. After retiring as a player he took on a coaching role back at Dumbarton.

King's Park finished eighth in the 1932-33 season, their inconsistent form perhaps best summed up by the two matches played against Raith Rovers. As mentioned above, Haddow scored all six in a 6-0 win in December. The Stirling club had opened the new season with a 9-1 defeat against Raith, at that point, their record League defeat. In mitigation, they were handicapped by a loss of a player early on, Regan, their inside-right was taken to hospital in Kirkcaldy for treatment to a cut head.

The following season they went one place better, finishing in seventh place and they matched that in the 1934-35 season. This campaign was notable for a club record winning streak in the League and a marathon Scottish Cup tie against First Division Ayr United. On the 22nd September 1934 King's Park beat Leith Athletic 2-1, coming from behind to win the game when a draw was the fairer result. This win started a run of seven League wins in a row that lasted until early November. Included in this run was a 9-4 win over Edinburgh City at the end of September, in which Bryce, their centre-forward, scored four. The Parkers moved up from sixth place to the top of the table and opened up a three point lead on eventual champions Third Lanark. The run ended in a 4-2 loss in Greenock against Morton in which they conceded two penalties and had Baird, their centre-half, ordered from the field. Things began to unravel during December as they went down 7-2 at Cowdenbeath. They led twice in this game but an injury meant they then had to play the majority of the match with ten men and before the break they conceded three goals in as many minutes. Later in the month they also lost at promotion rivals St Bernard's and new leaders Third Lanark and at the turn of the year they had slipped back to fifth.

Having knocked Edinburgh City out of the Scottish Cup in the First Round King's Park drew Ayr United of the First Division. The two clubs shared a marathon Cup tie which took four games to separate them, played between the 9th February to the 19th. Nearly 10,000 spectators watched their first match at Somerset Park, where Ayr United, who were struggling at the bottom of the First Division, took the lead after 23 minutes. King's Park equalised seven minutes before the interval to earn a replay. A defensive mix-up between Ayr's keeper Hepburn and his back Currie, where they collided, allowed Bryce to take control of the ball and play in Lang to score into an empty net.

The following Wednesday, the 13th, the two sides met at Forthbank and over 7,000 watched the replay. The home team dominated early on but a mistake by Milton in the King's Park goal allowed United to take the lead. Baird then equalised before half time. King's Park now took the lead when Young headed home on 58 minutes but with twenty minutes to go McGibbon levelled. With the score level at 2-2 at 90 minutes an additional half an hour was played. The referee awarded King's Park a penalty for handball during extra time but controversially changed his decision after consulting a linesman. The tie remained undecided even after extra time, with the eventual winners of the contest being drawn away to Airdrieonians.

On the Saturday the 16th February, the League programme was resumed and the two sides had contrasting fortunes. King's Park beat Brechin City 8-1 despite making six changes, with Bryce scoring four. Ayr United suffered a blow to their relegation battle losing 7-1 at Aberdeen. On the Monday night the two sides met on neutral territory in Glasgow for a second replay. The game was played at Firhill in front of a crowd of 6,000 and after another two hours the two sides were still level. King's Park got off to a flying start and took the lead after a quarter of an hour through Lang and then five minutes later doubled their lead through Young from a corner kick. Ayr were awarded a penalty, for handball, and scored and McGibbon equalised the score so that at half time it was 2-2. The second half had only been seven minutes in progress when Lang restored the lead but less than ten minutes later Ayr drew level again and at full-time the score was 3-3. In extra time Ayr took the lead through McGibbon in the 101st minute but King's

Park immediately attacked and incredibly Fowler equalised and the game ended 4-4. At the end of the game it was decided that the two teams would stay on in Glasgow and meet again the following day, although this time at Hampden Park.

After playing seven hours of football in which 17 goals were scored, King's Park finally defeated Ayr United in their fourth meeting, winning 2-1. *The Scotsman* reported that "at one stage it looked as if Ayr United would gain a mastery which would secure victory. They were confronted, however, by a resolute and skilful defence, in which Hillan, a shrewd tactician, was outstanding. Even when King's Park found themselves a goal in arrears, they were always fighting with a chance, and it was this unflinching spirit which ultimately changed what looked like defeat into a brilliant victory." McGibbon scored yet again, opening the scoring for Ayr United in the 18th minute. Seven minutes later a penalty was awarded to the Forthbank side, which was surprisingly missed by Bryce. Two minutes before half-time a second penalty was awarded to King's Park, and they must have thought it wasn't going to be their day when Baird missed this one as well! Both spot kicks had been awarded for handball. In the second half King's Park scored two quick goals. In the 56th minute Young set up Andrew for the equaliser. Two minutes later Bryce harassed the Ayr defence and the ball ran loose for Lang to pounce on and cross. The Ayr keeper spilled the cross and Andrew drove home the ball. Over 14,000 fans watched the tie eventually be settled. Total attendance at the four matches was 37,000 and nearly £1,400 was taken (close to £100,000 in today's money). Just four days later the Third Round tie was played, King's Park losing 6-2 at Airdrieonians, although the game was not as one-sided as the score suggests. The Parkers were only one down at the interval and not surprisingly ran out of steam, still feeling the effects of their four games with Ayr.

King's Park resumed in the League with two defeats in early March and although these were followed by a 5-1 win over Montrose in which Bryce scored a hat-trick, they were now in sixth, ten points behind second place with only four games to play. Two wins and two defeats in these matches saw them eventually placed in seventh for the second season in a row. They would never again achieve such heights.

The club won their opening two games of the 1935-36 season but then lost 5-1 at home to Stenhousemuir and this was followed by an 8-0 thrashing at the hands of Cowdenbeath. Their hosts stormed into a lead by scoring three times in the first eight minutes and they added a fourth goal midway through the first half. Cowdenbeath eased off but after the resumption they added further goals. Milton was an absentee from the King's Park goal, and the poor display of his Purdon, his replacement seemed to demoralise his backs. In October they lost 4-0 at East Stirlingshire and 6-1 at Dumbarton and in early November they were beaten 5-0 at perennial strugglers

Edinburgh City, a result that left them 14th. They picked up a few wins across the remainder of 1935 but on the 18th January 1936 they suffered their record SFL defeat when Falkirk beat them 10-2 at a snowy Brockville. *The Scotsman* reported that "the game at Brockville Park proved to be a very one-sided affair, Falkirk beating King's Park with the greatest of ease by ten goals to two. On the snow covered, frost-bound pitch, the Stirling team were never happy, whereas Falkirk, once they got properly into their stride, played sparkling football, proving as effective at close quarters as they were attractive in the open. It was a sorry day for the King's Park defenders, although Milton, in goal, takes no blame for the heavy defeat. Indeed, but for his brilliant work the Falkirk score might have been higher still….At the start there was no suggestion that Falkirk were to have a runaway victory, for King's Park made quite a lively start, and went within an ace of opening the scoring. When the home men got going, however, they moved to grand purpose, although it was not until the 26th minute that they claimed the first goal…Keyes following two minutes later with a second, and adding a third soon afterwards. Two minutes before the interval Cowan registered a fourth but this was followed immediately by a penalty goal for King's Park, Strathie scoring. In the second half Falkirk toyed with the opposition and collected six goals…Keyes, displacing Haddow at centre-forward for the day, scored five [overall]…while Miller got King's Park's second point." King's Park suffered further heavy defeats, although none were quite so bad, going down 8-1 at St Mirren and 9-2 at East Fife in March. They picked up four points in their last three matches and eventually came in 14th place, having conceded over 100 goals for the season. They finished six points ahead of Raith Rovers, who, together with Dumbarton, were re-elected unopposed.

This fate befell them in the 1936-37 season as they finished in the bottom two, along with Edinburgh City, both teams being re-elected as no other clubs applied. They lost their opening game 4-2 at home to Dundee United, Arthur Milne scoring all four. Milton, the former King's Park goalkeeper was playing against his old side. In mid-September they lost 8-3 at home to Cowdenbeath but in early October they secured back-to-back wins, beating Leith Athletic 6-4 and Raith Rovers 5-1. Defence was again their Achilles heel and they again conceded over 100 goals and in December they conceded six in consecutive matches, 6-1 at St Bernard's and 6-0 at Morton and they ended 1936 in eleventh place.

On the 2nd January they beat bottom side Edinburgh City 4-1 (who only earned seven points all season) and then drew 3-3 at Dundee United a week later. On the 16th January they lost 3-1 at home to Stenhousemuir, the first of seven League defeats in a row, which included a 6-3 loss at Dumbarton and 5-0s versus Forfar and against Ayr. In between, on the 13th February, Hearts recorded their biggest ever win in the Scottish Cup when they beat King's Park 15-0. Willie Walsh, their big bustling centre-forward, scored a club record eight goals in this game, including a first half hat-trick. Hearts led 9-0 at half-time and Walsh scored seven consecutive goals (eight through to fourteen). The other scorers were Tommy Walker (2), Andy Black (2), Jimmy Dykes, John Harvey and Freddie Warren. Hearts were managerless, the game being played only a few days after David Pratt had resigned over internal wrangling at the club. Willie Walsh was sold to Millwall later that year for a fee of £2,500.

King's Park didn't win again until the 10th April, only the shocking form of Edinburgh City keeping them off the bottom. They eventually beat Brechin City 2-1, thanks to two penalties, their first win since the 2nd January. At the League's AGM on the 26th May King's Park were re-elected along with Edinburgh City, as both clubs were unopposed.

The 1937-38 season was a marked improvement as the club came in 12th. They lost their first two games, fielding a makeshift team, but then won 6-2 at Cowdenbeath, McDowall scoring a hat-trick. They then went on to lose 6-0 at East Stirlingshire and this inconsistency would plague them throughout the season – winning 4-2 one week, but then losing 5-1 the next. In February 1938 a strange episode occurred that resulted in the chairman of the club and two players being banned. The incident arose following a League game between King's Park and St Bernard's. The two teams had already met twice in the Scottish Cup, the Edinburgh side winning 4-3 in midweek in Stirling in the replay. St Bernard's also won the League game at Forthbank, 1-0, following a penalty for handball. At the interval during this game the referee was alleged to have heard the Chairman of King's Park, Tom Fergusson, telling his players to get rough and not to worry about any fines for being sent-off, as he would cover them. The official subsequently referred to this in his official report. Two months later, on the 12th April 1938, *The Scotsman* reported that "the Referee Committee of the SFA met yesterday afternoon and continued the investigation of the report by Referee R E Carruthers regarding the statement alleged to have been made by a director of King's Park FC at the interval of the League game between that club and St Bernard's on February 19 at Forthbank, Stirling. Further evidence was taken, and at the conclusion of the meeting the Press were informed that the Committee had arrived at the following decisions: - Director T H Fergusson suspended from taking any part in football until 16th May 1939. Players W Deans and W Clark (both of King's Park) suspended until January 1, 1939, on account of the Committee being dissatisfied with their evidence." Thomas Henry Fergusson was a local businessman who had founded Fergusson Coal, located on Wallace Street, in 1926. As Chairman of the club he would go on to have a major part to play in the club's demise…along with the German Luftwaffe.

The 1938-39 season was the club's last full season in the Scottish Football League. The made another poor start, drawing their opening game by throwing away a two goal over Edinburgh City, before losing the next five, until a 6-0 win over Brechin City on the 24th September gave them their first win of the season and lifted them off the bottom. On the 8th October they caused a major surprise by beating Forfar Athletic 11-3. Keenan was the only King's Park forward who failed to score. Kennedy (3), Paterson (3), Ferguson (2), and Duncan did score, as did Holland, with two penalties. At the end of the month they beat Montrose 7-1, Paterson scoring another hat-trick. After two wins in early November they failed to win again in 1938 and they went into 1939 in 14th place.

In January 1939 King's Park were in Scottish Cup action and were knocked out by Babcock & Wilcox of Renfrewshire, a boiler works team, after a replay. The Parkers led 2-0 but went into the interval 4-2 down and were trailing 5-4, saving their blushes by equalising in the last ten minutes. However, they lost the replay 3-2. In February they beat Morton 6-5 back in the League. The club had six different scorers in a game of fluctuating fortunes in which the margin between the teams was never more than a single goal.

They continued to feature in a number of high scoring games. In early March they beat St Bernard's 5-0, Paterson and Walker each scoring two. A month later they beat Forfar 6-5 away in an amazing game. Walker netted the deciding goal in the closing seconds, scoring five overall and Keenan had the other. Reid of Forfar also netted five but ended up on the beaten side. At the end of April, in the final game of the season, they lost to Dunfermline 7-1, playing part of the game short-handed. Walker got their goal.

The 1939-40 season only lasted four matches before the League was suspended due to the outbreak of the Second World War. Their last game before the SFL was suspended was on the 2nd September 1939, the day before war was declared. King's Park hosted East Stirlingshire and shared the points in a 2-2 draw in what would eventually prove to be their last ever SFL game. The visitors took an early lead but goals from Ferguson and Anderson gave King's Park the half-time lead. East Stirlingshire equalised three minutes from the end. The King's Park team taking that field that day was: Glannandrea; Bourhill, Naismith; Reay, Harrison, Moffat; Stewart, Kennan, Anderson, Ferguson and Duncan. When war broke out King's Park were sitting equal third, enjoying a decent start with six points from four games.

In October the League restarted with two regional divisions of 16 clubs apiece and King's Park played in the Eastern Division. They played their first fixture on the 21st October, beating Arbroath 2-0. They eventually finished eleventh, although Cowdenbeath withdrew mid-season.

King's Park became a casualty of the Second World War in a very direct way. Censorship of the German Luftwaffe bombing raids means that details are sketchy but it appears that in the early hours of Saturday 20th July 1940 a plane, on a possible raid on Clydebank, dropped a couple of bombs on Stirling. One missed completely, landing harmlessly in a field, but the other landed on Forthbank, destroying one wing of the grandstand and leaving a deep crater, 18 feet deep and 30 feet in diameter in the pitch.

In the spring of 1945, with hostilities drawing to a conclusion, the club's future came up for discussion. Tom Fergusson, wanted to purchase the Annfield Estate, a stone's throw away from the old Forthbank, and re-establish senior football as soon as possible. However, the majority of the King's Park board wanted to wait for war compensation before re-starting the club. Fergusson decided to go his own way and established Stirling Albion FC. Annfield opened on the 1st August 1945 and the first game played at Annfield was Stirling Albion's Eastern League game against Edinburgh City on the 18th August 1945, which Stirling Albion won 8-3. Fergusson was the manager of the new club until 1960 and he remained a director until his death in 1967.

Stirling Albion were admitted to the new third level Division 'C' for the 1946-47 season. This ten team division included three reserve sides and they won their opening game on the 10th August 1946 4-1 away at Dundee A. Stirling Albion went on to win the division, losing only one game all season, leading to their promotion to Division Two (or 'B').

It was not until 1953 that the War Office settled King's Park's claim, which went entirely to pay off their creditors after which the club was formally wound up. On the 8th August that year, under the headline "Bombed out club pays a dividend", the *Evening Times* reported that "the final echo of the bomb that blasted King's Park FC, the former Stirling Second Division club out of existence in the early part of the last war and indirectly led to the formation of Stirling Albion was heard today. It was contained in an announcement that at a meeting of the shareholders of King's Park FC (in liquidation) the liquidator intimated that his committee had approved the payment of a first and final dividend to the creditors of 19s per £1. No surplus was available to the shareholders. The funds from which the distribution is being made arise from compensation received from the War Damage Commission as a result of a claim for damage to Forthbank ground and stand by enemy air action during the last war." King's Park and St Bernard's of Edinburgh, were the only pre-war clubs not to re-appear.

In 1993 Stirling Council constructed a new Forthbank Stadium to replace a now deteriorating Annfield, on the outskirts of the town, situated about two thirds of a mile from the location of the original King's Park's ground of Forthbank Park.

The old Stirling club, won precisely nothing during its 18 year Scottish League career, although they were four times winners of the Stirlingshire Cup. Their best season came in 1927-28, when they just missed promotion by one point.

SEASON	LEAGUE	P	W	D	L	F	A	P	POS
1921-22	SCOT-2	38	10	12	16	47	65	32	17/20
1922-23	SCOT-2	38	14	6	18	46	60	34	12/20
1923-24	SCOT-2	38	16	10	12	67	56	42	6/20
1924-25	SCOT-2	38	15	8	15	54	46	38	10/20
1925-26	SCOT-2	38	14	9	15	67	73	37	13/20
1926-27	SCOT-2	38	13	9	16	76	75	35	12/20
1927-28	SCOT-2	38	16	12	10	84	68	44	3/20
1928-29	SCOT-2	36	8	13	15	60	84	29	15/19
1929-30	SCOT-2	38	17	8	13	109	80	42	6/20
1930-31	SCOT-2	38	14	6	18	78	70	34	14/20
1931-32	SCOT-2	38	14	5	19	97	93	33	15/20
1932-33	SCOT-2	34	13	8	13	85	80	34	8/18
1933-34	SCOT-2	34	14	8	12	78	70	36	7/18
1934-35	SCOT-2	34	18	2	14	86	71	38	7/18
1935-36	SCOT-2	34	11	5	18	55	109	27	14/18
1936-37	SCOT-2	34	11	3	20	61	106	25	17/18
1937-38	SCOT-2	34	11	4	19	64	96	26	12/18
1938-39	SCOT-2	34	12	2	20	87	92	26	13/18
1939-40	SCOT-2	4	2	2	0	11	7	6	ABAND

Leith Athletic

Formed: 1887
Colours: Navy blue (black from 1905) and white vertical striped shirts, navy blue shorts
Ground: Bank Park (renamed Beechwood Park), Hawkhill Recreation Ground, Old Logie
Green, New Powderhall, Marine Gardens, (Old) Meadowbank, New Meadowbank
Entered League: 1891. Elected to First Division. 1924 Elected to Third Division. 1927
Elected to Second Division. 1946 Reinstated to Division 'C' (third tier)
Number of League Seasons: 45 (across four spells-24+2+12+7)
Highest League Finish: 4th in Division One 1891-92
Honours: Second Division Champions 1905-06, 1909-10, 1929-30
Left League: 1915. Second Division disbanded. 1926. Third Division abandoned. 1939.
League suspended due to war. 1953. Expelled. Folded in 1955.

Leith is best known as the port of the City of Edinburgh, home to the Scottish
Executive, the last mooring of the Royal Yacht Britannia and as the title of a song by the
group the Proclaimers: *"Sunshine on Leith"*. Few would recall that the port of Leith
once had a top flight football team, with nearly a half-century of completed seasons
and with three Second Division titles to their credit.

Leith Athletic, were formed in 1887 and had joined the Scottish Football League for its
second season, 1891-92, replacing Cowlairs. They became Edinburgh's second team to
gain admission, their entry pre-dating that of Hibernian, with Hearts being one of the
original founding members. The club's colours were black and white striped shirts and
black shorts and they played their games at a variety of grounds including Hawkhill,
Bank Park, Logie Green, Powderhall, Marine Gardens, and Meadowbank.

 In their debut season they finished fourth, one place below Hearts but above Rangers.
In the process they beat former Cup holders Vale of Leven 10-0 in September 1891. The
club was unable to sustain its excellent start and they lost their top flight status after
just four seasons. They had been re-elected in 1894 but secured only three votes the
following year. They did go onto win two Second Division titles, in 1906 and 1910
(shared with Raith) and were runners up on four occasions. However, promotion was
by election as there was no automatic promotion until 1921 and the club were
overlooked.

Leith Athletic didn't immediately return to the League after the Great War, and eventually returned to the recently formed Third Division in 1924. When this collapsed just two years later they were denied a place in the Second Division and lost their League status yet again. They didn't have to wait as long this time as they were successfully voted back a year later, re-joining for the 1927-28 season. They won a third Second Division championship in 1930, this time gaining automatic promotion to Scotland's top flight. Life was hard in the First Division and they were relegated after two seasons, conceding a record number of goals in the 1931-32 season. Up until the outbreak of the Second World War they mainly finished in mid-table in the Second Division.

On the resumption of League football after the war Leith Athletic were unhappy at being placed in the 'C' division, which was a mix of clubs and reserve sides. The following season the decision was taken to expand the Second Division from 14 to 16 clubs and Leith were elected to one of the vacancies having finished third in League Division C. Unfortunately they finished bottom of Division B and dropped back down again into the third tier. This division was restructured for the 1949–50 season when the number of reserve sides was significantly expanded and the Division divided into two sections, Leith joining Division C (North & East). They played on for four seasons, continually agitating for expansion and election to the Second Division. When they failed to make any headway they took the unusual step of refusing to play their games. Leith Athletic were eventually expelled in August 1953 for refusing to fulfil any Division C games. In a supreme irony, the two regional Division Cs were abandoned a couple of years later, and in 1955, just as Leith had wanted, the non-reserve sides were admitted to the Second Division. In the same year Leith Athletic folded.

Leith Athletic were formed in 1887 and played their home games at Bank Park, which was located near Lochend Road and Hawkhill Avenue. They made their debut in the Scottish Cup in September of that year, losing 4-1 to Bo'ness on the 3rd September 1887. Just over a week later they also appeared in the East of Scotland Shield for the first time. They beat Haddington Rangers in the First Round before being knocked out by Hibernian 1-0 in the next round. Results of matches from this time also reveal the existence of a Leith Harp and Leith Wanderers. In the 1888-89 competition they knocked Hibs out in the First Round in a run to the final, where they were beaten by Hearts, 5-2, in a match played at Easter Road on the 2nd March 1889. In their second appearance in the Scottish Cup they were thrashed by fellow Edinburgh side St Bernard's 7-0 in the First Round.

In the 1889-90 season they reached the final of the East of Scotland Shield for the second time. Their opponents were once again Hearts, and this final was lost as well, Hearts winning 2-0. Of more significance was their run to the Scottish Cup Quarter-finals in the same season. Local teams such as Adventurers, Edinburgh University and Broxburn were all knocked out before they knocked out Ayr FC after a replay to meet the then eight time winners Queen's Park for a place in the Semi-final. Leith put in a fine display with Laing coming close on a number of occasions in an even first half. The second half followed a similar pattern with *The Glasgow Herald* commenting that "the Queen's were clearly not in good form; they lacked their usual dash, combination and shooting at goal...The Athletic men continued to play up with increasing energy, and fairly outplayed the Queen's by their splendid passing, rapid runs, and surprising goalkeeping. Indeed, for a long time they had the best of the play...and it looked like the home team were going to be beaten, so well were the visitors playing, and so indifferently were the Queen's showing up." However, with only a few minutes remaining Queen's Park scored an undeserved winner. Their opponents went on to lift the trophy but the Leith team won plenty of admirers with their display, the *Glasgow Herald* commenting that "the Leith men, by their smart play and splendid defence, especially in goal, won golden opinions, and will no doubt be heartily welcomed when they return to Glasgow."

The following season saw the formation of the Scottish Football League, with Hearts as the only representative from the east of Scotland. Leith Athletic matched their run to the Quarter-finals of the Scottish Cup and in the Third Round registered a club record win of 12-0 over Adventurers of Edinburgh, *The Scotsman* simply reporting this as a "phenomenal score." In the next round they recorded a fine win over seven-time finalist and three time winners Vale of Leven, who were also one of the founding League members. Despite miserable weather a crowd of 2,000 came out to Bank Park for the game. The match kicked off late due to the late arrival of the visitors. Leith won the game 3-1 but by the end, and with dusk approaching, the players were barely discernible. Vale lodged a protest on these grounds, which was quite astonishing given it was their late arrival which had caused the delay in the first place!

After receiving a bye in the Fifth Round they drew League opposition in the shape of Abercorn of Paisley, who they hosted on the 20th December 1890. Due to a frost there was a pitch inspection with the Bank Park pitch hard in places. The visitors scored two goals in the first half but early in the second half Leith succeeded in equalising. Nearing the end, and during the absence of M McQueen, who had "incurred the displeasure of the referee" (*The Scotsman*), Abercorn scored the winning goal to progress to the Semi-final. Leith subsequently lodged a protest on a number of grounds including "on account of the state of the ground, which, they allege, the referee at first declared unplayable, but ultimately gave way to the representations of the Abercorn captain...and in consequence of McQueen being ordered off the field without a previous caution." On Tuesday the 6th of January 1891 the SFA met and Leith's protests were dismissed.

Better news followed when, on the 28th March 1891, inside left Robert Clements and Matthew McQueen played for Scotland against Ireland in Glasgow. McQueen had been capped the year before against Wales. The two strong Scottish Cup runs and the presence of Scotland internationals in their side meant that the cub could make a compelling case to join the League. At the end of the League's first season and at the SFL AGM held on the 5th June 1891, Leith Athletic were elected to replace Cowlairs from Glasgow. Renton returned having been expelled and Clyde were added to provide an expanded League of 12 teams. Leith Athletic therefore joined the Scottish Football League for its second season and finished a very respectable fourth, completing vindicating their participation. This would turn out to be their best placed finish, achieved in their first ever season.

On the 15th August 1891 Leith Athletic played their first ever Scottish League game, winning 3-0 away at Third Lanark. Centre-forward Robert Laing scored their first League goal after 20 minutes and they led 1-0 at the interval. A Hugh McQueen strike and an own goal gave them a convincing opening victory. Their first ever League line up was: Robert Burnside; Robert McCartney, William Anderson; Matthew McQueen, George Anderson, E Stevenson; Alex McLeod, Robert Clements, Robert Laing, Alex Mathieson and Hugh McQueen.

Clements and Matthew McQueen were already Scotland internationals. Matthew McQueen played for the club 1885-87 and 1890-92 and in-between played for Hearts. He joined Liverpool in 1892 along with his younger brother Hugh. He went on to manage Liverpool between 1923 and 1928. Centre-half Geordie Anderson also left Leith in 1892 to join Blackburn Rovers and later played for Blackpool. Robert Laing later played for St Bernard's. In April 1893, while at Leith he played for the Scottish League versus the Irish League.

On the 22nd August Leith Athletic played their first home League game at Bank Park in front of a crowd of around 5,000. Leith were beaten 3–2 by Renton; Renton's James McCall scoring the first-ever penalty kick in SFL history during the game. Leith scored first through an own-goal. Renton got level via the penalty kick, *The Scotsman* describing the historic moment: "a continual pressure was kept up on the home goal and in a scrimmage near the goal mouth G Anderson fouled the ball. As a result, the new rule was brought into requisition. J McCall, the Renton captain, took the kick and with a well-directed shot sent the ball well out of Burnside's reach, thus placing the teams on terms of equality." Renton took the lead but then Leith missed their own penalty kick, the paper reporting that "a foul similar to that in the first half was given against the visitors. M McQueen took the kick and though his shot was a good one, Lindsay very adroitly knocked the ball over the bar." The visitors then made it 3-1 before Laing scored to set up pulsating finish but the home team couldn't convert their chances.

Mixed fortunes initially followed, best illustrated when they lost 6-0 at joint champions Dumbarton, only to win 10-0 the following week at home to Vale of Leven. Reporting on the second of these matches, *The Scotsman* wrote "at Bank Park, the Leith Athletic secured a great victory over the once famous Vale of Leven by the large score of ten goals to nil. The visitors came without their renowned goalkeeper, Wilson, and three others of their customary eleven. The Leith Club tried a new centre in Scott of the Cameron Highlanders, but his play generally was somewhat unsatisfactory. The attendance was only about 1500 when the Leith men started the game against the wind. They had decidedly the best of the argument in the opening stages. Two corners in quick succession were forced by H McQueen from Henderson. No gain to the Athletic came by these…[then]…the Vale assailed continuously for a lengthy period, and there was no mistake that they were having the home team at every point. Ultimately, Hugh McQueen again got away…and forced a corner. Another followed, and as a result Blessington drew first blood twenty minutes after the start. Up to this point the play, in short, had been tame. The Vale retaliated strongly, but the Athletic were now fairly under weigh, and a prolonged attack on the back division of the visitors followed. Sturdy was the defence…but the goal was doomed to fail, and with a grand attempt M. McQueen put on the second point. The Athletic had the better of improved play up to half-time, when the score was: Leith Athletic, two goals; Vale of Leven, nil. On the game being restarted the Vale led the way…A grand throw-in by McQueen gave Scott a chance which he availed himself of, but the Highlander was off-side on appeal to the referee. Soon after G Anderson made no mistake, and while the Vale were playing with but ten men, Busby having a minute previously been rendered hors de combat, the third goal was scored amid much enthusiasm. A few minutes later Mathieson gained the fourth from a pass by Blessington and the fifth was scrimmaged through by Scott, whose play, though it left much room for improvement, was fast becoming more effective. Busby returned to the field to see the Athletic press harder than ever and a marked improvement visible in the Leith play generally. On the right, Laing and Blessington worked wonders. From the attack G Anderson got the sixth goal from twenty-five yards out, and a somewhat similar one brought the seventh from H McQueen. W Anderson, from a foul kick close in, scored the eighth, and the ninth came by Scott. In the last thirty minutes of the game the Leith men were continuously around Henderson [in the Vale goal]. The double figure followed just on time, and the game resulted:-Leith Athletic, ten goals; Vale of Leven, nil." Their record highest scoring win thus came very early in their SFL history. The Leith team who set this record was: Burnside; W Anderson, McCartney; Stevenson, G Anderson, M McQueen; Blessington, Laing, Scott, Mathieson, and H McQueen. One notable change in this line-up was the inclusion of James Blessington who would controversially join Celtic in the summer of 1892 and who would later gain four caps for Scotland against England and Ireland between 1894 and 1896.

The result against Vale of Leven was the first of four consecutive wins, with the other victories coming over St Mirren, Cambuslang and Rangers. These results took them up to fourth but any hopes of a championship challenge were quickly dispelled when a 3-1 defeat at Hearts was the first of three straight losses. In mid-December they suffered a blow when they were knocked out of the Scottish Cup in the Second Round by non-League Annbank, 2-1. However, a strong finish during the hot spring of 1892 saw Leith finish in fourth in the League in their very first season, justifying their election to the League. They were well supported as well and near to the end of the season, a record crowd of 6,000 watched a 2-1 win over Celtic.

Leith Athletic kicked off their second season as a Scottish League club on the 20th August 1892 by beating Clyde 3-0. *The Scotsman* commented that "a successful start was made by the Leith Athletic on Saturday with their League engagements for the season, their opponents, the Clyde, being defeated by three goals to nil. Throughout, notwithstanding the absence of Blessington, who is understood to be in the western city, they gave an exhibition of the game which proved highly gratifying to their supporters" The goals were scored by Henderson, McLeod and George Anderson - all in second half.

The reference to the absence of Blessington being in the "western city" refers to his disputed transfer to Celtic. Blessington wanted to transfer from Leith to Celtic but his request had been refused. The player then turned out for a Celtic IX who played against Johnstone in a friendly a few days later and he formally signed for Celtic on the 27th August. Leith subsequently protested and the transfer was investigated by the authorities. *The Scotsman* reported that "an important adjourned meeting of this body was held in Glasgow last night to consider an application from the Celtic Club for the transfer of a player named Blessington from the Leith Athletic, on the strength of a statement made to Leith by that player. The Athletic objected to that transfer. After a long discussion, the League suspended Blessington for one week, after which he is eligible to play for Celtic." Blessington subsequently made his debut for Celtic, against Rangers, on the 24th September. Celtic went on to be crowned champions. During the time of this transfer saga Leith suffered five consecutive defeats and at the 1st October 1892 they were joint bottom.

On the 8th October Leith beat Renton 3-2 away and this kick-started a run of four consecutive wins which included a 5-1 win over St Mirren and a 3-0 win over the champions Dumbarton. This was achieved against a background of turmoil in the team line-up as the brothers McQueen left to join Liverpool and Geordie Anderson went to Blackburn Rovers. Reporting on the situation, *The Scotsman* noted that "prior to the match the composition of the Athletic team was freely discussed, the secession of the McQueens and Anderson being looked upon as likely to weaken the Leith team considerably. The officials experienced some difficulty getting an eleven together, but eventually were successful, although they hardly looked for favourable results. It must therefore have been a matter for satisfaction to them to witness the brilliant play of their chosen ones and the manner in which they completely outplayed their opponents." In their next game, Leith beat Dumbarton 3-0 at Bank Park, although *The Scotsman* commented that "the score did not accurately represent the display of the teams, for the west country players had slightly the better of matters." Cox, in the Leith goal, made a string of fine saves and "gave an exhibition of goalkeeping such as is seldom witnessed." Leith took an early lead through Henderson before the visitors lay siege to their hosts' goal, only Cox standing between them and parity. Gradually Leith asserted themselves and Laing scored a second after the break, with Russell adding a third from a swift counter-attack near the end. "The performance of the Leith team, despite recent defections, was a highly creditable one, and greatly pleased their enthusiastic supporters. Saturday's victory was the fifth in succession for the Athletic." By the end of November Leith had climbed to fifth. They beat Renton 6-2 in April, their opponents turning up an hour late after missing their connection in Glasgow. *The Scotsman* reported that "the return League engagement between these teams was played at Bank Park before a pretty large gathering of spectators. The match was advertised to start at four o'clock, but it was nearly an hour after that time before the Renton put in an appearance, their explanation for the delay being that the train was late...The Athletic rearranged their team, no fewer than six second eleven men being promoted to the senior team. The changes made by the Leith officials wrought admirably, Renton being completely outplayed and defeated by six goals to two." The two sides swapped goals in the first half and went into the break level at 2-2. Continuing its report *The Scotsman* observed that "the second half calls for little description, as there was clearly only one team in it. In fact, Renton have seldom got such a decided defeat by an eastern club; and although the Athletic were materially assisted by the wind, their forwards dribbled splendidly." Leith went on to finish in sixth place.

In the Scottish Cup, Leith beat Orion of Aberdeen 11-2 in the First Round Played at Central Park, Aberdeen, in a match played on the 25th November 1892. Leith won the toss and kicked off with the advantage of the slope. Hislop scored first for Leith before the hosts equalised. C. Henderson restored Leith's advantage and then Hislop scored a third. Close to half-time Orion got one back. "The second period opened with bright prospects for the local men. With only one go down, and the incline and a slight breeze in their favour, it looked like the Orion being able to pull off the match. The Leith men, however, started in a determined fashion, and played for all they were worth." (*The Scotsman*) Leith completely dominated the second half and scored goal after goal, scoring eight in the half, and ran out with an emphatic 11-2 victory. There would be no extended Cup run though, as they went out to eventual winners Rangers in the next round.

In the 1893-94 season Leith Athletic finished in ninth place, in a ten team top division. Although a new Second Division had been formed there was no automatic promotion or relegation so they faced an election at the League's AGM at the end of the season. The new season opened promisingly with a 2-0 away win against city rivals Hearts with second half goals from John Scott and James Henderson. But they then lost four in a row before another city rival win, this time 4-2 over St Bernard's. Leith continued to struggle in the League and won only four games all season, the last of these being a 5-0 win over newly crowned champions Celtic on the 17th March. The game also saw a change of venue, as described by *The Scotsman*: "complaints having been made by some clubs that owing to the uneven nature of the surface of Bank Park the Leith Athletic were given an advantage over opposing teams, Hawkhill football ground, which had again been leased by the Company, was opened on Saturday under the most auspicious circumstances - the home team defeating the League champions by the tall score of five goals to nil before 3000 spectators. No other victory could have so thoroughly silenced those who contended that the Athletic were given a decided advantage when playing at Bank Park, for the football pitch at Hawkhill is as good as any in the kingdom. Though the Celtic were without the services of two such able men as McMahon and Doyle, who were reported to be on the injured list, this in itself was not a sufficient reason for the severe reverse, which can best be explained by at once stating that the Athletic were the superior team. ...the Celtic...had to retire pointless, and with a defeat, the like of which they have seldom, if ever, sustained in a League encounter."

Leith reached the Final of the East of Scotland Shield, where they were again beaten by Hearts. The initial game in February was affected by the weather and a poor pitch so the final was rescheduled and played in May, Hearts winning 4-2.

At the Scottish League's AGM, held on the 1st June 1894, Leith were successfully re-elected to the First Division with 8 votes. Dundee (also re-elected) and Clyde, from the Second Division (who effectively replaced Renton) each had 14. The unsuccessful clubs were Cowlairs (who got 4 votes), Renton (who got 3) and the very first Second Division champions, Hibernian (who could only muster 1 vote).

If the club's 1893-94 performance and subsequent involvement in a re-election vote was a warning, then Athletic didn't heed it. At the end of the 1894-95 season they found themselves in exactly the same situation, only this time they couldn't raise the support needed to stay in the top flight. Leith won only three games this time, setting a new club record for the fewest wins in a League season and gained just seven points, matching the poor performance of Dumbarton. Leith faced a second successive re-election vote and this time the club was relegated to the Second Division.

For the new season their ground was renamed Beechwood Park. They lost their opening game here 2-1 against St Mirren on the 18th August 1894 and lost the next five as well, only registering their first points in a 3-2 win over Third Lanark on the 22nd September. They led this game 3-2 at half time and in the second half Thirds lay siege to the Athletic goal but were unable to beat goalkeeper Archie Kay. Leith secured their second win by the same scoreline against Dundee in mid-October, a victory that lifted them off the bottom, above Dumbarton, and now level on points with Third Lanark.

The following month they beat Abercorn 5-1 in the Scottish Cup but the Paisley team lodged an appeal on the grounds that Leith had played a man (Fraser) who had infringed the professional rules. Leith were unaware of this but it was agreed that the game be replayed at Paisley, which Abercorn won 4-1. During this time they suffered five straight League defeats including a 7-1 loss against Third Lanark on the 22nd December, a result which left them bottom with just four points, level with Dumbarton, with both clubs six points adrift at the bottom.

Due to adverse weather Leith didn't play again in the League until the 2nd March 1895 when they recorded their third and final win in the League, beating Clyde 2-1, taking advantage of the visitors having a man ordered off. The win moved them off the foot of the table above Dumbarton.

They lost 4-0 at Parkhead against Celtic later in March and the two sides, in the reverse fixture, were involved in an eleven goal thriller. This game was Leith's penultimate fixture, *The Scotsman* reporting that "the visit of the well-known Glasgow combination to Beechwood Park, Leith, drew out a good attendance of spectators; but, unfortunately, the game which took place was not of a very high order. The ground was in a very sloppy condition when the Athletic started, fifteen minutes after the advertised hour, the delay having been caused by the Celtic. The opening was of a pretty sensational order, and in two minutes each side had scored a goal. A couple of accidents just after delayed proceedings, but all through this period the struggle was merely a scramble, and at the interval each side had put on four goals. The second portion began in brisk fashion, and some really fine play was witnessed. Play ranged from end to end, and from another kick the Irishmen gained the lead. A few minutes from the finish they increased their total to six, but a great rush by the Athletic forwards in the last second or so terminated in a goal. In the closing stages the Leith Athletic played with ten men, Boyd being ordered off for rough play." Celtic played the game without first choice 'keeper McArthur and back Doyle, who were representing Scotland at Parkhead against Ireland. All of the forward line for Leith scored: Marshall, Walker, Allan, Boyd and Dobie. Leith's last game was also their one and only draw. The two bottom clubs obtaining a point each from a 1-1 draw, with Dumbarton equalising with five minutes remaining. This time Leith were not re-elected, having survived a vote the year before. They came bottom of voting with just 3 votes. Dundee, with 14, and Dumbarton with 10 were both re-elected. Hibernian, who had again won the Second Division, perhaps had the moral high ground, and got 11 votes and replaced them.

Over the next four seasons Leith finished as Second Division runners-up three times but on each occasion were not elected back into the First Division. They began life in the second flight on Saturday the 17th August 1895 with a 3-1 win over Kilmarnock at Beechwood Park. The visitors caused a sensation by scoring in the first minute but Leith lay siege to their opponents' goal and eventually equalised through Marshall. Leith scored twice in the second half through Boyd and Donnie. Leith then won 4-1 at Airdrie but then suffered a surprise 4-0 defeat at home to Renton. However, they bounced back with a 6-1 home win against Port Glasgow Athletic in early September that took them top. Their visitors arrived half an hour late and were seemingly ill-prepared. Port Glasgow got their revenge, winning 6-2 in the reverse fixture in early December but once again Leith bounced back, beating Partick Thistle 7-0 the following week. At half-time they only had an own goal to show for their efforts but they scored at regular intervals in the second period. This result placed them in second, three points behind leaders Renton but having played three games fewer. Continuing their inconsistent form, the following week they lost at eventual champions Abercorn 4-0.

As the season went into 1896 Leith suffered a very disappointing Scottish Cup exit, losing 6-0 at Third Lanark. However, the following month they got their League campaign back on track with another fine win, beating Motherwell 6-1, scoring four in the first half. They went top of the table as a result, a point ahead of Renton who were involved in Scottish Cup action, although Abercorn, five points behind had three games in hand. The followed this up with a 5-3 victory away at Partick, to go three points clear, but then lost back to back games in March against Linthouse and Kilmarnock which left four clubs tied at the top on 21 points - Leith, Abercorn, Kilmarnock and Renton. However, Abercorn had only played 15 games, whereas the other three had played 17 and had just one game left to play. On the 28th March Leith beat Airdrieonians in their closing League fixture of the season. Only a crowd of around 750 watched them go 2-1 behind at the break but they completely dominated the second half and won by 5 goals to 2. Abercorn also won but none of the other two were in action. Renton subsequently lost against Abercorn, who won their remaining fixture as well to finish four points clear at the top, with Leith Athletic in second.

The bottom three from the First Division – Clyde, St Mirren and Dumbarton – now faced a vote against the top three in the Second Division – Abercorn, Leith Athletic and Renton. A number of clubs felt that the Second Division champions should automatically go up and there were a number of unsuccessful attempts to get this enshrined in the League rule book. What this meant was that there was a great deal of sympathy for Abercorn, and they were elected to the First Division at the expense of Dumbarton. The votes cast for each club was as follows: Clyde 14, St Mirren 13, Abercorn 8, Leith Athletic 4, Dumbarton 2 and Renton 1.

Leith Athletic finished as runners up in the Second Division for a second consecutive season for 1896-97, again finishing four points behind the champions, this time Partick Thistle. They recorded 13 wins from 18 matches and compiled a club record 27 points for the season, four more than the previous season. They won eight of their first nine fixtures, scoring four goals in a game on five occasions, and a 3-2 away win against Renton on the 10th October gave them a massive eight point lead, although eventual champions Partick, sitting in fifth, were ten points behind but with five games in hand.

On the 24th October they beat recently relegated Dumbarton 7-1 and in December Leith Athletic beat Partick Thistle 3-1 in what would turn out to be the only League defeat the Jags would suffer all season. Covering the game, *The Scotsman* noted that "the League fixture between these two clubs created some interest in football circles in view of the chances which the combinations held of gaining the Second Division championship. A crowd of about three thousand was present at one stage of the game, and a splendid contest was furnished, although in the second half, accurate football was placed beyond possibility by the heavy rain and consequent soft ground. The Partick Thistle started, and their opponents at once attacked. The start was a little sensational, for in a minute or two the Leith Athletic scrambled the ball into the net. The fast rushing tactics of the home lot broke up the Glasgow defence and Laidlaw was successful in adding another two goals to the Leith score. Up to the interval the Patrick Thistle were confined much to their own quarters. The first item of note in the second half was a goal for the visitors. The following play was very lively, and if anything, the Thistle had the pull of matters. Numerous chances were allowed to slip owing to the insecure footing. No further scoring taking place, the game ended: Leith Athletic, three goals; Partick Thistle, one goal." In the Scottish Cup Leith were involved in a lengthy battle with Dumbarton, where it took three matches to eventually separate them. Dumbarton went on to reach the Final, where they lost to Rangers.

At the beginning of March Leith beat Motherwell 6-3 and they were still top, now by two points, with two games left. However, Partick in second, had two games in hand. The two sides met the following week at Partick's Inchview ground with Leith knowing that a win would deliver a heavy, if not a knockout blow, to their host's championship aspirations, whilst boosting their own. With the game having such a massive bearing on the Second Division championship there was a crowd of 5,000 present to witness the game. After a keenly contested opening period with chances on both sides Thistle opened the scoring and they went on to add a second before the interval. Leith made strenuous attempts to reduce the leeway but spurned their chances. Early in the second half Partick added a third which resulted in a sustained period of pressure from Athletic but which was ultimately unproductive. Partick added two more and only the goalkeeping of Gillespie saved Athletic from a heavier defeat. Partick subsequently won their three remaining games during which time Leith weren't in League action. By the time they played their last fixture, on the 3rd May, when they beat Port Glasgow Athletic 5-0, Partick were already confirmed as champions. At the Scottish League's AGM held on the 1st June 1897 Partick Thistle replaced Abercorn in the First Division. The other two First Division sides, Third Lanark and Clyde, were successfully re-elected. Leith Athletic, along with Kilmarnock, sought election but neither club received any votes.

Leith Athletic kicked off the 1897-98 season with a 4-0 home win over Renton, although their opponents subsequently withdrew from the League in October. The results were allowed to stand and Hamilton Academical were voted in and took on Renton's fixtures. The club lost early games against Abercorn and future champions Kilmarnock. Killie also inflicted their club record Scottish Cup defeat at Rugby Park where Leith put on a poor showing. Drummond opened the scoring for Leith after ten minutes of play but Kilmarnock soon equalised and although the play was keenly contested, they succeeded in adding three more before half time. Kilmarnock had things all their own way in the early stages of the second period and took the score up to 7-1. Fotheringham then got one back for Leith. Kilmarnock added two more, the last from a penalty to run out 9-2 winners.

Their best win of the season was a 6-3 home victory over Airdrieonians towards the end of the season, and in the context of the two previous finishes, fourth place was something of a disappointment. There had also been disappointment in the East of Scotland Shield. Leith had reached the final for the fourth occasion but once again faced their nemesis, Hearts, who had beaten them in each of their previous finals. History repeated itself, although there was the scant consolation of taking Hearts to a replay this time. The first final, played in February had seen Leith leading 2-1 in the second half, when they missed a penalty, Hearts coming back to equalise near the end. The final was replayed on the 19th March and the opportunity had gone, Hearts winning 2-0 this time.

The 1898-99 season saw Leith Athletic claim their third runners up spot in four years. Kilmarnock hadn't been elected to the First Division as champions the previous season and they won the title for the second year in a row. Killie were unstoppable, going the whole League campaign unbeaten (P18 W14 D4). In that context, Leith coming in second, five points behind, was a commendable effort. Port Glasgow Athletic were a close third. Leith won their opening game of the new season, 3-1 against Hamilton and then secured back-to-back 5-0 wins away at Morton and home to Motherwell in September. The match against Morton had a disappointing and dull opening half an hour and J Walker finally opened the scoring for Leith just before half-time. On the resumption Morton pressed but from a counter-attack Willie Walker scored. Leith then dominated the game, adding three more. A week later Leith entertained Motherwell and an evenly contested first half ended goalless. The second half had barely started when Gardner raced away for Leith down the right and crossed for Jim Laidlaw to head home. Two minutes later J Walker made it two. Motherwell went down to ten men for the last twenty minutes due to injury and Leith made the most of the extra man, adding further goals from Gardner, Fotheringham and Laidlaw.

These large wins were followed by a narrow win over Airdrieonians in early October. Leith then conceded five themselves, as they lost 5-3 away at Kilmarnock. *The Scotsman* reported that "great and special interest was manifested in the meeting of these teams at Rugby Park, Kilmarnock. Each had participated in four League matches without dropping a point, but though Leith Athletic had the best goal record, Kilmarnock were favourites. As events turned out, the Ayrshire team fulfilled expectations." Kilmarnock bossed the early part of the game and quickly established a two goal lead, but "gradually the Leith players got over the effects of their railway journey" and got back on level terms. Close to the call of half-time their hosts retook the lead. The second half opened rather quietly but eventually Kilmarnock extended their lead, which more or less settled the game. Kilmarnock finally added a fifth after a string of fine saves by James Oswald in the Leith goal and in the last five minutes Leith scored a consolation.

Leith appeared to suffer a bit of a hangover from their game with Kilmarnock as the following week they lost 8-5 away against Port Glasgow Athletic. Seven goals were scored in the first half, the odd number belonging to their hosts. Port scored after five minutes and a few minutes later made it 2-0. Brown pulled one back, but Port responded immediately by restoring their two goal advantage. Jim Laidlaw scored a second for Leith and before the interval each side added another goal, Leith scoring through Walker. Port scored within two minutes of the restart to make it 5-3 before Fotheringham hit the bar. Laidlaw then scored a fourth to make it 5-4. Leith played the second half with only ten men so it was no surprise when Port Glasgow went 6-4 ahead. Leith kept hanging in there and Brown added a fifth before Port Glasgow scored two more to run out 8-5 winners.

Leith Athletic responded by nearly going the rest of the League season unbeaten. They went eleven games unbeaten from the 22nd October 1898, only losing their final League fixture against Hamilton on the 22nd April 1899 – six months later! Part of that sequence included six consecutive victories, so that by mid-December they were second in the table with 21 points, one behind leaders Kilmarnock and one ahead of Port Glasgow in third. The highlight of this incredible run was an 8-2 victory over Abercorn on the 12th November. Two goals from Fotheringham and then strikes from Gardner, Dryburgh and Laidlaw gave the Port side a 5-0 half-time lead. Leith continued to dominate the second half but some time had elapsed before they added to their score, Armstrong scoring from the penalty spot following a handball. Laidlaw accepted a pass from Fotheringham for number seven and Fotheringham then secured his hat-trick for 8-0. During the last minute of the game the visitors burst away and scored a consolation goal. The club's fortunes weren't so good in the Scottish Cup, as they went down 7-1 away at St Mirren in the First Round.

On the 15th April the top two clubs met at Beechwood Park with unbeaten leaders Kilmarnock visiting Leith. The club trailed Killie by a point and Kilmarnock also had a game in hand so a Leith victory was imperative in terms of the destination of the championship. This was also to be the final League match played at Beechwood and a crowd of 4,000 was present. *The Scotsman* covered this important match, reporting that "as the winning of the match would still keep Leith in the running for the championship, while a draw would ensure that honour to Kilmarnock, more than usual interest attached to the game....At once Leith took up the running, and thrice in quick succession they visited Craig. Some neat passing by Kilmarnock was smartly broken up by Boyd, who let his men nicely away, with the result that Armstrong scored, the ball

473

glancing off Busby. Spirited play by both teams followed, but at length Reid found an opening and placed the teams level. Again Leith assumed the lead from a well-placed foul kick by Armstrong, but before half-time Campbell from a scrimmage in front of Oswald, placed the teams level, and with two goals each they crossed over. Leith were unsteady on resuming, and Oswald had to negotiate a difficult shot from Campbell. At the other end Leith kept Craig busy for a time…The game was being very keenly fought out, a brilliant run by Fotheringham giving Leith the lead for the third time. The Athletic now looked winners all over, but Kilmarnock came again, and after repeated attempts at length scored through Findlay, a hard fought game ending in a draw of three goals each." The Leith Athletic side is listed as: James Oswald; White, Boyd; Armstrong, Wood, Lowe; Alex Gardner, Walker, Anderson, Bell and Fotheringham. Right half Gardner left Leith to join Newcastle United at the end of the season, making over 300 appearances for the Toon between 1899 and 1910. The game ended 3-3 and Leith would have been disappointed to have had the lead three times and yet not claim victory.

The following week Killie secured the title with an empathetic 5-0 win over Motherwell; whereas Leith lost 4-1 at Hamilton, for who Eglinton scored a hat-trick. An injury to a Hamilton player then left them a man short but nevertheless they extended their lead before Fotheringham scored for Leith. At the Scottish League's AGM held on the 30th May Kilmarnock were elected to the First Division with 15 votes and took the place of Partick who only secured 5 votes. Dundee were re-elected with 10 votes. Leith disappointingly only got 2 votes, despite their third second-placed finish in four seasons.

At the end of the season the club left Beechwood Park, because of the North British Railway building a new line into Leith Central across the site. The club moved to the nearby Hawkhill Recreation ground and hosted their home games here for the 1899–1900 season. Leith opened the new campaign at Hawkhill but only 500 watched the 3-1 win over Hamilton. A better crowd of 2,000 came for their second home game against Partick, which they won 2-1 but in-between there had been two away defeats. At the end of September they suffered a particularly bad defeat on the road, losing 7-1 at Port Glasgow. Leith started well and striker William Walker, who had played the previous season for Liverpool, opened the scoring after eleven minutes. However, by half-time Leith were 3-1 down and conceded four more in the second half. The following month they won back-to-back away games, their only ones of the League campaign, and eventually finished a mid-table fifth place, their lowest League finish to date.

The 1900-01 season marked their tenth anniversary as a Scottish Football League club but they finished an even more disappointing eighth place. Problems off the pitch were evident in the fact that Leith led a nomadic existence, variously playing their home matches at Easter Road, Logie Green and Hawkhill. Leith won their opening game, a narrow 1-0 victory over Airdrie with Walker scoring the only goal of the game. By the end of October they were in mid-table but they picked up only four points across November and December and so by the turn of the year they were eighth. On the 22nd December they had been beaten 5-1 at Abercorn but they bounced back well in January when they beat Ayr FC 4-1. They eventually finished in joint eighth place with Hamilton, and one point above bottom side Motherwell.

In the Scottish Cup Leith beat non-League Forfar Athletic 4-0 away in the First Round before losing 3-0 at home to fellow Second Division Port Glasgow Athletic in the next round. Despite a terrible season Leith somehow picked themselves up to win the East of Scotland Shield for the first time. Having lost their previous four finals they finally emerged victorious against the odds in the final played on the 18th May. A crowd of 3,500 at Easter Road saw Hearts take the lead but Leith responded well and equalised through Walter Hutchison. However, Hearts restored their lead with the last kick of the half. The second half was pretty even but Leith snatched a late leveller through Willie Walker. They then stunned their opponents with a last minute winner scored by Alex McAulay.

On the 30th May 1901 Leith were re-elected, along with Hamilton and Motherwell. Arthurlie beat Raith for the remaining place. Despite being re-elected this was an unsettling time for the club. Their financial situation was not good and there was confusion as to what ground they would be playing on. When the new railway line was being built into Leith Central the club had been forced to move and play their games at the Hawkhill Recreation Ground. However, the rent was high and this was a contributory factor behind their financial difficulties.

The new season opened on the 15th August with Leith due to play St Bernard's, but the match didn't go ahead. On the 26th August 1901 *The Scotsman* reported that "a general meeting of the Leith Athletic Football Club (Limited) was held last night in the Leith Liberal Club - Mr Hill presiding - when it was resolved that the club should go into liquidation. It was further resolved that a public meeting be held on Friday night, when the support of the public should be asked for an attempt to form a new club. The question of acquiring a suitable Park was remitted to a committee."

A well-attended public meeting was held in the Kinnaird Halls in Leith on the 4th September which unanimously resolved to form a new senior club in place of the Leith Athletic, in liquidation, and a preliminary committee was appointed to get a ground and arrange a team to play a Scottish Qualifying Cup match against West Calder on the forthcoming Saturday. The club succeeded in putting a team out but conceded three goals in the first half. Their opponents had submitted a protest before the game on the basis that this "reconstituted" club was not the same club they had been drawn against but in the end it didn't matter as they beat Leith anyway. Play in the second half was more evenly contested and there was no further scoring with the match ending 3-0. On the 11th of September the Scottish Football League Second Division Committee met in Glasgow and the principal business was the application of the reconstituted Leith Athletic Club to proceed with the fixtures, and this was unanimously granted.

A month after the season had started Leith finally played their opening fixture, on the 14th September, away against Port Glasgow Athletic. The first half was evenly contested and at the interval the score was 1-1, but the home team scored soon after the restart and added four more goals in the last twenty minutes to win 6-1. The *Edinburgh Evening News* commented that "Leith should not be disheartened by Saturday's result. The silver lining of their cloud must soon appear, for with but a few alterations their team will do, and scores against them such as Saturday's will be rare."

There was still the issue of being without a ground and Hibs came to the rescue and Leith's early League fixtures were played at Easter Road. The first of these was played on the 21st September when Leith beat East Stirling 1-0. A week later they also played at Easter Road, this time beating Motherwell 3-0. In early October they returned to Hawkhill where they played out a 1-1 draw with Ayr. Leith then negotiated the lease of a ground at Logie Green in the Canonmills area of Edinburgh, *The Scotsman* reporting on the 11th November that "on Saturday the Leith Athletic opened the new ground at Canonmills, Edinburgh, which they recently acquired, by engaging the Port Glasgow Athletic." The game ended in a 3-3 draw. The following week they beat new club Arthurlie 2-1 and then made it three wins in a row when they beat Clyde 3-1. At the end of December they beat Abercorn 5-0, having only been one up at half-time and they eventually finished in seventh place, out of the now 12 teams.

The 1902-03 saw an improved showing for Leith Athletic, who, for a time, were in contention at the top of the table. They lost their first two fixtures, conceding seven goals and scored only once themselves, before going on an eight game unbeaten run that was rudely broken by a 5-1 defeat at Hamilton. In their first three matches in December they scored four goals in each of their games and were placed second at the turn of the year, although a number of teams behind them had games in hand. Airdrieonians were the runaway leaders but any hopes of finishing as runners-up were dealt a blow when they lost 5-1 at East Stirlingshire on the 3rd January. They finished their programme on the 21st March with a 2-1 win over Hamilton and ended on 27 points. Airdrie also completed their League matches and were uncatchable on 35 points. Motherwell and Ayr both had 25 points but had three and two games respectively still to play, and both teams eventually overhauled Leith, who were placed fourth at the season's end. Leith reached their sixth East of Scotland Shield final and met Hibs at Easter Road on the 25th April. In glorious spring sunshine Hibs won a memorable game 4-3, although Leith led 2-0 at one point.

Leith made a good start to the 1903-04 season and were unbeaten after five matches to be joint top. However, a 3-2 loss at Arthurlie was followed by a 5-1 defeat at Falkirk. Although they then beat East Stirlingshire 4-0, and later beat struggling Ayr Parkhouse by the same score, they struggled after the turn of the year and eventually finished in seventh. In the Scottish Cup they had some success and knocked out First Division Port Glasgow Athletic and Motherwell before losing 3-1 at home to Morton.

Leith Athletic started the 1904-05 season by entertaining Hamilton on the 27th August 1904 and *The Scotsman* was on hand to provide a report: "Leith Athletic opened their enclosure at Logie Green on Saturday, when, before 2000 spectators they defeated Hamilton Academicals, the champions of the Second Division last season, by two goals to one. It was a hard game all through, Leith attacking in the early stages, but failing to score from a penalty." They were made to pay when Hamilton opened the scoring mid-way through the first half. Early in the second half Walker equalised and Penman scored the decisive goal after a fine run by Dow.

Athletic briefly threatened a championship challenge and were joint leaders at the beginning of November. By the beginning of the following month though they were down to third, although just two points off the lead, but by the turn of the year they had slipped back to mid table. On the 21st January 1905 they recorded a season's best 7-0 win over fellow mid-table side Albion Rovers at Logie Green. Leith took the lead after just seven minutes when Walker crossed to Dow who beat the Albion 'keeper Muir. Dow soon added a second, Cameron a third and Grant a fourth, before half-time. Although they had a commanding lead they didn't relax and soon after the restart Walker scored a fifth. Cameron then converted two crosses by Dow to secure his hat-trick.

Inconsistent form from here on in mitigated against any championship push and they eventually finished in fourth place, some way behind champions Clyde, Falkirk and Hamilton. This didn't stop them from making an attempt at being elected to the First Division though. In fact the top four clubs in the division, plus mid-table Albion Rovers and Aberdeen, applied and took on Morton and Motherwell in the re-election vote held on the 22nd May at the League's AGM. In a surprising move, although Clyde were four points clear at the top of the Second Division, runners-up Falkirk and seventh place Aberdeen were elected into the expanded First Division, with the existing clubs re-elected. Leith, along with Albion Rovers and Hamilton secured no support in the voting. Having failed once again in the end of season voting, Leith Athletic was wound up and a new limited company was formed to take over the old club's assets.

The following year the club secured their first major honour by winning the Second Division championship. They only lost three games all season and finished three points clear of Clyde, the previous years' champions. The club played their first five fixtures of the season away from home whilst the new limited company agreed the lease at Old Logie Green and the club lost their first two matches but won the next three. They didn't play at home until the 18th November when they hosted Raith Rovers, winning 1-0. They then went eight games without defeat before losing the return at Raith on the 30th December 1905. By this time they were only placed a mid-table fifth, eight points behind leaders Albion Rovers (who would eventually finish third) but with four games in hand.

Leith then went unbeaten across the five games played in the first two months of 1906. Entering March the club was up to third place with their next two fixtures against the two teams above them. On the 3rd March they drew 0-0 at leaders Clyde. Clyde now had 29 points but only one game left to play. Second placed Albion Rovers had 27 points with two matches left and Leith had 24 points but with five matches left. A week later they won 1-0 away at Albion Rovers. This twice postponed game went ahead on a sodden pitch and given the state of the division was played out in front of 4,000 spectators at Whifflet. Leith scored in the first half and although their opponents lay siege to their goal in the second period Leith went on to win 1-0. Overall Leith won their last four games, and the 4-1 home win over Arthurlie on 24th March took them top for the first time. In this match Leith went ahead early on before the Barrhead goalkeeper broke a finger and had to retire.

On the 31st March Leith beat Albion Rovers again, this time at home, to move three points clear of Clyde with one to play. *The Scotsman* reported that "before an attendance of 4000 spectators, these clubs met at Logie Green, Edinburgh, in their return League match. By defeating their opponents Leith Athletic became champions of the Second Division for the season just ending. The game was a keenly contested one throughout. The Rovers opened play with a sharp attack on the home goal. This lasted for little more than a minute, and throughout the remainder of the first half Leith Athletic kept matters moving in the opposing half of the field. Henderson, at outside left, put in a lot of telling work, but the teams crossed over with no goals scored. Soon after resuming the Athletic forwards missed a likely chance, and, play returning to the centre, Duguid burst away, and opened the scoring for the Rovers. Henderson was making good headway on the left when he was fouled. A penalty resulted, and Moffat kicked a goal. This put more heart into the Athletic and twice in succession Blackburn was let down on the right. On the first occasion Dewar took his pass, and then made his way through the opposition, and scored. On the next Penman turned the ball nicely into the net, after Blackburn had sent it across the goal mouth. Result: Leith Athletic, three goals; Albion Rovers, one." Leith won their final match at Hamilton and finished three points clear of Clyde to win their first major honour.

At the League's 1906 AGM held on the 21st May the decision was taken to expand the First Division from 16 to 18 teams. Both Kilmarnock and Queen's Park were first re-elected to the top flight and then six Second Division clubs lobbied for the two new spaces. Leith Athletic applied as champions, along with Clyde, Albion Rovers and Hamilton Academical from the top four. Raith Rovers and Cowdenbeath, who had finished in eighth and ninth place respectively, also applied, but came in the bottom two in the voting. Hamilton, who had finished fourth and eight points behind Leith topped the ballot with 10 votes and were elected. Runners-up Clyde and third placed Albion Rovers tied on 7 votes and went through to a run off ballot, and Clyde were voted up. Leith were eliminated with 6 votes. Two replacement clubs joined the Second Division – Dumbarton returned and were joined by Ayr Parkhouse.

For the next three seasons Leith Athletic finished in mid-table. In the first of these, the 1906-07 season they briefly challenged. On the 12th January 1907 they were at home to Vale of Leven in a top of the table clash. Moffat scored two for the hosts but an injury to Willie Walker meant that Leith played a man short for the whole of the second half, conceding three. Walker didn't line up the following week and on the 23rd January *The Scotsman* reported the sad news of his death, caused by the injuries he sustained on the football pitch. The paper reported that: "William Walker, the well-known player of the Leith Club, died yesterday afternoon in Edinburgh Royal Infirmary as the result of an accident sustained on the football field. Less than a fortnight ago he was badly hurt when playing at Logie Green in a Scottish League match with the Vale of Leven. That match was a particularly keen one, and it may be noted that a penalty kick was given against the Vale when Walker was brought down. He was taken to the Infirmary after the accident, but was so well after a few days that he was able to be removed to his home at Broxburn. On Saturday, however, he had again become so ill that he had to be taken back to the Infirmary, and he did not long survive an operation performed on Tuesday. His injuries, it is stated, were caused by a kick in the stomach. Walker was originally connected with the Broxburn clubs, and except for a year, which he spent with Liverpool, he had been with Leith for some twelve years. He was most popular, both with his colleagues and his opponents, and a fairer and more gentlemanly player could not be got. Veteran though he was, he was still one of the best in the Leith ranks, His tragic death will be deeply regretted by a wide circle of friends."

This tragic incident overshadowed the rest of the season and Leith eventually came in fifth. This prompted another failed attempt to join the First Division at the 1907 AGM. As Port Glasgow Athletic, Kilmarnock and Hamilton had all finished bottom with 21 points, it was decided not to arrange a three-way play-off to decide who would apply for re-election and all three stood. Leith applied along with Dumbarton, Raith Rovers, St Bernard's and Vale of Leven but the three existing clubs were re-elected. During this time they reached the Final of the East of Scotland Shield on two more occasions, losing both finals – to Hearts and to Hibs (after a replay) respectively.

In the 1909-10 season they won the Second Division championship for a second time, this time sharing the title with Raith Rovers. Before 1915 clubs finishing on equal points would normally play-off for the title. At the end of the season Leith and Raith both finished with 33 points but it was decided not to play-off for the title and they were therefore declared joint champions. Leith opened their 1909-10 campaign on the 21st August 1909 with an easy 3-0 win over Arthurlie at Old Logie Green. The club then went unbeaten in their first nine games and suffered their first defeat in the 1910 New Years' game 3-1 away against Abercorn. At this point it was hard to assess progress from the League table as there was quite a disparity in the number of games played. Leith, in fifth place, had only played ten games whereas for Abercorn this was their 18th. Leaders Raith had played 15 and St Bernard's and Vale of Leven, in second and third respectively, had each played 17 matches.

Throughout the next six weeks Leith started to catch up on games played and points gained so that by mid-February they were only four points behind leaders St Bernard's and three behind Raith Rovers with six games in hand on the leaders, but just one game in hand on Raith. On the 26th February Leith won away at Albion Rovers, a saved penalty ensuring that they got both points instead of just one – this would ultimately prove crucial in the final standings. On the same day Raith beat Ayr FC to go top. Raith were now three points ahead of Leith having played a game more.

On the 5th March the top two clubs met and drew 1-1. There was no scoring in the first half but eight minutes after the resumption Paterson put Leith ahead with a low hard drive but Raith got back on level terms. A week later both sides won, Leith 2-1 at home to Dumbarton and Raith 1-0 against Ayr Parkhouse. On the 19th March, and with Raith not playing, Leith won away 3-1 against Vale of Leven. The following Saturday Leith outclassed East Stirlingshire 3-0, Raith again didn't play so Leith now went top for the first time with 30 points, one ahead of Raith, who now had a game in hand.

On the 2nd April fellow Edinburgh club St Bernard's did them a favour by beating Raith 2-1, which meant the two sides were now level on games played with 20 matches played each, with two fixtures to go. Leith were ahead on points - 30 plays 29. A week later both sides won, Leith winning 4-0 at home to Cowdenbeath, while Raith won 4-2 against Arthurlie. On the 16th April Raith won 2-1 away at East Stirlingshire, scoring the winning goal ten minutes from time to finish their programme on 33 points, one point ahead of Leith. Leith were due to play the same opposition, also away, knowing that if they could match Raith's result at East Stirling they would be crowned champions.

Leith travelled to Falkirk on the 30th April and *The Scotsman* covered the action, commenting that "considerable interest was manifested in this match, the winner of the Second League championship having to be decided. The home team started in a manner that quite non-plussed their opponents. Cram opened the scoring, and although Leith protested strongly that the player was offside, the point was allowed. Against the sun and wind Leith put up a strong game, but Colombo, who took Paterson's place for the day, was weak at centre-forward, and many chances were lost. Ivory put the home team further ahead, and again there were protests that the point had been registered from an offside position. Half-time: East Stirlingshire, two goals; Leith nothing. Having found their bearings, Leith played determinedly after the interval, but half an hour had gone before Stewart scored from a penalty. David Lindsay put the teams on an equal footing ten minutes from the close. Until the finish Leith had all the play, and should have won. As it was there was no further scoring, and Leith and Raith Rovers now tie for first place. Result: Leith, two goals; East Stirlingshire two." Both teams ended up on 33 points. Leith had lost only two games, one less than Raith. They had also conceded only 18 goals, two less than Raith and had scored eight more. In other words, they had both the better goal average and goal difference but neither measure was yet in place. The League decided against a play-off and the Second Division title was awarded jointly to Leith Athletic and Raith Rovers. Leith did not contest election to the First Division but Raith did, and were elected to replace Port Glasgow Athletic.

Leith came fourth in the 1910-11 season, which was the start of declining fortunes on the pitch. They won their opening game 3-2 away at Dundee Hibernian but then lost 6-4 at home to Ayr United, although at one point the score was 3-3. At the end of February they were in tenth place but they only lost one more game to the end of the season and steadily climbed the table. Leith reached the Final of the East of Scotland Shield and held Hibs to a 0-0 draw. However, four weeks later they lost 3-0 at Easter Road in the replay, conceding three first half goals. 1911-12 was a forgettable season with the club finishing in seventh place. Dunfermline Athletic and Johnstone joined as the Second Division expanded from 12 to 14 clubs.

Three years after jointly winning the title Leith were involved in the end-of season elections once again but this time they had finished in last position and their place in the League was at stake. They won only five games in the 1912-13 season and finished with 18 points, one behind Arthurlie and three behind St Johnstone and Vale of Leven, with the bottom two sides facing re-election. They made a great start going seven games unbeaten and topping the table in mid-October. They experienced mixed fortunes during the autumn but by end of November were second with 24 points from 13 games. However, in their remaining 13 games they only gained four further points - all from draws – and they failed to win from early December to the end of the season. They lost five in a row without scoring throughout December and the New Year period including a 5-0 defeat at Vale of Leven, in a display described as "wretched" by *The Scotsman*, which was attributable to lots of changes in personnel. They eventually scored and got a point in a 2-2 draw at home to Dumbarton in mid-January and picked up a couple of draws during early February. On the 22nd February they lost 4-1 at home to League leaders and eventual champions Ayr United and were now second from bottom, one point above Abercorn. They finished their fixtures with a 1-1 draw against Abercorn, with both of these sides with 18 points, but Abercorn still had two games to play and picked up a point in one of these to condemn Leith to finishing bottom - having been top five months earlier and second at the halfway stage. At the SFL AGM on the 2nd June 1913 Leith Athletic and Arthurlie saw off the challenge of Dumbarton Harp, East Fife, Galston, Kirkcaldy United, Peebles Rovers and Wishaw Thistle and were both re-elected to the Second Division.

Their terrible run crossed over into the new season as they made a poor start to the 1913-14 season and didn't win until mid-November, registering only five draws in this time. Only 500 spectators watched in wretched weather as they beat Johnstone, their opponents playing all of the second half a man down. The result moved them away from the bottom and the victory was the start of a run of three consecutive wins which carried them up as high as fifth at the end of 1913. However, they then failed to win in the first two months of 1914 and suffered a 5-0 loss at Arthurlie and conceded six (although scored four themselves) away at Albion Rovers. They only won once more and dropped down the table to finish in tenth place, six points above the two re-election places.

Once again Leith carried this poor run of form into the start of the 1914-15 season, losing two of their three opening matches. Form picked up after that and a 4-0 away win at Albion Rovers at the beginning of October signposted their championship credentials. Reporting on the game *The Scotsman* commented that "the visiting club was superior in every department. During the first half Hyde scored a capital goal from twelve yards' range. Even against the wind in the closing portion Leith were in rampant form, and could do nothing wrong, so much so that Meaney, Smith and Hyde scored in turn. The Rovers failed to count, and Leith retired winners by four clear goals. The Leith defence was excellent, with Dornan the outstanding man on the field. The forwards moved in perfect unison. Hyde and Gordon were the most troublesome to the Rovers' defenders. The game was one of thrills, and the good form of the visitors took the Rovers and their supporters by surprise." The victory moved them up to third, behind Cowdenbeath and Clydebank.

Although they lost their next match, away at Clydebank, they then went six games without defeat, culminating in a 5-0 Edinburgh derby win over St Bernard's in which Taylor scored a hat-trick. The club was now in second place but suffered a devastating loss at Clydebank where they were trounced 9-2. Reporting on the game *The Scotsman* notes that "the wind was a powerful factor in the game. Clydebank utilised to such an extent that in the first half they scored seven times to Leith's once. The odds were too great for Leith to face."

Leith went the rest of the season unbeaten. A 5-0 home win over Lochgelly United on the 2nd January 1915 saw Smith and Taylor score two first half goals each. At the end of the month they travelled through to Cowdenbeath for a top of the table clash. A draw would have been a fair result but Leith scored through Taylor midway through the first half and survived a Cowdenbeath onslaught to edge the game 1-0. Reporting on the match the *Daily Record* noted that "Cowdenbeath's failure against Leith has lent the Second League competition added interest. The Fifers were not the favourites of fortune; indeed they were superior to Leith, who obtained an early goal, which gave them confidence. To make matters worse, Cowdenbeath rattled the woodwork two or three times, and Birrell failed to improve a penalty kick. Although still three points better ahead of Leith, the leaders must not lose more than one game if they are to secure the championship."

Both sides won their next matches and on the 6th March Leith drew at Abercorn to close the gap to two points, although now they had played a game more. A week later, and with Leith not in action, fellow Edinburgh side St Bernard's did Leith, and themselves a favour, by beating the leaders 1-0. Cowdenbeath now had 37 points with one game left to play; Leith had 35 points, also with one match to play; and St Bernard's were now in the championship picture, with 33 points, and with three games left to play.

On the 20th March Cowdenbeath completed their fixtures with another defeat, this time at St Johnstone. However, St Bernard's failed to take advantage when they lost themselves 2-1 at Johnstone. A week later St Bernard's beat St Johnstone 3-1 to draw level with Leith on 35 points. On the 3rd April Leith beat East Stirlingshire 1-0, Hume scoring the all-important goal in the first half, with *The Scotsman* commenting that "in the second half Leith had the advantage, but their forwards could not augment the total. Latterly Leith were hard put to hold on to their slender lead, but eventually retired victors after a hard game." Leith were now tied at the top with Cowdenbeath on 37 points. Goal average was not yet in existence, let alone goal difference so the SFL ordered a play-off game, which took place at a neutral ground, East End Park Dunfermline on Saturday 10th of April. Leith were beaten 2-1, with *The Scotsman* reporting that "Leith's championship prospects have become less bright as the result of their meeting with Cowdenbeath at Dunfermline, where victory lay with the Fifers in deciding the tie, both clubs having finished equal in the League. Cowdenbeath were the more aggressive lot in the first half, though their lead of two goals at the interval did not accurately indicate the trend of play. In the second half Leith had a vastly improved display, but weakness in finishing negatived the otherwise clever work of the forwards, though in the Cowdenbeath backs they had opposition to face which was not to be easily beaten. Tait and Taylor were Cowdenbeath's marksman, while Taylor, Leith's inside left, scored for his team from a penalty."

Any celebration by Cowdenbeath was quickly muted when news came through that St Bernard's had beaten Lochgelly United 6-0 to join both clubs on 37 points and thus earned the right to participate in a three way tie. The SFL had no choice but to extend the play-offs to a round robin with the Cowdenbeath versus Leith result standing. A week later, on Saturday 17th April Leith avoided elimination by beating St Bernard's 2-1 at the neutral venue of Easter Road, watched by a crowd of 5,000 spectators. St Bernard's didn't deserve to lose having dominated possession and Leith were indebted to Wilkinson in goal who saved his side from defeat. Peter Hyde scored the opening goal for the Port side and thereafter Saints lay siege to the Leith goal. Their city rivals had two penalty shouts not given but eventually equalised. Early in second half Saints twice struck the woodwork. Meaney headed home late on, converting a cross from Black to keep Leith in the running and opened up the possibility of a triple tie. St Bernard's still had to play Cowdenbeath. Should the Fifers, who had already beaten Leith, win or draw, they would be assured of the championship, but if they lost the triple tie would remain undecided, *The Scotsman* reporting that ""by defeating the St Bernard's at Easter Road by 2 goals to 1, Leith have created an interesting situation for the Second Division Championship. Thus, if the St Bernard's win over Cowdenbeath on Saturday next, the three teams concerned will be on an equality with a win each."

The SFL must have been praying for Cowdenbeath in the final game of the three as a win for St Bernard's would leave each of the three teams with a win apiece in the playoffs. The following Saturday, the 24th April, again at Easter Road, the League were spared any further deliberations as Cowdenbeath deservedly beat St Bernard's 3-1 to take the championship title, although a draw would have been enough. Leith Athletic were classified as runners-up, for the fourth time in their history. This was their sixth time in the top two since entering the Second Division in 1895 but they had never been elected back to the First Division. The Leith team that year was Wilkinson; Campbell, Gromart; Denholm, Gordon, Grieve; Smith, Meaney, Hyde, Taylor and Black.

In 1915, it was decided to suspend the Second Division due to the First World War, but allow its members to form two regional leagues, Western and Eastern. Leith played in the twelve team Eastern league but dropped out after one season having finished eighth. Over time the number of clubs competing declined although the Western League continued. After the anticipated restoration of the Second Division failed to materialize, the Western League continued in 1919-20 with an increased membership. In 1921 the Second Division was eventually reformed with a number of clubs leaving the Western League and Leith Athletic joined the Western League despite coming from Edinburgh. They played for just the 1921-22 season and also participated in the Scottish Cup, losing 6-0 at Third Lanark in the First Round.

For the 1922-23 season Leith returned to the Eastern League and applied unsuccessfully at the end of the season to re-join the League. The SFL then started a Third Division but Leith were not one of the clubs. They instead joined the Scottish Alliance for the 1923-24 season, a competition almost wholly made up of reserve or 'A' sides. They also featured in the Scottish Cup where they drew 0-0 at League opposition Vale of Leven in the First Round, before losing the home replay 2-1 in a match played at Wardie Park.

On the 23rd May 1924 *The Scotsman* reported that "a public meeting was held in the Kinnaird Hall, Kirkgate, Leith, last night for the purpose of stimulating interest in the Leith Athletic Football Club, and so placing it on a sound financial footing...The Chairman appealed for increased support for the club, which, he remarked, would probably be playing in the Third Division of the Scottish League next season. They must all do their bit to see that the club was sufficiently supported." On Wednesday 25th June, at meeting of the SFL Management Committee, Leith were readmitted as a member and joined the Third Division for its second season.

On the 16th August Leith played their first game back in the League and in its new third tier. They kicked off against one of the new clubs, Nithsdale Wanderers, a game which they lost 3-2. When the club returned to the SFL they returned to Old Logie Green to play their matches and the first game staged, was on the 23rd August, when the club beat Clackmannan 2-1. Their best result of the season was a 5-1 win over Galston on the 31st January 1925. On a sodden pitch, Laidlaw, a triallist and then Charles Orr gave them a 3-0 half-time lead and Telford added two more in the second half. The club never put any kind of run together though and never got in any kind of position to challenge for promotion, and they lost their final League match 5-0 away at Beith, eventually finishing sixth in the sixteen team division. They did reach the Final of the East of Scotland Shield, which was played at Easter Road on the 27th April 1925. They lost 3-0 in front of a crowd of 9,000 and never reached final again as the competition began to be completely dominated by Hearts and Hibs.

Leith kicked off the 1925-26 season on the 15th August with a 6-1 win over Montrose at Old Logie Green. The Port side only led 2-1 at the interval and centre-forward Telford and Jim Laidlaw each scored two goals and Anderson and Charles Orr got the others. However, Leith then didn't win again until mid-September, when they won five in a row, including a 5-3 win over Helensburgh on the 25th November. Leith completed a remarkable comeback as they were 3-0 down at half-time. Elliott scored ten minutes after the restart and then Leith were on level terms with goals by Orr and Brown (from a penalty). Another penalty converted by a Brown gave his side the lead and Lindsay got a fifth goal ten minutes from time. Helensburgh had a man sent off. In the New Years' Day game they registered a club record SFL win when they beat Peebles Rovers 6-0 away.

In March Leith lost vital games at promotion rivals Forfar Athletic and Helensburgh and at this point were nine points behind the leaders Forfar, but with five games in hand. By this time though it was also clear that a number of Third Division clubs were struggling to fulfil their fixtures. Galston had dropped out a couple of months previously and so Leith were unable to play the reverse fixture against them. In the eight games they did play to the end of the season they recorded six wins and two draws, including five wins in a row in April. A 4-1 win over Johnstone on the 17th April took them into third in the table, two points behind Forfar and Helensburgh, but with games in hand. They scored four away at Brechin City and Beith and on the 24th April they played their last fixture, a 3-3 draw at Clackmannan. *The Scotsman* reported that "three goals were scored in the first ten minutes. Cook scored but Elliott for Clackmannan scored two in quick succession. Like in the first half, goals came quickly after kick off and this time two were scored within five minutes of the resumption - one for each side, Walker and Laidlaw finding the net. Davidson equalised. Only ten minutes remained when Clackmannan equalised with the final score." Leith Athletic finished one point behind Helensburgh who had played all of their games, but Leith had the one game not played. Forfar, in third, were two further points back, but with two games to play. In all, nine fixtures had not been completed.

In view of the fact that 14 clubs had not completed the competition the Scottish Football League Management Committee, at a meeting in Glasgow on the 29th April 1926, decided that in accordance with the rules, that no Third Division Club was entitled to promotion and also that in view of the unsatisfactory state of the competition that no championship flag would be awarded. The decision was a blow to Leith Athletic who could have topped the table.

On the 20th May the Scottish Football League's AGM was held in the rooms of the SFA at Carlton Place, Glasgow. At the meeting Leith Athletic made an application for promotion but the motion failed to carry. Bathgate and Forfar Athletic were elected instead to complete the Second Division, with Broxburn United failing to secure readmission. Under the headline "No Promotion For Leith - League AGM Decision" *The Scotsman* reported on the events surrounding the demise of the Third Division, with the League's annual report stating that "with regard to this competition, the Committee regret that, instead of progressing, it has been even worse than last season. Starting with 16 clubs, the Galston club, after playing 15 games, tendered their resignation, and before the season closed, Beith, Clackmannan, Peebles Rovers and Vale of Leven, with 2, 3, 3, and 2 games respectively to play, intimated their inability to continue, with the result that, Helensburgh played 30 (including two with Galston which they won), earned 38 points; Leith Athletic played 29 (including one with Galston, which they lost), earned 37 points; and Forfar Athletic played 28 (including one with Galston, which they won), earned 35 points. In view of the fact that 14 clubs did not complete the competition the Committee, in accordance with the rule, decided that no Third Division club was entitled to promotion, and, further, in view of the unsatisfactory state of the competition also decided to declare the competition null and void, and to withhold the championship and the badges and flag which accompany the same."

Denied promotion Leith then decided to contest the end of season elections for the Second Division. The end of the Third Division meant no automatic promotion/relegation so instead a re-election vote was held involving Leith and three other leading teams from the last season of the Third Division and the bottom two clubs from the Second Division - Bathgate and Broxburn United. Leith topped the first ballot as Broxburn, Helensburgh and Dykehead were all eliminated, and so it became a three way tussle for the two vacant spots. In an extraordinary tight contest only one vote separated the top three clubs on the first ballot and Leith went into a second round of voting against Bathgate and Forfar. The second ballot was slightly more definitive with Bathgate securing re-election with 23 votes to Forfar's 21 and Leith's 20. In the third ballot run-off for the remaining place in the Second Division Leith tied with Forfar on 16 votes apiece with the Chairman's casting vote going to Forfar Athletic. The thinking was that if Leith and Forfar had each won their respective remaining games Forfar would have topped the table.

As a result Leith Athletic left the Scottish League for a second time, along with all the remaining Third Division clubs. They re-joined the Scottish Alliance for a season and the club moved grounds again, this time to New Powderhall. At the end of the season they successfully re-joined the Scottish League following the League's AGM on Thursday the 26th May, where they were elected in place of Nithsdale Wanderers.

After a year's absence Leith played their first game back in the Scottish League on the 13th August 1927. *The Scotsman* reported that "King's Park performed the official opening ceremony at Powderhall Grounds, and the occasion, the re-entry of a Leith Athletic into League Second Division Football, was taken advantage of by some five thousand spectators. It was well on in the second half before the Athletic side took command of the game, and made the points secure. Early on such a success did not seem probable, the King's Park defenders breaking up all the endeavours of the Powderhall attack to combine. When the first goal came along, it was through Reid, the Athletic centre-half, whose shot, from a free-kick, the Stirling goalkeeper could not hold. A header, just before the interval, from Granger put the sides level. When Orr headed a cross from Elliott into the net, the home side, especially the front line, got going, and monopolised the play. Goals followed from Young and Lindsay."

Despite this victory Leith generally struggled and the highlight of the season came in mid-November when they beat bottom side Armadale 5-0 with Elliott and Orr both scoring two goals. Orr suffered a long term injury in a match against East Fife in December 1927 which didn't help their cause. They ended up finishing in 13th place in the twenty team division with another highlight being when they beat the newly crowned Second Division champions, Ayr United, 2-1 in the last game of the season.

After only a season at New Powderhall, the club moved to Marine Gardens, where they remained until 1936. On the eve of the 1928-29 season the *Edinburgh Evening News* reported that "an added interest is given locally to the Second Division by the establishment of Leith Athletic in their new headquarters at the Marine Gardens. The lowly position of the club last season was, in part at least, attributable to matches lost at home, the circumscribed pitch at Powderhall affecting the play of the team. They will have a better chance at the Marine Gardens, and they will have the advantage of being a young team of players who were for the most part associated last season, and should make a good combination. The average age of the players is 24, and they are practically a local combination, nine being natives of Greater Edinburgh, two of the County, and three of Fife." A trial match of two club elevens was played at Marine Gardens on the evening of Thursday the 2nd August, and 3,000 fans came along. A second trial game was held in which Leith played against the newly formed Edinburgh City, who would share the ground on alternate Saturdays.

After a number of turbulent seasons the 1928-29 season saw the club make a big step forward as they finished in fifth place. Bert Marshall joined from Hearts as an addition to the forwards and they opened the new season with a 4-2 away win at Alloa Athletic on the 11th August. Alloa scored first, Steele being beaten by an angled drive. But the tables were soon reversed as Nicol, within the next five minutes, scored twice. The second half saw Alloa get back on level terms and for a while their hosts were in the ascendancy. Leith were indebted to the tackling of half-back Barclay who then turned provider for Johnstone to score, which was quickly followed by another from Laidlaw. Three days later Hibs marked the opening of Marine Gardens in an East of Scotland Shield tie, in which a crowd of 5,000 turned out, but who watched a drab 0-0 draw. The following Saturday they played their first League encounter at Marine Gardens, drawing 1-1 with Dunfermline. During the season they beat East Fife 5-2 and Arthurlie 6-1 in successive matches but also conceded six against Albion Rovers and five at Dundee United and this erratic form cost them, never really challenging for promotion.

They certainly challenged the following season, earning promotion by winning the Second Division championship for the third time in their history. Leith went an incredible twenty League games without defeat, their first reverse being inflicted on them by Albion Rovers on 28th December 1929. They won 13 matches in a row from the end of August to the end of November, including a 5-0 win over Clydebank; a 6-2 triumph over Dumbarton; a 5-1 win against Bo'ness; and a 4-0 victory versus King's Park. They only lost four games all season, the first in the second round of games and then at Christmas, and then also at the beginning of April. In the Scottish Cup they played a marathon Cup-tie against First Division Falkirk, which went to four games before they went out.

On the 1st March 1930 they recorded a season's best win against Alloa Athletic, winning 7-1. The result left them a point clear of East Fife at the top of the table, having played two games fewer. Third placed Albion Rovers were a further two points back, on the same number of games. Leith then suffered a little wobble, with four draws in their next five matches and then a fourth defeat of the season, their first at home, against Arbroath. Fortunately for Athletic their nearest rivals East Fife also lost so Leith retained top spot. The situation was now tense. The two sides were now level on 53 points, although Leith had the superior goal average, and a game in hand. Albion Rovers were now only two points behind them and had a game in hand on Leith.

On the 12th April Leith won 3-2 away at East Stirlingshire. East Fife also won, taking their season's tally of goals up to 111, but Albion Rovers were held to a draw. A week later Leith beat Stenhousemuir 5-1 and East Fife won their last game. Albion Rovers went down heavily 6-2 at Raith and so the other two sides were promoted as they were five points ahead and Albion Rovers only had two matches left. Leith were more or less guaranteed a third Second Division title. They could afford to lose their remaining match, they just needed to avoid a heavy 5-0 defeat due to their superior goal average.

Leith lost their final League game but avoided the heavy defeat and were crowned the Second Division champions on goal average from East Fife. They played Third Lanark on the 23rd April 1930, losing 2-1, with *The Scotsman* reporting that "Glasgow got its first glimpse of the new First Division team from the Marine Gardens last night. Though Leith Athletic went under to Third Lanark in the Second League encounter at Cathkin Park, enough was seen of the capabilities of the Athletic to indicate that, with more experience, they will justify their place in the new sphere. There was undoubted cleverness, craft, and confidence in their method, and had it not been for the fact that Carruthers was injured early in the game and was naturally handicapped as a result, it is safe to say the points would not have gone to Third Lanark. The Athletic, who fought back with pluck and perseverance, had also to play for the last quarter of an hour without Marshall, who received a leg injury. When those factors are considered, it will be realised that there was no stigma in the defeat." Leith Athletic thus returned to First Division after an absence of 35 years, having won a club record 23 League games in a season, scoring a record of 92 goals and amassing a club record number of points (57).

Leith Athletic played two seasons in the top flight, narrowly avoiding relegation in the first season before finishing bottom in the season after. The 1930-31 season saw them have a brush with relegation, finishing just two points above the drop zone in 17th place. Leith marked their return to the First Division on the 9th August 1930 with a 2-2 draw against Falkirk at Marine Gardens in front of a crowd of 10,000. At one point they were two goals behind and only resolute defending by Mitchell and Jamieson and the goalkeeping of Steele kept the scoreline down. Laidlaw managed to open Leith's account just before half-time and in the second period Leith came into their own. Laidlaw scored the equaliser and they were unlucky not to snatch the winner such was their dominance in the second half. According to *The Scotsman*, "the players should be able to do sufficiently well to make the name of the club respected."

Leith lost their next two matches before recording a 1-0 win at Easter Road against Hibernian in front of a crowd of 25,000. The win was secured against the balance of play with Leith's goal coming as early as the 11th minute, when a slip allowed Nicol to break clear and score. After that Hibs lay siege to the Leith goal and were unlucky when they hit the woodwork. Leith beat Queen's Park the following Saturday, but then failed to win any of their next eleven matches, the last of these on the 22nd November, being a 7-1 thrashing at the hands of Cowdenbeath, conceding five goals in fifteen first half minutes. Cowdenbeath were as high as fourth in the table and only two points off the top, whereas the result left Leith in 18th place, just above the relegation zone, three points ahead of Ayr United, with East Fife a further three points back.

At the end of November they recorded a rare win with a 2-1 victory over Partick Thistle but the following week they lost 6-0 at Dundee. By the time they had been dumped out of the Scottish Cup 7-0 by Clyde they had edged up a couple of places and were five points clear of the drop zone. At the end of January they crushed bottom of the table East Fife 6-1, Jimmy Young scoring a hat trick. A 2-1 win over Hearts the following month saw them move seven points clear of the relegation zone and to apparent safety. However, they only won once more to the end of the season, finishing in 17th place, just two points above Hibernian who were relegated, along with East Fife.

For the 1931-32 season there certainly was no sunshine on Leith, just dark clouds. In that season the club were relegated from the First Division, losing a record 28 League games in a season and conceding a divisional record of 137 goals in their 38 League games. The season didn't get off to a great start when the club was beaten 7-1 away at Motherwell. The Well finished as eventual champions so perhaps there was no disgrace in this result. Leith were consistent - every month they would suffer a heavy defeat. In October they lost 8-2 away at Airdrie. On the 7th November they lost 9-1 at Morton, which was a club record SFL defeat. Morton's win and Ayr's draw at Cowdenbeath lifted both clubs above Leith and left Athletic at the foot of the table. Black and Lyle each scored four goals for Morton and Leith's only goal was an own goal. In December they lost 6-0 at Celtic and Jimmy McCall, who had been appointed player manager was one of eleven players freed in January 1932 and did not stay on as manager. He was replaced by Hearts and Hibs veteran Peter Kerr, who initially came as player-manager.

As is often the case, problems off the field caused problems on it. Leith's problem was one of finance. The city of Edinburgh at this time was supporting four senior clubs. Leith's home game against Airdrie attracted gate money of just £69. Their match guarantee to the opposition side was £100. The club was simply losing money and things came to a head in January 1932. The Board met with the players and agreement was eventually reached to release half of the players, with those remaining taking a cut in wages. The *Daily Record* reported that George Smart, the Chairman, had put their difficulties down to "the whole economic position, the weather and the fact that the

League fixture arrangement had put them in opposition to the Hibernian at Easter Road."

In the New Year they fared no better. Knocked out of the Scottish Cup by Albion Rovers, January also saw a 6-1 away defeat at lowly Ayr. In February they lost 5-0 at home to Motherwell, and 7-0 at Hamilton. March though was a particularly bad month. With players released and amateurs drafted in to replace them they lost all their games, three of them heavily and two of them were against fellow relegation battlers. It was these games then that sealed their fate and set them on the way to the unenviable record. They lost twelve games in a row from the start of 1932 until the end of March.

On the 5th March 1932 Leith hosted Dundee United. This was an important game for both clubs as it involved two struggling teams fighting relegation. Going into the game, Leith trailed United by three points and Falkirk by six. In the proverbial "six-pointer" (or "four pointer" in old money) Dundee United boosted their survival chances, whilst severely denting Leith's, with a 5-1 demolition at Marine Gardens in front of just 500 people. According to *The Scotsman* "The score…did not greatly flatter the winners. Dundee United were the better-balanced team, and they used their scoring chances well…The Athletic had the assistance of two amateurs in D H McKenzie, goalkeeper from Leith Amateurs, and A Miller, a left-back from Edinburgh City. They also had a new outside-left in Hutchison, transferred from Bo'ness. Of the three, Hutchison gained the greatest prominence, and he scored a fine goal. As a side, however, the Athletic never pulled well together, keen though the players understandably were." In blustery and rainy conditions Dundee United weathered some early onslaughts as the three debutants appeared to lift Leith. However, in the closing minutes of the first half the United wingers Brant and Bain both scored, the latter claiming a deflection of the Leith centre-half Hamilton. Five minutes into the second half Jackson scored to make it 3-0, soon followed by Jim Dyet who made it 4-0. Hutchison, marked his debut for Leith by scoring "from well out", six minutes from the end to pull one back but "close on time a blunder between McNeil and the goalkeeper allowed a ball from Logie to enter the net." In a crucial relegation match Leith had been roundly beaten, 5-1 at home and it was their ninth successive reverse at Marine Gardens. They had now conceded 114 goals in 33 games and found themselves five points adrift of United and six behind Falkirk, who didn't play.

The following Saturday the tally of goals against topped 120 as Athletic conceded six away at Kilmarnock. What was remarkable about this game though was that Leith actually took a 3-0 lead before eventually losing 6-3. Under the headline of "Extraordinary Scoring at Kilmarnock" *The Scotsman* reported that "with the wind behind them to begin with, the Leith team put in three goals inside the first twenty minutes, the scoring actually being done in eight minutes. Kilmarnock knocked one off the Edinburgh side's lead before the interval and then staggered the visitors by piling on three goals in nine minutes after play was resumed. Another two goals were called by Kilmarnock before the finish and they also failed to convert two penalty kicks." The extraordinary turn of events can be explained by the wind, which was a distinct aid to each team in turn. Leith's play in the first half was a revelation. It appeared they could do nothing wrong in a display that contradicted their lowly league position and form. "Nicol was a dashing leader, and Laidlaw and Coutts were clever and resourceful inside-forwards. Thomson also showed a fine turn of speed on the right but Hutchison was inclined to double back too much on the left." At the end of the first period Athletic led 3-1, thanks to two goals by Nicol and one from Coutts, with Maxwell pulling one back for the home side. After some early pressure, in which Laidlaw had hit an effort narrowly over the bar, Leith took the lead when Nicol played a pass to Coutts, who cut inside and unleashed a shot past Bell. Three minutes later, Nicol, showing great tenacity made it 2-0 and Athletic scored their third in seven minutes when Nicol netted again. *The Evening Times* reported that "three goals in seven minutes was great work, and in not a single instance was there any semblance of fluke." If truth be told, Leith were playing well and it required the steadying influence of McEwan and the promptings of Maxwell, a local shoemaker, to keep Kilmarnock in the game. Connell, McLeod and Aitken combined before the latter had a shot that flashed wide but on the stroke of half-time Killie pulled a goal back. With the wind at their backs in the second half the home side dominated. The visitors were quickly overrun and never recovered from the loss of three quick goals early in the second half. Todd, the Leith goalkeeper was beaten five times in the second period, once again by Maxwell and twice each by Connell and Aitken. Kilmarnock showed renewed resolve from the off, Maxwell forcing Todd into a save. Two corners followed as the home side kept up the relentless pressure, which paid off when Maxwell grabbed his second from close range just three minutes after the resumption. This was quickly followed by one from Connell, who drew the home team level when he received Aitken's cross from the left and, unmarked, smashed the ball into the net. Soon after Connell, a lace worker, scored a second, pouncing on a rebound to put Kilmarnock ahead 4-3. In a remarkable turnaround in fortunes, Kilmarnock now bristled with confidence and the men of Leith appeared shell-shocked. In the 68th minute McLeod was brought down in the box but Maxwell missed the spot kick, shooting straight at the 'keeper. Five minutes later Aitken scored a fifth before another penalty was awarded to the home side – Duncan was pulled down but incredibly McEwan missed this time. In the final minute Aitken notched his second and Kilmarnock's sixth to complete an extraordinary comeback.

On Saturday 19th March Leith lost 2-0 at home to Morton, a result that represented something of an improvement. But the month of March, that had come in as a lamb, didn't go out as a lion. On the last Saturday of the month Leith had a humiliating experience at Brockville, where Falkirk, third from bottom and fighting for retention of their place in the First Division, won 9-1, a result that sealed their fate. Almost 4,000 spectators were present for this key relegation battle. According to *The Scotsman* "The score…might have been larger, so great was the disparity between the sides. The Athletic were a poor lot, especially in defence. The forwards showed dash and cleverness at times… [especially]…Coutts." The size of this defeat equalled their record SFL defeat set just four months previously. Requiring just a point for safety, Falkirk carried the game to their opponents and dominated the early play, creating a couple of good chances. The early pressure paid when Falkirk went ahead in the fifth minute. A poor clearance came out to Radcliffe who subsequent low drive beat Todd. But parity was restored immediately. Leith's goal was scored immediately from kick-off on the resumption and no Falkirk player touched the ball as it was moved swiftly round the Leith forward line. Laidlaw made progress and crossed to Coutts who connected first time, his low shot surprising Thomson in the Falkirk goal. Thomson made amends, saving well from Gallacher, before Falkirk regained the lead in the 14th minute. Radcliffe's run and cross saw the ball deflect off Miller in the Leith defence. Todd kept the ball out but was only able to parry it and Gall nipped in to score. Falkirk then proceeded to dominate the game as Falkirk's second appeared to knock the stuffing out of the visitors and the home side went in at the interval 5-1 up. Miller knocked in a third after an error by Todd and Hamill unleashed a terrific drive for the fourth. Just before half-time Beath's 25 yard effort took a deflection past the surprised 'keeper for 5-1. Four further goals were scored in a one-sided second period as Leith showed no stomach for a fight. Hamill scored the sixth and Stevenson the seventh from a free-kick. In the 70th minute Miller connected with Radcliffe's cross for 8-1 and Stevenson made it 9-1 towards the end. *The Evening Times* concluded that the game was "just what the score suggests – a debacle. Falkirk…overwhelmed a team that never showed the slightest confidence and only a small measure of skill."

Leith did pick up their first point in twelve games by drawing 2-2 at Dundee but finished their campaign with a 4-1 home reverse against Clyde. In total they had conceded 137 goals, including 88 goals from 19 away matches, at an average of 4.63. They had an away record of no wins, and just four draws from 19 away fixtures. Leith's last win in the League had been on Boxing Day when they had beaten Third Lanark and they finished three points behind Dundee United but nine points adrift of Falkirk and safety. It was not a great time to support a side from the capital outside of Hearts or Hibs, for in the same 1931-32 season, Edinburgh City, playing in the Second Division conceded a record goals against for any division of 146.

There would be no immediate bounce back as in the 1932-33 season they finished a lowly 16thplace. Under Kerr's leadership the club then recorded six mid-tables finishes, with a highest finish of eighth place in the 1934-35 season. They experienced a particularly bad patch in the autumn when they lost 6-1 at East Fife, which was followed by a 4-0 loss at King's Park, an 8-2 defeat at Brechin City and a 6-0 loss at Dunfermline Athletic on the 3rd December which left them in 15th place. They eventually finished one place lower but comfortably above the bottom two. In the Scottish Cup they took a modicum of revenge on Brechin, beating them 5-1, before losing to First Division Clyde, but only after a replay.

In the 1933-34 season they had an improved showing, finishing 12th in the League, with the highlight being a 5-0 win over Montrose, who played a man short. They went out of the Scottish Cup in the First Round, beaten 1-0 at home by First Division Cowdenbeath. The improvement continued the following season as they nudged up into the top half, finishing in eighth, with the highlight being when the beat city rivals Edinburgh City 6-0 at the end of March. They were again knocked out of the Cup in the First Round, this time 3-2 at Brechin.

The 1935-36 season featured a number of high scoring, one-sided contests. Leith lost both matches against a St Mirren side that would earn promotion, losing their matches 5-0 and 6-0. They also lost 8-2 against Dundee United but did beat Dumbarton 6-0 and they eventually finished just a place lower in ninth. They made it past the First Round of the Scottish Cup this time, knocking out Buckie Thistle, but only after a replay and having been held 3-3 at Marine Gardens. They eventually went out to Third Lanark, who went on to reach the Final.

At the end of the 1935-36 season Leith left Marine Gardens for Meadowbank and a crowd of 2,000 came out for the ground's opening on the 15th August 1936, when they beat Dumbarton 2-1. The club dropped back a few places in finishing in eleventh place and also went out of the Scottish Cup at the first hurdle. The 1937-38 season was more a less a carbon copy as they finished in tenth place and made a Cup exit in the First Round at the hands of Queen of the South. After three seasons of mid-table finishes Leith fell back to 16th place in the 1938-39 season. During this season, on the 22nd October 1938, Leith suffered their record SFL home loss, 7-1 at home to Airdrieonians. In this match they conceded first, but then equalised before the visitors found the net on another six occasions. They also lost to Airdrie in the First Round of the Cup. They also lost 7-0 against Dundee in February 1939 and 6-1 at Dundee United a month later.

The 1939-40 season started badly as Leith lost their opening three games against Dumbarton (home), King's Park (away) and Dunfermline Athletic (home). On the 2nd

September they earned their first points of the new campaign by beating Dundee United 2-0 away and moved off the bottom and into 15th place. However, the 1939-40 season only lasted four matches before the League was suspended due to the outbreak of the Second World War.

After the hostilities were over, the now homeless Edinburgh club St Bernard's proposed a merger with Leith but this went nowhere. Leith's Meadowbank ground was also out of action, requiring rebuilding, and Leith spent the 1946–47 season at the adjacent New Meadowbank. Their ground had been taken over by the Army during the war and used as a transport depot and when the League was resumed in 1946, Leith were forced to play their home matches at the neighbouring New Meadowbank. When the original Meadowbank was reopened, it was renamed Old Meadowbank.

On the resumption after the War the League had another go at a three division structure. Post-war seasons saw the divisions renamed 'A', 'B' and 'C' with the last section also including reserve sides. Leith were unhappy at being placed in this 'C' division for the 1946-47 season. They finished the season in third place, five points behind the new Stirling Albion, who had replaced King's Park, but only the champions of the division were promoted. However, for the following season the decision was taken to expand the Scottish Second Division from 14 to 16 clubs and Leith topped the poll with 25 votes, beating East Stirlingshire, Montrose, Edinburgh City, Forfar and Brechin City, and were elected to one of the vacancies.

However, after just one season in 'B' Division they were relegated having finished 16th and bottom at the end of the 1947-48 season. Leith lost their opening game 1-0 at home to East Fife at Old Meadowbank but then won their next two games and also qualified from their League Cup section before being beaten 8-2 by Aberdeen in the Quarter-Final. On the 11th October they were beaten 7-1 away at Stirling Albion for whom George Henderson scored a first half hat trick and ended up with four. Eddie Broadley scored Leith's goal. From the end of October they went 16 games without a win conceding five or more on five occasions. They eventually won again on the 14th February with a 3-0 win over Alloa. It took Leith a while to capitalise in their first half superiority and they eventually opened the scoring from a penalty. Robertson was brought down in the box in the 38th minute and Somerville dispatched the penalty. Skinner added a second on the hour mark and Somerville got his second right at the end. Leith remained bottom following this, only their fourth win of the season. Dundee United got a point so they were now four points behind United with seven games left. A 3-1 home win against Dunfermline in mid-March drew them level with Dundee United at the bottom on 18 points but having played two more games. They only picked up one more point from their remaining two games and finished three points behind Dundee United and were relegated to Division C.

They missed out on an immediate return by finishing as runners-up in the third and final season of this short lived division that featured reserve teams. Forfar Athletic won the title by two points and were promoted. In the early stages of the season Leith recorded some big victories, including 5-0 at Edinburgh City, 7-1 against Queen's Park Strollers and 10-0 away against Dundee United A. On the 8th January 1949 they beat Dunfermline Athletic A 7-1 and a week later they beat Raith Rovers A 5-3. The following week a crowd of 11,500 saw them narrowly lose 1-0 at home to Raith's first team in the First Round of the Scottish Cup, *The Scotsman* reporting that "Leith Athletic are due a measure of sympathy for their narrow defeat by Raith Rovers, the B Division leaders. They put up a gallant fight, and had they scored from a penalty in the first half, they could have gone on for a deserved win. As it was, the all-important counter went to Rovers, though it was generally agreed that Brady's winner was hardly warranted on play. Leith paid the penalty for putting too much work on the ball, and they also showed a fatal hesitancy near goal." As the League season reached its climax Forfar, Brechin and Leith were all in contention. Forfar led on 33 points with Brechin on 30 and Leith on 29, with two games to go. Leith beat Brechin City 3-0 in the penultimate round of games but Forfar beat Montrose 4-2 to claim the C Division title and the sole promotion spot. Leith secured the runners-up spot when they themselves beat Montrose the following week.

The competition was restructured for the 1949–50 season when the number of reserve sides was significantly expanded and the Division divided into two regional sections, the South-East (soon renamed the North-East) and South-West. Leith played four seasons in the Division C North East section, finishing in the bottom four in each season.

In the 1949-50 season they made an appearance in the Scottish Cup, playing St Johnstone on the 28th January 1950. Leith took a 3-1 half-time lead through an own goal and two from Dalziel, and briefly threatened a Cup upset but Buckley scored four of his side's six second half goals as St Johnstone ran out 7-3 winners. In the 1951-52 competition over 9,000 spectators at Meadowbank saw them take a 1-0 lead into the interval against Dundee United. McCall's penalty in the 42nd minute hit the crossbar but Dalziel reacted quickest to put the rebound into the net. Frank Quinn equalised before a Peter McKay hat-trick gave their opponents a comprehensive 4-1 win. In the 1952-53 Scottish Cup they were thrashed 8-1 at home to Airdrieonians in the First Round. This game was played at Old Meadowbank before a crowd of 3,000 on the 24th January 1953. Leith suffered an injury blow before the game as veteran and pre-War

Raith legend Ernie Till was absent from their line-up. First Division Airdrie took the lead after 27 minutes and scored a second six minutes later. Ten minutes before half-time the visitors made it three but just before half-time Blackie converted from a Swan lay off to make it 3-1 at the break. Early in the second half Airdrie made it four and they doubled their tally by scoring four in ten minutes in the final quarter of the game.

Leith Athletic continued to agitate for fuller membership of the SFL. In 1950 they had submitted a motion that they, along with Brechin City, East Stirling and Montrose should be admitted to the 'B' Division but not participate in the League Cup but this was defeated 22-15. In 1951 they applied to join the Second Division at the League's AGM but only got 6 votes in the last ever re-election vote - both Stenhousemuir and Alloa were comfortably re-elected.

By the summer of 1953 the club had had enough. They informed the League by letter on the 22nd of July of their decision not to play any more fixtures, but that they were not relinquishing their League membership, arguing that other clubs such as Dundee United and St Johnstone had withdrawn sides from the reserve section without sanction. The Management Committee of the SFL informed them on the 28th of July that failure to fulfil their first fixture of the new 1953-54 season on the 8th of August would risk expulsion. The club had sought to get a re-structure or expansion of Division B by promoting the non-reserve Division C clubs and argued that it wasn't economically viable for them to play matches while in that division. Leith Athletic were eventually expelled on the 28th of August 1953 for refusing to fulfil any of their Division C fixtures. On the 4th of November 1953, a special meeting of the League upheld the Management Committee's earlier decision by 25 votes to 12 (Airdrieonians were absent), and Leith Athletic were formally expelled from the Scottish Football League.

The club continued to play in the Scottish Cup as they remained members of the SFA. On the 30th January 1954 they played what would turn out to be their last match, going out to Fraserburgh in the First Round. The match was played at Fraserburgh's Bellsela park ground in front of a crowd of over 2,000. The game was fairly even to begin with although their hosts started to get on top as the game progressed. Somewhat against the run of play Finnie opened the scoring for Leith but two minutes later Fraserburgh were level. Only the heroics of Nolan in the Leith goal kept them on level terms before the break. In the second half McKenna, Doig and Peat all added goals for Leith but unfortunately Fraserburgh scored four times to win 5-4. The last ever Leith line up was: Nolan; Barton, Masterton; Doig, Hailstones, McNellis; Dalziel, McKenna, Peat, Vannet and Finnie. Fraserburgh drew Hearts in the next round which would have been a more fitting end for Leith if they had made it through.

Ironically the League structure was abandoned at the end of the 1954-55 season. The following season saw the League being re-organised into two divisions with the five non-reserve teams who had played in the Division C the previous season being admitted into the Second Division (Berwick Rangers, Dumbarton, East Stirlingshire, Montrose and Stranraer). If only Leith Athletic had held on for two more years!

With nowhere to go Leith Athletic disbanded in 1955. They had a turbulent SFL career having been elected three times and having left the League twice due to war, once on the abandonment of the Third Division, and then by having been the first club since Armadale in 1932 to be expelled. They had a Scottish Football League career spanning 45 seasons across four spells. They had three Second Division two titles to their name and the unwanted record for the most goals conceded in a First Division season.

In 1996 a new Leith Athletic FC was formed and in 2008 they merged with Edinburgh Athletic, continuing to play under the Leith name. This merger enabled them to take the latter's place in the East of Scotland League. Leith were promoted to the Premier Division of this competition in 2011 and won it in the 2015-16 season. Promotion to the Lowland League is via a play-off between the winners of the East of Scotland Football League and South of Scotland Football League but the club didn't meet league membership criteria around membership of the SFA or around owning its registered ground. The reformed club had originally played at Leith Links and Muirhouse Playing Fields before moving to Meadowbank. In late 2017 the club has played its matches at the University of Edinburgh's Peffermill 3G pitch.

SEASON	LEAGUE	P	W	D	L	F	A	P	POS
1891-92	SCOT	22	12	1	9	51	41	25	4/12
1892-93	SCOT	18	8	1	9	35	31	17	6/10
1893-94	SCOT-1	18	4	2	12	36	46	10	9/10
1894-95	SCOT-1	18	3	1	14	32	64	7	9/10
1895-96	SCOT-2	18	11	1	6	55	37	23	2/10
1896-97	SCOT-2	18	13	1	4	54	28	27	2/10
1897-98	SCOT-2	18	9	2	7	39	38	20	4/10
1898-99	SCOT-2	18	12	3	3	63	38	27	2/10
1899-00	SCOT-2	18	9	1	8	32	37	19	5/10
1900-01	SCOT-2	18	5	3	10	23	33	13	8/10
1901-02	SCOT-2	22	9	3	10	34	38	21	7/12

1902-03	SCOT-2	22	11	5	6	43	41	27	4/12
1903-04	SCOT-2	22	8	4	10	42	40	20	7/12
1904-05	SCOT-2	22	10	4	8	36	26	24	4/12
1905-06	SCOT-2	22	15	4	3	46	21	34	1/12
1906-07	SCOT-2	22	10	4	8	40	35	24	5/12
1907-08	SCOT-2	22	8	5	9	41	40	21	7/12
1908-09	SCOT-2	22	10	3	9	37	33	23	6/12
1909-10	SCOT-2	22	13	7	2	44	19	33	1/12
1910-11	SCOT-2	22	9	6	7	42	43	24	4/12
1911-12	SCOT-2	22	9	4	9	31	34	22	7/12
1912-13	SCOT-2	26	5	8	13	26	47	18	14/14
1913-14	SCOT-2	22	5	9	8	31	37	19	10/12
1914-15	SCOT-2	26	15	7	4	54	31	37	2/14
1924-25	SCOT-3	30	13	5	12	48	42	31	6/16
1925-26	SCOT-3	29	16	5	8	73	41	37	2/16
1927-28	SCOT-2	38	13	9	16	76	71	35	13/20
1928-29	SCOT-2	36	18	7	11	78	56	43	5/19
1929-30	SCOT-2	38	23	11	4	92	42	57	1/20
1930-31	SCOT-1	38	8	11	19	52	85	27	17/20
1931-32	SCOT-1	38	6	4	28	46	137	16	20/20
1932-33	SCOT-2	34	10	5	19	43	81	25	16/18
1933-34	SCOT-2	34	12	8	14	63	60	32	12/18
1934-35	SCOT-2	34	16	5	13	69	71	37	8/18
1935-36	SCOT-2	34	15	3	16	67	77	33	9/18
1936-37	SCOT-2	34	13	5	16	62	65	31	11/18
1937-38	SCOT-2	34	16	5	13	71	56	37	10/18
1938-39	SCOT-2	34	10	4	20	57	83	24	16/18
1939-40	SCOT-2	4	1	0	3	4	7	2	ABAND
1946-47	SCOT-C	18	11	3	4	57	33	25	3/10
1947-48	SCOT-B	30	6	7	17	45	84	19	16/16
1948-49	SCOT-C	22	15	3	4	76	29	33	2/12
1949-50	SCOT-CNE	30	8	8	14	55	73	24	13/16
1950-51	SCOT-CNE	30	6	5	19	43	73	17	14/16
1951-52	SCOT-CNE	30	5	7	18	46	88	17	15/16
1952-53	SCOT-CNE	28	5	6	17	41	87	16	15/15

Linthouse

Formed: 1881
Colours: All navy blue
Ground: Langlands (sometimes known as Govandale) Park
Entered League: 1895. Elected to Second Division
Number of League Seasons: 5
Honours: None
Highest League Finish: 5th in Division Two
Left League: 1900. Resigned

Linthouse were one of the early teams from Glasgow, and although not founder members, they did join the League just five years on from its creation. However, that delay was significant, as Rangers FC were by this time well established and their geographical proximity meant that Linthouse were somewhat overshadowed by their burgeoning neighbour. Linthouse is part of the Govan district of Glasgow, a shipbuilding area south of the River Clyde, and the district takes its name from the Linthouse Burn. The football club, known as the "Linties", were formed in 1881 and were one of a number of clubs emanating from the districts of Glasgow. The club originally played at Langlands Road before moving a short distance to Langlands Park.

Linthouse competed in the Scottish Cup for nine successive seasons prior to League admittance from 1885 onwards and made their debut in the Cup on the 12th September 1885, losing 4-1-away at fellow Glasgow side Northern. In the 1889-1900 competition they progressed as far as the Fourth Round. In the First Round they had beaten Fairfield of Glasgow 7-2, their biggest ever win in the Scottish Cup. Shortly after the start of play Linthouse opened the scoring but Fairfield equalised soon after. For the next 15 minutes play was even but then Fairfield scored a second. Before half-time McIntosh equalised for Linthouse and the sides went in level at 2-2. In the second half of the game the Linties totally dominated the play and scored five more goals. In the next round they knocked out fellow Glaswegians Cowlairs after a replay. Their Third Round tie against Wishaw Thistle was remarkable for having thirteen goals scored in it. This game took place on the 19th October 1889 at Wishaw with a match report appearing in *The Scotsman*: "Shortly after commencement, Watt and Lyle, of the Thistle, had a combined run up the left, which resulted in a corner, and Watt having taken the kick, Lyle sent the ball through the Linthouse goal. The visitors equalised immediately afterwards, one of the Thistle players inadvertently kicking the ball through his own goal. Subsequently the game became very fast, but Linthouse had much the best of it, and, chiefly by smart, accurate shooting, put on goal after goal till half-time, when the score was six to one against Wishaw. At the beginning of the second half, each team scored once, after which the character of the game completely changed. The Thistle completely hemmed in Linthouse, and scored three goals in succession, but the capital defence of the visitors frustrated their efforts to equalise. Linthouse broke away shortly before the close, and defeated the home custodian for the eighth time, the game ending in the defeat of Wishaw by eight goals to five." Linthouse were knocked out 2-0 by the holders Third Lanark in the next round.

The following year they made it to the Third Round, securing another five goal winning margin along the way, this time against Maryhill of Glasgow in the Second Round. In the first half each side scored two goals but in the second half Linthouse scored five. They lost 4-3 at home to Abercorn, then competing as founder members of the SFL, so almost a giant killing of sorts. The *Glasgow Herald* reported on the game: "As this was the first visit of the Paisley Club to Langlands Park considerable interest was taken in the event. Fully 3000 spectators were present." Abercorn scored first after 15 minutes but Linthouse then scored two in quick succession to briefly lead before Abercorn drew level and then edged ahead just before half-time. The second half was goalless for thirty minutes before Abercorn made it 4-2. The *Glasgow Herald's* report continued, saying that "the Linthouse exerted themselves to their utmost to improve matters, and were successful in obtaining a third goal, McIntosh doing the needful. They strove hard to equalise, but time sounded without any further scoring."

On the 23rd March 1891, William Bowie, became the only Linthouse player to be capped for Scotland while on the club's books, playing in the 2-1 win over Northern Ireland. Playing at inside right, Bowie had a powerful physique which enabled him to dominate his opponents. Later in the same year Linthouse became founder members of the Scottish Football Alliance and they won the competition in its inaugural season, topping the 12 team table that included Kilmarnock, Morton, Airdrieonians and Partick Thistle. They also suffered their biggest Scottish Cup defeat that year, losing 6-0 at home to Bathgate Rovers in the First Round. Linthouse were missing a number of players and conceded twice in the first five minutes and never recovered from the shock. The score was 5-0 at half-time. The second half was dominated by Linthouse but they couldn't fashion an opening.

In July 1893, the Scottish Football League decided to form a Second Division. On 10th July, Abercorn and Clyde, who were not re-elected at the initial AGM, were granted a place in the new Division, as were Hibernian. Cowlairs, Morton, Partick Thistle, Port-

Glasgow Athletic, Northern and Thistle (all from the Scottish Alliance) and Motherwell (Scottish Federation) were also selected to form the new division. The other members of the Alliance, including Linthouse, were unsuccessful.

A year later the club made another attempt to join the SFL. At the AGM on 1st June 1894 Morton and Northern found themselves up for re-election and Linthouse applied along with four other clubs – Airdrieonians, Dundee Wanderers, Kilmarnock and Royal Albert – for the three vacancies, Thistle having decided to not re-apply. Linthouse came bottom of the poll with just seven votes as Morton (30 votes), Dundee Wanderers (23) and Airdrieonians (19) were elected.

In 1895 Linthouse were finally elected to the Second Division at the third attempt. This time Abercorn, Cowlairs and Dundee Wanderers were up for re-election and Linthouse faced competition from the Alliance champions Wishaw Thistle, Kilmarnock and Raith Rovers. At the AGM held on the 3rd June Linthouse jointly topped the poll with Kilmarnock with 24 votes and replaced Cowlairs and Dundee Wanderers who could only muster 3 votes apiece, whilst Abercorn were re-elected with 22 votes. Despite an impressive Alliance winning campaign, Wishaw Thistle only secured 6 votes.

Linthouse only completed five seasons in the SFL and their first season in the League was not a successful one, with the club finishing bottom of the ten club division. On the 17th August 1895 they played their first ever SFL game, a home match at Langlands Park against Airdrieonians. A crowd of 2,000 saw them start League life with a 2-1 win. Linthouse were the first to press but Williams shot wide of the post. After half an hour of play Logan scored Linthouse's first ever League goal. King then equalised for Airdrie but before half-time Williams headed the men from Govan back into the lead. Airdrieonians tried hard to equalise in a well contested and even game but Linthouse held on for the win. The team taking the field that day was: McGowan; McNaught, Mathieson; McIntosh, Steel, McLaine; McFarlane, Simpson, Williams, Smith and Scott.

Linthouse also won their next game, away at Morton at Cappielow by the same score, courtesy of two goals inside the first fifteen minutes to temporarily top the table. Two more wins followed but these were sandwiched by three consecutive defeats in which they conceded eleven goals. After a further 1-0 win over Morton on the 30th November, which took them up to sixth place, they then went seven games without a win, picking up a solitary point. The last game in this sequence was a heavy 6-1 home defeat at Govan against Abercorn on the 29th February 1896, which left them joint bottom, level on nine points with Morton. Linthouse picked up two further points from their remaining fixtures (a 3-2 win over Leith Athletic) whereas Morton picked up three, meaning Linthouse finished bottom. Both clubs though faced a re-election vote, only surviving re-election after a third ballot in which they defeated Wishaw Thistle.

The AGM was held on the 26th May 1896 and after tying in the first ballot, Linthouse retained their place by defeating Wishaw in a deciding vote. *The Scotsman* reported that "following the election of the new clubs, the members then went on to consider the applications for places in the second division, the three retiring clubs being Motherwell, Linthouse and Morton. Besides those three, applications were put in by Ayr, Raith Rovers, East Stirlingshire, Falkirk, Wishaw Thistle and Dundee County (a new organisation)...On the final count Motherwell and Morton were re-elected. Linthouse and Wishaw Thistle tieing for the remaining place. Linthouse secured the verdict by 21 votes to 19."

Their second season saw a marked improvement as they came in seventh but they would have finished in the top half but for being docked four points for fielding an ineligible player. They started with home wins over Motherwell and Leith Athletic but conceded four at Morton and six at Port Glasgow Athletic in early December. They also conceded five in the 5-2 home defeat in the Boxing Day fixture against Morton. Linthouse had the best of the early exchanges, taking the lead before Morton took the game in hand and scored two in quick succession. Linthouse got back on terms from a free-kick but Morton responded and again scored two quick goals to lead 4-2 at half-time. After the interval the play was evenly contested with Morton scoring a scrambled goal near to the end. The result left them with only five points (from the opening two wins and a draw against Dumbarton) from ten games and they went into 1897 eighth in the table, above Motherwell and Dumbarton.

Linthouse won five of their next six matches, only losing to leaders and eventual champions Partick Thistle and included in that run was a 6-2 win over Renton. Of more significance was a narrow 2-1 win over Port Glasgow Athletic on the 20th February. Included in the Linthouse line up was a player listed as 'Anderson', who turned out to be J Steel of Third Lanark. On the 3rd March the Management Committee of the Second Division held their usual monthly meeting in their chambers, at West Regent Street in Glasgow. Taking up the story, the *Glasgow Herald* reported that "the Port-Glasgow Athletic representative brought up the question of the eligibility of J Steel, late of Third Lanark, and now of Linthouse, who played for the latter club against the Port a fortnight ago in a Second League game. After some discussion it was found that as Steel had played more than four First League games for Third Lanark, the Linthouse had violated rule 12 in playing him without having him formally transferred." It was ultimately decided to deduct Linthouse four points for fielding an ineligible player, which cost them two places in the final table.

Their third season in the SFL saw them achieve their best placed finish of fifth in the Second Division. The 1897-98 season opened with a 4-1 win away at Ayr FC and they later went on to score seven in a ten goal game at Langlands against Airdrieonians on the 23rd October, their highest scoring SFL win. However, they also lost 5-0 on the road against eventual champions Kilmarnock in the November. A 4-0 win over Motherwell in early March 1898 had them up as high as third place but leaders Kilmarnock and second placed Morton were not catchable. In any case Linthouse lost their last two matches to eventually finish in fifth place.

The 1898-99 season was when the decline set in. And the rot set in pretty quickly. Linthouse lost four of their first five games, conceding four or five in each game. On the 5th November 1898 they were thrashed 8-0 by leaders Kilmarnock, the *Glasgow Herald* reporting that "the ground was in a miserable condition and against good play. The home team, however, played strongly, and registered five goals in the first half, while the Linthouse only occasionally got over midfield. In the second half the visitors made a better show, and the play was fairly even for half an hour, after which Kilmarnock broke away and added three goals before the whistle was blown." The result, their heaviest ever League defeat, left them in ninth place, second from bottom with just four points, two points ahead of bottom club Abercorn, who, like them, were struggling in the shadow of a large neighbour. The three games they played in December were all lost heavily, 4-0 at Airdrie, 6-1 at Motherwell and 7-1 against bottom side Abercorn. In this game they were three down at half-time and although they scored straight from the resumption of play through Bell they failed to mount a more serious comeback and Abercorn scored four more. The result left the two clubs level at the bottom on points with just six. In the 12 games played to this point, Linthouse had only scored 15 goals, yet conceded 49, averaging four a game. Linthouse did win their last home game, against Ayr FC who finished eighth, a result that ensured they didn't finish bottom. In front of a meagre attendance of only 500, Pearson and Smith giving them a 2-0 half-time lead. Smith made it 3-0 but then there was a comeback from Ayr who scored two in quick succession. McNeish then settled any nerves by making it 4-2. Pearson and Smith notched the last two goals to win 6-2.

At the League AGM, held on the 30th May, 1899, Linthouse again faced re-election, having finished in the bottom two and once again they were successful. In the voting they topped the poll with 37 votes and were re-elected along with Abercorn who got 32 votes. Their nearest challengers were Raith Rovers, of the then East of Scotland League who got 13 votes. Dundee Wanderers and Orion of Aberdeen also applied but failed to find a seconder.

The endorsement from the other clubs at the AGM was all very well, but the writing was already on the wall for the club. Gates that had been around 2,000 had dwindled to around the 500-1,000 mark as they struggled with competition from Rangers, who had lifted the Scottish Cup in 1897 and 1898 and who had won the League title in 1899, as well as reaching a third successive Cup final (which they had lost against Celtic).

The 1899-1900 season would be the club's fifth and last in the SFL. This time they finished bottom and resigned to their fate they didn't seek re-election. They won only two games all season, failing to win at home, as both victories came on the road. They only picked up nine points, three from three drawn games at home and six on their travels. Their first six games didn't give a clue as to what was to follow - two wins, two draws and two defeats, had them sitting reasonably comfortably in sixth in the table. The reality was that they wouldn't win another game.

The 4-3 away win against Abercorn on the 28th October 1899 was their last ever SFL victory. In this game Linthouse had raced into a three-nil lead with goals from Bell, Drysdale and McIntosh, but by half-time Abercorn had reduced the arrears and the sides cross over at 3-2. Their hosts strove hard to equalise, which they eventually did ten minutes from time but Linthouse snatched the win following a goal mouth scramble. Linthouse went the remaining twelve games of the season without winning and lost eight games in a row from the 2nd December 1899 until a draw on the 10th March 1900. In this sequence they lost 5-0 home and away against Morton, 6-0 at home to Abercorn, and 8-1 away against Partick, the Second Division leaders. The match on the 2nd December, the 6-0 home defeat to Abercorn, was their biggest losing margin at home. A week later, they conceded eight, although despite conceding in the first minute, Linthouse did compete, but failed to take their chances. Partick were much more clinical in front of goal and went into the break 4-0 up. On restarting they immediately added a fifth. At this point Linthouse stepped up their effort and playing with more purpose lay siege to the Thistle goal. The pressure eventually culminated in a penalty, converted by Drysdale. But this only served to bring out the latent powers of Thistle who scored three more in quick succession. The eight game losing streak eventually ended in what was to be the last ever SFL game at Langlands Park. Played on the 10th March 1900, Linthouse secured a 2-2 draw with Motherwell.

When they finished in last place the board decided enough was enough. It was clear that they would never be able to compete with their close neighbours, Rangers and so the club withdrew from the Scottish Football League. When the League AGM was held on the 16th May 1900 Linthouse did not seek re-election and East Stirlingshire beat Raith Rovers in the battle to replace them.

Linthouse were without a league competition for 1900-01 but they did enter the Scottish FA Cup and were eliminated in the Second Round without kicking a ball. Clydebank forfeited their first round tie and Linthouse then scratched from the next match against Motherwell. Shortly afterwards Linthouse went out of business and the ground was subsequently redeveloped for housing.

SEASON	LEAGUE	P	W	D	L	F	A	P		POS
1895-96	SCOT-2	18	5	1	12	25	48	11		10/10
1896-97	SCOT-2	18	8	2	8	44	52	14	*	7/10
1897-98	SCOT-2	18	6	4	8	37	39	16		5/10
1898-99	SCOT-2	18	5	1	12	29	62	11		9/10
1899-00	SCOT-2	18	2	5	11	28	68	9		10/10

*Four points deducted

Lochgelly United

Formed: 1890
Colours: Black and gold striped shirts, black shorts
Ground: Recreation Park
Entered League: 1914. Elected to Second Division. 1921. Founder members of the reformed Second Division.
Number of League Seasons: 6
Honours: None
Highest League Finish: 10th in Division Two
Left League: 1915. Second Division suspended due to the Great War. 1926. Division Three abandoned. Wound up 1933

Lochgelly United were a football team that competed six seasons in the Scottish Football League, across two spells, but predominantly in the 1920s. Having agitated for League admission they were unlucky to be finally admitted in 1914, the onset of war bringing a premature suspension to their League involvement. Having re-joined the League in 1921 they were again unfortunate to be relegated to the ill-fated Third Division which was abandoned in 1926, an episode that brought to an end their short League career. During their six seasons they achieved a highest finish in their first season, 1914-15, when they came in tenth place in the Second Division, a position they subsequently matched in an expanded division in the 1922-23 season.

Lochgelly is a town in Fife, located near to Cowdenbeath, which takes its name from a loch of the same name, which is Gaelic for 'Loch of Brightness'. From the 1830s until the 1960s Lochgelly was a mining town. The football club was formed in 1890 by the merger of two local clubs, Lochgelly Athletic and Fifeshire Hibernian and initially played at Schools Park. Athletic had been formed at first from the Melgund Pit and played at Cooperhall Park. Fifeshire Hibernians had been formed by a group of Irish immigrants into the town in 1889. In 1901 the club moved to Reids Park and then onto the Recreation Park in 1910. The ground was located to the west of the town, accessed off Bank Street. Nicknamed the 'Happylanders' the club played in black and gold striped shirts and black shorts.

The team played in the Northern (1895-1909), Central (1909-12 and 1913-14) and Eastern (1912-13) Leagues and were admitted to the SFL in 1914, and were then a founder member of the reformed Second Division in 1921. They made their first of six pre-League Scottish Cup appearances in the 1895-96 season when they beat Raith Rovers at home 2-1 on the 11th January 1896. They drew Second Division Hibernian in the next round but before that game could be played Raith lodged a protest, which was discussed at a meeting of the SFA on the 28th January. *The Scotsman* reported on the proceedings and the outcome: "Raith Rovers submitted a protest against Lochgelly United, who they declared played an ineligible man – David McLaren – under the name of David Anderson, he having taken part in the first round of ties for Lochee United against Dundee Hibernians. A letter was read from McLaren stating that he did not inform Lochgelly of his real name when he played for that club. The tie was ordered to be replayed on the ground of the Kirkcaldy club. McLaren was suspended until the end of the present season." Raith won the replayed game 5-2, although the scores were level at 2-2 at half-time. Hibs beat Raith 6-1 a week later and went on to reach the Cup final, where they were beaten by Hearts 3-1.

Lochgelly exited at the First Round stage the following season, 2-1 to King's Park of Stirling and then didn't play in the Cup again until 1902. In their next four appearances they only got past the First Round once, in 1905, when they knocked out Inverness Caledonian, going out to Celtic in the Second Round.

In the 1905-06 season they finished second bottom of the Northern League but still made an application to join the Scottish League at the AGM on the 21st May 1906. Due to League expansion two additional places were made available and 11 non-League clubs applied and not surprisingly, Lochgelly's bid failed as they secured only 3 votes.

In the 1913-14 season, Lochgelly, now playing in the Central League, submitted a second bid. On Thursday 4th June 1914, at the AGM of the SFL, a proposal by Celtic and Third Lanark to increase the number of clubs in the Second Division from 12 to 14 was carried. Johnstone and Vale of Leven were re-elected and Clydebank, along with Lochgelly United were admitted to the Second Division as the new clubs. Lochgelly were elected to the Scottish Second Division after a series of elimination ballots (they won through in the third round). They survived the initial elimination ballot involving seven clubs, tied in third place. They also came third in the next ballot involving five clubs, with the top two elected. They then went into a third round of voting with Bathgate and Johnstone and won with 23 votes. (Bathgate 17, Johnstone 15). Lochgelly United won the last place despite finishing bottom of the Central League, Bathgate (3rd place), East Fife (4th) and Forfar (6th) being rejected.

Lochgelly United joined the Scottish Football League Second Division for the 1914-15 season, although this division was subsequently suspended due to the onset of the First World War, so they only completed one season before a six year hiatus. R Bain was their manager and they finished tenth out of 14 clubs, their best League placing. On the 15th August 1914 they made their League debut against county rivals Cowdenbeath. Lochgelly made an inauspicious first appearance losing 4-0 at home to Cowdenbeath (who would go on to be the champions, after a series of play-off matches with Leith Athletic and St Bernard's). The first League line-up for Lochgelly was: Finnerty; Hopkins, Paterson; Kennedy, Kellock, Young; 'Another', Meechan, Grant, McLaren and Prentice.

In their next game they suffered a heavy defeat, losing 5-1 in Perth against St Johnstone. *The Dundee Courier* reported that "two of the Saints' goals were scored while Finnerty, the United goalkeeper, was in the pavilion injured....Lochgelly United players must improve greatly before reaching Second Division standards. Young, the left back was a hero, and bore the brunt of the fight. The halves were week in feeding, their placing of the ball being invariably over the heads of the forwards. McDonagh, the right winger scored a pretty goal, and Hopkins, the centre, was occasionally noticeable."

Lochgelly only picked up one point in their first five games and on the 10th October they finally got their first ever SFL win at their sixth attempt, beating Albion Rovers 1-0. The *Daily Record* reported that "it was not *a* brilliant game at Lochgelly, where Albion Rovers met the United under Second League auspices. Still, there was great jubilation over the deserved success of the home team, who recorded their first victory in the competition. Lochgelly, who introduced Ramsay, late of Windygate Rangers, did the bulk of the pressing, but weak finishing and clever goalkeeping by Harrigan were responsible for a blank scoring sheet at the interval. Seven minutes after the resumption Lochgelly forced a corner, which was well taken. Harrigan made to clear, but the ball was deflected into the net. Near the end the Rovers' attack improved, and Watson was given a rare opportunity to equalise, but failed. The defences were the strong parts in either team. Trainer and Wallace played grandly for the Whifflet club, especially in the first half." The Lochgelly team earning their first ever SFL win was: Hallwood, Young, Lindsay, Taylor, Brown, Bennett, Milne, McLean, Ramsay, Pattison and Wishart. The win moved them off the bottom of the table, one place ahead of Arthurlie and they stayed there for the rest of 1914 in 13th place, despite a run of five games unbeaten.

1915 didn't start so well, as they lost 5-0 to second placed Leith Athletic in Edinburgh. They were trailing 4-0 at the interval and but for good goalkeeping by Hallwood, Lochgelly would have received a bigger beating. On the 27th February they recorded a good win of their own. The game against East Stirlingshire was played in a blizzard and was called off early with United leading 6-1. In April 1915 they recorded their heaviest ever SFL defeat but also their biggest winning margin. On Saturday 10th April they lost 6-0 in Edinburgh against joint leaders St. Bernard's. They gave away an early penalty and despite the home team playing the greater portion of the match without their left back, they conceded five more. A week later they beat a feeble Johnstone 6-0 where Scott scored a hat-trick and Hallwood had very little to do. By this time the club had thirteen players on active service, the most of any Second Division club, and including four of the line-up that secured their first ever win. Lochgelly eventually finished 10th which was their best placed League finish.

The Second Division was suspended for the duration of the war. These clubs, plus a number of non-League clubs, formed two regional leagues, the West of Scotland League and the Eastern League. Lochgelly played in the Eastern League, and then joined the Central League in 1919 when the Second Division was not re-started. In 1921 this competition was incorporated into the Scottish League as the new Second Division.

The 1921-22 season was the first season of automatic promotion and relegation in the League. The League had also decided on reducing the number of clubs for the following season to 40, with two divisions of 20 clubs. To facilitate this the bottom two clubs of the Second Division would automatically drop out of the League, with no re-election vote. Under the stewardship of ex-Falkirk and Celtic left-winger John Brown, their player-manager, Lochgelly struggled and finished in 18th place, narrowly retaining their League status by three points, with Dundee Hibs and Clackmannan dropping out.

They played their first game back on the resumption of the Second Division on the 20th August 1921, losing 4-3 at Cowdenbeath. Kirkby scored their first goal but then gave away a penalty for handball, Little beating Paterson with a strong shot, and the two sides were level at the break. Three goals were scored in the first three minutes of the second half, Cowdenbeath taking the lead, Lochgelly equalising through Reid and then Cowdenbeath re-taking the lead once more. Tonner again brought things level before Cowdenbeath scored again. The match attracted considerable interest with a crowd of 10,000.

The following Saturday Lochgelly beat St Johnstone 2-1 to get their first points of the new season, but the visitors were worthy of a draw. All the goals were scored in the first half with Berry and Forbes scoring for United. St Johnstone pushed for an equaliser but the Lochgelly defence held firm and Paterson was rarely troubled. After this game they struggled to score and in their next five matches scored only one goal and consequently dropped to second bottom. The sequence ended with a relative goal-fest and a 4-2 win over Forfar Athletic which lifted them to 17th place. They had signed a new centre forward called Ferguson, and he got a hat-trick and Tonner got the fourth. The following week they lost 4-0 at Dundee Hibs and then a 3-1 defeat at Dunfermline Athletic at the beginning of December left them bottom of the division, with their League status under threat.

Lochgelly ended 1921 with a rare away win though, beating Bo'ness by the odd goal in seven at Bo'ness. Here the home side raced into a two goal lead before Reid reduced the deficit before the interval. In the second half, with Bo'ness pressing for more goals Tonner twice set up Sinclair to score. Bo'ness got it back to 3-3 but Sinclair capped a fine performance by scoring the winner and getting his hat-trick. In February 1922 they recorded two, consecutive 4-0 wins, against strugglers Clackmannan and Stenhousemuir. Lochgelly had four different scorers in each game in which Tonner was outstanding and all the goals followed from his clever work. The following month they beat second placed Cowdenbeath in a local derby in front of a 7,000 crowd by 2-1. They led 1-0 at half-time through Reid and Tonner added a second on the hour mark. Cowdenbeath got one back through a penalty but United deserved the win. The win saw them up to 16th in the table with a five point cushion from the bottom two places, which was just as well, as form after this win was disappointing. Lochgelly went winless in their last five games, picking up only one point and scoring only two goals and they slipped to third from bottom, but avoided dropping out of the League. It was too close for comfort for the Board though, and player-manager John Brown was axed, with Tommy Timmons taking the reins, combining the managers' role with that of club secretary.

The following season they matched their best ever League finishing, coming in tenth again, although arguably this was a better finish than that in their first season, as this was in a 20 team division as opposed to one with 14 teams in it. Five of their first six games in the new season all ended with just one goal scored and the other was goalless. This parsimony of goals changed in October with the first three games played that month registering four each time. At the beginning of December they lost 5-0 at Bathgate and obviously disliked playing West Lothian teams as they conceded five against Armadale as well the following month. Following this defeat they went unbeaten in five games, a run that took them up as high as fifth in the table. However they then lost 4-0 at Cowdenbeath and then lost 5-0 at home to second placed Clydebank, a record losing margin at home for them in the League. This defeat was the start of a run of five straight defeats which ran through to the end of the season with them also conceding five in the last game of the season away at Dumbarton. Celtic were the visitors in the First Round of the Scottish Cup in front of 9,850 spectators and United went ahead through McIntosh after seven minutes, drawing much excitement from the home crowd. Celtic hit two quick goals before United equalised again through McIntosh but with five minutes to go Celtic got the winner much to the despair of Lochgelly, *The Scotsman* commenting that "the Lochgelly team gave their famous opponents a fright."

Their improved showing didn't last and in the 1923-24 season they finished 20th and bottom. John Brown had returned for a second spell as manager but they had a disaster of a season, setting two unwanted records for the old Second Division – most defeats in a season (30) and fewest League goals in a season (21). The club though retained its League status as they were relegated to the Third Division (which had been formed the previous season).

They opened the new campaign on the 18th August 1923 with a 1-0 win over Bathgate, thanks to a goal from Meechan. They then went 15 games without a win only picking up two draws, a sequence finally ended on the 8th December when they beat Armadale 1-0 to record their first victory since the first day of the season. In the Armadale game the visitors were superior and Orr in goal for Lochgelly made a number of good saves. Lochgelly's outside-left Neilson scored from distance and from then on Lochgelly had the best of the game and pressed for a second but were unable to add to their score.

In January 1924 they suffered heavy defeats away at Dunfermline 6-1 and away at leaders St Johnstone, 6-0, for who Coyle scored a hat trick. These left them nine points adrift at the bottom. A Scottish Cup tie at Ibrox in front of 48,000 saw United go down 4-1 but helped boost their finances. Back in the League, on the 16th February they scored two goals in a game for the first time that season, but unfortunately promotion challengers King's Park of Stirling scored eight! The Happylanders home form this season had been noted for low scores with the club and their visitors sharing only 22 goals in 18 of the 19 matches. However, in this one match, the club lost 8–2, nearly half the total of all the others put together. The Stirling team scored two goals within the first five minutes. They added a third later in the half, before Young converted a penalty to reduce the arrears at half-time to 3-1. Lochgelly scored a second, another penalty, this time taken by Collins because Young had missed a second penalty, but their opponents then scored five more. The defeat was their highest scoring home loss and was their equal highest losing home margin.

In early March Lochgelly secured back-to-back wins away at Bo'ness, 2-0, and then 1-0 at home to Albion Rovers, but it was too little too late and relegation was confirmed. They only picked up one point from the last four games in April and finished 19 points behind Vale of Leven, who were also relegated. Lochgelly only gained 12 points, from four wins and four draws. They lost 30 games and scored a paltry 21 goals, nearly half of the next lowest club, which was Vale of Leven.

Manager John Brown was given the chance to redeem himself but a promotion challenge never really materialised and Lochgelly finished fifth in the Third Division. The club never really got close to the three southern clubs of Nithsdale Wanderers, Queen of the South or Solway Star at the top of the division. Vale of Leven, the other relegated club came in fourth. This was an achievement of sorts though as the club had released all of their players at the end of the season and played with mostly amateur players who worked in the local mines.

Lochgelly had a tough start to life in the Third Division, playing a number of the teams who would challenge for promotion, picking up only one point, although they did beat Dykehead 5-1. At the beginning of October they beat Dumbarton Harp 6-0, brothers John and Thomas McLean scored the first two and Paterson and John McNeil each had a brace. The result took them to fifth but was ultimately excluded from the record books when Harp's records were expunged. *The Sunday Post* commented "a feature of Lochgelly's play was the penetration of the front rank, the whole five being speedy and always on the move. Paterson's goals were scored with rocket shots when on the run."

In February 1925 they gave a good account of themselves in the Scottish Cup when they were drawn against Dundee, only going out 2-1, *The Scotsman* commenting that "the Fifers were noteworthy for their pluck, and did not confess themselves beaten until the very end. Indeed, in the closing minutes they came very near to equalising the score on several occasions." The following month, back in League action, they put six past Galston without reply, with Cuthbert ordered off the field for the visitors.
By the end of March they were in fifth but crucially seven points behind the team in fourth, with only four games left to play. They finished strongly in April beating Brechin, Royal Albert and Helensburgh before losing their final match in Shotts against Dykehead.

The 1925-26 season would prove to be their last in the League and they finished a mid-table ninth place, which would represent their lowest ever placed finish. P Henderson was their manager for this season only. The Third Division came to an ignominious end, with a number of games uncompleted. Lochgelly managed to complete 29 of their 30 games, missing the away game at Galston who had resigned by then, and they started their campaign at home to the same team, and led 2-0 at half-time following goals by Young and Ramsay. Guthrie scored both of the visitors' goals in the last ten minutes to grab a point. In early September they got a good 3-0 win in Lockerbie against Mid-Annandale and scored five a month later in a 5-3 win over Peebles Rovers.

The Happylanders then suffered a bad run in the autumn, losing five in a row, albeit all away games, and scoring only once. Included in this sequence was a 5-0 loss to Peebles in the reverse fixture, a 4-0 reverse at Brechin and 5-1 defeat at Beith. In December they also lost 5-0 at Royal Albert but they also beat Clackmannan 5-0, *The Sunday Post* reporting that "Lochgelly thoroughly deserved their big win over Clackmannan, and, had they not slackened off considerably in the latter part, the score against the men from the "Wee Coonty" would have been even greater. The home team had Penman, of Bowhill Juniors, on trial at centre forward, and he signalised his appearance by scoring three fine goals. The first was secured by Don twenty minutes after the start, and a few minutes later Penman netted another two. The second half had just started when Penman scored again, this time with an overhead kick that took McPhail by surprise. The fifth goal was registered by Newman from a free kick." A fortnight later they lost 8-2, away at Vale of Leven, who went top with this win. Urquhart scored four of his sides goals, while Penman scored both of the Lochgelly goals.

The club started 1926 very strongly with a run of seven games without defeat which started when they beat bottom side Brechin City 7-2, although the five goal winning margin flattered them. Brechin actually opened the scoring but goals by John McLean, Penman and two by James McNeil gave the home team a 4-1 lead at half-time. The second half was only a few minutes old when Brechin pulled one back for 4-2. After this Lochgelly got three other goals through Penman, John McNeil and McGurk. The following month they beat Royal Albert 6-0, and again the papers highlighted the score line was not indicative of their superiority. *The Sunday Post* reported that "Lochgelly United have now a reputation for high scoring, and against Royal Albert, in a Third League match yesterday they ran up six goals. They, however, were hardly superior to the extent the score indicates, for in the second half there was little or nothing to choose between the teams. In the first half they were all over the Royalists, and at half-time led by five goals. Young and McTurk had one each, and Penman had two, while the other was accounted for by a Royal Albert defender heading into his own goal. Young got Lochgelly's sixth just after the restart." By now Galston had resigned from the League and other teams were unable to fulfil their fixtures, struggling with gate receipts that did not cover their expenses. Lochgelly were forced to sell their best players to keep the club afloat with William Miller sold to Liverpool for £200 and Penman was snapped up by Stoke City for £300.

On the 24th April 1926 Lochgelly played their last SFL game at the Recreation Ground against Solway Star, where the spoils were shared in a 1-1 draw. No goals were scored in the first half. Hutchison scored for the visiting side and ten minutes later John McLean equalised and scored Lochgelly's last ever League goal. The following month the Third Division was abandoned when it became clear that the financial costs of the competition exceeded the means of its members. Lochgelly spent one season in the Scottish Alliance Northern Section before the expulsion of the ex-Third Division clubs. They decided to concentrate on Cup-ties for the 1927-28 and went out of the Scottish Cup in the First Round to Brechin City.

They made two further appearances in the Scottish Cup in the early 1930s. In the 1931-32 season they were drawn against Hearts in the First Round. Lochgelly surrendered home advantage and sixteen goals were scored at Tynecastle. The match, on the 16th January 1932, was played in a gale force wind and with heavy rain, leading to a sodden pitch and the conditions did not favour spectating. *The Scotsman* commented that Lochgelly "had given away ground advantage, but did not reap much monetary reward, as only 5600 spectators paid for admission" Lochgelly only held out for five minutes before Barney Battles got three in the next quarter of an hour – the first a header; the second a shot following a poor clearance by Cameron; and the third after the 'keeper misjudged a cross in the wind. Bob Bennie then made it four. Three more goals were then scored in the last five minutes of the first half, by Bennie, Johnstone and Battles, to give Hearts a 7-0 lead at the interval. Lochgelly surprised Hearts by scoring the opening goal of the second half through Breslin. Smith then retaliated for Hearts. McFadyen then got a second for the Fifers and Smith then got his second to make it nine. Battles then took the home score into double figures, scoring his fifth, before Breslin scored to make it 10-3. Jock White. Willie Murray, and Bob Bennie's third completed the scoring. The *Edinburgh Evening News* ran with the headlines "A Baker's Dozen" and "Battles' Nap Hand." The Lochgelly United team was: D McKinlay; McAndrew, Cameron; Collins, J McKinlay, Duncan; Breslin, Whyte, Rarity, Davies and McFadyen.

The following year, the 1932-33 season, they made their final Cup appearance, in a First Round exit to First Division Kilmarnock on the 21st January 1933. Lochgelly gave a good account of themselves and did well to keep the score to a margin of three goals to one. Killie dominated in the first half and reached the interval with a three goal lead. Lochgelly did much better after the break and gave the home team a shock by scoring just three minutes after the restart through McAllister. *The Scotsman* commented that "this encouraged the visitors to go about their work more boldly, and the home defence was more often in action. The Lochgelly attack was too light, however, to do any further damage, although Bain, McGurk and Gallacher carried through some smart raids. The defence was the best part of the team, and defied the Kilmarnock sharpshooters during the whole of the second half. A McKinlay gave a confident display in goal, and McKettigan and McNeil, at back, gave him every assistance. The half-backs also lent a hand in defence, Russell doing well at centre-half. The three forwards already mentioned were the pick of a line that had few opportunities."

Lochgelly United were wound up at the end of the season but the Recreation Park continued to be used for football until 1934. The ground was eventually sold to the town council for £400 in 1935 and it was later redeveloped for housing. The street that cuts through the old ground site is called Timmons Street, honouring the club's secretary turned manager. The adjacent street is called Henderson Street, after the club's last League manager.

SEASON	LEAGUE	P	W	D	L	F	A	P	POS
1914-15	SCOT-2	26	9	3	14	44	60	21	10/14
1921-22	SCOT-2	38	11	9	18	46	56	31	18/20
1922-23	SCOT-2	38	16	5	17	41	64	37	10/20
1923-24	SCOT-2	38	4	4	30	20	86	12	20/20
1924-25	SCOT-3	30	15	4	11	59	41	34	5/16
1925-26	SCOT-3	29	9	9	11	58	63	27	9/16

Meadowbank Thistle

Formed: 1974
Colours: Gold shirts and black shorts (originally hooped shirts of gold and black)
Ground: Meadowbank Stadium
Entered League: 1974. Elected due to SFL re-construction
Number of League Seasons: 21
Highest League Finish: Runners-up in Division One (2nd tier)
Honours: Second Division Champions 1986-87 (3rd tier)
Left League: 1995. Relocation and name change – to Livingston

Meadowbank Thistle played in the Scottish League between 1974 and 1995 and are the forerunners of the present day Livingston FC. They have both their origins and their demise in a name change. They were originally formed in 1943 as Ferranti Amateurs (later Ferranti Thistle from 1948), the works team of the giant Edinburgh based electronics firm, Ferranti. In 1953 they entered the East of Scotland League, as Ferranti Thistle and they moved to the old Edinburgh City ground of City Park in 1969 and they competed in the early rounds of the Scottish Cup when they gained full SFA membership in 1972.

On the 16th December 1972 they made their debut in the Scottish Cup playing Duns from the Borders. The Ferranti line up was: Simpson, McDonald, Sivewright, Bell, Brock, Nisbet, Crawford, Thompson, Martin, Mains and Birrell. Ferranti got off to a great start and inside-left Mains scored in off the underside of the bar in the first minutes from a great shot. There was no further scoring in the first half. In the second period Crawford scored twice for Thistle and Kerr scored for Duns, with the final score 3-1, with the game played out in front of only 150 spectators. They suffered a Second Round defeat to Elgin City, but only after a replay. The first game was tied 2-2 and they lost the replay on the 13th January 1973 by 2-1, this time in front of 2,000 fans. In the 1973-74 Scottish Cup they had the distinction of being the last remaining non-League team in the competition, reaching the Third Round. Here they lost 6-1 to Patrick Thistle at Firhill on the 27th January 1974 with Ronnie Glavin scoring a hat-trick.

This Cup run would prove to be timely. Since 1967 and the demise of Third Lanark, the Scottish Football League had consisted of 37 clubs and with League reconstruction under debate a decision was taken to fill the vacancy and applications were invited to be the 38th club. Seven clubs competed for the slot including then Highland League teams Ross County, Elgin City and Inverness Thistle, as well as Forres Mechanics, Gateshead United (from England) and Hawick Royal Albert. Their main rivals were all from the Highlands and this divided the vote for the North of Scotland applicants. Ultimately it came down to a straight choice between Ferranti and Inverness and Ferranti prevailed by 21 votes to 16 and became the city of Edinburgh's third club – for the first time in 25 years. Ferranti's admittance to the SFL was only confirmed when they fulfilled the twin conditions of a new ground and, as sponsorship wasn't permitted, a new name. Edinburgh City Council provided use of Meadowbank Stadium, which had been built as a venue for the 1970 Commonwealth Games. As they couldn't have the original company name in their title they took the name of the stadium, whilst retaining 'Thistle' and Meadowbank Thistle was born. Other footballing events overshadowed their elevation to SFL status such as Scotland's participation at the World Cup finals in West Germany where the national team played Brazil, Yugoslavia and Zaire and also David Hay's transfer from Celtic to Chelsea for the then massive sum of £250,000.

Manager John Bain kept faith with the players who had been instrumental in the club's progress for their debut season in the Scottish Football League. Their first match as a League club was played on Friday the 9th August 1974 against Albion Rovers in a League Cup tie. The tie was switched to a Friday night to avoid clashing with a Hibs match the next day. With an entry fee of just 30p, Meadowbank's senior debut attracted a crowd of 3,000, although the game ended in a 1-0 defeat. The first Meadowbank Thistle team to take the field was: Derek Gray, Dave Cathcart, Alan McDonald, Kenny Bell, Alan Robertson, Neil Nisbet, Robert Scobie, Derek Fotheringham, Ian Martin, George Hall and Jim Sivewright, and the substitutes were Charlie Crawford and Denis McGurk. *The Scotsman* reported on the game with the headline: "Thistle get the cheers, but no points". Their report went on to say: "Meadowbank Thistle, the first senior team to make their debut in Edinburgh for over 40 years, got most of their sums right for their inaugural League Cup tie against Albion Rovers at Meadowbank last night. The only thing wrong was the result, a second half goal by Albion Rovers' Dickson which upset the celebrations. There were about 4,000 spectators and with the stand drawing 30p a head (20p for old-age pensioners) the takings would be about £1,200. Doubtless the blonde go-go dancer who appeared before the start and at the interval helped to swell the crowd but there were other gimmicks. Programmes were given away free and the disc jockey's choice of records was with it. Meadowbank Thistle, on this evidence, have the right ideas and the crowd appreciated the enterprise. Once the game had started they were generous in their applause of good moves by Thistle. The goodwill had been created. Meadowbank's future rests with football, and while the Albion Rovers had superior looking players such as Rice, Brogan, Coughlin and Shields, Thistle were in control throughout the first half. On the massive expanse of Meadowbank, so different from the grounds they had been used to, they slowed the pace to suit their game. Goalkeeper Gray had a first-class game and made several tremendous saves. Sivewright got a great ovation for forcing Thistle's first corner in senior football in the seventeenth minute. He also came near to scoring for Thistle with a tremendous free-kick. Martin looked a tremendous little striker and Fotheringham is one we could be hearing more about. Just on the interval he and Martin took part in a neat little double act to force a corner. Just when Thistle were beginning to string their passes together effectively, Gray made his only mistake of the game and it cost them a goal. In the 58th minute he misjudged a cross from his right and Dickson nipped in to head home. Apart from that Thistle's defence, led by ex-Hib, Alan Robertson, did surprisingly well for the first venture into this class of football. John Bain, the Thistle manager, said after the game: 'The lads were a bit nervous and perhaps they lacked a little professionalism and guile which would have been needed to win, but we were very pleased with our opening performance. At this stage it is all largely experimental. Tom Fagan, chairman of Albion Rovers commented: 'We have received one of our biggest cheques in years, proof surely that the League's choice of Meadowbank Thistle and not Inverness Thistle was fully justified." Derek Gray, Meadowbank's first goalkeeper went on to play for Thistle 155 times. The final attendance figure was confirmed as 2,818, a very healthy start. Thistle lost their remaining four games in the League Cup including a 4-1 loss at home to Brechin City, this time watched by a lowly 360 crowd.

On Saturday the 31st August 1974 they made their Scottish League debut away at Stranraer, losing 3-1. Their first home League game was on Wednesday the 11th September. Alloa Athletic were their guests and the visitors won 1-0 with the crowd put at 680. Meadowbank did not win their first match until October, having suffered nine straight losses, including 8-1 at Alloa and 5-0 at Cowdenbeath. By this time they were the only senior side across the three Divisions in Scotland and the four in England to be without a single point and with a record of played nine, lost nine, goals for three, goals against 29. Their first League win (and points) eventually came on Saturday 12th October 1974 at Glebe Park, away against Brechin City. Brechin were slightly better having gained five points. Having cleared a home effort off the line with Gray well beaten, winger Charlie Crawford confirmed his hero status by putting Thistle ahead after the interval and they duly held on to secure the points. The Thistle team to earn their first ever SFL points was: Gray, McVey, Sivewright, Jones, Cathcart, Hunter, Crawford, Hancock, Fotheringham, Scoular and Mackinson.

A month later Meadowbank beat eventual champions Falkirk, who at that time were sitting in mid-table, at home 1-0 watched by 856 spectators. Back-to-back win against

Albion Rovers and Forfar at the end of November and the beginning of December saw them briefly off the bottom, going above Forfar Athletic, but this was followed on 14th December 1974 by another heavy defeat when they lost 8-0 against Hamilton. A mini three game unbeaten run during the rest of December (Cathcart scoring in the 1-0 win over Clydebank) saw them end 1974 in 17th place in the twenty team division. An eventual 18th place finish in a 20 team division, winning nine matches, did represent a triumph of sorts as they overhauled first Forfar (who would become the Division's whipping boys, winning only one game all season), and then Cowdenbeath. They hadn't finished bottom, and they had not been humiliated. Scoring goals was their main problems, scoring only 26 in 38 games. It was all too much for John Bain though, who resigned at the of their first League season after 20 years in charge. He was replaced by Willie MacFarlane, the ex-Hibs full-back and then manager.

The 1975-76 season saw Meadowbank finish 14th but this was not an improvement as this was the first season in the new, three-tier setup of a premier division consisting of 10 team, then two divisions of 14 clubs. Effectively they were bottom of the now third tier. The next four seasons saw them continue to struggle and they finished 11th, 13th, 14th (bottom) and 12th. Highlights during this time were their Scottish Cup runs of 1977-78 and 1978-79, where they reached the Fourth Round on each occasion. In the second of these, a crowd of over 5,000 watched them lose 6-0 to Hibs. Macfarlane was sacked in early 1980 and his assistant Terry Christie took over and presided over the club's most successful period. Christie had previously played for Stirling Albion and had managed non-League Newtongrange Star before becoming MacFarlane's assistant.

There were no immediate signs of improvement as the club finished 13th (and second bottom) in Christie's first full season in charge and only one better the following season. By this time gates were down to around 300-400 and an evening game on Tuesday 8th September 1981 at home to Albion Rovers attracted a crowd of only 152. In the same season Meadowbank again reached the Fourth Round of the Scottish Cup knocking out Clyde and Arbroath along the way, before losing to Dundee and missing out on a lucrative Quarter-final tie against Rangers.

In the 1982-1983 season Christie led Meadowbank to second place in the Second Division and promotion to the First Division, an outstanding achievement for a club who had never previously finished outside the bottom four places of Scottish football. In a dramatic turnaround in fortunes they finished only one point behind champions Brechin City, and were five clear of Arbroath in third. Meadowbank won their first five League games and lost only one of the first 16 games before a surprise 5-0 defeat at Bayview against East Fife. By the turn of the year they had a four point lead over Brechin and Arbroath. Back-to-back 5-0 victories over Montrose and Berwick Rangers in early February 1983 left them six points ahead of Brechin City, although the team in second had two games in hand. Perhaps more importantly they were eight points ahead of Arbroath in third and with a game in hand on them and a +7 better goal difference. A couple of defeats followed as did a 3-0 home reverse against Arbroath but they continued to pick up sufficient points so that by the end of April, with two rounds of games to play for each team, they were second on 51 points, two points behind new leaders Brechin and four clear of Arbroath. They therefore needed only one point from their two remaining games to earn promotion. Both of these were away games, one which was against the leaders and the other against mid-table Cowdenbeath. On the 7th May 1983 Arbroath won 5-2 at home to Stenhousemuir but Meadowbank got the point they needed with a 1-1 draw against Brechin at Glebe Park to gain promotion for the first time in their League history. A maiden trophy was out of their grasp though as they were two points behind Brechin and with a vastly inferior goal difference (21 goals). They beat Cowdenbeath in their final game of the season but Brechin drew away at Stenhousemuir and they missed out on the title.

Meadowbank were expected to struggle in the First Division but in the end they finished a very creditable 11th place (out of 14 teams), finishing three points above Raith Rovers and eight points above Alloa Athletic, both who were relegated. They lost the opening League game of the season 4-1 at home to Morton but bounced back a fortnight later to beat Alloa 1-0 away. This was followed by a home win over Airdrieonians by the same score but they then failed to win in their next six games until they beat leaders Partick Thistle 2-1 in mid-October. At the end of the same month they lost 5-1 at home to Ayr United but they continued to accumulate points. A 4-1 away win at Falkirk at the end of February was followed by a 2-1 win over second bottom Alloa and these results gave them some breathing space and a five game unbeaten run in the spring guaranteed them another season of First Division football.

The 1984-85 season brought mixed fortunes. The club were relegated back to the bottom tier but not before embarking on a fantastic run in the League Cup, seeing off Greenock Morton and Premier League sides Hibs and St Johnstone to reach the last four of a major competition for the first time in their history. A crowd of just over 400 was present at the Meadowbank Stadium on the 11th August 1984 to see the club kick off the new season in a League match at home to Airdrieonians, which they lost 3-0. The following Saturday they conceded three goals again, this time at Falkirk, but an Adrian Sprott hat-trick meant Meadowbank scored three of their own to register their first point of the season. Only three draws came from their next six League matches and so by the end of September they were the only winless team in the First Division, although it was Kilmarnock and St Johnstone that occupied the two relegation places at this time. They finally won in the League on the 6th October when they beat Kilmarnock 4-0 with a brace from Smith and Sprott.

By this time they were already faring match better in the League Cup, having recorded victories over Morton and Premier Division side Hibernian. They met St Johnstone in the Quarter-finals and won 2-1. Alan Lawrence was the man who got the decisive goal, heading in just two minutes after Thistle full-back Paul Leetion had been sent-off for a second yellow card. All the goals came in the second half with the Perth side taking the lead before Armstrong converted a penalty. This set up a two-legged Semi-final against the mighty Rangers. This tie was effectively ended with a 4-0 defeat in the first leg. The *Glasgow Herald*, under the headline "Sad Ending to Meadowbank Bid" commented that "the Skol Cup fairytale run of Meadowbank last night turned into a kind of Hitchcock horror in the semi-final first leg at Ibrox where a second half collapse saw them left with virtually no chance of progressing to the Hampden final. They fought just as hard and maybe even more bravely than they had done in previous matches against Morton and Hibernian but the effect of containing a strong and speedy Rangers side were all to plain during the last half hour. They had held Rangers to just one goal by Ally McCoist until midway in the second half, but when Ian Ferguson and McCoist struck again their chance had gone. Just to rub in the agony they lost fourth near the end to Cammy Fraser, and it is now almost certain that the holders Rangers will go back to Hampden to defend the trophy. But one consolation for the Edinburgh side came when their centre-half Jim Stewart was given the man-of-the-match award for a gritty performance in marshalling a defence under heavy pressure." The unfortunate 'keeper on the night was Dougie McNab. They got a very creditable draw in the second leg, 1-1, going out 5-1 on aggregate.

Back in the League they continued to pick up points, losing only once in the first five games in December before a crashing 5-0 defeat away at Airdrie on the 29th. Under the headline "Meadowbank Pay for Arrogance" the *Herald* reported that "Meadowbank Thistle pranced on to Brookfield on Saturday, took possession straight from the kick-off, and ushered the ball back into the depths of their own defence. There they proceeded to knock it about in text-book style, you know, neat triangles and tidy, tight circles. It was all very continental and pretty. How could such artists be bottom of the first division? Surely it should have been Airdrie, the league leaders, out there stroking the ball around with such arrogance. Instead they stood back watching the silky display: Jim Rodger fidgeted nervously; Dave McCabe scowled; and Jamie Fairlie, the captain, spat on the turf. There was no visible sign from him, but suddenly his troops surged towards the Edinburgh maestros. Just under 90 minutes later the Diamonds had done the business again, and Thistle, 0-5 down, could not even find the ball. Or perhaps the poor souls just didn't want to any longer. Airdrie, you may have gathered,

do not take kindly to visitors who try to play the smart Alex, and their retribution was swift and hard. They took it upon themselves to teach Thistle some respect, they also taught them how the game should really be played. It is all very well being able to huddle in defence and roll the ball around when the opposition are holding off on the halfway line. The rest of the trick, is being able to do it when the other team are climbing all over the top of you. Meadowbank have clearly not reached that stage in their development, and they were made to suffer for their shortcomings."
Meadowbank were now bottom with 15 points, although it was tight at the foot of the table with only three points separating the bottom five, the other clubs involved being Patrick Thistle, Kilmarnock, St. Johnstone and Ayr United.

Meadowbank failed to win any of their League matches in January although did beat fellow strugglers Patrick 4-2 in the Third Round of the Scottish Cup. They were knocked out by Motherwell at home in the next round but a week later recorded a first League win of 1985 with a 2-0 away win at St Johnstone which lifted them off the bottom above the Perth Saints. In mid-March they recorded back to back League wins, beating Kilmarnock 2-1 (Graeme Armstrong 2) and then incredibly winning 5-3 at third placed Airdrie. Reporting on this game, the *Herald,* under the headline "Meadowbank find will to survive" commented that "Airdrie can consider themselves lucky. Had Meadowbank Thistle been mean enough they might have finished up playing with only nine men instead of 10. There is no telling how badly beaten Airdrie would have been if Thistle had resorted to such cruelty. Trailing 2-3, the Edinburgh side seemed to draw strength from the dismissal of David Conroy, sent packing for a show of retaliation against Willie McGuire, and went on to win 5-3. It is a ploy which might be worth using next time the going gets tough. They seemed perfectly happy with fewer than the regulation number. It reduced their options, gave them less to think about, and made them more direct, which seemed to bring out the best in those who remained." Airdrie had raced into a 2-0 lead and then allowed Meadowbank to level before regaining the lead. Then came Conroy's dismissal and Meadowbank went on to win 5-3, the goals being scored by Robertson, an Armstrong penalty, Sprott, an own-goal, and Hendrie. Unfortunately, relegation rivals Kilmarnock and Partick Thistle also won and St Johnstone picked up a point. They were off the bottom though. Thistle had 24 points, St Johnstone 23, and ahead of them were Kilmarnock with 25 and Partick with 27 points - with seven games still to go.

Meadowbank followed this up with a third successive win, winning 1-0 away at Motherwell, to give their supporters hope of escaping relegation. However, they couldn't keep it going and they then lost consecutive home matches against Clydebank and promotion chasing Falkirk, meaning that they remained in the bottom two, three points above St Johnstone, but two behind Kilmarnock and five behind Patrick, with four matches left. Back-to-back away wins against Brechin and Clyde left them second from bottom, two points behind Kilmarnock, and three behind Partick and East Fife with two games to play. On the 20th April Sprott and Chris Robertson had scored as they beat Brechin City 2-1 away in what the *Glasgow Herald* describes as "Meadowbank's stubborn refusal to go quietly". St Johnstone had been relegated and only three points separated them, Kilmarnock and Patrick with three games to go. A week later they won at Clyde 1-0 thanks to a goal from Robertson, but Killie won at already doomed St Johnstone 4-2 and Patrick Thistle won at East Fife, the *Glasgow Herald* commenting that "for genuine nail-biting tension...Meadowbank, Kilmarnock and Patrick Thistle are all fighting the good fight against relegation. St Johnstone have already gone and there is an understandable reluctance to accompany them into the largely forgotten world of the Second Division. None of this trio can be confident of survival since only three points separate them."

On Saturday the 4th May 1985 Kilmarnock's safety was assured as they beat Clyde 2-0. Meadowbank lost 4-2 at home to Hamilton and made an immediate return to whence they came. The *Herald* reported "well wasn't that an eventful afternoon" and went on to say "It was all a bit sudden really the way the first division promotion and relegation issues were settled. It had been such a nervy and drawn out slog that most had fully expected the fates of those clubs involved to be still hanging in the balance in the dying seconds of next week's final matches. But Motherwell, Clydebank, Falkirk, Kilmarnock, and Meadowbank decided enough was enough and ended the suspense in Saturday." A week later Meadowbank concluded their fixtures, winning 3-1 at Ayr United. They had won three out of their last four League fixtures, all of the victories coming on the road, but this hadn't been enough.

Meadowbank almost bounced straight back in the 1985-86 season, finishing in third place, but six points adrift of Queen of the South in second and eight points behind champions Dunfermline Athletic. They began life back in the third tier with away defeats against Cowdenbeath and Arbroath before beating Stirling Albion. Their season kick-started with a 5-1 away win at Stenhousemuir followed by a 4-1 home win over St Johnstone, a game in which Alan Lawrence scored all of his side's goals. A 6-0 win over Raith Rovers in early November was the beginning of four consecutive victories and they went into 1986 in third place, four points behind Queen of the South in second and six behind leaders Dunfermline. A shock Scottish Cup exit to Nairn County in early January seemed to also impact on their League form as they fell further behind and slipped to fifth. A 4-1 win over Stirling Albion in early March saw them close the gap on the second-placed Pars to six points, but they missed an opportunity when the two sides drew 2-2 at the Meadowbank Stadium, the hosts twice coming from behind through goals from Lawrence. A 1-0 win over leaders Queen of the South at the end of the month offered some hope, but this was followed by two 1-0 defeats. Their slim chances were boosted by a 4-0 win over Dunfermline in early April, but the games were running out, with the gap at seven points with only five left to play. Meadowbank won all five games to take a maximum of ten points but Queen of the South and Dunfermline picked up eight and seven points respectively to comfortably earn promotion.

Meadowbank made no doubts the following year, winning promotion for the second time, this time as Second Division champions, the club's first senior honour. They opened their season on Saturday 9th August 1986, winning their opening game 5-1 away at Muirton Park against St Johnstone. The *Glasgow Herald* headline was "Injury-hit Meadowbank still too good for Saints" and the paper noted that "It is just as well for St Johnstone that Meadowbank were hit by injuries, with the club's 38-year old physio Arthur Duncan on the substitutes' bench on Saturday. As it was, Meadowbank had enough good, fit players to stroll to a 5-1 won, and stake their claim as the team to beat in the Second Division this season. The main executioner was Darren Jackson, with three goals and an assist." Jackson began his footballing career with Meadowbank while he worked part-time as a printer. Scoring over twenty goals, the 19 year old earned a move to Newcastle United and later played for Dundee United, Hibernian, Celtic and Hearts as well as being capped 28 times for Scotland.

Meadowbank had to play a couple of home games at Ochilview as the stadium was hosting an athletics meeting, beating Stranraer and rather ungratefully, Stenhousemuir 1-0. On their return to their home they again scored five the following month at home to Albion Rovers in a 5-0 win. Top scorer Darren Jackson had a hand in four of the goals beginning with a 15th minute cross that allowed John McGachie, signed from Hamilton, to head home. It was in the second half when Meadowbank ran riot – Jackson broke clear and took a return pass from McGachie for the second; McGachie crossed to give Graeme Armstrong a free header; Jackson's speed and control set up McGachie to tap in for the fourth; and Armstrong converted a penalty after Jackson had been tripped.

This emphatic victory was followed up by four more wins which took them joint top with Alloa Athletic. However, they then failed to win any of their next four games picking up just a solitary point so that by mid-November they had dropped down to fourth, with Raith, Alloa and Albion Rovers ahead of them. On Saturday 29th November they scored five in a match for the third time with a 5-0 win over Stenhousemuir, McGachie scoring four, taking his season's tally to 13 and Roseburgh scoring the other. At this point only three points separated the top six clubs, and Meadowbank finished 1986 just outside of the promotion places in third place, just a point behind St Johnstone and a further point behind leaders Raith Rovers.

The beginning of 1987 saw a run to the fourth round in the Scottish Cup. Having accounted for Stirling Albion and Ayr United in the previous rounds they took Premier Division Dundee to three games. In the first game away at Dens Park on Saturday 21st February they took a shock 8th minute lead through an unchallenged Roseburgh header but Dundee equalised in the second half and the game ended 1-1. The replay a few days later ended by the same score, after extra time. The *Glasgow Herald* reported that "Meadowbank gave Dundee a hard time, and then some overtime, in the Commonwealth Stadium last night but will have to do even better to win their place in the quarter-finals. After surviving an early pummelling the Second Division side went on to outplay their Premier Division opponents for long spells and can count themselves a little unlucky to be forced into a third game next week. They rocked Dundee in this replay, as they had done at Dens Park, this time taking the lead in 33 minutes through Tom Hendrie. Although the equaliser from Ross Jack came soon afterwards they proceeded to dominate the second half during which the Dens side were decidedly unsure of themselves. It was clear almost immediately that Donald Park [formerly of Hearts], who has paid his dues in the cup over the years, would be an important player for the Second Division side. In the first few minutes he was one moment up in attack and at another back in defence...[after half-time]...Thistle came out in great heart and indeed took the gamer to Dundee, producing some neat football in the process. One excellent move ended with a good McGachie shot that was only a foot or so the wrong side of a post." The team that took Premier Division opposition to a second replay was: McQueen, Hendrie, Roseburgh, Boyd, Tierney, Armstrong, Lawrence, Lawson, Callachan, Park and McGachie. They eventually went on to lose the second replay at Dens 2-0.

Back in the League, Meadowbank went undefeated throughout their six fixtures in the month of March and ended it with a 1-1 draw at promotion rivals Raith. That run had seen them hit the front and they went into April top of the table on 45 points, two points ahead of four teams (Raith Rovers, Stirling Albion, Ayr United and St Johnstone). Meadowbank continued their good form in the new month and won all four games in April. On Saturday 25th April Vic Kasule put them ahead just before the interval at home to East Stirlingshire. Their opponents headed an equaliser but David Roseburgh made sure of the two points for the leaders. With their two closest rivals Ayr and Raith sharing the spoils in a 0-0 draw this gave them a four point lead over Raith in third and a plus six goal difference more or less confirmed promotion. A draw at Stirling, or at Alloa the following week would make it mathematically certain. A win would give them the championship.

On Saturday 2nd May the unbeaten SFL run of 11 games came to an end as they lost 3-1 at Stirling Albion. Somewhat anti-climatically, Raith's draw at St Johnstone promoted

Meadowbank, the *Glasgow Herald* reporting that "Meadowbank are up despite going down." They conceded after just eleven minutes and Stirling remained solid in defence and eventually made sure by a second in the 74th minute. A third soon followed before McGachie got a 90th minute consolation, ending the season with 22 goals. In the final game Meadowbank made sure of the title with a 1-0 at Alloa with Roseburgh scoring the goal, his 13th of the season. Three points behind them Raith, Stirling and Ayr all ended on 52 points with Raith accompanying them to the First Division on goal difference.

Many pundits expected Meadowbank to struggle, especially with the sales of strikers Darren Jackson and Alan Lawrence to Newcastle United and Dundee respectively, which raised £100,000. The club defied all predictions by finishing as runners-up in the First Division, but they were not promoted due to League reconstruction. A reduction of the Premier Division from 12 clubs to 10 saw three clubs (Falkirk, Dunfermline Athletic and Morton) relegated with a solitary promotion place going to First Division champions Hamilton Academical, who finished four points ahead of Meadowbank.

They kicked off the new campaign at home on the 8th August 1987 with a five goal thriller against Partick in front of a 1,040 crowd. In the battle of the inter-City Thistle's, Meadowbank fought back to win 3-2. Alan Prentice, on his debut, and goals from last season's main scorers Roseburgh and McGachie secured the win. Meadowbank won the next game by the same score, away at Dumbarton. They went the first six games of the new campaign unbeaten, to sit in second place, before a 2-1 home loss against Airdrieonians. This started a run of five games without a win, a sequence that was ended with a 2-0 win at Queen of the South on the 3rd October 1987.

At the end of October they surprisingly beat leaders Hamilton 5-1 away from home in a midweek evening kick-off with a hat-trick from Allan McGonigal, who had signed from East Stirlingshire. This defeat prompted the *Glasgow Herald* to ask "how does a good, seemingly invincible team turn into a shambles overnight? Answers on a postcard, please, to John Lambie, manager, Hamilton Academical. "In the following game, also away, they had another fine goal-scoring performance at Kilmarnock. McGonigal took his tally to seven in four games with one of the goals in Thistle's 4-2 victory. These two results put Meadowbank second in the table, one point behind leaders Hamilton, at the end of October. At the end of the following month, they thrashed Queen of the South 5-0 with David Roseburgh and Vic Kasule scoring a brace but injuries began to take their toll as they went into the winter. A 3-1 home defeat in the Boxing Day game against Kilmarnock saw them end 1987 in third place, three points behind Raith and six points behind leaders Hamilton.

Meadowbank went unbeaten in their first six Scottish League games of 1988, the last of these being a 2-0 win over leaders Hamilton. This victory was a nice wedding present for boss Terry Christie who had been married the day before. Neil Irvine scored his first goal since signing on loan from Hearts and Alan Logan clinched the points with a deflected shot 11 minutes from the end to take Thistle to within three points of Accies, but with a game more played.

Going into the last three rounds of games Meadowbank were in second, four points behind Hamilton. On Saturday 23rd April 1988 both Thistle and Hamilton lost at home by the same 1-0 scoreline. With Meadowbank losing to Clyde in Edinburgh, Hamilton should have been celebrating. But Forfar scored four minutes from time at Douglas Park to take matters into the penultimate round of matches. Meadowbank needed to win and hope Hamilton lost to take things to the last game of the season. Clydebank did their bit, beating Hamilton 3-1 but Thistle surprisingly lost 4-2 at home to bottom club Dumbarton, thus handing Hamilton both the title and promotion to the Premier Division. Christie's side drew their last game with Hamilton. Their opponents let spectators in for free and a bumper crowd of 5,000 saw the champions receive their trophy and medals. The game ended in a 1-1 draw.

Having secured their best ever Scottish Football League finish Meadowbank now entered a period of perennial struggle to avoid relegation to the Second Division. They finished the 1988-89 season tenth in the First Division (out of 14 teams), two points from safety. It was a largely uneventful League campaign, but they did knock out Premier Division strugglers Hamilton in the Third Round of the Scottish Cup 2-0. Goals were a problem and their top scorer was Bobby Forrest with ten (eight of those for Arbroath!).

There was an improved showing in the League the following year as they finished in seventh place but they were knocked out of each Cup on their first appearance. They lost their first three League matches, including two at home, but eventually recovered. The highlight of the season was a 2-1 away win at leaders and eventual champions St Johnstone in February 1990, where they came from behind with goals from Walter Boyd and Brian McNaughton.

In the 1990-91 season they slipped back in the League finishing just above the relegation places, coming in eleventh place, although they were six points clear of the relegated Clyde and nine clear of bottom side Brechin. They had won their opening game 1-0 against Kilmarnock but then had failed to win in their next eight League games until a 6-1 win over Brechin City on the 20th October. This was the start of a nine game unbeaten run. They entered the Scottish Cup at the Third Round stage and thrashed Ross County, then of the Highland League, 6-1 in February 1991 before being knocked out by fellow First Division side Morton in the next round. As the League season drew to a close they disappointingly lost 8-1 at home to Kilmarnock in April 1991.

Although not immediately apparent, the future direction of the club would change dramatically in the summer when businessman Bill Hunter was invited to join the board of directors. It wouldn't be until after 1993, once a controlling interest was gained, that plans would be implemented that would ultimately lead to the disappearance of the club.

Also off the pitch, Scottish League reconstruction meant the new 1991-92 season saw a reduction in the number of First Division clubs to twelve. Meadowbank Thistle finished in tenth place, just above the relegation places, finishing three points clear of Montrose, who dropped down along with Forfar Athletic. Thistle won their opening League game against Raith but then lost the next three. The first signs of their struggle to avoid relegation became apparent in mid-September when they were thrashed 7-0 at Ayr United. They beat fellow strugglers Forfar 2-0 on in early October but then failed to win any of their next nine matches, before a surprise 2-0 win at promotion challengers Partick Thistle on the 30th November. They went six games unbeaten in early 1992 and by the beginning of April had a six point cushion over Montrose, with only five games left to play. The two sides met at the Meadowbank Stadium where the visitors came away with a narrow 1-0 win to set the nerves jangling. Both sides lost their next two games but this suited Meadowbank more. On the 25th April they guaranteed their safety in the penultimate game by surprisingly beating promotion chasing Partick Thistle 2-1 away whereas Montrose could only draw. This couldn't help manager Terry Christie though. With the relationship with Hunter at best described as strained, he was sacked after the game, with former player and now coach Donald Park taking the managerial reins.

Having flirted with relegation the proverbial chicken came home to roost in the 1992-93 season as Meadowbank's stay in the First Division finally came to an end after six seasons. They won their opening League game away against Ayr United 2-1 and later in August beat Cowdenbeath 5-1, also away from home. Cowdenbeath though would be the division's whipping boys, ending the season firmly at the bottom with just 13 points and with only three wins from 44 matches. Meadowbank beat Clydebank 1-0 in mid-September but then failed to win in their next nine League matches until they met strugglers Cowdenbeath again on the 14th November and won 2-0. This appeared to give them a boost as they followed this with two more wins and a draw before coming back to earth with a bump and a 5-0 loss at leaders Raith on the 5th December 1991. At the end of March 1992 Meadowbank drew 2-2 at Stirling Albion and these two clubs later entered the month of May level on 30 points with three matches left to play. On Saturday the 1st May Meadowbank lost 2-1 at home to Ayr United but Stirling beat the newly crowned champions Raith 2-1. Relegation was confirmed the following week when the same sequence of results repeated itself – Stirling won at Morton but Meadowbank lost 3-2 at Raith.

In the 1993-94 season Meadowbank finished fourth in the 14 team Second Division. Only the divisional winners were promoted but Meadowbank finished sufficiently high in the table to retain their place in the Scottish Second Division when another restructuring created a fourth level. The bottom eight clubs were joined by two new teams (Inverness Caledonian Thistle and Ross County) as the League reconstructed into four ten team divisions. They opened with a 2-1 win at fellow relegated club Cowdenbeath and then, following a 3-1 home loss against Stranraer, who would go on to dominate the division, they went unbeaten in their next six games, drawing the first and then winning five in a row. Meadowbank scored five in a 5-3 win over Montrose in Mid-November but a few weeks later conceded five themselves, losing 5-1 at Queen of the South. Manager Donald Park left shortly after and was replaced by ex-Cowdenbeath manager John Brownlie who took charge until he resigned just over a month later citing business reasons. He was replaced by former player Micky Lawson at the beginning of February 1994.

The 1994-95 season would be the last for Meadowbank Thistle as they were re-branded and re-located to Livingston for the 1995-96 season. They opened their League campaign on the 13th August 1994 with a 5-1 win away against Brechin City, but their team selection would prove to be costly. Five days later they received a £5,000 and fine had three points deducted for fielding Paul Rutherford while he was suspended. A week later they played their first home League game of the season, losing 1-0 at to Morton, watched by less than 400 spectators.

Meadowbank lost five in a row across September and October and at the beginning of November lost 4-0 at eventual champions Morton. By this time crowds were down to several hundred. For example a crowd of only 210 came to the home match against Dumbarton in mid-November and a month before the crowd had been even lower against Brechin City when only 149 spectators came to that home game on Saturday the 22nd October.

The club had been fully bought over by Bill Hunter, a local businessman in 1993. He believed that Edinburgh wasn't big enough to sustain three senior league clubs and that Meadowbank had no future trying to compete with the likes of Hearts and Hibs, playing in a stadium built for athletics. These gates seemed to vindicate his position. As a result, Hunter began to look for untapped areas which could sustain a successful football team. Hunter's initial plan was to move to Musselburgh, but he was unable to come up with an agreement with the local authority to facilitate a move. The next possibility arose when Hunter had a meeting with the Livingston Development Corporation, who felt that West Lothian lacked a senior football club. The Livingston Development Corporation offered to provide a purpose built all-seater stadium for the club, but the deal was dependent on a change of name to incorporate the new West Lothian location. Livingston Thistle was muted at one point but the move infuriated Meadowbank's small but committed core support.

In mid-January Meadowbank embarked on a Scottish Cup run to the Fourth Round. After beating leaders Morton 1-0 they then beat Forfar 1-0 away before scraping past Berwick Rangers. They drew 1-1 at home and, then 3-3 away, before winning 7-6 on penalties to earn a glamour tie at Celtic. Under the headline "Meadowbank on a Final Mission" *The Independent* reported that "Hampden would be a fitting place for the Scottish Cup chapter of Meadowbank's history to end - even if it is with defeat by Celtic on Saturday rather than parading the trophy in May. Edinburgh's third club - who joined the Scottish League 20 years ago - are set to leave the capital for nearby Livingston next season, changing their name to that of their new home town in the process. So if Saturday's fourth-round tie follows form, it will be the last time the name Meadowbank appears in the Scottish Cup records. Apart from the newcomers Caledonian Thistle, Celtic are the only team that Meadowbank have never faced since coming into the League (they have met Ross County in the Scottish Cup). Celtic's is the only ground they have not visited and, even though Saturday's tie takes place at the Glasgow giants' temporary base, the Meadowbank party will have the chance to view Parkhead, which is under reconstruction. That is because Celtic have invited the part-timers to have their pre-match meal at the stadium before they head for Hampden and the Cup-tie. It will be a particularly poignant occasion for the 83-year-old honorary president and former chairman, John Blacklaw, who has been involved with the club since their early days. Perhaps optimistically, Meadowbank have booked Hibernian's nearby Easter Road ground for the replay." Easter Road wasn't needed as Pierre van Hooijdonk was among the goalscorers as Celtic won 3-0.

After their Cup exit the club lost four in a row. Although Lawson had been given a two and a half year contract he left after just over a year and Jim Leishman took over on the 24th March and managed the transition of the club to Livingston. Meadowbank beat Queen of the South and Dumbarton in their next games but then lost next three to confirm their relegation. On the 29th April in their game against Brechin City, only 144 people came to watch, both sides having already been relegated.

On Friday the 5th of May 1999 Meadowbank Thistle played their last home game. They beat Stenhousemuir 1-0 in front of a bigger crowd than usual, with 463 spectators present. On Saturday the 13th May the club played its last ever SFL game as Meadowbank Thistle, losing 1-0 at Cappielow against Morton. They finished in ninth place, eleven points ahead of Brechin who were bottom, but eight points behind East Fife in eighth place.

Despite fan opposition Meadowbank Thistle became Livingston FC in the summer of 1995 and in November moved to the then named Almondvale Stadium (having continued to play at Meadowbank Stadium until their new home was ready). Controversially the club's new name completely broke with the past. There was a change of colours and club crest at the same time to form what was essentially a brand new club. Their move to West Lothian was deeply divisive. Disenfranchised and disenchanted by the demise of Meadowbank Thistle, many supporters opted against following the club to Livingston and turned instead to an alternative club. Edinburgh City had previously been a member of the Scottish Football League, and could legitimately stake a claim once more to be an alternative to Hearts and Hibs in the city. Edinburgh City had played in the Scottish Football League between 1931 and 1949 before closing down in 1955. Having reformed they made a failed bid to join the League in 2002 from the East of Scotland League. They tried again in 2008 to replace Gretna, but secured only one vote and were eliminated, Annan Athletic being voted into the League. In 2013 they entered the newly created Lowland league and were champions in the 2014-15 and 2015-16 seasons. At the end of the 2015-16 season they defeated East Stirlingshire in a Scottish Football League play-off and became the first team to earn promotion into the League. League football thus returned to Meadowbank Stadium in 2016.

The new entity of Livingston won promotion and the Third Division title, finishing nine points clear of Brechin and 15 points clear of third place. They came third the following year and two years later, in the 1998-99 season, were promoted as Second Division champions. They continued their rapid rise when they were promoted again at the end of the 2000-01 season, as First Division champions and they joined the top flight SPL just six years after relocating to Livingston. There have been some ups and down since then, including a third placed finish, European football and a League Cup victory, but also two sets of administration, relegations, demotions, and a series of disastrous foreign ownership of the club before rebirth, successive promotions and a return to the Premier League via a play-off victory in 2018.

SEASON	LEAGUE	P	W	D	L	F	A	P	POS
1974-75	SCOT-2	38	9	5	24	26	87	23	18/20
1975-76	SCOT-2	26	5	6	15	24	53	16	14/14
1976-77	SCOT-2	39	8	16	15	41	57	32	11/14
1977-78	SCOT-2	39	6	10	23	43	89	22	13/14
1978-79	SCOT-2	39	8	8	23	37	74	24	14/14
1979-80	SCOT-2	39	12	8	19	42	70	32	12/14
1980-81	SCOT-2	39	11	7	21	42	64	29	13/14
1981-82	SCOT-2	39	10	10	19	49	62	30	12/14
1982-83	SCOT-2	39	23	8	8	64	45	54	2/14
1983-84	SCOT-1	39	12	10	17	49	69	34	11/14
1984-85	SCOT-1	39	11	10	18	50	66	32	13/14
1985-86	SCOT-2	39	19	11	9	68	45	49	3/14
1986-87	SCOT-2	39	23	9	7	69	38	55	1/14
1987-88	SCOT-1	44	20	12	12	70	51	52	2/12
1988-89	SCOT-1	39	13	10	16	45	50	36	10/14
1989-90	SCOT-1	39	13	13	13	41	46	39	7/14
1990-91	SCOT-1	39	10	13	16	56	68	33	11/14
1991-92	SCOT-1	44	7	16	21	37	59	30	10/12
1992-93	SCOT-1	44	11	10	23	51	80	32	11/12
1993-94	SCOT-2	39	17	13	9	62	48	47	4/14
1994-95	SCOT-2	36	11	5	20	32	54	35	9/10

Mid-Annandale

Formed: 1910
Colours: Gold and black vertical striped shirts, black shorts
Ground; Kintail Park
Entered League: 1923. Founder members of the Third Division
Number of League Seasons: 3
Highest League Finish: 6th in Division Three
Honours: None
Left League: 1926. Division Three abandoned. Wound up 1936.

Mid-Annandale were another of the ill-fated clubs that featured in the experimental Third Division in the 1920s. The club started out as Vale of Dryfe FC in 1896 and played in Lockerbie, a small market town only 20 miles from the English border (and some 70 miles south of Glasgow), and now infamously known for the plane disaster of December 1988, when the PAN AM flight 103 exploded over the town as a result of a terrorist bomb onboard the flight and the wreckage crashed onto the town.

The original club was wound up in 1906 and subsequently reformed as Mid-Annandale 1910. 'The Mids, a rather uninspiring nickname, played their games at Kintail Park in Lockerbie, having originally played at Livingston Place Park.

Prior to League admittance they made four appearances in the Scottish Cup between 1888 and 1892. They made their debut in the Cup on the 22nd September 1888, a 3-1 defeat away against Vale of Nith from Dumfries. In the following year's competition they lost heavily against the 5th KRV (Kirkcudbright Rifle Volunteers) of Maxwelltown, near Dumfries. The match was played on the 7th September 1889 and Mids lost 11-3. The following September the two sides met again, but this time in a Second Round tie. In the First Round they met a newly formed club, Rising Thistle of Lochmaben, at Lockerbie, and beat them 15-1. When they met 5th KRV, they again lost heavily, 9-1.

They reached the Second Round again in the 1891-92 competition. In the First Round they had played a team from Aberdeen at Stirling and triumphed 6-2. In the next round they played against former SFL side Cowlairs of Glasgow and lost 11-2. The two sides met on the 19th December and the *Glasgow Herald* reported on the match: "Mitchell [of Mid-Annandale] set the ball in motion, and the visitors made off with a rush, but McLeod cleared. Bishop got on the ball, and from a beautiful pass Campbell scored first. Keeping up the pressure, and in two minutes more, Burke scored again. A third point was gained by Shanks immediately after. This was too much for the visitors, and Adamson got away in fine style, and carried the ball right through the goal. Getting into close quarters again, Campbell defied the efforts of Adamson. A penalty kick for Cowlairs came to nothing. Play for a time was confined to the visitors' territory, and they had hard lines in not adding to the score. Two corners in succession were fruitless. The Annandale defended grandly at this point. They found an opening at last. After the ball had been passed across the field twice, Shanks managed to head it through. Nothing daunted, the Dumfries men kept pegging away, and J Steele, after a smart run, sent in a beauty which rather surprised McLelland. A foul in the goal mouth saved the strangers and half-time was called before the kick could be taken, the result standing – Cowlairs, 5 goals; Mid-Annandale, 2. On restarting, the home team again took up the running, and in less than five minutes Bishop rushed the ball through. The home forwards were in fine form, and simply carried all before them. Result:-Cowlairs, 11 goals; Mid-Annandale, 2 goals." The Mid-Annandale team was: McKinnon; McCallum, Jardine, Carruthers, F Ross, J Ross, R Steele, J Steele, Mitchell, W Ross and Adamson.

Mids didn't play in the Scottish Cup again until 1921 when they lost in the First Round to SFL club Albion Rovers 3-1. Later in the same year the Mids joined the revived Southern Counties Football League, with teams drawn from across Dumfries and Galloway. Mid-Annandale completed all of their fixtures and topped the table but other fixtures remained unfulfilled. Nevertheless, Mids were awarded the title and they successfully retained it the following year. They also featured again in the Scottish Cup, losing once more to Lanarkshire opposition, this time Airdrieonians. They gave a good account of themselves though, only losing by the odd goal in three, although they had Varrie, their goalkeeper to thank, for a string of fine saves.

Their title winning success in the Southern Counties League led to the club to being invited to join the new Third Division in 1923 and they were the only team originating from this League. On the 18th August 1923 they made their first Scottish Football League appearance, winning 2-1 away at Peebles Rovers. McClaine, their centre-forward, opened the scoring in the first half and added a second after the interval before Peebles got a late consolation. *The Sunday Post* reported that, "almost diminutive in comparison with Mid-Annandale, the Rovers suffered sorely in the matter of inches on a rain-sodden pitch, and the advantage was always with the big fellow. The only goal of the first half was got by McClaine, the Mid's Centre, and the same player counted just after the interval. The Rovers showed up well in the closing stages, and from a magnificent cross by Ritchie, Turner reduced the leeway with a header."

On the 25th August 1923 Kintail Park hosted its first League game. In front of a crowd of 950 Mids won a seven goal thriller 4-3. Groves scored for Mids after just seven minutes to score the first League goal at Kintail. Helensburgh equalised before McClaine made it 2-1 at half-time. In the second half Groves made it 3-1 before Helensburgh got one back. Seven minutes from time the visitors equalised again but Groves was then downed in the box and carried off, so couldn't take the penalty for a chance for a hat-trick. Instead, Robb scored from the spot and won the game for Mids.

On the 3rd November 1923 a record crowd of 2,500 watched the 3-1 home defeat by Queen of the South. Later in the same month Mids secured their biggest ever SFL win, beating Clackmannan 6-1. This was the start of a run of four consecutive wins but they couldn't sustain this form and slipped back into mid-table. In their last game of the season they matched their record win, beating Brechin City 6-1 on the 26th April 1924, with Tennant scoring a hat-trick and they eventually finished eighth in the 16 team division.

Mids suffered from a second season syndrome as in the 1924-25 season they finished second bottom, just one point ahead of Montrose. Leith Athletic joined the division but Dumbarton Harp dropped out half way through so the club is classified as having finished 15th. Things started badly for Mids as they went the first 13 games of the new season without a win. Included in this run was their biggest ever SFL defeat, an 8-3 defeat against Beith in October. A 5-0 loss at Brechin City on the 22nd November left them bottom of the table.

Their first win eventually came on the 6th December and was a surprise 4-2 victory over high flying, and eventual champions, Nithsdale Wanderers. Edgar, one of their forwards, scored three goals. Their form picked up in 1925 and they recorded five more wins. They ended the season with 3-2 away win at Royal Albert on the 18th April but still finished 15th and second bottom.

Mids changed their manager for the 1925-26 season with J Graham taking charge and he led them to their best ever finish of sixth place, in what was to be the last season for the fledging division. It took a little while for things to change on the pitch though as Mids lost their first five games of the new season and they were the only team that were pointless at the beginning of October.

On the 17th October Mid-Annandale beat Dykehead 4-1, coming back from conceding the first goal and producing a terrific second half display where they fully merited their victory. However, the following week they lost heavily at Johnstone by 6-2. But now the revival well and truly got underway. They won three out of four games in November, including a 3-1 win over Vale of Leven, so that by the beginning of December they were up to tenth place. Four consecutive wins across December and January saw the club rise up to sixth and they went six games unbeaten during February and early March.

Saturday 20th March 1926 saw what would turn out to be the last ever Scottish League home game at Kintail Park. Brechin City were the visitors and the game ended in a 1-1 draw. Brechin scored through Milne in the first half at Lockerbie and Lennox got the equaliser five minutes from the close. Mids were now up as high as third in the table, a far cry from October when they were bottom. In the 18 games since the 6-2 defeat against Johnstone they had won 13 of them and lost just three.

On Saturday the 10th April Mids played their last SFL game ever, away at Leith Athletic, where they lost 4-0, having been 3-0 down at half-time. On this day, all other results were overshadowed by the Scottish Cup Final, where St Mirren beat the holders Celtic, lifting the Cup for the first time. Mids completed all but one of their games, the only fixture not fulfilled being the reverse game against Galston, who had already dropped out of the League. By the time the season ended with a large number of games uncompleted Mid-Annandale were in sixth place, their highest ever placing.

Whilst crowds of over 2,500 turned up for Mid-Annandale's derby game against Queen of the South in November 1923 and Nithsdale Wanderers in September 1925, attendances at this level were the exception rather than the norm. Like most Third Division sides, the Lockerbie-based club faced expenses that were not covered by gate receipts against teams that were unfamiliar to local supporters and which failed to draw in the crowds.

With the demise of the Third Division Mid-Annandale dropped down into the Scottish Alliance, southern section. Following the expulsion from the Alliance of the former League clubs at the end of the 1926-27 season the remnants of the ill-fated Division decided to set up a new League, called the Provincial League. Mids started off in this competition for the 1927-28 season but on the 17th March 1928 *The Sunday Post* announced the club's resignation under the headline "Mid-Annandale FC Collapse – Impossible to Carry On Any Longer." The club reported that "a letter from Mid-Annandale FC to the secretary of the Scottish Provincial League discloses an unhealthy state of provincial football. The collapse of mid-Annandale is announced – 'I am sorry to inform you that the committee cannot see their way, owing to financial losses, to fulfil their remaining League fixtures. Gates have been so poor- a loss of £40 on the last two home games – that you will agree it is impossible to carry on. The committee are very sorry indeed to take this step, but to carry on would be to sink into debt; with very little prospect of getting out of it. We have tried everything to help the funds of the club, but have lost on all. A supporters' club was formed at the beginning of the season, and it looked as if funds would be provided to enable the club to carry on, but unfortunately the project fell through on account of lack of support, and now the supporters' club is defunct.' "The Provincial League itself ended after just one season, with the clubs concentrating on cup ties instead.

Mids continued to feature in the Scottish Cup and played on four more occasions up until 1931. While in the Alliance, in the 1926-27 season, they reached the Third Round, knocking out Forres Mechanics and then the saved, former Third Division club, Forfar Athletic, who were now in the Second Division. A crowd of 1,100 at Kintail Park witnessed the Cup upset on Saturday 5th February 1927. When the clubs had last met at Lockerbie, in the Old Third Division, in December 1925, Mids had won the game 2-1 and play was very even. This Cup-tie followed a similar pattern and just on the stroke of half time Mid-Annandale took the lead. Stewart, the home outside-left was brought down in the box by a Forfar defender, and Lennox smashed home the penalty. *The Scotsman,* reporting on the second half said that "with their goal lead the Mid-Annandale resumed with dash and determination, and under the heavy strain of repeated onslaughts the Forfar team's defence began to waver, and further goals by Dawson and Lennox gave Mid-Annandale the victory, which, on their second half display, they fully deserved."

Their reward was a tie at Brockville against First Division Falkirk, who would finish sixth in the table. A fortnight later the game was played with Falkirk winning 3-0. *The Scotsman* commented that "the visitors gave a splendid account of themselves" and *The Sunday Post* had the deadlines "Plucky Fight by Mid-Annandale" and "No Cake-Walk for Falkirk at Brockville" and in the report that followed stated that, "though beaten, Mid-Annandale left behind them the impression that at Lockerbie they would have stretched the best."

 The Cup run of 1926-27 would be the high point of their ex-League career. The following year, they had a heavy First Round exit, losing 7-3 at Cappielow against Morton. *The Sunday Post* reported that "Morton had an easy hurdle to negotiate and the only consolation which Mid-Annandale got from the encounter was that for a brief sepll in the second half they had the home team temporarily in doubt as to whether their lead would be of sufficient use." Morton had raced into a 3-0 lead inside the first ten minutes and led 4-0 at the break. The home team made it five soon after the resumption before a mini-revival from Mids saw them score two goals – one from Durham and the other from a penalty kick by McCrindle. But Morton scored two more, and sandwiched between these two goals Stewart scored Mid-Annandale's last ever goal in the Scottish Cup.

On the 18th January 1930 Mids lost 5-0 at home to Ayr United in a First Round tie. A crowd of 5,500 saw Mids hold Ayr in the first half, with all of the goals scored after the interval. Their final Cup appearance came on the 17th January 1931, when they went out in the First Round to Montrose 2-0.

The club eventually disbanded in 1936. Kintail Park was subsequently used for housing and there is now a road and playpark of that name in the town, sandwiched between the B7076 to the west and the B723 to the east.

In 2003 the club was resurrected and joined the South of Scotland Football League. The modern club plays at King Edward Park in Lockerbie in the gold and black colours of their predecessor.

SEASON	LEAGUE	P	W	D	L	F	A	P	POS
1923-24	SCOT-3	30	13	5	12	59	48	31	8/16
1924-25	SCOT-3	30	7	7	16	47	70	21	15/16
1925-26	SCOT-3	29	14	3	12	50	54	31	6/16

Nithsdale Wanderers

Formed: 1897
Colours: Blue and white horizontal striped shirts and white shorts
Ground: Crawick Holm
Entered League: 1923. Founder members of the Third Division
Number of League Seasons: 4
Highest League Finish: 12th in Division Two
Honours: Third Division Champions, 1924-25
Left League: 1927. Failed re-election. Folded in 1964

Nithsdale Wanderers were based in Sanquhar, Dumfries and Galloway, a royal burgh located on the River Nith, 26 miles north-west of Dumfries, where the river flows through this town on its way to the Solway Firth. The town has a population of about 3,000 and in the 19th Century was an important centre for wool and weaving. With the town's small population the naming of the club was a direct appeal to the wider area taking in places along the river such as Thornhill to the south and Kirkconnel to the north.

They played their games at Crawick Holm, moving there in 1920, the ground taking its name from the nearby Crawick Water which flows into the Nith north of the town around the village of the same name. Playing in blue and white horizontal striped shirts and white shorts, Nithsdale joined the Scottish Football Combination in 1909 and were joint winners for the 1909-10 season (they tied with Girvan but no play-off game was arranged to decide the title). In 1911 the Combination folded and Nithsdale joined the Scottish Union, playing there until the onset of the First World War. In 1922 Nithsdale Wanderers joined the Western League, one of the regional competitions set up by the former Second Division sides in 1915, and then transferred across to the League's new Third Division in 1923.

Nithsdale Wanderers won the Third Division title in 1925 and with it, promotion to the Scottish Second Division. After a comfortable mid-table finish in 1926, 'Dale finished last in 1927, nine points adrift and had to seek re-election, since the Third Division had been abandoned the previous year. At the Scottish League AGM, Nithsdale were voted out and replaced by former League and Edinburgh side, Leith Athletic. Nithsdale

Wanderers have the dubious distinction of being the last Scottish Football League club to lose their place because of a failed re-election vote.

Dale's best performances in the Scottish Cup came in the years just prior to League admittance. In both the 1920-21 and 1922-23 competitions they reached the Third Round stage. The second of these Cup runs was notable for a couple of scalps they took along the way. In the First Round they beat Second Division strugglers Arbroath 4-0. *The Scotsman* commenting that "Arbroath played disappointingly at Sanquhar, and were never like winning their tie with Nithsdale Wanderers, who scored twice in each half. The goals were got by Ballantyne, Ness, Keggans and McConnell. This was the first Scottish Cup tie played at Sanquhar since 1910." In the next round they beat Dundee Hibs, who had been a League club the year before, 1-0 away in front of a 7,000 crowd at Tannadice. Jim McConnell scored the only goal of the game after 75 minutes. They went out to Second Division Bo'ness 2-0 in the Third Round.

On the 18th August 1923 Dale began life in the Scottish Football League. They won their opening game, a 3-1 win away at Clackmannan at Chapelhill Park. Jimmy McConnell scored all three in the first half after the home team had taken the lead. On the 25th August 1923 they played their first home League game at Crawick Holm and beat Brechin City 5-0 in front of a crowd of 1,100. This would be their best win of their debut season and McConnell scored another hat-trick in a game in which "Nithsdale did pretty much as they pleased" (*The Sunday Post*).

Nithsdale also won their third game, 3-2 away at Galston to briefly top the table. An attendance of 1,500 spectators watched the derby game versus Queen of the South the following month, with the game ending in a 1-1 draw. Their unbeaten start to League life came to an end in Larkhall at the end of September, going down by the odd goal in three against Royal Albert. By the turn of the year they were in fourth place and they eventually finished a respectable sixth out of the 16 teams.

At the end of the 1924-25 season Nithsdale won the Third Division championship. They were unstoppable at home, winning 14 out of 15 home games and going through the season unbeaten at Crawick Holm. They only lost five games and clinched the title with an 8-0 win over Montrose on the final day of the season. The promotion battle was a regional affair as Queen of the South came in second and Solway Star of Annan were third. Only Mid-Annandale of Lockerbie let the region down finishing second from bottom.

Queen of the South had topped the goalscoring charts with 64 goals in the first season of the Third Division, in finishing third. Nithsdale scored 62 goals - just at home -

averaging four goals a game. They scored six goals or more on four occasions. Three of the teams on the receiving end were Peebles, who lost 7-1, and Royal Albert and Vale of Leven, who each conceded six. The win over Vale was particularly impressive as their opponents had won 14 out of their first 16 matches and had topped the table for five months. The key player here was their prolific centre-forward James "Jimmy" McConnell. Born in Ayr in 1889. McConnell began his football career in June 1920, when he played one game, scoring one goal, for Kilmarnock. In May 1921 he signed for Nithsdale and he would go on to score 45 league goals in their championship winning season.

Dale opened the new season with a 3-2 win over newcomers Leith Athletic and followed this up with a 4-1 away win at Dumbarton Harp. Commenting on this match *The Sunday Post* said "it was no tuneful Harp at Dumbarton, where the men from Sanquhar helped themselves to four goals and all the points. Nithsdale are going all out for promotion, and on yesterday's display must surely go well forward. Ballantyne and McConnell shared the winners' goals between them." Overall Nithsdale went the first six games of the new season unbeaten before a 2-1 reverse at Queen of the South. Following this first defeat they then won the next five in a row, with McConnell regularly finding the net. This run was surprisingly ended by the one team in the region not having a good season – Mid-Annandale. They were struggling, winless at the bottom, but surprisingly beat Dale 4-2 in early December to record their first win. From then on they went on a 13 game unbeaten run in the League, lasting from mid-December to mid-March.

One of the most notable results in this run came on the 10th January 1925 when they beat Peebles Rovers 7-1. *The Sunday Post* reported that "Nithsdale gave a dazzling display against their border rivals at Sanquhar, and from start to finish were masters of the situation. They displayed great dash at the start, and inside fifteen minutes were three goals ahead." McConnell headed the first from a corner, Allan dashed in for a lovely second and Ballantyne beat Wilson in the Peebles goal with a thunderous unstoppable drive. With a three goal lead at the interval Nithsdale were in total control and only some goalkeeping heroics by Wilson kept the score down. Eventually Peebles succumbed to another Ballantyne drive and McConnell added a fifth from a low left-footed shot after being set up by Allan. The Nithsdale centre was in rampant form and scored another two goals to take his personal tally to four. Near the end Lang raced clear and got a late consolation, the match ending 7-1.

Three weeks later a 6-2 win over Royal Albert, and leaders' Vale of Leven's 0-0 draw with Solway Star, meant that Nithsdale were now only a point off the top. *The Sunday Post* reporting on their win noted that "Nithsdale Wanderers gave no quarter and asked none against Royal Albert at Sanquhar. The Wanderers were in irresistible form, and, with the forwards displaying positively dazzling form, the Albert never looked like stopping the locals. James McConnell had a field day, and his three goals stamps him as a sharp-shooter when the chance does come along to him." Allan scored two and Mountney the other. A week later, with the leaders in Scottish Cup action, a 2-0 win over Queen of the South saw them go top. McConnell scored both goals although Nithsdale had Randell sent off on the hour mark.

A fortnight later the top two sides met at Crawick Holm. The ground was covered with a slight dusting of snow as Reid opened the scoring for the visitors against the run of play, before two from Ballantyne gave the Wanderers a half-time lead. The second half saw the Vale in difficulties as Grove scored from a header and then a second half hat-trick from McConnell, scored in ten minutes, gave Dale a resounding 6-1 victory. Nithsdale now took the lead in the Division, going two points clear of their defeated opponents, and Queen of the South.

Their magnificent run came to an end with consecutive defeats at the end of March, the first a narrow 3-2 defeat against Peebles in an ill-tempered game where both teams were reduced to ten men and two of the five goals were penalties. Their second loss, 4-0 against Helensburgh was their biggest defeat of season. Only Armour in goal kept the score to level terms at half-time but once Helensburgh scored on the resumption they ran away with it. This stumble was somewhat mitigated with both Vale of Leven and Queen of the South also losing, so with three games to go Dale led the Third Division by three points - Nithsdale played 27, 39 points; Vale of Leven played 27, 36 points; Queen of the South played 28, 36 points; and Solway Star played 27, 35 points.

The first of these three games was a crucial 1-0 win away against Clackmannan where the home team lay siege to the Wanderers' goal for large parts of the game and only the heroics of Armour kept parity. As is often the way Nithsdale scored with a rare foray just after the interval with McConnell lobbing the home keeper McDonald, who scarcely touched the ball otherwise, the ball glancing into the net off the upright. Queen of the South and Solway Star also won whilst Vale of Leven didn't play. The win though meant Queens couldn't catch Dale but the other two sides still could.

Nithsdale lost their penultimate match 3-0 against Beith. Vale of Leven and Queen of the South both won but Solway Star could only draw at home to Dykehead. All of these results meant Nithsdale were guaranteed promotion but they could still be caught for the title by Vale of Leven. Nithsdale had 41 points with one game remaining; Queen of the South had finished their fixtures with 40 points,: vale of Leven had 38 points with two to play; and Solway Star also had 38 points, but with just one game to play.

Nithsdale secured the title in emphatic style with an 8-0 win over Montrose on the final day of the season. This was 'Dale's biggest ever win and their opponents finished the game with only eight men as three of their players gave up and left the field in a torrential downpour in the second half, a story taken up by *The Sunday Post* under the headline "Montrose Players Seek Shelter." "Nithsdale made the Third Division flag secure by a great display against Montrose. The weather was stormy. An early goal by Grove seemed to take the sting out of Montrose, and when McConnell followed with a second from a free kick the 'Dale were on the velvet. Before the interval McConnell made the issue safe by scoring another two goals. The second half had only been a minute in progress when Mount rushed through a fifth goal. The Montrose team was soon depleted by several of their players seeking the shelter of the pavilion, and the game became a pure farce. Nithsdale added another three goals through Grove, McConnell and Ballantyne. Montrose finished with eight players." McConnell's four goals in the match took his season's total to 45.

Queen of the South also gained promotion as a result of Vale of Leven losing 2-0 at Leith Athletic (they also lost their last game). Although Solway Star won to match them on points Queen of the South were far more proficient in front of goal and were promoted on goal average. In the end Nithsdale won the title by three clear points.

Nithsdale made a good showing at the higher level in the Second Division, finishing a very comfortable 12th place out of 20 teams (Queen of the South finished 17th). They more than held their own and once again they were indebted to Jim McConnell's contribution of 37 League goals.

On Saturday 15th August 1925 they opened their campaign away at Dunfermline Athletic, losing 4-1 in front of 9,000 spectators. Armour kept the home team at bay initially but Dale eventually succumbed and were trailing 3-0 when McConnell slipped the home defence and beat Muir with a good shot. Under the headline "Nithsdale Fare Badly" *The Sunday Post* commented that "Nithsdale Wanderers fared badly in their first Second Division game, but their play on occasion gave promise of better things in store, and, if one or two improvements are effected, the team may yet be seen to much better advantage." The Nithsdale team was: Armour; Vance, Gourlay; McManus, McLaren, Cree; Allan, Ballantyne, McConnell, Wilson and Houston.

Nithsdale were seen to "much better advantage" when they surprisingly recorded five wins on the bounce: 3-1 at home to East Stirlingshire with a crowd of 3,000; 4-2 away at Armadale; 5-1 at home to Dumbarton; 4-2 away at Alloa Athletic; and 3-2 at home to Queen of the South in front of 5,000 people. They then lost 3-0 away at Stenhousemuir before winning another three games on the trot. A 2-0 away win at Broxburn Untied on 10th October, both goals from McConnell, saw them go top of the Second Division. They cemented top spot a week later with a 1-0 win over promotion chasing Third Lanark, with a goal by none other than McConnell.

They couldn't sustain this form, however, and they failed to win in six games across October and November (four draws and two losses) including a 6-1 defeat at Ayr United. They had a good Christmas and New Year with a 4-0 win over Broxburn United and a 3-0 away win on New Year's Day against Queen of the South in front of a 6,000 crowd. The score was 0-0 at half-time but the home team had to play with nine men in the second half due to injuries, McConnell taking advantage to notch a hat-trick. These festive fixtures left them fourth in the table, three points behind leaders Dunfermline Athletic but with a game in hand.

Between the 16th January and the 13th March 1926 Dale unfortunately went nine games without a win including a 4-1 loss at Bo'ness and a shock 5-2 defeat at home to King's Park, especially after taking a 2-0 lead. Part of this sequence was a match against Arthurlie on the 13th February in which the two sides shared a dozen goals in a remarkable match at Barrhead. The draw was a fair result with each team scoring three goals in each half. Arthurlie at one time had a two goal advantage, leading 3-1 before Dale got it back to 3-3 and then to lead 4-3. On this occasion McConnell only scored once, with W Ballantyne scoring four for Nithsdale, two in each half. *The Sunday Post* reported that "Arthurlie and Nithsdale played very different types of football at Barrhead, but the result would indicate that both were equally successful. Twelve goals were equally divided. Nithsdale adapted the open game, and kept the ball swinging...Arthurlie played a more intensive game. Later in the same year, although in a new campaign, Arthurlie scored seven against them, conceding just the one in return.

On the 20th March they finally won again, beating fourth placed Stenhousemuir 5-1, McConnell and Ballantyne each notching a brace. By this time they has slipped to ninth place and they went on to lose eight out of their last ten fixtures to drop down the table and finish in 12th place.

Nithsdale had amassed 24 points in the first half of the season but only 13 in the second, which was relegation form. Unfortunately they carried this recent form into the new season where they only accumulated 23 points, finishing nine points adrift at the bottom and concededing exactly 100 goals, winning just 7 of 38 matches. By this time the ill-fated Third Division had been scrapped and therefore the club effectively finished bottom of the League structure and had to apply for re-election.

Surprisingly they won their opening game 2-1 against Third Lanark and drew their next two before suffering the first of a series of heavy losses. On the 4th September 1926 they lost 7-2 at Firs Park against East Stirlingshire. Their hosts opened the scoring but near the interval McConnell was on hand to register the equaliser. In the second half East Stirlingshire stepped up a gear and scored five times in just ten minutes, W Ballantyne scored added a late consolation right on the call of time. Two months later they suffered their biggest ever SFL defeat, losing 7-1 against Arthurlie at Dunterlie Park. Arthurlie deserved to win, although but not by such a wide margin. Arthurlie took their chances whereas Nithsdale were weak in front of goal. Malloy, recently signed from Celtic, scored two as Arthurlie built up a substantial 4-0 lead at the break. Jessiman, who had scored one of the first half goals, added two more to register a hat-trick. W. Ballantyne scored Nithsdale's solitary goal.

In December 1926, McConnell was lured away to play in the United States Soccer League, where he joined the Springfield Babes. He played only three games with Springfield before being sent to Providence. In August 1927, McConnell moved to Bethlehem Steel where he scored seven goals in his first eight appearances. He later played for a team called J&P Coats, where he scored 12 goals in 23 games. In 1928, McConnell would move back to Britain, joining English side Carlisle United where he became a club legend, scoring 124 goals in 149 games. He later played in England for Crewe Alexandra (1932-33) and then Rotherham United before retiring from football in 1934. The club found it hard to replace such a prolific goalscorer and their fortunes took a turn for the worse.

Dale endured a run of six consecutive losses across December and January before a 4-3 win away at Stenhousemuir. This rare win was followed up with a 6-2 away defeat against Dumbarton and a 4-0 loss away at Ayr United. In their last ten games they only picked up five points, the last of these on the 9th April 1927 in a home 1-1 draw with Bo'ness. They played their last home game on the 30th April, a 4-3 loss to Clydebank in front of 1,000 spectators.

Nithsdale now had to seek re-election as there was no relegation to a now defunct Third Division. They and Arbroath faced a re-election vote against Leith Athletic, who had missed out the year before on the Chairman's casting vote. At the League AGM held on the 26th May 1927 Arbroath secured re-election with 33 votes but Leith were preferred to Nithsdale, securing 27 votes to Dale's 12. Nithsdale Wanderers are the last Scottish Football League club to fail a re-election vote. Nithsdale joined the ill-fated Provincial League for the 1927-28 season. They also featured in the Scottish Cup, where somewhat ironically, they knocked out Arbroath in the First Round before going out to Partick Thistle. At the end of the season they applied to return to the Scottish League.

The two clubs seeking re-election were Bathgate and Armadale and they secured 27 and 23 votes respectively against Nithsdale's 14.

With the demise of the Provincial League after just one season Nithsdale joined the Scottish Alliance and the club applied to regain their League status the following year as well. There was no re-election vote this time due to the resignations of Bathgate and Arthurlie. Instead, Nithsdale applied along with ex-Third Division sides Brechin City and Montrose for the two vacant places but came third in the ballot with 17 votes (Montrose 31, Brechin City 24). Both sides had competed in the Scottish Alliance with Nithsdale finishing fourth, whereas Brechin were 13th and Montrose 17th.

Nithsdale made three further unsuccessful attempts to re-join the SFL but could not attract sufficient support. At the 1930 AGM, held on the 29th May they lost out to the two clubs facing re-election, Brechin and Alloa. In 1931 and now playing in the Southern Counties League, Nithsdale, along with Edinburgh City lost out in a vote against the two clubs facing re-election, Clydebank and Bo'ness. When Clydebank subsequently disbanded in late June 1931 a vote was held to replace them with Nithsdale going up against Edinburgh City, losing out 25-7 in the voting. They made their last attempt in 1932 when they were up against Edinburgh City and Brechin. These two clubs, who had previously beaten them to entry to the League, faced re-election. Nithsdale lost the vote by a big margin only garnering six votes (Edinburgh City 36, Brechin City 33).

Nithsdale continued to feature in the Scottish Cup during this time. In 1930 they beat St Andrew's University 6-1, a club record win in the competition, with Atkinson scoring five goals for Wanderers. The following year they suffered their record Cup defeat, a 14-0 drubbing at the hands of Dundee United. In 1939 they were involved in a high scoring draw against Buckie Thistle, in which a crowd of 600 saw the two sides share ten goals. The result though was overshadowed by Hearts beating Penicuik Athletic 14-2 and more importantly holders East Fife, the holders being knocked out by Montrose. The tie at Crawick Holm proved to be one of the most exciting games ever played at the ground. Nithsdale galloped into a three goal lead inside the first 17 minutes, but once the Buckie side got going they created opportunities and by half-time had reduced the margin to one goal. Encouraged by their showing the visitors completed a remarkable turnaround by drawing level within five minutes of the restart. Nithsdale regained the lead when the experienced McGowan, once of Dunfermline and Kilmarnock converted a penalty, and the tie seemed settled when they increased their lead to 5-3 and the game entered its final few minutes. But drama was to follow as a late rally by Buckie saw them reduce the lead in the 88th minute and right on the final whistle they drew level at 5-5. The draw for the next round offered the prospective of a non-League side in the Third Round as the winners of the replay were drawn away to Blairgowrie. Buckie won the replay 5-2 a week later and also beat Blairgowrie, after a replay, before being thrashed 6-0 by Third Lanark.

Nithsdale Wanderers made their last appearance in the Scottish Cup in the 1947-48 season in a Second Round match played on the 7th February 1948. They lost 5-0 to Aberdeen, the Cup holders, who had to make a long journey almost the length of Scotland. A crowd of 2,600 saw them hold out for 55 minutes, thanks to the heroics of their 16 stone skipper Arthur Phillips. Under the headline "16 Stones of Inspiration" *The Sunday Post* reported on "the story of gallant Arthur Phillips and his Merry Men of Nithsdale who, with the help of Crawick Holm's tantalising turf, held the Dons at bay for more than half the game. By his ponderous example, this 16-stone railwayman skipper, using his bulk at every crucial moment, gave his lads the inspiration they needed. Their response was terrific. Into the battle went everything they had. Storm-tossed and outpaced, they gritted their teeth and held on." Eventually Aberdeen ground them down and ten minutes into the second half a long raking ball set Archie Kelly, the Don's centre-forward, through and he opened the scoring by shooting past the outcoming Anderson, the Nithsdale goalkeeper, once of Queen of the South. Within a minute Kelly scored another and the Dons began to breathe more easily. Six minutes later another route one pass saw Tony Harris make it three and a minute later Jimmy Stenhouse made it four in nine second half minutes. Stenhouse, on debut made it five with a quarter of an hour left.

The Nithsdale team that made their final appearance was: Anderson; Phillips, Maxwell; Fleming, Lorraine, Saddington; McCourty, Milligan, Keggans, Coupland and Chisholm.

Nithsdale played on at senior level until 1951 when they adopted junior status and they kept playing on until 1963-64 when the club folded. In 2001 a new senior club was formed and currently plays as Nithsdale Wanderers in the South of Scotland League. A route therefore now exists back to the League via promotion first to the Lowland League and then via the play-offs

SEASON	LEAGUE	P	W	D	L	F	A	P	POS
1923-24	SCOT-3	30	13	7	10	42	35	33	6/16
1924-25	SCOT-3	30	18	7	5	81	40	43	1/16
1925-26	SCOT-2	38	15	7	16	79	82	37	12/20
1926-27	SCOT-2	38	7	9	22	59	100	23	20/20

Northern

Formed: 1874
Colours: Halved shirts of light and navy blue, navy blue shorts
Ground: Hyde Park
Entered League: 1893. Founder member of the Second Division.
Number of League Seasons: 1
Honours: None
Highest League Finish: 9th in Division Two
Left League: 1894. Failed re-election. Wound up 1896

In what would be one of the shortest Scottish Football League careers, lasting only one season, Northern joined the Scottish Football League in 1893 when the Scottish Alliance was incorporated into the new Second Division. They finished second from bottom and had to re-apply, losing out in the re-election vote by just one vote. Northern were another of the early Glasgow teams and they played at Hyde Park in the industrial Springburn district of the city, which was also home to rivals Cowlairs.

Glasgow Northern were formed in 1874 and have their origins as a works team for the Neilson & Co. locomotive manufacturers, based at their Hyde Park Works, and the ground of the same name was located opposite the factory. Unlike the other Glasgow "compass" teams – Eastern, Southern and Western – they did not participate in the first two Scottish Cups, making their debut in 1875, from when they became regular participants. In their first match, on the 30th October 1875, they beat Ramblers of the Gorbals area of Glasgow 4-0, before losing to the holders (and that season's winners) Queen's Park 5-0 in the next round.

The following season they recorded their best ever Scottish Cup run, advancing to the Fourth Round, which included a 12-0 win over Telegraphists of Glasgow. They were again knocked out by Queen's Park, this time 4-0. Queen's Park were knocked out by eventual winners Vale of Leven. Other notable results in the Scottish Cup included a 9-1 win over Luton, of the Possilpark district of North Glasgow, at Lorne Park, Plantation on the 1st October 1881. Northern scored four times in the first half and five times in the second, Luton scoring once. On the 25th October 1884 they suffered their biggest defeat in the Cup, losing 9-2 to the eventual winners Renton.

An eventful game took place on the 19th October 1889 between Northern and Carfin Shamrock at Hyde Park in the Third Round of the Scottish Cup. In a keenly fought contest Robb opened the scoring for the home team and Northern added a second before the visitors were rewarded for a period of pressure with a goal from Naughton, and they kept this up but were kept at bay. The *Glasgow Herald*, picks up the story: "on restarting Carfin began to press and were having the best of it, when an unfortunate circumstance occurred which brought the tie to a sudden termination. Party feeling, which was very high during the first half, got the better of the crowd, who broke through the ropes and engaged in a free fight. The referee and three or four of the Northern team were severely handled; and some of them seriously injured". This game is often erroneously recorded as 22-1, an example of an original error being compounded by plagiarism across the ages. A replay was ordered due to the crowd disturbance which Carfin won 4-3.

Another replay was ordered the following year, in the 1890-91 competition. In the First Round Northern had beaten Clydesdale 5-0, Riddoch had scored two first half goals and then Northern had added another two goals in quick succession at the start of second half, and a fifth came near to time. Clydesdale lodged a protest with the SFA for Northern having played an illegible man and it was unanimously agreed that the match should be replayed. It was also decided that J Riddoch, the player in question, should be suspended for twelve months. The replayed tie ended in a 7-1 win for Northern, with Mitchell opening the scoring after ten minutes. Northern were five up at the break. Northern lost 5-1 to Queen's Park in the next round.

In 1891 and 1892 Northern made First Round exits to Broxburn Shamrock and Leith Athletic respectively but of more significance was the club becoming founder members of the Scottish Alliance in 1891. This league competition was set up following the successful first season of the Scottish Football League. Northern finished fifth in the twelve team competition in its first season and this prompted an attempt to join the Scottish Football League. The odds weren't in their favour though. First of all, the SFL was reducing the number of teams from twelve to ten clubs so there were already three retiring clubs from the League chasing one place. Second, two other teams from the Scottish Alliance, Kilmarnock and St Bernard's also applied, and both had finished higher. At the AGM held on the 3rd June, Northern's bid was indeed unsuccessful, and they failed to secure any support.

Northern finished seventh in the Scottish Alliance at the end of the 1892-93 season. In July the SFL decided to expand and form a second tier with ten clubs. Northern were among the clubs who joined the Scottish Football League at the end of the season when the Alliance was incorporated into the new Second Division. On the 12th August

1893 Glasgow Northern played their first ever game in the Scottish Football League, although they didn't get off to a very auspicious start, losing 6-1 at Port Glasgow Athletic. The two sides were evenly matched for the first twenty minutes of their encounter before Athletic scored and two further goals were scored by McNeill and Martin to leave the half-time score as 3-0. After the restart Smith added a fourth before Northern scored their one and only goal. Athletic got two more goals scored by Martin and McCorkindale and ran out 6-1 winners. Port Glasgow would later be deducted seven points for playing D McNeil against Northern (and also Clyde), when he was ineligible to play. The first Northern team to play a League match was: Burnside; Buist, Gossland; Sinclair, Fraser, Mathieson; Gossland, Kyle, Graham, O'Brien and Russell.

On the 26th August Northern played their opening home game at Hyde Park against Clyde. The *Glasgow Herald* reported on the game: "Hydepark was opened for the season by a League (Second Division) fixture with the Clyde....There was no scoring in the first half. On restarting, the Northern after once assumed the offensive, and O'Brien scored within three minutes, amid great excitement. Hydepark men now did the pressing, and some beautiful shots were saved by McCorkindale [in the Clyde goal]. From a scrimmage, McKenzie equalised. Encouraged by their success, the visitors worked hard, and for a time looked as if they would score again. A free kick brought the East-Enders nearer Burnside [in the Northern goal] and...[he was] caught napping...a third goal was scored....five minutes before the finish."

Northern's disastrous start would see them lose six of their first seven games, including a club League record 7-0 away defeat to rivals Cowlairs. This game, their third, took place on the 9th September and *The Scotsman* covered the game: "Played at Springvale Park. Cowlairs kicked off, and immediately made a raid on Burnside, who saved cleverly. The Northern next had a trial; but Kyle grazed the post. From a free kick McPherson scored for the home team. The game then became lively. The Northern strove hard to equalise, but half-time was called without further scoring. On resuming the Cowlairs began pressing, but the strong defence of the Northern's backs kept them well in check. About twenty minutes from the start Burnside was the means of scoring against his own side by striking the ball against the post and sending it through. During the rest of the game Cowlairs seemed to settle down for scoring, Scott adding two goals within a few minutes. A hard game ended Cowlairs, seven goals; Northern, nil."

Northern's first League point came in their fourth fixture on the 30th September, a 2-2 draw at home against eventual divisional champions Hibs. *The Scotsman* colourfully describes an exciting game: "These clubs met for the first time in the Second League competition at Hyde Park, Springburn. The Northern field, even in good weather, is not the best, and on Saturday it was very soft. Prompt to time, Martin [the Hibs captain] led his team on to the field and was greeted with loud cheering, he being an old Hyde Park man. The Northern winning the toss, Kennedy started play for the Hibernians in presence of a fair crowd. Burnside got a visit just at the start, but before many minutes the ball was at the other end, and rallying round Cowan [the Hibs goalkeeper] the Northern surprised him by sending the ball through. McGeachan passed to Howie, who was making straight for goal, when Burnside intercepted him and allowed the ball to pass. From a rush Smith equalised. A corner against the Hibernians looked dangerous but Rooney cleared in time. The Hibernians thought they had an easy win but so far the Northern kept them well at bay, they having fully the most of the play. The game became very fast, the ball travelling from end to end time after time, and both sides missing good chances by bad shooting. Pulling together a bit, the Northern kept Cowan at it, and latterly Neave scored the second goal with a quick low shot. Another shot was sent in, but it struck the bar and passed over. The game became very slack, both sides being pretty well done up, but the whistle at half-time brought relief with the Hibernians one goal down. On restarting the Hibernian assumed the aggressive, and were making way when the game was stopped by a Northern player being injured. Keeping up the pressure, after several unsuccessful attempts, Smith put on the equalising goal, just as Mathieson came on the field again. The superior staying powers of the Hibernians were beginning to tell, shot after shot being put in, but all being misjudged. Breaking away they again gave Cowan a visit, and two corners fell to the lot of the Northern, but without success. The Hibernians were slack at back…Ten minutes from time a penalty came to the Hibernians, and Murphy taking it struck the bar and missed out….The game ended in a draw – two goals each." The Northern team securing their first ever SFL point was Burnside; Buist, Gossland; Sinclair, Fraser, Mathieson; Fyfe, Kyle; A Gossland, Neaves and McBride.

Still winless, the Glasgow derby game on the 14th October against fellow strugglers Thistle offered an opportunity to break their duck. Play was very even and end-to-end before Thistle took the lead. Fyfe of Northern had two sharp shots but couldn't beat the 'keeper before Thistle doubled their advantage. The game was again even on the balance of play but the Northern forwards spurned their chances and Thistle made them pay for their profligacy in front of goal by scoring a third for a rare win.

It wasn't until their ninth game, halfway through the season, that they recorded their first League win, a narrow 2-1 win over Partick Thistle, on the 23rd December 1893, in front of 1,000 spectators. *The Scotsman* reported that "in the first half play was very even, both sides rushing a lot, but without success." Northern opened the scoring just before half-time through Neaves. Shortly after the restart Partick got back on equal terms and mid-way through the second half Fyfe scored from a corner. Despite pressing from their opponents Northern held on for their first win with *The Glasgow Herald* reporting that "After a fast, and well-contested game, Northern retired with their first League victory."

At the turn of the year Northern were bottom of the table, just a point behind Morton and two behind Glasgow Thistle and Abercorn. In mid-February the bottom two met at Cappielow but Northern lost heavily 7-1 despite only being 2-1 down at the break. Northern had scored first but Morton had equalised almost immediately. *The Scotsman* reported that "Morton made a fine show on resuming, and they quickly scored goal after goal" Morton now had six points and Northern five. On the 10th March 1894 they won their second game, beating Abercorn 5-2. Northern were in the ascendancy in the first half and led at half-time 4-1. Play was more even in the second half with each side scoring a goal apiece. In their short SFL career this would be their best ever win, a result which temporarily elevated them to seventh place.

On the 7th April they travelled through to Edinburgh to play leaders Hibs. They turned up late and probably wished that they had not turned up at all! *The Scotsman* reported that "a poor attendance turned out to witness this second division League contest at Easter Road. The weather was miserable and it was half an hour after the advertised time before the visitors put in an appearance. The game was a poor one almost throughout, and, with the exception of a few minutes in the first period, never any doubt prevailed as to the ultimate result. Early in the first half the Irishmen scored a couple of goals, but did not manage to add to this number up to the interval. In the second portion, however, they pressed incessantly, and scoring another four goals, won a poor game by six goals to nothing."

The season was now drawing to a close and four teams were involved in a battle to avoid the three places that would require a re-election vote – Northern were competing against Port Glasgow Athletic (who had a seven point deduction), Morton and Thistle. On the 21st April Northern beat Port Glasgow 3-1 to register their third win of the season. The teams had been level at 1-1 at the interval but Northern had the better of the second half. The result took them level with their beaten opponents on nine points in joint seventh place. Morton were in ninth place with seven points, although with a game in hand on Morton and Thistle were bottom, and had completed their fixtures.

On the 28th April, Northern and Morton met at Hyde Park in a crucial game. Northern led 2-1 at half time but were completely over powered in the second half and were thrashed 7-2. Morton went above them as a result of this win. This game would ultimately turn out to be the last ever League game staged at Hyde Park. The following

Saturday Port Glasgow thrashed Morton 10-1 to condemn both Morton and Northern to a re-election vote. On the 19th May 1894 Northern played what would be their last ever SFL game, a 2-0 defeat at Dalziel Park against Motherwell and the last Northern line up was: Burnside; Mathieson, Graham; J Fraser, A Fraser, Lamont; Kyle, Watson, Donaldson, McBride and Neaves.

Prior to the AGM of the Scottish Football League Glasgow Thistle indicated that they would not be standing for re-election having taken the decision to disband due to their perilous financial position. At the meeting on the 1st June, Northern, along with Morton, faced competition from five other clubs for the three League places available. The other applicants were Airdrieonians and Royal Albert from the continuing Scottish Alliance, Linthouse, once of the Scottish Alliance, Kilmarnock from the Ayrshire Combination, and a new club, Dundee Wanderers. Morton were re-elected, topping the voting with 30. Dundee Wanderers came in second with 23 votes and the third and final place went to Airdrieonians by just one vote. Airdrie got 19 votes whereas Northern got 18!

Northern returned to the Scottish Alliance but resigned part way through the 1896-97 season and the club was wound up. Their Hyde ground was later built upon, being used for an expansion of the locomotive works.

SEASON	LEAGUE	P	W	D	L	F	A	P	POS
1893-94	SCOT-2	18	3	3	12	29	66	9	9/10

Peebles Rovers

Formed: 1893
Colours: Maroon shirts, white shorts but from 1924 white shirts and navy blue shorts
Ground: Whitestone Park
Entered League: 1923. Founder members of the Third Division
Number of League Seasons: 3
Honours: None
Highest League Finish: 8th in Division Three
Left League: 1926. Division Three abandoned. Wound up in 1927. Later reformed as a Senior Club 1928-1963

The Royal Burgh of Peebles is situated in the heart of the Scottish border country about 30 minutes' drive from Edinburgh and an hour from Glasgow. The Borders is perhaps best known for its rugby clubs but in the 1920s a football club from Peebles competed in the experimental Third Division first set up for the 1923-24 season, playing for the three years of its existence.

The football club was formed in 1893 and joined the Border League in 1902. They played their home games at Victoria Park, Walkershaugh, before moving the short distance to Whitestone Park in 1906. This was situated off the Innerleithen Road, across from the Peebles Hydro hotel.

The club didn't make their Scottish Cup debut until the 1907-08 competition when were drawn away to Celtic in a match played on Saturday 25th January 1908. *The Scotsman* reported that "from the start the Celtic took a good grip of the game, but despite their pressing, the Parkheaders always had to reckon with MacPherson, who kept a magnificent goal for Peebles. He repelled shot after shot for Peebles, and saved his charge when goals seemed certain. The Peebles forwards had one or two good runs, but they failed to make any impression on the Celtic defence. At half-time there was no scoring, but the second half was not long in progress until Celtic opened the scoring. The Peebles backs put up a great defence, but even had to submit to a superior lot." Celtic added another three goals to win 4-0.

Peebles played in the Scottish Cup five more times before League admission and reached a best of the Third Round in both the 1912-13 and 1913-14 competitions. In the 1912-13 season they were again knocked out by Celtic, this time losing 3-0 at home in a match played on the 22nd February 1913.

In 1909 they had joined the Scottish Football Union and they won it in the 1910-11 season. In 1912 they then joined the Eastern League and played here until the War. At the Scottish Football League AGM in 1912 Peebles Rovers applied unsuccessfully to join the Second Division when this division was being expanded by the addition of two new teams. Peebles came bottom of the poll and Dunfermline Athletic and Johnstone were elected instead. The club tried again the following year but failed in a vote in which eight teams were involved. Arthurlie and Leith Athletic were the successful clubs this time. After the War they re-joined the Borders League in 1919, before going on to play in the Eastern League (1921-22) and then the Western League (1922-23).

While playing in the Western League they took Hibernian, then sixth in the First Division, to a replay in the Second Round of the Scottish Cup. The first game was played on the 27th January 1923 with Peebles gaining a 0-0 draw at Easter Road in front of a 14,000 crowd. The result was a special one, not solely to do with the heroic defence and stout resistance, but also because of them having to play men short due to injuries. Under the headline "Peebles Rovers' Impregnable Defence" *The Scotsman* reported that "once the first fifteen minutes were over, the game at Easter Road, Edinburgh, developed into a struggle between the Hibernian attack and the Peebles Rovers' defence, and, in the end, the honours lay with the visitors, who refused to be beaten, and never allowed their opponents to settle down to a standard of play that was within measurable distance of their usual form. The Hibernians, were undoubtedly the stronger and better side, but the visitors earned their draw, if only for their plucky and able defence. Allison, Hodge, Maxwell and Veitch were outstanding. Early in the game Hannigan injured his knee, and had to go off, and though handicapped in that manner, the Rovers offered stout resistance. On crossing over it was seen that Duncan, the Rovers' centre-half, was suffering from a strained back. Hannigan resumed later, but was of little use, and though the Hibernians were almost continually in the goalmouth, they failed to get the ball into the net." The Peebles result was somewhat overshadowed by the fact that Hearts were knocked out of the Cup by Bo'ness on the same day. The replay was held the following Tuesday, also at Easter Road, as Peebles agreed to surrender home advantage and play again in the city. The two sides met again on the 30th January in front of a lower crowd of 8,000. The game followed a similar pattern to the first game with Hibs dominating play but the indifferent form of their forwards and the stout defence of Peebles kept the scoreline lower than it might have been. Hibs got an early goal but couldn't be comfortable until they got a second approaching the end and victory was made certain when they netted a third.

In 1923, eleven of the twelve Western League teams were incorporated into the Scottish League as the new Third Division. Peebles Rovers, were the only team entering from the Borders. They had an undistinguished career, finishing 14th (out of 16), 8th (out of 17) and were lying 14th (out of 16) when the competition was abandoned at the end of the 1925-26 season.

The first Scottish Football League match at Whitestone Park was played on the 18th August 1923, a 2–1 defeat by Mid-Annandale of Lockerbie in front of only 800 spectators. *The Sunday Post* attributed the defeat to the height of their players. Under the headline "The Wee Rovers" they reported "Almost diminutive in comparison with Mid-Annandale, the Rovers suffered sorely in the matter of inches on a rain-sodden pitch, and the advantage was always with the big fellow. The only goal of the first half was got by MacLaine, the Mid's centre, and the same player counted just after the interval. The Rovers showed up well in the closing stages, and from a magnificent cross by Ritchie, Turner reduced the leeway with a header."

Peebles Rovers lost their next game on the road against Solway Star before registering their first League win, 3-1 over Montrose on the 8th September 1923. This was followed by only one point in the next seven games, losing six and picking up a solitary point at Clackmannan, a poor run which left them second from bottom by the beginning of November, with only three points from the first ten games. The reverse fixture against Clackmannan at home resulted in a 4-0 win to end the sequence. Goals from Watson, Kane and Ritchie (2) gave them a well-deserved victory. But by the end of 1923 only Brechin City were below them in the table.

An upturn in fortunes occurred in the New Year, including a 5-2 win over Helensburgh in January, in which Allan scored a hat trick and Wilson, the Peebles' goalkeeper saved a penalty. This was followed by three consecutive wins in February 1924. They did, however, fail to score in their next four games, ending the season with a 2-0 defeat at Beith, Wilson, the 'keeper was the saviour of his side, making a string of saves to defy the opposition forwards. In their first League season Peebles finished a lowly 14th, with only Helensburgh and Brechin below them.

The following season proved to be their best in their short three year stay in the Scottish League as they finished in the top half in eighth place. They went the first six games unbeaten, although this included four draws, before they lost at home to Queen of the South who scored a late winner, somewhat against the run of play (the Dumfries team would finish second and be promoted). Four consecutive wins in the run up to Christmas saw Peebles briefly up to sixth but erratic form in January, in which they lost 7-1 to eventual champions Nithsdale one week, but then won themselves the next week 5-0 against Helensburgh put paid to any promotion challenge. This in turn was followed by a 6-0 loss to Queen of the South.

Their 7-1 record defeat against Nithsdale Wanderers came on the 10th January 1925. Nithsdale scored three in the first 15 minutes, McConnell heading home the first from a corner, followed by goals by Allan and Ballantyne, the latter with a fierce drive. Gossman and Jamieson tried in vain for Peebles but rarely troubled Armour in the Nithsdale goal. Wilson defied all efforts to add to the score and four times in rapid succession turned shots over the bar before succumbing to another Ballantyne driven shot. McConnell added a fifth from a low left-footed shot after being set up by Allan. McConnell added two more, bringing his total for the game to four and for the season to 26. Near the end Lang raced clear and got a late consolation for Peebles, the match ending 7-1.

This poor result was followed by a 5-0 home win against Helensburgh. After a goalless first half the Rovers reorganised their front line and moved Gossman to centre-forward. He notched up a second half hat-trick with Rutherford and Dick the other scorers. *The Edinburgh Evening News* commenting that "Peebles Rovers had the thought which inspired a rearranged forward line to thank for their big vlctory....With the original arrangement of the first half, the Peebles men cut a poor figure, but a change on resuming, which allowed Gossman to take up the centre position saw the Rovers strike a game which yielded them five goals. Gossman himself, who made a brilliant leader of the attack, had the hat-trick. He scored in the first minute of the second half from a Dick pass, added a second from a Rutherford cross, and a third following a clever solo effort."

In the same month Whitestone Park's probable record attendance of 1,500 was set for a Scottish Cup First Round replay against St Cuthbert Wanderers of Kirkcudbright in Dumfries and Galloway on the 28th January 1925, with Peebles winning 5–0, Turner, the home centre forward scoring a hat trick. A few days later Peebles lost 6-0 in the League away against Queen of the South. *The Edinburgh Evening News* reported that "Rovers will not readily forget their visit to Dumfries. Queen of the South were their masters all the time, and, had the locals not eased off towards the finish, their victory might have been even more decisive." McDermid scored the first after a quarter of an hour for the home team, Hair scored a hat-trick and the other goals came from McAlpine and Gray.

Peebles Rovers went out of the Scottish Cup to Dykehead, 3-1 at Shotts in early February and their Cup exit was followed by four consecutive League defeats. They had a strong finish in April though, unbeaten in the four matches, where they recorded both their biggest home and away SFL victories. First, they won 5–2 away against Galston on 11 April 1925. Under the headline "Peebles' Fireworks" *The Edinburgh Evening News* reported on the match, saying that the game "at Portland Park, ended in a somewhat sensational victory for the visitors. The first half was hotly contested, and Galston did most of the running, and all the pressing." But it was Rovers who opened the scoring through Mitchell, who beat Christie in the home goal after the 'keeper had superbly saved his first effort. Peebles led at half-time thanks to this goal but soon after the resumption Cook equalised. Continuing the match report "the Rovers came in their might, and in the short space of fifteen minutes they had rattled on four goals" through Craig, Jamieson (2), and Rutherford from a penalty. Howat got one back but Rovers thoroughly deserved their victory. A week later their record home and overall biggest SFL victory was achieved, 7–1 against Beith on the 18th April 1925. Rutherford scored in the first minute to set them on their way and goals quickly followed from Jamieson (2), Mitchell, Craig and Dick - so that all players in the home front line had scored. At half-time Rovers led 6-0. In the second half Jamieson got his hat-trick and McLean scored for Beith.

Their final season started with a 2-1 away win against Beith but they then lost away at Helensburgh and at home to Vale of Leven. In October they won 5-0, twice, at home to Solway Star on the 17th and then against Lochgelly United on the 31st. In the game against the men from Annan all the goals came in the second half. With a strong wind behind them, Turner, their centre-forward scored a hat-trick and Craig got the other two. In the game against Lochgelly, Turner scored the only goal of the first half, and in the second period goals were added to the Peebles total by Craig (2), Turner and Findlay. *The Edinburgh Evening News* commented that "Lochgelly United were all but outclassed by the Rovers of Peebles in a game that had a lot of interest. The Rovers were most worthy winners. Lochgelly were not deficient in pluck, but had a feckless attack threw away many chances, particularly in the first half. The Rovers' superiority was very marked in the second half, during which they scored four of their five goals." The result took Peebles up as high as seventh but then Rovers twice conceded five away from home in two consecutive 5-3 defeats at Montrose and Lochgelly United. Games over the New Year period saw them lose both 6-0 and 4-0 against Leith Athletic and Beith respectively, and both were home games. Leith were going well but Beith were second from bottom. Rovers were the better side in the first half and were unlucky to go into the break one down before completely capitulating in the second period.

One bright spark was their form in the Scottish Cup where they registered their highest scoring win in the First Round against Keith, 7-3 (if not the biggest winning margin which was the 5-0 against St Cuthbert Wanderers from a year earlier). Turner, their centre-forward scored five but defensive lapses led them to concede three. This led to a tie against Second Division Albion Rovers who they held to a 1-1 draw in Coatbridge. The home team went in at half-time 1-0 up and missed a penalty in the second period before Turner got the equalising goal nine minutes from time. There was to be no fairytale Cup run though as they succumbed 4-0 at home in the replay at a wintry Whitestone Park.

Poor form in the League continued and a 7-1 record equalling defeat away against Solway Star in early March left them bottom of the 'active' table. By this time though, Galston had already folded, as financial problems beset many clubs in the Division. Ross opened the scoring for Star and Knox scored two before Findlay scored one from a penalty for Rovers. In the second half Ross added another three goals and W Alexander was the other scorer. *The Edinburgh Evening News* kindly reported that "Peebles gave a good display, but were outclassed."

What turned out to be Peebles Rovers' final home match in the SFL was played on the 17th April 1926, when they hosted Royal Albert of Larkhall at Whitestone Park and lost 4–1. They had only completed 26 games of their 30 fixtures, none of which were draws, and were placed 14th. The Third Division collapsed at the end of the season with multiple unfulfilled fixtures and was subsequently abandoned by the Scottish League.

Like many of the Third Division clubs Peebles Rovers joined the Scottish Alliance when the Division was abandoned, strangely competing in a Northern section, alongside the likes of Montrose and Brechin City. In the Scottish Cup they went out to Kilmarnock, but only 3-1. When the ex-Third Division clubs were expelled from the Alliance the following year Peebles decided against joining the Provincial League and the club subsequently folded and then reformed as a junior club, playing in the Midlothian Junior League in 1927-28. The following year they returned to Senior football and joined the East of Scotland League, where they played until 1963. Peebles Rovers won the championship in four successive years, between 1933 and 1936. Between 1963 and 1974 they played as a Junior club then joined the Border Amateur League (1976-78) before joining the East of Scotland League in 1980 as a Senior club using the title of Peebles FC. They continued to participate in the Scottish Cup during this time and suffered some heavy defeats. In the 1930-31 competition, a home crowd of 1,400 saw them lose 4-0 in the First Round against Falkirk. *The Falkirk Herald* reported that "the Bairns did not experience very great difficulty in accounting for Peebles Rovers, though the Borders amateurs proved a game lot, and refused to be overwhelmed. Falkirk established a safe lead of four goals in the first half, and that sufficed for them to win the tie." In the 1936-37 season they were again thrashed by Falkirk, 6-0 this time. Played in front of a small crowd at Brockville and in wretched weather, Falkirk won even more convincingly than the score line suggests. Peebles conceded after just six minutes and the tie was effectively over after ten minutes when the Bairns had added two more. No more goals were scored in the first half as Falkirk's intensity dropped. Ormiston, Rovers' centre-half was sent off before the interval and in the second half three more goals were added.

Their performances in the Cup in the 1950s were characterised by some decent runs, but also by some heavy defeats. In the 1951-52 season they lost 7-0 to Berwick Rangers in the First Round. Berwick had joined the SFL in 1951 in a regionalised Division C. In the 1953-54 season 1,500 watched a Second Round match against Buckie Thistle, with the match ending in a 1–1 draw. Rovers lost the replay 7-2. In the 1954-55 season they made it to the Fourth Round where they lost to Forres Mechanics 2-0. The following year they again made it to the Fourth Round where they were involved in a marathon tie with Brechin City. There was a 1–1 draw away, a 4–4 draw at home after extra time, 0–0 in a second replay at Easter Road, again after extra time, and finally they lost 6–2 in a third replay, at Tannadice on the 16th November 1955. On the 13th February 1959 they lost 10-0 at St Mirren in the Second Round, with Gerry Baker scoring four goals. St Mirren went on to knock out Motherwell, Celtic in the Semi-final 4-0, and go on to lift the trophy beating Aberdeen 3-1 in the Final. The following year they lost 6-1 against Ayr United and to cap them all, on the 11th February 1961 they lost 15-0 to Hibernian in a Second Round tie, Joe Baker, Gerry's brother, scoring nine that day. Their final appearance was better though, in 1965-66, they drew 2–2 at Dumbarton and took the Sons to extra time in the replay before losing 3–2.

SEASON	LEAGUE	P	W	D	L	F	A	P	POS
1923-24	SCOT-3	30	7	8	15	43	56	22	14/16
1924-25	SCOT-3	30	12	7	11	64	57	31	8/16
1925-26	SCOT-3	26	9	0	17	52	76	18	14/16

Port Glasgow Athletic

Formed: 1880
Colours: White shirts, navy shorts
Ground: Clune Park
Entered League: 1893. Founder member of the Second Division
Number of League Seasons: 18
Highest League Finish: 9th in Division One
Honours: Second Division Champions, 1902
Left League: 1911. Resigned, did not seek re-election. Wound up 1912

Port Glasgow is located west of Glasgow and four miles east of Greenock and was originally called Newark. A castle bearing that name stills stands alongside the River Clyde. It was formed as a port for nearby Glasgow in 1668 due to ships not being able to make it all the way up the shallow River Clyde and was renamed Port Glasgow in 1775. Glasgow merchants would import tobacco, sugar, rum and cotton amongst other things and the goods would be unloaded here and then transported by road to Glasgow. Port Glasgow became a centre for shipbuilding but the port declined due to dredging of the river which created deeper channels for ships to navigate. Today the shipbuilding industry has all but gone and only the Ferguson Marine Shipbuilders yard remains.

Port Glasgow Athletic FC was formed in 1880 although they originally played under the name of Broadfield and were based at Devol Farm, south of the town. A year later they changed their name and moved to Clune Park just off the old Glasgow Road and Gourock branch railway line, close to the shipyards. They were nicknamed 'the undertakers' because they played in dark shorts and white shirts.

Port Glasgow played in the Scottish Cup from 1881 and in 1891 became founder members of the Scottish Football Alliance. The majority of these teams became founder members of the new Scottish League Second Division in 1893. Port Glasgow played in the Scottish League from 1893 to 1911, playing in 18 seasons and they won the Second Division Championship in 1902. They then spent eight seasons in the top tier of the Scottish League, surviving three re-election votes before eventually being relegated in 1910. They only played one further season before resigning altogether due to financial problems. During their League tenure they also reached the Semi-finals of the Scottish Cup twice (in 1899 and 1906). During their first season in the Scottish League they had a record seven points deducted for rule infringements.

A team representing Port Glasgow played in the Scottish Cup between 1877 and 1879 and Port Glasgow Athletic formally made their debut in the competition in 1881. Their first game in the Cup was a 6-1 defeat away at Paisley Athletic on 17th September 1881.They played in the Scottish Cup every season after that up to their Scottish Football League admission. In the 1885-86 Cup competition they reached the Fifth Round eventually going out to beaten Semi-finalists Third Lanark after two drawn matches. A year later they went one stage better, reaching the last eight where they were beaten by Vale of Leven, winners of the Cup three times in succession between 1877-1879. During this Cup run they beat Johnstown Harp 10-1 and also knocked out St Mirren, Abercorn and St Bernard's. In the 1887-88 competition they beat Greenock Rangers 11-0 in a First round tie played on the 27th August 1887, although they subsequently only made it as far as the Third Round.

In 1891 Port Glasgow were founder members of the Scottish Alliance which was set up as a rival competition to the Scottish Football League. Two years later the club, along with five others from the Alliance joined the SFL as members of the newly-formed Second Division. This was by invitation only and four Alliance clubs missed out (including Kilmarnock and Airdrieonians).

 Port Glasgow Athletic made their League debut on the 12th August 1893, beating Glasgow Northern 6-1. The *Glasgow Herald* reported that "Athletic kicked off, and after several incursions by both teams into the territories of their respective opponents Athletic obtained the first count about twenty minutes from the start. For the same team A McNeill scored a second goal and Martin a third. The cross-over was made without further scoring. Smith scored a fourth goal for Athletic which was followed shortly afterwards by Northern scoring their first and only point. Athletic got two more goals, taken by Martin and McCorkindale."

The following week they drew 2-2 away at Clyde before beating Glasgow Thistle 4-3 at Clune Park a week later. In this game the club had their first brush with the footballing authorities. One of their players, J Smith, was censured for refusing to leave the field of play when ordered by the referee during that game against Thistle. Port led 3-1 at half-time, Smith having scored the third. The *Glasgow Herald* noted that "soon after play was resumed an unfortunate incident occurred. One of the Thistle players kicked a member of the Athletic. The Port man made an attempt to retaliate by squaring up to fight. The referee immediately brought the game to a standstill, and ordered the member of the Athletic off the field." Despite being a man short Athletic scored a fourth through McCorkindale before a determined Thistle, finally making the extra man count, scored two more goals but couldn't find the equaliser.

A week later their good start on the pitch continued after beating Paisley's Abercorn 5-4, coming from 3-0 down. They conceded after just two minutes. Repeated shots were sent in towards Connell in the Athletic goal who saved these but he was eventually beaten and then for a third time. Nisbet pulled one back with renewed determination from Athletic and McCorkindale scored just before half-time. During the first twenty minutes after the restart the teams were evenly matched. After 65 minutes McNeil levelled the scores and Athletic, with the momentum, scored two more, both from McCorkindale who ended with a hat-trick, to complete a remarkable comeback. With a few minutes left Abercorn got a fourth but Athletic saw out the win.

Port Glasgow now topped the division but then came disaster, courtesy of another run-in with the authorities. The club was deducted seven points for rule infringements having fielded an ineligible player. Daniel McNeil was played against Northern (12 August) and Clyde (19 August) while still registered with Clyde. On the 12th September the case came before the SFA and the *Glasgow Herald* reported that "the monthly meeting of the Scottish Football Association was held last night in their rooms, 6 Carlton Place, Glasgow – Mr Archibald Sliman in the Chair. The charge by the Clyde against Daniel McNeil, of Port Glasgow Athletic, of having signed a professional form for Clyde was under consideration and, after a lengthy discussion, the committee decided that he was a professional, and ordered him to keep his engagement with the Clyde." McNeil, who had signed professional terms with Clyde, attended the meeting in person and asked for reinstatement as an amateur. McNeil stated, according to *The Scotsman,* who also reported on the meeting "that he would lose his situation if he played as a professional, and therefore wished to be allowed to play as an amateur for his old club, the Port-Glasgow Athletic. The Committee decided that McNeill was a professional, and refused to release him from his engagement.

Port never really recovered from this set back and settled for mid-table. They finished sixth with 13 points. If they had kept the additional seven points earned they would have only finished one place higher. They ended their debut season both dishing out and being on the receiving end of a 10-1 score line. First, on the 5th May 1894 they beat local rivals Greenock Morton 10-1 in front of 4,000 spectators at Clune Park, but a fortnight later they then lost 10-1 against champions Hibernian, in what was the last game of the season. The first half was actually evenly contested with Hibs going into the interval only two goals to the good at 3-1. But in a one-sided second period Hibs put seven more goals past the Port Glasgow 'keeper Connelly, with the goals being shared around the Hibs forward line of Murray, Kennedy, Martin, Smith and Amos.

The 1894-95 season saw a massive improvement. Although Hibernian, who hadn't been elected to the First Division, again ran away with the championship, Athletic finished in third place. They started the new season with three straight wins but came down with a bump on the 18th September when they lost to newcomers Dundee Wanderers 9-1 at East Dock Street. This result was somewhat of a surprise as a week before they had beaten Partick Thistle 6-2 and Wanderers had lost their first three games. At the outset the game was equally contested but somehow they managed to go into the interval three-nil down. In the second half Port Glasgow collapsed and Dundee Wanderers piled on the goals putting another six past Connelly, the unfortunate 'keeper, before Athletic got a late consolation. The club bounced back with a 5-1 win over Abercorn and then a 9-1 win of their own against Morton but lost three of their last four games including a 5-0 defeat away at Patrick in the last game of the season.

The following season saw the club drop back to finish a disappointing seventh place. New clubs Kilmarnock and Airdrieonians performed well and Athletic made a poor start, losing four out of their first five matches. This included a 6-1 defeat at Leith Athletic where they arrived late at Beechwood Park and must have wished they'd never arrived at all! *The Scotsman* reported that "the visitors were late in arriving, and it was fully half an hour after the advertised hour when the game was started. For a time matters were evenly contested, but at length Boyd opened the scoring…This was quickly followed by another goal from the same player and before the interval they added a third. During the second half Leith continued to have the game completely in hand and won very easily." Port Glasgow didn't fare much better in the Scottish Cup, as they were thrashed 8-1 by Queen's Park in the Second Round.

The 1896-97 season was slightly worse as they finished in their lowest position in their League history to date, coming in eighth place in the ten team division. They only won one game in the first half of the season but were kept off the bottom by winless Dumbarton. A season's best 6-3 home win over Linthouse; a 5-2 home win over Kilmarnock and 5-1 home win against Morton lifted them up the table but they finished with three consecutive defeats in which they failed to score. At the end of the season they faced a re-election vote with four challengers. At the League's AGM on the 1st June the club was comfortably re-elected in second place with 27 votes. Motherwell came top with 34 and Ayr FC came third with 24 votes, beating Dumbarton, who had gathered only six points all season.

Perhaps the re-election vote was a wake-up call as Port Glasgow bounced back in empathetic style, winning 12 out of 18 games as they finished as runners-up to Kilmarnock. During the 1897-98 season they recorded thee big wins, where on each occasion they scored eight goals. First up was an 8-0 win over Renton in the October at Clune Park. Smith opened the scoring for Port which was followed shortly afterwards by a second. Renton couldn't get into the game and from a penalty kick, Martin made it three. Before the interval a fourth was added and the two sides cross over with Port Glasgow Athletic leading 4-0. The second half was a repeat of the first with the home team scoring four more goals without reply. They followed this up with an 8-2 win against Abercorn in December, *The Scotsman* noting that "in this match the Athletic had matters practically all their own way after the opening minutes, during which Lappin scored for Abercorn. At the interval the home team led by three goals to one, their points been got by Smith (2) and Tarbet. In the second half they scored five goals to Abercorn's one, and ran out winners by eight goals to two." Finally, in March 1898 they beat Airdrieonians 8-1.

In April 1898 they hosted leaders Kilmarnock who were well clear at the top of the table, with Port Glasgow in third. Athletic came from 1-0 to win 4-2 with the *Glasgow Herald* reporting that "the game was evenly contested, but Port were superior all over to Kilmarnock." The newspaper made no reference to any crowd trouble or incident but later Kilmarnock protested about the crowd and at how their players were treated at Clune Park. On Thursday 5th May the same paper reported that "a meeting of the Second Division Committee was held…the principal item on the agenda was the consideration of the protest lodged by Kilmarnock about the treatment received by several of their players at the hands of the Clune Park spectators in their League game with Port-Glasgow Athletic a fortnight ago. Much conflicting evidence was tendered by players of both teams and the referee stated that while the spectators did manifest a desire to ill-treat himself and the Kilmarnock players, he did not think that what had happened warranted him in reporting the matter to the League. The case was found not proven." Port Glasgow finished in second place and at the Scottish League's AGM held on the 30th May, the club applied for membership of the First Division, along with Second Division Champions Kilmarnock and third placed Morton. However, the three existing First Division clubs (St Bernard's, Partick Thistle and Clyde) were all re-elected. Kilmarnock lost out on a second ballot to Clyde.

The 1898-99 season was another successful one for Port Glasgow Athletic as they finished third in the Second Division and also reached the Semi-finals of the Scottish Cup for the first time. Kilmarnock again finished as champions, seven points ahead of Athletic, with Leith Athletic finishing above them in second. These two clubs were involved in an entertaining game in the October, which the *Glasgow Herald* –reported on: "this fixture, which created considerable interest, was played at Port Glasgow. A stiff easterly wind blew down field, and against this Port kicked off. The game was not far gone before it became apparent that there would be a hard struggle for the points. Leith were the first to get well over mid-field, but an air of determination was conspicuous with the ground team. In dashing form they recrossed the line. McNeill made a pass towards centre, and Smith headed to Hodge, who drove home some minutes from the start. Leith for a time we're forced to assume the defensive. Tosh passed in from the left, and a smart scrimmage in front of goal resulted in a lead of two goals for Port Glasgow. Still pegging at it, Oswald, Leith's custodian, got a stinger to deal with. The ball, it was quite apparent, was through, but this must not have been seen by Referee Walker, for prompter or juster refereeing could not be wished for. Indeed, in a game so fast and full of points and dash, the referee performed his duties admirably. Leith were by no means lying low. The backs and halves deserved all praise for their clever play. Centre forward Laidlaw was in champion form. Fotheringham had some clever tries at goal, but did not quite succeed in negotiating successfully the wind. The game was 20 minutes gone, when Laidlaw played first count for Leith. After this goals came fast and furious. Hodge banked home a third for Port Glasgow, and two minutes later, Laidlaw cleverly responded. McCorquodale put on a fourth for the homesters, and Walker, from a clever pass from Fotheringham, scored for Leith. Seven goals were thus registered in the first half, the odd numbers in favour of the Port. Laidlaw and Brown each placed a goal to the credit of Leith in the second half, while for the ground team Smith scored two and McCorquodale and Tosh one each. Leith were handicapped by playing ten men only in the second half. A grand game ended: Port Glasgow 8; Leith 5." The result moved Port Glasgow into second, two points behind leaders Kilmarnock and two ahead of their vanquished opposition Leith.

A month later the club was involved in another high-scoring encounter, this time beating Airdrieonians 8-2 to go joint top with Kilmarnock but having played two games more. The *Glasgow Herald* reported that "Athletic were early on the aggressive, and in the opening minutes the Airdrie goal ran a few narrow escapes. After a brief attack by Airdrie, the home forwards cleverly returned, and Hodge notched the first goal with a capital shot. The visitors worked hard for the equaliser, which came shortly afterwards from the foot of Kyle. Responding to the enthusiastic shouts, the Port simply toyed with their opponents, and did not halt till their total stood at five. Airdrie tried to get away on numerous occasions, but it was not till close upon half-time that their efforts were rewarded by Scott placing the ball out of the reach of Ward. The cross-over was effected with the ground team leading by 5 goals to 2. In the final 45, Port scored a sixth through Smith. Airdrie were seldom across the centre line, and on any occasion in which they got to close quarters they were successfully frustrated by the home defence. After 30 minutes play, Galbraith scored a seventh for Port and nearing the close Smith applied the closure by netting the eighth. Athletic in all had the ball in the net no fewer than ten times, two of which were struck off on the plea of off-side." Going well in the League, the 1898-99 season also saw Port Glasgow Athletic have their best run in the Scottish Cup, reaching the Semi-finals. They beat Renton and West Calder Swifts in the early rounds before beating Patrick Thistle in the last eight, 7-3 at Clune Park before a crowd of 4,000. In this game Partick drew first blood but that seemed to spur the hosts on who countered with two goals in quick succession. Play settled down and was evenly balanced before both McCorquodale and McMaster scored for Athletic who thus went into the break with the score at 4-1. Smith with a well-taken goal extended their lead and they added two more to threaten a rout. Partick kept going though and nearing the finish they had more success notching up two more goals.

The win set up a Semi-final against Celtic, played on Saturday 11th March 1899. *The Scotsman* reported that "this semi-final match in the Scottish Cup was played before a large attendance at Celtic Park, Glasgow. The game opened in favour of the Athletic, but the Celtic opened the scoring. The visitors were not long in equalising, and keeping up the pressure, McArthur was again beaten. Five minutes from time McMahon brought the scores level. Half-time:- two goals each. On resuming, the Celtic showed rare dash, and from a fine pass by Bell, Campbell scored. With the wind behind them, the Celtic were constantly troubling the Port's defence, and Divers added another point. Spasmodic efforts were made by the visitors." Celtic went on to beat holders Rangers 2-0 in the Final and lift the trophy for the second time.

Port concluded their successful season and League programme with a 6-2 win over Ayr FC on Saturday 1st April 1899. This was an even game for the first thirty minutes with the score at 1-1 before first Smith and then McCorquodale scored for Athletic. Ayr pulled one back just before the break but in the second half Athletic laid siege to the Ayr goal and ran in three more goals. Athletic couldn't catch Leith or Kilmarnock who were still one and two points ahead and who still had games to play. Due to a rule change now only the top two of the Second Division and the bottom two of the First Division contested re-election and so Port missed out despite scoring a club record 75 goals in the League for the season. This time Kilmarnock were elected, replacing Partick Thistle.

The 1889-1900 season was another good one as Port Glasgow secured a third successive top three finish, but again missed out on participating in a vote by finishing in third place behind Partick and Morton. Although placed third they were a long way back, finishing nine points behind Patrick and eight behind Morton. Interestingly, none of their 18 League matches ended in a draw. Their best result of the season was a 7-1 win over Leith Athletic but they also lost 8-2 at home to Ayr on the 6th January 1900, in their first game of the new century. The *Dundee Courier*'s report hinted at behind the scenes issues and noted that "matters at present are not going smoothly in the Port Glasgow camp, and the team's display against Ayr was on a par with the weather - miserable - and little else could be expected when backs and half-backs have to be utilised as forwards. The game was pure burlesque, and some explanation is certainly required from the Port Executive as to why such a scratchy lot did duty in a Second League engagement."

Unfortunately Port Glasgow couldn't maintain this consistency or push on and the following season they slipped back to a mid-table fifth place. The highlight of their season was another good Scottish Cup run where they beat Newton Stewart Athletic 7-1 before going out in the Quarter-finals at home to eventual winners Hearts 5-1, in front of 4,500 spectators.

Under the reins of Secretary/Manager Alex MacFarlane Port Glasgow Athletic celebrated their tenth season in the League by securing their first and only senior honour, winning the Second Division title, finishing just a point ahead of Partick Thistle. An increase in the First Division from ten to twelve teams also saw both clubs promoted to the First Division. Home form was key to them being champions as they went through the whole season undefeated, winning 10 out of 11 matches and only dropping points against promotion rivals Patrick Thistle in a 1-1 draw. They also set club records for most wins in a season (14), fewest defeats (4), and most points (32).

The season actually started poorly with three defeats out of four, although the defeats all came on the road. In September they scored six goals at Clune Park against both Leith Athletic and Clyde and went ten games unbeaten, the sequence only ending with a narrow 2-1 defeat in Edinburgh to St Bernard's. Despite this loss, they led the table, six points ahead of second placed Patrick. They soon bounced back with an 8-1 thrashing of Motherwell in early December, although their visitors were handicapped by the loss of a man through injury.

For the second consecutive season they were knocked out of the Scottish Cup 5-1 at home to the eventual winners, the previous year it was Hearts; this time it was Hibs in front of 4,000 spectators on the 25th January 1902. Back in the League and a 3-1 win in their last home game against Arthurlie on the 15th February led *The Scotsman* to report that "the Athletic led by one goal to nil at the interval, and playing the smarter game, eventually won by three goals to one. The Athletic have now 31 points to their credit, and cannot be passed by any other team in the League." A draw and a defeat in their last two games away from home saw their lead cut to just one point but they were crowned champions, although this was overshadowed by the Ibrox stadium disaster in April 1902.

At the Scottish League's AGM held on the 19th May 1902 the First Division was increased to 12 clubs with the inclusion of Port Glasgow Athletic. *The Scotsman* reported on the meeting, saying "it was unanimously agreed to increase the League to twelve clubs in each division, instead of, as present, ten in the first and twelve in the second. Port Glasgow Athletic and Partick Thistle were promoted, and along with the ten of last year, will form the first division. The Clyde and Abercorn were re-elected to the second division, and the vacancies caused by the promotion of Port Glasgow Athletic and Partick Thistle were given to Raith Rovers and Falkirk."

Port Glasgow Athletic spent the next eight seasons in the top flight of Scottish League football, rubbing shoulders with the likes of Celtic, Rangers, Hearts and Hibs. They generally found it tough going, securing a best finish of ninth place in the 1903-04 season. In their first season in the top flight they finished in eleventh place, second bottom, two points ahead of Morton. They won only three of their 22 matches, an unwanted club record of fewest League wins in a League season, which was subsequently matched in the 1909-10 campaign when they were relegated. This time the club avoided a re-election vote as the top division was again expanded, this time to 14 teams.

They played their first match in the top flight of Scottish football on the 16th August 1902, recording a creditable 2-2 draw at Love Street against St Mirren. Port scored first through Aitken but trailed at half-time having conceded two. Ross got them level twenty mins from time. The side taking to the pitch in their first ever top flight game was: Ward; Russell, Scott; Ross, Young, McNeil; J Black, Aitken, Clark, Bolton and G Black. A week later they played their first home game in the top flight watched by a crowd of 6,000 at Clune Park, *The Scotsman* reporting that "the occasion was the opening of the Athletic's extended ground, following upon their promotion to the First Division of the Scottish League, and the visit of the Cup holders was heralded in grand style. Across one of the thoroughfares hung bunting and banners bearing such inscriptions as 'Welcome to Hibernians' and 'Success to the Port'. The Second Division championship flag of last season was unfurled by Colonel Denny, the local Member of Parliament, who is an old Dumbarton player. He congratulated the Athletic on their promotion, and wished them all success. Afterwards, the game which was witnessed by fully 6000 people was begun, and in setting the ball rolling the home side were at little disadvantage, for there was scarcely any wind blowing. The opening passages were very fast and there was plenty excitement, as the local players showed their paces and troubled the Hibernian defence considerably. As the game progressed, the football was not of a high order and mainly by long kicking and following up were the respective goals visited with rapidity. Unable to settle down to their usual passing game, the Hibernians did not show to advantage, and indeed they were kept pretty busy keeping in check the home forwards....Just on half-time the Edinburgh side were unfortunate to lose the services of Glen, who had had a big say in the defence, the back having sprained his ankle badly....Shorthanded, the Hibernians were greatly handicapped, but the heavy ground and wet ball were against accurate shooting, and the home players were repeatedly at fault. As matters turned out the first and only goal fell to the visitors, who...eventually retired victorious one goal to nothing."

The following week another large crowd watched their 3-0 home defeat to Rangers. The Port improved considerably in the second half after conceding all three goals in the first period. The result left the newly promoted club already bottom of the Division after the first three matches. Worse was to follow with three more consecutive defeats. They had now played six, lost five, scored only three and had conceded 16. At the end of September they played fellow strugglers and local rivals Greenock Morton and recorded their first win of the season, by three goals to nil. A 4-0 win over Queen's Park in October lifted them off the bottom and above Morton which is where they stayed. At the League's AGM held on the 18th May 1903 the First Division was expanded to 14 clubs. Port Glasgow Athletic, along with Morton were both unanimously re-elected and Motherwell and Airdrieonians secured the two new places, having been elected from the Second Division.

The 1903-04 season was Port Glasgow's highest finish in the League as they came in ninth place in the newly expanded 14 team First Division. They opened with a surprising 3-1 win over champions Hibernian at Clune Park. Port led 1-0 at half-time through Galbraith and an early penalty in the second period, converted by McNicol, gave them some breathing space. Hibs missed a penalty before they did get a goal back from a long range effort. Hibs strove hard to equalise and hit the bar. Shortly afterwards McNicol scored again to give Athletic a great win, although there was only 3,000 there to witness it due to incessant rain.

Port Glasgow lost the first three games in September but then secured back-to-back wins at the end of the month, at Morton and Kilmarnock, which would be the only away victories they would register all campaign. They won the game at Rugby Park 4-0 with all of the goals coming in the second half, two from McNicol. They then went winless during October and November before beating Kilmarnock in the reverse fixture 4-1 in mid-December. They only secured two more wins to the end of the season and suffered an 8-1 defeat at Rangers in February, conceding six second half goals. However, the points accumulated earlier in the season helped them finish in ninth, ahead of the two new clubs Airdrieonians and Motherwell, plus Morton, Kilmarnock and champions Hibernian.

In the 1904-05 season Port finished two places lower, in eleventh place, finishing above Queen's Park, Morton and Motherwell. They lost their opening game narrowly 1-0 at Morton and then lost the opening game at Clune Park 4-1 against future champions Celtic. A good run of results in September saw them temporarily in the top half but they soon dropped back. They failed to score in four consecutive games in November and dropped to second bottom in the table by the turn of the year. 1905 brought an improvement in form and a season's best result, a 6-1 win over Partick Thistle coming in early January. The *Glasgow Herald* reported that "this First League fixture took place at Port Glasgow on Saturday in excellent weather, and on turf that was in fine condition. All through the home team had the best of play. The visitors kicked off with a slight wind in their favour, but from the start showed themselves quite unequal of the homesters' attack, and within eight minutes from the kick off the Athletic were leading by three goals. Hartley netted the first one, Allan put a second through a minute later, and before Thistle had quite recovered Robertson added a third. For the remaining portion of the first half the visitors showed slightly better form, and repulsed one or two attacks successfully. Shortly before half-time Hartley added a fourth for Port Glasgow. On resuming, play was for a time rather quiet, neither side doing anything of particular merit. After a considerable amount of uninteresting work Ross forced a corner, and Robertson headed in from O'Brien very neatly. At this point Melville [for Partick] was hurt by a strong kick, and had to be taken from the field. Hartley added another for the Port...About half a minute from time Ferguson scored the Thistle's only goal. For Port Glasgow Hartley was best man." Port Glasgow followed this up with a 2-0 win at Fir Park against Motherwell and secured further victories over Queen's Park and Dundee to finish in eleventh place.

For the 1905-06 season the top flight now consisted of 16 teams with the addition of Aberdeen and Falkirk, but Port continued to languish in the lower half of the table. They finished tied for second bottom, accumulating only 20 points although they did reach the Scottish Cup Semi-finals for the second time after knocking out Rangers. They opened their League campaign with a 2-1 win over newly promoted Falkirk but they then went seven games without a win. A 3-2 win over fellow strugglers Queen's Park in early January 1906 saw them briefly up to 12th.

Scottish Cup success then followed with a run to the Semi-finals for the second time having knocked out Rangers in the Quarter-finals. A record crowd at Clune Park of 11,000 watched their Third Round 1-0 win. Star player Gladstone Hamilton set up the winning goal in the first half for Cunningham. In the second half Rangers were the superior side and continually pressed but the Port defence held firm and "Ward was in great fettle, and repeatedly saved when all seemed the lost." (*The Scotsman*) Hamilton was subsequently capped for Scotland a week later, against Ireland, but was injured for the Semi-final which Hearts won 2-0 before an 8,500 crowd at Clune Park. Hearts scored in the first minute but it wasn't until three minutes from time that they made the game safe.

Port only picked up one further point from their remaining five League fixtures and then were involved in a play-off with Kilmarnock to determine which team would have to apply for re-election. On Tuesday the 15th May Athletic won 6-0 at Cathkin Park to avoid the dreaded vote. At the League's AGM held on the 21st May Kilmarnock and Queen's Park were both re-elected, each receiving 14 votes. It was agreed to further extend the First Division from 16 to 18 clubs and Hamilton and Clyde were voted into the division.

Port Glasgow again struggled in the 1906-07 season, earning just 21 points, as did Kilmarnock and Hamilton. As goal average wasn't used to separate clubs in important League positions, Port Glasgow, Kilmarnock and Hamilton all finished bottom. However it was decided not to arrange a three-way play-off to decide who would apply for re-election. All three clubs were re-elected at the League's AGM on the 27th May. The other applicants for admission were Raith Rovers, Dumbarton, St Bernard's, Leith Athletic and Vale of Leven.

In the 1907-08 season Port Glasgow Athletic finished bottom for the second consecutive season, losing a club record 22 out of 34 games and gaining only 17 points, finishing one point behind Clyde and five behind Queen's Park. They conceded six in their two opening matches, first, at home to Rangers, 6-1 on the 17th August and then, 6-0 a week later away at Motherwell. In all they conceded 98 goals in the League, a club record. There was an element of misfortune in the Rangers game. Drawing 1-1 at half-time Port had to play with ten men for the whole of the second half. There was no mitigating factor in the next game though, where they conceded three goals in each half.

Athletic's first points came in their fifth match, a narrow 1-0 win over Hamilton but this was immediately followed by a 9-0 thrashing at Brockville against Falkirk, in which they were six down at half-time. They also lost 5-0 four times - at home to Partick and Dundee, and away at Celtic and Hearts. In the Scottish Cup they beat Second Division Ayr Parkhouse 7-2 in the First Round before losing to Hearts 4-0.

At the League's AGM held on the 1st June 1908 the club narrowly survived another re-election vote. Port and Clyde faced the top four sides from the Second Division who all applied. Of these clubs, Raith attracted the most support with 8 votes. Port secured one more vote with 9. Clyde topped the poll with 12. *The Scotsman* noted that "a good deal of interest was attached to the meeting as it was believed that a strong effort would be made to secure places for two Second Division clubs in the First League. Raith Rovers and Dumbarton, who headed the Second Division, tabled applications for inclusion, as well as Clyde and Port Glasgow, who were the lowest in the First Division. Other applicants were Abercorn and Ayr. On a vote, Clyde secured 12, Port Glasgow 9, Raith Rovers 8, Dumbarton 2, Abercorn 1, while Ayr failed to get a supporter. Accordingly Clyde and Port Glasgow were re-elected in the First League."

The 1908-09 season brought an improved showing as they finished five places higher in 13th place. Patrick Thistle struggled earning only eight points all season. Things didn't start well with a 7-0 opening thrashing at Ibrox but they went five games unbeaten during late November and early December and early in 1909 they pulled off a shock 2-0 home win over Rangers, who were challenging for the title. The result still left them second bottom but they followed it up with three consecutive away wins to climb away from the foot of the table.

There was no such luck the following season as they finished bottom for the third time in four seasons. Port Glasgow won only three games, matching their record for the fewest wins in a season. They lost 26 matches, this time setting a new club record and they recorded just 11 points, finishing a massive 14 points adrift of Morton in 17th place. Port only scored 25 goals in 34 games and conceded 93. The season kicked off on the 21st August 1909 with a 3-0 home defeat at Clune Park against Aberdeen. They had the best of the early chances but were wasteful in front of goal. They went behind following an error by their goalkeeper Montgomery who let a weak shot through his hands. This reverse seemed to unsettle him as he was beaten by a long range effort just a couple of minutes later. After the interval Athletic huffed and puffed but couldn't make their possession count. Ten minutes from time Montgomery saved well but did not push the ball far enough from the goal and the rebound was converted.

Port Glasgow won away at Clyde in the next game but then went the next 14 games without a win, a sequence that included a 5-0 defeat at Cathkin Park against Third Lanark on 23rd October that left them bottom of the table with five points (level with Partick Thistle and Queens Park). On the 11th December they beat Queen's Park, who were second from bottom, to break their dismal run. They won 3-0 at a Clune Park to record their first home win of the season, thanks to goals from the Findlay brothers. They scored after just five minutes through T Findlay and this was followed immediately after by Robert Findlay. Speirs of Athletic was ordered off for attempting to kick Craigie but the Athletic held firm despite the numerical disadvantage. Near the close Hagan scored a third goal.

Gladstone Hamilton re-signed for the club but only contributed one goal in 18 appearances. In January 1910 Port suffered three consecutive heavy defeats - 4-0 at Rangers, 5-0 at home to Clyde and 4-0 at Celtic - and by the end of the month they were firmly rooted at the bottom with just nine points, seven points behind Queen's Park and eight behind Partick Thistle. A third, and what would be their last win over the season, came in early February with a 2-1 win over Hamilton Academical. However in March they conceded 16 goals in three games (losing 6-3 at Motherwell, 4-0 at Kilmarnock and 6-0 at Hearts).

Their final game of the season was ignominious as they lost 6-1 to Queen's Park in a midweek evening kick-off on the 26th April 1910. Robert Smith McColl, otherwise known as 'Toffee Bob' scored all six goals. By 1910 McColl was already established as one of the early greats of Scottish football. Known as the 'prince of centre-forwards', McColl possessed great speed, courage and above all else, ruthless finishing. He had made his debut for Queen's Park aged 17 and was a Scottish internationalist at 19, when he made his debut in March 1896. He scored three hat-tricks in his first five internationals including one in the 4-1 win over England in April 1900. He had signed professional terms with Newcastle United (1902-05) and then with Rangers (1905-07). He was re-instated as an amateur with Queen's Park in 1907 when he asked to return to the club to finish his career. McColl later set up a newsagents business with his brother Tom, under his name RS McColl, which survives to this day. The game in the first half was much more evenly contested than the eventual final scoreline suggests. The visitors competed well but lacked a cutting thrust near goal and were seldom dangerous. Queen's Park led 3-0 at half-time with the goals all scored by McColl and all finely taken. Port Glasgow Athletic opened the scoring in the second half when McCreadie beat Burnett to make it 3-1. But the home team continued to dominate and McColl scored three more times, the sixth from the penalty spot after he had been brought down. *The Herald* commented that "without the exception of McColl's great scoring feat the game was without special feature". The match represented the last game of the season for Port Glasgow Athletic who were anchored at the bottom of the table, having lost their last ten games. They had accumulated just 11 points and three wins – one of those being a 3-0 home win over the amateurs.

At the Scottish Football League's AGM held on the 7th June Port Glasgow Athletic did not seek re-election, resigning their First Division place and were relegated after eight years in the First Division. Morton were re-elected and Raith Rovers were finally voted in on their fifth consecutive attempt to join. Port Glasgow only played a single season in the Scottish Second Division, finishing eighth in a 12 team division and only coming three points ahead of Vale of Leven who finished bottom. The 1910-11 season would prove to be their last in the Scottish Football League as facing severe financial difficulties they resigned their membership.

They started life back in the Second Division losing 2-0 away at newly merged Ayr United. The following Saturday they won their opening home game 2-0 against Dumbarton. The following month they beat Cowdenbeath 5-1 and they won three games in a row in October to go level at the top on points with St Bernard's. They then lost three in a row, but a 1-0 win away against St Bernard's in mid-November lifted them back up to second place, behind new leaders Albion Rovers. The top two met at Clune Park the following Saturday and Port won 3-1. However, they then failed to win another game in 1910 (five matches) and dropped out of the promotion race.

On the 18th February 1911 they played their last home game, a 2-1 loss against Leith Athletic. Their opponents scored first and Cross got an equaliser but Leith won it in the second half. Only 300 spectators watched the game, an attendance described as "miserable" by *The Scotsman*. After a gap of a month the club played what would be their last ever Scottish League game on the 18th March, losing 4-1 against Dundee Hibernian in wintry conditions. Dunnian scored a first half hat-trick for the hosts. Cross scored their last ever SFL goal. The club finished tied in eighth place on 19 points with three other clubs (Arthurlie, Abercorn and Dundee Hibernian); three points ahead of bottom club Vale of Leven.

In a sign of things to come three players lodged complaints against the club for arrears off wages. The club was ordered to pay by the 28th March or face suspension. At a meeting of the SFA on the 11th April 1911 the club was duly suspended from the Association after they failed to clear the arrears. On the 30th May the suspension was lifted by the SFA after the complainants withdrew their application for arrears of wages. At the Scottish Football League's AGM on the 5th June Port Glasgow Athletic formally resigned due to their precarious financial position. They were replaced by St Johnstone who were the only club applying for the vacancy.

Port Glasgow left the League and joined the non-League Scottish Union for the 1911-12 season only. They continued to face severe financial difficulties and were wound up in 1912. Clune Park was then taken over by Port Glasgow Athletic Juniors. It was subsequently redeveloped into housing and one of the roads is called Clune Park Street.

SEASON	LEAGUE	P	W	D	L	F	A	P		POS
1893-94	SCOT-2	18	9	2	7	52	53	13	*	6/10
1894-95	SCOT-2	18	8	4	6	62	56	20		3/10
1895-96	SCOT-2	18	6	4	8	40	41	16		7/10
1896-97	SCOT-2	18	4	5	9	39	50	13		8/10
1897-98	SCOT-2	18	12	1	5	66	35	25		2/10
1898-99	SCOT-2	18	12	1	5	75	51	25		3/10
1899-00	SCOT-2	18	10	0	8	50	41	20		3/10
1900-01	SCOT-2	18	9	1	8	45	44	19		5/10
1901-02	SCOT-2	22	14	4	4	71	31	32		1/12
1902-03	SCOT-1	22	3	5	14	26	49	11		11/12
1903-04	SCOT-1	26	8	4	14	32	49	20		9/14
1904-05	SCOT-1	26	8	5	13	30	51	21		11/14
1905-06	SCOT-1	30	6	8	16	38	68	20		15/16
1906-07	SCOT-1	34	7	7	20	30	67	21		18/18
1907-08	SCOT-1	34	5	7	22	39	98	17		18/18
1908-09	SCOT-1	34	10	8	16	39	52	28		13/18
1909-10	SCOT-1	34	3	5	26	25	95	11		18/18
1910-11	SCOT-2	22	8	3	11	27	32	19		8/12

* Points deducted

Renton

Formed: 1872
Colours: Dark blue shirts and shorts.
Ground: Tontine Park
Entered League: 1890. Founder members of the Scottish Football League
Number of League Seasons: 6
Highest League Finish: 7th in Division One
Honours: Scottish Cup Winners 1884-85, 1887-88
Left League: 1897 Resigned. 1922 Dissolved

The small village of Renton lies midway between Dumbarton and Alexandria. It takes its name from Cecilia Renton, daughter-in-law of Tobias Smollett, a famous writer (1721-1771), after which the planned model village was named in 1762. His picturesque novels including 'The Adventures of Roderick Random' (1748) inspired future authors such as Charles Dickens. His face is one of 16 depicted on the Scott Monument in Edinburgh.

The team from this village in West Dunbartonshire competed in the first Scottish Cup, won the trophy twice and produced over a dozen internationals and became the first World Club Champions. And yet, despite being founder members of the Scottish Football League, Renton were out of the League before the 20th century came around and out of existence by 1922.

Vale of Leven FC were founded in August 1872 and Renton followed a few months later, the two sides developing a fierce local rivalry. Renton were the first of the two sides to reach the Scottish Cup Final, in 1875, but the Vale developed the early ascendancy and local bragging rights when they won the Scottish Cup three years in succession in the late 1870s. From 1878 Renton played their home games at Tontine Park, which was located near to the River Leven, to the south of the village and opposite the Dalquhurn Dye Works.

Renton were a prominent team in the early history of Scottish football. They were a two-time winner of the Scottish Cup prior to League formation and reached the Final on three further occasions (the last time as a Second Division club). One of the early powerhouses of Scottish football Renton were one of the eleven founder members of the Scottish Football League in 1890, but they were expelled soon after for breaching the regulations against professionalism. They returned to the League in 1891, but struggled financially and resigned in 1897 after further brushes with the footballing authorities. They continued to play in minor senior leagues before folding in 1922.

As one of Scotland's oldest football clubs Renton featured in the first ever Scottish Cup and in the first day of fixtures played on the 18th October 1873. Renton faced Kilmarnock on neutral territory at Crosshill, Glasgow, winning the game 2–0. As this was the first of three games to kick off in the Cup that day, this is believed to be the very first official competitive football match to take place in Scotland. Renton went on to reach the Semi-final, losing to eventual winners Queen's Park 2-0. The Renton team for the Semi-final against Queen's Park, played on the 13th December 1873 was: Turnbull, J Kennedy, Mackay, Campbell, McCrimmond, Brown, Melville, Glen, F Kennedy, McCrae and Dinwoodie.

The following season they went one step further, reaching the Final, but again lost to Queen's Park, this time by 3–0, all of the goals coming in the last fifteen minutes. This was the first of five times they would achieve that feat. They reached the Final after beating Dunbartonshire rivals Dumbarton 1-0 in the Semi-final, after a replay. On Saturday the 10th April 1875 they met the holders Queen's Park at Hampden Park, watched by a crowd of 7,000. With the wind in their favour Renton had the better of the first half but the Queen's Park defence could not be breached and the teams changed ends goalless. Now with the wind behind them the holders began to exert their own pressure on the Renton backs and after a succession of corners they eventually broke through. Turnbull in the Renton goal was eventually beaten by Angus MacKinnon with just fifteen minutes remaining. Renton's heads dropped whilst the tails were up for their opponents who ran in two further goals before the close, scored by Tom Highet and Billy McKinnon. *The Scotsman* provided a full report on the game, reporting that "the day was fine, the ground in excellent order, and a very large number of spectators witnessed the match. The team took the field at a quarter to four. The Renton had a decided advantage in point of weight. The Renton captain won the toss, and elected to play with the advantage of a slight breeze, although this was counteracted to some extent by having to play with the sun in their faces. During the first half of the game no goals were taken by either side, although Renton had rather the best of the play. A change of ends at half-time gave the wind to the Queen's Park and they at once took the ball up to their opponents' territory. They made no score, however, until within a quarter of an hour from time, when a corner kick by Weir landed the ball in front of the Renton goal, and McKinnon played it through. Five minutes only elapsed when another goal was placed to the credit of the home team, the ball being dribbled by McNeill and passed to Highet, who put it through. A third was taken shortly before time from a fine shot by McKinnon. The match all through was an exceptionally rough one; charging, which seems to be the speciality of the Renton men, being indulged in to a great extent. For the Queen's Park, the most prominent were Taylor and Phillips as backs, and Highet, A MacKinnon and N McKinnon as forwards; while Kennedy, a back, and Brown and McCrae as forwards, worked hard for the other side." The *Glasgow Herald* were quite scathing of Renton's play, observing that "we would counsel the members of the Renton Club to learn the art of dribbling. They seemed to have little acquaintance with it at present, their style being more appropriate in Rugby, than in Association play." The Renton cup-final team was: Turnbull; J Kennedy, McKay; Scullion, McGregor, Melville; MacRae, M Kennedy, J Brown, Glen and L Brown.

In the 1875-76 season Renton made a Second Round exit at arch rivals Vale of Leven and things got worse the following year when they were knocked out by Dumbarton in the First Round. In the 1877-78 season though they reached the Semi-final for the third time, losing to Third Lanark, but only after three matches. Rivals Vale of Leven retained the trophy and went on to win it for a third successive season whereas Renton were humiliated 6-1 at home by Dumbarton in the Second Round. In these times the early rounds were regional affairs and Renton came a cropper against Dumbarton the following season, losing 5-0 in the Third Round. Vale of Leven accounted for them in the 1880-81 competition, and they scratched from the competition the following year.

In the 1882-83 season Renton reached the Fourth Round and along the way recorded a 14-1 victory. They beat Southfield, a pit village near Slamannan, Falkirk on the 30th September 1882. They played away and the *Glasgow Herald* described the scene, saying "the ground was of the most primitive description, there being neither touch line nor ropes. The Renton soon made themselves at home, and the forwards, all playing a passing game, were always in the Southfield ground. They scored 6 goals in the first and 8 in the second half." Renton were surprisingly knocked out at home, 5-3 by Lugar Boswell of Cumnock, Ayrshire at the next stage.

Although Renton knocked out Dumbarton in the First Round of the 1883-84 competition, and followed this up by thrashing King's Park of Stirling 6-1 in the next round, they came up against their old adversaries Vale of Leven in the Third Round and were knocked out 4-1. The *Glasgow Herald* provided a very succinct report, saying that "the game was rough but well contested. The ground was in bad order, the turnout of spectators very numerous, and great interest was manifested in the game."

Renton lifted the Scottish Cup for the first time in 1885, beating local rivals Vale of Leven in the Final, which no doubt made the triumph somewhat sweeter. In the early rounds they registered some big wins. On the 4th October 1884, in a Second Round tie, they beat East Stirlingshire 10-2 away from home, having previously accounted for Vale of Leven Wanderers in the First Round. In the Third Round they beat Glasgow Northern 9-2. This game was evenly matched at the beginning and Renton twice had to come from behind to level, but during the remainder of the game Renton dominated. The big shock of the day though was Battlefield of Glasgow knocking out Queen's Park 3-2.

At the Quarter-final stage they drew Rangers. The game was played on the 27th December and Renton raced into a two goal lead. Rangers came back into the game and pulled one back after thirty minutes and then equalised just on half-time. In the second half Rangers picked up where they left off and went ahead for the first time in the match. Their lead was short lived though as Renton soon equalised. Towards the end Renton added two more goals to win 5-3.

At this time Semi-Finals weren't played on neutral grounds and they were drawn away at Hibernian and travelled through to Easter Road on the 24th January 1885. Hibs scored first, but then Thomson made it 1-1. Hibs retook the lead before McIntyre equalised for a second time, and the two sides went in level at the break. Renton scored the only goal of the second half. Prior to this Hibs claimed a goal but this was ruled out and Hibs protested. Renton's goal was also protested by Hibs, claiming handball. After the match Hibernian registered a formal protest which was heard at the SFA Meeting on the 10th February, but this was dismissed, and Renton were through to their second Scottish Cup Final. Vale of Leven, their local rivals were their opponents and were in the final for the sixth time, having won it already on three occasions. The *Glasgow Herald* noted that "the final game has invariably been played between Glasgow clubs or Glasgow and provincial clubs, and this is only the second occasion in the history of the Cup that two outside elevens took part in the final." Two year's previously Dumbarton had beaten Vale of Leven in a replayed Final.

The Final was played on the 21st February 1885, the first final at the second Hampden Park. Unfortunately the game didn't live up to expectations, no doubt affected by a hard pitch and a cold day with a strong wind. The very cold and blustery conditions were not conducive to a game of football, the *Glasgow Herald* commenting that "to players and spectators alike the day was disagreeable. The ground was hard and slippery. This made running a matter of some difficulty, not unattended with danger, while a strong wind carried the ball high over the cross-bar, and rendered futile all attempts at scoring. A fine exhibition of the 'dribbling game' was therefore out of the question" and that "the result met with the approbation of all neutral parties, as the capabilities of neither side were fairly tested." The game ended 0-0 with little goal mouth action. In the first half Vale were required to defend, Renton having the best of the play and on one occasion the ball just grazed the post. The second half was a repeat of the first but with the roles reversed, with the Vale on the offensive. "Towards the close it was remarked that a win by either side could only be regarded in the light of a fluke, and a draw appeared to be the fairest termination of the game."

The replay was staged a week later and was a bad tempered affair. The tone was set early on by an injury to a Renton forward following a clash with a Vale back that drew blood. After a goalless first half Renton took the lead just after the hour mark and added two more late on before Vale scored a late consolation. Describing the action *The Scotsman* reported that "at Hampden Park, these teams met again in the final tie for the Challenge Cup. There were between five and six thousand spectators, fully a third of who, had come from Dumbarton and the Vale of Leven. In the first half of the game, the ball being kicked off by the Vale, no goal was taken by either side, though Renton, playing fast and loose, signally failed to take advantage of several good opportunities to shoot between their opponents' sticks. After seventeen minutes play in the second half, Renton got the first goal, taken by McCall, and within ten minutes of time they scored two more goals, both shot by McIntyre, while the Vale managed to get one in the course of a scrimmage. Renton thus won the cup by three goals to one, this being the first time they have been successful." Renton's Scottish Cup winning team was: John Lindsay: Andrew Hannah, Archibald McCall: Bob Kelso, Donald McKechnie; Alexander Barbour; James Kelly, Andrew McIntyre, James McCall, A Grant, and J Thomson.

Renton FC produced a number of famous players and the club had over a dozen players capped for Scotland. The first of these were Bob Kelso and Alexander Barbour, who were both capped a month after winning the Scottish Cup, playing for Scotland on the 14th March 1885 against Ireland at Hampden. Scotland won 8-2 and Barbour scored the sixth goal just after half-time. Barbour was a powerful centre forward and his career peaked in 1885 when he won his single Scotland cap as well as winning the Scottish Cup. He also appeared in the Cup final team the following year and subsequently moved to Bolton Wanderers in May 1888. Robert "Bob" Kelso was capped seven times for Scotland (six as a Renton player) between 1885 and 1898. There was a ten year gap between his sixth and final cap. He won two Scottish Cups with Renton and appeared in the 1886 final as well. He joined Newcastle United in July 1888 and a year later Preston North End where he won the League title and then played for Everton before returning to Scotland with Dundee. Whilst there he captained Scotland in his final international appearance in 1898, a 3-0 win over Ireland on the 26th March.

Renton made a fine defence of the Scottish Cup and reached the Final but once again this ended in defeat against Queen's Park. In the First Round they beat Kirkintilloch

Athletic 15-0 on the 12th September 1885 in a match played at Townhead Park, Kirkintilloch, and in the Second Round they beat Dumbarton Athletic 7-2 away. In the Fifth Round Renton renewed their acquaintance with local rivals Vale of Leven. Renton knocked them out after a replay at Alexandria, the first game ending 2-2 at Renton. In the replay, after chances for both sides and end to end action Renton took the lead after 18 minutes. In the second half a poor goal kick by Wilson led directly to a second goal for Renton. Seven minutes from the end Renton scored a third which was hotly disputed by the Vale, with Renton winning 3-0.

In the Quarter-finals Renton received a bye, and in a repeat of last year's Semi-final they were drawn against Hibernian. The match was played on the 23rd January 1886, *The Scotsman* commenting that "last year, it may be remembered, the Renton, with identically the same team, threw out the crack Eastern Club, and in the final, carried off the cup. That this was no fluke the consistent form the Dumbartonshire men have since shown, amply testifies. On the present occasion, the Hibernians, who now got the opportunity they had longed for, were slightly the favourites owing to the heavy state of the ground and their playing at home....however, the wearers of the green were fairly beaten, though it must be added they had one or two bits of hard luck, and Renton repeated their last year's victory, leaving the field winners by two goals to nil." Renton scored two first half goals in quick succession, first through McIntyre and then Thomson.

The Cup holders came up against seven time winners Queen's Park in the Final, played on the 13th February 1886. The *Glasgow Herald* covered the match, reporting that "the scene during the earlier part of the game was one of the most miserable ever experienced by devotees of the sport. Not only did the rain fall in torrents, but it was driven before the wind right in among the unhappy mortals who were around the ropes, while the ground was very soft." Queen's, as the premier team and favourites dominated the play and hit the post and had another couple of good chances. From a corner kick they eventually took the lead. Barbour then had Renton's best opportunity of the half. Play was now much more even and both goalkeepers were called upon to make saves but there was no further scoring and the half ended with their opponents leading 1-0. At the start of the second half "the Renton men showed up well for some time and soon equalised matters, to the great delight of their partisans, of whom a large number were present." During the last half an hour the pace of play quickened as both sides chased the winner. Their illustrious opponents finally got the upper hand and scored two goals to win 3-1 to lift the trophy for the eighth time. Renton's Cup final line up was: Lindsay; Hannah, A McCall; Kelso, McKechnie; Thomson, Grant, Barbour, J McCall, H McIntyre and Kelly.

In the 1886-87 season Renton competed in both the Scottish and English FA Cups, exiting both at the Third Round stage. They were knocked out of the Scottish Cup by Third Lanark by three goals to one on the 23rd October 1886 and a week later beat Accrington Stanley 1-0 in the First Round of the English FA Cup. In the early stages of this game Accrington claimed a goal but the referee ruled it out. Then, in a blow to Renton, McIntyre went off injured and they had to do without his services for the rest of the match. Renton had a rare foray forward just before the interval but Barbour missed a good chance. Play was even in the second half but few chances were created and the game looked destined for a draw. Ten minutes from time McCall produced a pin point accurate corner which was headed towards goal by McNee and prodded home by Campbell to give Renton a 1-0 victory. Queen's Park, Hearts and Rangers also played that day in the FA Cup, only the latter progressing to the Second Round.

Renton overcame holders Blackburn Rovers in the next round. After a 2-2 draw at Tontine Park they travelled to Ewood Park and recorded a 2-0 upset. The tie was played on the 4th December and *The Times* reported that "several ties in the Association Challenge Cup were played off on Saturday, among which was the undecided match in the second round between the Blackburn Rovers (holders) and the powerful Renton team from Scotland. It will be remembered that the clubs met some time ago, and, after playing for two hours, left the field with the scores equal. Last Saturday the teams met again at Blackburn. Considerable interest was manifested, and about 6,000 witnessed the game. Both teams played vigorously, but at half-time nothing had been scored. Afterwards Renton got the better of the play as defeated their opponents by two goals to none." The goals were scored by McNee and Campbell. Their run in the English FA Cup came to an end when they fell 2-0 to eventual semi-finalists Preston North End.

Renton won the Scottish Cup for the second time in the 1887-88 season and in doing so recorded the biggest win in the Final in the history of the competition, beating Cambuslang 6-1. This feat has never been broken, but has been matched in by Celtic in the 1971-72 season when they beat Hibernian. Renton beat two Dumbarton teams, Union and Athletic in the first two rounds, beating the former 6-0, before thrashing Camelon 8-0 in the Third Round. In the Fourth Round they racked up a massive score, beating Lindertis of Kirriemuir 13-1 away. The scoreline was much closer in the next round when they beat St Mirren 3-2 away to set up a Quarter-final with Dundee Wanderers.

Renton had home advantage for the tie but conceded early. However, they recovered to lead 2-1 at the break and scored two goals early on in the second half and ran out comfortable 5-1 winners. Renton got the toughest opponents in the Semi-final when they were drawn to play Queen's Park but they had did have home advantage. They got their tactics spot on as they stifled their opponents and counter attacked swiftly to win 3-1 with Queen's Park only scoring near to the close of time. According to the *Glasgow Herald* their dominance was down to "the superior tackling powers of the Renton, combined with the speed which they showed when they got on the ball." Cambuslang beat Abercorn in the other tie after a replay and the two sides contested the final on the 4th February 1888.

There was no sign of what was to follow as with the wind behind them in the first half Cambuslang made most of the early running, and John Lindsay in the Renton goal made a number of fine saves. A rare attack from Renton led to a goalmouth scramble in which John McNee poked the ball home to open the scoring. Renton were now on top and having forced a series of corners doubled their lead when Neil McCallum slotted home. Cambuslang though hit back just before half-time to make it 2-1 at the break. With the advantage of the wind now in their favour Renton dominated the second half and James McCall got on the scoresheet with a low, hard drive and after a brief spell of possession from their opponents McCallum made it 4-1. McCall made it five and a few minutes later McNee completed the scoring to give Renton a 6-1 victory.

Providing a full match summary *The Scotsman* reported that "these clubs, having beaten all their previous opponents in the ties for the Scottish Football Association Cup, met on the ground of the Queen's Park Cup at Hampden Park to decide who would have the honour of holding the trophy for the season 1887-88. In anticipation of a good game there was an enormous attendance, it being computed that over 10000 spectators witnessed the match. The weather, though showery, did not interfere much with the play, while the ground was in fair trim. After the opposing teams had been photographed, they faced each other amid cheers. The game at the opening looked as if it would prove to be a close one, but such did not turn out to be the case, Renton in the second half holding their opponents safe, and ultimately winning by six goals to one - the largest score yet put on in a final tie for the Scottish Cup. Renton lost the toss, and J Campbell kicked off with the wind against his team. After a few minutes' play a foul was given against Renton close on the goal line, which, however, was unproductive. Cambuslang keeping up the attack several times gave the Renton backs some trouble. Ultimately J McCall put in a splendid run for Renton, which relieved the pressure. The relief, however, was only momentary, Plenderleith, the Cambuslang centre, dribbled the ball right to the goal. The shot, however, was cleverly saved by Lindsay. Immediately afterwards Lindsay was called upon again to save a shot from Gourlay. Campbell then put in a magnificent run for Renton, his final effort just grazing the uprights. Renton keeping up the pressure, kept the Cambuslang backs busy, Cambuslang, however, by superior forward play, retaliated for some time, Hannah and

McCall having all their work to keep their citadel intact. In turn Renton gave Dunn some bother, several shots being sent in which he cleared promptly and successfully. Give and take play followed, the ball travelling quickly from goal to goal; but it was some time till Renton, who were showing the better play, scored from McNee. Nothing daunted, Cambuslang worked with great energy, Lindsay, the Renton goalkeeper, being repeatedly called upon to put the ball out of danger, which he did magnificently. Several throws in helped the Renton considerably - Kelso in particular being prominent. The Cambuslang backs saved in good style, and for several minutes the play was of a desultory character. Proceedings were enlivened by a well-executed run by McNee for Renton, which after skilful manoeuvring forced Buchanan to give a corner. Although this came to nothing it was followed by a second and third, the upshot of the last being that McCallum notched the second goal for Renton. From this up to half-time, Cambuslang had if anything the advantage. Buchanan, junior, experienced hard lines, a beautiful shot from him just going past the upright. Eventually, almost on the call of half-time, Cambuslang scored by Gourlay, Renton thus crossing over leading 2 goals to 1. After the usual interval, Renton now having the advantage of the wind, at once asserted their supremacy, McCall scoring within a couple of minutes of the kick-off. On the ball being started from the centre, Cambuslang obtained a free kick from a foul in front of the Renton goal, but the place came to nothing. For a few minutes the Renton goalkeeper had a warm time of it, shots being sent into him with lightning like rapidity. The scene of operations was changed to the other end, where a shot from Gourlay just missed taking effect...Lively played followed, the respective teams doing their best. Renton especially strove hard to increase their score, while the Cambuslang, on the other hand, worked hard to make matter on a level footing...Renton by superior play put on a further point, McCallum fairly beating Dunn. The Renton after this had matters pretty much their own way, McCall adding another goal to their credit a few minutes later. This was quickly followed by another from McNee. Cambuslang completely collapsed at this stage, the remainder of the game being fought out on their territory. The whistle sounded with the score: - Renton, six goals; Cambuslang, one goal."

The same paper also reported on the team's triumphant return home commenting that "the victors' reception at Renton on Saturday night eclipsed any welcome previously accorded them. Early in the evening a huge bonfire was kindled on Carman Hill [an ancient Hill fort and landmark], which continued blazing for several hours. A waggonette was brought from Dumbarton to await the 9:40 train, fog signals were placed on the rails, and amidst the cracking of these, the display of fireworks, and the shouts of several thousands of spectators, the heroes were lifted into the waggonette, and preceded by the Renton band, were drawn by willing enthusiasts through the streets of the village. A short visit was made to Cordale House to receive the congratulations of their honorary president, Mr A Wylie, after which they were

587

entertained for a short time by some of their supporters." The team that won the Scottish Cup for the second time, and by a record score was: John Lindsay, Andrew Hannah, Archibald McCall, Bob Kelso, James Kelly, Donald McKechnie, Neil McCallum, Harry Campbell, John Middleton Campbell, John McNee and James McCall.

A month after the Scottish Cup Final four Renton players featured in the Scotland line-up to play England. John Lindsay made his debut in goal, James Kelly also made his debut and also in the team were Bob Kelso and James McCall. Unfortunately Scotland lost for the first time since 1879 and the 5-0 loss was also the first Scotland defeat at home. A week later Archibald McCall and Neil McCallum were also capped for Scotland, this time against Ireland.

Three months after their second Scottish Cup triumph, Renton played the English FA Cup holders West Bromwich Albion in a famous friendly challenge match billed as being for the "Championship of the United Kingdom and the World". When Renton won, organised football competitions around the world were rare, almost exclusively played by Scottish and English clubs. It was a World Cup Championship by default. Nevertheless that didn't stop the club proudly displaying a "Champions of the World" sign on the pavilion at Tontine Park. The match took place on the 19th May 1888 and the *Glasgow Herald* reported that "the weather was of the most wretched description, and the game had to be stopped on two or three occasions owing to the thunderstorm...it was next to impossible to play anything approaching football under such conditions." Renton had the best of the early exchanges but Albion grew into the game and Lindsay was called upon to make a couple of fine saves. After 25 minutes McCallum had the ball in the net for Renton but was clearly offside and the effort was disallowed. Continuing its' match report, the *Herald* noted that "the village boys did not seem the least disconcerted by the thunder and rain, and after hemming in the Englishmen, little McNee, with a cross shot, beat Big Roberts, thus scoring the first goal of the match for Renton amidst tremendous cheering. The thunderstorm became worse, and the rain poured down most unmercifully, necessitating a stoppage of the game 16 minutes from half-time. After a short interval the rain cleared away, and the game was restarted. The ground by this time was covered with water in some places, and the rain coming on again play was rendered almost impossible. Still Renton kept pegging away, and made the best of the adverse circumstances. It was only occasionally that the Albion could break away, and then the good defence of the village boys rendered their efforts of no avail."

At half-time Renton led 1-0 and due to the earlier interruption the second half was started without the two teams leaving the field. Soon after the restart West Brom ran the length of the pitch and scored "the softest goal ever witnessed on a football field."

Rain again began to fall heavily and the game was stopped for a few minutes. On resuming Renton were unlucky not to restore their lead as they struck the crossbar. "Not withstanding the heavy rain, Renton continued to have the best of it, and McNee beat Roberts for the second time, thus placing his team in the ascendancy by two goals to one. Some time afterwards McCall beat Roberts for the third time, amidst loud cheering." Renton now had the upper hand and Harry Campbell added a fourth near the end, as Renton won "a game that was without parallel in the history of football" 4-1 to earn the accolade of world club champions. The Renton team that day was: John Lindsay; Andrew Hannah, Archie McCall (Captain); Bob Kelso, James Kelly, Donald McKechnie; Henry Campbell, James McCall, John Middleton Campbell, Neil McCallum and John McNee.

However, the club's success had its drawbacks. The win alerted clubs from both Scotland and England to the talent at Renton and a number of players took up invitations to play elsewhere. A number of payers went to ply their trade in England and James Kelly and Neilly McCallum joined the newly formed Celtic. When the club kicked off in the Scottish Football League in August 1890 only the brothers McCall remained. Goalkeeper John Lindsay left the club in 1889 to play for Accrington Stanley but returned in 1891 and earned two more Scotland caps in 1893 when back at the club. Andrew Hannah, a right-back, was the skipper of the team and had three spells at Tontine Park. West Brom were so impressed with him after the World Champions match that they signed him but he returned homesick. He then joined Everton where he won a League championship medal in 1890-91 before again returning to Renton. Next he went to Liverpool, reuniting with former Everton manager William Barclay. Hannah played in Liverpool's first-ever League match and won the Second Division title with the club also earning the distinction of being the first man to captain both of the Merseyside teams. He was capped for Scotland on the 10th March 1888, in a 5-1 victory over Wales at Easter Road. Archibald "Archie" McCall, who, like his younger brother, James, stayed with Renton, had been capped for Scotland on the 24th March 1888 in a 10-2 win over Ireland. Younger brother James, an elegant inside-right, resisted all contract offers from a queue of English clubs. He was capped five times for Scotland and scored twice. He had scored on his debut on the 10th April 1886 in a 4-1 win over Wales. He also scored in March 1887 in a 3-2 away win against England, scoring the opening goal in Blackburn. He made his last appearance for his country in April 1890 in a 1-1 home draw with England. James Kelly was a mobile centre-half who joined the fledging Celtic in July 1888, making over 100 appearances for the Hoops, and who went on to be both club captain and then later chairman. Having made his international debut in March 1888 as a Renton player he was capped eight times in total. He scored on his fifth appearance in a 6-1 win over Ireland in March 1893. Donald McKechnie was a subtle left-half and one of a few players without an international cap. Already in his late twenties he went on to play the 1889 season at least in part at Newcastle West End but quickly returned, seemingly giving up football. Henry "Harry" Campbell went to Blackburn Rovers in June 1889. He was capped once while at Renton, on the 15th April 1889 away against Wales. John "Johnnie" Middleton Campbell, a 19 year old forward, was signed by Sunderland in June 1889 and went on to win 3 League championships with then, and scored in the 1895 World Club Championship between Sunderland and Hearts. Cornelius "Neilly" McCallum joined Celtic in June 1888 after the Cup final and World Champions game and is credited with scoring their first ever competitive goal. He later played for Blackburn Rovers and both Nottingham Forest and Notts County. He was capped for Scotland in March 1888, scoring the eighth goal in the 10-2 win over Ireland. John "Jack" McNee was a diminutive right-winger, and another player never to be capped. He also moved to England and joined Bolton Wanderers in 1889 and subsequently played for Newcastle United and Watford.

Renton made another fine defence of their trophy in the 1888-89, going all the way to the Semi-Finals before losing to the eventual winners Third Lanark. In the First Round, on the 1st September 1888 they beat Bowling 8-0, the visitors collapsing in the second half conceding six goals. Three weeks later they recorded another big win, beating Vale of Wanderers 10-2 at Alexandria. In the first fifteen minutes Wanderers made several attacks but Renton gradually asserted themselves and Harvey opened the scoring. Two more goals followed before half-time. However, the Wanderers kept going and scored two goals of their own in quick succession to set up an interesting second half. The *Glasgow Herald* reported that "in the second half Renton showed something like their well-known form, and although the Wanderers played with determination, still they wanted stamina for a prolonged campaign, and soon Renton piled up their score rapidly and gave their opponents a crushing defeat."

In the next round they had a fresh encounter with Cambuslang. Johnnie Campbell scored after an even first 30 minutes but an own goal made it 1-1 at half-time. Renton dominated the second half and scored three goals to win 4-1. In the next round they were drawn away to Lanemark, of New Cumnock, Ayrshire. The tie was played at Connel Park, South Boag and Renton scored after just two minutes from a corner. Their hosts then came close themselves but after 20 minutes Campbell increased their lead. Three minutes later McNee added another and a fourth was scored before half-time. Renton doubled their score in the second half winning 8-0.

The Cup run continued with Renton knocking out Arbroath, after a replay and then Dumbarton Athletic in the Quarter-finals. This set up a Semi-final away against Third Lanark at their Cathkin Park ground on the 12th January 1889. The first half's play was very even with the *Glasgow Herald* commenting that both sides were "playing in capital style, and it was quite evident the men had been trained to the hour." Thirds took the lead after 35 minutes when Marshall fed Oswald who shot past Lindsay and at the break their hosts led 1-0. Third Lanark scored a second within a minute of the restart, Hannah heading in. "The Volunteers were playing with great go and dash, but two goals up no doubt gave them great confidence." Thirds scored again but it was ruled offside and Renton then missed chances through Johnny Campbell and James McCall, both hitting their shots over the crossbar when well set. Continuing the *Glasgow Herald* noted that "the Renton men were simply outwitted...surpassed in their passing...and met with a stubborn defence." Towards the end Lindsay prevented Thirds increasing their score and the match ended in a 2-0 win for Third Lanark.

The following season Renton made an early exit at the hands of Dumbarton. Renton were keen to secure a guaranteed set of fixtures, and income, and were catalysts for the creation of the Scottish Football League. It was Peter Fairly, secretary of the club, who wrote to the representatives of twelve leading Scottish clubs requesting a meeting on the 20th March 1890 at 7.30 p.m. at Holton's Commercial Hotel in Glassford Street in Glasgow to consider the question of organising League matches in Scotland and the Scottish Football League was officially formed a month later on the 30th April and formally constituted at the beginning of June.

Dunbartonshire was a hotbed of the game in the early years of organised football in Scotland, with the county's three leading clubs of the era, Renton, Vale of Leven and Dumbarton all joining the SFL as founder members. However, Renton were soon expelled for breaching rules against professionalism and the League, which had started with eleven clubs was reduced to ten.

Things kicked off normally on the 16th August 1890, with Renton unexpectedly winning 4-1 at Celtic in front of 8,000 at Parkhead. *The Scotsman* reported that "Renton surprised everybody with their dash and the perfection of their combination. The Celts' defence was severely tested, and frequently nonplussed...and were baffled and chagrined beyond measure at the non-success of their efforts." The Renton goals came from Cameron, James McCall and James Brown before Hugh Gallacher pulled one back for the hosts before half-time. Renton eventually added a fourth in the 83rd minute and their first ever League line-up was: Gow; McLean, Campbell; Brown, Gardner, McNair; Hendry, Duncan, McArthur, James McCall and Cameron.

Renton failed to capitalise on this good start, only picking up one more point in the next four games. They drew 2-2 at St Mirren before losing 4-1 at Rangers and 4-2 at Abercorn. The last of these matches was a 2-1 home defeat against local rivals Vale of

Leven on 20th September 1890, before a poor crowd of only 1,500. A misunderstanding amongst the backs for Vale was capitalised on by McCall who opened the scoring after ten minutes. Vale then had a number of chances but Gow saved well until five minutes before the break when Vale equalised. Vale carried over their ascendancy into the start of the second period and took the lead after five more minutes play. Renton responded well but couldn't create any clear cut chances and Vale edged a keenly fought contest 2-1.

In between these League games Renton suffered a shock Scottish Cup exit at the hands of Kilsyth Rangers. This match, held on the 6th September 1890, was played at Garrel Garden Park and the *Glasgow Herald* reported that "a large concourse of spectators was present, and the two teams started in great spirit. The Wanderers in particular made a gallant fight, and during the first half scored two goals to their opponents' one. The second half showed some splendid play, Renton playing with great determination, and making a game effort to turn the tables. They repeatedly got the ball into close quarters, but the Wanderers with great pluck always repulsed them." On the 16th September Renton lodged two protests. The first, on account of the encroachment of spectators onto the pitch was dismissed on a technicality because the protest was not lodged on the day of the game. The second, that Kilsyth had been assisted by a player under an assumed name, was withdrawn at the meeting. Renton had suffered a serious blow to both pride and finances in this First Round Scottish Cup exit and worse was to follow. The club's first experience of League competition was to be cut short a month into the 1890–91 season when they were suspended from all football by the SFA for playing a friendly against a team billed as "Edinburgh Saints". This was, in reality, a thinly disguised St Bernard's, who had themselves been suspended following allegations of professionalism.

Before that came an indefinite suspension for James McCall for receiving a Renton benefit match. The SFA, regulating the League and perhaps resentful of Renton's role in forcing it upon them, implemented the rule which stated that only players who were retiring could receive benefits. On the 27th September Renton played a side called "Edinburgh Saints" in a hastily arranged home friendly. Few doubted this was a thin disguise for the St Bernard's team, who had already been outlawed over allegations of payments to players. The SFA ruled that the Edinburgh Saints were to all intents and purposes the same club as the St Bernard's and ruled that they couldn't play during the term of their suspension. However, Renton, expressing some sympathy for the plight of St Bernard's, played the game, *The Scotsman* reporting that "notwithstanding the decision of the Business and Professional Committee of the Scottish Football Association regarding the newly formed Edinburgh Saints, Renton fulfilled their fixture with that club at Renton. It was very doubtful even after the arrival of the Edinburgh team whether the game would be played, as some of the Renton committee, and several members of the teams were strongly against running the risk. The majority, however, were evidently in favour of going on with the game, as both teams played. Davie kicked off for Renton, and the home men at once assumed the aggressive, but a wild shot by Duncan sent the ball high over the bar. The visitors' left wing McMillan and McNab broke away with a fine dashing run, and the former passing the ball over to Williams, that player with a high angular shot scored the first point. Renton played up pluckily, and five minutes afterwards McCall, with a low swift shot put on an equalising point. Both teams strove hard to regain the lead, but the Renton men had fully the best of the play, and before half-time Gardner finished up a really brilliant run by putting on a second point., Davie in the nick of time charging Robertson [the Saints 'keeper] through [the] goal. The second half was but a few minutes old when Davie put on a third point for Renton, and five minutes later the same player added a fourth. The 'Saints' were conspicuously out of the game, and very rarely got within shooting distance of their opponents' goal. Renton, on the other hand, played with a dash and smartness that they have not hitherto approached this season. Before the call of time McNair added a fifth goal for Renton, and in the last moments of the game McNab added a second goal for the Saints. Renton thus won by five goals to two." The Renton team was: Gow; Mclean, Campbell; Brown, Gardner, McNair; Abraham, Duncan, Davie, McCall and Brady.

The *Glasgow Herald* commented that "Renton cannot be said to have gone into this matter blindfolded....Renton's committee were not unanimously in favour of playing, and several players were indisposed....The general opinion in Renton is that a conflict with the SFA is inevitable." Sure enough, on the 30th September 1890 Renton were suspended by the SFA for professionalism, and the club was subsequently expelled from the SFL with their record expunged. They had played five games, won one, drawn one and lost three. Ten goals had been scored, thirteen conceded and they had three points. *The Scotsman,* under the headline "Expulsion of Clubs and Suspension of Players by the Scottish Association" reported that "last evening, a meeting of the Business and Professional Committee of the Scottish Football Association was held in the Rooms, 53 Waterloo Street, Glasgow....In accordance with the constitution and rules number 11, sub-section b, the Renton Club were declared professionals, and expelled from the Association. The Renton Committee were prohibited from taking further part in football affairs in Scotland, and the Renton players who played against the Edinburgh Saints were suspended till 30th April next year. The St Bernard Club were also expelled from the Association, and the players who took part in the match against Renton at Renton last Saturday were suspended till 30th April next." On Wednesday the 1st October a meeting of the Management Committee of the SFL was held in Aitken's Hotel, Glasgow to consider the suspension of Renton by the SFA. It was decided that the League match scheduled for Saturday between Renton and Hearts could not go ahead and Hearts played Dykebar in a friendly match instead.

Renton were raging. In their view they had been summarily banned by the SFA, their League fixtures had been scrapped and their players effectively outlawed, all without a hearing. They therefore took the only action open to them which was to take legal proceedings. Under the headline "The Expulsion of the Renton – Threatened Legal Proceedings" *The Scotsman* reported that "acting on behalf of the Renton Football Club, Messrs Campbell & Mackenzie, solicitors, Glasgow, on Saturday issued written communications to the various league clubs with whom their clients have fixtures threatening that unless these fixtures are fulfilled the Renton club will hold them liable in whatever loss or damage may result. They have, at the same time, communicated with the Scottish Football Association asking that the Renton Club should have an opportunity afforded them of being heard in a general meeting regarding the recent decision of the Professional Committee expelling the club from the Association and suspending the players who played against the Edinburgh Saints until 30th April 1891....Messrs Campbell and MacKenzie...found nothing in the constitution and rules of the Association to justify the action of the committee, but, apart altogether from the merits or demerits of the case in hand, what they took special exception to was that the Committee, or any section of the Football Association, should take upon itself the high responsibility of expelling any club without consulting the whole body....They also took exception to the decision being arrived at without the club being afforded an opportunity of stating a defence to the charges, and they therefore had to ask the Association to convene a meeting of the whole Association to consider the charge or charges preferred against their clients. All their clients desired was that they should be afforded an opportunity of vindicating their position, and they would prefer that that should be done within the Association if at all possible. They believe that a few words of explanation would be sufficient justification, as not a single player who had been suspended could be held responsible, morally or otherwise, for what had taken place. In conclusion, they state that if they did not hear from the Association by Wednesday morning next they would assume that they were not willing to comply with their request to have a general meeting and would act accordingly."

The SFA met on the 7th October and a letter submitted by Messers Campbell & McKenzie solicitors representing Renton, and regarding the club's expulsion was not read - consisting of 35 pages. Instead the matter was referred to a sub-committee, with full powers to defend any action which might be taken against the association or its committees. At the same meeting a letter sent by the Edinburgh Saints was ignored on the grounds that the committee did not know of a club in connection with the SFA.

Faced with no other options Renton took their case to the Court of Session, claiming £5,000 in damages from the SFA over failure to give notice of the move to ban the club, or to provide an opportunity for the club to defend themselves. On the 17th October *The Scotsman* reported that "the Renton Club, with the unanimous consent of its members has brought an action in the Court of Session against the Scottish Football Association to have it declared that its expulsion from the Association was illegal. £5,000 damages will also be sued for. The summons, which was signed today, will be served upon the Association on Monday, and will be lodged in the Court about ten days hence." The amount sued for would be the equivalent of £600,000 today.

There was some sympathy for Renton, especially as the football authorities had been throwing their bureaucratic weight around. Both Cowlairs and Celtic had incurred a four points deduction in the League in that first season for allegedly fielding unregistered players. On the 18th November at an SFA meeting, a protest signed by Dumbarton, Hibs, Celtic, Clyde, Third Lanark, Abercorn, Hearts, St Mirren and Cowlairs (but not Vale of Leven) asking for a reconsideration of the Renton and St Bernard's case was read, and was unanimously dismissed as being extremely injudicious.

The case rumbled on in the courts but signs started to emerge of a negotiated settlement. On the 30th April 1891 the Scottish Football Association Annual Report was published and referenced the legal case: "The lawsuit Renton v. Association...is now pending before the Court of Session. The Association procured the services of three of the leading counsel at the Scottish Bar, and on their advice fought the case out on the preliminary pleas, which were decided against the Association. A very heavy proof on the merits of the case was fixed for July, but as this would entail an enormous outlay, from which, win or lose, the Association could gain nothing, therefore, with a view to save this expenditure, terms of compromise are under negotiation. The committee hope that before this report is submitted the settlement of the case will be 'un fait accompli'."

In reality the SFA had been losing the legal battle and were facing considerable costs when they made the decision to climb down and reinstate Renton, and provide legal costs of an estimated £300 (about £80,000 today). The original £5,000 claim was dropped as a compromise. On Tuesday the 5th May, the settlement was confirmed and the issue debated at the AGM of the SFA. Lots of questions were asked about whether it was worth it and the costs involved.

On Thursday the 21st May 1891 Renton played a friendly to celebrate their reinstatement, and perhaps somewhat provocatively played a match in Edinburgh against St Bernard's of all people. *The Scotsman* reported that "fully 2500 spectators attended at Logie Green last evening to welcome the reappearance of the famous Renton team. The village players brought a capital eleven with them....The Dunbartonshire men were accorded a warm reception on stepping on to the ground...Renton played grandly...and had easily the best of matters throughout. " Renton won the game 2-1 and the team that took to the field was Lindsay; Hannah, A McCall; Devine, MacKay, McBride; Abraham, Harvey, Davie, J McCall and Brady.

At the Scottish League's AGM on the 5th June 1891 Renton were formally reinstated. Cowlairs left the League and Leith Athletic and Clyde were voted in as the First Division expanded to twelve teams. On the 15th August Renton started their restoration to the League with a home game against Rangers, watched by 5,000 at Tontine Park. Reporting on the game, the *Glasgow Herald* said "the first of this season's League fixtures in the Vale of Leven was played on Saturday at Renton, when the home eleven met the Rangers on Tontine Park. This is the first match which the senior Renton team has played at home since their case with the Scottish Football Association was settled. Although comprising several former veterans, there were a good few fresh men in the team who had yet to win their laurels." Renton would prove no match for the joint champions, losing 4-1, McBride scoring their goal and Lindsay in goal keeping the scoreline down. The Renton team was: John Lindsay; Andrew Hannah, McQuilkie; Daniel Devine, George Davie, Jim McBride; John Duncan, John Murray, Abram, James McCall and Joe Brady. Included in their ranks was the returning Andrew Hannah.

Renton got their first win in their next game, 3-2 away at new club Leith Athletic, despite conceding after just 30 seconds. *The Scotsman* reported that "when the teams settled down it was at once observable that the Renton were a fine set of players and likely to uphold the past fame of the club." After sustained pressure James McCall the Renton captain, got them back in terms from the penalty spot. This was a little piece of history as it was the first-ever penalty kick in Scottish League history. *The Scotsman* described the historic moment: "a continual pressure was kept up on the home goal and in a scrimmage near the goal mouth G Anderson fouled the ball. As a result, the new rule was brought into requisition. J McCall, the Renton captain, took the kick and with a well-directed shot sent the ball well out of Burnside's reach, thus placing the teams on terms of equality." George Davie put Renton ahead just before the interval and McCall headed a third. Fine goalkeeping by John Lindsay kept Athletic at bay although they did eventually reduce the deficit.

At the end of August they won 3-0 at home to local rivals Vale of Leven. Vale lost one of their players early one, having to retire owing to an injury to the knee. Playing a man down the Vale were sorely pressed but did well to get to the break with the score goalless. In the second half Renton were awarded a penalty but James McCall's spot kick was saved. They eventually broke through and ran out 3-0 winners. The club settled into mid-table, neither threatening the leaders nor getting into a battle to avoid the re-election places. At the end of the season it was decided to reduce the League back to ten clubs, with the bottom three clubs facing a re-election vote. St Mirren were voted back in, but local rivals Vale of Leven, along with Cambuslang, dropped out of the SFL.

The club had a good run in the Scottish Cup in the 1891-92 season, reaching the Semi-finals, knocking out holders Hearts in the Quarter-Finals after two replays. In the first game, at home, they led 3-1 and then trailed 4-3, before the game ended 4-4. In the replay at Tynecastle they were 2-0 down, but two goals from James McCall, the second a penalty, took it to a third game. This was an ill-tempered game with several players coming to blows near the end. On the 6th February 1892, they met on neutral ground, with Hampden staging the second replay, with a crowd of 14,000. Joe Brady was the hero for Renton scoring a hat-trick in a game which Renton won 3-2. In the Semi-Final they met Queen's Park at Tontine Park and drew 1-1. They lost the replay rather tamely 3-0.

Renton had a much poorer 1892-93 season, finishing two places lower in the League (and in a ten team, rather than a twelve team League), and being in the bottom three faced a re-election vote. They also made a First Round exit in the Scottish Cup at the hands of Abercorn. On the opening day of the new season they lost a seven goal thriller away against champions Celtic. Renton came from 3-1 down to draw level at 3-3. However, Renton subsequently lost a player to injury, both sides had a man sent off and four minutes from time Celtic got the winner.

Renton subsequently won two and drew two of their next matches to sit mid-table including a season's best 4-1 win over Hearts on the 1st October, with two goals from John Murray and one apiece from James McCall and Thomas Towie. They suffered a heavy loss in the Third Round of the Scottish Cup, losing 6-0 at Underwood Park, Paisley against Abercorn on the 26th November 1892. Mathieson missed an early chance for Renton before the home team took the lead. McLeod for Renton had an effort tipped around the post and Renton lay siege to their hosts' goal for a while but no more goals were scored before the interval. On the resumption Abercorn totally dominated and scored three goals in quick succession. Haig, the Renton back, then suffered an injury and had to leave the field. Playing with a man advantage Abercorn scored two more goals before the end.

In February 1893 they avenged their Cup defeat with a 2-1 home win over the men from Paisley to be in sixth place in the table. However, they failed to win any of their remaining matches so that Leith and Dumbarton went above them. These results included a 6-2 loss at Leith and a 4-0 home defeat in the last match against Dumbarton. At the League's AGM on the 12th June 1893. Renton were successfully re-elected, coming joint top of the voting, whereas Abercorn and Clyde were placed in the new Second Division. These two clubs were replaced by Dundee and St Bernard's.

The following season Renton's League form continued to decline and they finished tenth and bottom of the First Division. In this instance they failed in the re-election vote and were relegated to the Second Division, never to play in the top flight of the League again. Renton had a terrible League campaign, picking up just four points all season from a solitary win and two draws. They finished six points behind Leith in ninth and a massive thirteen points from avoiding the vote.

They made a disastrous start to the 1893-94 season, losing all five of their first matches. Their first point didn't come until a 3-3 draw away at Third Lanark on the 30th September 1893. The end result would probably feel like a point lost rather than one gained as Renton actually went into the break 3-0 up. They had opened the scoring through James McCall. Then John McNee and John Bell increased their lead to 3-0. Thirds came back to level in a stirring second half comeback and in the last ten minutes either side could have won. Renton doubled their points tally the following Saturday with a 1-1 draw at home to Dumbarton, this time coming from behind to equalise through John Fleming.

Renton then lost nine in a row, the last of these on the 10th February 1894, when they suffered their heaviest defeat of the season against eighth placed Dundee, losing 8-1. They conceded five goals in the second half and got a consolation goal right at the end. Reporting on the second half *The Scotsman* noted that "in the second half play was even more one-sided. The Renton uprights were promptly besieged, and although Davie, the custodian, made a magnificent appearance, he was unable to cope with the attacks of the Dundee front rank." The only other game in which they picked up points came in their solitary win on the 17th February 1894, the day of the Scottish Cup Final, when Rangers beat Celtic 3-1. The win came in their penultimate game against second from bottom Leith Athletic. James McCall scored at both ends, his own goal equalising for Athletic before his powerful 20 yard shot secured the win.

Renton played their final League game in the top flight on the 3rd March 1894, losing 5-1 against Hearts. John McNee got late consolation. Covering the game the *Edinburgh Evening News* was quite scathing of Renton, commenting that "Renton by no means enhanced their reputation either by play or general conduct...we really must declare that they made a rather ignominious exit from their League connection....After

Saturday's experience , football officials in Edinburgh will be convinced that Renton is no more a "draw" and unless anything extraordinary is mushroomed the hitherto popular Dumbartonshire club will be seldom seen in the East."

Renton thus faced a re-election vote at the League's AGM on the 1st June 1894, with possible demotion to the new Second Division that had been formed at the start of the season. Reporting on the meeting *The Scotsman* noted that "the chief business was the selection of clubs to take the places of Dundee, Leith Athletic and Renton – the last three in the league table. Dundee were unanimously re-elected and Leith Athletic also secured their place; but it was decided to substitute Clyde instead of Renton. The non-inclusion of the Hibernians, champions of the Second Division, caused considerable surprise….It may be mentioned that Renton, who have now lost their place among the first ten, were the prime movers in the formation of the League." Renton came fifth in the voting and only got 3 votes. Dundee were re-elected with 14 votes and Clyde were elected with the same number, effectively replacing Renton. Leith Athletic were re-elected in third place with 8 votes. Cowlairs, the Second Division runners-up got 4 votes and Hibernian, the first Second Division champions surprisingly only got 1 vote.

Renton's first season in the Second Division had an element of controversy as they as failed to fulfil a fixture obligation and ran into trouble with the footballing authorities once more. They played a game less, failing to turn up for a game against Dundee Wanderers, preferring instead to organise a friendly with Queen's Park. On a more positive note Renton reached a fifth Scottish Cup Final and became the first SFL club from the Second Division to reach a final (Queen's Park continued to feature in Cup finals but didn't come into the Scottish Football League until 1900).

Renton started life in the Second Division against new SFL club Airdrieonians on the 18th August 1894 with a 2-1 win. But then three consecutive defeats provided a reality check about their prospects. As a village side, Renton had no hope of competing with the financial muscle of the big city clubs. The club sought to arrange a series of lucrative friendly matches instead and at the end of September they played a couples of friendlies in London against Millwall and the Woolwich Arsenal. They were due to play Dundee Wanderers over the September holiday weekend but failed to turn up in favour of playing a more money-spinning friendly against Queen's Park on the 29th September. Dundee Wanderers were eventually awarded the two points in mid-October.

By mid-November they were as low as seventh place in the table but they then won seven games in a row from the 17th November to the 30th March, including an 8-2 win over Abercorn on the 29th December. For this match the Paisley team turned up minus

599

their goalkeeper and had to play a substitute, *The Scotsman* commenting that "this player, unfortunately, was not much of a goal-keeper, and in the first half of the game, lost six goals." This run of victories had lifted Renton up into third place, but they were six points behind runaway leaders Hibs.

By this time they had reached the Final of the Scottish Cup for the fifth, and as it turned out, last time. The Cup run had started on the 24th November 1894 when they beat Slamannan Rovers away 3-2. However, at a meeting of the SFA on the 4th December a replay was ordered following a protest. *The Scotsman* reported that "Renton claimed their tie with the Slamannan Rovers, although the game was stopped six minutes before time. They alleged that the crowd broke into the field of play and maltreated their players, when they were leading by three goals to two. Slamannan Rovers answered that their players in no way interfered with Renton, although they received provocation, one of the Renton men challenging anyone to fight for £5. The referee said the game was a very rough one, and he had ordered two players off the field. The game was stopped by the crowd breaking in, and it was impossible to bring the match to a close before dark. One of the Slamannan men was hurt. By the casting vote of the chairman, it was agreed that the tie be replayed at Renton on Saturday first. The minority thought the tie should be replayed at Slamannan." Renton won a one-sided replay 4-0, the *Glasgow Herald* commenting that "Renton's play was worth a bigger score, but the exceptionally brilliant goalkeeping of Bell for a time almost defied Renton's attack. Minus the goalkeeping Slamannan's play was poor."

In the Second Round Renton beat the 5th King's Rifle Volunteers of Dumfries 6-0, although they were made to work harder than the final score might suggest. They only led 1-0 at half-time and their opponents missed opportunities to equalise before Renton piled on the goals at the end. In the next round Renton came from two goals down at half-time to win 3-2 in Ayr against Parkhouse. *The Scotsman* reported that "in the second half the visitors made a determined effort to retrieve their position, and they succeeded before the end of the half-hour in equalising the game, McLean and Gilfillan kicking the goals respectively. It looked like a draw till the very close, when just before the whistle blew, Renton put on another goal."

In the Semi-final, staged on the 16th February, Renton played Dundee and the two sides met initially at Dundee's Carolina Port. Dundee took the lead thanks to an own goal. Renton equalised near the end, the home 'keeper flapping at a cross which flew right in. Dundee were then awarded a penalty but shot wide and the game ended in a draw. A week later the replay was held. The clubs should have met at Tontine Park but the match was moved by mutual consent to Hampden, a move vindicated by a crowd of 25,000. At the interval Renton led 2-0 but Dundee roused themselves and got the game back to 2-2. Pryce restored Renton's lead after 78 minutes but a soft equaliser at the end meant the match ended in a 3-3 draw.

On the 9th March the Semi-final tie was replayed at Celtic Park in front of a bumper crowd of 30,000 and a lengthy and colourful report appeared in the *Glasgow Herald*: "The Renton were the first to appear, and were received with a perfect roar of applause. Dundee followed shortly afterwards, and had a fairly good reception; but it was nothing as compared with the ovation which their opponents received. Renton won the toss and played with the breeze in their favour...Amidst tremendous applause Renton at once raised the siege, Murray and McLean carrying the ball well down the field, but Dundee cleared. Again the Renton lads dashed along, and in less than five minutes from the start, Tait scored the first goal of the match amidst great applause. The Dundee backs were fairly taken by surprise. Barrett cleared but before he could realise it, Tait dashed in and cleverly scored. Dundee, feeling the loss of a goal which they could easily have prevented, played with stern reality, and after hovering around the Renton goal they were at length beaten back. The Renton lads were playing with great gusto, never flinching in their work, and tackling and brushing along with great energy. Dundee, however, were displaying the better football, their forward play, in particular, being very fine, and from a free-kick they all but scored. The pace, however, which the Renton lads were going seldom allowed the men from the north to settle down, and for a time at least they had to act on the defensive. Determined not to be taken by surprise again, the Dundee backs and half-backs were very watchful...Nothing, however, could withstand the pressure of the Renton lads. Away they came in a body and, being frantically cheered, they fairly stormed the Dundee citadel...and after a shot from W McColl, the ball was literally scrimmaged through. Two goals in such a short time was a big lead indeed; but the Dundee men were not in the least disheartened, and played as good football as ever. Indeed, they had desperately hard lines in not scoring one goal at least. Renton continued their rushing style of tactics, and the Dundee goal had some marvellous escapes. The game continued to be equally contested, but Renton suited themselves better to the circumstances, their rushing, fearless style being in strong contrast to the dallying tactics of the Dundee men....Dundee had the wind in their favour in the second half, and were expected to make good use of it....Even against the wind the Renton were more than holding their own...W McCall sent in a magnificent shot, which Barrett saved, but the effort might have been turned to good account but for one of Renton's left-wingers hurriedly shooting past. Murray was the most prominent forward on the Renton side, and his feeding of McLean and his general play was superb. Dundee were desperate in their efforts to score, and tried quick long shots which failed sometimes by inches. At length, however, Dundee did score; but Sawyers, who gave it the finishing touch, was said to be off-side, and the point was disallowed. Hard lines again for Dundee, who had been playing clever and good football all along. After twenty minutes' play, Pryce very cleverly scored Renton's third goal with a shot twenty yards out, and it was now clearly all over with Dundee. Pryce's goal was taken after a grand effort, and it was a long way the best of the three. Renton won by superior tactics and by making the most of the opportunities that came their way. Dundee made a dying effort, but all to no purpose. Renton could not be beaten; they remained sturdy and dour to the last."

The Scottish Cup Final, played on the 20th April 1895, pitted Renton against the opposition that had embroiled them in their earlier brush with officialdom. St Bernard's were now a mid-table First Division side and had caused a minor upset by defeating Hearts in the other Semi-Final. The match was keenly contested initially but gradually the Saints got into the ascendancy and made this dominance count with James Cleland scoring two goals in quick succession. Renton then pushed on and Robert Duncan fired in a shot that appeared to beat James Sneddon. The Saints claimed that the ball had gone in by the side of the net but the referee allowed it to stand and the half ended 2-1 to St Bernard's. As the game wore on Renton gave it a good go to get on equal terms but were kept at bay by Sneddon especially, following a succession of corners prior to the whistle being blown to end the match. A full match report appeared in the *Glasgow Herald*: "the final tie for the Scottish Cup between the Renton and the St Bernard's was played on Ibrox Park, the ground of the Rangers, on Saturday. The ground was in excellent condition, and everything bar a strongish wind favoured a good game. Considering that the charge of admission was 1s there was a good attendance, some 15,000 persons being present...Renton lost the toss, and the Saints played with the wind. Cleland and Crossan [for St Bernard's] were the first to get away, but they were held in check by Ritchie, and then McCall, with a long, well-timed shot, transferred the ball to the other end. Renton were further materially aided by a free kick, but the ball was sent over the goal line...The Saints were probably the smartest on the ball so far, and twice in succession Dickie was called upon to save. Amidst intense excitement the Edinburgh men were awarded a free kick close on the Renton goal...but Renton relieved and galloped down the field in great style. Duncan shot, and the crowd sent up a wild shout of delight, but they were sadly disappointed when the referee gave no goal, the ball having passed the post. The Renton men were playing fairly well, and the left-wing was shaping for goal when they were tripped up. However, nothing came of the advantage, Ritchie shooting the ball high over the bar. So far there had not been very much in the game, which was equally contested, and neither side could claim much advantage...The first goal of the match fell to the Saints after 23 minutes' play, Cleland heading the ball through from a pass from the right, amidst loud cheers from the Edinburgh crowd. The ball had no sooner been kicked off than the Saints pulled themselves together, and coming away in a body, the ball was passed from the right wing across to Cleland, who, with a steady shot sent the ball past Dickie for the second time. Two goals in 25 minutes, taken very early indeed, was a dispiriting outcome for the Renton. The second goal was scored when Dickie thought Cleland was offside, but he should have first saved the ball and then claimed...Cleland again tested Dickie with a high swift shot. This time the Renton goalkeeper made the effort, and just succeeded in tipping the ball away. As the game progressed it was quite evident that the St Bernard's were the better trained team...The Renton warmed up a bit and after some 36 minutes play, by characteristic dash, they scored their first goal. The ball was very easily slipped past the Saints half-backs, and Murray passed wide out to Duncan, who with a grand long kick, sent the ball through amidst indescribable scenes of enthusiasm. It was evident that the Renton were the favourites with the crowd. The Saints protested about the ball having gone through between the net and the goal post but referee James Robertson was decided in giving the goal. This success of Renton put a different complexion on the game, as fired with enthusiasm they played much harder and better. At half-time the feeling was that the team that could last longest would win. Renton had the wind this half, and were expected to take full advantage of it. Laing led off the attack for the Saints, and passed to Cleland, who shot, but one of the Renton backs headed out. Again the Saints attacked in spirited style, and Dickie saved a shot from the right. Renton retaliated in dashing manner, and a free kick was awarded them twenty yards out. McCall took the free kick but the Saints easily relieved, and play was once more in Renton territory. The play was stopped for a minute or so owing to an injury for Duncan, Renton's outside-left winger, who had unfortunately to be assisted off the field, evidently suffering considerable pain. Playing with ten men only, Renton were considerably handicapped, but did their very best in the circumstances. Duncan reappeared a minute or so later on, looking alright, and was loudly cheered. Renton replied in grand style...[and]...the play became exciting, and from a long return by McCall an exciting siege of the Saints' goal ensued...The Renton were putting a lot of go into their play, and Sneddon [the Saints goalkeeper], really for the first time, was called to beat out a smart shot, which he did promptly. At the other end too, Dickie also did well in catching a long shot and quickly getting rid of the ball. Renton again led the siege in gallant style, the whole of the forwards putting in some beautiful passing, but they parted with the ball too quickly, and allowed Sneddon too much time to clear his lines. The play improved vastly, at least it became faster and more interesting, each goal being visited in rapid succession, and Dickie distinguished himself in saving a scorcher from Cleland, who was doing nearly all of the shooting for the Saints. Determination was marked on the face of each player, the Renton putting forth desperate efforts to equalise, while the Saints nearly increased their score...Time wore on, and there was little prospect of Renton equalising. Their backs were defending well, especially Glen and McCall, but their opponents were giving Sneddon too much time to save. Renton rallied, and amidst intense excitement they nearly captured the Saints' goal on two occasions. It only wanted a minute a or two from time, and the excitement reached its highest point as time after time the village lads marvellously escaped equalising. Such excitement in the closing stages has seldom before been seen at a final. Renton had desperate hard lines, and contested every inch of ground right up to the finish…and all that can be said is that [they] right on to the finish, nobly maintained their ancient traditions for downright pluck against luck that would have disheartened any body of men." The Renton Cup final side was: Matt Dickie, John Ritchie, Archibald McCall, David Tait, William McColl, Robert Glen, John McLean, John Murray, John Pryce, David Gilfillan and Robert Duncan. Renton never reached the Scottish Cup Final again.

Goalkeeper Matt Dickie subsequently joined Rangers where he stayed for a decade, and was capped three times for Scotland between 1897 and 1900. Robert Glen also joined Rangers, in December 1896 and ended his career at Hibs where he made 140 appearances. He was also capped three times for Scotland and made his international debut as a Renton player in a 2-2 draw with Wales on the 23rd March 1895 in Wrexham. Fellow players John Murray and William McColl were also capped in this match but never played for the national team again.

Between the Cup Semi-Final and Final Renton had won three out of their four League games, keeping the pressure up on the top two clubs – Hibernian and Motherwell. On the 4th May, in their first game after their Cup final defeat they played leaders Hibernian. *The Scotsman* reported that "considerable interest was taken in this match, as it was the last which could have any bearing on the championship of the second division of the Scottish League. A crowd of 3,000 was present at Easter Road and gave the famous villagers a splendid welcome to Edinburgh. The Hibernians fairly carried everything before them and led at half time by half a dozen goals. Early on resuming a seventh was added; but playing up better, Renton succeeded in getting a goal. The closing stages again saw the Irishmen simply do as they please, and adding another couple of points won by nine goals to one. The result puts the championship of the League beyond a doubt."

Renton eventually finished in fourth place. Motherwell in second place only finished two points ahead of Renton. So, if Renton had fulfilled their fixture against Dundee Wanderers, who finished second bottom, and won, they could potentially have entered a re-election vote as Second Division runners-up, as well as beaten Scottish Cup finalists. Hibernian were subsequently promoted by election and took the place of Leith Athletic. Motherwell who came second also applied but could only muster four votes.

History repeated itself as Renton missed out on the runners-up spot by two points again in the 1895-96 season. It was almost a similar story in the Scottish Cup as well, as they had another great run but this time fell just short at the Semi-final stage. They kicked off their League programme on the 24th August with a home game against Partick Thistle, which they lost 6-2, conceding four goals in the first half hour. The *Glasgow Herald* covered the game but provided little information on the match itself, preferring instead to make comment on an improved ground, noting that "Renton opened their home fixtures in a match with Partick Thistle. Tontine Park, barricaded anew with galvanised iron, has been greatly improved. The new ground taken in affords additional standing room, which, unfortunately, on Saturday was in no way utilised." Their form improved and in October they won three games in a row, scoring ten goals and conceding none. In fact from mid-October to Mid-December they lost only once in seven games and following a 3-1 away win at Linthouse on the 14th December they were top of the division, leading Leith Athletic by three points.

At the beginning of 1896 Renton embarked on another great Scottish Cup run. Having beaten Cowdenbeath in the First Round they claimed two First Division scalps, first knocking out Clyde 2-1, and then Third Lanark after a replay to reach the last four. In the first game at Cathkin Park Third Lanark took an early lead before Johnstone equalised. Their hosts continued to dominate and Renton were lucky to reach the interval on level terms. In the second half, Thirds were, according to *The Scotsman* "repeatedly unfortunate in not scoring." Play then went from end to end with Thirds adding two more goals before Renton got one back. Right on the call of time Renton equalised and the match ended in a 3-3 draw. A large crowd of 5,000 watched the replay at Renton, who had to withstand a first half dominated by Thirds, but Dickie in goal and his backs stood firm and they made it to the interval unscathed. Renton started the second half strongly and scored twice in the first twenty minutes. The *Glasgow Herald* was somewhat derisive in its summary, commenting that "the game was scarcely up to the standard of the previous week, but all the same it was sufficiently exciting to maintain the interest of the spectators till the close."

Renton were drawn to play Hibernian, now in the First Division, away at Easter Road for the Semi-final, played on the 22nd February 1896. Renton took an early lead after five minutes play through Campbell. This seemed to unnerve their hosts and their defence was particularly shaky. However, they got past this early wobble and only the efforts of Dickie in the Renton goal kept the visitors in the lead. *The Scotsman* reported that "at length the Hibernians pulled themselves together and played in a more confident manner. Their forwards attacked with more precision, and the Renton backs were not so successful as they had previously been. Dickie still maintained his form, and it seemed as if he was going to prevent his opponents from equalising. The manner in which he got the ball away from a tight scrimmage under the bar was wonderful, but he was unable to stop the return from Murray, and amid enthusiastic applause the game was equalised." In the second half Hibs were camped in the Renton half and the Villagers were hampered by an injury to Ritchie, the right back. With the prospect of a draw looming Hibs snatched the victory their play probably deserved with just five minutes remaining.

At the end of the game Renton lodged a protest, alleging that John Thomas Roberston, the Hibs back, had taken part in a game between Kirkmuirhill and Larkhall on the 15th June 1895, and that, playing during the close season, he had been guilty of a breach of the professional regulations. Renton essentially claimed before the SFA that the Edinburgh club had fielded an ineligible player. It was a technical point, but Renton's case was undermined by what they later claimed was "fraudulent" testimony. Presented with hopeless contradictions in the evidence, the SFA dismissed the appeal. The protest was heard at a meeting of the SFA the following Tuesday. Roberston was brought before the committee and admitted that he had played in this game. He said he had been passing a field, and noticing a number of players in a football ground, he and a friend went into the park and had been invited to take part. So far as he knew, the match was not a pre-arranged one and he had only played about half of the game having got tired. Mr John Copland of the Kirkmuirhill club then testified to say the club was not a club in the ordinary sense of the term. At the match in question there was no gate money taken. The club was not under any Association and had no proper officials. He went on to say that the Larkhall players had only come over for an outing and that they played on Saturdays for the love of the game. However, other witnesses, and Nisbet, one of the Larkhall players, testified that gate money had been taken. This though was contradicted by a further witness who said there was no proper gate to the field and that people could freely enter via gaps in the hedges. Copland, who was recalled, denied taking any money, and stated that the club had no books to show money had been taken. At the close of evidence it was moved that as it had not been proved that money had been taken at the gates the protest should be dismissed. No amendment was proposed and the protest was dismissed unanimously. Robertson went on to play in the final, played at Old Logic Green in Edinburgh, which Hearts won 3-1.

Renton should have left it there. Instead, perhaps spurred on by their recent experience of litigation the club took out a Court of Session interdict in an effort to prevent the Hibernian versus Hearts final from being played. What had begun as a question of principle was escalating out of all proportion. When they lost the case there was no compensation and no recovery of costs, an expensive exercise in futility that the club could ill-afford.

Perhaps distracted by off-pitch events the club lost their next three League games played after the Cup Semi-Final and only drew their final game to slip down to finish tied in third place with Kilmarnock, behind new Second Division champions Abercorn and Leith Athletic. As there was no means for separating teams level on points a play-off game was held to decide third place and the last election place. Renton beat Kilmarnock 2-1 in a play-off at Cathkin Park in Glasgow on the 20th May 1896 but at the League's AGM held a week later they only secured one vote and came last out of the six competing clubs. Abercorn, the Second Division champions did take the place of Dumbarton (Clyde 14, St Mirren 13, Abercorn 8, Leith Athletic 4, Dumbarton 2 and Renton 1).

The next season Renton only achieved sixth place in the Second Division, winning just six of their fixtures and in the Scottish Cup they were dumped out in the First Round, 5-1, at the hands of St Mirren. The 1896-97 season would turn out to be their last full season as a Scottish Football League club. They lost their opening game on the 15th August 5-1 away at Kilmarnock. Only 500 spectators turned out at Tontine Park for the 4-0 win over Dumbarton in September, in which Murray scored twice. As a result the club began to face some financial difficulties especially in terms of meeting the minimum guarantee of £5 payable to the visiting opposition. When Renton won the return match against Dumbarton in November the club was lying in third place but they failed to win another game and just picked up one more point to drop to sixth.

Renton only lasted a few games into the new 1897-98 season in the Second Division before they were found unable to meet the new minimum guarantee of £10, which had been increased from £5 at the League AGM on the 1st June 1897. Their League career ended four games into the season when they tendered their resignation.

On the 20th October 1897, at a meeting of the Second Division clubs, Renton resigned for financial reasons, *The Scotsman* reporting that "Mr Fairley, a representative of the club was present, and explained that in consequence of the poor form of the team, the gates both at home and away were very poor, and the club was unable to pay the £10 guarantees. Trade was bad in the Vale of Leven district, and there was no prospect of any improvement in the attractive powers of the club. Several members of the committee expressed regret that circumstances had reduced Renton to such a position. On the motion of Mr Williams, Port Glasgow, it was agreed to recommend to the first division of the League that the resignation be accepted, and that Renton be exempted from the monetary penalty under which they are liable according to rule." The *Glasgow Herald* reported more fully on the debate that followed, as to how the division should proceed. "A special meeting of the committee of the Second League, to consider Renton's withdrawal from the competition, was held in the League Chambers, West

Regent Street….A letter was read from Renton FC intimating that, owing to financial and other difficulties, they were unable to fulfil their remaining fourteen League engagements, and soliciting permission to withdraw from the competition. The communication gave rise to a long and heated discussion, the members of those clubs which had already met and obtained points from Renton being desirous of bringing in a successor to the village club, but stipulating that the points gained by them against Renton should continue to count in their records; while another section of the committee, whose clubs had not yet met Renton, and who therefore resented being forced to meet a new and probably much stronger combination in their stead, urged that the competition be carried on with nine clubs, and that all points so far gained against Renton should be deducted."

A proposal that the Second Division carry on with nine clubs was rejected and the search for a successor was on. Suggestions for a replacement club were canvassed and it was agreed that the secretary of the League would write to a number of clubs asking if they were willing to join the Second Division and that a choice be made at a future meeting in a week's time. It was decided to consult with Scottish Combination clubs Hamilton Academicals, Albion Rovers, East Stirlingshire and Falkirk to ascertain if they were willing to fill the vacancy. Three other clubs that applied for the place – Arthurlie, Raith Rovers and Victoria United - were all deemed unsuitable. On the 27th October, Hamilton were elected, and took on Renton's fixtures. They tendered their own resignation from the Scottish Combination, having to pay a £20 penalty in the process.

Renton had played four games, and lost them all, scoring only two goals and conceding 19. The record of the four games stood and they were a 4-0 away defeat at Leith Athletic on the 4th September; a 4-1 home loss to Motherwell; an 8-0 defeat at Port Glasgow Athletic and on the 16th October, their final League fixture, and the last home League game at Tontine Park, a 3-1 loss in the reverse game against Leith, in which Renton had scored first through Crooks.

On the 4th November, *The Scotsman* reported that "a meeting of the Second Division of the Scottish Football League was held in the Rooms of the League, West Regent Street, Glasgow, last night…The representative of Hamilton Academicals, the club elected to fill the Renton vacancy, took his seat for the first time, and was welcomed on behalf of the members of the League by the Chairman." Hamilton Academicals took on Renton's remaining fixtures, playing their first League game on the 6th November 1897, when they lost 3-2 at home to Kilmarnock. They eventually finished ninth and were successfully re-elected at the end of the season.

For the following four seasons Renton played only cup and friendly games and in the

1898-99 season they participated in the Scottish Cup, going out in the First Round to Port Glasgow Athletic. In a very close game they went down 3-2, the winner only coming in the final minute.

In 1902 they joined the Scottish Combination, where Hamilton had been playing, and they finished as runners-up to Albion Rovers in their first season in the competition. The came second in the following season as well, this time behind Royal Albert of Larkhall, but they finished the 1905-06 season in last place. This didn't deter them from seeking to re-join the Scottish League though and at the AGM on the 21st May when the Second Division was being expanded by two teams. Renton were one of seven Scottish Combination sides to contest the election but only got three votes. Instead, Combination champions, and former League champions Dumbarton were elected back into the League, along with Ayr Parkhouse.

In 1906 a new league competition was formed from Combination and Alliance clubs called the Scottish Football Union. Renton were one of the founding members but failed to fulfil all their fixtures and ended the 1906-07 season with seven games unplayed. They had continued to participate in the Scottish Cup and achieved a final bit of fame in the 1906–07 competition when they put out St Bernard's, then leading the Second Division and then stunned Scottish football by knocking out Dundee, who were to finish second in the League championship that year. It took three matches to get past St Bernard's. The first game at Tontine ended goalless. Renton scored a second half equaliser at the Royal Gymnasium, to earn a second replay. The two sides met at Parkhead on the 9th February 1907 with Renton winning 2-0. Crawford scored after twenty-five minutes and Ritchie added a second after a goal mouth scramble shortly afterwards. St Bernard's lodged a protest against McLaughlin for alleged professional irregularities, but this was subsequently withdrawn.

In the Second Round Renton caused the sensation of the day by knocking out First Division Dundee. The match was played on the 23rd February and there was a crowd of 6,500 to witness the visit of the team who were lying in second place in the First Division. *The Scotsman* reported that "Renton kicked off, and were early called upon to defend. Dundee, however, were inclined to play too fancy football, with the result that the Rentonians more than held their own. The latter adopted the rushing tactics, which did not suit the style of the First Leaguers, and when McLaughlin scored, from a beautiful cross from Ritchie, after thirty-five minutes' play, it was no more than the homesters deserved. Keeping up the pressure, the Rentonians again scored through Whyte, but this goal was disallowed for off-side, and at the interval the groundsmen led by one goal to nothing. In the second half the First Leaguers showed good football in the early stages, but gradually he Rentonians wore them down, and Muir had to save his charge from further downfall." Renton went out to old adversaries Queen's Park, who were now in the SFL, but struggling at the bottom of the First Division. They conceded four first half goals and made desperate attempts to reduce the deficit in the second period but only had a solitary goal, scored by Travers, to show for their efforts, going out 4-1.

Perhaps buoyed by their Cup exploits they made another unsuccessful attempt to re-join the League at the SFL AGM on the 27th May 1907. They applied along with Dunfermline and were up against East Stirlingshire and Ayr Parkhouse. Both existing League clubs were retained, East Stirlingshire receiving 24 votes, Ayr Parkhouse 16, Renton got 8 and Dunfermline 6 votes. Two years later they made a third and final attempt to re-join the League at the AGM held on the 31st May 1909. Arthurlie (21) and Cowdenbeath (17) were both re-elected. Renton came fourth (out of six) with 8 votes.

Renton participated in the 1911-12 Scottish Cup competition but were thrashed 5-0 by Third Lanark in the First Round. Renton continued playing in the Scottish Union until 1915. After the outbreak of War in 1914, the Scottish League continued with a full programme of fixtures for both of its divisions. In 1915, it decided to suspend the Second Division, but they allowed its members to form two regional competitions, the Western and Eastern Leagues. Renton were among the non-League clubs who joined the ranks of the new Western League, competing alongside other founder members of the League Abercorn and Vale of Leven. In 1923 a number of Western League clubs were used to form the new Scottish League Third Division but by this time Renton had already disbanded.

Renton played for one more season in the Scottish Cup, participating in the 1920-21 season. The club received a bye in the First Round before being drawn against First Division Motherwell. Unfortunately Renton lost 3-0 although they held out for 75 minutes due to the heroics of Wilkinson, the Renton 'keeper, who also saved a penalty. Under the headline "Renton's Hero: A Dazzlingly Display of Goalkeeping" *The Sunday Post* noted that "early on the Renton keeper established himself a firm favourite with the crowd by his masterly saving. He saved time and again, and especially in the latter half gave a brilliant display of goalkeeping. The late goal encouraged the hosts but had the opposite effect on Renton and in the last ten minutes Motherwell scored two more. The last Renton team to play a senior match was: Wilkinson; Brown, Lees; Porteous, Cameron, Wallace; Ritchie, Paterson, Devine, Haddow and Blanchflower.

Renton, the one-time 'World Champions', entered the 1922–23 Scottish Qualifying Cup, but scratched from their match, finally folding in 1922. Tontine Park became a housing estate in 1928, located near to where the B857 road joins the A81 and A82. It is said that Archie McCall, one of the club's legends, was one of the bricklayers. One relic of the club is preserved. In a garden on the Tontine council estate is the original centre spot of the Renton pitch.

Renton were one of the pioneers of organised football in Scotland, winning the Scottish Cup twice. They were one of the prime movers behind the formation of the Scottish Football League and were also crowned as unofficial World Champions in 1888. They were also involved in lots of issues, hearings, protests and legal actions and seemed to court controversy as a club. All in all, Renton FC had one of the most colourful histories of any of the former League clubs.

SEASON	LEAGUE	P	W	D	L	F	A	P	POS
1890-91	SCOT	RECORD EXPUNGED							
1891-92	SCOT	22	8	5	9	38	44	21	7/12
1892-93	SCOT	18	5	5	8	31	44	15	8/10
1893-94	SCOT-1	18	1	2	15	23	52	4	10/10
1894-95	SCOT-2	17	10	0	7	46	44	20	4/10
1895-96	SCOT-2	18	9	3	6	40	28	21	3/10
1896-97	SCOT-2	18	6	2	10	34	40	14	6/10

Royal Albert

Formed: 1878
Colours: Black and white vertical striped shirts and black shorts
Ground: Raploch Park
Entered League: 1923. Founder members of the Third Division
Number of League Seasons: 3
Highest League Finish: 5th in Division Three
Honours: None
Left League: 1926. Division Three abandoned. Wound up in 1931

Royal Albert were a Scottish Football League club based in Larkhall, a town in South Lanarkshire situated 14 miles south-east of Glasgow and six miles from Hamilton. They were one of the founding members of the new Third Division formed in 1923 and left the League when this competition was abandoned in 1926.

Traditionally a mining, weaving and textile area the club was formed in 1878 as a works team, linked to local coal mines owned by a Captain Johns, with the name said to originate from the name of his boat, the *Royal Albert*. Royal Albert played at Raploch Park, the ground being on the north-western side of Raploch Street. Old maps show another football ground on the opposite side of Raploch Street with MacNeill Street to the south and this was Gasworks Park, the home of rivals Larkhall Thistle. The clubs were known as 'The Royalists.'

Royal Albert made their debut in the Scottish Cup as early as 1881, losing 5-0 away at Cambuslang in the First Round. This was to be the first of 16 Scottish Cup campaigns prior to Scottish Football League admission. In the 1883-84 season they reached the Fourth Round, after two big wins and a bye in the Third Round (8-0 against Shettleston and 8-1 versus Clarkston). In the 1889-90 competition they surpassed these wins with a 12-0 victory over Whifflet Shamrock.

In the 1890-91 season they achieved their best ever Scottish Cup run, reaching the Fifth Round. They beat Motherwell and then accounted for Fairfield (of Govan, Glasgow), Saltcoats Victoria and Burnbank Swifts (of Hamilton) before being drawn at home against Celtic, who had reached the final in 1889 (and who would win their first Scottish Cup in 1892). The 29th November 1890 is often recorded as the first match, which ended 2-2, with the following game a replay. In fact *The Scotsman* reported that "owing to the frost, a friendly game was played instead of the Scottish Cup tie. The game resulted in a draw-two goals each." The two sides met at Raploch Park in front of a record crowd of 5,000 for the rearranged tie, played on the 6ᵗʰ December. *The Scotsman* reported on the match, saying that "the Celts scored the first point shortly after the commencement of the game, and keeping up the pressure soon added another two goals to their credit. The home team's play improved towards the close of the first half, but they failed to score. On change of ends, play was more even, and each goal was assailed in turn. Ten minutes before time a slight accident occurred, and a rush by the spectators prevented the game being completed." In the aforementioned incident it was later reported that a Celtic player had struck an opponent. On Tuesday 9ᵗʰ December the SFA met to consider a protest from Royal Albert that the game was stopped 11½ minutes from time. There was some debate as to whether the tie should be awarded to Celtic on the grounds that the Larkhall club were responsible for the spectators' infringement as the host club. A vote was taken 12-8 in favour of a replay, to be played at the neutral venue of Ibrox.

The replayed game took place on the 13ᵗʰ December, *The Scotsman* reporting that "the third attempt to settle this a Cup tie was made in splendid weather. Play opened fast, but by no means pretty, and it was very evident that both teams had fairly gauged each other's play. But though the game raged from end to end and no scoring took place, the whistle blowing at half-time with the score unopened. In the second half, within the first five minutes the Celts scored from a scrimmage in the goal-mouth. Still they could not claim more than a fair share of a very give-and-take game. They certainly pressed most so far as shooting goes, but were only able to notch another point."

The year 1891 was a big one for the club. In March, one of their players, James Cleland, was capped for Scotland against Ireland, becoming the club's only international player in their history. It was also the year that the club first entered a league competition, becoming founder members of the Scottish Federation. They won the competition in its second season before leaving to join the Scottish Alliance in 1893, replacing a number of clubs who had gone on to form the Scottish Football League's new Second Division. In between, the club had enjoyed a notable Scottish Cup success, thrashing Cambuslang, the beaten finalists from four years ago. The match, played in November 1892 saw Albert beat Cambuslang 6-1 at Larkhall. Faulds scored after five minutes to give Albert the lead. Cambuslang then pressed but the home team on the counter scored a second through Thomson. Faulds sent in a hard and fast shot which Scoular in the Cambuslang goal allowed to slip through his fingers and then MacLuggage then had a run and evading all defenders, scored a fourth. The second half was more evenly contested, with both sides scoring, Douglas registering for the hosts. Just on the call of time Albert scored a sixth.

Royal Albert won the Scottish Alliance in the 1893-94 season, their first in the competition, and this prompted a bid to join the Scottish Football League. At the League's AGM held on the 1st June 1894, with three places available, the club only came in sixth place in the voting, with 11 votes. Despite being the Alliance champions, Airdrieonians, also of the Alliance got elected in third place with 19 votes.

In 1896 Royal Albert left the Alliance and became founding members of the Scottish Football Combination, playing in this competition for ten years, winning it in the 1903-04 season. This success prompted another attempt to join the SFL at the AGM on the 30th May 1904. Royal Albert got through the first ballot into a deciding ballot against the club seeking re-election, Ayr Parkhouse, and against two Northern League sides – Aberdeen and Cowdenbeath. Despite being Combination champions Albert got only 3 votes whereas Aberdeen, who weren't even the Northern League champions, won the place with 14 votes (Ayr Parkhouse got 6 votes and Cowdenbeath 1).

At the 1905 SFL AGM Royal Albert decided to have another go as the odds were better. This time there were four places available, two for re-election and with two new clubs joining due to League expansion. Abercorn and St Bernard's were both re-elected and were joined by Vale of Leven, who were the Combination champions, while Cowdenbeath also joined, having finished second behind Dundee 'A' in the Northern League. Royal Albert failed to find a seconder.

Undeterred, Royal Albert had a fourth attempt the following year as again there were four places up for grabs. A record thirteen clubs applied for a place at the AGM held on the 21st May, seven of which were members of the Scottish Combination. The two clubs facing re-election, Vale of Leven and East Stirlingshire, were both successful. Ayr Parkhouse were successfully returned to the SFL with 14 votes and Dumbarton, the new Combination champions took the final place with 12 votes. Royal Albert, who had finished fifth in the Combination got 7 votes and were seventh in the voting. Later that year they quit the Scottish Combination to join the new rival Scottish Union, which included a number of reserve teams.

Royal Albert played in the Scottish Union until 1915 but with little success. In 1915 the SFL decided to suspend the Second Division due to the War, but allowed its members to form two regional competitions, the Western and Eastern Leagues. The new Western League consisted of six ex-Scottish League clubs and six non-League clubs, including Royal Albert. It was as a member of the Western League that Royal Albert were finally admitted to the Scottish League. In 1923 Royal Albert became one of the founder members of the ill-fated Scottish Third Division, which was largely made up of Western League clubs.

J Gowans was the club's secretary/manager for their first ever Scottish Football League season and the club finished a respectable ninth in the 16 team division. Their first ever game in the League was a home match against Dumbarton Harp on the 18th August 1923. Under the headline "Harp Unstrung" *The Sunday Post* reported that "clever and interesting play was witnessed at the game between Royal Albert and Dumbarton Harp at Raploch Park yesterday. The Royalists front rank struck up a good understanding, and frequently harassed the visitors' defence. In sixteen minutes McFarlane opened the scoring for the Albert. In the second half the visitors were seen in the picture, but could not get the better of the Royalists' stubborn defence. The home lot added another two goals, the scorers being Buchanan and Barton. The Royalists were worthy winners." Royal Albert only lost three games at home all season but then only won three times on their travels. Their best win of the season was a 4-0 home win over Peebles Rovers and their biggest defeat was a 6-1 loss at Helensburgh.

In the 1924-25 season the Royalists again finished in ninth place. They won their opening game, a 3-0 win at Links Park away at Montrose. *The Sunday Post* reported that "it was a poor match at a Montrose where Royal Albert, from the start, displayed form a bit in advance of the locals. In all departments the Royalists were first, and on play their decisive win was well merited. From a melee in front of goal McLaren scored Albert's first point, and Pettigrew before the interval had made the total three. Montrose did better later on, but never reached the standard displayed by the opposition, and the best they could do was to prevent Albert from increasing their goal average." They then went eight games without a win which left them just one point off the bottom, a sequence that was ended on the 29th November with a 2-0 win over Solway Star. In contrast to what had gone before, on the 13th December, they thrashed Dykehead 7-0. *The Sunday Post* reported that "Royal Albert were in rampant form against Dykehead at Raploch Park yesterday, and simply overwhelmed their Lanarkshire rivals. In the first half Dykehead put up a good fight, but Albert were superior in all departments, and led at the interval by two goals, the scorers being Findlay and Ritchie. There was no holding the Albert forwards after the cross-over, and goals came rapidly. Findlay and Ritchie got another goal apiece, and the other marksmen were Forrester, Cullens and Dickson. Dykehead failed to convert a penalty. The Albert forwards, despite the heavy going, gave a great display, and the defence was always reliable and steady." A month later though they suffered their heaviest defeat of the season, losing 5-1 at Queen of the South. They already trailed 3-0 at half-time when McLavin was sent off for disputing an offside decision.

Their 7-0 League victory against Dykehead was surpassed in a 9-1 win over Stranraer in the First Round of the Scottish Cup. Stranraer had surrendered ground rights and the *Sunday Post* headline was "Slaughter of Stranraer." The match report went on to say that "Albert did pretty much as they pleased. Stranraer presented a feeble opposition...From the start of play they were a beaten team, and play was fearfully one-sided. The Royals piled on goal after goal, and allowed Stranraer to score just one. Not long were the Albert in drawing blood, Collins soon scoring from a corner. Then Goodwin popped on another with a drive. This was followed by goals from Ritchie and Forrester (two), and at the interval Royal Albert were five up. In the second half, Gillies scored twice and Murray and Ballantyne each once. Stranraer's only goal was got by McGeoch. It was no game at all. Criticism is not required, the Royal loads simply outclassing the enemy." Royal Albert were knocked out in the Second Round at home to Second Division Broxburn United, who were struggling in their division, but they did have the compensation of a large 3,000 crowd. In a game they lost 3-1, *The Scotsman* simply commented that "Royal Albert played hard but without method."

The season reached a low ebb when they lost 5-1 at home to bottom club Brechin City in what *The Sunday Post* called "the surprise of the afternoon." Smith, Brechin's centre-forward scored four. The teams were level 1-1 at the interval but "in the second half the Larkhall efforts to stem the tide of misfortune were feeble, and lacked method, and they have only themselves to blame for the heavy defeat they sustained." Both teams had a player ordered from the field. Royal Albert continued to have mixed fortunes and they eventually matched their previous season's finish of ninth place.

The 1925-26 season was both their best and their last in the Scottish Football League. They had a big win to start the season, beating Clackmannan 7-1 on the 15th August 1925. *The Sunday Post* commented that "against Clackmannan at Larkhall, Royal Albert were in rampant form, completely overwhelming their opponents, and winning by 7 goals to 1. The first half was fairly well contested, but it was early apparent that the Albert were superior for clever footwork and good combination. MacMillan counted first, and then Stirling scored with a splendid effort. Davidson notched the visitors' solitary point. In the second half Albert's aggressiveness continued unabated, and Stirling, with another two goals completed his hat-trick. Ray with a couple of counters, and Macmillan with another goal, raised the total to 7. All the Albert players did well, and if Saturday's form is maintained they will take a prominent place in the competition."

Their home form was superb as they won all 14 of their SFL games at Raploch Park. This included a 5-0 win over Lochgelly United and a 6-1 win over Brechin. They were let down though by their away form, where they lost 11 of the 14 fixtures played, including 8-2 at Dykehead, 6-0 at Lochgelly and 5-1 at Helensburgh, where they scored first but were behind 2-1 at half-time. Despite Helensburgh playing a man short in the second half they still added three more.

By this time the future of the Third Division was in doubt as the general economic situation was poor and the small clubs were struggling to survive on low gate receipts which had to cover wages, travel costs and match fee guarantees, and in the January Galston folded. This ill-conceived competition collapsed towards the end of the 1925-26 season with fixtures unfinished. Royal Albert still had two games to play – against Beith and Clackmannan. They were in fifth place with 33 points, five points behind leaders Helensburgh, who had completed their programme. Their last SFL home game at Raploch Park was held on the 10th April 1926, a game which they won 3-0. Their last ever Scottish League game took place a week later, when they secured a rare away win at Peebles Rovers by 4-1.

With the collapse of the Third Division Royal Albert were among the majority of clubs taken into an expanded Scottish Alliance where they played for the 1926-27 season in the southern regional section. Following the subsequent expulsion of the majority of the former Third Division clubs from the Scottish Alliance a year later they joined the new Provincial League, but this only lasted one season. Royal Albert made two brief appearances in the Scottish Cup, the last being a 16-0 thrashing away at Partick Thistle on the 17th January 1931. Soon after this they disbanded and reformed joining the Junior ranks.

Raploch Park was subsequently redeveloped for housing in the 1960s. Gasworks Park across the road is used by Larkhall Thistle, a rival Junior team and Royal Albert ground shared for a while. They currently play out of nearby Stonehouse.

SEASON	LEAGUE	P	W	D	L	F	A	P	POS
1923-24	SCOT-3	30	12	4	14	44	53	28	9/16
1924-25	SCOT-3	30	9	8	13	48	61	26	9/16
1925-26	SCOT-3	28	16	1	11	75	61	33	5/16

St Bernard's

Formed: 1874
Colours: Blue shirts and white shorts. Changed to blue and white horizontal striped shirts in the early 1920s.
Ground: New Logie Green (1893-1899), Powderhall (1900-01), Royal Gymnasium Ground (1901-1915), Old Logie Green and Tynecastle (1921-24), Royal Gymnasium Ground (1924-1939).
Entered League: 1893. Elected to First Division. 1921. Founder Member of the reformed Second Division.
Number of League Seasons: 40
Highest League Finish: 3rd in First Division, 1893-94
Honours: Scottish Cup winners 1895, Second Division Champions 1900-01, 1906-07
Left League: 1915. World War One. 1939. World War Two. Disbanded 1943.

The name of St Bernard's FC, in their time known as the Saints, may be unknown to modern day supporters, but this Edinburgh club was once a force to be reckoned with. St Bernard's are one of the most successful of the Scottish League's former clubs, one of only four defunct clubs to have lifted the Scottish Cup, which they won in 1895. Two years earlier they became Edinburgh's third club to join the Scottish Football League, in June 1893, entering at the First Division level, following on from founder members Hearts (1890) and then Leith Athletic (1891). Hibernian joined the SFL the same year (July 1893), but as members of the newly formed Second Division. St Bernard's were involved in a controversial episode when they were suspended for professionalism in 1890, which also led to the suspension of Renton, who were in the first season of the SFL. Despite a run to the Semi-finals of the Scottish Cup in 1938 the club played out its final years in the Second Division, before being forced to sell off its ground in 1943 which ultimately brought about its demise.

Like a number of teams, St Bernard's started life as a military team when they were formed in February 1874 as the Third Edinburgh Rifle Volunteers. This army connection ended in 1878 and the club was re-named after the famous St Bernard's Well sitting on the banks of the Water of Leith nearby. The club was based in the Stockbridge district of Edinburgh and originally played at The Meadows, which is still a large public park south of the city centre and bordered by buildings belonging to Edinburgh University.

They later moved to their own ground, firstly at Powburn Park in Newington, located south of The Meadows, in the direction of Dalkeith and then to John Hope's Park in Stockbridge, near the Royal Botanic Garden. In 1880 the club changed grounds yet again, playing their games at the large public park established in 1864 known as the Royal Gymnasium Grounds, or affectionately called the 'Gymmie'. The director of the park, William Lapsley, allowed the club to use its football pitch but the club moved again in 1883, because the ground was lacking in space, and they relocated to New Powderhall, located just south of the Water of Leith, at Beaverbank, less than half a mile away.

Prior to League admission the club played in the Scottish Cup between 1881 and 1893, reaching the Semi-finals in the 1892-93 season and the Fifth Round in the 1883-84 season and then in two successive seasons - 1886-87 and 1887-88. The early rounds of the Scottish Cup were regional affairs and their first appearance came against Hearts on the 10th September 1881 in a First Round tie, staged at the Royal Gymnasium. *The Scotsman* reported on the Cup tie, saying that "the event drew together a large number of people. The game was, of course, played under the Association code. It was splendidly contested throughout, and now and again loud applause was elicited from the spectators by bits of good play. Both goals were several times in imminent danger, but no advantage was gained until about the close, when one of the Stockbridge lads, by a well-directed kick, brought down the Hearts' fortress - a result which was followed by ringing cheers all-round the ground. As nothing more of a decisive character happened, the St Bernard's team were left victors. For about the last quarter of an hour, St Bernard's lost the services of one of their players, who had met with an accident." St Bernard's played their Second Round match on the 8th October when they lost 2-1 against Hibs.

In the 1882-83 competition they went out in the First Round, losing to Hearts after a replay. The following season they recorded their best Cup run to date, reaching the Fifth Round. In the First Round they secured an overall club record Scottish Cup win when they beat Dunfermline Athletic 13-1 away from home, in a tie played on the 15th September 1883. The *Glasgow Herald* simply reported that "this Cup tie was played At Dunfermline, in the presence of 2000 spectators. The strangers appeared with an excellent team, but The Dunfermline only succeeded in getting up a scratch defence." St Bernard's scored after five minutes, and this was soon followed by another, although the score was only 3-1 at half-time. The Saints scored ten goals in the second half, and rather uncharitably, the *Edinburgh Evening News* solely reported that "the Dunfermline had a miserable scratch team." The St Bernard's team that registered this record victory was: James Baillie; Wauch, Heathcote; Robertson, Collie; Wilson, Charleston, Denholm, Arthur Low and McBeath. After receiving a bye in the next round St

Bernard's went on to beat Benhar of Musselburgh 7-0 in the last of the regional rounds, before beating the 1879-80 runners-up Thornliebank of Glasgow 2-0. They lost their Fifth Round tie 3-0 at home to Rangers.

The Saints reached this stage of the Scottish Cup in successive seasons - 1886-87 and 1887-88. In the first of these they knocked out Bo'ness, then got another bye, then they put out Armadale, and in the Fourth Round beat Erin Rovers of Perth 5-1, before losing 6-2 to Port Glasgow Athletic. The following season they beat Armadale and Broxburn Shamrock in the regional ties, got a walkover against Dunfermline and then a bye into the Fifth Round where they were drawn against Abercorn. They travelled through to Paisley on the 26th November 1887 but came away with a heavy defeat, losing 9-0. Due to heavy rain the ground was very wet and there was some discussion around a postponement before the match got underway. The attendance was poor, perhaps due to the weather. Abercorn dominated the play from the off and James Baillie in the St Bernard's goal was called upon at least half a dozen times in quick succession. Reporting on the game, *The Scotsman* noted that "this beginning on the part of the Paisley team was followed up by rapid scoring in their favour." Baillie was eventually beaten by a long range shot and once they went behind the floodgates opened. Abercorn quickly put on six more goals and just on the call of half-time scored number eight. Soon after the resumption Abercorn made it nine, *The Scotsman* reporting that "with this large total against them, the St Bernard's played up with greater dash than they had been going, but they could not, though they made a number of spirited attempts, break through the Abercorn's defence. Good play on the part of Paterson and Heathcote, with Baillie's splendid goalkeeping, prevented the Abercorn from further adding to their score...During the last half of the match, and also during a portion of the first half, the St Bernard's played with ten men."

In February 1887 the first players from the club were capped for Scotland. Half-back James Hutton, and left winger James Lowe each made their sole appearance for their country on the 19th February against Ireland at Hampden. Lowe scored Scotland's fourth and last goal in the 4-1 win.

Their subsequent best performance in the Scottish Cup came in the 1888-89 season when they knocked out Keith, Norton Park and Kirkcaldy Wanderers, before losing 4-1 to Celtic in Edinburgh. They exited the competition at the First Round stage for the next four seasons until their run to the Semi-final in the 1892-93 season. Before that, the club went through the most controversial part of its history, when they were expelled from the Scottish Football Association.

The year 1890 was a momentous one for Scottish Football with the formation of the Scottish Football League but also one for St Bernard's. Although the club were involved in the preliminary discussions regarding the formation of the SFL they did not attend the meeting in Glasgow in the spring of 1890, although they were admitted in 1893. Later that year though, they fell foul of the footballing authorities when the club was expelled from the SFA for payment to players.

The events leading to their expulsion began with a First Round Scottish Cup tie against Adventurers of Edinburgh. The significant event was the inclusion of a player called Ross in their line-up. The game was played on the 6th September and *The Scotsman* reported that "the St Bernard's experienced little difficulty in ousting the Adventurers in the first round defeating them at Logie Green by seven goals to nil...The Saints started the ball and were not long in making themselves felt at the other end. Ten minutes from the start, Lowe put on the first point for the home team with a swift low shot with which the goalkeeper was completely at sea. Combe Hall, who from the beginning had been doing most of the offensive work for the Saints, was responsible for the second goal, which was the outcome of a splendid unaided run. For the first time the Adventurers now managed to endanger the Saints' citadel, which escaped only through ,miserable shooting...The St Bernard's soon returned to the attack, and after a long spell of play in front of the strangers' goal the ball was at last put through from a scrimmage, half-time arriving with the score at this stage. For some time after resuming neither team could claim any advantage...The Adventurers had several chances at this stage, but were unable to make use of them, their shooting being very wild. Ross shone in defensive work. The finest piece of play in the game was now witnessed, a magnificent dribble and shot by Hall resulting in a fourth goal...The character of the game changed greatly after this, the Adventurers now betaking themselves to rough play, which caused the referee to concede several free kicks to the Saints. These were taken advantage of to the full, and before the finish three other points were registered." The St Bernard's line up that day was: Baillie; Methven, Ross; Reid, Murdoch, Hutton; Lowe, Hogg, Baxter, Hall and McNab. However, the "fine defensive work" of James Ross, from Dunfermline, would come back to bite them as The Adventurers lodged a protest with the SFA on the grounds of professionalism.

A week later the club hosted Queen's Park and drew 2-2 but three days later the SFA met, on the 16th September in Glasgow and heard a number of protests in relation to the cup ties. Reporting on the St Bernard's case *The Scotsman* noted that "the Adventurers, Edinburgh, lodged a protest against the result of the cup tie with the St Bernard's on the ground of professionalism, it being alleged that the latter club induced Ross, Dunfermline, to leave that town and join them on the promise of paying him a weekly wage for playing football. Before Ross had made up his mind to leave

Dunfermline, it was alleged that he had been offered by the St Bernard's 10s. a match and a job. Mr McDowell, secretary of the Association, said he had only received the protest that afternoon, and had telegraphed for representatives of both clubs to appear at that meeting. Mr McIntosh, secretary of St Bernard's, who was called, stated that he had received too short notice for the case to go on that evening. It was decided that the whole matter be remitted to the Professional Committee."

Reporting on the following day under the headline "Suspension of the St Bernard's", *The Scotsman* wrote that "quite a sensation was caused in Association circles in Edinburgh...when it became known that the St Bernard's, a club of the highest reputation, has been suspended for professionalism by the Professional and Business Committee of the Scottish Association. It was midnight on Friday when the decision was arrived at. After examining Messrs Common (secretary, Adventurers F.C.), Brown and Clark (Dunfermline Athletic), A S McIntosh (secretary, St Bernard's F.C.) W Murray (treasurer, St Bernard's), Ross (St Bernard's) and T Paton (St Bernard's), the Committee, delivered the following finding:- Having heard the evidence, examined the cash-books, and other documents produced, sustain the protest, and reinstate the Adventurers; find the St Bernard's guilty of professionalism under rule 11, Constitution and Rules, sub-section b and g, and declare them suspended till 31st October; suspend the player James Ross till that date, and the members A B McIntosh, W Murray, and T Paton, and prohibit them from taking further part in football affairs in Scotland until said period expires. Ross, the player implicated, formerly belonged to the Dunfermline Athletic, and his suspension naturally gave rise to great jubilation in that town. In football circles generally, however, sympathy is felt for St Bernard's, who seem to have been severely dealt with. One result of the committee's decision is to bring nearer the legalising of professionalism unless a more vigorous effort is made in the future to stamp out the secret professionalism which is stated to prevail in a number of the leading clubs in Scotland."

The club circumvented the suspension by simply adopting the new name of the Edinburgh Saints. Although St Bernard's were suspended the newly named club played on Saturday the 20th September against Clackmannan. Their line-up was Baillie; Methven, Murdoch; Reid, Baxter, Hutton; Lowe, Corson, Hall, McMillan and McNab. This team showed only two changes from the St Bernard's side that had taken the field against The Adventurers, one of course being the exclusion of Ross. Reporting on the game *The Scotsman* commented that "it being necessary for the St Bernard's to adopt a new name till the 31st October, a meeting was held in the pavilion at Logie Green on Saturday when Clackmannan arrived. The latter, of course, could not play in the Shield tie, but had no objections to play a friendly game with the "Saints", as it was decided to call the club by that name. Clackmannan, however, were a few men short, and substitutes had to be picked up on the field. The game partook more of the nature of a practice game for the "Saints" who kept pressing during the most of the first half, which finished in their favour by three goals to two. In the second half the "Saints" scored two more points, while the visitors made no further progress, the game resulting:- "Saints", five goals; Clackmannan, two goals."

On the night of Tuesday the 23rd September the club met to discuss the situation. *The Scotsman* reported that "a meeting of the St Bernard's Football Club was held last night in the club-house at Logie Green - Mr T Fraser, president in the chair. There was a large attendance of members. After an explanation had been given of the proceedings at the meeting with the Professional Committee of the Scottish Football Association in Glasgow on Friday last, as already reported, the meeting agreed to minute their confidence in those officials who had come under the ban of the Scottish Football Association, in spite of the decision arrived at, and to send a copy of said minute to the gentlemen suspended. While protesting against the unjustness of the decision arrived at by the committee, in view of the evidence adduced, the meeting also agreed, seeing there could be no appeal against the decision, to accept the offer of the Edinburgh Saints for the ground at Logie Green during the time of suspension. A meeting was afterwards held of the Edinburgh Saints - Mr R H Christie presiding - when members' tickets were issued to the members of the new club. It was intimated that the first eleven of the Saints would play Renton at Renton on Saturday first, while the second eleven would meet the Hearts' Strollers at Logie Green."

The following day the East of Scotland FA met and were supportive of the club, citing double standards in the treatment of clubs from the west versus the east. *The Scotsman* reported that "a meeting of the East of Scotland Football Association was held last night at 80 Potterrow- Mr G Sneddon, president in the chair...In reporting on the consideration of the St Bernard's case by the Professional Committee on Friday last, Mr Sneddon stated that the meetings were held in private, so that representatives were not at liberty to give as full information with reference to what transpired as they could in the general committee meetings of that body. In reply to a question...as to what the St Bernard's were suspended for, the representative merely gave the rule and sub-sections. Pressed as to the grounds for the suspension, the representative stated that the committee did not consider that the cash-book was satisfactory....An application was submitted from the Edinburgh Saints requesting admission into the Association, and also that the first eleven be admitted to the second round of the Shield ties. [It was moved, by Mr Bingham, of Hibernians]...that the Saints be admitted...[and it was]...thought the committee would be doing no more than justice to the Saints in admitting them. Had the Scottish Association displayed the same zeal and the same anxiety to keep the game as pure in the west as in the east, they would have had a busy time of it. Why did they leave home, it was asked, and come so far away to look for corruption? In the city where they held their council there were some clubs steeped to their eyes in it, and well known to them." St Bernard's were admitted on a vote of 18-1, with some abstentions and it was also agreed by 19-6 to admit them into the second round of the Shield, where they were drawn to play away at Bellstane Birds on the 11th October.

Two days later, on the 25th September, a committee of the SFA put a spanner in the works. They ruled that they considered St Bernard's and Edinburgh Saints to be one and the same. They added that no clubs under the jurisdiction of the SFA could play either side during the term of the suspension of St Bernard's. Reporting on the meeting *The Scotsman* wrote "a meeting of the committee on professionalism of the Scottish Football Association was held in the Rooms, Waterloo Street, Glasgow, last night- Mr Park, president in the chair. One of the chief matters under consideration was the proceeding of the Edinburgh Saints in admitting the St Bernard's players to membership in their club during their period of suspension. The following resolution was agreed to:- 'In the opinion of the Business and Professional Committee, the Edinburgh Saints is the same club as the St Bernard's, and therefore they decide that clubs under the jurisdiction of the Scottish Football Association cannot play them during their term of suspension."

Their remained a good deal of sympathy for St Bernard's, and one of their most prominent supporters was Renton. In defiance of the Scottish football authorities Renton hosted the Edinburgh Saints on Saturday the 27th September. The Edinburgh Saints team was: Robertson; Methven, Fleming; Reid, Murdoch, Hutton; Williams, Corson, Hall, McMillan and McNab. *The Scotsman* covered the match, reporting that "notwithstanding the decision of the Business and Professional Committee of the Scottish Football Association regarding the newly formed Edinburgh Saints, Renton fulfilled their fixture with that club at Renton. It was very doubtful even after the arrival of the Edinburgh team whether the game would be played, as some of the Renton committee and several members of the team were strongly against running the risk. The majority, however, were evidently in favour of going on with the game, as both teams took the field at five o'clock. Davie kicked off for Renton, and the home men at once assumed the aggressive, but a wild shot by Duncan sent the ball high over the bar. The visitors' left wing McMillan and McNab broke away with a fine dashing run, and the former passing the ball over to Williams, that player with a high angular shot scored the first point. Renton played up pluckily, and five minutes afterwards McCall, with a low swift shot put on an equalising point. Both teams strove hard to regain the lead, but the Renton men had fully the best of the play, and before half-time Gardner finished up a really brilliant run by putting on a second point., Davie in the nick of time charging Robertson [the Saints 'keeper] through [the] goal. The second half was but a few minutes old when Davie put on a third point for Renton, and five minutes later the same player added a fourth. The "Saints" were conspicuously out of the game, and very rarely got within shooting distance of their opponents' goal. Renton, on the other hand, played with a dash and smartness that they have not hitherto approached this season. Before the call of time McNair added a fifth goal for Renton, and in the last moments of the game McNab added a second goal for the Saints. Renton thus won by five goals to two." The SFA were not happy at such defiance and on the 30th September they met and Renton were declared as professionals and expelled from the SFA. At the same meeting St Bernard's were also expelled from the SFA, having been merely suspended before, and the players who took the field against Renton were suspended until 30th April the following year.

The East of Scotland Football Association were now in a quandary and a special meeting was held on the 8th October at 80 Potterrow in Edinburgh to consider the events. This local association had admitted the Edinburgh Saints as members whereas the SFA had ruled they could not play other clubs. *The Scotsman* reported that "the Chairman explained that they were met in consequence of the development of events with regard to the Edinburgh Saints. He then proceeded to review in detail the circumstances which had elapsed since the date of the last meeting, when the Edinburgh Saints applied for and obtained admittance to the Association. The Scottish Association, through the Business and Professional Committee had decided that the Edinburgh Saints could not play against clubs in the Scottish Association., and having been admitted to that body it was for them to consider the decision of the Scottish Association. After considerable discussion, the Chairman explained that the position of their Association was that they must either rescind the finding of the last meeting or sever their connection with the Scottish Association."

A motion was moved to rescind but an amendment was brought with a wording that vindicated the local Association's decision and "that while regretting the finding of the Professional and Business Committee of the SFA, and still believing that their action in admitting the Edinburgh Saints to their membership in no respect violated the laws of the SFA, they resolved to acquiesce in the decision of the Professional Committee." This was carried by 18 votes to 6 and the Edinburgh Saints membership was rescinded. At this point, Mr Mathieson, the representative of the Edinburgh Saints, withdrew from the meeting. It was then agreed to return the Saints their subscription money. A further motion that the SFA be asked to receive further evidence on behalf of the Saints was rejected by 16 votes to 6.

On the 18th November at an SFA meeting, a protest signed by Dumbarton, Hibernian, Celtic, Clyde, Third Lanark, Abercorn, Hearts, St Mirren and Cowlairs (but not Vale of Leven) clubs asking for a reconsideration of the Renton and St Bernard's case was read, and was unanimously dismissed as being extremely injudicious. St Bernard's served their suspension while Renton, who had also been thrown out of the Scottish Football League, pursued the matter through the courts.

St Bernard's were subsequently readmitted to the SFA in the spring of 1891 and on Thursday the 21st May they played a friendly to celebrate, somewhat provocatively hosting a match in Edinburgh against Renton of all people. *The Scotsman* reported that "fully 2500 spectators attended at Logie Green last evening to welcome the reappearance of the famous Renton team. The village players brought a capital eleven with them….The Dunbartonshire men were accorded a warm reception on stepping on to the ground…Renton played grandly…and had easily the best of matters throughout." Renton won the game 2-1 and the St Bernard's team that took to the field was: Baillie; Methven, Phillip; Baxter, Murdoch, Edgar; McLeod, Lowe, Mackay, Sutherland and McNab.

St Bernard's were one of the original members of the Scottish Alliance, which was one of a number of leagues set up a year after the Scottish League was formed in 1890. St Bernard's finished fourth out of twelve teams in the 1891-92 season and made a failed attempt in join the SFL at that organisation's AGM held on the 3rd June. The odds were always against them as the SFL was going from 12 clubs to 10, with three existing League clubs up for re-election, and three other non-League teams also going for the place. In other words, seven teams were after one place. Perhaps their run in with the football establishment also counted against them as they received no support and no votes.

In the 1892-93 season St Bernard's finished as runners-up in the Scottish Alliance which prompted another bid to join the Scottish League. This time they received much more backing and came third, securing the last place. The AGM was held on the 12th June 1893 and the three retiring League clubs were Renton, Clyde and Abercorn. In the first round of voting Renton and Dundee (at that point a new club formed by the amalgamation of Our Boys and East End) tied joint top with 12 votes and were elected to the League. St Bernard's got 8 votes, Clyde 7, and Abercorn 2. Abercorn were then excluded and their two votes went to St Bernard's who were therefore replaced Clyde in the League. A number of other Alliance clubs had expressed an interest in joining the League, including the Alliance champions Cowlairs of Glasgow. A month later the League formed a Second Division, with six Alliance clubs (Cowlairs, Morton, Partick Thistle, Port-Glasgow Athletic, Northern and Thistle), Motherwell from the Scottish

626

Federation, Abercorn and Clyde, the two defeated clubs and the tenth club completing the division was Hibernian. The city of Edinburgh now had four League clubs participating in the 1893-94 season, St Bernard's joining Hearts and Leith Athletic in the First Division, and Hibernian competing in the Second. St Bernard's made an immediate impact, securing their highest ever Scottish League finish in their inaugural season. They finished in third place, six points behind the champions Celtic and three behind Hearts who came second. Leith Athletic finished in ninth place but survived a re-election vote. Hibernian won the very first Second Division championship but failed to be elected to the First Division.

On the 19th August 1893 St Bernard's played their first ever Scottish League match when they travelled through to Glasgow to play Third Lanark at Cathkin Park. The Saints got off to a dream start and led 3-0 at half-time with goals from Jimmy Oswald, Scott and Steel. However, they capitulated in the second half as their hosts ran riot, scoring five goals and they lost 5-3. The first ever league line-up for St Bernard's was: Lindsay; Arnott, Foyers; Sibbald, Baird, Murdoch; Scott, Steel, Oswald, Crossan and Adams.

Their first ever League point came the following week, in their first home game at New Logie Green, a 0-0 draw against Rangers in front of a crowd of 5,000. They followed this up with their first League win, away at Boghead against Dumbarton. The Saints won 5-1 with goals from Oswald (2), Jimmy McNab (2) and Crossan. Three more wins out of four meant that by the end of September the Saints sat in third place, just two points behind joint leaders Rangers and Celtic. During October they lost 5-2 at Celtic but they beat Third Lanark in their reverse fixture 6-2. In this game they were again leading 3-0 at the interval but this time making sure of the points, Jimmy Oswald scoring four.

By the beginning of November St Bernard's were in second place, level on points with Celtic but having played three games more. However, they then lost three in a row to quash any hopes of a tilt at the championship. They lost 8-1 against Celtic in the Third Round of the Scottish Cup but did score eight themselves when they beat St Mirren 8-3 at the end of March - Brady scored three and Crossan got two of the goals. Victories over Hearts and Rangers brought to a conclusion a highly successful first League season in which they secured third place, which would turn out to be their highest ever League finish.

As the Scottish League fixture list ran to only 18 games several clubs banded together to form supplementary regional competitions. One of these was the Edinburgh League which was formed in 1894 by Hibernian, Heart of Midlothian, Leith Athletic and St

Bernard's. It changed its name to the East of Scotland League in 1896 when Dundee and East Stirlingshire joined and it ran until 1908, although St Bernard's never won it.

Although the 1894-95 season saw St Bernard's regress in terms of their final League position, coming in sixth, it was also the season of their finest hour, as they went on to lift the Scottish Cup. St Bernard's lost their opening League games against Celtic and Rangers before winning three on the trot, including a 6-3 Edinburgh derby win over Leith Athletic in mid-September, thanks to a Brady hat-trick and two from Oswald. Early in the following month the lost a seven goal thriller against eventual champions Hearts, despite leading 1-0 at one point. In December they beat Dumbarton in gale force conditions, winning 5-0 with five different scorers (Wilson, Oswald, Murdoch, Baird, and Laing). On the 2nd February 1895 they beat Clyde 6-2 in a friendly game, played when the pitch was considered unplayable for their Quarter-final cup tie. The postponed game was played on the 23rd March and St Bernard's won 2-1.

For the Scottish Cup Semi-finals St Bernard's got the toughest tie, drawn against League leaders Hearts, whereas Dundee and Renton were the other Semi-finalists. Hearts were drawn with home advantage so the two sides met at Tynecastle on Saturday the 9th March 1895. This closely contested game ended 0-0, *The Scotsman* commenting that "both teams proved unequal to the task of getting the ball late into the net and latterly they seemed to rest content with a draw." The two sides met a week later at Logie Green for the right to play Renton, the 1888 Cup winners, who had beaten Dundee 3-0 in the other Semi-Final. The replay was played on the 16th March, and *The Scotsman* reported that "so great was the interest manifested in Edinburgh over the replayed semi-final tie in the Scottish Cup competition between these clubs that there assembled at Logie Green fully 18,000 spectators - £387 being drawn at the gates, and over £100 at the grand stand. It will be remembered that at Tynecastle the preceding Saturday the match was drawn, neither side scoring. This result was unexpected by the Heart of Midlothian, and during the past week, by assiduous training, they determined to put the issue out of doubt by winning the match. In this, however, they failed, for the St Bernard, despite the fact that they were without the international forward, Oswald, and Wilson, not to mention Brady, secured a popular and, in the circumstances, a well-earned victory by one goal to nil....The game was started punctually, and instantly the excitement of the partisans of the respective clubs got full play as each goal was early visited. In fact, for a considerable time neither side could claim the advantage....Towards half-time the Hearts got the first corner of the match but the Saints bore off, and were around Fairbairn [in the Hearts goal] when half-time was called, there being then, as on the previous Saturday, no scoring. The second half was opened in rare style by the St Bernards, for whom Cleland...almost scored with a grand long range shot. About thirty yards out [the Saints] were awarded a free kick.

From this Murdoch shot the ball into goal with a terrific force, and glancing off the head of Hall in its progress, it lay in the net for the first and only time, and the Saints were a goal to the good. Their plucky efforts were duly recognised – sticks, hats and handkerchiefs being flourished in the air amid deafening cheers…The Hearts had much the best of the subsequent play in mid-field, but again and again were baffled by the superb play of the St Bernards' backs and halves, who held out gamely to the end, and had a large share in what to the club was the greatest victory in its annals." The St Bernard's team that day was: Sneddon; Foyers, Baird; McManus, Robertson, Murdoch; Laing, Paton, Hall, Crossan and Cleland. Hearts got revenge in the League the following month, winning 3-0 and took the League title, with St Bernard's coming in sixth place. A fortnight later St Bernard's lined up to take on Renton at Ibrox, on the 20th April 1895, in the Final of the Scottish Cup.

It was somewhat ironic that their opponents should be Renton. Just five years earlier both sides had been embroiled in issues of professionalism and both had been expelled. When St Bernard's were finishing third in 1894 Renton were coming bottom, failing in the resulting re-election vote and were now a Second Division club, and who were fielding a very young side (only two of their players were over 20 years old). Having beaten the favourites Hearts, St Bernard's were now the resounding favourites, and they justified that tag, winning the final 2-1. *The Scotsman* reported that "for the first time in their history, the St Bernard's became custodians for the year of the much coveted trophy. For the third time in the history of the competition the Scottish Cup has found a resting place for the year in Edinburgh. The Hibernians and Heart of Mid-Lothian have both had the honour of bringing that much coveted trophy to the East, and it was only fitting that the St Bernard's, considering the prominent positions they have long held in Scottish football, should also have a share of the honour. There are few more popular teams in Scotland, and though the extent of their following cannot compare with that of the Heart of Mid-Lothian the popularity of their win was very evident by the cordial reception which awaited them on their arrival in Edinburgh. The present is the first occasion on which the Saints have even got the length of the final in the national competition, their opponents being Renton, who are perhaps deserving of even more credit from the fact that they occupy a position at present in only the second division of the League. Though Renton were undoubtedly favourites with western people, the St Bernard's were generally looked upon as being the more likely team to carry off the trophy, and this anticipation they justified by running out winners by two goals to one."

Ibrox was chosen as the venue for the Final and in contrast to previous finals the crowd of 12,000 was a small one. St Bernard's were missing their captain William Urquhart Baird and his place was taken by Combe Hall with George Murdoch as captain. The game was keenly contested initially but gradually the Saints got into the ascendancy and made this dominance count with James Cleland scoring two goals in quick succession. First he headed in from a beautiful cross from Oswald and then converted following a pass from the same player. Renton then pushed on and sent in a shot that appeared to beat James Sneddon. The Saints claimed that the ball had gone in by the side of the net but the referee allowed it to stand and the half ended 2-1 to St Bernard's. A mazy run by Oswald at the start of the second period appeared to be ended by a foul in the box but the referee made no signal. Oswald continued to be the main outlet for the Saints but as the game wore on Renton gave it a good go to get on equal terms but were kept at bay by Sneddon especially following a succession of corners prior to the whistle being blown to end the match.

Less than five years after being expelled from the competition and the SFA, Captain George Murdoch now lifted the Scottish Cup trophy. *The Scotsman* reported that "after the match the teams dined together in the Alexandra Hotel, Glasgow, where the Cup was presented to the winners. Mr W.M. Lapsley, as president of the club, taking the custody of it. At the station there was a scene of much enthusiasm on the departure both of the special train and of that bearing the team and officials: while at the Waverley Station, on the arrival of the team in Edinburgh, the scene was one to be remembered. Proceeding afterwards to the Hotel Metropole, Hanover Street, the team, officials, and a number of supporters further toasted the club on its success." Renton subsequently protested the result of the Cup final on the grounds that Barney Crossan had participated in an unauthorised match: Edinburgh Fish Merchants v Butchers in the summer of 1894, in which admission had been charged, thereby alleging professionalism. St Bernard's produced witnesses stating a case of mistaken identity, and produced a lookalike who was being confused with Crossan and the appeal was dismissed. Come the summer of 1895, all three Edinburgh clubs were enjoying what was at that point their finest hours. Heart of Midlothian had won the Scottish League for the first time, Hibernian had won the Second Division again and this time, promotion, whilst St Bernard's had won the Scottish Cup.

The St Bernard's Cup winning team was: James Sneddon; Robert Foyers, Combe Hall; George Murdoch, Thomas Robertson, Patrick McManus; Robert Laing, Daniel Paton, James Oswald, Bernard Crossan and James Cleland. Both Scottish and English clubs snapped up the club's best players to the extent that only five of the Cup winning team played in the Semi-Final the following year, when they again met Hearts, this time losing 1-0. Robert "Bob" Foyers, a full-back, played for St Bernard's between 1890 and 1895. He was capped for Scotland twice, both against Wales, in 1893 and 1894, first at the Racecourse Ground, Wrexham in an 8-0 win for Scotland and then at home at Rugby Park, Kilmarnock. Foyers signed for Newcastle United in 1895 for a fee of £100 and was appointed club captain. He returned to St Bernard's in 1897 before ending his career with short spells at Clyde and Hamilton Academical. Combe Hall was in his second spell at the club having started his career at St Bernard's before playing for Blackburn Rovers between 1890 and 1894 and won the FA Cup with them in 1891 against Notts County (who had Jimmy Oswald in their line up). Thomas "Tom" Robertson played for Cowlairs, Aston Villa, Queen's Park, and then St Bernard's and played for Scotland three times when at Queen's Park. After retiring as a player, Robertson was a football referee and became president of the Scottish Football League. Daniel "Dan" John Ferguson Paton had also previously played for Aston Villa and was capped by Scotland, once, on the 21st March 1896 against Wales in a British Championship match at Carolina Port, Dundee, and Paton scored the third goal in a 4-0 win. James "Jimmy" Oswald was the undoubted star of the team. He had started his career at Third Lanark and won the Scottish Cup with them in 1889. He moved to England and joined Notts County, playing and scoring in the FA Cup final with them in 1891, although ending up on the losing side. He was first capped for Scotland in April 1889 when at Third Lanark and scored Scotland's equalising goal as they came from behind to beat England 3-2. He returned to Scotland to play for St Bernard's and scored ten goals in the 1894-95 season. He was capped twice more for Scotland, in April 1895 as a Saints player, and then in March 1897. By this time he had joined Rangers, in August 1895, and won two more Scottish Cups before later playing for Raith Rovers and Morton. Bernard "Barney" Crossan had started his career at Celtic but left in 1891 and joined Preston North End. He came back to Scotland and played for Third Lanark and then joined St Bernard's for the 1894-95 season. His performances impressed his former club and he re-joined Celtic in June 1895. James Cleland was a tricky dribbler with a good shot. He had also played for Third Lanark before joining St Bernard's in December 1894. By this time he had already been capped for Scotland, his solitary appearance coming on the 28th March 1891 against Ireland. He subsequently played for Abercorn and Partick Thistle. Missing from the line-up was William Urquhart Baird. He had previously played for Dundee and was later capped for Scotland in March 1897 against Ireland at Ibrox.

Only Sneddon, Murdoch, Paton and Hall started in their opening 4-1 defeat at Hearts on 10th August 1895, with Oswald now at Rangers and Crossan playing for Celtic. The club won three of their next four fixtures, drawing the other, to sit in third place, just a point behind leaders Celtic. On Monday the 16th September 1895 they beat eventual champions Celtic 3-0, *The Scotsman* reporting on the game: "the holiday attraction at Logie Green was provided by the visit of Celtic. Owing to the counter attraction at Easter Road [Hibs were playing Rangers on the same day], the crowd was not an exceedingly large one, there being between three and four thousand persons present when play opened. The Saints, losing the toss, kicked off, and they made a sensational opening, being within an ace of scoring in the very first minute of the game. The Celts, more by good luck than anything else, cleared their goal, and the game then raged at the other end. Here the Celtic had several attempts at goal, but the defence was too good for them, and gradually the scene of play veered round again to Celtic territory. Cleland here sent in a beautiful shot, which struck the cross-bar and then seemed to rebound into the net. McArthur [in the Celtic goal], however, caught the ball as it rose from the ground and fisted out, and the referee seemingly being of the opinion that the ball had not been through, allowed the game to proceed. From this point the Celts for a time assumed the ascendancy, but their efforts were of no avail, and the opening score came from the St Bernard's by a grand shot from Paton. Following upon this, the Celtic pressed, but the Saints played up with more confidence, and about a quarter of an hour later, after some fine play near goal, they put through a second point from the head of Brown. Great cheering followed this second point, and the Saints thereafter played with renewed dash. Nothing further resulted, however, before half-time, and the Saints crossed over leading by two goals to nothing. Starting the second half, the home team lost a splendid chance of increasing their lead, but failed owing to the inability of McKnight in the centre. The Celts, however, made a determined effort to redeem their position and pressed severely for a time. It fell to the lot of the Saints, however, to register the next point, which went to the credit of Wilson. This was all the scoring, and the game ended in a victory for the Saints by three goals to nothing. It is understood that the Celtic lodged a protest with the referee, owing to him refusing to allow them a penalty kick for an alleged infringement."

St Bernard's subsequently lost 5-0 at home to Hearts, a club record home SFL defeat. The game was played on the 21st September and *The Scotsman* reported that "the most important match under Scottish League auspices was that played at Logie Green between last year's champions and the holders of the Scottish Cup. As both teams had created quite a sensation by brilliant victories over such redoubtable opponents as the Celtic, so much interest was manifested in the encounter that fully 7000 spectators paid for admission." Chances came at either end before Hearts took the lead. The second half had just started when Sneddon gifted a goal, trying to punch a ball clear but seeing the ball spinning back off his hand and into the net. This goal seemed to knock the stuffing out of St Bernard's and Hearts put the issue beyond doubt with a third. St Bernard's weren't in the contest after that and Hearts added two more goals before the close. The St Bernard's team that day was: James Sneddon; George Wilson, Hugh McKinnon; George Murdoch, William Baird, Thomas Tennant; Jock Wilson, Dan Paton, John McKnight, Alex Brown and James Cleland. Jock Wilson, the outside right scored 25 goals in 47 matches across two seasons before heading to England. Alex "Sandy" Brown scored 21 goals from 43 appearances and had success with Preston

North End, and especially Tottenham Hotspur, for whom he scored for in the FA Cup final in 1901.

The following Saturday the Saints lost 5-0 at Clyde with Baird retiring injured at the start of the second half with the score at 2-0. St Bernard's lost all four games played in October to slip down the table and towards the end of the year they lost 6-0 away at Hearts. Willie Taylor scoring a hat-trick. They were now down in seventh place, but comfortably above the re-election spots occupied by St Mirren, Dumbarton and Clyde.

Their defence of the Scottish Cup was much better. On the 11th January 1896, in the opening round, they beat Clackmannan 8-1. The game was supposed to be played at Clackmannan but the Saints committee persuaded them to switch grounds. They beat Queen's Park 3-2 at Hampden in the Quarter-Final and there were three Edinburgh teams in the draw, Hearts and Hibernians joining them, along with Renton. This time they lost 1-0 to Hearts in another closely fought contest which was only settled in 87th minute when Willie Michael scored for the Maroons. Just five of the Cup winning team were left in the line-up. (Murdoch, Robertson, Hall, Paton and Laing). Ironically, St Bernard's went on to host the 1896 Scottish Cup Final. With the other finalist being Hibernian, the SFA allowed the match to be played at New Logie Green, the only time the Scottish Cup Final has been held outside Glasgow. Hearts won the final 3-1. In March 1896 Duncan McLean was capped for Scotland against Wales. He had left Renton in 1890 and played for Everton and Liverpool before leaving Anfield in 1895 and ended his career with St Bernard's in 1899. While with St Bernard's, McLean played for Scotland twice, the second time in 1897 against Ireland.

After three very eventful seasons, 1896-97 was a bit of an anti-climax. St Bernard's exited the Scottish Cup at the Third Round stage at the hands of Dumbarton, and came seventh in the table for the second year in a row, finishing thee points clear of the re-election vote spots. None of their 18 League games ended in a draw. Following on from their Scottish Cup dominance, Hearts and Hibs finished first and second in the League. The main highlights of the season were a 6-0 win over Abercorn on the 19th December, in which Provan scored a hat-trick and there were Scottish caps in March 1897 for James Andrew McMillan against Wales and William Urquhart Baird, at centre half versus Ireland.

Under the stewardship of Louis Gumley in the 1897-98 season St Bernard's finished a poor second bottom but were reprieved from demotion by the votes of their fellow top flight clubs. In their worst performance to date they secured only nine points, four ahead of Clyde who were bottom, but also four from avoiding the re-election vote. The Saints only picked up one point in their opening four League games, which included a 7-

2 defeat away at St Mirren in mid-September. Their first victory came at the end of the month, a 3-2 win home against Hibs which lifted them off the bottom, ahead of both Hibs and Clyde. In this game they came from 2-0 down, getting the winner through Dan Paton, his second, with just a couple of minutes left.

They suffered a really bad autumn, losing 5-1 away at Hearts in early October due to a Willie Michael hat-trick and a week later they lost 6-1 away at Hibs to drop to the bottom with just three points from eight games with six defeats. A month later they lost the return home game against Hearts, also 5-1, this time Willie Taylor scoring a hat-trick. On the 4th December they recorded their second win, an emphatic 9-1 victory at home to Partick Thistle, to go above Clyde and therefore off the bottom. *The Scotsman* commented simply that "the St Bernard's, whose performances in this year's competition have been very disappointing, secured an unexpected and remarkable victory by nine goals to one." Jimmy Houston and McInnes each got a hat-trick, Bobby Houston scored two and the other was scored by Kinghorn. This was followed up by a 4-1 win over Dundee in which Houston scored two. But after these back-to-back wins they suffered two consecutive losses, losing 5-1 at Celtic and then 6-0 at Third Lanark over the Christmas period.

A 3-1 New Years' Day win over Clyde briefly gave them hope, but this was their last win and points. A Second Round Scottish Cup exit 5-0 at home to Queen's Park was followed by a humiliating 8-1 loss away at Rangers. Rangers scored four in each half. This was their record SFL defeat to date and would last for 30 years. Saints finished ninth and second from bottom with four wins and a draw from 18 matches. At the League's AGM held on the 30th May 1897 St Bernard's and the other two First Division clubs facing re-election, Clyde and Partick Thistle (who had lost a play-off with Dundee to decide the third club), were successfully re-elected to the First Division (Clyde beating the Second Division champions Kilmarnock on a second ballot).

The same four First Division teams occupied the bottom four places in the table for the 1898-99 season, although this time it was St Bernard's who avoided the vote, although starting from this season it was agreed that the number of clubs required to apply for re-election in both divisions was reduced from three to two. St Bernard's, now managed by John Banks, came in seventh, with Dundee and Partick only picking up four and six points respectively. Rangers won the championship, winning every single one of the 18 matches they played. St Bernard's lost their opening games against Hearts and Hibs before picking up their first point in a 1-1 draw at Dundee at Carolina Port, which was followed by a 3-0 away win at Partick, these two opponents finishing in the bottom two. After these games they won only one of their next ten games, losing the other nine, eventually defeating Clyde. They had a strong finish and were unbeaten in their last three games.

The 1899-1900 season saw the Saints slip to ninth and second bottom which meant a further re-election vote. The Saints lost their opening four games before defeating Dundee 2-0 on the 7th October. The following Saturday they lost 5-0 at Hearts and in the last weekend in October the club lost 5-0 at Celtic. Three wins across November and December, including the double over Clyde, saw them move within a point of St Mirren and two to Dundee as they went into the new century in ninth place.

In 1899 their lease expired at New Logie Green and they played their games at Powderhall. On the 30th December 1899 they drew 3-3 with St Mirren and owing to Powderhall being required as part of the New Year pedestrianisation this match was played at Tynecastle. Saints took the lead after five minutes through Lee but near to half-time the Paisley Saints equalised. Almost immediately Cameron scored a second goal for St Bernard's but St Mirren equalised again and the two sides went in level 2-2 at the break. Lee put them ahead for third time but again St Mirren got level. This would turn out to be a significant result and a missed opportunity as the two clubs would be tied at the end of the season.

On the 13th January they played their first game of 1900, a home First Round Scottish Cup tie against Arbroath on what *The Scotsman* called "Mr Lapsley's ground at Powderhall, Edinburgh." They won 1-0 but were knocked out in the next round by Partick Thistle. Back in League action the Saints drew their penultimate game at Hibs, 1-1 and played their last League fixture on the 3rd February when they lost 4-1 to Rangers. This was technically a home tie but the match was switched to Ibrox to avoid a clash with a replayed Cup tie between Hearts and Hibs. St Bernard's ended the season with 12 points, the same as St Mirren. They had a marginally inferior goal average and goal difference (having scored a goal fewer and conceded one goal more) but neither was in operation at the time. A play-off game was arranged by the SFL to decide who would occupy the second re-election place and this was held on the 7th April and staged at Dundee's Dens Park. After a nervy goalless first half Bobby Houston scored for the Saints but the Paisley Saints responded and raised their game to equalise and then went on to score the winning goal following a goal mouth scramble.

On the 3rd May *The Scotsman* reported on the club's financial difficulties and details of the offer made by the Board to the club's creditors. It reported that "a meeting of the creditors of the St Bernard's Football Club was held in Dowell's Rooms, Edinburgh, last night...when an offer was submitted as to a settlement of claims. The offer was to the effect that the committee of gentlemen who have indicated a willingness to carry on the club were prepared to make a cash payment to creditors of 5s. in the £1. After some discussion, Mr Gumley moved that the creditors accept 6s. 8d. per £1 in full of all claims, payable within a fortnight, and no counter proposal having been submitted, it was decided to inform the general body of creditors to this effect."

At another significant meeting, the Scottish League's AGM, held on the 16th May, Partick and Morton, the top two sides from the Second Division, challenged St Bernard's and Clyde for the First Division place. Sadly, St Bernard's were eliminated on the first ballot getting just 5 votes. Morton, the Second Division runners-up secured 13, Clyde 8 and Partick Thistle 6. In the second ballot Morton picked up 3 more votes and Partick 2. Morton were thus elected in place of St Bernard's. Partick and Clyde now tied on 8. Lots were drawn and Partick were elected. Queen's Park were also admitted to the Scottish Football League and were fast-tracked into the First Division, which now consisted of eleven clubs. St Bernards were therefore relegated to the Second Division and the 1899-1900 season was the last time Saints would be a top flight club, despite subsequently winning the Second Division championship on two occasions in the following decade.

The first of these championship wins came immediately as St Bernard's won the Second Division at their first attempt. For a few seasons they adopted the primrose and pink racing colours of the Earl of Rosebery, and it was wearing these colours that they finished three points ahead of Airdrieonians. The Saints won their three opening home games at New Powderhall winning against Port Glasgow Athletic, Clyde and Leith Athletic. They also won their first two away games to have a 100% record after the first five matches. Their first defeat came in mid-October when they lost 3-1 away at Airdrieonians, who would be their main championship rivals. A 3-3 draw at Motherwell on the 15th December, together with an Airdrie win, saw their rivals go top but St Bernard's regained top spot after a 4-3 win over Airdrieonians on the 22nd December. This win was part of an unbeaten run in their last seven games, which included a 5-0 win over East Stirlingshire in mid-January 1901.

Although St Bernard's won the Second Division at the first attempt, they were not elected to the First Division by the other clubs. They made an unsuccessful bid for election back to the First Division at the Scottish League's AGM, held on the 30th May 1901. However, League reconstruction counted against them. The First Division was being reduced to ten clubs and the Second Division was being expanded to twelve. Partick Thistle as the bottom side in the First Division were automatically relegated and Arthurlie joined the Second Division. St Mirren and Hearts from the First Division were then re-elected despite the challenge from St Bernard's and Airdrieonians.

The next three seasons brought mid-table finishes with Saints coming in sixth, fifth and then eighth. On the 19th August 1901 St Bernard's hosted an East of Scotland League game against Hearts, which marked the opening of their Royal Gymnasium Ground. *The Scotsman* reported that "these teams opposed each other last evening before an attendance of 4000, on St Bernard's new ground, Royal Gymnasium, Eyre Place, Edinburgh. The match was the first fixture on the new field, and the opening ceremony was performed by Bailie [a civic officer of the council] Murray, who from the grandstand delivered a brief address, in which he congratulated the club on its enterprise, and wished it success in the future." The ground is now part of the King George V Park and the grandstand backed onto Royal Crescent.

The first Scottish League fixture was played there on the 31st August 1901 when St Bernard's hosted Ayr FC, *The Scotsman* reporting that "these teams met on Saturday at Royal Gymnasium Park, Edinburgh, the new enclosure of the St Bernard's." Goals from Lee, Prior (2) and Grace gave the Saints a 4-0 lead at half-time and they eventually won 4-1. Over the next two months St Bernard's conceded five against Partick Thistle and Port Glasgow Athletic. They put a good run together during November and December to reach the turn of the year in third place, but a poor run in saw them drop to sixth place in the twelve team division. The Saints finished a place higher the following season, but never challenged for the championship, with the only notable victory being an 8-3 win over Falkirk. Almost immediately after the start of play Falkirk went down to ten men due to an injury and for the whole of the second period they played two men short.

In 1903 events off the pitch cast a shadow over the club with the death of William Lapsley, the driving force behind the club and their major financial backer. He was killed when his cab crashed after the horse bolted. As for events on the pitch, the 1903-04 season was largely uneventful, as the club finished in its lowest League position, coming in eighth. Things got worse in the 1904-05 season as St Bernard's existence as a League club came under threat as they reached a new low by finishing 12th and bottom. Now they were facing a re-election vote for their very survival as a Scottish League club. The new season started badly with a 4-0 loss at the divisional championship holders Hamilton on the 20th August. They recovered from this early setback and three wins in in October against Ayr FC, Abercorn and Raith Rovers saw them mid-table by the end of the month. Things then went badly wrong as they suffered a club record ten consecutive defeats, including 4-1 at Leith on the 31st December, 5-1 at Ayr FC on the 7th January and 5-0 at Clyde a week later. Following their loss at Shawfield they were now anchored at the foot of the table, five points adrift of East Stirlingshire and Aberdeen.

The sequence was finally ended with a 1-1 draw at Pittodrie, Aberdeen in their next game, *The Scotsman* reporting that "the Saints were assisted by five men residing in the north, four from Peterhead and an Aberdeen junior. There is no mistaking they materially helped to make the game what it proved to be." The Saints picked up a further three draws in their last three games but only gained 11 points overall from their 22 matches (W3, D5) and finished bottom, six points behind Abercorn, and eight behind Raith Rovers in tenth place. At the League's AGM on the 22nd May 1905 they survived the re-election vote, although they were partly indebted to the League's expansion of the First Division, which had a consequence of creating two vacancies in the Second Division. There were four places available and St Bernard's and Abercorn were challenged by eight other clubs. Both existing League clubs were re-elected, St Bernard's topping the poll with 23 votes and Abercorn getting 19. Cowdenbeath, the runners-up in the Northern League to Dundee 'A' joined at this time with 18 votes and Vale of Leven made a re-appearance, coming in as the Combination champions with 17 votes. The six unsuccessful clubs were Ayr Parkhouse, Stenhousemuir, Beith, Dumfries, Royal Albert and Bathgate.

Saints bounced back with an improved showing in the 1905-06 season. They lost their first two matches but eventually recorded a League win on the 9th September when they beat Hamilton away 4-0, the home team missing a penalty at the start of the second half with the score goalless and Saints then going up the other end and immediately scoring. They also won the return fixture against the Accies 4-0 in November and a 5-1 win over second placed Ayr FC on the 9th December, with the score being only 1-1 at halftime, lifted them up to fifth in the table, which is where they eventually finished. Inconsistent form, and then losing a double header against eventual champions Leith at the end of season, prevented any possibility of pushing on.

Push on they did though in the following season as at the end of 1907 they were crowned Scottish League Second Division champions for a second time, but once again they failed to gain election back to the First Division. They opened with a 3-0 win over Dumbarton on the 18th August all three goals scored by their new centre-forward Sandy Hall who joined Newcastle United at the end of the season for a fee of £200. Hall was a member of Dundee's 1910 Scottish Cup winning squad and turned out for Canada in the 1904 Olympics despite being born in the north-east of Scotland and incredibly won a gold medal in the football tournament. His goals were a major factor in the Saints winning the Scottish League Second Division championship. He made little impression at Newcastle and returned to Scotland to play for Dundee. He later played for Portsmouth, Motherwell and Dunfermline.

Backed by Hall's goalscoring prowess Saints won their first seven League games, conceding only three goals in the process, and their first defeat came in mid-December when they went down 1-0 at the Old Logie Green against city and promotion rivals Leith. They also suffered a 5-1 reverse at Arthurlie in the first game of 1907 but later they went undefeated throughout March 1907 and their 0-0 draw at the end of the month at home to Albion Rovers left the top three sides of Saints, Arthurlie and Vale of Leven all on 27 points, although the other two had now completed their programmes, whereas St Bernard's still had a remarkable four fixtures to play.

On Monday 1st April Saints secured the point that guaranteed them top spot and the championship at Stark's Park, away at Raith. Hall scored in the first half before they conceded a penalty ten minutes from time. They surprisingly lost 5-3 at home to bottom side Ayr Parkhouse on the 6th April but finished with two wins to take the title by five points. Port Glasgow Athletic, Kilmarnock and Hamilton all finished bottom of the First Division with 21 points. Goal average wasn't used to separate teams and the precedent was for a play-off. However it was decided not to arrange a three-way play-off to decide who would apply for re-election and all three clubs stood, against five challengers from the Second Division, including St Bernard's. At the League's AGM on the 27th May all three First Division clubs were re-elected and the Saints missed out yet again. At the same meeting a motion by Hearts which proposed automatic promotion and relegation was rejected by 11 votes to 6.

The following seasons in the run up to the First World War were largely characterised by mid-table finishes with the highlights being the 1909-10 and 1914-15 campaigns where they came in third. They only featured four times in the Scottish Cup between 1907 and 1915 and never went beyond the First Round. In the 1906-07 competition they contested three matches with Renton before going out and it was the same story in 1907-08, although the opposition was Queen's Park this time. In the 1910-11 Scottish Cup they lost 7-2 at Partick Thistle and their best performance probably came in the 1912-13 season when they took First Division Hamilton to a replay.

After two seasons of finishing in the lower half of the Second Division table, the 1909-10 season saw an upturn in fortunes as St Bernard's finished in third place. Edinburgh rivals Leith Athletic were crowned champions along with Raith Rovers, Saints finishing six points behind them. At the beginning of October they beat Vale of Leven 6-1 and in early December they also scored six against East Stirlingshire. Graham scored a hat-trick in the 6-2 victory as the Shire had to play all of the second half with ten men conceding five but scoring two themselves. The result left Saints lying in second, just a point behind leaders Raith. However, they then lost 1-0 away at Leith and 2-1 away at Raith to lose top spot to the side from Kirkcaldy. Although they regained top spot following a 4-0 win against Albion Rovers both Raith and Leith each had a handful of games still to play whereas St Bernard's only had two. Saints played no games during the month of March during which time their two rivals moved ahead of them and they eventually finished third.

At the end of the 1913-14 season, despite finishing a mid-table seventh, the club were one of seven teams putting themselves forward for election to the First Division, which was being expanded from 18 to 20 clubs. Champions Ayr United and sixth placed Dumbarton were elected on the 2nd June. The bid by St Bernard's didn't receive a seconder so they took no part in the voting.

In the 1914-15 season St Bernard's were involved in an extraordinary three way play-off for the Second Division title. St Bernard's, along with Leith and Cowdenbeath, finished on 37 points and the League ordered a three-way "play-off" to decide the championship. At the start of the campaign St Bernard's won their first three matches but then lost four of their next five, and when they lost 5-0 at Leith at the end of November they were in sixth place in a 14 team division. 1915 saw the club hit a purple patch of form as they won a club record eight consecutive matches starting with a 5-1 victory over Dundee Hibernian on the 23rd January. A week later they beat Arthurlie 6-0, with Coupar scoring four. On the 20th February they registered another six goal winning margin, beating Vale of Leven 7-1 away from home. Although they conceded the first goal, this setback seemed to shake the Saints up and goals from Cox (2), Coupar (2), McDougal (2) and A. Ross took them up to fourth, still ten points behind leaders Cowdenbeath but having played four games fewer. Their fine run eventually ended on 20th March with a 2-1 defeat at Newfield Park against Johnstone, but they then bounced back with a 3-1 win against St Johnstone.

Things were really getting exciting at the top of the table. Cowdenbeath finished their programme at the end of March with 37 points from their 26 matches. Leith Athletic, two points behind, played East Stirling on the 3rd April and won to be tied at the top. Goal average was not yet in existence let alone goal difference so the SFL ordered a play-off game, which took place at a neutral ground, East End Park Dunfermline on Saturday 10th. Cowdenbeath took the initiative and established a two goal advantage in the first half. Leith put on an improved display but their finishing was wasteful. They did eventually get a goal back through a penalty but lost 2-1. Any celebration by Cowdenbeath was quickly muted when news came through that St Bernard's had beaten Lochgelly United 6-0 to join both clubs on 37 points. Their victory over Lochgelly was even more remarkable in that they played most of the game a man short due to injury. *The Scotsman* reported that "it was a surprisingly good account which the St Bernard's gave of themselves in their game at the Gymnasium, Edinburgh, with

Lochgelly United, and their six goals victory is all the more meritorious when it is borne in mind that they were for the greater portion of the match without Penman, their left back, who had met with an accident. The opening goal scored by McGarrity was a penalty one. The scorers of the remaining goals were A Ross (2), Coupar, Bennett and McDougall."

The SFL had been far too premature in organising a championship play-off match and now had no choice but to extend the play-offs to a round robin with the Cowdenbeath versus Leith result standing. A week later, on Saturday 17th April Leith avoided elimination by beating St. Bernards 2-1 at the neutral venue of Easter Road. *The Scotsman* reported that "by defeating the St Bernard's at Easter Road by 2 goals to 1, Leith have created an interesting situation for the Second Division Championship. Thus, if the St Bernard's win over Cowdenbeath on Saturday next, the three teams concerned will be on an equality with a win each...The St Bernard's had about three fourths of the play but failed badly at goal. Leith were disjointed, but they made the most of their opportunities. Early on Hyde scored from a cross by Smith [for Leith], but before the interval Weir equalised. As in the first half, the St Bernard's did most of the attacking, yet they were actually defeated." St Bernard's didn't deserve to lose having dominated possession and Leith were indebted to Wilkinson in goal who saved his side from defeat. Early in the second half Saints twice struck the woodwork. Leith's win kept them in the running and opened up the possibility of a triple tie if St Bernard's beat Cowdenbeath.

The following Saturday, on the 24th April, again at Easter Road, the Scottish Football League were spared any further deliberations as Cowdenbeath beat St Bernards 3-1. *The Scotsman* reported that "Cowdenbeath beat St Bernard's by reason of adapting themselves to the conditions and playing hard on the weaknesses of their opponents. The St Bernard's had the greater share of the play, and during the second half particularly the times when the Fife lot crossed the half-way line could have been counted on the fingers of one hand. But in front of goal the Cowdenbeath men were most dangerous, and Phillip, in the first half, snapped the chances made for him by Aitken, who was often too much for Morrison. Persistent attacks by St Bernard's in the second half yielded a point just before the finish through A Ross, but prior to that, Aitken, from a breakaway, had added to the Cowdenbeath total." Cowdenbeath thus topped the playoff group with four points and were classified as champions, Leith Athletic took two points and were second, and St Bernard's were placed third.

At the end of May 1915 the Second Division was disbanded due to the First World War and the clubs affected joined a number of non-league clubs in forming two regional leagues, the West of Scotland League and the Eastern League. St Bernard's competed in the latter and in its first season finished as runners-up to Armadale. The following season they came third but a number of clubs dropped out, including St Bernard's. When the Second Division wasn't reformed by the Scottish Football League in 1919 St Bernard's were one of a dozen clubs to lose their League status. They then joined the Central League, where they competed for two seasons, and coming in seventh place on each occasion.

A number of players from the club saw active service in the War. One example was inside-left David McDougal, who had scored 10 goals in just 16 appearances. He was killed in action in at Flanders, Belgium in 1918 aged 24. John Ferguson was killed at the Battle of Somme in October 1916, aged 24, and posthumously awarded the Victoria Cross. Alex Kay who played for the club between 1898 and 1900 was killed in 1917. John Frail, John Fleming and James Hastie never returned but Harry Simpson, who was wounded at Gallipoli in 1915 survived.

The Royal Gymnasium was used by the War Department, and when the club were given it back the pitch was destroyed and the ground damaged. It was not until 1922 that the War Office offered compensation and not until November 1924 that the Royal Gymnasium was fit to play on again. In the meantime St Bernard's secured a five year lease at Old Logie Green from Leith Athletic and the Saints played their home matches here and also at Hearts' Tynecastle ground.

At a Scottish Football League meeting on the 11th May 1921 the League finally agreed to the restoration of the Second Division, including automatic promotion and relegation. The Central League disbanded and its clubs became members of the Scottish League for the 1921-22 season. St Bernard's made a terrible start to their resumption of League football, picking up only one win during the first months of August and September. The reinstated Second Division now consisted of 20 teams and the bottom two clubs would drop out of the League as part of creating two divisions of 20 clubs each (the First Division had 22 clubs with three clubs going down and only the Second Division champions going up). After the first six games St Bernard's were joint bottom with Clackmannan with only three points.

Results were much better during the autumn. In October the Saints recorded victories over St Johnstone, Alloa Athletic (the eventual champions) and Stenhousemuir. Four of their five games played in December ended 1-0 with the spoils shared. On the7th January 1922 they beat Johnstone 6-0 in which Donachie (2), Cox, Brown, Wilson and Robertson all scored past Eden, the Johnstone goalkeeper. However, mixed fortunes during the rest of 1922 saw St Bernard's settled in mid-table and they eventually came in ninth place, finishing their League programme with a 2-1 loss to already promoted

Alloa on the 29th April.

The next three League seasons were really poor, as the Saints finished in the bottom four. In fact St Bernard's were never out of the bottom half of the table for the next six seasons with a best placed finish of 13th in the 1926-27 season. For the 1922-23 season John Hay returned at full back from Bradford City but Cox the right winger went to Hamilton and Archibald, their goalkeeper, went to Newcastle, replaced by Mason, a Burnbank junior. The team made a solid start and by mid-October they were just in the top ten, in eighth place. However, they failed to win in the League across December and January to slip to 14th place. In mid-January they beat Dalbeattie Star 8-1 in the First Round of the Scottish Cup, with hat-tricks from both Lawrence and Pettigrew, although they went out to Dundee in the next round, but only after a replay. The Saints beat eventual champions Queen's Park 1-0 on the 17th February 1923 with a last minute goal but then failed to win in their next eight games and slid down the table to eventually finish in 18th place. On the 29th April 1923 they were deducted two points for fielding D L Anderson in four games from the 16th March while he was ineligible.

The 1923-24 season brought with it the prospect of relegation to the newly formed Third Division and St Bernard's only narrowly avoided the drop, finishing in 18th place, just one point ahead of Vale of Leven, who were relegated along with Lochgelly United. Thomas Heatlie was appointed as manager but lasted just the one season. Mark Paterson, who had made over 400 appearances for Hibs, joined the club for the season also, where he ended his career aged 36. The Saints started with three consecutive draws and only won one of their first eight games before recording a second win of the season on 6th October with a 1-0 win over bottom club Lochgelly United. A 3-0 defeat at Stenhousemuir in the last game of 1923 left them in 18th place going into the New Year. Five wins during January and February, including a 4-0 away win against struggling Vale of Leven, in which the Saints centre-forward Archie Young scored a hat-trick, took them up to 15th in the table.

The Saints were also going well in the Scottish Cup. They had beaten Fraserburgh 3-0 and then had knocked out Stenhousemuir, who were going well in the same Division, after two replays. They were now drawn to visit Raith Rovers, at that point a First Division side, who were going really well and who would achieve their highest ever League placing in finishing third. A crowd of over 10,000 at Stark's Park saw St Bernard's pull off a Cup shock by winning 1-0 with *The Scotsman* observing that "St Bernard's accomplished one of the best performances in their history" and that "on play, they were fortunate to come out on the right side, as during both halves, they were penned to their own portion of the field for a considerable part of the time. Their defence, however, never wavered, and, though often in difficulties, always managed to clear their lines safely, and to them must be given all the credit of a sensational victory."

Raith Rovers completely dominated the first half but could not score, mainly due to the heroics of Tommy McAlpine in the St Bernard's goal. Only towards the end of the first half did St Bernard's look dangerous, forcing a succession of corners. The second half ran along similar lines with St Bernard's defending stoutly. Eight minutes from the end the unexpected happened as the Saints centre-forward Archie Young, formerly of Hibs and Hamilton, darted in to intercept a sloppy back pass and score, but in doing so first collided with the Raith goalkeeper and then the post, breaking his arm in the process. With a man advantage Raith then made a desperate effort to get level but the Saints held firm. Summarising the *Sunday Post* noted that "the Saints played a steady game. They did not show so many frills at Raith, but method and purpose were apparent on every occasion. It would be unfair to individualise in such a level lot. The Rovers simply could not finish their outfield work, so an opportunist in Young finished their career in the competition for this season." The victorious St Bernard's team was: McAlpine; Law, Dunsmuir; Paterson, G Henderson, McLeod; Leitch, J Henderson, Young, Lauder and Penman. In the Scottish Cup Quarter-finals St Bernard's were drawn away at First Division Aberdeen and lost 3-0. They failed to reproduce their best form and effectively lost the tie in the first half, conceding goals at regular intervals in the 12th, 25th and 40th minutes. The second half was much more even but both 'keepers made good saves.

Their Cup run seemed to negatively impact on their League form as after their victory over Raith they failed to score in any of their next four League games. They broke this barren spell in fine style, beating East Fife 4-3 in mid-March. In this game they were behind 3-1 going into the last twenty minutes but goals from Leitch, Penman and Kane gave them a much needed victory. They failed to win any of their next four games and suffered a setback in the last of these, when they lost 2-1 at home to relegation rivals Broxburn United. With Lochgelly United already down, only two points separated the next four teams – Vale of Leven, Arbroath, Broxburn had 28 points with two fixtures left, whereas St Bernard's had 30 points, but with just one game left to play. The other three sides played their games on the 19th April and all won, so that the four sides were now all on 30 points. The last round of matches was played on Saturday the 26th April. Broxburn won 3-1 at Albion Rovers and Arbroath thrashed King's Park 5-1. St Bernard's entertained Johnstone and *The Scotsman* reported that "an early penalty goal scored by Young gave St Bernard's confidence to go and win in their important game with Johnstone, and win they did so that they retain their position in Second League football. It was a strenuously contested game from beginning to end, and there is no doubt that the points went to the better team on the day's showing." Johnstone were already under strength and an injury to McDonald shortly after the start reduced them to ten men. Johnstone nearly drew level but Dunsmuir made a goal line clearance. The Saints scored a second goal through Lauder late on in the second half. In the final match, Vale of Leven could only draw 1-1 at Bo'ness and therefore accompanied Lochgelly down into the Third Division.

The club avoided the drop by just one point but better news came on the 1st May 1924 when *The Scotsman* reported that "negotiations were concluded this week by the St Bernard's Football Club for the purchase of the Royal Gymnasium Ground, Eyre Place, Edinburgh, which is to be converted into a modern football enclosure in readiness for the beginning of the next season. The St Bernard's held a yearly tenancy of the ground, but have not played on it since the beginning of the war, at which time it was taken over by the military authorities as a drill ground. Since the end of the war, the St Bernard's have occupied the Logie Green ground on a five years' lease, which has now expired. The new pitch will run east and west, and a stand is to be erected on the south side. A drill hall included in the purchase is to be utilised to provide stripping and office accommodation."

The new ground wasn't available for the start of the 1924-25 season but the Saints made a solid start playing their home fixtures at Tynecastle. With Hearts playing away at Cowdenbeath on the 16th August they started the season hosting Armadale, as reported on by *The Scotsman*, who reported that "playing at Tynecastle, Edinburgh, until their new ground is ready, the St Bernard's won with little to spare against Armadale. From first to last the game was hard fought, and both sides showed wonderfully good form considering that new players outnumbered those carried forward from last season. Armadale had the pull at the outset. For twenty minutes they worried the Edinburgh defenders until Smellie brought out a merited goal. Almost immediately a St Bernards' improvement took place, and Young, gathering a left wing cross, scored a good equaliser. That fairly represented the run of the first half, but a surprise occurred when Fordyce, from a free-kick, gave St Bernard's the lead just before half-time. Another fine goal by Young early in the second half strengthened the St Bernards' position. Armadale, however, rallied splendidly...[to reduce]...the leeway and there was a lively finish with the visitors just failing to divide the points. The St Bernard's appear to have recruited well, and the new team made a promising appearance, good features being the sturdy back play by Dunsmuir and Donaldson, and the forcing work of Fordyce and Ramage at half-back."

St Bernard's played seven matches at Tynecastle, winning five, and by mid-October were sitting in seventh place. However, they suffered a heavy 6-0 defeat away at Bo'ness and slipped down into the bottom half of the table over the next four weeks. Saturday the 15th November 1924 saw the re-opening of the Royal Gymnasium ground, with Arthurlie the guests. *The Scotsman* reported that "after a lapse of ten years the St Bernard's resumed playing on their old ground at the Royal Gymnasium, Edinburgh, which they acquired by purchase six months ago. Keen as they were to excel in the first game, however, the St Bernard's had to surrender both points to Arthurlie, who secured a soft goal in the early stages, and hung on to the lead till the finish...There were about 3000 spectators, including Mr Patrick J Ford, MP for North Edinburgh, who prior to the game, declared the new ground open, and wished the club success in their efforts to reach the First Division."

The club's first points back at the Gymnasium came a fortnight later, in a 2-2 draw with Clyde but it wasn't until the 27th December that they recorded their first win back there, when they beat Albion Rovers 2-0. They won their next two home fixtures as well but at the end of January 1925 lost 5-1 away at Armadale. They recorded a season's best 5-1 win against strugglers Johnstone in early March, where inside the first ten minutes, three crosses from Boyd out on the right had all been converted, two by Graham and the other by Duncan. Five minutes into the second half Alston made it four and the same player scored a fifth from a corner. In the closing minutes Johnstone got a late consolation. They then failed to win any of the next five games, earning just a single point, but the bottom two clubs Forfar and Johnstone were relegated to the Third Division, with a game to spare, St Bernard's ultimately finishing in 17th place, four points clear of the drop zone, the margin being bigger thanks to a final day 2-0 win over Arbroath.

For the 1925-26 season St Bernard's recruited Davy Gordon as their new manager. He had played for Leith, Hibs and Hull City and had then gone on to manage Hibs between 1919 and 1921. He made a number of signings recruiting Cummings from Ayr and Steve Mitchell from St Rochs in the backs, along with Willie Birrell from Cowdenbeath at centre-half. Main was signed from Aberdeen and Gilmour from Dundee United but most significant was Peter Simpson, signed from Leith. He scored 12 times in his first seven games for Saints and eventually totalled 33 goals for the season.

Having lost their opening game 2-1 away at Stenhousemuir the Saints bounced back with an 8-0 victory at home to Broxburn United on the 22nd August. Under the heading "St Bernard's Swamp Broxburn" *The Scotsman* noted that "during the first half there was no hint of the coming collapse by the visitors...but a run of scoring by Simpson, the St Bernards centre-forward quickly changed the aspect of the game." *The Sunday Post* reported that "with both teams on the losing side last week, it was no surprise to find St Bernard and Broxburn United going all out for victory at the Gymnasium. Play was even enough in the first half, but afterwards the Broxburn men collapsed like a pack of cards, and the Saints found goals easier to get than they have done for many a long day. Eight they got past McKinlay, seven of these in the second half, Simpson, at centre proved himself a rare opportunist, and had half of the goals. Duke had two, and Pollock and McCulloch had the others. It is difficult to account for Broxburn's rout. The forwards certainly were very poor, and this threw a lot of extra work on the half-backs, and allowed the Saints to push on the game uninterruptedly. McKinlay in the Broxburn goal, had not much chances with any of the shots that beat him. It can at least be said for Broxburn that they never lay down. The Saints had a fine pair of backs in Muir and Mitchell, who quite took the heart out of the opposition. The half-backs settled down to an effective game, and the forwards played with fine understanding and precision."

In early September St Bernard's beat East Stirlingshire 6-1. During the first half the Saints were clearly the better side, scoring four goals – Simpson had two, Duke and Muir one apiece, the latter from a penalty. The visitors scored once in the opening period, also from a penalty. In the second half East Stirlingshire missed a penalty, before Cumming and Main took the total to six. A fortnight later they beat Armadale 6-2 with *The Scotsman* commenting that the "St Bernards continue to be prolific scorers on their own ground." They reported that "the team work of the St Bernards was well balanced, though the defence wavered occasionally when hard pressed. Birrell, the centre-half, played well in defence and attack, and the forwards never missed an opportunity of shooting, with the result that they were three goals up inside the first fifteen minutes, Gilmour and Duke (2) being the scorers. Simpson got a fourth before the interval, and Armadale's response was a goal by Anderson. Armadale improved in the second half, but their forwards were weak in front of goal. Duff scored their second goal, but not before Muir and Main had put the Saints further ahead." These two fine wins moved the club up to seventh in the division but by the turn of the year they had slipped into the bottom half.

In their first match of 1926 they beat struggling Broxburn 7-4 away from home. The hosts made a good start and opened the scoring but their early advantage was short-lived as St Bernard's assumed the ascendancy and the Saints led by the odd goal in five at the interval. In the first fifteen minutes of the second half they blitzed their opponents, scoring five more goals to lead 7-2 before United got two back near the end. *The Scotsman* commented that "the Edinburgh team played with plenty of dash, and showed opportunism in turning scoring chances to account." Simpson scored four goals with the others coming from Ramage, Gilmour and Muir. However, set against these wins were a 6-3 loss at Bo'ness and a 5-1 defeat at Armadale. At the end of January they lost 8-1 at First Division Aberdeen in the First Round of the Scottish Cup. They followed this by winning four in a row in the League from mid- February to mid-March but then failed to win again and they eventually finished a disappointing 14th place.

The 1926-27 season only saw a marginal improvement as the club finished one place higher. They lost 5-1 at Raith in September and conceded five at home to champions Bo'ness in a 5-3 loss. Their best League win came near the end of the season with a 6-3 win over Bathgate. The general economic downturn hit a number of lower League sides and part way through the season top goalscorer Peter Simpson was lured away to play for English non-league side Kettering Town, and then Crystal Palace, having scored 78 goals in 58 appearances for the Saints.

St Bernard's opened the 1927-28 season with an entertaining 4-4 draw against what would be runaway champions Ayr United. *The Scotsman* commented that "St Bernard's had a difficult task for an opening engagement, but they came out of the game with good credentials. A well-earned point was won from Ayr United at Somerset Park after a strenuous tussle for supremacy." Ayr opened the scoring after three minutes but Saints led at the interval by the odd goal in three. Had McKnight converted a penalty kick just before the interval for St Bernard's the result may have been different. This would probably be the high point of what would otherwise be a poor season with a lot of heavy defeats.

Four of these heavy defeats came during the winter of 1927. On the 12th November Saints lost 9-2 at Forfar Athletic, a new record loss – still a seven goal margin of defeat but surpassing the 8-1 loss against Rangers on goals conceded from 1897. *The Scotsman* commented that "St Bernards were heavily trounced in their match with Forfar Athletic at Station Road, Forfar, and much of the blame for the defeat was due to the visiting backs, who were unsteady. Boyne played well in goal, and could hardly be blamed for the Forfar total. The Edinburgh forward line was a good attacking force, and, had their backs been as strong, Forfar's win would not have been so big." Forfar rattled in seven goals in the first half, whilst Walker and Boyle scored for St Bernard's.

A week later they lost 6-3 at Queen of the South, Gray scoring four goals. Saints conceded first but equalised through a brilliant effort by McCaig, while playing a man short due to an injury to Swanson. However by half-time they were losing 4-1. St Bernard's were on top from the resumption and in the first twenty minutes of the second half scored through Mitchell and McCaig, which reduced the host's lead to one. Queen of the South finished strongly, however and added two more, Gray taking his tally to four. They could have scored more but for some brilliant saves by Boyne. A month later, on the 17th December, St Bernard's lost 7-1 at Clydebank. Boyne kept them in the game for the first quarter of an hour but was then beaten twice in the next fifteen minutes before Moffat reduced the arrears, but Crawford completed a first half hat-trick to give Clydebank a 3-1 half-time lead at Clydeholm. Mitchell, the St Bernard's right-wing was injured and didn't play in the second half during which Thomson also scored a hat-trick for Clydebank. On the 31st December the Saints lost 6-1 at promotion chasing Third Lanark, *The Scotsman* noting that "the St Bernards were no match for Third Lanark at Cathkin Park, Glasgow, and the score in no way exaggerated the home team's superiority. On the snow-covered pitch, the winners showed remarkably accurate ball control, and a combination which kept the Saints' defence on the run from start to finish." Wilson scored five first half goals for Thirds, who visibly eased off in the second half. Near the finish St Bernard's scored a consolation goal by Walker.

By this time St Bernard's sat second from bottom in the Second Division, three points above Armadale at the foot of the table but just one point behind Morton and Clydebank. It was a new low. A change of year brought a change of fortune and within the first week of January the Saints had recorded three consecutive wins. These wins moved them up three places in the table. On the 24th March they recorded their best win of season, winning 8-2 against Queen of the South. In this match the visitors were unlucky as their left-back suffered a collision early in the game and spent the rest of the game confined to hobbling along the touchline. Eadie, the Saints centre-forward scored four and also missed a penalty. McCaig (2), Swanson and McKnight also scored for the home side, five goals coming in 17 second half minutes. By this time Armadale were ten points adrift at the bottom but only two points separated the next five clubs, which included St Bernard's, with four games left to play.

The Saints went down 6-2 at Albion Rovers in their next match, which left them, Bathgate and Morton all on 31 points and second from bottom. A crucial 2-0 home win over fellow strugglers Bathgate eased their re-election fears, the return of Duke at inside right after a three month absence, being key. In their penultimate game they lost 8-1 at King's Park. *The Sunday Post* reported that "King's Park had the record victory of their League career when, at Forthbank yesterday, in the last home match of the season, they trounced St Bernard to the tune of eight goals to one. Three of the eight came in the first half and five in the second, and all were due to the dashing tactics of the home front rank, who time and again went through the defence, the home halfs and backs giving no rope to the Edinburgh club's forwards, who only made occasional attempts at scoring with no combination or method in them." Toner scored four goals for the Stirling outfit, with Eadie scoring for the Saints. Other results meant St Bernard's were safe. On the 21st April they concluded their League programme with a 1-0 win against Clydebank, Eadie scoring in the 86th minute from the penalty spot after Duke had been brought down. St Bernard's finished 17th but conceded a club record 101 goals for the season. This match was the last game as manager for Davy Gordon after three years in charge.

James Kirkwood took over as manager and oversaw a big improvement in the club's performance in his first season. Saints started the 1928-29 season with a 1-1 draw with Queen of the South, *The Sunday Post* commenting that "there are more strangers in the St Bernards…eleven than in most of the Second Division teams, and it was not to be expected that [they] would strike a game right away." Included in the line-up was a new goalkeeper, R Leonard Small. He was an Edinburgh University Divinity student and was nicknamed "The Holy Goalie." He was later forced to give up the game by Church authorities and in later years he became Moderator of the Church of Scotland in 1966 and was awarded an OBE.

It took the new team some time to gel and it wasn't until the 22nd September, and their seventh fixture, before they registered a win, a 2-1 victory over Forfar Athletic, in which Eadie scored twice. When they beat Armadale 5-1 at the end of October, Ramage and Robertson both scoring two, against an opposition side that was reduced to nine men due to injury, that was only their third win and they were 13th in the table. This big win heralded in a great run of form where they also beat King's Park 4-1, in which Meagher, a new signing, scored twice on debut; Arthurlie were beaten 5-1 in an eventful game in which Eadie scored a hat-trick, St Bernard's missed two penalties and two players were sent off after a melee; and Morton were defeated 7-3, with goals from Eadie (3), Meagher (2) and Robertson (2). The Saints scored 24 goals in five home games in a run that took them up to sixth by the turn of the year. St Bernard's only lost twice in their first ten matches of 1929 but any hopes of a promotion challenge were ended by a 4-1 reverse at Morton who went on to finish second to Dundee United. They eventually finished in sixth, their highest placing since their return to the League in 1921.

The improvement wasn't sustained, however, and in the following season they slipped back into the bottom half, coming in 14th. St Bernard's never really recovered from a poor start in which they lost five of their opening seven games. Later in the season they won three games in which they scored five from December 1929 onwards, against Dumbarton, Armadale and Arbroath but ultimately it was a disappointing season given the improved showing the year before. The one highlight was a 5-3 victory over Third Lanark in the First Round of the Scottish Cup. Three times Saints came from behind in front of a 10,000 crowd. They drew Hearts in the next round, and conceded five themselves, in a 5-1 loss, although only after a replay when the first match was drawn 0-0.

The 1930-31 season only saw a marginal improvement in their final League placing. They lost their opening game of the new season 2-0 away at would be champions Third Lanark. In their first home League game they thrashed Clydebank 6-1, their opponents fielding seven amateurs. Two of the goals were scored by new signing Rab Walls, who scored 23 League goals in 36 games for the season. In total he went on to score 29 goals in 66 appearances before joining Hibs at the end of the 1931-32 season. Saints then lost four out of their next five games, including a 5-1 defeat at St Johnstone. By the time they played out an entertaining 4-4 draw with Arbroath in mid-December they were in the bottom four. In their first game of 1931 they beat Alloa Athletic 5-0, with Walls scoring two. Another 4-4 draw, this time against Albion Rovers in mid-February was the beginning of a run of nine games without defeat which included a 7-2 win over Montrose. They also beat Arbroath 8-0 in their final League game of the season and this strong finish saw them climb up to an 11th place finish. The game against Arbroath, on the 25th April, brought Kirkwood's three year spell as manager to an end.

Bob Innes, a former referee took charge of the Saints and remained as manager until October 1939. Hibs had been relegated and Edinburgh City were a new team elected into the League so there were lots of Edinburgh derbies in the 1931-32 season. St Bernard's started their League campaign at home with a 5-1 over Brechin city on the 15th August but lost four in a row soon after. On the 5th September St Bernard's recorded a 4-2 away win at Easter Road against Hibs in front of nearly 10,000 spectators. This was a day when football was marred by accidents. At Ibrox, the Celtic keeper John Thomson received injuries that proved fatal. Another incident, although not so series occurred in this game with Blyth, the Hibernian keeper breaking his leg.

A heavy home defeat against leaders and eventual champions East Stirlingshire in November, by four goals to nil, left the Saints in mid-table, where they stayed until the spring of 1932. A 6-1 away win at Powderhall against strugglers Edinburgh City was part of a run of five consecutive wins. The run came to an abrupt halt with a 5-1 loss at East Stirlingshire but they won their last three remaining fixtures, including two 4-0 wins over King's Park and Dunfermline, as they finished in fifth place, two ahead of Hibernian. Although Walls didn't reproduce his scoring from the previous season he still attracted interest from other clubs and at the end of the season he moved to city rivals Hibs.

Leith Athletic had been relegated from the First Division so the 1932-33 seasons started with four Edinburgh teams in the Second Division. St Bernard's won their opening game 4-1 against Albion Rovers but then conceded four a week later in a 4-0 loss at East Fife. On the 3rd September the won 6-3 away at Bo'ness although this result was later expunged when their opponents were expelled from the League. A week later they won one of many Edinburgh derbies, beating city strugglers Edinburgh City 8-1 with Davidson and Eadie scoring three apiece. They also scored eight in the reverse fixture, this time winning 8-2 on the 27th December and they ended 1932 in eighth place.

Willie Ferguson, an ex-Queen of the South and Chelsea winger, returned to Scotland after a decade in London and played 17 games in the second part of the 1932-33 season with St Bernard's. The Saints went undefeated in their first six fixtures of 1933, which included an 8-0 win over strugglers Brechin City at the beginning of March, the visitors having a man ordered off after half an hour's play and Murray scored four. The run was ended with a 6-0 loss at Dumbarton and a fortnight later they lost 4-1 against city rivals and champs-elect Hibs, but were handicapped by an injury to their centre-forward Murray. They lost two of their three remaining fixtures 4-0 against Forfar and Dunfermline and slipped down to finish in 12th place.

In the 1933-34 season St Bernard's recorded some big wins during the season but were plagued by inconsistency and had another mid-table finish. In early September they scored five when beating Edinburgh City away from home. A month later they doubled that score in a surprise win over the current leaders Morton. Under the heading "St Bernard's Amazing Feat", *The Scotsman* reported that "not for years has such a feast of goals been provided at the Gymnasium as was the case in the St Bernards Morton game, and the 2000 spectators got full value for their money by seeing no fewer than eleven goals scored, ten of which were claimed by the home team. It was a truly amazing feat on the part of the Saints, especially when it is taken into consideration that they were opposed by the League leaders, but such was their form in the first half that few teams of their class could have stood against them. Opposed to the methodical attacks of Murray and his wings the Greenock defence simply became demoralised. Eight goals were conceded up to half-time. Throughout the first 45 minutes the Saints played well together as a team, but the man of the match was undoubtedly A Brown, who gave a brilliant display of shooting. He scored five goals, four of which were magnificent efforts. The other came from a penalty kick. With Campbell, he made up a fine left wing, and the outside man, besides finding the net once, contributed many fine runs and generally made the most of his partner's astute moves. Murray with three goals, was also a lively leader, and Forbes, whose goal made up the total, if not so prominent as usual, nevertheless was a good winger. He seemed unable, however, to work harmoniously in conjunction with King, who was not always happy at inside-right. The other departments in the team gave the Morton side no time to settle, and but for a mistake of judgement on Kennan's part, it is questionable if Vandelear's drive would have eluded the goalkeeper's vigilance." This win on the 14th October 1933 was a club record SFL victory.

A month later St Bernard's beat Alloa 5-1 and in the New Years' Day game they won 5-0 against Edinburgh City, Murray, their centre-forward, scoring a hat trick and also missing a penalty. In March they won 7-2 versus Dumbarton. Forbes, their outside-right, scored two, as did Murray and Russell. However, despite these big wins, across the course of the season the Saints lost as many as they won (15 apiece) and finished in tenth place.

St Bernard's scored 75 League goals in the 1933-34 season but in the following camapign they scored over 100 goals, setting a new club record for a League season. This attacking ethos would be sustained as the Saints scored over 100 goals in each of the next two seasons as well. With this weight of goals Innes's team were regular challengers for promotion. After losing their opening game of the 1934-35 season at home to Edinburgh rivals Leith 1-0, the Saints followed this up with four big wins. A 5-2 away win at Arbroath was followed by a 4-1 home win over Stenhousemuir and on the 1st September they played at Central Park where they thrashed Cowdenbeath 10-1, setting a new club record away SFL win. *The Scotsman* reported that "the St Bernards maintained their recent good form on the occasion of their visit to Cowdenbeath. Close on 1500 spectators saw the Edinburgh team, playing with great dash and cleverness, obtain ten goals against the loss of one. In comparison with the virile play of the winners, the Cowdenbeath side lacked guile and team-sense, and they were completely over-run long before the end." Weir headed the opening goal for St Bernard's from a corner kick after 12 minutes and Murray added a second just two minutes later. Hay scored a third and Murray and Noble made it 5-0 at half-time. In the second half Hay made it six with a brilliantly taken goal before Cowdenbeath got one back and then contrived to miss a penalty. The rout continued with Murray (2), Hay and Laidlaw raising the total to ten. The fourth big victory came in a 5-1 home win over Brechin City in which the Saints were three up within 13 minutes, Murray's speed and alertness being the main feature of the game. He scored four of the goals, two in each half.

These four victories were part of a nine game unbeaten run which was eventually ended by a 4-2 loss in Stirling against King's Park on the 20th October. Across November and December they scored five or more on four occasions, starting with a 6-2 win over Raith on the 10th November, in which Eadie scored two penalties. This was followed a fortnight later by a 6-1 win over East Fife. Again, Eadie converted two penalties and their opponents had two players ordered off. At the beginning of December they beat Dumbarton 5-0, Russell scoring a hat-trick and the other two came from Murray. Finally, at the end of the month they beat Edinburgh City 6-2 away at the Marine Gardens, Portobello to move into second place, two points behind leaders Third Lanark and level on points with Arbroath and Stenhousemuir (who had each played a games less).

The Saints scored four in wins over King's Park and Montrose over the New Year period going unbeaten in January to consolidate second place, especially having beaten promotion rivals Stenhousemuir 2-1 at Ochilview, Larbert. By mid-February Third Lanark remained top on 40 points, St Bernard's were second, just a point behind on 39, and Arbroath were third, on 38 points – all having played 27 matches. On the 2nd March they suffered a blow losing 1-0 against Morton at home. Having gone behind they hammered away at the Morton defence from start to finish and repeatedly hit the woodwork. The result dropped the club down to third, a point behind Arbroath. They bounced back the following week as they beat the leaders Third Lanark 3-2 to keep themselves in the running for promotion. With a lot riding on the game for both sides it was a keenly fought contest witnessed by a crowd of 6,000. St Bernard's showed great character by twice coming from behind. Thirds took an early lead but Eadie equalised five minutes later from a penalty. But just another three minutes had elapsed before Thirds regained the lead. Shortly after their opponents had an effort crash against their crossbar. Russell got them back on level terms again and the two teams went into the interval level at 2-2. The second half saw end-to-end action but both defences repulsed their opponents' attacks. In the 81st minute Russell scored to put St Bernard's ahead for the first time. Late drama was to come as Thirds, pushing for their own equaliser, were awarded a penalty as a result of Fitzsimmons using his hands to stop a near certain goal, but the resulting spot-kick was missed, costing Thirds a point.

A week later St Bernard's lost ground as both their rivals won and they shared the spoils in an entertaining eight goal thriller at Forfar. They let slip a two goal lead at 3-1 but then went ahead to lead 4-3 before conceding again. The following Saturday they met promotion rivals Arbroath at the Gymnasium in front of 8,000 spectators, hoping to reduce the leeway but were held to a 0-0 draw leaving them two points behind Arbroath and three behind Thirds, with three games left to play (Third Lanark 46, Arbroath 45, St Bernard's 43).

Their promotion hopes were dealt a fatal blow a week later, on the 30th March, when they lost 3-0 away at Raith and Thirds and Arbroath both won. Under the headline "St Bernard's Challenge Fails" *The Scotsman* noted that "the promotion hopes of the St Bernard's received a severe set-back at Kirkcaldy, where the Raith Rovers administered this season's heaviest defeat to the Edinburgh team. While the home club deservedly won, a three-goal margin was flattering. In the outfield the St Bernard's were much smarter...The visitors' backs were not so good as usual, and their positional work was poorly executed...The St Bernard's forwards missed too many scoring chances." There was no scoring in the first half of the match, with St Bernard's having the best of the play. Raith scored two goals early in the second half and got a third ten minutes from the end. The Saints were now four points behind Arbroath and five behind Third Lanark with two games left, so they needed to win both and for Arbroath to suffer two defeats. The following weekend, with St Bernard's not in action, Arbroath drew to get the single point they needed to secure promotion. On the 13th April the Saints played their penultimate game, winning 7-0 against East Stirlingshire and in doing so reached 100 goals for the season. Noble, Russell and Murray each scoring two. They won their last game, 3-2 at Brechin to finish third and end on 103 goals for the season.

In the following 1935-36 season St Bernard's surpassed this goals total, this time scoring a club record 106 goals, but disappointingly failed to mount a sustained promotion challenge, coming in fifth. They started well, going unbeaten in their first five games which included a 6-3 away win against Stenhousemuir, in which Brooks scored four. They followed this up with a 6-2 win at Leith, thanks to a Noble hat trick and for a while were joint top, along with St Mirren and Falkirk. Two further big away wins were recorded in October, 6-1 against Edinburgh City and 8-2 at Brechin. In this game six goals came in second half and Mitchell scored a hat-trick, with Noble and Russell each scoring two. In early November they won 6-2 against Raith, scoring two in the first four minutes, but at the end of the month they lost 3-2 at home to Falkirk, who would be the eventual champions. This defeat was the start of a run of three consecutive losses which also included a 4-2 reverse at their other promotion rivals St Mirren.

In January 1936 St Bernard's introduced a teenage David Nelson into the first team as a wing-half. He scored seven goals in 12 appearances during the second half of the season and left the club in May 1936 to join Arsenal. The Saints won all four League games in January to sit in fifth place, eight points behind the leaders, but then lost their next three games in February including a devastating 7-1 defeat at Falkirk. *The Scotsman* reported that "victory was made easier for Falkirk by the fact that in the absence of their regular goalkeeper through injury, the St Bernard's fielded a deputy, who found the occasion too much for him....The result did not in any way reflect the run of the play or the general merits of the teams. Falkirk would, however, probably have won even if their opponents had been better served in goal." The following week they also lost 4-1 at Raith Rovers to leave them in sixth place although a massive 13 points off second place.

They bounced back and a 5-2 win over city rivals Leith Athletic was followed by a 7-0 win over bottom club Dumbarton at the Gymnasium. The Saints scored in the first minute, when Noble scored from a penalty and further goals from Nelson, Noble and two from Hay made it 5-0. In the closing stages Russell and Nelson brought the total to seven. The result was somewhat overshadowed by Falkirk (scoring 8) and St Mirren (also scoring 7). Both of these clubs had been relegated the year before and both went on to make an immediate return.

St Bernard's won their next two as well, including a 2-0 home win against St Mirren. Nelson opened the scoring and it was his aggressive following up that put a St Mirren defender under pressure, resulting in them putting the ball past his own goalkeeper. This goal was their 104th for the season, surpassing the previous year's total. This good run was halted in early April when they lost 6-2 at third placed Morton. *The Scotsman* commented that "St Bernard's fell in surprisingly easy fashion. A four goal margin, however, flattered Morton." Noble and McPherson had given the Edinburgh side a two goal lead inside the first half an hour but by half-time Morton had taken the lead. Resuming 3-2 up their hosts scored three more times despite play being of a fairly even nature. St Bernard's lost their last game and finished in fifth place, with a new record total of 106 League goals.

In the 1936-37 season St Bernard's mounted more of a promotion challenge and it was the third consecutive season that they scored 100 League goals. They had contrasting fortunes in their first two games, handing out and being on the end of a thrashing. St Bernard's began the new season on the 8th August in fine style with a 7-1 win over Montrose at the Gymnasium in front of a crowd of 2,000. The Saints took command from the beginning and scored after a minute against an opposition team featuring seven newcomers. Newcomers in the Saints line-up included Tommy Smith in goal. He had made over 140 appearances for Queen's Park and played for the Saints for two seasons. Also making his debut was Peter Flucker, an ex-Hearts and Hibs centre-forward, one of a handful of players to play for three Edinburgh clubs. In this opening game Flucker scored two on debut before Brooks then scored two of his own. In between Montrose got one back but they played all of the second half a man short due to injury. Langton scored a fifth and Noble then scored two, both from penalty kicks.

A week later St Bernard's were beaten 6-1 at Bayview against East Fife. Two quick goals inside the first fifteen minutes gave the home team confidence. Saints reached the interval four-nil down but did not deserve to be so heavily in arrears. Soon after the interval they got a goal back, an own-goal after Flucker had put the defender under pressure. However, they couldn't add to their total and it was East Fife who added two more in the closing stages. Saints went on a good run during the autumn including an 8-1 win away at Forfar in September. Perhaps more significantly was a close 2-1 win over Morton in a top of the table clash the following month. St Bernard's went joint top with Morton as a result, both clubs on 16 points from 11 matches. *The Scotsman* reported that "the Second Division promotion race, which looks like providing one of the best tussles for many seasons, was further improved by St Bernards' win over Morton at the Gymnasium, Edinburgh. The win brings the Edinburgh club level with Morton at the top of the table...St Bernard's made the most of a wind advantage in the first half of their match, and crossed over in the lead by a goal from Russell. This they augmented by a second score by Flucker, shortly after the restart, and although Morton fought back strongly, they could do no more than score once…The outstanding player was Strathie, the home club's stalwart centre half-back." In November the Saints beat strugglers Brechin City 6-0, although a number of goals came near to the end. Ayr United topped the table with 24 points, St Bernard's had 23, as did Morton and Airdrie had 21 points. The win set up an important fixture the following Saturday with the leaders set to visit the Gymnasium. The two sides met on the 28th November with St Bernard's going down rather easily, by five goals to two, inflicting a blow on St Bernard's promotion hopes. Their opponents scored three goals in the first half an hour. Ayr's centre forward McGibbon scored a hat-trick. Airdrie beat Morton 1-0 so that these two teams plus St Bernard's were all level on 23 points in second, three points behind Ayr United.

A fortnight later St Bernard's avenged an earlier defeat in Stirling in some style, beating King's Park 6-1, scoring three goals in each half before their opponents got a late consolation goal. The result took them from fourth to second as Morton lost and Airdrie drew. With Ayr now five points clear it looked like a three-way battle for the remaining promotion spot. St Bernard's won their next four games to consolidate second position and lead the other two teams by two points. A surprise defeat away at second bottom Stenhousemuir in early January wasn't too costly as it was a day of surprises with two of the other clubs around them also suffering surprise defeats. At the end of the month the Saints put up a good showing in the First Round of the Scottish Cup, going out 3-1 to Hearts.

In early February they were beaten by a 5-2 scoreline by Ayr for the second time that season but they continued to pick up vital wins and in mid-March they dealt one of their promotion rivals a blow. St Bernard's beat Airdrieonians 6-1 with six different goal scorers - Philip, Strathie (from a penalty), Grant, Johnston, Dawson and Pinkerton. *The Scotsman* commented that "the home club have never played better all season and were superior to their opponents in every division." Morton got a draw at Ayr so St Bernard's moved a point ahead of Morton and into second place. St Bernard's had four games left to play, but Morton, due to still being in the Scottish Cup, had an extra game to play.

It was "as you were" for in the next two rounds of matches St Bernard's beat Alloa and Dundee United, both by the same 3-0 scoreline, while Morton won their games 6-0 and 4-1. St Bernard's remained one point ahead but had played a game more. This set up a virtual promotion decider as Morton now hosted St Bernard's at Cappielow in a Wednesday night rearranged game. *The Scotsman* covered this crucial midweek game and reported that "Morton and St Bernard's, who have been amongst the foremost clubs for promotion for several years have had to fight it out near the finish this season. In the past they have been fated to deal each other vital blows, while last night's game had a precedent in that when the Greenock club gained promotion in 1929 it was the result of a 4-1 victory over St Bernards. Last night there was scarcely that much between the teams, but there was no doubting the home club's superiority. Morton were faster, especially forward, and had a steadier defence. St Bernards never struck their best, and lacked the resource to beat down vigorous opposition. Much of this vigour was misplaced, and what good football was apparent was often ruined by an undue amount of pushing and jostling. A climax to this was the ordering off of Allan, the left back of St Bernards, who, though by no means an early or constant offender, was too downright in showing his viewpoint in a scene near the close of the game. This incident, however, had little to do with the result. The match appeared to be won and lost by the interval, when the home side were two goals ahead as a result of clever, quick moves after 35 and 37 minutes play. St Bernards had been having a level share of the play, but lacked success on the wings to press home their advantages...Three minutes after the restart St Bernards reduced the arrears. Their wingers improved, and Pinkerton made headway on the left to lob the ball across goal for Grant to head into the net." But Morton hit back and scored two goals in quick succession, the match report observing that "the scoring of the third and vital goal coincided with the appearances a black cat, which gambolled down the pitch and around the goal, to add merriment to the enthusiasm of a record Greenock mid-week crowd of over 13000....St Bernards played a hard game and fought back pluckily, but they were struggling throughout to reach teamwork, which is always a difficult matter on an admittedly tricky pitch. T G Smith, their amateur international goalkeeper, did very well with several brilliant saves. Weir played a strong and thoughtful game at left half-back, while Flucker at centre-forward was always lively, and would have done well with support. On the showing of this match, however, the better team are likely to be promoted." This 4-1 loss was a massive blow as Morton now went a point ahead of them, and with a game in hand. The position now was that Morton, even in the event of St Bernard's winning their one remaining game at Airdrie, would require only one point from two matches - against Dumbarton at home and away at King's Park - to make promotion certain as they had a vastly superior goal average. On Wednesday the 21st April Morton played their game in hand and secured promotion along with Ayr United by thumping Dumbarton 5-0. St Bernard's played their last game two days later, to avoid a clash with the Scottish Cup final, and lost 4-2 at Broomfield against Airdrie. Morton surprisingly lost 2-1 at King's Park in their last game but ended three points ahead of the Saints.

The 1937-38 season saw another promotion challenge and perhaps more famously a Scottish Cup run to the Semi-Finals, their best Cup run for forty years. In the League they dropped a place, although again they were only three points off promotion. On the 14th August 1937 they opened their League campaign against Dundee United at Tannadice. *The Scotsman*, previewing the match wrote "St Bernard's, who just failed with last season's bid, have an unenviable opening at Tannadice Park, for Dundee United, whatever else, generally maintain a good home record." Perhaps it was a massive surprise then when the Saints opened their campaign with a 7-1 win. *The Scotsman* commented "there were several outstanding performances in the Second Division which give strength and optimism of a good and lasting promotion struggle. St Bernard's, strongly in the running in the past three seasons, and perhaps unfortunate last April, started off in great style by scoring seven goals against Dundee United, repeating a 7-1 opening last season, when they defeated Montrose at home...[they]...had an easy win...where they displayed a fine understanding, and after crossing over with a two goal lead they scored five goals in the second half, two of them from penalty kicks. The scorers were: Flucker (2), Grant (2), Dawson and Johnston (2, from penalties). A good feature was the play of the young inside left Dawson, whose improvement with experience should now solve a problem caused last season by the transfer of Noble." Also in the side was Jerry Kerr, who had played for Armadale, Motherwell and Alloa and who would captain the team. Somewhat ironically, he would go on to successfully manage Dundee United.

Mixed fortunes followed and a low point was reached when they lost 5-0 at previously relegated Albion Rovers at the end of October, conceding three goals in the first twenty minutes. The following Saturday they beat Alloa Athletic 6-1. George Grant, deputising for the injured Flucker at centre-forward, scored a hat-trick. Johnston converted two penalties and Dawson scored the other. However, successive defeats against promotion rivals Raith and Dunfermline in November saw them drop down to sixth. Five consecutive wins across the remainder of November and December lifted them back into the promotion race and they ended the first week of 1938 in fourth place, four points off East Fife in second place and six behind leaders Raith, but with two games in hand.

The Saints now embarked on a superb Scottish Cup run. A narrow win over Vale of Leithen and a replay victory over King's Park was followed by a bye in the Third Round. They were then drawn against Motherwell, who were going well in the First Division. The two sides met on the 19th March 1938 at the Royal Gymnasium for their Quarter-final tie. Motherwell took the lead after a quarter of an hour but two minutes later Flucker equalised and the score was 1-1 at half-time. Nine minutes after the restart St Bernards were gifted a goal scored by Grant due to a defensive mix-up. As the game wore on Motherwell became anxious and tried long range shots. In the 85th minute Flucker sealed the tie. *The Scotsman* reported that "St Bernard's defeat of Motherwell at the Gymnasium in the fourth round of the Scottish Cup, unexpected as it was, was no fluke. If ever a team deserved to be beaten, Motherwell did. Their experienced First Division players were unable to counter the fiery onslaughts of the St Bernard's men, who played real Cup-tie football - hard and fast, but always fair." Contrasting the two teams' performances, the *Glasgow Herald,* under the headline "St Bernard's spring Scottish Cup Surprise," commented that "the Motherwell passed out of the Cup competition ingloriously at the Gymnasium Ground. They gave a disappointing display, every section of the team being affected, and never once did they get a real grip of the game. St Bernard's were permitted to determine the trend of affairs, and they kept moving with such energy, skill, and real team harmony as to thoroughly merit victory. It was no haphazard success. Motherwell's methods partly contributed to their own downfall. In the early stages they were inclined to adopt a slight air of superiority, and later, when under stress, they completely lost their balance." In reviewing the team performance of the Saints, *The Scotsman* said that "the whole St Bernard's team played the game of their lives. Every man pulled his weight, but above them all stood Russell, whose cool judgement in defence was the main reason for the failure of the Motherwell attack. Aird and Kemp were a little behind. T G Smith was in great form in goal and Kerr and Allan played splendidly. The forwards all worked hard, but Flucker and Grant were the match winners. Grant did some grand running on the wing, and Flucker showed splendid opportunism, his second goal being a delightful effort." The giant-killing Cup team was: T G Smith; Allen, Kerr; Aird, Russell, Kemp; Grant, Johnston, Flucker, Dawson and Pinkerton. The only disappointing feature of the game was the low crowd of only 3,000. The other Quarter-finals all had over 20,000 spectators. St Bernard's had doubled the price, ostensibly on the grounds of safety but this backfired with the low crowd. St Bernard's were now in the Scottish Cup Semi-finals, their best Cup run for forty years. The last time they had reached this stage was in 1896, as the holders. Remarkably, within five years of this achievement they would cease to exist.

Their Semi-final would be an all Second Division affair as they were drawn to face one of their promotion rivals - whoever won out between Raith and East Fife, who had drawn 2-2 at Methil, with the Semi-final set to be staged at Tynecastle. In the other, Kilmarnock or Ayr United would play Rangers at Hampden. East Fife won at Kirkcaldy and St Bernard's then played out an epic tie involving three matches, watched by a total crowd of nearly 100,000, all played at Tynecastle, with the guarantee that a Second Division club would be in the Scottish Cup Final.

East Fife started the favourites although St Bernard's had earned three of the possible four points from their League encounters. The two sides first met at Tynecastle on Saturday the 2nd April before a large crowd of 36,000. *The Scotsman* covered the game, saying that "in a fairly even struggle, the Edinburgh club were just slightly ahead in point of pressure. For this they may have had the weather to thank. A more stronger team, they proved to be more adaptable upon a heavy, treacherous pitch and with a swirling ball affected by a gusty wind. They missed chances, but also gave East Fife a trying spell in the closing minutes." Johnston scored for the Saints but East Fife equalised almost immediately. Pinkerton had a chance to win it for St Bernard's near the end but the chance was cleared off the line. Meanwhile, in the other Semi-final, Kilmarnock beat Rangers by the odd goal in a seven goal thriller.

The two sides met again in midweek but the tie ended still undecided as to who would now meet Kilmarnock at Hampden on the 23rd April. The match was going to be replayed on the Monday at Tynecastle, but clashed with a Tommy Walker benefit match when Hearts were playing Derby County. East Fife had suggested Stark's Park as an alternative venue but St Bernard's did not agree so the game was played on Wednesday at 5:30. St Bernard's had the better of the first game and it was much the same in the replay, *The Scotsman* commenting that "the element of Cup-tie luck was clearly shown when St Bernard's outplayed their opponents, but could do little better than shoot against the cross-bar and the post-eight times in all." There was a turning point in the game ten minutes after the interval when a shot by Flucker struck the underside of the crossbar. The referee signalled a goal but was then challenged by the East Fife players. The referee subsequently consulted a linesman and revered his decision, *The Scotsman* observing that "this appeared to have some effect upon the Edinburgh players. To most people it did look like a goal, but the disappointment of having one awarded and then withdrawn apparently affected the Saints." East Fife had the ball twice in the net towards the end of the ninety minutes but both times the strikes were ruled out for earlier infringements. The game went to extra-time and in the 97th minute East Fife took the lead. Flucker headed the equaliser from a cross by Kerr and the replay, watched this time by a crowd of 30,000, ended in a 1-1 draw.

Both sides were in League action on the following Saturday and they replayed for a second time at Tynecastle on Wednesday the 13th April, this time in front of a 35,000 crowd. The *Glasgow Herald* reported that "in the first half the Edinburgh side had sufficient chances to run up a substantial lead, but half-time came without any scoring." In the 17th minute Flucker's header from a free kick from Kerr beat Milton in the East Fife goal but cannoned back off the upright. Saints continued to have the better chances, Pinkerton and Grant both passing up good opportunities. Shortly after the interval and just after the hour mark East Fife took the lead. Smith then pulled off a good save to keep the Saints in it and fifteen minutes from the end Johnston was pulled down in the box. Kerr took the penalty, Milton getting his hand to it, but the shot was so powerful it went in. Just when it seemed that extra-time would be needed again, East Fife scored. For this replay they had borrowed a Falkirk player, McKerrell, and he scored the winning goal six minutes from time, although Smith got a hand to it his effort was in vain. Reviewing the game *The Scotsman* observed that "the margin between the clubs was very narrow. Play was tremendously hard, and in the end the club who played the cleverer football just got through. Saints, however, should have had the game won in the first half, when they had many chances to score and failed to profit from them they had hard luck, too, but in the end the superior forward tactics of the Fifers gained them the day."

By this point in the League season Raith were up and confirmed as champions, leading by nine points with four games to go. They would go on to score a League record 142 goals for the season. Airdrieonians, in second, were three points ahead of St Bernard's; Albion Rovers were two ahead, and also in contention were Scottish Cup Finalists East Fife and Cowdenbeath. St Bernard's won their next three games, but so did Albion Rovers; Airdrie winning two but losing the other. Matters were therefore out of their hands going into the last round of matches: Albion Rovers had 47 points, Airdrieonians 46 and St Bernard's 45. In the final round of games Albion Rovers were surprisingly held to a one-all draw by Montrose in Coatbridge but this was enough to take them up. Ten goals were equally shared at Tannadice between Airdrie and Dundee United. Meanwhile, in Edinburgh, St Bernard's were shocked by King's Park, losing by the odd goal in seven, to ultimately finish fourth.

In the 1938-39 season that followed St Bernard's finished seventh, in what would prove to be their last full season in the League. They opened with an Edinburgh derby game at home to Leith Athletic in which Johnston, their new inside-right, snatched the winning goal in the last minute. Also playing were Libberton, a young goalkeeper from the Borders and they re-signed Brooks, a speedy winger, who had moved to play for Clyde. At the end of August they beat Brechin City 7-1, Brooks scoring four. A run of six games without defeat during September and early October saw them up to fourth, just a point off the top. At the end of October they beat Morton 5-0 thanks to new inside forward Alex Dawson. *The Scotsman* reported that "undoubtedly the feature of the match at the Gymnasium was the splendid appearance made by Dawson of Stoneyburn Juniors at inside-right for St Bernards. He was signed by the Edinburgh club after the game, in which he scored three goals. The recruit is a brother of Dawson, Rangers' international goalkeeper. In addition to his scoring feat, Dawson indicated that he is a player of some ability, and he fitted in well to a sprightly St Bernards front rank, who displayed punch which has been lacking far too often this season. Brooks had the other Saints' goals."

The following week a crowd of 7,000 was at the Gymnasium for the visit of leaders Cowdenbeath but the Saints went down 2-1, when they deserved a draw, the winner coming five minutes from the end. Poor form followed in December when they lost four out of five League fixtures, including a 6-1 loss at Alloa, to drop down to ninth place. This time there would be no Scottish Cup heroics either, as they lost 2-0 at Dundee in the First Round.

On the 18th February the St Bernard's centre-forward Jimmy Johnston scored all six of his side's goals in their 6-2 win over Forfar Athletic. Johnston scored four goals in the first half an hour and added two more in the second half. The *Edinburgh Evening News* observed that "the Saints' changes were made for improvement, and none more so than the playing of J Johnston at centre-forward. His six goals showed fine opportunism." During the early exchanges the best chances fell to the Saints, but Mair, in the Forfar goal pulled off a series of saves. However, after 12 minutes he was beaten when Johnston converted a cross from close range. S Johnston then missed two sitters before Jimmy Johnston demonstrated to his namesake how to take your chances, scoring a second after 18 minutes of play. A rare attack by Forfar on the half hour mark was broken up by Flucker and a swift counterattack led to Johnston scoring his hat-trick. Three minutes later he scored a fourth and the sides crossed with St Bernard's four nil up. The start of the second half pretty much mirrored the first with even play and chances on both sides before Johnston made it five from an Aird cross. Saints seemed to relax after that. About 15 minutes from the finish a Kemp cross was only partially cleared and Johnston was on hand to force home the ball for his double hat-trick. That wasn't the end of the scoring though as Forfar scored two late consolation goals. The *Sunday Post* choose to highlight the performance of 20 year old Dave Brown, who had previously been loaned out to Gala Fairydean. He was the chief architect "by his accurate passing, unselfishness and pluck," although they did note that "the game's big feature was the scoring of a double hat-trick by Jimmy Johnston. His shooting was neat and accurate. But he owed much to the splendid purveying of his mates. Still, he never scorned a scoring chance - and that's what is wanted." Just a fortnight later the Saints lost 5-0 in Stirling against King's Park and by the end of March they were in seventh place, which is where they eventually finished.

The 1939-40 season kicked off as normal on Saturday 12th August with St Bernard's travelling to play Brechin City, where they played out a goalless draw, although Philip missed a penalty for them. The following weekend they beat Forfar Athletic 6-2 but they then lost 5-1 at East Fife. On the 2nd September they played what would turn out to be their last ever Scottish Football League game, which was a 0-0 draw at home to Queen's Park. The St Bernard's team that day was: McKay; Dick, Gilchrist; Philip, Flucker, Aird; S Johnston, J Johnston, 'Newman', Dawson and Kemp. Two days earlier Nazi Germany had invaded Poland and on the same day as the match, Britain formally declared war on Germany.

World War Two saw the suspension of the Scottish Football League for a short while and the Saints did not travel the following weekend to play Edinburgh City. In October the League restarted with two regional divisions of 16 clubs apiece and St Bernard's joined the Eastern Division, although Edinburgh City and Leith Athletic were not included in the new setup. On the 21st October they played their first game in the new competition, losing 4-0 at Cowdenbeath. The team that day included six of the players who had lined up against Queen's Park. The Eastern Division was suspended at the end of 1940 and was eventually replaced by a North Eastern League for the 1941-42 season. As this was an eight team competition the league ran the competition over two series. Saints came fifth and then bottom in the 1941-42 season. Their last match was on the 16th May 1942, a 3–2 home defeat to East Fife. The line up for that game is listed as: Matthews; 'A N Other', James Duffy; Gillies, Murphy, Gilbert; Dougall, Dingwall, Moodie, 'Junior' and John Duffy.

This competition also came to an end but worse was to follow in 1942 when one of the directors, a coal merchant called Cooper, died that year, and the Executors of his Will demanded the immediate repayment of a loan he'd given the club. With no means of income and no substantial capital reserve, the club was forced to sell the only asset it had - the Royal Gymnasium ground. With no income and no ground the club effectively folded and was one of only two clubs not to re-emerge after the war (the other being King's Park).

The site of the Royal Gymnasium Ground became part of the King George V playing fields. The stand was dismantled in 1947 and the new park opened in 1950. Parts of the old terracing can still be seen and there is a commemorative plaque and an information board in the park about this largely forgotten Edinburgh Scottish Football League club, who most famously won the Scottish Cup in 1895.

SEASON	LEAGUE	P	W	D	L	F	A	P	POS
1893-94	SCOT-1	18	11	1	6	53	41	23	3/10
1894-95	SCOT-1	18	8	1	9	39	40	17	6/10
1895-96	SCOT-1	18	7	1	10	36	53	15	7/10
1896-97	SCOT-1	18	7	0	11	32	40	14	7/10
1897-98	SCOT-1	18	4	1	13	35	67	9	9/10
1898-99	SCOT-1	18	4	4	10	30	37	12	7/10

1899-00	SCOT-1	18	4	4	10	29	47	12	9/10
1900-01	SCOT-2	18	10	5	3	41	26	25	1/10
1901-02	SCOT-2	22	10	2	10	30	30	22	6/12
1902-03	SCOT-2	22	12	2	8	45	32	26	5/12
1903-04	SCOT-2	22	9	2	11	31	43	20	8/12
1904-05	SCOT-2	22	3	5	14	23	54	11	12/12
1905-06	SCOT-2	22	9	4	9	42	34	22	5/12
1906-07	SCOT-2	22	14	4	4	41	24	32	1/12
1907-08	SCOT-2	22	8	5	9	31	32	21	8/12
1908-09	SCOT-2	22	9	3	10	34	37	21	8/12
1909-10	SCOT-2	22	12	3	7	43	31	27	3/12
1910-11	SCOT-2	22	10	2	10	36	39	22	6/12
1911-12	SCOT-2	22	9	5	8	38	36	23	6/12
1912-13	SCOT-2	26	12	3	11	36	34	27	7/14
1913-14	SCOT-2	22	8	6	8	39	31	22	7/12
1914-15	SCOT-2	26	18	1	7	66	34	37	3/14
1921-22	SCOT-2	38	15	8	15	50	49	38	9/20
1922-23	SCOT-2	38	8	15	15	39	50	29 *	18/20
1923-24	SCOT-2	38	11	10	17	49	54	32	18/20
1924-25	SCOT-2	38	14	4	20	52	70	32	17/20
1925-26	SCOT-2	38	15	5	18	86	82	35	14/20
1926-27	SCOT-2	38	14	6	18	70	77	34	13/20
1927-28	SCOT-2	38	15	5	18	75	101	35	17/20
1928-29	SCOT-2	36	16	9	11	77	55	41	6/19
1929-30	SCOT-2	38	13	6	19	65	65	32	14/20
1930-31	SCOT-2	38	14	9	15	85	66	37	11/20
1931-32	SCOT-2	38	19	7	12	81	62	45	5/20
1932-33	SCOT-2	34	13	6	15	67	64	32	12/18
1933-34	SCOT-2	34	15	4	15	75	56	34	10/18
1934-35	SCOT-2	34	20	7	7	103	47	47	3/18
1935-36	SCOT-2	34	18	4	12	106	78	40	5/18
1936-37	SCOT-2	34	22	4	8	102	51	48	3/18
1937-38	SCOT-2	34	20	5	9	75	49	45	4/18
1938-39	SCOT-2	34	15	6	13	79	79	36	7/18
1939-40	SCOT-2	4	1	2	1	7	7	4	ABAND

* 2 points deducted for fielding an ineligible player

Solway Star

Formed: 1911
Colours: Gold and black horizontal striped shirts and white shorts
Ground: Kimmeter Green Park
Entered League: 1923. Founder members of the Third Division.
Number of League Seasons: 3
Honours: None
Highest League Finish: 3rd in Division Three
Left League: 1926. Division Three abandoned. Folded 1947

The alliterating and quixotically named Solway Star were based in Annan, a small port on the Solway Firth, 17 miles south-east of Dumfries. They were formed from the amalgamation of several Annan based clubs in 1911 and played in gold and black horizontal striped jerseys and white shorts. In their first decade they played mainly friendly games and a couple of forays into the Scottish Cup in the early 1920s led to heavy defeats - 5-1 at home to East Stirlingshire and 7-2 away at St Mirren.

Solway Star joined the Southern Counties League in 1914 but with the onset of the First World War the competition was suspended. The Southern Counties League was revived in 1921 and in the same year the club moved from their original ground at Summergate Park to their new ground, Kimmeter Green Park, located to the east of the town, beyond the railway station. Despite no club completing their fixtures, the title was awarded to Mid-Annandale, even though Solway Star were unbeaten in second place, just two points behind Mids having played three fewer games. Star left that competition after just one season, moving to the Western League for the 1922-23 season. In June 1923 the Western League clubs were incorporated into the Scottish League in a new Third Division.

Star played their opening Scottish Football League game on the 18th August 1923 away in Ayrshire against Galston, losing 2-0. *The Sunday Post* reported that "in the opening stages a Galston had all the play, and Watson beat Little with a fine header. In the second half play continued strong and McGarvie scored a second for Galston. The best players for Solway Star were Little, Robinson, Alexander and Thom." The following Saturday, they hosted their first ever Scottish League match at Kimmeter Green Park, entertaining Peebles Rovers, who they beat 2-1. Under the headline "Ascending Star" *The Sunday Post* reported that "Devlin and Thom scored for the winners...the greasy ground was against good football...[and] Star's defence was excellent. Little, Robinson, Ferguson and Mitchell were outstanding. Devlin was poor at centre forward."

Star then lost four of the their next five games so that by the end of October they were 13th in the 16 team competition and had suffered their heaviest defeat of their inaugural season, 5-1 away at Montrose. Following a narrow 2-1 home win against Helensburgh on the 1st December 1923, Star then went ten games without defeat, a run which was finally ended at home by Nithsdale Wanderers on the 23rd February 1924 in a 1-0 reverse. The team ultimately faded after that losing five of their last six fixtures to eventually finish in eleventh place in their first League season.

The 1924-25 season proved to be their best in their short-lived Scottish League history. They went the whole of the campaign unbeaten at home and lost only five times overall, missing the runner-up spot and promotion place on goal average. As well as a promotion challenge they also had a decent Scottish Cup run, securing a glamour tie with Celtic. They opened the new season at home on the 16th August 1924 against the previous year's bottom side Brechin City winning convincingly 4-1. *The Sunday Post* commented that "Solway Star made no mistake about seeing Brechin City off the premises. From the outset they took a grip of the game and held on to it. Alexander had the first goal for the Annan men, and McGeechan, Higgins and Duncan, the last-named from a penalty, improved on the good work." Star went on to match their ten game unbeaten run from the previous season with seven wins and three draws, during which the goal scoring from of Higgins was particularly prominent. A 1-1 draw in the derby game against Queen of the South on the 11th October 1924 attracted a League record attendance of 3,500. Again the unbeaten run was halted by Nithsdale Wanderers, with a 3-0 defeat away on the 8th November 1924, but later in the same month Solway Star recorded their biggest ever League win, a 7-1 win over Dumbarton Harp. Unfortunately this club went out of business and their records were expunged. Higgins and Jack both got hat tricks, *The Sunday Post* noting that "the Star of Solway gave no quarter, and in the end the Harpists were thoroughly trounced."

Star had missed out on Scottish Cup qualification for the 1922-23 and 1923-24 competitions but did get through to the 1924-25 Scottish Cup, where they beat Second Division side Stenhousemuir 4-2 in the First Round before overcoming former winners and fellow Third Division side Vale of Leven in the Second Round Two after two replays, the second of which saw a record crowd of 6,000 at Kimmeter Green. Their reward was an away match against then ten time winners Celtic and a team that included goal scoring legend Jimmy McGrory.

The teams met on the 21st February 1925 in front of a crowd of about 7,000. Right from the start Celtic took control but their finishing on this occasion was not good. Alec Thomson eventually opened the scoring with a header and near the interval Jimmy McGrory made it 2-0 to Celtic. In the second half, Solway Star did come back into the match but their finishing was as erratic as the home team and Celtic held out fairly comfortably for a 2-0 victory. *The Sunday Post* though, felt like it was a missed opportunity. They opened their match report saying "if Solway Star had imparted more vim into their forward play at Celtic Park yesterday they might have given Celtic a shake. The Annan defence, if not artistic, was wholehearted; but the forwards were, for the most part, a straggling line. There were glimpses of ball control from Higgins and Black. Accurate passing seemed beyond them. It was faulty passing which ruined any chance that Solway had. Celtic were rarely tested. Perhaps this was just as well, for the First League team had many apparent weaknesses. Cleverness of manipulation abounded in the forward line, but the close formation attacks broke down upon a defence which, if often outplayed, always came up for more. The two goals scored came in the first half. After twenty-five minutes' play McLean sent in a centre from near the goal line. Muir could only fist clear. Thomson headed the ball first time, and Celtic were one up. McGrory was the other scorer. The centre very cleverly got the ball under control, and shot low into the corner. Muir had no chance with either point. The second half was not long in progress when McGrory retired, suffering from a strained leg. The duties of pivot descended upon Patsy Gallagher, and his display in that position tended to brighten things. Thomson was most effective on the Celtic side. He was the only one not to overdo trickery. Best for Solway were Muir, Duncan, Higgins and Black." The Solway Star team was: Muir, Robinson, Harkins; Graham, Duncan, Hardie; W Alexander, Higgins, Edgar, Black and Smith. Celtic went on to lift the trophy for the eleventh time with a 2-1 win in the Final over Dundee.

Back in the League Solway Star went unbeaten in their final eight games but there were four draws in that sequence and ultimately that proved costly as they missed out on promotion on goal average. The promotion battle was a regional affair with Queen of the South and Nithsdale in the mix, along with Vale of Leven. A 3-2 away win against Leith Athletic at the end of February, with two goals from McDavid, left Star in fourth place, four points off second place. Three consecutive draws in March, followed by a narrow 1-0 win over Lochgelly United on the 28th of March, left them still in fourth, but now only one point off second, thanks to defeats for their promotion rivals.

A week later a 2-0 away win up the road at Lockerbie against Mid-Annandale moved them up to third, just a point behind local rivals Queen of the South but with a game in hand. A further point behind them though were Vale of Leven who themselves had a game in hand on Star. It was all getting very tight! Nithsdale though looked set to be crowned the Third Division champions so it was effectively a three-way fight for the one remaining promotion place.

In the next round of games on the 11th April Queen of the South beat Helensburgh 2-0 to end their programme and Vale of Leven beat Brechin 4-0, but Star couldn't match these results from their rivals as they were held 1-1 by Dykehead. *The Sunday Post* reported that "at Annan, Solway Star were extremely unfortunate not to extract full points from Dykehead...Solway pressed hard for the winning goal, but were denied the success they deserved." This dropped point at home would ultimately prove costly. Star slipped to fourth, two points behind Queen of South with just one game to go, but with a far inferior goal average.

The issue for the club was in the forward line as whilst they conceded a similar number of goals as the others they had only scored 40 (with a game to go) whereas Queen of the South had scored 67 and Vale of Leven 61. Vale of Leven at this point could still have overhauled the Dumfries team with the same two point deficit, with two games still to play, but they lost both fixtures. Solway Star won their last game, 1-0 against Royal Albert to match Queen of the South's forty point mark but missed out on promotion on goal average (67:32=2.094 v 41:28=1.464).

I'm labouring a point here but this is about fine margins. If Solway Star had got the winner against Dykehead they would have pipped Queen of the South to the second promotion spot. The Doonhammers went up instead to the Second Division, missing the demise of the Third Division and went on to have continuous membership of the SFL except for the seasons interrupted by the War. Solway Star, by contrast, were one of fifteen clubs to leave the SFL in 1926 with the abandonment of the Third Division and one of the twelve who never returned.

The 1925-26 League season started badly for Star with a 6-1 home defeat against Vale of Leven on the 15th August 1925, a recording losing margin. *The Sunday Post's* headline was "Solway Star Eclipsed." Solway Star were 4-0 down at half time but played better in the second half and scored through Alexander, but only after Vale had scored two more goals. This margin of defeat was equalled with a 5-0 defeat away against Peebles Rovers in October. Following a 4-2 away defeat at Montrose on the 21st November 1925, the team went eleven games without a win, a sequence that was finally ended with a 2-1 away win against Vale of Leven in the last week in February

1926. By this time the future of the Division was in doubt as the general economic situation was poor and the small clubs were struggling to survive on low gate receipts which had to cover wages, travel costs and match fee guarantees, and in the January, Galston had folded.

On the 6th March 1926 Solway Star got revenge on Peebles Rovers for that earlier heavy defeat with a record win of their own, a 7-1 scoreline which matched the expunged win over Dumbarton Harp from the previous year. *The Sunday Post* reported that "Peebles Rovers were routed at Annan, where Solway Star scored seven times to their once. Ross scored after ten minutes for the Star. Knox had two before the interval, and Findlay reduced the leeway from a penalty. Assisted by a strong wind in the second period, Star took matters completely in hand. Ross added another three goals, and W Alexander was the other marksman." The final Scottish League match at Kimmeter Green was played on 3 April 1926, a 3–2 defeat by Johnstone. *The Sunday Post* commented that "it was a poor game at Annan. Solway Star twice took the lead through Baxter and Knox, but defensive blunders allowed Braidwood to restore equality. In the second period Watt obtained the winning goal. Solway were very disappointing."

On the 24th April Solway Star played their last ever SFL game, a 1-1 away draw at Lochgelly United. Hutchison scored their last ever League goal and ten minutes later McLean equalised. Solway Star were eleventh in the table, having played all their matches except the reverse game at Galston who had quit the League.

With the collapse of the Third Division Solway Star were among the majority of clubs taken into an expanded Scottish Alliance where they played for the 1926-27 season before joining the Provincial League for the 1927-28 season. After that they joined the reformed Southern Counties League before resigning in 1933 after which the concentrated on Cup games and friendlies.

They continued to make occasional appearances in the Scottish Cup, all ending in defeats. In January 1929 they lost 5-0 at Aberdeen, and the following year they hosted Montrose, and in front of a 1,300 crowd lost 8-0. *The Sunday Post* described their performance as "plucky but ineffective". Kicking off and playing with the wind the visitors kept the home team at bay for the first 30 minutes. The newspaper reported that the Annan men barely crossed the halfway line. The Gable Endies eventually broke the deadlock and added a second before the interval. On the resumption they quickly added two more and despite visibly easing off scored another three times. *The Sunday Post* added "they could easily have scored another half dozen but they did not take advantage of the Star's leg weariness." Their next appearance was in 1933 when they lost at Hearts 3-0 and they lost to the same opposition in 1935, this time by 7-0. The 1936-37 season was their last Scottish Cup campaign and they recorded a rare victory, beating Larbert Amateurs 3-1 away in the First Round. On the 13th February 1937 they travelled to Cowdenbeath for their Second Round tie. The Annan team started well with Beattie scoring for them after just seven minutes. It didn't take the home team long to get on equal terms and only a good display by McBride in goal prevented Cowdenbeath leading by more than 2-1 at the interval . The second half was a different story though. Malloy the home centre-forward scored four and Boag at outside-left scored three as Star succumbed 9-1.

The club eventually folded in 1947 and the town is now represented by Annan Athletic, who joined the Scottish League in 2008, replacing nearby Gretna. Kimmeter Green was originally returned to agricultural usage and is now part of the Stapleton Road Industrial Estate, with the name living on in the adjacent residential street of Kimmeter Place.

SEASON	LEAGUE	P	W	D	L	F	A	P	POS
1923-24	SCOT-3	30	9	9	12	42	48	27	11/16
1924-25	SCOT-3	30	15	10	5	41	28	40	3/16
1925-26	SCOT-3	29	9	6	14	50	62	24	11/16

Third Lanark

Formed: 1872
Colours: Scarlet shirts and white shorts.
Ground: Cathkin Park
Entered League: 1890. Founder members of the Scottish Football League.
Number of League Seasons: 70
Highest League Finish: League Champions
Honours: Scottish Cup Winners 1888-1889, 1904-1905. First Division Champions 1903-04. Second Division Champions 1930-31, 1934-35.
Left League: 1967. Bankrupt.

Third Lanark are one of the biggest and high profile names to disappear from the Scottish Football League and also the most successful of the now defunct clubs. Founder members of the Scottish League, they won the championship in 1904 and made six appearances in the Scottish Cup Final, winning it twice in 1889 and 1905 (beating Celtic and Rangers respectively). They also won the Second Division title twice in the 1930s when they alternated between the two divisions. Third Lanark also has the most capped Scottish internationals of any defunct team with over 30 players going on to play for Scotland.

In 1936 they reached the Scottish Cup final for the sixth and last time, losing out to Rangers 1-0. After 1945 Thirds reached their first ever League Cup final, although they lost it to Hearts 2-1, and in the 1960-61 season came third in the League. And yet, the club would be relegated at end of the 1964-65 season having lost 30 of their 34 matches and ending up with only seven points. Third Lanark lost their last 21 League games that season and the first two the following season for a total of 23 in succession, a record only recently beaten by East Stirlingshire. Sadly, within two years, the club was declared bankrupt, thrown out of the League and dissolved in the courts.

Like a number of teams, Thirds started life as an army team. The club was formed as the Third Lanarkshire Rifle Volunteers at a meeting held on the 12th December 1872 in the Regimental Orderly Room in East Howard Street, Glasgow. The old regiment was eventually amalgamated under a series of army reforms and the team was renamed as the Third Lanark Athletic Club in 1903. They played their games at Cathkin Park from

1875, having originally played on the Regimental drill ground at Victoria Road, Glasgow. The original Cathkin Park was located just to the east of Dixon Halls on the east side of the Cathcart Road, near modern day Govanhill Park. The original Cathkin Park hosted the Scottish Cup final in 1882 and was used again for the 1886 final. The panoramic views from their ground may have given rise to the club's unusual nickname of the 'Hi Hi.' In 1903 the club moved grounds, taking over the original Hampden Park from Queen's Park, and renamed the ground "New" Cathkin Park. The site of the original Cathkin Park was subsequently used for housing.

Under the leadership of manager-secretary R Moodie, Third Lanark played in the early Scottish Cup competitions, reaching the final in 1876 and 1878. The club was one of three defunct League clubs to play in the very first Scottish Cup competition (along with Renton and Vale of Leven). They secured a walkover in the First Round against Glasgow Southern and made their first appearance on the 8th November 1873 against Clydesdale of Glasgow. The match was played at Kinning Park and Clydesdale scored in the first half, with W Dick, the captain of Thirds equalising. The 3rd LRV team was: Haswell; J Glas, John Hunter; J Donald, W McOney; W Dick (c), J Stewart, William Miller, T Lawrence, J Wilson and Drinnan. A week later a replay was held, again at Kinning Park, and this also finished as a draw, 0-0, with the match ending in near darkness. The second replay was eventually staged on the 6th December. Clydesdale scored two goals in the first half an hour and despite all of their efforts the Volunteers couldn't score. Clydesdale went on to contest the first Scottish Cup Final, losing to Queen's Park.

On the 7th March 1874 full back John "Jack" Hunter made his international debut for Scotland against England at the West of Scotland Cricket Ground, Hamilton Crescent, Glasgow, in just the third ever international match, aged just 19. He played in Scotland's next two matches as well but retired in 1878 due to ill-health having contracted tuberculosis and later succumbed to pneumonia in November 1881, aged just 26.

In the second running of the Scottish Cup competition Third Lanark reached the Third Round, or Quarter-final stage. They beat Barrhead Rangers in the First Round, after a replay, and needed a replay also to get past Standard of Glasgow. In the next round they went down narrowly against Dumbarton, losing 1-0.

In the third Scottish Cup competition Third Lanark went all the way to the Final. Thirds knocked out Havelock from Glasgow before Rangers beat them 1-0 in the Second Round on the 30th October. However, a replay was ordered after Third Lanark protested about the fact that Rangers had kicked off in both halves. Their protest was upheld and the two sides met again, on the 23th November, with Thirds winning this time, 2-1. This time it was the turn of Rangers to protest. They objected to the lack of distinguishing colours worn by the Thirds goalkeeper and against the crowd invading the pitch but these were both dismissed. Levern of Renfrewshire were beaten 3-0 away in the next round and in the last eight Third Lanark beat Western of Glasgow 5-0, although several of the Western's first eleven were unable to play. Third Lanark needed three matches to reach the Final eventually overcoming Dumbarton 3-0 after two 1-1 draws.

On the 11th of March 1876 they came up against the major power of the day, Queen's Park, the only winner of the trophy so far, and into their third consecutive Final since the competition's inauguration. The Final was played at the West of Scotland Cricket Ground in Hamilton Crescent in Glasgow. Thirds took a surprise lead after just two minutes when Drinnan scored and they held onto this lead at the interval. Tom Highet equalised for Queen's Park in the second half and the match ended as a draw.

The replay was held a week later and took place at the same venue. This time Queen's Park took an early lead, after a quarter of an hour's play, with Highet again scoring for his side. The same player made it a hat-trick of Cup Final goals when he added a second as Third Lanark went down two-nil. The 3rd LRV Cup final team for both matches was: J Wallace; John Hunter, Watson; White, Davidson; Crichton, Drinnan, Scoular, Walker, William Miller and McDonald. William Miller impressed in the final with his dribbling and had already been capped the week before against England in a match Scotland won 3-0. This was his only international cap and the right winger retired from the game in 1879. John Hunter was also in the Scotland side.

In the 1876-77 competition Thirds reached the Third Round, going out to Vale of Leven, who went on to break Queen's Park's early monopoly and record the first of their own Cup wins. The two sides met again the following year, this time in the Final! Having knocked Clyde out in the First Round Thirds won a one-sided match 11-0 against Derby of Shawfield, Glasgow. This match, played on the 27th October 1877 was the club's biggest ever win in the Scottish Cup. Their reward was a Third Round tie against the mighty Queen's Park played on the 10th November 1877. The weather was bleak and there had been a lot of rainfall in the days preceding the match. However, despite the conditions a crowd of between three and four thousand was present. Queen's Park put Thirds under immediate pressure with Wilf McKinnon particularly prominent in their attacks. However, captain and goalkeeper J Wallace was in fine form, with the *Glasgow Herald* noting that he "proved himself equal to the occasion." There was little respite for Thirds and Kennedy now came to their rescue with a fine clearance. After half an hour, and against the run of play, Third Lanark took the lead. A counter attack and a one-two between Kay and Miller saw the latter shoot at goal, although the attempt lacked any power, and it was easily gathered by Anderson in the Queen's Park goal. In going to kick the ball out the 'keeper slipped, and lost his balance, the ball falling and coming off his knee. This enabled Miller to pounce and open the scoring. Queen's Park protested to the referee that Kay had been offside but as the final touch came of the goalkeeper the referee allowed the goal to stand. Queen's Park immediately resumed the offensive but couldn't breakthrough by the time that the interval was called. In the second period the *Herald* noted that the "Volunteers now played a more even game with their opponents, and seemed determined to hold the advantage they had gained...A noticeable feature of their play during this half was their long passing, which certainly was more effective, considering the condition of the ground, than the close passing and dribbling of the Queen's Park, which was productive of many slips and misses." Thirds held onto to their lead and inflicted a surprise defeat on Queen's Park. Their victorious team was: J Wallace; W Somers, J Hunter; J Kennedy, McKenzie; W Miller, A Hunter, R Lang, Peden, McCririck and Kay.

Reviewing the enormity of the result, the *Glasgow Herald* commented that "Saturday will long be remembered in the annals of the association game in connection with the defeat of the Queen's Park by the 3rd L.R.V. Since its formation nine years ago the Queen's Park Club has had an almost uninterrupted successful career - the only occasion on which they were defeated being by the Wanderers in London two years ago, and by the Vale of Leven on Hampden Park last season. As in the latter case the match on Saturday is all the more disastrous for the Queen's Park seeing that it is a cup tie competition, while on the other hand the 3rd L.R.V. is all the more to be congratulated on their success in having got rid of such a formidable opponent."

Third Lanark went on to beat Govan Athletic 7-0 and Beith 4-0 before losing to South Western of Glasgow 1-0 in the Quarter-Finals on the 12th January 1878. *The Scotsman* reported that "this cup tie came off on the ground of the latter at Copeland Road, Govan. When time was called the South-Western were the winners by one goal to nothing. We understand the 3d L.R.V. have protested against this result, having, as they allege, taken two disputed goals." The SFA ruled in the club's favour and a replay was ordered, Thirds winning this time 2-1. *The Scotsman* reported that "this tie, which was won by the South-Western on Saturday the 12th inst, by one goal to nothing, was, owing to a protest lodged with the Association to the effect that the spectators interfered with the game, played over again in Copeland Park, Govan. A very exciting game was the result and at the termination the Volunteers were declared the winners by two goals to one."

In the Semi-Finals Third Lanark drew Renton away and won the initial tie but in an age of protests a replay was ordered. Renton scored first and look set to be victorious but two minutes from time Thirds equalised. The two clubs agreed to play another half an hour but no further scoring occurred. On the 16th March, and now with home advantage, Third Lanark beat Renton 1-0 to reach their second Scottish Cup Final. John Peden headed in to give Thirds a first half lead. Renton thought they had equalised but the score was cancelled due to a foul in the build-up.

On the 31st March 1878 Third Lanark met the holders, Vale of Leven in the fifth Scottish Cup Final. Reporting on the occasion *The Scotsman* commented that "the Vale of Leven and the 3d L.R.V. clubs met at Hampden, the ground of the Queen's Park, to play off their final tie for the Association challenge cup and the championship... From the form which both clubs have shown this year, and the fact that the 3d LRV have defeated the Queen's Park this season, great interest was taken in the match, and a large number of spectators turned out to witness the game. The play, however, was disappointing, very few of the fine points of the game being brought out. In the first half the 3d played with the sun in their faces, and a slight wind against them. For a short time the 3d acted on the defensive, but a fine run by Peden right into the Bale's goal caused Parlane to through the ball over his own lines. From the corner kick McCririck headed the ball right into the goal, but Parlane again put it over the line for safety. A second corner was similarly dealt with, Lang heading it right in again, but Parlane this time managed to send the ball to Baird, who effectively raised the siege. After this till about fifteen minutes from half time the play was very even on both sides. At this stage [the Thirds 'keeper] Wallace kicked off from his own goal, and the forwards not lying up the field well, the Vale backs managed to give McDougall possession of the leather, who immediately made straight for the 3d's goal. He finished up his run with a long, low shot, the ball glancing off J Hunter's foot on its way. This diverted it slightly off course, and before Wallace could stop it, it had passed through his goal close to the bar. In the change of ends the 3d assumed the offensive, and the splendid goal-keeping of Parlane alone prevented the downfall of his citadel. The result was that at the call of time the Vale were declared the winners of the game and the cup for 1877-78. The beaten Third Lanark Cup Final team was: J Wallace; John Hunter, William Somers; Alexander Kennedy, McKenzie; Kay, McCririck, James Lang, John Peden, Archie Hunter and William Miller.

The club's Scottish Cup successes helped swell the ranks of players who were capped for Scotland. Joining Hunter and Miller were Lang, Somers and Kennedy. James Joseph "Jimmy" Lang had originally been capped in 1876 when playing for Clydesdale. He moved to the club in 1877 and won his second international cap on the 23rd March 1878 against Wales. He scored Scotland's ninth and last goal in a 9-0 victory. He left the club in 1879 to join Sheffield Wednesday. Right-back William Scott Somers was capped against England on the 5th April 1879 at the Kennington Oval and then three days later versus Wales in Wrexham. He started at Glasgow Eastern, then spent a year or two at Third Lanark and was with Queen's Park from 1879 until his early retirement in 1881. He won the Scottish Cup with Queen's Park in 1880. Alexander "Sandy" Kennedy won six caps. He had already been capped three times when playing for Glasgow Eastern between 1875 and 1876. He earned his last three caps as a Third Lanark player, the first of these on the 2nd March 1878 against England. He was also capped against Wales in 1882 and won his sixth and final Scottish cap against the same opposition in March 1884.

In an ever-expanding Scottish Cup competition Third Lanark reached the Fifth Round in the 1878-79 season. They recorded a couple of big victories in the first two rounds, beating Havelock 7-1 away and then Wellpark of Crossmyloof, Glasgow, 8-1. However, they were then beaten heavily by Queen's Park 5-0. They went one round further the following year, reaching the Sixth Round or Quarter-Final stage. Having accounted for Union of Dumbarton, Possil Bluebell, Glasgow University and Kirkintilloch Athletic they then received a bye and were drawn against Thornliebank, going out after a replay. Their opponents went on to contest their one and only Scottish Cup Final, losing to Queen's Park 3-0. On a brighter note, winger James McAdam earned international recognition on the 27th March 1880 and scored Scotland's fourth goal in a 5-1 win over Wales, although he was never capped again.

The 1880-81 Scottish Cup competition saw Thirds exit at the First Round for the first time in their history, beaten 3-1 by Glasgow Northern. They also went out early the following year but in the 1882-83 season they reached the Quarter-Finals. South Western, Clyde, Airdrie and Dunblane were all knocked out before they surprisingly lost against Pollokshields Athletic of Glasgow. The two sides first met a few days before Christmas and played out a closely fought draw. In a goalless first half Thirds had the best of the play. Mid-way through the second period the visitors took the lead but John Marshall equalised soon afterwards. Thirds protested against a disallowed second goal but the result stood and they went on to lose the replay 5-2.

The next two seasons saw comparatively early exits with their next decent Cup run coming in the 1885-86 season. Before that John Marshall earned the first of four caps for Scotland against Ireland. An outside right who had earlier turned out for local Glasgow sides Wellpark and Harmonic, he scored Scotland's fourth in an 8-2 win on the 14th March 1885. He played against Wales in 1886 and made two more international appearances in 1887. After he finished his playing career he stayed in the game and became a referee.

R Moodie's 13 year tenure as manager-secretary ended and he was replaced by J Thomson who held the position for eight years. In his first season the club reached the Semi-Finals of the Scottish Cup although the season ended in controversy. In the First Round of the competition Shawlands of Glasgow were easily dispatched 9-1 on the 12th September. Auld opened the scoring after ten minutes and this was followed by Tait, Thomson, McIntyre and Johnston in quick succession. Shortly before half-time Thomson made it 6-0. In the second half Marshall, Tait and McIntyre all scored. Just before the call of time Shawlands scored from a long range effort. Thirds kept up their good shooting form when they thrashed Glasgow Uni YMCA 8-1 away from home in the next round and they then went on to equal their best ever Cup win in beating St Andrews 11-0 on the 31st October. In the Fourth Round they beat Ayr 3-2 but a replay was ordered and that game ended in a 3-3 draw. Back at Cathkin they won 5-1. The game was evenly contested before Thomson scored, followed by Tait and Miller two minutes later. Marshall scored two in the second half. Just before the whistle Ayr scored. The *Glasgow Herald* commented that "the Volunteers should make a good bid for the Cup this year if they keep up their present form."

It took Thirds another three games as well to get past their Fifth Round opponents Port Glasgow Athletic. The first match was drawn 1-1 and a week later at Port's Clune Park ground the replay ended with the same score. Port Glasgow thought they had taken an early lead. Although the Thirds 'keeper Campbell caught a shot, the home team alleged that the ball was fully a yard over the line but it was not allowed. Thirds took the lead courtesy of an own goal. The home team thought that they had equalised from a corner but Thirds protested about a foul and the referee agreed and disallowed the effort. But Port Glasgow kept up the pressure and got a deserved equaliser before the interval. According to the *Glasgow Herald* "a protest has been made by the Athletic. They claim two goals which were not allowed, and they allege that the game was stopped a minute before time, and that the referee be disqualified by being a member of the Cambuslang Club, who are still in for the cup."

As it was the two sides met again, at Cathkin Park on Boxing Day. Thirds started quickly and a Marshall centre was converted by Miller to give them an early lead. Port Glasgow responded but from a counter Marshall made it 2-0. Thirds then went a man down when Weir had to be carried off the field after a clash with an opposing player. Despite this Third Lanark extended their lead before the break following a goalmouth scramble. On the resumption Thirds were restored to eleven men with the reappearance of Weir. Athletic though had all of the possession and it was another swift counter attack that led to McIntyre scoring a fourth. Athletic kept going, despite this setback, and their persistence paid off with a consolation goal. The *Glasgow Herald* reported that "for the Volunteers the forwards in particular were in grand form. Marshall and Thomson, by their swift runs and general dodging play, proved quite a beat, and required a great deal of watching. Johnstone and McIntyre - particularly the latter - puzzled sorely the opposing backs; while the half-backs and backs played an admirable defensive game...Though the game was not characterised by such brutality as that of last Saturday at Port-Glasgow, still questionable and injurious practices were often resorted to by the visitors, and if permitted to go, such tactics will only tend to injure the game in the eyes of every sensible person."

In the Quarter-finals Third Lanark received a bye and were drawn against the mighty Queen's Park in the Semi-final. Thirds had home advantage but were without Marshall and Weir. The game was played on the 16th January 1886 in poor weather conditions. The match ended in controversy when Third Lanark refused to play the second half on account of the conditions. Reporting on the tie the *Glasgow Herald* commented that "much interest had been taken in the game as both clubs were in the best of form, and had been playing splendidly all the season, particularly the Volunteers, who have of late been showing up exceptionally well, and aspiring determinedly to the high position they occupied some time ago...Unfortunately the weather was of the worst possible description for football. The ground was wet and slippery, and covered with snow, making really good play out of the question. To add to the general misery of the scene, snow fell pitilessly throughout, which combined with the intense cold, made things rather disagreeable alike to players and spectators. Such atmospheric conditions were no doubt the cause of the limited attendance; and surprise was expressed by those who did turn out that instead of being postponed the match should have been gone on with." The game was stopped part way through the first half in order to decide whether to continue as the snow was falling heavily - "several of the players expressed a hearty desire to retire, and justly so, but the spectators were decided in their manifestations to play on, which was done."

The match continued with Queen's Park having the better of it and they finally made their dominance count. Once the first goal went in the floodgates opened and Queen's Park added two more. Continuing their coverage the *Glasgow Herald* reported that "the teams adjourned to the pavilion for shelter, and it was there seriously debated whether the match should be proceeded with, as both teams were benumbed with cold, and the snow was still falling fast. Indeed, several of the Volunteers were so knocked up that restoratives had to be applied, and rather than face up with a diminished team they decided not to go out. The Queen's Park, on the other hand, though not inclined to resume in such boisterous and disagreeable weather, were evidently anxious to finish off the match. The referee was appealed to repeatedly, and a long and spirited wrangle, in which high feeling was manifested on both sides, ended in the Queen's Park turning out in the field and kicking a goal. The spectators were much disappointed, and exhibited their wrath against the Volunteers in various ways.

The protest of the 3rd L.R.V. will be considered at a meeting of the Scottish Association this week. The tie will in all likelihood be played over again, as there must have been some misunderstanding in playing off the match on such a miserable day." The club's protest was considered by the SFA Business Committee on the following Thursday and was dismissed and Queen's Park went on to lift the trophy for an eighth time.

Third Lanark kept up their good performances by reaching the Quarter-finals in the 1886-87 season. The club beat Glasgow clubs Northern and then Linthouse, both 4-1 away, before beating Renton 3-1 and securing a bye in the Fourth Round. In-between they played in the English FA Cup, beating Higher Walton 5-0 before losing to Bolton Wanderers 3-2. In the Scottish Cup Fifth Round they beat Clyde, after a replay to reach the last eight. The surprise of the Quarter-finals was the victory of Hibernian over Thirds in Glasgow in late December 1886. *The Scotsman* reported that "the weather was of the most miserable description with showers of rain and sleet falling continuously during the game. As regards the ground, it was in the worst condition possible. There had been a pretty sharp frost overnight and several pools of water that had gathered on the field during the week were covered with ice, and all over the ground was frozen hard. At one time it was thought that the tie would not be gone on with, but on consideration the clubs determined to have it played." After an even start "grand forwards play by the Edinburgh Shareholders followed, and by one of their usual dashes they swept through...and by a nice, low shot brought about the downfall of the Volunteers' goal." Hibs were on top and soon scored a second. Rain and sleet now started to fall and Thirds now started to dominate, McIntyre almost getting a goal back. Eventually, a fine run by Marshall resulted in a pass to Johnstone, who scored for Thirds. In the second half "D McIntyre, Johnstone and Auld put in grand work for the Volunteers, but though they several times were within an ace of scoring they could not send the ball through." Thirds kept up the pressure but the Hibs defence held firm and there was no further scoring, Hibernian winning 2-1. Hibs went on to lift the Scottish Cup for the first time in their history.

A couple of months later, on the 19th February 1887, half-back John Weir won his single Scottish cap against Ireland. Weir subsequently moved to Everton. Also in the Scotland team was William Johnstone, who went on to earn three caps in total, the last in 1890. He scored Scotland's third in a 4-1 win. A month later, on the 19th March 1887 John Robertson Auld won the first of three caps versus England in a 3-2 away win in Blackburn. Two days later he also played against Wales in Wrexham. He made his third and final international appearance against the same opposition two years later. A fine defensive centre-half, Auld began his career with Kilmarnock and Lugar Boswell before joining Third Lanark and then Queen's Park in November 1884. He returned to Thirds in 1885 and then joined Sunderland in 1890 where he played until 1895, and where he won two League Championships. He subsequently left Sunderland for their arch rivals, Newcastle United.

The following season Thirds were knocked out by Cowlairs of Glasgow at the First Round stage but this time the club lodged a successful protest. In the original game Cowlairs came from behind to win 2-1 but Thirds protested on the grounds that Cowlairs had played McLeod and Robertson, despite them both having played for a Nottingham club. They also protested against Calderwood on the grounds of professionalism. *The Scotsman* reported that "after examination of several witnesses, it was unanimously agreed not to sustain the protest with regard to McLeod and Robertson. Calderwood, however, was convicted of professionalism and suspended for a period of two years, this being his second offence. A motion was made to disqualify the Cowlairs Club on account of employing Calderwood, but by a large majority it was decided that the club had played him not knowing him to be a professional. The Cup tie in which they played Calderwood was then arranged to be replayed on Saturday on the ground of the protestors." Days later the match was played again,
The Scotsman reporting that the game "ended in the [Cowlairs] emphasising their victory of the previous week by scoring four goals to one." McIntyre put Thirds ahead early in the game but Cowlairs equalised after a quarter of an hour. Cowlairs were now on top and pressured the Thirds goal for the rest of the half. Just as it looked like Thirds might weather the storm Cowlairs scored. Keeping up the pressure added two more, one just before the break. There was no scoring in the second half and Cowlairs deservedly progressed to the next round.

In the 1888-89 season Third Lanark secured their first major honour by winning the Scottish Cup. It was another campaign that had a dose of controversy, both en-route to the Final, and in the Final itself. They met Celtic in their third Final, a match they won but which had to be replayed after a protest by Celtic over the state of the pitch. After a walkover in the First Round they met Kelvinside Athletic of Glasgow, their opponents giving up home advantage. Reporting on the Cup tie, the *Glasgow Herald* noted that "as usual in matches of this kind the Volunteers took matters too easily, and the strangers for a time had the best of the play, which was not very interesting." Marshall scored after ten minutes and then added two more before the end of the first half. In the second period Thirds kept up a continual siege of their opponents' goal and won 8-0.

In the next round they drew Queen's Park once more. The two sides met on the 13th October and the *Glasgow Herald* commented that "in the Glasgow district there was only one match in which the result was at all doubtful, that between the 3d L.R.V. and the Queen's Park, but it commanded an amount of interest which is almost unprecedented at such an early stage in the national cup ties...Both teams had an unbroken record for the season, and the supporters of each were confident of victory. But fortune, which has so often smiled upon the premier club, withdrew her favour, and after a keenly contested game the Volunteers emerged triumphant by two to one. That result fairly represented the game; for while the Queen's have been seen to better advantage, their rivals had a magnificent combination, and their play was almost faultless. We understand that the Queen's Park have lodged a protest against Love being allowed to play in the opposing eleven. The question will be brought before the association." In the match itself Marshall put Thirds ahead after ten minutes although their opponents claimed offside. After half an hour Queen's Park equalised but two minutes after the restart Marshall scored with an unstoppable shot.

The Queen's Park protest was upheld and the tie ordered to be replayed at Cathkin Park. Two members of the committee resigned in protest but the re-ordered match was played a fortnight later. The protested tie drew lots of interest and there were 12,000 spectators at Cathkin Park for the game. Covering the replay, the *Glasgow Herald* reported that "it will be remembered that the premier club protested against the 3d L.R.V. having played a man whom they alleged had figured previously in a Cup tie for another club. The committee of the association, by a large majority, sustained the protest, and ordered the tie to be replayed. The decision of the association committee, whether rightly or wrongly, had caused a considerable amount of ill-feeling, which was given vent to on Saturday in no unmissable terms, the Volunteers being clearly the favourites by a large majority of the crowd. As for the game, not much need be said. The strong wind from the south-west completely spoiled all correct calculations in shooting for goal, and at the same time there was a sad absence of anything approaching pretty play. In fact, it was a rough and tumble game, in which determined, forcible play was more conspicuous than passing and dribbling."

In blustery conditions, Thirds had the wind in their favour in the first half and scored three times, all of which were taken by Oswald. Queen's Park scored once. Their opponents were a player short due to injury in the second half. According to the *Glasgow Herald* "the early play indicated that the Queen's Park men were in excellent fettle, but the Volunteers were as lovely and determined as ever." After 17 minutes of play Thirds opened the scoring. After a period of sustained pressure Oswald's shot struck a Queen's Park defender and rebounding, slipped in between the posts. Eight minutes later they extended their lead. Lochhead sent over a fine throw in and Oswald was in hand to head it in. Queen's Park now responded strongly and Downie was twice called upon to make saves. Their opponents then suffered a blow as one of their players was forced to leave the field of play with a knee injury. Playing with ten men Queen's Park astonishingly pulled a goal back. However, Thirds then scored again before half-time, with Oswald netting once more. Queen's Park resumed the second half back up to full strength. The game was very even, with chances on both sides, before Marshall, with a strong shot scored a fourth for Third Lanark. Midway through the second half Queen's Park made it 4-2. By this time the wind had strengthened considerably which made life difficult for the players. Although Queen's Park had the best of the play "it must be admitted that they had hard lines in at least not gaining a third point." With only five minutes left "the play degenerated somewhat, and the faces of the Third's supporters beamed with delight, as it seemed impossible for the Queen's to equalise."

In the next round Third Lanark were drawn at home to Hurlford and Thirds ran out emphatic 7-1 winners. The Ayrshire team had the best of the early play when the two sides met at the beginning of November. After 40 minutes Thirds scored through Oswald. However, Hurlford silenced the Cathkin crowd a minute later and the two sides went into the break level at one apiece. Hurlford started the second half the strongest, but breaking away from defending a corner Thirds scored through Johnstone and five minutes later Morrison registered a third. Hannah quickly added two more as Thirds made it four goals in fifteen minutes. The *Glasgow Herald* noted that "the game was now virtually over, but the enthusiasm of the spectators was sustained by the spirited play of the Hurlford men, who, however far behind, never slackened their efforts of opposition. These efforts, however, were not sufficient to prevent Morrison adding a sixth goal and Thomson a seventh."

In the Fifth Round Third Lanark were involved in a marathon Cup tie with Abercorn of Paisley. The two sides first met on the 24th November. The *Glasgow Herald* reported that "against Abercorn the Volunteers were looked upon as favourites...As the result shows, the city eleven only managed to pull through by the narrow majority of five goals to four." The two sides were level at 2-2 at half-time. In the second half Thirds made it 3-2, then 4-2 and ten minutes from time Johnstone made it 5-2. The team from Paisley then scored two goals in quick succession. According to the *Herald*, "darkness by this time had set in, and it was with the greatest difficulty that the ball could be seen. The prevailing opinion was that had there been a little more time the Abercorn would at least have succeeded in making a draw of it...It is understood that the Abercorn have protested on account of the game being finished in darkness." The protest was upheld and on the 8th December the protested Scottish a Cup tie was replayed at Cathkin. Abercorn led 2-0 at half-time but Thirds completely hemmed in their opponents in the second period and deservedly drew level. Thirds appealed against the original ruling and submitted a counter protest, requesting that they be awarded the original tie. This was dismissed by eight votes to two. A week later the sides met at Paisley but the two sides couldn't be separated so a third replay was needed. On the 22nd December the sides met for a fourth time at the neutral venue of Ibrox. In this game Thirds had the best of the play and took the lead through Hannah and eventually won 3-1. *The Scotsman* reported that "towards the close Lochhead (Third Lanark) and Buchanan (Abercorn) exchanged blows, and a fight ensued between the pair. The game immediately stopped, and the malcontents were surrounded by their friends, who soon put an end to the unseemly disturbance. The referee...interfered, and promptly ordered both men to leave the field." Both players subsequently appeared at Govan Police Court where they were charged with a breach of the peace. According to *The Sporting Life* Robert Buchannan, who seemed to be the instigator of the altercation was offered 33 days' imprisonment or a fine of two Guinea's. Lochhead was offered 25 days' imprisonment or a fine of thirty shillings. Both fines were paid.

A week later Third Lanark were in Quarter-Final action against Campsie. Their opponents had already accounted for Falkirk and Hearts but Thirds had no difficulties progressing to the last four, winning 6-1. Thirds were two up after twenty minutes through Oswald and Johnstone and early in the second half they doubled advantage. Their opponents got one back before Oswald secured his hat-trick and Marshall completed the scoring in the 78th minute. In the Semi-finals Third Lanark were drawn at home to the Cup holders Renton and in the other Dumbarton hosted Celtic. On the 12th January Thirds beat Renton 2-0 in front of a 10,000 crowd at Cathkin. After a good start by Renton, Oswald junior scored. Hannah headed Thirds a second five minutes after the restart. It was a very even first half, the *Glasgow Herald* commenting that both sides were "playing in capital style, and it was quite evident the men had been trained to the hour." Thirds had took the lead after 35 minutes when Marshall fed Oswald who shot past Lindsay. Thirds scored a second within a minute of the restart, Hannah heading in, and "the Volunteers were playing with great go and dash, but two goals up no doubt gave them great confidence." Thirds scored again but it was ruled offside. Renton then missed chances through J Campbell and J McCall, both hitting their shots over the crossbar when well set. "The Renton men were simply outwitted...surpassed in their passing...and met with a stubborn defence." Towards the end Lindsay prevented Thirds increasing their score and Thirds beat the Cup holders 2-0. In the other Semi, Celtic won 4-1 to reach their first Scottish Cup Final.

The Final was played on the 2nd February 1889 and became known as "the snow final." As the teams arrived at the ground snow started to fall and there was a covering of a couple of inches. A pitch inspection decided it was playable but the snow became heavier after the decision to go ahead had been made. With ankle-high snow on the pitch the club's agreed to just play a friendly match and rearrange the Final for another date. However, the referee did not agree to this request on the basis that the fans had already arrived expecting to see a cup final. The match proceeded and Thirds won the Cup Final 3-0, with goals by John Marshall, John Oswald and James Hannah. Celtic lodged a protest with the SFA and demanded a replay due to the poor weather conditions. The SFA eventually agreed, much to the disgust of Third Lanark.

The replayed Final was staged a week later. Celtic dominated early on but Thirds grew into the game and opened the scoring after 25 minutes had been played through Marshall, after a goalmouth scramble. Half time was reached with them leading 1-0. Celtic started the stronger on the resumption and eventually made their pressure pay by equalising in the 67th minute. With momentum on their side Celtic now pressed for the winner but couldn't find a way through. Instead it was Thirds who scored from a breakaway, John Oswald scoring in the 79th minute, which appeared to knock the stuffing out of the Celtic players. Reporting on the match *The Scotsman* commented that "the match all way through was most stubbornly contested, but the superior combination of the Third told, and to this their success may in large measure be attributed. The 3rd Lanark lodged a protest against the finding of the Association at their last meeting, and also on account of the state of the ground, but having won the match these objections fall to the ground....Play soon raged fast and furious, and an early visit was paid by the Third to their opponents' quarters. The ball was sent past, and Tom Maley, aided by his brilliant speed, made for the Third's goal. Thomson defended superbly, but another good run by Maley enabled McCallum to send the ball through but as the referee's whistle had previously blown, the point was of no value. After this narrow escape, the Volunteers replied with telling effect, Marshall after a clever run, all but capturing Kelly's charge. A corner fell to the Volunteers, but Groves fixed on the ball and ran it the whole length of the field amid the greatest enthusiasm. Tom Maley received the ball from the Celt crack, but missed a remarkably easy chance. It was now the turn of the Volunteers, grand combination in front carrying the ball past all opposition, but Kelly proved a successful custodian, repelling all attacks. Thomson, however, missed with the goal at his mercy. The game was proceeding on fast and open lines, and was thoroughly enjoyable from a spectator's point of view. Groves, and then McCallum, might with luck have scored but they invariably met with a stubborn defence from Auld and Thomson. A foul at the Celts' goal caused their supporters much uneasiness, and amid a scene of indescribable excitement, the ball was sent through, the Third thus scoring twenty-five minutes from the start. This roused the Celtic to renewed efforts, Groves and Maley initiating a beautiful run, but McCallum's shooting was at fault. The Third had an open goal at their mercy, and how the Celts escaped was a mystery. The Volunteers still kept up the pressure, the "green and white stripes" not having settled down to their usual play. The latter's defence was thus severely tested. At half-time the Third led by one goal to nothing. The game was soon restarted. The Celts kept their adversaries busy. The combination seemed more effective than in the first period, with the result that Downie's abilities were much tried. Hannah, after some clever work, sent in a stinging shot, which Kelly caught and threw out in a wonderful fashion. After this near shave the Celts redoubled their efforts, and Groves gave McCallum a grand opportunity, which he again failed to take advantage of. A foul against the Volunteers further assisted the Celtic, but McFarlane and Auld were impassable. The Celts kept their opponents continually on the defensive for some time, and a rare shot by Maley was taken to the Volunteer goal, and McCallum equalised amidst a scene which simply baffles description. This put new life into the Celtic, the whole team playing as one man. McKeown being cheered over and over again for his superb kicking. The Celts continued to hem their opponents within their territory and a continual bombardment was kept up on Downie. The Irish form, compared with the beginning of the game was simply astounding. Try as they liked, however, they could not increase their score. The Third, on the other hand, by some excellent passing, carried the play in front of Kelly and Oswald sent the ball through amid wild excitement. The unexpected reverse seemed to chill the ardour of the Celtic players, and their prospects of success with time close at hand looked gloomy indeed. This proved correct, and when Mr Campbell blew his whistle the Volunteers had secured the Cup." The Third Lanark side that lifted the Scottish Cup was: Robert Downie; Andrew Thomson, James Rae; Alex Lochhead, John Robertson Auld, McFarlane; John Marshall, John Oswald, James Oswald, James Hannah and William Johnstone

Two months after their Scottish Cup triumph six players from the club featured in the international against Wales in Wrexham on the 15th April 1889. Auld won his third and last cap and Johnstone was capped for the second time. The club also supplied four debutants: Andrew Thomson, John Rae, James Hannah and Alex Lochhead. Of these, only Rae played again for his country. He also played against Ireland in March 1890 and subsequently moved to England. James "Jimmy" Hannah left the club in 1889 and moved to Sunderland where he won the English League title in 1893 and 1895. He returned to Scotland to play for Third Lanark between 1897-99, before returning south once more to play for Queen's Park Rangers. Alex Lochhead moved to Everton in February 1891 but failed to settle and returned to Scotland, first with Third Lanark, and then with Clyde. A few days before the Wales match James Oswald had played for Scotland against England at the Kennington Oval in London. He scored Scotland's second equalising goal in a 3-2 win as Scotland came from 2-0 down. Oswald later moved to Notts County, playing and scoring in the 1891 FA Cup. He returned to Scotland in 1893 to play for St Bernard's of Edinburgh where he earned a second cap. In 1895 he moved west and joined Rangers where he won his third and final Scottish cap. He left Rangers in 1899 and moved to Raith Rovers and then Morton.

Third Lanark reached the Semi-Finals in defence of their trophy in the 1889-90 season. After beating Patrick Thistle 3-2 they then thrashed Maryhill 9-3. They then beat Dumbarton, after a replay and then Linthouse of Glasgow before receiving a bye into the Quarter-Finals. Here they met Kilbirnie of North Ayrshire on the 21st December at Milton Field in front of a crowd of 3,000. Thirds scored three quick goals through Marshall and W Thomson (2), the first after just seven minutes. The home team got one back before the interval and Marshall sustained an injury early in the second half and had to leave the field. As the pitch began to cut up badly Thomson scored his third and Third Lanark progressed to the Semi-Finals by four goals to one. In the last four they drew Vale of Leven but lost to the three time winners 3-0 at Alexandria on the 27th January 1890.

At the end of March 1890 the original meeting to form the Scottish Football League was held and Third Lanark were one of the eleven founder members. They were one of only four clubs that joined who had triumphed in a Scottish Cup, the others being Vale of Leven, Dumbarton and Renton. Cambuslang, Celtic and Rangers who had all reached a Scottish Cup final also joined. On Saturday 23rd August 1890 Third Lanark played their first ever SFL game at home to eventual joint champions Dumbarton. *The Scotsman* reported on the game, saying that "these clubs met at Cathkin Park in favourable weather and before a large crowd. The Third Lanark in this fixture made their debut in the League competition, but it was Dumbarton's second appearance. The Volunteers introduced several new players into their team - Scott (Thornliebank) and Dewar (Thistle) at back, and McIntosh (Linthouse) in front. The Volunteers faced the wind in the first half, and the play started brisk and in the ground club's favour. After half an hour's play Dumbarton from a corner kick scored rather luckily, and a few minutes after the Volunteers made amends by equalising. The play quietened down before crossing over. Against the wind Dumbarton showed improved form. In twenty minutes they scored a second point, and a few minutes later...a third. The Third made several efforts to lessen the difference but McLeod was all there and twice saved miraculously. The play, which was never very bright, was occasionally needlessly rough, and the dominating feeling oftentimes reprehensible. Towards the close it was most uninteresting. The score at the finish was in favour of Dumbarton, who won by three goals to one." The Third Lanark team making their Scottish League debut was: Downie; Scott, Dewar; McFarlane, Love, Lochhead; McIntosh, Thomson, Lapsley; Johnstone and Burke.

Thirds beat Celtic 2-1 at home in their next League game before two consecutive 8-1 wins in rounds two and three of the Scottish Cup. In the first of these they beat Kilmarnock Athletic, scoring seven in the first half, and in the next round they thrashed Summerton Athletic (of Govan, Glasgow), despite their opponents scoring early. Thirds led 3-1 at half-time and scored five second half goals. Thirds eventually reached the Semi-final of the Cup for the third season in a row, knocking out Queen's Park in the Quarter-final after a second replay, before losing to eventual winners Hearts 4-1. Hearts would go on to beat Dumbarton 1-0 in the final. Dumbarton though would go on to jointly lift the first Scottish League championship with Rangers. As for Third Lanark, they finished a mid-table fifth place, despite incurring a points deduction. They were one of three clubs to have four points deducted for fielding ineligible players that season.

In the League's second season Thirds secured another mid-table finish, placed sixth, with the key highlight being a record SFL win in the Boxing Day fixture against Vale of Leven. The *Glasgow Herald* reported that "the Vale opened with some clever play, but were not allowed to become closely acquainted with Downie. Blair robbed Paton of the ball, and tipping it over to McVean, that player forced a corner, from which Andrew Thomson scored with a shot 20 yards out. Time - three minutes. The ball was no sooner set in motion than McVean and W Thomson fastened on it, and in a minute more the latter registered goal No. 2. The Vale thereafter opened out a bit, and treated the spectators to pretty play. It did not last long, however, for the Third's half-backs were in grand form, more especially Murdoch, whose play was really brilliant. The Third's forwards again formed themselves in a line, and W Thomson gave the finishing touch to a combined attack. The Vale could make little or no headway. They were sorely hampered, and at this time their goal fell for the fourth time, McVean scoring with a header. At length the spell was broken, and the Vale found themselves a few yards from Downie. Bad luck dogged their footsteps, for one of the players accidentally handled the ball. Andrew Thomson took the free kick, and after some fancy work by the home team's forwards Woodburn scored a fifth goal. Again the Vale got well up the field but here they became feeble, disorganised and timid. Smith stepped in amongst them, and with a powerful kick, transferred the play to the Vale's goal, which Wilson saved in splendid style. At half-time the Third led by 5 to 0. The Third opened brilliantly, and in five minutes times scored three goals, taken by Graydon, Murdoch and Woodburn, all against the wind, too. At this time the Vale were playing with ten men, and they continued to give the Thirds' defence some trouble. When they got a chance to score there was a lack of 'go' about their efforts, and the Third consequently had no difficulty in clearing. The Volunteers had a few more tries at Wilson, this time without success, and the Vale came away with surprising dash, and, getting a free kick for a foul near Downie, Gillies scored with an extremely swift shot. The game was now interesting, the Vale, with the assistance of the wind, playing with commendable dash, but when they were likely to become dangerous Smith and Thomson generally accounted for them. The Third again took the game in hand, and McVean registered a ninth goal. This was all the scoring, and the game finished as follows: - Third Lanark, 9 goals; Vale, 2 goals." Vale didn't win a single game all season. The Third Lanark team was: Downie; A Thomson, Smith; Burrell, Murdoch, Blair; McVean, W Thomson, Graydon, Woodburn and Crossan. One of the club's stars in this match was Malcolm McVean. Although never capped by Scotland he was signed by newly formed Liverpool in 1892 and as well as scoring their first ever goal, McVean was also Liverpool's captain. When Liverpool were admitted to the Football League a year later, it was McVean who scored their first ever goal in the League. McVean subsequently moved to Burnley in 1897 and returned to Scotland soon afterwards, playing for Dundee. Another highlight of the season came in March 1892 when goalkeeper Robert Downie was capped for Scotland against Wales on the 26th March at Tynecastle. He won just this one cap.

In the 1892-93 season Third Lanark achieved their best placed finish to date coming in fourth place. They lost their first game 4-1 at home to Hearts but then won the next two by the same 4-1 score line. On the 1st October they recorded a big win against Abercorn of Paisley who they hosted in front of a small crowd of about 1,000. After an evenly contested first 15 minutes, Thirds scored three quick goals. This knocked the stuffing out of the visitors and the play was all in favour of Third Lanark who won 8-0. The *Glasgow Herald* reported that "the game for some time was pretty equal until the Third, by judicious play, got down to Jamieson [in the Abercorn goal], and after hanging about goal for a few minutes Boyd sent the ball through. Without much effort Ellis managed to beat Jamieson, and in less than a minute Boyd put on a third point for the Volunteers. The Abercorn, although playing passably well, were no match for the home team, and at half-time the Volunteers were leading by 3 goals to nil. The second half requires no description, as it was all in favour of the Third, who won by 8 goals to 0."

Later in the same month Thirds beat Renton 6-2. Early Renton pressure with balls into the box were neatly cleared away by the Third's backs. Thirds weathered the storm and after 30 minutes play took the lead and they added a second before half-time to lead 2-0 at the interval. On the resumption Renton scored the goal that on the balance of play they deserved. This had the effect of stirring up the Thirds team who responded by restoring their two goal advantage. Renton came back again to make it 3-2 and had a chance to equalise but fluffed their chance. This seemed to spur Thirds on and towards the end of the game, as Renton continued to push forward, Thirds raided their opponent's goal, time and again, to eventually run out comfortable winners, although the 6-2 final scoreline flattered them. The result moved Third Lanark up to fourth in the table.

At the end of January 1893 Thirds recorded a 4-1 win over Clyde. They played two new signings from Thistle - Allan and Rae - but finished the first half without Love due to injury. He didn't appear for the rest of the match and despite this Thirds still won.

However, they then lost four out of their next five matches, picking up a single point, the last of these being a 6-0 home defeat by Celtic at the end of April. In this game they were only 1-0 down at half time but a couple of injuries in the second half severely handicapped them. Thirds bounced back by scoring six of their own in a 6-1 win over St Mirren, where they raced into a 3-0 lead within the first 15 minutes. They gained a measure of revenge over Celtic as both teams concluded their League programme in a midweek fixture on Thursday 18th May - a 5-2 away win at Celtic Park - although Celtic were already the League champions and had reached the final of the Scottish Cup. Doyle of Celtic was ordered off the field in the first half and Thirds made the numerical advantage count, although parity of players was restored in the second half when Smith of Third Lanark also received his marching orders. Thirds finished fourth on 19 points, one behind third placed St Mirren, but ten behind the champions Celtic.

The 1893-94 season saw Third Lanark slip back in terms of their final League placing, finishing in sixth place, although they did reach the Semi-Finals of the Scottish Cup once more. The new season saw the introduction of a Second Division and a First Division limited to ten teams. There was no automatic promotion and relegation but the bottom three would face a re-election vote. Thirds finished just outside the bottom three, coming in seventh place, finishing two points ahead of Dundee in eighth.

Bill Abel replaced J Thomson as the manager and the club opened their new League campaign with a heavy 5-0 defeat away against the champions Celtic, but scored five themselves the following week when they beat St Bernard's of Edinburgh 5-3. With Renton struggling at the bottom a series of defeats left Third Lanark competing with Leith Athletic and Dundee to avoid the other two re-election spots. The Scottish Cup proved to be a nice distraction as at the end of November Third Lanark recording a whopping 9-9 win over Inverness Thistle in the First Round. Thirds had nearly all the play and were leading 5-0 at half-time. Inverness Thistle showed up better in the second half, which they only lost by four goals to three. Thirds then accounted for St Mirren and Port Glasgow Athletic and went on to reach the Semi-Final which they lost 5-3 at home to Celtic, who in turn were beaten 3-1 in the final by Rangers. Back in the League, vital away wins at Renton and Leith Athletic, and a draw at Carolina Port against Dundee ensured the club would secure their First Division status again by avoiding the re-election vote. At the end of the season right winger Andrew Stewart became the latest Third Lanark player to be capped for Scotland, when on the 24th March 1894 he played against Wales at Rugby Park, Kilmarnock. Stewart was never capped again and subsequently played for Queen's Park and St Bernard's.

In the fifth season of the League Third Lanark improved on the pitch and matched their best League placing of fourth, although they were again ten points behind the eventual champions Hearts. It was against Hearts that they opened the 1894-95 League season, losing 6-3 at Tynecastle. Thirds came back from 3-1 down to level at 3-3 but this stung the home team into action. They beat Celtic 2-1 at Cathkin Park in their next game but then suffered four consecutive defeats to be joint bottom with just two points from their opening six fixtures. A 4-2 away win at St Bernard's in mid-October kick started a run of only one League defeat in ten matches. Included in the run was a 6-3 win over bottom club Dumbarton and a 7-1 victory over Leith Athletic, another club that was struggling. The visitors opened the scoring and then, according to *The Scotsman* "the Third Lanark asserted themselves after this, but showed great want of judgment in front of goal." Bell eventually equalised and John Herbert Fyfe added a second. Thirds were now in the ascendancy and scored three more times before half-time, Fyfe completing a first half hat-trick and Blair getting the fifth. In the second half Thirds kept up incessant pressure and only the goalkeeping of Kay for Leith kept the score down. He was, however, between twice as Third Lanark won 7-1. However, during the course of this great League run they also suffered a shock Scottish Cup exit. On the 24th November 1894 they played Annbank, the *Glasgow Herald* reporting that "the ties in the first round of the final stage of the Scottish Cup competition brought out at least one big surprise, and that was the defeat of the Third Lanark by the Annbank, at Annbank. It is difficult, indeed, to account for the overthrow of the Glasgow team by Annbank, especially as at one period of the game in the second half they were leading by four goals to two. The ground we know is not of the best, but that cannot wholly explain it away. There must surely have been something tantamount to a complete collapse in the closing stages of the game, because the local men scored three goals in succession, and amidst the greatest excitement actually won by five goals to four." Thirds finished their League campaign with a record number of wins (10) and this helped lift them up to fourth place. Half-back James Simpson won three caps in 1895, all in the same international season and winger John Herbert Fyfe played in the first of these games, against Wales in Wrexham on the 23rd March, although this was his only cap.

There now followed a series of mid-table finishes over the course of the next eight seasons with occasional Cup runs and notable victories. The 1895-96 season started in terrible fashion as Thirds lost 7-2 at home to Hibernian but they later beat Rangers 4-0 at Ibrox and beat Clyde 6-2 at home and 7-2 away and they eventually finished tied for sixth place, two points above the bottom three placings. William Blair became the latest club player to be capped against Wales in Dundee, on the 21st March 1896. He originally played for Greenock Morton and this was his only international appearance.

The following season they found themselves in the bottom three for the first time and therefore faced a re-election vote. They lost 12 of their 18 League matches, a new club record, although they did beat bottom side Abercorn 8-3. They also scored eight in the Scottish Cup, beating Newton Stewart Athletic 8-1 in the First Round. They then went on to knock out Hearts, who would go on to be the League champions, before losing to Second Division Kilmarnock. Left back David Richmond Gardner, was capped for Scotland in a 2-2 draw against Wales in Wrexham in March. He started his footballing career with Third Lanark before moving south to play for Newcastle United in 1899 and Grimsby Town 1902 and in 1904 he joined West Ham United. At the League's AGM held on the 1st June 1897 Third Lanark were successfully re-elected, topping the poll with 14 votes.

In the 1897-98 season Third Lanark had an improved showing, coming in fifth, but the highlight of the season was in reaching the Scottish Cup Semi-Finals. Thirds knocked out Clyde, Celtic and Hibernian, all First Division sides, before being drawn to play Rangers. It took three matches to separate the sides, the first being played at Ibrox on the 19th February 1898 in front of a crowd of 15,000. Thirds took the lead in the first half through Hannah. Thirds were then awarded a penalty but Dickie saved from Johnstone. Rangers equalised after ten minutes play in the second half and an evenly contested game ended with no further scoring. A week later the teams met at Cathkin where 15,000 also gathered for the replay. As in the first match Thirds opened the scoring through Johnstone, Rangers soon equalised though. A misunderstanding between the visitors' backs let in Johnstone who squared for James Gillespie to restore the lead for Third Lanark. Just before half-time Rangers were awarded a penalty but the resulting kick was blazed high over the bar. In the second half the game lost any rhythm due to persistent fouling and it was a foul that led to another penalty for a Rangers. The same player who had missed their first spot kick, Neil, took the penalty, but Milne was equal to it and parried it out of danger. Just when it looked like they were going out and would be left to rue those penalty misses, Rangers got an equaliser just before the end. The second replay was played on the 12th March and this time Rangers won 2-0. A poor clearance by the 'keeper, Milne, enabled Rangers to score early. This was then followed by end to end play but no further scoring resulted. The game continued in a similar vein in the second half with both goalkeepers called into action. Smith of Thirds collected a knee injury and had to leave the field leaving his team with a numerical disadvantage. Shortly afterwards a penalty was awarded against Thirds, leading to a second goal for Rangers. Smith returned after ten minutes but by this time the game was beyond Third Lanark and it was Rangers who advanced the final to play Kilmarnock - which they won 2-0.

On the 19th March 1898 James Gillespie scored a hat trick on his international debut in a 5-2 win over Wales at Motherwell's Fir Park. He wasn't picked a week later for the match against Ireland or then England in the home internationals and this turned out to be his only cap. He had originally started his playing career at Renton but moved to Sunderland in 1892 where he won two English League titles. He returned to Scotland in 1897 with Third Lanark and despite scoring a hat-trick he was never capped again for his country.

Three wins and three defeats in the first half dozen matches set the tone for the 1998-99 season in which Thirds finished a mid-table 6th place. In the Scottish Cup they beat Arthurlie 4-1, which was a season's best victory but lost in the next round 2-1 at St Mirren. Their inconsistency was again evident in the 1899-1900 season and is well illustrated in their opening four matches. They lost their season opener 5-1 at home to Rangers before beating St Mirren by the same scoreline, hitting four goals in the second half. The following week the winning team again scored five, Thirds going down 5-2 at Celtic before scoring five once more in a 5-0 win over Clyde. The sequence of the winners scoring five was ended in the next match when Celtic won 3-0. Thirds settled into mid-table and finished in seventh place. In the Scottish Cup they reached the Third Round, beating Raith Rovers and Motherwell before Hearts came from behind to beat them 2-1 at Cathkin Park.

For the 1900-01 season the First Division was expanded to 11 teams with Queen's Park finally deciding to join and being fast-tracked into the top flight. Other than a new League opponent, the new season was largely uneventful for Thirds. They lost their opening game 4-0 at Ibrox against Rangers and the following month they went down 5-1 at Celtic and were in seventh place. A good run in the autumn saw them edge up a place to finish sixth. In the Scottish Cup they beat Douglas Wanderers 5-0, then Abercorn after a replay, before going out to St Mirren after a second replay.

In the 1901-02 season the First Division reverted back to an even number of clubs with Partick Thistle being relegated and no clubs coming up. Two wins and two draws in the League were followed by four consecutive draws. In mid-November they then recorded two consecutive 4-1 away victories, first, surprisingly at Rangers and then at Morton. Thirds also beat Morton 4-1 at Cathkin, a result that lifted them up to fourth, which is where they finished. William Maxwell finished as the League's top scorer with 12 goals. In the Scottish Cup they beat Morton after a replay but lost 4-1 to Hearts in the next round.

The 1902-03 season, although not successful on the football field, did see some significant changes off it for the club. First, the club severed their links with the military and got incorporated as a company. After turning professional in 1893 links with the regiment became more tenuous and in 1903 they were severed altogether, the club re-registering with the Scottish FA as Third Lanark Athletic Club. Secondly, they took over the stadium that Queen's Park had owned before, and renamed it New Cathkin Park, reverting later to simply 'Cathkin Park'. Third Lanark's final League game at the old Cathkin Park was played on the 4th April 1903, with the club losing 1–0 to Dundee. Their opponents finished as runners-up to Hibs but were distinctly lucky in taking both points. The club came in seventh in the League at the end of the season. James Johnstone (10 goals) and William Wardrope (7 goals) were the club's leading goalscorers. They beat St Johnstone 10-1 at Perth in the First Round of the Scottish Cup in January 1903. The home team actually opened the scoring but Thirds soon equalised and by half-time they had added another two goals to their score. The visitors took complete control of the game in the second half. Thirds reached the Quarter-Final stage where they were knocked out by eventual beaten finalists Hearts.

Third Lanark are the only ex-Scottish Football League club to have won the ultimate honour of League champions and they achieved it in the 1903-04 season. After a decade of mediocrity in terms of League finishes it came somewhat as a surprise that they should win the ultimate accolade. Key to their success was the appointment in August 1903 of Frank Heaven as manager, who replaced Bill Abel who had been in charge for a decade. He had managed West Bromwich between 1896 and 1902. There have been lots of Scottish managers who have been successful in the English game but very few the other way about and he is the only English manager to have won the Scottish League title. He successfully blended experience and youth and largely played a settled side. What is also remarkable about their championship winning season was that it was achieved despite them playing their "home" matches away from Cathkin Park. Thirds used the new Hampden Park for much of the season whilst building work was carried out at New Cathkin Park.

On the 15th August 1903 Third Lanark lost their opening game of the 1903-04 season 4-3 at Ibrox in which Rangers led three times before finally winning in the last minute. They then went an amazing 16 games without another defeat, running from the 22nd August to the 4th January 1904, some four months. During this unbeaten run they won seven games in a row from the end of October to the beginning of January. This included home and away wins over Celtic, a 2-0 away win at defending champions Hibs and an 8-2 away victory at Queen's Park on the 12th December, which was a club record SFL away win. In this match the first half was an even affair and the sides went into the break level at 2-2 with no signs of things to come. Reporting on the game *The Glasgow Herald* said "It was in the second half that some most surprising football was shown by both sides. The Third surprised everyone by the all-round brilliance of their work; while the Queen's, save for a few spasmodic rushes, gave an impotent display. Goal after goal was put on by the Third, and more than one of these gave rise to heated arguments on the field. The referee kept a firm hold of the game, and did his duty

694

admirably under trying circumstances…The Queen's were thoroughly outplayed in the second half during which the Third's display was superb."

A 2-0 away win at Motherwell, coupled with Rangers drawing 1-1 at Port Glasgow Athletic meant that Thirds ended 1903 two points behind leaders Rangers but having played three games less. However, they lost consecutive games at the end of January, first to Morton and then away at Hearts in early February. A 4-0 away win at Airdrieonians followed by a 3-0 home win over Motherwell in early March 1904 took them level at the top with Hearts on 37 points and one ahead of Rangers, having played two games fewer. And both of their rivals only had one more game to play. Celtic were in fourth place, three points behind and like Thirds, still had three games remaining.

Before the League could reach its denouement Third Lanark were in Scottish Cup action where they had carried their League form into the Cup and had gone deep in the competition. A walkover in the First Round against Newton Stewart Athletic had been followed up with victories over Alloa Athletic and then Kilmarnock. In this Quarter-final tie they had won 3-0, their visitors turning up twenty minutes late. On the 19th March their double hopes were dashed in the Semis when Celtic beat them 2-1 at Parkhead in front of a 35,000 crowd. The two sides had already met at Parkhead early on in the League season resulting in a 3-1 away win for Thirds. Fairly early on, McLeod, the right-back for Celtic had to retire injured and while he was absent off the field Thomas McKenzie opened the scoring following a poor clearance by Orr that left him one-on-one with the 'keeper Adams. Third continued to make their man advantage count and dominated the game but things changed when McLeod returned to the field and evened up the numbers. Celtic squandered a few chances to equalise but were eventually given the chance to get back on level terms via the penalty spot. However, Orr's kick was easily saved by Raeside and Thirds went into the interval one goal to the good. The game was resumed in torrential rain and *The Scotsman* commented that "Third Lanark had all the play, and though facing the breeze, they seemed certain scorers. Celtic, on the other hand, surprised their supporters by the spirit of their play, never falling away, even when they were most severely pressed." Eventually Celtic fashioned an equaliser, a curling shot from Quinn just evading Raeside's despairing leap. The goal had a galvanising effect on the home side who now had all of the play and Quinn gave them the lead. Although Thirds had one or two chances towards the end they couldn't get back on level terms and Celtic progressed to the Final, where they would beat Rangers 3-2.

On the 26th March Rangers concluded their fixtures by beating Airdrieonians 5-0 and Celtic beat Motherwell. Rivals Hearts were not in action but Thirds beat Kilmarnock 3-2, twice coming from behind. Thirds were without Wilson and McKenzie, having picked up knocks in the Cup Semi-final whereas the visitors were at full strength. Thirds conceded early but eventually equalised through Graham but before half-time bottom club Kilmarnock went ahead again. Five corners in succession for Thirds ultimately led to Comrie equalising. A minute later Graham gave them the lead and Thirds held on to secure a vital win. Third Lanark now couldn't be caught by Rangers and only needed one point from their remaining two games to be crowned as champions.

On Saturday 2nd April their two rivals for title, Hearts and Celtic, met at Tynecastle. *The Scotsman* noted that "the contest was an important one for both clubs, as the winner secured second position on the League table, and in the event of Third Lanark losing their two remaining games, became rivals of the Cathkin club for the Championship. The Hearts, as a result of strong and effective play throughout, won by the odd goal." The 2-1 victory meant Hearts drew level at the top with Thirds on 39 points having completed their fixtures whereas Third Lanark still had two games to play against fifth placed Dundee and tenth placed Hibernian, both at home, having beaten both these clubs away.

On Saturday 23rd April Third Lanark beat Dundee 4-1 to secure the League championship title - the only former club to have won the Scottish League title. Wardrop gave them the early lead before Johnstone beat the on-rushing Muir for 2-0. In the second half Neilson scored with a long range effort before Lennie had an effort disallowed for offside. Wardrop then made it four and just on time Cowie scored for the visitors. The *Glasgow Herald* reflected that it was "an honour they richly deserve on their season's play, for although the team does not possess that richness in individual stars which some clubs have it has the more profitable quality of general utility and balance. With fewer reserves than most first-class clubs, Third Lanark have gone through a hard season's work, and by strenuous effort and praiseworthy enthusiasm have reached their present position. Much of their success has been due to the wise policy of blending judiciously youthful energetic players with men of experience and tried ability."

On Saturday 30th April the club concluded their League fixtures with an academic 2-0 win over Hibernian. The new champions met the old champions at New Cathkin and Thirds took the opportunity to try out George Archibald and Thomas McMurdo who made their first appearances. Both had a part in the goals as Archibald set up Johnstone and in the second half a goal mouth scramble saw McMurdo score the second goal. To put Third Lanark's League title into perspective it is worth noting that after 1904 it took the other clubs 28 years to break the Celtic and Rangers duopoly, when Motherwell won the League in 1931-32.

The League title was basically won by twelve players, with another five only participating in a few matches. The key players were: James Raeside; Robert Barr, William McIntosh; John Cross, Thomas Sloan, John Neilson; William Wardrop, Robert Graham, Thomas McKenzie, John Campbell, Hugh Wilson and James Johnstone. Third Lanark's best goal scorers were McKenzie, Graham and Wilson, who all netted eleven goals each.

James "Jimmy" Smith Raeside was the goalkeeper and an ever-present in the championship winning side. He had made his debut for the club in August 1899 and went on to make nearly 150 League appearances for Third Lanark. A cool, agile and resourceful 'keeper he was capped once for Scotland in March 1906 against Wales at Tynecastle, a 2-0 defeat, and joined Bury in 1906. In front of Raeside was the reliable pairing of backs Robert Barr and William McIntosh. This dependable trio had the best defensive record in the League with just 26 goals conceded and with eleven clean sheets from 26 matches. William Forbes McIntosh was capped in March 1905 against Ireland at Celtic Park, and he later emigrated to Canada.

The half-backs were John Cross, Thomas Sloan and John Neilson. John Halliday Cross made close to 200 appearances for the club and also played for Petershill, Queens Park Rangers and Wishaw Thistle. He won one cap for Scotland against Ireland in 1903 when the Irish recorded their first ever win. He left the club in 1904. Glasgow born Thomas "Tom" Sloan played his entire career for Third Lanark, where he served as club captain. He won a full international cap for Scotland when he played in a 1-1 draw with Wales at Dens Park, Dundee, in March 1904. After his playing career was over he served as a Third Lanark club director. John Neilson previously played for Abercorn and was the only one of the trio not capped at international level. He subsequently joined Bristol Rovers but later returned to Scotland with Royal Albert and then Kirkcaldy United and Raith.

The forwards were a mix of youth and experience. The latter came from Hugh Wilson, Johnny Campbell and William Wardrope. John James Campbell was a prolific goalscorer who began his career at Celtic, where he played between 1890 and 1895. He won two League titles and a Scottish Cup before moving to England in the summer of 1895 where he won successive English League titles. He returned to Celtic in 1897 and won another Scottish League title and two more Scottish Cups. At the age of 32 he joined Third Lanark and scored 12 goals across three seasons before retiring in 1906. He was first capped for Scotland in his first spell with Celtic in 1893 and was capped 12 times in total across a ten year span, scoring four international goals. Hughie Wilson had joined Sunderland from Newmilns, Ayrshire in the summer of 1890 and won English League titles with them in 1892, 1893 and 1895, making over 250 club appearances. He was first capped by Scotland in March 1890 whilst still in Ayrshire, scoring in a 5-0 win over Wales. He played for Scotland again seven years later. He signed for Third Lanark in 1901 and earned two more caps while at Third Lanark, against Wales in 1902 at Cappielow, Greenock and then against Ireland in March 1904. He ended his career at Kilmarnock. William "Willie" Wardrope started his career with Motherwell and Linthouse before moving to England in August 1895 when he signed for Newcastle United, helping them earn promotion to the First Division. He later joined Middlesbrough where he repeated the feat with his new club. In 1902 he returned to Scotland when he joined Third Lanark. After two seasons he returned to England with Fulham and then Swindon Town. He returned once more to Scotland to join Hamilton Academical in 1907 and ended his career in 1908 at Raith.

These old heads were complemented by promising young strikers Thomas Mackenzie, Robert Graham and James Johnstone. MacKenzie joined at the start of the season and joint top-scored with 11 goals in 21 games. He scored 34 goals in 61 appearances between 1903 and 1905 before leaving to join Sunderland in October 1905. He later went on to play for Plymouth Argyle. Robert Graham also scored 11 goals and James Johnstone went on to score 58 League goals between 1901-09. The team also featured 22-year old James Comrie, who made his debut that season, playing in only four of the matches, scoring one goal. He had another two seasons at Cathkin before moving to England to play for Reading, Glossop, Bradford City, Lincoln City and then Burnley. On the outbreak of War in 1914 he enlisted and tragically died in action on the 9th August 1916.

Manager Frank Heaven left at the end of the season on the grounds of ill-health and sadly passed away on Boxing Day 1905. He was replaced by Samuel Wyllie who won the Scottish Cup in his first season. Third Lanark opened their title defence with a keenly contested 2-1 home win over Rangers on the 20th August 1904. They lost their next game, 4-1 away at Hearts and in September and October they lost both home and away against Celtic, who would go on to depose them as League champions. At the end of November they took revenge on Hearts, beating them 7-1 in interesting weather conditions. *The Scotsman* reported that the game was played "in a fog....so dense was the mist that it was not until the time for kicking off that the referee...decided to go on with the game, and it was only then that the gates were opened. During the first half the fog was not thick enough to interfere seriously with the game, but for the greater part of the second it was impossible for the spectators to follow the movement of the players, and how the officials in charge allowed it to proceed was difficult to understand. Towards the end matters had become farcical in the extreme, and from the press-box, where the work had to be done in candlelight, it was impossible to know what was taking place. One player could not be distinguished from another, and how the goals were obtained it was impossible to say; indeed, it was only be the shouting of those behind the posts and the lining up of players at the centre that it was known that goals were being recorded. The Hearts started well, but could not score, and after the Third had got a goal through MacKenzie the home team had the game pretty well in hand. They only led by one point however at the interval. After the change of ends the Third soon obtained the mastery, and another two goals were registered. Then Corbett scored for the Hearts and the 'Volunteers' replied with a fourth. After that the Hearts lost the services of G Wilson, who was hurt, and the home team hit another three points, and ultimately won by seven goals to one." Thirds couldn't back this result up though and failed to win any of their next four games. They won their last match of 1904, a 4-1 home win over Hibernian on Hogmanay to sit in third place with 24 points. Celtic led with 31 points and Rangers were second on 27.

Third Lanark started 1905 very strongly recording a 6-0 win over Airdrieonians, despite the handicap of an injury to Johnstone. Thirds had easily the better of their opponents and scored four times in the first half. *The Glasgow Herald* adding "the winners played a dazzling game, and as an index to the game it may be remarked that they had the ball in the net no fewer than 10 times." They also recorded a 5-0 win over Morton in January and a 6-1 victory over Partick Thistle in February, scoring three in each half. In fact they went the rest of the season in the League unbeaten to finish in third place, finishing six points behind Celtic and Rangers, who were tied on 41 points. A play-off for the championship was held in which Celtic beat Rangers 2-1. A month earlier Rangers were involved in another showdown for a domestic trophy, this time in the Scottish Cup Final, where they played Third Lanark, appearing in their fourth Final.

Third Lanark's run to the Scottish Cup Final had started back at the end of January when they beat Leith Athletic 4-1. They subsequently beat Motherwell 1-0 and then Aberdeen 4-1. They met Airdrieonians in the Semi-final on the 25th March 1905 at Cathkin Park in front of a crowd of 12,000. The early action was end to end with *The Scotsman* commenting that "both keepers...continued to withstand and distinguish themselves in all the onslaughts made by the forwards." Raeside made another save but the ball was only cleared 15 yards out and Thomson fired home to give the visitors the lead on 35 minutes. Thirds then dominated the remainder of the half and several chances went begging before Hugh Wilson forced the ball home and the two sides went into the break with the score level at 1-1. There was little flow to the second period as it was disrupted by a series of injuries, as described by *The Scotsman*: "McMenzie's (Third Lanark) knee first of all gave out, and he had to retire...Then Tarbert (Airdrie) and Sloan (Third Lanark) collided, and the latter had to be assisted off, and later Thomson (Airdrie) and Sloan went down together, and both had to be assisted to the pavilion." Only six minutes were remaining when the winning goal was scored. James Johnstone got free and fired a low angled shot which beat Duncan in the Airdrie goal and hit the inside of the post and went in.

In the other Semi-final Rangers beat Celtic 2-0 and the two sides met on the 8th April, *The Scotsman* providing a full report: "At Hampden Park, Glasgow, these teams met on Saturday to decide which would be the possessors of the Scottish national trophy for season 1904-05. The enormous interest taken in the final tie was reflected in the huge attendance, which at one time threatened to shake the record set up by the Celtic-Rangers final of a year ago on the same ground...the crowd...might be put down at 33000. Nor was the tie settled, the drawn game necessitating a replay, and next Saturday it has been decided the teams will meet on the same ground. If on the cold side, the weather was favourable...Winning the toss, the Rangers captain sacrificed the wind advantage, and, with the Third Lanark pressing from the outset, excitement was early at a high pitch. In the Rangers goal Sinclair had no easy task warding off the opposition, and the custodian had several ticklish shots to deal with before the game was many minutes old...Next it was the turn of the Rangers to show their paces, and the way the "light blues" beat up against the wind was quite in accordance with reputation...The Third Lanark backs had plenty to do, while occasionally Raeside got a fright, notably from a shot from Smith which travelled at a terrific pace across the goal. It was fortunate for the Cathkin side that it was a shade wide. The wind, naturally, kept the Third Lanark the more aggressive...[but]...the "Light Blues" stuck to their work grandly, and thoroughly deserved a goal, which, however, despite several good, at times brilliant, efforts, would not come...and the teams crossed over with a clean sheet. With the wind over their shoulders, the Rangers at once took up the running on resuming, but were beaten back, and a halt had to be called to permit of McKenzie recovering from a light injury. It was an uphill task the Third Lanark had now, but they faced it well, and their defenders stuck to their guns manfully, and completely upset the best laid plans of attack the Rangers could devise. Still the latter fell away badly, the forwards doing well enough in the open, but poorly when they got to shooting range. For the most part the second half was composed of runs and counter runs. As each set of forwards broke away, the opposing defence pulled them up, and the respective goalkeepers for a time had comparatively little to do. That sort of thing continued, and the crowd had little to become enthusiastic over, save a couple of appeals for penalty kicks, which were disregarded- one on each side. The chance of the match fell to Hamilton (of Rangers), who unaccountably failed to pop the ball into the net when in front of goal, with Raeside lying on the ground. The play in the second half neutralised all the good points of the first period, and the game finished up tamely, and was generally rated a very indifferent one."

Summarising the final, *The Scotsman* commented that "Saturday's finalists for the Scottish Cup are old rivals, but singularly enough the present is the first occasion upon which the two clubs have met in the last stage. The Rangers are experienced finalists; on the other hand, the Volunteers have repeatedly failed to do themselves justice in the national competition, and one has to go back as far as season 1889-90 to find them in Saturday's position as Scottish Cup finalists. Saturday's match was a distinct disappointment. All the credit for the replay rests with the respective defences, which, against the wind particularly, rarely made a mistake. The Rangers should have won."

A week later the two sides tried again and on the 15th April 1905 Third Lanark won the Scottish Cup for the second, and last time, beating Rangers 3-1 in the replay. *The Scotsman* reported that "this replayed tie to decide whether the cup would go to Cathkin or Ibrox took place on Saturday on the ground of the Queen's Park at Hampden Park, Glasgow. The weather was fine, and the game attracted another large crowd of spectators, estimated at 40,000. On the Rangers side Hamilton was left out, Low taking his place, but the Third Lanark team was the same as last Saturday. The Rangers kicked off against a fair breeze, and right from the start the players infused plenty of go into their play, and the first half was hotly contested. The ball travelled rapidly from end to end...the Rangers beat up finely against the wind, and time and again a goal seemed likely to fall to them. But Raeside had to be dealt with, and to beat him the Rangers tried hard enough, but to no purpose, the Cathkin custodian being in his best form...To the attack the Rangers came, but the Third defence prevailed...The field was well opened out...and the Third forwards made the most of their chance. From Johnston the ball was run on to McKenzie, who in turn played along to Munro. The left-winger passed to the veteran Wilson, who manoeuvred for a bit, and then from twenty yards' range drove a grounder into the net past the side of the post. Hitherto the Rangers had had the best of the exchanges, and seemed the more likely lot to score. The remaining few minutes were fought out determinedly by both teams, but without advantage to either, and the interval arrived with the Third leading by a goal to nothing. With the wind behind them in the second half, the 'Light Blues' were expected to at least retrieve their position, but the Third fairly upset calculations by their dash. A free kick was given them on the left touchline at about eighteen yards from goal. After a pass or two the ball was tipped along to Johnston, who, lying right in the way of the goal, dodged Craig and shot into the net. From that point onwards the 'Volunteers' looked the winning side, and against their still more determined onslaught the Rangers' defence wavered perceptibly. At length after a spell of pressure, Wilson again got on and drove from thirty yards' range right into the goal., the keeper being powerless to stop the shot. That was seventeen minutes after the restart, and practically settled the destination of the Cup. But the Rangers were not yet done, although they could make very little progress against the Third's half-backs and backs. At the same time...Raeside was not idle...The custodian was confident in his clearances, however, but once or twice he resorted to the somewhat risky practice of kicking out. Latterly a score came the way of the Rangers, Smith sending the ball into the net from the second of two corners. The Rangers continued to storm the 'Warriors' goal, but their attack was not clever enough for the strong defence against it, and no further scoring took place....It was not a great game by any means, but it was an improvement on last week's. It retained the characteristics in respect that the Rangers played the more artistic football, while the Third adopted the strong, rushing game. The Rangers on play should have led at the interval, and in view of their exhibition up to that point it was expected that they would soon make up what they had lost...The Third's superiority was in their defence, and in the fact that they had a player in the veteran Hugh Wilson, who knew how to take advantage of an opportunity when it presented itself. The Rangers' defence failed them. Forward, they were the better side, but their short, dainty passing was not the style of football to make for success in the hard, strenuous life of a cup-tie. The Cup now goes to the Third for the second year in their history." The Third Lanark Scottish Cup winning line-up for both matches was: Raeside, Barr, McIntosh, Comrie, Sloan, Neilson, Johnstone, Kidd, McKenzie, Wilson and Munro.

After their League and Cup triumph the period up to the onset of the First World War saw the club struggle to compete and they slipped down to mid-table mediocrity in the League, with the occasional Scottish Cup run. In particular they made a fine defence of their Scottish Cup, reaching a fifth Final. They started the regular League campaign by losing 3-2 at Hearts, almost snatching a point in coming from three-nil down. They won their next three though, including a 6-1 win over Motherwell at the start of September. They had only led 1-0 at half-time but a Robert Graham hat-trick gave them a comfortable win. Hearts and Airdrieonians had a 100% record but the club was placed third in the table at this point. Thirds recorded a 6-3 win over Queen's Park in October, James Comrie scoring a first half hat-trick and then back-to-back 5-0 wins in early December over Kilmarnock and then away in the reverse against Queen's Park, Comrie again scoring three. They were now in fourth place but they lost three out of four games at the end of December/beginning of January to drop to seventh and they eventually came in a place higher. Towards the end of the season, on the 17th March 1906, David Alexander Hill, the club's left back, won his one and only Scotland cap against Ireland in Dublin.

The Scottish Cup holders began their defence of the trophy in fine style, beating Galston 5-0 on the 27th January 1906. They proceeded to knock out Hamilton, after a replay and in the Quarter-finals beat Hibernian 3-2 to set up a Semi-final in Paisley away against St Mirren, where it took three matches to settle the tie. The teams first met on the 31st March and drew 1-1. The Paisley side suffered three injuries during the course of the match but had taken the lead in the first half. Johnston equalised for Thirds and the replay took place a fortnight later at Cathkin. A crowd of 20,000 saw a hard fought game end goalless. Their third meeting took place a week later at the neutral ground of Ibrox Park. Thirds started strongly and forced a succession of corners but the Cup holders drew a blank. St Mirren started the stronger in the second period but Third Lanark eventually opened the scoring from a breakaway. Hugh Wilson fired in a long range effort that was only partially cleared, Johnston following up to net the ball. St Mirren strove hard to get on equal terms but failed. Three time Cup winners Hearts beat Port Glasgow Athletic 2-0 in the other Semi-final and the two teams met at Ibrox on the 28th April to contest the 33rd Scottish Cup Final.

The Scotsman provides an extensive report on the Cup final, reporting that "on Ibrox Park, Glasgow, on Saturday, the Heart of Midlothian and Third Lanark met in the thirty-third final for the Scottish Cup, and after a game, which was keen, though never brilliant, the Edinburgh team annexed the national trophy by the narrow victory of one goal to nothing...On the respective showings of the finalists , who met for the first time in the joint capacity, the Hearts were favourites, and their win, which was generally expected, gives them the cup for the fourth time...The Hearts, playing in blue jerseys, turned out at full strength, but at the last moment, the Third Lanark announced a change, Reid, of Greenock Morton, being brought in at centre forward for McGrain...In the opening stages the Hearts completely hemmed the Cathkin side in their own quarters, and the fine passing to his wings of Menzies prepared the way for his forwards. G Wilson had a couple of tries, Cross clearing in the first instance, and the ball going behind in the second. Later on the finest shot of the early stages came from G Wilson. Raeside alone avoiding a score with a great save at the expense of a corner. After Thomson had a shot over from a free kick, an exciting scrimmage took place in front of Raeside, there being danger in every kick, but the attack ended owing to a mis-kick by Dickson. With the interval nearing, the Third took a more prominent part in the game, their forwards opening out in a better fashion, and Reid had a likely try, the ball going a little too high. Neither side, however, managed to secure a point, and the interval arrived with no scoring...In the second half, the Hearts...immediately forced the pace, and G Wilson almost rushed the ball through. Two corners were conceded by the Warriors, but the sound defence of the Cathkinites got them out of severe difficulties on both occasions...The Third Lanark then took up the running, and Reid broke away nicely, but was robbed of his chance...For a time the game proceeded on fast lines, attack and counter attack being the order...both custodians having to save smartly. Both sides struggled on determinedly, but could not score, but the misfortune which befell the Hearts in the shape of an injury to Menzies, who was carried off the field, seemed to open up the way for the Volunteers. But such was not the case, for the Hearts with their handicap initiated a more vigorous game, and a moment or two later they snatched the only goal of the game. A pass forward by Thomson let Walker dash between the backs, and Raeside, leaving his goal to intercept Walker, gave G Wilson a chance, which he promptly improved upon to the accompaniment of great cheering. To the end the Third tried hard to equalise, but the Hearts, who now had Menzies again, managed to hold out, and the game, which was on the whole, disappointing, gave the Hearts the victory and the cup to Edinburgh." George Wilson's deciding goal for Hearts came in the 81st minute. The vanquished Third Lanark Cup side was: Raeside; Barr, Hill; Cross, Neilson, Comrie; Johnstone, Graham, Reid, Wilson and Munro. It would be another thirty years before Third Lanark would be in the Scottish Cup final again.

Third Lanark started the 1906-07 season well and were unbeaten in their first four games to briefly jointly top the table with Celtic, but they then lost at both Airdrieonians and Celtic to drop to seventh place. Four wins in a row lifted them back up to fourth but they then lost three in a row to fall back again. By the time they beat leaders Celtic 2-1 in March in front of a crowd of 10,000 at Cathkin they were back up to fourth but they had played more games than the teams around them and despite winning their two remaining fixtures they were eventually overtaken when the other clubs finished their programmes to secure another sixth place finish. In the Scottish Cup they beat a then non-League St Johnstone 4-1, although their opponents' centre-forward broke his leg, but in the Second Round they went out 3-1 to Queen's Park.

In contrast the club made a poor start to the 1907-08 League season picking up a single point from their first three games and losing two home games. They lost all five games played in November and also went winless in the five games in December although they did get two draws. They eventually won again after two months in the New Year's Day game when they beat Hamilton 1-0 at Douglas Park, thanks to the brilliance of Brownlie in the Thirds goal, by which time they occupied one of the re-election places. A couple of further wins in January lifted them out of the bottom two and three points clear of trouble. At the end of January they were knocked out of the Scottish Cup in the First Round by St Mirren, 3-1, but they followed this by going unbeaten in the League for the rest of the season, a total of ten games. Included in this run was a 3-0 win over Airdrieonians, a 1-1 draw at eventual champions Celtic and in their last game they beat Kilmarnock 6-3, Griffiths scoring a hat-trick to eventually be placed ninth. Cup winning manager Sam Wyllie left at the end of the season and was replaced by Ned Tarbat, who remained in charge until 1917.

Thirds made a terrible start to the new season, losing their first four matches without scoring a goal. A first goal and point came in a 1-1 home draw against Morton. A 2-0 loss followed away at Celtic but having scored only one goal in their first six games they inexplicably scored seven away against Partick at the beginning of October. Their opponents were bottom with no wins from their first six fixtures and the game was played at Celtic Park. McPhee and Robert Ferguson scored in the first half and Thirds added five goals in the second half. Three weeks later Thirds beat Hamilton 6-1. James Richardson scored two and Bob Hosie added a third in the first half. Richardson scored two more in the second period, with McPhee scoring in-between. Hamilton got a late consolation before Richardson took his personal tally up to five. James Richardson went on to score 54 goals for the club between 1907 and 1910. He subsequently moved to England and played for Huddersfield Town and Sunderland, with who he won the English League title and played in the 1913 FA Cup Final. He returned to Scotland in 1914 with Ayr United and scored 111 goals from 159 appearances before retiring in 1921.

Despite Richardson's goals, by the beginning of 1909 Third Lanark were in 14th place, only two points clear of the bottom two. At the end of January they were thrashed 6-1 at Aberdeen but a fortnight later they emphatically beat strugglers Partick Thistle once more, this time 7-1 (to effectively make it 14-1 on aggregate). Thirds took the lead after five minutes and scored five more first half goals. According to *The Scotsman* "after the resumption the home team played with more restraint" and both sides scored a goal, Thirds running out 7-1 winners. After such a fine win they surprisingly lost 4-0 at home to Port Glasgow Athletic in a snow affected game. However, a six game unbeaten run which included a 1-0 win over Rangers and 1-1 draw at the eventual champions Celtic saw them rise up to finish in eleventh place. In the Scottish Cup they beat Brechin City 5-1 and Aberdeen 4-1 before Falkirk knocked them out.

On the 15th March 1909 goalkeeper James "Jimmy" Brownlie became the club's third goalkeeper to be capped by Scotland as he kept a clean sheet in the 5-0 win over Ireland at Ibrox. Brownlie would go on to be the club's most capped player. He became Scotland's first choice 'keeper for many years, being an ever present in the Home Internationals championships for three successive seasons between 1912-14, and ended up with 16 caps. In the 1910 home internationals he kept a clean sheet in all three matches as Scotland won the title for the tenth time outright. Almost his entire professional playing career, was spent with Third Lanark, who he joined, aged 20, in 1906, having started his career at Blantyre Victoria. In 1923, after 17 years at the club, he joined Dundee United as player-manager for Dundee United and then as manger only. He enjoyed some success as the club as they won two Second Division titles, before leaving in 1931. He returned for two further spells in the 1930s.

The 1909-10 season saw a modest improvement in Third Lanark's final League position as they finished in seventh place. They lost their first two matches but won the third against Kilmarnock 7-0 on the 4th September. In a one-sided first half they scored five

705

without reply, and they were all different goal scorers: Prentice, Johnstone, Ferguson, Richardson and Rankine. In the second half the goals were scored by Richardson and Johnstone. Towards the end of October they beat strugglers Port Glasgow 5-0, Rankine scoring a first half hat-trick. McDonald scored a fourth and then Rankine added a penalty for his fourth and his team's fifth. In Scottish Cup action they beat Killie after a replay before being knocked out by Celtic in the Second Round. Back in League action in late February they beat Morton 6-2. Tom Fairfoul, who played seven seasons for the club and who went on to play in the 1914 FA Cup Final for Liverpool, opened the scoring, before Richardson took over and scored a second half hat-trick. However, when they lost 1-0 at Rangers at the end of March they were in 15th place and only two points clear of the bottom two. Thirds then went unbeaten in their last six games of the season to rise up the table and finished in seventh place.

The club dropped a place in the final standings in the 1910-11 season. They only picked up a single point from their first four matches before a 2-1 away win at St Mirren started a run of six games without defeat. Included in this run was a 5-1 away win at Kilmarnock and a 4-1 away win at Hamilton. By mid-October they had settled into seventh place and they eventually finished a place lower. The club had a disappointing Scottish Cup performance, going out in the First Round 1-0 at home to Hamilton.

Thirds made a decent start the following season, winning their first three games but form dipped after that and by the turn of the year they were in eighth place. Their biggest low came in a 7-0 defeat to Falkirk on the 2nd March 1912. Brownlie was absent, playing in goal for Scotland against Wales, and Ewart took his place. He had an unfortunate experience and was beaten seven times. Thirds also played during the second half with nine men, following injuries to Fairfoul and Thomson, and ended with just eight men when Raitt also had to leave the field.

Third Lanark eventually finished in eleventh place but this was tempered by a fine run to the last four of the Scottish Cup. Their Cup run got off to a fine start with two big wins. In the First Round they beat former winners Renton 5-0 at the end of January. Renton actually had the better of the early play and Brownlie was called upon, more than once, to keep his side in it. On the stroke of half-time Third Lanark were awarded a penalty which Ferguson scored. After changing ends Thirds had matters pretty much their own way and Raitt soon doubled their lead. Whittle added a third and soon after Raitt scored again. Scouller scored a fifth near to the end. In the Second Round they won 6-1 against Broxburn Athletic. Their opponents conceded home advantage and so the game was played at Cathkin, albeit in front of a small crowd. After fifteen minutes Allan scored and Hosie and Whittle scored soon after. After this Broxburn improved and Brownlie was beaten before half-time. In the second half Thirds totally dominated the play and scored three more to win 6-1.

Third Lanark drew Motherwell in the last eight and won 3-1, scoring their three goals in the first half through Mainds, Rankine and Ferguson. Thirds drew Clyde in the Semi-finals while holders Celtic played Hearts. Their match was played on the 9th March at Hampden in front of a crowd of 25,000. Clyde were the favourites, as they were going well in League, sitting in third place behind the Old Firm, whereas Thirds were in eleventh place. In the match itself Thirds survived early pressure from Clyde and eventually asserted themselves, with Tom Fairfoul opening the scoring with a long, straight drive. Clyde started the second half as they had the first, and this time got their reward, Brownlie being beaten from a tight angle. The Shawfield team were now in the ascendancy and deservedly went ahead, before putting the game beyond doubt by scoring a third. Clyde went on to lose in the final against Celtic.

The 1912-13 season was a poor one, although it started well with a 4-1 away win at Hibs, Willie Whittle at centre-forward scoring all four goals in the second half. However, on the following Saturday they hosted Morton and lost 5-1 at Cathkin, despite leading 1-0 at the break. Thirds then failed to win any of their next six matches although four of them were draws. A 0-0 draw in the first game of 1913 against Hamilton was the first of three no-score draws. By the time they had been knocked out of the Scottish Cup at the Second Round stage by St Mirren they sat in 14th place, although they were only three points above the bottom two. They eventually finished a place lower, four points ahead of Partick Thistle in 17th, with Queen's Park finishing bottom.

1913-14 was another mediocre season in the League, although they had an improved showing in finishing just inside the top half in eighth place. Their best result was a 5-0 victory over Queen's Park. They saved their best performances for the Cup though and enjoyed another run to the last four, their second in three seasons. Having got past Dumbarton and Raith Rovers to reach the Quarter-finals they came up against non-League Stevenson Athletic of Ayrshire, who had got past Kirkcaldy United and Peebles Rovers to reach the last eight. With a home tie they were expected to progress but were surprisingly held at home to a goalless draw on the 7th March. A fortnight later they replayed at Stevenson's Warner Park, in front of a crowd of 8,000, but this ended in a 1-1 draw. The second replay took place at Cathkin just three days later and was played on the Tuesday afternoon in front of a crowd of 15,000. The first half was goalless and *The Scotsman* reported that in the second half "both teams strove hard to obtain a lead, and towards the expiry of the ninety minutes signs of the strenuous nature of the game were clearly evident. When the whistle was sounded the desired goal was still wanting, and an extra half-hour was played. Early in the second fifteen minutes Montgomery [the Stevenson United goalkeeper] was beaten by a shot from Smith that went over his head, and this proved to be the only goal of the match." Thirds were unfortunate to draw Celtic in the Semi-finals with the other tie pairing Hibernian with St Mirren.

Third Lanark played their Semi-final just four days after their second replay against Stevenson. The match was staged at Ibrox and a crowd of 46,000 witnessed an even first twenty minutes. A misplaced pass by the Thirds back Lennon allowed Celtic in to score and not long after this their opponents doubled their lead. Thirds started the second half well but soon faded and rarely troubled the Celtic defence or 'keeper, *The Scotsman* noting that "the Parkhead side qualified for the final very easily. Third Lanark disappointed badly, particularly in the second half, when a revival was looked for." Celtic went on to complete the League and Cup double.

Thirds struggled in the next two seasons. They didn't win any of their first five fixtures in the 1914-15 season but improved to win five out of six across late September and October. In December they beat Dundee 7-0. Thirds scored two quick goals and continued to dominate and an own goal added to their lead by the interval. In the second half "the Third Lanark showed superior tactics in all departments, and fittingly scored several times, although one of them was registered by the goalkeeper against himself when trying to avert a corner kick." (*Glasgow Herald*). However, they only won one of their first ten games played in 1915 and eventually finished in 16th place. Although the Scottish League First Division continued to be played during the First World War the Scottish Cup was suspended.

In their 1915-16 League campaign Thirds failed to score in their first three games and in five of their first six matches. They got their first win in early October and won only two more games by the halfway stage. In January they beat Aberdeen 6-2. Thirds gave a debut to a new forward in Weir (from Renfrew Juniors) and he scored three goals. Thirds won their next two as well although in March they lost 6-0 at Ayr United and they eventually finished a place lower in 16th, although this was now in a 20 team First Division rather than 18 sides.

In the 1916-17 season Third Lanark finished in fifth place, their best placed finish for a decade. They only lost once in their opening eight matches to be in fifth place which they maintained without ever challenging any higher. On the 12th August 1917 George Morrell was appointed as manager of Third Lanark, replacing Ned Tarbat after nine years in charge. Tarbat had enlisted in the army and was at that time stationed at Maryhill Barracks, Glasgow.

In 1917, because of the financial hardship caused by the War, the League requested that the three most northerly clubs - Aberdeen, Dundee and Raith - withdraw. Clydebank were then elected to even up the division to 18 clubs. In contrast to the previous season, Thirds only won once in their opening eight matches (the solitary win being 5-0 over Queen's Park) to be in the bottom three. They stayed there and ended 1917 second from bottom. A 5-3 New Years' Day win over Partick Thistle at Firhill was the start of a run of four win on the trot which eventually lifted them up to a 13th place finish.

Thirds started well in the following season, going unbeaten in their first six games including a 5-1 at Hibs and a thrilling 5-4 win at Brockville against Falkirk. A 3-1 defeat at Celtic started a run of four games without a win and poor form continued through the remainder of 1918 as they slipped from fifth to 15th place. A 6-1 away win against Airdrieonians in early January was the start of a run where they only lost once in eight matches and they finished the season in 12th place.

For the 1919-20 season the number of teams in the Scottish League was increased from 18 to 22. Those clubs who had been asked to retire for geographical reasons at the end of the 1916-17 season — Aberdeen, Dundee and Raith Rovers — all returned, while Albion Rovers were elected. Third Lanark started with a 2-0 win over Hibs but were beaten 6-1 by Rangers in November and then 5-1 by Morton in December. They reached the turn of the year in a lowly 17th place. Performances showed no sign of improving in 1920 and two months in they were two places lower having only won once in the New Year. A 2-1 away win at Airdrieonians on the 13th March was the start of an eight game unbeaten run, which included seven successive wins, as they finished the season strongly to climb to eighth place. The Scottish Cup was not competed for between 1914 and 1919 and on its resumption Thirds reached the last eight. Having beaten Inverness Caledonian, and former League clubs Vale of Leven and Lochgelly United in the earlier rounds they were knocked out by Morton.

Thirds started the new 1920-21 season with a thrilling 4-4 draw at home to Kilmarnock and won three and drew two of their first six matches to sit in eighth place. They lost four in a row in the autumn but recorded a fine 7-3 win over Airdrieonians, with Welsh scoring four, which was the start of four wins in a row and they finished 1920 still in eighth place, which is where they went on to finish. In the Scottish Cup they drew Hibs and it took three matches to find a winner, with Hibs progressing 1-0 in the second replay played at Ibrox.

For the 1921-22 season the Second Division was finally reinstated and automatic promotion and relegation was introduced this season, as well as goal average. It was also decided to reduce the number of clubs in the First Division from 22 to 20 with three clubs being relegated at the end of the season with only the champions of the Second Division being promoted. Under new manager Alex Bennett, the ex-Celtic, Rangers and Scotland forward, Thirds lost their opening game, 3-1 at home to Rangers, and failed to win any of their first five games before a 4-1 win over Clydebank at the end of September, Allan scoring a hat-trick. They then didn't win again for a month before winning their last four games of 1921 to end the year in a mid-table 11th place. They didn't win in the League again until a 3-1 away win at Motherwell in mid-February but they finished really strongly, only losing one of their remaining 13 fixtures to finish in ninth place. In the Scottish Cup Thirds registered a season's best 6-0 win over former League side Leith Athletic, scoring five in the second half. They drew Celtic in the Second Round and had a close tussle at Cathkin going down by the only goal of the game. Forward Frank Walker was capped for Scotland on the 4th February 1922, in a 2-1 defeat against Wales in Wrexham. He played for the club for eight seasons from 1919 onwards, scoring 68 goals in nearly 200 appearances and was forced to retire in 1927 due to a broken leg.

The next three seasons saw Thirds at the bottom of the table and battling to avoid relegation to the Second Division. Astonishingly, each of these three seasons they ended up with the same final record – played 38, won 11, drew 8, lost 19 and finished with 30 points. In the first two seasons this record was good enough to stay in the First Division as they finished in 17th and then 18th place respectively. However, in season 1924-25 they finished bottom with this record and were relegated to the Second Division after 35 years in the top division.

Third Lanark started the 1922-23 season with their heaviest defeat of the whole campaign, losing 5-1 at Ibrox against Rangers on Saturday the 19th August. Their opponents were so superior they played the second half a man short but still scored three times. Thirds then lost their first home game, 1-0 against Hibernian but then won the next two. They then won only once in eleven League games across November, December and January before beating champions Celtic 1-0 in mid-January.

In the Scottish Cup they needed replays in each of the first two rounds to account for Partick Thistle and Vale of Leven. In the Third Round they beat Ayr United and then it was back to replays (two of them) in eventually knocking out Dundee in the Quarter-finals to set up a Semi-final against Hibs at Tynecastle. In the second replay against Dundee, played at Ibrox, Third Lanark scored after twenty minutes from a goalmouth scramble. Thirds had the better of the first two games and *The Scotsman* reported that "all over...were the better side. Their forwards were all clever, but were not strong finishers; they had a good trio of halves, and a reliable pair of backs." Just four days later Thirds met Hibernian in the Semi-final, *The Scotsman* reporting that "against Third Lanark at Tynecastle, Edinburgh, in the semi-final round [Hibernian] had their sternest fight, out of which they emerged victors by the narrow margin of a goal to nothing. There was not more between the sides, and the balance lay with the Hibernians, because they showed a better conception of team play, because during the opening twenty minutes they were definitely the better side, and scored then the goal that won the tie, and because they gave the impression that it was their opponents, and not they, who were struggling against the collar all of the time. The two teams played a different kind of football. The Third Lanark halves contented themselves with breaking up the Hibernian attack, and made little attempt to supply the ball to their forwards, who were soloists, pure and simple. The best of the five were Reid and F Walker. Their straight go-ahead running held much danger, and but for fine saving by Harper in the closing phase of the game, Frank Walker would have equalised." Following their Cup exit Thirds only won one of their seven remaining League games to drop down to 17th finishing one point ahead of Hamilton and four clear of the two relegation places.

The 1923-24 season saw the club more directly involved in a relegation battle. Right from the off they were in trouble as they lost their first four League games their first point coming in late September with a 0-0 home draw with Airdrieonians. At this point they had only scored one League goal in five matches. They then scored two against Partick in their next match but unfortunately let in four! On Saturday the 6th October they finally recorded their first win of the new season, beating Hearts 2-1 with goals from Jimmy Johnston and Alex Reid, Hearts only getting one back late on. They were assisted by the inclusion of Cringan at the back, who had been transferred by Celtic, and who steadied the Cathkin defence. Johnston went on to score 58 goals for the club. Outside-right Alex Reid, had joined the club in December 1920 from Airdrie and scored 44 goals before signing for Aberdeen in June 1925 for a fee of £1,500. He played for the Dons for two seasons before attracting the attention of Preston North End.

This victory lifted them off the bottom, above Clydebank, but they then lost 6-1 at Raith, Jennings scoring four. Thirds then won three in a row with victories over Aberdeen, Clyde and Ayr United to move out of trouble and up to 16th place. However, they then went over two months and ten games without a win from the end of December to the end of February and only three points separated the bottom six. Thirds beat joint bottom Clydebank 5-1 on the 1st March to ease their relegation fears, Tom McInally scoring four inside the first twenty minutes. Unfortunately from mid-March the club lost five in a row. By this time Clydebank 's chances of avoiding relegation looked remote but Thirds had got sucked into a battle with Clyde and Queen's Park for the other spot – Clydebank had 22 points, Clyde 26, Queen's Park 27 points (with two games in hand) and Third Lanark also had 27 points. By the time Thirds earned a vital point at Motherwell on the 19th April Queen's Park had got to safety and Clydebank had been relegated meaning it was a straight battle between Clyde and Third Lanark to avoid the drop. Both teams were on 28 points although Thirds had the superior goal average (Clyde 0.558, Third Lanark 0.671).

On Easter Monday, the 21st April, the relegation question was settled when Clyde only secured a point while Thirds were getting two. Clyde drew with Hearts 2-2, *The Scotsman* commenting that "on the run of the game Clyde should have won", although they twice came from behind. Thirds played Hamilton and won 3-2, watched by a crowd of 10,000, *The Scotsman* reporting that "by defeating Hamilton Academicals in the holiday match at Cathkin Park, Third Lanark made certain of retaining their place in the First Division. Their victory was fully deserved. In the second half, especially, they were clearly superior." Only eight minutes had gone when Frank Walker got nicely away on Third Lanark's left, and from his cross, Higgins lobbed the ball into the net. Hamilton equalised after 33 minutes and just before the interval a poor clearance let their opponents take the lead. Restarting a crucial 45 minutes, Thirds came out quickly and Brown levelled the match from a penalty and 15 minutes later Tom McInally scored the vital winning goal. Thirds had avoided relegation by a single point. At the end of the season manager Alex Bennett left with club secretary P A Berry taking over the reins.

Clubs can often flirt with relegation for only so long before finally succumbing and this fate befell Thirds in the 1924-25 season. It was a close run thing as only two points separated the bottom six and three teams finished on 30 points, goal average deciding who went down. Third Lanark actually started the new season well, going unbeaten in their opening three games before going down 3-0 at Airdrieonians. This started a run of eight games without a win, which was finally ended on the 25th October when they beat Aberdeen 4-0, a result which lifted them off the bottom. This started a good run of five games without defeat which lifted them up as high as tenth place and they actually reached the turn of the year three places higher.

On the 5th January 1925 they were thrashed 7-0 by Celtic, although in mitigation they were down to eight men for some of the time, *The Scotsman* reporting that "Third Lanark lost three men all at once – McInally, who was ordered off for what appeared to be an interference with the referee during a throw up; Higgins, who was injured in a collision…; and Finlay, who retired after wrenching himself on the slippery ground. Fortunately for the visitors, Finlay and Higgins returned after a short period." Third Lanark went out of the Cup to the same opposition, 5-1 at home, and following this they lost 4-0 at St Mirren and 5-1 at Hibernian. These defeats came at the start of a run of ten games without a win where they only picked up a single point. Also included in this run was a 7-1 home defeat against leaders Airdrieonians, *The Scotsman* commenting that "Third Lanark cut a sorry figure." This result equalled their heaviest home SFL defeat. Ten days later they suffered their heaviest ever SFL defeat (subsequently equalled in 1947 and 1965) when they lost 8-0 at Motherwell, *The Scotsman* noting that "the first half display of the Cathkin team was woeful, their defence especially being weak." Thirds lost 1-0 at home to Ayr United the following week to sit in 15th place but only a point separated them and Falkirk in the drop zone.

When Third Lanark lost 5-2 at Rangers in their penultimate game they dropped into the relegation places for the first time. Queen's Park were bottom on 27 points and Third Lanark had 28 points. Above them were Kilmarnock and Motherwell, both on 29 points and then Ayr United and Aberdeen on 30 points. In midweek both Queen's Park and Kilmarnock won and on Saturday the 18th April Thirds beat Falkirk 4-0 in their final game, Tom McInally scoring all four, to go to 30 points. Motherwell and Queen's Park both drew to also move to 30 points. Six teams were all on 30 points but Third Lanark had finished their League programme whereas others still had a game to play. In addition, Thirds had the worst goal average of the six clubs (Third Lanark 0.6310, Ayr United 0.6719, Queen's Park 0.6761, Aberdeen 0.7857 Falkirk 0.7925, Motherwell 0.8852) prompting *The Scotsman* to say that "Third Lanark's easy win over Falkirk at Cathkin Park proved an unavailing success, and they are now certain of a period in the Second Division." On the 25th April Queen's Park, Falkirk and Aberdeen all won their final matches to move to 32 points. Ayr and Motherwell both lost to remain on 30 points with Third Lanark and only a superior goal average saved Motherwell. Third Lanark's goal average remained at 0.6310. Ayr's declined marginally to 0.6615 and Motherwell's was much better on 0.8571.

John Richardson, former Raith Rovers manager, took over as manager but Third Lanark didn't make an immediate return, spending three seasons in the Second Division. In their first season out of the top flight they finished a disappointing sixth place, although for the majority of the season they were in contention. They started life in the Second Division with a 4-0 home win over East Fife, winning their first four games and five of their first six to be joint top with Dunfermline by the end of September. They then suffered a series of defeats against the likes of Bathgate, Nithsdale Wanderers and Arbroath before beating Dunfermline (the eventual champions) 3-2 at the end of October to be placed fourth in the table. Their good form continued across the remainder of the year and they were placed third going into 1926, two points behind the joint leaders Dunfermline and Stenhousemuir. Their form then became a bit erratic across January and they then went on to lose 3-0 in a bad-tempered game at Armadale in mid-February, which also involved a pitch invasion, to drop out of the running, eventually finishing in sixth place, seven points behind second-placed Clyde.

In the Scottish Cup Third Lanark recorded some high scoring in the early rounds, starting with a 7-0 victory over Moorpark of Renfrew in the First Round. Their opponents' goalkeeper dislocated a finger and one of the backs donned the goalie's jersey, "play thereafter was farcical" (*The Sunday Post*). In the next round they beat Leith Athletic of the relatively new Third Division 6-1, Blair scoring a hat-trick. They then beat another Third Division side Brechin City 4-0 and were drawn to play First Division Aberdeen in the Quarter-finals. Third Lanark had home advantage and held their opponents to a 1-1 draw, *The Scotsman* commenting that "on the whole a draw was a fair result. Although Third Lanark held an advantage on play, the Aberdeen defence was very good and the Cathkin forwards could find few opportunities for shooting." In front of a crowd of 17,000, Thirds had hit the post in the first half and four minutes towards the end looked destined for a place in the Semi-final when McWaters scored. However, just two minutes later a slip by their defence let Smith through to equalise. A week later Aberdeen decisively won the replay at Pittodrie scoring three goals in the first half, *The Scotsman* noting that in the second half Thirds "played with great vigour and determination but found themselves opposed by a defence giving nothing away." Towards the close Hilley and an Aberdeen player were ordered off the pitch.

In the 1926-27 season Third Lanark got closer to a return to the top flight, finishing in fourth, five points behind Raith Rovers in second place, with Bo'ness the surprise champions. Thirds came with a late surge after a poor start in which they lost three out of their first five matches and went six games without a win across September and October, so that after three months of the new season and eleven games in they were joint bottom with just seven points. They picked up a couple of wins in November and won three out of four matches played in December. By the time they beat second placed Arthurlie 3-2 in the New Years' Day fixture they had moved up to 12th in the table, and were still a long way off mounting any semblance of a promotion challenge. Following a First Round Scottish Cup exit at the hands of King's Park, Thirds then recorded two big League wins. First, Bathgate were beaten 5-0 away from home in a snowstorm on the 29th January and a week later they beat struggling Arbroath 6-0. These two wins came at the start of a run of eleven games unbeaten which also included a 5-1 win over Ayr United. With Bo'ness already promoted Thirds had narrowed the gap to Raith in second place to four points, but were running out of games. When the run came to an end with a 2-1 defeat at Armadale in mid-April Raith's 6-3 win over East Stirlingshire saw the Kirkcaldy club promoted.

Third Lanark finally booked a return to the First Division in the 1927-28 season by being promoted as runners up to Ayr United - although they left it late. They won their first four matches, including the season opener 4-0 versus Clydebank, in which Wilson from Kelty, making his debut at centre-forward, scored four and they then beat King's Park 5-1. After such a great start it was somewhat of a surprise for them to then go six games without a win. On the 5th November they lost 6-2 at leaders Ayr United to drop into the bottom half of the table, although a week later they beat Dundee United 5-1, despite playing much of the game a man short due to injury, to move back into the top half of the table. On the 18th November manager John Richardson left the club to take up the vacant manager's position at First Division Falkirk. In December Thirds appointed John Morrison, a former Falkirk centre-forward and manager at East Stirlingshire as his successor.

Under Morrison, Thirds ended the year with an emphatic 6-1 win over St Bernard's. Under the headline "Five goals for Glasgow Player" the *Glasgow Herald* reported that "the St Bernard's were no match for Third Lanark at Cathkin Park, Glasgow, and the score in no way exaggerated the home team's superiority. On the snow covered pitch, the winners showed remarkably accurate ball control, and a combination which kept the Saints' defence on the run from start to finish. Wilson opened the scoring four minutes after the start, and five minutes later the same player added a second goal for Third Lanark. Ten minutes afterwards Mill put the home side three goals ahead. It was after that that the Third Lanark men came on to their game, and before half-time, Wilson, their centre-forward added three more goals, thus bringing his own total to five. In the second half the St Bernard's were more in the game as an attacking force, but it was only on sufferance, for Third Lanark lacked an incentive, and did not exert themselves to any great extent." The result saw Thirds go into 1928 sitting in tenth place, although in a tight division they were only four points behind King's Park in second, with Ayr United the runaway leaders.

Following a 4-2 loss at King's Park in early January the club went on a seven game unbeaten run which included a 5-0 win over Alloa Athletic (Wilson scored two), a 6-1 win over Bathgate (including a Wilson hat-trick) and a 5-0 victory against East Stirling (Wilson scoring another two). This unbeaten run saw Thirds rise up to fourth in the table and enter the promotion race, behind King's Park and Dundee United. The run came to an end against the worst possible team, a thrilling 4-3 loss against promotion rivals Dundee United. *The Sunday Post* reported that "the 7000 enthusiasts who braved the weather conditions to go to Tannadice Park yesterday saw a game which had not a stale minute in it. The score stood at three goals each with seven minutes to go, when Hutchinson [of Dundee United], tacked Moyles [the Third Lanark goalkeeper signed from Rangers] successfully, and walked the ball through for the winning goal." Five goals were scored in the first 21 minutes with Thirds twice coming from behind to then lead 3-2 at the interval. The defeat left them four points behind their victors with six games left.

On the 24th March Third Lanark bounced back in emphatic style thrashing bottom side Armadale 10-3, the club's highest scoring League win. White opened the scoring early on before Hamill scored a second with a long range effort. Parry crossed for Muir to head beautifully into the far corner for the third goal. Armadale then scored two goals to haul themselves back into the game but Parry scored for the home team and Mill scored from a free kick. Next Sam Brown scored from the penalty spot given for foul on Hamill. Thirds led 6-2 at the break and the second half was only four minutes old when they brought their score up to seven through McNeil. Two more followed by Muir and McNeil respectively. Dale got one back from the penalty spot before, with only two minutes to go, McNeil scored a tenth. The day got even better for Thirds, as both Dundee United and King's Park lost. Thirds then won 3-2 away at Leith Athletic before playing second placed East Fife on the 8th April. Under the headlines "Third Lanark Triumph In Vital Game for Promotion" and "Defensive Lapses Cost East Fife the Points" *The Sunday Post* reported that "first blood came early - and simply to Third, Flannigan drove goalwards. The ball bounced out from the crossbar, and Muir had an easy task to head to the net...A nice movement by the Fife attack brought about the equalising goal - and this after Third had enjoyed a monopoly of attacking." Four minutes later though Thirds were back in front, a poor clearance falling to Wilson, whose shot crept into the corner. In the second half Third Lanark established a two goal lead, Hamill capitalising on another defensive error to volley into the net. Minutes later the margin was reduced back to one but Thirds held on, *The Sunday Post* confirming that "the points went to the better side - the side with more snap and more skill."

Third Lanark now moved into the second promotion spot for the first time although only two points separated five clubs. Crucially Thirds had three games to play whereas all the other teams had just two. Two days later they played that game in hand, drawing 3-3 with the champions elect Ayr United. During this game Jimmy Smith, in scoring two for Ayr, set a new goal scoring record, moving onto 61 goals, two more than George Camsell of Middlesbrough. Smith ended up scoring 66 goals, a British record that still stands. His goalscoring prowess earned a move to Liverpool where he was the club's top scorer during the 1929–30 season, scoring 23 goals in all competitions.

All the teams had now played 36 matches and the points situation looked like this: Third Lanark 43; Dundee United 42; Forfar Athletic 41; East Fife 40; King's Park 40. On Saturday the 14th April two of their rivals won, but two lost. King's Park thrashed St

Bernard's 8-1 and East Fife won at Leith. Ayr United did them a favour by beating Dundee United 7-1 and Forfar were beaten at Queen of the South. Thirds didn't play as they had rearranged their home fixture to avoid a clash with the Scottish Cup Final between Celtic and Rangers (won by Rangers 4-0). The points situation was now: Third Lanark 43; East Fife 42; King's Park 42; Dundee United 42; Forfar Athletic 41. Thirds' game in hand was home to mid-table Stenhousemuir and they duly won 3-1 to secure promotion. The promotion winning side was: Moyles; Joe Brown, Weir; Mill, Mitchell, Flannigan; White, Archie Muir, Willie Wilson, Hugh Hamill and Perry.

In the Scottish Cup Third Lanark thrashed former League side Clackmannan 10-0 on the 21st January 1928 in their First Round tie. Mill opened the scoring after just four minutes and within the next ten minutes Muir had scored a hat-trick. Two further goals from Wilson either side of a Flannigan effort gave Thirds a 7-0 lead at the interval. Taking their foot off the gas Thirds added three more in the second half through Hamell, Mill and Wilson, who secured Thirds' second hat-trick of the match. However, there would be no extended Cup run as Thirds lost 2-0 at home to Hibernian in the next round.

The club's return to the top flight after three seasons was brief as they were relegated straight back down again at the end of the 1928-29 season. Thirds made a great start and went unbeaten in their first six games, scoring four goals in four of those matches. After a 5-2 win over Falkirk at the end of September they were as high as third place. In October they lost 5-2 at home to Rangers and 6-1 at Hibernian which was part of a wider run of poor form in which they failed to win in nine matches. The last of these, a 4-1 defeat at Hearts in the 1st December, in which they were three-nil down after the first half an hour, saw them now in 12th place in the table. A couple of wins in both December and January saw them recover slightly and by the time that they beat Clydebank 6-2 in Scottish Cup First Round action they were a place higher. In this match Thirds led 4-1 at half-time and James Thomson and Tom Callaghan each scored two. Thirds disappointingly went out in the next round 1-0 at home to St Mirren.

Following their exit from the Cup they went a further six games without picking up a single League point. In mid-March they lost 5-0 at St Mirren with the *Glasgow Herald* reporting that "a severe blow was dealt to Third Lanark, and their display against St Mirren, who won by the substantial margin of five goals, [this] indicates the Cathkin club as the most likely to accompany Raith Rovers to the Second Division." The result left the club second from bottom, in 19th place, seven points ahead of Raith, and level on points with Dundee, although with an inferior goal average. Ayr United were a further point ahead.

On the 23rd March they got a ray of hope when they beat Cowdenbeath 3-1. Archie Muir put them ahead after just two minutes and 1-0 was the half-time score. Neil Harris scored two goals in the second half, one from a penalty and Cowdenbeath got one back from their own penalty. The result moved Thirds out of the bottom two and onto 25 points. Ayr had 24 points and Dundee 23 but both clubs had two games in hand. Thirds subsequently lost to Celtic and drew at home to Hearts 2-2, twice coming from behind as Hugh Hamill scored both of their goals. This was to be the only point they would gain from their last four League matches. Thirds now had 26 points, with two to play, whereas Dundee had 25 points but with five games left. By the time Thirds played again nearly three weeks later Dundee had moved a point ahead of them and still had an extra game to play.

Any lingering hope was extinguished on the 20th April 1929 when an 8-3 defeat at Queen's Park effectively relegated the club. The *Glasgow Herald* commented that "it seemed probable that the closing games in the League tournament would determine whether Third Lanark or Dundee would descend with Raith Rovers to the Second Division, but the overwhelming defeat inflicted by Queen's Park upon Third Lanark on Saturday, and a fine stand by Dundee that earned them a point at Motherwell, put the issue beyond reasonable doubt. Should the Cathkin club win their last game next Saturday and Dundee fail to secure a point from their remaining two matches a tie in points would occur between the clubs. Even then, however, Dundee will retain their place on goal average. Their superiority in that respect is so pronounced that Third Lanark would require to win their last game by almost 20 goals to save their position. The Glasgow club will therefore return to the Second Division, from which they secured promotion only last season. Their descent will occasion regret among their followers, but on Saturday's display against Queen's Park it was obvious that the Cathkin team is not of First Division standard." As to the match itself, Queen's Park scored in the first minute and were very quickly three goals to the good before Thirds opening their account through Jack. Early in the second half the home team made it 5-1. Thirds scored again through Halliday but Queen's Park scored three more goals. Near the end a penalty was awarded to Thirds which Harris converted. Thirds finished their campaign with a 5-2 home defeat against Patrick Thistle. At the end of the season manager John Morrison left to join St Mirren and was replaced by Russell Moreland. Moreland had spent five years at Queen's Park and then a single season at Hamilton before joining as a player for the 1928-29 season. From 1929 up until 1933 he became player-manager and manager only for the 1933-34 season.

Back in the Second Division Third Lanark made an inconsistent start to the 1929-30 season. However, they then won four in a row in October, the last of these, a 4-0 away win against Queen of the South, lifting them up to fourth place. At the end of

November they beat King's Park 5-1 and in the New Years' Day fixture they beat Queen of the South 6-2 to remain in contention for a return to the top flight, five points off the second promotion spot. This win was the second of five consecutive victories, the last of these being a 5-0 win over Forfar. Although they then lost 2-1 at East Stirlingshire they went on to win three more in a row, including 5-3 at Dunfermline. By the beginning of March they were still in fourth, still five points off the promotion places with eight games left. A return of only one point from their next four games ended their promotion hopes. They won their last four games, including 6-3 against Brechin City and 4-0 versus Albion Rovers, but it was too little, too late, and they finished in fourth place, five points short of occupying the promotion places. They made an early exit from the season's Scottish Cup, beaten by fellow Second Division side St Bernard's 5-3.

In the 1930-31 season Third Lanark won the Scottish League Second Division under Russell Moreland, to secure a return to the top flight after just two seasons. They only lost four games during the campaign and scored a club record 107 goals. They went the opening ten games without defeat and on the 1st November 1930 beat Stenhousemuir 6-0 away, Neil Dewar scoring a hat-trick which would take his tally for the season up to 14 already. Curiously second placed Dunfermline won by the same score at home to Albion Rovers. A week later Thirds also beat Raith 6-0, Dewar scoring four more, to take his total for the season up to 18, with only a third of the season completed. Two weeks later Third Lanark beat Clydebank 9-3 in a top versus bottom contest. Having lost a couple of matches Thirds beat Forfar Athletic 5-0 in mid-December which was the start of another good unbeaten run, this time of 12 games.

On the 21st March the inevitable was confirmed when they beat bottom Bo'ness 3-1, with goals from Blair (2) and Breslin, and with Raith, in third place, losing, they were promoted with five games to spare. A fortnight later, with Dunfermline losing, Third Lanark's draw with Clydebank saw them confirmed as champions. In this game they came from two goals down to earn a point in a 3-3 draw against the Bankies which gave them the Second Division title. They celebrated in style two days later when they thrashed Montrose 6-1, *The Scotsman* commenting that "Montrose wilted before the power of the champions, and were overwhelmed as decisively as a reading of the score would indicate...Dewar, the Cathkin centre-forward, had the distinction of recording five of the six goals. Bruce Clark was the key man in the Third Lanark side. His scheming and destructive tactics were admirable, and laid the foundation of success. Blair and Breslin comprised an elusive west wing, and overshadowed their men on the other side of the field." In their penultimate game they recorded a 5-0 win over Alloa Athletic to establish a new record haul of 61 points for the Second Division. Alloa, strangely enough, previously held the record with 60 points, in the 1921-22 season. In the

Scottish Cup they reached the last eight, knocking out Buckie Thistle 6-2, Airdrieonians and Arbroath, before going out to St Mirren after a replay.

The Second Division championship winning team comprised of Willie Waugh; James Simpson, James Warden; Bruce Clark, John Clark, Russell Moreland; Johnny Lynas, Francis Jack, Neil Dewar, John McKenzie and Joseph Breslin. Goalkeeper Willie Waugh later made his name at Hearts where he spent a dozen years, and won a cap for Scotland in 1937. Half-back Bruce Clark joined Fulham in 1934 and made over 100 appearances for the Cottagers. Winger Johnny Lynas had spent a season at Bo'ness and then Sunderland before joining the club and centre-forward Neil Dewar would go on to be capped for Scotland. Dewar had signed for Third Lanark in October 1929, as a 20 year old and in his debut season had scored 40 goals for the club.

Unlike in 1929 when the club made an immediate return to the Second Division on being promoted, Third Lanark lasted three seasons back this time. On the 8th August 1931 they kicked off the new season back in the First Division, *The Scotsman* reporting that "Third Lanark made a favourable re-entry into First Division football by defeating Hamilton Academicals by the odd goal in five." John Lynas and Dewar put Thirds two up after a quarter of an hour. Hamilton got one back before Blair put his side two ahead once more. The second half was almost all Hamilton but they only got one back. Third Lanark then won their next three as well to take maximum points from all four of their games - quite a feat for a newly promoted team.

Thirds lost their next game at home to Kilmarnock but soon after drawing 3-3 with Celtic had a rude awakening with a 5-0 loss at Morton and a 6-0 defeat to eventual champions Motherwell (Willie McFadyen scored five), the first champions outside the 'Old Firm' since Third Lanark's League title in 1904. Six goals were also conceded in a 6-3 loss at Dundee to bring a thoroughly miserable September to an end. By this time they had dropped to sixth in the table, which was still very commendable for a promoted side. Thirds scored five on two occasions in October, first in a 5-3 win over Cowdenbeath and then in a 5-2 win over Airdrieonians in which they scored from two penalties. John Lynas, the Cathkin right winger, scored two and "his tenacity, coolness, and elusive feinting were admirable, while he carried a deadly shot."(*The Scotsman*)

Thirds went one better the following month, scoring six in a 6-1 win over Dundee, Dewar scoring a hat-trick, these results taking them up to third in the table, behind Motherwell and Rangers. In December Thirds lost 5-0 at Celtic and 2-0 at home to the leaders Motherwell and had slipped down to seventh place at the turn of the year. The year 1932 started on a high note with a 6-2 win over Morton in the New Years' Day game and in which Cathkin Park witnessed two hat-tricks scored by Francis Jack and

Dewar. A 4-2 away win at Clyde followed which made the 4-0 Scottish Cup exit at the hands of the same opponents difficult to swallow. A 6-1 defeat at Rangers in the League followed a month later but Thirds finished the season strongly, winning five of their remaining seven fixtures. One of these wins was a 4-3 victory over Rangers which effectively dashed Rangers' hopes of winning the League for the sixth consecutive year. Third Lanark eventually finished in fourth place, their best finish for a quarter of a century and Neil Dewar continued to bang in the goals, scoring 35 goals in 37 games, and was rewarded with an international call up. He made his Scotland debut on the 9th April 1932 in a 3-0 defeat against England at Wembley. A month later he scored a first half hat-trick in a friendly against France. He also scored Scotland's first in a 5-2 home defeat against Wales at Tynecastle on 26th October 1932. This was his last international appearance, having scored four goals in three matches.

After two great seasons the 1932-33 season was a big disappointment. Third Lanark hosted newly promoted St Johnstone in the season's opener and were lucky to get a 2-2 draw, being indebted to Dewar who scored once in each half. Thirds then lost three in a row including a 6-0 defeat at Kilmarnock, the *Glasgow Herald* acerbically commenting that "in dealing with Third Lanark it is well-nigh impossible to modify one's criticism. Their general bearing and conception of the game was extremely disappointing. Team sense was also entirely absent." Their first win came in their fifth match, a 4-0 victory over winless Falkirk, all of the goals coming in the second half, and Dewar netting two. A 5-0 loss at Rangers followed but a fortnight later Thirds registered a season's best 6-0 win over Queen's Park, Dewar scoring a hat-trick.

Thirds were unable to string a run of performances together, winning one week, losing the next and by the time they suffered a terrible 7-1 defeat at Falkirk on the 7th January 1933 they were a mid-table tenth place. A poor run in, where they only won once in their last five matches, saw them eventually placed 13th. Neil Dewar's goalscoring had attracted the attention of a number of clubs south of the border and in February 1933 he signed for Manchester United for a fee of £4,000. He only played one season for the Reds before transferring to Sheffield Wednesday. In the Scottish Cup Thirds knocked out Queen of the South in the First Round but succumbed to another Second Division side, Stenhousemuir, in the next round, losing 2-0 in one of the shocks of the day.

In the 1933-34 season Third Lanark were relegated for the third time from the top flight of Scottish League football and for the third occasion in the last ten seasons. They drew their opening League game 3-3 at Falkirk, coming back from 3-1 down with only ten minutes to play, David McCulloch taking Dewar's place. McCulloch went on to score 22 goals in 34 matches before joining Hearts for the 1934-35 season where he was capped for Scotland. He then moved to England and spent three seasons with Brentford where he earned three further caps for Scotland in 1936.

Third Lanark then beat Kilmarnock in their next game but went on to lose their next six games in a row, including on the 22nd August, in a midweek game, a 7-3 home defeat against Ayr United. In this match the home side had to battle for the majority of the game with ten men, their goalkeeper being injured in making a save. Thirds took the lead in the first minute through a low 20 yard shot by John McKenzie and five minutes later McCulloch made it two. Ayr hit back though, and were level by the 21st minute. Soon after, in saving a hard driven shot, Andrew Taylor, the Third Lanark 'keeper, injured his arm and had to leave the field. James Simpson, the right back, took his place between the sticks. Ayr took the lead after half an hour to lead 3-2 at half-time. Despite the handicap Thirds drew level early on in the second half through James Breslin. However, in the closing stages their defence capitulated and they conceded four goals, Terry McGibbon, Ayr's centre-forward scoring six goals in the match.

They then picked up three consecutive draws in late September and a second win came in a 3-1 win over Airdrieonians in mid-October. However, they followed this with a 7-2 loss at Love Street against St Mirren, mainly due to another injury to the Third Lanark goalkeeper Jimmy Sharp in the first half. Three wins across November and December saw Thirds reach the end of 1933 in 16th place, three points clear of the drop zone. Thirds went winless in January 1934 to drop to 18th, just a point above Airdrieonians, with Cowdenbeath a further four points back at the bottom. In the Scottish Cup Third Lanark knocked out Stenhousemuir, after a replay, but went out to Rangers in the Second Round.

A poor 4-1 home defeat against St Johnstone in the League at the end of February saw them drop into the relegation zone but a crucial 2-1 win at Airdrie in early March saw them swap places with their opponents. A 5-1 win over bottom side Cowdenbeath, together with Airdrieonians 6-3 loss against Motherwell saw Third's advantage grow to three points with six games to go. However, Thirds failed to win any of their next five matches. The last of these, a 3-1 loss at Hibs saw Airdrieonians go above them as they themselves beat already relegated Cowdenbeath.

Going into the last set of matches the Lanarkshire side were better placed, but if they were to lose at home to Ayr United and Third Lanark were to beat Partick Thistle at Cathkin, goal average would settle the matter in favour of Thirds. Airdrie, however, only required a draw to make their position secure. Although Third Lanark beat Partick Thistle on the 28th April they accompanied Cowdenbeath to the Second Division on account of Airdrie's draw with Ayr United. At Cathkin, the home centre-forward George

Hay scored a hat-trick. Over at Broomfield, Ayr took the lead after 55 minutes but in the 72nd minute Airdrieonians equalised to relegate Third Lanark.

Third Lanark bounced back immediately, as champions, losing only five League games all season. George Hay, who had signed for Third Lanark from local club Newtongrange Star scored a club record 46 goals in the season. He subsequently signed for Queen of the South in 1937 and played for them until the Second World War. Thirds started their campaign on the 11th August 1934 with a 3-0 win over East Fife and went the first ten games unbeaten. During this run they beat Dundee United 5-0, Hay scoring all five, *The Scotsman* commenting that "already Third Lanark are thinking of their return to the First Division, and their victory over Dundee United at Cathkin Park, Glasgow, was achieved in a way which suggests bright times ahead for the club." They also beat Arbroath 5-2, and it was Arbroath who inflicted their first League defeat in the reverse game in mid-October.

Following a further defeat against Forfar at the beginning of a November Thirds won six in a row, including a 5-0 win over Leith Athletic which took them to the top of the table, closely followed by Arbroath, St Bernard's, King's Park and Stenhousemuir. Manager Russell Moreland suddenly resigned, to take over at Clyde, who we managed up until 1937, and on the 13th December Tom Jennings, the former Raith Rovers and Leeds United centre-forward was appointed as his replacement.

In the Scottish Cup Thirds beat Creetown 6-2 in the First Round, scoring five first half goals, before drawing Rangers and going out 2-0. Back in League action Thirds beat Alloa 6-1, Hay scoring a hat-trick, and by the end of February they had opened up a three point lead over St Bernard's. These two sides met on the 9th March with the Edinburgh side winning 3-2 despite Thirds being twice ahead, the winner coming in the last ten minutes.

There were now four games left, and Third Lanark won all four to make it certain they would be Second Division champions for the second time in five years. They started with a 4-0 win at home to Brechin City on the 16th March. The score was 0-0 at the break but a Tom Jennings inspired team talk saw Thirds score three within ten minutes of the restart, despite resuming a man short. They were next in action at the end of the month, when they visited East Fife, and they won 3-1, with *The Scotsman* reporting that "Third Lanark made certain their return to the First Division by defeating East Fife at Bayview, Methil, by three goals to one. The Cathkin team displayed greater resource and coolness than their opponents, and were sound winners of a keenly contested game." Thirds went behind against the run of play after twenty minutes but then scored twice in quick succession, with both goals being scored by Hay. The same player was then brought down and Howe converted the penalty to go further ahead. There was no scoring after the interval. Their win secured promotion, especially as St Bernard's lost, and they were now five points clear of St Bernard's in third with two matches left. In the race for the title they were one point ahead of Arbroath and with a superior goal average.

To avoid a clash with the Scotland versus England international Third Lanark played the following Friday, beating Dumbarton 1-0 to extend their lead over Arbroath to three points. Arbroath drew on the Saturday which was enough to secure promotion to the First Division for the first time in their history, but it left them two points behind with a vastly inferior goal average. The following week, with Thirds not in action, Arbroath completed their programme with a 5-0 win over East Fife, to draw level on points. On the 27th April 1935 Thirds played Forfar simply needing to avoid an eight goal defeat. *The Scotsman* reported on the match saying that "by their defeat of Forfar Athletic at Cathkin Park, Third Lanark achieved the distinction of winning the Second Division championship without the necessity of having to depend on goal average." Forfar took a surprise lead just before the interval but within a minute of the restart Thirds were level through McLellan. Eight minutes from the finish Hay gave them the lead and the centre-forward emulated the feat four minutes later. The Second Division championship winning side was: McCormack; Jimmy Carabine, Harvey; John Blair, Jimmy Denmark, McLellan; John Lynas, Stewart, George Hay, Pat Gallacher and Robert Howe. One of the stars was centre-half Jimmy Denmark who had started playing football with junior clubs Tollcross Clydesdale in 1929 and Parkhead Juniors in 1930 before moving to Third Lanark in 1931. He moved to Newcastle United for £2,550 in May 1937.

The main aim for the 1935-36 season was to consolidate their position in the First Division and they achieved that quite comfortably, finishing in eleventh place. This was also the season of their last great run to the Scottish Cup Final. They initially struggled on their return to the top division, losing three out of their first four fixtures including, at the end of August, a 6-0 loss at Celtic. September was much better with two wins and a draw and the last of these victories was a 5-1 home win over leaders and unbeaten Aberdeen, with Ritchie scoring a hat-trick. By the time they lost the New Years' Day game 1-0 at Queen's Park they were in tenth place in the twenty team division and they eventually finished one place lower.

In the Scottish Cup they beat Hearts and Leith Athletic in the first two rounds and got a third home draw against Dumbarton in the Third Round. They went into the game having lost their last four League games but had no difficulty against their opponents, beating them 8-0 in a match played on the 22nd February 1936. Dumbarton made more of a fight of it than the final score line would suggest. Nevertheless they were eventually outclassed despite a strong showing in the first hour's play after which they were only losing 2-0. Hay, the centre-forward scored three for Thirds.

In the Quarter-finals Third Lanark deservedly beat Morton 5-3 at Cappielow on the 7th March. Hay gave Thirds the lead after nine minutes but Morton soon equalised. Kennedy restored Third Lanark's lead in the 18th minute and fifteen minutes later he scored a third. Hay then burst through to score a fourth goal. The contest wasn't over yet though and Morton got one back just before the break. Their hosts came out strongly but from a breakaway Howe scored a fifth. Morton were now beaten although did get a consolatory third goal. According to *The Scotsman* "Third Lanark were well served in every department. Muir and Carabine stood out as grand defenders. Blair and Denmark were seen at their best when they went up with the forwards. Hay, at centre, was a continual menace...Kennedy and Kinnaird were clever."

In the Semi-finals played on the 28th March, Third Lanark drew Falkirk, who were going well and leading the Second Division. *The Scotsman* reported that "Third Lanark were worthy winners by three goals to one of the Scottish Cup semi-final tie with Falkirk, before a surprisingly big attendance at Tynecastle Park, Edinburgh, but the game was so poor that the Cathkin club's challenge to the Rangers in the final does not appear to be very strong." Nearly 48,000 witnessed Falkirk deservedly take the lead having dominated the play in the first thirty minutes. Muir kept Thirds in the tie with a couple of good saves, and when he was beaten, the woodwork came to his rescue. Third Lanark equalised five minutes before the interval, Carabine converting a penalty. Thirds, with the momentum, had the better of the play in the second half, but it wasn't until fifteen minutes from the end, that McInnes, exploited a gap in the Bairns defence, and ran through before firing in a low shot that went in off the post. Kennedy then added a third. Off the pitch a barrier gave way on an embankment causing a crush which resulted in 60 spectators being injured.

Rangers comfortably beat Clyde 3-0 in the other Semi-final and most commentators made them overwhelming favourites to lift the trophy. Previewing the final, the *Glasgow Herald* noted that "since they have now only a slender chance of retaining the League Championship, Rangers will be especially keen to win the Cup for the third year in succession, and while one has no wish to underestimate the quality of the Third Lanark side, it is admitted on all hands that everything points to Rangers accomplishing their object. It would certainly be a notable feat for Third Lanark to carry off the Cup in the first year after gaining reinstatement to the First Division, but when it is recalled that they have lost both League games to Rangers, and they have won eight points only from the 13 League engagements they have played this year, it will be realised that their prospects are dim....If they strike their best form, there is always the possibility that they will upset their more fancied opponents." One good omen for Thirds was that when they last won the Scottish Cup in 1905 their vanquished opponents were Rangers.

The Final was staged at Hampden Park on the 18th April 1936 and there was a crowd close to 89,000 present. Rangers, although the favourites, had an unexpectedly hard fight, only winning by a solitary goal, scored by Bob McPhail in the first minute of the game. A quick burst by David Meiklejohn down the right saw him float in a cross that McPhail brought down, under control, before driving it past Muir. Rangers were considered a little fortunate to maintain their lead, especially towards the end when Third Lanark made strenuous efforts to equalise. The *Glasgow Herald* reported that "Third Lanark showed admirable steadiness after losing a goal in the first minute of the game, and, in the second half especially, they tested to the full the sterling qualities of the opposition defence. It is probable that even all the skill and resource of the rear division would not have saved Rangers from at least a replay had the finishing of the Third Lanark forwards been equal to their forcing work in the outfield." Reviewing the performance of the Third Lanark players, the paper noted that "Third Lanark had at least one outstanding player in Denmark, the young captain of the side. He was at fault in the scoring of the goal, but atoned for that mistake by giving Smith a great deal of trouble for the remainder of the game. Blair and McInnes were not quite so resourceful as the Rangers' wing half-backs, but their aggressive work near the end created a good impression. The backs covered well and, generally speaking, were never out of their depth against the opposition attack, while Muir dealt confidently with all he had to do in goal. Gallacher and Kennedy, especially the latter, were the best of the forwards, who at times stormed their way through a strong defence, only to hesitate and waste opportunities when within scoring range." In winning the trophy Rangers equalled the earlier feats of Queen's Park and Vale of Leven by winning the Scottish Cup for three years in a row. The Third Lanark Cup Final team was: Willie Muir; Jimmy Carabine, Bob Hamilton; John Blair, Jimmy Denmark, Jimmy McInnes; Robert Howe, Pat Gallacher, George Hay, Sandy Kennedy and A Kinnaird. This would be the last time that the club would reach the Scottish Cup Final.

Third Lanark's form was mixed at the start of the 1936-37 season. Thirds started the following season well with three wins and a draw from their first five matches but they went five games without a win and after two months they were a mid-table tenth place. They then registered seven wins in a row from the 3rd October to the 14th November, including a 6-3 win over Dunfermline. The run saw them rise steadily up the table to fourth place, just four points off the top. Their superb run came to an abrupt halt when they lost 6-3 at Celtic. Celtic took a 2-0 lead but Thirds hit back to stun the champions, by leading 3-2. Celtic hit back though, and with Jimmy McGrory scoring a hat-trick. On Boxing Day they scored two in the first four minutes to beat Queen of the South 4-1 in their last game of 1936 and were fifth in the table. Three defeats followed as they slid down to eighth place and they recovered a bit to finish in sixth, finishing the season with a 4-2 win over Celtic and then a 4-0 win over Dundee. In the Scottish Cup they only reached the Second Round. Montrose were beaten 5-0 in a replay after drawing 1-1 at Links Park but they were knocked out by Aberdeen, 4-2, who reached the Final, as well as finishing as runners-up in the League.

In May 1937 centre-half Jimmy Denmark left the club to join Newcastle but on the 19th July 1937, Neil Dewar re-signed for Thirds in a club record breaking £1800 deal. He went on to play a further three years of League football at Cathkin Park before retiring having scored over hundred goals for the club. Thirds made another good start the following season and were unbeaten in their first three League games. However, they then won only two of their next ten games by which time they had dropped to tenth place. They then went five games unbeaten before they unexpectedly lost 5-0 at home to St Johnstone at the end of November, *The Scotsman* commenting that "Third Lanark's heavy defeat was attributable to the inability of the forwards to do anything to counteract the pressure applied by the Perth team's front line." Shortly afterwards they beat Motherwell 5-3, with Dewar scoring a hat-trick and they settled into a mid-table position and they eventually finished in ninth place, and in a tight division, only three points ahead of the club in 19th place. There was no good Scottish Cup run to fall back on as they made a First Round exit at home to Celtic. In May 1938 right-back Jimmy Carabine was awarded the first of three international caps for Scotland when he played against the Netherlands in Amsterdam on the 21st May. He played again for his country five months later against Northern Ireland and earned the last of his caps against England in 1939. He played for the club from 1931 until 1947, making over 200 appearances for them before managing them between 1946 and 1950.

The 1938-39 campaign was the last full season before the Second World War. Thirds had a poor season in the League but had a good Scottish Cup run. They lost the opening game of the season 4-1 at Cathkin against Hearts, which was followed by a heavy 6-1 defeat at Aberdeen. They moved off the bottom with a 5-0 win over Raith, who would finish a long way adrift at the bottom, Johnny Jones, the home inside-left scoring three times in eight minutes. A fortnight later they also scored five against Queen's Park, who would be relegated alongside Raith, Jones again on the scoresheet and Dewar grabbing two. Heavy losses were suffered against Rangers (5-1) and Celtic (6-1) before a 5-0 victory away at Arbroath at the beginning of November. Dewar scored a hat-trick with all of the goals coming in the first half. The victory left them in 13th place. At the end of November they suffered a heavy defeat at Motherwell, 5-1, and when they lost at home to Partick Thistle a week later they were down in 17th place. Manager Tom Jennings left shortly afterwards. Under the headline "Third Lanark Surprise" *The Scotsman* reported that "Tom Jennings has resigned the managership of Third Lanark, and at a meeting of the directors on Thursday night his resignation was accepted. This surprise move follows a period of unrest behind the scenes. The shareholders of the club held a meeting on Tuesday night and a deputation of six was appointed to approach the directors with a request 'that the affairs of the club be investigated.' The meeting also gave unanimous approval to an ultimatum in the form of a requisition calling for an extraordinary general meeting if the directors refused to meet the deputation." George McMillan took over, but not until February 1939. Thirds went five games without defeat to move up to 14th but a poor run during the spring of 1939 left them just three points above the drop zone. A 2-0 win over Hibernian in their penultimate game settled any nerves as they eventually finished in 15th place, five points ahead of Queen's Park in 19th, with Raith Rovers finishing bottom.

In the Scottish Cup they reached the last eight. They beat Clachnacuddin 8-2, Dewar scoring five, and then beat Cowdenbeath 3-0, the goals only coming after the opposition 'keeper had to leave the field injured having collided with his own centre-back. In the Third Round they beat the only remaining non-League side Buckie Thistle 6-0 away at Victoria Park, John Jones scoring four. It was an all-Glasgow Quarter-final tie as they were drawn away to Clyde, who had knocked out Rangers 4-1. With home advantage Clyde were the favourites and a crowd of 26,000 at Shawfield saw Thirds hold their opponents, but Clyde got the winning goal three minutes from the end. Clyde went on to win the Final, Beating Motherwell, the conquerors of Celtic 4-0.

The outbreak of the Second World War on the 3rd September 1939 caused the suspension of the League after five rounds of games had been played. Thirds lost 2-1 at Cowdenbeath on the 12th August before drawing 2-2 with Hamilton a week later. They then beat Cowdenbeath 4-2 in a midweek fixture before beating Kilmarnock 1-0 away. On the 2nd September they played what would be their last fixture, losing 2-1 at home to Rangers. Dewar scored for Thirds, who were only denied a point by the brilliant goalkeeping of Dawson. The Thirds team that day was: McAffrey; Carabine, McCulloch; Blair, Black, Sinclair; Hart, Mason, Dewar, Jones and Stephenson.

Regional leagues were formed during the hostilities and Third Lanark joined the West Division, with football restarting on the 21st October when they beat Kilmarnock 3-2. *The Scotsman* reported on the match, saying that "perhaps the most exciting match of the day was at Cathkin Park, Glasgow, where Kilmarnock were two goals ahead of Third Lanark with fifteen minutes to play and cracked in the face of a fierce onslaught, to be beaten by the odd goal in five. With Carabine, the international full back at centre forward, and Dewar in form at inside left, the home side showed greater enthusiasm, and performed one of the big feats of the day." Thirds finished 12th out of the 20 teams in the Western division before the regional leagues were reorganised into a North-East and Southern sections. Thirds played a further six seasons in the southern division. Their best-placed finish was eighth (out of 16 teams) in the 1941-42 season. In the 1943-44 campaign they finished bottom, losing 20 out of 30 matches and conceding exactly 100 goals.

After the Second World War, Third Lanark played in Division "A" (top tier) until they were relegated in 1953. They finished ninth on the resumption out of 16 teams. Third Lanark started poorly losing 3-0 at home to Aberdeen on the 10th August 1946, conceding three in the last quarter of an hour. Their team was: John Petrie; Matt Balunas, John Kelly; Bobby Bolt, John Black, Malcolm Sinclair; George Henderson, Jimmy Mason, Adam McCulloch, Alex Venters and Davie Kinnear. Venters had previously been capped for Scotland in 1936 when playing for Rangers and joined for the 1946-47 season only before joining Blackburn Rovers. Matt Balunas went on to make over 220 appearances for the club between 1946-55 and ended his career at Stranraer.

Thirds lost each of the next three games by the same 4-1 scoreline before being thrashed 8-1 by Rangers at the end of August, a fifth consecutive defeat. Willie Thornton, Scotland's centre-forward, and Cassie each scored a hat-trick. Bobby Mitchell scored for Thirds first and the scores were actually level at 1-1 after half an hour's play. Mitchell went on to be the League's top goalscorer with 22 goals. Thornton scored the equalising goal and netted a first half hat-trick. George McMillan left his post as manager shortly afterwards with Hugh Good, the first team coach taking temporary charge until Jimmy Carabine was appointed manager in November. Their first win and points came in a 4-1 in over Partick Thistle. Thirds scored the same number of goals in this match than they had previously in their first five matches. They won all five games in November to rise up the table and eventually finished a mid-table ninth. In the Scottish Cup they reached the Third Round going out to Dumbarton. In the new League Cup the club didn't get out of their section.

The 1947-48 season opened with them losing a sectional League Cup tie 5-0 at Dundee and they also conceded five in their first League game, a 5-2 defeat at Rangers. On the 8th November they lost 8-0 at Hibernian which equalled their heaviest ever SFL defeat. Hibs were going well in second place and Smith scored five and Linwood three. A month later they lost to Falkirk 8-1. Willie Reid scored first for Thirds after 20 minutes and the half-time score was 1-1 but Falkirk scored three goals in ten minutes early on in the second half and then added four more in the last ten minutes. Archie Aikman scored three and would finish as the League's top scorer in the 1947-48 season with 20 goals. The defeat left Thirds in 14th place (out of 16), just one point ahead of the two clubs occupying the relegation places - Airdrie and Queen's Park. Two further defeats saw them drop to the foot of the table by the end of December. Fortunes turned in January where they were undefeated in six matches and they climbed away from the foot of the table to finish in eleventh. In the Cups they again went out in the group stage of the League Cup and went out of the Scottish Cup to Motherwell having entered at the Second Round stage.

The 1948-49 season saw a significant improvement following their flirtation with relegation the year before. They won their opening game against Aberdeen and in their third match they beat Queen of the South 6-1. After beating Celtic 3-2 in mid-November they didn't win again in 1948 and dropped to 12th in the sixteen team division. They regularly picked up points in the next three months and finished the campaign strongly, winning their last four games to finish in seventh. In the Scottish Cup Thirds beat Aberdeen before going out to Hearts and in the League Cup they failed to get out of their section once again.

One highlight of the season was striker James "Jimmy" Mason being capped for Scotland on the 23rd October 1948 against Wales in Cardiff. He scored Scotland's equalising goal in 3-2 win against Northern Ireland at Hampden a month later. He won his third cap against England at Wembley in 1949, scoring Scotland's first in a 3-1 win as Scotland won the home international title. He went on to win four more caps between 1949 and 1951, so seven in total, and scored two more goals to double his international tally. He is the second most capped Third Lanark player and made over 200 appearances for the club.

The new 1949-50 season started with the six sectional League Cup games but the club failed to progress once more. They started their League campaign on the 10th September with a 2-0 win at Clyde. Following a 3-0 win over Hearts in mid-October, that took them up to eighth place, they then lost seven out of their next eight games, picking up a solitary point. Consequently they went crashing to the bottom of the table, and faced the possibility of relegation from the top flight once more. Their poor run ended on the 17th December with a narrow 1-0 win over Dundee and they won again three weeks later when they beat Aberdeen 3-1, the result lifting them off the bottom on goal average. Three teams - Thirds, Queen of the South, and Stirling Albion - were all on 12 points and only two points separated the bottom six.

In the Scottish Cup Thirds knocked out Arbroath in the First Round to set up an all Glasgow clash with Celtic, securing a 1-1 draw, before losing the replay 4-1. Back in the

League Thirds recorded victories over St Mirren and away at Hibernian before a Felix Staroscik goal gave them a vital 1-0 win over Celtic. Thirds were now clear of the relegation zone but in mid-March they crashed 7-2 at home to Partick Thistle. Their visitors scored a goal inside two minutes and Alec Scott scored a hat-trick. Thirds got their two goals only when Partick were seven goals up and were reduced to ten men due to an injury to Willie Hewitt, John Cuthbertson scoring both Third Lanark goals from headers in the 86th and 89th minutes. Three wins and a draw in their last four games saw them climb to 12th place, although by this time Jimmy Carabine had submitted his resignation on the 30th March, although he agreed to stay on to the end of the season.

Alec Ritchie was appointed as the new manager in May 1950. The 1950-51 season again started with the six sectional League Cup games but in a group that included Celtic they failed to progress. They opened their League campaign in early September with a 2-0 win over Motherwell and in an uneventful campaign they soon settled into mid-table obscurity, eventually finishing in 13th place. They again failed to make any headway in the Scottish Cup, beating Forfar in the First Round before going out to Aberdeen.

In the 1951-52 season, although their final League position was a disappointing 12th, Third Lanark had a great run to the last four of the Scottish Cup. Once again Thirds didn't make it out of their League Cup group which included Celtic, Airdrie and Morton. The last of these games was a 5-0 win over Airdrieonians and the two sides met again a week later to start the League programme, Thirds winning 4-0 this time. Inconsistent form followed and from the end of October they went eight games without a win and by the end of the year they were in 18th place, just above the relegation zone, occupied by Airdrie and Stirling, with just a point separating the three sides. A couple of wins were recorded in January but they were still in the relegation zone at the end of the month. They then went unbeaten in the League from the end of February until the very last game of the season.

In the Scottish Cup they surprisingly beat Celtic 2-1 after a First Round replay. They also beat Hamilton in a replay in the next round before beating Albion Rovers and Falkirk (both in the Second Division) to set up a Semi-final against Dundee at Easter Road. The match took place on the 29th March 1952 and with fine League form behind them Thirds came into the tie with some momentum, even though Dundee were a few places ahead of them. In swirling snow Dundee took a two goal lead in the first half and held onto their lead to win 2-0. Dundee were then beaten 4-0 by Motherwell in the Final, who lifted the trophy for the first time.

Third Lanark's struggles in the League finally caught up with them and after three bottom half finishes in the First Division they were relegated at the end of the 1952-53 season. They won only eight League games, losing 18, although they had a much better performances in both Cup competitions, once again reaching the Semi-finals of the Scottish Cup, and succeeding in going past the sectional phase of the League Cup. Thirds finally progressed from their League Cup group, consisting of Queen of the South, Falkirk and East Fife and drew Rangers in the last eight. They drew 0-0 at Ibrox in first leg but succumbed at Cathkin a few days later, losing the return 2-0. Between the groups and the Quarter-final matches they started their League campaign with a 3-2 home defeat versus Hearts. Their first League points came on the 4th October when they beat Queen of the South 5-0, John Cuthbertson and Jimmy Docherty each scored two in the first half for Thirds. On the 8th November Thirds were involved in a remarkable nine-goal thriller away against Celtic. Their hosts scored after a quarter of an hour but Cuthbertson equalised just a minute later and after half an hour Peter "Wattie" Dick fired in from 20 yards to give Thirds a 2-1 half-time lead. Dick played for the club between 1949-55 and scored 75 goals in nearly 150 appearances before joining Accrington Stanley. Celtic were soon level within five minutes of the restart but two goals in three minutes from Dick and Cuthbertson gave them a 4-2 lead. Celtic got the score back to four all with fifteen minutes to go and scored a last minute winner from a corner to win 5-4.

A 5-1 defeat at Falkirk in the New Years' Day game left Third Lanark in 13th place, and only out of the relegation zone on goal average. Three more League defeats followed as they dropped to the bottom but at the end of January they beat Motherwell 5-1 at Fir Park to move off the bottom. Two more wins followed but they then suffered two 3-0 defeats at the end of March to drop back to the foot of the table. With three games left to play they had 20 points. Queen of the South had 21 points but had five games still to play; Falkirk had 22 points with three to play; and Motherwell and Raith Rovers each had 23 points. Thirds lost all of their remaining League fixtures, 5-2 at Clyde, which relegated them, and 7-1 at leaders Hibernian and 4-2 at Airdrie.

In the Scottish Cup Thirds knocked out non-League sides Elgin City and Wigtown and Bladnoch before narrowly getting past a Hamilton side going strong in the Second Division in the Third Round. In the Quarter-final they were drawn away against Clyde, who were sitting in fourth in the First Division. The match took place at Shawfield on the 14th March and Thirds started well when a Jack Liddell shot after only five minutes beat the 'keeper but cannoned back off the upright. Two minutes later Liddell headed a Dobbie corner into the net. Clyde responded well and deservedly equalised. Two minutes before the break Liddell scored a second. Thirds' defence was stubborn but Clyde were unfortunate when a shot hit the inside of the post, with Jocky Robertson beaten, and then rebounded across the face of the goal. Thirds now grew into the ascendancy and deserved their win.

Third Lanark were drawn against Aberdeen in the Semi-finals, and their opponents were favourites for the tie. The *Evening Times*, in previewing the game, noted that "Third Lanark's appearance in the semi-final At Ibrox is just one of those things which make football such a queer business. Here we have the old Cathkin club with one foot in the second division and the other in a Scottish Cup semi-final...Everything points to an Aberdeen success." Thirds dominated the early exchanges and a couple of chances for centre-forward John Cuthbertson went begging. Aberdeen's first corner nearly resulted in the game's opening goal but Matt Balunas cleared an inbound header from off the line. Aberdeen were now enjoying a spell of possession and kept Thirds penned back in their half and they were glad to reach the interval with the game goalless. Chances came at both ends after the restart but on the hour mark Aberdeen took the lead. A mis-judgment by Adam Forsyth allowed Aberdeen in and the effort went in off Robertson. In the 78th minute Thirds drew level when Cuthbertson got in the end of a free kick by Forsyth, atoning for his earlier error, and scored from close range. A few minutes later a Cuthbertson header from a free kick by Jimmy Duncan looked to have won the match for Thirds but Martin in the Aberdeen somehow got across to save brilliantly.

The replay was staged a few days later, on Wednesday 8th April, again at Ibrox. Dick scored for Third Lanark after 30 minutes but Aberdeen equalised a minute later. The sides seemed evenly matched but in the 71st minute Aberdeen went ahead. In the 83rd minute a Cuthbertson cross was flicked on by Dick but George Dobbie, six yards out, snatched at the chance and Martin was able to save. As it was, the glorious chance to take the tie to extra time was missed. Rangers beat Hearts in the other Semi and went on to lift the Scottish Cup for the 14th time when they beat the Dons, after a replay.

On the last occasion that Third Lanark had been relegated they made an immediate return, but this time they spent four seasons in the B or Second Division. They did mount a promotion challenge in their first season, but came up short, finishing in third place. They received a big boost when they won their first game of the season 10-0 away against Alloa Athletic in a sectional League Cup game played on the 8th August 1953. The *Evening Times* reported that Alloa had to make a last minute signing in order to put out a full team. They only had ten retained players re-signed and only got an eleventh man fixed up the night before the game. Walter Dick scored after seven minutes to give Thirds an early lead. After that play settled down and it wasn't until after 34 minutes that George Dobbie scored a second from close range. A minute later

Ally McLeod added another goal to give Thirds a 3-0 lead at half-time. Eleven minutes after the restart Dick scored again and in the 65th minute Dobbie scored a fifth. Jackie Henderson added a sixth and McLeod a seventh before Dobbie got his hat-trick in the 76th minute. Thirds added two more to win 10-0. Third Lanark also recorded a 7-0 win over Cowdenbeath to qualify from their section and earn a Quarter-final two-legged tie versus Hibernian. Unfortunately they lost the first leg at home 4-0 and lost the away leg by the same score to go out 8-0 on aggregate. In-between the two legs they started their League campaign with a defeat, losing 1-0 at Albion Rovers.

On the 26th September the club's high scoring feats in the League Cup transferred into League action when they thrashed Dundee United 9-1. Thirds led 6-0 at the interval with goals from Ally MacLeod, a Jackie Henderson hat-trick, George Dobbie and Jimmy Docherty. In the second half further goals were added by Dobbie, Wattie Dick and MacLeod. However, a month later they lost 6-1 away at St Johnstone and indifferent form saw them down in 13th place, only two points off the bottom. Thirds then put a good run together across December and January, going seven games unbeaten, before the run came to a juddering halt with a 7-3 home loss against Morton. Both sides were chasing promotion and after an even start Robertson made a couple of good saves, but Morton's pressure eventually told and nine minutes before the interval they took the lead. Morton pushed for a second and Robertson thwarted them with a string of saves but four minutes from the break Morton eventually doubled their lead to go in two-nil up at the interval. Early in the second half Morton added a third but Thirds got one back through MacLeod after 57 minutes. However, four minutes later Morton scored again. Thirds continued to fight and Dick scored a second. Morton scored three more times and just on time Sam Phillips scored Third Lanark's third goal with a penalty.

On the 6th February Thirds beat Ayr United 6-0 away from home to get their promotion bid back on track. They took the lead after just seven minutes when a corner kick by MacLeod was headed on by Bobby Kerr for Jimmy Docherty to smash home from five yards. Robertson then saved brilliantly to preserve their lead and Ayr kept up the pressure for the rest of the half. However, just three minutes from the interval MacLeod was brought down as he raced through on goal and Docherty converted the resulting spot kick to give Thirds a 2-0 half-time lead at Somerset Park. On the hour mark Kerr ran through to make it three from a counter-attack and two minutes later Dick made it four with a fine lob. Thirds added two more before the end to run out 6-0 winners. The victory started a run of ten games without defeat which also included a 9-2 win over St Johnstone a fortnight later. In this match Thirds made a blistering start, scoring six goals in the first half an hour's play. The *Evening Times* noted that "there is nothing like a good start, and within two minutes played Thirds were two goals up." An unmarked Docherty headed home from the first cross of the day and then a high shot/cross from Kerr was fumbled by the opposition goalie under a challenge from Docherty and the ball dropped behind him and across the goal line. St Johnstone then pulled one back but a minute later, on the quarter of an hour mark, Kerr made it 3-1 in a more orthodox fashion. After 21 minutes Matt Barclay crossed for a Docherty to make it 4-1 and two minutes later a mazy run from MacLeod made it five. After 27 minutes Kerr was unmarked from a MacLeod cross and made it 6-1, getting his hat trick in the process. St Johnstone then got another back but six minutes from the break Dick took advantage of a defensive mix up to slot home and give Thirds a 7-2 half-time lead. Play was more even with chances on both sides before a disastrous back-pass by a Saints defender was pounced on by Kerr who scored his fourth in the 69th minute. One minute from time Kerr scored a fifth and his side's ninth goal and the result moved the club into fifth place, five points behind the second promotion place.

Although this win was part of a long unbeaten run, this sequence included six draws. On the 12th April they beat Forfar 3-0 at Cathkin to go third but a 1-1 draw at second placed Kilmarnock five days later was a match they really needed to win. Another draw, at home to Dunfermline on the 19th April, ended their promotion hopes with two games to spare, as they finished third, six points behind second place. In the Scottish Cup Third Lanark knocked out Stenhousemuir and then Highland League side Deveronvale 7-2 before being drawn at home to Rangers. On the 27th February they held Rangers 0-0 and then astonishingly drew the replay 4-4. However, they narrowly lost the second replay 3-2.

Sadly, manager Alec Ritchie died in office on the 13th July 1954 after a short illness and was replaced by Jimmy Blair who had played for the club 1931-44. Third Lanark again mounted a challenge for promotion but once again this fizzled out and Thirds finished in fifth place, nine points away from the second promotion place. The club won three and lost three of their League Cup group fixtures and therefore failed to progress. The League season started on the 11th September with a 2-2 draw at Morton, which was followed by a 3-1 home win over Queen's Park. At the beginning of October they lost 5-1 at Hamilton but form picked up and on the 4th December 1954 they recorded their biggest ever SFL win when they beat their injury hit opponents Ayr United 9-0. Dick headed home the first after just five minutes and Norman Brolls smashed home the second after fifteen minutes, both goals assisted by Barclay. Dick added a third five minutes later and Brolls then got his second. Six minutes from the break Dick completed a first half hat-trick and Barclay deservedly added a sixth before half-time, when a long range effort on the stroke of half-time deflected in off an Ayr defender. One minute after the restart Ally Miller made it seven, becoming the fourth of the forward line to score- only Bill Armstrong was a non-scorer. The same player converted in the 68th minute after the ball had rebounded off the crossbar. In the 76th minute Dick scored his fourth, and his side's ninth and the big win moved them up to second in the table.

Third Lanark ended the year with a 4-1 home win over Morton, a victory that left them in third place on 19 points, level with Hamilton in second, with Airdrieonians five points clear at the top. Mixed form in January, where they won two but lost two, saw them slip down to fifth, four points off second place. Inconsistency continued to dog them and when they lost their last two matches in March they were effectively out of the promotion race, eight points off second place with only five games left. Following a 3-2 win over Arbroath at the beginning of April they were in fourth place but they failed to win any of their last four games and they eventually finished fifth, nine points behind Dunfermline in the second promotion place. In the Scottish Cup they entered at the Fifth Round or last 32 stage, beating Queen of the South 2-1. In the Sixth Round they were beaten 3-1 at home by Motherwell.

In 1955 the seeds of their demise were sown with the initial appearance on the scene of one William Hiddelston (often incorrectly spelt as Hiddleston). Relatively unknown at the time, Bill Hiddelston is the character who is generally accepted to be the villain of the piece. He originally joined the club as Director-Manager in November 1955 when Jimmy Blair left as manager. Thirds started the new League season with a 6-2 win over Stranraer but they only won one game in six from the beginning of October and a 6-1 defeat at Morton on the 5th November led to the managerial change. Later in the same month they lost 5-1 at home to Cowdenbeath, fielding a much changed side with five new players. The result left them second from bottom in the table and off the pitch the situation was also bleak, with the club admitting to being thousands of pounds in the red.

In early December the club recorded back-to-back League wins and at the end of the same month they equalled their biggest ever League win, set the year before, when they beat bottom of the table Montrose 9-0. Their opponents had lost 13 out of their 19 games played and Thirds scored after just three minutes and were four up after twenty minutes. In this match both Bobby Craig and Norman Brolls scored hat-tricks. Brolls had joined the club from Hurlford United in 1953 and went on to score 25 goals in 49 appearances before moving to Bradford Park Avenue at the end of the season. Bobby Craig played for the club between 1955 and 1959 and scored 61 goals in 124 matches. He subsequently moved to Sheffield Wednesday and had brief spells at Blackburn Rovers, Celtic, St Johnstone and Oldham Athletic. He returned to the club in 1967, making 9 more appearances, scoring once. He was actually in the line-up for Third Lanark's last ever League game. The following week Thirds beat Hamilton 6-1 but then conceded six themselves when they were thrashed 6-0 by St Mirren in the

Scottish Cup. At the beginning of March Third Lanark beat Albion Rovers 7-0 as they steadily moved away from the bottom and they eventually finished a mid-table tenth place.

For the 1956-57 season Division B reverted to being called the Second Division. Third Lanark won promotion finishing as runners-up to Clyde who stormed to the title, losing only one game and scoring 122 goals in the process. Thirds notched up a century of goals themselves, scoring 105 times, their highest total in a League season since winning the Second Division in 1931. The campaign started with an 8-2 thrashing of Stenhousemuir in a sectional League Cup match. However, this was their only win in six group games and they therefore failed to progress. The League season started with a 5-2 away win at Berwick Rangers. They suffered a couple of defeats at the end of September but bounced back with a 6-1 thrashing of Montrose at the beginning of October, which was the first of four successive wins. On the 1st December they again thrashed Stenhousemuir 7-0, with centre-forward Johnny Allan scoring a second half hat-trick. Allan had started his career at Dunfermline, where he spent two seasons and had played the previous season for Aberdeen, scoring 15 goals in 22 games. He spent two seasons at Cathkin, scoring 28 goals in 37 games before moving to England, playing for Bradford Park Avenue and Halifax Town before finishing his career in the 1962-63 season at Brechin City. The result against Stenhousemuir moved the club into third place, two points behind Cowdenbeath and five behind the leaders Clyde.

Bill Hiddelston gave an interview to a reporter from the *Evening Times* on the anniversary of his takeover as he outlined his ambitious plans for the club. In a report published on the 1st December 1956, and under the headline "Third Lanark hit on first class ideas" Hiddelston told their reporter about his progress and his plans: "Big news comes out of Cathkin today – news which proves beyond doubt that Third Lanark are more determined than ever to get back to First Division football and stay there as equal partners with Rangers and Celtic…The good tidings for the immediate future is that Reuben Bennet, the former Ayr United manager, and the man who as coach has helped to bring Motherwell right to the front of the League Championship race, has been invited to take over as full time coach at Cathkin. Mr Bill Hiddelston, the Third Lanark boss, told me today that he expects to have the deal all signed and sealed within the next few days. The job will be one of the 'plums' in Scottish football. With it goes a house and a salary which would turn many a manager green with envy. That's bright news item No. 1. News flash No. 2 is that the new Third Lanark board are looking far ahead. They are planning to make Cathkin Park one of the biggest and best stadiums in the country – one of a size and comfort which will be able to compete with Ibrox and Hampden for international and Scottish Cup games. The ground can now hold something over 55,000, but it is to be increased by at least another 10,000 by the erection of a magnificent new grandstand. Although the ambitious scheme will not be started right away, plans for the stand are already being drawn up, and when the whole project is completed Cathkin will also be equipped with new up-to-date offices, dressing rooms, and training area…Mr Hiddelston told me of these plans for the future…when we did a little bit of stock-taking on his year of office as honorary manager of Third Lanark. Twelve months ago the old club was sinking fast. Gates were down near the 1000 mark, and the team was in such a bad way that when the players were put up for sale two brought buyers at £25 each. Since that day last November Mr Hiddelston has worked practically day and night – all for love of Third Lanark. He has searched all over Scotland and into England too, for players - £5000 have been spent in the transfer market and a completely new team has been built up. Mr Hiddelston's signings to date include – Bobby Craig, John Brown, Joe McInnes, Jimmy Walker, Johnny Allan, Bill Lewis, John Kelly, Tommy Wark, Joe Roy, Ron Maybury, Peter Dallas and Blair Aitken. So far, the results have not been sensational…[but]…the old Hi Hi's are still well in with a chance of winning promotion in Mr Hiddelston's first full year of office. But even if Third Lanark are not back in Division I in April and the directors will keep on building and building until they do win promotion and put a famous club back where it belongs." However, Hiddelston's elaborate plans turned out to be pipe dreams. Yes there were short term improvements as the club secured promotion back to the First Division, consolidated their place and then achieved a superb third placed finish and reached the final of the League Cup. But the foundations of the recovery were proven to be built on shifting sands and the club began selling their prized playing assets to stay afloat and the club swiftly collapsed in an ignominious end of unpaid bills, the water supply being cut off and raids on the slot machines in order to pay the wages.

Just a few months after this interview Hiddelston surprisingly quit the board with the club in debt, although he then made an abortive takeover bid the following year. Always a bit of a maverick, Hiddelston had started to take actions without the knowledge or permission of the rest of the board, and this had led to boardroom unrest. Reuben Bennett, a former goalkeeper with Hull City and Queen of the South, and manager at Ayr United had joined as Hiddelston's coach (then called trainer) in December and stepped up as caretaker manager. An excellent late season run of 13 wins from 17 games carried them to the promotion that accompanied a runners-up spot. On the 12th January they beat Forfar Athletic 6-1, despite only leading 1-0 at half-time and a fortnight later they thrashed Dumbarton 7-0, with Jimmy Walker scoring a hat-trick. In their next game Thirds lost 5-0 at Albion Rovers, conceding four second half goals, as their victorious opponents went above them in the table. They then won their next four games and when they beat Brechin City 5-1 on the 6th April, they moved into the promotion places ahead of Cowdenbeath, who had been beaten at Alloa.

738

Thirds won four of their remaining five matches and eventually finished six points clear in second place.

Bennett`s team made a good start to the new season as they won their League Cup group, progressing unbeaten out of their pool which included Morton, Stirling Albion and Stenhousemuir. They were drawn against Celtic in the Quarter-finals and went out heavily in the two-legged affair, losing 9-1 on aggregate. They then had a rude awakening in September losing their first three League games. Third Lanark lost their opening League game back in the First Division, losing 4-2 at Starks Park against Raith Rovers. They continued to struggle and only picked up one win and were in 16th place in early October. Bob Shankly was then appointed as manager on the 10th October 1957 with Bennett reverting to his coach role. Bob Shankly was the older brother of the Liverpool legendary manager Bill Shankly and had made over 230 League appearances for Falkirk at centre-half but it was as a manager that he made his name. He managed Thirds until 1959 when he moved to Dundee, where he won the Scottish League title and he later managed Hibs between 1965-69. Shankly and Bennett formed a strong partnership and Thirds won four out of five League matches in November, including 5-1 at home to Dundee and 6-0 away at struggling East Fife. After taking the lead Thirds scored three goals in the last four minutes of the half. Soon after the club made it to the last eight of the Scottish Cup, beating Lossiemouth 6-1 and Queen's Park 5-3. They lost to the eventual beaten finalists Hibs 3-2 at Easter Road. Third Lanark eventually finished in 14th place in the 18 team First Division, seven points clear of the drop zone.

The 1958-59 season saw them improve three places in their final League standings and go one stage further in the Scottish Cup. They drew their opening League game, earning a 2-2 draw at Ibrox having gone two up inside the first twenty minutes. In their first home game they thrashed Queen of the South 7-1, their opponents going on to finish bottom. They were on the receiving end of a heavy defeat themselves, late in September, when Hearts beat them 8-3. Willie Bauld scored three in the first nine minutes, and five overall. Thirds missed two penalties, one in each half. The Third Lanark scorers were Tommy Dick, Dave Hilley and Matt Gray. A fortnight later they conceded eight again, this time losing 8-1 at Motherwell. By this time they had the second worst defensive record in the division, although they were placed 10th. Wins followed against the newly promoted clubs, Stirling Albion and Dunfermline Athletic, but victories were hard to come by, and by the time they beat Queen of the South 5-2 in Dumfries in the New Year's Day fixture they were down in 14th place, only two points clear of the relegation zone. Thirds won three more matches in January, drawing the other, to go unbeaten in the first month of 1959, and moved away from danger. By this time Reuben Bennett had been approached by Liverpool and in the December he had left the club to join them.

Third Lanark then embarked on a fine Scottish Cup run. Thirds started by beating Dundee United 4-0 at Tannadice, scoring a penalty after two minutes before adding three second half goals. Alloa and Hibernian were then accounted for before the club was drawn against Aberdeen in the Semi-finals. Celtic were drawn against St Mirren in the other tie. The week before they were due to be in Cup action, on the 28th March, Third Lanark warmed up nicely by beating struggling Dunfermline Athletic 7-1. The Pars were second from bottom and went behind after just ten minutes when Bobby Craig slammed home from Matt Gray's cross. Gray then collided with the Pars full-back Bain and both went down injured, Gray leaving the field but returned limping. After just under half an hour's play Connachan, in the Dunfermline goal, dropped a ball under no challenge and Dick nipped in to fire into an empty net. Ten minutes later Hilley headed home from a Kelly cross from the right to make it 3-0. Manager Bob Shankly withdrew the hobbling Gray, no doubt with one eye on their forthcoming Cup tie, and two minutes before the interval Hilley made it 4-0. Thirds added two more goals in the second half. Hilley was tripped in the box and the resulting penalty was slammed home by Craig and later on George Christie made it six. The two sides then traded goals near the end.

On Saturday the 4th April Thirds met Aberdeen at Ibrox for a place in the Scottish Cup Final. Thirds started in sensational style by scoring after just 90 seconds. Dick capitalised on hesitancy in the Don's defence, when trying to clear a rebounded cross from Hilley, to nip in and score. However, Aberdeen equalised after fifteen minutes. Thirds dominated the second half with Hilley a constant threat on the right with his runs and trickery. Kelly hit the bar from 30 yards with the 'keeper beaten but the game ended 1-1. St Mirren beat Celtic 4-0 in the other match. Thirds were made to rue those missed opportunities when they lost the replay a few days later, 1-0, also played at Ibrox. Aberdeen lost the final to St Mirren.

The 1959-60 season saw the club finish in the bottom half of the First Division for the third season running. Although their League place was disappointing, and they were knocked out of the Scottish Cup in the First Round, they did reach their first ever League Cup Final. In this competition Thirds qualified from their section which included fellow First Division sides St Mirren, Clyde and Dunfermline Athletic and were drawn against Falkirk of the Second Division in the two-legged Quarter-final. The Bairns had won a play-off against First Division Dundee United to qualify. Thirds won the home leg 2-1 and were much more comfortable at Brockville, where they won 3-0 to progress 5-1 on aggregate. In the draw for the Semi-finals, Thirds got Arbroath, who were struggling in the First Division having been promoted the year before. Cowdenbeath of the Second Division played First Division leaders and would be champions, and League

Cup holders, Hearts in the other. The match was staged at a neutral venue and was played at Ibrox. On the eve of this important match Bob Shankly left the club to go to Dundee (having given notice to quit before then) and George Young took over, having been appointed on the 28th September. Young is best remembered for his long playing career at Rangers, for who he made over 300 appearances and where he won six League titles and four Scottish Cups, and also for being the first player to receive more than 50 caps for Scotland. He hung up his playing boots in 1957. In the match itself, stout defence by Arbroath kept the Thirds forwards at bay and the score was 0-0 at half-time. Four minutes after the restart Joe McInnes scored from 18 yards out. Later, Bobby Craig, hit a swerving shot that struck the underside of the bar and then the far post before settling into the net and Ian Hilley added a third as Third Lanark ran out 3-0 winners to set up a final at Hampden against Hearts in three weeks' time.

The League Cup Final was played on the 24th October in front of a crowd of 58,000 and the favourites Hearts made the worst possible start as they gifted the 'Hi-Hi' the lead, McInnes capitalising on a defensive error after just two minutes to score. A McInnes ball forward was misjudged by the Hearts 'keeper Marshall who allowed the ball to drop through his hands and Matt Gray raced in to ensure the ball was over the line. Jocky Robertson in goal was the Third's hero, making a string of saves in the first half to keep the lead intact going into the break. According to the *Glasgow Herald*, "Robertson leapt and dived and saved shots and headers high and low; Young came within inches of scoring at least four times and both Hamilton and Crawford were balked of goals by the great agility and sure grasp of the stocky little goalkeeper. Fortune often favours the brave, and Robertson had a remarkable stroke of luck when, seven minutes after half-time and during a tremendous barrage of attack, Young flicked a header out of his reach and the ball hit the base of a post and bounced upwards into the goalkeeper's arms." But it was the turn of Hearts to get lucky in the 58th minute when Hamilton's 30 yard shot, hit a defender and was deflected just past Robertson's despairing fingertips. A minute later Hearts were in the lead through Young and this turned out to be the winner. In the last minute Thirds had a golden chance to draw level and force extra time. A free kick taken by McInnes was sent over and the Hearts keeper again misjudged the flight of the ball which Gray then headed agonisingly wide. An equalising goal though would have been undeserved. The Third Lanark side that contested the 1959 League Cup final was: John Robertson; Billy Lewis, John Brown; James Reilly, George McCallum; William Livingstone Cunningham, Joe McInnes, Bobby Craig, David Hilley, Matt Gray and Ian Hilley.

Things looked promising for Thirds. The financial prospects of the club were again looking healthy. The club reported a doubling of profits up from £2,226 to £5,553, on the back of the good cup run. In the same year they spent £10,000 on installing new floodlights and a year later work began on a new stand. The club was now being managed by Rangers and Scotland legend George Young. The club had assembled a fine team including Alex Harley, who would finished as the League's top scorer in the 1960-61 season with 42 league goals; Dave Hilley, Joe McInnes, Jim Goodfellow and Matt Gray – a forward line the envy of many a team and at the back was the imposing figure of John 'Jocky' Robertson in goal. The club also possessed a good ground in Cathkin Park, with significant crowds and a devoted support. The 1960-61 season built on the club's success in the League Cup as Thirds finished in third place, their best finish since the resumption of the League in 1946 and their best ever since 1905. And yet, within six years they would be out of business.

In the League Cup Thirds failed to get out of their section but this included both Rangers and Celtic, plus Partick Thistle. They opened their League campaign on the 24th August with a 5-2 win over Airdrieonians. They won their next two as well before then losing three in a row. In mid-October they edged a nine-goal thriller at Fir Park against Motherwell, McInnes and Harley both scoring two. The first signs of a successful League campaign came on the 5th November 1960 when Thirds beat Dundee United 6-1. Joe McInnes made two dashing runs in the first five minutes to wreak havoc in their opponents defence but no one was on hand to supply the final touch. In the tenth minute Fin McGillivray played a cross field pass up to Harley, who volleyed first time into the net, completely surprising the United 'keeper. Undeterred United then dominated the play but were made to pay when Hilley made it two. In the 26th minute Dundee United were awarded a penalty which they converted but Thirds restored their two goal lead just five minutes later when Harley scored. In the 55th minute Gray headed a fourth from a Goodfellow cross and seven minutes later Harley made it five. Seven minutes from time Hilley scored a sixth. This was the first of four consecutive wins in November that took them from ninth to third in the table - only two points behind the leaders Rangers.

Form then hit a bumpy patch as they lost four out of the five games they played in December, including, on the 24th, an 8-4 loss at Hibernian, Joe Baker scoring four for Hibs including a hat-trick in four first half minutes. Thirds were in third place going into the game and Hibs were fourth from bottom. After just two minutes Thirds were ahead through Goodfellow. Joe Baker then volleyed past Jocky Robertson to equalise in the eighth minute and went on to score three goals in as many minutes. Before the quarter of an hour mark had been reached Goodfellow reduced the leeway with a well taken goal from Gray's header. *The Evening Times* commented that "this only inspired the Hib-hib-hilarious Hibs" who scored again to make it 4-2. In the 54th minute Baker scored his own fourth and Hibs' fifth goal. Three minutes later McInnes made it 5-3 but only two more minutes had elapsed when Hibs restored their three goal margin. A seventh goal came in the 65th minute. Two minutes later Thirds were awarded a penalty but McInnes' effort was saved. Hilley then did score a fourth but Hibs got another near the end to run out 8-4 winners.

On the 7th January 1961 Third Lanark beat Celtic 3-2 away, Harley scoring twice and Goodfellow getting the other. They twice came from behind in the first half and only took the lead for the first time in the 67th minute. The victory took them up to fifth in the table. A month later they beat Aberdeen 5-1, McGillivray scoring two penalties and Harley also scoring two. At the beginning of March they devastatingly lost a Scottish Cup tie against St Mirren 8-0 but they bounced back in the League winning all five games played in March. One of these victories was a 6-3 away win at Raith in which Matt Gray scored a hat-trick. At the beginning of April they beat Clyde 7-4, to move into fourth place, although they were 13 points behind the leaders Rangers, but were level on points with Motherwell in third. On the last day of the 1960-61 season they took revenge by beating Hibernian 6-1, Harley getting a hat trick which included two penalties, to reach 100 goals for the season, finishing in third place in the First Division, their best finish since 1905.

After their top three finish the season 1961-62 was a disappointment. Instead of pressing on and mounting a title challenge - that honour went to Dundee - they slipped back down the table to finish in eleventh place. They failed to progress out of their League Cup group, which included champions Rangers, future champions Dundee and Airdrieonians. Unfortunately the opening game of the season at Cathkin against Rangers in the League Cup was marred by rioting, as thousands of fans still queuing outside as the game kicked off, rushed the gates.

The League campaign started on the 23rd August with a 3-0 win over Airdrie. Later in the season, at the beginning of October, they beat Dundee United 7-2, Alex Harley scoring five and they went unbeaten across the month of October to sit as high as fifth place. Performances then became inconsistent across the remaining two months of 1961 although they were still in seventh place when they beat St Mirren 5-2 in mid-December, Harley scoring a hat-trick and Matt Gray the other two. Thirds only won twice in the League in the first two months of 1962 and slipped down to tenth place and following a narrow 1-0 win over Hearts in mid-March only won one of their remaining six fixtures. In the Scottish Cup Thirds reached the Quarter-finals, beating Berwick Rangers (6-2 away), Hamilton and Inverness Caledonian (6-1) before drawing Celtic. The two sides played out an entertaining 4-4 draw before Thirds lost the replay 4-0 at home, the *Glasgow Herald* commenting that "so decisively and convincingly did Celtic win that many of the crowd must have been mystified that the two teams drew on Saturday."

The 1962-63 season saw the first signs of the club's decline. Top players were sold in 1962 to help finance a new stand and you can't take players of the calibre of Dave Hilley and Alex Harley out of your forward line and expect the same results. Alex Harley, who had scored 68 goals in just 85 appearances, including 42 goals in the 1960-61 season, was sold to Manchester City for £20,000. He only had one season at Maine Road, and despite scoring over 20 goals, the club was relegated. He then joined Birmingham City for £42,000 and played briefly for Dundee in 1964-65. Dave Hilley moved to Newcastle for five seasons and then moved onto Nottingham Forest and Matt Gray also handed in a transfer request. David Grant and former Hearts player Robin Stenhouse were signed as replacements and Finlay "Junior McGillivray" replaced Jim Reilly as captain, making him the youngest captain in the First Division.

The club played their League Cup matches and their first League game of the 1962-63 season at Hampden while the building works were completed a Cathkin. Thirds were drawn in League Cup Section Four with Rangers, Hibs and St Mirren and finished bottom, losing five of the six matches and drawing the other. Thirds drew their first three League games and on Saturday 23rd September they hosted Dundee United at the revamped Cathkin Park, *The Evening Times* reporting that "no attendance records were broken when Third Lanark hanselled their new stand for their first match of the season at Cathkin Park. The crowd was less than 5000 at the start." Dundee United took a deserved lead after half an hour but Grant equalised five minutes before the interval and there was no further scoring.

Having now drawn their first four matches the club extended their winless run to ten matches. By the beginning of November they were in the bottom two, with just five points, all draws. They were kept off the bottom by Raith, who were also winless, with just two points. Their poor run ended on the 10th November 1962 when they won 4-1 at Airdrie with goals from David Grant, Joe McInnes, Matt Gray and Ian Spence. This victory lifted them out of the bottom two and up three places. They also scored four in wins over Dundee (4-3) and St Mirren (4-2) and followed these with a 2-0 win over Celtic and a 5-3 win at Falkirk to climb up to eleventh place.

In December 1962, reviewing the club's position, the *Daily Record* praised the current board saying "five years ago...[when they]...took over the club...[it was]...close on £20,000 in the red. Now they have a substantial bank balance, a new stand and a bunch of youngsters who look like making a successful team." Mind you, the clubs coffers had been swollen by the sales of Harley and Hilley.

December 1962 would prove to be a fateful month. At a shareholders meeting on the 12th December civil war broke out at the club, caused by former director Bill Hiddelston fighting his way back onto the board. Hiddelston had been intensively buying up shares prompting a take-over bid and it was his actions that led to the mass resignation of officials the evening of the meeting. Hiddelston's re-appointment to the board led to the resignation of directors Bert Martin, Willie McLean, Secretary James Murray and perhaps most importantly of all, manager George Young quit as well. Martin made a prophetic statement to the press on leaving the club, warning of bad times ahead for the club. Young was eventually replaced by Airdrie boss Willie Steel as manager at the end of January 1963.The club's good League form fell away and they lost six of their last seven games to finish in 14th place in the 18 team division. Raith Rovers, who finished bottom and were relegated from the First Division, knocked them out of the Scottish Cup in March 1963.

At the end of the season 19 players were sacked or sold as rumours circulated about Hiddelston's alleged aim to sell the ground to a property developer. Among those freed were Sammy Baird plus survivors of the 100 goal season – John 'Jocky' Robertson, Jimmy Goodfellow, Joe McInnnes and Billy Lewis, Jim Reilly, and Willie Cunningham. Winger Jimmy Goodfellow, who had scored 30 goals in 117 appearances moved to Leicester City and Matt Gray finally got his move, joining Manchester City, after netting 94 goals in 166 appearances for the club. The core of the team, its very heart, was ripped out in an act of self-inflicted sabotage. Third Lanark were effectively scuttled.

In the 1963-64 season Third Lanark were involved in a relegation battle right from the off. They recorded only one win during the first three months of the season and by the end of October they occupied the relegation places. They picked up two wins in November but off the pitch boardroom wrangles continued. First vice-chairman Robert Spence quit. Then, in November 1963 four more directors, including George Foster resigned and a new board was formed with John Scanlon as chairman. Amazingly amidst all this boardroom turmoil the playing squad, stripped of its key players, avoided relegation. A fortuitous 1-0 win on New Years' Day at Firhill against Partick, courtesy of a deflected own goal, saw them start 1964 in 14th place, although only two points from the relegation places occupied by East Stirlingshire and Queen of the South. They failed to win again until the end of February and were knocked out of the Scottish Cup by Stranraer. With East Stirling more or less doomed, Third Lanark secured a vital 4-2 away win at second bottom Queen of the South in mid-March, coming from one nil down to win thanks to braces from Mike Jackson and Maxwell Murray. Inside-left Jackson had joined from St Johnstone in 1963 and played for two seasons. Centre-forward Murray signed from West Brom and scored 19 goals in 61 appearances across two seasons before joining Clyde in 1965. On the 4th April they suffered a heavy loss, going down 7-3 at home to Falkirk. Thirds actually took the lead in the 11th minute through Jackson but their visitors were on level terms less than five minutes later.

Jackson restored their lead just before the half hour mark and Thirds led 2-1 at the break. Falkirk scored two goals in the first ten minutes of second half to take the lead for the first time but an own-goal brought Third level at 3-3 with an hours' play gone. Falkirk then scored three goals in ten minutes and added another near the end. By this time the club was actually safe from relegation and they eventually finished in 16th place, nine points clear of trouble. In April 1964 Scanlon and fellow director Bert Haugh left the club along with more players and manager Willie Steel followed in June.

Steel was replaced as manager by Celtic and Scotland legend Bobby Evans who was previously a player/coach at the club. Evans was in charge for the 1964-65 season which saw Thirds reach their nadir on the pitch. They would reach rock bottom having lost 30 of their 34 matches (including the last 21 in a row) and ended up with only seven points. Four years earlier they had finished third in the League and had scored 100 goals. The speed of their decline was shocking but then never had a club been so systematically dismantled as evidenced by the fact that only McGillivray and McCormack were left as players from the 100 goal season four years earlier.

This particular League season opened on the 19th August 1964 with a 3-1 away defeat at Kilmarnock followed by a 2-1 home reverse against Morton. The first point came on the 12th September courtesy of a 3-3 draw at Motherwell thanks to two from Charlie Cullen and one from 'Maxie' Murray. The squad was reduced still further in the autumn of 1964 with the departures of Joe Davis, who would go on to captain Hibs, and Fin McGillivray. The following week Thirds went down 5-1 at home to Hearts but October was a better month of sorts, with their first win coming at the start of the month. Aberdeen were the victims, going down 4-1 at Cathkin Park, with two of the home goals scored by former Celts Bobby Evans and Mike Jackson. The other two came from Maxie Murray and Doug Baillie, the vastly experienced ex-Airdrieonians and Rangers centre-half, who was making his debut for the club. Later in the same month Murray was again on target as Thirds won away 1-0 at Partick.

This away win was followed by four straight defeats including a 5-0 defeat at Hibs. On the 21st November Thirds beat St Mirren at home 2-1, thanks to goals from Bobby Black and Charlie Cullen. At this stage, after 13 games their analysis stood at three wins, one draw and nine defeats. Incredibly this would be their last league win of the season – in November – as they lost the next 21 League games in a row. Included in this sequence were 5-0 defeats at Rangers and St Johnstone and 4-0 losses away at Kilmarnock and Morton. Thirds also lost 4-0 at home to Airdrie and Clyde but also only lost by one goal at home on four occasions. A victory was recorded, in the Scottish Cup, when the club won 5-1 away at Highland club Inverness Caledonian in February. The club were then knocked out by Dunfermline in the next round, but not until after two matches had failed to separate them. Dunfermline would go on to contest the Final, going down 3-2 against Celtic.

It would be Dunfermline who would administer the biggest defeat of Thirds in this terrible season, equalling their heaviest defeats of all time. The club had lost 8-0 to Motherwell in 1925 and then to Hibs in 1947 and a few years earlier they had lost 8-0 against St Mirren in a Cup replay. On Saturday 20th March Thirds went down 2-0 at home to Hibs but on the following Monday night, the 22nd, they travelled to East End Park and were gubbed 8-0. Thirds made three changes from the side that had lost on Saturday – Jim Little for Bobby Evans, Bobby Black for Jim Kilgannon and James Geddes for George Fyfe – but the changes made no difference as Dunfermline overwhelmed Third Lanark. The *Glasgow Herald* reported on "a night of personal triumph for Melrose, who scored four goals and had a hand in the leading-up work for two others." Harry Melrose already had a track record as a goalscorer, having scored six in a game for Dunfermline against Partick Thistle in 1959. Melrose scored all three of Dunfermline's first half goals, the first in 13 minutes, the second two minutes later from a John Sinclair cross and the third a header from an Ian Hunter cross after 43 minutes. Dunfermline "increased the passion in the second half" and George Peebles made it four after 55 minutes. Eight minutes later Sinclair prodded home a Peebles corner and Alex Smith then beat Williams from 20 yards out to make it 6-0 with 20 minutes left. In the last few minutes Melrose claimed his fourth from a corner and Sinclair slotted home an eighth. The win lifted Dunfermline up to third in the table, where they would eventually finish. Goalscorer Harry Melrose left the Pars in October 1965 to join Aberdeen, although he did return, this time as manager, in 1975. The Third Lanark team that suffered that day was: Sam Williams, Tony Connell, Don May, Mike Jackson, Jim Little, Alan MacKay, Willie Todd, Bobby Black, Maxie Murray, Jim Geddes and Harry Kirk. Goalkeeper Sam Williams, who had joined Thirds in October 1964 from Vale of Leven had a night to forget. But he would enjoy better times as he went onto play for Celtic in their championship winning sides of the early seventies, leaving Thirds in March 1966.

Thirds would lose their remaining six games of their 1964-65 campaign, including a 6-1 defeat at Dundee, finishing bottom of the table with a paltry seven points and having lost 21 consecutive games. Goalscoring was a key problem, with only 22 league goals scored. The distinction of being the club's topscorer was shared by 3 players – Maxie Murray, Bobby Black and Jim Kilgannon - and the total was a meagre seven. A lack of continuity on the pitch was also a problem, with over 30 players used and on only two occasions during the season did the same team feature in consecutive games.

The next two seasons were a lingering slow death for the club characterised by mediocrity on the pitch and discontent off it. Thirds, having retained the bulk of their team, made a decent enough start to life in the Second Division beating Alloa 7-1 in the September with goals from George Fyfe (a hat-trick), Kilgannon, John Kinnaird and a brace from Ian Henderson, the former Morton centre-forward who had joined the club in the August. However, despite the goalscoring trio of Fyfe, Kilgannon and Henderson, who scored 52 goals between them (Fyfe finishing top scorer with 23), the club could only finish 14th. A disastrous run of just one win in 15 games between December and April dictated their fate. Towards the end of the season a number of senior players left including goalscorers Bobby Black (to Stenhousemuir in February 1966) and Maxie Murray (freed in April 1966 after 78 appearances and 26 goals).

The club used 33 different players in the 51 games played during the 1965-66 season so there was a lack of understanding and continuity amongst the players that didn't help the club's cause. Bobby Evans had left the club during the close season to join Raith, having previously taken on the managers role with the departure of Billy Steel. Team affairs were now being managed by Hiddelston again and this period saw the steady off-loading and churning of players, which with hindsight was also an early sign of financial difficulties. A new stand had been built in 1963 to accommodate thousands of spectators that never materialised. With the club now in the Second Division gate receipts had fallen as they were not enough people coming through the turnstiles. At this time rumours also surfaced about relocating the club to one of the new towns." On the 8th January 1966, the *Glasgow Herald* announced in a front-page story that the Cathkin board were investigating the possibility of moving Third Lanark to the new town of East Kilbride and selling Cathkin Park for housing.

An early indication of financial irregularities at the club had come in February 1966 when an EGM was called. One of the resolutions tabled was to approach the Board Of Trade to investigate the failure of the auditors to ascertain the exact costs associated with the building of the new stand. Rumours of boardroom corruption were rife and it appeared to supporters that the club was being deliberately run down. Allegations were made that the club had stopped keeping records and accounts. Bills were going unpaid, and money coming into the club from gates just disappeared with no paper trail. A case in point was the monthly club lottery. Lots of entrant money was received but there are no records of anyone actually winning the first cash prize.

What would turn out to be Thirds last season kicked off with a 2-0 defeat at Arbroath in their League Cup section on the 13th August 1966. The club was now under the charge of former Raith player Francis Joyner. They kicked off their last League programme against Hamilton, which they won 3-2. The club went on to win three of their first four games to go fourth but a poor run, including six losses in a row during December and January saw them slump to 14th place. This poor run coincided with further departures amongst the playing staff including Mike Jackson, the former Celtic and St Johnstone defender who left In September and George Fyfe, who had scored 36 goals in 62 games, who was allowed to join Airdrie in the November.

Ironically, 1967 saw a modest upturn in the playing fortunes of the club. Bobby Shearer, the former Rangers full back who had been acting as a player-coach at Queen of the South (and who had made over 400 appearances for the Gers between 1955 and 1965, and was their captain in the second domestic treble season of 1963-64) took over the reins on the 10th January 1967 replacing Joyner and was to be the last manager of Third Lanark. As an indication of the lack of stability at the club he was their sixth manager in as many years and Third's 15th manager since the 1920s. In contrast, Celtic and Rangers in the same period had three. When Shearer took over they were near the foot of the Second Division but he had now got them to mid-table. He had signed a number of experienced professionals on short term deals such as Bobby Craig and had also uncovered a talented youth player called Drew Busby.

By the spring of 1967 the club's finances were in a perilous state. They had numerous unpaid bills and visiting clubs complained about the lack of hot water at Cathkin. Rumours abounded that the players' wages were no longer being paid out in notes but from coins from the slot machines and further players were being released. On the 11th April a petition for the winding up of the club over unpaid debts was brought before the courts by William Walker Rae, a Chartered Surveyor.

A few days later, on Saturday 15th April, Third Lanark recorded their lowest ever home League attendance of 297 spectators for the visit of Clydebank. The *Evening Times* reported that "with Cathkin staging the only senior game in the city today, Third Lanark had Glasgow to themselves. However, from an attendance point of view they did not benefit greatly for there could not have been more than 250 spectators." Thirds dominated the play in the first half yet the match was goalless at the break due to their profligacy in front of goal. On resuming, Third Lanark stepped up the pressure and they eventually got the breakthrough in the 67th minute when John Kinnaird scored from close range. Third Lanark won 1–0 and this would turn out to be their last League victory.

The players continued to demonstrate pride for the club with a four game unbeaten run during April. Busby had scored both goals in a 2-0 win away at Stenhousemuir and after the 1-0 home win over Clydebank they drew 3-3 against Brechin City. On the 25th April the club played what would turn out to be their final home game, a 3-3 draw with

Queen of the South. Brian McMurdo of Queen of the South scored the last ever League goal at Cathkin. The Third Lanark goals came from John Kinnaird with two, and Hugh McLaughlan with the other; Thirds had ended the first half 3-1 up. The final attendance at Cathkin Park was given as just 325 spectators.

On the night of Friday 28th April 1967 the 'Hi-Hi' played their last ever Scottish League game, away against Dumbarton. The Boghead side won the game 5-1 (with goals from Kirk (2), McMillan (2), and McCormack) with Drew Busby scoring the club's last ever League goal. The club finished in eleventh place. The Third's team line up for that last game was: Bobby Russell, Tony Connell, George Heaney, Garry McLaughlin, Jim Little, Gordon McEwan, Hugh Rundell, Bobby Craig, Drew Busby, Don May, and John Kinnaird. Goalkeeper Bobby Russell, who had joined from Stenhousemuir in March 1966 spent two further seasons with Morton after the club folded before being freed in April 1969. Tony Connell, the full-back who played 33 of the 38 League games in the club's last season, and who had made over 100 appearances for the club, joined St Mirren on the 24th June 1967. He was part of the team that won promotion to the First Division and he spent four seasons at Love Street before ending his career at Queen of the South, having made over 300 career appearances. Fellow full-back George Heaney, who had only joined the club in December 1966 and who made just 12 appearances was released two days after the last game against Dumbarton. Garry McLaughlin joined St Mirren along with Connell and spent five seasons there and then ended his career at Queen of the South. Jim Little, who played in all bar one of the final League programme and who made over 130 appearances for the club, dropped out of the game when the club folded. Gordon McEwan made just 13 appearances before disappearing out of football. Hugh Rundell, who had only joined the club at the beginning of April and played seven League games, dropped down to junior football. Inside-right Bobby Craig was in his second spell with the club, having spent five seasons with them in the Fifties. He had subsequently moved onto Sheffield Wednesday, Blackburn, Celtic, St Johnstone and Toronto in Canada. The diminutive, 5ft 5 player had re-joined Thirds in February 1967 and played nine times, netting once. He was freed by the club on the 30th April and continued his travels, playing for Johannesburg Wanderers in South Africa. Striker Drew Busby, just 19 years of age and scorer of the club's last goal, went on to play for Airdrie and then Hearts over a 10 year period, ending a long career in which he played over 450 times at Morton and then Queen of the South. Donald May was freed after the last game and joined opponents Dumbarton for a season. John Kinnaird was also freed after the last game, having made 47 appearances for the club over two seasons, scoring 9 goals. As for their last manager, Bobby Shearer, he went on to manage Hamilton after the club folded.

A few weeks after the humiliating defeat against Dumbarton the board of Third Lanark announced that they had negotiated the sale of Cathkin Park to the Glasgow Corporation for housing and a new stadium for Thirds would be built in Bishopbriggs for the club (needless to say this stadium was never built). On the 22nd May 1967 Third Lanark were drawn into Section 5 of the League Cup in preparation for the new season. However, by this time a firm by the name of Peter Thaw and Sons of Duke Street, Glasgow, had joined the petition, claiming that the club owed them money for work done on the new stand at Cathkin Park dating back to 1963.

On the 7th June 1967, the Rt Hon Lord Fraser of Carmyllie, in the Court of Session in Edinburgh issued a winding-up order against the club and appointed an official liquidator. On the 16th and 23rd of June official notices appeared in the *Edinburgh Gazette* noting that "Lord Fraser has, by interlocutor dated 7th June 1967, ordered that Third Lanark Athletic Club Limited, having its Registered Office at Cathkin Park, Crosshill, Glasgow, be wound up under the provisions of the Companies Act 1948 and nominated and appointed Thomas Peter Cowan Taylor, Chartered Accountant, 87 St Vincent St, Glasgow, to be Official Liquidator of the said Company with the usual powers all in terms of the said statue and of law." The club was declared bankrupt with liabilities exceeding its liquid assets by £40,000. On 26th June 1967, it was announced that Third Lanark's membership of the Scottish Football League had ceased and that their remaining players were up for transfer. Stranraer were moved into their League Cup section and took their place. It was too late to elect a replacement so the Scottish Football League ran with 39 clubs until 1974 when Meadowbank Thistle were elected.

Cathkin Park was sold for housing during the 1967 close season, but Glasgow City Council refused planning permission. The ground subsequently fell into disrepair and became derelict until 1977 when the Glasgow City Parks Department bought the site and converted it into a municipal park. The remains of the banks of terracing together with barriers are still visible on three sides although they are somewhat overgrown as nature reclaims the site.

A Government report in the form of a Board of Trade inquiry was published in 1968 and confirmed a situation characterised by player squabbles, internal wrangles for power and financial irregularities. As a result the Directors were censured and fined for not keeping proper accounts. The Report went on to state that £10,000 was apparently "mishandled" and that there were strong grounds for suspecting that money was misappropriated by Mr Hiddelston or misapplied for his benefit. Although no criminal proceedings were instigated the report concluded that Third Lanark was run as an "inefficient and unscrupulous business" with regard to company law and shareholders' interests and the investigating panel concluded that the demise of the club merited police inquiry. Some have alleged that Hiddelston deliberately engineered the club's collapse so that he could profit from the sale of Cathkin Park for housing development. And yet, Cathkin has never been developed, with the partial remains of the terraces still visible and is now owned by Glasgow City Council. All we have by means of an explanation for the demise of Thirds is what we know from the report from the Board of Trade's investigations. Only Bill Hiddelston really knows what happened, but on the 16th November 1967 he was deemed to have cheated justice when he died of a heart attack, aged 44 at his home at Lytham St Annes near Blackpool, before the findings were published.

Supporters of the defunct club remain and attempts to revive the name have been muted. 1967 was one of the best years in Scottish football history, when the national team beat the world champions and Celtic were crowned the champions of Europe but the one sour note was the demise of one of the founding League clubs and former winner of the Scottish Football League and Scottish Cup. The swiftness of their decline is the startling thing and has only been matched in recent times by that of Leeds United in England (from Champions League to the third tier of English soccer via administration) and by Gretna in Scotland. Again, financial mis-management and impropriety off the pitch was the key factor. The real travesty here was that Thirds, one of the founder members of the Scottish League, were just five years away from celebrating their centenary when they went out of business.

SEASON	LEAGUE	P	W	D	L	F	A	P	POS
1890-91	SCOT	18	8	3	7	38	39	15 *	5/10
1891-92	SCOT	22	9	4	9	44	47	21	6/12
1892-93	SCOT	18	9	1	8	54	40	19	4/10
1893-94	SCOT-1	18	7	3	8	37	45	17	7/10
1894-95	SCOT-1	18	10	1	7	51	39	21	4/10
1895-96	SCOT-1	18	7	1	10	47	51	15	6/10
1896-97	SCOT-1	18	5	1	12	29	46	11	8/10
1897-98	SCOT-1	18	8	2	8	37	38	18	5/10
1898-99	SCOT-1	18	7	3	8	33	38	17	6/10
1899-00	SCOT-1	18	5	5	8	31	38	15	7/10
1900-01	SCOT-1	20	6	6	8	20	29	18	6/11
1901-02	SCOT-1	18	7	5	6	30	26	19	4/10
1902-03	SCOT-1	22	8	5	9	34	27	21	7/12
1903-04	SCOT-1	26	20	3	3	61	26	43	1/14

1904-05	SCOT-1	26	14	7	5	60	28	35	3/14
1905-06	SCOT-1	30	16	2	12	62	39	34	6/16
1906-07	SCOT-1	34	15	9	10	57	48	39	6/18
1907-08	SCOT-1	34	13	7	14	45	50	33	9/18
1908-09	SCOT-1	34	11	10	13	56	49	32	11/18
1909-10	SCOT-1	34	13	8	13	62	44	34	7/18
1910-11	SCOT-1	34	16	7	11	59	53	39	8/18
1911-12	SCOT-1	34	12	7	15	40	57	31	11/18
1912-13	SCOT-1	34	8	12	14	31	41	28	15/18
1913-14	SCOT-1	38	13	10	15	42	51	36	8/20
1914-15	SCOT-A	38	10	12	16	51	57	32	16/20
1915-16	SCOT	38	9	11	18	38	56	29	17/20
1916-17	SCOT	38	19	11	8	53	37	49	5/20
1917-18	SCOT	34	10	7	17	56	62	27	13/18
1918-19	SCOT	34	11	9	14	60	60	31	12/18
1919-20	SCOT	42	16	11	15	57	62	43	8/22
1920-21	SCOT	42	19	6	17	74	61	44	8/22
1921-22	SCOT-1	42	17	12	13	58	52	46	9/22
1922-23	SCOT-1	38	11	8	19	40	59	30	17/20
1923-24	SCOT-1	38	11	8	19	54	78	30	18/20
1924-25	SCOT-1	38	11	8	19	53	84	30	20/20
1925-26	SCOT-2	38	19	8	11	72	47	46	6/20
1926-27	SCOT-2	38	17	10	11	67	48	44	4/20
1927-28	SCOT-2	38	18	9	11	99	66	45	2/20
1928-29	SCOT-1	38	10	6	22	71	102	26	19/20
1929-30	SCOT-2	38	23	6	9	92	53	52	4/20
1930-31	SCOT-2	38	27	7	4	107	42	61	1/20
1931-32	SCOT-1	38	21	4	13	92	81	46	4/20
1932-33	SCOT-1	38	14	7	17	70	80	35	13/20
1933-34	SCOT-1	38	8	9	21	62	103	25	19/20
1934-35	SCOT-2	34	23	6	5	94	43	52	1/18
1935-36	SCOT-1	38	14	5	19	63	71	33	11/20
1936-37	SCOT-1	38	20	6	12	79	61	46	6/20
1937-38	SCOT-1	38	11	13	14	68	73	35	9/20
1938-39	SCOT-1	38	12	8	18	80	96	32	15/20
1939-40	SCOT-1	5	2	1	2	9	8	5	ABAND
1946-47	SCOT-A	30	11	6	13	56	64	28	9/16
1947-48	SCOT-A	30	10	6	14	56	73	26	11/16
1948-49	SCOT-A	30	13	5	12	56	52	31	7/16

1949-50	SCOT-A	30	11	3	16	44	62	25	12/16
1950-51	SCOT-A	30	11	2	17	40	51	24	13/16
1951-52	SCOT-A	30	9	8	13	51	62	26	12/16
1952-53	SCOT-A	30	8	4	18	52	75	20	16/16
1953-54	SCOT-B	30	13	10	7	78	48	36	3/16
1954-55	SCOT-B	30	13	7	10	63	49	33	5/16
1955-56	SCOT-B	36	16	3	17	80	64	35	10/19
1956-57	SCOT-2	36	24	3	9	105	51	51	2/19
1957-58	SCOT-1	34	13	4	17	69	88	30	14/18
1958-59	SCOT-1	34	11	10	13	74	83	32	11/18
1959-60	SCOT-1	34	13	4	17	75	83	30	12/18
1960-61	SCOT-1	34	20	2	12	100	80	42	3/18
1961-62	SCOT-1	34	13	5	16	59	60	31	11/18
1962-63	SCOT-1	34	9	8	17	56	68	26	14/18
1963-64	SCOT-1	34	9	7	18	47	74	25	16/18
1964-65	SCOT-1	34	3	1	30	22	99	7	18/18
1965-66	SCOT-2	36	12	8	16	55	65	32	14/19
1966-67	SCOT-2	38	13	8	17	67	78	34	11/20

Thistle

Formed: 1875
Colours: Thin blue and white horizontal striped shirts and white shorts
Ground: Braehead Park
Entered League: 1893. Founder member of the Second Division
Number of League Seasons: 1
Honours: None
Highest League Finish: 10th in Division Two
Left League: 1894. Disbanded.

The least successful of the forgotten League clubs based on tenure, and the level they played at, Thistle, or Glasgow Thistle were founder members of the new Second Division in 1893. They managed only one season, finishing bottom with just two wins, and folded before the re-election vote at the League's AGM.

Thistle were formed in 1875 in the Outlands district of Glasgow, on the southern bank of the River Clyde and their main rivals were Clyde. Known as the 'South-Siders' they played their League games at Braehead Park from 1892 having originally played at Shawfield and Beechwood Parks. They were one of many clubs to spring up in and around Glasgow and they were regulars in the Scottish Cup from the 1878-79 competition, playing for 14 successive years in the competition prior to Scottish Football League admittance.

Thistle made their debut in the Scottish Cup on the 21st September 1878, beating a team from Possilpark, Glasgow, 2-0 and they knocked out local neighbours Clyde 4-1 in the Second Round. They then disposed of Partick Thistle and Stonelaw of Rutherglen, but both of their vanquished opponents were reinstated after Thistle were disqualified from the competition for fielding ineligible players.

The following season they made an early exit to fellow Glasgow side Northern, but in the 1880-81 competition they enjoyed a run to the Fifth Round. Having got past Lenzie, Tollcross, Glengowan and Airdrie they were drawn away against three times winner Vale of Leven, in a match played on the 4th December 1880. Unfortunately they were beaten 7-1 by the Vale, mainly as a result of playing the game short a player short. *The Glasgow Herald* reported that "the game commenced with great spirit, both teams playing with considerable dash. Within five minutes from the start the Vale scored, and although the strangers played at times a splendid defensive game, the home forwards broke through them and secured another two goals during the first half of the game. At this point one of the Thistle players got slightly injured and had to leave the field. Minus a man they played with great determination, and not only defended their goal successfully for some time, but once cleverly ran the ball past the Vale backs and scored. After this the home team settled down better to work, and in rapid succession added four other goals to their credit. While the back play and goalkeeping of the strangers was very good, still seven or eight corner kicks within 20 minutes showed that the Thistle players had to kick behind for safety rather frequently."

In the 1881-82 season they made it to the Fourth Round, the most notable result being in the Second Round when they beat Uddingston 10-0, on the 1st October 1881. The two sides met at Thistle's Shawfield Park ground and according to the *Glasgow Herald*, "after five minutes play Gilchrist placed the first goal to the Thistle's credit. Goal after goal followed, no fewer than seven being registered before half-time. On change of ends the play was of much of the same nature, another three goals being placed...the goaltakers being Gilchrist 3, Wallace 2, and J Taylor, R Taylor, Little, Crawford and Beveridge one each." Thistle suffered a heavy defeat of their own the following year when they were drawn away against holders and six-time winners Queen's Park. The two sides met on the 9th September 1882 and they were thrashed 12-1.

In the next two seasons they failed to get past the Second Round and although only making it to the Third Round in the two seasons after that they did notch up some big wins. In the 1885-86 competition they beat Westbourne of Hyndland, Glasgow, 11-1 in a First Round tie held on the 2nd September. The *Glasgow Herald* reported that Thistle, taking advantage of the strong wind after winning the toss, scored six first half goals and that "the Westbourne were too anxious and nervous to give themselves any chance to score" and "the home forwards played a splendid passing game." Thistle scored another five goals in the second half. They beat Clyde in the next round before being beaten by Dumbarton in the Third Round. In the 1886-87 competition they beat Blairvaddick of Govan, Glasgow 13-0 in the First Round and St Andrews (of Pollockshields), 12-0, in the Second, before being knocked out by Albion Rovers 4-2 in the next round.

In the 1887-88 competition they again got as far as the Fifth Round, starting off their Cup run with another fine win. On the 3rd September 1887 they beat Carrick of Partick, Glasgow, away 10-0. *The Scotsman* reported that this "Scottish Cup tie was played at Possil Park in the presence of a fair sprinkling of spectators. The Carrick won the toss, and Dunbar started the ball for the Thistle. At half-time the score stood - Thistle three goals, Carrick nothing. In the second half the Thistle continued to press, and at the call of time the score stood - Thistle ten goals, Carrick nil." Having reached the Fifth Round they lost at home, 9-2, to Vale of Leven Wanderers - not to be confused with former winners Vale of Leven. Played on the 26th November the *Glasgow Herald* reported that "the Thistle...succumbed rather easily to that comparatively unknown combination the Vale of Leven Wanderers. The young team deserve their success, for the East End club evidently underestimated their powers."

Thistle were not involved in the setting up of the Scottish Football League in 1890 but they did join the Scottish Alliance in 1891, although they finished 12th and bottom in its first season. The following year they improved to fifth place and on the 10th July 1893 the Glasgow-based Scottish Alliance clubs were incorporated into the new Second Division, and Thistle joined the Scottish League, along with Cowlairs, Northern and Partick Thistle.

Their first SFL season ended up just like their first in the Alliance league, as they finished bottom in tenth place. They played their first League game on the 12th August 1893, a Glasgow derby defeat, losing 4-2 at Cowlairs (who would finish second). Thistle conceded in the first few minutes of the match. Mortimer equalised thereby scoring their first League goal but by half-time they were losing 3-1. Mortimer also scored a penalty for the South-Siders to make it 3-2 and briefly raise hopes but close to the end the home team scored a fourth to make sure of both points. The first ever Thistle team line up was Neil; Haig, Jackson; Mackie, Ross, McCracken; Clarken, Scott, Mortimer, Wark and Cameron.

On the 19th August they played their first home SFL game at Braehead Park, disappointingly watched by only 500 spectators. They lost the game 2-1 against opponents Hibernian, who would go on to win the first ever Second Division championship. *The Scotsman* reported on the game, saying "from the start it was evident that the Edinburgh men meant business, and they soon surrounded Neil's charge, which he had some troubles in saving, A quarter of an hour after the start Murray put on a first point and after a similar interval Howie again scored. With this lead the visitors seemed content, as they had frequent grand chances, which, however, they dallied over."

On the 2nd September the home derby game against Clyde attracted a gate of 2,000 but Thistle lost 3-1 and they had also lost their game the week before, a 4-3 loss at Port Glasgow. Thistle finally got their first League points and win in their fifth match, on the 9th September, a 2-1 win over Greenock Morton. Morton scored first, before Hannah equalised, and the sides went in level at the break. *The Scotsman* reported that "both teams now played well in order to get the winning point...Mortimer sent in a warm one which just missed by inches. Collins [in the Morton goal] at last was beaten by Gemmell. Morton had hard lines several times but Neil seemed to be in grand form. A good game ended Thistle, two goals; Morton, one goal". The result lifted Thistle into eighth place, above the two pointless teams of Morton and Northern (who had played three games each). This win though would be one of only two all season as they amassed only seven points from 18 matches.

On the 7th October they suffered a 6-1 defeat at Barrowfield Park against Clyde. The hosts scored first but Blair, from a counter-attack equalised. *The Glasgow Herald* commented though that "the Thistle were playing a very erratic game" and Clyde soon gained the ascendancy and scored four more times before the break. Play was more even in the second half with Clyde only adding one more goal to the score. The result dropped Thistle to second from bottom, two points above Northern who were still yet to win.

The following week the bottom two met at Braehead Park with Thistle winning 3-0, in a contest that was more evenly matched than the score suggests. *The Scotsman* reported that "play continued very even for a time, each goal being visited in turn. The first goal fell to the Thistle....McCracken was playing a splendid game for the Thistle...The Thistle were having the pull over their opponents, a couple of corners falling to their lot, but nothing resulted. The Northern opened out a little, and gave the Thistle backs a good deal of bother, but they were weak at goal. After a bit of hard pressing by the Thistle McCracken shot the ball through." The result moved Thistle up as high as seventh place, above Morton, Abercorn and the vanquished Northern.

Glasgow Thistle were struggling. Off the pitch issues were impacting on the pitch. The club were hard-pressed financially and one impact of this was that they were having problems fielding teams. When Partick Thistle visited Braehead towards the end of October they found the place in disrepair. A poor crowd attended the game, which only compounded things. A week later they were thrashed 7-0 by Celtic in the Glasgow Cup but worse was to follow when they were knocked out of the Scottish Cup, at home, in the First Round by non-League Battlefield of Glasgow by three goals to one.

On the 16th December they played their last game of 1893, a trip to Dalziel Park to play Motherwell. Despite the two teams going into the interval goalless, Motherwell ran away with the game in the second period, scoring six times to win 6-2. Notwithstanding the heavy loss, they ended 1893 in joint seventh place on five points with Abercorn, Morton had four points and Northern just two. However, Thistle had completed 12 of their 18 games whereas the other three sides were only halfway through their fixtures. In addition, Thistle had only two home games left.

Thistle played their penultimate home game on the 10th February 1894, although it would turn out to be their last actual home SFL game at Braehead Park. Their opponents were Cowlairs and they lost 3-1 in a game in which they scored first and led 1-0 at half-time, but the visitors had the upper hand from the restart and ran out 3-1 winners. A month later their season reached a new nadir when they lost 13-1 against Partick Thistle at Inchview Park, Whiteinch. Glasgow Thistle's early season problems were worsening and the scoreline was the highest recorded in a Scottish League match up to that point (it has only been exceeded by Dundee Wanderers' 15–1 loss to Airdrieonians the following season). Three Partick Thistle players scored hat-tricks in this match – Willie Fairbairn, Willie Paul and William Proudfoot.

On the 24th March Thistle nominally played their last home game against Motherwell. Although the game is shown as a home game it was actually played at Motherwell's Dalziel Park ground. The *Glasgow Herald* reported that "the return League game between these teams (which should have been played off at Glasgow), for financial reasons took place on Dalziel Park, Motherwell, in splendid weather and before a good attendance of spectators....The Thistle had to face a strong end, but, nevertheless, pressed. After about five minutes play they score very luckily, the ball, from a drop kick by the home custodian, striking one of the opposing forwards and rebounding through the goal. Galloway equalised three minutes later, and before the game was quarter of an hour old a second point was scored [for Motherwell] by Watson from a corner. Before half-time was called Motherwell had again scored, the teams' crossing over – Motherwell 3 Thistle 1. The play in the second half was mostly in favour of the home team, who ran up their total to eight goals...The Thistle failed to find an opening and retired defeated."

A month later, on the 21st April, Thistle played what would be their last ever SFL game, when they visited Morton. Thistle scored in the first half and Morton in the second and the points were shared with a 1-1 draw. The last Thistle team to take the field was: McHarg; Haig, T Campbell; McCulloch, Hannah, J Campbell; Woods, Johnstone, Bryce, Munro and Combston. Only Haig, one of the backs, remained from the original Thistle line-up at the start of the season.

Thistle finished bottom, with just seven points and only two wins, the victories being achieved against the teams placed immediately above them – Morton and Northern. All three clubs were due to face a re-election vote at the League AGM on the 1st June but Thistle decided to dissolve prior to this due to their financial problems. On the 12th May 1894 they played a friendly against Clyde, *The Scotsman* reporting simply "these teams met at Barrowfield for the last time previous to the dissolution of the Thistle.

Result: Four goals each. Braehead Park was subsequently absorbed into the wider Richmond Park, a city park opened in September 1899.

SEASON	LEAGUE	P	W	D	L	F	A	P	POS
1893-94	SCOT-2	18	2	3	13	31	74	7	10/10

Vale of Leven

Formed: 1872
Colours: Navy blue shorts and white shorts
Ground: Milburn Park
Entered League: 1890. Founder members of Scottish League. Re-entered 1905 in Second Division. 1921 re-joined Scottish League as Second Division reformed.
Number of League Seasons: 17 over 3 spells. (2 + 10 + 5)
Highest League Finish: 9th in Division One 1890-91
Honours: Scottish Cup Winners 1877, 1878, 1879
Left League: 1892. Not re-elected. 1915. Second Division suspended. 1926 Third Division disbanded. Folded 1929.

We end our journey around the former Scottish Football League clubs by returning to the area that was an early powerhouse of football in Scotland, namely West Dunbartonshire. We end at one of the most successful of all of the defunct clubs and winners of three Scottish Cups – that's the same as Kilmarnock, St Mirren and Hibernian and more than Motherwell, Falkirk and both Dundee and Dundee United.

Vale of Leven were one of the early forces in the Scottish game. Prior to the formation of the Scottish Football League they had won three Scottish Cups in a row (1877-79) and competed in four further finals, the last one in a replayed final in 1890 prior to League admission. It was therefore natural they would be one of the founder members of the League although by that time they were a fading force. The club also has the second most capped players of any defunct team representing their early dominance in the Scottish Cup.

In their second season in the League they failed to win a single game and finished last. They were the last senior Scottish club to suffer this ignominy until Brechin City in 2018. Rather than face re-election for a second time, the club withdrew and joined the rival Scottish Alliance where they played for a single season. Between 1893 and 1902 the Vale played only friendly matches and cup competitions before joining the Scottish Football Combination.

In 1905 they applied successfully for readmission to the Scottish League when the Second Division was extended with two additional places. They played there for ten years finishing second in the 1906-07 season and third in 1908-09 but they did not receive the votes they needed to be elected to the First Division. However, in their last five seasons before the First World War they struggled finishing in the bottom three on each occasion and actually finishing bottom in the 1910-11 and 1914-15 seasons. When the Second Division was suspended in 1915, Vale joined the Western League.

On the resumption after the Great War in 1921 they returned to the Scottish League for a third time and finished fourth with a record points tally, but two years later in 1924 they were relegated to the Third Division, which had been formed for the 1923-24 season. For much of the season they were promotion contenders but in the end they finished fourth in the Third Division, despite equalling their record number of League wins in a season (17) and in the last year of the Third Division they were seventh although they only completed 26 out of their 30 matches. This ill-fated competition was abandoned in 1926 when it became clear that the cost of meeting match guarantees and additional travel expenses were beyond the means of its members and Vale of Leven lost their League status for good after a total of 17 seasons, across three spells.

Formed in 1872, Vale of Leven were based in Alexandria, a town in West Dunbartonshire, situated on the River Leven, four miles north-west of Dumbarton. Their local rivals were Renton and Dumbarton and they played their matches at Millburn Park, which was opened in August 1888 when Vale of Leven moved from their original North Street Park ground. Their new ground was situated alongside the river on the West Bank of the River Leven with a pavilion in the south-eastern corner. It was located north of the former ferry point across the River Millburn and is sited near to the modern Vale of Leven academy school.

Vale of Leven entered, but did not play, in the Scottish Cup competition in its first two seasons, 1873-74 and 1874-75. Vale were one of the three Dunbartonshire teams that entered the first, sixteen team, Scottish Cup for the 1873-74 inaugural competition. They were duly drawn to play local rivals Dumbarton as their First Round opponents. However, in each of these years their opponents protested about the professional status of one of the Vale's outstanding players, John Ferguson. On 18th October 1873 they should have played but Dumbarton successfully protested about Ferguson, and had their protest upheld by the SFA. In October 1874 they drew 0-0 at runners-up Clydesdale but resigned before playing their replay following a protest by Clydesdale.

When the third Scottish Cup competition was held in the 1875-76 season the number of entrants had swelled to 49 teams being included in the draw which was conducted on regional lines in the early rounds. Vale were allowed to compete this time and benefitted from a walkover of their own against Vale of Leven Rovers in October 1875. They won their first actual Scottish Cup tie on the 13th November 1875 when they beat Renton 3-0 at North Street Park. This was followed by a 6-0 win over Mauchline at Victoria Park to reach the last eight, where they were victorious over Rovers of Glasgow by two goals to nil. In the Semi-Final they were drawn against the all-conquering Queen's Park, winners of the first two Scottish Cups, and they put up a good show in only going down 2-1 in the match played on the 8th January 1876.

Queen's Park won the Final against Third Lanark after a replay meaning they had won the first three competitions. Vale broke the early dominance of Queen's Park and went on to have a dominant period of their own, matching Queen's Park in winning the Cup three times in a row. The 1877 Final was the first not to involve defending champions Queen's Park, who lost 2-1 to Vale of Leven in the Quarter-finals. Prior to this meeting Vale knocked out Helensburgh, Vale of Leven Rovers (7-0) and then met the previous years' runners-up, Third Lanark, on the 18th November in a Third Round tie. A crowd of 4,000 gathered at Alexandria and watched a close fought tie which Vale just edged 1-0. In the next round Vale beat Busby of Renfrewshire 4-0 to set up that Quarter-Final tie with the mighty Queen's Park at Hampden.

On the 30th December 1876 someone finally beat Queen's Park in a Scottish Cup game, and that club was Vale of Leven. *The Scotsman* was there to record this historic feat and reported that "this game, notwithstanding the condition of the ground, caused by heavy rain, was one of the fastest ever played on the Queen's Park grounds. For the first time since the formation of the Queen's Park Club in 1871, they on Saturday sustained a defeat from a Scotch club, and that too in an Association tie. The Vale of Leven, which has gained this coveted honour, has been for the last three years considered the most dangerous rival of the Queen's Park in the West, but their former efforts only resulted in their defeat, the last tie between the two clubs last year ending in a victory for the Queen's Park by two goals to one. On Saturday, however, the result was vice versa." Queen's Park opened the scoring after 20 minutes after an evenly contested opening to the game. After the goal Queen's Park remained in the ascendancy but the splendid work of the Vale backs kept them in the game. In a change in the balance of play, Vale dominated from the resumption and John Baird equalised in the 65th minute. With fifteen minutes to go Baird scored a second to give Vale the lead, although the Queen's Park players protested about a foul in the build-up. The Vale of Leven team that day was: W C Wood; Archie Michie, Andrew McIntyre; Will Jamieson, Sandy McLintock; John Ferguson, John Baird, John McGregor, Bob Paton, Davie Lindsay and John McDougall.

The *Glasgow Herald's* Alexandria correspondent wrote that "about half-past four o'clock a crowd had gathered in front of the Alexandria Post Office eagerly expecting the telegram with the result of the contest. On its being read aloud a hearty cheer was given, when all ran off to spread the news, and in an amazingly short time 'Hurrah for the Vale' was echoed and re-echoed everywhere throughout the district. At 10 o'clock, on the arrival of the train with the team, the station was besieged, and the conquerors of the world-renowned 'Queen's Park' received a most enthusiastic ovation, the players being borne shoulder-high amid the cheers of the crowd. On til midnight the streets were busy with lots of the natives discussing the great football match of the season."

In the Semi-final, played on the 13th January 1877 Vale thrashed Ayr Thistle 9-0 at Kinning Park. The *Glasgow Herald* described the action as "one-sided" and "thoroughly unequal." The Vale goalscorers were, in order: John Baird, Bob Paton, John McGregor, Sandy McLintock, McGregor, Paton, Andrew McIntyre, and two more from McGregor.

There was going to be a new name on the Scottish Cup after Queen's Park had won it for the first three years. Vale of Leven became the second club to have their name engraved on the trophy when they defeated Rangers in a twice replayed Final and after a titanic struggle, played out over five hours of football. The first Final was played on the 17th March at the ground of the West of Scotland cricket club at Partick. The best chance of the first half fell to Vale, a corner kick from McLintock being headed over by McIntyre. In the second half ten minutes of early pressure from Vale saw them go ahead. After Baird had a shot well saved, a free kick taken by McLintock saw Paton score. Rangers were level though within five minutes when John McDougall inadvertently headed a Rangers free-kick into his own net. Rangers had the momentum and only the heroics of Wood in the Vale goal kept them out, *The Scotsman* commenting that "the Vale of Leven did not seem to be in as good form as we have seen them this year."

The replay was held on Saturday the 7th April at the same venue and Vale were unchanged. Very early Rangers pressure from kick off resulted in them taking the lead this time, after just seven minutes. Bill Dunlop scored, and "lowered the Dumbartonshire colours" (*The Scotsman*). Vale of Leven "freed their citadel, and the play was mostly confined to the Rangers' ground until ends were changed." Soon after the interval McDougall got on the end of a free-kick and his low shot, fired in after a goalmouth scramble brought Vale back on level terms. "Though strenuous efforts were made on either side, the usual hour and a half's play ended without any side having the advantage, and it was agreed to play half-an-hour extra." Both teams were anxious to get a conclusion to the tie and this was the first time extra time had been played in a Scottish Cup Final.

The game ended in drama in the second period of extra-time, with Rangers on the attack. Reporting on the action *The Scotsman* described that "Dunlop made a fine run down upon the Vale's lines and from the west corner took a beautiful screw shot right into the goal mouth. The ball struck the lower side of the bar, and, bounding off amidst loud shouts of 'goal' struck the ground, and in the rebound was knocked out by Wood. While the umpires and referee were conferring together the spectators rushed on to the ground shouting for the goal, and it was found impossible to clear the ground. It was ultimately decided that the Rangers had not gained a goal."

Summarising the performance of the Vale of Leven side, the *Glasgow Herald* commented that "on the side of the Vale the half-back play of Jamieson was certainly the feature of the game, this gentleman seldom allowed the ball, when it did come in his way, to pass on to the backs of his own team. McLintock's merits as a halfback scarcely require to be mentioned, save to remark that his exertions on Saturday afternoon were of the greatest service to the Vale players. Baird played best of the forwards, while Ferguson and Paton occasionally made commendable runs."

Following the pitch invasion it was decided to switch the venue to Hampden Park, the game being played on a Friday evening – the 13th! *The Scotsman* reported on the match as follows: "for the second time in the annals of the Scottish Football Association Challenge Cup, the final contest for the possession of the coveted prize had been fought over three times before a decisive result was come to. Yesterday the Vale of Leven and Rangers met, for the third time, at Hampden Park. The ground was in splendid condition. The dribbling of Baird and McDougall for the Vale of Leven...was very good...The Rangers pressed their opponents strongly till a good dodging run by Baird and McDougall relieved them. A hand by McLintock enabled the Rangers to rear the ball up, and the play was of a give-and-take nature for about twenty minutes after the kick-off, when Marshall [of Rangers] relieved his goal in good style, but the ball being well returned, Watson [of Rangers], in endeavouring to punt it out, sent it into goal and Watt [the Rangers 'keeper] was cannoned through, the success of the Vale being loudly cheered by their partisans....Half time was called without anything of consequence taking place. About 15 minutes after the kick off M McNeil getting the ball after a short run passed to Campbell, and the latter finished a good run by a long slow shot. The ball ran along the ground and Wood missing, made matters equal....After 10 minutes' play the ball, coming out of a scrimmage, was taken up by W McNeil and swiftly put through the posts. After this reverse the Vale of Leven pulled themselves together, and Baird, after a good run, took a flying shot from the side, the ball passing obliquely through the Rangers' goal. Matters were again even. In about five minutes Baird made a good shot; this Watt averted by leaving his goal, but he did not get the ball away. It was quickly passed over to Paton, who scored the third goal for the Vale of Leven [scored in the 88th minute]. After the kick-off, the Rangers beset their opponents' goal, and a shot from Campbell struck the bar, and a very exciting scrimmage ensured. The Vale of Leven, however, kept the goal till time was called, and won by three goals to two." The Vale of Leven Cup winning team was: W C Wood; Archie Michie, Andrew McIntyre; Sandy McLintock, Will Jamieson; John Ferguson (c), Bob Paton, David Lindsay, John McGregor, John McDougall and John Baird. Seven of these players would go on to earn international recognition with Scotland.

In the 1877-78 competition Vale successfully defended their trophy, beating Third Lanark 1-0 in the Final. They had a walkover in the First Round before meeting Dumbarton. They drew 1-1 at Boghead and won the replay 4-1 at North Street Park in front of a crowd of 5,000 in late October 1877. Lennox were beaten next, 3-0, before a meeting with Rangers at Kinning Park, which ended in a goalless draw. Vale won the replay 5-0 and then, on the 22nd December in stormy conditions, beat Jordanhill 10-0 for a place in the last eight. In the Quarter-finals they continued their high scoring wins, beating Parkgrove of Govan, Glasgow 5-0. For the Semi-Final they were fortunate to receive a bye to the Final, whereas it took three matches to split Renton and Third Lanark.

The Scottish Cup Final was played on the 30th March 1878 and *The Scotsman* reported that "the Vale of Leven and the 3d LRV clubs met at Hampden, the ground of the Queen's Park, to play off their final tie for the Association challenge cup and the championship. Since the inauguration of these contests the Queen's Park held the Cup for three years in succession, but last year the Vale of Leven wrested it from them, having to play the Young Rangers three times in the final before a decisive result could be arrived at. This year however, they have managed to beat their opponents (the 3d LRV) at their first meeting, a thing that has only been achieved once before since the Cup was offered for competition, and they will accordingly hold possession of the trophy for another season, along with the position of the Premier Scottish Association Club. From the form which both clubs have shown this year, and the fact that the 3d LRV have defeated the Queen's Park this season, great interest was taken in the match, and a large number of spectators turned out to witness the game. The play, however, was disappointing, very few of the fine points of the game being brought out. In the first half the 3d played with the sun in their faces, and a slight wind against them. For a short time the 3d acted on the defensive, but a fine run by Peden right into the Bale's goal caused Parlane to throw the ball over his own lines. From the corner kick McCririck headed the ball right into the goal, but Parlane again put it over the line for safety. A second corner was similarly dealt with, Lang heading it right in again, but Parlane this time managed to send the ball to Baird, who effectively raised the siege. After this till about fifteen minutes from half time the play was very even on both sides. At this stage [the Thirds 'keeper] Wallace kicked off from his own goal, and the forwards not lying up the field well, the Vale backs managed to give McDougall possession of the leather, who immediately made straight for the 3d's goal. He finished up his run with a long, low shot, the ball glancing off J Hunter's foot [a Third Lanark back] on its way. This diverted it slightly off course, and before Wallace could stop it had passed through his goal close to the bar. In the change of ends the Third assumed the offensive, and the splendid goal-keeping of Parlane alone prevented the downfall of his citadel. The result was that at the call of time the Vale were declared the winners of the game and the cup for 1877-78." The Vale Cup winning team was: Robert Parlane; McIntyre, McLintock; Jamieson, John McPherson; John Campbell Baird, McDougall (c), James Baird, McGregor, Johnny McFarlane, and Ferguson.

In the 1878-79 season Vale of Leven matched Queen's Park's record of three consecutive Scottish Cup trophy wins. Vale recorded three consecutive big wins in the early rounds. Having beaten Alclutha of Dumbarton 6-0 and then Renton Thistle 11-0 they played a local team, in the Third Round, beating Jamestown 15-0, the *Glasgow Herald* reporting that "the senior team were in fine form, and played beautifully together; while the juniors though all the time playing a losing game, yet worked so pluckily throughout that it may be said they deserved a less crushing defeat." At the end of November they were drawn at home to Govan Athletic. The ground was blanketed in snow and the match was covered by the *Glasgow Herald* who reported that "five minutes had not elapsed when J C Baird lowered the colours of the visitors, and the same thing was repeated shortly afterwards. The game now settled into a tough give-and-take nature, which continued for fully twenty minutes, after which goal No. 3 was scored from a long kick by Ferguson. A fourth goal was the result of a beautiful passing manoeuvre between J C Baird and McDougall – the latter passing the ball through. The first half ended as McDougall scored No. 5 goal in the midst of a melee. Scarcely had the ball been set a rolling again than McPherson, by a long and sure kick, dropped the ball betwixt the posts. Play continued with great energy all round, but the Vale was not to be denied – its captain now scoring goal No.7. Though playing a losing game here, a bit of deserved fortune fell to the lot of the strangers, by which Gray scored their only success. Another four goals followed for the home players by James Baird, McFarlane, McDougall and J C Baird, the game thus ending in their favour by eleven goals to one."

Vale went on to beat Beith 6-1, and then Dumbarton in the Quarter-final, before defeating Helensburgh, a surprise Semi-finalist, 3-0. Vale of Leven met Rangers again in the Final. This was Rangers' second final and Vale's third consecutive Final. After a 1-1 draw in the original match, the replay was scratched and Vale of Leven were awarded the Cup when Rangers objected to a goal being disallowed in the original match and refused to play.

The Final itself was played on the 19th April 1879 at Hampden. Rangers had the best of the early exchanges and two efforts shaved the crossbar before they deservedly opened the scoring after ten minutes through Willie Struthers. Rangers then had a second effort ruled out before Vale came back into it but they trailed at half-time. Picking up the commentary the *Glasgow Herald* reported that "with energy and eagerness on both sides the game went on apace, and although the goals were frequently in great danger the defending team managed to free themselves." As time advanced Vale became increasingly desperate and resorted to a series of long range efforts. However, into the last five minutes the Vale successfully worked the ball forward and scored through Ferguson. The *Glasgow Herald* commented that "towards the close the Vale penned their opponents, and after a long-sustained assault the Rangers' citadel was reduced - the ball, out of a loose scrimmage, rolling slowly through. Only a minute or two remained, and the match ended in a draw - one goal each." The Vale team was: Parlane; McLintock, McIntyre; James McIntyre, McPherson; McFarlane, Ferguson, James Baird, Peter McGregor, John C Baird and McDougall.

There was a protest after the game by Rangers, claiming first that an effort in the first half had crossed the line and rebounded back into play and second   around an offside goal. On the evening of Monday 19th the SFA Committee dismissed their appeal and ordered the replay to be played on the upcoming Saturday, April 26th - the referee's original decision had to stand. The Vale team put in an appearance at Hampden Park on Saturday afternoon, presumably with the expectation that the Rangers would be there to meet them. However, the Rangers did not come forward, the *Glasgow Herald* reporting that "the undecided match between the Vale of Leven and Rangers for the final Cup tie, did not come off on Saturday. The Rangers considered they had gained the cup by a disputed goal, but the Association decided that the match should be played again. On Saturday morning the Vale of a Leven Club announced that they would appear at 3:30 PM, on the Hampden Park to play off the final Cup tie disputed match. None of the Ranger Club members appearing, the Vale captain kicked off the ball, which was passed through the goal. They now put in a claim for the cup." The referee awarded the game and the Cup to the Vale. That decision needed to be ratified by the SFA, and a few days later the SFA duly award the Cup to the Vale.

At the SFA AGM three days later Rangers submitted a further letter of protest stating that "the competition had provoked an amount of ill-feeling between certain clubs, which was as uncalled for as it was disgraceful." The meeting dismissed the protest and Vale kept hold of the trophy. Rangers didn't play in another Final until 1894 - which they won. Vale matched Queen's Park's three consecutive Scottish Cup wins but never won the Cup again, despite reaching four more Finals. Ironically, in one of these, five years later, Vale themselves did not appear for a Final replay.

A key feature of the Vale's Cup winning teams was the predominance of local men, a number of them working in the local textile works such as at Dalquhurn. Consistent Scottish Cup success also brought with it international recognition for a number of players. Of the seventeen players who lifted the Cup in 1877, 1878 and 1879, nine of them went on to represent their country. The first of these was forward John Ferguson. He was the first Vale player to be capped in Scotland's third ever international on the 7th March 1874. This was a 2-1 friendly win against England at the West of Scotland Cricket Ground, Hamilton Crescent, in Glasgow. Ferguson scored his first international goal against Wales two years later and went on to score two against England in March 1877 and two against Wales in 1878 in his last international appearance. All in all he made six appearances for Scotland, the second most by any Vale player, and scored five goals. He was the player at the centre of the 'professionalism' controversy that kept Vale out of the first two Scottish Cup competitions. Another player who was already an international before the club's Cup triumphs was Sandy McLintock. He was capped in Scotland's fourth ever match, a year after Ferguson in a friendly match against England at the Kennington Oval, London on the 6th March 1875, which ended in a 2-2 draw. He was capped three times, the last in 1880. He was a full back in all three Cup winning teams and later moved to England and played for Burnley. Also capped before their Cup success was John Campbell Baird. He made his international debut against England in March 1876 and played on two more occasions, in 1878 and 1880, scoring in each match. A few weeks prior to their first Scottish Cup victory John McDougall and Johnny McGregor were both capped. They both featured, first against England, and then a few days later against Wales. McDougall was the first player to score a hat-trick in an international game, scoring three goals for Scotland against England in a 7–2 win on the 2nd March 1878 and captained Scotland in April 1879 in his last international appeared against Wales in Wrexham, which resulted in a 3-0 win for Scotland. He was capped five times in total and scored four goals. McDougall featured at centre forward in all three Cup winning teams and was the Vale club captain. McGregor was capped four times and scored once, in the 7-2 win over England in March 1878. McGregor played in the first two Cup finals, but not in the 1879 one.

Following their Scottish Cup triumphs international recognition followed, first for Andrew McIntyre and then for Robert Parlane. McIntyre was capped against England on the 2nd March 1878 and played for his country on one other occasion in 1882. He played in all three Cup finals. Robert Parlane took over the goalkeeping gloves from W C Wood for the 1878 and 1879 finals. He was capped three times by Scotland and made his debut in a 9-0 win over Wales in March 1878. The two other players from the Cup winning teams that were capped by Scotland were Robert 'Bob' Paton and John Campbell McLeod McPherson. Paton was a forward in the 1877 Cup winning team and earned two caps against England and Wales in 1879. McPherson was Vale's most capped player winning eight caps between April 1879 and 1885.

Vale's trophy defence began with a tough match against local rivals Dumbarton. They were beaten 4-3 on the 6th September 18979. Most references have the score as 4-3 to Dumbarton but the report in the *Glasgow Herald* has it as a 4-3 win to the Vale. Anyway, it's Dumbarton who played in the next round against Helensburgh and not Vale.

In the 1880-81 Scottish Cup competition Vale enjoyed a run to the Semi-Finals. They beat Renton, Helensburgh and Arbroath in the early rounds before meeting Glasgow Thistle in the last sixteen. In this game, played on the 4th December 1880, Vale scored early and added two more before the break. The Thistle resumed a man short due to injury. Taking up the commentary, the *Glasgow Herald* reported that "the game commenced with great spirit, both teams playing with considerable dash. Within five minutes from the start the Vale scored, and although the strangers played at times a splendid defensive game, the home forwards broke through them and secured another two goals during the first half of the game. At this point one of the Thistle players got slightly injured and had to leave the field. Minus a man they played with great determination, and not only defended their goal successfully for some time, but once cleverly ran the ball past the Vale backs and scored. After this the home team settled down better to work, and in rapid succession added another four goals to their credit." Vale won 7-1 and in the Quarter-Final saw off Arthurlie 2-0 to set up a Semi-Final with Dumbarton.

The two sides met on the 5th February 1881 with Vale having the home advantage. Covering the game the *Glasgow Herald* reported that "this important Cup tie which has caused intense excitement and which has been looked forward to with great interest in all football circles, came off at Alexandria. In addition to the ordinary trains from Glasgow, which were crowded, there was a special from Glasgow, and one from Dumbarton, both of which were filled to their utmost capacity. The crowd which witnessed the game was the largest ever seen on the Vale ground, and would number about 6000. Dumbarton has many things in their favour. Securing a good team early in the season, they have by constant practice and good matches brought their play to great perfection. The Vale team individually could hardly be excelled, but they never had played together in a single match this season. Saturday's game conclusively proved that without constant practice as a team it is next to impossible to be successful in a first-class match." After the early exchanges Dumbarton look the lead after ten minutes. Vale then enjoyed a good spell with some fine runs by James Baird and Paton before a shot by John C Baird grazed the crossbar. However, a counterattack from Dumbarton led to their second goal, scored after 35 minutes and the first half ended with the visitors 2-0 up. The anticipated Vale comeback did not materialise, as "the want of combination and a thorough understanding on their part became evident. Whereas Dumbarton were playing with a perfection which we have seldom seen equalled." Both goals were repeatedly besieged but no further scoring took place, with Dumbarton securing a well-earned 2-0 victory and a place in the Final. This was Dumbarton's first Final but they lost it, after a replay, against Queen's Park, who won the competition for the fifth time. At this point, the only winners of the Cup were Queen's Park and Vale of Leven.

The following year Vale also lost 2-0 to Dumbarton, this time in the Second Round. In the following season Vale reached the first of three consecutive Finals, all of which were lost, with the middle one being one where Vale would be on the wrong end of a second walkover. In the 1882-83 Scottish Cup competition they beat Milngavie Thistle 16-0 in the Second Round which was the club's record Scottish Cup win. In the following round they thrashed Hearts 8-1 before knocking out Edinburgh University and Lugar Boswell (after a replay). In the Quarter-final they beat Patrick Thistle 4-0 away and on the 24th February 1883 they met Kilmarnock Athletic in the Semi-finals. At this point in history these ties were not played at a neutral ground and Vale had the home advantage and were therefore favourites to progress. The two sides met on the 24th February with *The Scotsman* noting that "the strangers were in excellent form, and played with a dash and combination which took the spectators you surprise." Vale scored a goal after twenty minutes but this was immediately equalised and a well contested game ended in a draw. The two sides replayed the tie on the 17th March, which was played at Holm Quarry, home of the Athletic. Following a goalless first half an injury occurred to a home player who had to leave the field. Vale made the man advantage count to reach the final. In the Final they met Dumbarton, who reached their third consecutive Final, having lost the previous two.

The first game was drawn 2-2, but in the replay Dumbarton beat the Vale 2-1. This was first and only occasion on which Dumbarton have won the Scottish Cup. The first match was played on the 31st March 1883 with the *Glasgow Herald providing* a full match report: "The Vale of Leven and Dumbarton clubs met on Hampden Park on Saturday in the final tie for possession of the Association Challenge Cup, and the match, like several former final games, resulted in a draw, each club having scored two goals. Another meeting is thus rendered necessary, when it is hoped the players will be fortunate in securing more favourable weather. On Saturday a strong wind which blew across the field interfered considerably with the play, and the game was consequently far from being an open one. The Dumbarton eleven, with the wind at their backs, during the first half pressed their opponents, while on changing ends they in turn had hard work to defend their goal....It was rather unfortunate that neither club was represented by its best eleven, though in this respect the Alexandria men suffered perhaps more than their opponents...The Vale lost the services of Brown and Logan - two excellent forwards....The Vale of Leven players having lost the toss, started the game against a stiff breeze...Despite the wind, the play was confined to mid-field for some time, till a desperate scramble took place near the Vale goal...For some time McLintock was kept busy kicking off from goal, but all the efforts of the Dumbarton men to score proved futile...McIntyre and Forbes were of great service, and but for their exertions the Dumbarton forwards would undoubtedly have scored on more than one occasion....Again the Vale goal was assisted, McLintock cleverly catching the ball as it fell and sending it into play. 'Hands', however were given against the Vale in front of their posts, and the ball being sent back to Paton, the latter neatly scored the first point for Dumbarton thirty minutes after the kick-off. In five minutes the Vale forwards got the ball, but the Dumbarton men, apparently under the impression that their opponents had made a foul, did not try their usual to prevent them from scoring. Johnston, who was making the run, thus had little opposition, and on nearing the Dumbarton goal rushed the ball through. The Dumbarton captain protested against the score, but it was allowed, the decision being received with mixed cheers and hisses. Towards the close the Dumbarton forwards pressed their opponents, and a minute from half-time succeeded in scoring a second goal. The second half of the game was keenly contested. The Vale, who were a goal behind, made strong efforts to equalise matters, and though they were repeatedly in front of the Dumbarton posts, 25 minutes elapsed before they managed to elude the vigilance of McAulay [in the Dumbarton goal]. The goal was, however, at that time neatly captured by McCrae, and the result was received with deafening cheers....The excitement was very great as the game drew to a close, the ball being kept hovering in front of the Dumbarton goal; but though on several occasions it seemed as if they would be beaten, no further scoring took place, and an evenly contested game ended in a draw. The Vale of Leven Cup final team was: A McLintock; A McIntyre, J Forbes; J McPherson, D McLeish; M Gillies, R McCrae, D Friel, W B Johnston, A Kennedy and J McFarlane.

The two sides met again on the 7th April with Vale unchanged. *The Scotsman* reported that "in fine weather in the presence of 12,000 spectators, these teams played for the Scottish Association Challenge Cup, at Hampden Park, the final tie having resulted in a draw on the previous Saturday. In the first half not a goal was had by either side, though the Vale of Leven, favoured by the wind, had several fine chances of scoring. On ends being changed for the second half, Dumbarton was early at the Vale of Leven posts, and Brown (#2) after a smart run sent the ball clean through amid loud applause. For some time afterwards the game was pretty even, till Brown (#1) made a shot from the centre, taking the Vale of Leven goal, this being the second goal for Dumbarton. About ten minutes before time, the Vale of Leven, by a splendid run on the part of Friel, McLeish and McPherson, scored a goal, the ball being shot by the first named player. After this both teams did their utmost to secure an additional goal, but neither was successful, and the cup was gained by Dumbarton by two goals to one."

In the 1883-84 competition Vale started the early regional rounds with a thumping 12-0 win over Levendale, also of Alexandria, before receiving a bye in the next round. In the Third Round the club met their deadliest rivals, Renton, who had already knocked out the holders Dumbarton. In front of what is only described as a "huge" crowd at North Street Park, Vale beat Renton by the surprisingly comfortable margin of 4-1. In the next round they beat Dundee Harp 6-0. The game was goalless at half-time despite constant Vale pressure. However, playing with the wind behind them in the second half Vale scored six. They then beat Arthurlie and Pollockshields Athletic which took them to a Semi-Final, again at North Street Park (there were no neutral venues for semis in those days), against Rangers. The two sides met on the 19th January 1884 before a crowd of 7,000 at Alexandria, and Vale took the lead after half an hour although there was some discussion about whether or not the ball crossed the line. Five minutes later Vale scored again but this time there was no doubt, C McIntyre scoring a beautiful goal with an angled shot. Rangers had opportunities, both before and after half-time but they were wasteful. They were made to pay when less from ten minutes from the end Johnstone made it 3-0.

The Scottish Cup final was scheduled for Saturday the 23rd February. However by Wednesday the 20th it was clear that because of bereavement, illness and injury, three Vale first team players would be unavailable, and to make matters worse, their three reserves were also injured or indisposed. On the eve of the final the *Scottish Athletic Journal* reported that "the Vale of Leven have approached the Queen's Park in order to try and affect a postponement of the final tie, which is to be played tomorrow. The reason given is that a near relative of Forbes died this week, which should prevent him playing. The Queen's Park, owing to their numerous arrangements, were compelled to decline to grant the request; neither would the Business Committee of the Association interfere. While everybody will sympathise with Forbes, it is hardly the thing to postpone a well- advertised match because one man may be absent. It is not improbable, however, Forbes will take part in tomorrow's game." John Forbes was a key player in the Vale team. He had already been capped for Scotland on the 26th

January 1884 against Ireland in Belfast in the inaugural British Home Championship and went on to play in all three fixtures. He went on to win five caps in total for Scotland and subsequently joined Blackburn Rovers in 1888. Forbes lost his mother in the week of the match and the funeral was arranged for the same day as the Final. Vale, who also had some illness and injury, sought to alter the date of the game but the SFA refused and in protest Vale of Leven declined to participate in the match and forfeited the trophy.

The following day *The Scotsman* reported that "the final tie between Queen's Park, Glasgow, and the Vale of Leven for the Scottish Football Association Cup, which was to have been played at Glasgow this afternoon, has been declared off, owing to the inability of the latter to raise a sufficiently good team. The probability is that he Vale, not being able to play their tie on the day appointed by the Association, will be declared out of the match, in which case the trophy will go to the Queen's Park."

On the 3rd of March the matter was taken before the SFA with the *Glasgow Herald* reporting that "a meeting of the Scottish Football Association was held in the rooms, Carlton Place, on Saturday...After discussion it was agreed to award the Queen's Park the Challenge Cup in respect that the Vale of Leven failed to meet them on the day set apart by the Association for playing off the final tie."

Vale reached their third Scottish Cup Final in a row in the following 1884-85 season where they met Renton in front of the smallest crowd so far to watch a Cup Final. The game ended in a goalless draw, and in the replay Renton outplayed the Vale to win 3-1. Vale's run to the Final started slowly as they needed a replay to get past Jamestown before they went on to thrash Campsie Central of Lennoxtown 14-0. Vale then beat Yoker and Arthurlie before receiving a bye to the Quarter-Finals where they were drawn away to Glasgow side Thornliebank, who had reached the final in 1880. In an evenly matched game played on Boxing Day, Vale took the lead after just two minutes but their hosts hit back with two goals in twenty minutes. However, Vale responded and scored two of their own to lead 3-2 at the break. Each side scored another goal in the second half with Vale therefore edging it 4-3.

Vale received a home draw for the Semi-final against opponents Cambuslang and a crowd of 4,000 was present to witness a 0-0 draw. After an even start the game changed on thirty minutes when Vale's McLeish sustained an injury and had to be carried from the field, with the *Glasgow Herald* commenting that "with this misfortune matters looked serious for the home team, but they played with greater determination than ever...When play was resumed [in the second half], Vale, without the aid of one of their best men, not only succeeded in preventing the strangers scoring, but confined play very much in Cambuslang territory." Repeatedly the Vale forwards fashioned opportunities but the Cambuslang backs and goalkeeper were in fine form.

In the replay Cambuslang dominated the early passage of play and besieged the Vale goal for the first twenty minutes. Wilson made some fine saves but eventually the pressure told and Cambuslang took the lead. A few minutes before the interval a rare foray upfield by the Vale saw Galloway equalise. Taking up the story, the *Glasgow Herald* wrote "this equalised matters, and it was now evident that with the change of ends and the wind in their favour, the strangers would press the home team very hard. This proved to be the case, although the game did not turn out so one-sided as was expected. The Cambuslang men worked with great determination, and exhibited clever passing, but the strong back play of their opponents rendered all of their efforts futile. The Vale's forwards made frequent attacks on their opponent's goal, but the stalwart custodian was on the alert, and succeeded in flating the ball away. The strangers, however, were not to be denied." A goalmouth scramble saw Galloway force the ball home and although Cambuslang then enjoyed a lengthy spell of possession they crafted few chances. With ten minutes remaining Vale sent in several shots and they booked their place in the final against local rivals Renton when D McIntyre fired home to make it 3-1.

Vale were appearing in their sixth Final and were three time winners. Renton, their local rivals had only once reached the final, ten years ago, when they lost 3-0 at the hands of Queen's Park. The Final had invariably involved a Glasgow club and this was only the second occasion in the history of the Scottish Cup that the Final had not involved a team from Glasgow. Two years previously Dumbarton had played Vale of Leven. The Final took place on the 21st February 1885 and the game was played on a hard pitch, on a cold day, and in blustery conditions. The conditions were not conducive to good football and the game ended in a 0-0 draw, necessitating a replay. Covering the match, the *Glasgow Herald* wrote: "the final tie in the Scottish Football Association Cup competition was played on Saturday on Hampden Park, and resulted, as has frequently happened in the first attempt to decide the final, in a draw. Neither side managed to score a single point. To players and spectators alike the day was disagreeable. The ground was hard and slippery. This made running a matter of some difficulty, not unattended with danger, while a strong wind carried the ball high over the cross-bar, and rendered futile all attempts at scoring. A fine exhibition of the 'dribbling game' was therefore out of the question." In the first half Vale were required to defend, Renton having the best of the play and on one occasion the ball just grazed the post. The second half was a repeat of the first but with the roles reversed, with the Vale on the offensive. "Towards the close it was remarked that a win by either side could only be regarded in the light of a fluke, and a draw appeared to be the fairest termination of the game." The Vale line up was: James Wilson; A McIntyre, J Forbes; J Abraham, John Wilson; J Galloway, D McIntyre, J Ferguson, W Johnstone, M D Gillies and D Kennedy .

Seven days later the two sides met again on the 28th February in better weather conditions, but being a derby match, the play was rough with persistent fouling. McPherson replaced John Wilson for the replay in the Vale team. Covering the match *The Scotsman* reported that "at Hampden Park, these teams again met in the final tie for the Challenge Cup. There were between five and six thousand spectators, fully a third of who, had come from Dumbarton and the Vale of Leven. In the first half of the game, the ball being kicked off by the Vale, no goal was taken by either side, though Renton, playing fast and loose, signally failed to take advantage of several good opportunities to shoot between their opponents' sticks. After seventeen minutes play in the second half, Renton got the first goal, taken by McCall, and within ten minutes of time they scored two more goals, both shot by McIntyre, while the Vale managed to get one in the course of a scrimmage. Renton thus won the Cup by three goals to one, this being the first time they have been successful."

In the following year's competition Vale were knocked out by the Cup holders. In the Second Round they had beaten Bonhill 10-0, scoring five in each half and in the Fourth Round they had beaten Dundee Harp 6-0. Renton knocked them out after a replay in the Fifth Round at Alexandria, the first game ending 2-2 at Renton. In the replay, after chances for both sides and end to end action Renton took the lead after 18 minutes. In the second half a poor goal kick by Wilson led directly to a second goal for Renton. Seven minutes from the end Renton scored a third which was hotly disputed by the Vale, with Renton winning 3-0.

In the 1886-87 season Vale continued their good showings in the Scottish Cup by reaching the last four, being beaten in the Semi-Final by the eventual winners Hibernian. In their run to this stage they beat Lenzie 13-0 and Campsie 7-4 before travelling through to Edinburgh on the 22nd January 1887. Hibs had been knocked out at the Semi-Final stage for the last two years and were hopeful of making it third time lucky. *The Scotsman* covered the tie, reporting that "this tie, which had to be postponed owing to the hard character of the ground last week, was brought to an issue at Easter Road on Saturday. The tie was one looked forward to with no little interest in football circles from the fact that it was considered that the clubs were just about equal, and that the winning team would likely prove the ultimate possessor of the trophy. The teams, knowing what they had in hand, went under special preparation for the struggle, and this was apparent from the fine condition of the players when they entered the field...The interest taken in the game was shown by the crowds that flocked to the ground...and could not have been far short of six thousand." The match was a thrilling one with action passing from one end of the pitch to the other before Nicol finally opened the scoring for the Vale. A minute before half-time Hibs equalised. The second half followed the same pattern as the first with chances falling at both ends and both keepers making fine saves. "The play now became very exciting, the players, urged on by the shouts of their supporters, playing all they could to try and increase their score, and at one time it looked as if the Hibernians would take the lead as they kept Wilson penned for a considerable time, and in saving a shot he fell, and there followed something akin to a Rugby maul, the whole players being engaged in it, but Wilson managed to roll behind with the ball. The Hibernians immediately afterwards, however, out of a scrimmage, scored, and put themselves in the ascendancy by two goals to one, amid loud cheering. This success seemed to nerve the Hibernians to renewed exertions, and they completely mastered the Vale at all points, and were rewarded with a third goal...The few minutes that remained of play was one prolonged assault on the Vale goal, but no further scoring took place, and thus for the first time in the Scottish Cup competition an Edinburgh club has run into the final." Hibs went on to win the competition for the first time after they beat the holders Dumbarton 2-1 in the Final.

In the 1887-88 Scottish Cup the Vale reached the Fourth Round, surprisingly going out 3-2 to Ayr FC. The *Glasgow Herald* reported that "in Association circles the greatest surprise on Saturday came from Ayr, where the local team and the Vale of Leven played off their tie in the fourth round of the Scottish Cup. While nobody expected that the Dumbartonshire men would have a 'walk over', yet it was looked upon as a certainty that they would win. Luck, however, was against them, and everyone will regret their having to retire from the competition without being given an opportunity to try conclusions with a more pretentious team than the Ayr. After their defeat of the Dumbarton, the Vale were to some extent looked upon as the favourites for the cup, and on this account the result of Saturday's tie will be all the more regretted. It seems that the home side were somewhat disorganised in the first half, and when ends were changed the strangers were one goal to the good. Then came the surprise, for the Ayr put on three points in rapid succession. The Vale tried their utmost to equalise, but were only able to score once, and that towards the close of the game, for the defence of their opponents could not be broken down."

At the end of the season the club moved from North Street Park to Millburn Park, work commencing in May 1888 and the new ground was officially opened on the 18th August when the Vale hosted Dumbarton. *The Scotsman* reported that "the beautiful new ground of the Vale of Leven Football Club was opened on Saturday in beautiful weather, but too hot for football. The field is called Millburn Park, and is situated to the south of the village, and about five minutes' walk from the station. The playing pitch measures 120 yards by 70 yards. It is surrounded by a cinder path a quarter of a mile in length and 5 feet in breadth, except at the finishing straight, where it is 25 feet broad. The whole is enclosed by a fence of corrugated iron. The old pavilion and grand stand have been erected at the north-eastern corner. The total cost will be over £700. The ground was in good order for the opening match with Dumbarton, and about 4000 spectators were present. The proceedings were enlivened by the instrumental band and pipers of the 1st Dumbartonshire Rifles. Before the game commenced the two teams and the officials of the clubs and friends assembled in front of the pavilion, when Mr W E Gilmour of Woodbank made a short speech, complimenting the Vale Club on the beautiful field which they now possessed, and which he believed in course of time would be the finest in the West of Scotland. He then, amidst great cheering, kicked off the ball, and the two teams settled down to what proved a very pleasant and evenly contested game [which ended 2-2]...In the evening tea was served in the Albert Hotel, Alexandria, when there were present, besides the teams, representatives from the leading clubs in the West of Scotland." Unfortunately the new ground saw no Scottish Cup action in the 1888-89 season. The club went out to Dumbarton Athletic 4-2 as early as the Second Round having received a Bye in the First Round.

Vale of Leven reached their seventh and last Scottish Cup Final in the 1889-90 season but lost their fourth Final in a row to Queen's Park. They knocked out Rangers in the Third Round at the end of October after a replay, after drawing 0-0. In an eventful first quarter of an hour Rangers took an early lead, but Sharp equalised soon after. Dan Bruce then gave Vale the lead. The two goal scorers were then involved in Vale's third. Bruce sent in a long range shot which the goalkeeper parried, and Sharp was on hand to convert the rebound. Rangers came out strongly in the second half and scored in the opening ten minutes. Picking up the action *The Scotsman* commented that "in the last fifteen minutes the Rangers did magnificent work at goal, and it for the exceptionally brilliant goalkeeping of Wilson they must have scored more than once. The international custodian was never seen to greater advantage. The game ended in a win for the Vale by three goals to two. The home team got quite an ovation, several of the Vale men being carried triumphantly from the ground to the pavilion."

In the next round Vale beat Grangemouth 7-1 away and drew Hearts in the last sixteen. Despite missing Sharp, their half-back, Vale scored in the first minute from a scramble before Hearts then had the better of the play. It wasn't until the 70th minute that Vale could start to feel comfortable when James Paton added a second. Hearts got one back with ten minutes left and lay siege to the Vale goal but Vale then broke away, *The Scotsman* reporting that "with magnificent dash [Hearts] worked for a draw, and when this seemed almost within their grasp, McLachlan and Paton bolted down the field, the former centred to the latter, and he with a grand shot put in the third goal for the Vale just before the call of time."

Vale met East End of Dundee on the 21st December in their Quarter-final tie, and this was an evenly contested game for the first 30 minutes before McLachlan scored twice to make it 2-0 at half-time. An injury saw East End go down to ten men for the second period and they defended in numbers, a goalmouth scramble eventually leading to Vale's third. Bruce scored a fourth right on the call of time with a cross-cum-shot. Vale drew Third Lanark in the Semi-finals with the tie being played on the 18th January 1890. James Wilson, who had been laid up for some time, got out of his sick bed against doctor's orders to keep goal. Paton though was missing, Graham was deputising. After even play a centre by Bruce was converted by Graham. The second half followed the pattern of the first with chances at both ends. Thirds lost a man to injury which led to Vale taking the offensive and the numerical advantage counted when Graham scored again. Thirds then suffered another injury, temporarily going down to nine men. Both injured players eventually returned but time was running out and the tie was settled when Bruce scored Vale's third.

The Scottish Cup Final was set for the 8th February at Ibrox, with Queen's Park as their opponents. Hard frost and heavy fog meant the match was postponed for a week and the two teams met instead a week later. The pitch was in a poor state and there was some concern about whether the game could go ahead. Queens Park totally dominated the game and were camped in Vale's territory for much of the game, *The Scotsman* reporting that "the contest was not long in progress before it became obvious that the Queen's Park were much the superior team. Time after time they bore down on their opponents' fortress, only to see the ball go past or be returned by the ever-watchful Wilson." It was therefore against the run of play when it was Vale who took the lead after 35 minutes, when McLachlan headed in from a free kick. The second half followed the same pattern with Queen's Park making most of the running, with the occasional forage by the Vale. As the game entered the final quarter of an hour the Vale goal was under siege, *The Scotsman* commenting that Queen's Park "bombarded their opponents' goal, but the ball could not be got through. The magnificent goal-keeping of Wilson had a good deal to do with state of matters, the international custodian ring cheered to the echo for his masterly display." Taking up the commentary, the *Glasgow Herald* reported that "the excitement became great, as within a minute from the call of time the Queen's Park crowded round the Vale's goal, and a loud shout proclaimed the fact that the Queen's had scored from a foul, and thus equalised the game. The scene which followed was enthusiastic in the extreme, hats, sticks and handkerchiefs being waved in the air."

The replay was held at the same venue a week later and Vale of Leven were "unluckily defeated" according to *The Scotsman*. "The Vale of Leven appeared to be much quicker on the ball than their opponents, and that prevented the Queen's from combining in the manner usually associated with their play. The Dumbartonshire lads, as a result, gradually forced their opponents back, and compelled them to act on the defensive for some time." Vale eventually broke the deadlock through a terrific shot from Bruce and on a number of occasions nearly doubled their lead but had to settle for a one goal advantage at the break. *The Scotsman* commented that "Vale were now playing in superb style, and a victory for Queen's at this point of the game at any rate, appeared a very remote contingency." As it was, their opponents grew into the second period, and forcing a corner, headed the equalising goal. The game had hardly been restarted when Queen's continued a remarkable turnaround by taking the lead from a long range shot and Queen's Park then held on to win their ninth Scottish Cup. The Vale of Leven Cup final team that featured in both matches was Wilson; Murray, Whitelaw; Sharp, McNicol, Osborne; McLachlan, Rankin, Paton, Bruce and McMillan.

The Vale line-up included several players who were capped for Scotland. Goalkeeper James Wilson was first capped for Scotland on the 10th March 1888 against Wales at Easter Road and made one appearance each year over the following three years, earning four caps in total. Full back Andrew Whitelaw had been capped on the 19th February 1887 against Ireland in the fourth Home Championships and was capped once more in 1890 before later moving to Notts County. The other full back, John Winning Murray, who had started his career with Cowdenbeath, was capped on the 22nd March 1890 against Wales. He subsequently left the club and joined Sunderland. Winger Dan Bruce also featured against Wales and in 1891 he signed for Rangers. A week after Murray and Bruce were capped, Gilbert Rankin made his debut, scoring the first and last of Scotland's four goals as they beat Ireland 4-1 in Belfast on the 29th March 1890. He played one more time for Scotland the following year.

A few days after losing the Cup Final replay the Vale received a letter from Peter Fairly, the Secretary of Renton. It was an invitation to a meeting at Hilton's Commercial Hotel, 28 Glassford Street in Glasgow, to be held on the 28th March 1890 "to consider the question of organising League matches in Scotland." As one of the most successful clubs in Scottish football it was no surprise to see Vale of Leven being invited to join the Scottish Football League as a founder member, although by this time they were already past their prime. They only spent two seasons in the SFL though, facing a re-election vote each time. In their second season they failed to win a single game and finished last. They were the last senior Scottish club to suffer this ignominy until Brechin City in 2018. Rather than face re-election for the second time, the club withdrew.

It is such a shame that by the time the three time Scottish Cup winners joined the Scottish League they were a declining force. They opened their Scottish League account on the 16th August 1890 away at Cambuslang. In the match played at Whitefield Park they were trounced by eight goals to two. They were losing 5-0 at half-time although they did manage to score two in the second period although their scorers are not recorded. The Vale of Leven team taking the field in their first ever SFL match was: McCullum; Bell, McKenzie; W Graham, A Graham, Cormack; McIntyre, James Buchanan, McLeod, A Paterson and John Cowan.

In their second match, also played away, they lost 3-2 against Cowlairs. Vale conceded in the first minute but recovered to be level at the interval. In the second period it was all Vale and they deservedly went ahead. Cowlairs desperately strove to equalise and eventually got level. With time drawing to a close both teams sought the winner and the excitement was intense. Just as time was up Cowlairs luckily put on a third goal to snatch the win.

Milburn Park finally hosted Scottish League football on the 30th August 1890 when Vale played hosts to Abercorn of Paisley, who were making their League debut. Vale of Leven secured their first ever League points in front of a crowd of 2,000 with a 2-1 victory with goals from John Nicol and James Buchanan. Vale of Leven weren't in League action again until the 20th September, when they travelled to local rivals Renton, whom they beat 2-1. Confusion amongst the Vale backs allowed Renton to capitalise and open the scoring. Vale then lay siege to the Renton goal but only equalised five minutes before the interval through Cowan. Five minutes after the restart a brilliant run by Bruce was only ended by him being tripped from behind. A resulting goalmouth melee resulted from the free kick and the ball was forced home. This was followed by a series of attacks at either end, and Wilson made a couple of fine saves to ensure Vale won. However, when Renton dropped out of the League the result was subsequently expunged.

In the Scottish Cup Vale beat Kilsyth Wanderers in the Third Round, their opponents being the side that had beaten Renton in the opening round. All of Vale's goals were scored in the second half. The following week they lost 8-1 at Tynecastle against Hearts highlighting their contrasting fortunes in the Cup and the League. Hearts had six difference scorers, with Tommy Graham grabbing an 87th minute consolation. Vale registered back to back League wins in late January/early February over Celtic and Cowlairs. They beat Celtic 3-1 but a factor was that Celtic only played with ten men as one player failed to turn up. They continued to struggle though and on the 7th March they lost 6-0 at Abercorn and in early May Celtic got revenge thrashing them 9-1, *The*

Scotsman noting that "the Celtic played magnificently and were not too severely stretched." They ended the season with a 4-2 home defeat against Hearts, Vale scoring first (John Cowan) and last (John Darroch).

Vale of Leven faced a re-election as they finished in ninth place, second bottom, along with Cowlairs who finished at the foot of the table, and St Mirren. This would be the first of a record seven re-elections required by the club. On the 5th June they were successfully re-elected along with St Mirren. Cowlairs were not and were replaced by Leith Athletic. Renton returned and Clyde were added to an expanded First Division of 12 clubs. Vale's second season was an unmitigated disaster, as they finished bottom, with no wins from their 22 matches, all of their five points coming from draws. Vale lost all 11 away games, including 8-0 at champions Dumbarton (12th December 1891), 10-3 in the opening game of the season at Clyde (15th August 1891) and 10-0 at Leith (19th September 1891). They conceded exactly 100 goals - which would be their worst season in their history and as well as a record low number of points they also set a record for the most League defeats in a season (17).

The opening game of the season, on the 15th August 1891, set the tone for the season. They lost 10-3 at Barrowfield Park against newcomers Clyde, who had been elected to the League. Vale scored first immediately from kick off through Bruce but Clyde equalised two minutes later from a corner. Vale re-took the lead after a goalmouth scramble through Dan Friel but Clyde got back on terms again before scoring twice more while Vale added only one. Clyde scored five times in the first fifteen minutes of the second half and totally dominated the second half with Vale playing a defensive game as they played with only ten men.

This opening loss was followed by three consecutive defeats in which they failed to score and then three really heavy defeats. Vale lost their first nine matches in a terrible run which included a 6-1 home defeat against Rangers (12th September 1891). On the 19th September they lost 10-0 away against the other newcomers Leith Athletic at Bank Park. The result was a club record SFL defeat. *The Scotsman* wrote "at Bank Park, the Leith Athletic secured a great victory over the once famous Vale of Leven by the large score of ten goals to nil. The visitors came without their renowned goalkeeper, Wilson, and three others of their customary eleven...the Vale assailed continuously for a lengthy period, and there was no mistake that they were having the home team at every point. Ultimately...[though, it was Leith who]... drew first blood twenty minutes after the start. Up to this point the play, in short, had been tame. The Vale retaliated strongly, but the Athletic were now fairly under way and a prolonged attack on the back division of the visitors followed. Sturdy was the defence...but the goal was doomed to fail, and with a grand attempt M. McQueen put on the second point. The

Athletic had the better of improved play up to half-time, when the score was: Leith Athletic, two goals; Vale of Leven, nil. On the game being restarted the Vale led the way... [but]... while the Vale were playing with but ten men, Busby having a minute previously been rendered hors de combat, the third goal was scored amid much enthusiasm." Their opponents then added four more goals in quick succession. "In the last thirty minutes of the game the Leith men were continuously around Henderson [in the Vale goal]. The double figure followed just on time, and the game resulted:-Leith Athletic, ten goals; Vale of Leven, nil." Vale then went on to concede six goals in Paisley twice, first against St Mirren and then against Abercorn. In the match against St Mirren at Westmarch they actually scored four goals, although not until they were 4-0 down. Rice got one back before the break and Bruce scored two to get the score to 5-3, with McFarlane scoring their fourth.

The club's first point of the season eventually came in their tenth game, after nine consecutive losses, with a 2-2 draw at home to Clyde on the 17th October. After an even start a mistake on the part of Cornoch, the Vale back, enabled Harvie to score for Clyde. After several chances had gone begging for Vale, Walter Bruce eventually equalised on the half hour mark and the two sides went into the break level at 1-1. The home team lay siege to the Clyde goal but it was the away team who retook the lead. With less than 15 minutes to go David Tait managed to beat Fortune in the Clyde goal to equalise. Both teams strove to win the game leading to an exciting finish.

 A week later they conceded six against Celtic, John Madden scoring a hat-trick. Two consecutive home draws followed against Hearts and St Mirren before two heavy defeats in the two games they completed in December. First came an 8-0 thrashing away against joint champions Dumbarton at Boghead on the 12th, *The Scotsman* reporting that the game was played "in a perfect storm of sleet and rain. Neither team was fully represented. The Vale played with the elements in their favour in the first half, but in the opening minute Taylor had a goal for Dumbarton. The Vale men got several corners in succession, but they were nearly all badly placed, and the home team again took up the running. Twenty minutes after the start Miller got a second point, and immediately after Bell was the means of piloting through a fine pass from Thomson. Before half-time a nicely placed ball from McDonald was scrimmaged through. Although the Vale had an immense advantage with the storm at their backs Dumbarton had the game almost wholly in hand. Half time: Dumbarton four; Vale nil. Just after the kick-off Taylor again notched for Dumbarton, McNaught (2) and Thomson raised the total to eight, and when twenty minutes of this half had gone the Vale gave up the game to Dumbarton. The storm was pretty severe at this time, but the referee would not stop the game and the Vale were very wise to give up playing." This was followed by a Boxing Day mauling at the hands of Third Lanark where Vale lost 9-2.

Thirds scored two early goals and add more at regular intervals, leading 5-0 at half-time. As in the first half Thirds scored early on, adding three more within the first ten minutes. Vale now responded and scored twice and also hit the bar before Thirds scored a ninth near the end.

Two home defeats followed in the first games played in the New Year and they failed to score in their first four games of 1892, losing 7-0 at Rangers in February, which left them facing a re-election vote with just three points from 19 games. Vale concluded their travels with another 7-0 defeat, at Tynecastle against Hearts on the 19th March and they finished their programme with two home draws, bringing their total of points up to five, but finishing winless and 11 points adrift of Cambuslang in eleventh position. Their last League game was a 1-1 draw against Renton on the 7th May 1892, in which they came from behind with Bryan scoring the equaliser.

At the League's AGM on the 3rd June 1892, it was voted that the number of competing clubs would reduce from 12 to 10 for the next season. The usual bottom three clubs had to apply for re-election but for only one place. The League also received applications from four non-league clubs: Kilmarnock, Cowlairs, Northern and St Bernard's. In the election, St Mirren received 11 votes and Cambuslang 7. All the other applicants, including Vale received no votes. As St Mirren got the most votes they retained their League status meaning Cambuslang and Vale of Leven, two of the original founding clubs, lost their League places. Cambuslang never returned but Vale of Leven would make a return in 1905.

Vale of Leven had suffered the ignominy of becoming the first club to go the entire League season without a win. This unwanted record was only shared 126 years later in the 2017-18 season when Brechin City of the Championship (second tier) went the entire League season without victory in being relegated to League One. Vale withdrew from the League with debts of £500 and played in the Scottish Alliance for the 1892-93 season, finishing eighth in the ten team competition. But with crowd levels barely covering expenses they dropped out, and between 1893 and 1902 they played only friendly matches, which helped to relieve their financial situation. They made a couple of Scottish Cup appearances, on both occasions going out in the First Round. In 1893 they lost at home to Dumbarton 2-1 and in 1902 they lost 4-0 at home to Partick Thistle. By the time of this second Cup tie they had joined the Scottish Football Combination, a competition that had been formed in 1896. They finished bottom in their first season but improved significantly the following year, coming in third.

Vale of Leven eventually re-joined the Scottish Football League in 1905, entering the Second Division following the expansion of this division, when two new teams were added. At the Scottish Football League's AGM held on the 22nd May 1905, four places were available –the two clubs contesting re-election were St Bernard's and Abercorn, plus there were two new places due to League expansion. Ten clubs contested these four places. St Bernard's topped the voting with 23 votes and were re-elected along with Abercorn who received 19 votes. Cowdenbeath, who finished second behind Dundee 'A' in the Northern League, secured 18 votes to take the first of the additional places and Vale of Leven, as the reigning Scottish Combination champions, secured the last place with 17 votes, comfortably coming ahead of Ayr Parkhouse who came in fifth with 7 votes.

Vale of Leven competed in ten League seasons in the Second Division up to the 1914-15 season, twice finishing as runners-up, but also in the last five seasons never finishing any higher than eleventh place. Vale didn't make a great return to life as an SFL club, finishing second from bottom in the 1905-06 season. They played their first match back on the 19th August 1905, when they drew at Merchiston Park, Falkirk, 1-1 against East Stirlingshire, Vale coming from behind with Ritchie setting up Robertson for the equaliser. A week later Millburn Park saw League action once more, as they beat St Bernard's 3-2. Alex Galbraith gave Vale a 1-0 half-time lead. Immediately on the resumption centre-forward Ritchie made it 2-0 with a low shot. Smith got a third before an injury to McGimpsey saw the inside left carried off. Playing a man short St Bernard's scored two goals but Vale clung on for the brace of points.

Having picked up a win and a draw in their first two games Vale then lost five in a row culminating it in a 5-1 defeat at Ayr FC, played in rough stormy weather. The visitors led 1-0 at half-time but conceded five in the second half, not helped by again going down to ten men due to injury. The club recovered a bit after this reverse against Ayr in early October by taking five points from their next three games so that by the beginning of November they were sixth in the table. However, they failed to win across the month of November before eventually beating bottom side Abercorn in early December. Despite conceding after just three minutes Vale were on equal terms by half time and took full advantage of the visitors playing with ten men for most of the second half with McGimpsey scoring a brace, and Stewart, an ex-Hibs player scoring from a penalty kick.

The club only picked up one more point on their travels, failing to win any of their away games, and despite a couple of home wins in January 1906 they eventually finished second bottom, four ahead of East Stirling at the foot of the table and just one behind Cowdenbeath and Abercorn. At the League's AGM held on the 21st May Vale were successfully re-elected, coming first in the voting with 22 votes. Their cause was assisted with further League expansion so that four places were available, for which a record 13 clubs applied. East Stirlingshire were also successfully re-elected and Dumbarton returned to the League. Making up the quartet were Ayr Parkhouse, who beat Alloa Athletic and Dunfermline to the last place.

The 1906-07 season saw a much improved performance as Vale of Leven finished as runners-up. They were particularly strong at Alexandria, winning nine of their eleven home matches. They started well, winning four out of their first five games, with the only defeat being a 5-4 loss at Arthurlie, where they had led 2-1 at the break. They then won their next three matches, including two away wins at Abercorn and Ayr FC, the 2-1 away win at Ayr seeing them go top of the division. They experienced mixed fortunes during the autumn and a dodgy spell during November and early December saw them only pick up one point from four games. Three consecutive wins in December saw them in a three way tie at the top with Leith Athletic, Dumbarton and themselves all on 21 points, although St Bernard's in fourth were five points behind but had played six games less. However this run came to a sudden end with a 5-0 loss at Raith Rovers, although they immediately bounced back with a win in their first match of 1907, where they recorded their biggest SFL win to date, a 6-0 victory over Albion Rovers with braces from both Brown and O'Brien. In their next game they beat Division leaders Leith away 3-2 to go top again. Leith led 2-0 at half-time but as a result of playing the second half with only ten men Vale scored three. The following Saturday they beat Cowdenbeath 6-0, with O'Brien and Brown again both scoring two apiece, to go four points clear of Leith, although St Bernard's also won.

The weather disrupted the League programme and Vale didn't play at home again for nearly two months. During this time St Bernard's picked up three points from three matches to close the gap at the top to four points, and they still had six games in hand! The two sides met on the 16th March which would be Vale's last League game of the season, and they effectively surrendered the Second Division title with a 1-0 loss. The result left St Bernard's just two points leaders Vale with six games still to play. St Bernard's drew their next three games, the third of these at Raith securing them the championship honour, with the Vale eventually finishing five points adrift, finishing level on points with Arthurlie in second. At the League's AGM held on the 27th May Vale of Leven made an unsuccessful attempt to be elected to the First Division, along with Dumbarton, Leith, Raith and St Bernard's, as the three existing First Division clubs – Hamilton, Kilmarnock and Port Glasgow Athletic – were all returned to the top flight.

Vale experienced a bit of a see-saw in performance as the following year they finished a lowly tenth place. Although they won their opening game 4-0, beating East Stirlingshire with goals from Robertson, Carr, Fitzpatrick and McCallum, they proceeded to lose three out of their next four games, including a 3-0 loss at Starks Park against eventual champions Raith Rovers. They only won once more in their next ten games but recovered with a 4-1 win over Albion Rovers at the end of November and they beat Abercorn 2-1 in their last game of the calendar year to finish 1907 in sixth place. They only recorded one more win in their remaining nine games and drew each of the last four matches to drop to tenth place in the twelve team division, narrowly avoiding the need for a re-election vote.

In the 1908-09 season Vale of Leven made a sustained challenge for the Second Division title, taking the championship race into the penultimate game. They only lost six League games all season, a club record, and conceded a club record low of 25 goals. Vale won their first three games without conceding a goal, beating Ayr FC, Arthurlie and Cowdenbeath. They didn't play again during the months of October and November and then repeated the feat in December. A 4-1 win in the New Years' Day fixture over Arthurlie saw them in fourth place in the table, nine points off the top but having played no less than six games fewer than those above them. The following Saturday they thrashed Albion Rovers 5-0, scoring four goals in the first half.

On the 6th February 1909 the Vale travelled through to Paisley to face the leaders Abercorn. Long in goal made some crucial saves and they were fortunate to come away with a 1-1 draw. A fortnight later they beat another title contender, Raith Rovers, coming back from conceding in the first five minutes to win the game 2-1. The result saw them up to fourth place but they still had 6-7 games in hand on the teams above them. At the end of February they played the return home game against the leaders. In front of a 2,000 strong crowd Vale took the lead in the first half and did most of the pressing in the first fifteen minutes of the second half. Abercorn pushed all out for a deserved equaliser but Vale held on to win 1-0. They were now six points behind the leaders but with six games in hand. However, Vale had a poor March and dropped points in draws against Leith and East Stirlingshire. On the 20th of the month they lost 2-1 away at Ayr FC suffering a real blow to their title hopes. They took the lead in the first half but Ayr scored twice in the second and they tried hard for the equaliser but on balance Ayr deserved to take home both points. On the same day Abercorn beat the other side from Ayr, Parkhouse, 4-0. Vale bounced back with a 2-1 home win over Leith to move up to 27 points with two games remaining. Abercorn had finished their programme and led on 31 points and likewise, Raith had finished their matches and had amassed 28 points. Vale of Leven's task was simple – win both of their remaining matches to tie with Abercorn.

On the 17th April Vale played the first of these two matches which would determine the fate of the Second Division championship. They hosted Ayr Parkhouse and were expected to win given that Abercorn had beaten them 4-0. Covering this match *The*

Scotsman reported that "fully two thousand spectators assembled at Alexandria to witness the return game between these teams in the race for the Second League Championship. Parkhouse, with the wind in the first half, scored through Hutchieson. Then Findlay equalised from a penalty kick, and at the interval the score stood one each. The Vale had the better of the second half, but they failed to beat down a stubborn defence, the match ending in a draw - one goal each. By this result the Vale are now out of the running for the Second League Championship, which now falls to Abercorn." With their title hopes gone Vale played a weakened team in their final fixture, losing 5-0 at Albion Rovers. At the League's AGM only Raith Rovers and Dumbarton applied for membership of the First Division but the existing clubs - Morton and Patrick - were retained.

Vale couldn't repeat a promotion challenge in the 1909-10 season, despite good home form. Any hopes were undermined by their away form as they only picked up one win on their travels. At the beginning of October they lost 6-1 in Edinburgh against St Bernard's but they then only lost one of eight games after that and at the end of November they were the joint leaders with Raith, although they had played four more games. In their last game of 1909 they beat Cowdenbeath 2-0 with a goal in each half from Browning and Robertson to stay in second place. They only had five games left to play in 1910 and unfortunately they didn't win any of them, picking up a solitary point to drop down to sixth place.

In their last five seasons before the First World War the club struggled, finishing in the bottom three on each occasion and actually finishing bottom in the 1910-11 and 1914-15 seasons. In the first of these they only won four games all season in a campaign where goals were few and far between. They only scored 21 in their 22 games but then only conceded 28. They didn't suffer any heavy defeats and eight of their ten defeats were by a single goal. Vale failed to win any of their first eight games, only picking up three draws. They got their first win at the end of October, staging a late comeback at Cowdenbeath, with Sneddon and Robertson scoring the goals near the end of the game to win 2-1. At the end of November they beat Dundee Hibs and then narrowly beat second placed Port Glasgow Athletic 1-0 with a goal by Anderson. They lost 2-0 on Hogmanay away at St Bernard's, although they didn't deserve to lose a close game in which Anderson had a goal ruled out for an earlier infringement. By this time they were in eighth place, having played 17 games - only one less than Leith and East Stirling combined - the two teams at the bottom.

The weather disrupted fixtures in early 1911 and when the matches recommenced Vale lost three of their last four fixtures. On Saturday the 8th April 1911 Vale played their last game of the season as they hosted Leith Athletic. Vale were second from bottom on 16 points with just this game to play. Below them were Abercorn on 15 points, but with three games to play. Above them, and currently avoiding the need to face a re-election vote was East Stirlingshire, on the same number of points as Vale, but also with three games still to play. The game was therefore a must win one for Vale of Leven. The visitors scored twice in the first twenty minutes before Howat got one back just before the interval. Trailing 2-1 they made the worst possible start to the second half, conceding after two minutes. The Vale strove hard to get back on level terms but fortune was against them and they lost 3-1. Other results went against them as the teams around them, with games in hand, won their matches. East Stirling beat Dumbarton 2-0 and Abercorn beat Albion Rovers 1-0 which guaranteed that Vale would finish bottom, regardless of how the remaining games went.

Vale were re-elected unopposed at the League's AGM but made no improvement the following season, finishing joint bottom with Albion Rovers with just 13 points. They scored the fewest number of League goals in a season, notching up only 19, less than a goal per game. They won their opening game against Cowdenbeath on the 19th August 1911. In the early stages it was their hosts who made all the running and so when they opened the scoring it was against the run of play. A second goal soon followed and a third, via a penalty kick, was scored in the second half, all of the goals coming from Vale's centre-forward Anderson.

Vale then proceeded to lose five of their next six matches, the last of these a 5-0 defeat in Edinburgh against St Bernard's. This result left them second from bottom with three points from seven matches (five defeats), just a point above Cowdenbeath, who had played three fewer matches. A 1-0 away win against Dundee Hibs brought 1911 to a close on a positive note and placed them ninth, the win putting some daylight between them and their vanquished opponents – Vale were now four points clear of both Dundee Hibs and Albion Rovers at the bottom. The club lost all four games played in 1912. The last of these was played on the 2nd March and Vale went into the game just outside of the bottom two. Albion Rovers and East Stirlingshire were at the bottom on 11 points, with Vale and Dundee Hibs two points ahead. Like Vale, Albion Rovers were playing their last games whereas East Stirling still had five games to play. Vale were away at East Stirling for their last game and lost 2-0, both goals coming in the second half. In the only other game Albion Rovers beat Dumbarton 2-1. Four teams were now on 13 points but Vale and Albion Rovers had finished their programmes and were placed in the bottom two. Both were re-elected unopposed at the League's AGM on the 3rd June as the Second Division was increased in size to 14 teams with Dunfermline Athletic and Johnstone joining the League.

At the beginning of the 1912-13 season Vale secured a win and a draw before losing heavily at the reigning champions Ayr United 6-0, their hosts scoring three in each half in a one-sided encounter. They continued to struggle although in their last game of 1912 they did beat Leith 5-0 at Millburn Park, Miller, the Vale centre-forward scoring a first half hat-trick. In the second half Ballantyne and Horn added two more goals and Miller had two efforts ruled out for offside. The result took them up to fourth, just two points off the top spot, but this was an artificial placing, as they had played three or four more games than all of the other teams in the division. As the season progressed they were gradually overhauled and at the end of February they lost 5-0 at Whifflet against Albion Rovers. They eventually finished in 12th place, above Arthurlie and Leith.

The Second Division reverted back to 12 teams for the 1913-14 season following the promotion of champions Ayr United and Dumbarton into a First Division now expanded to twenty teams. Vale only won five matches and finished second bottom with 13 points, just one ahead of Johnstone. In a largely uneventful season they lost four-nil on three occasions. The first time occurred in just their second match of the season, away at St Johnstone at the end of August. A month later they repeated the score line, this time away at Abercorn. Vale lost four of their last five games, including a 4-0 loss at bottom side Johnstone, picking up only a single point.

At the end of the season Vale faced a re-election vote and this time it was contested. Due to League expansion there were four places available and the two clubs facing re-election were joined by four Central League clubs – Bathgate, East Fife, Forfar Athletic and Lochgelly United – and Clydebank. At the League's AGM on the 5th June Clydebank, who had only been formed the previous February, surprisingly topped the first ballot, beating Vale of Leven by one vote. Vale were successfully re-elected in the second ballot, topping a five club poll with 29 votes. Johnstone were also re-elected and Lochgelly United entered the League.

Vale continued their poor run of finishing in the bottom three in the 1914-15 season and finished bottom or joint bottom for the third time in five seasons. The Second Division was once again up to 14 teams with the addition of Clydebank and Lochgelly United. Vale won only four times and equalled the club record of most defeats in a season with 17, and they lost all 13 away matches. On the 14th November they suffered a heavy loss, losing 7-2 at Dunfermline Athletic. The *Edinburgh Evening News* reported that "the Athletic were superior in all departments, and especially in the second half gave the Vale no chance. It was unfortunate that so much feeling was displayed amongst the players, and it would have been much better had the referee taken up a much firmer attitude from the commencement. The rough play and disregard for the rules culminated in Cairns (Dunfermline) and Bell (Vale) being sent off the field." Their best win of the season came in mid-January 1925 with a 5-1 win over Abercorn. Little over a month later they suffered a record club home SFL defeat, losing 7-1 at Alexandria to St Bernard's. "Vale were in straits for a team...[but gave St Bernard's]...a shake up by scoring the first goal" (*The Scotsman*). Conceding the first goal did indeed give the Edinburgh side a shake as they went on to score four first half goals in reply and then added three more in the second period. A week later they made it a dozen goals conceded in two matches when they lost 5-1 at bottom side Arthurlie. This was only Arthurlie's fourth win of the season and they moved ahead of Vale, eventually finishing three points clear of them at the bottom. Both sides were re-elected unopposed at the League's AGM on the 31st May as there were no applicants from any non-League clubs.

At the end of May 1915 the Second Division was disbanded due to the First World War and the clubs affected joined a number of non-league clubs in forming two regional leagues, the West of Scotland League and the Eastern League. Vale of Leven competed in the new Western League which consisted of six ex-Scottish League clubs - Abercorn, Albion Rovers, Arthurlie, Clydebank, Johnstone and Vale of Leven, former League members Renton and five non-League clubs - Dykehead, Royal Albert, Wishaw Thistle, Stevenston United and Dumbarton Harp. Vale were champions of the new competition for the 1915-16 season.

When the Second Division wasn't reformed by the Scottish Football League in 1919 Vale of Leven were one of a dozen clubs to lose their League status and they continued to play in the Western League. Vale played in the Scottish Cup in the 1919-20 and 1920-21 seasons. In the first of these they threatened an upset when they led 1-0 away against Third Lanark, and only lost to a late winner. The following year they lost 3-0 at home to Celtic in front of a crowd of 3,000. The game was scoreless at half-time and both sides missed a penalty.

At a Scottish Football League meeting on the 11th May 1921 the League finally agreed to the restoration of the Second Division, including automatic promotion and relegation. Vale of Leven were reinstated into the Scottish League for the 1921-22 season and they played for five more seasons between 1921-26. In 1924 they were relegated to the new Third Division after three seasons, which would ultimately seal their fate as a League club, when this division was abandoned in 1926.

Vale made a good start to their resumption of League football, finishing fourth with a club record points tally of 44 and a club record of most League wins in a season (17). They opened their campaign on the 29th August 1921 when they beat Forfar Athletic 5-0 at Milburn Park in front of a crowd of 3,000. The match had a sensational opening with a Jimmie Donald, the Vale's outside-right scoring in the opening sixty seconds. Four minutes later Tommy Burns scored a second from a corner and Donald added a third on the half hour mark with a left-foot drive. The second half also had a lively start with McAulay, the inside-left scoring a couple of goals within five minutes of the restart. The team taking the field on the resumption of the League was: Hagen; Brown, Clark; Blander, McCallum, Livingston; Donald, Burns, Jackson, McAulay and McMillan.

Vale lost their next game but won the next three and were unbeaten throughout October, and a 2-0 away win at Tannadice against Dundee Hibs (goals from Jackson and Charlie McCallum) on Hogmanay left them in third, six points behind runaway leaders Alloa Athletic but only three off second placed Cowdenbeath. Three consecutive draws and a 4-0 loss at Alloa (in which Crilley scored a hat-trick) in January 1922 saw them slip down to fifth. They lost 4-0 away at leaders Alloa in late January and went out to the same team in the Second Round of the Scottish Cup, after a replay. Back to back defeats in early February away at Johnstone and Armadale and a 0-0 draw at home to Cowdenbeath in March saw them end of any hopes of finishing as runners-up and they eventually finished in fourth place, one point behind Armadale in third, three behind Cowdenbeath in second and a whopping 16 points behind champions Alloa.

For the 1922-23 season Vale fielded a much changed team with only Charlie McCallum and Jimmie Donald featuring from the team that started the previous season. They lost their opening game against Cowdenbeath before beating Clydebank 2-1. Clydebank later had two points deducted for playing John Swan against Vale while he was ineligible. They also won their next match 4-3 against East Stirlingshire to briefly top the division but mixed fortunes followed with a 5-1 win over King's Park at the beginning of November the highlight, with Willie Walker their centre-forward scoring a hat-trick to leave them mid-table. This would turn out to be their last victory of 1922 as they went the next nine games without a win, which meant that by the turn of the year they had dropped to 16th place. They beat Dunfermline on the 2nd January by the odd goal in a nine goal thriller but continued to struggle. Home wins in March against Broxburn and St Bernard's saw them eventually finish in 17th place, only narrowly avoiding a re-election vote, although this was superseded by the creation of a new Third Division.

Another season of struggle would mean relegation and sure enough, Vale finished second from bottom, and were relegated into the third tier of Scottish League football. Form was mixed to begin with but they had built up a reasonable cushion over the bottom sides. When Browning, an ex-Celtic player had scored the only goal of the game on a frost bound pitch at East Fife at the end of December 1923 the Vale were in 16th place, seven points clear of Arbroath in 19th position. Vale went winless for their next seven League matches so that by the time that sequence was ended with a 2-1 away win at bottom club a Lochgelly United, on Wednesday 20th February 1924, they were third bottom, one point ahead of Arbroath with 20 points, with Lochgelly detached at the bottom on just seven points. Vale dropped into the bottom two on the 8th March after suffering a 5-0 loss at Albion Rovers, suffering a double-whammy with Arbroath winning 3-1 at Johnstone.

Vale then recorded consecutive wins at the end of March, beating King's Park and Stenhousemuir. On the 5th April the Vale made it three wins in a row when they beat relegation rivals Broxburn. The game was goalless at the break but there was no mistaking Vale's superiority in the second half. McLardie opened the scoring after 56 minutes and the same player scored a second six minutes later, with Fleming making it 3-0 in the last ten minutes. Lochgelly United at this point were already doomed. With St Bernard's losing, and with three games left to play, the final relegation place would come from one of Vale, Arbroath and Broxburn who were all level on 28 points or St Bernard's who had 30.

A week later their good run came to an end when they lost 4-1 away at Johnstone, McDonald scoring a hat-trick for the hosts. In the other matches Broxburn beat St Bernard's to join them on 30 points but Arbroath also lost 3-0 at Bo'ness. On the 19th April, in the penultimate round of games, Vale got a crucial victory over Armadale, winning 3-2 despite playing part of the second half with ten men. However, there were positive results for their rivals as well. Arbroath also won beating Alloa 1-0 and Broxburn secured safety with a 3-2 win over Lochgelly. The result of all of this was that Vale, Arbroath and St Bernard's all went into the final game on 30 points. However, Vale's goal average was worse, having scored fewer and conceded more. They therefore needed to better the results of the other two clubs in the final round of matches.

On the 26th April Vale of Leven travelled through to Bo'ness. Their hosts dominated possession and led 1-0 with ten minutes to go. At this point the Vale centre-forward Angus Urquhart got an equaliser, which set up a frantic last ten minutes but unfortunately they couldn't force a winner. It would have all been academic though as both Arbroath and St Bernard's won their games and the Vale finished a point behind them and were relegated to the new Third Division.

Vale played in the second season of the new Third Division and opened life as a third tier team with a 4-1 away win at Helensburgh on the 16th August 1924. Burns opened the scoring for Vale and although Laurie equalised for Helensburgh from the penalty spot the Vale continued to dominate and Wyllie scored twice and Reid added a fourth.

Vale were tipped as one of the favourites and this was cemented with a 3-0 home win over Galston. They then unexpectedly came down to earth with a bump with a 4-1 loss against Dykehead. This defeat seemed to spur them on and the Vale then won nine games in a row between the 6th September and the 1st of November – a club record. They hit the top of the division with a 1-0 win at Palmerston Park against Queen of the South on the 20th September and a week later they registered their biggest win of the season at the expense of Montrose, *The Sunday Post* reporting that "the feature of the game was the clever play of Urquhart, the Vale's centre, who scored five of the six goals for his side. The visitors counted first, through McCoy, but Urquhart scored twice before the interval for the Vale. In the second half, Urquhart (3) and McCabe put the Vale further ahead, and near the close McCoy again scored for Montrose." As part of their winning run they also beat Beith 5-2, Urquhart and Jackson each grabbing a brace, and on the 1st November they achieved their ninth win in a row with a 6-0 victory over Clackmannan, in which Jackson scored four and Urquhart got the other two. They now had 11 wins from 12 matches and were five points clear of Solway Star in second. *The Sunday Post* commented that "whatever may happen later on, there can be no denying the fact that Vale of Leven are going to take a lot of stopping on their way to the Third Division flag." The only downside was that Vale of Leven were twice censured by the League and fined and ordered to pay compensation to Galston and Montrose for reducing gate admission prices.

On the 8th November the Vale surprisingly failed to make it ten wins in a row as their winning sequence was ended by a surprising 4-2 loss at third bottom Brechin City. *The Sunday Post*, reported that "the game was keen and vigorous throughout and the locals deserved their victory because of sustained virile play. There was no denying the superiority of the locals in the first half, even against the incline, but later it was more even...Urquhart was well watched." Vale's last game of 1924 was the reverse game against Helensburgh where they were held 2-2 but they still ended the year two points clear at the top. They continued to be promotion contenders in 1925, competing against the Dumfries and Galloway trio of Nithsdale Wanderers, Queen of the South and Solway Star. They lost their first game of 1925, 3-0 away at Clackmannan and lost again later in the month away at Galston so that by the end of January their lead was down to a point and only four points separated the top four.

Vale were then involved in a titanic struggle against fellow promotion rivals Solway Star, this time in the Scottish Cup, where it needed three games across February in order to separate them, before the Vale eventually went out. The sequence of League games that followed would prove vital as they played each of their promotion rivals. On the 21st February the top two met at Crawick Holm, the home of Nithsdale wanderers, with the two teams level on points at the top. Vale took the lead through

Reid from a corner, against the run of play. Their hosts then scored twice before the break and only the heroics of Broadley, their goalkeeper, formerly of Third Lanark, kept them in it. They were, however, completely overran in the second half as Nithsdale won 6-1 and supplanted them at the top of the table. The matches against their promotion rivals continued as Vale bounced back to beat Queen of the South 1-0 and then drew with Solway Star 0-0. Leaders Nithsdale won 4-1 away to stretch their lead at the top to three points. Vale came next with a one point advantage over Queen of the South, who had also played a game more. Solway Star were in fourth, a further three points back.

With six games left to play Vale effectively blew it. They only picked up three more points out of a possible twelve and in the end they finished fourth, despite equalling their record number of League wins in a season (17). On the 14th March they had a quick chance for revenge as they now played at home to Nithsdale Wanderers, although they missed an opportunity by being held to a 2-2 draw. *The Sunday Post* reported that "to force Vale of Leven to a draw at Alexandria was a very smart achievement on the part of Nithsdale Wanderers, and the Sanquhar men now have every reason to feel very hopeful of joined the charmed circle of the Second Division. Vale had high hopes on conquering the leaders yesterday, but Nithsdale held out to the end, and this valuable point gives intense satisfaction to their happy followers....The locals scored early on through Urquhart, but the visitors responded gamely, and Mountenay achieved a clever bit of work when he registered the equaliser. Vale, however, wanted the leading point, and when Burns scored they probably thought they were right for a victory. Ballantyne, however, came along with the equaliser, and to the end the game was fought out on the keenest lines. Urquhart came very near to getting the winning goal for the Vale. Armour played splendidly in Nithsdale's goal, and had a lot to do with the draw." Third placed Queen of the South surprisingly lost at Montrose, and Solway Star drew again, so that Vale remained three behind the leaders but were now, two ahead of Queen of the South and four ahead of Solway Star.

There were now five games remaining and Vale lost four, starting with Beith. They conceded two first half goals and although the second half was keenly contested Vale couldn't find a way to get back into the game. Although leaders Nithsdale lost 3-2 at Peebles, Queen of the South closed the gap by thrashing Galston 8-0. Solway Star were held 0-0 at home to Clackmannan. A week later only Solway Star of the top four picked up any points. Vale narrowly lost at Peebles 1-0 (who had beaten the leaders Nithsdale the week before), The *Sunday Post* reporting that "a solitary goal scored in the last second of the first half decided the issue...Craig was the scorer, his shot leaving Broadley with little chance. Despite the dearth of goals, the game was a highly entertaining one to watch. It was conducted in excellent spirit, and both teams displayed clever football. The defences were the outstanding departments in both teams, and while the forward play was quite praiseworthy the honours of the day rested with the men behind. There was not a great deal between the teams, but on the whole the Rovers' display quite warranted them winning." The leaders Nithsdale stumbled again as Helensburgh beat them 4-0, Queen of the South lost at Leith and the main beneficiaries were Solway Star who beat Lochgelly 1-0.

With three games to go Nithsdale had 39 points, and held a three point lead over Vale and Queen of the South, with Solway Star a further point back. On the 4th April, with Vale of Leven not in action, their three rivals all won, away from home. Nithsdale won 1-0 at Clackmannan, Queen of the South won 1-0 at Dykehead and Solway Star won 2-0 at Mid-Annandale. As a result Vale dropped out of the top two for the first time since the early stages of the season, although they had a game in hand on Solway and two on Queens. A week later Vale concluded their home fixtures with a 4-0 win over Brechin City, with Angus Urquhart scoring all of the goals. Brechin played the whole of the second half with ten men due to injury but they were already 3-0 down by half-time. Nithsdale were going through their own sticky patch and lost again, this time 3-0 at Beith. Queen of the South beat Helensburgh 2-0 to finish their programme and Solway Star drew 1-1 at home to Dykehead.

The top four were now only separated by three points. Nithsdale remained the leaders on 41 points, with a game to play and couldn't finish outside the top two and were assured of promotion. Queen of the South had 40 points and had concluded their fixtures. Vale of Leven were on 38 points but with two to play, and theoretically could still be crowned champions, and Solway Star also had 38 points, with one game left. With the teams so tightly bunched on points their respective positions in terms of goal average could prove significant. Here Queen of the South had the advantage, with a goal average of 2.09 (67/32), compared to Vale's 1.61 (61/38) and Solway Star's 1.43 (40/28). Due to their inferior goal average as compared to Queen of the South, Vale of Leven really needed three points from their remaining games, otherwise they needed an implausible net gain of 19 goals. Before they played again Solway Star beat Royal Albert 1-0 to move ahead of Vale and level on points with Queen of the South. This completed their programme and so it was now down to Nithsdale and Vale of Leven.

On Saturday the 18th April Nithsdale thrashed Montrose 8-0 to win the Third Division championship. Meanwhile Vale's promotion hopes were shattered at Logie Green as they lost to Leith Athletic 2-0. *The Sunday Post*, under the headline "Vale Not Going Up" reported that "requiring three points from their last two matches to beat Queen of the South for promotion, Vale of Leven turned out at Logie Green determined in victory. Leith, however, were in no mood to lie down, and, after holding their opponents for the first half, scored twice in the second, and settled the Vale's promotion aspiration." The best that Vale could now hope for would be to be tied in joint second place with Queen of the South and Solway Star on 40 points, but they would need to beat Royal Albert by an improbable 21-0 to earn promotion on goal average. The two sides met on the 25th April and Vale lost 3-0. Missing out on promotion was huge disappointment and their poor form at a crucial time was the key factor. Little did the club know of the massive consequences of missing out. A year later the Third Division was abandoned with the clubs involved losing their League status.

The 1925-26 season was Vale of Leven's last in the League although this wasn't known when the new season got underway. Vale made a convincing start on the opening day, winning 6-1 away at Solway Star on the 15th August. Vale scored in the opening minutes through Urquhart and McLachlan and although Star strove to get back on terms, Urquhart and Campbell netted again before half-time to give the away team a commanding lead. Urquhart got his hat-trick in the second half and McLachlan added his second and his side's sixth before Alexander got a consolation for Star. Vale also won their next two to briefly top the table before losing away at Royal Albert and at home to Leith.

At the end of September the Vale won a nine goal thriller, defeating Brechin City at Glebe Park 5-4. Brechin were unlucky as they lost Colin Hampton (a former Chelsea goalkeeper, playing his first game for club), to injury and he was off the field for most of the first half. Vale took full advantage and Moffat and McNab (2) scored to lead 3-1 at half-time. Urquhart and Moffat scored further goals as Vale moved into third place as the division's top scorers with 21 goals from six games. At the end of the following month Vale recorded their biggest ever SFL away win when they won 7-1 at struggling Clackmannan. O'Neill in goal made some important saves early on to deny the home team who were initially in the ascendancy. Halloran then opened the scoring after ten minutes from McLachlan's fine cross with the visitors' first real attack. Vale only held a slender lead at the break but in the second period Urquhart scored five and McLachlan got the other. A penalty was awarded against Hendry in the closing minutes for a late consolation for the hosts. The victory lifted Vale into second, just a point behind leaders Forfar, who lost at Leith, and who had played two games more.

On the 19th December Vale recorded their biggest overall SFL win when they beat Lochgelly United 8-2 on a snow covered pitch. Under the heading "Fifers Snowed Under", *The Sunday Post* reported that "as the score indicates, the Vale won as they liked. The match was played on a snow-bound pitch, and it took the home team twenty minutes before Urquhart gave them the lead from a scrimmage. Fifteen minutes later Hyslop added a second goal from a Campbell pass, while three minutes later Urquhart added a third goal with a lovely header, again from a Campbell cross. Two minutes from the interval Moffat made the total four, following good work by Campbell. Fifteen minutes after the restart Hyslop made Vale's nap hand, following further clever play by Campbell. The Fifers came more into the picture after this...[and scored two goals]... Granger had a sixth goal for the Vale, and in the last five minutes Urquhart helped himself to two other goals, making the Vale's total eight." Due to the snow a number of other fixtures were postponed, and with Helensburgh losing Vale went top by a point.

Vale lost the New Years' Day game 6-2 at promotion rivals Forfar. Vale did well in first half but were over run in the second and Forfar thoroughly deserved their win. Forfar took over the top spot from Vale who were now one point behind the Loons but with a game in hand. Vale hit back by scoring five against Montrose in their next match. Urquhart scored two of their goals in the 5-3 win but was carried off injured. On the 16th January Vale, now in third place, played second placed Helensburgh and won, 5-1 away from home, inflicting Helensburgh's first home defeat of the season. James Crawford scored first for Vale after ten minutes and Reid scored a second from a free kick and Lauderdale added a third before the home team got one back. Crawford scored twice more in the second half. The teams were actually evenly matched and the difference was O'Neill in the Vale goal. The result moved Vale above Helensburgh into second, a point behind leaders Forfar and with a game in hand.

As winter continued during January 1926 many of the teams found themselves facing a worsening financial situation. The general economic situation was poor and clearly was a mitigating factor. However, from the outset it became apparent that the small clubs involved would struggle to survive on meagre gate receipts given the travel costs and match fee guarantees required. On the 14th January 1926 fellow Third Division side Galston submitted a letter to the Management Committee of the League meeting being held in Glasgow intimating their resignation from the Scottish League. Another club, Johnstone, were only kept afloat following donations from supporters.

At the beginning of February Vale of Leven beat Johnstone 6-3. Urquhart, their goal scoring centre forward was again missing, with Hyslop playing at centre forward. After half an hour of play Lauderdale scored from a Campbell pass and a few minutes later McLachlan made it two. Craig got one back for the visitors just before the interval. The second half was only a couple of minutes old when a Lauderdale shot deflected off the boot of Miller, the Johnstone right back into the net for a 3-1 lead. Johnstone got another one back before Lauderdale added a fourth. Hyslop scored a fifth and McLachlan got a sixth before Gilchrist scored the visitors' third goal.

Vale then surprisingly lost their next two matches, 3-1 at Beith and 2-1 at home to Solway Star and by the time they earned their next point in a 1-1 draw in Shotts against Dykehead they were down in fourth place. They then lost a lost vital home game against Forfar at the end of March, *The Sunday Post* reporting that "Forfar were a trifle fortunate to take both points from Vale of Leven. The Alexandria men were clever in outfield work, but the inside forwards finished poorly and good chances were lost. Forbes scored the only goal of the game half an hour from the start, giving O'Neill no chance from close range."

On the 3rd April 1926 what turned out to be the final Scottish Football League match was played at Millburn Park with Vale of Leven drawing 2–2 with Mid-Annandale. Mids took the lead before Moffat equalised five minutes before half-time. The visitors went ahead again in the second half but Lawson quickly drew Vale level. At this point Vale still had four games to complete but a number of clubs were struggling to fulfil fixtures. A week later *The Scotsman* reported that "the Vale of Leven were unable to fulfil their fixture with Montrose at Montrose. Owing to the dull trade in the Vale of Leven and the extra expense caused by the long railway journeys, the directors of the club have found it difficult to carry on this season. Last Saturday week, against Mid-Annandale at Alexandria, they did not draw the guarantee, with the result that several of the players who did not receive their wages for that game refused to travel to Montrose on Saturday. In addition to that several of the players were injured and suffering from influenza. The return fare to Montrose was 16s 1d and the club were not able to meet the expenses. That, added to the fact that they could not raise a team, left the Vale officials no alternative than to put the match off. For several seasons now the district has been badly hit through the lack of employment. A few years ago the Vale club erected a covered terracing at Millburn Park, Alexandria, and against that there is an overdraft at the bank amounting to £800. That overdraft has been a great drawback to the club. The affairs of the Third Division of the League appear to be in serious condition. Most of the clubs are carrying on under difficulties, and it is known that several of them will not continue in it next season under the existing conditions."

The following day, under the headline "Vale of Leven FC Revolt - Players go on strike for wages", *The Sunday Post* reported that "Vale of Leven, after their long history, are in a very bad way. Yesterday they were unable to muster a team, the reason being given as 'financial difficulties'. The cause of the trouble is that the players, not having been paid for their last week's services, are in revolt. Last Saturday the Vale played Mid-Annandale, and drew as gate money the sum of £13 2s 19d. From this they paid the visiting club £10, £5 short of the Third Division guarantee, and after meeting the referee's fee and other expenses they were left with 2s 10d to pay the players' wages. A hurried search was made, but the wherewithal could not be found, so the players had to depart empty-handed. On Tuesday evening the players held a meeting to consider what action they should take, and apparently they decided to go on strike, for yesterday four players turned up at Buchanan Street Station in time for the ten o'clock for the North, and these four were not present at the players' meeting earlier in the week. The Supporters' Club also held a meeting on Thursday evening, but feverish activity on the part of this organisation, which has done much to help the finances of the football club, failed to find any means to alleviate the club's pecuniary embarrassment." The Third Division ultimately collapsed with a number of teams unable to fulfil all of their fixtures. Although their last season, and obviously overshadowed by the division's demise, the 1925-26 season produced Vale's best overall Scottish League win, their best away League win, and their most goals in a season, 78, despite only completing 26 out of their 30 matches.

At the Scottish League's AGM in May 1926 it was decided that no championship would be awarded due to the number of fixtures unfinished. The Third Division was abandoned despite attempts led by Helensburgh to keep in going in a regionalised format, with a south-western and north-eastern divisions, augmented by teams from the Second Division. Vale of Leven joined the Scottish Alliance after the Scottish Third Division was abandoned. Goalscorer Angus Urquhart joined Dumbarton and scored 35 goals for them in the 1927-28 season. When the majority of the ex-Third Division clubs were expelled from the Alliance a year later they decided to set up their own league, known as the Provincial League, but it only lasted a season. Vale then moved into a local league before disbanding in 1929.

Vale of Leven appeared in the Scottish Cup for two more seasons. In the 1926-27 competition they beat another former League club, Johnstone, in the First Round. Played on the 22nd January 1927, Vale won the game 6-2. Hendry, a left back, was called on to play at centre-forward for the Vale, and scored three goals, while Finlayson had two. In the next round they went out 4-1 at Dundee United. Their last appearance was in the First Round of the 1927-28 season when they lost 2-1 at home to Leith Amateurs. Only 230 spectators turned out in wretched weather in Alexandria, with the winner coming five minutes from time.

Milburn Park continued to be used as a football pitch and played host to matches played by Vale OCOBA (Old Church Old Boys Association). This team, regarded by many as a continuation of Vale of Leven by another name, participated in the Scottish Cup for four seasons in the 1930s, never progressing beyond the First Round. In the 1933-34 competition they went out 4-1 at Albion Rovers. The following year Scottish Cup football was again played at Millburn Park when they hosted Dumbarton. A crowd of 5,000 saw them go down 6-1, with Haddow scoring four. On the 1st February 1936 Vale

OCOBA hosted Hibs at Millburn Park, declining an incentivised offer to switch the tie to Easter Road. A crowd of 2,600 saw the visitors score first but Vale equalised a few minutes later. Hibs scored two close to the end of the first half and although they had much the better of the second half they couldn't increase their score. They made their last appearance the following year, losing 8-0 against Clyde.

In 1939, representatives from Vale OCOBA attended discussions around reforming the Scottish Alliance, although it was actually a reformed Vale of Leven FC that joined. This club played some fixtures as a senior club but the war intervened and they the stepped down to become a junior side, which they remain to this day. In 1953 this new Vale of Leven side won the Scottish Junior Cup. The Semi-final was played on the neutral territory of Ibrox against the much fancied Ashfield of Glasgow. A massive crowd of 33,000 saw centre-forward Willie Cassidy score a hat-trick as Vale won 3-0. These goals were in addition to the two goals which he had scored in a Quarter-final 2-0 win over Dunbar United at Millburn Park. On the 23rd May an even bigger crowd of 50,000 saw Cassidy score the one and only goal in the Final. The *Glasgow Herald* reported that "the goal by which Vale of Leven won the Scottish Junior Cup at Hampden Park on Saturday was one of the few bright features of the match. In 63 minutes, Gailey, the Vale left-half, swept the ball into the penalty area, where Cassidy, the centre-forward, for the first time in the game, tricked the Annbank United centre-half, and shot low into the net. Within minutes of the goal the Ayrshire left wing partners wasted simple opportunities of scoring at close range. Those misses emphasised United's main weakness - inability to seize their chances....Nor were Vale of Leven impressive in attack. The forwards failed to recapture the sparkling form they had shown in defeating Ashfield in the semi-final."

Vale of Leven continue to play in the Scottish Junior Football Association, a far cry from the days when they were one of the dominant clubs in Scottish football, winners of the Scottish Cup three times in a row and one of the founding members of the Scottish Football League. As such, they make this a perfect way to end this history of the League's former clubs.

SEASON	LEAGUE	P	W	D	L	F	A	P	POS
1890-91	SCOT	18	5	1	12	27	65	11	9/10
1891-92	SCOT	22	0	5	17	24	100	5	12/12
1905-06	SCOT-2	22	6	4	12	34	49	16	11/12

1906-07	SCOT-2	22	13	1	8	54	35	27	2/12
1907-08	SCOT-2	22	5	8	9	25	31	18	10/12
1908-09	SCOT-2	22	12	4	6	39	25	28	3/12
1909-10	SCOT-2	22	8	5	9	36	38	21	6/12
1910-11	SCOT-2	22	4	8	10	22	31	16	12/12
1911-12	SCOT-2	22	6	1	15	19	37	13	11/12
1912-13	SCOT-2	26	8	5	13	28	45	21	12/14
1913-14	SCOT-2	22	5	3	14	23	47	13	11/12
1914-15	SCOT-2	26	4	5	17	33	66	13	14/14
1921-22	SCOT-2	38	17	10	11	56	43	44	4/20
1922-23	SCOT-2	38	11	8	19	50	59	30	17/20
1923-24	SCOT-2	38	11	9	18	41	67	31	19/20
1924-25	SCOT-3	30	17	4	9	61	43	38	4/16
1925-26	SCOT-3	26	14	2	10	78	55	30	7/16

Appendix

Appendix 1 - Movements in and out of the League

Year	Clubs Joining the League	Clubs Leaving the League
1890	Abercorn, Cambuslang, Cowlairs, Dumbarton, Glasgow Celtic, Glasgow Rangers, Heart of Midlothian, Renton*, St Mirren, Third Lanark and Vale of Leven – Formation of League	*Renton – expelled after 4 games but reinstated for the following season
1891	Leith Athletic, Clyde – Elected	Cowlairs – Not re-elected
1892		Cambuslang, Vale of Leven - Not re-elected
1893	Dundee, St Bernard's Joined Division One Clyde, Cowlairs, Hibernian, Morton, Motherwell, Northern, Partick Thistle, Port Glasgow Athletic, Thistle - Formation of Division Two	
1894	Airdrieonians, Dundee Wanderers – Joined Division Two	Northern, Thistle – Not re-elected
1895	Kilmarnock, Linthouse - Joined Division Two	Cowlairs, Dundee Wanderers – Not re-elected
1897	Ayr, Hamilton Academical – Joined Division Two	Dumbarton – Not re-elected Renton - Resigned
1900	Queen's Park – Joined Division One East Stirlingshire – Joined Division Two	Linthouse – Not re-elected (didn't apply)
1901	Arthurlie - Joined Division Two	
1902	Falkirk, Raith Rovers - Joined Division Two	
1903	Albion Rovers, Ayr Parkhouse - Joined Division Two	
1904	Aberdeen - Joined Division Two	Ayr Parkhouse – Not re-elected
1905	Cowdenbeath, Vale of Leven - Joined Division Two	
1906	Ayr Parkhouse, Dumbarton – Joined Division Two	
1910	Dundee Hibernian – Joined Division Two	Ayr & Ayr Parkhouse – Merged
1911	St Johnstone – Joined Division Two	Port Glasgow Athletic - Resigned
1912	Dunfermline Athletic, Johnstone – Joined Division Two	

1914	Clydebank, Lochgelly United – Joined Division Two	
1915	Albion Rovers – Joined Division One	Second Division suspended affecting:- Abercorn, Arthurlie, Clydebank, Cowdenbeath, Dundee Hibernian, Dunfermline Athletic, East Stirlingshire, Johnstone, Leith Athletic, Lochgelly United, St Bernard's, St Johnstone, Vale of Leven
1917	Clydebank – Joined Division One	
1921	Alloa Athletic, Arbroath, Armadale, Bathgate, Bo'ness, Broxburn United, Clackmannan, Cowdenbeath, Dunfermline Athletic, Dundee Hibernian, East Fife, East Stirlingshire, Forfar Athletic, Johnstone, Kings Park, Lochgelly United, St Bernard's, St Johnstone, Stenhousemuir, Vale of Leven - Re-formation of Second Division	
1922		Clackmannan, Dundee Hibernian – League reconstruction – reduction in clubs
1923	Dundee Hibernian – Joined Division Two Arthurlie, Beith, Brechin City, Clackmannan, Dumbarton Harp, Dykehead, Galston, Helensburgh, Mid-Annandale, Montrose, Nithsdale Wanderers, Peebles Rovers, Queen of the South, Royal Albert, Solway Star - Formation of Division Three	Dundee Hibernian – Name change to Dundee United
1924	Leith Athletic – Joined Division Three	Dumbarton Harp – Folded mid-season
1926		Galston – Folded mid-season Broxburn United – Failed re-election Beith, Brechin City, Clackmannan, Dykehead, Helensburgh, Johnstone, Leith Athletic, Lochgelly United, Mid-Annandale, Montrose, Peebles Rovers, Royal Albert, Solway Star, Vale of Leven - Division Three Dissolved
1927	Leith Athletic – Joined Division Two	Nithsdale Wanderers – Not re-elected
1929	Montrose, Brechin City - Joined Division Two	Arthurlie, Bathgate - Resigned
1931	Edinburgh City - Joined Division Two	Clydebank - Resigned
1933		Armadale, Bo'ness - Expelled

1946	Stirling Albion – Joined new Division C	Kings Park, St Bernard's – failed to re-emerge after Second World war
1949	Stranraer – Joined Division C	Edinburgh City - Resigned
1951	Berwick Rangers – Joined Division C	
1953		
1964		Leith Athletic – Expelled
		East Stirlingshire – Name change to ES Clydebank
1965		ES Clydebank – Name change to East Stirlingshire
1966	Clydebank II – Joined Division Two	
1967		
1974	Meadowbank Thistle – Joined 3rd tier of League	Third Lanark - Bankrupt
1994	Inverness Caledonian Thistle, Ross County – Joined 4th tier of League	
1995		
		Meadowbank Thistle – Name change to Livingston
2000	Elgin City, Peterhead - Joined 4th tier of League	
2002	Gretna - Joined 4th tier of League	Airdrieonians – Bankrupt Clydebank II – Name change to Airdrie United
2008	Annan Athletic - Joined 4th tier of League	Gretna - Folded
2016	Edinburgh City – Promoted to 4th tier of League	East Stirlingshire – Relegated to Lowland League
2019	Cove Rangers – Promoted to 4th tier of League	Berwick Rangers – Relegated to Lowland League

Appendix 2 - Club A-Z

Club	First Season	Last Season	Reason
Abercorn	1890-91	1914-15	Disbanded – effectively from 1921 due to being unable secure a new ground
Armadale	1921-22	1931-32	Expelled
Arthurlie	1901-02	1928-29	Resigned
Ayr FC	1897-98	1909-10	Merger with Ayr Parkhouse to form Ayr United
Ayr Parkhouse	1902-03	1909-10	Merger with Ayr FC to form Ayr United
Bathgate	1921-22	1928-29	Resigned during the season
Beith	1923-24	1925-26	Abandonment of Third Division
Berwick Rangers	1955-56	2018-19	Relegated
Bo'ness	1921-22	1931-32	Expelled
Broxburn United	1921-22	1925-26	Failed Re-election
Cambuslang	1890-91	1891-92	Did not seek Re-election
Clackmannan	1921-22	1925-26	Abandonment of Third Division
Clydebank I	1914-15	1930-31	Resigned
Clydebank II	1965-66	2001-02	Administration followed by name change
Cowlairs	1890-91	1894-95	Failed Re-election
Dumbarton Harp	1923-24	1924-25	Resigned during the season
Dundee Hibernian	1910-11	1921-22	Name change
Dundee Wanderers	1894-95	1894-95	Failed Re-election

Dykehead	1923-24	1925-26	Abandonment of Third Division
ES Clydebank	1964-65	1964-65	Name change
East Stirlingshire	1900-01	2015-16	Relegated
Galston	1923-24	1925-26	Resigned during the season
Gretna	2002-03	2006-07	Entered administration and then resigned
Helensburgh	1923-24	1925-26	Abandonment of Third Division
Johnstone	1912-3	1925-26	Abandonment of Third Division
King's Park	1921-22	1938-39	Failed to re-emerge after the Second World War
Leith Athletic	1891-92	1952-53	Expelled
Linthouse	1895-96	1899-1900	Did not seek Re-election
Lochgelly United	1914-15	1925-26	Abandonment of Third Division
Meadowbank Thistle	1974-75	1994-95	Name change
Mid-Annandale	1923-24	1925-26	Abandonment of Third Division
Nithsdale Wanderers	1923-24	1926-27	Failed Re-election
Northern	1893-94	1893-94	Failed Re-election
Peebles Rovers	1923-24	1925-26	Abandonment of Third Division
Port Glasgow Athletic	1893-94	1910-11	Did not seek Re-election
Renton	1890-91	1896-97	Resigned
Royal Albert	1923-24	1925-26	Abandonment of Third Division
Solway Star	1923-24	1925-26	Abandonment of Third Division
St Bernard's	1893-94	1938-39	Disbanded 1943
Third Lanark	1890-91	1966-67	Bankrupt
Thistle	1893-94	1893-94	Disbanded

	1890-91	1925-26	Abandonment of Third Division. Folded in 1929
Vale of Leven			

Appendix 3 - Honours of the Forgotten Clubs

15 former clubs of the Scottish Football League have won a League Divisional championship or a Scottish Cup. The most successful club is Third Lanark, the only former club to have won the overall League title, which they won "by strenuous effort and praiseworthy enthusiasm" (*Glasgow Herald*). They top the overall list with five trophies. Vale of Leven won three Scottish Cups in a row and Renton won two Scottish Cups, and still jointly hold the record winning score in a Scottish Cup Final (6-1). The only other former club to have won the Scottish Cup is St Bernard's, who also won two Second Division titles. Gretna picked up three successive Divisional championships in their climb to the Premier League and the other multiple championship winners are Leith Athletic, who were Second Division champions on three occasions; founding members Abercorn who won the Second Division twice; East Stirlingshire have a Second and a Third Division title to their credit; and likewise, Berwick Rangers have been champions of both the Second and Third Divisions. Port Glasgow Athletic and Bo'ness can each boast a single Second Division title and Arthurlie, Nithsdale Wanderers, Clydebank and Meadowbank all have a third tier championship title to their name. The full list of honours by club is:

Third Lanark - First Division Champions (SFL Champions) 1903-04. Scottish Cup 1889, 1905 (and four times runners-up). Second Division Champions 1930-31, 1934-35.

Vale of Leven - Scottish Cup winners 1877, 1878, 1879 (and four times runners-up).

Renton - Scottish Cup winners 1885, 1888 (and three times runners-up).

St Bernard's - Scottish Cup winners 1895 (and once a runners-up), Second Division Champions 1900-01, 1906-07.

Gretna - First Division Champions (2nd tier) 2006-07, Second Division (3rd tier) Champions 2005-06, Third Division Champions (4th tier) 2004-05. (also runners-up in the Scottish Cup)

Leith Athletic - Second Division Champions 1905-06, 1909-10, 1929-30.

Abercorn - Second Division Champions 1895-96, 1908-09.

East Stirlingshire – Second Division Champions 1931-32, Third Division Champions 1946-47

Berwick Rangers – Second Division Champions (3rd tier) 1978-79, Third Division Champions (4th tier) 2006-07.

Port Glasgow Athletic - Second Division Champions 1901-02.

Bo'ness - Second Division Champions 1926-27.

Arthurlie - Third Division Champions 1923-24.

Nithsdale Wanderers - Third Division Champions 1924-25.

Clydebank - Second Division Champions (3rd tier) 1975-76.

Meadowbank Thistle - Second Division Champions (3rd tier) 1986-87

Cambuslang reached a Scottish Cup final

Bibliography

Newspapers
The primary source of my material has derived from the newspaper archives available in the National Library of Scotland in Edinburgh, The Mitchell Library in Glasgow and the Airdrie Public Library. The main titles I have used are the Glasgow Herald, The Scotsman, the Evening Times and the Sunday Post. Other titles have included the Daily Record, the Edinburgh Evening News, the Dundee Courier and the Airdrie and Coatbridge Advertiser.

Books
The Breedon Book of Scottish Football Records: includes all League, Scottish Cup and League Cup results and League tables by Gordon Smailes, published by Breedon Books.

A Record of Scottish League Football. In Four Parts: Dates, results and final tables of every Scottish Football League game since its inception, including both wars and Division Three by Gordon Smailes, published by Basildon

The Evening Times' Wee Red Book - various editions

The Ultimate Directory of English & Scottish Football League Grounds by Paul Smith & Shirley Smith, published by Yore.

Gaffers by David Ross is a who's who of Scottish football managers and is published by Lulu.

Magazines
The Scottish Football Historian is a quarterly publication and various articles have been reviewed

When Saturday Comes is a monthly football magazine and articles have been reviewed on those club's being relegated from the Scottish League since 2016.

Forth Naturalist and Historian - Volume 35 2012 - A Brief History of King's Park Football Club - Nigel Bishop

Online Resources

The three primary web-based sources of information have been:

www.scottish-football-historical-archive.com
www.scottish-league.net
www.londonhearts.com

The first site has a plethora of information, especially around the League's AGM and re-election votes. The second is more forum based and provided lots of background information on various club managers and players. The third site provided lots of details around the results of each club, season by each season.

The statistics by season at the end of each chapter have been sourced from the Football Club History Database at www.fchd.info.

The information about each of the club's primary playing colours has been sourced from www.historicalkits.co.uk. This site has also provided some of the early history for a number of clubs.

The BBC Sport website has provided match reports on the most recent clubs to exit the Scottish League - Clydebank, Gretna, East Stirlingshire and Berwick Rangers.

Club websites for some of the most recent clubs to drop out of the League – Clydebank (archive section) East Stirlingshire and Berwick Rangers.

The late Neil Brown's Post War English & Scottish Football League A - Z Player's Transfer Database provided details of the players for the clubs that left the League after the Second World War.

The heritage site www.valeofleven.org.uk has provided information on the history of both the Vale of Leven and Renton clubs.

The website www.rsssf.com, the Rec. Sport Soccer Statistics Foundation, has a wealth of statistics, and provided details of Scotland's international matches and line-ups. This was supplemented by the Scottish FAs own website, www.scottishfa.co.uk, which provided biographical details on players capped for Scotland.

The Scottish Courts and Tribunals Service provided details of cases where litigation was undertaken, most noticeably with Clydebank and the Steedman's, and details can be found at www.scotcourts.gov.uk. Details of the financial position of those clubs listing their accounts can be found at www.companieshouse.gov.uk.